We the People

A Brief American History

Peter N. Carroll
Stanford University

Australia • Canada • Mexico • Singapore • Spain • United Kingdom • United States

WADSWORTH

THOMSON LEARNING ™

WADSWORTH

THOMSON LEARNING ™

History Publisher: Clark Baxter
Senior Development Editor: Sue Gleason
Assistant Editor: Kasia Zagorski
Editorial Assistant: Jonathan Katz
Executive Marketing Manager: Caroline Croley
Print/Media Buyer: Karen Hunt
Permissions Editor: Stephanie Keough-Hedges
Production Service: Johnstone Associates
Text and Cover Designer: Lisa Devenish
Photo Researcher: Susie Friedman

Maps: Thompson Type
Map, p. 138: Pat Rogondino
Cover Image: © Scala/Art Resource, NY. Currier & Ives (19th C) Rocky Mountains. Color lithograph. Museum of the City of New York, NY USA.
Cover Printer: Phoenix Color Corporation
Compositor: Thompson Type
Printer: QuebecorWorld, Taunton
For photo credits and further information on chapter-opening photos, see the Photo Credits on page 764.

Wadsworth/Thomson Learning
10 Davis Drive
Belmont, CA 94002-3098
USA

For more information about our products, contact us:
Thomson Learning Academic Resource Center
1-800-423-0563
http://www.wadsworth.com

International Headquarters
Thomson Learning
International Division
290 Harbor Drive, 2nd Floor
Stamford, CT 06902-7477
USA

UK/Europe/Middle East/South Africa
Thomson Learning
Berkshire House
168-173 High Holborn
London WC1V 7AA
United Kingdom

Asia
Thomson Learning
60 Albert Street, #15-01
Albert Complex
Singapore 189969

Canada
Nelson Thomson Learning
1120 Birchmount Road
Toronto, Ontario M1K 5G4
Canada

Library of Congress Cataloging-in-Publication Data
Carroll, Peter N.
    We, the people : a brief American history / Peter N. Carroll.
        p. cm.
    Includes bibliographical references and index.
    ISBN 0-534-59355-0
    1. United States—History. I. Title

E178.1 .C317 2002
983—dc21   2001057461

*This book is dedicated to my coworkers
at the Abraham Lincoln Brigade Archives,
a nonprofit educational organization.*

Brief Contents

Contents

CHAPTER 4

The Emergence of Colonial Cultures, 1675–1765 • 71

CHAPTER 5

Patriarchal Politics and the Colonial Crisis, 1689–1776 • 91

CHAPTER 23

The War Against Fascism, 1931–1945 • 521

CHAPTER 24

Cold War Society, 1945–1952 • 549

Peter N. Carroll was born in The Bronx, New York, and received his A.B. from Queens College and his history Ph.D. from Northwestern University. He has taught the U.S. history survey course at the University of Illinois, the University of Minnesota, and San Francisco State University; consulted on dozens of textbooks; and worked with survey course teachers for the National Faculty in the 1990s. He has also taught U.S. cultural history, American studies, and creative writing at the University of Minnesota, Stanford University, the University of San Francisco, and the University of California at Berkeley. Carroll's publications include *It Seemed Like Nothing Happened: America in the 1970s,* rev. ed. (Rutgers University, 2000); *Keeping Time: Memory, Nostalgia, and the Art of History* (University of Georgia Press, 1990); *The Odyssey of the Abraham Lincoln Brigade: Americans in the Spanish Civil War* (Stanford University Press, 1994). In addition, he co-authored *They Still Draw Pictures: Children's Art in Wartime* (University of Illinois Press, 2002). Carroll and his partner, author Jeannette Ferrary, live in Belmont, California.

A Preface for Instructors

We the People is written for contemporary college students who are inhabiting a world of unprecedented cultural complexity. They have grown up in a society of racial and ethnic diversity, are participating in a technological revolution based on electronic globalization, and look somewhat askance at the promises and bromides of their leaders. Many instructors lament the "aliteracy" of this generation, but this book presents the nation's history from a fresh perspective that will resonate with current undergraduate interests.

What are this book's priorities?

- Good, clear writing
- Brevity and succinctness (leaving abundant reading time for outside assignments)
- The integration of political, social, and cultural history, with a clear political chronology framing the major economic, social, and cultural topics
- The human dimension: a multicultural perspective that reflects the demographics of today's student experience
- Brief quotations that illuminate the concerns of both political leaders and plain folk

At the dawn of the twenty-first century we no longer need to justify a multicultural approach to U.S. history. Today's students expect no less. Besides, historians know that America has always been a pluralistic land. Even before Columbus's ships touched these shores, Native Americans spoke about 2,000 languages, some as different from each other as English is from Chinese. Yet, despite vast linguistic diversity, the word that each of them used to describe its own group, society, or nation was equivalent to the English words "the people."

We the People, as the title suggests, presents the history of diverse cultural groups as a basic ingredient of the national narrative. In this book, women, minorities, and ordinary people find their distinctive voices, often in vivid, pithy language, along with the more familiar words and ideas expressed by politicians, business leaders, and other prominent citizens. Rather than isolating different groups, this book invites comparisons among them by describing issues and themes that affected them all.

For reasons of clarity and simplicity, *We the People* follows a political chronology, assuming the structure of most U.S. history survey courses. Students will follow a familiar sequence of events from the pre-Columbian societies of North America through the founding of the United States and its social, economic, and political development in the nineteenth and twentieth centuries. Yet the book's multicultural perspective also encourages an intertwining of what historians call "social history" within that political framework. Rather than placing social, economic, and cultural topics in separate chapters, *We the People* carefully blends those subjects into the nation's political history. In every chapter, politics, society, economics, and culture form the threads of a single tapestry— a coat of many colors—that tells the story of this country's diverse inhabitants.

Within this broad structure, *We the People* addresses several specific themes that are woven through this nation's history. First, the history of the United States has always been a pluralistic experience, a complicated interaction of women and men from diverse ethnic and cultural groups, involving many races, religions, and national origins. The relationships among these groups have changed dramatically during five centuries of history. The sheer diversity of the population has obliged all cultural groups to accommodate one another and thereby redefine their own identities. Second, because the history of this people involves members of diverse economic and social groups, this book endeavors to describe connections between society and politics, between ordinary people and their leaders. It explores how the country's political system has reflected and represented larger social and economic trends. Third, this book asks the reader to consider how interactions among groups have produced changes in the larger common culture. Taken together, these themes describe the evolution of a distinct national identity and enable us to discuss what it is to be a nation, to have a history, and to live in a specific time and place. From this common past, we can begin to answer the question, asked from the very beginnings of our country's history: What is an American? Going further: Who are we? What do we stand for? What is the meaning of our society, of our culture, and of our individual lives?

For the Instructor

Instructor's Manual and Test Bank

Prepared by Laura Matysek Wood, Tarrant County College, this manual features chapter outlines, lecture/discussion topics, student projects, multiple-choice and essay questions, Web addresses that link you to additional resources, and a *Resource Integration Guide* that features chapter-by-chapter ideas for instruction, as well as suggestions for incorporating CD-ROMs, print resources, and Internet and video resources into your course. With this easy-to-use tool, you can quickly compile a teaching and learning program that complements both the text's coverage and your own personal instructional style.

ExamView®

Cross-platform computerized testing. Create, deliver, and customize tests and study guides (both print and online) in minutes with this easy-to-use assessment and tutorial system. ExamView offers both a Quick Test Wizard and an Online Test Wizard that guide you step by step through the process of creating tests, while its "what you see is what you get" capability allows you to see the test you are creating on the screen exactly as it will print or display online. You can build tests of up to 250 questions using up to twelve question types. Using ExamView's complete word processing capabilities, you can enter an unlimited number of new questions or edit existing questions.

U.S. History Transparency Package

This package contains nearly 200 color transparencies that include maps, charts, graphs, and cartoons from the text and other sources. The transparencies are keyed to chapters of the text for ease in lecture planning.

Historic Times: The Wadsworth History Resource Center (http://history.wadsworth.com)

Both instructors and students will enjoy this Web-based resource center. From this full-service site, instructors and students can access such selections as a career center, lessons on surfing the Web, and links to great history-related Web sites. Students can also take advantage of the online Student

Guide to InfoTrac® College Edition, featuring lists of article titles with discussion and critical-thinking questions linked to the articles to invite deeper examination of the material. Students can access chapter-by-chapter resources for this book (including interactive quizzes), and professors can browse Historic Times to learn more about our other history texts and supplements.

We the People Web Site

Provocative, exciting, and interactive, this site has something for everyone: instructors, students, and U.S. history buffs. Includes a wealth of documents and visuals with related activities, tutorial quiz questions, hyperlinks, and Internet and InfoTrac College Edition exercises for each chapter. Also features link searches for American Journey Online (see below) for each chapter of the text, as well as extended descriptions of the text's chapter-opening photographs. Each chapter opener in the text carries the Wadsworth History Resource Center address to remind readers of the availability of these American Journey searches. http://history.wadsworth.com.

WebTutor™ on WebCT and Blackboard

A great study tool, a great course management tool, a great communication tool! For students, Web-Tutor offers real-time access to a full array of study tools, including flashcards (with audio), practice quizzes, online tutorials, and Web links. Use Web-Tutor to provide virtual office hours, post your syllabi, set up threaded discussions, track student progress with the quizzing material, and more. WebTutor provides rich communication tools, including a course calendar, asynchronous discussion, "real-time" chat, whiteboard, and integrated email system. Professors who have tried WebTutor love the way it allows students—even those in very large classes—to participate actively in class discussions online. This student-to-student interaction has enormous potential to enhance each student's experience with the course content.

WebTutor is filled with preloaded, text-specific content (including interactive simulations, Power-Point files, and much more) and is ready to use as soon as you and your students log on. At the same time, you can customize the content in any way you choose, from uploading images and other resources, to adding Web links, to creating your own practice materials. Contact your Wadsworth/ Thomson Learning representative for information on bundling options.

Multimedia Manager for U.S. History: A Microsoft® PowerPoint® Link Tool

This cross-platform digital library and presentation tool is available on one convenient multi-platform CD-ROM. With its easy-to-use interface, you can take advantage of Wadsworth's already-created text-specific presentations, which consist of map images, slides of art and architecture photos, interactive map and timeline images, and much more. You can even customize your own presentation by importing your personal lecture slides or other material you choose. The result is an interactive and fluid lecture that truly engages your students.

The Wadsworth U.S. History Video Library

This completely new selection of videos, from Films for the Humanities and Sciences and other sources, includes a variety of titles, including *Colonialism, Nationalism, and Migration; From Workshops to Factory; Revolution, Progress: Politics, Technology, and Science;* and many more. Contact your Wadsworth/Thomson Learning representative for additional information on requesting videos. Available to qualified adopters.

American Heritage Reader

In partnership with *American Heritage,* the preeminent magazine of the American experience, Thomson Custom Publishing is offering instructors the opportunity to build their own Custom *American Heritage* reader. The process is simple: contact our Custom group at 1-800-335-9983 or ask your Thomson Sales Representative for details. From there we can share a list of articles available for the reader. For nearly half a century, *American Heritage* has been the nation's memory, telling our shared story with verve, humor, passion and, above all, authority. Our wars and our songs, our heroes and our villains, our art and our technology—all are brought to vivid and immediate life through incisive prose and a wealth of original images.

For the Student

Study Guide

Prepared by Mary Ann Heiss, Kent State University, this valuable resource for students includes chapter summaries, chapter outlines, chronologies, identifications, matching, multiple-choice, fill-in-the-blank, questions for critical thought, and map exercises. Available in two volumes.

American Journey Online (http://www.americanjourney.psmedia.com)

The landmark events of American history recorded by eyewitnesses, the great themes of the American experience according to those who lived it—these are captured in the fifteen primary source collections that make up American Journey Online. Each key topic in American history and culture addressed by the series encompasses hundreds of carefully selected, rare documents, pictures, and archival audio and video, while essays, headnotes, and captions by scholars set the sources in context. Full text searchability and extensive hyperlinking provide fast and easy access and cross-referencing. The scope of the collections and the power of online delivery make American Journey Online a unique and unprecedented tool for historical inquiry for today's researchers. For more information and sample searches, see the inside back cover of this volume.

InfoTrac® College Edition

Ignite discussions or augment your lectures with the latest developments in history. InfoTrac College Edition provides free online access to hundreds of journals and periodicals. A free four-month subscription to this extensive online library is enclosed with every new copy of the book, giving you and your students access to the latest news and research articles online—updated annually and spanning four years! This easy-to-use database of reliable, full-length articles (not abstracts) from hundreds of top academic journals and popular sources is available twenty-four hours a day, seven days a week, and includes such journals as

- *American History*
- *Antiquity*
- *Biography*
- *History Today*
- *Past & Present*
- *Smithsonian*
- and many more!

(Available only to college and university students.)

American History Atlas

An invaluable collection of more than fifty clear and colorful historical maps covering all major periods in American history. Please contact your local sales representative for information.

History: Hits on the Web

Recently revised for 2002, Hits on the Web (HOW) is an exciting, class-tested product specially designed to help history students utilize the Internet for studying, conducting research, and completing assignments. HOW is approximately eighty pages of valuable teaching tools that can be bundled with any Wadsworth textbook at an affordable price. Available through Thomson Custom Publishing.

Acknowledgments

I have benefited immensely from the advice and suggestions of many active teachers, including: Terry L. Alford, Northern Virginia Community College; Stephen Armes, Fresno City College; Thomas E. Blantz, University of Notre Dame; John D. Buenker, University of Wisconsin—Parkside; Tony Edmonds, Ball State University; Carolyn Eisenberg, Hofstra University; Shirley M. Eoff, Angelo State University; Emmett M. Essin, East Tennessee State University; Melanie Gustafson, University of Vermont; Mary Ann Heiss, Kent State University; Chuck Hope, Tarrant County College, Southeast; Lisa M. Lane, Miracosta College; Gaylen Lewis, Bakersfield College; Barbara Melosh, George Mason University; Carl H. Moneyhon, University of Arkansas at Little Rock; James O'Donnell, Marietta College; J'Nell L. Pate, Tarrant County College, Northeast; Daniel Pope, University of Oregon; R. B. Rosenburg, University of North Alabama; David Sloan, University of Arkansas at Fayetteville; Ron Stocker, Tarrant County College, South; Richard M. Ugland, Ohio State University; Ken Weatherbie, Del Mar College; Lynn Weiner, Roosevelt University; Daniel Wilson, Muhlenberg College; David Wilson, Southern Illinois University; Laura Matysek Wood, Tarrant County College, Northwest.

I thank David A. Horowitz of Portland State University, who read an early draft and gave valuable advice, and especially acknowledge the help of Michael Batinski of Southern Illinois University, whose support made this entire project possible. My editor, Sue Gleason, earns special thanks for her astute criticism of the manuscript and imaginative suggestions for its improvement. Judith Johnstone provided excellent copyediting and overall production management. Hal Humphrey at Wadsworth extended many courtesies. Clark Baxter, former student and now editor, merits a medal for loyalty. My daughter, Natasha Carroll-Ferrary, who passed AP U.S. history while this work was in progress, cleansed the book of literary clichés, such as "tip of the icebeg" and "scratching the surface." Jeannette Ferrary, as ever, was a stalwart friend, a wise critic, and (come to think of it) everything else that matters.

Peter N. Carroll
Belmont, California

When a book advertises itself as a history of the American people, readers are entitled to ask, "Which people?"

"We the people," I answer. "All of us."

"We the people," the first words of the U.S. Constitution, tell much about the nation's values, expectations, and history. The phrase is inclusive, rather than exclusive. It suggests that all citizens have a voice and should be heard. We know, to be honest, that the signers of the Constitution did not listen to the voices of all Americans, but later amendments to the document broadened its meanings to bring more people into its framework.

This history seeks the same inclusiveness. To speak about "the American people," *We the People* uses a multicultural approach that embraces all people—rich and poor, men and women, and the rainbow of ethnic groups. From its historical beginnings, long before Columbus sailed in 1492, the land that became the United States supported many different cultures. Migrations from Europe, Africa, and Asia added to that multiplicity. Because of this historical diversity, Americans have struggled with questions of self-definition. In other parts of the world, most people do not question which nation or culture they belong to: "French," "Korean," or "Egyptian" suffices as a self-descriptive term. For those who inhabit the United States, however, self-definitions have been more complex. Part of the story that follows examines changing self-definitions.

It is important to remember that every history has three elements. First, there are the *people,* those who inhabit the realm of history. Second, history is about *place,* where events happen, how one place relates to another, how places change over time as people pass over them. Third, history is about *time,* chronology, sequence, putting first things first and second things second. Dates make this mental operation easier, especially because some events occur simultaneously, and others may cause additional events to follow. This book presents these three elements as a constantly changing interaction, a juggling act, as people experience time and place during five centuries and more.

Because of the great diversity of their origins and their willingness to intermix, the *people* who call themselves "Americans," "North Americans," or "U.S. citizens" have been uncertain about how to define their national identity. In fact, to speak about Americans requires thinking in plural terms which include Native Americans, African Americans, European Americans, Asian Americans, Latin Americans, male Americans, female Americans, and so on. Even more important, we need to remember that being American is not an absolute, unchanging category, but an evolving, often-ambiguous concept that enables us to define ourselves as part of a larger national group and as part of the human species.

The *place* of this book is the portion of North America that today is called "The United States of America." Yet the borders of that place have changed over the centuries as various peoples have come to consider America their home. Part of the story that follows involves the changing meaning of America as a place. To some extent, these changes involve redrawing the lines on a map, establishing boundaries with other nations, creating internal borders (colonies, states, territories), and transforming the land for different economic and social purposes (reservations, cities, suburbs). A major theme of this book examines how places have changed as populations have migrated from sea to shining sea. Such migrations also involve different types of transportation (from prehistoric canoes to railroads and automobiles), communications (oral messages, telegraph, mass media), and ideas or values (the things people say or believe). Underscoring this theme of place over the passage of time, we have inserted in the front of the Comprehensive Volume and Volume 1 of this textbook two acetate overlays of the 48 contiguous states. These volumes cover the period before which most present-day state boundaries had taken shape. You may place these acetates over specially labeled maps in the textbook to help you determine, for example, which current states arose out of the Louisiana Purchase.

As for the discussion of *time,* this book follows a familiar chronology—the dates that give history a logic and a sequence, though *not* a sense of inevitability. Life does not change abruptly every December 31 or at the end of each decade and century. *People,* not dates, make history. Indeed, human beings generally stress the continuity of their lives—their connections to ancestors and descendants, their heritage and their expectations for the future.

History, however, also involves those occasions when abrupt events disturb the ordinary flow of time. For Americans, the date 1492 immediately implies the idea of a "before" and an "after." So does December 7, 1941, the "day of infamy" that brought the United States into World War II. Other dramatic events—George Whitefield's preaching that sparked the Great Awakening in the 1740s or Henry Ford's development of mass production during the first decades of the twentieth century—may not be pinpointed so precisely, but they highlight the discontinuities of time, the sense of before and after, that illuminate historical change.

At the same "time," events occur at different places that may or may not be related to each other. Who creates those events or witnesses them often determines whether they are considered historically important. On the day Neil Armstrong became the first human being to touch the surface of the moon, his country was fighting a war in Vietnam. Two human events have never occurred so far away from each other—yet one date, July 20, 1969, binds them inextricably together. And both events, seemingly so far apart, reflect the same industrial-technological culture of the 1960s.

This book also deals with the changing meaning of time itself. From the cultures of Native Americans, who measured time by observing the changing natural cycles and seasons, to our world of digital watches and clocks, which divide time into linear microseconds, Americans have increasingly rationalized the use of time. This growing consciousness of time has helped Americans define themselves. Captain John Smith had to institute martial law to make the first Virginia colonists work six hours a day; a century-and-a-half later, Benjamin Franklin extolled the efficiency of an eight-hour work day. In the nineteenth century, factory owners imposed a twelve-hour day on their workers. By the twentieth century, labor unions forced a reduction of the work day so that workers would have more leisure. Yet, in today's society, people are busier (that is, are *choosing* to have less "free" time) than ever before. One must ask: How does the use of time reflect other cultural and historical values?

Issues of time and place help to define a people's common identity, the sense of living as part of a community. Although each person is as different as his or her fingerprints and DNA, we all coexist and share our individuality with social and cultural groups. In the times and places described in the pages that follow, Americans defined themselves by who they were and who they were not. To be an "American" meant different things, depending on a person's race, gender, class, or values, and these meanings changed greatly over time and in different places. This history, then, is about us, all of us: where we have come from, where we are heading.

Such ideas help us to understand not only the people of the past but also "We the people" today. Our own identities—as students and teachers, historians all—reflect our own sense of time and place: where we live, where we came from, who we are.

We the People

A Brief American History

In the Beginning: The World of Native Americans

CHRONOLOGY

35,000 B.C.	Lowering sea level exposes Beringa subcontinent
13,000 B.C.	Global warming raises sea level; land bridge flooded
12,500 B.C.	Oldest fossil evidence of humans in Americas
11,200 B.C.	Clovis spear tips used in New Mexico
7,000 B.C.	Earliest evidence of agriculture in Mexico
2,500 B.C.	Maize (corn) cultivated in central Mexico
1,500 B.C.	Lima beans domesticated in Peru
A.D. 100	Mayan culture flourishes in southern Mexico
A.D. 600–1200	Anasazi culture appears in Southwest
1100	Incas emerge in Peru
1100–1400	Mississippian cultures flourish in Ohio and Mississippi valleys
1451	League of Iroquois Nations created
1492	Columbus touches land in Bahamas
1519–1521	Cortes leads Spanish into Mexico; epidemic among Aztecs
1540	Coronado meets Zunis in Southwest
1607	English plant settlement at Jamestown, Virginia
1609	Henry Hudson establishes Dutch claims to New Amsterdam
1616–1618	New England epidemic claims 90% of local population
1776	Spanish expedition explores San Francisco Bay

In the beginning, there were only Earthmaker and his creations. Standing on a plain in the midst of the void, facing his maker, Coyote howled aloud on behalf of his fellow beings:

"How, I wonder—how, I wonder—
in what place, I wonder—
where, I wonder—
in what sort of place might we two see a bit of land?"

"Each of you will have a place to be," replied Earthmaker to his children. "Each and every one . . . will have a name." He went on:

"You are creatures who speak differently—
creatures who look different.
You also will have a place of your own. . . ."

Then he divided out the lands among them.

"You take the land over *that* way,
And you others, go to *that* country.
All of you various creatures will be called different things."

So it was sung, as part of a creation myth of the Maidu people, who inhabited the northern ridge of the Sierra Nevada, in what is now California.

The Maidu creation story emphasizes how diverse was human life in the Western Hemisphere long before Europeans, Africans, and Asians reached what became known as America. By 1492, when Europeans first landed on American shores, the population of the Western Hemisphere was considerable. Statistical estimates, based on archeological evidence, European observations, and belated oral testimony, remain inexact. Yet the total population of the American continents in 1492 probably approached 50 million people (the combined present-day populations of California and New York State), about one-half of whom inhabited Central America. Residents of North America reached 5 to 10 million. The Algonquian-speaking nations of New England numbered well over 100,000 before the arrival of French and English explorers. Around Chesapeake Bay, the groups led by Powhatan totaled at least 20,000. The Cherokees of the Southeast comprised some 30,000 people; Florida's rival nations, the Timucuas and Apalachees, together reached 75,000. Farther inland, Huron and Iroquois villages contained 1,500 to 2,000 residents at a time when most European villages held about 500 persons.

The American continent, in other words, was hardly a vacant territory waiting to be discovered, but was the home of many diverse organized societies. This dense population included thousands of different cultures and subcultures, each pursuing distinctive activities and values. Terms like *Native American* and *American Indian* tend to obscure such differences, just as the word *European* refers to a diversity of Catholics and Protestants, rich and poor, Spanish, French, Italian, English, and Dutch.

As the Maidu creation story indicates, Native American peoples had a strong sense of place; they knew where they belonged. This knowledge of place enabled them to interact well with their natural en-

The American continent was hardly a vacant territory waiting to be discovered.

vironments—exploiting local resources, integrating human culture into natural cycles, changing the land as it changed them. The harmony between nature and the native cultures may seem idealized, but relations among geography, climate, and society were not static. Droughts, poor harvests, disease, and warfare could quickly destroy any sense of security; all too frequently, natural disasters provoked the fear—and sometimes the reality—of extinction.

The diversity of Native American life invites comparison and contrast among the multitude of tribes and nations that inhabited the Western Hemisphere. Indeed, to acknowledge that the Native American population in 1500 comprised so many people, speaking at least 2,000 languages, some as different from one another as English is from Chinese, suggests the magnitude of the subject. Among Native American groups, differences of size were most obvious. Some bands, such as the Ute-speakers of the desert plains, numbered only in the dozens as recently as the 19th century, reflecting the difficulty of sustaining large populations in arid territory. Other Native American communities, such as the Mississippian moundbuilding people at Cahokia, just east of modern St. Louis, enjoyed a beneficent environment that supported a community of 20,000 around A.D. 1000. Such numbers imply diversity, not a hierarchy of superior and inferior groups. Many small groups, such as the Utes, were still flourishing when the Europeans arrived; some large ones, like the Mississippian moundbuilders, had disappeared.

After contact between Europeans and Native Americans, startled observers on both sides were preoccupied by their similarities and differences—by the very existence of strange beings from distant worlds. And such primary contacts recurred constantly as men and women, exhibiting biological and cultural differences, met again and again over a vast landscape of time and place. The shock was always mutual, and focused on unexpected physical appearances, social customs, and inferred attitudes. Yet both sides attempted to locate common human qualities. Indeed, the desire to *understand* the other—however futile or dangerous—emerges as a major theme of cross-cultural contact.

The First Migration

Ironically, Europeans and Native Americans shared the experience of long journeys. Although Native peoples stressed their deep attachments to particular places, their creation myths and traditional storytellers often depicted their origins with legends of distant migrations, guided by spiritual visions, that led their ancestors to their "natural" homes. Such tales reinforce the most recent archeological and anthropological evidence about the origins of the first Americans. For Native Americans were not truly "native" to America; at least no fossil evidence has been found to indicate the presence of ancient types of human beings in the Western Hemisphere. Rather, the first Americans appear to have been modern *Homo sapiens,* who migrated to a "new" world during the later stages of the last Ice Age, beginning about 15,000 years ago, but possibly even 10,000 years before that.

Geological evidence supports the theory that the first Americans came from Asia. During the last Ice Age, when huge glaciers absorbed oceanic waters, the levels of the seas fell, creating a 750-mile-wide subcontinent, known today as Beringia, where the Bering strait now separates Siberia from Alaska. This grassy, shrubbed land bridge between Asia and North America attracted large mammals such as mammoths, mastodons, and bison, as well as smaller animals, including seals and birds. Asian hunters apparently pursued these animals across this temperate territory, eventually entering the American continent as the largest glaciers melted and created overland routes toward the east. Such migrations occurred in waves, interrupted by climate changes and the wanderings of the mammals. Indigenous peoples such as Eskimos and Aleuts, who currently inhabit the most northern regions, probably arrived during the last waves of migration. When the glaciers finally melted 10,000 to 15,000 years ago, the land route from Asia was submerged, as it remains today.

Archeological evidence also reinforces the theory of Asian origins. Until recently, the oldest evidence of a human presence in America was a distinctively shaped type of stone spear point that was first excavated at Clovis, New Mexico.

These so-called Clovis points were found embedded in the bones of a mammoth killed by prehistoric hunters. Measuring the rate of radioactive carbon disintegration of the mammoth bones dated the Clovis site as 11,200 years old. The discovery of similar Clovis points throughout North and Central America reinforced the theory that the first hunters spread through the hemisphere in search of mammals. Not until 1996 did archeologists working in Siberia discover similar Clovis points, which were dated 8,300 years old. Since by then Beringia was under water, this discovery suggests that Asia was indeed the source of Clovis points and of the people who used them. Other biological data—common shovel-shaped incisor teeth, a few rare blood enzymes, and some typical body characteristics such as sparseness of facial hair—support the view that the first Americans originated in Asia.

Because glacial conditions prevented direct overland migration south from Alaska, archeologists

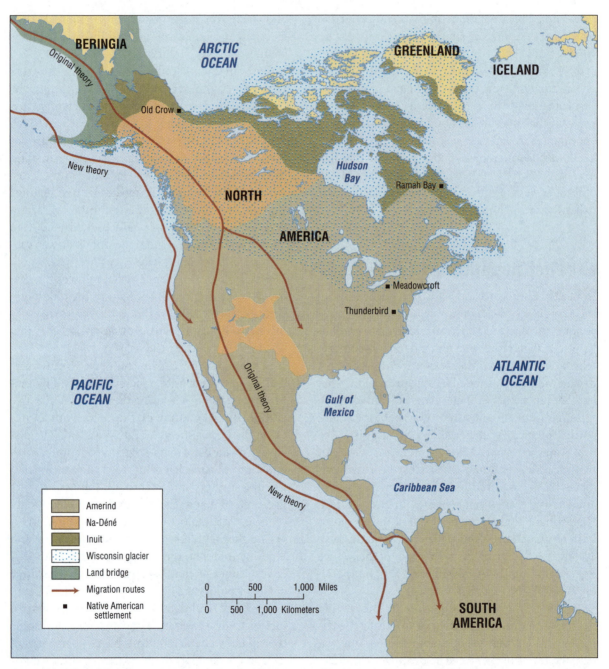

Early North American Migrations and Settlement. There have been two prevailing theories of the settlement of North America. According to the old theory, the original Americans traveled across the Bering Strait from Mongolia. However, the new theory holds, based on new archaeological finds, that migration moved by both land and sea from Asia.

These distinctively shaped stone tips, known today as Clovis points because they were found at Clovis, New Mexico, were attached to wooden shafts and used to hunt animals.

have long believed that the first American hunters migrated east across Beringia, then south and east of the Rocky mountains to places as diverse as Clovis, New Mexico, the Atlantic seaboard, and the southern reaches of South America. Over the years, tantalizing evidence of earlier human occupation has called into question the theory of overland migration but never with convincing proof. But in 1997, archeologists confirmed the dating of a site called Monte Verde in southern Chile to be 12,500 years old, more than 1,000 years older than Clovis. Evidence at this site included DNA specimens from a mastodon, seeds and nuts, and the single footprint of a human child. Since geologists believe that northern glaciers prevented an overland migration at that time, the hunters or their ancestors who arrived in Chile probably followed a coastal route that took them by sea from Beringia to South America. In 1998, archeologists discovered two sites in coastal Peru, both 12,000 years old, that provided evidence that humans lived on seabirds and small fish. Another recent discovery of 9,700-year-old human bones in an Alaskan coastal cave, together with seal bones dated 17,565 years old, suggests the possibility that mammals could have survived and traveled by a water route. Perhaps, then, other claims that humans occupied America 25,000 to 30,000 years ago may not be wrong.

More recently, archeologists have found other pre-Clovis sites in Pennsylvania, Virginia, and South Carolina. These discoveries are forcing a reevaluation of migration theories. The sites, which have been dated up to 17,000 years old, contain the oldest stone tools found in America. Their existence, dating to a time when glaciers would have prevented overland migrations, raises questions about the origins of the first humans in America. Rather than accepting the theory that all prehistoric Americans originated in Asia, some archeologists speculate that some migratory people began their journeys in Europe and traveled in boats near the icy shorelines westward across the North Atlantic to the east coast of America. Low sea levels would have minimized long voyages on the open seas. Whether such people survived, became extinct, or mixed with other humans from Asia is unknown. Archeologists now believe that multiple migrations probably occurred, some from Asia or Polynesia and others, perhaps, from Europe.

Establishing Local Cultures

Long-distance migrations over many centuries brought the first Americans into diverse environments, which in turn stimulated the development of multiple local cultures. Archeological evidence has suggested human occupation in the Ohio River valley near Pittsburgh at least 12,000 years ago; excavation of a man's gravesite near Sarasota, Florida, demonstrates human habitation there 10,000 years ago. Such wide and rapid geographical dispersal suggests that these early American residents were opportunistic migrants, seeking animals to hunt, fish to snare, or wild plants to gather. Around 11,000 years ago, moreover, climatic warming and human hunters hastened the extinction of the largest mammals, such as mammoths and mastodons. To survive, humans had to adapt to smaller sources of food. Instead of searching widely for big game, they learned to exploit the varieties of local regions. As hunters and gatherers of edible vegetation, Native Americans became a settled people.

Diverse California Communities

The diversity of local habitats can be seen even in a single area, such as modern-day California. "You will live here," Earthmaker told the Maidu to explain their settlement in a land of abundance. "Living in a country that is little, not big, you will

"Living in a country that is little, not big, you will be content."

be content." And when he created more people, Earthmaker promised them "a small country [called] by different names." California, apparently known even in prehistoric times for its good climate and ample food, attracted diverse groups. The region's languages reflected their separate origins. At the time Europeans first met Native Californians, the population spoke over 100 languages. Some of these languages were related to those spoken in Canada; some came from the southwestern regions of what is now the United States; other dialects were similar to the Algonquian spoken on the east coast. Whatever the geographic origins or linguistic roots, each Native American group simply called itself "the people."

The first settlers of North America's Pacific coastal regions made their lives in a land of plenty. In the high country of the Maidu, thick forests sheltered abundant populations of deer, elk, rabbits, and mountain lions, and produced crops of protein-rich acorns that provided the dietary staple. Armed with chiseled stone arrows, spears, and woven snares, Maidu men pursued their primary occupation of hunting. They prepared for the hunt with ritualistic smokehouse ceremonies—fasting, purifying themselves, appealing to the spirits of the animals to ensure the success of their task. Then, wearing animal heads and skins as camouflage, the hunters approached the game for the kill. The slain animals became communal property to be shared by all, and the carcasses were treated with utmost respect—the hunters never chewed the bones or carelessly discarded remnants—lest the animal spirits become offended and withdraw from the forests.

California Native American Languages

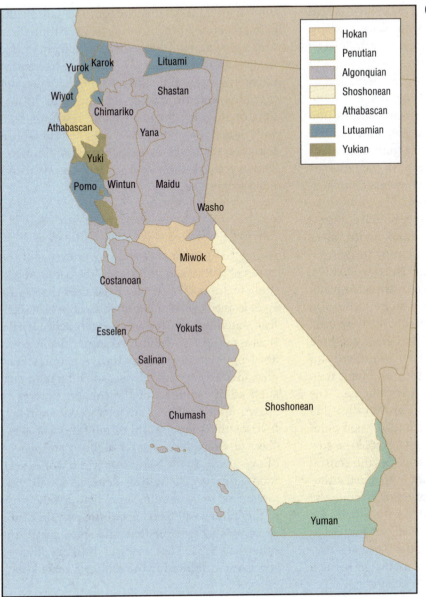

Legend:
- Hokan
- Penutian
- Algonquian
- Shoshonean
- Athabascan
- Lutuamian
- Yukian

Map labels: Yurok, Karok, Lituami, Wiyot, Shastan, Chimariko, Athabascan, Yana, Yuki, Wintun, Maidu, Pomo, Washo, Costanoan, Miwok, Esselen, Yokuts, Salinan, Shoshonean, Chumash, Yuman

Most women of the Pacific region assumed responsibility for the vegetable harvest. Their task began in the spring with the gathering of willow shoots and stringy roots. After participating in religious ceremonies that gave them spiritual visions, the women wove the plant fibers into beautiful baskets, some patterned after the skins of snakes, lizards, or deer. Woven so tightly that water did not leak out, the baskets served as utensils for cooking and carrying. To heat water in this nonmetallic society, the women made fires, heated stones, and dropped them into the water baskets. Women also gathered the acorn harvest, placed the dried seeds in baskets lined with herbs to repel insects and mold, and stored them underground or in granaries built on stilts. For food, women pounded acorns with stone pestles into fine powdery flour, leached out the bitter tannins with hot water, and cooked the grain into a watery mush or made acorn bread. In the fall, harvests of wild seeds such as fennel made pungent and easily preserved seed cakes.

Native California architecture revealed diverse interrelations between the natural environment and the customs of the inhabitants. In the redwood and pine forests near the Northwest coast, for example, the Karuk people constructed plank houses by splitting logs with stone wedges to form flat boards; lacking metal nails, they used knotted wild grapevine roots and gravity to hold the structures together. Here families gathered for meals and communal activities, although men slept apart from women in their sweathouses. The Miwok people of California's central valley dug circular houses into the earth, joined wood poles at the top to form a steeple, and covered the surface with soil to keep out water. On the central coast marshlands, the Ohlones built small circular houses from the native tule grass, while the Chumash of Santa Barbara used willow poles for houses that accommodated as many as fifty occupants. Some groups erected other special structures, such as huts in which menstruating women were segregated from contact with men.

The architecture of transportation was equally varied. At the mouth of the Klamath River, the Yuroks cut tough dugout canoes from redwood logs, sturdy enough to withstand the pummeling of coastal rocks and gravel river bottoms, yet, according to one observer, "smooth as if they had been sandpapered." The Modocs, by contrast, built light, thin-shelled dugouts to sail on the calmer waters of the interior lakes. Around San Francisco Bay, the Ohlones went fishing in canoes made from woven tule grass, the same fibers used for their houses and skirts. California's premier mariners were the Chumash, who built 30-foot long oceangoing boats of plank, sewn together with deer sinew and caulked with natural asphalt found on the beaches. In such vessels, Chumash sailors embarked on voyages as far as sixty-five miles from shore.

The Spirit World of Native California

Native Californians were astute students of the cycles of nature and understood the habits of natural creatures. Those who lived near the Pacific coast learned to exploit the abundance of fish, shellfish, waterfowl, and the occasional beached whale, thus assuring a generous food supply that encouraged population growth. Native peoples even measured the calendar by seasonal phenomena, such as the running of the salmon upriver to spawn (an excellent time to trap the abundant fish) or the annual autumn migration of geese (best lured by decoys and caught in nets woven of tule grass). In the Native American world, such food-gathering activities demanded spiritual awareness: the communication between the spirit of the hunter and the spirit of the prey, in which there was agreement that one should kill, the other be killed. That was why hunters adopted strict rules prohibiting the indiscriminate killing of game.

Underlying this sensitivity to natural cycles was the belief held by most Native American peoples that all the world was alive. "These mountains, these rivers hear what you say," a Modoc woman learned from her parents, "and if you are mean they will punish you." Native Californians treated not only animals but also plants and inanimate objects as living entities. "This rock did not come here by itself," declared a Yuki holy man. "This tree does not stand here of itself." Rather, human beings were surrounded by aspects of the natural creation. And if everything was alive, created by an Earthmaker, then animals were related to humans as kin.

In contrast to Europe's Judeo-Christian traditions and the Bible's Book of Genesis, which said that humans "have dominion . . . over every living thing," Native Americans saw themselves as members of animal clans. They identified, for example, with the families of Bears or Hummingbirds or Turtles, each of which had their own special qualities. Animal clans helped define who were a person's relatives and whom one could marry. Believing in spiritual communication with other species, humans might sing to animals or plants. Indeed, many songs had no words, but their melodies were sung or played on bone whistles or flutes to be understood by different animals. Many tunes have vanished and only the lyrics remain: "I dream of you," sang the Ohlones.

> I dream of you jumping.
> Rabbit. Jackrabbit. Quail.

The Rise of Agriculture

In areas of natural abundance, such as California, hunter-gatherer societies had sufficient food to survive without drastically altering the environment around them. Observation of natural phenomena enabled some men and women who were considered healers to use the medicinal properties of native vegetation to treat illness and injury. Indeed, Native American medicine men and women identified over 170 pharmaceutical ingredients that are still used today. Such botanical wisdom eventually led to a major transformation of some societies. Experimenting with wild seeds, prehistoric Americans learned the ways of agriculture—planting, weeding, and irrigating to produce larger crops. Domestic agriculture offered a stable food supply, stimulated population growth, and encouraged more settled habits, at least during the planting and harvest seasons. Yet few societies relied exclusively on agriculture. Most continued to gather wild foods and to hunt. Having different sources of food protected human groups from natural calamities such as drought or the disappearance of game. And, within most societies, certain groups became more expert in exploiting specific resources. Typically, women worked at agriculture while men specialized in hunting.

Early Agricultural Societies

The cultivation of maize, or yellow corn, probably began in central Mexico about 4,500 years ago. Domesticated lima beans appeared in Peru 3,500 years ago, and green beans emerged in the Andes 1,000 years later. As native farmers developed improved varieties of these crops, food supplies increased dramatically. The absence of written records has left huge gaps in the historical chronology, but archeological remains show that by about 2,000 years ago agriculture was supporting a flourishing Maya civilization in southern Mexico and Guatemala. With sufficient resources for a dense population, the Mayans built temples and cities, established wide trade networks, encouraged skilled artisans to produce silver and gold jewelry, and included intellectuals who invented a written hieroglyphic language and sophisticated astronomical calendars that could predict eclipses for centuries.

Supported by its extensive agricultural base, Mayan wealth attracted other groups. Among these newcomers were a migratory people called the Toltecs, who invaded from the north about 1,000 years ago and reigned in the region for about 200 years. Another migratory people, the Incas, entered the Andes region about 900 years ago, established extensive trade routes, built lavish cities, and flourished for 400 years.

Other invaders penetrated Central America, including the long-migrating Aztecs, who followed the spiritual guidance of the Hummingbird god into Toltec territory in Mexico. After acting as mercenary warriors for the Toltecs, the Aztecs intermarried with a royal family. But when they executed a Toltec princess in the expectation that she would become a goddess, the Toltecs expelled them. The Aztecs then moved to the shores of a swampy lake and proceeded to build a magnificent city called Tenochtitlan on the site of today's Mexico City. By the 15th century, the Aztecs were rulers of the region, dominating the core city with a population of a quarter of a million and demanding tribute from subordinate peoples of Central America. Elaborate irrigation systems made possible seven crops each year, and engineering feats included aqueducts, roadways, masonry buildings, and the fabulous Great Temple where human sacrifices took place. Aztec leaders enjoyed great wealth, exotic foods, and fine crafts and literature. Subject peoples faced mass religious sacrifices to satisfy Aztec gods; over 20,000 were killed in one celebration. Such subordinates were all too willing to betray their Aztec masters when later invaders arrived.

North American Agriculture

Agricultural knowledge probably moved from Central America in a northeasterly direction. Maize cultivation appeared in the southwestern areas of what are now Arizona and New Mexico about 3,000 years ago, followed soon after by squash and beans. About 1,500 years ago, the Hohokam people introduced irrigation to the desert lands to harvest crops twice annually. Five hundred years later, the Anasazi

people ("old ones" in Navajo) adopted irrigated agriculture, developed an elaborate road system, and dominated southwestern culture. Anasazi architecture included *kivas,* underground circular chambers in which men held religious ceremonies, and rectangular apartment-style dwellings still imitated by their Pueblo descendants. Archeologists believe that soil erosion and droughts forced the Anasazi to abandon their pueblos and migrate to other parts of the Southwest.

Agriculture also supported thriving societies in the Ohio and Mississippi river valleys. Beginning about 2,500 years ago, groups known to anthropologists as the Adena and Hopewell peoples established extensive community networks. Mixing hunting, gathering, and farming, these societies built large earthen mounds, apparently as religious sites and fortifications. By about 1,000 years ago, this so-called Mississippian culture dominated what is now the southeastern United States. Most of these settlements remained small villages, but at least one site at Cahokia in western Illinois contained an extensive metropolitan culture with a population density of 4,000 people per square mile.

At Cahokia, hundreds of acres of crops (maize, beans, squash) provided food for residents of the urban center, who also domesticated turkeys and tended herds of deer. Living in square wooden and mud houses, these Mississippians constructed enormous earthen pyramids, some 100 feet high, on which the chiefs and religious leaders lived. A continental trade network linked Cahokia to copper from Lake Superior and conch shells from the Atlantic seaboard. But wood supplies ran short, and the population began to decline 700 years ago. Drought, food shortages, and conflicts with neighboring groups led the Mississippians to migrate to the Southeast about 500 years ago. Their descendants continued as the Natchez, Choctaw, Chickasaw, Creek, and Cherokee peoples. Evolving as separate cultures, these southeastern groups developed societies based on agriculture and hunting, with a division of labor based on gender.

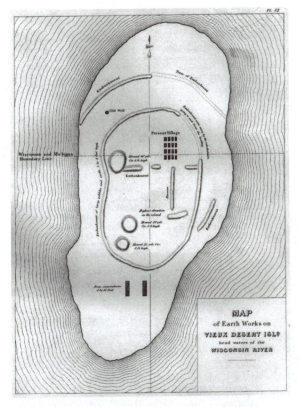

MAP
of Earth Works on
VIEUX DESERT ISLE
head waters of the
WISCONSIN RIVER

Map of the earth works discovered on Vieux Desert Isle, at the headwaters of the Wisconsin River, at the boundary of Wisconsin and Michigan. This encampment appears to have been designed as a retreat and a stronghold. No enemy could approach it except by water, and an elliptical embankment at its center seems to have served as the foundation for pickets. There were small mounds or barrows within the enclosure.

Among the Cherokees, for example, agriculture was a female task and hunting was male. Consequently, Cherokee men and women had equal economic and spiritual importance.

The Settled Cultures of the Northeast

Native societies in the Northeast also mixed agriculture and hunting. According to the Algonquian-speaking people who lived east of the Appalachian mountains, a sacred crow brought them the first kernels of corn and beans. Northeastern men still pursued animals to hunt, but women coordinated the tasks of planting, watering, and weeding with the responsibilities of childcare. Reliance on agriculture and gathering meant that women often contributed more to the household's diet than did men. Among these Algonquians, agriculture affected both social relations and their broader cultural outlook. Thus, while hunting tribes such as the Micmac regulated their social activity by the annual changes among animal populations (naming lunar months with reference to salmon runs, the migration of birds, or the hibernation of bears), New England agricultural people adopted a calendar describing activities involved in growing crops.

Agricultural communities in this region remained mobile, however, not only to accommodate the men's hunting and fishing seasons but also because it was easier to abandon old fields than to fertilize the soil. (The practice of using fish heads as fertilizer, a technique taught to the Pilgrim settlers in the 1620s, appears to have been unusual, partly because of the difficulty of transporting fish to fields.) In winter, entire communities moved from the planted areas into wooded valleys, where fuel was more convenient. The frequency of moves from field to forest encouraged the development of simple wigwam structures, which could easily be dismantled, moved, and reassembled.

Although the Algonquians' spiritual outlook encouraged the protection of natural resources, hunters and farmers left their mark on the land. To clear fields for agriculture, the men burned the woods twice annually to remove underbrush and dead wood. Such practices made it easier to track game and encouraged the growth of pine trees, which survived the fires to become the tallest trees in New England, some as high as 250 feet. Burning had the ecological advantage, probably unknown to the hunters, of accelerating the recycling of nutrients into the forest floor, opening areas to sunlight, killing plant diseases, and eliminating such omnipresent pests as fleas.

As in California, the hunters of the eastern woodlands understood the migratory habits of fish,

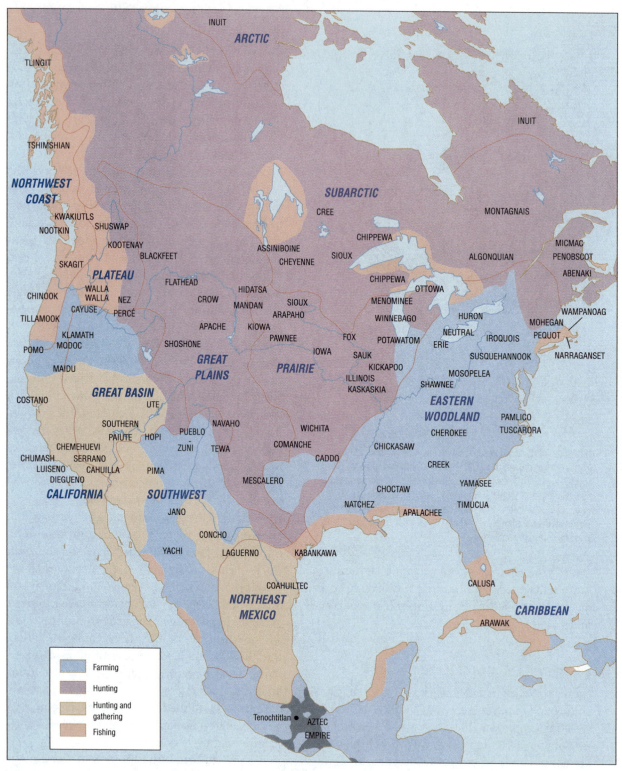

Native American Regions, 1492   OVERLAY 2

fowl, and other animals. At one remarkable site in Boston, dating from about 2,500 B.C., the inhabitants built a fish trap made of 65,000 stakes and intertwined brush that covered two acres. Fishermen of the Southeast developed poisons made from buckeyes or walnut bark that, when dumped in small lakes, temporarily paralyzed the fish. Native hunters simply scooped the floating fish into their nets. The pursuit of larger game, deer or bear, required equally subtle strategies—stalking, trapping, working as teams to drive the prey toward ambushes of tribesmen. The catch provided large quantities of meat that, when smoked or dried, could feed the people all winter. Women fashioned animal skins into clothing and moccasins.

The mixed economies of hunting, gathering, and agriculture reinforced a sense of territoriality. Although Native Americans considered the personal ownership of land as absurd (how could anyone own the natural creation?) they believed that organized groups possessed the right to use the resources of a specific geographic area. Custom dictated tribal boundaries. Claims to the land gave a people rights to hunt, fish, farm, and gather natural resources. Outsiders did not enjoy such privileges. A hungry stranger might be permitted to kill animals for food, but not for the skins. Usually, natural geography—a river, mountain, or valley—defined borders, and the perennial harvesting of resources justified the continued presence of a people. Native American maps, later copied by Europeans, reveal considerable knowledge of distant places, far beyond the range of an individual's personal travel.

Leadership and Warfare: Political Organization in Native Groups

Within their territorial communities, Native peoples accepted the leadership of a select few, but even hereditary leaders ruled by earning the respect and consent of their people; they could not coerce people to obey, relying instead on the power

Inhabitants built a fish trap made of 65,000 stakes and intertwined brush that covered two acres.

of persuasion. "Neither anger nor fury shall find lodgement in their minds," a European described the Iroquois chiefs, "and all their actions shall be marked by calm deliberation." Many societies deferred to their older men and women, acknowledging the wisdom of age.

This idea of a community consensus did not extend to outsiders who threatened precious natural resources. Among the eastern groups, warfare was violent, cruel, and seemingly perpetual, largely because conflict had both spiritual and political meaning. "They firmly believe," a European said of the Catawba, fierce fighters of the Carolina hill country, "that the spirits of those who are killed by the enemy, without equal revenge of blood, find no rest, and at night haunt the houses of the tribe to which they belonged." Among the Iroquois, another people feared as warriors, warfare served literally to revitalize the community by replacing the dead with captives, who might be either adopted into an Iroquois family to replace a recently deceased member or ritually tortured to ease the grief of a dead person's family. Native American warfare preceded the arrival of Europeans; palisaded villages and circular fortifications were part of the landscape throughout the eastern woodlands. But, while warfare was brutal, it did not involve extermination or genocide. Women, children, and the elderly were usually spared from death, and even enemy warriors were preferred as captives.

Among the most complex political arrangements in North America was the Iroquois Confederation, whose territorial influence ranged from the Adirondack Mountains to the Great Lakes. Consisting of five major societies or nations—Mohawk, Onondaga, Oneida, Cayuga, and Seneca (and later a sixth nation, the Tuscarora)—the Iroquois League emerged in the 1400s as an alternative to intertribal warfare and persistent blood feuds.

According to Iroquois tradition, a supernatural creature named Dekanawidah appeared before the Mohawk chief Hiawatha and proposed a union of the tribes that forbade blood revenge. Persuading other chiefs of his vision, Hiawatha developed a plan of confederation for the separate villages. A council of forty-nine elders assumed responsibility for diplomatic affairs, although it could not interfere with the internal problems of the separate groups. In this way, the Iroquois achieved a powerful unity to challenge the neighboring Hurons and Algonquians, with whom they were chronically at war. Later, when Europeans entered their territories, the Iroquois could offer a united front against the newcomers.

Central to Iroquois society was a matrilineal family system, or "fireside," in which social relations followed the female line. Married men entered the households of their wives, and women alone could initiate divorce. Networks of related women formed the clans. Women also participated in political decisions. The female elders named the 49 male representatives on the Iroquois council. Men dominated political speeches, but the matriarchs advised and consented about political matters. Women could also initiate wars by sending male war parties to capture an enemy to replace a dead member of the extended family, and women could determine the fate of the captive, either death or adoption. Women could also replace the male counselors or veto military attacks. Shared power between men and women underscored the values of consensual government.

The World View of Native Americans

Political consensus strengthened group identity. Since the Americas were so large and the local en-vironments so diverse, each location encouraged a unique sense of place and reinforced the distinct development of each group. Yet, despite great variations of language, customs, and spiritual ideas, most Native Americans shared similar beliefs that framed their cultural views. Living close to the natural world, Native Americans held a holistic image of life, believing that all aspects of the universe were interconnected like the threads of a web. Time could be measured by moons and seasons; societies could be divided into clans that shared an identity with animals; individual development followed the biological life cycle of birth, growth, decay, and death. Such a perspective deemphasized individuality, but valued communal obligations. Native Americans saw the world as cyclical, moving from season to season and birth to birth, because, as one Native American prophet put it, "everything is round." Yet because their world appeared complete, Native Americans were unprepared for their encounters with utterly different peoples and failed to appreciate the threat that Europeans posed to their way of life.

Respect for Place

Among Native peoples, group identity was closely linked to where they lived. When they thought of history, they emphasized place rather than time. *Where* things happened appeared more important than *when*. "Instead of records and chronicles," explained one observer of the New England inhabitants, they used the physical environment to stimulate oral traditions. "Where any remarkable act is done, in memory of it, either in the place or [nearby], they make a round hole in the ground." When others passed the hole, "they inquire the cause and occasion of the [hole], which being once known, they are careful to acquaint all men . . . ; and lest such holes should be filled or [overgrown] by accident, as men pass by, they will often renew the same; by which means many things of great antiquity are fresh in memory." Residents of the Appalachian region made small piles of stones to commemorate historical events. Thus history was not about chronological time—a date or year—but a recognition of an important place.

Native Americans also embraced the past by respecting traditions. They were conservative people, dedicated to preserving the "truths" of their elders, because local custom reflected accumulated wisdom and contributed to their survival. Abundant food in most of North America assured adequate subsistence. In New England, adults consumed about 2,500 calories daily, comparable to the modern U.S. diet. But seasonal shortages and crop failures reinforced the values of mutual support for survival. And so proven traditions—customs, habits, "the old ways"—assumed paramount importance for preserving a society. Men hunted the same way their great-grandfathers hunted, and caught the descendants of the animals their great-grandfathers had killed. Innovation and independence were less valued than perfecting the known arts and crafts, observing community restrictions, and accepting one's place in the cosmic order.

Family Relations

Marriage also forged connections to the past, serving to bind together not only two individuals but also their families. Native couples sang love songs and experienced the pangs of passion. "I am a fine-looking woman; still, I am running with my tears" were the words of a traditional Maidu song. Successful marriage required the approval of both families and was sealed by the exchange of gifts, which symbolized the mutual obligations of the two clans. Because marriage was a shared commitment, either spouse could usually initiate a divorce. And, rather than establishing independent households, newly married

Native couples sang love songs and experienced the pangs of passion.

couples took up residence in one of their parents' homes, depending on whether that community emphasized fathers' or mothers' lines of descent. These extended families reinforced community loyalties for mutual assistance.

"Single fornication they count no sin," observed one European of the Rhode Island Narragansetts, "but after marriage . . . then they count it heinous for either of them to be false." Sexual relations were usually controlled by strict rules. Understanding that unrestrained sexuality could be disruptive, societies imposed restraints, or taboos, that obliged people who were preparing to hunt or participate in religious ceremonies or collect medicinal herbs to avoid sexual contacts. Nursing mothers, concerned about producing sufficient milk, abstained from sexual relations, sometimes for years. Native women also used herbs and medicines to avoid pregnancy or induce miscarriages and, in times of war or famine, might practice infanticide.

Warnings about reckless sexuality appeared frequently in tribal folklore, such as the Maidu story of the young mother who left her child to pursue a beautiful butterfly, only to have the insect turn into a man, who led her into strange valleys where she was lost. "When people speak of the olden times," was the moral of the story, "people will say that this woman lost her lover, and tried to get others but lost them, and went crazy and died." Even with these strict heterosexual codes, many tribes permitted certain men (rarely women) to dress and live as members of the opposite sex. According to French observers, such people might be "as much esteemed as the bravest . . . men in the country."

Among the Cherokees, men who crossed customary gender boundaries became the objects of jokes—a way of reaffirming traditional roles. But Cherokee women who took male roles (as warriors, for example) might be honored.

Most Native mothers clung closely to their children. Soon after birth, infants were swaddled tightly in soft skins and attached to a cradleboard, which could be carried on the mother's back. Women used the fluff of cattails or the powdery core of rotten wood to keep the babies dry and clean. Some cultures saw beauty in the flat shape of the face and literally molded the skulls of their offspring to create the desired appearance. Children were breast-fed for years and weaned on a porridge of boiled corn. In the absence of domestic cows and goats, Native people lacked a milk substitute and it was unusual to use wet nurses. Even today, people of Native American descent are more likely than the descendants of Europeans to develop allergies to dairy products.

Contrasts of Childhood.

In most Native American cultures, the end of childhood came with a naming ceremony. "They never invent new names," observed a French traveler, explaining that each clan used certain names to reinforce kinship ties. Yet a person's name did not necessarily remain the same through an entire lifetime. Instead, names indicated not only one's individual identity but also a social role or status as a member of the community.

Native American naming practices contrasted with European customs. In medieval Catholic countries, at a time when Paris and London were no larger than Cahokia, families usually named their offspring after saints or holy figures, and children celebrated their birthdays on the nameday of their saint. By the 1500s, however, parents in some parts of Protestant Europe, such as England, began more frequently to name their children after themselves or some favored secular person. To assure the perpetuation of a particular

name at a time of high infant mortality, some English families even gave two children the same name. At about the same time, England instituted formal birth registration. With secular names and legal records, birthdays became personal events rather than occasions to celebrate the sacred calendar of the saints. Unlike Native American practices, which linked names to communities, Europeans increasingly stressed individuality.

Native Americans also differed from Europeans in rejecting corporal punishment of the young. At a time when European parents believed that to spare the rod spoiled the child and used beating to discipline the youngest children, Native American parents relied on more gentle practices to instill respect. Splashing water on a child's face was considered an ultimate penalty, which gave great shame to the young. Typically, elders held up positive role models for children to imitate and gave greater latitude in personal behavior.

Contrasting Rites of Passage.

Elders also supported their children through personal rites of passage. "You are a girl no more," sang the Wintu of northern California as part of a menstrual ritual. "The chief, the chief, honors thee." Throughout Native America, elaborate ceremonies brought young women through puberty into adult status. Believing that menstruation gave women extraordinary powers—not just the capability of procreation, but also magical energy that could inflict harm or illness—many societies required a woman to live apart during her period, to abstain from certain foods and sexual relations, and to avoid eye contact with everyone. The husband of a menstruating woman might be prohibited from hunting because her condition could weaken his prowess or turn his luck.

Such magical beliefs about menstruation had analogies in European customs. Traditional Jews required women to undergo a ritual bath after menstruating and before resuming sexual relations with their husbands. In medieval Christianity, a menstruating woman was considered spiritually unclean and could be refused religious communion. After childbirth, women were required to undergo "churching," or purification, before returning to normal life. Only with the rise of Protestantism in the 16th century did reformers begin to challenge rituals that implied that sexually active women were unclean. Criticizing Catholic traditions, one Protestant asked indignantly, "Why do they separate her? Why do they cleanse her? Why may she not return to Church . . . before her month be expired?" These protests show that magical beliefs, not very different from those of Native Americans, persisted in Europe.

Other contrasts could be seen in male rites of passage. Except for the sons of aristocrats, European boys engaged in manual work as soon as they were able. Poorer families usually gave their children as apprentices or servants to other families. For boys in England, apprenticeship began at about age 7, and youngsters were expected to serve a master until reaching adulthood. Yet, because of limited economic resources in Europe, boys were not considered men until they could support an independent household. Although statistics are imprecise, the average age of marriage for men in England was in the late twenties, around age 28. For women, it was slightly younger, about 26. English children thus endured a long period of dependence before they could claim to be full-fledged adults.

Among Native Americans, boys also began preparation for adulthood at a young age, learning hunting skills with small bows and arrows and forming a friendship with a male comrade who would become a constant companion. The onset of puberty brought more elaborate rituals, some requiring extraordinary ordeals by which a boy proved his manhood. Taken blindfolded into the forest at night by an older male relative, a New England boy would be left alone to survive by his own ingenuity for an entire winter. Then he would undergo a ritual purging by drinking a brew made from poisonous herbs. "If he is able to stand it all well, and if he is fat and sleek, a wife is given to him." The first successful hunt was another important male rite of passage.

Hallucinogenic drugs also initiated young men into tribal mysteries. Among southern California peoples, such as the Luiseno and Chumash, boys were taken at night to consume *toloache,* a beverage made from Jimson weed, and then they danced until they lost consciousness. This state might last for days, during which the initiate experienced visions. As the heightened sensitivity was prolonged by weeks of fasting, the elders taught young people sacred songs, dances, and wisdom. As a final rite, the men produced sand paintings on the ground to depict the universe and lectured about the meaning of astronomical and natural phenomena. The influence of *toloache* can still be seen in the colorful Chumash rock paintings, found in caves and outcroppings throughout southern California.

On the opposite side of the continent, the Powhatans of Virginia and the Carolinas selected their religious and political leaders by putting boys through rigorous tests called *huskanaws,* which included the use of intoxicating drugs that caused amnesia. "This violent method of taking away the memory," a visitor was told, "is to release the youth from all their childish impressions. . . and unreasonable prejudices which are fixed in the minds of children." Purged of personal bias, a man could then qualify as a political leader. Such impartial men assumed responsibility for dividing food, settling disputes, and initiating diplomacy and war.

The World of Spirits

Besides respecting their political leaders, Native Americans recognized the power of spiritual guides, or shamans. These religious leaders served as intermediaries between humans and the world of spirits. Their skills could be used for good or ill—they could cure or curse—and were seen as extremely dangerous and potent. Bear shamans might not only prophesy a successful hunt but also participate by luring the animals out of their retreats. In regions of drought, the weather shaman would conduct rituals to hasten the arrival of rain. Shamans also conducted religious ceremonies (such as annual mourning rites), treated those afflicted by ghosts, and preserved traditional spiritual practices.

Shamans were valued, above all, for their power to cure. Among Native Americans, illness was seen as a physical entity ("pain," "poison") deposited in the body by an enemy or evil spirit or because the sick person had violated a rule. To remove such ills, the shaman used herbs or animal parts, or manipulated sacred objects such as a secret amulet. Cuts might be made between the eyes to heal headache or other pains. Blowing tobacco smoke into an ill person's face might cure a fever. Among the Yurok and northwestern California people, most shamans were women who underwent rigorous trials, fasting and dancing for ten days until unconscious, before they claimed control of the sacred powers. These practices mirrored unorthodox religious behavior throughout medieval Europe, where "wise men" and "wise women" employed astrology, made amulets, and dispensed herbs to cure disease, change the weather, or predict the future.

The Meeting of Unexpected Peoples

Religion, spiritual prophecy, and a sense of cosmic unity enabled people of all cultures to explain the world according to their beliefs. When the Italian navigator Christopher Columbus saw the naked Taino people in the Caribbean in 1492, he concluded that he had met exactly what he had been looking for: "Indians" from East Asia. Meanwhile, the Taino, Columbus reported, "believe very firmly that I, with these ships and people, came from the sky." Similarly, when Spanish explorers encountered Zuni elders in the southwestern desert in 1540, they reported that "it was foretold . . . more than fifty years ago that a people such as we are would come, and from the direction we have come, and that the whole country would be conquered." Native prophets on the Mississippi River and the Atlantic coast recalled similar predictions of the coming of "a white race."

Such impressions reflected the difficulty of explaining the existence of mutually unknown beings. Prior to direct contact, both Europeans and Americans considered their worlds complete and finished. Just as Christianity assumed that God had created the world in six days, so the Maidu believed that the Earthmaker had shaped the primordial waters into familiar patterns of life. Or, to use another example, the Iroquois of northeastern America thought the Great Spirit ordered the Great Turtle "to get from the bottom of the waters some slime on its back" to form an earthly foundation. Even today, many "Indians" call America "Turtle Island."

The European "discovery" of new humans raised basic questions about the Garden of Eden and the descendants of Adam and Eve. One Spanish writer even proposed the theory of an ancient land bridge connecting the "old world" and the new as a way of preserving his faith in the known universe. Some writers suggested that the natives were one of the "lost" tribes of Israel. Like the Europeans, Native Americans incorporated new beings into their world view by perceiving the strangers as heavenly spirits (*manitous,* in the Algonquian vocabulary) who could communicate with humans.

A Clash of World Views

One day in 1609, the Delawares and Mohicans who inhabited the area of what is now New York and

New Jersey observed something immense floating in the water and debated whether it was an animal or a house. They concluded that "the great Mannitto [the great or Supreme Being]. . . probably was coming to visit them." While the spiritual conjurors wavered "between hope and fear," the women prepared a welcoming feast. Soon the crew of Henry Hudson's *Half Moon* was among them. The sight of the first Dutch visitors provoked wonder at the whiteness of their skin. But the chiefs hesitated to drink the strangers' mysterious brew—believing it to be blood or poison—until one man, fearing that such a rejection would infuriate the Great Spirit, drank the offered cup of wine.

The resulting intoxication proved amazing. For people already fascinated by dream-visions and spiritual quests, alcohol opened a realm of mind-altering substances. Later, alcohol abuse would contribute to the loss of cultural integrity, but initially Native Americans believed that the European traders were gods. A subsequent exchange of gifts, iron axes and stockings from the Europeans, established friendly relations. Yet while the Americans admired European goods, they adapted them to their needs, wearing the axe heads as ornaments around their necks and using the stockings as tobacco pouches. Significantly, the Iroquois word for *European* translated as "ax-maker."

Even a century later, encounters between Native Americans and Europeans continued to be characterized by fear and bewilderment. "We came upon a poor Indian who was coming very carelessly along, carrying a bunch of grass such as they eat," reported a Spanish priest who accompanied an exploratory expedition south of San Francisco Bay in 1776. "But as soon as he saw us he manifested the greatest fright that it is possible to describe. He could do nothing but throw himself at full length on the ground, hiding himself in the grass in order that we might not see him, raising his head only enough to peep at us with one eye." When a Spaniard approached with glass beads, the Ohlone "was so stupefied that he was unable to take the gift. . . . Completely terrified, and almost without speaking," the man offered his bundle of grass to the strange creatures on horseback, "as if with the present he hoped to save his life, which he feared was lost. He must never have seen Spaniards before," concluded the priest, "and that is why we caused him such surprise and fear." Indeed, the Ohlone had never seen a horse either, and probably believed that the man on horseback was not even human.

Early commercial relations between Native Americans and Europeans underscored profound differences of cultural perspective. Even simple transactions, such as trade and barter, revealed complex distinctions. Just as Europeans saw Americans as a source of natural resources (animal skins, access to gold mines, valuable plants such as sassafras), Native traders saw Europeans as a source of kettles, guns, and fishhooks. But for Native Americans trade was not merely an economic transaction; it was also a form of gift giving, representing friendship and alliance, mutual obligations, and trust. To engage in commercial relations, therefore, Europeans had to give gifts, ranging from beads and "trifles" to manufactured goods, to tribal leaders. The chiefs then dispensed these goods to others in their communities to strengthen their own social relationships. Europeans also had to learn how to measure goods by American standards—an arm's length of beads, for example, or a mouthful of rum. Reciprocal gifts sometimes gave European men access to women as wives or temporary partners. Although these personal arrangements resulted in economic advantages, Native Americans complained frequently that Europeans considered only profits, not communal responsibility, in business relations.

Measuring Place and Time

Cultural differences shaped the way people literally looked at their worlds. European explorers well understood the importance of reliable compasses in navigating the oceans and trekking through unknown country. Indeed, the invention in the 15th century of the astrolabe, a device that measured longitude by the stars, greatly facilitated ocean voyages. Europeans also relied on their own bodies to express direction. "From the summit of this range we saw the magnificent estuary, which stretched toward the southeast," wrote the first Spaniard to see San Francisco Bay. "We left it on our *left* hand, and, turning our *backs* on the bay, advanced to the south-southeast." By contrast, Native Americans never used the egocentric "left-hand, righthand" to give directions. A person walking north might say a mosquito had bitten her "east hand"; later, walking south, she would scratch her "west hand." Native American maps did not locate north at the top, but used the course of the sun from east to west to depict both direction and distance. Equally common was the use of geographical landmarks to describe directions: upriver/downriver might mean north/south; or specific places would be used instead of universal compass points.

The sense of living close to the natural world also influenced the Native Americans' measurement of time. While European traditions emphasized the linearity of time—the chronological calendar moving forward day-by-day, year-by-year—Native Americans generally perceived a cyclical pattern in which time moved with the changing seasons. Each year began in the spring. In fact, Europeans in the age of Columbus shared that perspective. Not until 1582 did Pope Gregory introduce a new calendar that began the new year on January 1 rather than at the spring equinox in March. Protestant countries did not accept the changes until the 18th century. During most of the English colonial period, Anglo Americans used a double-year system; for example, 1630/31 would be used in 1631 between January 1 and the spring equinox. Native Americans, moreover, marked time by seasonal events; among southeastern people, the herring month was equivalent to March, the strawberry month was June.

Native Americans and Europeans also expressed different views about the spirituality of the land. Although some Native rituals occurred inside specific structures—underground kivas and sweathouses, for example—these edifices were located on geographical places that were endowed with spiritual meaning. But many ceremonies took place outside human architecture. Europeans no longer worshipped outdoors. Instead, they marked religious places with consecrated buildings (churches, chapels, shrines), many of them built on sites considered sacred since pre-Christian times. By 1600, the European countryside had sprouted some 500,000 Christian structures. The first European explorers saw no comparable architecture in America and, without evidence of Christian churches, concluded that Native Americans lacked any religion. "I believe that they would easily be made Christians," wrote Columbus of the first Americans he encountered, "for it appeared to me that they had no creed." The Italian navigator Amerigo Vespucci, for whom the continent was eventually named, agreed that "they are worse than heathen; because we did not see that they offered any sacrifice, nor yet did they have [any] house of prayer." Later, when Europeans did learn of Native American religious practices, they concluded that these heathen worshiped the devil and vowed to convert them to the "true" faith.

Encountering Strange Diseases

Differences of culture and perspective led to multiple misunderstandings, confusion, and disappointment, but nothing after 1492 more powerfully dramatized the collision of worlds than the arrival

An epidemic in 1616–1618 killed 90 percent of the population, effectively exterminating the Massachusetts people.

of deadly diseases for which neither Native American shamans nor European "doctors" could offer a cure. "A few days after our departure," wrote one 16th-century English explorer, "people began to die very fast. . . . The disease . . . was so strange that they neither knew what it was, nor how to cure it." From the first major epidemic that swept through the Caribbean islands and Mexico in 1519, Native Americans succumbed in huge numbers to respiratory infections, typhus, diphtheria, smallpox, measles, mumps, and other illnesses against which their immune systems had no antibodies.

Mortality figures are at best rough estimates, but the population of Aztec Mexico probably dropped from 25 million to 16 million in a single decade. Inhabitants of many Caribbean islands became extinct. In New England, an unspecified epidemic in 1616–1618 killed 90 percent of the population, effectively exterminating the Massachusetts people and removing most of the Native claimants to the land. People "died on heaps, as they lay in their houses," reported one European colonist, who saw human "carcasses lie above the ground without burial."

Native medicine compounded the problem. The custom of crowding around a patient, blowing smoke, and sharing a sweathouse merely exposed more people to infection. Moreover, because the shamans dutifully responded to the needs of the sick, they too became victims, dying suddenly and disrupting the expected treatment of illness. When they saw that Europeans showed no signs of disease, Native Americans concluded that these god-like creatures indeed held powerful weapons that could destroy them at a distance. Ironically, Europeans accepted that interpretation of divine intervention, claiming that the epidemics proved God had cleared away the Native rivals for their settlements.

A Shattered World Survives

Raging epidemics destroyed the very structure of Native societies, killing leaders and followers, shamans and chiefs, adults and children. In addition to foreshadowing the arrival of more strangers who held powerful technological inventions (firearms, fishhooks, knives, cloth, beads, and alcohol), the appearance of diseases without cure created profound demoralization. A world that had seemed orderly and spiritual quickly became fragmented and chaotic.

"There was then no sickness," remembered the Aztec survivors of a lost age. "They had no aching bones; they had then no high fever; they had then no burning chest; they had then no abdominal pain; they had then no consumption; they had then no headache." Instead, sang the Aztecs, "the course of humanity was orderly. The foreigners made it otherwise when they arrived here." A century later, in the 1640s, a New England Narragansett repeated the lamentation: "Our fathers had plenty of deer and skins, our plains were full of deer, as also our woods, and of turkeys, and our coves full of fish and fowl. But," he exclaimed, "these English having gotten our land, they with scythes cut down the grass, and their hogs spoil our clam banks, and we shall all be starved." Ninety years after that, the Natchez leader Tattooed Serpent complained that before the French came "we lived like men who are satisfied with what they have; whereas at this day we are like slaves."

The competition between Native Americans and Europeans for the land and resources of North America would last for centuries. In the beginning, the outcome was not so clear, for the indigenous peoples had developed flourishing societies and lived in harmony with the environment. The early European arrivals, uprooted from their homes and familiar places, depended heavily on the Native Americans' generosity, knowledge of the country, and eagerness to exchange gifts and produce. Neither people expected to abandon their beliefs, but neither could avoid the presence of the other. Steadily, however, European diseases, technologies, and an expansionist ideology shifted the balance of power from Native Americans to invading colonizers. In the end, Europeans and their descendants prevailed, though not completely, and the histories of the rival cultures remained forever intertwined.

INFOTRAC® COLLEGE EDITION EXERCISES

For additional reading go to InfoTrac College Edition, your online research library, at *http://web1.infotrac-college.com.*

Subject search: early Native Americans

Keyword search: maize

Keyword search: Anasazi

Keyword search: Stone Age America

Keyword search: Amerindian

Keyword search: Indian converts

Keyword search: Aztec

Keyword search: Maya

Keyword search: Iroquois

ADDITIONAL READING

The First Migration

Brian M. Fagan, *The Great Journey: The Peopling of Ancient America* (1987). An archeological analysis of the first Americans, though the most recent discoveries have modified the author's chronology.

Establishing Local Cultures

Alice B. Kehoe, *North American Indians: A Comprehensive Account* (1992). A thorough anthropological survey of the history and culture of diverse societies and peoples; a basic resource for the field.

Diverse California Communities

Malcolm Margolin, *The Ohlone Way* (1978). Written for the lay reader, this work examines Native Americans who inhabited the region around San Francisco Bay.

The World View of Native Americans

Colin G. Calloway, *New Worlds for All: Indians, Europeans, and the Remaking of Early America* (1997). The author explores the interaction of environment, biology, and culture.

Theda Perdue, *Cherokee Women: Gender and Culture Change, 1700–1835* (1998). The first chapters describe the world view of one southeastern nation.

Marion Schwartz, *A History of Dogs in the Early Americas* (1997). A survey of Native Americans' views and uses of the only domesticated animal in America before 1492.

The Meeting of Unexpected Peoples

William Cronon, *Changes in the Land: Indians, Colonists, and the Ecology of New England* (1983). Contrasts Native American and European views of the natural environment.

Alfred W. Crosby, Jr., *The Columbian Exchange: Biological and Cultural Consequences of 1492* (1972). This pioneering work describes the impact of European diseases on Americans and the diffusion of plants and animals between Old World and New.

Karen Ordahl Kupperman, *Indians and English: Facing Off in Early America* (2000). Depicts the earliest cross-cultural encounters between Native peoples and English and how they viewed each other.

Daniel K. Richter, *The Ordeal of the Longhouse: The Peoples of the Iroquois League in the Era of Colonization* (1992). This study of Iroquois culture and diplomacy explains underlying values and changes induced by Europeans.

Anthologies of Primary Sources

James Axtell, ed., *The Indian Peoples of Eastern America: A Documentary History of the Sexes* (1981).

Malcolm Margolin, ed., *The Way We Lived: California Indian Reminiscences, Stories, and Songs* (1994).

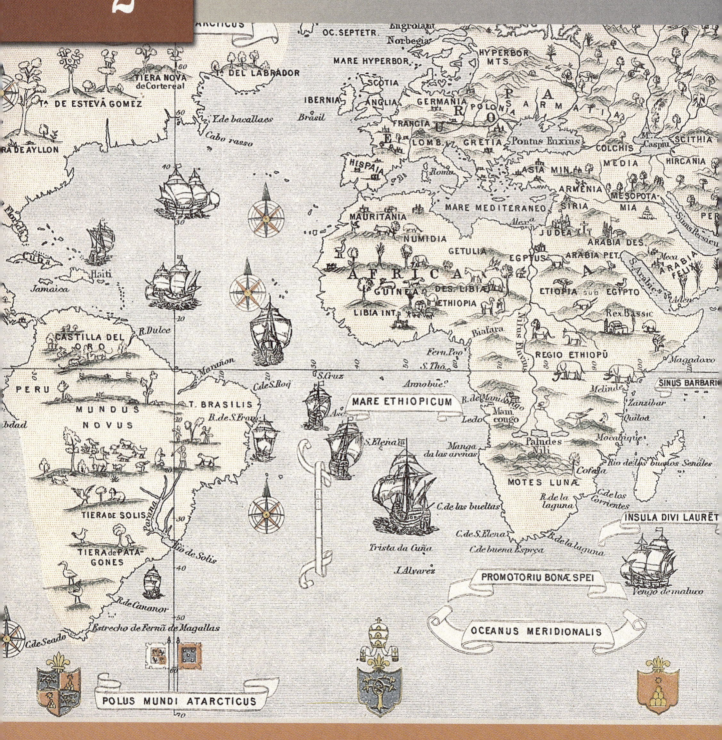

Europe's Quest for Empire in America

"What is it for?" inquired Queen Isabella peevishly in 1492.

A member of the royal court, who had just presented her with the first printed grammar of the Spanish language, was taken aback for a moment.

"Your majesty," responded the donor, with all the presence a courtier could muster, "language is the perfect instrument of empire."

Although the young queen could not have known it in 1492—the year Spain's monarchs sponsored Christopher Columbus's historic quest for a water route to the "Indies"—Spanish names were destined to appear in all corners of the globe. Soon the words of the Spanish empire would be stamped on places called "San Salvador" in the Caribbean, "La Florida" in southeast North America, and "California" on its western coast.

This quest for empire, dramatized by the startling "discovery" of America in 1492, reflected a longer process of European expansionism. Unlike most Native American peoples who exploited local natural resources, Europeans had probed beyond their own continent for centuries, seeking commerce, commodities, and technology from distant lands. This interest in expansion stemmed in part from the lack of a self-sufficient economy in Europe, and from the desire to obtain valuable products from Asia and Africa, such as spices to preserve food.

Geographic expansion also expressed a competitive impulse as Europe's Christian monarchs undertook military and religious crusades to end Muslim domination of the Mediterranean world. Indeed, European Christians assumed that God approved their worldly conquests and they needed no further justification for waging wars against the "infidels." Expansionism also reflected persistent rivalries within Europe, particularly conflicts among the monarchs about national wealth, political prestige, and religious truth. After the Protestant Reformation shattered the religious uniformity of Europe in the early 1500s, Catholics and Protestants competed aggressively to expand the "true" religion around the world.

Expansionism inevitably involved cultural confrontation. Just as the Europeans who first penetrated the Western Hemisphere carried cultural and biological baggage (metal swords, infectious diseases) that transformed Native American life, so the natural resources of the Western Hemisphere (gold, silver, tobacco, maize, animal skins, human labor, and the often-fatal syphilis bacterium) changed European society. The importation of gold and silver from America to Spain, for example, produced an inflation of prices in western Europe, which encouraged landlords to raise rents. Many poor agricultural workers lost their homes and wandered the countryside in search of work. Believing that Europe had a surplus population, some writers advocated colonization to ease the misery of the poor. Yet, ironically, the first cargo of workers to cross the Atlantic in 1495 sailed from west to east. These were the enslaved Caribbeans who were shipped to Spain.

European contacts with the peoples of Africa stimulated similar exchanges of commerce and culture and produced similar problems. Trade for west African peppers, gold, and slaves enriched both European and African rulers and the merchants who transacted overseas business. But the result was the enslavement of vast numbers of Africans, of whom more than 10 million were shipped across the Atlantic to populate America and exploit its resources. The overwhelming majority went to South America and the Caribbean; about half a million—5 percent of the total—landed in North America.

Native Americans, Europeans, and Africans thus shared an intricate relationship in America's development. Biological differences among them included skin color, facial characteristics, blood enzymes, and antibodies against various diseases. But intermarriage and sexual relations, voluntary or forced, soon diluted the genetic purity of all races. Among this multitude of groups, moreover, differences in social structure, culture, and political organization could be matched by innumerable similarities. Hereditary monarchies, for example, existed in England, Mexico, and the Kongo; meanwhile, trading empires flourished among the Dutch of northern Europe, the matriarchal Iroquois who inhabited the northern Adirondack regions in North America, and the Ibibio-speaking Efiks of Biafra in western Africa. Yet, in America after 1492, the steady expansion of European political power over Native Americans and Africans created unequal relationships. Political institutions that were imposed by European kings, bishops, and merchants limited the cultural independence of other peoples, as well as of European men and women who lacked a political voice.

The Cultures of West Africa

Africans shared with Europeans and Native Americans an enthusiasm for commerce. The diversity of African societies had encouraged trade for centuries. In the region between the Senegal and Gambia rivers, for example, one of the first areas reached by the Portuguese during the 15th century, inhabitants of Mali had long exchanged "clothes of fine cotton" for salt brought by coastal traders. Although Africans spoke some 800 distinct languages, many had related grammars and vocabulary that were mutually intelligible, and politically separate groups often participated in trade networks along the rivers. Even when groups were linguistically diverse, such as the people of Upper Guinea, their shared Islamic influences and geographical proximity facilitated trade. In Lower Guinea, the Yoruba language and traditions prevailed on the coast, while those of Benin dominated the interior, in each case establishing a common culture for trade. On the Angola coast, by contrast, similar Bantu languages encouraged cultural homogeneity, but strong political rivalries produced continuing conflict and warfare.

A World of Spirits

Christian and Muslim traders often sought to gain the religious conversion of African "heathens" to facilitate commercial transactions, and some African leaders, such as the king of the Fetu, became Christians to gain access to western goods. But most west Africans resisted such efforts, because they already held religious views that acknowledged a supreme being, or creator, and a world of spirits that included the living and the dead, plants and animals, and even inanimate objects. Although some groups, like the Ashanti, built shrines to the high god, Africans generally revered the lesser spirits, particularly those of ancestors and elders. Central to the African world view was respect for the past and for the founders of the lineage clans with which each individual identified. Like Europeans, Africans named their children after grandparents and other elders who defined their place in the clan.

West African religions linked individuals with ancient ancestors as well as recently deceased relatives. According to African beliefs, such predecessors remained intimately involved in the affairs of this world, for good or evil. Communication with the spirits of the dead required knowledgeable priests, skilled in magic and medicine, who made offerings to these ancestors. Like Native American shamans, these spiritual guides used amulets, charms, and herbs to negotiate with the spirit world, to counter witchcraft, and to treat those afflicted by evil ghosts. Centuries later, some Africans in America placed glass bottles in trees to ward off bad spirits.

West African religious ceremonies involved intense musical expression, including dancing, clapping, drumming, and singing. Africans believed that each spirit responded to personal melodies or rhythms. Among the common elements of west African cultures was the circular counterclockwise dance (following the direction of the sun in the Southern Hemisphere), which appeared in the rituals of the life cycle associated with birth, coming of age, and death. Such beliefs, shared by many different cultures, would endure in America and

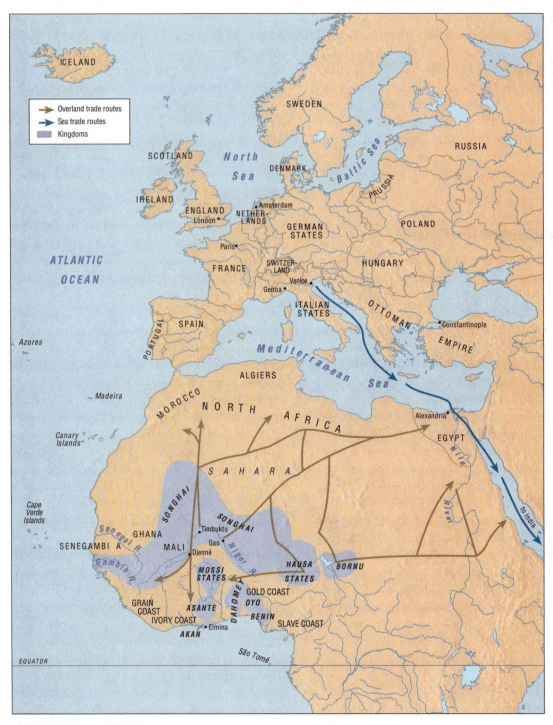

Africa's Trade Routes, 15th Century

establish common grounds for diverse Africans to form an African American identity.

Political Diversity and Commercial Rivalry

Despite their shared spiritual universe, west African societies remained politically fragmented. Some were little more than a cluster of villages claiming a common ancestry and a central place where elders met to settle disputes. Others developed broader geographical ties and emerged as kingdoms and empires. Most Africans lived in decentralized political units with a population ranging from 3,000 to 30,000. This small scale underscored the importance of belonging to a particular place—having a sense of home ground—where, upon death, a person's spirit was believed to return. Most west African societies were hierarchical, controlled by a single ruler or ruling family with extensive power. Yet political diversity encouraged competition between villages and regional groups for trade. Commercial rivalry, in turn, provoked persistent warfare, even before the arrival of European merchants whose desire for African commodities, including slaves, intensified competition.

Slavery and Africa

Long before they had contact with Europeans, many African states accepted slavery as a social institution. The Ashanti, for example, used five different words to describe degrees of servitude. A criminal might be sentenced to slavery or a debtor might settle a payment through voluntary enslavement; more frequently, prisoners of war became slaves of their captors. Usually slavery implied some type of kinship between owner and captive, a relationship involving mutual responsibilities that did not necessarily pass on to the children of slaves. As in many Native American societies, a prisoner might be adopted by the captor and permitted to intermarry and raise children who participated in community life. Yet such a person would remain subordinate within the captor's family. African slaves also retained basic rights to earn wealth and own property, even to inherit their owner's assets.

Slavery and long-term servitude flourished in African societies because cultural values permitted limited opportunities for individuals to acquire wealth. As in Native American cultures, African law generally rejected private ownership of land. Rather, land belonged to the state or community and was appropriated according to its use by particular households. But a family could increase its economic productivity, and thus improve its wealth, status, and power, by using slaves to tend larger fields or weave more cloth. Often slaves captured in war might be conscripted into the armies of their conquerors, and some were employed as public officials. Rather than joining a family or clan, public servants became slaves of the ruling household.

Because slaves might easily escape to their home countries, African leaders often took the precaution of trading their captives to more distant places. Before Europeans arrived in west Africa, a substantial overland trade in gold and slaves linked that region with the Muslim states of northern Africa. In fact, the very expansion of trade created a demand for labor to produce commodities and transport them to market, a demand that stimulated the sale and purchase of human beings.

European Involvement in the Slave Trade

European involvement in the Atlantic slave trade built upon African precedents and required the cooperation of African merchants. Although early European slave traders simply kidnapped Africans from coastal areas, by 1450 Europeans generally purchased African slaves from previous African

TABLE 2.1	
Portuguese Slave Imports, 1450–1870	
1450–1500	33,500
1500–1600	241,400
1600–1700	560,000
1700–1810	1,909,700
1810–1870	1,445,400
	4,190,000

Source: James A. Rawley, *The Transatlantic Slave Trade*, New York, 1981.

owners, who acquired slaves specifically for the purpose of resale.

The Portuguese first acquired African slaves by purchase from caravans heading north, effectively diverting the human traffic from the Sahara to the Atlantic coast. Even though the European market for slaves remained limited, the Portuguese traded about 2,500 per year during the 15th century; by 1500, Portuguese exports totaled 33,500 slaves. During the next century, the Portuguese traded 240,000 slaves. And, despite increasing competition from other European nations, Portuguese purchases exceeded half a million slaves during the 17th century and doubled again in the next hundred years (Table 2.1).

The most obvious change wrought by Europe's entry into the slave trade lay in the racial and religious differences between white Christian owners and black non-Christian slaves. The growing market for slaves also intensified competition among African slave catchers. "Every day people are kidnapped and enslaved," complained the Kongo's King Afonso in 1525, "even members of the king's family." Like earlier Muslim slave traders, the Catholic church accepted slavery as a fair punish-

ment for prisoners taken in a "just" war. Now African leaders fought wars simply to acquire slaves for Europeans.

By treating African slaves as economic commodities, rather than as family members, European traders could disregard traditional cultural restraints on the treatment and status of slaves. Of course, it was in the economic interests of merchants to protect their investments. But a growing demand for slave labor greatly increased the profitability of the slave trade, so that Atlantic merchants could focus on gross benefits rather than the condition of individuals. In any event, the journey of slaves from Africa to Europe, to the Atlantic islands, and eventually, for most slaves, to the lands of the Western Hemisphere—the so-called Middle Passage—proved extremely brutal.

The Ordeal of Enslavement

During the four centuries in which the Atlantic slave trade flourished, 10 to 12 million Africans were forcibly uprooted from their homes and shipped to America. Mortality rates, which varied according to the length of voyage (typically from one month to six weeks, or more), ranged from 5 to 20 percent. So appalling were conditions aboard slave ships that even European crews died at high rates. Tightly packed in suffocating quarters below decks, shackled slaves lacked fresh air and sufficient space to lie on their backs. Slave women, fewer in number, were sometimes permitted to remain on the decks, but fell prey to sexual assault by European sailors. Faced with dehydration, malnutrition, and such diseases as smallpox, dysentery, measles, scurvy, yaws, and worms, even the strongest slaves experienced profound suffering during the passage to America.

"What heart could be so hard," wrote Gomes Eannes de Zurara, a courtier who witnessed the arrival of the first African slaves in Portugal in 1444, "as not to be pierced with piteous feelings to see that company? For some kept their heads low, and their faces bathed in tears, looking one upon another. Others stood groaning very dolorously, looking up to the height of heaven, fixing their eyes upon it, crying out loudly, as if asking help from the Father of nature; others struck their faces with the palms of their hands, throwing themselves at full length upon the ground; while others made lamentations in the manner of a dirge, after the custom of their country."

Three hundred years later, an Ibo man named Olaudah Equiano described the same sense of fear and despair, believing that he "had gotten into a world of bad spirits, and that they were going to kill me." Observing a large copper pot boiling with water "and a multitude of black people of every description chained together, every one of their countenances expressing dejection," he was convinced that he would be eaten by the crew. Some slaves were stunned into melancholy by the ordeal and refused to eat; others jumped overboard to die and thus facilitate the return of their spirits to Africa before they lost their way. Still others attacked their captors, which led ship captains to keep the men (seldom the women) in chains through the entire passage. Once landed, the weakened slaves endured additional indignities, such as branding, whipping, and separation from family and friends.

Sugar and Slaves

Despite the high death toll of the Atlantic slave trade, profits in America promised to more than offset any economic losses. Within only two decades of Columbus's first voyage to America, Spain's colonial settlements in the Caribbean were returning great wealth by satisfying Europe's sweet tooth, the craving for sugar. Portugal and Spain first developed profitable sugar manufac-

An Ibo man named Olaudah Equiano was convinced that he would be eaten by the crew.

turing on the Atlantic islands. The formation of colonies in America merely increased the economic opportunities. Indeed, Spain's Caribbean colonies of Santo Domingo, Jamaica, and Puerto Rico and Portugal's Brazil offered unprecedented profits for European sugar investors, but only if the American plantations could find an adequate supply of labor.

Having already developed the slave trade in west Africa, Portugal and Spain looked there for a labor force to work the sugar plantations in America. Although Spain's Catholic monarchs promulgated many laws against Native American slavery, few Spaniards objected to the enslavement of Africans. Since the Middle Ages, Spanish law had permitted the enslavement of Muslims and other "heathen," and Muslims in turn had seized Europeans to become slaves. Beginning in the 15th century, both Portugal and Spain had used African slaves to manufacture sugar for decades. Ironically, the Africans' immunity to yellow fever and malaria, due to a genetic factor known as sickle-cell hemoglobin, made them hardier tropical workers than either Native Americans or Europeans. By the early 1500s, the Caribbean islands had become a profitable market for African slaves; by the end of that century, the demand for sugar workers had spread from Spain's island plantations to Portugal's Brazil.

The economics of sugar production intensified the misery of African workers. In 1530, in a typical mix of cultures, 3,000 African slaves worked on sugar plantations in Puerto Rico, but only 327 Europeans inhabited the island. The vastly outnumbered Europeans had little personal interest in their laborers. The slave population was overwhelmingly male and not expected to live long. But rather than seeking a sexual balance to encourage natural reproduction, sugar planters found it much cheaper to import new slaves to replace those who died. Nor did the planters wish to waste profitable sugar acreage by growing food, preferring to import dried fish and other commodities, even though the resulting poor diet increased mortality rates. High sugar profits easily offset the labor costs. For the next three centuries, sugar and slaves were inextricably connected, enriching European investors while consuming African workers.

The Origins of European Expansionism

European expansion of the slave trade was inseparable from Europe's political expansion into the Western Hemisphere. During the 15th and 16th centuries, several factors stimulated exploration, trade, and colonization beyond Europe's borders. This expansion first emerged among the centralized monarchies, which were capable of expending large national resources to finance overseas endeavors. That was one reason why Portugal and Spain initiated colonial development, why England and the Netherlands, delayed by domestic upheavals, came later, and why other countries, such as Italy and Germany, barely participated in the great adventure. Colonies, in other words, were an extension of national power.

Successful expansion also depended on new commercial practices, which could produce the capital and credit to support such expensive and risky undertakings. Overseas investments initially promised to add to private and national wealth. In addition, the search for new trade and new

lands expressed an intellectual curiosity associated with a cultural movement known as the Renaissance, a rebirth of learning during the 15th and 16th centuries. The desire for more knowledge about the world, for technological innovations, and for new experiences created the mental impulse that made European expansion possible. Trade and colonies rewarded those who made daring choices.

Finally, these expansionist values presumed the absolute superiority of western European culture. "Colonies degenerate," advised an English promoter of overseas settlement, "when the colonists imitate and embrace the habits, customs, and practices of the natives." Europe remained the standard by which explorers and colonizers measured the peoples of the world. European modes of thought—European ideas about food, clothing, and shelter; European notions of time, place, and justice—defined their relationships with the inhabitants of other parts of the world.

Western Europe Takes the First Steps

Geographical location prompted Portugal and Spain to embark on the road to empire in the 15th century. Both nations had competed for centuries with Islamic peoples on the Iberian peninsula and in North Africa for political dominance and control of Mediterranean trade. Religious differences between Catholic and Islamic rivals added intellectual and emotional intensity to European expansionism. Both Spain and Portugal had participated in religious crusades to free Jerusalem from its Islamic occupants. These endeavors had introduced Europeans to valuable commodities from Asia: silk, spices, gold, sugar, and precious stones. But commerce to Asia was dominated by merchants in the Italian city-states, such as Venice, who operated between western Europe and the Middle East and made immense profits as middlemen. Because of the Italian control of this trade, Asian products remained scarce and expensive in western Europe.

To break the Italian trade monopoly, the monarchs of Portugal and Spain sought an alternative route to the riches of Asia. Portugal's Prince Henry the Navigator, a visionary empire builder, also wanted to bypass the Muslim merchants of Morocco, who controlled trade with sub-Saharan west Africa, particularly to gain access to the celebrated gold fields and the "grains of paradise" (peppers) that grew on the Atlantic coast. During the early 1400s, Portugal and Spain began to explore and settle the Atlantic islands—the Canaries, Madeiras, and Azores. In the mid-1400s, Portugal occupied the uninhabited Madeiras and Azores, and Spain seized the Canary Islands, enslaving the native population. Taking advantage of the fertile lands, both countries established sugar plantations and wine production and imported African slaves as a labor force. Meanwhile, Portuguese sailors advanced along the west coast of Africa, reaching the Senegal River ("river of gold") and Cape Verde in 1444. By the end of the century, Portuguese navigators had rounded the Cape of Good Hope at the southern tip of Africa and found a direct water route to the Indian Ocean.

The Portuguese on the African Coast

This gradual expansion along the African coast introduced Europeans to vast commercial opportunity. Portuguese maps described the shoreline by its commodities: the Grain Coast, the Ivory Coast, the Gold Coast, the Slave Coast. Portugal's success came from superior navigational technology, including new ocean-going vessels, such as the speedy caravel, which sailed efficiently into the head winds; an improved box compass, borrowed from Arab sailors; the astrolabe to measure latitude; and sophisticated charts of ocean currents and maps of the Atlantic coast.

Such technological advantages allowed the Portuguese to attack west African shores and raid coastal communities for gold, pepper, and slaves. But although European ships could dominate the high seas, Africans successfully defended coastal waters from the invaders. The tropical disease environment caused high mortality among Europeans, further discouraging military raids. Unlike the Atlantic islands, west Africa could not be conquered and settled by Europeans. (Thanks to a lucky accident, however, Portugal's expansion toward Africa did lead to a single colony in America. Blown off course in a storm in 1500, a Portuguese crew landed in South America, establishing claims to what later became Brazil.)

Unable to conquer Africa, Portugal's empire consisted of a network of trading posts. Africans participated equally in this coastal trade, collecting tribute and customs duties for local transactions. African preferences for European textiles, metal products (iron knives, copper bowls), shells, and beads—items which were already available in Africa—underscore the voluntary nature of this trade. To conduct business, European visitors had to follow African protocol, bring gifts to rulers, obtain permission, and pay taxes.

While African rulers negotiated commercial arrangements with Portuguese officials, they also conducted business unofficially with private traders, known by the Portuguese word *lancados*, who settled in small numbers along the coast. Intermarrying with African women, these Afro-Portuguese traders and their mulatto descendants served as intermediaries in coastal commerce and came to dominate the local markets. They established trade networks along the African river systems that led into the interior of the continent. By exchanging European goods for commodities that previously had gone overland by caravan to Morocco, the Portuguese accomplished their plan to break Muslim control of the African trade. By the

16th century, Portugal had extended its commercial transactions into east Africa on the Indian Ocean and to the islands still further east in Asia.

Spain Challenges the Portuguese Empire

Portugal's burgeoning empire—the sugar plantations on the Atlantic islands, the spice trade near Senegal, and a thriving slave trading center on the island of Sao Tome—brought immense profits and excited Europe's interest in exotic commodities. Among the most ambitious dreamers of expanding global trade was a Genoese mariner, Christopher Columbus, who had sailed three times under the Portuguese flag to the Guinea coast. Like all educated sailors of his time, Columbus knew the world was round and speculated that he could find a water route to the Asian markets by sailing west across the Atlantic. But unlike most geographers, he drastically underestimated the circumference of the globe. The Portuguese court, content with its commercial success, promptly rejected Columbus's plans. He took them to Spain, where he obtained royal approval from Queen Isabella and King Ferdinand to launch three ships in search of Asian markets.

Columbus was unaware that other European sailors had preceded his western voyage. According to archeological evidence and oral tradition, Norse explorers led by Leif Erickson had landed in "Vinland" (today's Newfoundland, Canada) in the 11th century, but made no effort to build a settlement. Four hundred years later, Basque sailors had probably discovered the rich cod fisheries off the Newfoundland coast and may have built smokehouses and traded with local inhabitants. Such contact remained haphazard because Europeans lacked an incentive to develop trade or settlement on such isolated terrain. Columbus's promise of access to Asian commodities, by contrast, appealed to an existing demand. Indeed, in the decade prior to Columbus's voyage, merchants in Bristol, England, had sent exploratory vessels westward across the Atlantic toward a place they called "Brasil," though the voyages proved futile.

The Search for Wealth

Columbus's four voyages to America followed the pattern of Portuguese exploration and commerce. Like his first employers, Columbus's Spanish sponsors were interested less in establishing colonies than in opening trade. Soon after landing in what he thought were the "Indies" (really the island of San Salvador in the Bahamas), Columbus began to search for valuable commodities, especially gold, and for places to build fortified trading posts like those he had visited in west Africa.

As for the native inhabitants he encountered, Columbus quickly tested the market advantages. On the very first day of contact, he recorded giving the Taino natives red caps and glass beads "in which they took so much pleasure." Later, the Taino reciprocated with parrots, cotton threads, and spears, for which the Europeans exchanged small glass beads and bells. Columbus was obviously disappointed by their limited resources, describing them as "people very poor in everything." They had no iron and knew nothing of arms; when the Spanish showed them swords the Taino grasped the blades with their hands and cut themselves. Yet even in these deficiencies, Columbus perceived commercial opportunities. "They ought to be good servants," he wrote in his journal. "Our Lord pleasing, I will carry off six of them at my departure. . . in order that they may learn to speak." When Columbus departed for Spain, he carried thirty Taino aboard ship; only seven survived the voyage.

Having discovered no obvious wealth, Columbus was already envisioning another type of com-

"They ought to be good servants. Our Lord pleasing, I will carry off six of them at my departure . . . in order that they may learn to speak."

mercial enterprise, similar to the Portuguese and Spanish settlements of the Atlantic islands. The natives "are fit to be ordered about and made to work, plant, and do everything else that may be needed," he assured the Spanish monarchs, "and build towns and be taught our customs, and go about clothed." After receiving a royal reception in Spain, Columbus began to prepare for a second voyage. Instead of viewing America as a unique place with a distinctive environment, the Spanish planned to remake the Western Hemisphere in the image of Europe. Among the cargo on the second voyage would be horses, cows, goats, sheep, and pigs; seeds for vegetables and fruit trees; and wheat to serve as a food staple. New Spain would become an extension of the Old World.

News of Columbus's voyage aroused Portuguese protests against intrusion into its empire. But in 1493 the two Catholic monarchies accepted mediation from the Pope, who drew a demarcation line dividing the heathen world between the two kingdoms. In 1494, the Treaty of Tordesillas gave control of the African and Asian trade to Portugal and confirmed Spain's claims to most of the Western Hemisphere. The boundary line left a large portion of South America to Portugal, the area later claimed because of the accidental landfall in 1500. Other European nations, not parties to the treaty, simply ignored it.

Spain's Early Colonization

On his second voyage to the Caribbean in 1493, Columbus brought 1,500 Spanish settlers to His-paniola in the Caribbean and planned to establish regular trade with Spain, including the sale of Native American slaves, whom he described as cannibals. Resistance from the native Caribs resulted in the first struggle between Americans and Europeans, which the Spanish won. Columbus subsequently gave one captured woman to his friend Cuneo, who recorded the ensuing rape with clinical amusement. By 1515, the Spanish had planted settlements on the islands of Puerto Rico, Jamaica, and Cuba.

To encourage development of these settlements, the Spanish crown established a system of forced labor, known as *encomienda*, and gave private citizens rights to use both the land and the labor of the inhabitants. As an *encomienda*, an entire native village might be assigned to work for a single landowner. Intended to Christianize and civilize the native peoples, the system instead brought calamity, forcing the Native Americans to perform hard labor in agriculture, mining, road building, and public works. As a result of overwork and vulnerability to European diseases, the Native American labor force began to decline. Of a Caribbean population that numbered about 1 million in 1492, fewer than 50,000 survived 30 years later.

Some Catholic missionaries, most famously the friar Bartholome de Las Casas, protested the mistreatment of native peoples. The Spanish monarchy shared those concerns and rejected the enslavement of Native Americans, viewing them instead as subjects to be converted to the Catholic faith. But the royal authority could not prevent abuses in distant America. In 1530, two Spanish judges reported that Native Americans "treat slaves as relations, while the Christians treat them as dogs."

Spaniards continued to seek easy wealth. Still believing that the newfound lands were a part of Asia, explorers embarked on numerous voyages to find a water route to the Indies. In 1513, Vasco de Balboa crossed the Isthmus of Panama and became

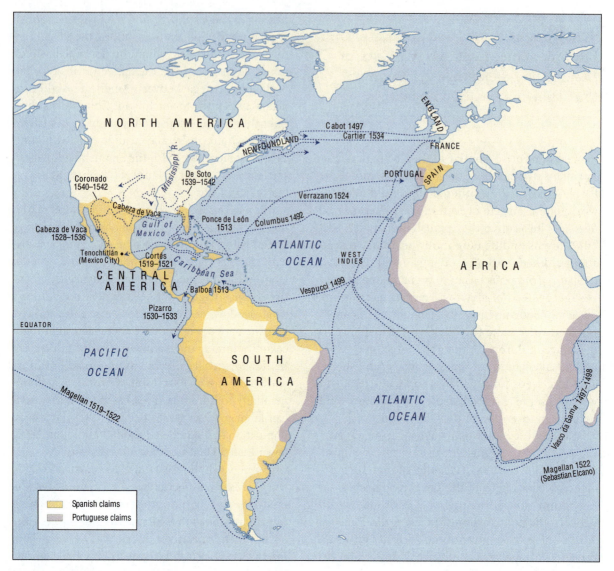

European Explorations, 1492–1542

the first European to glimpse the Pacific Ocean. But the first explorer to suggest the existence of a separate continent was Amerigo Vespucci, a Florentine navigator who sailed under Spanish flags; by the second decade of the century, he had placed his name on maps of the New World. Yet only after Ferdinand Magellan sailed through the straits of South America into the Pacific and proceeded to circumnavigate the globe between 1519 and 1522 did Europeans generally understand that America was a separate continent with potential riches far more valuable than the spice trade with Asia.

Other Spanish adventurers, members of the lower aristocracy who became known as *conquistadores* (conquerors) came to America to find wealth by plundering the more affluent Native American societies. In 1519, a Spanish official, Hernan Cortes, led an expedition to the coast of Mexico, where the native peoples told of the vast wealth of their Aztec rulers. Forming alliances with these dissatisfied subjects and benefiting by the Aztecs' belief that the Spaniards were mythical white gods, Cortes overpowered the Aztec capital at Tenochtitlan. The Spanish conquest succeeded because of some technological advantages, particularly European guns and soldiers who rode on horses, animals previously unknown in America. But the decisive factor was the presence of a microscopic virus, smallpox, which devastated Mexico's population. "The streets, squares, houses, and courts were filled with bodies," said one observer. "Even Cortes was sick from the stench in his nostrils."

The splendor of the Aztec metropolis, with its elaborate aqueducts, silver and gold statuary, and masonry buildings, astonished the invaders. "Some of our soldiers even asked whether the things that we saw were not a dream," declared one of the victors. Cortes proceeded to confiscate the precious metals and jewels, destroy the temples where the Atzecs had conducted human sacrifices, and enslave the survivors. By 1521, the Aztec emperor Moctezuma was dead. Out of the ashes of the capital, Spain's Mexico City would rise. And the quest for gold continued. In 1531, Francisco Pizarro led an expedition against the Incas of Peru, accomplishing the conquest of this rich empire with the aid of European diseases.

Competition for North America

As Spain extracted great wealth from Central and South America and founded a sugar empire in the Caribbean, the hope of finding precious minerals lured explorers into the unknown territories of what is now the United States. Spain's interest in North America also emboldened other Europeans—French, Dutch, and English—to seek similar acquisitions. Like the Spanish and Portuguese, these interlopers searched primarily for trade advantages, particularly a sea route to Asia, and only belatedly recognized the economic and political benefits of colonization. Viewing America as a map rather than a landscape, they drew artificial boundaries, made extravagant territorial claims, and disregarded the prior rights of the Native peoples.

Spain Explores North America

Despite fabulous tales told by Native Americans to Spanish explorers, none of the *conquistadores* found the mythical cities of gold in North America. Their efforts did inspire great sagas of adventure. Ponce de Leon, for example, landed on the Florida coast in 1513, seeking gold and the "fountain of youth," but met resistance from the native Calusas and withdrew without finding any treasure. When he returned eight years later, the Calusas again repelled the invasion. Later Spanish *conquistadores* raided the South Carolina coast for Native American slaves, and Spaniards built houses and a church among the Guales in Georgia in 1526, but soon abandoned the colony. Exploratory voyages by Juan Cabrillo along the Pacific coast during the 1540s extended Spain's claim to the western shores of North America.

By the mid-16th century, Spanish explorers were penetrating the interior of the northern continent. "They wore coats of iron, and war bonnets of metal, and carried for weapons short canes that spit fire and made thunder," remembered the Zuni people who lived in what is now New Mexico. In 1540, the arrival of a Spanish expedition on horseback, led by Francisco Vasquez de Coronado, prompted a Zuni attack with bows and arrows. The invaders retaliated with gunpowder, enabling Coronado to occupy the Native village he called "Cibola," which consisted of adobe apartment-like structures. The party proceeded to explore surrounding regions, including the Grand Canyon, but found no gold and abandoned the search in 1541. Meanwhile, an expedition under Hernando De Soto marched from Florida to the Mississippi River, plundering Native villages, raping, maiming, and murdering with impunity. Seeking gold, these campaigns acquired little systematic information about North American geography, except that the interior of the continent was vast and diverse.

Rival Claims to North America

"Without settlement," warned a 16th-century Spanish official, "there is no good conquest." Focusing on the plunder of Native American societies, fabled water routes to the Indies, and the mythical cities of gold, Spain claimed rights to all of North America, but failed to establish colonial settlements to protect its authority. Soon other countries arrived to challenge Spanish claims. Like Spain, these European rivals sought wealth through theft or trade with Native Americans rather than the creation of permanent settlements. During the 16th century, most European activity in North America involved temporary territorial encroachment and military raids. Looking at America as a map, European soldier-explorers enabled their countries to claim ownership of areas that were already inhabited by other people, mostly Native Americans. Possession of those lands was another matter.

Since Spanish treasure ships sailing from Mexico passed close to Florida's shores, French pirates used the peninsula as a base of attack. But the first

efforts at French settlement appeared on the coast of what is today South Carolina in 1562. As French Protestants, known as *Huguenots*, sought refuge from religious persecution at home, an expedition of 150 men built a fort at "one of the greatest and fairest havens in the world." Two years later, another group of French Huguenots landed at Fort Caroline on the St. John's River in Florida.

Responding to these territorial threats, Spain sent Pedro Menendez to start a settlement at what is now St. Augustine, Florida, in 1565. Believing that Huguenots and Native Americans "held similar beliefs, probably Satanic in origin," Menendez decided to become "free from this wicked sect." Two weeks after landing, he attacked the French, killing even those who surrendered. The next year, Spain eliminated the French settlement in South Carolina. While continuing to search for precious metals, Menendez planted small garrisons around Florida, most of which failed to survive. By the end of the century, St. Augustine stood as a lonely outpost of the Spanish empire.

While Spain and France engaged in petty warfare on the Atlantic coast, 2,000 miles to the west in the desert country near what is now Albuquerque, a Spanish official named Juan de Onate stood among the native Pueblo peoples in 1598 and invited them to become subjects of Spain in the new province of New Mexico. The Spanish hoped that the settlement would lead to the discovery of silver mines and provide access to the Pacific Ocean, an expectation that soon clashed with the geographical reality. Spanish oppression of the Pueblos also provoked retaliatory attacks, which brought even harsher retribution. But limited natural resources and the difficulty of survival in the dry environment discouraged further settlement. Onate was recalled to Mexico in disgrace, partly for abusing the Pueblos, and the outpost was left to Franciscan missionaries to Christianize the natives. Spain's North American colonies would grow slowly during the next two centuries.

The French Seek Permanent Settlement

While Spain concentrated on the southern areas of North America, close to the colonies of Central America, France tried to build permanent colonies in the Northeast. French exploration began with the 1524 voyage of Giovanni da Verazzano, who sailed along the Atlantic coast seeking the "Northwest Passage," a direct water route to Asia. Ten years later, Jacques Cartier sailed around Newfoundland, then entered the St. Lawrence River, believing he had found the elusive waterway. In 1541, the French erected a fortified settlement in Canada, but conflicts with the local peoples and outbreaks of disease ended the experiment. Yet, by 1600, French fishermen were exploiting the cod waters off Newfoundland, while fur traders tapped the market for beaver skins along the St. Lawrence.

Seeking an extensive trade network with the Native Americans for fish and furs, Samuel de Champlain founded the first permanent French settlement at Quebec in 1608. From this base, French explorers, traders, and religious missionaries followed the river routes inland to acquire the precious beaver furs and to redeem the souls of the local Hurons. Later in the century, French explorers traced the Mississippi River to its mouth in the Gulf of Mexico and built trade networks that extended through the Great Lakes and the Mississippi valley. Forming commercial alliances with native inhabitants and accepting intermarriage between Europeans and Native Americans, the French established their dominance of eastern Canada and the hinterland even though their numbers remained fairly small. As in west Africa, where the *lancado* offspring of interracial marriage conducted the slave trade between Europeans and African rulers, in French America, a class of half-French, half-Native Americans, called *metis,* served as intermediaries of French-Native culture and trade.

The Dutch in America

Competition for empire also attracted the Low Countries of northern Europe. Superiority in shipbuilding, navigation, banking, and military aggression enabled the small Dutch nation to emerge as a powerful commercial rival. Having rebelled from the Spanish empire in 1580, the Dutch created the East India Company, which successfully challenged Portuguese business in Asia, while the Dutch West India Company broke the Portuguese slave trade monopoly in Africa. Lacking sufficient population to colonize extensively, the Dutch built trading communities on the African Gold Coast, on islands in the Indian Ocean, in Brazil, in Barbados in the Caribbean, and along the Hudson river (named for Henry Hudson, who explored the region in search of the Northwest Passage in 1609).

Planting a town named New Amsterdam at the foot of Manhattan Island in 1624, and a trading post at Fort Nassau (now Albany) in the Hudson valley, the Dutch West India Company competed with the French for control of the northern fur trade. Limited by a small population, the company tried to attract settlers by offering large land grants (called "patroonships") to investors who, in turn, promised to transport tenant farmers to the colony. But few colonists wanted to be tenants when free land abounded. Yet, because the Dutch trading empire reached across Europe, Africa, Asia, and the Caribbean, the New Netherlands colony attracted a multiethnic population, including Jews, Catholics, Africans (free and slave), and other European nationalities. Yet the establishment of a Swedish trading settlement at the mouth of the Delaware River alarmed the Dutch leaders, who sent a war party to annex the region to New Netherlands. During the 1640s and 1650s, persistent wars with Native Americans accentuated the colony's vulnerability. Despite economic success, the Dutch could not prevent the settlement of Long Island by English colonists nor defend themselves against the English navy.

England Reaches for America

England was late in entering the race for empire in America. Although King Henry VII sponsored a voyage of exploration to North America by John Cabot in 1497, just five years after Columbus's first voyage, dynastic problems during the 16th century distracted England from pursuing colonization. When Henry VIII broke with the Roman Catholic church in 1534 in order to divorce his wife, Catherine of Aragon, he placed England on the side of Protestants who denied the spiritual leadership of the Catholic pope and refused to accept Spain's claims to America.

The English monarchy also encouraged foreign trade. By the mid-16th century, English merchants were forming privately owned "joint-stock companies," the predecessor of the modern corporation, to pool their investments and share the risks and profits of overseas enterprise. By 1600, English trade with Spain and the West Indies brought great profits to adventurous merchants. Although foreign trade encouraged English landowners to shift to wool production, thereby displacing many agricultural workers, merchants claimed that commercial profits would benefit the entire nation. Influential writers such as Richard Hakluyt, who wrote a *Discourse Concerning Western Planting* in 1584, supported colonization as a way of increasing foreign trade while relieving England of its landless population.

Interest in overseas colonies aggravated the rivalry between England and Spain. The conflict

The Roanoke colonists wasted their energy searching for gold instead of planting fields.

flared during the reign of Elizabeth I (1558–1603), who supported attacks on Spanish shipping in the Atlantic. During the 1560s, the buccaneer John Hawkins violated Portugal's trade monopoly in west Africa to acquire slaves and then ignored Spain's commercial prohibitions to sell his cargo in the Caribbean. Hawkins's cousin, Francis Drake, also raided Spanish treasure ships during the 1570s, in one voyage burning Florida's St. Augustine, in another capturing Spanish gold ships in the Pacific, refitting on the California coast near San Francisco, and proceeding to circumnavigate the world (1577–1580).

In defying Spain, Elizabeth also supported colonization in North America during the 1580s under the auspices of Humphrey Gilbert and his half-brother Walter Raleigh. With a royal charter from the queen, Raleigh planted the first English colony on Roanoke Island off the coast of North Carolina in 1585. The artist John White, who accompanied the settlers, produced drawings to document Native American life, while the naturalist Thomas Hariot wrote detailed descriptions of the vegetation and animals. But the Roanoke colonists wasted their energy searching for gold instead of planting fields. When Francis Drake visited the colony the next year, the settlers abandoned the effort and returned to England. Raleigh sent a second expedition to Roanoke in 1587, though once again the colonists quarreled with the local tribes and imperiled their food supply.

While the Roanoke colonists clung precariously to their island outpost, England lost contact with the settlement. In 1588, Spain responded to English

The English artist John White visited Roanoke Island in 1585 and drew careful illustrations of the Native people. The circular palisaded village provided protection from enemies and suggested a preference for circles rather than squares.

attacks in America by sending its fleet, known as the *Armada,* to war against England. But in a remarkable victory, the English navy defeated the Armada, opening the way for colonial development in North America. But, because of warfare with Spain, no ships sailed from England to Roanoke until 1590. When English ships reached the colony, they found no settlers, only the word CROATOAN, the name of a nearby island, scratched on the bark of a tree. Whether the English had been killed, died of natural causes, or joined a Native community remains unknown. But the failure of the "lost colony" demonstrated the importance of maintaining contact between colonial outposts and the home coun-

try and providing adequate resources in planting overseas settlements.

The Ideology of Empire

"Religion stands on tip toe in this land," wrote the English poet George Herbert, "ready to pass to the American strand." In speaking about the colonization of America, promoters in every country emphasized trade, commodities, economic profit, and the resulting expansion of national power. Equally prominent in every country's justification of overseas settlement was the language of religion. Whether Catholic or Protestant, Europeans viewed the world through a religious lens. Just as Native Americans and Africans saw connections between the visible world on earth and an invisible world of spirits, so Europeans believed that God ordered the universe, scrutinized human behavior, and judged individuals worthy of everlasting immortality or damnation. Of course, not everyone had the same religious beliefs: Catholics and Protestants, though Christians, hated each other. But it was precisely because Europeans took religion so seriously that they were prepared to wage bloody wars against those who worshiped in a different faith or, like Native Americans and Africans, who seemed to Europeans to have no faith at all.

Naming the Land

This sense of a God-given superiority allowed Europeans to dismiss the competing claims of other peoples. Wherever European adventurers discovered unfamiliar geography—rivers, lakes, islands, or mountains—they instantly affixed their own names to the lands and waters, even to the people, they encountered. Thus the Caribbean Taino became the first Americans to be labeled "Indians" and their home was called "San Salvador" in the vocabulary of Spanish Christianity. Three decades later, Verrazzano summarily dealt European names to the islands of the north Atlantic coast: "Arcadia" and "Le Figli di Navarra" (daughters of Navarre). When the English settled the same portions of North America, they paid homage to their own royalty, naming Virginia for Elizabeth I, the virgin queen, and other coastal areas—Maryland, New York, and Carolina—for other aristocrats.

This naming suggested important power relationships. Spain's elimination of French settlers in Florida in 1566 transformed "Fort Caroline" into "San Mateo." After the English defeated the Pequots in New England, they promptly renamed Pequot village "New London" and called the nearby river the "Thames." When the Spanish explorer Juan Bautista De Anza punished a runaway servant with a severe whipping near the Gila River in Arizona, his soldiers named the place El Azotado for "the one who got the beating." As the names of European places and princes dotted the maps of North America—New Amsterdam, Boston, New Orleans, Albuquerque—Europeans not only established continuity of their culture and values but also strengthened their claims to the land.

Maps and National Power

Given the Europeans' ignorance of American geography (to his dying day, for example, Columbus never accepted the fact that he had failed to reach the Indies), naming the land became a means to control the unknown, the so-called terra incognita. Detailed maps established claims of ownership and political rights. During the 15th century, maps assumed new importance as European nations competed for knowledge of uncharted seas and places. Portugal's Henry the Navigator treated his maps as state secrets, threatening the death penalty for any mariner who divulged cartograph-

To his dying day, Columbus never accepted the fact that he had failed to reach the Indies.

ical information to a foreigner. Although Native American guides drew sketches and maps for European visitors, explorers like Captain John Smith not only ignored Native place names but also drew maps that left vast areas blank. Thus, the continent appeared largely uninhabited. And empty lands validated European claims. "In a vacant soyle," wrote an English preacher, "he that taketh possession of it . . . his Right it is."

After the invention of the printing press by Johann Gutenberg in the 15th century, European travel accounts spread rapidly in intellectual circles. These writings often blurred reality with fantasy, but a major topic in this literary genre was the description of exotic commodities—plants, such as sassafras and tobacco; an abundance of birds, fish, and fur-bearing animals; and the fertility of the land, which also became a commodity. Maps, such as the 16th-century Mercator Projection, not only reduced the unknown world to manageable proportions but also provided Europeans with valuable information about distant places. Thus maps, ocean charts of winds and currents, and travel literature became crucial ingredients in the continuing pursuit of overseas trade and national power.

A Passion for Colonization

To Europeans, the ideology of empire expressed the sense of cultural superiority. Such beliefs did not inspire toleration of others. Rather, Europeans continued to believe in a singular world view, which could embrace all knowledge, all truth, all

The 16th-century Flemish mapmaker, Gerardus Mercator, created a linear format for picturing the globe, but his pattern exaggerated the size of the Northern Hemisphere.

beings. When they discovered aspects of the world that did not fit their beliefs, they did not change their minds, but instead sought to change the world. This arrogance enabled European adventurers to endure incredible hardships to fulfill deeply held beliefs. To be sure, exploration, trade, and colonization required careful calculation, economic wisdom, and distinct material objectives. But it also demanded passionate commitment from those who risked not only material possessions but also life and limb—and, in their eyes, immortal souls as well.

The first European explorers, traders, and colonizers to reach America had no idea of the vastness of the continent or the difficulty of fulfilling the goals of conquest and settlement. Indeed, most individuals had smaller objectives, such as profit from trade in furs, sugar, spices, and slaves, though some, no doubt, sought the promised immortality of success. Like Columbus, they expected approval by European standards—a title, a coat of arms, hard cash, and a great reputation.

But most Europeans failed to find what they sought; most did not even survive to return home. Although European expansion brought gold and glory to a lucky few, exploration and colonization also created misery and suffering for millions of Native Americans and Africans as well as for those anonymous sailors, traders, and colonists who disappeared from history in faraway places. Yet Europeans continued to sail to unknown lands in increasing numbers, built beachhead communities on the Atlantic shores of the western world, and eventually, by the 17th century, even began to call America their home.

INFOTRAC® COLLEGE EDITION EXERCISES

For additional reading go to InfoTrac College Edition, your online research library at http://web1.infotrac-college.com.

Keyword search: Portugal history

Subject search: slave trade

Subject search: Spanish colonies
Subject search: British colonial
Keyword search: colonial France
Subject search: Vikings in America
Subject search: triangular trade
Keyword search: Jamestown
Keyword search: Coronado
Keyword search: Spanish Armada
Subject search: East India Company
Keyword search: Walter Raleigh

ADDITIONAL READING

European Involvement in the Slave Trade

John Thornton, *Africa and Africans in the Making of the Atlantic World, 1400–1680* (1992). The author analyzes the role of Africa in the formation of European empires, examining the slave trade and its consequences.

James A. Rawley, *The Transatlantic Slave Trade: A History* (1981). A detailed analysis of slavery in the commercial activities of the major slave-trading nations.

Hugh Thomas, *The Slave Trade: The Story of the Atlantic Slave Trade: 1440–1870* (1997). An overview of slave trading that emphasizes the industry's economic complexity and discusses the struggle for its abolition.

The Origins of European Expansionism

J. H. Parry, *The Age of Reconnaissance* (1963). An overview of European expansionism, linking ideology, exploration, trade, and empire.

David B. Quinn, *North America from Earliest Discovery to First Settlements: The Norse Voyages to 1612* (1977). A comprehensive account of exploration and colonization, including a thorough bibliography.

Spain Challenges the Portuguese Empire

William D. Phillips, Jr. and Carla Rahn Phillips, *The Worlds of Christopher Columbus* (1992). With a critical eye, this study places Columbus's career in the context of his times.

Spain Explores North America

David J. Weber, *The Spanish Frontier in North America* (1992). A thorough description of Spain's colonial activities north of Mexico.

England Reaches for America

Harry Kelsey, *Sir Francis Drake: The Queen's Pirate* (1998). A lively account of the voyages of England's premier sailor.

David Harris Sacks, *The Widening Gate: Bristol and the Atlantic Economy, 1450–1700* (1991). A detailed study of one of England's major port cities, examining the expansion of trade and its impact on one community.

Maps and National Power

Emerson W. Baker, et al., eds., *American Beginnings: Exploration, Culture, and Cartography in the Land of Norumbaga* (1994). This collection of essays examines Europe's image of the Atlantic coast and the development of northern New England and Canada.

Colonial Competition and Cultural Struggle, 1598–1700

CHRONOLOGY

Long at sea and weary of seeing little but waves and sky, two English sea captains, Philip Amadas and Arthur Barlow, at last approached the coast of North Carolina as part of the doomed expedition to Roanoke in 1584. The lush green coastline beckoned with its low, sandy beach.

They later recalled, "We smelt so sweet, and so strong a smell, as if we had been in the midst of some delicate garden abounding with all kind of odoriferous flowers. . . . [We landed on a beach,] very sandy and low towards the water's side, but so full of grapes, as the very beating and surge of the sea overflowed them."

It seemed they had found paradise itself. Soon welcomed by the native people, "We were entertained with all love and kindness, and with as much bounty (after their manner) as they could possibly devise. We found the people most gentle, loving, and faithful, void of all guile and treason, and such as live after the manner of the golden age."

http://history.wadsworth.com

Such explorers' reports sent from America to Europe during the 1500s may be seen as an early form of mass advertising. Although published descriptions of the "new world" often depicted the absence of "civilized" institutions—no churches, farms, or settled towns—most commentators praised the natural bounty of uninhabited lands waiting to be developed. An abundance of gold and silver awaited visitors. Claimed Sir Walter Raleigh of Guiana, "The graves have not been opened for gold, the mines not broken with sledges, nor their images pulled down out of their temples." Such chronicles usually downplayed the presence of native inhabitants and whetted the European appetite for colonies in North America. Colonists from western Europe seized the bait. By the end of the 17th century, Spain had settlements in Florida and New Mexico; English men and women lived along the Atlantic coast; French colonists inhabited eastern Canada and the Mississippi River valley; and the Dutch held outposts in what are now New York and New Jersey.

The hopes that prompted colonization often collided with American realities. For the first colonists, survival in a strange land remained problematic, with success or failure often depending on their relationships with Native peoples. As in England's "lost" colony at Roanoke, antagonism between settlers and the indigenous people could spell disaster. Relations with Native American groups also reflected the policies of the home countries that sent colonists overseas. Indeed, each European nation had a distinctive approach toward the native inhabitants. Thus, Spaniards in New Mexico characterized the Pueblo people under their control as "stupid" and "of poor intelligence." Accordingly, the conquistadors expected them to adopt European dress, religion, and customs. By contrast, the French colonists in Canada, fewer in number and lacking the power to impose their will on the native villages, treated

their Huron and Algonquian neighbors as allies and trading partners and emphasized their voluntary cooperation. Meanwhile, English and Dutch encroachment on Native American lands frequently provoked quarrels, violence, and warfare. By the end of the 17th century, however, the balance of power between Europeans and the coastal tribes had shifted forever, and the colonial outposts worried less about survival than about competition from neighboring colonies.

As Europeans gained control of the Atlantic territories, the colonists increasingly exerted their cultural domination. The introduction of European manufactured goods such as guns, iron kettles, and woven shirts demonstrated technological advantages that encouraged Native peoples to participate in vigorous trade relations. Such products altered traditional tribal practices; for example, to satisfy the European demand for beaver pelts, Native hunters no longer limited their kill to those animals that could be eaten, but began to overkill the animals for their furs. The European demand for leather and venison drastically reduced the number of white-tailed deer in the Chesapeake area; as early as 1699, the southern English colonies enacted laws banning the hunting of white-tails during certain seasons. Such conservation laws appeared infrequently during the colonial era, but indicated how quickly the pressure of European trade threatened the environmental balance. And, wherever Europeans went, the accompanying diseases devastated the human population.

The technological dominance of Europeans also revealed fundamental differences in cultural perspectives among the colonists, Native Americans, and Africans. One of the mechanical wonders brought to New France during the 17th century was a clock that chimed the hours. According to a French priest, when as a joke one of the Frenchmen "calls out at the last stroke of the

As Thomas Harriot put it, "Manie other thinges that we had, were so strange unto them, and so farre exceeded their capacities to comprehend . . . that they thought they were rather the works of gods than of men."

hammer, 'That's enough,' and then it immediately becomes silent," the amazed Native observer believed that the clock could hear. Similarly, the Virginia slave Olaudah Equiano found himself in his master's bedroom with orders to fan the sleeping man. "The first object that engaged my attention was a watch which hung on the chimney," he recalled. "I was quite surprised at the noise it made, and was afraid it would tell the gentleman anything I might do amiss." Meanwhile, in Spanish New Mexico, Franciscan missionaries sounded bells to summon Native Americans to religious worship. To Native Americans and Africans, accustomed to living by the natural time of sunrise and sunset, who ate when hungry and slept when tired, European timekeeping seemed inherently authoritarian. Indeed, the Algonquians in French Canada called the chiming clock "the Captain of the day" because the timepiece dictated when social activities, such as prayers and meals, would

occur. Yet, by the 17th century, Europeans considered clock time natural and used the measurement of hours to discipline their own lives as well as those of the Africans and Native Americans under their control. Timekeeping, in other words, became a form of cultural domination.

The Europeans' authority and power—their control of time or seizure of the land—created severe tensions with other peoples. While both Native American and African traditions denied that individuals should own the land, European nations claimed land titles from "sea to sea," drew straight boundary lines on their maps, and occupied Native American territory. And, since land in America usually had no value to Europeans unless it was "improved" to produce crops, the effort to reap agricultural profits justified the enslavement of Africans and Native Americans as a labor force. By the end of the 17th century, moreover, land itself had become a commodity.

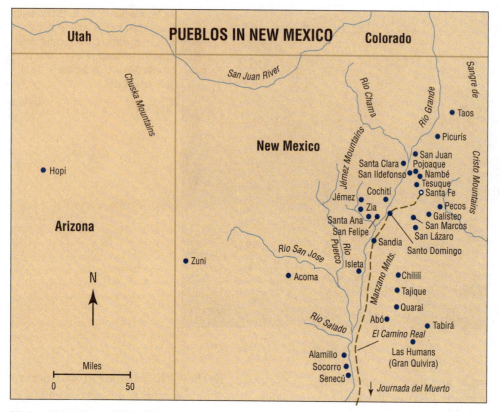

Missions in New Mexico, 1650–1675

Unlike Native Americans, who saw the land as a home, or Africans, who regarded their homelands as sacred places to which their souls would return, European colonists saw the land as real estate—property to be bought, used, and sold. Since Europeans shared this cultural perspective, rivalries among nations (English, French, Dutch, and Spanish) produced constant competition and conflict. Government policies made in Europe, such as royal land grants to colonial investors or treaties that artificially divided natural geography, determined which country's settlers could claim American land and how they would exploit its value. This persistent discord about the land and its resources meant, finally, that some European nations would lose their colonies in America and others would determine the future of the continent.

Spain's Empire of Souls

After the first conquistadors failed to find gold on the dry lands of New Mexico, the sparsely settled area offered few attractions for Spanish settlement. In 1573, the Spanish monarchy disavowed military conquest of Native peoples and demanded that further discovery "be carried out peacefully and charitably." The Pueblos thus emerged as ideal targets for Spain's religious missionaries, the Franciscan monks who resolved to convert the "heathen" on

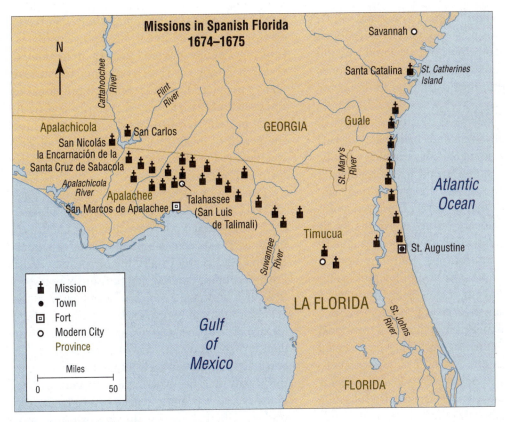

Missions in Spanish Florida 1674–1675

Missions in Florida, 1650–1675

the northern fringes of the Spanish empire. Establishing the first mission in New Mexico in 1598, the Franciscans built some fifty churches and baptized 85,000 individuals during the next thirty years. Meanwhile, on the eastern side of the continent, the Franciscans established missions in northern Florida and along the Atlantic coast of Georgia and South Carolina. Such religious expansion bolstered Spain's North American claims; missionaries rather than soldiers protected the northern frontiers.

Imposing Spanish Culture

Spain's missionary goals made few allowances for the traditions of indigenous peoples. Instead, the Franciscans forced the Pueblos to construct the mission churches: men under Spanish supervision performed the carpentry; women made the adobe walls. Even church design reflected a conflict of cultures. Where the Pueblos traditionally worshipped in circular underground chambers called *kivas*, Catholic architecture—indeed, the very adobe bricks used to build the structures—was uniformly rectangular in shape. The churches also brought sacred ceremonial space indoors and sheltered religious ritual from the natural environment. Thus, while Pueblo religions observed the cycles of seasons and the movement of celestial bodies, Spanish church bells summoned converts indoors at fixed hours and marked sacred time by calendars and holidays ("holy days"). Of course, the Pueblos never completely abandoned their own spiritual beliefs, but accepted a fusion of ceremonies. Thus Franciscan Christmas rituals became mixed with Pueblo ceremonies honoring the winter solstice.

The mission schools taught the elements of Christianity to both adults and children but focused on converting the young. Besides teaching Catholic catechism, prayers, and hymns, the missionaries demanded that the Pueblos "live in a civilized manner," which meant that they wear European clothing and shoes, cultivate European crops such as wheat and fruit trees, and raise domesticated animals imported from Europe, including horses, cattle, sheep, and pigs. Although Spaniards emphasized that conversion to Christianity was a voluntary act, they used elaborate gifts to entice converts and undermine the authority of traditional spiritual leaders. Moreover, once a person accepted Christian baptism, the convert became subject to Catholic discipline. Converts who violated religious rules, neglected the mass, or participated in Native ceremonies were severely punished.

Oppression and Resistance

Emphasis on religious conversion severely disrupted Pueblo society, dividing communities between converts and traditionalists. Worse, the missionaries inadvertently brought diseases that killed in epidemic numbers. By 1680, the Pueblos had been reduced by half; the Florida Apalachees had dropped 60 percent. High mortality compounded the difficulties of mission life. As subjects of the Spanish crown, the Pueblos were required to pay tribute in the form of goods and labor to the landowners. Public works projects, such as the building of roads, forts, and the town of Santa Fe, obliged the Pueblos to perform extraordinary labor. In addition, Spanish settlers violated royal orders by occupying Native lands, enslaving non-Christian people, and sexually assaulting Pueblo women. Recent archeological research among the skeletal remains of Florida's Native peoples shows that Spanish missionaries imposed a new cornbread diet in place of traditional protein-rich fish-based foods, weakening the health of local inhabitants. The use of well water instead of natural streams also increased the Natives' illness and mortality.

Resisting such changes, Native groups in Florida and New Mexico organized rebellions. In 1680, the Pueblos staged a surprise uprising, coordinating some 17,000 people from numerous communities and culture groups. Led by the spiritual leader Popé, whom the Spanish had previously punished in a witch hunt, the Pueblos killed a quarter of the Spanish settlers and drove the survivors out of New Mexico. The uprising particularly targeted Christianity. Pueblo converts destroyed Spanish churches and religious objects and plunged into rivers to wash away their baptism. During the same period, Florida's Native peoples, goaded by nearby English traders, rebelled against the Spanish missions, killing Christianized Natives as well as Spanish settlers. Among the rebels were some who rejected their baptism, slapping their foreheads and shouting "I am no Christian!"

The Spaniards fought their way back into New Mexico in 1693, using military force to overcome Pueblo resistance. In Florida, Franciscans and soldiers clung to isolated bases at St. Augustine and Pensacola. Thus the Spanish empire in North America remained fragmentary, dispersed, and sparsely populated by Europeans through the next century. These military outposts, which by the 1770s extended into Texas, Arizona, and northern California, served primarily as territorial claims against Spain's European rivals. But the poverty of the Spanish settlements offered little competition to English and French traders, and the mission system proved immeasurably oppressive to Native peoples. Visitors compared the regimen of mission life to the slave plantations of the West Indies; others noted that the Natives wore their hair singed short—a sign of mourning. "I have never seen one laugh," wrote a French observer. "They look as though they were interested in nothing."

English Colonies on the Chesapeake

The sparseness of New Spain's settlements in North America would eventually contrast with the growth of England's colonies, but from the beginning both nations faced similar problems of attracting residents. Although England had failed to establish a permanent colony at Roanoke during the 1580s, English commercial investors continued to view Virginia as a site for colonial development. Such a colony would assert Protestant England's challenge to Catholic Spain, while offering the prospect of trade in the region's natural resources, which included lumber, sassafras (believed to be a cure for syphilis), and gold. Interest in colonization also expressed long-term economic developments that were changing England from a rural society into an expanding capitalist nation. As English merchants increasingly traded manufactured goods overseas for spices, sugar, and other commodities, landowners shifted from growing crops to raising sheep for wool to be made into cloth. Consequently, many farm workers lost their lands and migrated to English cities; London tripled in size between 1560 and 1625. Widespread poverty made colonization attractive to people without prospects of betterment at home.

The Background of English Colonization

The political situation in England also encouraged colonization. After Henry VIII separated from the Roman Catholic Church in 1534, the monarchy wavered between accepting Protestantism or returning to the Catholic faith. Queen Elizabeth (1558–1603) adopted a middle course, strengthening the national Church of England while rejecting extreme Protestants who wished to eliminate certain prayers and church offices that remained from Catholic days. Those who wished to purify the Church of England by removing all traces of its Catholic heritage were called *Puritans*. Significantly, puritanism had a strong appeal among those English people who experienced social uprooting. By emphasizing godliness over materialism, spiritual purity over worldly corruption, puritanism offered unfortunate people religious security in the next world, if not on earth. Such self-assurance would inspire many English Puritans to pursue their beliefs in America.

Despite widespread social upheaval, most people in Elizabethan England idealized the harmony and orderliness of society. As William Shakespeare wrote, all the elements of the world "observe degree, priority, and place." Elizabethans assumed that certain people were naturally better than most and expected these superiors to rule their inferiors. Status distinctions divided English society into a hierarchy. At the top stood the ruling monarchy and aristocracy; then came the well-to-do gentry—gentlemen and gentlewomen— who did not have to work with their hands; below them were the yeomen, who owned land but had to work on it; and finally the landless poor, the overwhelming majority of whom could not vote and barely earned enough to survive. These status distinctions remained patriarchal at all levels. Men were considered heads of their households; women assumed the status of their fathers or husbands.

Although the privileged aristocracy and gentry amounted to only 5 to 7 percent of the population, Elizabethans claimed that the interests of

English Colonies in Maryland and Virginia, early 1600s

ciety and politics would be transferred to England's colonies during the 17th century.

Founding Virginia

In 1607, a 60-year old Algonquian leader named Powhatan claimed authority over 14,000 people who lived in small groups around Chesapeake Bay. That year, the Virginia Company, a London-based joint-stock investment corporation sent three ships with settlers and supplies to plant a colony north of Spain's Atlantic settlements. Their objectives were to establish English claims in the area, find precious metals, seek the fabled Northwest Passage to the Pacific, and convert the Algonquians from the worship of devils to Protestant Christianity. Selecting a site on the newly named James River, the English constructed a base at Jamestown and laid claim to Powhatan's territory. The leader, fearful of the armed intruders, maintained friendly but cautious relations, exchanging goods and information to avoid open conflict.

When Powhatan's generosity wavered, however, Virginia leaders such as Captain John Smith used military force to take the food they wanted. Jamestown's settlers also copied Algonquian architecture, using bark and grass mats to insulate their drafty dwellings. But when Smith returned to England in 1609, the colonists' discipline collapsed. As the ill-prepared, mostly male colonists paid less attention to planting fields and more to raiding Native-grown crops, Powhatan withdrew his support. The "starving time" commenced during the winter of 1609–1610, when, without Native assistance, the English died of famine and disease, and some resorted to cannibalism. Of 900 English settlers, scarcely 60 survived until the arrival of reinforcements in the spring. According to the relief group, the survivors "looked like anatomies, crying out, we are starved, we are starved."

all groups could be protected by these wealthy few, who were responsible for preserving fair prices for food and fuel. Only male property holders with a stake in society were allowed to vote, and they elected their betters to represent them in the national Parliament. These ideas about so-

The Virginia Company continued to send fresh colonists and instituted martial law to force them to work. Even then Captain Smith required only six hours of daily labor, leaving the rest of the day for "pastime and merrie exercises." But as Powhatan's people continued to withhold supplies, the English used military force to seize lands along the James River. In 1614, Powhatan accepted a truce and permitted his daughter Pocahontas to marry John Rolfe, symbolizing the uneasy alliance between the two peoples. Her death of disease while visiting England indicated the fragility of such relationships. Saddened by her loss, the elderly Powhatan transferred his authority to his brother Opechancanough.

By 1613, Powhatan's English son-in-law, John Rolfe, had laid the basis for the colony's survival. Experimenting with a locally grown plant, he introduced Virginia's first profitable commodity: tobacco. As the demand for tobacco increased in England, Rolfe's hybrid variety brought revenue to the Virginia Company's investors. But to maximize tobacco production, the company needed additional laborers and began to offer fifty acres of land to anyone who paid the passage of a worker—an arrangement known as a "headright." The policy enabled wealthy merchants and ship captains to acquire large land holdings by transporting servants to Virginia. Between 1619 and 1622, 3,000 new settlers arrived in the colony. By 1622, however, the total number of surviving colonists was only 1,200.

The high colonial death rate encouraged Virginia leaders to seek an alternative labor supply. By 1619, people of African descent were working in the colony. That year John Rolfe reported that a Dutch ship had deposited a cargo of "twenty Negars." Whether these Africans were slaves or free, or what became of them in Virginia, remains unknown. Through the first four decades of Virginia's settlement, the legal status of Africans remained extremely fluid, varying greatly in individual cases. Certainly, given England's tradition of social hierarchy and a belief that black Africans were inferior to white Europeans, those first black Virginians entered a society that treated all workers as commodities to be bought, traded, and sold.

Although tobacco provided some financial security for landowners, the plant rapidly depleted the soil, usually within three years. Virginians found it cheaper to acquire new lands than to fertilize old soil, and the colony began to expand along the rivers, maintaining proximity to ocean-going vessels. To consolidate the colony, the Virginia Company ordered the summoning of the first legislative assembly, the House of Burgesses, in 1619. Composed of two delegates from each geographic district, this legislature participated in company decisions, an early example of representative government.

As tobacco planters continued to encroach on Algonquian territory, the Native people recognized the threat to their way of life. In 1622, the Powhatans attacked the settlements, killing over 300 colonists, including the leading missionary, and forced the survivors to retreat to fortified sites. The colonists soon retaliated, slaughtering people, destroying crops, and smashing villages. Now Virginians could claim Algonquian lands by "right of conquest." Yet one casualty of war was the Virginia Company itself. Although more than 8,500 colonists had sailed to Virginia by 1624, the surviving population numbered only 1,300. Frustrated by the colony's failure to prosper, the king revoked the Company's charter in 1624, making Virginia a royal colony. Hereafter, a governor appointed by the crown would govern the colony, assisted by an appointed council and the elected House of Burgesses.

After a decade of warfare, Opechancanough agreed to peace and withdrew beyond the edges of colonial settlement. During the 1630s, the English population began to grow, devouring fertile acreage along the rivers for tobacco. By 1640, Virginians numbered 10,000, about the same as the declining Powhatans. In 1644, Opechancanough launched another attack, killing nearly 500 colonists. But Virginians under Governor William Berkeley suppressed the uprising, executed the Native leader, and imposed a punitive peace that forced the Powhatans to migrate to the western part of the colony. By 1675, when Virginia's colonial population exceeded 40,000, the remaining Powhatans totaled 2,000. Fifty years later, they would number in the hundreds.

Maryland, a Proprietary Colony

While Virginians struggled to build a tobacco economy, King Charles I granted the northern portions of Chesapeake Bay, later named Maryland, to George Calvert, Lord Baltimore, in 1632. Unlike Virginia, which was first controlled by an investment company and then by the king, Maryland was the private property of the proprietor. Calvert owned all the land, controlled trade, and held extensive political power. First settled at St. Mary's in 1634, the colony produced good harvests of corn and wheat but, as in Virginia, tobacco emerged as the main crop. By 1640, Calvert introduced headrights to encourage the transportation of workers. Although the Catholic proprietor intended the colony as a haven for his co-religionists, most settlers were Protestants. Forced by the colonists to establish a local legislature, Calvert attempted to protect the Catholic minority with the Toleration Act of 1649, a landmark law that established religious liberty for all Christians.

The tobacco economy defined not only the nature of work in the Chesapeake region but also the geography of settlement. Since overland transportation was difficult, the local river systems provided convenient lines of communication.

Nearly all colonists lived within a half mile of a river, and most were even closer. In laying out property sites, surveyors used the riverfronts as one boundary line and drew rectangular straight lines for the other three sides. Each 1,000 acre holding entitled a landowner to a mile and a half of riverfront. This type of settlement encouraged population dispersal. Most households had few close neighbors or common buildings, such as churches. Unlike village society of England or crowded London, Chesapeake settlers were more isolated and had fewer obligations to society.

Chesapeake Society

Settled along rivers and based on commercial agriculture, Maryland and Virginia produced similar economic and social patterns. As in the mother country, 17th-century English settlers believed that society was naturally hierarchical, though conditions in the Chesapeake encouraged greater social mobility. In England, a titled aristocracy governed the country, held most economic wealth, and enjoyed the privileges of high social status, but few aristocrats migrated to the colonies, and most of those who did died soon. Indeed, the extraordinarily high mortality rates, due to unfamiliar diseases and malnutrition, left few propertied colonists to prosper during the early decades of colonization.

Most 17th-century immigrants to the Chesapeake were propertyless young adults whose primary asset was the ability to work. Most journeyed to America by becoming indentured servants, meeting the cost of their transportation by contracting to work for a master for a period of time (usually around five years) after which they would receive their freedom and a small payment. About 40 percent of those indentured did not live long enough to collect. Colonists who had the money to pay the passage of other settlers not only acquired the services of indentured workers but also accumulated substantial acreage through head-rights. Such landowning investors, who controlled agricultural supplies and food, also controlled the lives of their workers and could sell their labor contracts to others.

Most indentured servants were males in their late teens or early twenties, and they faced back-breaking labor six days a week. At the end of their contracts, servants achieved freedom to work for themselves, but few had accumulated sufficient wealth to purchase their own lands. However, since tobacco prices remained high until about 1660, a free worker might save enough during a year's labor to afford modest acreage. In this way, a poor English immigrant might become a person of property—a goal that was much harder to achieve in England. Despite opportunities for so-cial mobility, most former servants improved their position only slightly, if at all, in one generation. Chesapeake society remained only slightly less stratified or hierarchical than England's and be-came even less fluid during the 17th century as new leaders consolidated their wealth.

One important difference between England and the Chesapeake was the sexual composition of society. In England, where sex ratios were ap-proximately equal, economic limits forced young people to delay marriage until they could afford independent households, usually in their mid- to late twenties. With limited years of marital fertil-ity, English families had from five to seven live births, of whom perhaps half lived to adulthood. By contrast, most Chesapeake colonists were un-married young adults, with at least three times as many men emigrating as women. In early Mary-land, 70 percent of males died before age 50; for women, who were particularly vulnerable to malaria while pregnant, life expectancy was even shorter. Few marriages lasted ten years before one spouse died. Since women who came to the colony

as servants had to delay marriage until they fin-ished their indentures—penalties for pregnancy included additional years of servitude and some-times the seizure of their babies—they enjoyed fewer years of marital fertility than English women and had fewer children. Yet the scarcity of females encouraged widows to remarry, sometimes more than once. A woman might thereby inherit con-siderable property. Indeed, a good marriage was one way a former indentured servant of either sex might ascend the social ladder. The precariousness of life thus produced a volatile social order that would explode before the end of the century.

French North America

Unlike the Spanish and English colonies in North America, French settlements in Canada remained lightly populated by Europeans, largely because their home population felt little pressure to leave Europe. But French Protestants, known as *Huguenots,* did face religious persecution, both in France and in French colonies, and they frequently sought refuge in the colonies of other countries, such as New Netherlands. Because the French lacked the numerical strength to dominate Native American people as the Spanish or English did, their colonies emphasized economic and cultural reciprocity, par-ticularly with the Algonquians and Hurons of the Northeast and the Choctaws of the lower Missis-sippi valley. Although the French sent Jesuit mis-sionaries to convert the American "heathen" to the Catholic faith, they also permitted French fur traders and trappers, known as *coureurs de bois* ("travelers of the woods"), to form partnerships with Native American traders and to marry Native American women.

After Samuel de Champlain established Que-bec in 1608 (see Chapter 2), French traders sup-ported the local Huron nation against the Mohawk

Iroquois to gain access to the interior beaver trade. During the 17th century, French fur traders extended their influence around the Great Lakes and the Ohio River valley. By 1672, the Jesuit Jacques Marquette and the trader Louis Joliet explored 1,200 miles of the Mississippi River; a decade later, the explorer Sieur de La Salle reached the Gulf of Mexico and claimed the Mississippi valley for France, naming the territory *Louisiana* after King Louis XIV. By the end of the century, the French were planting small outposts near the mouth of the Mississippi, close to the present site of New Orleans.

These extensive commercial networks discouraged concentrated settlements in Canada. Royal plans to establish agricultural estates in the St. Lawrence valley failed to develop because of a chronic shortage of labor, and efforts to stimulate the immigration of indentured servants to work the land could not compete with the attraction of fur trading. French fur traders, who spent long seasons among the Native Americans of the interior, remained loosely attached to the colonial government in Quebec.

Based on alliances with Algonquians and Hurons, the French fur traders remained vulnerable to attacks from the aggressive Iroquois. Decimated by European diseases, the Iroquois nations embarked on war against the Hurons in order to repopulate their clans with captives. Such violence threatened Canadian trade and led the French to give military aid to their Huron allies. The Mohawk Iroquois responded by attacking New France. By 1650, the Mohawks had crushed the Hurons, opening the way for peace negotiations with the French. But frequent violations of the truce led the French government to dispatch a military expedition that destroyed several Iroquois villages. Further weakened by epidemic diseases, the Iroquois accepted peace, enabling the French fur trade to prosper. But the Iroquois remained implacable foes of French expansion and allied themselves with other Europeans to limit French influence.

Puritanism Comes to New England

Unlike the Spanish missionaries, who focused on converting the native peoples, or the dispersed tobacco growers of the Chesapeake, or the scattered fur traders of French Canada—all of whom were overwhelmingly male—the founders of New England migrated to America to build stable communities. Governor John Winthrop called New England "a city upon a hill" to demonstrate to the world (especially a decadent England) the values of a godly Puritan society. Thus, the Puritans transplanted strong social institutions, including families, churches, and town government to assure common standards of behavior. But not all New England colonists were Puritans, and many quarreled with the leadership. Some Puritans also challenged specific religious doctrines and departed to establish colonies in Connecticut and Rhode Island.

The Origins of Puritanism

Puritanism arose within the Church of England during the late 1500s as a protest against the continued use of Catholic prayers and officers such as bishops. Influenced by the Protestant theologian John Calvin of Geneva, reform-minded ministers in England sought to simplify religious services and establish the independence of each congregation. They insisted that a person's salvation depended not on church rituals but on the quality of an individual's faith in God. Their opponents called them *Puritans* as a term of scorn.

Besides its religious argument, puritanism expressed strong emotional elements. Making a distinction between those people whose souls were saved for all eternity and those who were destined for eternal damnation, Puritans insisted that the

Their opponents called them *Puritans* as a term of scorn.

issue remained entirely in God's hands. This idea of *predestination*—the belief that a person's fate was determined before birth—could cause great anxiety. But from that inner stress most Puritans discovered in a moment of religious conversion that they were among the Elect, those chosen by God for salvation. And while Puritans believed that their fate rested entirely with God, they taught that individuals should strive to "prepare" themselves to receive God's grace. It was the conversion experience, the realization of one's total dependence on God and the sense of a spiritual rebirth, that ever after separated the "saved" from the damned. Those who were saved formed Puritan congregations in England and denied that the bishops should oversee their affairs. While demanding reforms of the Church of England, most Puritans did not believe that the national church was beyond redemption; those extremists who did were called *Separatists*.

Although puritanism began as part of a theological dispute, the movement spread rapidly during the reign of Elizabeth I. Puritanism appealed especially to people whose lives had been affected by the dislocations of English society. Although Puritans admitted that no one could ever know God's will, most were confident about their own salvation. Thus puritanism created a feeling of community. This enthusiasm, the feeling of divine inspiration, gave Puritans courage to criticize England's religious practices and to found godly communities in America.

The Pilgrim Colony

To Puritan eyes, God's grace could be seen in the effects of an epidemic that killed "great multi-tudes of natives" in New England in order to "make room for us." So reported a leader of the group that sailed aboard the *Mayflower* and landed at Plymouth on the Massachusetts coast in 1620. The group's leaders were Separatists, or *Pilgrims*, representing a form of puritanism that rejected the Church of England as totally corrupt. These religious dissenters had lived in the Netherlands since 1607 before deciding to establish an independent community in America. They had obtained a grant of land from the Virginia Company, and their financial support came from a joint-stock company, a mix of London investors and actual settlers who traded their labor for a share of stock. Only one-third of the *Mayflower's* passengers were Separatists (the others were called "strangers") but the colony leaders persuaded all to sign the "Mayflower Compact," by which they agreed to abide by laws of their own making. The agreement enabled the Pilgrim minority to exercise some control over the outsiders.

Touching Plymouth Rock just as winter descended, the Pilgrims were scarcely prepared for the hardships of settlement. Only the timely assistance of Massasoit, a local Native leader, and his translator Squanto, who had learned English after being kidnapped by earlier explorers, saved the Pilgrim community from starvation. Some Pilgrim merchants tried to develop trade in furs, fish, and lumber; most settlers turned to small-scale farming. Few outsiders were attracted to the colony, and the population grew slowly. Eventually, the Pilgrim colony merged with a larger settlement at Massachusetts Bay.

The Great Puritan Migration

As Separatists from the Church of England, the Pilgrims left Europe to escape from religious corruption, but the ascension of King Charles I in 1625 aroused concern among even the non-Separatist Puritans, who still hoped to purify the Church of

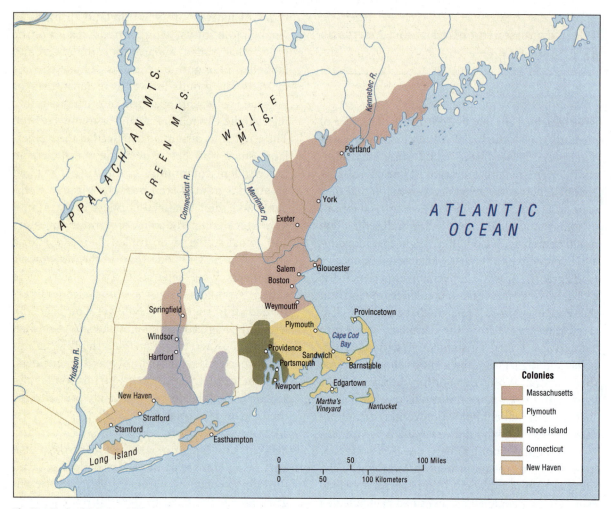

The New England Colonies, 1640

England. As the king silenced Puritan ministers and ignored protests in Parliament, Puritan leaders made plans to migrate to America to preserve their religious principles, perhaps as a model for England to imitate. In 1630, the Puritans began the "great migration" to New England when 1,000 settlers landed near Boston under the leadership of John Winthrop. Within a decade, 20,000 English had flocked to Massachusetts Bay and extended settlements into Rhode Island, Connecticut, and the towns of western Massachusetts. This remarkable growth reflected not only the power of Puritan idealism—the desire to create a "wilderness zion," a spiritual community in America—but also the related decision to migrate as families, rather than as individuals.

Unlike the Chesapeake colonies, which were settled by young, unattached people, the Puritans carried strong community values. Seeking to live in geographic clusters, they granted land not to individuals but to townships consisting of families and a minister, who then subdivided the land among the settlers. As in the southern colonies, New Englanders expected their "betters" to own more land than the common sort, but local leaders remained closely connected to the towns in which they dwelled. By law no one could live more than a mile from a church or "meeting house."

The government of Massachusetts originated in the joint-stock Massachusetts Bay Company. Corporate rules permitted only stockholders, known as *freemen,* to vote. But Puritan leaders preferred a consensual type of government that would bind people to community decisions. In 1631, the definition of freemen was altered to mean "citizen," which expanded the base of political participation. Yet Puritans allowed only church members to become freemen with full rights of citizenship such as voting and holding office. And, although religion and government remained legally separate, Puritans controlled who could become full church members. After 1634, men had to testify publicly to having had a conversion experience before they could join a church; women could describe such personal experiences privately. As in England and other English colonies, women, whether or not they were church members, could not vote. On the town level, where open meetings supervised local government, all property-holding men could vote or hold office, and in 1634 the colony legislature ordered the towns to elect delegates to a representative assembly.

Puritan Families

The social basis of Puritan government began in the family. Puritans saw their households as a microcosm of society and required all unmarried people to live in "well-governed families." They assumed that parents were superior to children, husbands to wives, and masters to servants. Puritan leaders believed that such a hierarchy assured a balance of obligations and responsibilities. "The husband should love, provide for, and be tender-hearted to the wife," a Puritan minister explained. "The wife should reverence the husband, obey him, and endeavor to be an help[mate] for him."

As in England and the Chesapeake, the legal status of married women was subsumed by their husbands. Married women could not own property independently; married women therefore were not responsible for their debts, even when contracted prior to marriage. Ironically, when a wife was fined for sexual misbehavior with another man, her husband was required to pay her fine. In protecting these patriarchal households, Puritans treated the rape of a married woman more seriously than other sexual offenses, even the rape of a child, because such crimes threatened their basic social unit. In contrast to the Chesapeake colonies, where the family structure was constantly shifting because of high mortality and frequent remarriages, the Puritan governments considered household life subject to public scrutiny. Thus Puritans viewed sexual misbehavior by either gender as both sinful and criminal.

The healthy environment in New England—a sharp contrast with the Chesapeake colonies—encouraged population growth, and the abundance of land encouraged people to marry younger, averaging in their early twenties. With a longer time of marital fertility, the birthrate in 17th-century New England increased, averaging from six to eight children per family. Believing that even babies were naturally evil because of Adam and Eve's Original Sin, Puritans emphasized discipline of young children.

From early childhood, youngsters learned moral lessons along with the alphabet from the

A page from the *New England Primer*, first published in 1690.

New England Primer: "In Adam's fall / We sinned all" and "The idle fool / Is whipt at school." Puritan attitudes toward sexuality were not necessarily "puritanical." Evidence from Puritan diaries shows that marital sexuality was welcome, and even premarital sexuality between engaged couples was often considered acceptable.

Expanding into Connecticut

New England's growing population created pressure for geographical expansion. Although epidemic diseases had eliminated the coastal tribes, numerous interior peoples occupied the fertile acreage coveted by Puritan farmers. Among these groups were the

Puritan attitudes toward sexuality were not necessarily "puritanical."

Pequots of Connecticut, who had developed extensive trade with the nearby Dutch settlements. Using the murder of an English trader as an excuse, the Puritans sent a military expedition against the uncooperative Pequots and proceeded to burn their village, killing inhabitants as they tried to escape. Pequot men who survived the ensuing battle were executed; captured Pequot women and children were enslaved and sold in the West Indies. There they were traded for the first African slaves to arrive in New England, in 1638. But small farms and cohesive family life limited the economic viability of slavery in the northern colonies. A few Pequots who survived the massacre lived on as stragglers, too few in number to resist the migration of Puritans from Massachusetts, who founded separate colonies at Connecticut and New Haven.

Puritan aggression against the Pequots reflected a wider European intolerance of cultural differences. Believing that Native Americans worshiped false gods, if not the devil, Puritans, like other European colonials, professed a desire to convert them to Christianity. Yet, unlike the Franciscans of New Spain and the Jesuits in French Canada, only a few Puritan missionaries attempted to preach to Native groups. Apostles like Massachusetts' John Eliot baptized some converts, and Eliot even translated the Bible into Algonquian in 1661. But Protestants no less than Catholics expected the converts to abandon their own culture, move into "praying villages," and accept European values.

Expressing Religious Dissent

Although the Puritans sailed to New England to protect their religious beliefs, they opposed extending similar liberties to other dissenters. When the pastor at Salem, Roger Williams, demanded a complete separation of church and state (because, he argued, politics would inevitably corrupt religion), Governor Winthrop arranged for his expulsion. In 1635, Williams fled to Rhode Island, where he took refuge among the Narragansetts and later purchased land to establish an independent colony dedicated to religious toleration. His book *A Key into the Language of America* (1643) remains a valuable source for Native American historians and anthropologists. Rhode Island became a haven for other Puritan nonconformists.

Another challenge to Puritan orthodoxy emerged in 1636 when a parishioner of the Boston church, Anne Hutchinson, began to hold private religious meetings in her home and included women in the discussions. Hutchinson even dared to question the ministers' emphasis on "moral" behavior, such as attending sermons, as a condition for salvation. Her position was a logical extension of puritanism, for it assumed that God's grace, not a person's actions, determined who would be saved. But in two ways Hutchinson challenged Puritan authority. First, she stated that God had spoken to her directly (a heresy known as *antinomianism*) and so diminished the importance of the ministers. Second, she defied the traditional subordination of women to the male clergy. "The woman is more subject to error than a man," announced her pastor, John Cotton. "You have stepped out of your place," said another minister. "You have rather been a husband than a wife, and a preacher rather than a hearer, and a magistrate rather than a subject." For defying the social order, Anne Hutchinson was banished from Massachusetts in 1638. She fled to Rhode Island, where she gave birth to a deformed fetus, which the Puritans considered proof of her diabolical purposes. Massachusetts also expelled a group of Quakers and executed a few, who, like Williams and Hutchinson, expressed heretical religious views.

Although the Puritans placed great emphasis on instilling their religious values in the young and founded Harvard College in 1636 to provide educated ministers, they discovered that the proportion of young people who qualified for church membership by undergoing a conversion experience was steadily declining. Perhaps the social conditions that inspired puritanism, religious anxiety, and conversion experiences had vanished in America. By mid-century, Puritan ministers were bemoaning the decline of religion and the rise of material values. Meanwhile, the outbreak of civil war in England during the 1640s reduced interest in colonial affairs and slowed immigration, precipitating an economic depression in New England and a feeling of spiritual loss among Puritans. While old England struggled with internal problems, New England remained a distant outpost, no longer the beacon on the hill.

The Restoration Touches America

In the Old World, the English civil war pitted Charles I against a pro-Puritan Parliament, which demanded the right to control taxation and criticized the king's religious views. The execution of the king in 1649 opened a brief era of parliamentary rule under the Puritan Oliver Cromwell. But in 1660, Parliament agreed to restore the monarchy in the person of the dead king's son, Charles II, whose subsequent reign was called the *Restoration*. Having defeated his opponents, the restored king proceeded to tighten royal control over England's growing empire in America. At the king's bequest, wealthy aristocrats received title to vast tracts of land on the Atlantic seaboard to establish colonies, including the Carolinas, New York, and Pennsylvania. The crown also gave more attention to regulating trade between the colonies and the mother country.

Settling the Carolinas

Charles II repaid his political supporters by giving them large "proprietary" grants in America. The first of these gifts, given to a group of eight lords in 1663, comprised the region known as Carolina. Expecting to produce expensive exports, such as silk and wine, the proprietors envisioned a country of large estates. Their secretary, the philosopher John Locke, proceeded in 1669 to draft a blueprint, known as the Fundamental Constitutions, proposing a hereditary nobility based on large landholdings and slave labor. This scheme was never implemented because few colonists wanted to live as peasants rather than on their own lands. Already the northern part of Carolina around Albemarle Sound had attracted small farmers from Virginia who rejected proprietary rule. This area later formed the independent colony of North Carolina in 1712.

The Carolina proprietors did attract another class of settlers who already had wealth in America, particularly sugar planters from Barbados, who migrated with their slaves to the area around Charles Town (later Charleston) in 1670. Some began raising cattle, using Africans who had acquired herding skills in their homelands of west Africa. More profitable was the trade for deerskins with the populous Southeast nations—Creeks, Chickasaws, Chocktaws. By 1700, Carolina's commerce extended to the Mississippi River, where the English competed with Spanish and French fur traders.

Carolina merchants found even greater profits in the slave trade among Native Americans. Encouraging rival tribes to war among themselves, white Carolinians offered firearms and other manufactured goods in exchange for Native American captives. Beginning in the 1670s, Carolina's Yamasee and Creek allies conducted slave raids against the Spanish missions in Florida. But because Native American captives often fled into the woods, Carolinians preferred to ship these slaves to other colonies. By 1710, Charleston had exported 12,000 Native American slaves to Virginia, New England, and the West Indies. Warfare and European diseases took an additional toll on the Native inhabitants. Between 1685 and 1700, the Native population dropped 25 percent, to about 15,000. Thirty years later, with continuing slave raids and wars, only 4,000 survived. Thus passed such thriving groups as the Westos, Savannahs, Tuscaroras (who found refuge among the Iroquois of New York), and Yamasees. Meanwhile, Carolina merchants built fortunes to invest in rice plantations in the next century.

Seizing the Dutch Colonies

Consolidating English possession of the mid-Atlantic seaboard, Charles II sent a military expedition in 1664 to seize the single outpost of Dutch competition in North America, the small colony of New Netherlands. Linked in a fur trading alliance with the Iroquois confederacy, the Dutch were competing effectively against French traders in Canada, who aligned with Algonquians. But the colony was sparsely populated and unable to defend itself. Already New Englanders had taken Dutch territory in Connecticut. The English fleet proceeded to conquer the Dutch colony without firing a shot, and Charles II granted proprietary rights to the area to his brother, the Duke of York. The Duke then granted the southern portions of his domain (now New Jersey) to two other proprietors. In 1670, the Dutch would recapture New York, but they later returned it as part of a peace settlement with England.

English rule brought little change to the settlements on the Hudson. With a heterogeneous population and a shared commitment to commerce, Dutch and English coexisted peacefully throughout the colonial period. However, the replacement of Dutch legal traditions with English customs altered the status of married women. Under Dutch law, married women could own property independently of their husbands, and wives maintained rights to half their family's estates. The conquest of 1664 did not immediately change Dutch practices, but as Dutch families adopted English customs, the English limits on married women's rights prevailed.

New York and New Jersey continued to attract land-hungry settlers from New England as well as English Quakers seeking religious freedom. By the end of the 17th century, over 10,000 settlers inhabited the two colonies. New York's primary economic activity was trade, first in beaver furs brought by Iroquois allies and later in the export of wheat and corn. By 1700, New York City was already a thriving metropolis.

Founding Pennsylvania

To settle another political debt, Charles II granted a proprietary colony to William Penn, a wealthy English Quaker, in 1681. The Society of Friends, or Quakers, had emerged in England as a radical offshoot of the Puritan movement; but, instead of emphasizing Original Sin and the limits of human achievement, the Quakers stressed the "inner light" of divinity within each person and the importance of achieving a spiritual community on earth. Believing that all humans were spiritual equals, the Quakers rejected worldly authority, refusing to tip their hats to their betters or to engage in warfare. Quakers also acknowledged the spiritual equality of women, who spoke freely at the Friends' religious "meetings." Such beliefs had led to their persecution both in England and New England. Now, in Pennsylvania, William Penn hoped to create a godly society and a sanctuary for his co-religionists.

To administer the colony, Penn granted a charter called the First Frame of Government in 1682,

which established the principles of religious freedom and representative government. Penn also took pains to purchase the lands given to him by the king from the Delaware people who inhabited the area. Such fair dealing earned Penn the appreciation of the Native groups and facilitated subsequent trade for furs.

Penn's religious toleration, together with liberal opportunities for land purchase, attracted colonists throughout Europe. By 1700, German and Scottish settlers contributed to Pennsylvania's heterogeneous population. Since most immigrants arrived as families, the colony boasted a high birthrate comparable to New England's. By 1700, the population numbered 12,000. Penn planned the colony's chief city, Philadelphia, as a grid with right-angle intersections and park areas, typical of his desire for orderly development. With choice agricultural land to grow wheat, corn, and rye, and the port at Philadelphia to ship exports abroad, Pennsylvania emerged as America's breadbasket during the 18th century.

Mercantilism and English Commercial Policy

Although private proprietors controlled the Restoration colonies, the English government recognized the great economic value of colonial development. During the civil war, English merchants had worried about the loss of commerce in America to Dutch traders who bought West Indian sugar, Virginia tobacco, and North American furs and sold European commodities and African slaves. Such interloping by foreign traders violated the economic principles of *mercantilism*, which held that a nation's wealth depended on the amount of gold and silver it possessed. Mercantilists believed that countries could become richer at the expense of other countries by engaging in trade that produced more exports than imports. Accordingly, colonies could serve as sources of raw materials and as markets for products of the mother country. Such trade promised prosperity to both trade parties, and any apparent conflicts of interest between specific groups would be compensated by the economic benefit to the nation as a whole. Parliament therefore responded to Dutch competition by passing the first Navigation Act in 1651. The law required that all goods shipped to and from the colonies be carried by English or English colonial ships; furthermore, all non-English products, including colonial exports such as tobacco, had to be brought directly to England from the point of origin. By including English colonists as bona fide shippers, the measure supported colonial merchants and shipbuilders.

After the restoration of the monarchy in 1660, Parliament passed a second Navigation Act in 1660, eliminating some loopholes in the original law. English vessels now had to be manned by crews of which three-quarters were English or English colonials. The law also "enumerated" certain colonial products (tobacco, sugar, cotton, indigo) that could only be exported to England. Later navigation acts added to the enumerated list to include rice, furs, iron, lumber, and naval stores. But, because colonial producers could sometimes sell these items illegally to other countries at greater profit, many shippers ignored the law, much to the frustration of English officials. To prevent such violations, Parliament passed additional laws of enforcement. These included provisions that required all European trade headed for the colonies first to pass through English ports before being trans-shipped (1663); required merchants to post bonds assuring that goods would not be shipped to illegal destinations (1673); and created naval courts (which omitted juries) to punish smugglers (1696). These various navigation acts, though frequently ignored by colonists and royal officials alike, represented a conscious effort by English administrators to coordinate colonial policy.

The mercantile system thus forced the colonists to trade with the mother country, but such trade probably would have occurred anyway. In an age when most commercial activity required familiarity with trusted agents overseas, English-speaking merchants would most likely have created arrangements with people of similar backgrounds. Moreover, England's manufactured products were of superior quality, were much preferred over other European goods by both colonists and Native American traders, and were much cheaper. The enumeration of goods also gave England's colonists a monopoly of the English market for such products as tobacco, naval stores, and indigo. Although some of these products might have been sold at higher prices in other countries, the total cost was not excessive. Yet economic analysis shows that England's navigation system had its greatest impact on the colonies at the end of the 17th century, when law enforcement was strict and the young economies were most susceptible to extra costs.

English intervention in the colonies during the late 17th century also brought new political problems, especially in Puritan New England. After the Restoration, a royal commission, sent to investigate New England's trade policies, found widespread violations of the navigation acts. To exercise greater control, the crown revoked Massachusetts' charter in 1684, removing the legal basis of self-government. When the Duke of York ascended the throne as King James II, he incorporated the New England colonies and New York in a larger administrative unit known as the Dominion of New England. This political system lacked a representative government. English officials also threatened New England's independence by questioning the legality of old land grants, enforcing the navigation acts more strictly, levying new taxes, and allowing the Church of England to hold services in Puritan Boston.

By 1689, therefore, New Englanders welcomed the news from England that Parliament had overthrown the king in a so-called Glorious Revolution. New Englanders spontaneously supported

Parliament by revolting against the Dominion of New England and seeking a new royal charter from the new monarchs, William and Mary. Residents of New York, equally hostile to the Dominion, joined the rebellion. In America, the Glorious Revolution stood as a benchmark in political liberty, long a reminder that royal power had to respect colonial rights.

The Clash of Cultures

By 1689, the growth of colonial society was impressive. At the beginning of the century, Powhatan had reminded John Smith that "we can plant anywhere. . . and we know that you cannot live if you want [i.e., lack] our harvest, and that relief we bring you." Two generations later, an English negotiator could reverse the claim, telling an Iroquois leader "You know that we can live without you, but you cannot live without us." By then, Iroquois hunters had come to depend on European goods, such as guns to hunt animals and defend themselves from equally supplied enemies. Yet despite their dependence on European weapons, the Native American nations remained a potent factor in the development of the colonial economies.

Nothing showed the power of Native Americans more clearly than the continuing competition for the fur trade. Although the French in Canada had developed ties with the Hurons and Algonquian groups to dominate the Great Lakes beaver supply, by the mid-17th century the rival Iroquois, armed by Dutch and English colonies, threatened this valuable commerce. Moreover, after the Iroquois defeated the Hurons in 1650, scattering their tribal remnants into the Ohio valley, French traders had difficulty maintaining the lucrative commerce. Under Iroquois control, beaver furs moved in greater quantity toward the Dutch and English traders of Albany, New York, rather than to New

> **"You know that we can live without you, but you cannot live without us."**

France. Hostility between Iroquois and Algonquians thus paralleled the rivalry between England and France, laying the basis for intercolonial warfare that would last for another century.

King Philip's War

The strategic position of the Iroquois played an important role in the defeat of a major Algonquian uprising against the Puritan colonies. Since the Pequot war of 1637, New England colonists had avoided warfare with the local peoples, though war scares occurred frequently. Territorial disputes between New England and the Narragansetts finally erupted in open warfare in 1675, when the colonists responded to the murder of an English settler by invading Native lands, burning villages, and destroying the growing crops. When the local tribes fought back, organizing coordinated attacks against English towns, New Englanders realized they were fighting for the right to live in western New England.

Under the leadership of Metacomet, known to the English as King Philip, the Wampanoags were joined by many other Algonquian groups to attack colonial settlements, killing and kidnapping inhabitants, and burning English homes and fields. Exposed to surprise attack, the colonists abandoned twenty-five towns, more than half of all their communities, and feared for the survival of the English colonies. Although the colonial militia organized counterattacks, Metacomet avoided entrapment for more than a year. But his hope of creating a Native American alliance against the English failed to gain support from the rival Iroquois, who wanted to preserve their fur trade with the colonists. Instead of supporting the uprising, Iroquois warriors helped the Puritans pursue Metacomet, killing him in battle in 1676. Then the Iroquois joined the English in forcing the Algonquians to accept a harsh treaty that took away their lands. Despite the Puritan victory, New England suffered 2,000 casualties and severe economic losses that retarded colonial development for decades.

The Iroquois Covenant Chain

In 1677, Iroquois and English negotiators agreed to a formal alliance known as the "Covenant Chain," which protected peace between these trading empires for nearly a century. Meanwhile, the French restored commercial relations with scattered Algonquian groups, who had resettled west of the Iroquois in the Ohio valley. In this competition for the fur trade with Europeans, the Native chiefs demonstrated considerable diplomatic skill, forcing both the French and English to make concessions. Successful colonial traders recognized the importance of ritualistic language and gift giving in forging alliances with their trading partners. All parties understood that allies were independent and could be swayed by competitors to become deadly enemies. When, for example, the Iroquois learned that the French were building a fort at Detroit, they expected the English to challenge their common enemy. Indeed, the English failure to act persuaded the Iroquois to sign a peace treaty with New France in 1701.

An Emerging North American Society

The clash of cultures in 17th-century North America thus involved high political stakes for the competing European empires as well as for the Native American nations that struggled to benefit from this international conflict. But as the complicated diplomatic drama unfolded, most colonials were more concerned with their mundane activities—farming, raising children, and building communities. Although most colonists who landed on the Atlantic coast expected simply to transplant familiar social customs and economic practices, their great distance from Europe forced the settlers to create societies different from the ones they had left behind. The cultural diversity that appeared in many colonies—the presence of people from different areas of the home country as well as strangers from other parts of Europe and Africa—required adjustments of traditional views. Moreover, the lack of established traditions (the absence of churches in 17th-century Virginia, for example, or titled aristocrats in New England) encouraged the colonists to improvise as they organized new societies. Such changes created a distinct provincial environment and the sense of being only a small part, a province, of a larger empire.

INFOTRAC® COLLEGE EDITION EXERCISES

For additional reading go to InfoTrac College Edition, your online research library, at http://web1.infotrac-college.com.

Keyword search: Spanish colonization

Subject search: Champlain

Keyword search: colonial Spain

Keyword search: Puritans

Subject search: Pilgrims

Subject search: Anne Hutchinson

Keyword search: Oliver Cromwell

Keyword search: mercantilism

ADDITIONAL READING

Spain's Empire of Souls

Ramon A. Gutierrez, *When Jesus Came, the Corn Mothers Went Away: Marriage, Sexuality and Power in New*

Mexico, 1500–1846 (1991). An excellent analysis of cultures in conflict, depicting Spain's impact on the Pueblo peoples.

David J. Weber, *The Spanish Frontier in North America* (1992). Describes Spanish colonization from Florida to New Mexico and California.

The Background of English Colonization

David Hackett Fischer, *Albion's Seed: Four British Folkways in America* (1989). Focusing on four regions in Britain, this book examines the social origins of English colonial customs.

Founding Virginia

Kathleen M. Brown, *Good Wives, Nasty Wenches, and Anxious Patriarchs: Gender, Race, and Power in Colonial Virginia* (1996). Tracing the transfer of English values to Virginia, this book describes the emergence of white male leaders at the expense of women, Africans, and Native Americans.

Edmund S. Morgan, *American Slavery, American Freedom: The Ordeal of Colonial Virginia* (1975). Examining the labor system of early Virginia, this volume reveals the rigors of early settlement that paved the way for slavery.

Chesapeake Society

Gloria L. Main, *Tobacco Colony: Life in Early Maryland, 1650–1720* (1982). Based on probate records and demographic statistics, this work provides a lively analysis of social life on the Chesapeake.

Timothy Silver, *A New Face on the Countryside: Indians, Colonists, and Slaves in South Atlantic Forests, 1500–1800* (1990). Studies the human impact on southern natural resources during the first two centuries of European settlement.

French North America

James Axtell, *The Invasion Within: The Contest of Cultures in Colonial North America* (1985). A lively analysis of English and French competition among Native Americans.

Puritanism Comes to New England

Edmund S. Morgan, *Puritan Dilemma: The Story of John Winthrop* (1958). This classic biography of the Massachusetts governor offers a lucid explanation of Puritan objectives in New England.

Puritan Families

Mary Beth Norton, *Founding Mothers and Fathers: Gendered Power and the Forming of American Society* (1996). A study of gender values in English America, exploring the legal and political implications of 17th-century attitudes.

The Clash of Cultures

Jose Antonio Brandao, *Your Fyre Shall Burn No More: Iroquois Policy toward New France and Its Native Allies to 1701* (1997). A study of Iroquois warfare, emphasizing the cultural context of Native American diplomacy.

Francis Jennings, *The Ambiguous Iroquois Empire: The Covenant Chain Confederation of Indian Tribes with English Colonies from its beginnings to the Lancaster Treaty of 1744* (1984). An exhaustive study of diplomacy that stresses the ability of the Iroquois to negotiate with Europeans.

Francis Jennings, *The Invasion of America* (1975). A detailed analysis of Puritan relations with native tribes, stressing the role of European aggression and greed.

Jill Lepore, *The Name of War: King Philip's War and the Origins of American Identity* (1998). Analyzes the cultural context of the deadly New England war.

James H. Merrell, *The Indians' New World: Catawbas and Their Neighbors from European Contact through the Era of Removal* (1989). Discusses the interaction of the southern tribes and English settlers in the Carolinas.

Neal Salisbury, *Manitou and Providence: Indians, Europeans, and the Making of New England, 1500–1643* (1982). A careful study of competition for land and resources during the formative period of colonization.

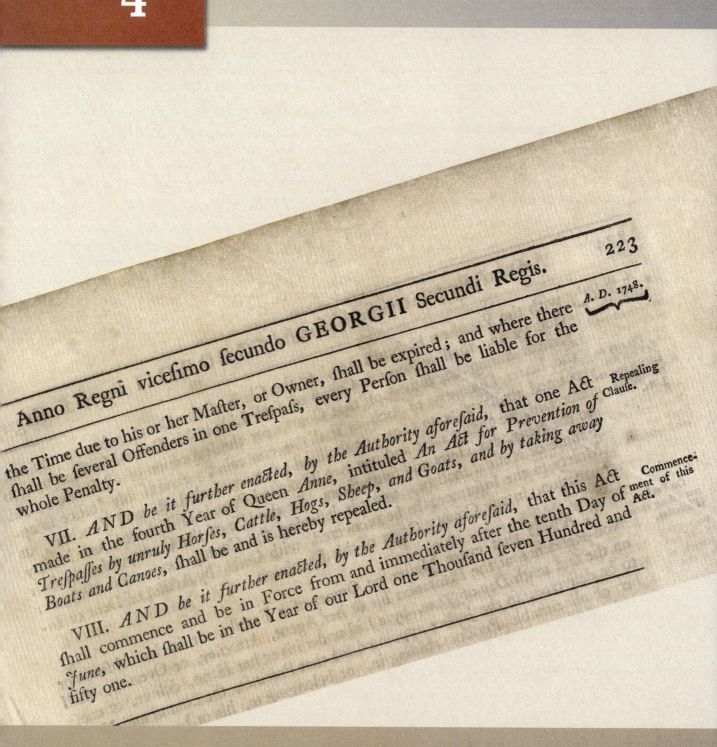

4

223

Anno Regni vicefimo fecundo GEORGII Secundi Regis.

A. D. 1748.

the Time due to his or her Mafter, or Owner, fhall be expired; and where there fhall be feveral Offenders in one Trefpafs, every Perfon fhall be liable for the whole Penalty.

VII. AND be it further enacted, by the Authority aforefaid, that one Act made in the fourth Year of Queen Anne, intituled An Act for Prevention of Trefpaffes by unruly Horfes, Cattle, Hogs, Sheep, and Goats, and by taking away Boats and Canoes, fhall be and is hereby repealed.

Repealing Claufe.

VIII. AND be it further enacted, by the Authority aforefaid, that this Act fhall commence and be in Force from and immediately after the tenth Day of June, which fhall be in the Year of our Lord one Thousand feven Hundred and fifty one.

Commencement of this Act.

The Emergence of Colonial Cultures, 1675–1765

Looking out upon his flock from the heights of a rough-hewn pine pulpit, Connecticut pastor Samuel Wakeman turned his eyes heavenward. Where was the humility that faith demanded of his people?

He could see the more richly clad of the colony's leaders seated comfortably, footwarmers at their toes, in the front pews. Toward the rear, in the chillier reaches of the church, sat the humbler ones with aspirations to the front. More and more, these folk, he thought, felt that "every nobody would be a somebody, and that persons of a commoner rank look. . . too earnestly towards the upper end of the world: men know not their places. . . . Men's conditions sit uneasy, and their callings suit them not." He felt, in short, that people had forgotten their proper places in society, in God's eyes.

Although the first colonists had struggled to transplant their familiar society in America, they could never reproduce what they had left behind in Europe. Population dispersal, the mixture of cultural groups, and shortage of labor—all brought changes to the social order. The absence of a hereditary aristocracy, for example, allowed men of lesser status to assume leadership, causing resentment among those who were expected to defer to their "betters." At the opposite end of the hierarchy, the introduction of slavery created a new caste that divided workers along racial lines. How colonials adjusted to these social changes usually depended on the benefits and losses they experienced.

During the first century of settlement, the North American colonies developed a new social order. New leaders emerged and consolidated their wealth and power. By 1750, they formed an established colonial elite that claimed the respect and allegiance of people of lesser status, at least among whites. "A man who has money here," remarked a Rhode Island colonist, "no matter how he came by it, he is everything." Although the distance between the richest and the poorest was not as wide as in Europe, property holding remained the prime standard of citizenship, a category that excluded women, slaves, and other economic dependents who could not legally own property. Yet even small property holders could aspire for success as merchants, politicians, or "gentlemen."

Colonial society also differed from Europe's in the diversity of its population. In 1700, 250,000 non-native people inhabited British North America; three-quarters of a century later, the population had multiplied tenfold to 2.5 million. Only one-quarter of this growth resulted from immigration; the remainder reflected natural increase, which created denser communities and encouraged internal migration to unsettled areas.

This population explosion involved complicated changes in social composition. As the number of Africans increased tenfold, whites in all colonies met west Africans of diverse backgrounds who spoke dozens of dialects and possessed distinct cultural experiences. European immigrants included ever larger numbers from Scotland, Ireland, Wales, and the West Indies, who mingled with settlers who spoke German or Dutch or French. Native communities, especially those near the fringes of European settlement, often consisted of remnants and survivors of decimated groups, linked together by distant ties of kinship or political dependence. Yet the leadership in British North America remained overwhelmingly English, eager to imitate the values of the mother country.

Transforming Chesapeake Society

The transformation from a European social order could be seen clearly in colonial Virginia during the last quarter of the 17th century. In 1675, the colony's royal governor, Sir William Berkeley, stood at the apex of society. As the highest government official, Berkeley and his appointed advisers in the colony's council dominated the tobacco economy. They controlled all grants of land, collected export revenues, and levied taxes. This powerful group consisted of those who had survived the ravages of colonization: economic uncertainty, conflict with the Powhattan natives, and high mortality. By vigorously exploiting the labor of white indentured servants and black slaves and by using their connections with royal power they had amassed large landholdings, taken control of the fur trade with the Susquehanna hunters, and exported much of the colony's annual 15 million pound tobacco crop to England. Despite their great wealth and power, however, Virginia's leaders were "new men," products of rapid social mobility rather than the inherited status that prevailed in England.

Bacon's Rebellion

Challenges to the leadership group began in the 1660s. The end of the English civil war had encouraged immigration to the Chesapeake at the same time that many indentured servants were completing their terms of labor. The result was an overproduction of tobacco, which brought a drop in prices. Yet new planters and former servants continued to seek land to become tobacco farmers. They soon confronted two obstacles: first, Governor Berkeley and his entrenched advisers opposed the ambitions of potential rivals; second, the Susquehannas and their allies, who traded animal skins with the English, resisted a further loss of their land. When Virginia settlers encroached on Native territory in 1675, minor disputes flared into violence. Angry Chesapeake colonials, under the leadership of a recent well-born immigrant named Nathaniel Bacon, marched against the Susquehannas, seeking an opportunity to seize their lands.

Governor Berkeley refused to provide military assistance to Bacon and his allies, opposing their desires to obtain western lands. Bacon then led his armed followers to Jamestown, where he defied the governor's authority and forced the House of Burgesses to enact laws providing for tax reforms and authorizing an attack on the Susquehannas. Backed by indentured servants who coveted western lands and African slaves who fought for their freedom, Bacon's insurrection threatened both the legal government and the social order that had evolved during the first generation. But Bacon's sudden death from illness and the arrival of British military forces ended the up-

"Like one of the patriarchs, I have my flocks and my herds, my bond-men and bond-women."

rising. Berkeley proceeded to crush the remaining rebels, executing twenty-three for treason, re-enslaving Africans and bond servants, and confiscating the rebels' property.

Although Bacon's rebellion indicated widespread dissatisfaction with the colonial leadership, the old order triumphed and persisted. After 1676, the House of Burgesses would share authority with the governor and council in making grants of land. But the Burgesses also reversed recent laws that permitted all free white men to vote and limited suffrage to "freeholders," that is, to property owning free men. Maintaining control over land and trade with Native peoples, affluent planters continued to dominate political power, and in time their leadership came to appear stable and respectable. With wealth and power, leading families intermarried and formed the "first families" of the colony. This elite self-consciously imitated the English gentry, building elegant capitals at Annapolis, Maryland, and Williamsburg, Virginia, founding the College of William and Mary in 1693, and adopting English fashions and architectural models. By 1726, one Virginia planter could boast: "Like one of the patriarchs, I have my flocks and my herds, my bond-men and bond-women, and every sort of trade among my servants, so that I live in a kind of independence of every one, but Providence."

The drive of the Chesapeake leadership to consolidate wealth, power, and status was made easier by other changes in society. If Bacon's rebellion expressed the frustrations of landless workers and slaves, the decline of tobacco prices during the late 17th century further diminished Virginia as a land of opportunity. With new colonies opening in the Carolinas and Pennsylvania, fewer white laborers migrated to the Chesapeake region. To the established leadership, reduced migration meant less competition, but it also aggravated the colony's labor shortage. The result was a major transformation of tobacco society and culture.

Defining Slavery in the Colonies

Virginia's labor problems prompted a reconsideration of the colony's African residents. The status of the first Africans in Virginia and Maryland remains uncertain, though like all servants, whether slave or free, most were males, and their conditions were undoubtedly poor. Probably most Africans entered the colony as slaves; but within a few years some had obtained both freedom and property, perhaps because they were treated as indentured servants. Whatever their exact status, surviving court records suggest that the legal system treated blacks differently than whites and occasionally punished black offenders with lifetime servitude. Africans, unlike European settlers, were generally listed only by their first names in the local census. Such practices reflected English ideas about the inferiority of nonwhite peoples—the belief that Africans lacked both Christianity and civilization, that their skin color indicated both sin and savagery. When, for example, a New Englander criticized another white woman for "the black side of her actions," she meant that the behavior was evil. When Africans came to be treated as slaves, their social debasement perpetuated these cultural prejudices.

During the mid-1600s, Chesapeake law steadily undermined Africans' civil rights. In 1643, Virginia imposed a tax on landowners who employed African women, thus placing black women (but not white women) in the same category as male

workers both black and white. At around the same time, Maryland prohibited Africans from bearing arms. Both colonies banned interracial sexual relations, with a Maryland law of 1664 stating that all "English women [who are] forgetful of their free condition and to the disgrace of our nation do intermarry with Negro Slaves . . . shall serve the master of such slaves during the life of her husband." The children of such women also became slaves. In 1669, Virginia legislated that a master who killed a slave while administering punishment would not be charged with murder.

The political consequences of a permanent slave population emerged during Bacon's rebellion. The interracial insurrection, allying white indentured servants and black slaves, was especially dangerous to political leaders, not only because of the number of organized rebels but also because by then African Americans had the least to lose by rebelling. Indeed, of the last 100 rebels who confronted Governor Berkeley, 80 were black.

As more English immigrants settled in other colonies, where opportunities for owning land were better, the decline of indentured servitude encouraged a rise in the number of black slaves. In 1660, Africans in Virginia numbered 1,700; twenty years later, they comprised 4,600; in another twenty years, their number had grown to nearly 13,000; and by 1710, the figure touched 30,000. To put it another way, in 1680 Africans represented 7 percent of the total Chesapeake population; by 1720, they comprised 25 percent.

During this period of increasing slave importation, the Chesapeake colonies adopted additional measures to restrict slave activity. Serious slave offenses were tried by separate tribunals. Slaves convicted of capital crimes, such as violence against whites, were often hanged or burned alive, their bodies dismembered and displayed publicly as a warning to others. Chesapeake laws declared that conversion to Christianity did not liberate a slave;

nor could free Africans, mulattos, or Natives own another person, except of their own "complexions." In 1699, Virginia ordered all free Africans to leave the colony, though the measure was seldom enforced. In 1705, these various statutes were reenacted as a comprehensive slave code.

The effect of Virginia's slave laws was not just to keep Africans in a subordinate position. More subtly, laws that restricted blacks reminded free whites of who they were *not*. Although poor whites had aligned with black slaves during Bacon's rebellion, by 1700 even the most oppressed white could claim a superior position to virtually any black person. During the 1680s, moreover, interracial sexual relations became illegal, and white women were prosecuted for having intercourse with black men (but the rape of black women by white men was not treated as a crime). In 1723, even free Africans were denied the right to vote. By the middle of the century, only 4 percent of Virginia's population consisted of free Africans, most of whom lived in female-headed households because slaveowners emancipated more women than men.

Slave Trading. Although the first slaves imported into the Chesapeake originated in the West Indies, tobacco planters disliked these "refuse" or "rogue" slaves, who had apparently been rejected by sugar planters for reasons of poor health, old age, or bad behavior. After 1680, as British merchants dominated the Atlantic slave trade, North Americans imported most slaves directly from Africa. Some colonies, such as New York and South Carolina, taxed slave imports from Africa at a lower rate than those from the West Indies. Yet until 1697, the Royal African Company, chartered by the English crown, held a monopoly of England's slave trade and limited sales in North America to keep prices high. Once English and colonial merchants broke that monopoly, slave prices fell and imports rose.

In purchasing slaves from Africa, colonial slaveowners expressed distinct ethnic preferences, favoring Africans from the Gold Coast and Windward Coast to those from other areas. Slaves who were Calabar or Ibo were less attractive because colonials believed they were more likely to commit suicide or try to escape. Southern planters preferred strong young men capable of hard field work, while whites in urban areas looked for younger boys and girls who could be trained as domestics or artisans.

In the Carolinas, African slaves had a great influence on the colony's economic development. Carolina's first planters came from the Caribbean, bringing slaves who had learned about herding and stock raising in Guinea along the Gambia River. Their skills, including seasonal burning of forests to stimulate the growth of grasses, enabled the planters to prosper. Later, as Carolina planters searched for a staple crop suitable for the colony's semi-tropical lowlands, west Africans contributed their experience with rice cultivation. The Africans' resistance to malaria and yellow fever also enabled them to survive in the swampy rice fields. Using African types of hoes and dikes, Carolina's slaves made rice the major cash crop after 1700. Exports jumped from 1.5 million pounds in 1710 to 20 million in 1730. Carolinians also used slaves to cultivate indigo dyes, based on the experiments of a white woman named Eliza Lucas, but that crop depended on continued economic subsidies from England. Reliance on African labor turned South Carolina into a black majority (about 60 percent), while Charleston became a slave trading center. Nevertheless, a high percentage of small farmers, especially in the western regions of the Carolinas, owned no slaves.

Unlike Carolina, the colony of Georgia, founded in 1732 by James Oglethorpe as a philanthropic experiment, explicitly prohibited slavery. But slow economic growth led the colonists to protest the ban. Arguing that it was "simply impossible to manufacture the rice by white men," and that blacks were "as essentially necessary to the cultivation of Georgia, as axes, hoes, or any other utensil of agriculture," the colonists won the right to own slaves in 1750. Carolina rice planters, eager to expand their holdings, promptly moved south with their slaves. By 1773, Georgia's African population numbered about 15,000—about the same as the white population.

Slavery in the North. Northern slaveowners experimented with Native American slaves imported from South Carolina, but found these servants "malicious, surly, and revengeful" and banned this trade in 1715. Africans comprised only 3 percent of New England's population: 10–15 percent in the middle colonies, but nearly 20 percent in the cities (Newport, Rhode Island; New York). On family farms, blacks worked closely with whites and shared their meals and housing, and so had fewer opportunities for privacy and anonymity than slaves on larger southern farms. Most northern Africans were male; most surviving Native Americans in the northern colonies, free or slave, were female. Intermarriage resolved those demographic imbalances, though not without arousing strong objections from white political leaders.

In northern cities, African occupations included skilled trades, such as sail making, brewing, and carpentry, as well as hard dockside labor and domestic servitude. Because of the relatively small African population, the northern colonies permitted more mobility to slaves. But certain crimes—sexual relations with whites, for example—were punished severely, and a Massachusetts law banished convicted Africans to the West Indies. Northern slaveowners showed their disdain for Africans by giving them, as one writer reported, "such-like names they give their dogs and horses." In the cities, where there were small populations of free blacks, African behavior was limited by curfews and prohibitions of alcohol. During economic slow-

Cotton Mather, who said of early smallpox inoculations "ye Method of Inoculation, I had from a Servant of my own, an Account of its being practiced in Africa. Enquiring of my Negro-Man Onesimus, who is a pretty Intelligent Fellow, Whether he ever had ye Small-Pox, he answered Yes and No; and then told me that he had undergone an Operation, which had given him something of ye Small-Pox, and would forever preserve him from it."

downs, competition between white workers and black slaves sometimes produced violent conflict. Yet cultural exchange occurred frequently. Indeed, it was an African slave who taught Boston's minister, Cotton Mather, the secrets of smallpox inoculation that, when introduced in Boston during an epidemic in the 1720s, limited the mortality rate.

Creating an African American Culture

Africans in America found themselves among people who spoke different languages and dialects. Those from neighboring African homelands tended

"If my slaves go to heaven, must I see them there?"

to group together, speaking "creole" languages that blended English and African tongues. But conditions of slavery determined which African traditions survived. In the scattered rural areas of the north, Africans remained isolated, meeting others only occasionally. Yet, even with few blacks around, Puritan churches maintained racial segregation during religious services and in churchyard burials. Southern Christians also established racial segregation in their churches, leading one troubled parishioner to ask "If my slaves go to heaven, must I see them there?" But in the southern colonies, where large numbers of Africans lived close together, racial segregation encouraged the preservation of African cultures and traditions. Within the separate slave quarters, Africans from diverse backgrounds were obliged to construct new lives. Exposure to different African languages, marriage into new kin networks, the sharing of work and leisure—all had a homogenizing effect, laying the basis for a common African American culture.

African American Kinship

In the decades before 1720, slave importations created a lopsided male population in North America. With few African women to marry and with prohibitions on interracial sex, most slaves lacked the opportunity to form families, and the African birthrate remained low. Yet Africans took pains to travel between plantations, sometimes walking as many as thirty or forty miles, to gather in the evenings, on Sundays and holidays or, as one planter complained, "beating their Negro drums by which they call considerable numbers of Negroes together in some certain places." Since enslavement drastically disrupted networks of family, kin, and clan, Africans developed extended relationships with neighbors and friends, who offered emotional support, assistance, and cultural continuity. "Uncles" or "Aunties" who were not blood relatives served as surrogates and role models for children in the event of the death or sale of a parent.

Around 1720, as declining tobacco prices reduced slave imports, the gender balance among Africans improved, and the African birthrate began to rise. In 1700, the African population of British North America totaled 28,000; by 1776, it exceeded half a million. That growth, far higher than increases in other parts of the slave world, reflected a healthier environment, better nutrition, and a sex ratio that stimulated natural increase. Because of work obligations, male slaves often resided apart from their wives and children, leaving childrearing to the women. Despite laws prohibiting interracial sex, slave women were vulnerable to sexual exploitation by their masters. Mulattos, children born to slave women by white men, followed their mothers' status into slavery. Meanwhile, slaveholders denied the legality of slave marriages, and allowed mothers with infants to be sold "together or apart." Yet Africans respected their family ties, choosing names for their children that established parental lineage. Advertisements for runaway slaves in Virginia before 1775 reveal that one-third had departed in search of their relatives.

African American Religion

"Talk to a planter about the soul of a Negro," wrote a traveler in 1705, and he will respond that although the body is worth twenty pounds, "the souls of a hundred will not yield him one farthing [penny]." Slaveholders feared that conversion to Christianity might stimulate interest in freedom. Consequently, most Africans had little exposure to organized Christianity, and most preserved the spiritual beliefs of their own cultures.

The racial segregation of burial grounds, seen at George Washington's Mount Vernon plantation, enabled African Americans to preserve their traditional burial customs. The monument's inscription reads "In memory of the Afro Americans who served as slaves at Mount Vernon this monument marking their burial ground dedicated September 21, 1983, Mount Vernon Ladies' Association."

The survival of African religious beliefs took many forms. Believing that spirits abounded in the natural world and could intervene in human activities for good or evil, Africans resorted to conjurors (people skilled in magical powers) to calm antagonistic spirits with charms, amulets, or herbal potions. (Similar magical beliefs existed among some European colonists, particularly those who did not belong to traditional churches; cross-cultural beliefs regarding witches would later form common ground for accusations of witchcraft in New England.) Because of the importance of ancestor worship, Africans took pains to uphold their traditional funeral rites and burial services. Long funeral processions, alive with song and dance, escorted the dead to their graves. This practice was outlawed in Boston because it was considered both unseemly and un-Christian. Recent excavations of an 18th-century African cemetery in New York City revealed that the dead were buried with care—shrouded, placed in wooden coffins, and aligned as in Africa with their heads toward the west.

Despite claims that slavery would Christianize the "heathen," English churches made few converts among transplanted Africans. In New England, requirements for baptism demanded both theological knowledge and Christian deportment, a formality that did not exist in African traditions and discouraged membership in Puritan churches. In the southern colonies, interest in converting Africans conflicted with the fear that Christianized slaves would claim spiritual equality and demand their freedom. Moreover, since slaves lived in large groups segregated from whites, they had more freedom to define their religious life. Missionaries who did preach among slaves usually emphasized the importance of Christian obedience and humility. To be baptized in South Carolina, a slave had to swear to remain obedient.

Evangelical preachers, who tapped African traditions of spiritual rebirth and whose sermon styles evoked African call-and-response rhythms, won many Christian converts in the mid-18th century. During a larger religious revival known as the "Great Awakening," Africans responded to a familiar feeling of spirit possession marked by dancing, clapping, shouting, and singing, and came forward in large numbers to be baptized. "They feel themselves uneasy in their present condition," remarked Samuel Davies, a white revivalist preacher, "and therefore desire a change."

Interpreting Christianity selectively, Africans drew parallels between going to heaven and returning to the spirits of their ancestors. In the emerging Baptist churches, moreover, whites and blacks, free and slave, created mixed congregations that permitted equal participation in church affairs. By the end of the colonial era, some of these churches, together with the Quakers, were calling for an end to slavery. Yet the overall proportion of slaves who became Christians remained very small.

Resisting Slavery

Christian sermons typically advised slaves to submit to their owners, but Africans demonstrated considerable skill, both personal and collective, at thwarting the demands of their masters. By controlling the pace of their labor, slaves could define their daily lives. Black slave drivers, respected leaders within African communities, emerged as intermediaries between workers and white overseers, ensuring the reasonableness of the work. On rice plantations, a task labor system focused on the completion of specific tasks, leaving slaves free time to tend their own gardens. Such produce would be used for personal consumption or traded in markets. Masters who ignored customary holidays (Sundays, summer nights, harvest feasts, Christmas) faced retaliation such as arson that imperiled an entire season's work.

Efforts to escape from slavery were omnipresent. Newly arrived Africans tended to flee in groups, while slaves who were familiar with the English language usually ran off alone. African-born slaves were more likely to become fugitives; American-born slaves were less likely to be caught. Newspaper advertisements for runaway slaves often mentioned their ethnic origins, reinforcing white opinions that certain African areas, such as Angola, produced less compliant slaves. Angolans, with some knowledge of Portuguese, often fled from the Carolinas to Spanish Florida, gaining sanctuary with Native Americans in mixed ethnic communities. Members of the Catawba nation that lived on the western fringes of the Carolinas sometimes acted as slave catchers, protecting their relations with white settlers by returning fugitives. Punishment for running away might include bodily mutilation, which served as a warning to others.

The dispersal of Africans inhibited slave rebellions in North America, but wherever slaves lived in dense communities, owners faced (and feared) the possibility of insurrection. A group of twenty slaves in New York City, including women and Native Americans, fomented an uprising in 1712, burning buildings and killing whites, before being crushed by military forces. The ensuing penalties—torture, execution, or deportation to the West Indies—and passage of a new slave code that curtailed blacks' activities pacified the city. But in 1740, rumors of another slave plot to destroy the city set off investigations, backed by torture, that produced confessions from accused Africans. Although dozens were executed and punished, evidence of conspiracy remained sketchy.

Some uprisings were less ambiguous. In 1739, slaves near the Stono River in South Carolina organized a mass rebellion, seized weapons and ammunition, and attracted dozens of recruits by beating drums. The rebels headed south toward

Florida, but a white militia intercepted them and defeated the fugitives in battle. It took months before all the rebels were caught and killed. After the Stono rebellion, rumors and fear of slave uprisings circulated in all the colonies.

Economic Expansion and Social Conflict

The widespread use of slavery in North America underscored the commercial basis of colonial society. With the exception of a small minority of household servants, who comprised only 5 percent of all bound workers, most slaves worked to produce goods that were sold in an expanding Atlantic marketplace. Such commercial activity obviously preoccupied their employers. Even small farmers, who prided themselves on being "self-sufficient," were dependent on neighbors and crossroads markets for certain products and trade. During the 18th century, colonial enterprise developed an international network that linked North American markets to England, continental Europe, the West Indies, and West Africa. And, although English navigation acts endeavored to regulate and restrict this trade (see Chapter 3), colonial merchants showed remarkable initiative in exporting American goods such as lumber, grain, fish, and rum around the world, while importing finished products from England, sugar from the West Indies, and slaves from west Africa.

Economic activity permeated colonial society. Slaveowners harnessed workers to produce tobacco, rice, and indigo, and small farmers labored to maximize agricultural production. Farm households in all regions typically had women working with men in barns and fields, at least during harvest time, in addition to performing domestic chores. During the 18th century, farm women specialized in dairy and poultry products (butter, cheese, eggs, feathers for bedding) for sale in the marketplace. In this way, small-scale agriculture was tied to market activity.

The search for economic success won reinforcement in the popular writings of Philadelphia's premier self-made man, Benjamin Franklin. His widely read *Poor Richard's Almanack,* first published in 1732, and his pamphlet *The Way to Wealth,* offered practical advice for business success. His famous aphorisms, such as "A penny saved is a penny earned," emphasized values of individual initiative and personal advancement. Franklin also advocated the strict measurement of daily time to ensure the improvement of one's life.

Franklin's advice appealed to an ambitious society because he insisted that America, in contrast to England, was a land of opportunity. "The only principle of life propagated among the young people," agreed one of Franklin's New York friends, "is to get money, and men are only esteemed according to what they are worth—that is the money they are possessed of." Most leading families had achieved their status during the early years of colonization, a time of social fluidity, and later generations consolidated their positions. To be sure, rapid social mobility remained possible. Franklin had begun his career as an apprentice printer and rose to become a leading tradesman, politician, and intellectual. Virginia's George Washington had obtained a fortune through land speculation and marriage to a wealthy widow. But most colonials could only hope for modest advancement.

The relative ease of achieving land ownership in America encouraged the appearance of small independent farmers. In the cities, artisans and shopkeepers formed a thriving middle class, though urban dwellers comprised only 5 percent of the total population. Beneath middle-class property owners on the social scale were propertyless farm workers (including, in descending order of wealth, tenants, free workers, and indentured servants)

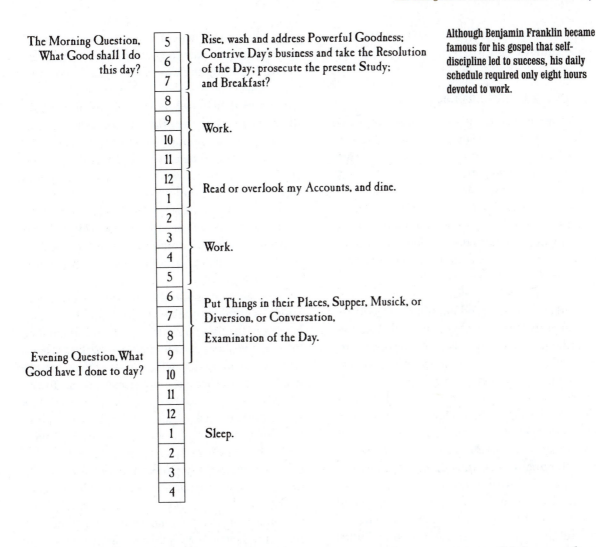

The Morning Question, What Good shall I do this day?	5	Rise, wash and address Powerful Goodness; Contrive Day's business and take the Resolution of the Day; prosecute the present Study; and Breakfast?
	6	
	7	
	8	Work.
	9	
	10	
	11	
	12	Read or overlook my Accounts, and dine.
	1	
	2	Work.
	3	
	4	
	5	
	6	Put Things in their Places, Supper, Musick, or Diversion, or Conversation,
	7	
	8	Examination of the Day.
Evening Question, What Good have I done to day?	9	
	10	
	11	
	12	
	1	Sleep.
	2	
	3	
	4	

Although Benjamin Franklin became famous for his gospel that self-discipline led to success, his daily schedule required only eight hours devoted to work.

and, in urban areas, day workers and apprentices. Lowest in the social order were racial minorities, free as well as slave. Although women worked on family farms and city shops, they assumed the social status of their fathers and husbands. Widows, particularly those with young children, were usually the poorest individuals, though some successfully continued their husbands' businesses.

Colonials well understood and respected these degrees of status and rank. In New England, for example, seating in the meeting house reflected a per-son's social position; so, too, did the annual ranking of students at Harvard and Yale. In the southern colonies, middle-class farmers, even nonslaveowners, recognized a leadership of wealth and assumed their own superiority to Africans and Native peoples. These assumptions enabled the wealthy minority to claim the privileges of a "natural" aristocracy. Yet, precisely because the colonial leadership was based on wealth and not inherited aristocracy, contention sometimes exploded into social conflict. Such outbursts were rare and short-lived, indicative of frustration but seldom a real threat to colonial authorities.

Social Stress in New England

Concern about changing social values appeared dramatically in New England at the end of the 17th century. Unable to develop a staple cash crop, early New Englanders had gone to sea, exporting huge quantities of Newfoundland cod to feed slaves on the sugar plantations of the West Indies, and shipping lumber from local forests to build barrels for tobacco, rum, rice, and other goods. This commerce stimulated a shipbuilding industry as well as bringing profits to shippers. Successful Boston merchants emerged as a wealthy elite who owned choice urban real estate and houses, mahogany furniture, imported linens, and fine clocks that chimed quarter hours. Meanwhile, as a high birthrate created population pressure on old lands and encouraged younger generations to migrate to new towns, land prices rose and speculators reaped profits. By the 1690s, the top tenth of New England society controlled 40 percent of local wealth.

Although Puritan ministers continued to uphold communal values, the pursuit of profits and the disparities of wealth disturbed the traditional social order, resulting in local conflicts about taxes, political representation, and the sites of new churches. Such contention occasionally led to accusations of witchcraft. Belief in witchcraft permeated the folk culture of all colonies, and witchcraft cases had appeared sporadically. But the patterns of the accusations indicated unspoken conflicts involving gender relations, especially in Puritan New England. In 1692, such tensions exploded in Salem, Massachusetts, when over 200 people were accused of witchcraft—and twenty were sent to their deaths.

Although men were occasionally accused of sinful contact with the devil, the overwhelming majority of accused witches were women. One of them, Katherine Harrison of Connecticut, defended herself by saying she was "a female, a weaker vessel, subject to passion." As her words reveal, women were believed more likely to succumb to the devil and, like the original Eve, seduce others into sin. Such assumptions reinforced women's subordination within the churches and the larger society. Indeed, while most of the *accusers* were young women, most of the *accused* were middle-aged women who were considered misfits by their neighbors. The accusers were poorer, often widowed, and known for abrasive conduct; some of the so-called witches had publicly criticized their neighbors' uncharitable behavior.

The Salem trials also illuminated new economic conflicts within colonial society. Some historians have seen the Salem case as an example of conflict between two types of communities—backward agricultural Salem Village, where most of the accusers lived, and prosperous commercial Salem Town, where most of the accused resided. These scholars speculate that social resentment may have provoked rural villagers to criticize the more worldly townspeople. Other historians have emphasized the decline of economic opportunity as population growth caused greater competition for available land. Many accused witches had been involved in legal disputes with family members and neighbors about inherited property. Their economic independence, or the possibility of their achieving such independence, threatened the interests of competing families and challenged the prevailing belief that women should remain subordinate to men. Thus the witch trials could be seen as efforts of male authority figures to keep women in their place.

What distinguished the Salem outbreak were not the accusations, but the number of people implicated, including members of wealthy families. The case thus aroused the interest of the colony's leaders, an elite composed of wealthy merchants,

> **The witch trials could be seen as efforts of male authority figures to keep women in their place.**

who intervened to halt the trials. Thereafter, charges of witchcraft abruptly ceased. Old Puritans might dislike the materialism of New England society, but they no longer looked to the devil to find an explanation for their problems.

Conflicts in Boston appeared less subtle. During the 17th century, New England towns had regulated the price of food and fuel to protect the poor. But when a leading Boston merchant ignored this tradition in 1710, acquired a monopoly of grain, and caused bread prices to soar, a mob attacked his warehouses and took the stored grain. Although a conservative townsman claimed that the rioters were "not God's people, but the Devil's people," the poor had effectively challenged the new law of supply and demand. None were prosecuted for the violence. Commercial values continued to triumph, however, and Boston society became increasingly polarized between rich and poor. The old "publick spirit," one clergyman subsequently complained, had been replaced by a "greedy desire of gain." New England preserved its hierarchical character to the end of the colonial era.

Pluralism and Conflict in the Middle Colonies

Society in the middle colonies appeared more heterogenous than New England's, but also experienced growing stratification. William Penn's liberal offers of land and religious toleration attracted considerable non-English immigration, particularly among German religious groups such as the Moravians and Amish, who fled persecution and European wars. In addition, Scots-Irish Presbyterians

from northern Ireland also migrated to Pennsylvania, New York, and New Jersey in search of economic opportunity. Coming initially as indentured servants, many Germans and Scots-Irish provided manual labor in Philadelphia; New York City, by contrast, relied more on African slaves. Immigrant farmers obtained cheap land and produced corn, wheat, beef, and pork for export. As eastern areas became crowded, later settlers moved west toward the Appalachians and then south into the Carolinas and Georgia. Their desire for land often led to conflicts with Native Americans such as the Catawbas, who traded deerskins with colonial merchants.

Other non-English Europeans included French Huguenots and Mediterranean Jews, who settled as merchants in the port cities. Along with Quaker and English merchants, they participated in the Atlantic trade, exporting food to the West Indies and Europe, selling beaver fur to England, and importing slaves to the colonies. Such merchants also traded with England's French and Spanish colonial rivals, even in times of war. By the mid-18th century, immigration and natural increase saw Philadelphia and New York emerge as major cities, bringing prosperity to shopkeepers and skilled artisans like Benjamin Franklin. Yet city workers faced seasonal unemployment and price inflation and found small opportunity for social mobility. During the colonial era, these cities experienced greater social stratification as wealth became concentrated in fewer hands and the poor became more dependent on public assistance.

Mixed populations contributed to social conflict. Pennsylvania's German immigrants tended to cluster in cohesive communities, avoiding the English language, the English legal system, and English-speaking churches. Their economic success troubled Anglophiles like Franklin, who feared that the colony would become Germanized. Other ethnic and economic rivalries created political crises. In 1763, the Scots-Irish who lived in western Pennsylvania demanded military assistance from the pacifist Quaker legislature to wage war against the Delaware people. When Quakers hesitated to support these frontier farmers, Scots-Irish rebels, known as the Paxton Boys, massacred a village of peaceful Conestogas, then marched to Philadelphia to protest their lack of representation in the legislature. Only Franklin's negotiations thwarted an insurrection against the government. Meanwhile, in New York's Hudson valley, where wealthy Dutch landlords rented property to English tenant farmers, eviction orders provoked an armed rebellion in the 1760s, which was finally crushed by the British military.

Anxieties in Southern Society

Society in the southern colonies appeared more stable as commercial agriculture dominated social relations. Tobacco planters with access to the rivers served as merchants for their neighbors—exporting crops and importing finished goods, and thus made urban centers unnecessary. Overproduction continued to lower tobacco prices, and planters responded by intensifying cultivation, only lowering prices more. Although large landowners with more than five slaves comprised less than 5 percent of the population, they owned nearly 50 percent of the total wealth. This elite built spacious brick houses, employed slaves as domestic servants, and purchased luxury items (furniture, libraries, silver dinnerware) to show their high status. Their assets set the tone of Chesapeake society, and smaller farmers deferred politically to these leaders. "Before a boy knows his right hand from his left," remarked one visitor about the children of the rich, "he is a Gentleman."

By the mid-18th century, however, Chesapeake planters lived amidst ever growing debt to English and Scottish merchants who sold them imported goods. Whipped by fluctuating tobacco prices, some frustrated planters, such as George

Washington, finally abandoned the crop to plant more wheat and corn, but most grew tobacco out of habit and its implied prestige. Virginia planters also engaged in land speculation, using political connections to profit from westward expansion. But despite their best efforts, falling tobacco prices and rising consumption of English goods created a crisis of indebtedness, which was aggravated after 1760 when British creditors began to demand payment.

Planters in South Carolina and Georgia enjoyed more stable prosperity, exporting rice, indigo, deerskins, and naval stores. To avoid the malarial lowlands, wealthy landowners resided in Charleston and Savannah, employing overseers to manage their holdings. Supported by commercial agriculture and surrounded by a black majority of slaves (in some areas more than twice the white population), this elite of planters, merchants, and lawyers pursued an aristocratic lifestyle and supported diverse cultural activities. But the western regions of those colonies were settled by small farmers who objected to the eastern elite's indifference to their problems. Angered by dishonest tax collectors and a poor judicial system, western farmers in North Carolina formed a "Regulator" movement in the 1760s and challenged government authority. The Carolina leadership used the militia to crush the rebellion, but the protests, together with constant fear of slave revolts, created a mood of intense insecurity among southern leaders.

Social tension thus percolated through the English colonies, occasionally erupting in urban riots to protest bread prices or election frauds, and sometimes prompting western farmers to disobey laws against selling alcohol to Native people. Such outbursts were exceptional, symptoms of stress rather than rebellious intentions. Most inhabitants of British origin accepted the hierarchical social order and allowed their "betters" to rule. Yet by English standards, the self-made leadership groups in America appeared as pseudo-aristocrats, big fish in a small pond, rather than members of a hereditary elite. Ironically, many American leaders shared that feeling of inferiority. By the mid-18th century, the sense of being provincial—cultural outsiders compared to the English aristocracy—defined the identity of the colonial leadership.

The Paradoxes of Colonial Culture

The sense of provincialism was accentuated by the flourishing commerce between American wharves and the mother country, which involved not only economic goods but also ideas and values. Imitating English leaders, the colonial elite read English books, magazines, and newspapers, copied English fashions and architecture, and reproduced English curricula in American schools and colleges. American scientists, such as the Quaker John Bartram and Benjamin Franklin, who together founded the American Philosophical Society in Philadelphia in 1743, still communicated their research to the Royal Society of London. Provincialism—the sense of England's cultural superiority—thus served as an intellectual common denominator, whether a colonial lived in a Boston townhouse or presided over a Virginia plantation.

Although the colonial elite took pride in its cultural sophistication, few Americans were really qualified to discuss the contemporary Enlightenment. Basing their ideas on the scientific theories of Sir Isaac Newton, Enlightenment thinkers viewed the universe as a clock, which God had wound up at the Creation and which ran eternally according to the natural laws of physics. Accordingly, they believed that God no longer had to intervene in human affairs. But while a small intellectual elite pondered these ideas, most colonials simply accepted the Protestant faiths. By the mid-18th century, the spirit of religion had flattened; proportionately fewer people attended worship services. Criticism of religious indifference permeated the

land, but most inhabitants ignored the preaching, allowing their spiritual feelings to subside.

These subdued passions suddenly erupted into a major religious revival when an English evangelist named George Whitefield arrived in America in 1739, urging sinners to "fly to Christ." Earlier revivals in the middle colonies and in Jonathan Edwards' church at Northampton, Massachusetts had touched local congregations. But Whitefield's public oratory (Franklin estimated in one open-air meeting in Philadelphia that his voice could reach 25,000 people) sparked what was known as the "Great Awakening." Whitefield's message stressed the futility of achieving worldly success without obtaining spiritual redemption. Instead, Whitefield and his "New Light" disciples summoned individuals to experience a religious rebirth and create a Christian community on earth.

Such preaching, filled with hellfire and brimstone, aroused many colonials from spiritual sleep. Facing eternal damnation, frightened souls shouted out "Oh, I am going to hell! What shall I do to be saved?" And they experienced a spiritual "rebirth" from sinner to saint, joining the churches in great numbers. Although the revivalists were effective in all regions and among all classes, they proved most successful in areas undergoing rapid change, such as newly settled parts of Connecticut, or among groups facing particular problems, such as epidemics or the prospect of war. Since women outnumbered men in church membership (a shift from the early days of colonization), new converts were disproportionately male, young adults in their late twenties. Perhaps the problems of finding one's place in a new society (what today might be called an identity crisis) explains why young men responded to the evangelical call. The Awakening also attracted young women, often during pregnancy when the fear of death was close. "I was . . . brought to the very brink of eternity," said one woman of her conversion, "and then I received comfort." In churches that embraced the revival, women sometimes assumed greater responsibility in church affairs. The revival also attracted Africans, who discovered a parallel between the Christian rebirth and African beliefs of continuing spiritual revelation.

The Awakening's promise of spiritual equality challenged the religious status quo. "It is impossible to relate the convulsions into which the whole country is thrown," complained one clergyman, "for men, women, children, servants, and Negroes are now become (as they phrase it) exhorters." Revivalists boldly rejected traditional styles of worship, even holding services outdoors. As Christians debated the revival, the Presbyterian and Congregational churches split into bitter factions—anti-revivalist "Old Side" Presbyterians and "Old Light" Congregationalists versus evangelical "New Sides" and "New Lights"—resulting in a proliferation of denominations and sects. Methodists and Baptists, who embraced the revival, increased substantially, particularly in areas that previously lacked churches. The willingness of Baptists to accept African American converts as spiritual equals also defied religious justifications for enslaving "heathen" peoples.

Denominational competition inspired the founding of new colleges: the College of New Jersey (now Princeton) by evangelical Presbyterians; King's College (Columbia) by Anglicans; Brown by Baptists; and Queen's College (Rutgers) by Dutch Reformed. Such competition indicates that colonial Americans took religion seriously, even passionately. But when, eventually, these denominational rivals realized that no one group could achieve religious supremacy, they grudgingly accepted the reality of religious pluralism, at least for Protestants. (Only Rhode Island and Pennsylvania accepted religious freedom in principle.) Thus religious toleration—not equality—gradually emerged in American society. Although privileged churches continued to receive tax support, dissenters began to demand separation of church and state.

Preserving a Native American Identity

Colonial Protestants and white ethnic minorities learned to coexist, but toleration did not often cross boundaries of race. Colonial law and social custom kept Africans in subordinate positions, while Native peoples, when they were not enslaved, remained either dependents or cultural outsiders. By 1700, the coastal groups had virtually disappeared, decimated by disease and war or driven by colonial expansion to seek homes beyond the fringe of white settlement. Other Native nations continued as partners in the fur and skin trade with English, French, and Spanish merchants, contributing to the flow of goods overseas. They also served as military allies of the warring European colonies, balancing their own interests in a struggle to maintain their cultural independence.

Dependent Peoples

The coastal peoples, or what was left of them, faced grave problems of maintaining a group identity. Defeated in warfare during the 17th century and plagued by disease and social upheaval, groups like Massachusetts' Nantuckets or Carolina's Catawbas reluctantly sought refuge near colonial settlements, accepting subordination as the price of survival. Known as "settlement Indians" in the southern colonies and "praying Indians" in New England, they exchanged their autonomy for protection from their enemies and accepted marginal employment as hunters, traders, tanners, transporters, and slave catchers. Many lived in mixed groups, composed of members of different nations, a situation that complicated their cultural identity.

Targeted by Christian missionaries, these Natives absorbed European beliefs and habits, but usually within a Native context. In New France, for example, Catholic priests instituted masses, prayers, and confession, but Iroquois converts continued to use shamans, charms, animal sacrifices, ecstatic dances, and festivals to express spiritual concerns. Such mixing of customs reflected not only pragmatic accommodation but also a permanent loss of cultural continuity. "They have forgot most of their traditions," explained one Carolina settler of the southern nations in 1710. "They keep their festivals and can tell but little of the reasons: their Old Men are dead."

Surviving members of the disrupted groups became targets for exploitation by unscrupulous traders, who used alcohol, sexual violence, and dishonest dealing to reduce Native peoples into indebtedness, claimed their labor, and stole their land. With irregular boundary lines separating Native and colonial settlements, common crimes such as trespassing, poaching, and squatting exaggerated tensions. Native disrespect of private property—the killing of livestock, burning of fences, and petty theft—caused conflicts with farmers, while colonials encroached on Native territory to cut wood or feed their livestock.

Inhabiting the Borderlands

While some Native groups surrendered their autonomy, others migrated into the interior to form new communities, hoping to preserve their economic independence and identity. By the 1720s, Shawnees, Delawares, Senecas, and other multi-ethnic tribes had found refuge in the Ohio valley, an area rich with game and fertile acreage, seemingly remote from European intruders. These tribal clusters established self-sustaining kinship-based societies. Women engaged in agriculture and men pursued hunting. During the next three decades, male leaders continued to trade with colonial merchants, exchanging furs for manufactured goods. And, although colonial traders used rum and extended credit to make the Ohio Natives dependent on their goods, the resettled tribes formed stable communities and profited from this commerce.

These inland settlements did not long preserve their independence. As early as 1699, the French had begun to settle the Louisiana territory at the mouth of the Mississippi River. The small colony, based on African slave labor and trade as far east as Carolina and west to Texas and Nebraska, anchored France's southern claims to North America. To the north, French settlements on the St. Lawrence formed an elaborate trade network with the Native peoples around the Great Lakes and in Illinois. Together, France's colonies created an arc of settlement that effectively contested English expansion west of the Appalachians. Thus when English traders from Virginia, Pennsylvania, and New York entered the Ohio valley to deal with the resettled nations, they knowingly threatened France's territorial claims. By the 1740s, the French government began to send military expeditions to block English colonial interlopers. The Ohio nations now found themselves caught in the middle of an explosive imperial rivalry. Soon war would come to the Ohio valley, forcing them to choose sides.

Competing for the Continent

In contrast to the sparsely populated French settlements, some of which were little more than trading posts, the English colonies had achieved considerable economic and cultural strength during the 18th century. Yet the land still appeared overwhelmingly undeveloped. In Virginia, for instance, the dense woods between tobacco plantations served as an alternative territory for African slaves, a sheltered place to hold religious ceremonies and feasts or simply a refuge to hide from their owners. Even around the tamest communities of New York and New England, Native peoples remained a presence, if not a threat to peace.

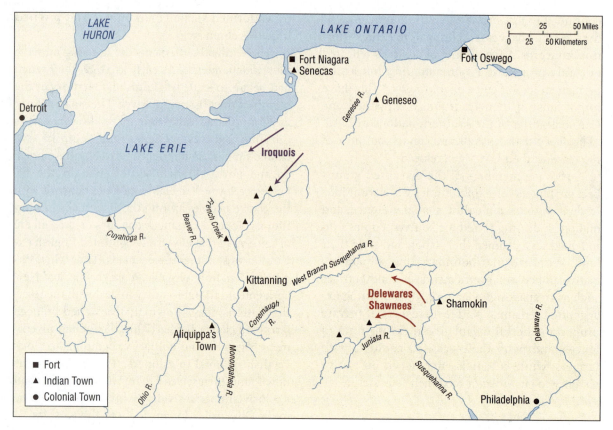

Native American Migrations to the Ohio Country, 1724–1745

Thus as English provincials emphasized their advanced social development, they perched precariously on the edges of the continent, looking more to Europe for trade, values, and purpose than to the western interior. Facing the Atlantic, they referred to the West as the "back country." With their eyes on England, moreover, colonial leaders remained acutely dependent on merchants and politicians in the mother country who could threaten their political and economic interests. Yet by the mid-18th century, western lands were increasingly summoning colonial surveyors and speculators, traders and settlers, to seek opportunity. As England and France simultaneously looked to the future in the Ohio valley, colonists and native inhabitants understood the stakes of this competition. The winner would control the continent.

INFOTRAC® COLLEGE EDITION EXERCISES

For additional reading go to InfoTrac College Edition, your online research library at *http://web1.infotrac-college.com.*

Subject search: William Berkeley

Keyword search: Bacon's Rebellion

Subject search: slavery

Subject search: slavery, religious aspects

Keyword search: slave culture

Subject search: colonial America

Subject search: Great Awakening, related subjects

Keyword search: American philosophy

Keyword search: wars of religion

ADDITIONAL READING

Jon Butler, *Becoming America: The Revolution before 1776* (2000). A convenient summary of colonial social history.

Bacon's Rebellion

Stephen Saunders Webb, *1676: The End of American Independence* (1984). An analysis of Bacon's rebellion, placing colonial conflicts within the context of British and Native American affairs. See also Edmund Morgan's *American Slavery, American Freedom,* listed in Chapter 3.

Defining Slavery in the Colonies

Ira Berlin, *Many Thousands Gone: The First Two Centuries of Slavery in North America* (1998). A comprehensive study of the development of slavery in the Atlantic colonies and Louisiana. See also Philip D. Morgan, *Slave Counterpoint: Black Culture in the Eighteenth-Century Chesapeake and Low Country* (1998).

Michael A. Gomez, *Exchanging Our Country Marks: The Transformation of African Identities in the Colonial and Antebellum South* (1998). Analyzes ethnic diversity in Africa and its continuities among American slaves.

Winthrop Jordan, *White over Black: American Attitudes toward the Negro, 1550–1812* (1968). A classic study of the origins and forms of race prejudice and slavery in North America, whose focus is on white thinking about blacks.

Economic Expansion and Social Conflict

Richard L. Bushman, *From Puritan to Yankee: Character and the Social Order in Connecticut, 1690–1765* (1967). Describes social changes in rural Connecticut and their effect on religion and politics.

Jack P. Greene, *Pursuits of Happiness: The Social Development of Early Modern British Colonies and the Formation of American Culture* (1988). A comparative analysis of colonial history, linking economic changes to social structure.

Rhys Isaac, The *Transformation of Virginia, 1740–1790* (1982). The author explores the interaction of social relations, religious controversy, and political values.

Gary B. Nash, *The Urban Crucible: Social Change, Political Consciousness, and the Origins of the American Revolution* (1979). Focusing on Boston, New York, and Philadelphia, Nash explains the relationship of economic and social issues to the emergence of political conflict.

Laurel Thatcher Ulrich, *Good Wives: Images and Reality in the Lives of Women in Northern New England, 1650–1750* (1982). This book, studded with details about everyday life, describes the life cycle of ordinary colonial women.

Social Stress in New England

Carol F. Karlsen, *The Devil in the Shape of a Woman: Witchcraft in Colonial New England* (1987). This analysis of New England witchcraft emphasizes underlying gender issues.

Preserving a Native American Identity

John Demos, *The Unredeemed Captive: A Family Story from Early America* (1994). Focusing on a Puritan girl who was captured by Iroquois warriors, the book examines the ensuing cultural interactions.

Daniel R. Mandell, *Behind the Frontier: Indians in Eighteenth-Century Eastern Massachusetts* (1996). Examining the period after King Philip's War, this book describes the cultural pressures faced by Native survivors.

Michael N. McConnell, *A Country Between: The Upper Ohio Valley and Its Peoples, 1724–1774* (1992). Describes the complicated Native cultures west of the Appalachians.

Richard White, *The Middle Ground: Indians, Empire, and Republics in the Great Lakes Region, 1650–1815* (1991). A thorough study of Native American society, politics, and diplomacy, emphasizing cross-cultural relationships.

5

Patriarchal Politics and the Colonial Crisis, 1689–1776

CHRONOLOGY

1689–1697	King William's War fought against New France
1701–1713	Queen Anne's War waged against French Canada and Spanish Florida
1744–1748	King George's War embroils England against France
1754–1763	Seven Years' War results in expulsion of France from North America
1754	Benjamin Franklin proposes plan of union at Albany congress
1761	James Otis argues against writs of assistance
1763	Proclamation Line limits western expansion
1763–1764	Pontiac leads uprising against Anglo American posts
1764	Parliament passes Sugar and Currency acts
1765	Stamp Act provokes colonial protests
1766	Declaratory Act affirms Parliament's right to legislate
1767	Townshend acts seek alternative source of revenue; John Dickinson publishes protest
1770	Conflict with British troops sparks Boston Massacre
1773	Parliament passes Tea Act; Boston stages "tea party"
1774	Passage of Coercive acts prompts first Continental Congress
1775	Minutemen battle redcoats at Lexington and Concord; Second Continental Congress convenes
1776	Congress approves Declaration of Independence

On a sunny Thursday morning in 1765, thirty-nine of Virginia's most powerful leaders sat transfixed in the chamber of the House of Burgesses, the colony legislature. The 29-year-old delegate from Hanover, Patrick Henry, stood before them, his voice ringing through the hall, his words stirring their hearts.

In vivid patriotic language, like none ever before uttered in the legislature, Henry eloquently defended his countrymen's exclusive right to tax themselves rather than accept the latest proposals of the English Parliament. He urged his colleagues to remember that history's tyrants, including the kings of England, had always faced strong opposition. Now, in a new moment of peril, he hoped simply that "some good American would stand up in favor of his country."

But, just as Henry paused to take a breath, another more-cautious representative startled the delegates: "Treason! Treason!" he shouted.

http://history.wadsworth.com

That verbal duel underscored the immense changes in colonial politics since the founding of England's colonies in the previous century. The 3,000 miles that separated Americans from Europe had encouraged the birth, and growth, of a distinct political perspective. As the mother country pursued a policy of "salutary neglect," the colonists developed considerable self-government—in practice, if not in principle. Most colonies had established a political order based on England's system of government. They celebrated a heritage that preserved individual legal rights, such as trial by jury, and constitutional protections, which limited the power of the monarchy with an elected representative legislature. But, ironically, these much-honored "rights of Englishmen" would eventually lead colonials to defend their *own* rights when challenged by the mother country. From being loyal Englishmen, colonials like Virginia's Patrick Henry and Thomas Jefferson, Massachusetts's Sam Adams and John Adams, Maryland's Daniel Dulany, and Pennsylvania's Benjamin Franklin, would slowly but surely become loyal *Americans*.

This evolving political identity mirrored the colonists' social views. The key to understanding colonial politics could be found in the belief that the family was a miniature of society. "Families are the nurseries for church and commonwealth," said one New England minister. "Ruin families, and ruin all. Order them well and the public state will fare better." To people living in colonial America, both family and government existed as patriarchal institutions dominated by powerful father figures. Fathers were expected to rule their households, just as political leaders governed society and the state. The Fifth Commandment—"Thou shalt honor thy father and thy mother"—established the moral underpinnings of both private and public life. Yet, to colonials, a patriarchal society was

not oppressive—indeed, just the opposite. Fathers, whether biological or political, were expected to protect the entire family.

Although political leaders assumed that families, societies, and governments should be hierarchical (that is, that some should be higher than others) they believed that no segment of society could flourish unless the entire society did. Such views justified, in their eyes, colonial dependence on the patriarchal king and the mother country. Even when the English Parliament passed laws that were unpopular in America, colonial leaders usually expressed affection for the king and appealed to him to correct injustices. Only as a last resort did Americans attack King George directly. And then, in 1776, leading colonists announced to the world that the Anglo American political family no longer satisfied the needs of all its members. The result was political divorce and American independence.

Patriarchy and Political Power

Patriarchal politics had its roots in local governments—the towns in New England and counties elsewhere—that were most closely tied to family life. Local officials, including sheriffs, justices of the peace, and coroners, provided all the government services that most people needed. Their duties included the probate of wills, assessment of taxes, dispensing of charity, and supervision of elections to the colonial legislatures. According to English custom and provincial laws, political leaders were chosen from the local elite; they were men of property who acted as "fathers" of their communities. Because land ownership was widespread among free white men, English colonials formed a larger electorate than in other countries. Yet voters accepted a patriarchal view of government and chose their "betters" to exercise power.

Gender and Politics

"Parents should be very careful to uphold a prudent government of their children," remarked a New Englander in 1737. "A steady, mild, yet close and taut government is the best." Believing that infants were born corrupted by original sin, many colonial parents began to discipline their children at a very young age. Children of both sexes were dressed in gowns or petticoats, which covered their feet and so restricted their mobility. At the age of about six, boys began to wear the breeches or pants of adult male garb. The change was significant, for while boys achieved greater liberty of movement, girls' skirts hobbled their ability to run and ride. Boys obtained more education; male literacy remained substantially higher than female during the colonial period: 85 percent of males to 50 percent of females in New England; 60 percent to 25 percent in the other colonies.

The division of male and female roles reflected popular assumptions about gender differences. According to conventional wisdom, men possessed "wisdom, strength and courage, fit to protect and defend," whereas women appeared "weaker . . . more fearful, and more affectionate [i.e., more emotional]." The consequences of such beliefs were substantial. Men were seen as active, women as passive; men were expected to be leaders, women their followers. In advising his son to prepare for public

Colonial portraits pictured children as miniature adults. Such images reinforced the idea that even youngsters were burdened by the "original sin" of Adam and Eve and were not born innocent.

life, Maryland's Charles Carroll urged the young man to find a wife who was "virtuous, sensible, good natured, complaisant, complying, and of a cheerful disposition."

Colonial laws, based on English precedents, reinforced this emphasis on female passivity by restricting women's legal identity. Upon marriage, a woman's property legally passed to her husband, her income belonged to him, and anything she inherited became his. Fathers controlled the custody of their children, which was in significant contrast with Native practices (and sometimes an impediment to legal marriages between Native women and English men). Colonial inheritance laws gave widows the use of one-third of their husbands' property, but seldom the independent ownership of that property; children received the remainder. Sons received larger amounts than daughters, whose inheritances passed to their own husbands. Since divorces and legal separations were extremely difficult to obtain, colonial women understandably worried about their marital choices. "If we happen to judge wrong," complained the widowed South Carolina indigo planter Eliza Lucas Pinckney, "there is an end of all human felicity." Yet the independent, educated, and spirited Mrs. Pinckney would, on her own, successfully manage her extensive plantations and raise two sons, Charles and Thomas, to become political leaders and statesmen.

Local Politics and Political Participation

Patriarchal politics began on the local level of government, where property qualifications restricted the right to vote. The ease of land ownership in America (only New York, New Jersey, and Maryland had large numbers of tenant farmers) enabled most adult white men to meet the voting requirements (75 percent in the northern colonies, 50 percent in the southern colonies). By comparison with other countries, including England, Americans enjoyed wide suffrage. But nearly all women, servants, tenants, day laborers, slaves, and children—individuals who were dependents on a male head of household—could not vote because they owned no property and therefore did not have sufficient "stake" in society. For reasons of religious bigotry, most colonies denied the vote to Jews, Catholics, and other non-Protestants.

Since local officials oversaw the voting process, patriarchal assumptions diminished the importance of the right to vote. Most political candidates came from the local elites, either because of higher property qualifications for holding public

office or because their neighbors already recognized the nominees as leaders. Lacking significant political choices, many eligible voters simply did not vote. Those who did found their options limited. During the 18th century, most legal affairs, even the filing of court documents, were conducted orally. So, too, was voting. A voter approached the polling place and was greeted by the rival candidates, asked to express his choice aloud, and then treated to a glass of rum by his preferred candidate. Such open balloting hardly encouraged defiance of local leaders. Yet except at times of crisis, voters seldom protested this system of elite rule. Slaveowning rice planters in the Carolinas, tobacco aristocrats on the Chesapeake, wealthy landlords in the middle colonies, Atlantic merchants in Philadelphia, New York, and Boston—in all colonies, a respectable leadership emerged to dominate local governments.

The power of patriarchy in the English colonies contrasted with a more balanced gender system in many Native American communities. The Cherokees who lived on the borders of Georgia and the Carolinas, for instance, had a matriarchal clan system in which women played a major role in community decisions. Since control of property and crops followed the mother's lineage, women had considerable voice in determining how resources would be distributed. Cherokee men, who traditionally controlled trade in deerskins and diplomacy, had more contact with colonial leaders. When a Cherokee head man met with the South Carolina government in 1757, he was surprised at the absence of women in the council meeting, remarking in confusion to the governor that "White men as well as Red were born of women." Colonial leaders preferred to negotiate with male warriors and traders, and their views eventually altered Cherokee customs. As Cherokee men became more economically important in tribal life, women's status declined. Thus for Cherokees, as for Anglo Americans, control of property was linked to political power. Lacking the Cherokee women's access to land ownership, colonial women had no public voice.

The Structure of Provincial Power

The political system in America deliberately paralleled the structure of power in the mother country. Most colonies operated with a three-part government, consisting of a governor, council, and assembly, echoing the English system of king, House of Lords, and House of Commons. The governor (usually appointed by the crown or, as in Pennsylvania, by the proprietor) acted as the executive branch. Governors were responsible for approving legislation, enforcing the navigation acts, and serving as commanders-in-chief of the militia. Governors selected members of the council, who acted as the upper house of the legislature. The Council served with the governor as the highest court of appeal, authorized land grants, and confirmed judicial appointments. Yet, the councilors' dependence on the governor's favor limited their legislative independence. Political leaders who did not curry favor or enjoy the governors' friendship often sought political power in the elected assembly (lower house of the legislature).

While the governors defended the king's power, the lower house strove to protect colonial rights. (It was, for example, no surprise that Patrick Henry challenged the rights of Parliament in Virginia's assembly, the House of Burgesses.) These legislative bodies consisted of elected representatives, chosen by the adult white men in the towns and counties. During the colonial period, the assemblies had consciously imitated Parliament and won the right to enact taxes to finance government activities. With that right, the legis-

latures could challenge the governors' efforts to impose royal policies. By controlling taxes, for example, the assemblies could withhold approval of specific expenditures—even the governor's own salary—until he agreed to their terms.

In nearly every colony, the assemblies fought with the governors at one time or another about taxes, the payment of salaries, land grants, the appointment of government officers, issuance of paper money, access to trade with Native peoples, and military defense. These issues were closely related to economic success, since passage of a law could make the difference between a family's prosperity or failure. Land grants, for example, promised great profits as population increased and residents sought land for their children to inherit. Issuance of paper money, which usually was worth less than its face value, could become a bonus for those who had to repay debts. The appointment of friendly tobacco inspectors might benefit particular planters, and a wartime contract for warm blankets might reward cloth merchants.

More important than the advantages of specific laws, however, was the way colonial politicians viewed these political struggles. Among the most popular reading in the British colonies were the essays titled *Cato's Letters,* by John Trenchard and Thomas Gordon, first published in 1733 and frequently reprinted in colonial newspapers. The two writers had not benefited by the patronage system in the mother country and warned Englishmen on both sides of the Atlantic that conspiratorial politicians were attempting to undermine the English constitution. Suggesting that the king's advisors were using patronage to influence the other branches of government, they reminded readers that legislators had to remain independent of executive pressure to preserve the constitutional balance. The title of one of Cato's letters expressed their extreme suspicion of the political system:

"What Measures Are Actually Taken by Wicked and Desperate Ministers to Ruin and Enslave Their Country." To preserve the beloved English "liberty," they urged citizens to exercise utmost vigilance against the expansion of royal power.

English Interference in Colonial Affairs

Such advice made sense to colonial politicians, who lived 3,000 miles from the centers of power in England. Despite the efforts of provincial assemblies to assume the same rights that the British parliament enjoyed, colonial politics remained subordinate to England's interests. Patronage issues in the mother country often caused the recall of the royal governor and the appointment of his replacement. Many colonial assemblies hired agents to look out for their affairs in London. Even so, new royal governors arrived in America with fresh instructions to levy taxes, enforce trade laws, or raise an army without considering colonial concerns. Such arrivals and departures disrupted the political process, as colonial politicians formed coalitions to work with or against the governors. In addition, British regulations required that all legislative acts be approved in England before they could become law. Although the king's Privy Council seldom vetoed these laws, delays and uncertainty stirred colonial fears of the abuse of power.

English supervision of colonial politics also had economic consequences. The theory of mercantilism assumed that the advantages of empire would be reciprocal: both the colonies and the mother country would benefit from the regulation of trade. Thus the navigation acts had stimulated shipbuilding in New England and supported South Carolina's indigo industry with English bounties. But sometimes English policy threatened colonial prosperity. When falling tobacco prices prompted Virginia legislators to limit production by stopping the slave trade in the 1730s, the English Privy Council vetoed the measure, explaining that only Parliament could enact laws of trade. To protect English merchants from having to accept depreciated paper money as payment for imported goods, Parliament restricted the use of paper money, first in New England in 1750 and later in all colonies. The Hat Act (1732) favored England's hatmakers by halting colonial manufacture of finished hats, while the Iron Act (1750) limited colonial production to merely bar and pig iron. Such measures underscored the subordinate economic role of England's colonies.

Although many colonists disliked English interference and secretly defied some restrictions by smuggling and by bribing officials to close their eyes to violations (such as trade with French colonies), colonial protest usually remained only rhetorical and theoretical. In fact, colonial leaders typically asserted their allegiance to England's monarchy, reiterating their "obligations to duty, loyalty, and affection" in exchange for the king's "paternal care." Nonetheless, by the mid-18th century, colonial leaders well understood their subordinate position in the British empire.

Other colonials, less well placed than the political elite, could not always afford to accept England's authority. Although most 18th-century Americans accepted elite rule, economic or political grievances sometimes spurred political action outside the legal system. During the 1740s, for example, the royal navy provoked popular opposition in Boston by forcing colonial sailors to serve on British warships. On several occasions, spontaneous but purposeful crowds used violence to interfere with this British policy. Similarly, disputes about paper money in Boston created so much hostility among workers that when the house of a leading politician, Thomas Hutchinson, mysteriously caught fire, a crowd surrounded the blaze, cursed the unpopular leader, and roared "Let it burn! Let it burn!"

Such cases of organized violence were exceptions to the rule of voluntary obedience. Africans in the north also created an unofficial political system to settle disputes. On colony election days, Africans voted for their own "governors" and "kings," respected leaders who would provide guidance for their community. Only partly a satire of colonial rituals, these elections allowed Africans to choose leaders to resolve internal problems.

Imperial Wars Disrupt the Public Order

The general acceptance of the English colonial system could be seen in the colonists' sacrifices during time of war. As loyal subjects, Americans accepted the crown's control of foreign diplomacy and rallied to the king's defense. Four times between 1689 and 1763, the mother country engaged in war with European rivals, especially France; four times Americans shared the burdens of these wars. Because the European powers drew Native allies into these struggles, the wars also affected Native societies, disrupting trade, threatening territorial boundaries, and causing countless deaths. Among colonials, the wars had a strong economic impact, fostering brief booms and inflations that were followed by layoffs and depressions. Most important, these imperial conflicts underscored the colonies' dependence on English policies; decisions about war and peace were made in Europe, never in America. The colonials might well share English victories, but just as surely would they fear and suffer from military upheaval.

Europe's American Wars

The first colonial war, King William's War (1689–1697) pitted England against France on the northern borders of New England and New York. When English plans to invade French Canada failed in 1689, the conflict turned into a series of border raids. English, French, and Dutch settlers suffered grievous losses when Native warriors burned towns or kidnapped civilians to replace their own dead. Although some European captives managed to escape, becoming famous for preserving their faith amid "savage" conditions, many spent the remainder of their lives among their captors, assimilating into Native communities.

King William's War also brought heavy losses to the Iroquois, whose Algonquian and Abenaki enemies continued to fight even after the European treaty formally ended the war in 1697. By 1701, the weakened Iroquois negotiated with the French and their Native allies to preserve access to the western fur trade in exchange for limiting their military alliance with England. Despite losing 20 percent of their population, the Iroquois would remain an important military presence on the borders between New France and New England.

The second colonial war, Queen Anne's War (1701–1713), revived English-French hostility in the northern colonies and English-Spanish conflict between Florida and South Carolina. Once again, civilians on the outskirts of settlements suffered attacks, murders, and kidnappings. In colonial cities, war profiteering by wealthy merchants caused an inflation of prices and shortages of food. But the peace treaty gave England control of Hudson's Bay, Newfoundland, and Acadia (Nova Scotia), which had the effect of protecting New England's lucrative fishing industry.

In 1739, a dispute over trading rights in the West Indies (which became known as the War of Jenkins' Ear because a Spanish officer allegedly mutilated the English Captain Jenkins) erupted into a third conflict between England and its enemies, France and Spain, known as King George's War (1744–1748). As England organized military campaigns against Spanish shipping and Canadian towns, the colonial economy benefitted by shipbuilding, privateering, and war contracts. Three thousand Massachusetts men, a rough band drawn heavily from among Boston's poor, enlisted in an expedition against the French fortress at Louisbourg. All colonials celebrated their victory in 1745.

From England's point of view, however, glory in America was worth less than achieving dominance in Europe. To the dismay of colonials, the peace treaty of 1748 returned all conquered territories to their previous claimants. The social costs were less easily remedied. Recent estimates suggest that Massachusetts lost 2 percent of its population, 8 percent of its men over the age of 16. Such heavy casualties, the result of disease and malnutrition more than enemy bullets, left large numbers of widows, many with children, who became destitute. Such problems encouraged public efforts to help the poor. But when Boston caretakers introduced a textile workhouse for poor women, the beneficiaries rebuffed the scheme, preferring to spin wool at home, where they could labor in a familiar environment, supervise their children, and earn a meager living by taking in laundry and boarders. Although prosperity returned to the colonies in the 1750s, unemployment remained high in Boston.

The War for Empire

The peace was short lived. The outbreak of the Seven Years War (1754–1763) reminded colonials that the cherished rights of Englishmen demanded sacrifice. As France moved to protect its access to the rich fur trade of the Ohio valley and English colonials penetrated the same region for settlement and trade with the Ohio nations, both European powers understood that the contest involved nothing less than control of the continent. At the remote borderlands of the Ohio river valley, on territory occupied by various refugee peo-

Here was the threshold to all the natural riches of America.

ple including Delawares, Shawnees, and Mingos, but claimed by Iroquois, French, Virginians, and Pennsylvanians, the two European rivals drew lines on a map and fought to protect their claims. Here, after all, was the threshhold to all the natural riches of America.

In 1749, King George II had granted unknown acreage to the Ohio Company of Virginia, a private investment company, which employed a young land speculator named George Washington to survey the area. Pennsylvania's land speculators soon moved to secure their own claims to the region. Both colonial groups had dealt directly with the small Ohio nations, ignoring the Iroquois, who claimed to speak for their Ohio "cousins" and who also wanted a share of the interior trade. English activity in the region prompted the French to send an army to begin building a chain of forts in 1753 to keep English colonials east of the Appalachian mountains. Amid these competing interests, one view emerged clearly: the local Ohio nations wanted to remove all invading groups—English, French, or Iroquois—and tried to juggle their neutrality for their own benefit. Washington's appointment as a Virginia militia officer merely antagonized the Ohio people because of his tendency "to Command the Indians as his slaves."

Negotiations to form an alliance with the Native groups climaxed when seven English colonies sent delegates to Albany, New York, in 1754 to meet with the Iroquois and plan for mutual defense. Frustrated by intercolonial rivalry and broken promises, the Iroquois refused to join an alliance. Benjamin Franklin took the opportunity to introduce a "Plan of Union," proposing the cre-

The mortally wounded Major General Edward Braddock retreating with his army after being attacked by French and Indian forces near Fort Duquesne on July 9, 1755.

ation of a Grand Council that would represent all colonies to administer military defense, coordinate land and trade relations with Native nations, and levy taxes. Although approved by the Albany congress, the plan challenged the existing political leadership and was rejected by the colonial assemblies. In any event, royal officials in England had no intention of turning over such profitable business to colonial politicians.

In 1754, skirmishes between English and French troops signaled the outbreak of open warfare. Both European nations promptly transported their armies to America. But when the English General Edward Braddock notified the Ohio nations that "no Savage should inherit the land," Native leaders decided that English expansion represented more of a threat than French forts and trading posts. The result was a British military disaster. As Braddock marched his troops toward the French forts in western Pennsylvania in 1755, French and

> **"Our exalted ideas of the prowess of British regulars had not been well founded."**

Native warriors sprang from an ambush and forced the redcoats to retreat. "This whole transaction," Franklin later wrote, "gave us Americans the first suspicion that our exalted ideas of the prowess of British regulars had not been well founded."

In addition to humiliating Braddock and the English, the flight of English forces from the Ohio region gave the French great power over the Native nations. Threatening to destroy their villages, the French coerced the Natives to join them in attacking English settlements in Pennsylvania, Virginia, and the Carolinas. This alliance gave the conflicts its popular name: French and Indian War.

Pennsylvania Quakers, famous for their pacifism, faced pressure from their Scots-Irish and German neighbors to vote for taxes to finance retaliatory attacks. Although Quaker leaders quickly approved funds "for the king's purposes," a few Quakers resigned from the assembly to preserve their pacifist consciences. The Quakers also insisted on peaceful negotiations to end the brutal warfare. Indeed, Quaker criticism of previous unfair dealing with the Delawares and generous gifts to Native leaders eased tensions on the colony's western borders. "In all the desolation on our frontiers," remarked one pacifist politician in 1758, "not one Friend we have heard of has been slain nor carried captive."

The early failure of English military forces enabled the French to gain control of the borders of New York and Canada. But French success alarmed the Iroquois and Ohio nations. A complete victory by one European power would mean that the Native nations would fall subordinate to the victor and lose their independence. By 1758, Native leaders were eager to negotiate a neutral position with the English. Their withdrawal from the war coincided with the rise of a new English leader, William Pitt, who reinvigorated British military activity. Instead of sending fresh troops to America, Pitt agreed to finance the cost of the war if the colonies provided the manpower. Under the leadership of British officers, colonial militiamen recaptured the French forts in western Pennsylvania, New York, and Canada. The hostilities climaxed in the battle of Quebec, where General James Wolfe defeated the French General Montcalm in 1759. Four years later, the Treaty of Paris ended the war; France surrendered all its American possessions except for two sugar islands in the West Indies.

Benjamin Franklin delighted in the colonial contribution to England's victory. "The growth of the children," he gloated, expressing pride in America's sacrifices, "tends to increase the growth of the mother." The colonists had also gained considerable benefits. War contracts had brought prosperity to colonial cities; farmers found markets for their produce. And, once colonial privateers had swept the French navy from the seas, merchants resumed the profitable illegal trade with the French and Spanish sugar islands. But when Parliament attempted to stop such smuggling by permitting the issuance of general search warrants, called "writs of assistance," colonial merchants rose in protest. Attacking the use of such writs in 1761, Massachusetts lawyer James Otis suggested that Parliament lacked the *right* to legislate for the colonies. Although the Massachusetts courts ruled against him, Otis's argument foreshadowed new challenges to Parliament's power.

Not everyone in the colonies had profited from the war. In Maryland, Catholics (presumed allies of the French Catholics) were shouldered with double property taxes to finance the war. Boston soldiers again suffered heavy casualties, leaving large numbers of widows and orphans. From South Carolina, the Catawbas had sent warriors to battle with the English, only to have them return infected with smallpox that devastated the population. Drastically reduced in numbers and dependent on colonial trade, the survivors accepted reservation lands in the western parts of the colony as a way of preventing complete encroachment by colonial settlers.

Colonial Expansion Provokes Resistance

Other Native groups also faced an uncertain future. Although the removal of France from North America promised to end border warfare in the Ohio valley, the diverse Native nations now had to confront uncontested English power. To the dismay of Delawares, Shawnees, Ottawas, Miamis, Chippewas, and Iroquois, British General Jeffrey Amherst did not follow the defeated French in retreat from

British soldiers presented the Delawares gifts of blankets and handkerchiefs that had deliberately been contaminated with smallpox.

Fort Duquesne; instead, he built an English fort on the ruins at Pittsburgh. The British even violated the custom of diplomatic reciprocity, such as gift giving. During negotiations with Delaware diplomats, British soldiers presented gifts of blankets and handkerchiefs that had deliberately been contaminated with smallpox. "I hope it will have the desired effect," reflected a British soldier coldly.

Nor could British officials curb the appetite of colonial land grabbers. As colonials illegally occupied Native territory, one Delaware warrior complained that "the white people covets the land and eats them out by inches . . . which [is] against the will of God." Property disputes between colonial settlers and Native peoples provoked violence and intensified racial hatred. Meanwhile, the royal government in England also coveted Native lands and tried to restrict colonial land speculation and trade with Native groups. The royal government now issued the Proclamation of 1763, which prohibited colonial settlement west of the Appalachian mountains. The policy ignored both Native and colonial claims in the region.

"If you suffer the English among you, you are dead men," warned the frustrated Delaware prophet Neolin. "Sickness, smallpox, and their poison will destroy you entirely." Pointing to the disappearance of deer herds, the seizure of tribal lands, and the English refusal to trade gunpowder, Neolin called for a revitalization of traditional values, the rejection of "white people's ways and nature," including rum, and the display of friendship by shaking hands with the left hand, not the European's customary right hand. "Drive them away," Neolin urged. "Wage war against them."

During the spring of 1763, Native hostility spread through the Ohio valley, igniting another war. Under the leadership of the Ottawa chief Pontiac, Native groups in the Ohio valley attacked British forts and trading posts as well as frontier settlements in Pennsylvania and Virginia. But without French assistance, Pontiac's rebellion collapsed once British troops arrived. Although the royal government still hoped to control the western lands, colonial speculators won some revisions of the Proclamation Line. Colonials continued to stake claims in Kentucky and Tennessee, but legal title to these lands remained uncertain, contributing to dissatisfaction with England's policies.

England's Imperial Crisis

England's victory over France, instead of bringing peace and security to America, actually inspired new grievances that set the colonies on the road to independence. Of course, no one in 1763 actually spoke about the separation of the colonies from the mother country, nor did anyone envision the long and tricky route that led to the Declaration of Independence thirteen years later. Indeed, it would be a mistake to assume that the creation of an American nation was inevitable. And yet the French and Indian War had revealed serious problems within the British Empire. Despite the military emergency, the colonies had been slow to support England's efforts. Yet the war had increased England's indebtedness, and royal officials resolved to tax the colonies to pay for future military defense and administrative costs. England also had decided, even before Pontiac's rebellion, to station 10,000 regular troops (redcoats) in America, at the colonies' expense.

England's plans came at an inopportune time. The war's end had brought with it an economic depression that slowed business, lowered wages, and eliminated jobs. As credit contracted, English merchants demanded that colonists pay their outstanding debts; one result was a financial crisis in Virginia, where heavily indebted tobacco planters scrambled to avoid bankruptcy. Concern about British interference in colonial affairs surfaced when the king's Privy Council vetoed a Virginia law that would have lowered the salaries of clergymen. Defending the bill in 1763, an impassioned Patrick Henry denied the king's right to veto colonial laws, calling him a tyrant. Moved by the speech, a jury awarded the clergymen a single penny in damages; Henry soon won election to the Virginia House of Burgesses.

England Seeks Revenue, Colonists Dissent

Objections to Parliament's control of the colonies became precedents for further protests when England resolved to introduce new taxes to pay for colonial defense. Reasoning that the colonists who had benefited from the war with France should share the costs of empire, Parliament passed the Sugar Act in 1764—for the first time using a navigation law *not* to regulate trade but to raise revenue. Although the measure lowered customs duties on imported molasses, it also attempted to increase revenue collections with better enforcement provisions to end colonial smuggling. Yet the law deprived shippers of the traditional legal protections, such as trial by a local jury and presumption of innocence rather than guilt. Despite protests from colonial merchants, an indifferent Parliament also passed the Currency Act of 1764, which prohibited the use of paper money and thus reduced the supply of currency just as English creditors were recalling debts and tax collectors were seeking more revenue.

Parliament then passed a broader tax law, the Stamp Act, in 1765. Requiring revenue stamps to be attached to legal documents, such as wills and deeds, newspapers, and printed matter, the law proposed to tax colonials without relying on the colony legislatures, which customarily had approved all revenue bills. Parliament also passed the Quartering Act of 1765, requiring colonials to provide food and housing for British troops in America. Since the redcoats were notoriously abusive to civilians, the law seemed doubly obnoxious: colonials would have to pay for protection they did not want or need. In fact, only New York faced a significant tax burden and finally simply refused to comply with the law.

The new taxes aroused storms of protest, particularly from the lawyers, merchants, and printers who would have to use the new revenue stamps. The Maryland lawyer Daniel Dulany led the attack. In a widely read pamphlet, *Considerations on the Propriety of Imposing Taxes in the British Colonies* (1765), he argued that by passing new taxes Parliament threatened a basic right of Englishmen. Although Parliament claimed that it "virtually" represented the entire empire, Dulany insisted that only "actual" representation by specific delegates was legal (though no one really wished to send delegates to England), and he declared that Parliament's interests no longer coincided with colonial rights.

In Virginia, Dulany's constitutional arguments translated on the popular level into a fear that English politicians intended to destroy colonial self-government. The Stamp Act prompted young Patrick Henry to advocate resolutions that denounced Parliament's supremacy. His fiery condemnation of the king made him instantly famous in all the colonies. Other protesters did not stop with words. Aware of the economic impact of the new taxes, merchants, artisans, and workers in the port cities formed secret groups called "Sons of Liberty" to prevent the use of the government stamps. In Boston, New York, Newport, and Philadelphia, angry crowds visited the appointed stamp officials and demanded their resignations. When the government officials refused, the mobs attacked their property and threatened their lives. Once again, the unfortunate Thomas Hutchinson lost his Massachusetts house to mob violence. In New York, another mob tore apart a theatrical playhouse frequented by the wealthy. Backed by such popular sentiment, nine colonial assemblies sent delegates to a Stamp Act Congress in New York in 1765, which drafted a Declaration of Rights and Grievances, denying Parliament's right to tax the colonies.

Adding muscle to these protests, colonial merchants agreed to boycott English goods until the Stamp Act was repealed. Believing that luxury imports contributed to a loss of morality, supporters of the boycott promised not only to persuade Parliament to repeal the law but also to restore the public virtue. More practically, the nonimportation and nonconsumption agreements threatened English commercial interests that had considerable influence in Parliament. To reinforce such pressure, the assemblies also appointed colonial agents to lobby Parliament to rescind the unpopular taxes.

Parliament Defends Its Sovereignty

By 1766, this combination of economic pressure, political lobbying, and constitutional argument convinced Parliament to repeal the Stamp Act. Americans rejoiced at the news. But England's reversal also fueled colonial suspicions of the mother country. Reasoning that Parliament would not have repealed a good law, colonials concluded that their fear of an evil conspiracy among English politicians had been correct. "We always have had enemies," declared a wary preacher. "We may depend upon it that they will lay new schemes." Such skepticism seemed confirmed when Parliament passed the Declaratory Act in 1766, affirming its right to legislate for the colonies. Although Parliament conceded the failure of the Stamp Act, the principle of legislative sovereignty remained in place.

The argument started again in 1767, when Parliament, still seeking revenue from the colonies, adopted a series of laws known as the Townshend

Burning the Stamps.

American colonists protesting the Stamp Act by burning the British tax stamps in a bonfire in 1765.

acts. Making a distinction from the Stamp Act, which levied *internal* taxes, the new laws claimed merely to enact *external* taxes, that is, taxes on trade and commerce, which Parliament had always controlled. The first new law introduced customs duties on such products as glass, paper, and tea; the second tightened enforcement of the navigation system by permitting trials without jury of suspected smugglers; the third permitted the use of customs taxes to pay government salaries, thus bypassing the colonial assemblies that had traditionally voted for such funds; the fourth, which was not related to taxes, suspended the New York Assembly for its earlier rejection of the Quartering Act. By the time news of the laws reached the colonies, New York had already complied with the Quartering Act, but Parliament's attack on a colonial government seemed menacing to all colonies.

Rejecting Parliament's Rights

Colonial leaders quickly challenged the new laws. In 1767, a Philadelphia lawyer named John Dickinson published twelve essays, entitled *Letters from a Farmer in Pennsylvania*, which provided a legal argument against the Townshend acts. Dismissing any difference between an "internal" tax, such as revenue stamps, and an "external" tax, such as a trade law, Dickinson denied that Parliament had the right to legislate for the colonies or to raise money without the consent of the taxpayers. Political leaders in Massachusetts authorized two Sons of Liberty, Samuel Adams and James Otis, to write a "Circular Letter" in 1768 to the other colonies, denouncing Parliament's threat to self-government while "expressing their firm confidence in the king our common head and father." Meanwhile, to pressure English merchants, colonial businesses renewed the nonimportation agreements, appealing to popular dislike of luxury goods and their implied immorality.

Such peaceful boycotts drew women into the political crusade. "The great difficulty of all," remarked South Carolina's Christopher Gadsden, "is to persuade our wives to give us their assistance, without which it is impossible to succeed." While refraining from purchasing such products as tea, women also organized spinning bees to increase domestic production of cloth and so reduce dependence on English trade. The entire graduating class of Yale College came to the 1769 commencement "wholly dressed in the manufactures of our own country." But ironically, in light of women's central importance to the effort, political leaders like Mass-

achusetts's John Adams defined the boycott as an assertion of "manly and warlike virtues" against the English "elegance, luxury and effeminacy" that threatened American virtue. Meanwhile, in Boston and New York, street mobs coerced reluctant importers to respect the boycott.

As colonial leaders waged moral warfare against Parliament, city merchants continued to smuggle goods into the ports, although they encountered greater obstacles from England's newly appointed customs collectors. Street crowds occasionally recaptured confiscated goods. One night in 1768, a mob attacked the customs officers who had seized Boston merchant John Hancock's vessel *Liberty* for failing to pay a duty on wine. Such violence moved the English government to send four regiments of redcoats to Boston. These troops further antagonized the city's workers by taking odd jobs during their free time. Street brawls between soldiers and civilians erupted sporadically, climaxing on March 5, 1770, when the redcoats fired into a crowd, killing five people, including the mulatto sailor Crispus Attucks. To colonists, this Boston "massacre" epitomized the tyranny of English authority.

While Boston mourned its dead, news arrived in America in 1770 that Parliament had repealed the Townshend duties, retaining only the tax on tea as a sign of legislative supremacy. Jubilant colonials, vindicated in their defiance of English policy, resumed business as usual—except for the boycott of English tea. As one anonymous woman wrote,

Let the Daughters of Liberty, nobly arise,
And tho' we've no Voice, but a negative here,
The use of the Taxables, let us forbear.

"Thus acting," she added with a pun, "we point out their Duty to men."

With provincial trade expanding, however, tranquility returned to American politics. But the peace was fragile, easily disrupted by mutual suspicion. When the British patrol ship *Gaspée* ran aground while chasing smugglers in Rhode Island in 1772, a mob ignored the sacred English rights of property and set the vessel afire. To reassert royal authority, the governor of Massachusetts announced that the salaries of certain judges would hereafter be paid by the treasury rather than by the colony's legislature. The decision offended the colonial sense of justice. "An independent ruler," responded the indignant lawyer John Adams, was "a monster in a free state." Sensing an attack on colonial rights, Boston's Samuel Adams persuaded the town meeting to create a "committee of correspondence" to spread news and coordinate defenses with other communities. The scheme created a political network that extended through New England and eventually to other colonies, bringing political issues into the lives of ordinary citizens and laying the basis for intercolonial cooperation.

The Colonies Move toward Independence

As politicians in the separate colonies responded to the imperial crisis, common interests gradually coalesced into a shared identity as aggrieved colonials. To be sure, at the beginning of 1773 a cautious calm prevailed throughout North America; no immediate issue demanded resolution. But by then colonials had developed a political perspective that made them wary of British politicians. Their faith in Parliament's wisdom had evaporated years before. As loyal colonials, however, they perceived the monarchy, now embodied by King George III, as the legitimate head of the English political family. In their religious sermons, political speeches, and private letters, they continued to view England as their mother country, the king as their political father, and themselves as dutiful colonial children. But many agreed that political harmony, like good families, depended on mutual benefits. Against that standard, colo-

nial leaders took the measure of a new series of English laws.

Tea and Protest

In this atmosphere of mutual mistrust, the English government announced passage of the Tea Act in 1773 to save the East India Company from financial ruin. The law reduced the tax on tea, but it also granted the company a monopoly of tea sales, threatening to undersell both smugglers and independent shopowners who could not compete with the company's prices. Once again, Parliament seemed more concerned with protecting English interests than the colonials'. More serious, the tea tax showed no retreat from Parliament's claims to tax the colonies.

The arrival of East India tea in 1773 precipitated a crisis. Determined to prevent importations, mobs in the port cities refused to allow ships to unload. In Boston harbor, an orderly group of fifty men, disguised as Mohawks, slipped aboard the tea ship and, as thousands watched from shore, dumped forty-five tons of tea into the sea. The Boston Tea Party alarmed conservative Americans no less than English officials, for the perpetrators had not only broken the law but also destroyed private property.

An enraged Parliament promptly passed the Coercive acts (called in America the "Intolerable" acts) in 1774. The first law closed Boston harbor until the citizens paid for the tea. A second law changed the structure of Massachusetts's government, restricting town meetings and strengthening the royal governor. To protect British officials from local juries, a third law allowed the transfer outside the colony of certain legal cases, such as a British soldier's killing a civilian. A fourth measure reenacted the Quartering Act to station redcoats in Boston at the colonists' expense. News of a fifth law, the Quebec Act, unrelated to New England, also alarmed colonial opinion because it increased Canadian land claims in the Ohio valley, reaffirmed the unrepresentative French government, and mandated toleration for Roman Catholics. To shocked colonial leaders, Parliament's attempt to alter a colony's government violated the basic principles of the English constitution—the belief that royal power needed to be balanced by elected representatives to protect the rights of Englishmen.

A Continental Congress

The Coercive acts aroused colonial anger, ignited popular fear of tyranny, and prompted organized opposition. In September 1774, the first Continental Congress, composed of fifty-six delegates from twelve colonies, met in Philadelphia to adopt a common response to the imperial crisis. In this emergency atmosphere the delegates quickly voted to endorse Massachusetts's "Suffolk Resolves," which denied the legality of the Coercive acts and authorized defensive military measures in the event of an English attack. The congress also adopted a "Declaration of Rights and Grievances," which avowed loyalty to the king but rejected Parliament's right to make laws for America. Yet many delegates still opposed separation from England. Seeking a moderate alternative, one group, led by Pennsylvania's Joseph Galloway, proposed a plan of union that would give the colonial legislatures veto powers over parliamentary laws, but the Galloway plan failed by a single vote.

The delegates proceeded to add economic bite to their protests. Instituting an economic boycott, Congress adopted the Continental Association to end trade with England. Imports would cease at the end of 1774; but to protect southern tobacco, rice, and indigo planters, exports would continue until September 1775. Colonials also agreed not to consume English products that avoided the ban. Unlike earlier embargoes, moreover, the Association would not be voluntary. Congress recommended the formation of local committees of safety to enforce cooperation by confiscating contraband goods and boycotting defiant businesses. These committees, supervised by provincial councils, would form the basis of an extralegal government. Finally, Congress agreed to meet again in May 1775 if the controversy had not yet been settled.

While awaiting England's response to the protests, the colonials entered a period of public debate in the press and the pulpit. Adopting family metaphors, many conservatives opposed any "breach with the parent state," stressing the economic and military hazards of defying the mother country. "Even brutes do not devour their young," replied the uncompromising Thomas Paine, "nor savages make war upon their families." Meanwhile, the committees of safety enforced the economic boycott, sometimes using violence against reluctant merchants and consumers. When the king ordered more troops to New England, Massachusetts radicals formed militia companies, collected gunpowder, and prepared to fight.

The Second Continental Congress

"The shot heard 'round the world" exploded on April 19, 1775, when Massachusetts's military governor, General Thomas Gage, sent 700 redcoats to seize military supplies stockpiled at Concord. Warned by courier Paul Revere, the colony's militia (known as "minutemen" because of their readiness to fight at a minute's notice) exchanged shots with the British at Lexington. More skirmishes occurred at Concord, and the British retreated in a running battle back to Boston, taking heavy losses. As shocked Americans absorbed the news that military action had begun, the Boston militia readied for another battle. In Virginia the royal government guarded the public gunpowder, but in Vermont the Green Mountain Boys, led by Ethan Allen, captured the British forts at Ticonderoga and Crown Point on Lake Champlain.

On the threshold of war, the second Continental Congress opened sessions in Philadelphia on May 10, 1775. Of the sixty-five delegates, fifty had served in the first congress, evidence of the public's confidence in their elected representatives. Still hesitant to proclaim independence, the delegates agreed to send a conciliatory message directly to the king. This "Olive Branch Petition" pleaded to avert war but still demanded repeal of the Coercive acts and protection of colonial rights. But even as the appeal sailed to England, the congress assumed control of the provincial militias and dispatched the experienced military officer George Washington to Boston to act as commander-in-chief.

Before Washington arrived in Boston, New England troops had battled the redcoats at Bunker Hill in June 1775. Word of the engagement reached England by the end of the summer, destroying any interest in a political compromise. In October 1775, King George III told Parliament that the Americans "now openly avow their revolt, hostility, and rebellion." By the end of the year, king and Parliament declared America in a state of rebellion and forbade all commerce with the colonies. In January 1776, the colonists learned that England had hired German-speaking Hessian mercenaries to help subdue the rebels. Finally Americans began to see, in the words of Massachusetts's Abigail Adams, that England was "no longer [a] parent state, but a tyrant state."

Declaring Independence

"No longer piddle at the threshold," exclaimed Mercy Otis Warren to her friend, congressional delegate John Adams. "It is time to . . . open every gate that impedes the rise and growth of the American republic." But even as the king declared war on his American subjects, colonials hesitated to take the final step toward independence, still hoping that their benevolent political father, George III, would hear their pleas. The publication of Thomas Paine's pamphlet, *Common Sense*, in January 1776 helped overcome such illusions. The tract, which sold 150,000 copies in six months, proportionally rivaling today's bestsellers, drew no distinction between a bad parliament and a good king. According to Paine, monarchy itself was evil; George III was "the Royal Brute"! Urging immediate independence, Paine advocated the creation of a nonmonarchical form of government, a republic, in which citizens chose their own political fathers. As Paine's essay swayed public opinion and Americans prepared for a British invasion, the Continental Congress moved to decisive action. In March, Congress voted to send armed ships against "enemy" vessels. In April, the delegates opened American ports to all ships except England's. In May, Congress advised the separate colonial governments to draft new state constitutions that omitted any provision for royal power.

The next step was taken by Virginia, which authorized delegate Richard Henry Lee to present another resolution to the Continental Congress. On June 7, 1776, Lee introduced a motion declaring that "These United Colonies are, and of right ought to be, free and independent States." But Congress still hesitated to make the final move. Seeking to build a consensus of support, the delegates asked a committee of five, including Thomas Jefferson and John Adams, to draft a formal justification for this unprecedented step. Three weeks passed. Then, as encouragement poured into Philadelphia from local communities throughout the colonies, Congress voted to adopt Lee's resolution on July 2, 1776, formally creating the United States of America. The next day, Jefferson presented the document to Congress, and one day later the delegates approved the Declaration of Independence.

Jefferson's Declaration developed two lines of reasoning. The first drew on the political theories of John Locke and other English writer-philosophers, which held that governments existed by the consent of the governed and were intended to protect the natural rights of humankind, specifically the rights of "life, liberty, and the pursuit of happiness." When a government failed to protect such rights, "the people" had the right "to alter or to abolish" that government.

The second section of the Declaration contained a long list of examples of abuse, tyranny, and despotism by King George III to justify the decision to change the government. No word in the text referred to Parliament; it was sufficient to expose the failure of the evil political father, George III. In attacking the king, the Declaration personified the enemy and broke the last link of empire. Americans were now free to choose new political fathers.

The white male property holders who signed their names at the bottom of the Declaration did not intend to extend their "unalienable" rights to other social groups. As they all knew, the right to choose one's leaders did not exist widely in the 18th-century colonies. "I cannot say, that I think you are very generous to the ladies," remarked Abigail Adams to a signer of the Declaration, "for, whilst you are proclaiming peace and goodwill toward men, emancipating all nations, you insist on retaining an absolute power over your wives." Her husband, John Adams, merely laughed at the idea. And although some signers of the Declaration opposed slavery, they uncritically accepted the complaint that the king had "excited domestic insurrections," a reference to Virginia's royal governor, Lord Dunmore, who offered to liberate slaves who fled from their rebel owners. In defining the right to declare independence, the Declaration envisioned no social revolution, but merely a separation from the royal state.

The Legacy of Independence

As the founding document of a new nation, the Declaration of Independence achieved much more than the signers originally intended. The assertion that "the people" had the right to choose their leaders expressed a fundamental commitment to a representative, or republican, form of government. On July 4, 1776, no republic existed anywhere in the world, and it would take years of warfare with England before colonials won the right to build one. Nationhood and republicanism thus became inextricably intertwined, creating a unique identity for all citizens. By justifying independence in the universal language of "self-evident truths" and "unalienable rights," moreover, the Declaration presented a vocabulary that could be adopted by other groups of "the people" in different times and circumstances.

Although the so-called Founding Fathers had a narrow view of who was entitled to citizenship, other Americans and people around the world would later seize upon the Declaration to justify their own quests for self-government. In that vast ideological potential lay the great genius of Jefferson's words. But in 1776, the right of revolution was still a risky dream. To gain the government they wanted, colonials first had to win the war with England. That is why Jefferson added one final, solemn sentence to his document: "And for the support of this Declaration, with a firm reliance on the protection of divine providence, we mutually pledge to each other our lives, our fortunes, and our sacred honor."

INFOTRAC® COLLEGE EDITION EXERCISES

For additional reading go to InfoTrac College Edition, your online research library at *http://web1.infotrac-college.com*.

Keyword search: Patrick Henry

Keyword search: Seven Years' War

Keyword search: French and Indian wars

Subject search: Algonquians, reference book

Keyword search: Stamp Act

Keyword search: Boston Tea Party

Keyword search: Coercive acts

Subject search: Continental Congress

Keyword search: Thomas Jefferson

Keyword search: John Locke

ADDITIONAL READING

Gender and Politics

Philip Greven, *The Protestant Temperament: Patterns of Child-Rearing, Religious Experience, and the Self in Early America* (1977). A detailed interpretation of child-rearing practices that examines gender roles and their effects on religious beliefs.

Local Politics and Political Participation

Bernard Bailyn, *The Origins of American Politics* (1968). A thorough overview of provincial politics, emphasizing the built-in conflicts between colonists and royal authority.

Michael C. Batinski, *Jonathan Belcher: Colonial Governor* (1996). Following the research of the previous title, this biography studies provincial politics from the point of view of one royal governor.

Breen, T.H. *Tobacco Culture: The Mentality of the Great Tidewater Planters on the Eve of Revolution* (1985). A short study of the Virginia elite that explores the political and private problems of dependence on the English economy.

Richard L. Bushman, *King and People in Provincial Massachusetts* (1985). Focusing on one colony, this study explores public attitudes toward the English constitution and the growing conflict with royal power.

William D. Pierson, *Black Yankees: The Development of an Afro-American Subculture in Eighteenth Century New England* (1988). This study of African American life in the northern colonies includes a discussion of political activities.

Charles S. Sydnor, *Gentlemen Freeholders* (1952). A lively study of political practices in 18th- century Virginia. For more recent analyses, see John Gilman Kolp, *Gentlemen and Freeholders: Electoral Politics in Colonial Virginia* (1998).

The War for Empire

Fred Anderson, *Crucible of War: The Seven Years' War and the Fate of Empire in British North America, 1754–1766* (2000). A thorough history of the French and Indian War, emphasizing the global impact of the conflict.

Eric Hinderaker, *Elusive Empires: Constructing Colonialism in the Ohio Valley, 1673–1800* (1997). Examines French, British, and U.S. efforts to control trade and land in the Ohio valley.

The Colonies Move toward Independence

Bernard Bailyn, *The Ideological Origins of the American Revolution* (1967). Building on Bailyn's survey of provincial politics (listed above), this book examines the development of American attitudes toward the English government, arguing that the political system bred a fondness for conspiracy theories.

Edward Countryman, *The American Revolution* (1985). A brief survey of the coming of the war for independence and its impact on American society, this lucid book includes an overview of the secondary writings about the subject.

Woody Holton, *Forced Founders: Indians, Debtors, Slaves, and the Making of the American Revolution in Virginia* (1999). Examines how nonleadership groups affected the decision of Virginia politicians to seek independence.

Pauline Maier, *The Old Revolutionaries: Political Lives in the Age of Samuel Adams* (1980). Examining the careers of such revolutionary leaders as Samuel Adams and Richard Henry Lee, Maier links political values and personal development.

Declaring Independence

Pauline Maier, *American Scripture: Making the Declaration of Independence* (1997). A thorough analysis of the drafting of the nation's founding document that traces the Declaration's symbolic legacy for later generations.

The Pennsylvania Packet, and Daily Advertiser.

[Price Four-Pence.]   MONDAY, JUNE 22, 1789.   [No. 3242.]

Independence, Confederation, and the Republican Experiment, 1776–1787

CHRONOLOGY

1776	Washington avoids defeat in Battle of Long Island
	Pennsylvania adopts a democratic constitution
1777	Vermont constitution outlaws slavery
	Congress approves Articles of Confederation
	Burgoyne surrenders at Saratoga
1778	France joins military alliance with United States
	British army invades Georgia
1779	Spain supports United States
	George Rogers Clark defeats Native nations in Ohio valley
1780	British invade South Carolina
1781	States ratify Articles of Confederation
	Rhode Island blocks national tariff on imports
	Cornwallis surrenders at Yorktown
1783	Treaty of Paris ends war
1784	Economic downturn slows business
	Congress passes first Northwest Ordinance
1785	Land Ordinance creates grid land pattern in Northwest
1786	Virginia enacts statute of religious freedom
	Shays' Rebellion closes courts in Massachusetts
	Delegates attend Annapolis convention
1787	Northwest Ordinance creates territorial government
	Congress endorses constitutional convention

"**F**ather!"

Captain Pipe, leader of the Delaware people, looked carefully at the warriors attending a peace council near Detroit. Then he returned his piercing gaze to the commander of the British troops. His lips curled in sarcasm, he spoke directly to the man with an eloquence that was punctuated with a far-from-respectful form of address.

"Father! Some time ago you put a war-hatchet into my hands, saying, 'take this weapon and try it on the heads of my enemies, the Long-Knives [colonial Americans]. . . .

"Father!—At the time when you gave me this weapon, I had neither cause nor wish to go to war against a foe who had done me no injury. But you say you are my father—and call me your child—and in obedience to you I received the hatchet. I knew that if I did not obey you, you would withhold from me the necessaries of life, which I could procure nowhere but here.

"Father! You may perhaps think me a fool, for risking my life at your bidding—and that in a cause in which I have no prospect of gaining any thing. For it is your cause and not mine—you have raised a quarrel among yourselves—and you ought to fight it out.

***

"... I may, perchance, happen to look back to the place from whence you started me, and what shall I see? Perhaps I may see my father shaking hands with the Long-Knives; yes, with those very people he now calls his enemies."

Like the Delaware Captain Pipe, who seemed uncannily to foresee the events that would come to his people, Native groups residing near colonial borders had to choose between Britain and the United States, sometimes, as among the Iroquois, engaging in bitter disputes that sparked their own civil wars. And often, however they chose, these Native peoples would find themselves losers, abandoned equally by white allies and by the white enemies who coveted their lands.

The defense of colonial liberty also appeared hypocritical, if not absurd, to African slaves. As early as 1774, a young New England slave, Phyllis Wheatley, already a published poet, commented in a Boston newspaper that the colonists' "Cry for Liberty" masked "the reverse Disposition" to wield "oppressive Power over others." The next year, her owner set her free. Tens of thousands of other Africans took advantage of wartime disruptions to seek their freedom.

In declaring political independence from Great Britain in 1776, the American colonists went to war with the world's most powerful nation. But despite England's military superiority, the British government faced great obstacles in attempting to suppress the colonial rebellion, not least of which was the difficulty of transporting armies and supplies 3,000 miles across the Atlantic. The scattered, rural nature of American society gave the colonists important advantages. Colonial soldiers could be mustered from a friendly countryside and as easily dispersed after battle. Even decisive British victories, such as the military occupations of Philadelphia, New York, and Charleston, scarcely affected colonial troops elsewhere. Taking advantage of civilian supporters, General George Washington adopted brilliant guerrilla tactics to preserve the tattered Continental Army and avoid a major defeat.

But the dispersed American people were still far from united in 1776. Indeed, the war for independence resembled a civil war—a conflict not only between colonials and the mother country but also among social and political groups with different needs and expectations. Numerous Americans, known as Loyalists or Tories, opposed independence and remained loyal to the mother country. Even the desire to remain neutral was not always possible because the fortunes of war forced individuals and groups onto one side or the other. Certainly American political leaders worried about the lack of unanimity among colonials and acted harshly against suspected critics and enemies.

This demand for political conformity reflected important ideological beliefs. In separating from the British empire, the colonists had dismantled the existing type of political authority that linked citizens to the principles of monarchy. During the long struggle against royal power that led to the Declaration of Independence, Americans had discussed theories about non-monarchical republican governments—political systems based on the consent of the governed, in which free citizens chose their rulers. Republics seemed to offer maximum liberty to the citizenry, but political leaders debated whether large numbers of free people could be trusted to choose their rulers wisely. Only a highly moral citizenry, uncorrupted by material ambitions, they concluded, would overcome selfish interests and seek the benefit of the entire society. They doubted that all were so virtuous. From the birth of the American republic, the nation's leaders believed that morality and politics should be closely connected.

Political leaders also agreed that republican systems needed to keep government close to the people. In 1776, the same Congress that approved the Declaration authorized the separate states to create republican forms of state government. On the national level, Congress adopted the Articles of Confederation in 1777, deliberately establishing a weak federal system to prevent the abuse of power associated with the old monarchy. Under the Articles, Congress remained weak and the state governments became strong. But as unexpected political, economic, and diplomatic problems emerged in the 1780s, political leaders began to rethink these assumptions. The weakness of Congress and the independence of the states increasingly appeared as obstacles to effective government. By 1787, the political leadership was prepared to propose a new form of national government.

Choosing Sides: Social Divisions and Political Allegiances

"Rebellion is so odious," exclaimed one Massachusetts official. "It saps the foundation of moral virtue." Although colonial leaders, who called themselves patriots, overwhelmingly supported Congress and independence, a substantial portion of the population remained loyal to the king. Indeed, so vocal were the Loyalists in the months before Congress declared independence that the British government greatly exaggerated their strength. Believing that Congress consisted of rebellious conspirators rather than representatives of their communities, British strategists assumed that with armed support the Loyalist population would overthrow the rebels and return the colonies to the empire. But the strength of the Loyalists varied greatly: perhaps 6 percent in Connecticut, as many as half in New York. Elsewhere, regional pockets of strength reflected local issues and political disagreements. Overall, probably 20 percent of the colonists remained loyal to England.

Loyalism and Gender

Who were these Loyalists? Most royal government officials, such as Massachusetts's Thomas Hutchinson (whose home had twice been destroyed by colonial mobs) stayed with the king. So did merchants and large landholders who benefited from the government's patronage and grants. Recent British immigrants, including veterans of the Seven Years' War who had remained in America, retained allegiance to England.

Loyalism also appealed to social or cultural groups who felt oppressed by the colonial majority. In New England, worshippers in the Church of England resented tax discrimination by the Puritan Congregational churches, believed that English bishops could help them win tax relief, and tended to become Loyalists. Yet, ironically, New England Baptists, who also faced religious prejudice and tax discrimination, shared the Congregationalists' hostility to English bishops and so supported independence. Baptists thus gained greater respectability (though religious tax reforms would not come until the 1800s). Among non-English ethnic groups, assimilated colonists (such as English-speaking Germans and Dutch) supported independence, while isolated communities (such as Dutch-speaking members of the Dutch Reformed Church) backed the royal government. In New York, tenant farmers supported the king to oppose their landlords, who favored Congress; in the western Carolinas, small farmers were Loyalists in defiance of the wealthier planters who controlled their government.

Recognizing the strength of Loyalist opinion, Congress and the states tried to enforce political conformity. Some states banished Loyalists from their homes and exiled them to areas under British control. Other states passed laws confiscating Loyalist property. Even pacifists were suspect. The refusal of some Pennsylvania Quakers to support the war against England led to their banishment from the state. Members of the Shaker sect, a communal group led by the visionary Mother Ann Lee, faced arrest for refusing to support the fighting. By the end of the war, between 80,000 and 100,000 Loyalists followed the British armies into exile in

Some women served in the war as soldiers, by disguising themselves as men.

Canada, England, the West Indies, or the Spanish territories of Florida and Louisiana.

The persecution of Loyalists also affected women, who were presumed to share the political views of their fathers and husbands. Or course, women did chose sides during the war. Some, like Betsy Adams, the wife of Samuel Adams, shared the enthusiasm of their patriot spouses for independence; others, like Philadelphia milliner Margaret Hutchinson, aided British prisoners and carried messages for the redcoat army. Thousands of women made similar choices, serving in the war as cooks, nurses, washerwomen, and occasionally even as soldiers, by disguising themselves as men. Such involvement violated the widely held belief that women should not engage in political affairs. Yet some women used the presumed innocence of their gender to disguise their activities as spies and couriers. Women who rendered military service were often the wives of soldiers and followed the armies with their children. Others stood guard on the home front. "Imitate your husband's fortitude," wrote South Carolina's Eliza Lucas Pinckney to her daughter-in-law. "It is as much a female as a masculine virtue, and we stand in as much need of it to act our part properly."

Women's political views sometimes diverged from their husbands', and partisanship sometimes doomed their marriages. Such cases were rare, but significant. Whatever a woman's political views, the laws of most states assumed that married women shared the political positions of their husbands. Thus, with few exceptions, the confiscation of a Loyalist man's property included the possessions of his spouse, regardless of her politics. Patriot committees of safety, which tried to enforce a consensus among civilians, often ordered the wives and children of Loyalists into exile behind enemy lines. Without legal defense, such women lost their homes and property to the cause of liberty, and most never received recompense.

African Americans Choose Liberty

Among the Loyalists was a sizable proportion of Africans—approximately 25 percent of the total, or 20,000 people. Most were slaves who were compelled to accompany their pro-British owners into exile, but many had deliberately joined the British to gain their freedom. As early as 1775, Virginia's royal governor, Lord Dunmore, had offered emancipation to any slave who would fight for the king. In November 1775, the governor fielded a small army of ex-slaves who wore sashes declaring "Liberty to Negroes," but they were beaten by a patriot force. By the end of the war, Dunmore's proclamation attracted some 30,000 African Virginians who abandoned their masters. These included fighting men, but the entire slave population of a particular plantation often fled as a group. Similar offers of emancipation in other southern states encouraged thousands of slaves to take refuge behind British lines. Although some managed to keep their freedom and a few even returned as free people to west Africa, most were treated badly by the British and many were resold into slavery in the West Indies.

African Americans also fought for freedom in the patriot army and navy. Although free Africans had participated in the pre-war protests in northern cities, the slaveowning General Washington refused to allow Africans to serve in the Continental Army. Yet manpower shortages led the state militias to accept free Africans, although in some cases these recruits fought in segregated units. By the war's end, some 5,000 free blacks had served in the rebel ranks. Other African American soldiers were still slaves, sent as substitutes for their owners, and

some thereby obtained their freedom. For them, independence acquired a quite literal meaning.

Native Americans Choose Sides

The outbreak of war soon forced the various Native American nations to choose sides. Survivors of the coastal groups, surrounded by colonial settlers and dependent on local trade, usually supported the American cause. Mahican men from the praying village at Stockbridge, Massachusetts, for example, fought in the Continental Army and served as ambassadors to the nations of the Ohio valley; but the war did not improve their economic position and they migrated westward in the 1780s. By contrast, the Carolina Catawbas kept a precarious hold on their dwindling lands by joining the colonials against the hostile Cherokees.

Most Native groups, however, had no affection for the colonists. As 50,000 white settlers moved west of the Appalachians by 1774, the Ohio nations, such as the Shawnees and Delawares, and the Cherokees, Creeks, and Chickasaws of the south, fought to protect their lands from the colonial invaders. "The Rebels," a Seneca chief advised the Huron, "notwithstanding their fair speeches, wish for nothing more, than to. . . possess our lands, . . . which we are convinced is the cause of the present war between the king and his disobedient children." As a result, the British won many Native American allies and used their bases in Canada and Florida to provide ceremonial gifts, food, and ammunition. Even when a particular nation, such as the Iroquois Mohawks, preferred neutrality, colonial invasion of their lands propelled them to side with the British. The Great Spirit, one Cherokee told the Americans in 1777, "has given you many advantages, but he has not created us to be your slaves. We are a separate people!"

Colonial military tactics intensified problems within Native American communities. When Cherokee militants resisted colonial expansion by attacking border settlements, the militia retaliated violently, indiscriminately killing warriors and non-combatants, destroying Cherokee villages, and burning the growing crops. Americans waged similar wars of attrition against Iroquois and Shawnee villages, reporting the destruction of immense quantities of food. One campaign in Iroquois country in 1779 burned forty towns and 160,000 bushels of corn. The plundering of cornfields, timed late in the season to prevent replanting, brought widespread famine, suffering, and dispossession. It also upset the spiritual balance of groups like the Cherokees, Creeks, and Shawnees, who traced their origins to the corn goddess. Such attacks on Native life, while tactically successful, kept most Native American groups allied with the British and a continuing threat to the border settlers.

The alliance between the British and the Ohio peoples nevertheless failed to achieve a military victory in the west. In 1779, a colonial force under George Rogers Clark seized British supplies at Vincennes and prevented an attack by pro-British Shawnees. Americans then destroyed Shawnee villages and claimed title to the lands north of the Ohio River. Three years later, an American militia group gathered 96 Native American inhabitants from Moravian Christian villages at Gnadenhutten and slaughtered them all. Horrified survivors vowed that "no word of God should again be heard in the Indian land." Despite such bitterness, military victories strengthened American claims to Native lands, and the influx of American settlers continued.

The War for America

As the rebellious colonists prepared for a British military invasion, England faced problems of its own. King George may have had the best-trained soldiers in the world, but his military strategists used them poorly to suppress the rebellion in America. Since the British believed that most Americans were loyal to the empire, they ordered the redcoats into inhabited areas, expecting to be welcomed with open arms and civilian support. Instead, their very presence angered colonials and provoked rebel resistance.

Washington's Continental Army faced different problems. The colonial tradition of training adult men for militia duty provided adequate numbers of soldiers, but only for local defense. Throughout the war, the militias remained under state control, evidence that a national identity had not yet developed. To encourage recruitment of a national army, Congress offered bounties and promises of land after the war, but Washington never had enough reliable troops, and never more than 30,000 at one time. Still, the soldiers in the Continental Army repeatedly demonstrated courage and conviction, and as long as they fought somewhere the British could never claim victory.

The Early Battles

The ink on the Declaration of Independence was barely dry when Washington led the poorly trained 10,000-man Continental Army into battle against a superior force of redcoats on New York's Long Island in August 1776. Only the ineptness of British General William Howe permitted the defeated but resourceful American army to escape at night by evacuating to Manhattan. Stunned by this early failure, Washington explained to Congress that he was fighting a "defensive" war, retreating to buy time and trading territory to preserve the army. Howe pursued Washington north of New York City, forcing skirmishes at Harlem Heights and White Plains, but permitting an American retreat through New Jersey in the late autumn.

As the British went into winter quarters, Washington led a surprise attack against the king's Hes-

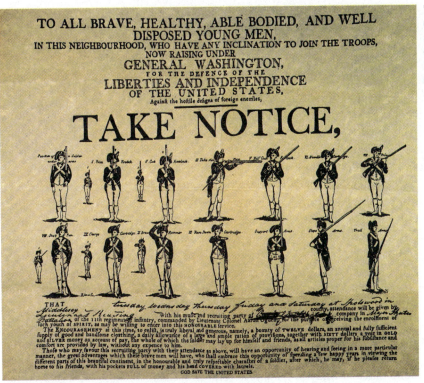

This recruiting poster summoned colonial troops to defend their liberty and independence "against the hostile designs of foreign enemies," which is how American leaders now viewed the mother country.

sian mercenaries at Trenton, New Jersey, by crossing the icy Delaware River on Christmas Day. He followed that triumph with a victory at Princeton three days after the new year. During the British occupation of New Jersey, the redcoats plundered civilians and raped young girls, politicizing the local population and gaining support for the rebel side. Washington's success boosted American morale and stimulated vigilance against the Loyalists. Thousands were sent into exile and others converted to the cause of independence.

In the spring of 1777, the British launched their next offensive in New York with an elaborate plan to split the colonies. Under the command of General John Burgoyne, a British force would march south from Quebec toward Albany, expecting to converge there with a smaller army of redcoats and Mohawks led by General Barry St. Leger coming from Montreal and Lake Ontario. Meanwhile, General Howe would bring his army north from New York City. The combined British forces would end the rebels' military resistance, restore the Loyalists to power, and effectively separate New England from the other states. British maps, however, showed little knowledge of the local terrain. Even skillful military leaders would have had difficulty penetrating the area's dense forests that were inhabited by a hostile population—and the British generals were neither skillful nor resolute.

Rather than following the plan to bring his redcoats up the Hudson River toward Albany, General Howe decided to seize Philadelphia, home of the Continental Congress. Although the political leadership fled to safety, the city's boardinghouse keepers, many of them women, had to exchange patriot tenants for unwanted British officers. Such inconveniences appeared wherever the rival armies passed. Depending on the course of war, Loyalist or patriot families fled as refugees, carrying children and furnishings to safety. As Burgoyne's army marched through New York in 1777, one woman, whose companions "scattered like a flock of frightened birds," wandered alone through the forest for days and lost her baby daughter. "Alas! the wilderness is within," she grieved. For Philadelphia's African slaves, the British occupation provided an opportunity for immediate freedom, and many left their masters. "The defection of the Negroes," observed a Pennsylvanian, using the language of the Declaration, "showed what little dependence ought to be placed on persons deprived of their natural liberty."

While Howe's army settled into Philadelphia, Burgoyne captured New York's Fort Ticonderoga and proceeded toward his rendezvous with St. Leger near Albany. But patriot fighters felled trees to impede his progress and shot from ambush at his troops. Meanwhile, as St. Leger's army passed through Iroquois country, Native leaders argued bitterly about whether to join the British. As the League of Six Nations veered toward its own civil war, the sacred council fire that had symbolized Iroquois unity for centuries was ritually extinguished. Although older chiefs pleaded for neutrality, younger warriors accepted the British invitation "to come and see them whip the rebels." In the end, when American troops met St. Leger's army at Oriskany, New York, during the summer of 1777, the Iroquois were drawn into battle, where they shared a bloody defeat. Consequently, Burgoyne was left stranded near Saratoga. The Iroquois were left with a bloody civil war as the pro-British Senecas took revenge on the neutral Oneidas and the Oneidas retaliated against the Mohawks. Ignoring such tribal distinctions, New Yorkers raised arms against all Iroquois, attacking villages and crops for the remainder of the war. With the peace, even the Oneidas, who fought as patriot allies, found they had lost their lands in New York.

The War Becomes International

When Burgoyne finally surrendered at Saratoga in October 1777, the direction of the war changed dramatically. By defeating the British army, Americans had proven their ability to wage war and their determination to remain independent. The king of France, still bitter about the loss of French colonies in North America in 1763, now resolved to support the United States against his old British enemies. Indeed, the French had secretly been sending aid to America and had allowed the former colonists to launch warships to attack British commerce. After Saratoga, the American ambassador to France, Benjamin Franklin, persuaded Louis XVI to grant formal recognition to the new nation. The gesture prompted the British government to rethink the war. Fearing the expansion of French power, England's prime minister, Lord North, offered to meet all American demands, except that for independence. But Parliament moved slowly, and British ambassadors for peace did not reach Philadelphia until the summer of 1778. By then, France had signed a commercial treaty granting trade advantages to American merchants and had accepted a formal alliance, in which both nations agreed to fight together until Britain conceded the independence of the United States.

The French alliance of 1778 altered the political stakes of war. Besides sending men, money, munitions, and supplies to America, France represented a threat to Britain in Europe, forcing the mother country to maintain a large home army. When France and Spain formed an alliance in 1779, Britain faced another enemy not only in Europe but also on the colonial borderlands. From bases in Louisiana, Spanish troops fought against the British and their Choctaw and Chickasaw allies

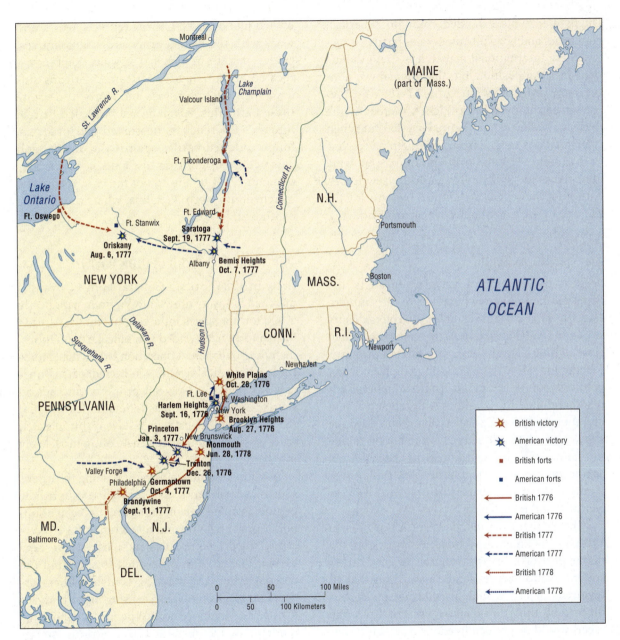

The War in the North, 1776–1778

in West Florida, destroying that colony as a refuge for Loyalist exiles and their slaves. The Spanish also moved against the Chickasaw capital at Natchez, ending pro-British interference with navigation of the Mississippi River. Britain's violation of neutral rights led other European nations to form a League of Armed Neutrality to protect their trade, a step that provoked war between Holland and England.

Dutch merchants extended credit to American companies and bought United States bonds.

These international maneuvers strengthened the American position, but the colonial war continued. During the winter of 1777-78, Washington's undernourished soldiers suffered in the frosts of Valley Forge, Pennsylvania. But when British troops moved from Philadelphia to New York in June 1778, the inspired Continental Army attacked successfully at Monmouth, New Jersey. Although the redcoats occupied New York City, the war in the north came to a virtual standstill.

The War Moves South

Seeking to encourage a rising of Loyalists, the British shifted military operations to the southern states in 1778. The invasion of the riverside city of Savannah, Georgia, brought the war home to slaveowning planters and their human property. Fleeing for safety to neighboring colonies, many planters took their slaves with them; others simply abandoned their holdings. Left behind, several thousand Georgia slaves, about one-third the state's total, fled to freedom, some taking refuge in remote areas, others trailing the redcoat army as noncombatant laborers. When American forces attacked the British armies, many Africans were captured and re-enslaved.

The British then invaded South Carolina in 1780. As the king's army attacked Charleston, the major port city, British General Henry Clinton stiffened Carolina's resistance by warning that all captured blacks would be sold as slaves, but promising that those who deserted from the rebels would be granted freedom. The policy outraged a plantation aristocracy already nervous about potential slave revolts. Thousands of Africans now escaped for freedom, some to serve with the redcoat army, others to seek refuge on abandoned plantations. After the British captured Charleston, the redcoats cynically returned those fugitives owned by Loyalists. Other fugitive slaves found work with the British army as artisans, nurses, guides, porters, or personal servants. Kept in segregated encampments, African Americans suffered high rates of disease and mortality. Despite these hardships, Africans accompanied British forces as the redcoats destroyed patriot farms, fought pitched battles against the militia, and defeated the Americans at Camden, South Carolina, in 1780. By the end of the year, the British marched into North Carolina, where the fighting continued.

THE WORLD TURNED UPSIDE DOWN

Early in 1781, British General Lord Cornwallis marched his army north into Virginia, with nearly 5,000 former slaves following his ranks. Already British forces had raided Chesapeake plantations, including one violent operation led by the famous traitor, Benedict Arnold. As the redcoats confiscated supplies, destroyed property, and seized slaves, Governor Thomas Jefferson, fearing that the British would instigate a slave revolt, pleaded with Washington to bring the Continental Army into battle.

Washington moved quickly, rushing the troops south from New York. As Cornwallis occupied the peninsula at Yorktown, expecting to receive support from the British navy, a French fleet intercepted the British rescuers and blocked an escape by sea. Washington proceeded to surround the redcoat army. The starving British soldiers ordered all blacks to depart, causing many to die of disease and malnutrition. When Cornwallis surrendered on October 19, 1781, patriotic Americans danced to the tune "The World Turned Upside Down."

The exhausted British empire, beaten by rebel forces, overwhelmed by war debts, confronted by France and Spain, now accepted the inevitability of United States independence. Negotiations among

The War in the South, 1778–1781

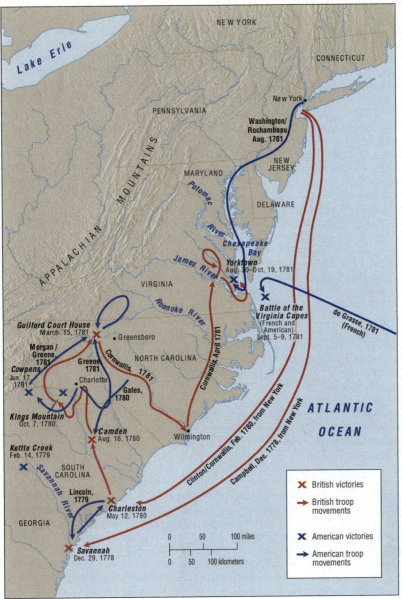

the British, the French, and three American agents (Benjamin Franklin, John Jay, and John Adams) opened in Paris in 1782, with various international claims complicating the question of territorial boundaries in America. The Treaty of Paris, formally signed in September 1783, reflected the facts of the American military victory. King George recognized the independence of the United States and agreed to remove British troops from his former colonies and territories.

The peace treaty established national boundaries: north to the Great Lakes, west to the Mississippi

Western Land Cessions, 1782–1802

River, and south to the 31st parallel in Florida (this latter line, a figment of cartography rather than geography, would remain a bone of contention between Spain and the new nation until 1795). The peace also protected New England's historic fishing interests in Canadian waters; assured both countries rights of navigation on the Mississippi River; and guaranteed payment of pre-war debts and compensation for property confiscated during the war. Significantly, the treaty omitted any reference to Native American sovereignty or their claims to western lands. Shocked by Britain's betrayal of these allies, a northern chief condemned "this act of cruelty and injustice that Christians *only* were capable of doing." Although Britain proved slow to remove military posts from the Ohio valley, the Native peoples were left alone to confront an invading population of farmers and merchants.

Governing a Free People

Although winning independence had taken seven long years of warfare, American leaders had not waited to begin the great experiment in republican government. The creation of a new political system involved two overlapping realms of power. The first, and most important in the early phases of the war, led to the formation of republican governments in the states. Based on newly written constitutions in each state, these governments embodied the idea that political power ultimately rested on the consent of the governed. The second aspect of government making involved the creation of a national union to coordinate and, in some cases, oversee government activities in the separate states. In 1777, Congress had approved a written constitution of national union, the Articles of Confederation; but this charter was not ratified by the states until 1781, less than a year before the British finally surrendered. Through most of the war period, therefore, the second Continental Congress, first chosen to represent the people in 1775, had regulated the national government. The absence of a formal central government reflected the limited development of a national identity; most Americans still identified more closely with their states and regions than with a national political system.

Republicanism in the States

The delegates who represented the separate states in Congress were the first Americans obliged to deal with national problems. They learned the art of government as the fortunes of war demanded, using standing committees and ad hoc groups to handle administration and propose policy. To supply Washington's armies, Congress asked the states for requisitions of supplies and money, borrowed $15 million by selling bonds at home and overseas, issued paper money, and sent ambassadors to treat with European and Native American nations. Such functions required national coordination, but the heritage of colonial politics had made political leaders suspicious of a strong central government. Most Americans believed that power belonged close to home, in the state governments. Two months before adopting the Declaration, Congress had instructed the states to create new governments based on republican principles. With two exceptions, each newly independent state proceeded to draft a constitution providing for a popularly elected government that attempted to balance the necessities of political power with the rights of a free people.

Republican politics thus began, not in Congress but in the states. Having resisted the power of monarchy and royal governors, political leaders took care to weaken the executive branches of the new state governments. Pennsylvania's constitution even eliminated the office of governor, creating an elective executive council. Most states only limited the governors' judicial and legislative functions and weakened the executives' powers of appointment. Demonstrating optimism about popular politics, the states gave greatest power to the elected legislative branch, including the right to oversee foreign relations, to make executive and judicial appointments, and to regulate financial affairs.

The preeminence of the state legislatures encouraged other cautions. While many Americans believed that republican government would guarantee liberty, others worried that such popular governments might endanger the rights of property. Thus although Pennsylvania approved a single legislative house, all other states created a bicameral (two-chamber) system in which the assemblies represented "the people," while an upper house or senate served as an aristocracy of talent to check the power of the masses. Some state constitutions established different property requirements for members of each house in an attempt to formalize a division of social classes; in fact, the social composition of the two houses usually reflected similar affluence. Still, the membership of the legislatures did reflect a loosening of the old colonial system. Compared to the colonial assemblies, the state legislatures attracted men of lesser wealth, including those who had first participated in politics during the colonial protests.

To ensure a representative government, most states increased the frequency of elections and enlarged the size of the lower house to make government more responsive to constituents. Recognizing the importance of an informed public, the governments encouraged newspapers to publish their proceedings. As a further check on legislative power, each state constitution included a bill of rights that defined the civil liberties of citizens. Among the political innovations of the era were provisions to protect religious minorities. Many states still gave benefits to particular churches, and Massachusetts and Connecticut used public funds to support the Congregational churches into the 19th century. But new measures, such as Virginia's 1786 statute of religious freedom, in the words of James Madison, "extinguished forever the ambitious hope of making laws for the human mind."

Property, Patriarchy, and Republican Women

Although the state republican governments derived their power from "the people," the new constitutions upheld the traditional concept of citizenship by limiting political participation to those who owned property. Moreover, the states often established even higher property ownership qualifications for those who sought public office. Such principles reflected the belief that voters had to remain completely independent in exercising political choices. By contrast, those who were dependent on others (the poor, children, servants, slaves, women) would not be able to make free choices. Even property-holding women were excluded from the suffrage on gender grounds—except in New Jersey, where the state constitution neglected to specify the gender of "free inhabitants." Because of this apparent oversight, some New Jersey women voted in local elections until an 1807 law explicitly disenfranchised both women and African Americans. Few Americans doubted that power belonged in the hands of propertied white male adults.

The commitment to property qualifications ironically stimulated other political reforms. Except in New England, colonial law had perpetuated two feudal types of land ownership: one, *primogeniture*, required that all inherited property pass to the first-born son; the second, *entail*, limited the division of estates among heirs. Such practices had effectively excluded widows and daughters from inheriting property, even though some colonial fathers made special provisions for younger sons. (New England's inheritance laws, by contrast, had customarily allowed widows one-third of a spouse's property.) Nearly all of the new state constitutions eliminated these feudal relics, making it easier for younger sons, daughters, and widows to acquire inherited property. Although women remained legally dependent on their husbands and fathers, changes in state property laws expanded their rights to control separate holdings, to enter contracts in the absence of husbands, and (in New England and Pennsylvania) to seek divorces. Most states still required private legislation for a couple to end a marriage or to live apart, and gave custody of children to the father.

By separating husbands from wives, the war encouraged women to exercise greater control over their households. "I hope you will not consider yourself as commander in chief of your own house," one wife wrote to her military spouse, "but be convinced. . . that there is such a thing as equal command." Although fathers still claimed a right to choose their daughters' husbands, women increasingly demanded more choice. Some evaded patriarchal authority by becoming pregnant and then marrying the man of their choice: during the late 18th century, a rising proportion of northern women delivered "seven-month" babies. A declining birthrate beginning near the end of the century suggests that married couples were deliberately practicing birth control, sometimes with syringes advertised in newspapers. With fewer children per household, parents could devote more attention to each child, a duty of growing importance for women in republican America.

As republican writers continued to emphasize women's domestic responsibilities, the burdens of family assumed a new political role. "Virtue alone," declared Pennsylvania's Benjamin Rush in 1778, ". . . is the basis of a republic." But if only a virtuous citizenry could be entrusted with liberty, republican leaders needed assurances that future generations would be worthy of their legacy. Republican mothers, viewed as the primary bearers

> **"I hope you will not consider yourself as commander in chief of your own house," one wife wrote to her military spouse.**

of moral lessons, appeared as the conveyors of republican morality.

Popular literature aimed at female readers advised mothers to assume responsibility for raising virtuous citizens. "The women, in every free country, have an absolute control of manners," declared a Fourth of July orator in 1790, "and . . . in a republic, manners are of equal importance with laws." Such ideas promoted an interest in women's education that, while preserving traditional female domestic roles, would contribute to a sound political system. Women's advancement as a group thus represented no threat to the patriarchal order. After the war, the expansion of female academies, mainly in the northern states, enabled women's literacy to reach equality with men's. Yet few women directly challenged the assumption that women's proper place was in the home. One exception was Judith Sargent Murray, who published essays, fiction, and poetry asserting women's intellectual equality. "Females," she noted tartly in 1786, "possess talents capable of extending their utility beyond the kitchen or the parlour." But even Murray made little effort to defy conventions within her own affluent Massachusetts family.

Slaves and the Ideal of Liberty

While educated women could find a vital, if subordinate, niche in republican America, the obvious inequality of African American slaves proved more difficult for republicans to excuse. Long before Jefferson spoke of the natural rights of human equality, Pennsylvania Quakers, believing in the inner light of each person's soul, had condemned ownership of human beings. Such humanitarian concerns coincided with a preference among urban merchants and artisans to employ free workers, who could be released during times of economic slowdown. African American participation in colonial protests against England proved their interest in the cause of liberty. As the African-born poet Phyllis Wheatley wrote in 1774: "In every human breast, God hath implanted a principle, which we call love of freedom." But when Congress discussed the status of slaves in 1776, the debate proved too explosive for compromise and the issue was dropped. Yet African Americans were keenly alert to the language of natural rights. "I have not yet enjoyed the benefits of creation," stated a Massachusetts slave women named Belinda in 1782. "I beg freedom."

The spirit of liberty moved some slaveholders, such as the Declaration signer Henry Laurens, to free their slaves; others provided in their wills for emancipation after their death. Such private emancipation increased in the 1780s, and in 1785 Virginia's College of William and Mary gave an honorary degree to antislavery activist Granville Sharp. In the Chesapeake states—Delaware, Maryland, and northern Virginia—declining tobacco production encouraged some planters to lease their slaves as urban workers, where they competed with free white labor. Sometimes the slaves would keep a portion of their wages and used these earnings to purchase their freedom. As rented labor, African American artisans mixed with free blacks and whites and enjoyed considerable freedom in their social activities.

Northern states, with smaller slave populations, also began to terminate slavery. Vermont became the first state to outlaw slavery in the constitution of 1777. In a series of legal cases brought by slaves, Massachusetts's courts ruled that slavery violated the state constitution of 1780. Other northern states, encouraged by local aboli-

tion societies, enacted laws mandating gradual emancipation. Choosing a particular date (often July 4), these laws declared that children born to slaves thereafter would be free, but only after serving their mother's owner for many years (21 for females, 28 for males). The parents of these children remained slaves for life. In 1810, there were 27,000 slaves in the northern "free" states. Gradual emancipation thus protected the property rights of slaveowners and meant that thousands of northern blacks remained slaves into the 1840s. All states prohibited the international slave trade, though some later repealed those laws.

As more African Americans obtained freedom, black communities sprouted around the country. Seeking jobs as mariners, day laborers, cooks, and domestics, African American men and women migrated from rural areas to the growing port cities such as Philadelphia, New York, and Baltimore. These ex-slaves moved quickly to stabilize family life, causing a surge in marriages. Emancipated slaves often marked their transition to freedom by choosing new names, most commonly English names—a sign of both independence and acculturation. "Robert," for example, adopted the surname "Freeman," and "Robin" became "Robin Justice." Others commonly took surnames that indicated their occupations, such as Carter, Mason, and Cook. Few kept slave names like Caesar or Pompey.

In 1787, ex-slaves in Philadelphia, the nation's largest free black community, founded the Free African Society; members of this organization established burial societies to continue traditional funeral rites, formed "African" churches, and supported mutual-aid groups. By 1790, nearly 60,000 African Americans, 8 percent of all blacks in the United States, were living free, and their number increased rapidly during the next two decades. As freed slaves continued to move to the cities for economic and cultural opportunities, however, most remained poor, experienced mortality rates twice as high as for whites, and faced discrimination in employment.

A Limited Revolution

Such changes appeared to contemporaries as "revolutionary." But to call the war for independence the "American Revolution" implies greater social change than actually occurred. Although the introduction of republican state governments encouraged citizens to reassess the relationship between property rights and liberty, most changes in American society appeared slight. While some African Americans achieved freedom, most—even those who followed the British into foreign countries—continued to labor as slaves. Women could claim some legal benefits and enjoy improved status as republican mothers, but full citizenship remained elusive. When republican governments confiscated Loyalist property, the lands were sold, not given freely to tenants or other claimants, and the beneficiaries usually were commercial land speculators who resold the real estate at a profit. Despite some laws that eased voting requirements, the electorate clung to old habits, choosing with few exceptions men of the "better sort" to represent them. Yet republican theories of government had great potential for social change, and that promise would emerge later as the powerful legacy of independence.

Launching the Confederation of States

Because of the preeminence of state governments in the lives of most citizens, few political leaders discussed a national union prior to the Declaration of Independence. But, as Congress led the nation into war with Britain, a committee headed by Pennsylvania's John Dickinson drafted Articles of Confederation to define an interstate or national union. The plan of government that emerged, and that unified the country from 1781 to 1789, is best known for the powers that it lacked, for its "weakness" in comparison to the government that followed under the Constitution. But for Americans of that time, so recently a part of the British empire, the Confederation expressed their political preferences well. Mindful of the problems of Britain's rule, the Articles made state sovereignty the first defense of political liberty. Yet practical problems of finance, diplomacy, and administration ultimately revealed the Confederacy's inadequacy. Less than four years after the war ended, most political leaders were advocating a new and stronger national government.

The Confederation

For almost all citizens, local and state governments provided all the services they would ever need. Although war and diplomacy required interstate cooperation, these issues were considered exceptional matters. Consequently, the Articles of Confederation stated that Congress could exercise *only* those powers expressly delegated by the states to the national government. These included declarations of war and peace; conduct of foreign relations, including the negotiation of treaties with Native American nations; borrowing money; and the establishment of uniform coinage, weights and measures, and a postal service. Congress could not pass national taxes nor regulate interstate commerce; those powers remained in the states. Within Congress, moreover, each state carried a single vote, and nine states of the thirteen had to approve all laws. The national government had no executive or judicial branch. Instead, congressional committees handled administrative affairs such as diplomacy and finance. This weak central government, with sovereignty derived from the states, reflected the public's fear of power at a distance.

These limitations on national power nearly destroyed the young republic. Congress's paper money, used to pay bills on the promise of future redemption, gradually declined in value as citizens lost faith in the republic's ability to fulfill its obligations. Toward the end of the war, frustrated army recruits mutinied for back pay, forcing Congress to negotiate discharges, bonuses, and reenlistments. In 1783, Washington's top officers, encamped at Newburgh, New York, even suggested a coup d'etat to force the awarding of congressional pensions, but the prestigious general simply stared them down. On the home front, shortages of goods and inflation of prices created conflicts between merchants and consumers that occasionally flared into mob violence. Contemporaries fretted about lawlessness and the difficulty of reconciling conflicts of interest. "The few . . . who act upon principles of disinterestedness," observed Washington, "are, comparatively speaking, no more than a drop in the ocean." Such voices wondered whether the frail republic could survive.

Approval of the Articles of Confederation, which took four years of wrangling among the states, revealed the difficulty of reaching political compromise. The major stumbling block involved control of the territory west of the Appalachians. Despite the claims of Native American nations, colonial charters had granted some states territory that stretched as far west as the Pacific ocean. Consequently, Maryland, a small state with dubious claims to western lands, worried that the larger states would obtain greater power in the republic and refused to approve the Articles unless *all* western land claims were transferred to the national government. But Virginia refused to make that concession. The deadlock lasted until 1781, when Cornwallis's invasion of the Chesapeake persuaded Virginia's planters to relinquish their claims to the west to ensure military assistance from the other states. Only then did Maryland ratify the Articles, launching the new nation in 1781.

> ## "The peacemakers and our enemies have talked away our lands at a rum drinking."

Diplomatic Disarray

The weakness of the new national government also undermined efforts to enforce the Treaty of Paris with England and Spain. Although both countries formally acknowledged the sovereignty of the United States, they ignored provisions of the treaty, and then dared to use their questionable policies as a basis for altering the treaty's terms. United States diplomats struggled to protect the nation's interests, but the new country lacked political respect abroad and the military power to back up its demands.

During the 1780s, Britain stubbornly refused to abandon its military and trading posts around the Great Lakes, a territory now part of the United States. Such violations benefited from Native American objections to surrendering their lands to either of the English-speaking rivals. "The peacemakers and our enemies," complained a Cherokee chief, "have talked away our lands at a rum drinking." Despite protests to England, the United States could not persuade the British to leave the region. Britain also refused to provide the promised compensation to American slave-owners for the slaves confiscated by the redcoats during the war. To justify its refusal, Britain emphasized that the Americans had failed to compensate the Loyalists for their losses and had ignored promises to pay pre-war debts to British merchants. That issue, too, pointed to the weakness of the Confederation, because Congress lacked the power to force the states to honor those obligations to Britain. England also forbade the profitable U.S. trade with the West Indies, a grievance that led Congress to send ambassador

John Adams to Britain to negotiate a new agreement. The British rudely rebuffed the offer.

On the southern borders, Spain threatened the nation's interests by refusing to permit American commerce on the Mississippi River, blocking Ohio valley farmers from bringing their produce to the port of New Orleans. In 1786, negotiations with U.S. ambassador John Jay complicated the crisis by proposing that Spain could close the Mississippi for 25 years if it opened Caribbean ports to U.S. shipping. The proposal, while beneficial to northern merchants and fishing interests, outraged southern and western farmers, whose prosperity depended on access to New Orleans. Although an angry Congress rejected the treaty, some frustrated Kentucky settlers proposed secession from the Confederation. The protest remained mostly talk, ending when Spain reopened the Mississippi in 1788.

Creating a Western Domain

The problems of western development remained the most pressing issue facing the Confederation Congress. Challenged not only by Spanish and British interests in the region, the new country also confronted the claims of Native American nations and a restless domestic population that wished to migrate west of the Appalachians. Without waiting for congressional approval, squatters and speculators flocked to the area. In western North Carolina and what is now Tennessee, illegal settlers organized a state called "Franklin"; by 1785, 30,000 migrants inhabited Kentucky. Conflicts over land, trespassing, and trade provoked innumerable acts of violence between U.S. citizens and Native Americans. When Native leaders protested the invasion of the Ohio valley, congressional agents replied that their nations had sided with Britain, "had desolated our villages and destroyed our citizens," and had, as a result, become "a subdued people." By right of conquest, the United States claimed the territory that England had ceded in the Treaty of Paris, even

though the same territory was still claimed by the Native peoples.

The seizure of 160 million acres of tribal lands north of the Ohio river temporarily satisfied the demand for fertile acreage while providing an easy solution to problems of public finance. Rather than allowing individual settlers to occupy this valuable territory, Congress passed three laws, or ordinances, to promote what one investor called "the systematical mode of settlement." The first measure, proposed by Thomas Jefferson, was the Northwest Ordinance of 1784, which established the republican principle that any states formed from the territory north of the Ohio River would enter the United States as equals of the original thirteen.

Congress then approved the Land Ordinance of 1785, which provided for the sale, not the give-away, of western lands to obtain revenue to run the government. This measure established a pattern for western development that mixed economic practicality with geographical symmetry. Whatever the particular contours of the land, surveyors would divide the public domain into square six-mile townships. These right-angle grids would then be subdivided into 640-acre (one square mile) sections. One section in each township would be reserved to support a school; four sections would be set aside for the United States; and the remainder would be sold at public auctions at no less than $1 per acre (equivalent to about $10 in today's money). So emerged the grid pattern of U.S. agriculture in the Midwest. But, since few farmers could afford to buy an entire section, wealthy investors reaped profits by purchasing sections and reselling the acreage in smaller parcels.

With western lands for sale, the Confederation extended political rights into the new territories. The revised Northwest Ordinance of 1787 divided the lands of the Shawnee, Mingo, and other Native American nations into no less than three and no more than five "territories." Jefferson's fanciful names for these units (Cherronesus, Assenisipia,

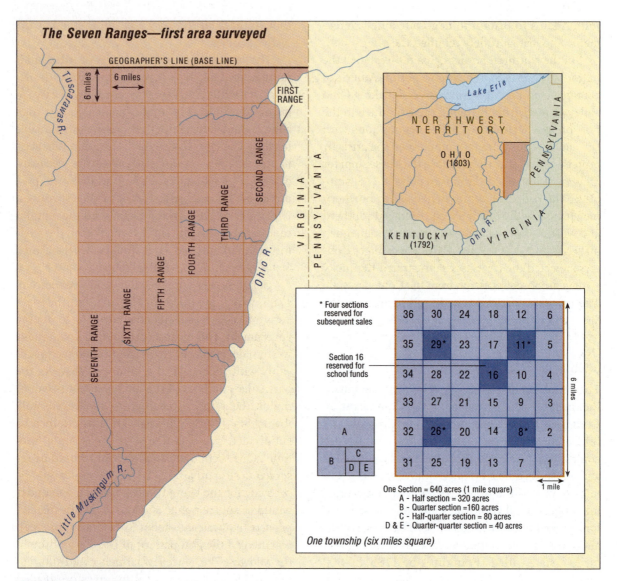

The Seven Ranges—first area surveyed

GEOGRAPHER'S LINE (BASE LINE)

6 miles

6 miles

FIRST RANGE

SECOND RANGE

THIRD RANGE

FOURTH RANGE

FIFTH RANGE

SIXTH RANGE

SEVENTH RANGE

Tuscarawas R.

Ohio R.

Little Muskingum R.

VIRGINIA

PENNSYLVANIA

Lake Erie

NORTHWEST TERRITORY

OHIO (1803)

PENNSYLVANIA

KENTUCKY (1792)

Ohio R.

VIRGINIA

* Four sections reserved for subsequent sales

Section 16 reserved for school funds

36	30	24	18	12	6
35	29*	23	17	11*	5
34	28	22	16	10	4
33	27	21	15	9	3
32	26*	20	14	8*	2
31	25	19	13	7	1

6 miles

1 mile

A

B

C

D E

One Section = 640 acres (1 mile square)
A - Half section = 320 acres
B - Quarter section =160 acres
C - Half-quarter section = 80 acres
D & E - Quarter-quarter section = 40 acres

One township (six miles square)

The Land Ordinance of 1785

Polypotamia, among others) eventually translated into Ohio, Indiana, Illinois, Michigan, and Wisconsin. Each territory would pass through three stages of political development. First, Congress would appoint territorial governors and judges; second, after the adult male population reached 5,000, citizens would elect a legislature and send a nonvoting delegate to Congress; and third, when the total population reached 60,000, the territory would achieve statehood by submitting a constitution for congressional approval. In another unprecedented step, the 1787 ordinance prohibited slavery in the

Northwest territories. While unwilling to eliminate slavery in the existing states, political leaders determined to restrict its expansion, hoping the institution would become unprofitable and disappear.

The Crisis of Money and Taxes

The Confederation Congress also confronted a deeper crisis of foreign trade. After the war for independence, new commercial relations with France, the French sugar islands, Holland, and even China expanded the U.S. marketplace. Optimists like Connecticut theologian Ezra Stiles saw the expansion of trade as part of the "great American revolution," in which "navigation will carry the American flag around the globe . . . and illuminate the world with truth and liberty." But the simultaneous loss of trade with Britain caused serious economic problems. To punish the ex-colonies, Britain barred U.S. fish and meat from the West Indies and permitted other imports only in British ships. Although northern shippers frequently violated these rules, the decline of business contributed to unemployment in the port cities. Without the protection of the royal navy, moreover, Mediterranean pirates preyed freely on American shipping.

During the war, the absence of British products had stimulated local manufacturing. On southern plantations from Virginia to Georgia, slave women learned the arts of spinning and weaving, establishing a local self-sufficiency that lasted until mass-produced textiles began to arrive in the early 19th century. Numerous northern farm families also began to manufacture local products (fermenting cider, nailing barrels, dressing animal skins) to supplement agricultural income. Even this resourcefulness could not satisfy consumer demands. As soon as the war ended, British merchants exported large surpluses, accumulated since the boycotts of 1775, into the warehouses of American importers. The merchandise

moved quickly, going to retailers in the cities and in rural towns and villages, who found customers among farmers and small artisans. To pay the bills, hard cash flowed rapidly to Britain.

The postwar boom ended abruptly. Without markets in the West Indies, American importers lacked sufficient hard money to pay for additional imports. They called in debts from their rural retailers. But most country merchants had been paid with agricultural goods because few farmers had enough cash to pay all their bills. As debts mounted, business slowed. Pressed by creditors in England, large merchants squeezed the retailers; they, in turn, pushed the indebted farmers. "It's a common saying," one Massachusetts trader told his brother, "business before friends."

The states seemed equally stubborn in rejecting proposed remedies. Efforts by Congress to establish a national tariff (a duty on imported goods) failed when prospering Rhode Island alone blocked the measure in 1781; a second proposal stalled in New York. Instead, the separate states individually enacted tariffs to protect local business; but because these lacked uniformity, trade moved to low tariff areas. Some states responded to the commercial crisis by issuing paper money, which eased the currency shortage. Some states also passed *stay laws,* which prevented the foreclosure of farm mortgages to pay debts, and *tender laws,* which permitted payment in produce rather than hard currency. But paper money caused inflation, angered creditors, and failed to help large merchants involved in international trade. Farmers who were accustomed to bartering their goods with neighbors now felt threatened by more impersonal creditors who were prepared to prosecute debtors in court, seize their farms, or send them to jail.

The problem crystallized in western Massachusetts in 1786, when the state government enacted high land taxes to repay wartime debts and required payment in cash. Facing property seizures

SCENE IN SHAYS'S REBELLION.

A Massachusetts blacksmith served with a writ of attachment for debt during Shays' Rebellion in 1786.

for nonpayment, farmers in Massachusetts rallied behind war veteran Daniel Shays, formed an armed citizens' militia reminiscent of the pre-war crowds, and forced the local courts to halt debt collection. Although Congress tried to muster federal troops against the insurrection, other states refused to legislate taxes to pay for the army. Horrified merchants and political conservatives in Massachusetts privately subsidized the state militia to crush the rebels. After several pitched battles around the New England countryside, many of the Shaysites fled the state; a few were condemned and executed for treason. The return of prosperity in 1787 eventually eased the problem.

Reconsidering the Confederation

The Shays rebellion reflected and helped to stimulate an important shift in attitudes toward state government, all of which culminated in a proposal to restructure the national government. Since independence, political leaders had emphasized the value of decentralized power with supremacy placed in a legislative branch that was responsive to public pressure. The framers of the Confederation had deliberately created a weak central government—so much so that delegates frequently resigned their seats in order to return to their home states, where politics seemed more important. To be sure, a few leaders—Robert Morris, the superintendent of finance; Alexander Hamilton, an aide to General Washington; and Virginia delegate James Madison—had long advocated a strong national government. But when peace came in 1783, even these three departed from Congress and returned to private life. Through the 1780s, therefore, Americans measured their satisfaction with government based on what happened on the state and local level. Shays' rebellion, along with outbreaks of rural violence in other states, raised an old but alarming question: Were republican governments stable enough to survive?

Fears about the future of the republican experiment impelled a group of nationalist-minded leaders to consider a revision of the Articles of Confederation. Although still overwhelmingly a nation of farmers, the United States had already entered the commercial age. More citizens—merchants, artisans, export farmers—had developed interstate interests that could not be regulated by a single state legislature. Even Daniel Shays and his neighbors in rural Massachusetts were affected by international credit. In the border states of Georgia, western Carolina, and Pennsylvania, settlers looked to a central government to protect their holdings from attacks by Native American warriors. And political conservatives everywhere worried that the state governments had become overly responsive to popular opinion.

Such people responded to the call to revise the Articles. The movement began when representatives from Virginia and Maryland met in 1785 to discuss navigational improvements on the Potomac River and proposed a conference of all states to consider problems of interstate commerce. Only five states sent delegates to the gathering at Annapolis in 1786, an embarrassment that precluded any political action. Hamilton suggested that another conference be held the next year "to render the constitution of the federal government adequate to the exigencies of the union." In May 1787, after Congress endorsed the meeting, 55 delegates from every state except Rhode Island began their journeys to Philadelphia. The ensuing constitutional convention would stabilize a generation of revolutionary politics.

INFOTRAC® COLLEGE EDITION EXERCISES

For additional reading go to InfoTrac College Edition, your online research library at *http://web1.infotrac-college.com*.

Keyword search: William Howe

Subject search: Battle of Trenton

Keyword search: American Revolution

Subject search: American Revolution, Loyalists

Keyword search: Yorktown

Subject search: Articles of Confederation, Reference

Keyword search: Shays' Rebellion [R]

ADDITIONAL READING

The War for America

Charles Royster, *A Revolutionary People at War* (1979). This innovative study of the military aspects of war stresses the political significance of the Continental army.

African Americans Choose Liberty

Sylvia R. Frey, *Water from the Rock: Black Resistance in a Revolutionary Age* (1991). Beginning with the effects of the British invasion on slavery, this study describes the evolution of black communities into the next century.

Native Americans Choose Sides

Colin G. Calloway, *The American Revolution in Indian Country: Crisis and Diversity in Native American Communities* (1995). A survey of the Native American response to the war for independence, emphasizing the variety of situations and the calamitous effects on Native peoples.

Property, Patriarchy, and Republican Women

Mary Beth Norton, *Liberty's Daughters: The Revolutionary Experience of American Women, 1750–1800* (1980). The first half of this pioneering book examines the private world of 18th-century women; the second half looks at their involvement in political issues.

Slaves and the Ideal of Liberty

Gary B. Nash, *Forging Freedom: The Formation of Philadelphia's Black Community, 1720–1840* (1988). Tracing the emergence of the nation's largest free community of African Americans, this book explores the impact of independence on black life.

Launching the Confederation of States

Jack N. Rakove, *The Beginnings of National Politics: An Interpretive History of the Continental Congress* (1979). Examines the political ideas of congressional delegates and how they shaped policy during the confederation.

Gordon S. Wood, *The Creation of the American Republic, 1776–1787* (1969). A thorough analysis of the drafting and ratification of state constitutions, focusing on changing attitudes toward republican governments.

The Crisis of Money and Taxes

David Szatmary, *Shays' Rebellion: The Making of an Agrarian Insurrection* (1980). Examining the clash between rural values and commercial interests, this study places the uprising in the context of changing political values.

7

THE AMERICAN MUSEUM, OR UNIVERSAL MAGAZINE,

For MAY, 1791.

CONTENTS.

ORIGINAL ARTICLES.

PROSE.

Building a Republican Government, 1787–1800

CHRONOLOGY

1787	Philadelphia convention drafts U.S. Constitution
1787–1788	Eleven states ratify Constitution
1789	George Washington inaugurated first president
	French Revolution overthrows monarchy
1790	Alexander Hamilton presents *Report on the Public Credit*
1790–1791	Native Americans defeat U.S. armies in Ohio
1791	States ratify first ten constitutional amendments (Bill of Rights)
1793	England and France go to war
	Washington issues Neutrality Proclamation
1794	Federal troops suppress Whiskey Rebellion
	U.S. troops win Battle of Fallen Timbers
	John Jay negotiates treaty with England
	Yellow fever epidemic rages in Philadelphia
1795	Treaty of Greenville ends warfare in Northwest territory
	Thomas Pinckney signs treaty with Spain
1796	John Adams elected president
1798	XYZ affair arouses public opinion
	Congress passes Alien and Sedition laws
1798–1799	Republicans offer Virginia and Kentucky resolutions
1800	Gabriel plans slave insurrection in Richmond, Virginia
	Thomas Jefferson elected president

His frilled neckpiece, wavy powdered wig, and serious expression placed him in the generation of the Founding Fathers, but Noah Webster's nationalism was more cultural than political. He grew from average colonial roots in a West Hartford, Connecticut, family engaged in farming and weaving. Despite financial shortages, Webster managed to attend Yale College (class of 1778), where he imbibed the patriotism of the war for independence and developed an intellectual passion for the new American nation.

As a young Connecticut school teacher, Webster became frustrated with the English books he had to use for his pupils, and in 1783 published his own textbook: *A Grammatical Institute of the English Language,* popularly known as "The Blue-Backed Speller." For 100 years it would teach children, including Ben Franklin's granddaughter, to read, spell, and pronounce words with a distinctive American syntax. Between its blue covers, Webster took up his lifelong mission of creating a unique "national language" with an American vocabulary and spellings. In the speller, as well as in his famous *American Dictionary of the English Language*

http://history.wadsworth.com

(1828), he used spellings like *color* instead of the English "colour," and *music* rather than "musick." He also added such uniquely American words as *skunk, squash, chowder,* and *hickory.*

"We ought not to consider ourselves as inhabitants of a particular state only, but as *Americans,* as the common subjects of a great empire," Webster urged. His ideas anticipated a time when the "United States" would be a singular noun—a country rather than a union of separate states. As Webster was developing his ideas about cultural nationalism, the Constitutional Convention of 1787 became a forum for discussing issues of political nationalism. The delegates who converged in Philadelphia to "form a more perfect union" struggled mightily to surmount traditions of local government and to replace state power with a stronger national government.

I n the 1780s, a sense of American nationalism remained an aspiration for the future. Most citizens still identified with state politics, and many political leaders doubted that a republican government, elected by "the people," could survive in such a widely dispersed country. The lines of national communication remained rudimentary. In 1790, there were just seventy-five post offices in the country, and fewer than 2,000 miles of roads. It took four days for news to travel from the nation's first capital in New York City to James Madison and Thomas Jefferson in Virginia.

The political leaders who traveled to Philadelphia in 1787 thus had to bridge wide local and regional differences about social, political, and cultural values. Not least of these, perhaps, was the matter of punctuality. Benjamin Franklin, the oldest delegate to attend the constitutional convention, had made a virtue of keeping regular hours (see Chapter 4). Yet the convention opened eleven days late, for want of a quorum. Most delegates obviously were not in a rush to change the Articles of Confederation. "These delays greatly impede public measures," complained George Washington, "and serve to sour the temper of the punctual members, who do not like to idle away their time." The delay had its productive side, however, as James Madison drafted detailed proposals for the tardy delegates.

The many differences among the delegates provoked important philosophical debates about the essence of a republican government. The Articles of Confederation had created a "federal" union in which the national government depended on the approval of the separate state legislatures. Amendments required unanimous consent of the states. Politicians who opposed any changes in the Articles,

The convention opened eleven days late, for want of a quorum.

such as Virginia's fiery orator Patrick Henry, simply refused to attend the convention. By contrast, the political leaders who did attend the convention had a more national view of politics. Understanding *interstate* issues, they accepted the importance of giving greater power to the central government.

These delegates, who later achieved immortality as the Founding Fathers, were relatively young, averaging 42 years of age. Most had matured during the war against England rather than in the colonial period, and they understood the value of interstate cooperation. But, as products of their time, they accepted the existing basis for choosing political leaders. They expressed no interest in changing the political system within the separate states.

Among the most sensitive of the differences among the delegates would be the status of slavery. Many northern states had begun to abolish involuntary servitude, but southern states saw their prosperity linked to slave-based agriculture. Nor did northern delegates, who represented the merchant class involved in the Atlantic trade, share the concerns of southern delegates about protecting free navigation of the Mississippi River. Local interests also influenced the delegates' positions about strengthening the national government. The Georgia delegates represented white farmers interested in seizing Creek and Cherokee land and wanted a strong government to provide military support on their western borders. Delegates from states without western lands, such as New Jersey and Delaware, worried that a strong national government might submerge the interests of less populous states.

Although the first national leaders adopted the motto *e pluribus unum* ("from many, one"), most realized the danger of political disintegration. Washington, the most prestigious national figure, worried that western migration would weaken the country to the advantage of European nations with claims in the western territories. "No well informed mind need be told, that the flanks and rear of the United territory are possessed by other powers," he wrote in 1784, "and how entirely unconnected should we be . . . if the Spaniards on their right, or Great Britain on their left . . . should invite their trade and seek alliances with them." Washington's point of view ("Spaniards on their right" [Florida]; "Great Britain on their left [Canada]") shows that the man chosen to preside at the constitutional convention was facing east, looking across the Atlantic, and for good reason. During the next decade, Europe would profoundly affect the domestic politics and stability of the American republic. The danger of foreign influence would stimulate the formation of political parties in the 1790s and would ultimately strengthen a sense of national identity.

Designing a National Union

"Every man thinks himself at least as good as his neighbors," observed a New Englander in 1791, "and believes that all mankind have, or ought to possess equal rights." Two decades of political discussion had created a consensus about republican government: "the people" were the true source of political authority, and government depended on the consent of the citizens. To preserve those principles, two additional beliefs had emerged: first, citizens had to be protected from the arbitrary power of their elected leaders, and second, the people's representatives had to be protected from the whims of changing majorities. Political power, which might threaten minorities or even the government itself, had to be divided and balanced to

George Washington's View of the United States, 1784

prevent one interest group from achieving dominance over the political structure. Although the constitutional convention decided not to reform the Articles of Confederation, but to create a new political system, the delegates agreed to preserve state governments, dividing the power to govern between the states and the central government. (Even at the convention, delegates voted as state blocs, one vote per state, and not as individuals.) Within the national government, moreover, power would be divided and balanced among separate branches, each with distinct but overlapping re-

sponsibilities so that no one office could claim complete power.

Representation and Compromise

The drafters of the Constitution shared many ideas about republican government, but because they represented states with different interests, they soon split into two competing groups, disagreeing about the form such a government should take. The debate began when Virginia's James Madison, probably the most ardent supporter of a strong central government, introduced a plan of government known as the "Virginia Plan." Madison's proposal gave primary power to a two-house national legislature, in which members of the lower house would be chosen on the basis of each state's population, and the lower house would elect the members of the upper house or senate. Voting within the legislature would be by individuals rather than state delegations. Madison's plan gave the legislature unlimited powers to make laws, pass taxes, and veto state legislation. The legislature would also elect officials of separate judicial and executive branches.

The Virginia Plan aroused objections from the smaller states, which opposed representation based on population. These delegates preferred a plan of government proposed by William Paterson of New Jersey. The "New Jersey Plan" was closer to the Articles of Confederation, proposing a single-house legislature in which each state had an equal vote and provided for separately chosen judicial and executive branches.

Since both plans proposed to strengthen the legislative powers of the national Congress, disagreement focused on the question of representation within the legislature. The protracted debates ended with the "Great Compromise," proposed by the Connecticut delegation. This version provided for the election of a lower house of representatives based on population and the creation of an upper house or senate in which each state government (not the voters) chose two delegates who would vote as individuals. The lower house would thus represent "the people"; the senate would represent the states. The election of senators by the state legislatures would also protect the states from national power. Although both houses would have to approve all laws, a third provision required finance measures, including taxation, to originate in the lower house to protect citizens from taxation without representation.

The problem of representation introduced another dilemma: Who would count as citizens?

Southern states with substantial slave populations wanted to count slaves as persons for purposes of apportioning representation; they were not eager to count slaves as persons to apportion taxes. But delegates from states with few or no slaves protested the idea of giving representation to slaves who lacked any civil rights. If slaves were "not represented in the States to which they belong," asked New Jersey's Paterson, "why should they be represented in the General Government?" Another delegate from Philadelphia warned that his constituents "would revolt at the idea of being put on [an equal] footing with slaves."

Northern criticism of giving representation to slaves (who would have no political voice in choosing those representatives) provoked some southern delegates to threaten rejection of the whole Constitution. To remove that threat, the convention struck another bargain, called the "Three-Fifths Compromise": for purposes of determining representation and taxation, five slaves would count as three persons. To further protect investments in slave property, the delegates barred any state from blocking the return of a runaway slave to another state. The convention also refused to permit the national government to interfere with the importation of slaves prior to 1808, at which time Congress might enact prohibitions. In embodying this compromise in what became the nation's highest law, the Constitution allowed slavery to persist in the states as a "domestic" institution not subject to national law. The debate about slavery also showed that the delegates disagreed about which residents of the United States were entitled to be treated as citizens of the republic.

Devising Checks and Balances

By September 1787, after a hot, muggy summer of debate, the Philadelphia convention had drafted the Constitution of the United States. This document shifted power from the state governments to a national government consisting of a bicameral (two-chamber) Congress, an executive branch, and an independent judicial system. Under the Constitution, Congress had power to enact taxes (for example, on imported goods), borrow money, regulate interstate commerce and trade with foreign and Native American nations, coin money, establish uniform weights and measures, maintain military forces, declare war, and pass "all laws which shall be necessary and proper" to fulfill the responsibilities of the national government.

These extensive powers called for additional checks and balances to prevent one branch of government from becoming too powerful. To keep political oversight close to the people, the states would establish the qualifications for voting for delegates to the House of Representatives who would serve two-year terms. To ensure stability of government, senators would be chosen by the state legislatures and serve six-year terms. The Senate would approve appointments made by the president and would have the power to ratify treaties by a two-thirds vote. Such treaties, together with the Constitution, would stand as the supreme law of the land.

Accompanying the balance of power between the two houses of Congress, the Constitution established an independent executive branch led by a president. To keep this chief executive officer independent of those who chose him, the Constitution created an "electoral college," consisting of electors chosen by popular ballot and equal in number to each state's congressional representation. Every four years, each state's electors would meet, cast ballots for president and vice president, and then disband forever. In this way, the drafters of the Constitution expected to prevent a permanent alliance of politicians who could influence presidential decisions. Like most 18th-century thinkers, the founders feared the formation of political parties, or factions, which were considered inherently divisive and contrary to the ideal of public harmony. They believed

that a good ruler should reject all factions and seek the welfare of the whole. Thus, the president would be independent of both the Congress and the mass of citizens. The notion of lasting interstate political parties, which emerged later, had no place in the Constitution.

The Constitution gave the president the power to execute all laws, to negotiate and sign treaties with foreign nations, to act as commander-in-chief of the armed forces, to appoint judges and executive officers (subject to ratification by the Senate), and to approve or reject laws passed by Congress (presidential vetoes could be overridden by two-thirds vote of both houses of Congress). This strong executive diverged from the fear of monarchy that had influenced both the state constitutions and the Articles of Confederation. Now, after Shays' rebellion of 1786, the constitutional convention had more reason to fear the disruptive effects of popular unrest. The delegates also expected the first president to be George Washington, whose commitment to a republican government was beyond doubt.

The Constitution also established an independent judicial branch (distinct from the existing court systems in the states), which today is called the "federal judiciary." Giving Congress power to create a supreme court and lower courts, the document granted federal judges lifetime appointments (assuming only their good behavior in office; otherwise they might be impeached by Congress). These judges were thereby freed from executive or legislative interference. Reinforcing the ideas of federalism—that is, the division of power between state and national government—the Constitution preserved the judicial systems of the separate states but granted jurisdiction to the federal courts to resolve constitutional issues, interpret congressional laws and foreign treaties, and decide cases involving the separate states or citizens of more than one state. The Constitution made no provision for judicial review of the law (the power of judges to declare laws null and void for being "unconstitutional"), but federal judges subsequently assumed that power in interpreting the supreme law.

The Amendment Process

Anticipating the need to revise the basic system of laws, the Constitution provided for a process of amendment. Unlike the Articles of Confederation, constitutional changes did not require a unanimous vote, but they still had to gain substantial approval. Amendments could first be proposed, either in Congress by a two-thirds vote of both houses, or in conventions whose delegates were elected by the citizens of two-thirds of the states. Proposed amendments then had to be ratified by three-quarters of the states, either by the legislatures or by elected conventions. The complexity of the amendment process discouraged frequent changes, adding to the Constitution's stature as the law of the land. In later years, constitutional amendments often came in clusters as political leaders addressed fundamental changes in U.S. society.

What the Constitution did *not* do is equally significant. Not only did the founders preserve state governments and state judicial systems, but they also specifically reserved all powers *not* granted to the national government to the states. The debates at the constitutional convention assumed that citizens, regardless of their occupations as merchants or farmers, had primary loyalty to a state rather than to an economic interest group. Accordingly, the powers of the states included basic responsibilities that affected the ordinary citizen: voting procedures, property rights (including slavery), domestic laws (marriage, divorce, inheritance), administration of local affairs, and a concurrent right to tax the public. Legal inhabitants of the United States thus held dual citizenship within state and national governments.

Although national law assumed preeminence, and although the national government could compel enforcement of its laws in the states, such powers remained more *potential* than actual in 1787. In this rural country, the lives of most Americans remained focused on local matters.

The Struggle for Ratification

Assuming that the new government derived its powers from the sovereignty of its citizens—from "We, the people," as the Constitution's opening statement declared—the Constitution provided for the popular ratification of this basic document of law. Rather than relying on the separate state legislatures to approve the Constitution, the framers proposed that popularly chosen conventions in each state make that decision. Ignoring the Articles of Confederation's requirement that all thirteen states had to ratify changes, the constitutional convention decided that only nine states would need to approve the Constitution for the new government to take effect.

What followed was an impassioned debate in all states about the nature of the American republic. Because most citizens remained loyal primarily to their home states, they preferred to retain state sovereignty; in a literal sense, they believed in a federal form of government as a league of independent states rather than an all-powerful centralized unit. Realizing the popularity of the term *federal,* those who supported the Constitution called themselves "Federalists," even though that document greatly increased the authority of the national government. Their opponents, who desired stronger state governments, found themselves called "Anti-Federalists." The language was paradoxical, but voters in the states well understood the issues. To simplify matters further, the drafters of the Constitution proposed that citizens either approve or reject the entire document; amendments, such as a bill of rights, would only be considered after ratification.

Anti-Federalists versus Federalists

Faced with the all-or-nothing choice, critics of the Constitution mounted their attacks in the state ratifying conventions. Anti-Federalists, such as Virginia's Richard Henry Lee and New York's George Clinton, saw themselves as New Yorkers, Pennsylvanians, or Virginians, rather than as Americans; they expressed, in short, a limited national identity. As state-oriented politicians, they viewed the Constitution as a threat to the states and feared that a strong central government would neglect local interests in favor of national issues. Having adopted state bills of rights in the years after 1776, they also objected to the absence in the Constitution of a national bill of rights to protect civil liberties. "My primary objections," stated Massachusetts's influential Elbridge Gerry, "are that there is no adequate provision for representation of the people—that they have no security for the right of election."

At a time when most citizens pursued small-scale farming, Anti-Federalists spoke for those with little or no economic interest beyond their local communities and states. Regionally isolated, such farmers feared government at a distance, especially with leaders chosen indirectly for long terms of office. Anti-Federalists believed that republican governments should represent all community interests; government must be a perfect miniature of society. According to Anti-Federalist thinking, therefore, republics could function well only in small, fairly homogeneous units that allowed citizens to keep a close eye on their rulers. "The largest states," concluded one Anti-Federalist, "are the worst governed."

The Federalists, by contrast, were committed nationalists, men with interstate interests who advocated strengthening the central government. New York's Alexander Hamilton, for example, had served with Washington in the Continental Army and had suffered from Congress's inability to raise taxes for the war. Others, like Madison, believed that a national government could best protect property rights from majority rule. Believing that the state governments were overly democratic, Federalist leaders saw the Constitution's checks and balances as a protection against any politician's mere popularity.

Federalist supporters emerged among urban merchants and commercial farmers who transacted business in more than one state and therefore understood how national economic policies and a strong government could protect international trade. In the port cities, workers and artisans backed the Constitution because their prosperity, too, depended on interstate commerce. Investors who had purchased bonds issued by the Confederation government favored a stronger national government that might repay public debts at face value. Newspaper editors, with interests and influence in more than one state, lined up behind the Constitution. (Anti-Federalist writers complained, for good reason, of the difficulty of getting their ideas into print.) Other Federalist supporters came from areas with special interests, such as Georgia's farmers, who wanted military assistance for their border skirmishes against the Creeks, the Cherokees, and their Spanish allies in Florida.

To support their position, the Federalists offered a new theory of republican government. Whereas Anti-Federalists insisted that republics could survive only in small societies, Federalists argued that the best safeguard of republicanism lay in broad, diverse communities. During the ratification controversy, three leading Federalists—James Madison, Alexander Hamilton, and John Jay—published a series of newspaper essays, *The Federalist Papers,* in which they theorized that the larger and more pluralistic a country, the less likely it was that any one group could achieve a majority and force its will on the whole society. "The only remedy" to majority oppression, said Madison, "is to enlarge the sphere." Instead of being problems, the geographic dispersal of the American people and their multiple differences of interest, said the Federalists, precluded the tyranny of a majority and protected citizens from the abuse of power.

Ratification and Its Aftermath

These arguments prevailed in the state ratifying conventions. With Federalists seizing the initiative, the necessary nine states approved the Constitution by June 1788. But in two centrally located states, Virginia and New York, the Anti-Federalists attracted substantial support, leaving the survival of the new union uncertain. In Virginia, where the popular Patrick Henry looked at the Constitution and "smelled a rat," Federalist support came from western settlers, who wanted the national government's assistance in their conflicts with Native peoples. The Federalist victory in Virginia in turn strengthened the cause in New York, where the Anti-Federalists held an apparent majority. When Hamilton suggested that pro-Federalist New York City might secede from the state, the tide shifted. New York entered the union in July 1788, ensuring implementation of the republican experiment; but North Carolina did not join until 1789, and Rhode Island (the last of the thirteen original states to do so) waited until 1790 to ratify the Constitution.

Despite the great potential of the new centralized government, the Constitution did not significantly alter politics-as-usual in the states. By permitting the states to establish voting qualifications, the structure of political power remained unchanged. The same white male property owners who qualified as citizens in the 1780s participated politically in the 1790s. Those white men who were full citizens, moreover, continued to pay most taxes to local and state governments, not to the national government, and voter participation in national elections remained lower than in state contests.

Meanwhile, women, slaves, Native Americans, and free African Americans won no additional liberties. Still described primarily by their domestic roles, white women measured their power by their ability to influence the next generation. African American slaves, such as Thomas Prosser's blacksmith, Gabriel, of Richmond, Virginia, exercised political power only by rebellious action. And Native Americans inhabiting the nation's borderlands fought bravely, but with mixed results, to keep their lands. Even free white men who lived far from the centers of power, such as the farmers of western Pennsylvania, possessed small power to oppose excise taxes that the new government imposed on whiskey production in 1794. Although denied equal rights by the Constitution, such people could hardly be viewed as invisible; indeed, their frustrations often drew violent attention from the leadership groups. Yet voters accepted the undemocratic elements of the new political system because the Constitution did not create, but merely expressed, the inequities of American society.

Equally striking was the absence of lasting recrimination. Once adopted, the Constitution became preeminent in the public mind, and the Anti-Federalists, as a group, disappeared from the political scene. Led by Madison, the first Congress soon approved ten constitutional amendments, known as the Bill of Rights, to guarantee basic civil liberties. Among property-holding white male citizens, the 1790s saw political participation increase as greater numbers voted, attended public meetings, wrote letters to newspapers, and held office. Although hardly democratic by today's standards, this rise of political activity quickly obliterated older traditions of monarchy and aristocracy. The Constitution's "We, the people" excluded many, yet strengthened the nation's commitment to an elected government. In time, too, this political in-clusion would broaden the number of people who adopted a national identity.

Population Expansion and Migration

The creation of the new government coincided with a rapid expansion of the American popula-tion. Indeed, in 1790, "We, the people" were al-ready diverse, though many areas remained homogenous. In New England, 80 percent of the people traced their ancestry to England (60 per-cent of the country's total population had an En-glish lineage). New York remained heavily Dutch, while Pennsylvania was 40 percent German. And about 30 percent of the people of Georgia, the Caro-linas, and Kentucky had roots in Ireland and Scot-land. Despite such diversity, the nation's political and legal system remained overwhelmingly En-glish, and British Americans dominated the na-tional leadership. Indeed, the idea of a *written* Constitution, in contrast to the unwritten legal tra-ditions that prevailed among Europeans and Native Americans, placed priority on literacy. Although the ability to read and write English was not a require-ment for citizenship, those possessing such skills had obvious advantages. High literacy rates en-couraged the expansion of newspapers, which spread information throughout the states. Yet un-written oral traditions, such as Native American interpretations of treaties, lacked legal standing and could be dismissed as "hearsay evidence."

Immigrants from Europe and slaves from Africa continued to land on American shores, but the surge in population from 4 million in 1789 to 9 million in 1815 primarily reflected a high birthrate. Rural white women in the north were delivering seven to eight children, most healthy enough to reach maturity. Life expectancy for white adults averaged about 45. But the mortality rate of African American children was twice as high as for whites and life expectancy for blacks was only 35. The rising population also disguised (perhaps even caused) a decline in life expectancy among all Americans as infectious diseases spread more rapidly and took a higher toll.

Geographic Mobility and Society

The population boom within farm families created land shortages in settled areas, stimulating two economic trends: children of eastern farmers looked for land in western regions; others turned to nonagricultural employment, sometimes tem-porarily until they inherited or could afford to buy land, sometimes learning trades that brought them into towns and cities. Total urban growth remained small, yet the population of New York and Penn-sylvania increased by 60 percent, while the rest of the nation grew 25 to 35 percent. Meanwhile, the price of public land rose to $2 per acre ($27 in today's money) for a minimum of 640 acres (or over $17,280 in today's money). Such prices pri-marily benefited land speculators who had money to invest. Migrants who settled the land bought smaller parcels at higher prices per acre.

In the coastal areas of the southern states, soil exhaustion encouraged tobacco planters to shift to grain production, while younger sons moved their families into the western foothills to transplant a tobacco economy there. Smaller farmers in west-ern regions, many with Scots-Irish backgrounds, turned to livestock, fattening cows and pigs to feed the coastal towns. Such family farms seldom could afford to employ slaves. By contrast, tobacco planters who moved west either brought along their slaves or purchased them from dealers who operated an active domestic slave trade between the Upper South and Lower South. As white farm-ers built tobacco plantations in western Virginia, Carolina, Georgia, Kentucky, and Tennessee, some 40,000 African Americans were uprooted from their homes during the 1790s. Efforts by Quakers in Maryland to block this trade brought assurances from slaveowners that African Americans would thrive in the Gulf states' "warmer and more congenial climate." The demand for slave labor also resulted in the reopening of the foreign slave trade. Between 1783 and 1808, over 100,000 African slaves, mostly men and boys, entered the country through Savannah, Charleston, and New Orleans.

The enthusiasm for growing cotton increased substantially following the introduction of Eli Whitney's mechanical gin, which facilitated the separation of oily seeds from the cotton fibers. Stimulated by demand from English factories, western Georgia and South Carolina were producing 30 million pounds of cotton annually by 1800. The cotton boom encouraged expansion into the Alabama and Mississippi territories, where rivers linked planters to Gulf of Mexico ports. By 1800, cotton was the staple crop of Mississippi, and half the population in the Natchez district was African American.

Resistance to Westward Expansion

In the 1780s, the nation's 4 million inhabitants (including 700,000 African American slaves) were already looking beyond the frontiers of the thirteen states into areas claimed by other nations. Over 100,000 had crossed the Appalachians into Kentucky, Tennessee, and Spain's Louisiana territory. Territorial expansion brought the new nation into conflict with those already inhabiting the western regions.

New Spain, now a tottering empire, reluctantly permitted immigration into Mississippi, promising, in the words of Thomas Jefferson, "the means of delivering to us peaceably what may otherwise cost us a war." Treaties with Spain in the 1790s transferred some territorial claims to the United States. The collapse of the Spanish empire also became apparent in the Pacific northwest, where Great Britain successfully challenged Spain's claims to Vancouver in western Canada.

AMERICAN COOKERY,

OR THE ART OF DRESSING

VIANDS, FISH, POULTRY and VEGETABLES,

AND THE BEST MODES OF MAKING

PASTES, PUFFS, PIES, TARTS, PUDDINGS, CUSTARDS AND PRESERVES,

AND ALL KINDS OF

C A K E S,

FROM THE IMPERIAL PLUMB TO PLAIN CAKE.

ADAPTED TO THIS COUNTRY,

AND ALL GRADES OF LIFE.

By Amelia Simmons,

AN AMERICAN ORPHAN.

PUBLISHED ACCORDING TO ACT OF CONGRESS.

HARTFORD

PRINTED BY HUDSON & GOODWIN,

FOR THE AUTHOR.

1796

Title page from Amelia Simmons's *American Cookery* (1796). Styling herself as "an American orphan," Amelia Simmons performed a service for those American women who now needed cookbooks, because they were less likely to be geographically close to the source of their mothers' advice.

Some Americans were already eyeing nearby California, seeing the area as hopelessly undeveloped under Spanish rule. "The characteristics of the Californians," announced Jedediah Morse in his

"The characteristics of the Californians are stupidity and insensibility . . . ; an excessive sloth and abhorrence of all labour."

ethnocentric book, *The American Geography* (1789), "are stupidity and insensibility . . . ; an excessive sloth and abhorrence of all labour."

More strenuous opposition to territorial expansion came from the Cherokees, Creeks, and Chickamaugas. American expansionists relied on trickery, whiskey, and force of arms to win their claims. ("I considered it in the interest of the United States to be . . . liberal," explained Tennessee's governor about dispensing corn liquor to a local chief and his thirsty party in 1793.) Military victories against Chickamauga towns on the Tennessee River, followed by the destruction of growing crops, effectively ended Native resistance. Forced treaties then gave Americans title to the lands in western Georgia, which rapidly became cotton fields.

Similar ambitions encouraged settlement of the Northwest Territory. "The original right of the aborigines to the soil," remarked a settler of western Pennsylvania, "is like the claim of children; it is mine for I saw it first." Making counter-claims, U.S. promoters stressed the superiority of developing the land for commercial purposes. As small farmers and organized land companies from New England claimed Native lands, Shawnee opposition provoked warfare. Between 1790 and 1796, the new nation spent five-sixths of the national budget for military action against the Ohio peoples. Expeditions in 1790 and 1791 brought U.S. defeats, and the victorious Shawnee warriors stuffed fertile soil into the mouths of slain U.S. soldiers to express their hatred of land hunger. President George Washington sent another army under General "Mad" Anthony Wayne, which won the

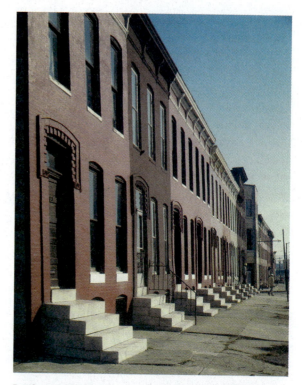

Row houses in Baltimore, built at the beginning of the nineteenth century. Each dwelling was constructed identically. With standard heights for roof lines, windows, and front steps, row houses revealed a cultural preference for geometric regularity.

Battle of Fallen Timbers in 1794 and then dictated the Treaty of Greenville to the Shawnees in 1795. The agreement gave the United States title to most of Ohio, and southern Indiana and Illinois. To preserve peace, Washington became the Shawnees' honorary "father" and agreed to provide annual payments to selected Native leaders.

Urban Geometry and Social Inequality

As some Americans migrated west, others headed for towns and cities. Here, problems of territoriality took different forms. "Curved lines symbolize the country, straight lines the city," observed Daniel Drake, a Cincinnati physician in 1794. Urban ar-

Andrew Ellicott's engraved map of 1792, based on Pierre L'Enfant's manuscript plan, which was adopted by the Congress as the final plan for the federal city of Washington. The plan deliberately placed the executive, legislative, and judicial branches of the government in separate parts of the city, mirroring the separation of powers in the Constitution.

chitecture of the period, the so-called Federal style, emphasized simplicity and uniformity. Municipalities initiated grid plans to facilitate real estate transactions and rationalize the use of urban space. New York introduced street numbering, with odds on one side, evens on the other. After political leaders agreed to move the nation's capital to the District of Columbia near the Potomac River in 1791, the new city's blueprint featured rectangular street plans and right-angle intersections.

The new urban growth underscored inequalities of wealth. As the nation's city population doubled during the 1790s and trade exports jumped fivefold, land values rapidly increased—by as much as 750 percent in Manhattan between 1785 and 1815. Few artisans and unskilled workers could afford to own a house; instead, they rented from more affluent landlords. The rising cost of housing provoked sporadic protests, but despite increasing rents, free African Americans migrated to the cities

to take a growing number of unskilled jobs as dock workers and domestic servants. Some free blacks entered the skilled trades as shipbuilders and carpenters, but whites did not welcome their competition for jobs. Indeed, white workers excluded free blacks from annual July Fourth street celebrations, lest the principles of liberty attract enslaved blacks as well. The demand for labor was encouraging an increase in the number of urban slaves. As Richmond, Virginia, grew from 3,700 residents in 1790 to 5,000 in 1800 and nearly 10,000 by 1810, for example, the demand for construction workers stimulated the hiring of slaves owned by tobacco planters whose lands were losing fertility and value.

The increasing number of urban blacks, free and slave, encouraged the emergence of distinct African American institutions. Since the Great Awakening of the mid-18th century, a small proportion of blacks, probably less than 10 percent of the total black population, had converted to Christianity, joined racially mixed Baptist congregations, and developed an identity as black Christians. Despite Baptist tenets of Christian equality, many whites disliked racially integrated congregations; one white preacher in Richmond was pejoratively called "Negro George." Such prejudices, together with a growing sense of racial community, prompted the formation of separate black churches during the 1790s. Within these segregated institutions, slaves and free blacks enjoyed greater social independence. In New York City, however, African Americans encountered a distinctive type of vertical segregation and were obliged to live in unhealthy quarters. According to a medical report about an epidemic, numerous blacks "living in 10 cellars" died in great numbers, "while . . . whites living immediately above their heads in the apartments of the same houses" did not succumb to the fever.

Economic inequality in the cities accentuated the vulnerability of poor women of all races. In a celebrated New York City rape trial in 1793, a wealthy man, accused of seducing a poor 17-year old girl in a "bawdy" house, deflected blame by charging his victim with prostitution. "Could she imagine that a man of his situation would pay her any attention," asked the rich man's lawyer, "unless with a view of promoting illicit commerce?" The all-male jury could not, and voted for his acquittal, whereupon an angry mob of workers attacked both the bawdy house and the lawyers. The verdict was not changed.

Social and economic patterns of the period—urban growth, western migration, disruption of Native American life—existed in a distinct, parallel realm from problems of national government and political forms, though politics and society remained closely interrelated. For most citizens and noncitizens, social and economic issues remained more important than the affairs of state. Yet the nation's diversity reinforced the commitment to republicanism. A political system based

> **In frontier Kentucky, "the women . . . would follow their cows to see what they ate [so] that they might know what greens to get."**

on "the people" promised not only to represent the country's inhabitants, but also to encourage their social and economic liberty.

Launching the New Government

Although social institutions changed slowly, geographic mobility and political innovation constantly forced citizens to confront new challenges. In frontier Kentucky during the 1780s, recalled a pioneer settler, "the women . . . would follow their cows to see what they ate [so] that they might know what greens to get." Such prudence enabled migrating Americans to survive in unfamiliar territory. National politicians faced an equally strange landscape. "We are in a wilderness," remarked James Madison in 1789, "without a single footstep to guide us." The Constitution provided the blueprint; the nation's founders took tentative steps and built precedents.

Forging Political Precedents

George Washington was unanimously elected president by the first electoral college and took the oath of office in New York City, the nation's first capital, in 1789. Political leaders quibbled about what to call him; John Adams, the first vice president, proposed "His Elective Highness." Washington rejected this relic of monarchism; the democratic "Mr. President" would suffice. Although the Constitution did not provide for a presidential cabinet, Congress established executive departments of state, treasury, justice, and post office in 1789 and granted the president the right to appoint and dismiss the heads of these agencies. In selecting his cabinet, Washington chose men from geographically diverse backgrounds, thereby fulfilling the Federalists' notion of dispersing political power.

To establish a national legal system, Congress passed the Judiciary Act of 1789, creating district and appellate courts as well as the Supreme Court. The law also ensured that state courts would retain the bulk of original jurisdiction. Other legal precedents emerged less systematically. When Washington arrived in the Senate in 1789 to seek the constitutionally mandated "advice and consent" about a pending treaty with the Creek nation, the ensuing discussion proved unsatisfactory. The president retreated with "sullen dignity," creating the precedent of consulting with the Senate only *after* treaties had been negotiated and signed.

Congress established other legal precedents that revealed political values not explicitly included in the Constitution. The Naturalization Act of 1790 required two-year residency before immigrants could become citizens and reserved citizenship for applicants who were of good character and "white." The Militia Act of 1792, aimed at recruiting soldiers for wars against the Northwest nations, limited enrollment to able-bodied free white males. The Fugitive Slave Act of 1793 permitted an owner to seize a runaway slave in another state merely by presenting a sworn statement (oral or written), whereas a criminal fugitive from justice enjoyed rights of due process. Such racially discriminatory legislation reflected the views of the nation's first political leaders.

Although the Constitution had omitted a bill of rights, many states' ratification conventions assumed that basic protections of civil liberties would be added as amendments, and Washington's inaugural address recommended measures to protect the "characteristic rights of freemen." Accordingly, in

the first session of the House of Representatives, Madison presented a dozen constitutional amendments to protect citizens from government. Ten were ratified by the states in 1791 and became part of the Constitution. These amendments, collectively known as the "Bill of Rights," guaranteed freedom of speech, the press, and religion; allowed the states to form citizen militias (to eliminate the need for standing armies); assured the right of trial by jury; protected citizens from unreasonable police search and seizure; and permitted individuals to refuse to give self-incriminating testimony. Together, they amounted to a defense of personal liberty against government power. During the 1790s, the Supreme Court extended citizens' rights to sue the states in federal courts. This expansion of federal judicial power alarmed Congress, leading to approval of the Eleventh Amendment, limiting such suits, in 1798.

Amendment XI (1798)

The judicial power of the United States shall not be construed to extend to any suit in law or equity, commenced or prosecuted against one of the United States by citizens of another state, or by citizens or subjects of any foreign state.

With the exception of the Twelfth Amendment of 1804, these were the last constitutional amendments until the 1860s, when the Civil War forced a redefinition of the rights of citizenship.

Hamilton's Financial Plan Provokes Debate

As political leaders formalized government operations, the nation's commercial interests looked to the new government to create a financial system that would ensure safe economic development based on foreign trade, primarily with England. The energetic and visionary secretary of the treasury, Alexander Hamilton, responded by designing an elaborate program to stabilize government credit at home and abroad. In 1790, Hamilton unveiled his ideas in a *Report on the Public Credit*. The plan proposed that the government pay or "fund" the entire existing national debt (the bonds and vouchers remaining from the Confederation government) at full face value. At a time when such paper money was worth a fraction of its printed value because few believed the Confederation would ever pay its debts, Hamilton's scheme would prove a windfall for speculators who had purchased these depreciated bonds at much less than their face value. By rewarding these wealthy citizens, Hamilton hoped his plan would marry the nation's business interests to the new government. In Congress, southern representatives, such as Madison, challenged the plan for its failure to reimburse the original holders of government bonds, among them war veterans who had been paid with promissory notes. In response, Hamilton emphasized the long-run advantages of stabilizing the nation's credit.

Hamilton's financial plan also proposed that the national government assume the outstanding debts of the state governments, even though those too were largely held by wealthy investors of the northeast. Yet Hamilton did not see his proposal merely as a benefit for Federalist business groups. He believed that the government's promise to pay the national debt would increase its credit—and so attract additional capital investment in the government. Since most southern states had already paid their debts, the debt-assumption plan aroused regional opposition. Hamilton eased those objections by making an agreement with the leading southern politicians, Madison and Jefferson. While New York and Philadelphia were competing to become the permanent capital of the United States, which would bring additional benefits to local businesses, Hamilton consented to move the capi-

tal to the banks of the Potomac in exchange for southern support of the debt-assumption program. The creation of the District of Columbia on federal lands further established the separation of the national government from state influence. The first Congress passed both the funding and debt-assumption measures in 1790. The resulting national debt would soon require Hamilton to propose new tax measures to balance the budget.

A third element of Hamilton's financial program emerged in 1791 with his request that Congress establish a national bank, the Bank of the United States, with power to raise $10 million by selling stock to the public. The government would hold one-fifth of the stock; investors would purchase the remainder. The bank would serve as a depository of government funds and would collect and dispense government monies. The bank's notes, backed by government deposits, would act as a legal currency. Thus the bank would both benefit stockholders and provide loans for business investment.

When Congress approved the Bank of the United States in 1791, however, President Washington raised questions about its constitutionality and sought the opinions of his cabinet. Secretary of State Jefferson, who believed that the nation's future lay in agriculture rather than in business, opposed the idea of using government funds to benefit private investors. He adopted a "strict" interpretation of the Constitution, arguing that anything the Constitution did not explicitly *permit* should remain outside the scope of government. Since the Constitution did not provide for a national bank, Jefferson denied its constitutionality. Hamilton, by contrast, adopted a "loose" interpretation of the Constitution and assured Washington that Congress could enact anything that was "necessary and proper" (in the words of the Constitution) as long as the Constitution did not explicitly *forbid* it.

The argument about the bank revealed rival ideas about the function of a republican government. To Hamilton, the issue hinged on stabilizing the nation; he did not care that certain business interests would benefit more than most citizens. To Jefferson, the matter involved the protection of the liberty of the citizens; he thought government should not play favorites. Washington listened to their pleas, then signed the bill into law. In the end, history vindicated both Jefferson and Hamilton. As Jefferson warned, individuals profited from doing the government's business; but, as Hamilton predicted, the expansion of credit boosted commerce around the country.

To complete the financial program, Hamilton issued a *Report on Manufactures* in 1791, stressing the advantages of tariffs (taxes on imports) to raise government revenue and to enable U.S. manufactures to compete against cheaper imported goods. Although Congress rejected high duties to stimulate manufacturing, the modest tariff of 1792 provided 90 percent of the national government's revenue. Most of that income came from duties on textiles and iron products imported from Great Britain. In this way, Hamilton's financial program linked the nation's budget with British trade. The merchants who dominated commerce with Britain, moreover, had benefited from Hamilton's funding plan. These connections would soon influence the nation's foreign policy. As Hamilton remarked to the British ambassador, "We think in English."

The Whiskey Rebellion

To keep tariffs low, Hamilton proposed a domestic excise tax on the manufacture of whiskey. Americans were famous for heavy drinking, but interest in whiskey reflected primarily the economics of transportation in rural areas such as western Pennsylvania. Farmers there relied on Ohio River flatboats to bring their produce to market and fermented their grain into whiskey to reduce freight charges. The 1791 excise tax, however, drew no distinction between home manufacturing and commercial distilleries. Struggling small farmers protested the new taxes, sometimes forming outlaw militias to harass government tax collectors.

Civilian violence alarmed government leaders, including the president, who thought the refusal to pay taxes was equivalent to sedition. To show the authority of the national government and prove its ability to enforce the law, Washington summoned the army in 1794 to suppress the so-called Whiskey Rebellion. Resistance quickly evaporated, but authorities imposed harsh penalties until Washington finally pardoned those convicted of treason. Soon afterward, the opening of the Northwest Territory to settlement eased the region's economic problems. Congress repealed the excise tax in 1800 and avoided such measures until the Civil War. But the turmoil over whiskey taxes demonstrated the limits of acceptable protest in a republican government.

Partisan Politics and Foreign Entanglements

Government fears about the Whiskey rebellion reflected a larger unease caused by the French Revolution of 1789, which dramatized class conflicts between the poor masses and their wealthy rulers. As president, Washington held the esteem of most citizens, and his birthday became a day of patriotic celebration. But when Hamilton proposed that Washington's face be stamped on U.S. coins, republicans objected to such "monarchical" poses, and Congress rejected the idea. Instead, a female representation of "Liberty" symbolized the new nation's ideology on U.S. money. The argument indicated a growing rift about other political issues. By the end of Washington's second term, his birthday had become a matter of partisan strife.

Conflicts over Foreign Policy

Foreign policy emerged as a prime topic of political disagreement. Although many Americans had welcomed the French Revolution as an extension of their own attack on King George III, the execution of the deposed French king in 1793 and the declaration of war between France and England forced a reappraisal of their initial enthusiasm. Washington issued a Proclamation of Neutrality in 1793 that rejected any obligations of the French alliance of 1778 and announced a desire to keep the country out of war. The arrival of the French ambassador Edmond Genêt soon afterward complicated the issue. Greeted as a hero by crowds as he traveled from Charleston to Philadelphia, Genêt overestimated the government's sympathy for revolutionary France. When the ambassador openly defied Washington's neutrality proclamation by outfitting ships to attack British commerce, the president demanded Genêt's recall.

The Genêt affair aroused public opinion. While the pro-British Hamilton organized mass meetings to denounce the French ambassador, pro-French sympathizers formed grassroots organizations, called Democratic Societies, to encourage support for France. Neutralists like Washington considered both sides potentially seditious. Since private political factions or parties were extralegal (that is, outside the constitutional system), these early steps in the formation of political parties appeared subversive to the nation's leaders. Ironically, both rival factions warned that their political enemies were threats to republican government. Both sides believed that any political discord endangered a republican system.

Yet the two political factions stood for different principles. The pro-French partisans claimed to defend republican principles of liberty (the "Spirit of '76") against a conspiracy of monarchist sympathizers. The anti-French partisans, such as Hamilton, claimed to defend the rights of property against radical revolutionaries. These differences involved not only political ideas but also strong emotions. Such passions intensified political debate and laid the basis of the first political party system: the pro-French "Democratic-Republicans" (later known simply as Republicans) versus the pro-English "Federalists."

The danger of radical politics crept closer to home when the slaves of Saint Domingue, a French Caribbean colony, erupted with violence in 1793. As French slaveowners (many with their slaves) sought refuge in North America, U.S. slaveholders worried that the spirit of insurrection would spread among their slaves. Saint Domingue, said Jefferson, was only "the first chapter." In New York City, a rising number of runaway slaves and outbreaks of arson fires terrorized the populace. In Philadelphia, a yellow-fever epidemic created an odd medical debate as anti-French doctors blamed the disease on the French refugees while pro-French physicians sought local explanations. Believing that Africans were immune to yellow fever, the nation's foremost physician, Dr. Benjamin Rush, persuaded blacks to assist the dying and remove the dead until they too began to succumb. Whatever the medical diagnosis, African Americans well understood the political crisis. Perhaps stimulated by the Caribbean revolt, cases of murder and poisoning of slaveowners rose dramatically and rumors of slave conspiracies abounded. Fear of slave revolts underscored the fragility of the nation's political structure. Throughout the decade, government leaders did not feel confident about the loyalty of their foes, whether slaves or free men.

The Jay Treaty and the Rise of Political Parties

Washington's policy of neutrality in the war between England and France increased U.S. shipping. Merchants took advantage of food shortages in Europe and expanded trade in the West Indies. But the risk of war increased when both Britain and France seized American ships on the high seas for trading with the enemy. Since the British navy dominated the seas, England's violations were more threatening to American interests. The two countries headed toward war.

To seek a peaceful settlement, Washington sent Ambassador John Jay to England. But British leaders showed little interest in negotiations, and Jay felt obliged to make concessions to avoid war. Instead of defending the principle that neutral nations could trade freely with warring countries, Jay accepted the British position that goods could not be carried to enemy ports and that trade with enemy colonies—the West Indies in particular—could not be legalized in time of war. England then promised reimbursement for lost cargoes and abandoned its claims to the Northwest Territory.

Jay's Treaty brought foreign controversy directly into domestic politics. As the ambassador's concessions to England inflamed public opinion, congressional opponents of the treaty clustered around the anti-British or "Republican" faction, led by Madison and Jefferson. Meanwhile, a pro-British "Federalist" faction, inspired by Hamilton, defended the treaty because it protected the lucrative trade with England. Both sides organized public rallies to petition the government; both used popular newspapers to sway citizen opinion. Both articulated distinctive political persuasions. The Federalists claimed that the commercial treaty would ensure stability and protect property; the Republicans pleaded for the commercial rights of a free nation and warned that the Federalists were monarchists who conspired with England to overthrow the republican experiment. What the two groups shared was a conspiratorial outlook, a belief that their opponents threatened the survival of republican government. Believing that factions were inherently subversive, neither side could accept the idea of a loyal opposition.

Beneath the rhetoric lay substantial differences of political interest. Federalist support for England obviously appealed to merchants who prospered with British trade. In New England, traditions of anti-French sentiment, dating to the colonial

wars against Canada, made the region a Federalist stronghold. Small farmers in isolated areas tended to follow Federalist conservatism. Republicans, by contrast, appealed to farmers and merchants who sought economic opportunity by extending trade beyond the British marketplace; in urban areas, smaller merchants, manufacturers, and artisans opposed the Federalist leadership and expressed pro-French sentiment. Despite such public disagreements, neither side believed that their opponents were sincere or that their differences were based on interests and principles rather than some conspiratorial intentions. In this atmosphere of intense distrust, the Jay Treaty slipped through the Senate by a single vote in 1794.

Political leaders expressed greater unity in accepting Pinckney's Treaty of 1795, which settled the Florida boundary dispute with Spain and assured U.S. shipping rights on the Mississippi River. But national politics remained edgy, taut, and suspicious. When Washington retired after two terms as president, his farewell address of 1796 criticized the spirit of political parties and advised Americans to avoid entanglements with foreign nations because they imperiled domestic harmony.

Even as Washington spoke, the elections of 1796 intensified conflict between Federalists and Republicans. In the cities, Republicans attracted Irish (anti-British) immigrants and French refugees from Saint Domingue. But most voting followed regional lines, with Federalists strong in the northeast and Republicans successful in the south, rather than sharp party alignments. Indeed, half the candidates never clearly expressed a party identity. Nevertheless, Federalist sympathizers captured both houses of Congress. The outcome of the presidential contest revealed less clarity. While the Federalists nominated John Adams and Thomas Pinckney for the highest offices, the Republicans endorsed Jefferson and Aaron Burr. But the Constitution had made no mention of party affiliations in the electoral college vote. Consequently, the candidate with the majority of electoral votes, the Federalist Adams, became president; the second highest tally, just three votes short, went to the Republican Jefferson, who assumed the vice presidency.

Challenges to the Adams Administration

Despite the warning in Washington's farewell address, foreign entanglements soon swamped the Adams administration. As French privateers attacked U.S. ships in the West Indies, Adams dispatched negotiators to France in 1797 to reach agreement about neutral rights. In Paris, U.S. diplomats confronted the sly minister Talleyrand, who suggested that, instead of demanding monetary damages, the Americans would do well to offer a bribe to three French agents (later known as X, Y, and Z). "We are not a degraded people," exclaimed Adams, upon bringing the news of the XYZ affair to Congress. Infuriated by the insult to national honor, public opinion supported preparations for war. Congress voted to terminate the French Alliance of 1778, created a Department of the Navy to build warships and license privateers, and approved an army. Yet when influential Federalist leaders, including the retired Washington, forced Adams to appoint his rival, Hamilton, to head the troops, the second president hesitated to demand war. Fearful of open hostilities and mistrustful of Hamilton's intentions, Adams weighed his options.

The Alien and Sedition Acts

As an undeclared naval war commenced against France, bringing moments of glory to the new navy, Republicans and Federalists clashed about extending hostilities. One Federalist newspaper called the pro-French Republicans "democrats, mobocrats

and all other kinds of rats" and claimed that they intended to install French anarchy on the American republic. Without waiting for the president's decision to go to war, the Federalist Congress proceeded to enact four laws, the Alien and Sedition acts of 1798, to ensure political conformity and reduce foreign influence in domestic politics. First, the Naturalization Act aimed at what Federalists called "hordes of wild Irishmen" and other "turbulent and disorderly" immigrant groups (that is, those who opposed England's interests) by extending the period of probationary residence for citizenship to 14 years. Second, the Alien Act permitted the president to expel unnaturalized foreigners deemed "dangerous to the peace," but the measure expired in 1800 without ever being implemented. Third, the Alien Enemies Act allowed the president to apprehend, restrain, or remove dangerous foreign nationals, but only in wartime. Unlike the other statutes, this measure remained a permanent law, used by twentieth century presidents to restrict foreign groups during the world wars.

The fourth law, the Sedition Act, struck closer to home. Assuming that political dissent constituted a threat to legal order, this Federalist measure declared that any citizen who was guilty of writing, publishing, or speaking anything of "a false, scandalous or malicious" nature against the government or a government official faced stiff fines and imprisonment. The administration promptly issued indictments against Republican newspaper editors, sending several to jail.

As Hamilton proceeded to build the army, and Federalists pushed for a declaration of war against France, Republican leaders gathered support in the state legislatures. Fearing government suppression backed by the army, Madison and Jefferson wrote two resolutions that were passed by the Virginia and Kentucky legislatures in 1798. These resolutions argued that a state government had the power to nullify and refuse to obey congressional laws that threatened the people's liberties and were thus unconstitutional. The Adams administration made no effort to challenge this assertion of states' rights, but Virginians made preparations to meet a Federalist-led military attack. The peril of civil war seemed real to Republicans and Federalists alike.

Peace with France

While the constitutional squabble threatened domestic order, news from France suggested that negotiations might settle the foreign conflict. "The end of war is peace," Adams remarked, agreeing to send another ambassador to France in 1799. His decision outraged less conciliatory Federalists who broke with the president and looked to Hamilton for leadership. But the resolute Adams allowed diplomacy to proceed. By the time the ambassadors reached France, Napoleon Bonaparte had seized power and was eager for a truce. The Convention of 1800 did no more than guarantee neutral rights during wartime (indeed, the agreement angered Federalists by neglecting the matter of damage payments) but a grateful administration offered the treaty as a better alternative to war. Unknown to Adams, Bonaparte's designs were more ominous, for the day after signing the Convention he secretly persuaded Spain to cede the Louisiana territory to France, preparing to challenge American control of the Mississippi valley (see Chapter 8).

The Election of 1800

As the war clouds disappeared, the country focused on the 1800 presidential election. With Federalists divided between pro- and anti-Adams factions, Republicans built a coalition among commercial farmers, aspiring merchants and artisans, and non-English immigrants, all of whom had opposed recent Federalist war preparations, high taxes, and political persecution. Once again, Jefferson faced Adams in the presidential contest, this time gaining a majority of eight electoral votes.

The Constitution, conceived before the rise of political parties, made no distinction between presidential and vice-presidential ballots, and Jefferson and his running mate Aaron Burr of New York received the same number of electoral votes. Following the Constitution, the choice between Jefferson and Burr then moved to the sitting House of Representatives. Here, Federalist influence remained strong, and thirty-five ballots brought an unyielding deadlock. Since the new Congress would not take office for nearly a year, some Federalists saw an opportunity for remaining in power. But Hamilton's hatred of Burr, a New York rival, finally moved him to support Jefferson, who was named president on the thirty-sixth ballot. (Burr would later have his revenge, killing Hamilton in a duel.) To prevent any similar constitutional crisis, the Twelfth Amendment, adopted in 1804, separated electoral college balloting for president and vice president.

Amendment XII (1804)

The electors shall meet in their respective states and vote by ballot for President and Vice-President, one of whom, at least, shall not be an inhabitant of the same state with themselves; they shall name in their ballots the person voted for as President, and in distinct ballots the person voted for as Vice-President, and they shall make distinct lists of all persons voted for as President, and of all persons voted for as Vice-President, and of the number of votes for each, which lists they shall sign and certify, and transmit sealed to the seat of the government of the United States, directed to the President of the Senate;—The President of the Senate shall, in the presence of the Senate and House of

Representatives, open all the certificates and the votes shall then be counted;—the person having the greatest number of votes for President, shall be the President, if such number be a majority of the whole number of electors appointed; and if no person have such majority, then from the persons having the highest numbers not exceeding three on the list of those voted for as President, the House of Representatives shall choose immediately, by ballot, the President. But in choosing the President, the votes shall be taken by states, the representation from each state having one vote; a quorum for this purpose shall consist of a member or members from two-thirds of the states, and a majority of all the states shall be necessary to a choice. And if the House of Representatives shall not choose a President whenever the right of choice shall devolve upon them, before the fourth day of March next following, then the Vice-President shall act as President, as in the case of the death or other constitutional disability of the President. The person having the greatest number of votes as Vice-President, shall be the Vice-President, if such number be a majority of the whole number of electors appointed, and if no person have a majority, then from the two highest numbers on the list, the Senate shall choose the Vice-President; a quorum for the purpose shall consist of two-thirds of the whole number of Senators, and a majority of the whole number shall be necessary to a choice. But no person constitutionally ineligible to the office of President shall be eligible to that of Vice-President of the United States.

A Fragile Republic

The election of 1800, heralded as a peaceful transition of power from Federalists to Republicans, nonetheless revealed the shaky state of republicanism in the new nation. Not only did party leaders disagree about policies and programs but they also continued to doubt the essential loyalty of their political rivals. Indeed, fear of subversion dominated political discussion in both parties. Believing that republican governments were fragile entities, political leaders were not yet prepared to trust their opponents or accept the legitimacy of two-party politics.

Tension within the political leadership appeared slight compared to the potential conflict between citizens and racial outsiders. During the 1800 election campaign, slaveowners in Richmond, Virginia, discovered a slave conspiracy led by a blacksmith named Gabriel. The carefully planned uprising, thwarted at the last minute by a black informer, involved hundreds, perhaps thousands, of blacks and exposed the explosive contradictions of a republican government built on foundations of slavery. Adopting the slogan "Death or Liberty," African American rebels planned to spare the lives of Quakers, Methodists, and French persons because they were "friendly to liberty." But one African American insurrectionist confessed, "I could kill a white man as free as eat."

The state of Virginia soon hanged 27 blacks and sold hundreds into exile. Subsequent laws limited the freeing of slaves and restricted the movements of free blacks. Virginia Federalists blamed the crisis on the Jeffersonians for imparting "the French principles of Liberty and Equality . . . into the minds of the Negroes." Republicans replied by accusing the Federalist press of fomenting an "electioneering engine." Such partisan rhetoric belied the essential uncertainty of political life. As Federalists feared an epidemic of liberty, Republicans equally suspected a monarchist plot. Two hundred years ago, the stability of the new nation appeared doubtful, at best.

INFOTRAC® COLLEGE EDITION EXERCISES

 For additional reading go to InfoTrac College Edition, your online research library at *http://web1.infotrac-college.com.*

Subject search: United States Constitution

Keyword search: Federalist Papers

Subject search: Hamilton and Jefferson

Subject search: Hamilton

Keyword search: George Washington

ADDITIONAL READING

Designing a National Union

Jack N. Rakove, *Original Meanings: Politics and Ideas in the Making of the Constitution* (1996). A careful analysis of the political ideas that produced the Constitution.

The Struggle for Ratification

Saul Cornell, *The Other Founders: Anti-Federalism and the Dissenting Tradition in America, 1788–1828* (1999). This study analyzes the opposition to ratification; see also the older but still-useful book by Jackson Turner Main, *The Antifederalists: Critics of the Constitution* (1961).

Geographic Mobility and Society

Joyce Appleby, *Inheriting the Revolution: The First Generation of Americans* (2000). Examines the liberating effects of republicanism on religion, business, and private life.

Malcolm J. Rohrbough, *The Trans-Appalachian Frontier: People, Societies, and Institutions, 1775–1850* (1978). Describes the American farmers who migrated into the Midwest.

Shane White, *Somewhat More Independent: The End of Slavery in New York City, 1770–1810* (1991). A study of the social and cultural conditions among African Americans in New York, contrasting with Gary Nash's *Forging Freedom* (1988), listed in the previous chapter.

Resistance to Westward Expansion

Gregory Evans Dowd, *A Spirited Resistance: The North American Indian Struggle for Unity, 1745–1815* (1992). This fine book links Native American resistance during the colonial period to conflicts during the early republic.

The Whiskey Rebellion

Thomas P. Slaughter, *The Whiskey Rebellion: Frontier Epilogue to the American Revolution* (1986). This analysis of rural America places the tax rebellion in the context of popular protest.

Partisan Politics and Foreign Entanglements

Stanley Elkins and Eric McKitrick, *The Age of Federalism* (1993). A thorough study of politics and diplomacy during the 1790s.

John R. Nelson, Jr., *Liberty and Property: Political Economy and Policymaking in the New Nation, 1789–1812* (1987). Describes the political and economic differences between Federalists and Republicans.

Simon P. Newman, *Parades and Politics of the Street: Festive Culture in the Early American Republic* (1997). This analysis of public symbols emphasizes the growing partisanship of public life in the 1790s.

James Roger Sharp, *American Politics in the Early Republic: The New Nation in Crisis* (1993). A study of partisan conflict that describes the tenuous stability of the republic.

A Fragile Republic

James Sidbury, *Ploughshares into Swords: Race, Rebellion, and Identity in Gabriel's Virginia, 1730–1810* (1997). An analysis of racial consciousness among African Americans, which explains the social dynamics of Gabriel's conspiracy. See also Douglas R. Egerton, *Gabriel's Rebellion* (1993).

8

The Connecticut Courant.

PRINTED AT HARTFORD, BY HUDSON & GOODWIN, OPPOSITE THE NORTH MEETING-HOUSE.

VOL. XXXV.]   MONDAY, MARCH 10, 1800.   [NUMBER 1833.

PUBLISHED BY AUTHORITY.

SIXTH CONGRESS, OF THE UNITED STATES,

At the first session, begun and held at the city of Philadelphia, in the state of Pennsylvania, on Monday the second of December, 1799.

CHAPTER I.

An ACT for reviving and continuing suits and proceedings in the Circuit Court for the district of Pennsylvania.

Sec. 1. BE it enacted by the Senate and House of Representatives of the United States of America, in Congress assembled, That all suits, process and proceedings, of what nature or kind soever, which were pending in the Circuit Court of the United States, for the district of Pennsylvania, at the time appointed by law, for holding a session thereof in October, one thousand seven hundred and ninety-nine, and which were discontinued by failure to hold the said court, shall be, and they are hereby revived and continued, and the same proceedings may be had in the same court, in all things relating to the same, as by law might have been had in the same court, had it been regularly holden, at the time aforesaid.

Sec. 2. And be it further enacted, That all writs, and other process, which may have been, and which shall be issued, by the clerk of the said court, bearing teste of April session or October session, one thousand seven hundred and ninety-nine, shall be held and deemed of the same validity and effect, as if the same court had been regularly held on the eleventh day of October, one thousand seven hundred and ninety-nine.

Sec. 3. And be it further enacted, That it shall be lawful for the Judge of the District Court of the district of Pennsylvania, to direct the clerk of the said Circuit Court to issue such process for the purpose of causing jurors to be summoned to attend at the session of the said Circuit Court, on the eleventh day of April next, as hath heretofore been issued for the like purposes, returnable to any preceding session thereof; and the persons so summoned shall, in case of non-attendance, be liable to the same penalties as if such process had been issued in the ordinary course of proceeding.

THEODORE SEDGWICK,
Speaker of the House of Representatives.

SAMUEL LIVERMORE,
President of the Senate, pro tempore.

APPROVED—December 24th, 1799.

JOHN ADAMS,
President of the United States.

CHAPTER II.

An ACT extending the privilege of franking ...

---

dwelling houses in the same sub-division, shall not be changed or affected.

Sec. 2. And be it further enacted, That the said commissioners may direct the additions or deductions as aforesaid, to be made out and completed by the several principal assessors, or if they shall deem it more adviseable, by their clerk and such assistants as they shall find necessary, and appoint for that purpose: Provided, That the compensation to be made to the said assistants shall not exceed the pay allowed to the assistant assessors, by the act to which this is a supplement.

THEODORE SEDGWICK,
Speaker of the House of Representatives.

TH: JEFFERSON,
Vice-President of the United States, and President of the Senate.

APPROVED—January 2d, 1800.

JOHN ADAMS,
President of the United States.

LANCASTER, (Penn.) Feb. 22.

FRACAS in the Chamber of the House of Representatives.

On Thursday evening last a very disagreeable fracas took place in the chamber of the House of Representatives of Pennsylvania. We have endeavored to collect the circumstances with accuracy, and believe them to be briefly as follows:

During the evening session of the House, Mr. Samuel W. Fisher was delivering his sentiments on a resolution which went to disfranchise all officers and soldiers under the United States. In the course of his arguments, Mr. Fisher was twice interrupted by a call for adjournment from one part of the House. Both calls were negatived. A third call was made, which Mr. Fisher and his friends acceded to, and the House adjourned.

As soon as the adjournment had taken place, Mr. Fisher observed to a number of the members who had repeatedly called for an adjournment, that they had acted cowardly, were unwilling and afraid to hear his arguments.

Mr. Logan remarked that such foolish, nonsensical arguments as those made use of by Mr. Fisher, were not worth attending to. The latter then replied that any man who would call his arguments foolish and nonsensical was a puppy. Dr. Logan rejoined and called Mr. Fisher a rascal; on this Mr. Fisher struck him. The Doctor returned the blow. The members on all sides immediately interfered, and the combatants were separated. A considerable deal of altercation took place among some of the members,—and indeed we feel happy in being able to say that the battle was not more general.

While Mr. Fisher was aiming a blow at the Doctor, Mr. Wilson of Dauphin suddenly thrust himself in its road, and received a small contusion in or near the eye.

Another gentleman received a blow on his cheek but could not find his man. It was candle light, which rendered confusion the more confused. The members after some difficulty, found their hats, and dispersed.

Doctor Logan did not appear in the house on Friday, but addressed the following letter to Mr. Weaver, the Speaker.

Lancaster, February 21st, 1800.

SIR,

As a member of the House of Representatives, I complain to you as Speaker of the House of Representatives, that yesterday, in the chamber of Representatives, in the time when ...

---

the petition was referred to the Committee of Claims.

A message was received from the Senate, by Mr. Otis, their secretary, informing the house, that the Senate had passed the bill, intitled "An act further to suspend the commercial intercourse between the United States and France," with two amendments, to which they requested the concurrence of this house.

The first amendment, to strike out that part of the 4th section, which enabled citizens of the United States resident in France, to repair to this country, with vessels and other property bona fide belonging to them, was concurred in by the house—ayes 10, noes 36.

Previous to taking the question on concurring in this amendment, Mr. Macon made a motion, which superceded it—viz. "that the amendments of the Senate be postponed until the first Monday in December next"—which was negatived, only 30 members voting in favor of it.

The second amendment was to strike out the 10th section of the bill, by which it was enacted, that the Consul or Agent of the U. States shall receive an annual salary of 2000 dollars, and be restricted from trade, &c.

Mr. Otis moved that the House concur.

Mr. Champlin hoped not—and proceeded by stating that great complaints had been made of the conduct of the agent at Hispaniola—that it had been insinuated he had entered into trade with the planters of that island, previous to public notice having been given that the trade was opened, and had monopolized a large portion of the produce, previous to the American merchant's having an opportunity of becoming purchasers—Mr. C. also mentioned the circumstance of a vessel having been overhauled by an American cruiser, who shewed a passport from Toussaint and one from Dr. Stevens, by which she was permitted to proceed—and thereby inferred that the vessel might have been employed in an illicit trade.

Mr. Smith also spoke in favor in continuing the section—It had been introduced upon the most mature consideration, to prevent what was considered a great evil, and was much cause of complaint. By the proclamation opening intercourse with St. Domingo, our vessels were restricted, Mr. S. said, from going to but two ports in that island, upon clearing out at our custom houses—viz. Port Republican and Cape Francois. Upon their arrival at either of those ports, if the supercargo wishes to seek farther for a market, application must be made to our agent for permission; and he may delay granting it, and in the mean time, send to the place for which it is requested, buy up all the produce, and compel the merchant to purchase of him at an exorbitant price—this he had been informed had been done—but in mentioning it, the agent was allowed to trade—he had no compensation from the government—and it was what every merchant in a similar situation might and would do. He tho't a perfectly fair mercantile transaction. Hence arose the necessity of the section now under consideration.

But there was another transaction, Mr. S. said, the papers relating to which he had deposited with the proper executive officer.—A passport had been granted by our agent at Hispaniola, permitting the vessel of his part-ner to trade direct from the United States to ...

An Expanding Society, 1801–1815

"The Revolution of 1776 is now and for the first time arrived at its completion," trumpeted a Republican newspaper in 1801, "the sun of aristocracy [has] set, to rise no more." In Washington, D.C., the nation's new capital, Thomas Jefferson surveyed the muddy, undeveloped streets yet spoke glowingly of the country's future. Envisioning "a rising nation, spread over a wide and fruitful land," he predicted the expansion of agriculture, industry, and commerce "beyond the reach of mortal eye" and he frankly humbled himself "before the magnitude of the undertaking." To Jefferson, as he once put it, "those who labor in the earth are the chosen people of God," by which he meant the people of the United States.

And yet, Jefferson's optimism showed little sympathy for those who did not share the rights of citizenship. He saw Native Americans as a people doomed to disappear. "The backward [Native peoples] will yield," he vowed, "and we shall be obliged to drive them, with the beasts of the forest into the Stony [Rocky] mountains." Like most of his contemporaries, Jefferson also dismissed the political role of women, except as a moral presence in the home. "Our good ladies . . . have been too wise to wrinkle their foreheads with politics," he remarked. "They are contented to soothe and calm the minds of their husbands returning ruffled from political debate." When a shortage of civil service workers led a cabinet official to propose hiring women, Jefferson replied, "the appointment of women to office is an innovation for which the public is unprepared, nor am I."

Although the widowed Jefferson maintained an enduring relationship with his slave Sally Hemings, with whom he fathered children, he doubted too that African Americans could share the national identity—at least not for many generations. "From the experiments, which have been made," he wrote, "to give liberty, or rather, to abandon persons whose habits have been formed in slavery is like abandoning children."

Jefferson, author of the Declaraion of Independence, embodied the contradictions of a republican society, stressing the rights of self-government—but only for white men. As he prepared to take the oath of office as the nation's third president, he remained an enemy of recent Federalist policies, but he had no interest in attacking the party he had defeated. Rather, he expected his political foes to end their opposition and support his policies. "Every difference of opinion is not a difference of principle," Jefferson announced calmly. "We are all Republicans, we are all Federalists."

The transfer of power from Federalists to Republicans in 1800 was made easier by the relatively limited power of the national government, which dealt primarily with foreign affairs. During the previous decade, the war between England and France had drawn the United States into international conflicts, problems that would continue until 1815. Territorial expansion would also affect national policy and oblige the national government to confront the Native American nations fighting for their lands. The U.S. Supreme Court would issue precedent-setting decisions that affected interstate commerce and the law of contracts. National politicians, Federalists and Republicans, would disagree about such matters. But most domestic issues of this period—population migration, commercial growth, innovations in manufacturing—were local issues and did not involve national policy. In short, economic issues did not follow clear party lines.

Although Republicans increasingly replaced Federalists in public office (so much so that the Federalist party was nearly extinct outside New England by 1815), political power remained in the grip of property-holding white men in all regions. Slaveholding tobacco and cotton planters ruled the

> ## "We are all Republicans, we are all Federalists."

Thomas Jefferson (like George Washington, James Madison, and James Monroe) embodied the self-confident values of Virginia's slaveholding planter aristocracy.

southern states, while wealthier merchants dominated politics in the North. Republican ideology encouraged enterprise and economic advancement, though in many states propertyless people did not even have the right to vote or hold office. But during the eight years of Jefferson's presidency, and eight more under his colleague James Madison, the United States would come to fulfill its vast agricultural promise, extend its territorial limits, and accelerate its commercial development.

A Jeffersonian Agenda

Devoted to ideals of political simplicity, Jefferson promised "a wise and frugal Government" which would allow citizens "to regulate their own pursuits of industry and improvements." His administration proceeded to dismantle the most objectionable Federalist measures, repealing excise taxes, reducing military expenditures, and making it easier for immigrants to become citizens. But Jefferson proposed no changes in Hamilton's financial system or the national bank. Instead, a surge of overseas commerce brought surplus revenues, which shrank the national debt. Jefferson also preserved the young navy, sending warships against the Muslim states of North Africa (Tripoli, Morocco, Algeria), who were extorting payments for safe passage and sometimes seizing sailors to sell as slaves. Skirmishes around "the shores of Tripoli" ended the worst outrages.

Judicial Conflict

Jefferson showed less patience with the highly partisan, Federalist-dominated judiciary. Both Washington and Adams had appointed Federalist judges, some of whom had vigorously enforced the sedition laws against Republican critics. Reacting to Jefferson's election, the lame-duck, Federalist-controlled Congress had passed the Judiciary Act of 1801, which expanded the federal courts in time for Adams to fill the vacant positions with Federalist judges just before his term expired. These "midnight" appointments led the next Congress to repeal the law, and Jefferson refused to issue the appointment documents that Adams had lacked the time to distribute. One of Adams's appointees, a judge named William Marbury, appealed Jefferson's refusal to the Supreme Court (asking, in legal language, for a writ of mandamus that would require Secretary of State Madison to deliver Marbury's commission to hold office).

Chief Justice John Marshall, himself a recent Adams appointee, did not issue a verdict in *Marbury v. Madison* until 1803. But the decision in this seemingly inconsequential case altered the course of the country's legal history. Ruling that Marbury deserved his commission under the law, Marshall held nevertheless that the Supreme Court did not have proper jurisdiction in the case and therefore could not order Madison to comply. In effect, the decision declared that an earlier law of 1789 (which gave the Court jurisdiction of such cases) had exceeded the power of Congress under the Constitution and was consequently "unconstitutional." Marshall thus created the legal precedent of judicial review of congressional laws. Not until 1857 did the Court rule against another act of Congress. In other cases, the Marshall Court would later affirm its right to judge the constitutionality of state laws.

Jefferson did not object to Marshall's assertion of judicial power and thus endorsed the principle of judicial review. But some Republicans did challenge Federalist judges for expressing partisan prejudices in legal cases. In the most important impeachment case, involving Supreme Court Justice Samuel Chase, a rigid Federalist, Republican accusers appeared no less partisan than the judge. But when a Republican Senate failed to convict Chase in 1805, the proceedings confirmed that the judicial branch should be protected from partisan interference; for another half century, Congress would impeach no other federal judges.

The Louisiana Purchase

Jefferson's belief in a strict interpretation of constitutional powers soon clashed with his commitment to building a nation of farmers. Believing that the virtue of free citizens depended upon preserving their economic independence, Jefferson hoped that the country's "vacant lands" would provide for population growth and ensure the self-sufficiency of its inhabitants. As a tobacco planter, moreover, Jefferson understood the value of agricultural exports for domestic prosperity and he sympathized with western farmers who demanded that the Mississippi River remain open for U.S. shipping. But, after 1800, France owned the Louisiana territory and controlled river traffic on the Mississippi. Indeed, the French emperor Napoleon Bonaparte had plans for restoring a French empire in North America. When French officials in New Orleans closed the port to U.S. trade in 1802, Jefferson sent ambassador James Monroe to France to negotiate the purchase of that southern trading center.

By the time Monroe arrived in France, Bonaparte's plans had changed. The failure of a French military expedition to recapture Saint Domingue from rebel slaves and the threat of another war with England persuaded the French emperor to abandon his colonies. To Monroe's surprise, Napoleon offered to sell not just New Orleans, but the entire Louisiana territory, an area equal in size to the existing United States. While Jefferson appreciated the windfall, he faced a constitutional dilemma. The Constitution made no provision for the acquisition of new territory, and Jefferson hesitated to exceed the law; he even considered a constitutional amendment to permit the purchase. But, fear that Napoleon might withdraw the offer stretched his thinking. The Louisiana purchase would guarantee abundant land for the nation's farmers. Jefferson set aside his legal scruples to complete the transaction. Ironically, Federalists who preferred a loose interpretation of the Constitution objected to the Louisiana purchase because it promised to disperse population and erode the political influence of New England, the base of Federalist power. Such fears seemed justified. Already Ohio had entered

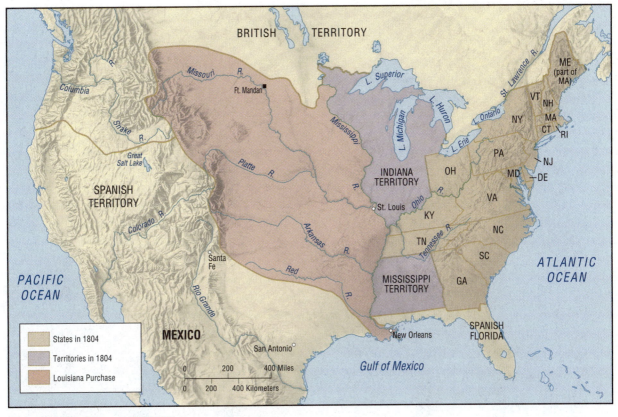

The Louisiana Purchase   OVERLAY 2

the union in 1803, and westward migration under-scored the Federalists' loss of national power. Yet Jefferson believed that the new territory would serve not to transplant independent farmers, but to resettle Native Americans west of the Missis-sippi, thus "filling up the eastern side, instead of drawing off its population."

Lewis and Clark Reach the Pacific

Jefferson's vision of western expansion, based on his philosophical speculation rather than geo-graphical knowledge, stimulated a bold govern-ment project to explore the Louisiana territory. Led by two military officers, Meriwether Lewis and William Clark, an expedition consisting of 50 men departed from St. Louis in 1804, sailed up the Missouri River, then crossed the western mountains and descended the Columbia River to the Pacific Ocean. During the two-year journey, the explorers traded with Native American groups for food and shelter, cartographic information, and guides (such as the Shoshone woman Saca-jawea, whose presence with her baby assured strangers of the group's peaceful purposes). Be-sides staking U.S. claims to the western shores, the expedition acquired geographical informa-tion, collected natural specimens, and served as early ethnographers, depicting the varieties of in-digenous cultures they encountered.

The Lewis and Clark Expedition

These discoveries in the heart of the continent mirrored the experiences of European explorers who had met the Atlantic coast peoples centuries earlier. Near the Missouri River, for example, the expedition observed the ruins of abandoned villages, remnants of a thriving Arikara population that had been devastated by smallpox just a decade before. These Plains people had thrived with mixed agriculture (corn, squash, beans) tended by women and buffalo hunting conducted by men. Living in dome-shaped earthen lodges, they had created compact villages that were surrounded by ditches and palisades as protection against the rival Sioux. By 1804, the Arikaras had dwindled to three large villages, composed of refugee remnants from numerous clans and kinship groups. Lewis and Clark assured "the red children" that "the great chief" of the United States, "impelled by his paternal regard," offered peace and profitable trade. Such messages were repeated on the long journey to the Oregon coast, as Jefferson's emissaries took the measure of Mandans, Shoshones, Nez Percés, and Chinooks along the way.

Reports of the Lewis and Clark expedition encouraged interest in western territories that were occupied not only by Native Americans but also by European settlers. By the beginning of the 19th century, Spain had planted twenty-one Franciscan missions in California, each a day's journey apart, plus a handful of military forts (presidios). But the non-Native population had climbed slowly from a mere 600 in 1781 to barely 3,000 thirty years later. "It would be as easy to keep California in spite of the Spaniards," remarked a visiting U.S. sailor, "as it would be to win it from them in the first place." Meanwhile, Great Britain used the 18th-century voyages of Captains James Cook and George Vancouver to claim the northwest regions, and Russian fur traders, seeking a food supply, planted a tiny colony in 1812 at Fort Ross, north of San Francisco Bay.

U.S. activity on the Pacific coast remained slight, though ships heading for China sometimes stopped for provisions. In 1816, two sailors, one an African American named Bob, took the opportunity to jump ship, be baptized as Catholics, take Spanish citizenship, and marry California women—apparently becoming the first U.S. settlers to stay in California. Farther north, the German immigrant John Jacob Astor planted a fur trading post, Astoria,

at the mouth of the Columbia River in 1811, but competition with British traders forced abandonment of the project.

Cultural Conflict on a Moving Frontier

Interest in the Louisiana territory and the Pacific reflected an acceleration of population migration from the settled states of the Atlantic seaboard. Jefferson himself believed that the newly acquired lands might become home to eastern Native Americans, who would surrender their traditional lands to migrating whites. Declining crop production, overcrowding, and a desire for land stimulated expansion across western New York and Pennsylvania and into the Ohio and Mississippi valleys. As Yankee farmers spread into Ohio and Indiana, pressing the Shawnees from their lands, southern migrants pushed across Creek and Cherokee country, bringing government roads that split Native lands. More ambitious southern planters headed to the Gulf plains, plowing cotton fields that tripled production in the first fifteen years of the century. By 1812, U.S. citizens who inhabited the area between the Appalachians and the Mississippi outnumbered Native Americans 7 to 1.

Western migration also brought conflicts between whites and blacks. Between 1800 and 1808, just before Congress voted to outlaw the international slave trade, 63,000 Africans entered the country, many of whom were transshipped into the western regions. In addition, slave traders moved over 100,000 Chesapeake blacks overland into the new territories. After Louisiana became American property, U.S. slaveowners joined French planters in boosting the region's sugar production. In this hot, humid climate, such manufacturing required strong male workers, who outnumbered women by a ratio of 3 or 4 to 1. In 1811, harsh labor conditions inspired the largest slave rebellion in U.S. history, when Charles Deslondes led as many as

A camp meeting in Indiana. As one observer described revivals, "A vast crowd, supposed by some to have amounted to twenty-five thousand, was collected together. The noise was like the roar of Niagara."

500 rebel slaves and fugitives in a bloody uprising against their masters. Armed militia finally ended the rebellion with violence and severe punishments. Whites in all the cotton states remained fearful of slave revolts.

Religious Revivalism

Geographic mobility also produced more subtle anxieties about social dislocation. By the 1820s, popular songs were expressing nostalgic lyrics, such as "How dear to this heart are the scenes of my childhood" ("Old Oaken Bucket") and "Be it ever so humble, there's no place like home" ("Home Sweet Home"). In newly settled areas, this concern about loss and a desire for stability contributed to a renewed interest in evangelical religions that stressed an individual's ability to find comfort in salvation. Seeking a personal religious conversion from sinner to saint, rural Americans increasingly moved away from the established Episcopalian, Congregational, and Presbyterian churches into less rigidly organized denomina-

tions, particularly the Baptists and Methodists, which emphasized a personal religious experience.

As itinerant preachers carried the gospel through scattered frontier villages, settlers sought spiritual expression in the electrifying Great Revivals at Cane Ridge, Kentucky, in 1801. These outpourings attracted some 20,000 enthusiasts, a dozen preachers, and converts by the hundreds. Within this evangelical Christianity, mobile people found not only a sense of personal salvation but also kinship and community, a voluntary joining of souls that merged an individualistic spirit with social responsibility. Congregations could scrutinize moral behavior, praise the faithful, and expel the sinful. Revivalism also stimulated the emergence of some women preachers, such as Harriet Livermore, known as "the Pilgrim Stranger," who in 1826 became the first woman to speak before Congress.

African American Christianity

The revival movement extended beyond white Christians and influenced the emergence of a distinctive African American Christianity. Responding to the Baptist and Methodist practices of communal prayer, exhortations, chanting, and clapping, which echoed the religious traditions of west Africa, blacks had joined those denominations during the late colonial period, often experiencing equality with fellow white parishioners. Even in southern states, some white evangelicals advocated the end of slavery. To blacks, evangelical Christianity had a familiar spiritual appeal. The practice of water baptism mirrored religious traditions in west African cultures, and the Christian belief of converting to a "new life" paralleled African beliefs in stages of spiritual development. The Christian idea of evil, though absent in African traditions, gave African Americans a context for understanding their enslavement. Nonetheless, only a small minority of slaves ever became Christians.

By 1800, southern evangelicals had retreated from supporting emancipation. Stressing the separation of church and state, these evangelicals described slavery as a strictly civil issue, not in the province of organized religion. While still emphasizing the universality of religious values, the churches created segregated congregations, seating black worshippers separately or holding different religious services for blacks and whites. From such pressure emerged the first African American Christian denominations, including the African Methodist Episcopal church founded by free blacks in 1816. Within their separate congregations, African Americans listened to female and male black preachers, preserved west African styles of prayer, such as call-and-response and the distinctive counterclockwise circle or ring dance, and perpetuated African funeral and mourning practices.

Christianity and Native American Conflict

Although migration across the Appalachians encouraged the mixing of diverse settlers, the westward movement brought newcomers into conflict with resident Native American communities. To aid white migrants, the U.S. government adopted a policy of divide-and-conquer, exploiting internal divisions within Native groups to seize their lands. In the Northwest territory, the national government began to make annual payments to selected "annuity" chiefs in exchange for tribal lands—a form of bribery that bitterly divided Native groups. With the white population spilling across the treaty boundaries of the 1790s, military officials and Christian missionaries pressed Native leaders to abandon their hunting economy and adopt agriculture. But since Native women traditionally attended to farming, Native men had no desire to assume female occupations; nor did Native women, who counted on men to supply skins for clothing and moccasins, wish to learn knitting and weaving. In other words, the proposed "civilizing" process, by which Native men adopted sedentary farming and women became "employed in our houses," involved a drastic reversal of gender roles. While some Native leaders who were beneficiaries of the government's annuity payments supported those changes, many leaders protested the abandonment of traditional beliefs.

One of the defenders of Native traditions was the Shawnee leader Tenskwatawa, known as the Prophet. Having experienced a religious vision around 1805, Tenskwatawa won a large following among the Northwest people by bringing a message from the Master of Life: "I will overturn the land," the prophecy declared, "so that all the white people will be covered and you alone shall inhabit the land." Under his guidance, imperiled Shawnees looked to traditional spiritual values to resist white expansion. Repudiating assimilation, the Prophet's supporters rejected the whites' food, alcohol, clothing, and utensils; curtailed sexual promiscuity with white traders; and resumed their traditional spiritual practices. Extinguishing what he considered

> ### "They have driven us from the sea to the lakes. We can go no further."

to be the corrupt tribal fires, Tenskwatawa ritually relit the flames at Greenville, Ohio, site of the ignominious treaty of 1795 (see Chapter 7). Young warriors, disgusted by land sales made by the annuity chiefs, flocked like pilgrims to the Prophet's camp. So numerous were the visitors, from places as distant as Wisconsin and across the Mississippi River, that the Shawnee spiritualist had to move his camp to a larger site at Tippecanoe on the Wabash River in Indiana.

While government agents watched with alarm as the movement grew, the Prophet's brother, Tecumseh, traveled among the Northwest peoples trying to build a coalition that would refuse to sell any more land to whites. Rivalry among competing groups undermined Native American unity. In 1809, General William Henry Harrison persuaded friendly chiefs to transfer another 3 million acres in Indiana. "They have driven us from the sea to the lakes," protested Tecumseh, "We can go no further."

As tensions between government agents and Native American revivalists mounted, Tecumseh visited the English in Canada to seek military assistance, then embarked in 1811 on a bold journey to gain support among the southern nations. By then, both the southern Choctaws and Chickasaws had adopted an agricultural way of life and rebuffed Tecumseh's offer to join a confederation. Some militant Creeks expressed sympathy, but their distance from the Northwest made cooperation virtually impossible. During Tecumseh's absence, moreover, Harrison moved his troops against the Prophet's settlements, routing his followers in the battle of Tippecanoe in 1811. Frustrated by U.S.

policy, Tecumseh's Shawnee allies would fight with the British during the War of 1812.

A New Spirit of Enterprise

While western migrants sought land and economic opportunity, more subtle economic changes began to affect the country's attitudes toward business relations around the turn of the 19th century. Some observers began to complain about a rise of materialism and lamented what author Washington Irving called "the almighty dollar." Others criticized the growing impersonality of the marketplace and warned about the risks of doing business with strangers.

On family farms, especially in the northeast, rural women began to devote larger portions of their time to making cloth, buttons, and straw hats, not just for home consumption but for sale or trade. As in the colonial period, local governments continued to regulate the economy, seeking to protect the public interest from selfish entrepreneurs. Yet, the spirit of enterprise often seemed an end in itself, a release of individual energy from social control. Innovative economic activity reflected a subtle loosening of traditional business constraints.

The Market Economy Alters Domestic Life

Throughout the colonial period, successful commercial farmers had sold their surplus crops in an international marketplace, exporting tobacco, grains, and meat to the West Indies and Europe. Even small farmers had engaged in an exchange economy, trading small surpluses, agricultural tools, or day labor to obtain goods and services they could not provide for themselves. But, while commercial farmers often lamented the problems of debt and credit, most business between neighbors and kin involved noncommercial values of friendship and mutual assistance. To be sure, colonials were not shy about taking their neighbors to court to settle disputes about land and other property. But, with cash in short supply, most trade involved borrowing or barter, and creditors would carry small debts for months, even years, without charging interest. Such informal arrangements differed from long-distance business transactions, such as transatlantic trade, which involved more detailed accounting and prompter payments.

By the early 19th century, as population increased, bringing a rise in nonagricultural work and geographical dispersal, economic relations gradually became more formal—and more profitable. One congressman boasted that his constituents were "bred to commerce." "Barter and sale are their delight. The spirit of business warms them." In both western New England and western Virginia, for example, the growth of livestock production created greater dependency on the drovers who took cattle and pigs to market. Meat producers increasingly dealt, not with consumers but with merchants and butchers who bought the animals to feed the towns and cities. In other words, more producers were becoming wholesalers, while retail merchants dealt directly with consumers. Livestock also stimulated the dairy industry, enabling farm women to produce surplus butter and cheese for sale. Seeking to maximize agricultural production, New England families harvested broomcorn, the natural ingredient of the broom industry, and sold their wares to rural and urban merchants. Although commercial transactions often remained informal and prices were usually negotiable, some large merchants introduced a new, impersonal business ethic. As one of them advertised in 1802: "No trust, no goods sent out, no samples given, no abatement in price first asked, no goods delivered until paid for."

These emerging economic trends affected the quality of domestic life. Economic protests during the war for independence and the loss of trade with England afterward had stimulated home manufacturing. In rural families, men increasingly filled slack times by making shoes, tools, or furniture for trade or sale, while women integrated spinning and weaving into their daily routines. In 1810, 90 percent of the nation's total textile output was made at home. Even the early industrial mills, introduced between 1790 and 1815, produced yarns, which were then distributed to weavers who worked at home. Such activity often made the difference between a family's profit and loss, but put great pressure on women's time. "A woman's work is never done," sighed one diarist in 1795, "and happy [is] she whose strength holds out to the end of the [sun's] rays."

Despite this rise in home manufacturing, most housewives continued to stress their contributions to childcare and the rearing of good citizens. "You may benefit a nation, my dear Papa," one young mother wrote to her politician father, but "I may improve the condition of a fellow-being." Among poorer families, the limitations of economic resources, particularly in eastern areas, began to force young couples to delay marriage. Such decisions caused, in turn, a reduction in years of marital fertility and brought a shrinking of the size of rural white families outside the South.

The declining birthrate enabled parents to focus more attention on each child. Together with the rise of evangelical religion, which emphasized the possibility of individual salvation, parents came to see their children, not as naturally sinful but as potentially perfectible. Attitudes toward childrearing also began to change. Instead of beating children to break their evil wills, parents now endeavored to shape their children with more moderate discipline. "It is the fashion of the times to be lenient, loose, licentious," observed a disapproving writer in 1814, "and parents, out of mere *parental affection*. . . give their children some portion of that indulgence, which they allow themselves." Ironically, as the drop in birthrates diminished the number of children, parents also lost the free labor of older siblings. In subsequent decades, overworked housewives gladly surrendered time-consuming domestic textile work to buy their cloth in village stores.

The Dawn of a National Economy

Even as household production prospered, manufacturing underwent subtle but significant change, particularly in northern towns and cities. Skilled male artisans—carpenters, shoemakers, tailors—continued to dominate the urban crafts. These master craftsmen produced mahogany furniture, fine dinner plates, gilt-edged mirrors, and accurate eight-day clocks for well-to-do consumers. But the growing market for inexpensive products altered the nature of skilled work. Even before the introduction of machinery for mass production, the demand for ready-to-wear clothing and cheap shoes for slaves, for example, led innovative tailors and shoemakers to change the manufacturing process to improve the quantity, rather than the quality, of their products. Instead of one skilled worker's making an entire shoe, the division of labor allowed two or three workers to specialize in specific parts of the process. Such specialization led to the introduction of distinct left and right shoes, an advantage to consumers. Meanwhile, the opening of the first shoestores further separated the shoemaker from the retail consumer.

New manufacturing techniques altered the nature of labor. Instead of signing a contract with an apprentice worker and agreeing to teach him a skilled craft, master artisans preferred to hire free workers, even child and women laborers, who

Eli Terry clock. During the first years of the century, Connecticut clockmaker Eli Terry built specialized, mass-production machine tools that operated with a small tolerance of error, thereby producing intricate, inexpensive, and fully interchangeable clock parts. Nearly every household owned a timepiece by mid-century. Yankee peddlers distributing these clocks around the country also spread new attitudes about the importance of accurate time keeping. Here was the technological base that would make punctuality a national virtue.

could be paid less than men and be taught only the rudimentary skills necessary to make so-called slop goods. Although workers complained bitterly about the decline of traditional crafts, day laborers formed a growing class of employees who lived in rented rooms and faced layoffs during lean times. The worst jobs were reserved for Irish and African American workers. Not accidentally, the early decades of the century witnessed the outbreak of the first labor strikes (which the courts usually held to be illegal conspiracies) as workers developed an identity distinct from that of their employers.

The expansion of domestic trade and commercial agriculture also stimulated a revolution in transportation. "Things which twenty years ago a man would have been laughed at for believing," stated a government report in 1812, "we now see." Traditionally, water routes were the cheapest mode of commerce, especially between port cities, but the inland river systems remained slow and unreliable. Private investors increasingly formed joint-stock companies, backed by state and local government investments, to finance the construction of public roads and bridges. State charters established minimal standards for each project and permitted investors to charge tolls to users.

By the second decade of the century, this marriage of government and business had produced a network of turnpikes that connected the major towns of the northeast. The national government also financed interstate roads, including the Federal Road, which cut through Creek country in Georgia, and the National or Cumberland Road, begun in 1811, which linked Cumberland, Maryland, with Wheeling on the Ohio River.

More dramatic were experiments with steamboat technology, culminating in 1807 with Robert Fulton's *Clermont*, the first commercially successful steamboat, which ran on the Hudson River. Steamboat traffic drastically reduced the cost of shipping. By 1814, the price of sending a barrel of flour between Albany and New York City had fallen from $2 to 25 cents. Meanwhile, other innovators were already planning artificial canals, which would transform domestic commerce in later decades.

The national and state governments also supported business by issuing charters for corporations and banks, numbering some 1,800 companies be-

"The market house, like the grave, is a place of perfect equality."

tween 1800 and 1817. Although a Republican Congress allowed Hamilton's Bank of the United States to expire in 1811, other banks mushroomed within the states, increasing from 29 in 1800 to over 200 fifteen years later. These banks not only invested capital at interest but also issued bank notes (a form of paper money), which served as a circulating currency so long as people were confident that their notes could be redeemed. Government aid to manufacturing remained minimal. Tariffs on imported goods served primarily to raise revenue rather than to protect domestic industry. But states granted water rights, land, tax incentives, and exemptions from nuisance laws to help specific enterprises.

This new "spirit of enterprise" brought mixed responses from contemporary observers. While many saw business expansion as a sign of progress, others lamented the loss of an older morality. "The market house, like the grave," quipped one observer, "is a place of perfect equality." But if economic development appealed to individualistic values, the new economy brought failure as well as success. Businesses failed with unnerving frequency, casting entrepreneurs into debt. Although western migration and business investment permitted economic advancement, a smaller proportion of the population controlled a larger share of the national wealth. In New York, the number of paupers in the city's almshouses tripled between 1790 and 1817. At a time when people still went to jail for debt, investors had reason to worry about excessive economic optimism.

"Multitudes are undone," warned a southern newspaper, "by taking, as well as giving too much credit." As cash transactions eroded an older ethic of unwritten agreements, critics of the new economy stressed the importance of individual responsibility and self-discipline to avoid financial temptation and deceit. Thus when "Parson" Mason Locke Weems, an ambitious, bestselling book peddler, published his immensely popular *Life of Washington* in 1800, he depicted the first president as the embodiment of virtue—hardworking, self-controlled, impeccably honest (hence the story of the cherry tree)—a perfect model for children to imitate.

Tightening the Law of Contracts

The fear of credit, debt, and inadvertent ruin reinforced the law of contracts. On the national level, John Marshall's Supreme Court rigidly defended the sanctity of contracts, even in the face of obvious fraud. Thus, in *Fletcher v. Peck* (1810), the Court rejected the Georgia legislature's repeal of a corrupt land transaction, explaining that the Constitution protected the original contract. Similarly, in *Dartmouth College v. Woodward* (1819), the Court ruled that the state of New Hampshire had violated a colonial charter (which the Court said was a type of contract) by attempting to turn the private school into a state college. Such rulings laid the foundation of a national legal system at a time of expanding domestic commerce and provided important precedents for government relations with private business.

Strict rules of contract extended even to the most private of matters. State courts increasingly treated marriage as a consensual arrangement rather than a property settlement and held that a breach of promise to marry violated the sanctity of contract. The injured party (usually the woman) thus was entitled to sue, in the words of one Massachusetts judge, for such "losses" as "the wounded spirit, the unmerited disgrace, and the probable solitude" that would result from a broken engagement. Rejecting a world of informal promises where a person's word was his bond, Americans moved toward a code of ethics based on written contracts. No wonder, then, that the number of lawyers in the country grew four times faster than the population between 1783 and 1820.

A Second War for Independence

The outbreak of a new war between England and France in 1803 underscored the nation's involvement in European trade. Jefferson's goal of minimizing government activity while encouraging economic development thus collided with the risks of international commerce. The European war initially brought a boom to U.S. trade. Happy to receive agricultural exports, England, still mistress of the seas, permitted the United States to trade with France and its colonies. But as Napoleon's French armies established dominance on the European continent, England shifted to economic warfare and tried to block foreign commerce from reaching France. Napoleon retaliated by establishing boycotts against countries that traded with England. And then both European belligerents began to seize and confiscate U.S. ships; by 1807, some 700 U.S. vessels had surrendered their cargoes.

Defending Neutral Rights

Britain's naval supremacy also aroused opposition to a practice that began in colonial days: the seizure of alleged British deserters aboard U.S. ships for impressment into the service of the royal navy. Complicating the issue was Britain's refusal to recognize naturalized U.S. citizens and the difficulty of proving an individual's status. American citizens were sometimes forced at gunpoint to serve in the British navy. The issue drew public attention in 1807 when, within sight of Virginia shores, the British warship *Leopard* ordered the U.S. *Chesapeake* to allow a boarding party to search for deserters. The American ship's refusal to comply brought a rain of fire and an embarrassing surrender. While an outraged public called for war with England, the cautious Jefferson opted instead for negotiations.

Reluctant to enter a war that would require military mobilization, higher taxes, and a disruption of trade, Jefferson adopted a policy of peaceful pressure. In 1807, he persuaded Congress to pass an Embargo Act, which prohibited U.S. commerce with foreign ports. Since Britain had already interrupted U.S. trade with France, the measure was clearly aimed at England, with the expectation that British needs for agricultural produce would force England to recognize U.S. commercial rights. More practically, the embargo kept U.S. ships off the high seas, safe from further trouble. Underlying the embargo rested another idea, old as the colonial protests before independence, that American frugality would prove stronger than Britain's addiction to the fruits of commerce.

By congressional statute, U.S. foreign trade came to a halt. To be sure, some enterprising merchants developed a substantial smuggling business through British Canada. Together with the rapid increase of exports from Canada to England, this illegal trade greatly reduced the impact of the embargo. But as U.S. ships rotted at the docks, urban unemployment rose, exports sank, and the only business seemed to be bankruptcy proceedings and imprisonment for debt. Hardest hit were the shipping centers in New England. The 1808 elections tolled the result. Although Secretary of State Madison won the presidential election, Federalists returned to Congress in force, determined to repeal the hated embargo.

Although both England and France violated U.S. neutral rights, Republican leaders remained committed to peaceful maneuvers. After terminating the embargo, Congress passed the Nonin-tercourse Act of 1809, which resumed commerce with all nations, except England and France, and then promised to open trade with either of those countries after they ended commercial restrictions. When the British ambassador accepted the U.S. offer, President Madison thought the negotiations had succeeded. Six hundred American ships raced for England to cash in on the peace. But the British government abruptly rejected the settlement. A frustrated Congress then passed another compromise law in 1810, known as Macon's Bill Number 2, which lifted all restraints on U.S. shipping, but promised that if either England or France ended its commercial restrictions the United States would restore an embargo against the other country. Since England controlled the sea lanes to Europe, Napoleon offered to stop French violations *if* England did the same.

Declaring War on England

Madison knew that Napoleon's diplomatic overture did not involve a change in French policy; indeed, the French continued to seize U.S. ships. But pushing his toe in the door, the president used Napoleon's promise to stop seizing U.S. ships as an excuse to restore the nonintercourse measure against England in 1811. Public opinion, already anti-British, supported this step. Madison also resolved to fight for U.S. honor, and the nation moved closer to war. In the spring of 1812, Congress approved a 60-day embargo—time enough to allow U.S. ships at sea to return safely home—in preparation for declaring war against England. And, at last, the pressure against English merchants had the desired effect. With business in a slump, English manufacturers, desperate for southern cotton, persuaded the British government to end commercial restrictions in June 1812.

Americans found little satisfaction in the diplomatic victory. By then, the president had already persuaded Congress to declare war on England. While Federalists bitterly depicted the impending evils of conflict, "war hawks" in and out of Congress emphasized the revitalizing effects of going to war. "Forbearance has ceased to be a virtue," announced a congressional war report drafted by the young South Carolina representative John C. Calhoun. "There is an alternative only between the base surrender of their rights and a manly vindication." Madison's war message also mentioned British assistance to the Native Americans of the Northwest. Such factors (anti-Native sentiment, the defense of national honor, the ideology of republican virtue) surely contributed to the decision to fight. But, at bottom, the United States went to war in 1812 to defend its maritime rights on the high seas—rights that not only protected the interests of shipowners, merchants, and sailors but also access to markets for farmers with goods to sell abroad.

The War of 1812 Begins

Madison now led an ill-prepared nation into war against the mighty British empire. Despite seven years of commercial and diplomatic conflict, neither Congress nor the citizenry had prepared for war. When Congress approved the creation of a 35,000-man army (white male citizens between the ages of 18 and 45), barely 7,000 enlisted. The nation turned to the state militias, but encountered divided leadership, inexperience, and an attachment to local interests that led some volunteers to refuse orders to fight. The navy, well tested in wars with France and North African pirates, would protect merchant vessels hurrying home, but could hardly match the royal navy at sea.

Frugal Republicans had also weakened the economic apparatus necessary to wage war. Customs duties remained the main source of government income, but the war reduced trade, which in turn reduced revenues. Excise taxes, never very popular, brought small funds. The government turned to borrowing money. But a Republican Congress had permitted the Bank of the United States to expire in 1811, and state banks lacked sufficient capital. In the second year of the war, the administration reluctantly issued treasury bonds and certificates, which circulated below face value. Meanwhile, Federalist merchants, who opposed the war because it disrupted their trade with Britain, refused to contribute to the cause. In Connecticut, Federalist towns filed nuisance charges against the army for playing martial music during recruitment rallies. By 1814, as the government veered toward bankruptcy, Republicans proposed higher taxes. Only the end of the war spared the country worse financial embarrassment.

Native Americans Side with Britain

The outbreak of war intensified conflicts with the Native American nations. As the United States made plans to invade British Canada, Shawnee leaders in the Northwest argued about which side to support. Although many annuity chiefs defended their ties to the United States, Tecumseh pleaded for "us Indians of North America to form ourselves into one great combination" to fight against the United States. Tecumseh then formed an alliance with British military leaders and again visited the southern Creeks to make plans for a coordinated attack against American forces. He returned to the Northwest territory just as the United States prepared to invade Canada.

The weakness of U.S. military efforts exaggerated Native American strength. When U.S. General William Hull led an expedition from Detroit toward Canada in 1812, Tecumseh's warriors cut his supply lines, forcing U.S. troops to retreat and

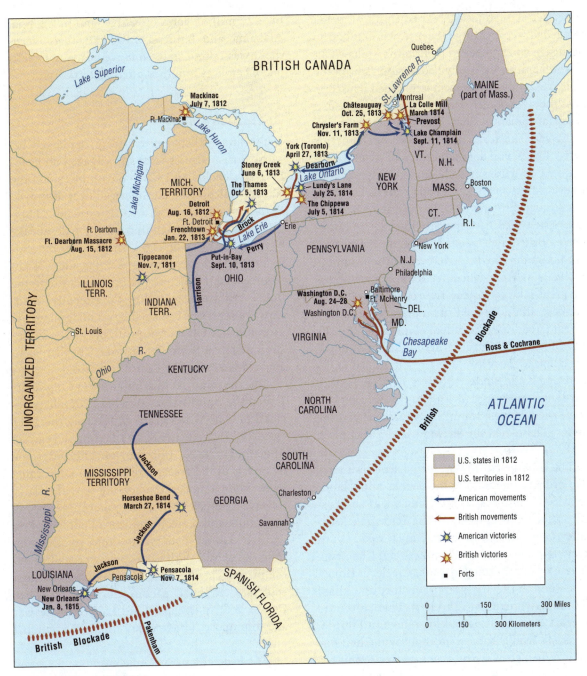

BRITISH CANADA

Quebec

MAINE
(part of Mass.)

Lake Superior

Mackinac
July 7, 1812

Châteauguay
Oct. 25, 1813

La Colle Mill
March 1814

Ft. Mackinac

Lake Huron

Chrysler's Farm
Nov. 11, 1813

Montreal

Prevost

Lake Champlain
Sept. 11, 1814

York (Toronto)
April 27, 1813

VT.

N.H.

Stoney Creek
June 6, 1813

Dearborn

Lake Ontario

MICH.
TERRITORY

Lake Michigan

The Thames
Oct. 5, 1813

NEW
YORK

MASS.

Boston

Detroit
Aug. 16, 1812

Lundy's Lane
July 25, 1814

CT.

Ft. Detroit

Brock

The Chippewa
July 5, 1814

R.I.

Frenchtown
Jan. 22, 1813

Lake Erie

Erie

Ft. Dearborn

Perry

PENNSYLVANIA

New York

Ft. Dearborn Massacre
Aug. 15, 1812

Put-in-Bay
Sept. 10, 1813

N.J.

Philadelphia

Tippecanoe
Nov. 7, 1811

OHIO

ILLINOIS
TERR.

Harrison

Washington D.C.
Aug. 24–28

Baltimore

Ft. McHenry

DEL.

INDIANA
TERR.

Washington D.C.

MD.

St. Louis

R.

VIRGINIA

Chesapeake
Bay

Blockade

Ross & Cochrane

Ohio

KENTUCKY

UNORGANIZED TERRITORY

NORTH
CAROLINA

TENNESSEE

ATLANTIC
OCEAN

Jackson

British

MISSISSIPPI
TERRITORY

SOUTH
CAROLINA

Horseshoe Bend
March 27, 1814

GEORGIA

Charleston

Jackson

Mississippi R.

Savannah

	U.S. states in 1812
	U.S. territories in 1812
←	American movements
←	British movements
✦	American victories
✦	British victories
■	Forts

Jackson

Pensacola
Nov. 7, 1814

LOUISIANA

New Orleans

Pensacola

SPANISH FLORIDA

New Orleans
Jan. 8, 1815

0   150   300 Miles

British   Blockade

0   150   300 Kilometers

Pakenham

The War of 1812 OVERLAY 1

surrender. A second U.S. expedition to Canada succeeded in capturing Queenstown, but had to disengage when attacked by Britain's Mohawk allies. Still a third U.S. army had to stop short of the Canadian border when local militiamen refused to cross the state border. The land war thus appeared as a great embarrassment to the United States.

At sea, the navy fought well, but superior British forces won dominance in the Atlantic, subject only to harassment by an extensive fleet of American privateers. On inland waters, however, U.S. seamanship prevailed. In the critical Battle of Lake Erie in 1813, Captain Oliver Perry eliminated a British fleet. General William Henry Harrison, famous for the slaughter of the Prophet's followers at Tippecanoe, ferried his army across the great lake to pursue the redcoats and their Shawnee allies. As the British prepared a further retreat, Tecumseh pleaded eloquently for the chance to fight. "Our lives are in the hands of the Great Spirit," he cried. "We are determined to defend our lands, and if it be his will we wish to leave our bones upon them." In the ensuing battle of the Thames, the U.S. army destroyed the enemy. There died the Shawnee leader Tecumseh in 1813.

Futile in the Northwest, Tecumseh's resistance also brought calamity to the Creeks and Cherokees in the southeast. After the Creeks successfully attacked U.S. forces in the Tennessee River valley, General Andrew Jackson organized a counterattack, supported by Cherokees and Choctaws. In 1814, Jackson trapped 1,000 Creeks at Horseshoe Bend in the Mississippi territory and killed 800 men, women, and children. Then, after the Creek survivors scattered for refuge in Florida, Jackson's troops turned on their own Cherokee allies. When government agents protested this betrayal, Jackson replied, "No confidence can be placed in the honesty of an Indian!" The punitive Treaty of Fort Jackson, imposed in 1814, claimed over 20 million acres of Native land in Georgia, Alabama, and Tennessee. By then, the government was taking steps to move peaceful Creeks and Cherokees into the Louisiana territory.

Mr. Madison's War

Such triumphs kept the war going, but largely because British armies were still engaged on European battlefields. In 1814, a British invasion from Canada failed when an American fleet destroyed British supply ships in a battle on Lake Champlain. But another landing on the Chesapeake overwhelmed U.S. defenses, enabling the redcoats to march on the nation's capital. President Madison escaped just before the British set fire to the public buildings, including the executive mansion. An intended British attack on Baltimore did meet resistance from troops at Fort McHenry (inspiring Francis Scott Key to write "The Star Spangled Banner") and the British retreated.

The burning of Washington, D.C., underscored the humiliations of what Federalists derided as "Mr. Madison's War." During the 1812 elections, Federalist critics of the war had carried numerous state elections in New England, some by means of the creative redistricting that came to be known as *gerrymandering*. But the party lacked a national base, failed to prevent Madison's reelection, and scarcely influenced public policy. Some frustrated Federalists spoke of secession from the union. With legal commerce stalled and the British occupying nearby Maine, Federalist leaders summoned a convention at Hartford, Connecticut, in December 1814 to protest the war and to propose "a radical reform" of the national union.

The Federalists' Hartford convention proposed a series of constitutional amendments, which would, in effect, preserve the political power of this conservative regional minority. Among the propos-

The term *gerrymandering* was first coined in 1812, when Massachusetts Governor Elbridge Gerry had his state legislature favor a fellow Republican by engineering the oddly shaped district shown here—half salamander, half "Gerry"-mander.

als was the apportionment of representation and taxation based on the size of the white population, thus voiding the Three-Fifths Compromise which had given slave states greater influence (see Chapter 7). Reflecting their fear of regional isolation, the delegates suggested that the admission of new states require a two-thirds vote of Congress, which would slow territorial expansion. Two other measures would protect New England's economic interests by requiring a two-thirds majority for Congress to enact embargoes or declare war. To weaken the influence of Virginia, which had already produced three of the first four presidents, another proposal would limit presidents to a single term of office. Yet another recommended that naturalized citizens be barred from holding public office, to preserve the ethnic homogeneity of the leadership. In sum, the Federalists attempted to re-

Overnight, Jackson and his frontier riflemen became national heroes.

verse history, stop national development, and restore the old colonial hierarchy. That was no longer possible.

Federalist frustrations soon vanished, however, when U.S. troops scored a stunning triumph against the British at New Orleans in January 1815. Defeating a force of 10,000 redcoats, Andrew Jackson's militia from Georgia, Tennessee, and Kentucky gave the country a victory that transformed public opinion about the war. Overnight, Jackson and his frontier riflemen became national heroes, citizen-soldiers who had saved the embattled republic. Politicians and newspaper publishers gushed their thanks in verse and song. Patriotic enthusiasts claimed that "God had tested Americans and their government" to prove the superiority of republican virtue.

The Fruits of Peace

Despite such boasts, both the battle of New Orleans and the Hartford convention occurred after diplomatic negotiations had formally ended the war in the Treaty of Ghent in December 1814. When news of the peace finally reached America the following month, joyous citizens paid little attention to its ambiguous terms. Neither side had gained additional territory, though precise boundaries between the United States and Canada would be settled later by joint commissions. Nor did the British concede questions of neutral rights or impressment. Rather, the end of the European wars effectively eliminated the grievances that had provoked hostilities in the first place.

The war, in short, brought no tangible benefits except the indefinable pride of having avoided defeat against the most powerful European country. "Let any man look at the degraded condition of the country before the war," suggested Speaker of the House Henry Clay in 1816. "The scorn of the universe, the contempt of ourselves; and tell me we have gained nothing by the war?. . . . Our character and constitution are placed on a solid basis never to be shaken." In peace, the nation achieved what it had lacked during the recent war: a sense of purpose, self-confidence, and stability.

After the War of 1812, political leadership passed to a new breed of politicians. John Quincy Adams, son of the second president, and his chief political rival, Andrew Jackson, were both born in 1767; Kentucky's Henry Clay came ten years later; South Carolina's John C. Calhoun and Massachusetts' Daniel Webster were five years younger. Unlike the Founding Fathers—Washington, Adams, Jefferson, and Madison—this younger generation of national politicians had grown up with republican institutions and ideals and had learned almost with their first breath the principles of self-government and majority rule, without qualms or fear. Proud of a newfound "national character," the new generation boasted of the country's growth, mobility, even diversity, and promised to extend their institutions across the continent.

INFOTRAC® COLLEGE EDITION EXERCISES

For additional reading go to InfoTrac College Edition, your online research library at *http://web1.infotrac-college.com.*

Keyword search: Anti-Federalist
Keyword search: Federalist
Keyword search: John Marshall
Keyword search: Marbury v. Madison
Keyword search: Lewis and Clark
Keyword search: James Madison
Subject search: United States History, War of 1812
Keyword search: Chesapeake
Keyword search: impressment
Keyword search: Tecumseh

ADDITIONAL READING

A Jeffersonian Agenda

Drew R. McCoy, *The Elusive Republic: Political Economy in Jeffersonian America* (1980). A study of economic values and ideas that links the republican tradition to political policy. See also Appleby's book listed in Chapter 7.

Lewis and Clark Reach the Pacific

James P. Ronda, *Lewis and Clark among the Indians* (1984). A study emphasizing the interaction with Native peoples; for a general overview, see Stephen E. Ambrose, *Undaunted Courage: Meriwether Lewis, Thomas Jefferson, and the Opening of the American West* (1996).

Religious Revivalism

Sylvia R. Frey and Betty Wood, *Come Shouting to Zion: African American Protestantism in the American South and British Caribbean to 1830* (1998). Traces the Christianization of African Americans from the colonial period through the great revivals of the early 1800s; see also the pioneering first chapter of Sterling Stuckey, *Slave Culture: Nationalist Theory and the Foundations of Black America* (1987).

Christianity and Native American Conflict

Allan W. Eckert, *A Sorrow in Our Heart: The Life of Tecumseh* (1992). A solid biography of the Shawnee leader; for a briefer study, see R. David Edmunds, *Tecumseh and the Quest for Indian Leadership* (1984).

R. David Edmunds, *The Shawnee Prophet* (1983). Examines the career of Tenskwatawa and explains the

Shawnee revival; see also Dowd's *Spirited Resistance,* listed in the previous chapter.

A New Spirit of Enterprise

Steven Watts, *The Republic Reborn: War and the Making of Liberal America, 1790–1820* (1987). This cultural history examines the expanding economy and its impact on American identity.

Nancy F. Cott, *The Bonds of Womanhood: "Woman's Sphere" in New England, 1780–1835* (1977). Based on women's writings, this book describes attitudes toward domesticity, education, religion, and sisterhood.

Cynthia A. Kierner, *Beyond the Household: Women's Place in the Early South, 1700–1835* (1998).

Depicts women's changing roles in the southern states. For the role of women in the northern maritime industry, see Lisa Norling, *Captain Ahab Had a Wife: New England Women and the Whalefishery, 1720–1870* (2000).

Jean V. Matthews, *Toward a New Society: American Thought and Culture, 1800–1830* (1991). A history of ideas, this book discusses such subjects as religion, science, art, and education.

A Second War for Independence

J. C. A. Stagg, *Mr. Madison's War: Politics, Diplomacy, and Warfare in the Early American Republic, 1783–1830* (1983). Examines the political background of the War of 1812.

The National Gazette
AND
LITERARY REGISTER.

PRINCIPLES AND MEN.

PHILADELPHIA, FRIDAY AFTERNOON, JUNE 7, 1822.

LINE OF
Packets for Liverpool.

Ship UNICORN,
S. W. M'Kown, master;
To sail 10th of 6th month (June.)
Ship TUSCARORA,
Wm. West, master;
To sail 10th of 7th month, (July.)

THE subscribers have agreed in con-
junction with their friends, to establish a line
of Packets from Philadelphia to Liverpool; one to
sail from Liverpool on the 8th of each month, except December, and from Philadelphia the 20th
of each month, except the 1st month (January.)
The line will commence at Liverpool on the 8th
of 6th month (June) and at Philadelphia, the 20th
of 6th month (August.) Until which time their
departure from Philadelphia will be as near that
date as practicable, of which notice will be regularly given.
Cabin passengers are taken at thirty pounds,
for which sum they will be furnished with beds and
bedding, and stores of every description, and the
owners will spare no expense to have every thing
complete and comfortable.
Two new ships are building expressly for this
line. Application for freight, or passage, to be
made to
Thos. P. Cope & Sons.
5 mo 11—tf

Packet for Liverpool.
The Ship MANCHESTER,
To sail the 20th June,
Is loading at the Bark Inspection wharf, but will
soon lay near Walnut street, opposite No. 51,
South Wharves.—(Liberal advances made on
bark, cotton and other goods shipped by this ves-
sel,) For freight or passage, apply to
J. Welsh.
No. 51, South Wharves.
Who has for sale,
Old Madeira Wine in pipes and } Entitled to
qr. casks
High Coloured Sattins in cases, } drawback
Glass Lights for vessels' decks.

Wanted to Purchase,
The Hull of a new Shallop or
Flat from 35 to 40 tons, drawing not
more than five feet and a half Apply as
above.   June 1—6t
The following described Real Estate, late the
property of Isaac Thomas, deceased, viz:

For Boston,
Union Line Schooner
REGULATOR,
Capt. Lu...
Will sail on Saturday next, 8th inst.
For freight or passage, apply to the captain on
board, at Perot's wharf, or

TEAS.
Just arrived in the Adriana, London Trader,
China, Scattergood, &c.
GUNPOWDER, half chests & boxes,
Do. in 2 lb. cannisters,
IMPERIAL, half chests and boxes,
Do. in 2 lb. cannisters,
HYSON, half chests and boxes,
Do. in 2 lb. cannisters,
YOUNG HYSON, chests and boxes,
HYSON SKIN,
SOUCHONG, fine and plain, in boxes,
PECCO, 10 catty boxes,
10 boxes Evening CUPS and SAUCERS.
For sale at moderate prices, by
John Field, jr.
5mo. 10—fmwtf   No. 13, South Front street.

Domestic Goods.
60 packages, consisting of—
3-4 and 7-8 Shirtings, brown and bleached,
4-4 and 5-4 Sheetings, do. do.
Plaids, Stripes, Denims, &c.
Landing and for sale, by
Cheever & Fales,
May 29—wfmtf   No. 17, South Front st.

Superfine Cloths.
4 bales German superfine BROAD
CLOTHS, Just received and for sale, by
Cheever & Fales,
April 24—wfmtf   No. 17, South Front st.

Just Received,
10 cases English Magnesia,
1000 lb. superior Gum Myrrh,
4000 do. do. Gum Gamboge,
500 do. do. Senegal,
500 do. do. Fetida, fresh,
350 do. fine Sponges.
And for sale by
John J. Smith, jr.
No. 131, Market street.
ALSO,
200 gallons Spirits Turpentine,
100 boxes 8 by 10 Glass, cheap,
100 lb. superior Sealing Wax,
30 cases Gum Shellac,
White and Red Lead, Liquorice Ball,
Rose Pink, Epsom Salts, Pint Bottles,
Gum Copal, do. Opium.   5mo. 4—fmwtf

CARRIAGES.
A COACHEE, a LIGHT WAG-
GON, for one Horse, and 2 GIGS, for sale
at the shop of
Conrad Hanse,
Corner of Fourth and Walnut street.
May 29—wfm7t

Philadelphia
BOOT AND SHOE STORE.

The National Gazette.

FOR THE NATIONAL GAZETTE.

THE FINE ARTS.

The Roman School is the most celebrated for beauty and correctness of design, elegance in composition, truth of
expression and intelligence in attitudes.
Its masters were fostered in the Greek
taste. They applied themselves less to
colouring, than to rendering with a kind
of solemnity, the grand ideas with which
they were penetrated; and in this they
have succeeded to a wonderful extent.
Rome has been, and must ever continue
to be, the best school for the fine arts,
so long as she retains the vestiges of
her greatness, and the monuments of
her former splendour and supremacy.
Where will the artist learn so well the
abridged history of Roman victory, of
the march of her legions, their banners,
and arms, and the costume of the nations
which she conquered, as on the trium-
phal arches of Severus and Constantine,
and the columns of Trajan and Antoni-
nus? In thus contemplating grandeur,
though amid ruins, his genius takes a
loftier flight, his mind is stored with
models for imitation, of a higher order,
and he labours in that spirit of enthusiasm which no other scenes could excite.
Let him walk through the halls of the
Vatican and Capitol, and his eye is met
by the personifications of divinity, high
and unbending in the Apollo, dignified
in the Juno, and graceful and lovely in
the Venus: the Emperor, the Philosopher and the Poet, are here present in
their busts and statues, which impart to
the spectator a portion of the respective
spirits which actuated them when living. Astonishment and admiration are
soon succeeded by a spirit of careful
discrimination, and a studious selection
of expressions, attitudes and disposition
of drapery: the memory filled with such
imagery and the internal sense rendered
acute, the hand soon executes what the
imagination devises, not the grotesque
vagaries of barbarism, but the sublime,
the beautiful and the true in nature. It
...as in looking at the Pantheon, that
Michel Angelo formed the daring idea
of raising the dome of St. Peter's to tower in the heavens, showing that not only

pupils. On the second story of these
lodges, in the first wing, are some of
his most celebrated productions, consisting of fifty two paintings, representing
some of the principal events recorded
in the old testament, and executed after
the cartoons of Raphael by Julio Roma-
na, Pietro del Vaga, Polidoro and Matu-
rin di Caravagio, and others. Of the
four first paintings that which is over
the door of the entry, and which repre-
sents the Almighty dispersing Chaos, is
entirely by Raphael. Few dare undertake such a subject, still fewer, none but
Raphael could have preserved in the
execution the sublimity of the concep-
tion. The Father is displayed darting
forward, in extending the arms and legs,
and by this single movement he separates the elements and arranges each in
its situation.
Between the first and second wing of
these lodges is a door opening into the
Rooms (Camere) of Raphael, containing
those paintings so celebrated in the an-
nals of the fine Arts, but which time,
humidity, and neglect, have much injured: the colouring is faded and of course
much of the effect must be lost, at least
the first impressions are not so favoura-
ble as would have been anticipated.
The greater part of these rooms was
already painted under Julius II. by Pietro da Borgo Bramante, of Milan, Pietro
Perugino and others, when at the instance of the celebrated Bramante Laz-
zari of Urbino, the Pope induced Raphael to come from Florence to Rome,
to paint also with the others a façade in
which he was to represent the Disputa-
tion on the Holy Sacrament. When
this work was finished, the Pope was so
much surprised and gratified that he
made all the other painters cease from
their labours, and even directed that the
whole of what they had done should be
effaced, and that Raphael should repaint
the entire series. This incomparable artist, however, out of respect to his pre-
ceptor Perugino would not suffer a ceiling
painted by him to be effaced. The
rooms are four in number, and named
after the subject represented in them.
The first is called the Hall of Constantine. On the wall opposite the windows is represented the victory of Constantine the Great, over the tyrant

Third room. One...
works of Raphael...
school of Athens on...
for the scene, is a fir...
in a magnificent sty...
This painting inclu...
which, while it displa...
of the ancient phil...
also a true school...
such is highly pri...
look upon it as of...
mance. In the fig...
sages, he has giv...
some of the person...
Archimedes who is...
ture, and marking...
a compass, we see A...
friend and relation...
young man who ha...
heart is Francis D...
Nephew to Julius I...
knee on the ground...
serve the last mem...
attention is Frederic...
tua.—The two figu...
roaster who holds a...
are intended for P...
Raphael himself, o...
countenance, and it...
cap.
The painting o...
of Athens represen...
the Holy Sacramen...
tioned, it is the fir...
Raphael, and one o...
fine composition, c...
and colouring.—Th...
in an altar in the m...
sun with the Holy...
above are seen the...
Virgin and St. Joh...
the sides of the alta...
tors of the Latin C...
fathers and saints w...
profound mystery.—...
to the right, over th...
Raphael, who has...
Mount Parnassus, w...
we see the nine M...
the midst of them, p...
different parts of t...
base are many of th...
modern, among wh...
race, Virgil, Ovid,...
Dante, and the...
poetess Sappho.

A Nation of Regions, 1816–1828

CHRONOLOGY

"The war was finished in a blaze of glory," exclaimed a Republican newspaper editor in 1815, "as though God had tested Americans and their government. . . . America now stands in the first rank of nations." A spirit of nationalism echoed in pulpits, schoolrooms, and political gatherings, and inspired enormous economic and social growth in the shape of territorial expansion, domestic commerce, and business development. The new national self-confidence also prompted the expansion of suffrage for white men. "Enterprise walks forth unrestrained," boasted the happy editor, *"and the people are free."*

After 1816, the decline of the Federalist party reinforced feelings of national unity. The Virginian James Monroe, elected in 1816 with hardly any opposition outside New England and reelected four years later with only one dissenting vote in the electoral college, presided over what was called in 1817 the "era of good feelings."

The new nationalism encouraged a spirited celebration of the country's brief history. When Congress commissioned the Connecticut painter John Trumbull to decorate the Capitol rotonda with historical paintings, the artist depicted life-sized scenes of the signing of the Declaration of Independence and the British surrender at Yorktown. In 1817, William Wirt's popular biography of Patrick Henry gave schoolchildren a model of republican virtue—and, along the way, rewrote the words of Henry's speech of 1765 (see Chapter 5) to become the stirring "Give me liberty or give me death!" Most celebrated was George Washington, immortalized in portraits by Gilbert Stuart, mythological biographies, and innumerable statues that showed the wooden-jawed Virginian in Roman togas (the 555-foot monument would come later). The Battle of New Orleans added Andrew Jackson to the list of national heroes. Like Washington, Jackson was a citizen-soldier, symbolizing the virtue of ordinary people. Such self-conscious nationalism appeared authentic and yet was deliberately manufactured in an effort to overcome people's attachments to their separate states.

Amid all this self-glorification, most citizens still clung to older habits of culture and politics, feelings of loyalty to their home states and regions. The new generation of political leaders—among them, Henry Clay of Kentucky, John Calhoun of South Carolina, and Daniel Webster of Massachusetts—spoke boldly of the nation's promise, but keenly guarded the interests of their local constituencies. Embracing the equality of all citizens, these younger politicians had put aside

George Washington before Yorktown, 1781, as depicted by Rembrandt Peale.

knee breeches, buckled shoes, and powdered wigs in favor of trousers, shoe laces, and short-clipped hair. Such democratic attitudes encouraged the expansion of the electorate, first in the Northeast in the decade after 1815, and later in the southern states.

Meanwhile, economic and social developments revealed increasing differences between regions of the country. In the South, the expansion of cotton reinforced slave agriculture; in the Northeast, textile manufacturing became more important and politically influential; in the Northwest, prosperous free-labor farming created surplus produce for export and trade. These trends forced national politicians to confront conflicts of regional interest. Legislation in Congress about economic policy or territorial expansion demanded extensive compromise; some differences, such as the status of slavery in the territories, truly imperiled national cohesion. And because regional differences had political consequences—and since the electorate grew substantially during this period—one-party politics soon disappeared. By the end of the 1820s, voters in the states and politicians in Washington had restored a vigorous two-party system.

The Politics of a National Economy

The spirit of nationalism that followed the War of 1812 encouraged Congress to address problems of a national economy. With the Federalist party in retreat, Republican leaders like President James Madison no longer worried about a monarchist conspiracy and accepted greater government power. Moreover, the recent war had exposed the problems of an uncoordinated financial policy. Thus, in 1815, Madison proposed the creation of a second national bank (to replace Hamilton's Bank of the United States, whose charter had expired in 1811); a tariff that would raise the price of imported goods and so protect the manufacturing businesses that had grown during the embargo and the war; and a program of federally financed internal improvements. In Congress, Henry Clay presented a similar legislative package, which he named the "American System."

The agenda appealed to the younger generation of politicians, not only because they embraced a stronger national government but also because the measures would benefit their home states. With manufacturers seeking protection for new industries, especially in New England, Congress passed the Tariff of 1816, which kept customs duties at the wartime levels. Clay, anticipating the growth of Kentucky's hemp industry, and Calhoun, imagining textile factories in South Carolina, supported the law. Congress also voted in 1816 to charter the second Bank of the United

States to centralize currency and credit as a check against unregulated state banks. No one now questioned the bank's constitutionality. Since dividends from the bank promised to provide new revenues for government expenditures, Congress proposed in 1816 to use the bank "bonus" to develop roads, bridges, and canals to improve transportation and ease commerce. "Let us bind the Republic together," said Calhoun. "Let us conquer space." Although Congress passed the measure, Madison vetoed the Bonus bill in 1817, three days before leaving office, claiming the Constitution did not permit such federal expenditures.

Building the Erie Canal

The most dramatic transportation project of the age, the Erie Canal, was funded not by the federal government but by the state of New York. Yet even this effort promised greater national cohesion; in the words of the canal's chief promoter, Governor DeWitt Clinton, the resulting commerce would eliminate "the distinctions of eastern and western, of southern and northern interests." Laid out on the route of the old Iroquois fur trade, the $7 million, eight-year project, completed in 1825, extended 363 miles, linking Albany and the Hudson river with Buffalo and the Great Lakes. Besides its impressive technological achievement, which required such innovations as light wheelbarrows, tree-cutting pulleys, new mortar, and 83 locks, the canal symbolized the conquest of the wilderness. At the groundbreaking ceremony on the symbolic day of national unity, July 4, 1817, politicians raised toasts to the mixing of western and eastern waters. Workers in New York City paraded to salute the spirit of enterprise and progress, while newspapers in inland towns celebrated the arrival, for the first time in history, of fresh Long Island oysters. In this age before public zoos, one canal boat (appropriately named *Noah's Ark*) transported a living menagerie

The Erie Canal, 1829. The watercolor drawing by John William Hall contrasts the peaceful rural landscape with the bustle of canal commerce.

Newspapers in inland towns celebrated the arrival, for the first time in history, of fresh Long Island oysters.

of western species, including animals, birds, and even Seneca people to awe urban New Yorkers.

The Erie Canal strengthened economic ties between the Northeast and the Northwest. The result saw a dramatic rise in canal freight as westerners shipped their agricultural surplus to metropolitan centers and beyond. By 1827, New York City's flour exports exceeded the total shipped through all other U.S. ports. Such success stimulated a burst of similar canal projects in other northern states.

The National Economy and the Marshall Court

The failure of Congress to fund such internal improvements reflected both constitutional scruples about the legality of such expenditures and local resistance to national regulation of economic affairs. At issue was the larger question of whether national laws took precedence over state and local laws. Disagreements about such matters eventually reached the United States Supreme Court and came under the scrutiny of John Marshall, the chief justice for thirty-five years (1801–1835) and the last Federalist to hold high office. In a series of cases, the Marshall Court reaffirmed the supremacy of national government over the states. When, for example, the Pennsylvania state legislature passed a law intended to invalidate a federal court ruling, Marshall ruled in the *Peters* case (1809) that states could not legislate against federal law. Other decisions determined that the Supreme Court could overrule the judgment of a state court. These rulings were not popular, but by 1825, Marshall's court had overturned laws in ten states.

In other cases involving economic development, the Supreme Court upheld the power of Congress to regulate a national economy. When the state of Maryland imposed local taxes on the second Bank of the United States, Marshall warned in *McCulloch v. Maryland* (1819) that "The power to tax involves the power to destroy" and denied the right of state governments to tax institutions created by Congress. The ruling reaffirmed the constitutionality of the bank and asserted the superiority of federal power. In a later decision that had important implications for commercial development, *Gibbons v. Ogden* (1824), the Court rejected a New York state-chartered steamboat monopoly, which limited competition, by defining commerce on the Hudson river as *interstate* commerce, thus giving the national government jurisdiction over commerce on rivers that touched more than one state.

The Panic of 1819

Despite Marshall's assertions of national power, political commitments to state and regional interests continued to affect national politics, particularly when the economy took a nosedive in what was called the "Panic of 1819." Although the second Bank of the United States had been designed to regulate economic expansion, optimism after 1816 encouraged a flurry of investment and speculation by state banks and private investors. As American farmers found larger markets in Europe after the devastation of the Napoleonic wars, food and cotton prices surged upward, encouraging greater development of western lands. But when European farmers resumed production, the demand for U.S. produce abruptly dropped, reducing both prices and exports.

The resulting economic collapse demonstrated that an interlinked national economy already existed. Cotton sank from 33 cents a pound to 14 cents; tobacco fell from 40 cents to 4. As trade dwindled, the central Bank tightened credit, setting off a domino wave of credit contraction among the state banks. When banks called in their loans, business slowed, forcing bankruptcies and defaults. Besides ruining merchants, wholesalers, and retailers, the downturn brought high unemployment among propertyless workers, who were forced to seek public relief. By 1820, commercial debtors (nearly 1,500 in Boston and 1,800 in Philadelphia) filled local jails.

This crisis, the first major depression in the nation's history, soon penetrated the rural economy. Farmers and land speculators, who had borrowed to expand agricultural holdings during years of prosperity, now faced eviction. Congress responded by revising western land laws to lower prices and permit farmers to liquidate some of their holdings to finance the remainder. State legislatures passed stay laws to prevent seizure of mortgaged property by creditors. These measures brought some relief, but the political consequences of the Panic endured. Cotton exporters and western farmers, for the first time facing the uncertainties of world markets, blamed their troubles on the national bank. Many became permanently anti-bank, and their feelings would affect later political alignments about rechartering the national bank.

Meanwhile, northern manufacturers, reeling from the loss of domestic markets and facing renewed foreign competition, appealed for higher protective tariffs (taxes that would increase the price of imported goods and so offer advantages to domestic products). However, southern interests realized that by raising the cost of finished goods, higher tariffs would only benefit the manufacturing states of the Northeast. Cotton, the South's main product, needed no protection. In 1820, southern senators defeated the proposed tariff. Four years later, a revised tariff bill added protection for western raw materials, such as wool and hemp, as well as northeastern textiles and iron products, thus creating a marriage of interests between western livestock producers and northern manufacturers. Although southern congressmen voted almost unanimously against the measure, Congress passed the 1824 tariff, which raised duties without offering benefits to southern agriculture.

Territorial Expansion and Regional Differences

Opinions in Congress about economic issues reflected the regional differences of specific constituencies, especially the contrast between the northern and southern parts of the western territories. With the return of peace in 1815, both areas attracted large numbers of settlers. Indiana entered the union in 1816, Mississippi in 1817, Illinois in 1818, Alabama in 1819. In the former Northwest territory, U.S. military actions had hastened the departure of Shawnees, Kickapoos, and other nations westward across the Mississippi River. In their place came farmers from New York and New England, seeking land and a free labor farm economy. Meanwhile, Andrew Jackson's defeat of the southern nations during the War of 1812 (see Chapter 8) opened Native American lands to cotton planters, who swarmed into the area and made Mississippi and Alabama slave states.

During the 1820s, 15,000 African American slaves were sold each year from the upper South to cotton plantations in the Gulf states. As a result, the cotton crop of Mississippi tripled to 30 million pounds annually between 1821 and 1826, and exports from New Orleans increased nearly tenfold during the decade. Although slaveowners dominated politics in the southwestern states, a majority of farmers in the region owned no slaves. Other white migrants from Kentucky crossed the Ohio River into southern Indiana and Illinois, where they converged with transplanted northerners to form "free" states. Yet African Americans in the Northwest remained second-class citizens, forced to post bonds for good behavior in Ohio and often laboring as contract workers for former

slaveowners in Illinois. Only a narrow vote prevented Illinois from legalizing slavery in 1824.

Free Society and the Paradox of Race

In contrast to the cotton planters of the Southwest, settlers in the Northwest tended to be more transient. Typical was Thomas Lincoln, father of the sixteenth president, who was born in Virginia, married in Kentucky, widowed and remarried in Indiana, and died on his second farm in Illinois. Government land surveys, which divided property into regular grids, facilitated real estate transfers. But although government land prices dropped to $1.25 an acre in 1820, prevailing wages made land purchases difficult. In Philadelphia, for example, day laborers earned only 75 cents per day and even along the booming Erie Canal workers could expect no more than a monthly income of $14 plus food, laundry, and a pint of whiskey. Families spent 80 percent of their income on food, clothing, and shelter. Although western settlers could buy a reasonable-sized farm for about $100, most frontier families could not save that much. Instead, they squatted on public lands for a limited time, then sold the "improvements" to a newcomer and moved on.

Despite this mobility, many western settlers migrated with or near other family members and friends, forming core communities that intermarried, built churches and schools, participated in political life, and shared "frolics," such as group corn-husking and house-raising. Early marriages in the new states encouraged high birthrates—6 to 8 children among first-generation settlers. Having small agricultural surpluses to sell, rural families engaged in a barter economy and worked hard. Those who owned their own land enjoyed both a sense of community and self-sufficiency.

The idea of a free society was nevertheless limited. Regional differences about the institution of slavery did not necessarily indicate differences about race prejudice. When a small group of African Americans in New England proposed a plan in 1815 to transplant free blacks to Sierra Leone on the west coast of Africa, white leaders gladly contributed to a project that would reduce the free nonwhite population. "We could be cleared of them," declared a white advocate of colonization; "we would send to Africa a population partially civilized and christianized . . . [and] blacks would be put in a better condition."

In 1816, leading national politicians, including Clay, Webster, Monroe, Jackson, and Marshall, joined in organizing the American Colonization Society to expedite the removal of free blacks to Africa. Significantly, the movement made no mention of emancipating slaves. The intent of white supporters was merely to remove part of the free black population. Moreover, most northern African American communities bitterly criticized the scheme. "Whereas our ancestors (not of choice) were the first successful cultivators of the wilds of America," declared a resolution approved by 3,000 black Philadelphians who crowded into the African Methodist Episcopal Church in 1817, "we their descendants feel ourselves entitled to participate in the blessings of her luxuriant soil." Although the federal government assisted colonizers in founding Liberia in west Africa, only 1,400 African Americans made the decision to migrate overseas during the 1820s; by 1856 the total number had reached only 9,500.

The Missouri Debates

The contrast between society north of the Ohio River, which was dominated by family farmers who cultivated grains and livestock, and southern society, which was dominated by cotton agriculture, provided the backdrop for a major debate about the status of slavery in the western territories.

Spurred by postwar expansion, over 60,000 whites, mostly small farmers from southern states, and 10,000 slaves had moved into the Missouri territory. In 1819, the territorial government petitioned Congress for admission into the union. This routine request suddenly exploded in the House of Representatives when New York's James Tallmadge ignored the views of territorial residents and presented two amendments to prohibit the importation of slaves into Missouri and to free the children of slaves already there when they reached the age of 25. These unprecedented motions aroused furious debate. In the House, where the more densely populated North had greater weight, the measures passed; but in the Senate, where North and South were equally represented, Tallmadge's amendments were defeated.

The Congress of 1820 soon faced Missouri again. As various state legislatures, county committees, benevolent organizations, slaveholders, and abolitionists transmitted opinions to Congress and the press, politicians in Washington debated the moral and constitutional issues. In the Senate, New York's Rufus King declared slavery "contrary to the law of nature, which is the law of God," while, according to John Quincy Adams, "the great slaveholders of the House gnawed their lips and clenched their fists as they heard him." Other senators described slavery as a benevolent institution: "Go home with me," said one to his northern colleagues, "and see the glad faces." The slave "is free from care," commented another. Southern politicians insisted that the Constitution protected slavery, and even northern critics were forced to agree: "our boasted Constitution connives" in slavery, admitted a New Englander. But now the issue exceeded constitutionality: "To tolerate slavery beyond the Constitution," stated the Congressman, referring to its extension into Missouri, "is a perversion."

Despite the moral arguments, the issue of Missouri appeared less a question of political principles

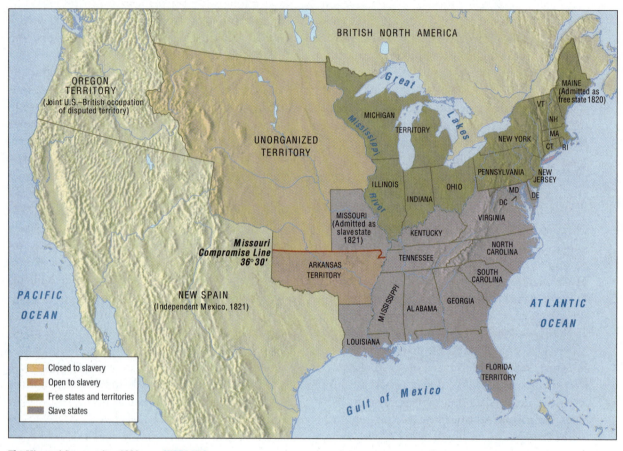

The Missouri Compromise, 1820   OVERLAY 2

than a matter of political power. The larger northern states already controlled the House of Representatives. But, in the Senate, the political match was clearly numerical: in 1820, eleven free states balanced eleven slave states. In the foreseeable future, only Florida and Arkansas promised to enter the slave column, whereas three free states waited in the wings. Missouri obviously held the future of southern power.

Reducing the Missouri question to such political numbers made the problem soluble. Since the district of Maine had also applied for admission to the union, politicians like Henry Clay saw a way of admitting the two states together—one slave, one free—to preserve the balance in the

Senate, at least for a time. But, to appease the antislavery forces, Congress compromised by prohibiting slavery in the remainder of the Louisiana territory north of the latitude 36°-30" (the southern border of Missouri). This imaginary line, which had nothing to do with the feasibility of growing cotton west of the Mississippi River, established a mental division that dominated U.S. politics for the next generation. By 1821, slaveholding Missouri was a full member of the union.

Political leaders and newspaper editors congratulated the architects of the Missouri Compromise; Henry Clay acquired a proud reputation as the "great compromiser." But other observers realized that slavery still imperiled the union. Thomas

Jefferson, living in retirement at Monticello, heard "a fire bell in the night," which, he said ominously, "awakened and filled me with terror."

The Vesey Conspiracy

Jefferson's fears about slavery reflected not only political divisions between free and slave states but also the social tensions caused by the subjugation of African Americans, both slave and free, and the possibility of racial insurrection. In 1822, such fears surfaced in Charleston, South Carolina. Denmark Vesey, a free African American carpenter, had closely followed the Missouri debates in Congress. As a person who had purchased his own freedom after winning a lottery, and as a member of the African Methodist church, Vesey held strong antislavery sentiments and had urged other blacks to seek their freedom.

The expansion of slavery to Missouri impelled him to action. With other blacks, both slave and free, Vesey organized a conspiracy to seize the local arsenal, burn Charleston, and flee from slavery to black-controlled Haiti in the Caribbean. The plot would begin on July 14, 1822, the anniversary of Bastille Day, when French revolutionaries had stormed that Paris jail in 1789. Before Vesey's rebels could muster their forces, however, a black servant betrayed the plot. The state government quickly summoned the militia to arrest the rebels, resulting in the execution of 35 African Americans and the banishment of 37 more. "Let it never be forgotten," exclaimed a worried Carolinian soon afterward, "that OUR NEGROES are . . .the common *enemy of civilized society,* and the barbarians who would, IF THEY COULD, become the DE-STROYERS of *our race.*"

As fear of slave insurrection permeated southern society, mysterious fires in Charleston kept the community on edge, and rumors of slave conspiracies abounded. Nor did the Missouri Compromise end the national debate about slavery. In Congress, various minor proposals (using profits from public land sales to finance emancipation or federal funding of colonization or restitution for damages to slave property) served as constant irritants that kept the argument alive. And free African Americans refused to be silenced. In 1827, black abolitionists in New York founded the newspaper *Freedom's Journal,* which stated "Too long have others spoken for us. . . . We abominate slavery, and all its advocates."

The Vesey plot and its anxious aftermath compelled many southern slaveowners to reconsider their involvement with human property. Since Vesey and his co-conspirators had belonged to an independent African American congregation, nervous southerners moved to discourage religious instruction, even Bible reading. Yet, as evangelical Christians, most southern leaders believed that eternal salvation, for black souls as well as white, depended on personal conversion. What did it mean, then, to deny religion to potential converts? Some relied on conservative preachers (rather than independent blacks) to emphasize biblical justifications of slavery. Others resolved the moral problem of slaveownership during the 1820s by defining slavery as a "necessary evil," a humane way of bringing Christianity and civilization to a supposedly inferior and degraded people. Others argued that emancipation was impractical: hundreds of thousands of ex-slaves could not be shipped to Africa nor left free in a white society. Significantly, few voices defended slavery as a positive good in itself.

Reshaping the Nation's Boundaries

The willingness of political leaders to colonize free black Americans in Africa coincided with efforts to expand the geographical borders of the republic. Like colonization, territorial expansion aimed at extending the power of free whites. Although southern expansionists wished to perpetuate slavery in the West, northern expansionists usually opposed the migration of free blacks. Such racial attitudes affected government policy about territorial expansion. On one hand, the United States recognized the power of the white nations of Europe by conducting legal negotiations and signing formal treaties that altered the nation's borders. On the other, white settlers and government officials disregarded the claims of the relatively powerless nonwhite nations of North America by engaging in illegal activities and violating formal treaties.

Negotiating with Britain and Spain

Negotiations with European nations, Britain and Spain, endeavored to remove competing claims to portions of the North American continent. Under President Monroe, Secretary of State John Quincy Adams developed a foreign policy to extend the country's territorial sovereignty and strengthen foreign commerce. In a series of treaties negotiated with Britain, Adams protected U.S. trading rights with British possessions and constructed a permanent peace along the Canadian border. The two countries agreed to demilitarize the Great Lakes, set the northern boundary of the Louisiana territory at the forty-ninth parallel, and subsequently provided for the joint occupation of the Oregon territory on the Pacific. Without consulting Native American groups, these agreements established precedents for westward expansion to the Pacific coast.

Adams also resolved differences with the Spanish empire about the status of Florida. That province had long served as a refuge for runaway slaves, who often entered Seminole society (sometimes as their slaves). Creeks fleeing U.S. armies also moved across the border. Hoping to limit U.S. expansion, these groups took assistance from Spanish authorities and British adventurers to raid U.S. settlements in Georgia. In 1818, Monroe ordered General Andrew Jackson to lead an expedition against Florida's Seminole-Creek-African communities. During the attack, Jackson seized Spanish garrisons and executed two British subjects who appeared to have instigated assaults against U.S. citizens. While some members of Congress denounced Jackson's aggression, fearing the incident would provoke hostilities with Spain and Britain, Adams defused the crisis by returning the Spanish towns and calming British outrage.

Jackson's expedition underscored the shaky state of Spain's remaining empire in North America. Already the Mexican province had rebelled against Spanish rule. Now Spain worried that the United States might seize not only Florida but also the northern portions of Mexico in Texas. Taking advantage of Mexican fears, Adams agreed to purchase eastern Florida for $5 million, which would be used to reimburse U.S. citizens for property damages. In exchange, the United States accepted a boundary division of Louisiana that assured Spanish control of Texas. But Adams bargained hard to persuade Spain to surrender claims in the far Northwest, beyond the Rocky Mountains, which gave the United States legal rights to the Pacific coast. This Adams-Onís treaty, also known as the Transcontinental Treaty, which was signed in 1819 and ratified two years later, formed the basis of the national empire. "A great epoch in our history," Adams wrote in his diary.

The Monroe Doctrine

Spain's concessions in North America reflected deeper fears of the upheavals occurring in the colonies of Latin America. After a decade of warfare, Mexico won its independence in 1821. As Spain faced other colonial rebellions, several European monarchs offered to support an army to reestablish Spanish control. Adams, already eyeing U.S. trade south of the border, saw no advantage in strengthening Spain's rule, and in 1822 encouraged Monroe to recognize the independence of the Latin American countries. The British

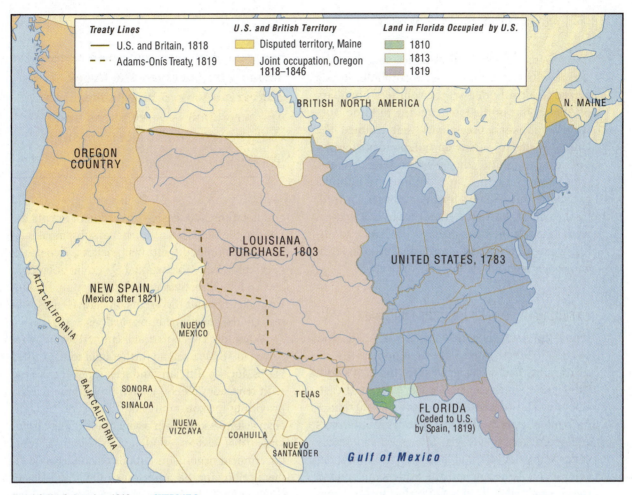

Treaty Lines
— U.S. and Britain, 1818
- - - Adams-Onís Treaty, 1819

U.S. and British Territory
Disputed territory, Maine
Joint occupation, Oregon 1818–1846

Land in Florida Occupied by U.S.
1810
1813
1819

BRITISH NORTH AMERICA

N. MAINE

OREGON COUNTRY

LOUISIANA PURCHASE, 1803

UNITED STATES, 1783

NEW SPAIN (Mexico after 1821)

ALTA CALIFORNIA

NUEVO MEXICO

BAJA CALIFORNIA

SONORA Y SINALOA

NUEVA VIZCAYA

COAHUILA

TEJAS

NUEVO SANTANDER

FLORIDA (Ceded to U.S. by Spain, 1819)

Gulf of Mexico

Spanish North America, 1819 **OVERLAY 2**

also wished to expand trade with Spain's former colonies and proposed that the Anglo-American nations cooperate in opposing European interference in South America, while repudiating any interest in annexing those countries. Adams quashed the idea. Recognizing that it was not in the United States' interests to support British trade with Latin America, nor advantageous to disavow any plans to annex areas of Mexico or Cuba, he also worried about recent Russian expansion on the Pacific coast. As the former minister to Russia, Adams knew about that country's fur-trading enterprises and colonial schemes in Alaska. The secretary of state also realized that whatever position the United States adopted, the

British navy would surely prevent unwanted military operations in South America.

Persuaded by Adams, the president announced what became known as the "Monroe Doctrine" in 1823. In his annual message to Congress, Monroe declared opposition to further colonization of the Western Hemisphere by any European power (a reference to Russian plans in the far Northwest), and renounced U.S. interference in European affairs (a reference to Greek and Spanish revolutions then occurring). More broadly, Monroe denied the right of European countries to interfere in political affairs in the Western Hemisphere.

The Monroe Doctrine had little immediate impact: the European monarchs made no serious effort to interfere in South America, and the colonial revolts ran their course. Meanwhile, Russia agreed to a treaty that set the southern boundary of Alaska. But in the long run, the Monroe Doctrine established precedents that enabled the United States to pursue an independent foreign policy throughout the Western Hemisphere, while promoting its own economic and political expansion into Spain's former colonies. Indeed, by the end of the 1820s, hundreds of U.S. settlers were entering Mexico's province in Texas, adopting Mexican citizenship and the Catholic faith, and scheming to overthrow Mexican rule.

Expelling the Creeks from the Southeast

Interest in developing new territory after the War of 1812 led the United States to repudiate several treaties that had been signed since the 1790s with the Native American nations of the Southeast. The war had forced these nations to surrender millions of acres to the United States, but farmers and speculators of Georgia, Tennessee, and nearby states wanted additional land for agricultural development. Although political leaders understood the contractual obligations of earlier treaties, government policy aimed at acquiring all Native lands, and as soon as possible. "The neighboring tribes are becoming daily less warlike, and more helpless and dependent on us," explained Monroe's secretary of war, John Calhoun, in 1818. "Our views of their interest, and not their own, ought to govern them."

Against the Creek nation, the government joined local officials, traders, and settlers (often the same individuals played all three roles) in depriving the tribal inhabitants of their land and formal treaty rights. By manipulating the agreed annual payments—for example, charging extravagant prices for manufactured cloth, treating personal debts as public credit, or distributing marked-up

Those who survived the Creek migration looked like "miserable and wretched . . . skeletons and their bones almost worn through the skin."

goods rather than cash—government agents defrauded the supposed recipients of substantial public sums and lined their own pockets. To be sure, Creek protests to the national government brought clear policy directives prohibiting certain fraudulent practices. But the agents on Native lands simply ignored government instructions.

When the Creek national council formally resolved in 1820 to sell no further land to the United States, local politicians and developers conspired with renegade "chiefs" to sign fraudulent treaties, providing for enormous land transactions in exchange for personal cash payments. Although legitimate tribal leaders repudiated these transactions, government negotiators submitted an illegal document calling for the surrender of all Creek lands in Georgia and Alabama to the U.S. Senate, which promptly ratified the deal in 1825.

Meanwhile, the government of Georgia, in an assertion of state sovereignty, initiated land surveys to expedite the removal of Creek inhabitants to areas west of the Mississippi River. Hastening to Washington, Creek leaders persuaded President John Quincy Adams to reconsider the fraud. But the revised Treaty of Washington of 1826 merely protected Creek claims in Alabama. Forced to abandon all their lands in Georgia, the Creeks agreed to move to tribal territory farther west. But the promised government assistance for the forced march failed to arrive, and those who survived the migration looked, as one white observer put it, like "miserable and wretched. . . skeletons and their bones almost worn through the skin." These uprooted Creeks remained in Alabama for nine years, until another round of white fraud, theft, and military force drove them farther west.

Cherokee Nationalism

The Cherokee people faced similar pressure to abandon their homes. Yet the Cherokees were divided between traditionalists, who rejected Anglo American culture, and assimilationists, many of them children of interracial marriages, who endeavored to overcome cultural differences and become citizens of the United States. Cherokee policy thus followed two distinct paths—one traditionalist, one assimilationist.

To avoid further conflict with whites, Cherokee traditionalists, a minority of the nation, surrendered claims to their lands in the Southeast and migrated to Arkansas, where they promptly fell into conflict with the resident Osage and Quapaw peoples, as well as with white squatters who asserted prior rights to the lands. Meanwhile, assimilationist Cherokees fought to save their homes in Georgia. When Secretary of War John Calhoun declared in 1819 that "the Great Spririt has made our form of society stronger than yours and you must submit to adopt ours if you wish to be happy by pleasing him," Cherokee leaders in Georgia took his advice. Introducing political and cultural reforms, they hoped to make the nation appear less alien and threatening to U.S. interests. An independent national identity, based on self-government and economic self-sufficiency, would not only minimize cultural differences but also fulfill Cherokee claims to political sovereignty.

During the 1820s, these accommodating Cherokees adopted a formal book of laws, a legal court system, and a representative bicameral legislature, which conformed with Anglo American traditions by excluding Cherokee women from suffrage. In addition, the traditional clan relations and matrilineal obligations were replaced by a patriarchal system. Inheritance, for example, which traditionally had followed female lines, now became male-oriented, and children became dependents of fathers rather than mothers. To protect patriarchal lines of descent, Cherokee women lost traditional control of their pregnancies, and abortion became illegal for the first time. New laws also prohibited multiple marriages by men and barred rape, a crime previously unknown in Cherokee history and perhaps introduced by non-Cherokee intruders. To further conform to Anglo American standards, the Cherokees held a constitutional convention in 1827, adopting a formal constitution modeled on the United States' founding document. By then, Cherokee women had largely lost their political voice, and Cherokee citizenship was limited to adult men.

Besides these political innovations, assimilationists strove to imitate Anglo American cultural practices. In 1821, Sequoia, a previously illiterate Cherokee, developed a written Cherokee language based on 86 spoken syllables, each with a distinct symbol. (Ironically, some Cherokee leaders hesitated to endorse the system because the pictographic language would suggest something less than total assimilation by Anglo American standards of literacy.) By the end of the decade, the *Cherokee Phoenix*, a bilingual Cherokee-English newspaper edited by Elias Boudinot, served community needs. Christian missionaries, particularly Methodists, won numerous converts among Cherokee youth. In addition, Cherokees increasingly adopted Anglo American economic forms—men becoming farmers and artisans, women learning to spin and to weave. Such changes encouraged economic individualism, including the acceptance of African American slavery. Although 18th-century Cherokees had treated blacks as equals, efforts to embrace white values prompted new laws that prohibited intermarriage with blacks, forbade free blacks from joining the nation, and limited the rights of blacks to own property. Indeed, the *Phoenix* printed advertisements about runaway slaves and opportunities to purchase slaves from Cherokee traders.

Despite such assimilation, Cherokees were no more successful than Creeks at persuading the U.S. government, the southern states, or land hungry settlers to respect this cultural transformation, much less their treaty rights. In 1828, a majority of the Georgia state legislature demanded all Cherokee land and enacted provisions for immediate surveys and sales. Promises by the federal government of a 7 million-acre reservation "forever" failed to raise interest in migration. Cherokee appeals to Washington evoked no sympathy. "We have been far more successful in the acquisition of their land," admitted President Adams in 1828, "than in imparting to them the principles, or inspiring them with the spirit, of civilization."

Transforming National Politics

The unresponsiveness of the U.S. government to the problems of Creeks and Cherokees and the limited interest in Congress about the status of slaves and free blacks reflected the prevailing assumptions of white male superiority in the political world. Yet the same principle encouraged the extension of equal rights of citizenship to virtually all adult white men, regardless of their standing in the white community. Even the poorest white man, merely by possessing rights of citizenship, embodied racial, ethnic, and gender superiority over those residents who were denied full citizenship. Few worried about those left outside the political household. "If the time should ever arrive when the African shall be raised to the level of the white man," a New York politician proposed, "when the colours shall intermarry—when ne-

groes shall be invited to your tables—to sit in your pew, or ride in your coach, it may then be proper to. . . remodel the constitution to conform to that state of society." But the supposed inferiority of such people justified, at least for the immediate future, their exclusion from the political process.

After the War of 1812, the expansion of equal rights for white males transformed national politics. The first state government constitutions, established during the war for independence, had usually limited voting rights to propertied male citizens. But as population increased and moved westward, as multiple religious denominations (Congregationalist, Presbyterian, Baptist, Methodist, Episcopalian, even Catholic) competed for American souls, and as economic changes increased the number of propertyless workers, a younger generation of political leaders challenged the continuation of political representation based on property requirements, religious affiliation, and indirect elections. The new states that entered the union during the early 19th century opened the vote to all adult white males, regardless of whether they owned property, and many states adopted secret balloting instead of public polling to assure fair voting. By 1815, older states felt pressure from propertyless workers, religious minorities, and younger politicians to adopt political reform. Many state governments now summoned constitutional conventions to change the political order.

Broadening the Vote

"The principle of universal suffrage, which is now running a triumphant career from Maine to Louisiana, is an awful power," complained an old Federalist at the New York convention, "which, like gunpowder, or the steam engine, or the press itself, may be rendered mighty in mischief as well as in blessings." Warning that "governments are becoming downright democracies," such conservatives fought to limit the changes affecting elections, taxation, and office holding. By contrast, the reformers demanded that the right to vote be expanded not only because "life was as dear to a poor man as to a rich man" and "so was liberty," as one Boston politician declared, but also because these new leaders better represented a diverse citizenry and, incidentally, expected to win popular elections.

These democratizing pressures brought significant reforms, broadening the suffrage to include most white male citizens, making more offices elective rather than appointive, and reducing property requirements for holding office. But political leaders also preserved important limitations on political democracy. As one delegate remarked of the principle of "universal suffrage": "Women are excluded—minors are excluded." So, too, were other minorities. In Massachusetts, for example, Congregational churches retained tax advantages, to the dismay of smaller denominations. The New York convention established taxpaying and residency requirements uniquely for men "of colour." Those two words effectively took the vote away from 30,000 free African Americans, leaving only 298 African Americans who could meet the qualifications. "The minds of blacks," one politician observed, were "not competent to vote." Besides, another delegate declared, extending suffrage to blacks "would serve to invite that kind of population to this state, an occurrence which I should most sincerely deplore." Such attitudes disqualified Native American "aborigines"—though many whites considered them "more acute and discerning . . . [than] the African race."

Changes in voting requirements were important in state and local elections, but did not immediately affect national politics. In 1824, competition among four presidential candidates (William Crawford of Georgia, John Quincy Adams of Massachusetts, Henry Clay of Kentucky, and Andrew Jackson of Tennessee) still focused on issues of "character" rather than political ideas or programs. All were well-known figures, but voters were unimpressed by the choice. Fewer than 25 percent of eligible citizens bothered to vote. Only Jackson, the popular hero of New Orleans, drew support outside his home region. None of the four, therefore, captured a majority of electoral votes. For the second time in U.S. history, the presidential election went to the House of Representatives, where each state held a single vote. Although Jackson had outpolled Adams, political maneuvering in Congress put the Tennessee soldier at a disadvantage. Speaker of the House Clay wanted no western rivals and remained sympathetic to Adams's nationalism. Clay's support gave Adams the election. When Adams followed his victory by naming Clay his secretary of state, Jackson's supporters claimed that their candidate had been denied election by a "corrupt bargain" in Congress. The Jackson camp began preparing for the next election.

A statesman rather than a popular politician, John Quincy Adams did not favor a broadened electorate and viewed party politics as "a baneful weed." Failing to understand that "party strife" reflected the conflicting views of various interest groups, the president tried to rise above the factions, refusing to use political appointments to build alliances within Congress. Yet his nationalist political agenda—federal internal improvements, government support of agriculture and manufacturing, the creation of a national university—accentuated regional divisions and aroused congressional opposition. New Yorkers, for example, usually supported improvements in transportation, but now wanted no competition for the newly opened Erie Canal; southerners, who saw no benefits for their region, raised constitutional questions about government projects. Adams further aroused southern criticism by proposing that the United States participate in a conference of the newly liberated Latin American countries in Panama, whose aim was to pressure Spain to recognize their independence.

In the wake of the Missouri debates and the Vesey plot, southerners wanted no official contact with delegates from black-controlled Haiti, lest it imply formal recognition of a slave revolution. Although Congress eventually provided the funds in 1826, the meeting ended before the U.S. delegate arrived.

Contesting the Tariff

Regional divisions surfaced more bitterly in 1828 during debates about revising the tariff. Initially, the tariff proposal offered to protect both the finished manufactured goods of the Northeast and the raw products of the West, such as hemp, wool, and flax. But New England interests, which imported raw materials to manufacture textiles, opposed protection of raw commodities that would raise domestic prices and introduced amendments to lower those duties. Southern politicians opposed all tariffs and hoped to defeat the measure by splitting western and northeastern interests. Instead of supporting amendments to lower tariffs on raw goods, therefore, southerners expected to kill the entire tariff by supporting the higher rates favored by westerners, believing that the Northeast section would then vote against the bill.

By 1828, however, the interests of northeastern manufacturers were committed overwhelmingly to a policy of tariff protection, even though it would mean high duties on raw materials. Reluctantly, northeastern congressmen joined westerners in passing the high Tariff of 1828, which raised tariffs on most products. To frustrated southern leaders, this "tariff of abominations" demanded protest. South Carolina's John Calhoun, recognizing the increasing isolation of his region, drafted an elaborate defense of political minorities in an anonymously published essay called "Exposition and Protest." Attacking the new tariff, the southern spokesman elaborated a theory of states' rights in the tradition of Madison and Jefferson's Virginia and Kentucky resolutions, justifying the nullification of congressional laws by acts of the separate state legislatures (see Chapter 7). Yet Calhoun's argument remained only an intellectual statement. Believing that the next presidential administration would revise the offensive tariff, he proposed no further political action.

Strengthening the Political Parties

Political alignments in Congress revealed not only regional conflict, but also basic changes in the nation's political structure. Although voter participation had remained only around 25 percent in 1824, largely because of a lack of competition within the separate states, the increasing number of eligible voters encouraged state leaders, notably New York's Martin Van Buren, to form political organizations or parties to maintain discipline among the electorate. Yet parties remained slightly suspect. Voters rallied around individual leaders (Adams and Jackson) rather than taking a distinctive name or identity. All parties considered themselves "Republican."

Two instruments stimulated the emergence of political parties during the 1820s: partisan newspapers, which announced political positions and defined the issues for the public; and patronage appointments, such as jobs in the post office or in customs collection, to reward political loyalty. Unlike the political party leaders of the 1790s, politicians no longer felt embarrassed about organizing support to achieve their political objectives. Rejecting the older politics of *consensus,* which assumed a natural harmony of political interests among all citizens (perverted only by corrupt politicians, demagogues, or monarchists), party leaders of the 1820s saw politics as an arena of competition, in which the opinion of a *majority* appeared sufficient. Rather than undermining the nation's political virtue, parties would express the interests of the voters. Candidates stood for political office not as personalities (though individual images remained critical for gaining votes), but as supporters of particular programs.

Adams's rejection of the new party politics doomed his bid for reelection in 1828. While the president, identifying himself as a "National Republican," kept his political base in the Northeast, Van Buren skillfully built a political alliance between New York and like-minded "Democratic Republicans" in the southern states. By "substituting *party principles* for *personal preferences*," he explained, "the planters of the South and the plain Republicans of the north" could rally behind Jackson not merely as a popular hero who could capture votes but also as the embodiment of a political position (what later would be called a party platform) dedicated to specific government programs.

The 1828 campaign left plenty of room for personal insult: Jackson's wife was accused of adultery, while Adams was charged with procuring a prostitute for the Russian tsar. But beyond personalities, the Democratic ticket of Jackson and Calhoun appealed to a coalition of western farmers interested in cheap land, southern slaveowners opposed to tariffs, and merchants in the middle states concerned with finance. With over 1 million voting—three times the number voting four years earlier—Jackson won 56 percent of the popular vote and two-thirds of the electoral college. The large turnout revealed not only the growth of the electorate but also greater public interest in national political issues. For the first time, questions of tariffs, internal improvements, banks, and western lands—subjects that had once seemed remote to ordinary citizens—had become topics of public debate.

Farewell to an Era

As Andrew Jackson ascended to power, the citizenry understood that they were coming to the end an era. The Founding Fathers' generation,

On the golden anniversary of the Fourth of July, the deaths of John Adams and Thomas Jefferson within hours of each other symbolized the end of an age.

which linked Americans of the 1820s to the birth of their nation, was rapidly passing from the stage. In 1825, the French patriot Lafayette returned to the land of his wartime triumphs, drawing crowds from Boston to New Orleans who gaped at this survivor of the French-American alliance. That year, on the fiftieth anniversary of the battle of Bunker Hill, the young Daniel Webster thrilled a crowd of tens of thousands by suddenly addressing the elderly war veterans standing on the slope before him. "Venerable men," he orated, "the great trust" of the republic "now descends to new hands." In 1826, on the golden anniversary of the Fourth of July, the deaths of John Adams and Thomas Jefferson within hours of each other symbolized the end of an age. Many wondered aloud whether the new generation could preserve the republican spirit of liberty. To keep the heritage alive, in 1827 Massachusetts became the first of many states to mandate instruction in American history in public schools.

The content of that schoolbook history extolled the progress of civilization from the landing of the Pilgrims at Plymouth Rock in 1620 to the construction of the Erie Canal by a "spirit of enterprise" that had "subdued the wilderness of the west." But some observers worried more about what was being lost by this passion for "progress" and individual achievement. New York novelist James Fenimore Cooper, born and raised in Erie Canal country, achieved literary fame by illuminating the darker side of progress. In *The Pioneers* of 1823, Cooper's first "Leather-Stocking" tale, his

THE

LAST OF THE MOHICANS.

BY
JAMES FENIMORE COOPER.

NEW YORK:
D. APPLETON AND COMPANY, PUBLISHERS.

James Fenimore Cooper's immensely popular Leatherstocking stories evoked the passage from "natural" society to "civilization."

frontier hero Natty Bumpo witnesses the wanton killing of enormous flocks of wild pigeons (passenger pigeons, which today are extinct) and remarks sadly: "This comes of settling a country!" The title of another popular Cooper novel, *The Last of the Mohicans* (1826) expressed the tragic plight of Native American cultures: "The pale faces are the masters of the earth," says the defeated chief. So, too, the New York poet William Cullen Bryant presented a saccharin farewell to a vanishing people: "A noble race!" he wrote, "but they are gone."

Such sentimentality greatly annoyed the writer William Apess, a New England Pequot, who had fought for the United States in the War of 1812. Comparing the "immortal Washington" to his own cultural hero, the Wampanoag King Philip, who led a bloody rebellion against the New England colonies in 1675 (see Chapter 3), Apess denounced the hero worship of his people's persecutors. His autobiography, *A Son of the Forest*, published in 1829, deplored the widely used and demeaning word *Indian*. "I could not find it in the Bible," he noted, "and therefore concluded that it was a word imported for the special purpose of degrading us." Apess was an exceptional person but not widely read. Rather, most readers shared the outlook of the nostalgic writers Bryant and Cooper, who like, Andrew Jackson, assumed that progress from wilderness to civilization was inevitable. Celebrating national values of territorial expansion, they saved their praise not for Native Americans, nor even for Leather-Stocking, who must depart toward the setting sun, but, as Cooper wrote, for "the march of the nation across the continent."

INFOTRAC® COLLEGE EDITION EXERCISES

For additional reading go to InfoTrac College Edition, your online research library at *http://web1.infotrac-college.com.*

Keyword search: James Madison
Subject search: Bank of the United States
Subject search: Missouri Compromise
Keyword search: Denmark Vesey
Keyword search: Monroe Doctrine
Keyword search: John Quincy Adams

Subject search: Cherokees, periodicals
Subject search: Creeks, periodicals
Keyword search: Martin Van Buren

ADDITIONAL READING

The Politics of a National Economy

George Dangerfield, *The Awakening of American Nationalism, 1815–1828* (1965). This volume introduces the major political events of the period.

Building the Erie Canal

Carol Sheriff, *The Artificial River: The Erie Canal and the Paradox of Progress, 1817–1862* (1996). This survey places the canal in the context of changing cultural values about the economy; see also Ronald E. Shaw, *Erie Water West: A History of the Erie Canal, 1792–1854* (1966).

The National Economy and the Marshall Court

Francis N. Stites, *John Marshall: Defender of the Constitution* (1981). This succinct biography places the major Supreme Court cases in historical context.

Territorial Expansion and Regional Differences

John Mack Faragher, *Sugar Creek: Life on the Illinois Prairie* (1986). A social history of one community, the book describes problems of settling new lands.

Free Society and the Paradox of Race

William W. Freehling, *Prelude to Civil War: The Nullification Controversy in South Carolina, 1816–1836* (1966). Analyzes the role of slavery in the political culture of the 1820s.

Edward A. Pearson, ed., *Design against Charleston: The Trial Record of the Denmark Vesey Slave Conspiracy of 1822* (1999). Besides a fine essay about slave culture, this volume includes a transcript of the legal proceedings.

Expelling the Creeks from the Southeast

Michael D. Green, *The Politics of Indian Removal: Creek Government and Society in Crisis* (1982). A detailed examination of U.S. policy toward the Creeks, emphasizing the role of racism and fraud.

Cherokee Nationalism

William G. McLoughlin, *Cherokee Renascence in the New Republic* (1986). Examining Cherokee society, this study describes the effort to avoid forced removal; see also Theda Perdue, *Cherokee Women* (1998), listed in Chapter 1.

Strengthening Political Parties

Donald B. Cole, *Martin Van Buren and the American Political System* (1984). Focusing on New York's premier politician, this book examines the emergence of party politics during the 1820s. For the role of informal politics in Washington, D.C., see Catherine Allgor, *Parlor Politics* (2000).

Farewell to an Era

Barry O'Connell, ed., *On Our Own Ground: The Complete Writings of William Apess, A Pequot* (1992). This anthology introduces the remarkable work of a long-forgotten Native American author.

Alan Taylor, *William Cooper's Town: Power and Persuasion on the Frontier of the Early American Republic* (1995).Describes community development in rural New York and its impact on the writings of James Fenimore Cooper.

10

Hudson River near West Point, N. Y.

The Politics of Northern Development, 1815–1840

CHRONOLOGY

A ragged man in antique dress, carrying a rusty fowling-piece on his shoulder, stumbled down from a green knoll in the Catskill woods overlooking the Hudson River. He was decked with leaves, his grizzled hair and beard hung down to his knees, and his eyes teared in the bright sunshine of this morning after his twenty-year sleep. He made his way slowly to his native village in New York, where he was immediately struck by the newly "busy, bustling, disputatious tone" of the place.

"Strange names were over the doors—strange faces at the windows—everything was strange," moaned Rip Van Winkle. "Instead of the great tree that used to shelter the quiet little Dutch inn" in the center of town, "there now was reared a tall naked pole, with something on the top that looked like a red night-cap, and from it was fluttering a flag, on which was a singular assemblage of stars and stripes." He recognized on the sign, however, the ruby face of King George, under which he had smoked so many a peaceful pipe; but even this was singularly metamorphosed. The red coat was changed for one of blue and buff, a sword was held in the hand instead of a sceptre, the head was decorated with a cocked hat, and underneath was painted in large characters, GENERAL WASHINGTON. The poor creature cried in despair, "Every thing's changed, and I'm changed, and I can't tell . . . who I am!"

When Washington Irving's famous character entered the literary scene in 1832, Rip's confusion became part of the nation's folklore, echoing as he did the concern of early 19th-century readers about the political and economic changes that were altering rural communities, towns, and cities alike.

These changes would eventually reshape the economy in every corner of the nation, but in the beginning they were most noticeable in the northeastern states. As that area became more urbanized and industrialized, its inhabitants developed an identity as entrepreneurs and workers. They saw themselves as diligent, disciplined Yankees and contrasted their way of life with less economically developed Americans elsewhere. Because the Northeast was the most densely populated region, moreover, people in other areas could not ignore this transformation. Southern and western farmers saw the same kinds of changes spreading toward their own homes, though they did not necessarily want or welcome the invasion.

The Expanding Market Economy

Some of the changes could be measured statistically: the national population in 1815 numbered 8.4 million; 25 years later the total had more than doubled to 17.4 million. New York City, the nation's largest metropolis, grew from 156,000 in 1820 (equivalent today to a modest community like Fort Lauderdale, Florida, or Oxnard, California) to 391,000 in 1840 (the size of a modern city like Omaha, Nebraska, or Honolulu, Hawaii). Only 7 percent of the country's residents lived in large towns, but in 1820, for the first time in U.S. history, the urban population began to increase at a faster rate than the population in rural areas, a trend that would persist until the census of 1980 found urban dwellers returning to the countryside in greater numbers.

More subtle changes lay beneath the statistical surface. When the Erie Canal opened in 1825, one politician boasted that the waterway would "bring a market to every man's door." Yet expanding com-

"Have I the right to make as good a bargain as I can?"

merce also brought more impersonal economic relations. Traditional social ethics had emphasized fairness, justice, and "character" in doing business, but transactions between strangers encouraged mere monetary concerns. One horsetrader, living near the Erie Canal and misled by the promises of a well-dressed customer he had never seen before, complained bitterly about the unexpected "sharp tricks of the day." Thus the widening marketplace forced increasing numbers of producers and consumers to confront issues of economic development. As questions of credit, bank notes, and transportation affected more citizens, economic issues entered the political arena and became subjects of political debate.

Americans also faced moral dilemmas about economic change. "Have I the right to make as good a bargain as I can?" asked New England's *Christian Almanac* in 1830. The answer was resoundingly negative. "No man has the right to do anything which causes needless suffering." Yet the question itself testified to important changes in values, suggesting that many entrepreneurs were indeed pursuing "as good a bargain" as they could, at the cost of older social ethics. While some reached solely for profits, others, like the editor of *Christian Almanac,* recoiled from purely commercial transactions, stuck to old values, and protested the changes. Fearing that the country was losing its virtue, many evangelical Christians appealed for a revival of economic and social morality. Based largely among middle-class groups, these reformers pressed for moral change in society.

Attitudes about economic growth had direct political consequences. With the expanded electorate of the 1820s and the rise of two-party competition in 1828, political leaders increasingly defined their differences about economic policies. Under President Andrew Jackson, the Democratic party questioned government support of economic development and opposed a strong national bank, high tariffs, and commercial "improvements." By contrast, Whig party leaders such as Henry Clay and Daniel Webster favored the central bank, modest tariffs, and congressional assistance for internal improvements. These political lines became clearer as the national economy touched the lives of more citizens. Yet regional economic differences—the South as slavery-based cotton producer, the Northeast as manufacturing center, and the Northwest as free-labor agriculture—continued to complicate national party alliances. On a broader level, these issues touched on competing definitions of the national identity: Were the American people merely materialistic? Could economic development be reconciled with traditional morality? Could two versions of the national identity coexist?

Economic Opportunity Stimulates Migration

The nation's growing population resulted primarily from a high birthrate, which despite a declining trend still averaged around five children per family. After the War of 1812, European immigration added to the growth, jumping tenfold from 8,000 in 1820 to 84,000 in 1840. Most newcomers in this period were skilled artisans from Britain and Germany, who could no longer compete with industrial factories, or farmers whose incomes suffered from declining food prices in their homelands. Such immigrants often traveled as families, though most were males. After a 4- to 6-week voyage at sea, most stayed in the ports where they landed, swelling the labor force of Boston, New York, Baltimore, and New Orleans. By 1840, over 40 percent of the residents of New York City and New Orleans were foreign-born (another 23 percent in New Orleans were African American slaves). Immigrants with cash often followed the river systems inland to the growing cities of Buffalo, Cincinnati, and St. Louis, and farmers bought acreage in the nearby hinterlands.

Economic opportunity also attracted the less fortunate. As high birthrates and land divisions caused overpopulation in Ireland, tens of thousands of single men and women sailed for American shores. Workers without money avoided the southern states, where slavery kept wages low. Most unskilled immigrants found jobs as manual laborers (such as digging the Erie Canal) or as domestic servants. By the 1830s, these propertyless Irish immigrants congregated in the cities, heralding the arrival of millions more when potato famines caused mass migration during the next decade.

Transportation and Mobility

The surge of population encouraged both geographical dispersal and innovative modes of transportation. The number of steamboats operating from New Orleans increased from 200 in 1820 to 2,000 in 1840. Meanwhile, the rage for canal building speeded western migration, as well as the shipping of agricultural products to inland ports and downriver cities. "Pork and Flour coming down—Tea and Sugar coming up," remarked a New York canal booster. "Things are as they should be; some up, some down." Canals also carried unhealthy cargo, such as the disease cholera, which raced in 1832 from the Atlantic seaboard to the Great Lakes in less than a month.

On July 4, 1828, the last surviving signer of the Declaration of Independence, Maryland's 91-year old Charles Carroll, flipped over a spadeful of sod to launch the Baltimore & Ohio, the nation's first railroad, boasting that the new technology would "perpetuate the union of the American

> **By 1840, railroad mileage had matched the total length of the nation's canals and would double that distance during the next decade.**

states." As Baltimore merchants reached for the Ohio River, Boston's tracks headed to the Erie Canal and Charleston's extended toward the cotton belt. By 1840, railroad mileage had matched the total length of the nation's canals and would double that distance during the next decade. Other advances in agricultural technology—Cyrus McCormick's reaper (1831), the wheat thresher (1836), and John Deere's plow (1837)—enabled farmers to increase production by intensifying cultivation and by opening the thick-grassed prairie lands of Illinois. On the shores of Lake Michigan, the new city of Chicago spearheaded a vast commercial revolution.

Such growth doomed the Native American presence east of the Mississippi. Although Creeks, Cherokees, and Choctaws continued to wage legal battle to save their lands (see Chapter 11), the last resistance in the old Northwest territory flared in 1832 when a large group of Sauk crossed the Mississippi into Illinois "to make corn" on their traditional lands. "Land cannot be sold," said their leader, Black Hawk, in a comment about market values. "Nothing can be sold but such things as can be carried away." Black Hawk's violation of old treaties brought out the state militia, including the young Captain Abraham Lincoln. The future president saw little fighting and played no personal role in what was to follow: the 15-week Black Hawk war ended with the slaying of 500 Sauk, the capture of the chief, and the forced surrender of Sauk claims in Iowa. "Farewell, my nation!" cried the defeated warrior. Black Hawk's "sun is setting, and he will rise no more."

Transforming Northern Working Conditions

The expansion of western farming, together with the transportation boom, had immense consequences for the northern economy. First, more fertile western farms in the old Northwest territory resulted in greater competition for the older, less profitable farms of the Northeast; second, the total agricultural surplus provided food for the growing numbers in the nation's towns and cities. In the rural Northeast, population pressure had already encouraged a trend toward nonagricultural work, such as the home production of textiles. After the introduction of machine spinning, factories produced cotton yarn, which was then "put out" to farm women, who wove the yarn into cloth. Middlemen delivered the raw materials to farm families and collected the finished work. By 1830, however, the introduction of power looms had ended this type of textile outwork.

The Rise of Factories

Northeastern farm families had become increasingly dependent on some nonagricultural income to preserve their economic independence. Many rural women (and, to a lesser extent, men) shifted to small-scale forms of home production, such as the hand-braiding of split palm leaves into straw hats and the binding of shoes, for trade or sale. Such tasks were integrated into the domestic economy of small farms. Since agriculture remained a major source of income, rural women performed home manufacturing in the time available after finishing their other chores. This work primarily occupied unmarried daughters, who contributed their earnings to the family economy. Home manufacturing also proved a means of subsistence for widows. Instead of receiving cash wages, domestic workers usually exchanged the finished products for goods at local stores, which served as distributors of the raw materials. By 1837, home production of straw hats in Massachusetts employed over 50,000 women and children, reaching an annual value of nearly $2 million.

Although domestic outwork persisted through the century, the centralization of textile manufacturing drastically altered the nature of industrial work. During the 18th century, English manufacturers had successfully introduced mechanized factories and had maintained a monopoly of textile machinery by forbidding its export. In 1789, however, Samuel Slater, an English mechanic, memorized the complicated plans and migrated to Rhode Island. Backed by the wealthy merchant Moses Brown, Slater reconstructed the English plans and launched the first American spinning mill in 1790. New England soon became a textile center. Its many rivers provided water power, commercial profits created investment capital, and declining agricultural incomes tempted workers to leave the farms. To keep down labor costs, early factories employed entire families, including their children. Rather than receiving regular wages, factory families obtained housing, credit in company stores, and payment of any remaining balance at the end of a contracted period. These early mills produced only yarn. Through the putting out system, whereby weavers who worked at home turned the yarn into finished cloth, the factories remained integrated with the rural economy.

Trade restrictions imposed during the War of 1812 inspired a radically new approach to factory production. Francis Cabot Lowell, heir to one of the country's commercial fortunes, organized a group of investors called the Boston Associates and in 1814 established a textile factory at Waltham, Massachusetts, which combined the entire manufacturing process into a single operation. Instead of simply spinning yarn for home production, the Waltham system produced finished cloth for cheap

Mill workers, Lowell, Massachusetts, ca. 1820. "Consider the girls in a factory," suggested Henry David Thoreau in *Walden,* his classic critique of material values, "never alone, hardly in their dreams."

mass consumption. The sheer size of the factory's capital and output enabled the manufacturers to purchase raw cotton at reduced prices, while extending credit to wholesale consumers. The economic result was amazing. In the first eight years, annual sales climbed from $3,000 to over $300,000. During the 1820s, the Boston Associates opened larger plants at Lowell, Massachusetts, turning that rural village into the nation's textile center, employing over 6,000 workers by 1836.

The Mill Workers of Lowell

The most innovative feature at Lowell was the recruitment of a female labor force. Reversing the pattern of outwork production, textile factories advertised for workers among New England's "active and healthy" farm girls and invited them to move to town. Unmarried young women, aged between their late teens and early 20s, eagerly took the well-paying jobs and relieved their families of their expenses. This out-of-house employment of young women threatened traditional family oversight, but the mill owners tried to protect the workers' moral environment by placing them in well-supervised boarding houses. Yet

Factories advertised for workers among New England's "active and healthy" farm girls and invited them to move to town.

working conditions were quite different from rural life. Regulated by factory time clocks, the mill girls labored 75 hours per week at fast-paced tasks. Their pay, based on the output of the machines they tended, averaged between 40 and 80 cents a day (equivalent to $9 today), about half the income of male workers. Unlike later industrial workers, the Lowell women saw themselves as temporary laborers, and indeed the average span of mill work was less than three years. Most married at a rate comparable to non–mill workers, though at a slightly older age.

Mill work offered new opportunities for female independence. The women's wages were their own, sometimes sent home to augment family incomes, but more often spent on books, clothing, and entertainment, or saved for their subsequent marriages. Amidst a community of single women,

Lowell workers shared social activities, attended popular lectures, went to church, talked, read, and wrote poetry and stories for the magazine *Lowell Offering*. The contrast with the rural lifestyle they left behind appeared in a letter from a young girl in Vermont to her sibling at Lowell: "I dreamed the other night that you. . . brought twenty-five hundred dollars home with you. I thought if that was the case I should go to Lowell."

The fantasy of easy money contrasted with the realities of the factory regimen. The novelty of the work, the repetitive pace, the noisy machinery— "like frogs and jewsharps all mixed together," said one Lowell worker—contributed to a physical and mental exhaustion that the women called "mill fever." Twice during the 1830s mill workers took collective action when their managers increased the workload, ordered wage cuts, and raised boarding fees in the company dormitories. Identifying themselves as "daughters of freemen still" (that is, not permanently part of an industrial working class), 800 mill women defiantly organized a strike in 1834 to protest "the oppressing hand of avarice."

The first mill strike lasted but a few days, weakened by lack of cohesion. A second walkout two years later seriously cut textile production. That strike ended when management evicted the women from their rooms. During the 1830s, other factory disputes, some involving child workers, erupted around the country, winning small concessions. But a severe economic depression in 1837 caused widespread mill closings and broke the union movement. During the next decade, male immigrant workers, desperate for jobs and willing to work for lower wages, would displace Yankee farm women from the mills and form a permanent industrial labor force.

Urban Day Laborers

The emergence of factory work in New England coincided with dramatic and enduring changes in the skilled crafts, such as tailoring, carpentry, and shoemaking. Independent artisans, who did not compete directly with factories, could still make good livings by producing custom-made clothes or furniture for affluent consumers. Such master craftsmen retained a public identity based on their occupational skills. In the frequent public parades that marked urban life, for example, skilled craftsmen (never women) clustered together and carried banners that proclaimed their unique contributions to society. Nevertheless, the increase of mass produced goods intensified competition within most trades and reduced opportunities for younger skilled workers.

As artisans tried to reduce their production costs, the system of apprenticed labor, which had centered in the households of master craftsmen, became fragmented. Instead of teaching young boys (or, less frequently, girls) the skills of a trade, artisans divided the work into separate parts and then hired piece workers to perform portions of the job. This division of labor speeded production and reduced the cost of training a skilled craftsman. Piece workers no longer lived within the masters' households, but resided in rented rooms where they performed their tasks.

The physical separation of master craftsmen from day workers paralleled a similar splitting of their economic interests. Instead of the traditional protections that apprenticeships assured young workers, the free marketplace offered no guarantee of food, clothing, shelter, or even tutelage in a skilled trade. Although day laborers benefited indirectly from mass production by being able to purchase cheaper consumer goods, their own incomes remained precarious and tended to decline. Competing against other workshops, master artisans strove to keep wages low, and real earnings dropped substantially during the 1830s. Women workers, who were paid at one-third to one-half the rate of men, sank toward desperation; for seven days labor from before sunrise to after sunset,

Half the children brought to New York's charitable House of Refuge were committed by parents who could not support them.

women shoe binders might earn only 50 cents (about $8 in today's money). Working families could survive only by putting their children to work, scavenging in the streets (a common juvenile crime, often prosecuted), crowding into cheap tenement apartments (the first multifamily dwelling was erected in New York in 1833), and cutting expenditures for necessities. Half the children brought to New York's charitable House of Refuge were committed by parents who could not support them.

Lowest on the urban economic ladder were the free African Americans, who were disproportionately female. Although black women had opportunities for domestic work, black men were often excluded from good jobs. Undisguised racial discrimination permitted northern municipal officials to refuse business licenses to aspiring blacks, while the skilled trades routinely rejected African American apprentices. Social segregation was common—in churches, streetcars, and cemeteries. Because black women outnumbered black men in the cities, there were fewer opportunities for blacks to marry and to have children. Despite their small numbers, northern blacks were politically active, staging public celebrations of northern emancipation, supporting the movement to abolish slavery, and expressing opposition for African colonization. Yet when New York blacks organized a referendum in 1837 to eliminate property qualifications for African American voters, the predominantly white electorate defeated the measure by a margin of 2.6 to 1.

Race prejudice also prompted the appearance of minstrel shows, the most popular form of public entertainment in 19th-century cities. Although theater owners usually required black spectators to sit in the segregated upper galleries, white audiences howled at the antics of white performers who blackened their faces with charcoal and presented musical comedies based on racial and sexual stereotypes. In 1832, a white actor named Thomas D. Rice captivated New York City audiences with the ridiculous dance steps of "Jim Crow," setting off a fad that dominated popular entertainment for decades. Using exaggerated physical gestures and contorted jumps, singing crudely in African American dialects, and brazenly depicting taboo topics of sexual promiscuity and cross dressing, white performers parodied the misunderstandings of a supposedly inferior people with names like Sambo, Zeke, and Zip Coon.

> I tell you what will happin den, now bery soon
> De Nited States Bank will be blone to de moon
> Dare General Jackson, will him lampoon,
> An de bery nex President will be Zip Coon.

Such song-and-dance routines allowed even the poorest whites to enjoy a sense of social superiority.

Early Trade Unions

Economic inequities encouraged white urban workers to form trade unions to protect their jobs. As early as the 1820s, labor unions, including a few women's trade organizations, went on strike in the larger cities to protest wage cuts and to demand a 10-hour workday. Such agitation was risky, not only because of the possible loss of jobs but also because the courts often held strikes to be criminal conspiracies.

Some middle-class reformers, who saw the emerging wage system as a threat to a republican society of equals, supported union demands. Workingmen's political parties appeared in Philadelphia and New York, appealing not only for economic benefits but also for free public education, abolition of imprisonment for debt, and lien laws to protect workers from employer bankruptcy. Headlining the crusade was the free-thinking socialist, Frances Wright, who electrified audiences by rejecting traditional female roles (she dared to lecture in public!) and condemned the inequalities of wealth and opportunity.

Such protests captured public attention, but brought few tangible reforms (though debt and lien laws were changed). During the 1830s, urban strikers successfully defended the 10-hour day, formed city labor councils, and established the National Trades Union. But, as in Lowell, the crushing depression of 1837 silenced the movement. Not until 1842 did a judicial decision in Massachusetts give labor unions legal standing and the right to strike.

Redefining the Middle Classes

The extremes of wealth and poverty that existed in the 1830s reflected a tightening of economic stratification, the increasing difficulty of achieving upward social mobility. Even the members of the middle classes—skilled workers, small merchants, and the emerging professions—felt the strains of economic change. As enterprising northern merchants and artisans became more involved in market activity, businesses tried to maximize profits and reduce economic uncertainty. In northern towns and cities, even in country stores, fixed retail prices replaced bargaining between buyer and seller. Hard cash, not country produce, became the preferred medium of exchange. As long-term credit arrangements between merchants and customers appeared undesirable, the first credit clearinghouse opened in New York City in 1841. Initially offering information about a borrower's personal "character," credit ratings

soon shifted to an assessment of a client's assets and wealth. Yet, most businessmen agreed that self-discipline was the surest way to protect one's access to credit: establish sober rational practices; adhere to firm rules; avoid needless risk.

The Changing Household

The decline of the apprentice system of labor also changed the structure of the middle-class household. With new business operations expanding the range of occupations to include clerks, managers, and professionals, middle-class men now departed their place of residence to work in shops. Even lawyers who kept offices at home established business hours to distinguish their private lives from their professions. Thus, the middle-class household lost its economic cohesion. Meanwhile, the lack of supervision of young workers underscored the separation of "home" and "work." Living in boardinghouses and residential hotels, young workers formed distinct communities and participated in a lively public youth culture, which involved "walking out" with members of the opposite sex, attending the risqué theater (where prostitution thrived on the third balcony), and consuming alcohol at the omnipresent taverns.

The mass production of clothing, shoes, and household goods also encouraged middle-class women to give up home manufacturing. Instead, they concentrated on unpaid domestic tasks and purchased more household goods. A large number of advice books now told them that it was their duty to make their homes shelters from the cold and heartless world of business. As the business household, which had once been filled with nonkin members, became a private home, family relations also changed. In the past, abundant farmlands had encouraged large families, but the growth of urban society, with crowded housing and greater economic uncertainty, brought a steadily declining birthrate, which fell below five children per family by mid-century.

The Cult of Domestic Purity

The separation of middle-class women from the world of business encouraged a new emphasis on domestic purity. "In America," observed the New England essayist Ralph Waldo Emerson, "out-of-doors all seems a market, in-doors an air-tight stove of conventionalism. Everybody who comes into the house savors of these precious habits: the men, of the market; the women of the custom." Middle-class writers described virtuous women as sexless creatures: "Ever timid," in the words of one male writer, "doubtful and clingingly dependent, a perpetual childhood." Such mothers emerged as the primary parents, dedicated to imparting lessons of morality to their children and preserving their homes as spiritual centers for their "worldly" husbands. "The success of democratic institutions," asserted Catharine Beecher, author of *A Treatise on Domestic Economy* (1841), "depends upon. . . the moral and intellectual character of the young, [which] is committed mainly to the female hand." Borrowing from the male work ethic, such reformers urged housewives to inculcate principles of efficiency, punctuality, and cleanliness into the household routine.

Colonial parents had opposed birthday celebrations as signs of "worldliness" (too much concern with human affairs instead of God's) but 19th-century mothers marked their children's birthdays as spiritual occasions, days of prayer, even fasting, to encourage the youngsters' religious development. The editors of *Mother's Monthly Journal* reported the result: "Well, Ma, if you will go down and take something to eat," exclaimed a 3-year old in 1838, "I will henceforth be a good girl!" Such precocious piety reinforced the evangelical Christian values that obliged adults to create a moral atmosphere in which virtue could flourish.

Middle-class families also expressed new attitudes toward sexuality. Although newspapers advertised various birth control products, including abortion remedies, couples increasingly practiced abstinence. One sign of this change was the decline of illegitimacy rates—the premarital pregnancies that in the late 18th century had led to marriage—which fell from about 33 percent to 23 percent for first births. Advice manuals, written by doctors and clergymen, warned young men of the dangers of masturbation, while medical literature viewed women's sexuality as diseased. In the cities, religious moralists targeted prostitution as a major evil. Meanwhile, male physicians, armed with obstetrical forceps and speculums, displaced midwives at middle-class births.

This emphasis on middle-class female purity encouraged more women, such as Catherine Beecher herself, to remain unmarried. Despite the negative connotations of "spinsterhood," over 7 percent of all American women (double that number in urbanized Massachusetts) opted not to wed. "A single lady, though advanced in life," rhymed one writer in 1817, "Is much more happy than an ill-match'd wife." Single women in the cities were usually among the poorest, but rising numbers of middle-class women found fulfillment (and low pay) as teachers, missionaries, social reformers, even pioneers in the professions. Among these was the educator Mary Lyon, who in 1837 founded Mt. Holyoke, the nation's first women's college. Another was Dorothea Dix, whose work as a Sunday school teacher exposed her to the poor treatment of insane people. Taking up their cause, Dix became an advocate for institutional reform, prompting the establishment of public asylums in several states.

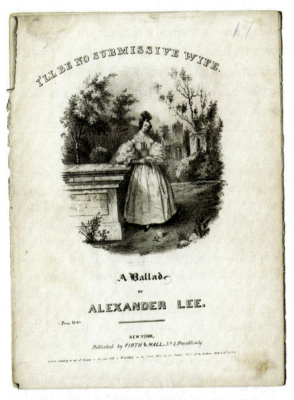

Cover of the popular song "I'll Be No Submissive Wife," which proclaimed, "Think you on a wedding day / That I said as others say / Love and honor and obey / . . . no no no not I. . . ."

Belief in a Perfectible Society

As the economy altered business relations and middle-class households, the prevailing religious values supported a secular creed of individualism, opportunity, and equality. By the beginning of the 19th century, the major Protestant denominations had moved in two directions. The first was a "rational" type of Protestantism, associated with the growing influence of Unitarianism and the Episcopal church among educated and affluent families. This religion emphasized the reasonableness of a benevolent God, freely offering love and salvation to those who pursued a good life. Such views made salvation appear possible for all godly citizens.

The second type was more "emotional" and emerged within evangelical denominations, especially the Methodists and Baptists. This type stressed God's power as well as his mercy, promised the possibility of religious conversion for all people, and inspired religious revivals throughout the country. "God has made man a moral free agent," declared the foremost evangelical preacher of the 1820s and 1830s, the Presbyterian Charles Grandison Finney. Since God had opened his heart to all sinners, Finney told his swelling congregations, the burden shifted to the sinners: They all could be redeemed if they would listen to the call, recognize their sinfulness, and avow a spiritual rebirth. Appealing to the possibility of individual self-improvement, Finney led a crusade through Erie Canal country and then into the poorest neighborhoods of New York City. Placing what he called an "anxious bench" in front of his congregation, the revivalist exhorted the unconverted to sit, focus on their peril, and come to God. Such pleas ignited spiritual fires, bringing a surge in church membership.

Finney's religion struck specific chords. First among Finney's converts were middle-class wives and mothers. Many kept the religious fires burning for years by encouraging their children to experience a feeling of salvation. Many women became religious missionaries, carrying a spiritual message to neighbors and strangers alike, as well as to their husbands. With religious self-confidence, rising businessmen could better face the uncertainties of a market economy and find justifications for their economic activities. "Only make it your invariable principle to do right and do business upon principle," Finney assured them, "and you can control the market." The gospel of self-discipline, sobriety, and avoidance of luxury and debt dovetailed with values of economic efficiency, orderliness, and good character.

Religion and Moral Reform

Belief in individual responsibility and the possibility of human perfectibility stimulated a movement to eliminate the ills and evils of society. Inspired by a sense of religious mission, middle-class women and, increasingly, men formed voluntary societies to bring Christianity to heathens and sinners. Some ventured to the Native American peoples, offering Christian schools to uplift Cherokees, Creeks, and other groups interested in assimilation; some boldly carried the gospel overseas. More frequently, evangelicals focused on the unconverted in the cities and countryside.

In the decade after 1825, the American Tract Society, backed by donations from the nation's richest merchants, such as Arthur and Lewis Tappan, printed and distributed over 30 million religious pamphlets, almanacs, and books. (The feat testified to the new technologies of steam-powered printing presses.) In addition, religious missionaries paid visits to the urban poor—giving away Bibles, kneeling in prayer, and offering relief to orphans, widows, and prostitutes. True to the evangelical creed, material assistance to the poor depended upon the recipient's moral character. Although rich evangelicals established charitable institutions, such as New York's Asylum for Lying-In Women, only expectant mothers with documentary proof of marriage could expect entry. Such moral criteria, however redeeming for the missionaries, barely affected the misery of the urban poor.

Evangelical efforts to curtail business on the Sabbath, including attempts to ban mail delivery on Sunday, failed to gain wide support. The single Erie Canal service that stood idle on the Sabbath

Workers commonly drank on the job; merchants conducted business over brimming glasses; working-class housewives interrupted their labors for a taste.

soon went out of business, and the proposed postal ban conflicted with the separation of church and state. But the marriage of business and moral reform did succeed in limiting the nation's thirst for alcohol. With whiskey prices as low as 25 cents (less than today's $5) per gallon, consumption of alcohol had soared. Workers commonly drank on the job; merchants conducted business over brimming glasses; working-class housewives interrupted their labors for a taste. In 1832, one New York worker beat his wife to death "because," he explained, "she was drunk & no signs of dinner." By 1835, ten years after the Erie Canal opened, 1,500 grog shops lined the right of way. Middle-class businessmen realized that drunkenness conflicted with rational business practices as well as evangelical morality. By 1830, a temperance crusade was trying to reform the nation's alcohol habits. As merchants and artisans banned alcohol from the workplace, religious groups launched local campaigns against Sunday tippling.

Most workers, accustomed to less disciplined labor habits, resisted efforts to impose sobriety, and voters usually rejected laws to prohibit alcoholic consumption. After the depression of 1837, however, workers responded to a campaign for voluntary abstinence and joined Washington Temperance societies, which mushroomed around the country. Women advocates formed Martha Washington societies. By the middle of the next decade, many members suffered relapses and the move-

The DRUNKARD'S PROGRESS,

OR THE DIRECT ROAD TO POVERTY, WRETCHEDNESS & RUIN.

The MORNING DRAM.

The CONFIRMED DRUNKARD.

CONCLUDING SCENE.

A temperance broadside expresses the viewpoint of a growing number of Americans in the 1820s.

ment disappeared. With this failure of voluntarism, reformers began to push for mandatory prohibition. Maine passed a prohibition law in 1846, and it was adopted by twelve states during the next decade. More impressive than legislation was the real decline in drinking. Where average annual alcohol consumption exceeded 7 gallons per adult in 1830, the quantity dropped to half in 1840 and half again by 1845.

The wide participation of middle-class evangelical women in moral campaigns expressed the limited range of female public life. Although it contradicted the domestic ideal that virtuous women should be sheltered from social vices, the missionary impulse enabled women reformers to assume public roles. Thus New York's Female Moral Reform Society, founded by evangelicals in 1833, sought not only to "rescue" prostitutes but also to shame their customers. Similarly, a few exceptional women (the African American Maria Stewart, for example, and the sisters Sarah and Angelina Grimké) rejected traditional roles to protest against slavery. These departures from so-

cial convention brought widespread criticism, which in turn contributed to a movement to improve women's rights in the next decade.

Reforming the Schools

Concern about public morality and business efficiency also inspired movements to create public schools for poor children. In 1825, New York City's business leaders persuaded the state to provide funds for eleven schools so "the indigent may be excited to emulate the cleanliness, decorum and mental improvement of those in better circumstances." Workers may have rejected such class snobbery, but they shared the belief that education offered an opportunity for social mobility. Most northern and western states now created public primary schools (only New England developed extensive public secondary schools) and extended the length of the school term. Yet no state made school attendance mandatory, and the quality of education varied widely. In the cities, racial segregation excluded most African American pupils

Pages from *American Pictorial Primer,* ca. 1845.

from public schools, though private classes provided elementary lessons for middle-class families. Well-to-do white families sent their children to private academies.

The nation's most prominent educator, Horace Mann, appointed head of the Massachusetts Board of Education in 1837, well understood that the lessons of public education served primarily to instill middle-class values among working families. "If the vicious and ignorant get possession of the [political] apparatus," said Mann of the risks of democracy, "the intelligent and the virtuous must take such shocks as the stupid . . . may choose to administer." Seeking to mold the character of the younger generation, William McGuffey's popular textbooks, which sold 120 million copies, offered a curriculum in patriotism, pru-

dence, and punctuality. "The good boy whose parents are poor, rises very early in the morning; and, all day long, does as much as he can to help his father and mother," read a typical story. "When he sees little boys and girls riding . . . in coaches, or walking with ladies and gentlemen, and having on very fine clothes, he does not envy them, nor wish to be like them."

Undemocratic Movements

The widely held values of individualism, opportunity, and equality did not always translate into practice, however. Although evangelical citizens celebrated the principle of voluntary association and formed a variety of societies, organizations, and political parties, they opposed groups that seemed to threaten egalitarian principles. During the 1820s, the Order of Masons appeared as one target. This secret male fraternal organization had hundreds of lodges with tens of thousands of members, including Washington, Jackson, and Clay. In 1826, a scandal erupted when an ex-member who was about to reveal the order's secrets was kidnapped and murdered with the collusion of government officials in western New York. The incident, showing signs of a widespread conspiracy, aroused public suspicions and inspired a popular anti-Mason movement, which spilled into local and national party politics. But why was Masonry seen as a threat? "IT IS POWERFUL," boasted one Mason. "It comprises men of RANK, wealth, office and talent, in power and out of power." To nonmembers, such a secret network of collaborators, working for self-advancement rather than an egalitarian community, seemed unduly conspiratorial.

Numerous Protestant groups viewed the Roman Catholic church with the same suspicion. In 1830, 300,000 Americans, only 3 percent of the population, were Catholics. Dating from colonial days, anti-Catholic feelings bubbled at the surface, evoking Protestant tirades against Catholic hierarchy, superstition, and alleged moral offenses committed in the secrecy of convents. To Protestants, the Catholic church appeared not only as a false religion but also as a threat to republican government—a foreign power cloaked in priests' robes and nuns' habits. As Catholic immigration increased in the 1830s, workers also saw a threat to their jobs. Ethnic antagonism provoked violence, dramatized one night in 1834 when a Protestant mob in Charlestown, Massachusetts, burned down the Ursiline convent and school. Respectable Protestants denounced the crime, but the climate of anti-Catholicism endured, feeding political movements in the following decades as Catholic immigration continued to climb.

Equally vulnerable was the Church of Jesus Christ of Latter Day Saints, known as the Mormons. This group had been founded in upstate New York in 1830 by Joseph Smith, who claimed to have been led by an angel to the hiding place of the Book of Mormon, where he discovered a divine revelation. The Mormons predicted that the creation of God's kingdom on earth would begin in North America. Unlike other evangelical churches, which appealed first to women, the Mormons initially attracted male followers, many of whom, like the prophet Smith, had been displaced by the new market economy. The Mormons' patriarchal communalism, permitting plural marriages, brought prosperity to members but attracted the hostility of suspicious neighbors. Facing attacks, the Mormons moved to Ohio, then to Missouri, and then to Nauvoo, Illinois, where they built a flourishing town in 1839. Violence followed them, culminating in the murder of Smith by a mob and the uprooting of the church once more as the new leader, Brigham Young, led 12,000 Mormons to Utah in 1847.

The social isolation of the Mormon church mirrored the experiences of other perfectionist groups that deliberately organized ideal or utopian communities outside existing social institutions. Often inspired by religious leaders, these groups withdrew from society to implement their ideals immediately and demonstrate that social perfection was possible. One social experiment began at New Harmony, Indiana, in 1825 when the English industrialist Robert Owen founded a socialist community that rejected private property, organized religion, and traditional marriage. New Harmony attracted wide attention, but internal divisions doomed the effort. One of Owen's disciples, the feminist Frances Wright, formed another community at Noashoba, Tennessee, which permitted African Americans to work for their freedom. Wright's radicalism offended potential supporters and this effort also failed.

Another example of perfectionism appeared when one of Finney's converts, John Humphrey Noyes, established a community at Oneida, New York, in the 1840s. Replacing private property with communal ownership and exclusive marriage with a system of "complex" marriage that permitted more than one partner, the Oneida reformers built a flourishing, self-sustaining community in rural New York that survived for decades. Other utopias were spiritually motivated, including the Amana Society, or "Community of True Inspiration," established near Buffalo, New York, in 1843. These diverse projects seldom succeeded, but they testified to a passionate desire among evangelical Americans to live in harmony with "natural" or divine principles. Their perfectionist impulse reinforced the idealism of the national identity, the widely held belief that Americans were a morally superior people.

Party Politics and the Market Economy

"It is said to be the age of the first person singular," noted the philosopher Ralph Waldo Emerson in 1827. As the expanding economy encouraged individual initiative and evangelical Protestantism emphasized personal responsibility for salvation, so the new national political parties, Democrats and Whigs, appealed to newly enfranchised voters to take stands on issues of economic development. The resulting political choices often reflected a citizen's position in the market economy. Facing new commercial activities, some citizens saw their fortunes decline, or feared that they would, and recoiled from the changes. Others rode the crest of financial speculation into realms of unimagined wealth or more modest middle-class occupations. Many more found themselves between those extremes.

In a nutshell, those who anticipated bettering themselves by means of commercial development (internal improvements, for example) supported policies to encourage change and found themselves aligned with what would be called, first, the National Republican and, later, the Whig party of Henry Clay and Daniel Webster. By contrast, people who felt threatened by government involvement in the economy (the regulation of credit by a national bank, for example) opposed public support of economic programs and aligned with Andrew Jackson and the Democratic party. Where Democrats supported a free-market economy and believed that people "looked to the government for too much," Whigs favored economic stimulation by tariffs and canal-building and proclaimed that the people were "entitled to the protecting care of a paternal government." Although local issues might affect voter opinion, party alignments cut across all regions. By the 1830s, both Whigs and Democrats competed for votes as *national* parties.

The Jackson Presidency

The inauguration of Andrew Jackson in 1829 demonstrated the power of political majorities. Having campaigned against the "corrupt bargain" that had deprived him of election in 1824, the new president claimed to embody the common citizenry. Jackson promptly redefined the meaning of a political "party" by opening the White House to inauguration day celebrants, according to one conservative "the most vulgar and gross in the nation," who got drunk, wrecked furniture, smashed china, and so introduced "the reign of King Mob." This welcoming of common people expressed the president's belief that "the duties of all public offices are . . . so plain and simple" that anyone of normal intelligence could perform them. Jackson proceeded to reward his political supporters with the "spoils" of politics—government jobs. Martin Van Buren, architect of the national party, became secretary of state, a rival to the succession of Vice President John Calhoun. Jackson also installed an informal "kitchen cabinet" of friends and supporters to give him counsel.

Jackson's political allies, chosen because of their position on party issues, nonetheless revealed the continuing role of personality and "character" in arousing political controversy. Indeed, party politics had nothing to do with Jackson's most debated appointment, Secretary of War John Eaton. What disturbed many contemporaries, including Calhoun and members of the cabinet, was the rumor that Eaton and his wife Peggy had had an affair while Mrs. Eaton's first husband was still alive. During the presidential campaign, Jackson's own wife had been accused of adultery and, when she died shortly after the election, Jackson blamed the rumormongers. As some administration wives started a moral crusade against Peggy Eaton, ostracizing the secretary of war from social affairs, a furious Jackson launched a personal campaign to restore her reputation. The issue, in this evangelical age, hinged on "virtue." Compromise proved impossible. The Eaton affair served mainly to split members of the administration, leaving Van Buren on the presidential side and Calhoun as an outsider.

Jackson and the Bank War

Jackson's suspicion of special privileges led him to oppose government support of economic development. Although the president praised the nation's commercial progress—while visiting the factories at Lowell, he marveled at the intricate machinery—Democrats questioned whether business interests deserved special government support. When Congress agreed to fund a turnpike linking Maysville and Lexington, Kentucky, in 1830, Jackson objected that the project was too costly and served only local needs. Van Buren, who desired no competition for New York's Erie Canal, drafted a veto message that challenged the constitutionality of such federal expenditures. Where politicians like Adams and Clay advocated ambitious programs to boost the market economy, Democrats opposed government favors to special interests.

This opposition came to a head in a "war" against the second Bank of the United States. Chartered for twenty years in 1816, the bank served as a depository of government funds and used its power to lend money to regulate the credit policies of smaller banks. But the bank had contributed to the sudden contraction of credit that had caused the Panic of 1819, creating abiding hostility among small businessmen and commercial farmers in the South and West. Jackson shared their antipathy to this "privileged" private institution and the benefits it brought to a "few monied capitalists." Yet by using its control of government revenues to extend credit, the bank had won supporters by stimulating economic development.

Among the defenders of the bank was Henry Clay, proponent of economic growth, who had his eye on the presidency. In 1832, four years before the bank's charter was scheduled to expire, Clay decided to make the institution an election issue. Passage of a recharter bill would assure continuation of Clay's program of economic development; a presidential veto, Clay believed, would offend the public and catapult him into the White House. With such assumptions, Congress passed the recharter bill four months before election day in 1832.

"Many of our rich men have not been content with equal protection and equal benefits, but have besought us to make them richer by act of Congress," Jackson replied in a ringing veto message that defined the fundamental conflicts of the age. Recognizing the growing importance of commercial activity, the president acknowledged the inevitable inequities caused by "superior industry, economy, and virtue." But government support of a particular bank, he said, introduced artificial advantages, favoring some citizens at the expense of others. "When the laws undertake . . . to make the rich richer and the potent more powerful," Jackson declared, "the humble members of society—the farmers, mechanics, and laborers—who have neither the time nor the means of securing like favors for themselves, have a right to complain of the injustice." Government, he said, should act as naturally, and neutrally, as the heavenly rains: "Shower its favor alike on the high and the low, the rich and the poor." Then, having thrown this challenge before Clay and the Bank of the United States, Jackson proceeded to throttle his opponents in the 1832 presidential election.

Voter endorsement of the bank veto expressed the public's ambivalence about economic development, desire for individual betterment coexisting with a fear of banks, credit, fluctuating prices, and the impersonal national economy. "You must recollect that the debt is due to the Bank, not to an individual," a nervous Virginia merchant informed his wife, "and we cannot get indulgence by promising to pay it tomorrow or next week, but it must be paid on the day it is due, or our credit must be ruined." To Jacksonians, the government-supported bank was evil, an artificial "Monster," that threatened "natural" economic operations. The bank reinforced those suspicions after the election by calling in loans and contracting credit. Fearing that the bank would destroy prosperity to save itself, Jackson resolved to withdraw government deposits and place them in state banks. He had to fire two secretaries of the treasury before finding a cabinet

> **To Jacksonians, the government-supported bank was evil, an artificial "Monster."**

officer, Attorney General Roger B. Taney, willing to implement the scheme. This unprecedented presidential action brought condemnations of "King Andrew I"; Jackson's opponents proudly adopted the name of those who had criticized King George III and called themselves "Whigs."

The Panic of 1837

Ironically, by distributing government deposits to state banks, which the Whigs called "pet banks," Jackson did kill the national bank, but he also accelerated the economic trends that he opposed. Backed by government money, these state banks increased their loans, setting off an expansion of credit that encouraged investment and speculation. At the same time, unrelated changes in international markets (high British purchases of cotton, foreign investments in canals, importation of silver mined in Mexico) added to bank reserves, which in turn encouraged even more expansion of credit. The ensuing inflation had large repercussions. Rising cotton prices triggered a boom in land sales—38 million public acres were sold in 1836–37—while the inflation of food prices hit workers in the eastern cities, provoking numerous labor strikes for wage adjustments. Worried about inflationary land speculation, Jackson issued a Specie Circular in 1836, requiring that investors, but not actual settlers, pay for land with gold and silver coin, known as specie, rather than with paper money or with credit.

Jackson's financial policies—the removal of government deposits from the national bank, the promotion of pet banks, federal land sales—provided ammunition for a political war between Democrats and Whigs. But economic development reflected more complicated changes in international finance. As British bankers responded to falling cotton prices by reducing investments in the United States, American bankers called in their loans, reduced credit, and provoked a severe economic downturn, the Panic of 1837. Problems in the cotton trade perpetuated the crisis, which affected businesses, large and small, throughout the country. "Men could run away from the cholera," remarked a helpless businessman about the epidemic of failures, "but they can't run away from this distress."

Building a Competitive Society

Jackson's inability to control the economy testified to the intricacy of market relationships. Even the desire to end government support of special interests might serve cross purposes. Consider the legal implications of the Supreme Court's *Charles River Bridge* case of 1837. Although Massachusetts had granted a private company the right to build a toll bridge between Boston and Cambridge in 1785, the growth of trade and population led the state legislature to approve building another free bridge nearby, thus imperiling the profits of the first company. Two decades earlier, the Marshall Court had upheld the sanctity of contracts in the *Dartmouth College* case (see Chapter 8). But the Jacksonian Court, led by newly appointed Chief Justice Roger B. Taney, ruled that the original company constituted a privileged monopoly, just like the Bank of the United States, whose private interests remained secondary to the larger public benefit.

Reinforcing the ruling was a realization that government no longer had to grant special privileges to encourage capital investment. The decision also encouraged basic changes in legislative regulation of new businesses. Instead of requiring a special law to create each private corporation, the states increasingly enacted general incorporation laws, which established uniform business codes that permitted virtually unlimited incorporation. In this way, the Jacksonian attack on privilege encouraged the types of commercial institutions (that is, private corporations) that Democrats usually opposed.

As the Panic of 1837 crippled the economy, Whigs and Democrats clashed about other economic issues. Believing that the federal government should support economic development, Whigs like Clay and Webster advocated government-funded internal improvements, tariffs, and the chartering of a third Bank of the United States. By contrast, Democrats saw monster banks and artificial privileges destroying the virtuous republic and demanded that government allow economic development to proceed without granting special favors. Yet neither party doubted that market values, for better or worse, pervaded society. "The question," explained an Indiana Democrat in 1838, "is not. . . whether the numerous family of banks should exist, but only whether government, out of that family, shall select one as a bride." One way or the other, business had become a crucial ingredient in the national identity.

The spread of commercial values highlighted differences of regional perspective. Although Democrats and Whigs won support in all sections of the country (both Tennessee's Jackson and Kentucky's Clay claimed to speak for the nation) business investment accentuated conflicts between the free-labor northern economy and the slave labor southern economy. If, for example, nonperishable southern cotton needed no haste to get to market, should southern politicians support federally funded roads and canals? If, for another example, western settlement depopulated the

Northeast and raised labor costs, should northeastern politicians approve cheap western lands? If, for a third example, northern manufacturers needed tariffs to compete with British imports, should westerners pay more for the clothes they wore? During the 1830s, leading politicians debated these issues of regional self-interest and economic development.

Equally divisive was the issue of slavery. As citizens in all regions confronted impersonal market values, the treatment of human beings as labor commodities—as units of production to be bought and sold—raised moral issues about the country's claim to be a government of "the people." Yet, southerners vigorously denied that slaves existed only as economic entities, insisting that patriarchal owners looked after "their people." Such arguments, discussed often on the floors of Congress, set the stage for a growing debate about the South's "peculiar institution."

INFOTRAC® COLLEGE EDITION EXERCISES

For additional reading go to InfoTrac College Edition, your online research library at *http://web1.infotrac-college.com*.

Subject search: United States economic history, reference

Keyword search: Erie Canal

Keyword search: Lowell mills

Keyword search: Horace Mann

Keyword search: Andrew Jackson

Keyword search: bank war

ADDITIONAL READING

The Expanding Market Economy

Christopher Clark, *The Roots of Rural Capitalism: Western Massachusetts, 1780–1860* (1990). Describes a subtle transformation of economic behavior among farmers increasingly drawn into marketplace relations.

Charles Sellers, *The Market Revolution: Jacksonian America, 1815–1846* (1991). This survey examines economic issues, cultural values, and political conflict.

Susan Sessions Rugh, *Our Common Country: Family Farming, Culture, and Community in the Nineteenth-Century Midwest* (2001). Focusing on a single Illinois county, this study describes the impact of market values on the community.

Transforming Northern Working Conditions

Paul E. Johnson, *A Shopkeeper's Millenium: Society and Revivals in Rochester, New York, 1815–1837* (1978). Examining a single community, the book examines economic growth, religious values, and community life.

Sean Wilentz, *Chants Democratic: New York City and the Rise of the American Working Class, 1788–1850* (1984). Focusing on skilled workers, the author describes the changing nature of work and its economic consequences.

James Oliver Horton and Lois E. Horton, *In Hope of Liberty: Culture, Community, and Protest among Northern Free Blacks, 1700–1860* (1997). A thorough discussion of African American life in the North.

The Mill Workers of Lowell

Thomas Dublin, *Transforming Women's Work: New England Lives in the Industrial Revolution* (1994). Moving beyond his pioneering book, *Women at Work: The Transformation of Work and Community in Lowell, Massachusetts, 1826–1860* (1979), the author offers case studies of women's work in the 19th century.

Christine Stansell, *City of Women: Sex and Class in New York, 1789–1860* (1986). A study of the lives of working women, this book depicts the difficulties of urban life amidst rapid economic change.

Redefining the Middle Classes

Mary P. Ryan, *Cradle of the Middle Class: The Family in Oneida County, New York, 1790–1865* (1981). This book analyzes the connections of gender roles, religious awakening, and economic change. See also

Catherine E. Kelly, *In the New England Fashion: Reshaping Women's Lives in the Nineteenth Century* (1999).

The Cult of Domestic Purity

Lee Virginia Chambers-Schiller, *Liberty, A Better Husband: Single Women in America, the Generations of 1780–1840* (1984). Whereas Ryan's study (above) explores the changing situation of married women, this book depicts the lives of women, mostly middle-class, who did not marry.

Amy Gilman Srebnick, *The Mysterious Death of Mary Rogers: Sex and Culture in Nineteenth-Century New York* (1995). Focusing on a celebrated murder of 1840, the author explores the changing nature of urban life.

Party Politics and the Market Economy

Harry L. Watson, *Liberty and Power: The Politics of Jacksonian America* (1990). A lucid explanation of the assumptions and interests that motivated political alliances of the period.

11

THE NEW WORLD.

PARK BENJAMIN,
EDITOR.

J. WINCHESTER,
PUBLISHER.

"No pent-up Utica contracts our powers; For the whole boundless Continent is ours."

QUARTO EDITION.   OFFICE 30 ANN-STREET. $3 PER ANNUM.

VOLUME IV......No. 8.   NEW-YORK, SATURDAY, FEBRUARY 19, 1842.   WHOLE NUMBER 90.

ISLAND AND RUIN ON LOCH LOMOND.
With Ben Lomond in the Distance.

For the New World.

Oh! loveliest spot beneath the sun
    You never looked so bright before!
We left the lake's romantic side,
    And treading high yon mountain way,
Looked o'er the hills and waters wide,
    And vallies fair that round us lay;
And now we spread our wingèd sail
Free to the glad and bounding gale,
And wake from out their sunny sleep
The ripples of that tranquil deep.
And now an isle of verdant hue
Stands forth amid the waters blue,
A favored spot—where every tree
That Scotland boasts the eye may see,
And every tender flower doth blow
That Lomond's dells and forests know,
And here a gentle refuge find
From withering sun and blighting wind.
Lovely thou art, yet not alone,
Sweet isle, for beauty of thine own,
My earnest eye would fondly stray
To thy wild shore and rocky bay,
Where, through the mist of rolling years
To fancy's dreaming gaze appears,
Seated beneath the aspen bough,
A friendly band long severed now,
And hearts from friendship long estranged
Are smiling there in eyes unchanged:
'Tis gone——but I awake to greet
An hour than all the rest more sweet,
Whose perfect joy forbids a sigh
For future time or days gone by.

With him for whom she scarce could grieve,

And dies in cadence sweet and low,
And the wild birds, in joyous crowd,
Soar upward to the summer cloud,
And warble forth their thrilling lays
To join the universal praise.

VIII.

We leave the hallowed spot behind,
And on before the dancing wind
Joyously sweep, till high appear
Their lofty peaks uplifting near
Yon mountains dark, whose craggy height
Makes barrier for those waters bright.
But ere we turn our sail once more,
And sadly leave this lonely shore,
Rest in our course, and pause awhile
Beside the lady Ellen's isle.
With turret rent and roofless hall
A castle rears its crumbling wall,
Where the wild rose its blossoms pale
Hangs forth to meet the summer gale,
And in the rough and moss-grown floor,
Where human step resounds no more,
Fit tenant of such dreary ground,
The darksome yew hath refuge found.
In vain ye list to hear the swell
Of martial pipe or matin bell—
In vain, at twilight's haunted hour,
Soft notes to list from lady's bower—
The wind that sweeps these chambers gray
But tells of death and dark decay,
And glory passed in dust away.

IX.

Slavery and the Southern Economy, 1828–1844

CHRONOLOGY

"Suppose," asked the white southern Reverend Charles C. Jones in his published catechism, "the Master is hard to please, and threatens and punishes more than he ought, what is the Slave to do? Answer: Do his best to please him."

"Is it right for the Slave to run away . . . ?" he further inquired. "Answer: No." Indeed, another white southern minister warned that resistance to slavery was a sin: "It is the devil who tells you to try and be free."

Such Christian ministers articulated the core values of a southern regional identity, taking pains to explain to African American slaves why servants should obey their masters. As they interpreted the Bible, God had commanded servants to be obedient, to accept lowly stations in this world, and to conduct themselves with patience and humility so that they would receive a just reward in heaven. In the eyes of most white southerners, blacks could never participate as equals in this world or share a place in the national identity.

Biblical justifications for slavery may have eased the consciences of Christian slaveowners, but slaves responded with less enthusiasm to the doctrine of submission. Although the circumstances of slavery diminished opportunities for resistance, enslaved African Americans were slow to embrace religious tenets that demanded complete obedience to their masters. To avoid punishment, however, slaves usually told their masters what they thought their masters wanted to hear.

This desire to say what was expected adds irony to a conversation between a Methodist minister and a slave in Alabama:

Question: What did God make you for?
Answer: To make a crop.

This simple dialogue between slaveowner and slave underscored the essence of the South's "peculiar institution." Slavery existed "to make a crop"—that is, it existed to make money. And that material objective showed just how much the slave South resembled the rest of the country.

By the 19th century, the growth of commercial enterprise had crossed all geographic boundaries, even penetrating southern regions that claimed to despise northern material values. Southern leaders often said that agriculture was more natural than commerce and industry, and they saw themselves as rural patriarchs rather than as businessmen. But, while northern investors built steam-powered textile mills and interstate banking systems, dug canals and laid railroads, the South invested primarily in cotton, the essential raw material that fueled the nation's economic development. Although scarcely 10 percent of the country's manufacturing occurred in southern states, and southern production depended on northern credit, insurance, and shipping, the export of cotton kept European capital flowing into the United States. By mid-century, cotton production approached 3 million bales (1.5 billion pounds) per year and constituted nearly two-thirds of the nation's exports. "We could bring the whole world to our feet," asserted a southern senator. "Cotton is King."

With such economic power, cotton planters could deplore factories and big cities and yet remain committed to economic growth and business efficiency. "Time's money, time's money," cried an Alabama cotton planter, worrying about his farm's productivity. During the 1830s, agricultural reformers advised southern planters to increase productivity by "scientific" management of their farms.

Using improved agricultural technology and fertilizers, southern planters also aimed to enhance the productivity of their slave laborers. Imitating northern textile manufacturers who used clock-time instead of sun-to-sun to regulate the work hours of factory employees, southern cotton planters timed bells and bugles to their household clocks or carried watches into the fields to regulate the labor of their slaves. Lists of southern household items showed a correlation between a planter's wealth and the ownership of accurate timepieces.

What distinguished the southern economy was not so much the supremacy of cotton (southern farmers actually planted more acres of corn than cotton) as the investment of profits to acquire more land and more slaves. As one observer reported, the logic of southern agriculture was perfectly circular: "To sell cotton in order to buy negroes—to make more cotton to buy more negroes." Yet, the high price of slaves meant that the majority of white southerners could not afford to purchase even a single human being. Wealth and property were thus intertwined with cotton production and slave ownership. As the wealthiest citizens, moreover, slaveowners emerged as political leaders. Whigs and Democrats alike supported slavery; both the Democratic Andrew Jackson and the Whig Henry Clay owned slaves.

Slave ownership not only distinguished rich and prominent whites from the poorer groups but also created a unique regional society. Although southerners, no less than northerners, aggressively pursued economic gain (while citizens of both regions expressed prejudiced views of African Americans), the difference between free labor and slave labor established rigid social divisions that limited economic mobility to whites. Every white citizen, no matter how poor, stupid, or immoral, could claim to belong to a superior social group. Such attitudes helped tie the interests of nonslaveholders to the slaveowning elite.

Expanding Cotton Society

Successful cotton cultivation required three factors: fertile land, green seeds that produced the favored short-fiber variety, and a frost-free environment for at least 200 days after planting. Material success also demanded a willingness to pull up stakes and head west. Such requirements stimulated the expansion of cotton agriculture onto the Gulf plains and into territories west of the Mississippi River. But westward migration confronted an unmoving legal obstacle. For centuries, the Creeks, Cherokees, Choctaws, and Chickasaws had claimed lands now coveted by cotton planters. Indeed, leaders of these groups had even imitated southern whites by acquiring black slaves.

During the 1820s, southern farmers, speculators, and politicians had pressured the Native people to surrender their land in exchange for western acreage (see Chapter 10). By 1830, President Andrew Jackson decided to expedite the removal of these so-called civilized tribes from the southern states. Disregarding previous treaties and ample evidence of Creek and Cherokee assimilation, the president viewed "savage" peoples as doomed to extinction unless they migrated beyond the reach of Anglo American civilization. Despite the protests of northern evangelical missionaries, who had converted many Native Americans to the Protestant religion, Congress passed the Removal Act of 1830, which provided permanent reservation lands west of the Mississippi. "If they now refuse to accept the liberal terms offered they can only be liable for whatever evils and difficulties may arise," said the paternalistic Jackson. "I feel conscious of having done my duty to my red children."

Forced Removal of Native Americans

The federal government proceeded to coerce Native American leaders (some of whom were only

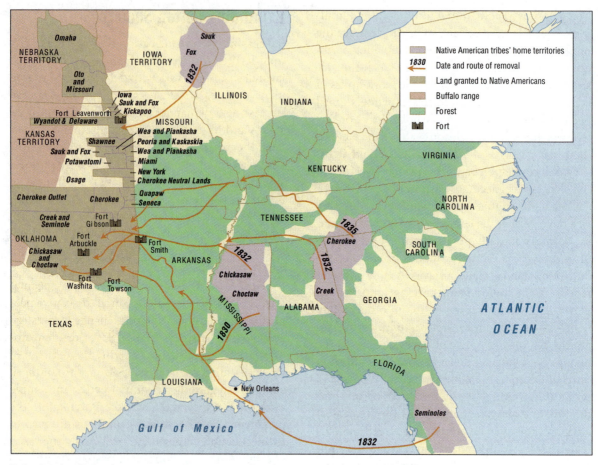

Native American Removals

self-appointed chiefs) to sign nearly seventy removal treaties. In 1831, Mississippi's Choctaws led the exodus to what is now Oklahoma. Inadequate food, clothing, and medicine brought immense suffering and high mortality en route, and when the Choctaws reached their destination, Jackson's promise of self-rule evaporated when federal officials refused to surrender supervision of tribal affairs. Meanwhile, the 7,000 Choctaws who had opted to remain on their lands in Mississippi fell victim to hostile squatters, fraudulent traders, and indifferent officials, who took advantage of local laws that forbade Native Americans

to testify against whites in court. A few half-bloods managed to hold onto their lands and even acquired slaves, but most Choctaws became landless agricultural workers who were treated no better than nearby African Americans.

In Georgia, efforts of the state government to establish sovereignty over Cherokee lands led to a legal battle that reached the U.S. Supreme Court. When a group of evangelical missionaries was arrested for violating a Georgia law that required whites living on Cherokee land to take an oath of allegiance to the state government, the pro-Cherokee defendants argued that federal

Suffering on the "Trail of Tears." Removed in a forced march to Oklahoma, one-quarter of the Cherokees lost their lives.

treaties superseded the state law. In 1832, John Marshall's Supreme Court agreed in *Worcester v. Georgia* that the Cherokees constituted a "domestic dependent" nation entitled to federal protection from Georgia jurisdiction. This statement of federal superiority should have won applause from Jackson, an avowed nationalist. But the president believed that no defeated Native American nation could claim sovereignty, and he ignored the Court's ruling. A treaty signed with a minority of Cherokees called for the departure of the entire tribe in 1838. "Doubtless it will be painful to leave the graves of their fathers," Jackson admitted. "But what do they [do] more than our ancestors did or than our children are now doing?. . . . Is it supposed that the wandering savage has a stronger attachment to his home than the settled, civilized Christian?" Despite Cherokee protests, Jackson's successor President Martin Van Buren, enforced the disputed removal treaty, ordering the military to compel the remaining Cherokees to leave their homes. The ensuing "Trail of Tears," a forced march to Oklahoma, brought starvation,

"Is it supposed that the wandering savage has a stronger attachment to his home than the settled, civilized Christian?"

disease, and 25 percent mortality. Georgia farmers promptly settled on Cherokee lands.

The South's Agricultural Economy

The urge to remove Native Americans reflected the vitality of southwestern agriculture. With the demand for cotton increasing about 5 percent annually and offering an 8 percent annual return on investment, the acquisition of land promised both quick profits and long-term financial security. Indeed, the profitability of cotton agriculture discouraged southern investments in the types of commercial and manufacturing enterprise that altered the northern economy. Fresh land seemed

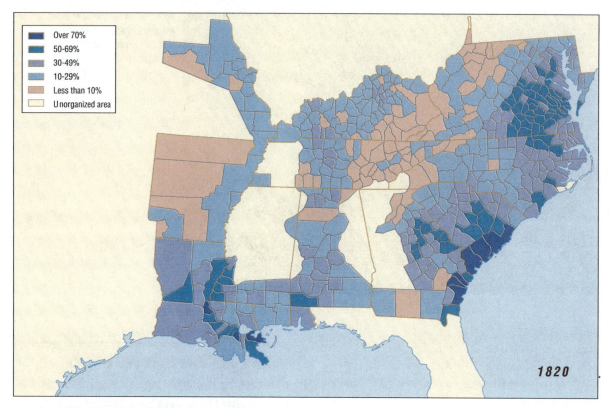

■	Over 70%
■	50-69%
■	30-49%
■	10-29%
■	Less than 10%
□	Unorganized area

1820

Percentage of Slave Population, 1820   OVERLAY 1

to offer its own reward. "The Alabama Fever rages here with great violence," remarked a North Carolinian who watched his neighbors migrating westward. "I am apprehensive . . . it will almost depopulate the country."

In this rural society, farming remained the primary occupation, and middle-class status depended on ownership of land. But ownership of slaves placed a farmer into a higher social category, and ownership of more than twenty slaves gave a farmer the prestigious status of "planter." In cotton-growing areas, 60 percent of all agricultural wealth took the form of slaves, while land and farm buildings contributed less than one-third of a plantation's value. Only about one-quarter of white families owned slaves, though slave owner-

ship in the cotton areas exceeded 40 percent. Half of all slaveowners held fewer than five slaves; three-quarters owned less than ten. Only 12 percent owned more than twenty. Yet this minority of white planters controlled the lives of a majority of the slaves and produced 75 percent of the region's cotton. Such economic power gave the planter elite disproportionate influence in southern society. Moreover, whether slaveowners were Whigs or Democrats, they had a larger percentage of seats in southern state legislatures than did nonslaveholding whites.

Outside the cotton regions, in the hill country of southern Appalachia (western Virginia, the Carolinas, and northern Georgia) farmers owned no slaves and concentrated on raising corn, live-

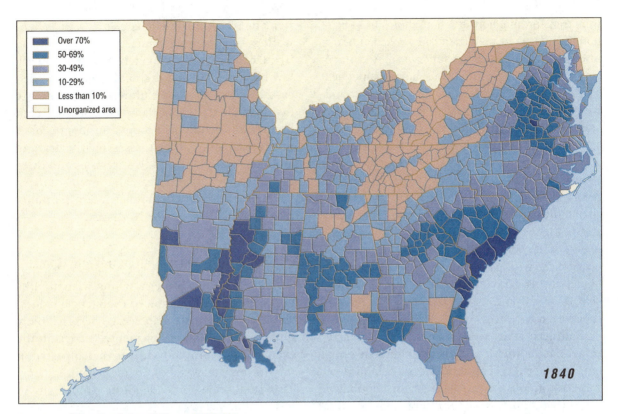

Percentage of Slave Population, 1840 OVERLAY 1

stock, and other subsistence crops. Less involved in commercial agriculture, these farmers grew crops to feed their households and exchanged small surpluses in local markets. Many were descendants of Scots-Irish immigrants who had come to America in the 18th century, and they created a distinctive self-sufficient society.

In plantation areas, by contrast, nonslaveholding farmers interacted closely with the larger cotton producers. They freely fished, hunted, and fed their livestock on any unfenced lands, treating such ground as common property. Smaller farmers also relied on nearby plantations to gin cotton, mill grains, and purchase their surplus produce. Some worked as overseers for wealthier planters; others rented slaves; most grew small quantities of cotton and aspired to enter the planter class. During the 19th century, this desire for upward mobility collided with rising prices for land and slaves. But shared values of white supremacy reduced class conflict. Small farmers acknowledged the leadership of slaveholding planters, voted them into political office, and accepted the legal responsibility to support the slave system, for example by riding in night patrols that enforced slave curfews.

Southern Households

Although cotton sales brought the planters into the market economy, rural life discouraged changes in domestic arrangements. While economic changes were transforming northern households from economic units where craftsmen had worked at home into domestic institutions supervised by women (see Chapter 10), southern households maintained a traditional rural character, in which men and women mixed agricultural tasks with domestic crafts. On small farms with few or no slaves, wives and daughters often worked in the fields, especially at planting and harvest times. Even on large plantations with numerous slaves, the household served as an economic center. Planters' wives managed a diverse domestic economy, tending cows and poultry, making dairy products, gardening, sewing, and cooking for masters and slaves alike. Because the workplace was not separate from the home, the plantation household remained patriarchal, even as women participated fully in domestic supervision.

Southern white women continued to marry earlier than northern women, extending the years of marital fertility. The continuing availability of western cotton lands may have inspired optimism about their ability to support large families and the absence of birth-control information in rural areas, in contrast to cities, precluded much choice. Thus the southern birthrate did not show the decline occurring in the northern states. White families with eight children or more were not uncommon. In busy households many expressed obvious ambivalence: "My [menstrual] courses came on," wrote the wife of a Virginia slaveholder. "I felt so thankful. God is good and kind to me a sinner."

Since slave families had no legal status, individual members could be bought, sold, and separated from each other. Indeed, the disruption of slave families contributed to their smaller size, even though African American women tended to have babies at a younger age than whites. This disparity probably resulted from the unhealthy environment in which slave mothers lived. Experiencing nutritional deficiencies as well as hard work during their pregnancies, slave women had frequent miscarriages or delivered babies with low birthweights and high vulnerability to diseases. Half of all slave children died before age five, about twice the mortality rate for white children. "Celia's child died about four months old," noted one planter diarist, assessing the death of an infant slave. "This is two Negroes and three horses I have lost this year." But even southern white families suffered higher infant mortality rates than did those in the Northeast.

The Domestic Lives of Southern White Women

Although most southern white women, like northern women, embraced evangelical values, southern Protestants emphasized personal piety rather than social improvement. As a result, the evangelical reform movements that appeared in the North won few followers in the South. In any case, rural society provided little opportunity to form voluntary organizations for social activity. Outside the wealthy planter class, a lack of public schools limited female education, producing higher rates of illiteracy among southerners. Moreover, the frequency of westward migration and the demands of supervising slave households isolated southern white women from relatives and friends. Multiple pregnancies endangered their health and often caused severe calcium deficiency. "You would be shocked to see how old I look with one of my front teeth gone," lamented one woman about a common rite of passage. Yet most southern women idealized marriage and motherhood, viewing that status as their highest virtue. While poor women and slaves relied on female midwives to assist at births, more affluent southern women, like their sisters in the Northeast, summoned male doctors. Their medical expertise did not appreciably improve survival rates.

At a time when married women could not legally own property independently of their husbands, and when divorces usually required special acts of the state legislatures and were only granted in cases of idiocy, impotence, or bigamy, women were dependent on fathers and husbands to protect their economic interests. Such powerlessness, together with the pressure of household management, frequent pregnancy, and rural isolation produced chronic depression—what contemporaries called "melancholia." "I am continually oppressed by a feeling of *inability* to do what I ought," cried a frustrated housewife. "All is confusion, *all is wrong*." Husbands were not necessarily sympathetic. "It is mere folly to be unhappy," wrote one annoyed spouse.

The Business of Slavery

While southern slaveholding women upheld values of domesticity, the slave economy continually threatened the bonds of African American families. Southern apologists claimed that most slave sales were made out of necessity to settle probate cases, but evidence of the slave trade between the Atlantic states and the cotton belt suggests that motives of commerce and profit were more common. Indeed, most sales occurred in times of prosperity. During the 1820s, 150,000 slaves were sold west, usually through a network of professional slave traders; in the next decade, the figure reached 250,000.

Contrary to slaveholders' claims, blacks did not typically move west with their owners or with kin. Twenty five percent of the interregional slave trade involved youngsters between the ages of 8 and 14, most of whom were purchased alone and separated from their mothers. About 10 percent of African American teenagers were sold from the Upper South, and 30 percent could expect to be transferred at least once during their lifetime. Children were seldom sold with their fathers, nor husbands with wives. When one state prohibited the importation of children under 10 without their mothers, the slave traders simply neglected to purchase the children in the first place, breaking up families at the initial place of sale.

For slaves, the possibility of being separated from their family instilled a pervasive fear and pain; the threat of being sold south or "down the river" served to discourage slave resistance. "Dear Husband," wrote a Virginia slave in 1840, "the trader has been here three times to look at me... . I expect I shall never see you all—never no more." "Dear Husband," wrote another Virginia slave, "A man . . . bought Albert and is gone. I don't know where." "Dear Husband," wrote yet another Virginia slave of her master's intentions, "I know not what time he may sell me, and then all my bright hopes of the future are blasted . . . for if I thought I should never see you, this earth would have no charms for me."

These sorrows, repeated innumerable times, contrasted with slaveowners' views of African American psychology. "The dance will allay his most poignant grief," observed a defender of slavery, "and a few days blot out the memory of his most bitter bereavement. His natural affection is not strong, and consequently he is cruel to his own offspring, and suffers little by separation from them."

The Conditions of Slavery

Such justifications could not disguise the essence of slavery: the control of human labor by compulsion and the lack of choice on the part of the enslaved. "We were worked in all weather," recalled the ex-slave Frederick Douglass. "It was never too hot or too cold; it could never rain, blow hail, or snow, too hard for us to work in the field. Work,

work, work. . . ." Such discipline commenced at an early age. "Us chillen start to work soon's us could toddle," recalled an ex-slave. "Iffen its freezin' or not us have to go to toughen us up."

Beyond this basic compulsion, the conditions of slavery varied immensely, depending on the nature of the work, the number of slaves, the temperament of the master, and the resourcefulness of the slave. One quarter of all slaves lived on small holdings of 1 to 9 slaves; half lived on larger holdings of 10 to 49 slaves; another quarter lived on big estates of over 50 slaves. The median number of slaves per holding was 32 in the cotton South and 23 in the region as a whole.

Most slaveholders viewed themselves as patriarchs, who used black labor not solely for their personal gain but also to regulate the lives of their supposedly inferior slaves. No rational person would deliberately imperil such valuable property—for economic, if not humanitarian, reasons. On small farms, slaves and masters often worked together, shared meals, and probably exchanged a degree of emotion. Slavery in those circumstances was personal, but whether relations were kind or brutal depended on intangible and capricious factors of personality. On small farms, slaves had less chance to develop families or unique institutions because of the day-to-day presence of their masters. Such owners were also less stable economically and more prone to sell their workers.

Slaves who did domestic work also interacted closely with whites. Freed from the drudgery of field labor, house servants enjoyed better food and clothing, but remained under the close oversight of master and mistress. In such proximity, it was easy to attract attention, and instant punishment. "I despise myself," admitted one planter's wife, "for suffering my temper to rise at the provocations offered by the servants." Believing that slaves were naturally lazy, slaveholders could

On small farms, slaves and masters often worked together, shared meals, and probably exchanged a degree of emotion.

justify their anger. Proximity to white men also exposed slave women to sexual assault. "I cannot tell how much I suffered, nor how much I am still pained by the retrospect," wrote ex-slave Harriet Jacobs of her experiences.

"If Cuffey won't work," went the slaveowners' motto, "you must make him work." While slaves on small farms or in plantation kitchens faced the spontaneous rage of masters and mistresses, field slaves were subject to the discipline of hired overseers. Whippings were frequent. "They'd never do any work at all if they were not afraid of being whipped," explained an overseer after thrashing a young woman with rawhide across her naked thighs. Even without violence, agricultural labor was harsh, from sun-up to sun-down, six days a week, a regimen that took women as well as men into the cotton fields. More arduous sugar production was largely male work.

Field workers wore slave-sewn clothing made from inferior "Negro" textiles or cheap ready-to-wear outfits and straw hats. Only in winter did slaves wear shoes, which were mass-produced and imported from the North. Slave cabins were drafty, windowless, crowded, and unsanitary. Slave diets, while usually sufficient in calories, lacked adequate protein and vitamins, causing chronic diseases that masters often attributed to laziness.

The desire for plantation self-sufficiency encouraged masters to allow some men to learn skilled trades (carpentry, masonry, blacksmithing), and their labor might be lent or leased to neighboring farmers. Women slaves sometimes acquired skill in spinning, weaving, and sewing. Artisans could occasionally negotiate to rent themselves out, earning money that they could use for self-purchase.

Slavery took a different form in towns and cities. One-fifth of southern slaveowners—artisans, merchants, lawyers, teachers, or doctors—lived in towns, but only 5 percent of the slave population were town dwellers. Urban slaves were usually domestic workers or tradesmen, sometimes factory workers. In the towns and cities, the proximity of slaveowners to each other served to reduce their brutality. "There is a vestige of decency, a sense of shame," explained the ex-slave Frederick Douglass, "that does much to curb and check those outbreaks of atrocious cruelty so commonly enacted on the plantation." Besides better food and clothing, urban slaves enjoyed the freedom to mingle with free blacks, attend churches, and experience public entertainment.

Defining African American Communities

In 1830, there were 2 million African American slaves in the United States. Although they traced their roots to diverse west African traditions, the conditions of servitude and work, for slaves and free blacks alike, had blurred their cultural differences. Just one generation after the legal closing of the African slave trade, African Americans had established a distinctive ethnic culture with unique patterns of language, religion, music, and family values.

Free Blacks in the South

Communities of free African Americans occupied most southern towns, even rural areas, and most lived in segregated sections that whites referred to by names like "Little Africa." In the Upper South, 20 percent of all blacks were free, but only 2 percent in the Lower South were free. The total number remained small—about 250,000 as late as 1860. Some free African Americans owned other blacks, though these were usually relatives or friends purchased from white owners. Half the free blacks in the southern states were mulattos, many of them liberated by their white fathers.

This free population encountered routine economic discrimination (they were the last hired and first fired) and constituted the poorest segment of southern society. Lighter-skinned women found work as domestics, darker-skinned as laundresses; free black men worked in fields or as casual laborers in town. Since more women than men were freed, most free black children inhabited female-headed households. During the 19th century, as slaveholders feared rebellions, the free population faced increasing restrictions on their movements. Free African Americans had to carry "freedom papers" to prove their status, and several states passed laws requiring emancipated slaves to migrate elsewhere. Free blacks had limited civil rights. They could not testify against whites in court, nor serve on juries.

Customary Rights and Slave Families

In most southern states, slaves could not legally marry, travel without permission, or learn to read and write, lest such activities disrupt the discipline of slave labor. Yet plantation slaves acquired many rights by custom. The selection of black slave drivers, respected leaders chosen informally by community approval, protected slaves from unusual burdens. Sunday work or nighttime work during the harvest time customarily brought extra rewards. Slaves also expected a traditional Christmas holiday, a labor-free week marked by gifts of food, clothing, and alcohol from their masters. Despite curfews and the vigilance of nightly patrols, slaves frequently traveled at night to neighboring plantations for social visits or religious meetings.

Viewing themselves as patriarchs, slaveowners routinely intervened in the private lives of their people. Most encouraged their slaves to form marriages, if only for convenience. On one plantation, a master arranged his newly acquired slaves in rows by sex, instructed each to find a mate, read aloud a marriage service, "and thus [saved] time by settling their matrimonial affairs." Such coercion was not typical. Plantation slaves usually chose their own partners, sometimes formally "jumping over a broom," a pagan European custom signifying that the relationship was more than casual. Nevertheless, plantation rules often undermined the creation of nuclear families.

Many slave families consisted of people owned by different masters. Such "abroad" marriages required permission from both partners' owners and often included strict rules preventing spontaneous meetings. Since children of slaves became the property of their mothers' owner, slave children usually lived with their mothers and their mothers' kin, and slave husbands traveled to visit their wives and children. To preserve a sense of family, many children were named after their fathers and grandfathers, and many slaves adopted surnames, often without their owners' approval, to signify family ties.

Long separations between husbands and wives encouraged serial relationships, which were sometimes monogamous, sometimes not. Since women slaves had work assignments, childcare passed to other female slaves, usually grandmothers or older children. When the young became old enough for field work, boys often moved into male dwelling units with or without their natural fathers, while girls undertook tasks that might separate them from

their mothers. To protect individuals from isolation, African Americans created elaborate networks of relationships with extended families or friends who served as kin and reinforced a sense of community.

African American Religion

Religion played an important part in African American culture. For most blacks, a belief in some aspects of African religion persisted, shaping a world-view that emphasized sacred elements of the natural world and the spiritual elements of human relations. Estimates suggest that between 10 and 20 percent of slaves brought from Africa were Muslims, some of whom surely continued to practice their religion in America. Masters sometimes assumed an obligation to instruct slaves in Christian doctrine, but so great was the fear that converted slaves might consider themselves spiritual equals and therefore deserving of freedom, slaveowners emphasized Christian virtues of humility, patience, and obedience. White missionaries occasionally visited slave plantations, preached a gospel of subjugation, and warned against stealing the masters' chickens. Slaves expressed little interest in such teachings and often preferred nonreligious owners who would be less scrupulous about punishing minor infractions. African Americans responded selectively to Christian teachings, embracing those principles that affirmed their humanity and offered the prospect not only of salvation but also of freedom. Within the slave communities, black preachers enjoyed both prestige and emotional power in interpreting religious subjects for fellow slaves.

Beyond formal church settings, slaves frequently held secret religious meetings in the woods at night, burying their dead with African customs that did not conflict with the daily work schedule of the plantations. In larger cities like New Orleans, free blacks and slaves continued the African tradition of elaborate funeral processions, marked by drumming, dancing, and singing through the streets. Other African religious practices, including call-and-response chants, ecstatic movement, and rhythmic cadence, clapping, and shouts, guided the slaves' religious experience. In addition, slaves chose aspects of Christianity that expressed the desire for freedom, preferring Old Testament stories about little David defeating Goliath, Moses leading the Hebrew slaves out of Egypt to the promised land, or Noah building an ark of deliverance from the sinful world. African American spiritual songs reiterated the chorus of freedom.

Slave Resistance

"Few people," wrote white South Carolina novelist William Gilmore Simms, were "so very well satisfied with their condition as the negroes,—so happy of mood, so jocund, and so generally healthy and cheerful." Singing, laughter, and storytelling among blacks might ease some owners' guilty consciences, but the content of African American culture reflected dual intentions, first, to assert the dissatisfaction with life under slavery and a hope for its abatement, and second, to distract the owners' attention from slave anger and resentment. The Br'er Rabbit stories, for example, which circulated during slavery days, typically described the success of weaker creatures outwitting stronger animals.

By pretending to be childlike, ignorant, or incompetent, slaves could thwart the masters' wishes without directly challenging their authority. Subtle forms of subversion abounded: damage to crops, broken tools, injury to farm animals, fires, pretended illness, self-inflicted injuries, and calculated laziness. "Negroes cannot, or will not— they do not—eat in as short a time as whites," complained a time-conscious planter, noting that what took him 10 or 15 minutes to eat required 30 to 45 minutes for his slaves to digest.

Slaves considered theft from their masters acceptable, even if they were punished when caught. The ultimate theft was to liberate one's labor, and oneself, by running away. Because they were more likely to have responsibility for their children, female slaves were less likely to run away than men. Hiding in nearby woods or swamps enabled runaways to avoid an impending punishment or burden, though masters responded severely to such infractions. Other runaways had specific destinations: to reach recently separated relatives, or the free states of the North. With the help of free blacks and southern Quakers, an "underground railroad" carried fugitive slaves into northern states or to Canada, where many became active in antislavery protests. Advertisements for runaway slaves also showed the brutality of slavery. In seeking their missing property, slaveowners identified personal characteristics—injuries, brands, or scars from whippings, as well as signs of intangible wounds such as stuttering or twitching.

Most runaways proved to be temporary fugitives, truants who returned after a few days of freedom or who were caught by slave trackers. Yet, despite the great difficulty of escaping through hostile territory, probably as many as 1,000 reached freedom each year. Other forms of resistance involved forceful confrontation with owners or overseers who, in the slaves' estimation, exceeded customary demands or punishments. Such spontaneous clashes were rare and could lead to severe punishment, even death. Sometimes the slaves prevailed, achieving an uneasy truce with their tormenters.

Nat Turner's Rebellion

"He who knoweth his master's will and doeth it not," slaveowners liked to quote from the scriptures, "shall be beaten with many stripes." One Bible-reading Virginia slave named Nat Turner put a different gloss on those words by taking God as his master. For years, the spiritual Turner had seen visions of retribution against slaveowners. In 1831, an eclipse of the sun, followed by atmospheric conditions that discolored the sky, came to Turner as an omen: "As the black spot passed over the sun, so shall the blacks pass over the earth." Turner struck in the late summer, leading fellow slaves in killing their masters and other whites, claiming sixty victims. Turner's ultimate goals remain unclear, but within two days slaveowners retaliated, capturing and executing about 120 rebels and selling others out of state. Turner hid in the woods for two months before he was caught. After a three-day interrogation, he was hanged for murder.

The Turner insurrection sent a chill through the South, alarming the nonslaveholding farmers, who questioned the wisdom of sustaining a hostile slave population. In 1832, anxious Virginia legislators debated a plan of gradual emancipation, much as northern states had once picked a future July 4 to liberate children of slaves. For a brief moment, the nonslaveholders challenged the value of slavery in southern society. But the slaveholders closed ranks and defeated the measure. Instead, Virginians encouraged free African Americans to depart for Liberia (see Chapter 10), though few accepted the offer of free transportation.

Meanwhile, in the wake of Turner's revolt, stricter enforcement of the slave codes limited slaves' travel, curtailed access to education, restricted church attendance, and made emancipation more difficult. "We must allay the fears of our own people," announced a southern newspaper. "We must satisfy them that slavery is of itself right—that it is not a sin against God—that it is not an evil, moral or political." Now slaveholders began to describe slavery not merely as a necessary evil but as a positive good. This change in attitudes about slavery foreshadowed a deepening conflict between southern and northern whites about the property rights of citizens.

The Antislavery Argument and National Politics

As the Turner rebellion undermined the confidence of slaveowners and showed that African Americans were not naturally content as slaves, antislavery reformers in the North expressed more militant criticism of southern society. Earlier critics of slavery, like Thomas Jefferson, had forecast the gradual eradication of slavery as African Americans acquired white civilization. But the spread of evangelical religion changed northern attitudes toward slavery. Sharing the slaveholders' belief that African Americans were inferior creatures and often incapable of moral choice, northern evangelicals nonetheless saw slavery as a sinful institution that corrupted the childlike slave. To be sure, many antislavery reformers had little experience with slaves or white southerners, and many northerners did not believe that slavery was unjust or morally wrong. In fact, northern businessmen made substantial profits selling cheap manufactured goods for slave apparel and shipped slave-grown cotton overseas without qualms. But for a small and passionate group of evangelical reformers, the commitment to creating a moral society demanded the *immediate* termination of the South's peculiar institution.

Free African Americans in the North moved to the forefront of protest. None was more bold than David Walker, a free black who had migrated from North Carolina to Boston and joined the antislavery Colored Association. His 1829 pamphlet, *Appeal . . . to the Colored Citizens of the World . . . and Very Expressly to Those of the United States of America,* minced no words. "The whites have always been an unjust, jealous, unmerciful, avaricious, and blood-thirsty set of beings," he wrote. Walker's solution was clear and simple. He advised American slaves to begin a rebellion: "Make sure work—do not trifle, for they will not trifle with you," he said. "Kill or be killed." Walker's *Appeal,* though reprinted three times, probably never reached Nat

TABLE 11.1

The Rise of Antislavery Societies, 1832–1838

	1832	1834	1835	1836	1837	1838
Maine	0	6	22	34	33	48
New Hampshire	0	9	12	42	62	79
Vermont	0	12	39	44	89	104
Massachusetts	2	23	48	87	145	246
Rhode Island	0	2	9	20	25	26
Connecticut	0	2	10	15	39	46
New York	0	7	42	103	274	369
New Jersey	0	2	3	6	10	14
Pennsylvania	1	2	6	32	93	126
Ohio	1	10	34	133	213	251
Michigan Terr.	0	0	2	4	17	19
Total	4	75	227	520	1000	1329

Source: Paul Goodman, *Of One Blood: Abolitionism and the Origins of Racial Equality,* University of California Press, 1998.

Turner. But his demand for immediate emancipation appealed to militant evangelicals, who believed that society was perfectible if only individuals would shun sin.

Evangelical Abolitionism

"I will be as harsh as truth, and as uncompromising as justice," declared the white abolitionist William Lloyd Garrison in launching his antislavery magazine, *The Liberator,* in 1831. "I will be heard." Garrison had initially supported both colonization of free blacks and gradual emancipation, but the election of the slaveholding Andrew Jackson in 1828 showed the strength of proslavery interests. "I am ashamed of my country," Garrison said. "I am sick of our unmeaning . . . praise of liberty and equality." Converted to evangelical Christianity, he saw slavery as a sin, which made any compromise morally unacceptable. Indeed, because the Constitution permitted slavery, Garrison considered it sinful and burned the document in public on July 4, 1834.

Such religious views informed the many antislavery societies that sprang up in the 1830s (Table 11.1), including the new American Antislavery Society founded in 1833. That year, the country's most popular woman author, Lydia Maria Child, shocked her readers by publishing *An Appeal in Favor of That Class of Americans Called Africans.* The first book to advocate immediate emancipation, Child's work underscored the plight of women slaves and their sexual exploitation. "The negro woman is unprotected either by law or public

Lydia Maria Child (1802–1880) was at the height of her literary success when she published her attack on slavery and racial discrimination, prompting a reader boycott that undermined her earnings.

opinion," wrote Child. "She is the property of her master, and her daughters are his property. They are allowed to have no conscientious scruples, no sense of shame." The book also demanded the repeal of laws prohibiting interracial marriages. Such abolitionists appealed primarily to the consciences of other whites, the reformers in the North and slaveowners in the South. Their objective was to end slavery by moral persuasion.

Antiabolitionism

Northern whites did not usually welcome the antislavery movement. Conservatives—indeed, even some abolitionists—viewed blacks as "docile" and "childlike," considered interracial social activities "unwise," and questioned whether ex-slaves could handle the responsibilities of freedom. During the 1830s, violent mobs attacked antislavery leaders in northern cities. In Boston, a crowd dragged Garrison through the streets with a rope around his neck, while in 1837 a mob in Alton, Illinois, murdered Elijah Lovejoy, an abolitionist newspaper editor. Most anti-abolition mobs included respectable citizens, many of whom believed that emancipation would encourage racial mingling and thus supported African colonization. Northern cities established segregated schools, churches, even cemeteries. What northerners opposed was not so much the abolition of southern slavery as the equality of African Americans in northern society. Complained one white father, "If you educate these young blacks, they will soon know as much as our children!"

Violence against northern abolitionists mirrored the treatment of southern whites who dared to criticize slavery and faced beatings, tarring and feathering, even murder (averaging thirty cases of homicide a year in the three decades after 1830). Such intimidation demonstrated the commitment of most southern whites, slaveowners and non-slaveowners alike, to the slave system. Although a numerical minority, slaveowners dominated southern politics at all levels. The slaveowners' power partly reflected their wealth; smaller farmers had both economic and ideological ties to their richer neighbors.

The Tariff and the Nullification Crisis

The prominence of slaveowners among southern politicians accentuated regional conflicts about economic development, political power, and the national identity. The 1828 "tariff of abominations," which raised duties on imported manufactured goods and so raised prices for southern consumers, remained a serious grievance. Although southern

Democrats voted for Jackson in hopes of lowering the tariff, the economy-minded president preferred to eliminate the public debt before reducing customs taxes. Meanwhile, Vice President John Calhoun, who privately had asserted the rights of states to nullify obnoxious federal laws (see Chapter 10), muted his criticism of the tariff, in hopes of succeeding Jackson to the White House. With cotton prices lower than average for two years, however, southern leaders protested the hardships of a high tariff. Jackson sympathized with their complaints. "Those who have vested their capital in manufacturing establishments," he told Congress in 1831, "can not expect that the people will continue permanently to pay high taxes for their benefit." With such presidential support, Congress passed a tariff measure in 1832 that lowered the rates by half, to the levels of 1816.

For some southern leaders, even that reduction was not enough. The conflict had moved beyond tariff reform to states' rights. As Calhoun put it, "the issue is no longer one of free trade, but liberty and despotism." With northern free states controlling a majority of the House of Representatives and abolitionists attacking slavery, southern spokesmen worried about other unwanted national policies involving banks, internal improvements, and interference with slavery. Seeking to forestall the expansion of federal power, South Carolinians defended the right of a state to nullify a national law. In 1832, during the same month that Jackson won reelection with a new vice president, Martin Van Buren, South Carolina summoned an elected state convention to consider the national tariff. Challenging the legality of congressional policy, the convention voted to declare the nation's tariff laws null and void and forbade the collection of federal customs duties in the state. Jackson responded with cries of treason, threatening to hang the nullifiers for turning the "perpetual union" into "a rope of sand."

As South Carolina radicals threatened to follow nullification with secession, Jackson tried to defuse the crisis by focusing on tariff policy rather than abstract principles of states' rights. In a proclamation to the citizens of South Carolina, Jackson denounced nullification and appealed for demonstrations of loyalty to the union, but he also asked Congress to lower the tariff. The resulting compromise tariff of 1833 did not result in a clear victory for the nullifiers. Customs duties would decline gradually over the next ten years. Congress also passed the Force Act, authorizing the president to use military force to collect customs revenues in South Carolina. However, the provisions of the new tariff effectively undermined the economic complaint, and anti-nullifiers within the state, mostly from nonslaveholding farm areas, quieted the protest. Outside South Carolina, every southern legislature repudiated nullification, leaving the movement without support. Facing Jackson's wrath, South Carolina repealed the nullification of the tariff; as an act of defiance, however, the state legislature proceeded to nullify the Force Act, a gesture that Jackson chose to ignore.

Congress and the Gag Rule

The frustration of powerlessness that had provoked the nullification crisis followed southern politicians into the halls of Congress, where they confronted a mounting campaign against slavery. While Jackson's Democratic party involved a political alliance between southern planters and northern merchants, northern evangelicals who were opposed to slavery tended to be Whigs. Believing that southern Christians could be made to see the evils of slavery, the American Antislavery Society commenced a new crusade in 1835 by publishing thousands of abolitionist tracts and mailing them to citizens of the South. Outraged by such uninvited communications, mobs that included respectable citizens stormed southern post offices, seized the offensive publications, and lit public bonfires to destroy the inflammatory documents.

Such protests did not disturb the Democratic administration. Jackson's postmaster general instructed local post offices to detain abolitionist mail, and the president subsequently told Congress that antislavery activity was "unconstitutional and wicked." Northerners did not necessarily sympathize with abolitionism, but they did worry about government censorship; limits on mail delivery impinged on the rights of free northerners. In 1836, Congress forbade postal workers from deliberately detaining the mails. But when southern state laws prohibited such deliveries, federal officials permitted local postmasters to obey local law.

The question of censoring antislavery statements erupted again in Congress in 1835, when abolitionists presented citizens' petitions demanding legislation to end slavery in the nation's capital. Women played a key role in these protests, because petitioning was one of the few political rights that they possessed. Although Congress did not have the power to legislate against slavery in the states, it did have the right to make laws for the District of Columbia. But southern representatives insisted that such petitions be rejected without any consideration or debate. "A war of religious and political fanaticism," said Calhoun, was being "waged not against our lives, but our character. The object is to humble and debase us in our own estimation." Such defensiveness revealed the moral power of antislavery. But in 1836 an alliance between southern politicians, both Whigs and Democrats, and northern Democrats managed to pass the so-called gag rule, which automatically used parliamentary procedures to ignore, or table, public petitions about the status of slavery. Many northern Whigs perceived the rule

Former president John Quincy Adams (1767–1848) was an outspoken abolitionist in the House of Representatives when he posed for this daguerreotype in 1845.

as an attack on the right of free debate, and former president John Quincy Adams, now a Whig representative from Massachusetts, agitated against the measure until gaining its repeal in 1844.

The Presidency of "Van Ruin"

The struggle over slavery in Congress, by linking the South with northern Democrats, fortified that party for the election of 1836. Martin Van Buren, Jackson's hand-picked successor, avoided the specific issues of tariffs, national banks, and antislavery. But the Whigs failed to agree on a candidate, and three nominees, each strong in a separate region, divided the opposition vote. Although Van Buren's anti-abolitionism remained popular in the North, southern Democrats distrusted his support of slavery, and Democratic votes declined drastically in the South. In the end, Van Buren captured just 50.9 percent of the popular vote.

Economic Crisis and the Panic of 1837

The new administration proved incapable of coping with the Panic of 1837 and the ensuing economic depression that struck just as Van Buren was entering office. By the summer of 1837, a wave of business failures brought rising bankruptcies and unprecedented unemployment in the cities. In New York City, thousands of idle workers protested in the streets and broke into warehouses to steal food. "Loud cracks in the social edifice," sighed the philosopher Ralph Waldo Emerson. The economy recovered briefly in 1838, then collapsed the next year when cotton prices plummeted, causing a wider depression that lasted into the 1840s. Both southern planters and northern merchants suffered from the downturn, as unsold cotton accumulated at wharves and warehouses and the value of slaves declined. In the crisis, Whigs blamed the Jacksonians for dismantling the Bank of the United States and undermining the nation's credit with hard money policies (see Chapter 10).

Believing, like Jackson, that private interests had corrupted the banking system, Van Buren proposed an "independent treasury" plan in which public funds would be separated from private banks by depositing government revenue in vaults or sub-treasuries around the country. The proposal also required that all payments to the government be made in hard money. But that provision would reduce the circulation of bank notes, contract the national currency, and retard economic growth. Whig politicians, more attuned than the Democrats to the market economy and scornful

> **In New York City, thousands of idle workers protested in the streets and broke into warehouses to steal food.**

of President "Van Ruin," thwarted the program until 1840. The long struggle showed the president's political weakness and his inability to meet the economic crisis.

Regional Discord: Texas, Slavery, and Race

Other aspects of Van Buren's policies revealed the difficulty of resolving fundamental regional differences. During the 1820s and 1830s, the expanding cotton economy had encouraged U.S. citizens to settle in the Mexican province of Texas. Many had joined the Missouri colonizer Stephen Austin, who obtained land grants from the Mexican government; others came as squatters. Both groups wanted slave-based agriculture, but Mexico outlawed slavery. Texans hoped that annexation to the United States would settle the dispute. Jackson shared that view. "The god of the universe," he had assured Van Buren in 1829, "intended this great valley to belong to one nation." Mexico, however, rejected Jackson's offer to purchase the territory. Frustrated by Mexican policy, Anglo Texans under the leadership of Sam Houston, declared independence from Mexico in 1836 and appealed to the United States for annexation as a state in the union.

As Mexico attempted to reconquer the newly proclaimed Republic of Texas, the Texas rebels, including Tennessee's Davy Crockett, took refuge in the Alamo, a mission in San Antonio. Mexico's General Antonio Santa Anna proceeded to attack the Alamo in 1836, killing all the rebels. Houston kept the insurrection alive by defeating other Mexican armies. In 1837, on his last day in office, Jackson recognized the independent Republic of Texas, but, fearing a war with Mexico, he rejected annexation. He left the Texas problem to his successor.

Under Van Buren, the Texas situation aggravated other regional disputes. Although southern expansionists supported the annexation of Texas to enlarge the domain of cotton and slavery, many northerners criticized an increase of slave territory. Caught in a crossfire, Van Buren opted to reject annexation, hoping to preserve his Democratic support in both regions. The result satisfied neither side. Van Buren's inability to bridge these regional differences did not indicate a lack of political skill, but rather the difficulty of achieving compromise on the issue of slavery in the territories.

Hesitancy to offend the South also shaped Van Buren's response to other controversial issues involving slavery and racial justice. When, for example, slaves aboard the Spanish ship, *Amistad*, rebelled in 1839 and brought the vessel ashore on New York's Long Island, Van Buren and proslavery members of his cabinet agreed to return the slaves to their owners in Cuba. Abolitionists challenged the decision, summoning John Quincy Adams to argue the case before the Supreme Court. Although the Court eventually ruled to release the slaves, Van Buren won applause in the South but earned the hatred of abolitionists.

Van Buren also continued Jackson's policy of removing the Creeks and Cherokees from their ancestral lands, overlooking the brutal Trail of Tears to tell Congress that the program had been "directed by the best feelings of humanity." Efforts to remove the Seminole people from Florida proved more difficult. Resistance by Seminole leader Osceola provoked open war in 1835. Although Osceola was captured and died in a federal prison, the Seminoles continued to fight under other leaders. The failure to achieve a military victory embarrassed the administration, and the use of bloodhounds against the Seminoles

aroused protests in the North. The war would continue into the next decade before the government could remove the Seminoles to Oklahoma.

Tippecanoe and Tyler, Too!

All Van Buren's problems—economic crisis, regional conflict, racial discord—crystallized in the election of 1840. When the Whig party passed over Henry Clay to nominate William Henry Harrison, victor in the battle of Tippecanoe against the Shawnees in 1811 (see Chapter 8), one disgruntled politician summed up the candidate: "Give him a barrel of hard cider and a pension . . . , [and] he will sit the remainder of his days in a log cabin." Intended as an insult, the image became a campaign theme, emphasizing Harrison's unpretentious democratic spirit. Whig enthusiasm exploded around the country with rallies and parades as well as slogans, cartoons, catchwords, and songs. "Farewell, dear Van / You're not our man: / To guide the ship, / We'll try old Tip." Women paraded, too, for the first time in a presidential campaign, carrying brooms to "sweep" the Democrats from office, baking cakes in the shape of log cabins, and vowing to marry "Whig husbands or none."

Issues were few, except for hard times and Van Buren's supposed aristocratic sensibilities. To attract southern votes, the Whigs chose Virginia's John Tyler, previously an avowed Democrat, as their vice-presidential candidate. About the campaign slogan "Tippecanoe and Tyler, Too!" admitted one Whig, "There was rhyme, but no reason." The election spirit was sensational. With a popular majority of only 145,000 votes, Harrison polled an electoral landslide, carrying Whig victories in both houses of Congress for the first and only time. A third presidential candidate, abolitionist James Birney, drew only 7,000 votes to the Liberty party in New York and Massachusetts, but even the existence of such a campaign indicated the growing sentiment against slavery in the North. Most significant, however, was the surge in public turnout. Up nearly 1 million voters from the last election, 2.4 million cast ballots in 1840, 80 percent of the eligible electorate.

The Politics of Stalemate

If the Whig Harrison carried a new agenda, it expired after he caught pneumonia during his inauguration and died just one month later. His successor, Tyler, still holding Democratic views against government support of economic development, had no interest in the Whig program of banks, tariffs, and internal improvements. Twice Henry Clay pushed legislation through Congress to establish a third Bank of the United States; twice Tyler vetoed the measure on constitutional grounds. The entire cabinet, except for Secretary of State Daniel Webster, denounced the new president and resigned from office. Webster stayed just long enough to complete negotiations with Great Britain about Canadian boundary disputes, extradition arrangements, and enforcement of laws against the slave trade. Then he, too, resigned. Thereafter, presidential vetoes and congressional deadlocks stalled most legislation. Indeed, the complicated political maneuvering in Congress testified to the strength of party discipline, as 90 percent of Democrats and Whigs voted as blocs on two-thirds of the votes.

The subjects of these legislative quarrels—banks, tariffs, and internal improvements—reflected fundamental disagreements between Whigs and Democrats about the nation's economic development and what each envisioned as the best type of society. Thus Whigs in all regions endorsed tariffs, banks, and internal improvements, praised economic nationalism, and promised that poor as well as rich would benefit by economic expansion.

Harrison caught pneumonia during his inauguration and died just one month later.

Democrats, in contrast, opposed government assistance to so-called privileged groups—bankers, manufacturers, and developers—who threatened independent farmers and merchants. Such disagreements partly reflected the regional differences between southern commercial agriculture and Northeast manufacturing. But southern Whigs and northern Whigs shared prodevelopment positions, just as southern Democrats and northern Democrats advocated low tariffs and free trade. Congress thus served as a battleground for competing interests. The stalemate under Tyler merely demonstrated the nearly equal strength of the rival positions.

Under Presidents Jackson, Van Buren, and Tyler, the art of politics hinged on compromise. Unlike their predecessors in the early years of the republic, politicians no longer expected to establish a broad consensus; mere majorities sufficed. Patronage, party loyalty, voter discipline—these threads enabled politicians to weave together national alliances that overcame regional differences. Political opponents no longer appeared as potential subversives but only as rivals for power; Whigs and Democrats could agree to disagree. Congressional politics could therefore reconcile disputes about banks, tariffs, and internal improvements.

The issues of tariffs, banks, and internal improvements drew the political lines between commercial opportunists and cautious farmers, between Henry Clay's Whigs and Andrew Jackson's Democrats. Yet both political parties claimed to speak for the nation, and both won support in all regions, despite obvious differences between the southern and northern economies. But, during the 1840s, as economic depression gave way to prosperity, investments in new technology (railroads, steamships, agricultural implements, telegraph lines) stimulated a surge of westward expansion. Geographic expansion, in turn, would imperil the two-party system.

Moral issues like slavery and abolition did not lend themselves to easy political compromises. Northern abolitionists condemned slavery as a sinful institution, and southern slaveholders defended their labor system as a positive good. These moral positions undercut the ground for political maneuvering. Van Buren's efforts to skirt the slavery issue weakened his strength in the North; his hesitation to defend slavery softened his standing in the South. Moreover, while party politicians tried to sidestep the slavery debate in the 1830s, the moral issues continually intruded into the political arena. Antislavery petitions aroused alarm in the South, just as the gag rule in Congress disturbed many in the North. Such tensions would not disappear. In the next decade, territorial expansion introduced new questions about the status of slavery and challenged Whigs and Democrats to reconsider their party loyalties. No longer a matter of political compromise, slavery emerged as a moral issue. The stalemate about how government could best promote economic development did not disappear, but the clash of regional interests increasingly focused not on wealth or poverty, boom or bust, but on slavery and abolition, matters of principle that could be neither ignored nor resolved.

INFOTRAC® COLLEGE EDITION EXERCISES

For additional reading go to InfoTrac College Edition, your online research library at *http://web1.infotrac-college.com.*

Subject search: Native Americans, periodicals
Subject search: plantation
Keyword search: plantation women
Keyword search: slave culture
Keyword search: slave life
Keyword search: slave religion
Keyword search: abolitionist
Keyword search: William Lloyd Garrison
Keyword search: gag rule slavery

ADDITIONAL READING

Expanding Cotton Society

Mark M. Smith, *Mastered by the Clock: Time, Slavery, and Freedom in the American South* (1997). An imaginative study of timekeeping in southern life, the book shows the importance of clock-time in regulating economic activities.

The Domestic Lives of Southern White Women

Elizabeth Fox-Genovese, *Within the Plantation Household: Black and White Women of the Old South* (1988). Based on diaries and letters, this book is a superb study of slaveholding women and their interaction with their slaves.

Suzanne Lebsock, *The Free Women of Petersburg: Status and Culture in a Southern Town, 1784–1860* (1984). Another study of a single community, this book describes the differing experiences of white and black women.

The Business of Slavery

William W. Freehling, *The Road to Disunion: Secessionists at Bay, 1776–1854* (1990). A thorough examination of southern attitudes and values about slavery, society, and the political controversies of the period.

Kenneth S. Greenberg, *Masters and Statesmen: The Political Culture of American Slavery* (1985). This essay about southern political values links social behavior, such as dueling, with demands for political equality.

Peter Kolchin, *American Slavery: 1619–1877* (1993). A lucid survey of slavery stressing the differing perspectives of masters and slaves.

Michael Tadman, *Speculators and Slaves: Masters, Traders, and Slaves in the Old South* (1989). A careful analysis of the interregional slave trade, describing the disruptive effects of this profitable business.

The Conditions of Slavery

Eugene D. Genovese, *Roll, Jordan, Roll: The World the Slaves Made* (1974). This ground-breaking study stresses the creative interaction between slaves and masters.

Customary Rights and Slave Families

Wilma King, *Stolen Childhood: Slave Youth in Nineteenth-Century America* (1995). Focusing on the experiences of children, the author examines the social and psychological effects of slavery.

Brenda E. Stevenson, *Life in Black and White: Family and Community in the Slave South* (1996). This study of a single Virginia county describes the variety of family relationships among slaves and masters.

Slave Resistance

Lawrence W. Levine, *Black Culture and Black Consciousness: Afro-American Folk Thought from Slavery to Freedom* (1977). This brilliant interpretation of African American music, stories, and folk culture depicts the creative opposition to slavery and racial injustice.

Evangelical Abolitionism

Paul Goodman, *Of One Blood: Abolitionism and the Origins of Racial Equality* (1998). This analysis of the northern antislavery community links the movement to evangelical reformism. See also Henry Mayer, *All on Fire: William Lloyd Garrison and the Abolition of Slavery* (1998).

Congress and the Gag Rule

William Lee Miller, *Arguing about Slavery: The Great Battle in the United States Congress* (1996). This book describes the congressional debates about antislavery and the gag rule.

12

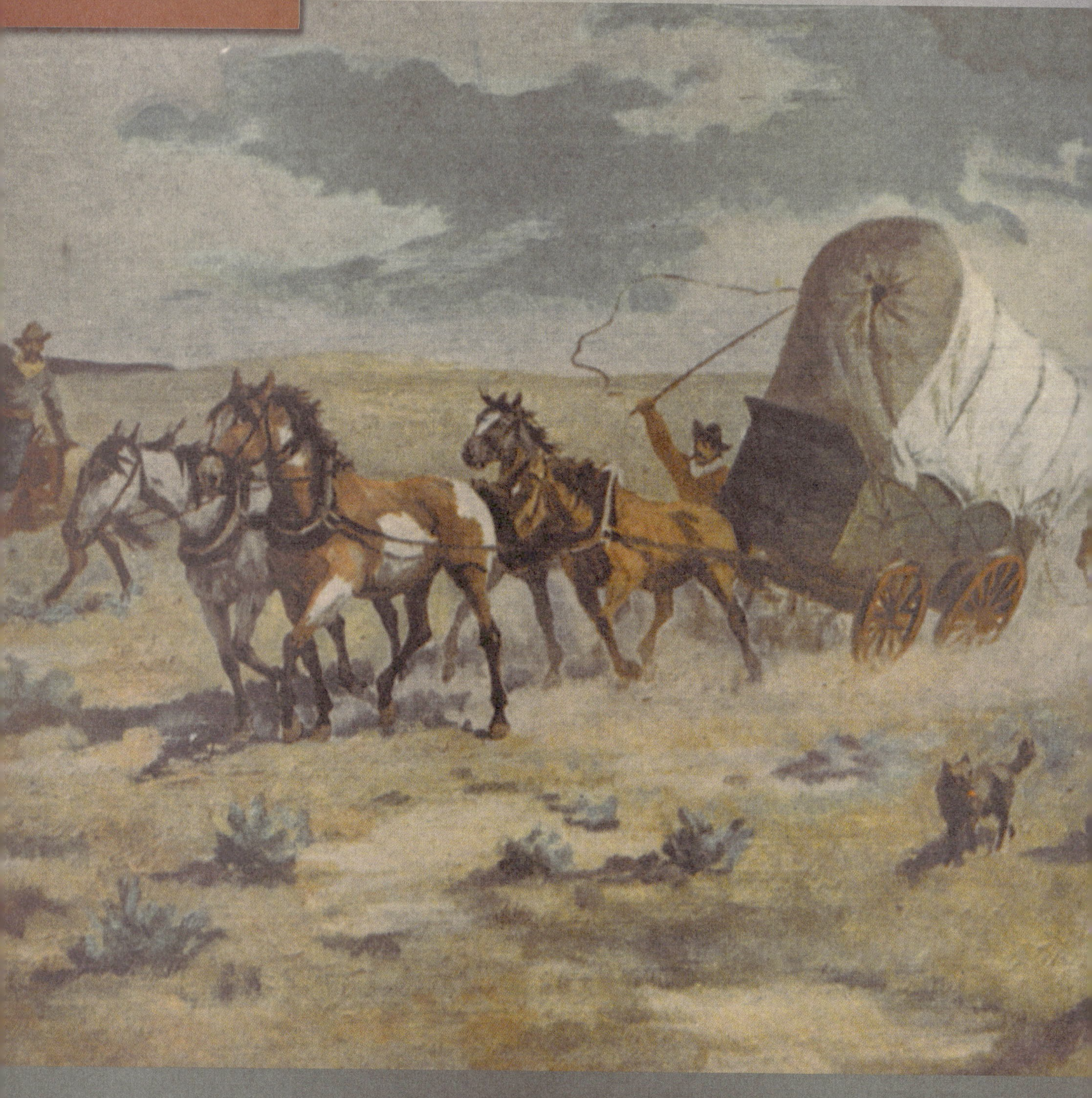

Manifest Destiny and the National Identity, 1844–1850

CHRONOLOGY

1844	Samuel Morse introduces telegraph
	James K. Polk elected president
	Treaty of Wangshia increases China trade
1845	Nativists gain political office in eastern cities
	Congress annexes Texas by joint resolution
1846	War begins between United States and Mexico
	U.S. settlers found Bear Flag Republic in California
	Congress ratifies Oregon treaty
	Wilmot Proviso seeks to prohibit slavery in new territories
1848	Treaty of Guadalupe Hidalgo ends Mexican war
	Californians discover gold at Sutter's Mill
	Women's rights convention held at Seneca Falls
1849	General Zachary Taylor inaugurated president
1850	Millard Fillmore succeeds Taylor
	Compromise of 1850 postpones crisis over slavery

Looking out over the green expanse of her Iowa home, now dotted with the blossoms of spring-flowering trees, the farm woman bewailed her husband's succumbing to an outbreak of "Oregon fever" in 1847.

"It seems to be contagious and it is raging terribly," she wrote. "Nothing seems to stop it but to tear up and take a six-month trip across the plains with ox teams to the Pacific Ocean."

"I said *O let us not go*," wrote another farmer's wife, "but it made no difference."

"I am going with him," yet another woman told her mother, "as there is no other alternative."

http://history.wadsworth.com

The successive waves of "Texas fever," "Oregon fever," and "California fever" that comprised westward migration brought a new perspective to the nation's identity during the 1840s. While surveying the western lands sixty years earlier, George Washington had put Canada on his left hand and Florida on his right as he looked across the Atlantic toward Europe (see Chapter 7). By the 1840s, the country had reversed direction. "Behold," exclaimed a public orator about the new citizen. "He plants his right foot at the source of the Missouri—his left on the shores of the Gulf of Mexico; and gathers into his bosom the ever-flowing abundance of the fairest and richest valley on which the circling sun looks down." From that position, easterners' eyes now looked west.

Optimism about westward migration translated into a belief that expansion was inevitable. As the Democratic newspaper editor John L. O'Sullivan stated in 1845, the United States had a "Manifest Destiny"—a self-evident fate—"to overspread and to possess the whole of the continent which Providence has given to us for the development of the great experiment of liberty." Believing that the country had received a divine mission to expand across the continent, politicians, preachers, and promoters stressed three unique national blessings that would accompany the migration, words that would become a virtual cliché, "civilization, religion, and liberty."

Each of these advantages was loaded with nationalist values. *Civilization* meant the imposition of rational order on the natural landscape: schools and churches would edify future generations, and the surveyor's grid would produce rectangular farms that facilitated real estate transactions. *Religion* signified the Protestant gospel which, as one minister stated, guaranteed "the moral destiny of our nation" in the struggle against Native American devils, the "childish mummery" of Mexico's Catholics, and the spiritual views of California's Chinese immigrants, who were disparagingly called "celestials." *Liberty,* to the expansionist mind, would bring republican institutions that assured equality—to white men. Such values justified settlement of the territories west of the Mississippi.

Having tied the national identity to the development of western lands, citizens discovered that geographic expansion aggravated tensions, not only with cultural outsiders but also among the most patriotic expansionists. To be sure, few complained that the annexation of Texas brought a war with Mexico and that the search for California gold created conflicts with the indigenous peoples of the Pacific coast (both Native and Mexican Americans) as well as with Chinese and South American immigrants. But political leaders were more disturbed by the growing conflict between northern and southern citizens over the status of slavery in newly acquired territories. Citizens of both regions believed in Manifest Destiny. But northern expansionists, dedicated to free labor and economic opportunity, saw the extension of slavery as a threat to their liberty, and southern expansionists, equally concerned about their rights, demanded constitutional protection of private property, including slaves. Such arguments had been submerged by the Missouri Compromise of 1820. By the end of the 1840s, the quarrel had resurfaced and threatened the survival of the union. The old party lines between Whigs and Democrats strained to contain this political conflict. Regional passions were finally cooled in 1850 by a political compromise, but only for a while.

Nature, Technology, and Expansion

Dozens of Native American nations inhabited the western territories in the 1840s, and Britain and Mexico challenged U.S. claims in the Pacific and Southwest. Still, the millions of undeveloped acres west of the Mississippi River appeared as a great temptation to eastern residents. "Everything . . . in

During the first half of the 19th century, the nation's population more than quadrupled, from 5 million to over 23 million.

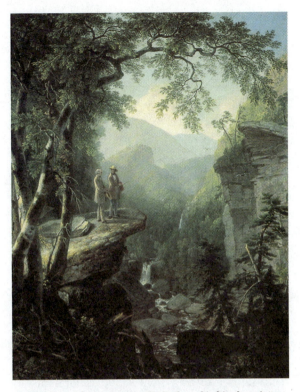

Asher Durand's Kindred Spirits (1849) places his friends, painter Thomas Cole and author William Cullen Bryant, amidst the natural grandeur of New York's landscape.

the natural scenery is on a scale so vast and grand," remarked an Ohio minister in 1846, "the majestic rivers, the boundless prairies, the deep forest . . . as to make man vast in his schemes, gigantic in his purposes, larger in his aspirations, boundless in his ambitions." To Whigs and Democrats alike, the West beckoned as a region for human improvement, a land to sustain both population growth and economic opportunity. During the first half of the 19th century, the nation's population had more than quadrupled, from 5 million to over 23 million. Politicians now promised to lead the country to the Pacific coast.

The Paradox of Progress

"Nature," remarked the New England philosopher Ralph Waldo Emerson in 1836, "is to stand as the apparition of God." Emerson's ideas, which belonged to a school of thought known as *transcendentalism,* emphasized the spirituality of the natural world and viewed social institutions as stifling of the human spirit. During the 19th century, the exploration of untouched natural formations west of the Mississippi—vast mountains, cascading waterfalls, untracked prairies and deserts—dazzled the imagination of explorers, travelers, and artists. These natural wonders, said the painter Thomas Cole, "are of God the creator—they are his undefiled works, and the mind is cast into the contemplation of eternal things."

Visions of natural glories awakened a sad foreboding, for it was obvious that "the axe of civilization" was destroying old forests and landscapes. The transformation of the wilderness into what one contemporary called "abodes of commerce and seats of manufactures" testified to the famous Yankee ingenuity. One Californian joked that "the Yankees will metamorphize the country over so that it will be showery the year round instead of [having a] rainy and dry season." The Hudson River painters, such as Cole and Asher Durand, saw no humor in the metamorphosis and resolved "to rescue" on canvas "the little that is left, before it is too late." Their paintings documented the price of technology.

The Wonders of Technology

Most citizens welcomed technology and its palpable improvements. "I hear the whistle of the locomotive in the woods," remarked Emerson. "Wherever the music comes it has a sequel. It is the voice of the Nineteenth Century saying 'Here I am.'" But to Emerson's literary friends Henry David Thoreau and Nathaniel Hawthorne, the whistle carried "the noisy world into the midst of our slumbrous peace." Women writers like Lydia Sigourney contrasted the subdued pleasures of domestic horticulture, "the sweet friendships of the quiet plants," with the "restlessness and din of the rail-road principle," which symbolized the pursuit of materialism. But most people simply expressed their wonder about technology, as did one little boy who was asleep when taken aboard for his first railroad trip in 1847, "and when he awoke," his mother wrote, "he looked around all surprised and said, 'Where is the horses?'"

Technology brought undeniable signs of progress. On the southern shores of Lake Michigan, the village of Chicago (named for the wild garlic used by the indigenous people) surged into a major metropolis, growing from 4,500 inhabitants to 30,000 during the 1840s. In the previous decade, a real estate boom encouraged Chicago builders to introduce a novel architectural design, known as the "balloon-frame" house. Built with pre-cut boards and nails, such structures could be made quickly and cheaply with a minimum of skilled labor. "We are proud of the flimsy, unsubstantial structures," boasted one local architect. "They are the homes of the people who will by-and-by build and own better ones." Chicago emerged as a major lumber center, where wood from midwestern forests provided not only homes and workshops but also the cross-ties for an expanding system of railroads.

The opening of the Galena and Chicago railroad in 1848, which was linked by canals to the Illinois river and to the steamships that sailed the great lakes, created a transportation network that turned the windy city into a year-round hub of economic enterprise. Financed by small farmers, who wanted to get their crops to market, the iron horse cut the

One little boy on his first railroad trip "looked around all surprised and said, 'Where is the horses?'"

journey to New York from two weeks to two days and eliminated seasonal slumps associated with bad weather. ("It's against the policy of Americans to remain locked up by ice over half of the year," quipped a railroad promoter.) Steam-powered grain elevators revolutionized the shipment of wheat, enabling Chicago to store and distribute 3 million bushels of grain annually by 1854.

Equally powerful was the telegraph introduced by Samuel F. B. Morse in 1844 with the haunting question "What hath God wrought?" Crowds flocked to telegraph offices to hear news of the 1844 presidential nomination, and newspapers predicted the "annihilation of time." For Chicago grain dealers, the telegraph initially enabled them to get price quotes from New York in 18 hours, but as wires followed the railroad tracks and became continuous, the interval was reduced to mere seconds. By 1860, the nation's 56,000 miles of wire were carrying 5 million messages a year. Few shared the pessimism expressed by the individualistic Thoreau: "We are in great haste to construct a magnetic telegraph from Maine to Texas," he observed; "but Maine and Texas, it may be, have nothing important to communicate."

Westward Migation and the Uprooted

Philosophical doubts about westward expansion could not compete with a popular desire to acquire land across the Mississippi. With federal land selling at $1.25 (about $19 in today's money) per acre for a minimum of forty acres, Congress passed the Preemption Act in 1841, which protected the

Deaths on the Oregon Trail averaged one every eighty yards.

claims of squatters, who could not afford to purchase their land but who "improved" its value by their settlement. "Come along, come along—don't be alarmed," said a popular song, "Uncle Sam is rich enough to give us all a farm." Westward migration nonetheless involved the pain of uprooting, as emigrants took their departures from family and neighbors, usually forever. More traumatic was the displacement of the Native Americans, whose lands were invaded, seized, and stolen. Although the federal government acknowledged the validity of some Native American claims in formal treaties, Manifest Destiny—the notion that expansion was ordained by God—permitted little respect for native cultures and jurisdiction.

Heading West

Heading west was usually a man's decision. Since most state laws considered the husband sole owner of family property, the sale of a farm and furnishings did not require the wife's agreement; some women learned of their imminent uprooting *after* their spouse had sold their home. Of course, many wives and daughters shared the men's enthusiasm, and many proved more than competent in assuming leadership when men died on the overland trails. All the same, women constituted only about 20 percent of those who moved west.

Migrants struggled to overcome their feelings of loss. Some admitted that their minds frequently wandered, "living once again the scenes of other days." Letters between emigrants and stay-at-homes included hair clippings, swatches of clothing, or photographs to preserve their connections. "Time, space, both are annihilated," wrote the

young poet Walt Whitman about the craze for photography in 1846. "We identify the semblances with reality." Within a decade, photographers were developing 3 million daguerreotypes annually, almost all of them portraits rather than interiors or landscapes, to satisfy a yearning for family memory.

Besides their recollections, travelers who crossed the mountains and desert areas that formed the Great Plains carried heavy provisions, tools, clothing, and utensils, as much as a ton per wagon, to sustain them during a 2,000-mile journey that could last from six to eight months. No preparations seemed adequate for the ordeal. Daily domestic duties exhausted the strongest women, while men staggered under the burden of steering the "prairie schooners" across rough terrain and dangerous rivers. The toll was high. Every traveler noted that the route west was dotted with graves—mostly the result of disease, accidents, exhaustion, and starvation. One estimate suggests that deaths on the Oregon Trail averaged one every eighty yards.

Marking the Trails

The perils of migration marked people and land alike. The custom of naming babies after features of western geography (Nevada, Gila, Columbia) indicated a pride of achievement, though all too many infants and their mothers died en route and were buried hastily to spare their corpses from wolves or thieves. Naming the land also offered a modicum of immortality. In 1838, the young Abraham Lincoln linked the efforts of the nation's founders to the national geography. "If they succeeded," he remarked, "they were to be immortalized; their names . . . transferred to counties and cities, and rivers and mountains." Western migrants added a democratic touch to the fetish. At the cliffs at Independence Rock in Wyoming, travelers paused to inscribe personal names, initials, and dates. "Nothing escapes that can be marked upon," noted one emigrant; "even the slabs

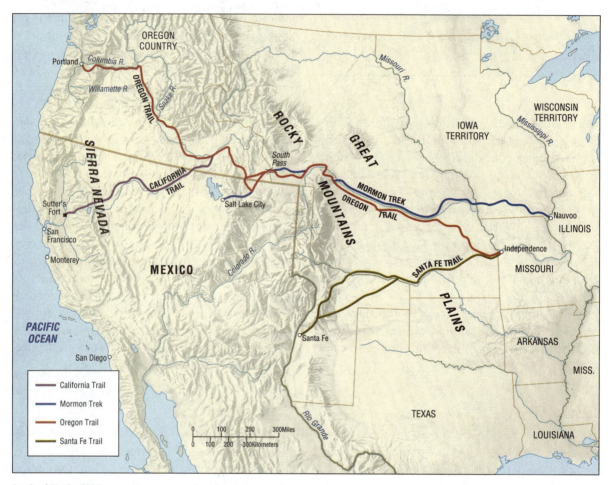

Overland Trails, 1846

of graves are all marked by this propensity for penciling." ("Each venturesome climber seems to wish to put his name above the last one," added the diarist. "One poor fellow fell and was killed.")

The graffiti proved less damaging to the landscape than the passage of thousands of wagon trains, together with flocks of sheep and herds of cattle, which in some years exceeded 150,000 head of livestock. Rotting carcasses of horses, mules, and oxen putrefied the air and water, while human excrement turned virgin canyons into stinking pits that spread cholera and other diseases. The prairies became junk heaps of broken wagons, furniture, and assorted household litter discarded to lighten the load. Cattle and sheep ravaged the land, competing with native buffalo for scarce water and grasses.

Disrupting Native American Life

Even more devastating was the male sport of random killing. "Not less than fifty buffalo were slaughtered this morning, whereas not three in all were used," noted a California-bound traveler. "But the desire by the emigrant of engaging once at least in a buffalo chase can scarcely be repressed." Such play endangered the economies of Native Americans, intensifying competition among the nomadic Sioux and the settled Pawnees. (Sometimes, western migrants found fun in shooting the indigenous people, though one migrant reported that a white man who killed a Native woman like "a wild animal" was turned over to her kinsmen, who "skinned him alive.") When the Sioux complained to Washington about the disruption of hunting grounds, a government official replied, with the logic of Manifest Destiny, that "the injury complained of is but one of those inconveniences to which every people are subjected by the changing and constantly progressive spirit of the age."

Although overland emigrants prepared for armed conflicts, violence occurred infrequently, a fact that did not reduce the level of anxiety. Cross-cultural contacts often proved invisible and subtler. In 1837, a smallpox epidemic reduced the population of the Plains people by half, wiping out the Mandans and Hidatsas. By the late 1840s, annual cholera epidemics not only weakened the Plains' survivors but also made them wary of further contact with whites. "We are armed to the teeth," said one California emigrant, "but . . . we carry with us in their imagination a protection more formidable: the dread scourge which has spread among them." In eastern Washington, the tendency of white children to recover from measles, while Cayuse children died, prompted Native leaders to murder the local missionaries Marcus and Narcissa Whitman. In the Southwest, Apache raiders attacked stragglers and kidnapped children. For most emigrants, assaults involved only the nighttime theft of horses and livestock. In the light of day, emigrants mostly encountered omnipresent beggars seeking gifts, or Native American

traders eager to swap sewn shirts for assistance crossing swollen rivers.

U.S. citizens also paid scant attention to the Spanish-speaking peoples of the Far West. "The greatest misfortunes of Spanish America," explained South Carolina's John Calhoun, "are to be traced to the fatal error of placing these colored races on an equality with the white race." Such racial attitudes justified their conquest, but drew a line at incorporating them into the national family. Northern expansionists shared Calhoun's views of Mexican inferiority. While attracted to California's outdoor festivals and "fandangos," eastern visitors like the author Richard Henry Dana concluded that "the women have but little virtue," an outlook that rationalized their sexual abuse. The absence of Yankee values—Protestantism, industry, and thrift—also persuaded expansionists that Californios were "an imbecile, pusillanimous race . . . and unfit to control the destinies of that beautiful country." By 1848, Yankee traders were exporting 6 million hides and 7,000 tons of tallow from California, a contrast with so-called California fever (laziness). As Dana exclaimed in his widely read *Two Years Before the Mast* (1840), "In the hands of an enterprising people, what a country this might be!"

Manifest Destiny, Ethnic Identity, and Social Reform

Since Manifest Destiny assumed the superiority of Anglo-Protestant culture, many political leaders worried that immigrant groups, especially Irish Catholics, would subvert the religious and political principles that defined the nation's identity. Protestants of all denominations viewed the Catholic church as an intolerant, undemocratic religion and questioned whether people who accepted the Pope's authority could be trusted to exercise republican rights of citizenship. Anglo-Protestants also doubted the ability of African Americans to become citizens. Although antislavery opinion increased in the northern states during the 1840s, criticism of the South's "peculiar institution" seldom acknowledged the equality of free blacks. When northern abolitionists did challenge such prejudices, they often provoked public hostility. In this way, women of the antislavery movement encountered discrimination against themselves, as women, and discovered the limitations of women's rights. Evangelical reformism thus linked the antislavery movement to a growing demand for women's equality.

The Rise of Irish Immigration

Public criticism of the Catholic church coincided with a surge of Irish immigration that rapidly increased the size of the Catholic population, especially in eastern cities. After 1815, economic depressions in Europe encouraged young Irish men and women to seek their fortunes in North America. Most were single people in their twenties who spoke English and wanted to acquire an "independence" instead of remaining landless tenants or underemployed trade workers. In the ten years after 1845, moreover, annual potato blights destroyed Irish agriculture, bringing famine that caused 1 million deaths and inspired nearly twice that number to seek refuge across the Atlantic. This wave of immigrants traveled as families, many suffering from malnutrition and shipboard diseases, and included non–English speaking people. Unlike most other immigrant groups, more than half the Irish newcomers were women. The simultaneous arrival of German immigrants, many fleeing the political rebellions that swept through Europe in 1848, aroused less concern because those newcomers were fewer in number, tended to be more prosperous, and settled in rural areas, not cities.

The famine-stricken Irish confronted an unfriendly economic and cultural environment. In the Atlantic port cities where they landed, Irish men

Slaveowners gave risky jobs in mining and construction to Irish workers to avoid endangering their slaves.

competed for low-paying manual jobs in construction and dock work; Irish women found domestic employment as maids, cooks, and laundry workers, displacing African American women from those occupations. Taking advantage of the transportation boom, many men found work building canals and railroads, which encouraged westward migration. When those jobs were finished, the Irish settled as farm workers or found occupations in the growing cities of the Midwest. Fewer Irish migrated to the southern states, where slaves and free blacks competed for manual work. Slaveowners sometimes gave more risky jobs in mining and construction to Irish workers to avoid endangering their slaves. For the Irish, traditional clannishness provided mutual support, but because they were the lowest-paid workers, their families often experienced the problems associated with poverty—alcoholism, violence, family desertion, and crime.

Skilled Irish immigrants also entered an economy of declining opportunity. As northern home manufacturing gave way to textile mills, Irish weavers had to abandon their trades for the routines and discipline of the factories. To support their families, the Irish accepted jobs at lower pay than native-born workers, often replacing New England farm girls in the mills. Meanwhile, the real wages of mill workers declined between 1830 and 1860. By the 1840s, entire families were forced to seek mill work, take in boarders to supplement their income, or find jobs for their children that included room and board. The low wages paid to Irish immigrants affected other groups as well: the distance between the richest and poorest Americans increased, reducing social mobility, and the competition for jobs among the poorest groups increased, sometimes provoking violent ethnic clashes.

Anti-Irish Nativism

Even before the floodtide of immigration, Irish Catholicism had aroused Protestant anger. Most citizens initially assumed that Irish "backwardness" reflected a deprived upbringing in Europe. "The sin of the Irish man is ignorance," declared a Harvard University commencement speaker in 1840, "the cure is Liberty." But as shiploads of Irish arrived in the 1840s, economic competition aggravated ethnic antagonism. In 1842, native-born citizens formed the American Protestant Association, an anti-immigrant group that opposed Irish Catholic culture, such as the reading of Catholic bibles in public schools. Street violence between anti-Catholic mobs and Irish gangs occurred frequently in the cities, climaxing in 1844 with organized riots in Philadelphia that left numerous dead and two Catholic churches burned to the ground. That year, a "nativist" candidate, campaigning to delay the naturalization of Catholic immigrants, won election as mayor of New York, prompting successful campaigns against immigration in other eastern cities.

Although many respectable citizens condemned the violence, anti-Irish views dovetailed with changing intellectual opinion. Instead of attributing Irish "deficiencies" to their environmental circumstances, during the 1840s nativist critics introduced racial and national characteristics to explain why the Irish appeared "ignorant . . . idle, thriftless, poor, intemperate, and barbarian." A stereotyped view of "Paddy" underscored physical differences in explaining ethnic behavior. Contemporary scientific theory reinforced such ideas. The popular fad of phrenology, involving pseudo-scientific measurement of skulls, suggested that

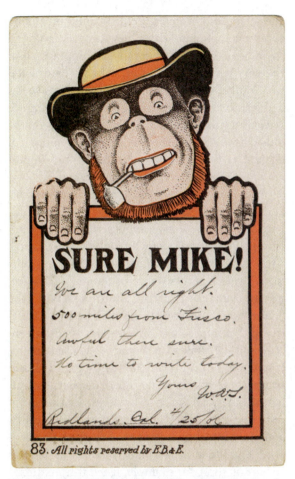

The influx of Irish immigrants prompted the stereotyped picture of an Irish "Paddy," with prominent nose and simian features.

psychological and cultural traits could be identified by the shape of the cranium and lent credence to the notion of permanent racial characteristics. More potent was the argument of Harvard's leading biologist, Louis Agassiz, who proposed a theory of *polygenesis*, the plural origins of mankind, which suggested racial differences among humans were God-given qualities of nature.

Native-born citizens usually viewed the Irish as an example of "otherness," of what they themselves were not. "All is noise and agitation, tumult and disorder," noted a Pennsylvania mechanic about the Irish immigrants he saw on a Mississippi steamboat; "nothing of composure or gravity, but the very reverse." Irish clannishness contrasted with Yankee individualism; their boisterous wakes and fraternal saloons clashed with the temperance crusade against alcohol; their shanty towns on the outskirts of town violated middle-class notions of domesticity; their tendency to support Democratic politics alarmed evangelical Whigs.

Irish family values, support of parochial schools, and ethnic societies offered protection and security for what one immigrant described as "a primitive people, wandering wildly in a strange land." After laboring for six days under harsh conditions, Irish workers wanted a Sunday of leisure, not an evangelical lecture about preserving the Sabbath. Yet, the desire to retain their ethnic identity did not preclude interest in assimilation. "Look to the Yankees as a model," advised one recent immigrant. "Imitate the energy, patience, and prudence of his character," said another. Assimilation and social mobility, however, depended not only on individual will but also on opportunity, and nativist attitudes kept the first generations of Irish outside society's mainstream. The federal census of 1860, for example, listed three national categories: "native," "foreign," and "Irish."

Challenging Racial Inequality

"I never hear an Irishman called Paddy [or] a colored person called nigger," wrote the abolitionist Lydia Maria Child in 1841, "without a pang in my heart, for I know that such epithets . . . are doing more to form the moral sentiments of the nation, than all the teachings of the schools." To evangelical reformers like Child, ethnic and racial discrimination contradicted the belief in human perfectibility. Yet if the Irish could anticipate a future time of cultural assimilation, African Americans faced deeper prejudices because of their race

and skin color. During the 1830s, evangelical abolitionism had injected a moral imperative into antislavery agitation. But since most northerners continued to view African Americans as culturally, spiritually, and biologically inferior, public support of abolitionism remained marginal. Partly for this reason, radical abolitionists like William Lloyd Garrison opposed political activity, fearing that public hostility would drown the effort. Garrison also insisted that the evil of slavery was beyond political debate. Instead, he emphasized spiritual appeals: the emancipation of slaves depended first on the moral regeneration of free people, who would then voluntarily liberate all slaves.

During the 1840s, other abolitionists began to advocate political participation. Although the antislavery Liberty party's presidential candidate, James G. Birney, received only 7,000 votes in 1840, political abolitionists continued to agitate for specific objectives. Acknowledging that Congress lacked the constitutional power to interfere with slavery in the separate states, the Liberty party targeted government support of slavery in areas where congressional authority appeared unquestioned: slavery in the national capital; the interstate slave trade; the use of slave labor to build public works and military fortifications. The Liberty party also opposed the admission of new slave states and insisted that Congress should reject slavery in federal territories such as Florida. Yet, by 1845, every state that entered the union from the Louisiana territory—Louisiana, Missouri, Arkansas, and Texas—was a slave state.

Recognizing that antislavery measures depended on winning the support of northern voters, the Liberty party challenged the belief that blacks were innately inferior, arguing that the environment of slavery, not natural or racial deficiencies, had limited African American development. Free African Americans, including Henry Bibb, Henry Highland Garnet, and members of the National Convention of Colored Men, endorsed the

Liberty movement, though they preferred more militant action. In an 1843 "Address to the Slaves of the United States," Garnet echoed David Walker's appeal for slave rebellion (see Chapter 10) and declared, "It is sinful in the extreme for you to make voluntary submission." By the mid-1840s, however, most abolitionists were focusing on tamer electoral politics, seeking not so much to gain public office as to control the balance of power between the major parties and so obtain passage of antislavery laws.

Antislavery Issues and the Rights of Women

By emphasizing the equality of all human beings, the abolitionist movement awakened second thoughts about other social institutions—marriage, family, and sexual relationships. Garrison's newspaper *The Liberator* included a "Ladies Department," illustrated by a slave woman kneeling in chains and bearing the caption "Am I Not a Woman and a Sister?" Evangelical women, such as Lydia Marie Child and the Grimké sisters, fought actively in the abolitionist crusade, writing articles and pamphlets, and creating female auxiliaries to all-male antislavery societies. Such involvement enabled women to participate in public life despite the middle-class belief that a woman's proper sphere remained in the home.

The incipient conflict about women's roles crystallized in 1837 when Angelina and Sarah Grimké, the daughters of South Carolina slaveholders, embarked on an antislavery speaking tour of New England. Their willingness to address mixed audiences of men and women troubled orthodox clergymen, who considered such behavior "promiscuous." A Congregational ministers association protested that a woman who "assumes the place and tone of man as a public reformer . . . becomes unnatural." Such attacks exposed the limitations of women's public status, and the Grimké sisters began to speak not only about abolitionism

but also about the rights of women. The ensuing public debate divided the antislavery movement. "Is it not forgetting the great and dreadful wrongs of the slave in a selfish crusade against some paltry grievance of our own?" asked the abolitionist poet John Greenleaf Whittier. Angelina Grimké replied, "Are we aliens, because we are women?"

In working to free the slaves, the Quaker Abby Kelley remarked, "we [women] found that *we* were manacled *ourselves.*" At the World Antislavery Convention held in England in 1840, male abolitionists voted against seating Lucretia Mott, Elizabeth Cady Stanton, and other women delegates, forcing them to attend the proceedings in a separate area. The insult reinforced their determination. "I was a woman before I was an abolitionist," said Lucy Stone. "I must speak for women."

During the 1840s, the Whig party took the lead in inviting women to form auxiliary clubs to campaign for presidential candidates. Evangelical women, who supported reform movements such as abolitionism and temperance, tended to be middle class and Whigs, and they used reform newspapers to argue for expanded political and legal rights. They wrote pamphlets, presented public lectures, and contributed to Amelia Bloomer's women's rights newspaper *Lily,* which by the mid-1850s reached a circulation of 6,000. Unsurprisingly, however, Bloomer acquired greater notoriety for proposing "short dress" costumes for women—loose fitting divided skirts called "bloomers" after their designer.

Women Democrats, in contrast, opposed government interference in private spheres such as the family, and generally opposed reform laws. So did most men in all parties. "Her speech like all others on Woman's Rights," remarked a Pennsylvania farmer who attended a feminist lecture, "was of very little practical use, being at least 5,000 years ahead of the time." Women often had a different reaction. "I really had thought we had all the rights that belonged to us," wrote a well-to-do

Bloomer acquired greater notoriety for proposing "short dress" costumes for women.

woman who attended a two-hour speech by Lucy Stone (who wore bloomers), "but . . . I find we are wronged and hope for a change in some respects."

The difficulty of altering male opinion inspired Stanton and Mott to organize a woman's rights convention at Seneca Falls, New York, in 1848. Seeking to appeal to women rather than men, the leaders nonetheless recoiled from drafting a manifesto ("as helpless and hopeless as if they had been suddenly asked to construct a steam engine," Stanton recalled) and persuaded Mott's husband to chair the meeting. The Seneca Falls convention soon found its voice. In a "Declaration of Sentiments," modeled on Jefferson's attack on King George III in the Declaration of Independence, the delegates offered an unwavering protest. "He," they declared, referring to men's treatment of women, "has endeavored, in every way that he could, to destroy her confidence in her own powers, to lessen her self-respect, and to make her willing to lead a dependent and abject life."

Having established that women were "aggrieved, oppressed, and fraudulently deprived of their most sacred rights," the Declaration of Sentiments demanded equal opportunities for professional careers and rights of citizenship. Among these was the right of married women to inherit and own property independent of their husbands. As women's rights meetings spread through the states, the movement clarified a critical element in the demand for political rights, including the vote: "We do not seek to protect women," an 1851 convention explained, "but rather to place her in a position to protect herself." By 1860, four-teen states had enacted legislation establishing married women's property rights.

The Politics of National Expansion

Women's rights, abolitionism, anti-Catholicism, and Manifest Destiny—all these impulses were rooted in the popular belief that individuals should be made free, liberated from patriarchy, slavery, religious hierarchy, and political oppression. Social reformers stressed the superiority of U.S. culture and sought to "perfect" its essential goodness. During the 1840s, these views coalesced with the nationalist spirit of westward expansion. Believing that the nation's institutions—government, churches, commerce, and families—were superior to those of other nations, political leaders argued for spreading those virtues across the continent to ensure the future happiness of the citizenry. By the end of the decade, some expansionists even envisioned American trade and culture crossing the Pacific, from the harbors of San Diego, San Francisco, and Puget Sound, to Hawaii, China, and Japan.

Expansionist ideas soon aggravated quarrels about the contradictions between southern slavery and the free-labor economy of the North. Political leaders in both regions claimed to uphold *national* values, including the principle of westward expansion. In the early 1840s, southern leaders like Virginia's John Tyler and South Carolina's John Calhoun supported the annexation of Texas to obtain additional territory for the cotton and slave economy, arguing that such a society reflected the values of the nation's founders. By contrast, northern leaders like New York's Martin Van Buren and Pennsylvania's David Wilmot favored expansion only if slavery, which they deemed the antithesis of liberty, would be prohibited in the newly acquired territory. Indeed, northerners feared that the spread of slavery would interfere with a free labor economy and stifle the prospect of upward mobility for poorer whites. Pro-slavery leaders replied that any limitation of slavery violated the constitutional rights of free men to own private property, imperiling their own liberty. But the issue ran deeper than legal argument. "It is not a question of national politics," observed a northern Whig, "but of national identity." In short, the nation now faced its troubling paradox: Was the United States a country in which all men—or only some men—were free?

Texas and Oregon

The issue of territorial expansion exploded in 1844 when proslavery President Tyler authorized Secretary of State Calhoun to draft a treaty calling for the annexation of Texas. When Calhoun linked Texas to the survival of slavery, Whigs denounced annexation and the Senate refused to ratify the treaty. Texas then became the prime topic in the 1844 presidential election. Although the northern front runner, Van Buren, expected the Democratic nomination, southern party leaders abruptly dumped him because of his refusal to back annexation. Instead, the Democrats chose Tennessee's James K. Polk, a fervent expansionist who promised to bring both Texas and Oregon into the Union. Meanwhile, as the Whig candidate Henry Clay waffled on the Texas issue, many northern Whigs deserted the party to back the Liberty candidate James G. Birney. That shift proved decisive. Birney's 65,000 votes drained enough ballots from Clay in New York to give Polk the state's 36 electoral votes and the presidency. "Slavery," remarked the Whig William Henry Seward, "is now henceforth and forever among the elements of political action. . . . the ground the public mind has traveled cannot be retraced."

Despite the narrow election results, lame-duck President Tyler, who was determined to acquire Texas, took Polk's victory as proof of the popular view and urged Congress to annex the Lone Star republic by a joint resolution, which required a simple majority rather than two-thirds ratification of the Senate. Anger at this parliamentary strategy spread through the North, leading some anti-Texas politicians to accuse a so-called slave-power conspiracy of threatening constitutional checks and balances. But Congress approved annexation and Texas became a state in 1845.

President Polk then pressed ahead with claims to Oregon as far north as the latitude of the Alaska border ("54-40 or Fight" was his campaign slogan). In 1846, the White House accepted a compromise with rival British claimants, establishing the U.S. border with Canada at the 49th parallel and bringing Puget Sound into the union. The farming families who settled in Oregon proceeded to create a nonslave territorial government.

Polk's willingness to compromise about the Oregon boundary contrasted with his stubbornness in negotiating with Mexico. After the United States accepted Texas into the union, Mexico broke diplomatic relations and threatened war to recover its lost province. The United States also inherited Texas's bitter warfare with the Comanches, Kiowas, and other mounted peoples, who resisted encroachment on their lands. After annexation, Texas requested federal military forces to remove the native inhabitants. Amidst violent boundary disputes, the Comanches ignored national borders to raid Mexican territory for livestock and adding to Mexico's grievances about annexation.

Rejecting Mexico's objections, Polk claimed that the southern boundary of Texas was not the Nueces River, as Mexico claimed, but the Rio Grande, and he ordered General Zachary Taylor to occupy the disputed area. With that provocative step, the president also dispatched a special ambassador to Mexico City with instructions to purchase New Mexico and California and to settle the Texas boundary at the Rio Grande. Mexico's refusal to negotiate its dismemberment goaded Polk further. He instructed Taylor to move U.S. forces south, then used a minor military skirmish as an excuse to claim that Mexico had shed blood on U.S. soil and asked Congress to declare war.

The War with Mexico

"We are waging a most iniquitous war," cried the abolitionist Theodore Parker. Although the Democratic majority in Congress swiftly supported Polk's war message, opposition to the war was widespread. Abolitionists and antislavery "Conscience" Whigs denounced Polk's failure to seek a compromise with Mexico. To protest the war, Henry David Thoreau refused to pay his taxes, went to jail and there wrote his classic essay *Civil Disobedience,* defending conscientious objection to immoral actions of government. In Congress, the Illinois Whig Abraham Lincoln introduced a resolution asking the president to identify the spot of U.S. soil on which blood had been shed; the nickname "Spotty" Lincoln was the sole result.

Anti-war sentiment scarcely disrupted the war effort. Polk took command of military plans, sending Taylor's army south from Texas to seize Monterey, Mexico, where U.S. troops defeated a larger Mexican force under General Santa Anna at Buena Vista. Taylor's sudden fame ignited his presidential prospects, which Polk decided to cool by ordering him to await further orders. To secure New Mexico, Colonel Stephen Kearny marched 850 miles from Kansas into Santa Fe and raised the U.S. flag above the city's plaza. Kearny made peace agreements with the Pueblos, Apaches, and Utes, but needed a show of force to gain a settlement with the Navajos. Despite numerous treaties, neither the local peoples nor the federal government would surrender their claims to the lands, and the southwestern border remained dangerous for both peoples for years.

Kearny's troops then headed for California, where U.S. settlers led by the explorer John C. Frémont had declared independence from Mexico and founded the Bear Flag Republic in 1846. Meanwhile, U.S. naval forces captured Monterey, California. Mexican defenders battled Kearny's cavalry in southern California, but by early 1847 the U.S. army controlled the province. Polk then prepared to invade Mexico City, but to stifle General Taylor's political ambitions, he gave command of the army to General Winfield Scott. Landing at Vera Cruz, Scott's 14,000 soldiers fought their way over the mountains and laid siege to the Mexican capital. Santa Anna's superior numbers engaged U.S. soldiers in several bloody battles, but in the autumn of 1847 Mexico was forced to surrender. The war claimed 13,000 U.S. lives—2,000 killed on the battlefields, the remainder taken by disease.

While Polk's ambassador negotiated a treaty of peace in Mexico, a sharp political debate was brewing in Washington. Some expansionists called for the seizure of all Mexico. But a vocal antislavery group, fearful of extending slavery, joined racial purists like Calhoun in rejecting the absorption of Mexico's "colored" population. The demand for all Mexico passed. Instead, the Treaty of Guadelupe Hidalgo of 1848 required Mexico to cede California, New Mexico, and the Rio Grande region in exchange for $15 million and the U.S. assumption of claims against Mexico. These Mexican acquisitions, plus Texas and Oregon, brought 1.2 million square miles into the union, including 1,000 miles of Pacific shores.

Confronting Slavery and Race in the West

The acquisition of Mexican territory seemed to fulfill the promise of Manifest Destiny but quickly sparked a debate between northern and southern

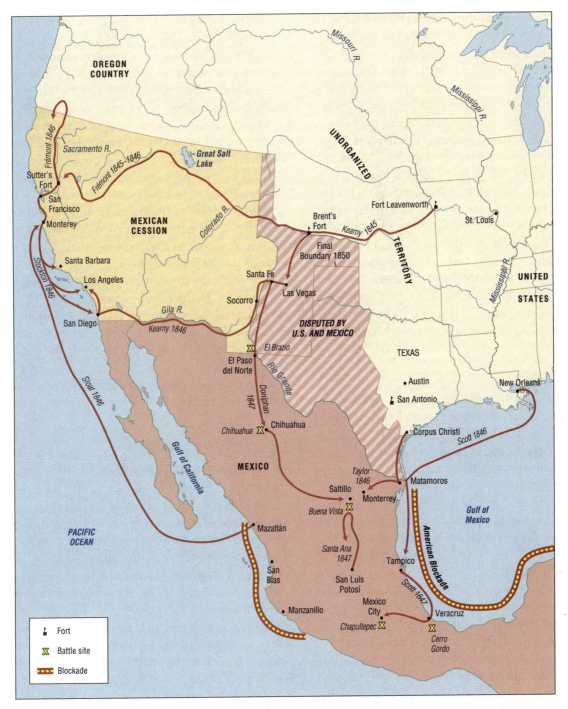

The Mexican War and Cession

versions of the national identity. The Missouri Compromise of 1820 had drawn a line through the Louisiana territory at the latitude 36°-30", prohibiting slavery north of that line. But, by the 1840s, northern opinion had turned against the spread of slavery anywhere. Rather than celebrating the acquisition of new lands, Congress became deadlocked in an effort to establish territorial governments. Complicating the crisis was the discovery of gold in California in 1848, which set off a mass exodus from around the world, brought new ethnic groups into the country, and underscored the importance of ending the congressional stalemate. Despite the presidential election that year, the national political parties failed to resolve the dispute. Not until 1850 did Congress find the basis for a compromise, trading political interests that offered a partial resolution of the territorial issue, but only for a decade.

Defining the Status of Slavery

"Slavery has within itself the seeds of its own dissolution," declared Pennsylvania Representative David Wilmot. "Keep it within limits, let it remain where it now is, and in time it will wear itself out." With such logic, the Democratic congressman introduced a resolution in 1846, known as the Wilmot Proviso, prohibiting slavery in all territory seized from Mexico. Disavowing any "morbid sympathy for the slave," Wilmot merely pleaded "the cause of white free men." As he assured his colleagues in the House of Representatives, "I would preserve to free white labor a fair country, a rich inheritance, where the sons . . . of my own race and color, can live without the disgrace which association with negro slavery brings upon free labor."

The ensuing debates revealed three competing views about the status of slavery in the territories. The first drew on the precedents of the Northwest Ordinance and the Missouri Compromise and insisted that Congress had the power and duty to prohibit slavery in the territories. President Polk, who proposed extending the Missouri Compromise line to the Pacific, took that position. The second view, articulated by pro-slavery leaders like Calhoun, argued that the Constitution protected personal property in territories no less than in states and that Congress had an obligation to protect slavery in *all* U.S. territories. In Calhoun's view, the Missouri Compromise was unconstitutional. The third position, expressed by two midwestern Democrats, Lewis Cass of Michigan and Stephen Douglas of Illinois, was later known as "popular sovereignty"; it proposed that the voters in each territory, not Congress, should decide the issue of slavery for themselves.

These irreconcilable views did not encourage compromise. In the House, where northern constituencies held a majority, Wilmot's proposal passed in 1846. But in the Senate, where southern states had equal power with the North, the measure failed to carry. Yet the principles of Wilmot's proviso would be revisited on many occasions; it was a point of difference that would not fade away.

Defining the Status of Citizens

The Wilmot debates illuminated the high value that 19th-century politicians gave to the rights of citizenship. Significantly, no political leader on any side proposed extending full citizenship to African American men, or to women of any race. To the contrary, 19th-century politicians believed that the privileges of citizenship belonged only to adult white men. Neither the Constitution nor congressional law had ever drawn moral distinctions between citizens. To southern leaders, therefore, Wilmot's proviso broke all precedents, saying "in effect to the Southern man," as one Virginian put it, "You are not my equal, and hence to be excluded as carrying a moral taint with you." To Calhoun, the proviso pushed the South "from being equals into a subordinate and dependent

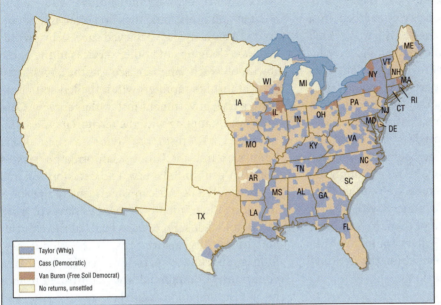

The Election of 1848

condition." This feeling of insult, of moral exclusion, of being denied the right to inhabit U.S. territory with one's private property in the form of slaves, threatened the foundations of republican politics, in which all white men possessed equal rights to life, liberty, and the pursuit of happiness. Even nonslaveholding southerners, interested in the opportunities of western expansion, shared this demand for equal status in the republic.

Northern politicians felt equally aggrieved by the proslavery leadership. Some, like Wilmot, objected to the immorality of slavery. Others opposed the increase of southern political power in Congress. The novel process of acquiring Texas by joint resolution, after the formal treaty had failed to win ratification, appeared to many northerners as an abuse of power. Then, the war with Mexico had brought vast territories into the union, most of which would prove inhospitable to cotton cultivation and slavery, but now proslave members of Congress were seeking to protect their power by admitting additional slave states. "They have trampled on the rights and just

claims of the North sufficiently long," a Massachusetts Whig wrote privately, "and have fairly shit upon all our Northern statesmen and are now trying to rub it in." Northerners might not share the abolitionist revulsion against slavery, but neither did they welcome competition with slave labor in the territories. "To contend that Congress should introduce, or engraft, Slavery upon territory now free," stated a northern Democrat, "is to ask the people of the union to consider and treat slavery as a positive benefit and blessing to be diffused and extended by the action of Congress."

As Washington remained deadlocked about territorial slavery, politicians prepared for the 1848 elections. Seeking southern votes, Democrats nominated the northerner Lewis Cass, whose support of popular sovereignty contradicted the Wilmot Proviso. The Whigs, by contrast, could achieve no unity on slavery and dodged the issue by nominating the military hero Zachary Taylor, who ran for president without a party platform. Thus the two major candidates had little appeal for Conscience

Whigs, antislavery Democrats, or Liberty party abolitionists. These dissenters converged in a third political party, the Free Soil party, which nominated the former Democrat Van Buren, who now endorsed the Wilmot Proviso. "The question is not whether black men are to be made free," averred a Free Soil Democrat, "but whether we white men are to remain free." African American leaders like Frederick Douglass welcomed the Free Soil movement as "the beginning [of] the end of . . . American slavery." And although the Free Soil party won no electoral votes, it held the balance of power in two states; with nearly 300,000 popular votes, half of them in New York and Massachusetts, Free Soilers spoke for one-tenth of the electorate. Meanwhile, the national majority elected General Taylor.

The California Gold Rush

Before Taylor or Congress could address the problem of new states, the California Gold Rush introduced a new element into the political equation. Ten days after Mexico surrendered California to Polk's diplomacy in 1848, a sawmill worker named James Marshall, employed by the entrepreneur John Sutter, had spotted gold nuggets in the sand near the American River. By 1849, the discovery had ignited an international race for fortune. "Forty-niners" flocked west by the tens of thousands, either along the overland trails or by ship to Panama and then across the isthmus and up the Pacific coast. In 1848, some 6,000 miners harvested gold worth $10 million; by 1850, the output had quadrupled to $42 million, and the number of miners had increased eightfold; in 1852, the peak year, gold values reached $81 million, but spread among 100,000 seekers.

The new Californians were overwhelmingly male—92 percent in 1850, and even higher in the mining camps. The shortage of women increased the value of what was usually considered women's work, such as cooking and laundry. Women who went to California could thus find economic opportunity, and many men achieved success by providing food, lodging, and other services in the boom towns, of which San Francisco was the largest.

California's rapid growth impelled settlers to form a civil government just at the moment Congress was grappling with the territorial issues. Encouraged by President Taylor to seek direct admission into the Union, California politicians voted to prohibit slavery. The decision assured freedom to 2,000 African Americans in the state, including those initially brought as slaves to work in the gold fields. Free status enabled them to create community institutions, such as churches, lodges, and newspapers. But, as the free black community complained, they continued to face racial discrimination, lacked the right to vote, and could not testify in state courts.

Even though California was a free state, political leaders made no effort to extend liberty to the indigenous population. State laws permitted the forced labor of any Native American found loitering, "strolling about," or "leading an immoral or profligate course of life." The state also approved a labor system that permitted white citizens to employ Native American children as involuntary "apprentices" at the minimal cost of giving them food, clothing, and "humane" treatment. Kidnapping proved a common way to acquire such youngsters to work as farmers, miners, ranchers, and domestic servants. With a shortage of white women, employers leased their female "apprentices" according to grade: "fair, middling, inferior, refuse."

Whites targeted "wild Indians" for violence, rape, and murder, and local governments offered bounties for their scalps. With such incentives, the Native American population of California dropped from 150,000 in 1845, to 100,000 in 1850, to 50,000 in 1855, to 35,000 five years later. Most died of imported illness (15 percent from sexually transmitted diseases) as well as alcoholism, murder, and

MINING LIFE IN CALIFORNIA.

CHINESE MINERS.

Chinese miners panned for gold on the American River in California in the 1850s.

abuse. Such distress aroused no interest from national politicians. When by the early 1850s federal officials appealed to Washington for aid in curbing these abuses, Secretary of War Jefferson Davis, a Mississippi slaveholder, declined to interfere.

East to Gold Mountain

One day a San Franciscan heard a man humming the homesick tune "Carry Me Back to Old Virginia," then looked twice to realize that the singer was Chinese. Forty-niners included several thousand men (very few women) who journeyed east to "Gold Mountain" from the province of Canton. Like Irish immigrants, Chinese peasants of the 1840s experienced overpopulation and food shortages caused both by drought and floods. China's opium wars with Britain in the 1840s and 1850s further disrupted the economy, while forced competition from foreign traders undermined local manufactures. Too weak to resist foreign pressure, China had signed the Treaty of Wangshia in 1844, opening several

ports to U.S. shipping. New York was already the home of a small Chinese community. Chinese merchants not only traded silks and other products but also sold the services of contract laborers who sailed to Australia, Latin America, and California.

"From far and near we came and were pleased," remarked an early Chinese merchant in San Francisco. But not for long. Protesting foreign competition in the gold fields, U.S.-born miners demanded restriction of the "Asiatic races . . . dissimilar from ourselves in customs, language, and education." In 1852, the state enacted a foreign miners' tax which targeted noncitizen miners, but particularly affected Chinese since a 1790 federal law had limited naturalization to white persons. By paying the discriminatory fees, Chinese miners provided nearly half the state government's annual revenue! After gold was discovered in Australia, many Chinese miners joined an outmigration. Those who remained in California worked in isolated, almost all-male communities. Spanish-speaking Forty-Niners from Mexico and Chile faced similar racial problems.

The Compromise of 1850

By 1850, the territories of California and New Mexico had drafted antislavery constitutions and applied for admission into the union. President Taylor's efforts to bypass the territorial stage (and so finesse congressional oversight of slavery) angered southerners of both political parties who saw the national balance of power tilting forever against them. Some extremists even spoke of leaving the union. Hoping to defuse another congressional deadlock, political moderates, led by Henry Clay, introduced a group of resolutions to permit the compromise of differences.

The resulting Compromise of 1850 provided for the admission of California as a nonslave state, but organized the remainder of the Southwest into a territory without restrictions about slavery; slaveowners could transport their human property into the region, but for reasons of climate and geography few expected to do so. The federal government would attach Texas's disputed western boundary lands to New Mexico, while assuming the state's public debt; this measure limited the size of Texas as a slave state, leaving the status of western Texas undecided, and satisfied Texas's northern creditors, who cared more about dividends than slavery. Two other key bills highlighted the impending conflict between northern and southern interests: one abolished the slave trade—but not slavery—in Washington, D.C.; the other mandated passage of a stricter fugitive slave law requiring free states to return runaways.

As the Senate, still balanced between slave and free states, considered the resolutions, the rhetoric of extremists in both regions exposed the fragility of the republic. "A single section, governed by the will of the numerical majority, has now, in fact, the control of the government," declared the aging John Calhoun; "the people of the southern states . . . cannot remain, as things now are . . . in the union." Jefferson Davis of Mississippi added a similar dissent. William Seward, a New York Whig, condemned the pending compromise, but for quite opposite reasons, decrying the refusal to confront the moral issue of slavery and declaring that there existed a "higher law" than the Constitution. Other senators spoke for the compromise, none more eloquently than Massachusetts' Daniel Webster, for which he earned the eternal malice of the abolitionists.

The sudden death of Zachary Taylor in 1850 abruptly removed presidential objections to the proposed compromise, and the new president, Millard Fillmore, backed Clay's proposals. Congressional managers swung into operation, dividing Clay's package into a series of distinct bills, each requiring a separate vote. The old party lines, dividing Whigs from Democrats, nearly disappeared. Southern Whigs and Democrats generally backed slavery; northern Whigs and Democrats largely opposed its extension. Consequently, neither region "compromised" its position. Instead, a small group of moderates held the balance on each measure, and the bills slipped through, one by one, each with a slim majority.

A Political Pause

Passage of the Compromise of 1850 generated a collective sigh of relief that echoed through the land. But no astute citizen could forget the tensions that had knotted Congress for more than a year. Regional politicians had not compromised their principles; they would monitor their opponents closely and demand that political promises to enforce the new laws be kept. Nor, ultimately, could lines drawn on the political map resolve the moral crisis that remained. "Slavery depends not on climate," observed the pedagogue Horace Mann, "but on conscience." The compromise thus brought not a resolution but only a temporary truce. What would happen when other western territories sought statehood? Exhausted political leaders could only wait.

INFOTRAC® COLLEGE EDITION EXERCISES

For additional reading go to InfoTrac College Edition, your online research library at http://web1.infotrac-college.com.

Keyword search: Manifest Destiiny

Keyword search: westward expansion

Keyword search: James K. Polk

Keyword search: Mexican War

Keyword search: Zachary Taylor

Subject search: Treaty of Guadalupe Hidalgo

Keyword search: Irish immigration

Keyword search: potato famine

Keyword search: Thoreau

Keyword search: Emerson

Keyword search: Wilmot Proviso

Subject search: Compromise of 1850

ADDITIONAL READING

William R. Brock, *Parties and Political Conscience: American Dilemmas, 1840–1850* (1979). A good overview of national politics, emphasizing the relationship of ideas, interests, and national identity; see also the titles listed at the end of Chapter 13.

Nature, Technology, and Expansion

Barbara Novak, *Nature and Culture: American Landscape and Painting, 1825–1875* (1980). Based on art and literature, this analysis suggests the 19th-century ambivalence about territorial development and "progress."

The Wonders of Technology

William Cronon, *Nature's Metropolis: Chicago and the Great West* (1991). An economic and ecological history, the early chapters focus on railroads, grains, and lumber; the study extends to the end of the century.

Heading West

Lillian Schlissel, *Women's Diaries of the Westward Journey* (1982). Based on women's writings, the book provides an engaging account of the epic migration.

Anti-Irish Nativism

Dale T. Knobel, *Paddy and the Republic: Ethnicity and Nationality in Antebellum America* (1986). A study of changing images of Irish immigrants, this provocative work may be supplemented with Kerby A. Miller, *Emigrants and Exiles: Ireland and the Irish Exodus to North America* (1985).

Challenging Racial Inequality

Richard H. Sewell, *Ballots for Freedom: Antislavery Politics in the United States, 1837–1860* (1976). This book provides a clear account of the role of abolitionism in the political arena.

Antislavery Issues and the Rights of Women

Blanche Glassman Hersh, *The Slavery of Sex: Feminist Abolitionists in America* (1978). Tracing the origins of feminism within the evangelical abolitionist movement, this analysis should be supplemented with the first chapter of Ellen Carol DuBois, *Feminism and Suffrage: The Emergence of an Independent Women's Movement in America, 1848–1869* (1978). See also the relevant chapters of Paul Goodman, *Of One Blood* (1998), listed in Chapter 11.

Texas and Oregon

David J. Weber, *The Mexican Frontier, 1821–1846: The American Southwest under Mexico* (1982). A thorough history of Mexico's northern provinces, analyzing the impact of U.S. expansion into the region.

The California Gold Rush

Susan Lee Johnson, *Roaring Camp: The Social World of the California Gold Rush* (2000). A multicultural perspective of the mining camps; for the impact on Native Americans, see also James J. Rawls, *Indians of California: The Changing Image* (1984).

Malcolm J. Rohrbough, *Days of Gold: The California Gold Rush and the American Nation* (1997). Using letters and diaries of California gold miners, the book depicts the migration west and its consequences for those who stayed east.

13

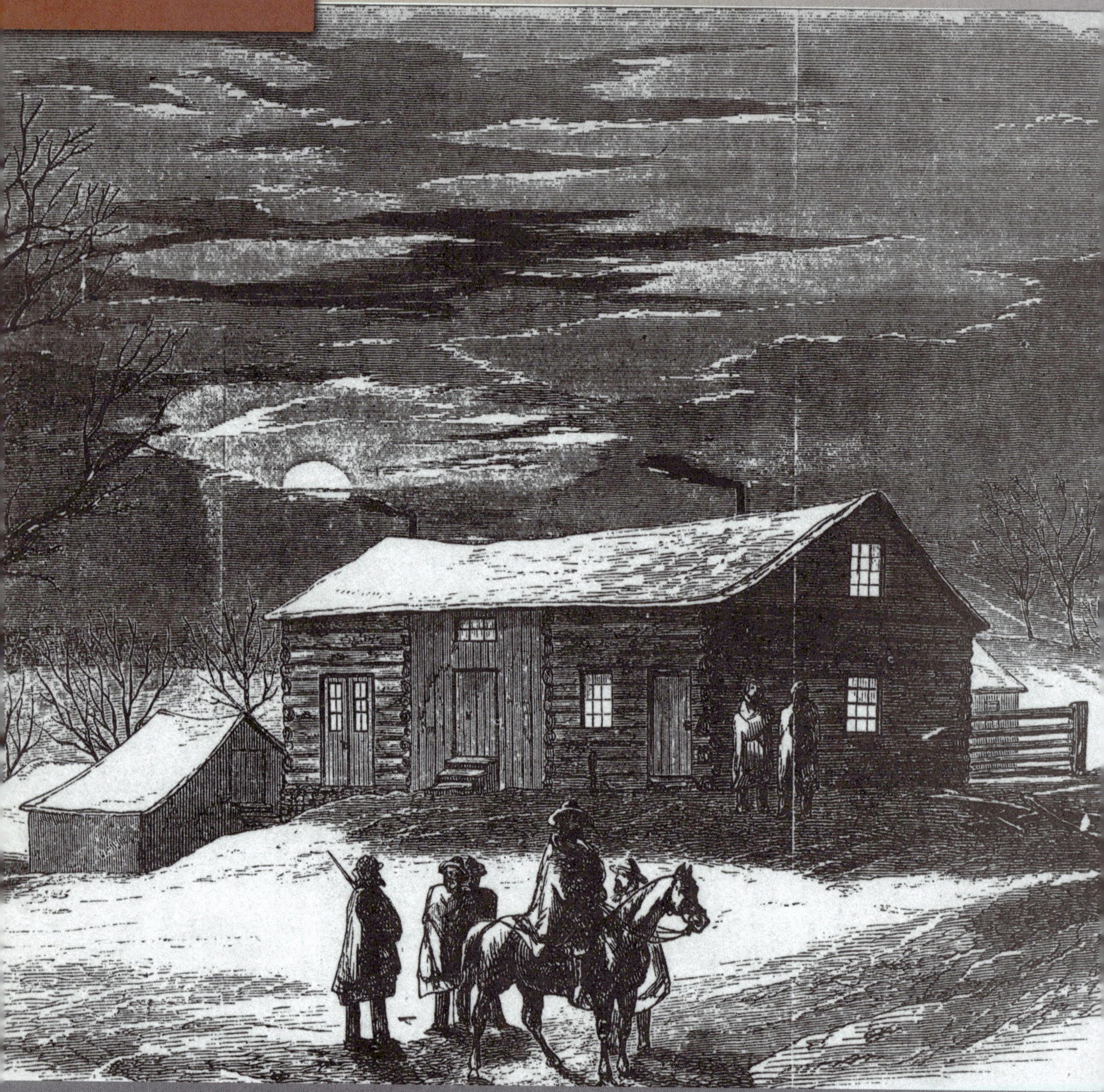

The Collapse of the Union, 1850–1861

CHRONOLOGY

Amid the strains of national politics in 1855, the country's foremost philosopher, Ralph Waldo Emerson, received from Walt Whitman a new book of poetry entitled *Leaves of Grass.* "I greet you at the beginning of a great career," he wrote the young author. While political leaders struggled to reconcile the contradictions of democratic sentiment—the divisions between southern and northern citizens, between cultures and classes—the 36-year-old New York poet's "Song of Myself" reveled in such paradoxes:

I am of old and young, of the foolish as much as the wise . . . ,

Maternal as well as paternal, a child as well as a man,

Stuffed with the stuff that is coarse, and stuffed with the stuff that is fine.

. . . .

A southerner soon as a northerner, a planter nonchalant and hospitable,

A Yankee . . . ready for trade.

. . . .

Of every hue and trade and rank, of every caste and religion,

Not merely of the New World but of Africa Europe
or Asia . . . a wandering savage.

. . . .

And am not stuck up, and am in my place.

Whitman's free verse celebrated the uncertainties of
the national identity—the coexistence of liberty and
slavery, of cultural toleration and intolerant nativism—
that made so many of his contemporaries uneasy. His
efforts to embrace all humanity seemed risky to a people fixated on "every hue and trade and rank." And
when the poet exulted, "I sing the body electric," he
touched on anxieties that were rooted both in the era's
sexual repression and in the "shock" of new technologies. Still, Whitman's work reaffirmed the uniqueness
of the country and its diverse inhabitants. "The genius
of the United States," he declared, "is not best or most
in its executives or legislatures, nor in its ambassadors
or authors or colleges or churches or parlors, nor even
in its newspapers or inventors . . . but always most in
the common people." This celebration of democracy
and cultural pluralism contrasted with the failure of
national politicians to resolve sectional disputes. Soon
after the decade ended, the poet's plea for union would
dissolve in a roar of cannons.

In his annual message to Congress in December
1850, President Millard Fillmore called the recent Compromise over extending slavery into
the new western territories "final and irrevocable."
His optimism was considerable, because most national politicians recognized that the political climate remained poisoned by regional conflicts.
Many northern leaders still refused to accept slavery in any unorganized territories, and southern
leaders equally condemned efforts to limit their
right to own slaves. Politicians in both regions
looked suspiciously at their opponents: some believed that a "slave power" conspiracy was seeking
to extend the South's peculiar institution; others
saw abolitionists laboring to deny the legitimate
rights of slaveholding citizens. The two regions
held different versions of the national identity;
each believed that the other's was immoral, if not
illegal. Yet, as government promoted westward expansion and citizens clamored for public lands, the
organization of new territories as either slave or
free could not be put off much longer.

Despite these tensions, most citizens of 1850
did not foresee a disruption of the union. Although slavery would dominate the nation's political life during the decade, a multitude of other
social issues competed for public attention. The
continuing immigration of foreign settlers, especially Catholic Irish and Germans, created social
tensions that affected voting alignments and political activity. Anti-immigration, or *nativism,* became a powerful political movement, attracting
voters from the old national parties. Whereas reformers of the previous decade had emphasized
moral persuasion alone to cure social and cultural
ills, during the 1850s citizens stressed legislative
solutions. Efforts to control foreign minorities
provoked both violence and political campaigns

to limit their influence. Yet, ironically, foreign immigration to free-labor states increased the North's population and its political representation in Congress, underscoring the South's minority status.

Political conflict about slavery, race, and ethnicity also obscured the decade's remarkable economic prosperity. California gold added a windfall to the nation's money supply, which, in turn, stimulated economic growth. In 1858, the discovery of gold in Colorado set off the cry "Pike's Peak or Bust!" The next year, silver finds in California and Nevada launched another mining boom. Economic optimism, in turn, encouraged investment in transportation, manufacturing, and commercial farming. Yet these economic developments, by stimulating western expansion, contributed to the sectional crisis. The question of slavery in the territories echoed behind every political issue.

The Ironies of Economic Prosperity

By 1850, half the nation's people lived west of the Appalachian Mountains. Most made their living in agriculture, but in two decidedly different economies. South of the Ohio River and extending toward Texas, the agricultural economy was based on cotton and slavery. Nonslaveholding southerners also migrated into this region, but many aspired to obtain land in order to improve their social position. Southwestern growers thus shared economic and cultural values with southeasterners. In the northwestern portion of the Mississippi valley, by contrast, free-labor agriculture prevailed, producing food crops for consumption in eastern cities and in Europe. Northern agricultural prosperity bene-

fited from the growth of transportation systems, especially railroads, which increasingly bound the economic interests of northwestern farmers to northeastern markets. The economic boom thus accentuated sectional differences between North and South. What the two regional economies shared, however, was a disregard for Native American land claims, which stood in the way of western settlement. During the 1850s, the federal government coerced the Plains nations to accept treaties that limited access to their traditional lands.

The Agricultural Boom

A boom in cotton fueled a decade of national prosperity. Between 1850 and 1860, southern output increased from less than 3 million bales a year to nearly 5 million. By 1860, the value of cotton exports reached almost $200 million per year, accounting for nearly two-thirds of the country's total export trade. Three other southern products—sugar, tobacco, and rice—enjoyed a similar boom.

Indicative of southern prosperity was the doubling of the value of slaves during the decade. Some historians suggest that southern planters were not "landlords" but "labor lords." As the price of slaves rose, the proportion of whites who owned slaves declined from one-third to one-quarter. In other words, the economics of plantation agriculture enabled a smaller segment of southern society to control more of the region's total agricultural assets, indeed, as much as 90 to 95 percent of its wealth. A defender of southern agriculture described the planters as "unquestionably the most prosperous people on earth." But one consequence of investment in slaves was a proportionally smaller ownership of manufacturing, banking, and transportation, which attracted northern investors (Table 13.1). Southern leaders frequently complained of their dependence on northern capital to maintain their agricultural economy.

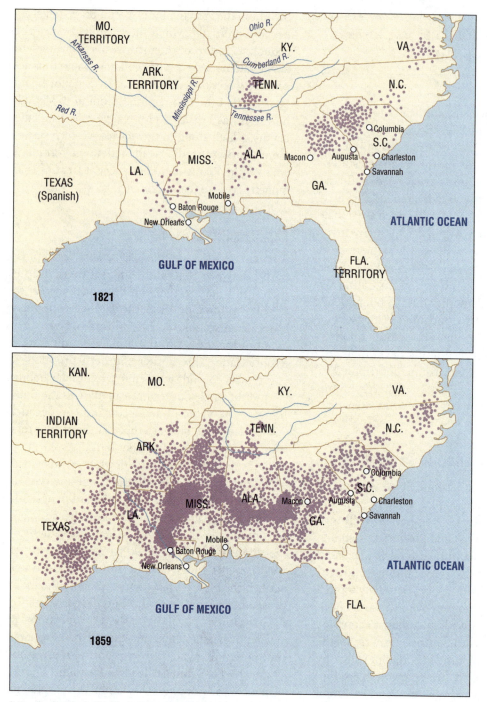

Cotton Production in the South, 1821 and 1859

TABLE 13.1

Regional Patterns of Manufacturing, 1850 and 1860

	Capital Invested by Manufacturing per Capita		Value of Manufacturing Output per Capita	
	1850	1860	1850	1860
New England	$57.96	$82.13	$100.71	$149.47
Middle States	35.50	52.21	71.24	96.28
Northwest	11.70	18.95	26.32	37.33
Pacific States	10.39	42.35	84.83	129.04
South	7.60	10.54	10.88	17.09
Cotton South	5.11	7.20	6.83	10.47
U.S.	22.73	32.12	43.69	59.98

Sources: U.S. Bureau of the Census, *Compendium of 1850 Census*, p. 179; Eighth U.S. Census, *Manufactures*, p. 725; Ninth U.S. Census, *Compendium*, p. 799.

Northern farmers were also affected by the operations of distant markets. The repeal of Britain's grain tariffs in 1846 and food shortages in Europe after the outbreak of the Crimean War in 1853 created new demands for northern corn, wheat, and pork. Since family farms, unlike southern plantations, faced perennial labor shortages, rising agricultural prices encouraged investment in farm machinery, which jumped over 60 percent to $250 million during the decade. Improved farming and crop specialization contributed to a doubling of production. Unable to compete with western grains, eastern farmers shifted to more specialized agriculture: vegetables, fruits, and dairy products. By 1860, local farmers were shipping nearly 200,000 quarts of milk to New York City every day. Areas of Massachusetts also enjoyed a small boom in tobacco production, though one college president expressed regret that tobacco farmers "sacrificed their luxuriant and lovely meadows to the growth of a narcotic."

The Economics of Railroad Expansion

Northern agricultural prosperity was closely tied to a boom in railroad construction, which reinforced the differences between the southern and northern economies. During the 1850s, railroad companies laid 20,000 miles of track worth $800 million of investments. The mileage of southern railroads increased 350 percent, but remained under one-third of the nation's total. By 1860, four major trunk lines linked the Atlantic ports of New York, Philadelphia, and Baltimore with the Ohio and Mississippi valleys. In 1856, the Chicago and Rock Island line opened the first railroad bridge across the Mississippi river, an engineering feat that required 1 million feet of lumber and over 300 tons of iron.

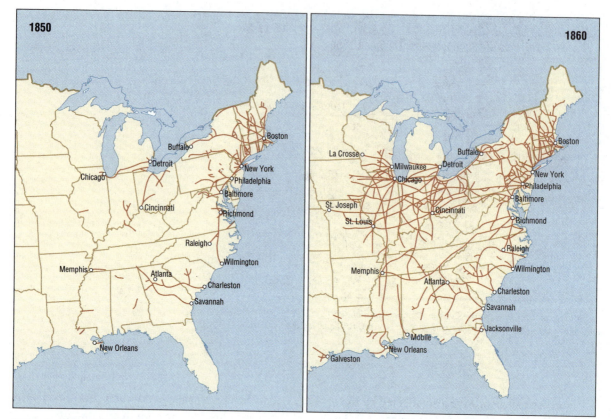

Railroads, 1850 and 1860

Meanwhile, the number of locomotives jumped from 3,000 to 8,500, and railroad employees increased from 4,800 to 90,000! Although freight traffic gradually surpassed passenger travel, the Erie line added a touch of professionalism by requiring conductors to wear uniforms. They were the first civilian employees so attired.

While the southern economy continued to rely on river transport to bring cotton to market, railroads began to weave inextricable ties between the Northeast and the Northwest. By 1860, eleven railroads and a hundred trains each day linked Chicago's massive grain elevators (with a total ca-

pacity of 4 million bushels) not only to transatlantic shipping companies but also to a commodities market that speculated in the future prices of grain. Similarly, the unprecedented amount of capital necessary to build the great trunk lines ($17 to $35 million each) required mass sales of railroad securities to domestic and foreign financiers. Boosted by railroad investment, by mid-decade the New York Stock Exchange was trading hundreds of thousands of shares each week. Meanwhile, new techniques of railroad finance—bond issues and subcontracted work—began to be used to fund northern municipal improve-

TABLE 13.2

Railroad Mileage in the United States, 1850–1860

Year	Miles of Line in Operation
1850	9,021
1852	12,908
1854	16,720
1856	22,016
1858	26,968
1860	30,626

Source: John F. Stover, *Iron Road to the West: American Railroads in the 1850s* (New York: Columbia University Press, 1978).

ments, enabling cities to pay for public works without raising taxes.

Track construction and railroad operations soon stimulated other industries. In rural Alabama, for example, woodburning locomotives and standard railroad ties demanded more logging and lumber mills. In the Great Lakes states, railroads virtually consumed the north woods. The shift to coal in the 1850s encouraged anthracite mining, particularly in Pennsylvania. Most important was the demand for iron rails. By 1854, investments in U.S. iron mills exceeded $10 million, achieving an industrial capacity of 100,000 tons a year. Yet railroads still had to import nearly twice that amount from British mills. Indeed, even with the low tariffs established in 1846, the duty on rail imports was large enough to produce a government surplus and a further lowering of tariff rates in 1857. Ironically, cotton exports supported this international trade, even though the immense profits from transporting the crop went to northern shippers and investors.

Railroads also had a cultural impact, stimulating a new preoccupation with timekeeping in all regions. "They come and go with such regularity and precision, and their whistles can be heard so far," remarked Henry David Thoreau in his 1854 book *Walden*, "that the farmers set their clocks by them, and thus one well-conducted institution regulates the whole country." By the 1850s, the nation's largest clockmaker was manufacturing 280,000 brass shelf clocks each year. Equally innovative was the mass production of pocket watches. Improving the technology of manufacturing 150 interchangeable parts, the Waltham Watch Company reduced the labor time for making each watch from 21 days in 1854 to 4 days in 1859 and advertised that broken parts could be replaced by mail with nothing more than the watch's serial number.

Despite the new national passion for punctuality, railroads still followed local sun time, which varied with geographical longitude, and efforts to standardize time zones were unsuccessful. Most citizens viewed timekeeping as a local, not a national, concern—an outlook that also applied to most political issues. Railroads would become an exception to local thinking, but not without consequences for sectional conflict.

Federal Support of Railroads

Railroads, claimed a Boston editor, "made the land a neighborhood," bringing local businesses into a national, even international, marketplace. Farmers and merchants living near projected rail lines became a major source of capital investment. By mortgaging their property to support railroad construction, farmers protected—indeed, increased—the value of their land and ensured their access to distant consumers. In this way, Chicago's aggressive railroad promoters overwhelmed the rival city of St. Louis, which relied on river transportation. While St. Louis doubled in size, the windy city quadrupled, as shipments of flour jumped sixfold and wheat increased five times. Chicago's merchants now sought to make their city the terminus of the nation's railroad network, especially for a transcontinental line that aimed west.

Because of greater distances and sparser populations, western railroad development required more funding than local sources could usually provide. State and local governments assisted new railroads with loans, tax exemptions, subsidies, and the purchase of stock. But, unlike the earlier government-backed turnpikes and canals, railroad companies rejected government regulation of fares and freight rates to protect private investors. Even state aid could not always satisfy the capital demands of extensive railroads. In 1850, Illinois's Democratic Senator Stephen Douglas persuaded Congress to give 2.5 million acres of land to the Illinois Central to construct a 700-mile railroad linking Lake Michigan with the Ohio and Mississippi rivers. With that precedent, the federal government proceeded to grant over 20 million additional acres of public lands (an area four times the size of Massachusetts) to eleven midwestern and southern states as well as a free right-of-way on the public domain during the decade. Such government gifts were quickly transformed into liquid assets. Besides using the land as security for railroad bonds, the companies sold the acreage to speculators and settlers. By 1859, the Illinois Central had disposed of 1.3 million government-bestowed acres at $12 each (a total of about $300 million in today's money).

Railroads and Territorial Expansion

Federal involvement appeared even more important as railroad investors envisioned a transportation system that would link commercial farmers with the Pacific coast and Asian markets. In 1853, eight years after Congress ratified a trade treaty with China, a squadron of U.S. warships, commanded by Matthew Perry, entered Tokyo Bay in Japan and forced the *shogun* leadership to establish diplomatic relations. The ensuing treaty ensured that U.S. commerce obtained, as one American put it, "the entering wedge that will . . . open to us the interior wealth of these unknown lands." The same year, Congress authorized the War Department to undertake geographical surveys of four projected railroad routes across the Great Plains to the west coast. Secretary of War Jefferson Davis, a Mississippi slaveholder, favored a southern route that would connect Texas to San Diego. After he noticed that this route dipped below the border with Mexico, the federal government dispatched former South Carolina railroad president James Gadsden to Mexico to negotiate the purchase of territory south of the Gila river. It was an area so desolate, said the explorer Kit Carson, "a wolf could not make a living from it." But in 1854, the Senate ratified the Gadsden Purchase, exchanging $10 million for 30,000 square miles of railroad country.

As Washington politicians drew railroad lines on territorial maps, the original residents confronted threats to their survival. "Since the white man has made a road across our land," protested the Shoshone leader Washakie in 1855, "and has killed off our game, we are hungry, and there is nothing for us to eat." Four years earlier, in 1851, federal authorities had summoned the Plains nations to a conference near Fort Laramie in Wyoming to propose a new policy. The 10,000 Native Americans who attended learned that the government planned to confine them within distinct territorial boundaries—tribal reservations—to separate them from U.S. emigrants and from each other. Promising gifts and future annuities in exchange for the land, federal officials overcame the objections of unhappy Native leaders. Through the 1850s, U.S. expansion onto tribal territory brought further federal intervention, which compelled the Plains peoples to surrender another 1.5 million

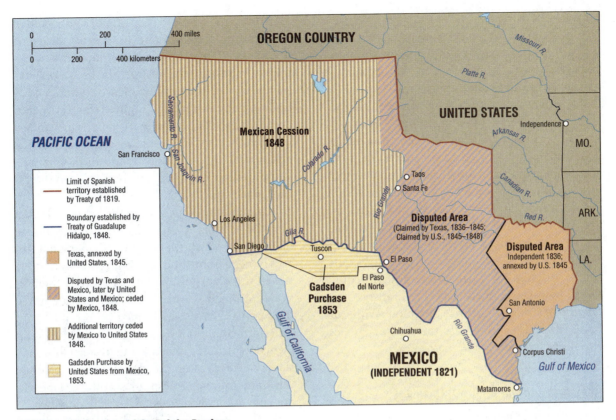

Southwestern Expansion and the Gadsden Purchase

> ## "Since the white man has made a road across our land and has killed off our game, we are hungry, and there is nothing for us to eat."

acres. Those concessions opened the region west of Missouri, known as the Kansas and Nebraska territory, to settlement by whites. Kansas and Nebraska would soon become familiar names throughout the country as plans to build a railroad to the Pacific reawakened the conflicts between North and South about the status of slavery.

Redrawing Political Lines

Regional disagreements also arose about expansionist schemes south of the U.S. border. Interested in acquiring territory suitable for cotton and slavery, southern expansionists spoke about seizing Cuba and portions of Central America. "The path of our destiny on this continent," declared one Virginian, "lies in . . . tropical America, [where] we may see an empire . . . representing the noble peculiarities of southern civilization." When Spain rejected U.S. offers to purchase Cuba, southern expansionists organized illegal invasions of the island. But military failures and lack of congressional support ultimately thwarted the efforts.

Many northern expansionists shared the view that the supposedly superior Anglo-Saxon "race" was destined to conquer the peoples of the tropical areas. Indeed, some hoped that expansion southward would redirect slavery away from the West, where free blacks were also unwelcome. During the 1850s, Indiana, Illinois, Iowa, and Oregon prohibited further settlement by blacks. The decade also saw renewed interest in transplanting freed African Americans beyond U.S. territorial limits to Central America, but such colonization schemes aroused opposition. "We are Americans, having a birthright citizenship," responded the black nationalist author Martin Delany in 1852. "We must not leave this continent." Interest in expansion south ultimately failed, however, because the issues of the western territories absorbed national attention. With railroads stretching from east to west, expansion south seemed remote and impractical.

Resistance to the Fugitive Slave Act

As southern expansionists touted the advantages of extending slavery through the Western Hemisphere, northern critics resolved to draw strict boundaries against its spread. At the beginning of the 1850s, the first border of contention was the Mason-Dixon Line, which had been drawn nearly a century earlier to mark the southern boundary of Pennsylvania and which separated slave states from free soil. The Compromise of 1850 had included a Fugitive Slave Act that was stricter than the statute of 1793 (see Chapter 7). The new law required free states to cooperate in returning runaway slaves. Southern politicians repeatedly stressed the importance of that law, both legally and symbolically, as evidence of northern good faith. "Upon a faithful execution" of that law, warned a southern leader, "depends the preservation of our much beloved Union."

Although southern politicians demanded northern cooperation and northern politicians like Daniel Webster promised compliance, a significant constituency of free blacks, slaves, ex-slaves, and antislavery whites honored a long tradition of resistance to fugitive slave laws. For decades, an informal network called the "underground railroad," operated by ex-slaves like the celebrated Harriet Tubman, southern Quakers, and northern sympathizers, had assisted the escape of fugitives, harboring them quietly in northern communities or speeding them to freedom in Canada. To prevent the kidnapping of free blacks, many northern states had enacted personal liberty laws guaranteeing the civil rights of fugitive slaves and obstructing efforts to return them to previous owners. After 1850, threats to enforce the Fugitive Slave Act alarmed northern African American communities. Thousands of blacks immediately fled to Canada, while respectable antislavery leaders announced their refusal to obey "an immoral and irreligious statute." Some did not rule out violent resistance. "The only way to make the fugitive slave law a dead letter," advised ex-slave Frederick Douglass, "is to make half a dozen or more dead kidnappers."

African Americans and their supporters soon forced northern citizens to confront the issue. In 1851, the arrest of a runaway slave, Frederick "Shadrach" Minkins, in Boston brought a mob of angry blacks into the courtroom, where they beat a federal marshal, seized the prisoner, and transported him to Canada. President Fillmore denounced the violence, but a defiant jury acquitted the perpetrators. Federal enforcement succeeded in a second Boston case involving Thomas Sims, but it required a small army, which ferried the accused south at four in the morning. Other incidents involved shootouts with would-be slave catchers, jailhouse rescues, and vigilante attacks on the courts. When a runaway from Virginia named Anthony Burns was ordered back to slavery after a week-long trial in 1854 and marched in chains through the streets of Boston under guard of 1,000 federal troops, northern outrage exploded. "My thoughts are murder to the state," said Thoreau. But a Georgia student at Harvard who witnessed the protests now wrote to his parents, "Do not be surprised if when I return home you find me a *confirmed disunionist.*"

For northern whites, however, fugitives like Anthony Burns, Thomas Sims, and Shadrach Minkins—or more famous runaways like Frederick Douglass, Harriet Tubman, and Harriet Jacobs—gave the anonymous slave a human face. So, too, did the popular songs of the 1850s written by Stephen Foster, such as "My Old Kentucky Home" and "Beautiful Dreamer." Despite their stereotypes, the lyrics described African Americans experiencing human emotions and feelings. "They are heart songs," said Douglass in 1855. "They awaken sympathies for the slave, in which antislavery principles take root, grow and flourish." The publication of numerous autobiographies by ex-slaves not only showed the evils of slavery but also answered southern claims that unsupervised blacks could not achieve their human potential.

These themes culminated in the appearance of a stunning work of fiction, Harriet Beecher Stowe's *Uncle Tom's Cabin,* in 1852. The book sold 300,000 copies the first year, 2 million in a decade, and it became a stage play that captivated audiences for the remainder of the century. Inspired by the fugitive slave cases, Stowe condemned the human suffering, presenting the slave Uncle Tom as a Christ figure who transcends worldly evil through spiritual redemption. Passionately written and read, the scenes of Tom sold away from his children or the slave mother Eliza crossing the icy Ohio river for freedom etched the agony of slavery onto the northern conscience. Southerners attacked the novel for its distortions, even published counter-

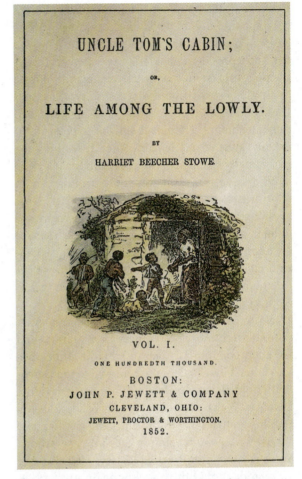

Title page of the 100,000th copy of the first edition of Harriet Beecher Stowe's *Uncle Tom's Cabin,* published at Boston in 1852.

novels to show the advantages of slavery. But Stowe's work remained a powerful indictment of the slave system, and she used her royalties to underwrite other antislavery protests.

The Weakening Party System

Despite the notoriety of the fugitive slave cases, most political leaders and voters hoped to preserve the Compromise of 1850. Off-year congressional elections in 1850 and 1851 showed support for the agreements, and in 1852 both national parties adopted platforms that accepted its principles. But the 1852 presidential election revealed strains in the political system, particularly among the Whigs. With the great compromisers Henry Clay and Daniel Webster dead in 1852, the Whig party had difficulty finding a candidate suitable to both southern and northern delegates. After 52 ballots, the party finally nominated the noncommittal General Winfield Scott over the pro-southern Fillmore to run for president. Scott would be the last Whig presidential candidate. Southern Whigs, frustrated at their failure to influence northern allies, began to abandon the party. The Democratic party also confronted a deadlock among competing factions before nominating New Hampshire's Franklin Pierce, a northerner with southern sympathies.

Both parties competed for the urban immigrant vote, though most newcomers from Ireland and Germany continued to identify with the Democrats. Van Buren's Free Soilers also returned to the Democratic fold. The splits in the Whig party gave the Democrat Pierce an electoral vote landslide, 254–42. But the popular vote was much closer, and in many areas eligible voters simply did not cast ballots. Voter participation reached its lowest levels since 1836 and would not be so low again until 1904. Some party regulars attributed the low turnout to the absence of issues. "General Apathy is the strongest candidate," remarked an Ohio politician. But it was the refusal of the national parties to address the real issues of the Compromise of 1850 that undoubtedly kept voters away.

"Party names of Whig and Democrat now mean nothing and point to nothing," observed a political commentator in 1853. The absence of national economic issues underscored the political intrigue of rival politicians competing for office. The parties had become "empty flesh, putrid mouths," said the poet Whitman, "the politicians standing back in the shadow telling lies." Cases of corruption emerged in local, state, and federal government, further weakening allegiance to the established parties. "Parties are broken up by local causes," lamented former President Fillmore at the end of 1853; only "some great national and centripetal force at Washington" could save them.

The Kansas-Nebraska Bill

National politics swiftly grabbed public attention in 1854 when Senator Stephen Douglas introduced legislation to organize the territories of Kansas and Nebraska. Seeking to secure Chicago's position as the terminus of the transcontinental railroad, Douglas saw no need to honor earlier pledges to protect the lands of the Plains nations, an omission that raised no congressional protests. But his willingness to tinker with the Missouri Compromise—under which both new territories would have become free states—soon aroused a political storm. The Missouri Compromise forbade slavery north of the line 36°30' but Southern Whigs, looking for an issue that would rejuvenate their party, now joined southern Democrats in demanding repeal of the Missouri line in exchange for their support of the Kansas-Nebraska bill. Douglas agreed to modify his proposal. Believing that neither territory was geographically suited to slave agriculture, he offered an alternative that he believed would satisfy southern demands for equal treatment in the West, while ensuring that the new states would adopt antislavery constitutions. His proposal reflected the idea of "popular sovereignty," which had already been part of the 1850 Compromise to regulate the New Mexico territory (see Chapter 12). Douglas proposed that the voters in each territory be allowed to decide the status of slavery. He never doubted the results: both Kansas and Nebraska would enter the union as free states.

Douglas underestimated the strength of anti-slavery opinion. Overnight, a group of antislavery Democrats, led by Ohio's Salmon Chase, published an "Appeal of the Independent Democrats," denouncing the proposed repeal of the Missouri Compromise "as a gross violation of a sacred pledge" and "part and parcel of an atrocious plot" to transform Kansas and Nebraska into slave states. To northern minds, the key word was *plot*; a conspiracy of slaveowners appeared ready to overthrow free republican institutions. "Past party lines will be obliterated with the Missouri line," predicted one politician—accurately, as it turned out.

The pro-southern Pierce administration worked with Douglas to muster a majority to pass the Kansas-Nebraska bill in both houses of Congress. Nevertheless, the Democratic party now began to divide along sectional lines. Meanwhile, Northern Whigs, realizing the unpopularity of the bill among antislavery constituents, voted against the measure. This trend prompted southern Whigs to announce "we will have no party association that will not . . . treat us as *equals*." Defending regional interests more than party ties, southern Whigs provided the critical votes needed to enact Douglas's plan into law. Frustrated northerners, Democrats and Whigs alike, began to form independent parties. Among these was the Republican party, born in the northern Midwest in 1854 and initially drawing support on a single issue: opposition to slavery in the territories. Thus passage of the Kansas-Nebraska act destroyed the Whigs as a national party and accelerated major political realignments.

Cultural Differences Become Political

As the slavery controversy disrupted both national parties, voters increasingly focused on political issues related to the changing ethnic composition of their communities. With 3 million immigrants arriving on Atlantic shores in the decade after 1845 (see Chapter 12), anti-foreign nativist politics assumed growing importance. When, for example, Irish and German immigrants showed indifference to evangelical temperance reformers, political leaders pushed for state legislation to outlaw alcohol consumption. During the 1850s, a dozen northern states passed prohibition laws. Ironically, the reluctance of traditional party leaders to take sides on prohibition contributed to the view that they were, as one reformer called them, "old fogies" who were oblivious to social problems. Protestant leaders frequently denounced a Catholic conspiracy against republican institutions, pointing, for instance, to Pierce's appointment of a Catholic postmaster general (a position with great patronage power) as a sign of impending subversion.

Growing anti-foreign sentiment encouraged a secret nativist club called the Order of the Star Spangled Banner to organize private lodges around the country, offering membership only to white Protestant men who had Protestant parents and who were "not united in marriage with a Roman Catholic." Members shared secret handshakes, passwords, and signals, strove for anonymity, and responded to outside inquiries by claiming to "know nothing." The Know Nothings, as they were called, sought to curb immigration and extend the probation period for naturalized citizenship. By early 1854, the Know Nothings tallied 50,000 members; half a year later, the secret group totaled over 1 million.

The election returns of 1854 awakened politicians to the strength of this political force, which many had not even realized existed. Selecting candidates from among their anonymous membership, the Know Nothings voted as a bloc in favor of temperance, against established politicians who depended on immigrant voters, and, in northern states, against repeal of the Missouri Compromise.

In Massachusetts, the Know Nothings captured the governorship, most of the state legislature, and the entire congressional delegation; in the South, many Whigs migrated to the movement as a way of competing with rival Democrats. The relationship between Know Nothings and slavery remained ambiguous. Southern Know Nothings supported slavery, but some northerners saw no difference between attacking slaveholders and Catholics. Others, like ex-Whig Republican Abraham Lincoln, wondered "How can any one who abhors the oppression of negroes be in favor of degrading classes of white people?"

Problems of Political Geography

By the mid-1850s, voters faced a widening array of political choices as new groups attempted to replace the Whigs as a national party and local issues complicated political alignments. In 1855, the nativist Know Nothings (now formally identified as the American party) tried to build a national organization by appealing to anti-immigration, anti-Catholic voters in all regions. Similarly, the small Republican party attempted to find allies among ex-Whigs, Free Soilers, antislavery Know Nothings, and anti-expansionist Democrats. "We are all very much in the dark as to the political future," confessed one politician.

While party leaders looked for a thread that would stitch national politics back together, one issue remained a powerful counterforce, ever dividing citizens along geographical lines: slavery in the territories. As more northern voters came to view slavery as a threat to wage labor, economic opportunity in the West, and civil liberties, and while southern politicians condemned the antislavery movement as a threat to property rights, slavery ignited deep passions that refused to be distracted by other issues. The one common concern of national politics, slavery split the country into two irreconcilable camps.

Bleeding Kansas and the Election of 1856

Stephen Douglas expected congressional approval of popular sovereignty to end the debate about slavery in Kansas. But the formation of a territorial government in 1855 triggered an explosion of violence that stunned the country and came to be known as "Bleeding Kansas." A majority of Kansas's settlers had migrated from free states and opposed slavery, but on election day slaveholders from Missouri rode across the state border to cast a majority of votes for a proslavery legislature to draft the state constitution. The legislature proceeded to enact proslavery laws, including one that prohibited antislavery men from holding office. This perversion of popular sovereignty outraged northern opinion. "We are for free Kansas," said an Illinois newspaper, "because we are for free white men." In Kansas, violence between proslavery and antislavery factions steadily escalated. Challenging the election fraud, the numerically larger antislavery settlers elected their own constitutional delegates and proceeded to form a territorial government in Topeka that prohibited slavery. Expressing widely held racist views, the same delegates also banned the immigration of free blacks.

President Pierce, now facing two rival constitutions, chose to support the proslavery legislature and warned the free-state claimants in Topeka that further opposition would be "treasonable insurrection." But violence between northern and southern settlers persisted. After a proslavery court in Kansas indicted antislavery leaders for treason, an armed proslavery posse attempted to arrest opposition leaders in the town of Lawrence, burned the Free Soil Hotel, and wrecked antislavery printing presses. Abolitionist

The Election of 1856

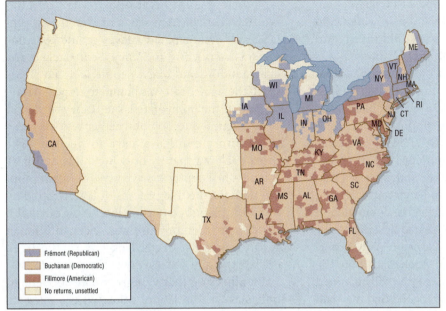

Frémont (Republican)
Buchanan (Democratic)
Fillmore (American)
No returns, unsettled

John Brown then took revenge by murdering five proslavery men at Pottawatomie Creek. Reacting to Bleeding Kansas, northerners and southerners cast blame on their opponents. In May 1856, Massachusetts's antislavery Senator Charles Sumner embarked on a two-day speech entitled "The Crime against Kansas." When Representative Preston Brooks learned that the senator's diatribe had insulted his cousin, South Carolina Senator Andrew Butler, he approached Sumner on the Senate floor and beat him into unconsciousness with a cane. It would take Sumner four years to recover from his injuries; northerners saw him as a martyr to the antislavery cause. Brooks emerged instantly as a southern hero.

The attack on Sumner infuriated the North, appearing as plain evidence of the barbarous effects of slavery and the threat to republican government: "Not merely an *incident,* but a *demonstration,*" said one politician, of a southern plan "to annihilate freedom." This sense of a southern conspiracy defined

the 1856 presidential election. The Democrat Pierce's acceptance of slavery in Kansas ended his hopes for reelection in the North. The election fraud in Kansas also belied Douglas's optimism that popular sovereignty would make that state free and weakened his support in the North. The Democrats then nominated Pennsylvania's James Buchanan, a northerner with strong southern leanings. As ambassador to Britain, Buchanan had avoided the sectional debate. Meanwhile, the American party nominated its first presidential candidate, former President Millard Fillmore, but his refusal to condemn the spread of slavery destroyed his northern support. The new Republican party, committed unequivocally "to prohibit in the territories those twin relics of barbarism—polygamy and slavery," nominated John C. Frémont, famous as a military explorer of the West.

"You never saw so much enthusiasm in the people," noted a Republican politician. Although Frémont had no chance to carry the South, northern voters saw his candidacy as an alternative to traditional politics. In writing a campaign poem supporting Frémont, the abolitionist Lydia Child found that the only word she could think of to rhyme with Pierce (pronounced "purse") was "curse." Seeing Frémont as a moral politician, northern women flocked to his campaign rallies. Despite rumors of the nominee's Catholic ancestry, Republicans also won support from former Know Nothings in the North, showing that antislavery remained a more potent issue than nativism. With the slogan "Free Soil, Free Speech, Free Men, Frémont," the candidate carried eleven of the sixteen free states. Buchanan dominated in the South, where Frémont was not a serious candidate. Fillmore took only Maryland. With 45 percent of the popular vote, Buchanan won the election. But Republican leaders carefully counted their gains in the North, understood that they had absorbed their former rivals, the nativists, and pronounced the result "a victorious defeat." After the election, the Know Nothings disappeared as a political party.

The Dred Scott Decision

"May we not, then, hope," said Buchanan in his inaugural address of 1857, "that geographical parties . . . will speedily become extinct?" Such wishful thinking reflected the president's expectation that an imminent Supreme Court decision would resolve the issue of slavery in the territories once and for all. Members of the Court had leaked the outcome of a pending decision to the president-elect. However, when Chief Justice Roger Taney, the son of a Maryland slaveholding family, publicly announced the verdict two days after Buchanan's inauguration, the ruling—and the public outcry—thwarted any hopes for a sectional truce.

The case involved the family of Dred Scott, a Missouri slave who had once lived with his master in free territory north of 36°30' and on that basis now sued for his freedom. The Court answered by denying that slaves or even the descendants of emancipated slaves could become citizens. According to Taney, Scott lacked any legal standing and black people had "no rights which the white man was bound to respect." Having settled the immediate issue, Taney turned to the theoretical question of whether residence in a free territory entitled a slave to freedom. The Court declared that by drawing a line at 36°30' Congress had deprived slaveowners of their property without the due process of law required by the Fifth Amendment; therefore, the Court said, the Missouri Compromise was unconstitutional. Congress, in other words, lacked the authority to legislate the status of slavery in the territories.

By affirming that Congress had no right to limit slavery, the Court validated the extreme southern view and persuaded southern Democrats that they had heard "the funeral sermon of Black Republicanism." Yet Douglas Democrats insisted that the Court had upheld popular sovereignty because enforcement of slaveownership would depend on local laws. Slaveowners obviously understood that logic, for they made no move to bring their slaves into free territory. By contrast, many northern politicians saw in the ruling the hand of a "slave power" conspiracy. Antislavery leaders denounced the verdict as having "as much moral weight as . . . the judgment of a majority of those congregated in any Washington bar-room."

Nor did the *Dred Scott* ruling end the struggle in Kansas. When the proslavery territorial legislature called elections for delegates to ratify the territorial constitution in 1857, antislavery settlers boycotted the polls. Proslavery delegates then met in the town of Lecompton, drew up a constitution that legalized slavery, and—with free soilers still boycotting the proceedings—ratified the document. When the constitution went to voters for ratification, free soilers ended their boycott and carried a majority that rejected the proposal. Nevertheless, the proslavery faction applied for admission into the union.

Congress now had to decide which vote was valid. Buchanan's pledge to support popular sovereignty quickly evaporated. Instead of challenging the dubious voting in Kansas, the president endorsed the proslavery Lecompton constitution. Northern politicians, enraged at Buchanan's dismissal of the majority vote, charged the president with being part of the southern conspiracy. Douglas, facing pressure from his northern constituents, broke with the administration. Despite intense presidential lobbying, the House voted to reject the admission of Kansas as a slave state. By then, Douglas had lost his southern support. Not until 1861, after several southern states had seceded from the union, did Congress admit Kansas—as a free state.

The Politics of Economic Crisis

With political tempers afire, a sudden economic downturn (one New Yorker called it "a clap of thunder in a clear sky") accentuated sectional grievances. The financial Panic of 1857, followed by a severe depression, reflected distant economic factors, particularly the end of the Crimean War, which reduced the market for U.S. agricultural exports, and shifts in European investments. As U.S. businesses fell into bankruptcy and banks suspended payments, the price of western wheat and southern cotton plummeted. The slump in demand for farm production, in turn, affected railroad traffic and abruptly terminated the boom in new construction. This unexpected stagnation reawakened southern condemnation of the nation's financial institutions, what one planter criticized as "the wild speculations of Northern and

To provide jobs for the unemployed, New York City launched the construction of Central Park.

Western corporations." Yet, thanks to European demand, the southern cotton economy proved more resilient than western agriculture. While wheat prices remained depressed for two years, southern exports recovered by 1858, reaffirming the adage that "cotton is King."

Poverty in the Cities

The depression of the late 1850s proved much harder for city dwellers than for farmers. With over 5,000 business failures, urban unemployment skyrocketed. Jobless workers massed in the streets of most major cities, crying "Bread or Blood!" Challenging pay cuts, shoemakers, miners, female mill operators, and Irish construction workers organized trade unions and went on strike to demand better wages. But companies lacked the cash even to offer back pay, and charitable assistance was hopelessly inadequate. In New York, 40,000 homeless and poor people sought shelter in police stations, and newspapers routinely reported cases of unemployed workers and children starving to death.

To provide jobs for the unemployed, New York City launched a major public works project, the construction of Central Park. The idea of an urban park also addressed worsening problems of population density, commercial traffic, and noxious living conditions. Drawing 20,000 immigrants a year, the city had doubled in size to 1 million during the decade. Even in prosperous times, many workers barely eked out a living, and disparities of wealth and property ownership increased. Prostitution,

A fashionable crowd gathers to socialize on a Saturday afternoon near the music stand on the mall in New York City's Central Park, 1869.

alcoholism, and crime abounded, while sanitation, sewage, and garbage removal were left to roaming pigs. To New York's merchant princes and middle class planners, a landscaped urban park promised an island of tranquility to ease what one gentleman called the "heart-hardening and taste-smothering habits" of urban life.

Under the guidance of landscape architects Frederick Law Olmsted and Calvert Vaux, construction began in 1857. The city spent $5 million and hired some 20,000 workers to build the 800-acre park in the middle of Manhattan. The project was truly staggering, requiring 166 tons of gunpowder (more than would be expended in the Battle of Gettysburg) to blast out the bedrock, 6 million bricks, 40,000 cubic yards of manure, and 270,000 trees and shrubs. What distinguished this extraordinary engineering feat was the aesthetic approach to the land. Avoiding the rectangular lines associated with the city's street grid, Central Park's arrangement of sloping hills and meadows, artificial ponds, and winding pathways offered refuge from the urban hubbub. But the park also placed a firm human hand on the irregularities of the natural landscape. Just as the entrepreneur P.T. Barnum presented "wild" animals in cages, so the urban park offered manicured "nature" to a people starved for sunlight and fresh air.

Reinforcing Regional Prejudices

The economic crisis in the North gave southern apologists cause for satisfaction. The problems of northern wage earners, a Virginia newspaper editorialized, contrasted with the "content and quiet" of southern slaves, who faced no "want and suffering." In a work entitled *Cannibals All!* Virginia's George Fitzhugh argued that northern wage labor lacked the inherent protections of a beneficent slave society. Southerners also used the Panic of 1857 as an opportunity to denounce northern business preferences, such as tariffs and western land speculation. The rapid recovery of cotton sales not only reinforced confidence in the southern economy but also convinced southern leaders that cotton was indispensable in the world market and that cotton importers, especially England, recognized their dependence on the crop.

Northerners also drew lessons from the economic crisis. Southern leaders had long supported low tariffs, including reduced rates in 1857. Northern business leaders blamed those lower rates for failing to protect industry and jobs and leaving the Treasury too depleted to ease eastern unemployment by financing internal improvements or encouraging settlement of the West. The belief that western lands could serve as a safety valve to absorb surplus free labor also reinforced northern opposition to extension of slavery in the territories. Responding to such pressure, the Republican party would endorse an economic program (higher tariffs, a homestead act to encourage westward migration, and internal improvements) that was opposed by most southern planters. In this way, economic regionalism reinforced the geography of political alignments.

Irreconcilable Differences

Sectional disagreements about the causes of the Panic of 1857, like the debate over slavery in the territories, reflected a polarization of opinion about recent laws. Although politicians in both regions shared political values about representative government, each side believed that its opponents had violated the principles of constitutional government. Accepting the *Dred Scott* decision, southerners perceived a conspiracy of northern extremists, fired by abolitionism, who refused to acknowledge, in the words of one politician, that

"southern opinion . . . is now the supreme law of the land." Antislavery northerners, frustrated by political defeats, saw a different conspiracy defeating the will of the majority. Challenging Stephen Douglas for the Senate in 1858, the Republican candidate articulated those fears. "When we see a lot of framed timbers . . . which we know have been gotten out at different times and places by different workmen—Stephen, Franklin, Roger, and James," remarked Abraham Lincoln (referring to Douglas, Pierce, Taney, and Buchanan), "and when we see these timbers . . . exactly make the frame of a house . . . we find it impossible to not believe that Stephen and Franklin and Roger and James . . . worked upon a common plan." In Lincoln's eyes, the secret plan aimed to bring slavery into the territories.

Lincoln versus Douglas

Lincoln's metaphor led into his famous statement that "A House divided against itself cannot stand" and that "this government cannot endure, permanently half slave and half free." Such moral rhetoric denied the ambiguous compromise language that, despite fundamental differences, had existed since the birth of the republic. Douglas's notion of popular sovereignty—the view that slavery and antislavery were equally valid political choices—attempted to perpetuate the advantages of imprecision and paradox.

In an 1858 public campaign debate at Freeport, Illinois, however, Lincoln forced Douglas to resolve the ambiguity. Could a territory voluntarily exclude slavery? asked Lincoln. To answer yes would cost Douglas his southern support; to say no would mean that he repudiated popular sovereignty and would cost him the north. "Slavery," replied Douglas, clinging to his ambiguous doctrine, "cannot exist a day in the midst of an unfriendly people with

An artist's reconstruction of the Lincoln-Douglas debates of 1858 during the campaign for senatorship of Illinois.

rel with white supremacy. He doubted that African Americans could achieve social and political equality, though he believed that black people had certain natural and economic rights. He favored colonization as a way of removing free blacks from the country. Yet, he saw the geographical spread of slavery as a threat to a free labor society, equal opportunity, and majority rule in Congress. Believing that southerners were conspiring to nationalize slave holding, Lincoln saw a political plot to make slavery legal everywhere, even in Illinois.

John Brown's Raid

Proslavery southerners, meanwhile, saw "Black Republicans" like Lincoln conspiring to end slavery—not only in the territories but also in the South. Such fears gained terrifying credibility one October night in 1859, when the zealous abolitionist John Brown led eighteen armed men in a raid on the federal arsenal at Harper's Ferry, Virginia, in hopes of igniting a slave rebellion. Local blacks showed no interest in the suicidal mission. Brown was soon captured, tried for treason, and hanged. The daring raid sent shock waves through the South, arousing nightmares of slave insurrection. The price of slaves began to fall. In the wake of Harper's Ferry, rumors of slave conspiracies raced through the southern states, instigating vigilante attacks on alleged abolitionist villains, African Americans, even Native American communities; most of those rumors, admitted a southern editor, "turned out to be totally false, and all of them grossly exaggerated." Although many northern politicians, including Lincoln, condemned Brown's raid, southern leaders were appalled to learn that many northern churches tolled John Brown's death as a martyrdom. "Nobody cares a damn if the union is dissolved,"

unfriendly laws." The Illinois state legislature, controlled by Democrats, soon sent Douglas back to his Senate seat in Washington. Northern Democrats still hoped that the ambiguity of popular sovereignty could bridge regional differences in the next presidential election, in 1860.

Lincoln's skillful oratory in his debates with Douglas catapulted him into presidential contention. The Illinois lawyer had entered politics as a Whig but, with the party's demise, he had followed his antislavery principles into the Republican party in 1856. Douglas's idea of popular sovereignty offended Lincoln's moral opposition to a slave society. To be sure, Lincoln had no quar-

snapped a slave trader bitterly. "Virginia can whip the whole North herself."

Women, Slaves, and White Male Dominance

The debate about slavery stimulated controversy about other so-called domestic institutions, such as marriage, the family, and household relations. "The black man and the woman are born to shame," Elizabeth Cady Stanton told the American Antislavery Society six months after Brown's execution. "The badge of degradation is the skin and sex—the 'scarlet letter' so sadly worn upon the breast." During the 1850s, women's rights advocates like Stanton and Susan B. Anthony assiduously petitioned state legislatures to pass laws for women's equality, seeking the right to divorce immoral men, to own property, and to vote. Such pleas brought widespread condemnation—but especially in the southern states, where slaveowning patriarchs defended their households. At the same time that some northern states passed divorce laws that protected women's claims to property, South Carolina prohibited legal divorce. Massachusetts became the first state to legalize interracial marriage in 1843, followed in the next decade by Iowa and Kansas. Southerners were horrified.

"The people of our Northern States, who hold that domestic slavery is unjust and iniquitous," said Virginia writer George Fitzhugh in 1854, "are consistent in their attempts to modify or abolish the marriage relation." Free women, no less than slaves, Fitzhugh insisted, required male authority: "Woman . . . has but one right and that is the right to protection." When one southern woman expressed concern that marriage would destroy her freedom, her fiancé quieted those fears by vowing to be her "protector and defender when all friends and relations fail." Like other troubled women, in the North as well as the South, this

"Woman [is] more fully identified with the slave than man can possibly be."

prospective bride accepted marriage without rights as better than its alternative, because, she said, "We poor women have no name or existence of our own, we pass silently down the stream of time without leaving a single trace behind—we die unknown."

In exchange for assuming responsibility for the "weaker" sex, however, men demanded women's subordination, what Fitzhugh called "the obligation to obey." Such ideas pervaded the country. "Woman [is] more fully identified with the slave than man can possibly be," Stanton told her northern audience. "She early learns the misfortune of being born an heir to the crown of thorns . . . , to womanhood." Ironically, the wives of slaveowners often agreed with this pessimistic view. Although Mary Chesnut, a well-to-do South Carolinian, wielded no small power over her slaves, she claimed that women like herself were oppressed by "a swarm of blacks about them as children under their care . . . hard, unpleasant, unromantic, undeveloped savage Africans." Another southern bride, twenty-two-year-old newlywed Tryphena Fox, explained her role: "Having two servants to do the work, I do but little myself and that particular things which I do not like to trust to them, but I have to watch them and tell them every little item to be done, for a negro never sees any dirt or grease, so if a *Southern lady* does not do much manual labor, she has head-work enough to keep her busy." Such racism made slaveholding women loathe the presence of slaves; yet these same women almost never challenged the institution of slavery. Rather, they shared with abolitionist women a sense of powerlessness over their own lives. Husbands, south and north, continued to rule the domestic realm.

The Election of 1860

In 1860, a presidential election year, southern leaders prepared to fight an expected attack on slavery. When the Democrats gathered at their nominating convention in Charleston, South Carolina, extremist delegates demanded a platform protecting slavery in the western territories. But Douglas supporters carried a majority in favor of popular sovereignty, and their victory provoked half the southern delegates to leave the Democratic convention. Unable to choose a candidate after fifty-nine ballots, the Democrats adjourned to a later meeting in Baltimore. When Douglas won the nomination there, the remaining southern Democrats quit the national party and chose their own candidate, Buchanan's vice president, John C. Breckinridge. The issue of slavery had torn apart the last national party. Although many southern rank-and-file Democrats remained loyal to the national party, Douglas could no longer expect to carry the southern states. Meanwhile, a splinter group of die-hard southern Whigs and nativists formed the Constitutional Union party and nominated Tennessee's John Bell.

To match Douglas's strength in his home region, Republicans nominated Lincoln. Although firmly opposed to the expansion of slavery, the candidate shared the racial views of his Illinois neighbors. "There must be a position of superior and inferior," he had declared in the recent senatorial election, "and I . . . am in favor of having the superior position assigned to the white race." Yet Lincoln had repudiated the racial exclusionism of the nativist movement, and he scoffed at the notion that "all men are created equal, except negroes, and foreigners, and catholics." Such ideas endeared Lincoln to the German farmers of the midwest. The Republican candidate also affirmed a commitment to free labor, describing himself as an example of someone who had risen from humble beginnings to national stature. To reinforce the message of economic opportunity, the Republicans adopted a party platform calling for a homestead law to promote free lands for settlers, a tariff to protect manufacturing and workers, and a transcontinental railroad.

The election of 1860 reflected the deepening sectional divisions. Douglas, understanding his chances were slim, nonetheless traveled south as well as north, defining himself as the only national candidate. Lincoln did not campaign in the South; his name did not even appear on most southern ballots. Breckinridge made no appeals in the North; his supporters warned that Lincoln's election would force the South to choose secession. That year, voters well understood the choices, and over 80 percent cast ballots.

In the South, Breckinridge defeated Bell everywhere except three border states; outside the South, Lincoln lost only the border state Missouri to Douglas. To be sure, Lincoln carried less than 40 percent of the popular vote to Douglas's 29.5 percent and Breckinridge's 18 percent. But the electoral score was decisive. Thanks to the dominance of the densely populated industrial states of the North, Lincoln received 180 electoral votes; everyone else's electoral votes totaled 123. "A party founded on a single sentiment . . . of hatred of African slavery," exclaimed a southern newspaper, "is now the controlling power."

Desperation shot through the South. "Nothing short of separation from the Union can save us!" cried one editor. Some were convinced that the Republican victory sounded the end of slavery. "Then every negro . . . will be his own master," warned a Baptist minister; "nay, more than that, will be the equal of every one of you." The

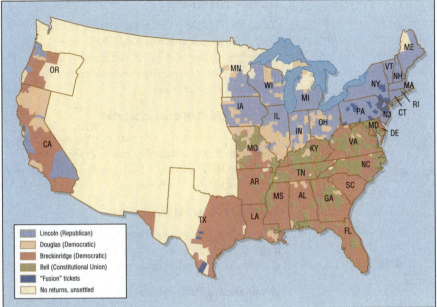

Lincoln (Republican)
Douglas (Democratic)
Breckinridge (Democratic)
Bell (Constitutional Union)
"Fusion" tickets
No returns, unsettled

governors of three southern states quickly summoned special conventions to consider secession from the union. One month after the election, South Carolina's convention voted unanimously to secede from the federal government, setting off a hooplah of fireworks, rallies, and parades. Within weeks, the six Deep South states of Mississippi, Florida, Alabama, Georgia, Louisiana, and Texas followed South Carolina out of the union. In February 1861, delegates met in Montgomery, Alabama, to found the Confederate States of America and choose Jefferson Davis to head the new republic.

A Failure to Compromise

Eight Border States remained loyal to the union. Hoping to heal the breach, Kentucky's John Crittenden offered resolutions in Congress to reestab-

lish the Missouri Compromise line all the way to the Pacific and enact a constitutional amendment to preserve slavery wherever it existed. But neither secessionists nor those opposed to extending slavery into the territories would compromise their principles. Lincoln, moreover, refused to allow the rebels to hold the government hostage. Already the seceding state governments had seized federal forts, customs houses, and other federal buildings. "If we surrender," said Lincoln, "it is the end of . . . government."

In his inaugural address of March 4, 1861, the new president reiterated his willingness to protect slavery in the southern states, and he promised to enforce the Fugitive Slave Act. "We must not be enemies," he pleaded. "Though passion may have strained, it must not break our bonds of affection." Through such peaceful gestures, the sixteenth president hoped to heal the nation's wounds. But, as Walt Whitman remarked about Lincoln, "the only thing like passion or infatuation in the man was the passion for the union of these states." Lincoln's commitment to constitutional government was unswerving, and he would go only so far to accommodate the secessionists. "The Union of these states is perpetual," he insisted.

Southern leaders showed no sign of retreat, no desire to reenter the union. As the crisis intensified during the winter of 1860–1861, the country perched on the edge of civil war. Herman Melville's *Moby Dick*, published nearly a decade earlier, had forecast the collision course. "Swerve me?" exclaims Captain Ahab ominously as the whaling ship pursues its own destruction. "Ye cannot swerve me. . . the path of my fixed purpose is laid with iron rails, whereon my soul is grooved to run."

INFOTRAC® COLLEGE EDITION EXERCISES

For additional reading go to InfoTrac College Edition, your online research library at *http://web1.infotrac-college.com.*

Keyword search: Harriet Tubman
Keyword search: Frederick Douglass
Keyword search: underground railroad
Keyword search: Harriet Beecher Stowe
Keyword search: Franklin Pierce
Subject search: slavery history
Keyword search: Bleeding Kansas
Keyword search: Kansas/Nebraska Act
Subject search: Dred Scott
Subject search: Lincoln-Douglas Debates, reference books
Subject search: United States history, Civil War

ADDITIONAL READING

David S. Reynolds, *Walt Whitman's America: A Cultural Biography* (1995). This exquisite study places the poet and his writings in the context of his times.

The Agricultural Boom

Gavin Wright, *The Political Economy of the Cotton South: Households, Markets, and Wealth in the Nineteenth Century* (1978). A statistical study comparing southern economic development with agricultural patterns in the free states.

Railroads and Territorial Expansion

Robert A. Trennert, Jr., *Alternative to Extinction: Federal Indian Policy and the Beginnings of the Reservation System, 1846–51* (1975). This book describes national policy toward the Plains nations.

Resistance to the Fugitive Slave Act

Albert J. Von Frank, *The Trials of Anthony Burns: Freedom and Slavery in Emerson's Boston* (1998). Depicts the capture and trial of a fugitive slave in 1854.

The Weakening Party System

Michael F. Holt, *The Political Crisis of the 1850s* (1978). A study of two-party politics describing the disintegration of the Democrat-Whig system and the emergence of new political alliances.

Cultural Differences Become Political

Tyler Anbinder, *Nativism and Slavery: The Know Nothings and the Politics of the 1850s* (1992). This careful analysis of party politics explores the emergence of the nativists and their relationship to antislavery issues.

Problems of Political Geography

Eric Foner, *Free Soil, Free Labor, Free Men: The Ideology of the Republican Party before the Civil War* (1970). A lucid study of the ideas that defined the nation's first sectional party.

William E. Gienapp, *The Origins of the Republican Party: 1852–1856* (1987). A detailed state-by-state study analyzing the emergence of Republican parties amid a welter of local and ethnocultural issues.

The Dred Scott Decision

Don E. Fehrenbacher, *The Dred Scott Case: Its Significance in American Law and Politics* (1978). Analyzes the constitutional implications of the landmark Supreme Court decision.

The Politics of Economic Crisis

James L. Huston, *The Panic of 1857 and the Coming of the Civil War* (1987). Describes the economic crisis and its political impact.

Poverty in the Cities

Roy Rosenzweig and Elizabeth Blackmar, *The Park and the People: A History of Central Park* (1992). A fine example of social and cultural history, examining the values that inspired the nation's first urban park.

Lincoln versus Douglas

Douglas L. Wilson, *Honor's Voice: The Transformation of Abraham Lincoln* (1998). Focusing on Lincoln's early career, this insightful study explores the background of a rising politician.

14

War for the Union, 1861–1865

CHRONOLOGY

1861   Abraham Lincoln takes office as sixteenth president
     Confederacy fires on Fort Sumter, South Carolina
     Confederates defeat Union army at First Battle of Bull Run
     U.S. Congress passes first Confiscation Act

1862   Union wins victory at Shiloh, Tennessee
     Gen. George McClellan leads Union army into Virginia
     U.S. Congress passes Legal Tender and Homestead acts
     Santee Sioux attack Minnesota farmers
     Union stops Confederate advance at Antietam, Maryland

1863   Emancipation Proclamation frees slaves behind Confederate lines
     Union wins at Gettysburg; Grant captures Vicksburg
     New York City workers riot against draft

1864   William T. Sherman takes Atlanta and marches to sea
     Lincoln wins reelection over ex-General George McClellan
     Colorado militia massacres Cheyennes at Sand Creek

1865   Lee surrenders at Appomattox Court House
     Actor John Wilkes Booth assassinates Lincoln
     States ratify Thirteenth Amendment

War clouds hovered over the nation's capital as the newly inaugurated President Abraham Lincoln adopted a firm stand against southern secession. One afternoon in March 1861, Ohio's Senator John Sherman introduced Lincoln to his brother, William Tecumseh Sherman, who might be of assistance should a war begin. Indeed, in expectation that war would soon commence, Sherman had resigned as head of the Louisiana Military Academy. "How are they getting along down there?" asked Lincoln. "They are preparing for war," replied the soldier. But apparently Lincoln was not yet interested in acquiring the services of the man who would prove to be an invincible military leader for the Union. "Oh, well," the president responded, "I guess we'll manage to keep house." After they had parted and William Sherman found a civilian job in St. Louis, he summed up his impression of the national predicament: "You have got things in a hell of a fix," he told his politician brother, John, "and you may get them out as best you can."

By then, the United States was already split in two, but whether the secession of seven southern states would lead to a permanent division of the Union remained uncertain. In February 1861, delegates from the seceded states had met in Montgomery, Alabama, formed an independent republic called the Confederate States of America, and elected former Mississippi Senator Jefferson Davis as president. Eight other slave states of the Upper South remained in the Union, but watched carefully as northern and southern leaders attempted to resolve the political crisis.

Hoping to keep the border states in the Union, Lincoln promised to preserve slavery where it existed. But he rejected the legality of secession and he vowed to "hold, occupy, and possess" all federal property within the seceded states. President Davis, for his part, defended the principle of states' rights and insisted that it was legal for a state to vote openly to secede from the Union and to form a new government. On these grounds, he refused to surrender federal property as a violation of his nation's sovereignty.

By April, the eyes of all citizens, North and South, turned toward an island in the middle of Charleston harbor in South Carolina, where the red-brick, federal Fort Sumter lay within range of Confederate artillery. As southern leaders demanded that Lincoln surrender the fort to the Confederacy, the fort's Union defenders informed the president that they lacked provisions to hold out much longer.

"The military excitement here is intense," Senator Sherman wrote from Washington, as Lincoln ordered a relief ship to bring food to Fort Sumter and prudently notified the state governor of his peaceful intentions. Davis countered by instructing Confederate commanders to take immediate control of the fort. When federal officers refused southern demands to surrender, Confederate artillery commenced firing on the morning of April 12. "Civil war is actually upon us," exclaimed Sherman, "and,

"Civil war is actually upon us and, strange to say, it brings a feeling of relief."

strange to say, it brings a feeling of relief: the suspense is over."

Thus the Civil War began as a contest of political rights between the North and the South. The two regions had already been separated by differences of society and economics; their residents held different views of what ought to be the national identity. As the North adopted principles of free wage labor and the South defended unfree agricultural slavery, their political differences became more difficult to compromise. Yet, to most contemporaries, slavery was only indirectly the cause of the war. Northerners and southerners alike saw themselves defending common political principles of citizenship and the rights of free white men. Indeed, even as the end of slavery eventually became one of the North's war goals, many northern unionists opposed the emancipation of blacks and expressed sentiments of white supremacy.

In firing the first shots of the Civil War, southern leaders defined their action as a defense of republican citizenship, including the right to create a government that protected private property in the form of slaves. In their speeches and letters, Confederates saw themselves defending "liberty" against northern "tyranny," and they appealed frequently to the spirit of 1776. "Sooner than submit to Northern slavery," declared a slaveowning South Carolina officer, "I prefer death." In the words of President Davis, the Confederacy fought for "the holy cause of constitutional liberty." Such patriotic rhetoric fired the consciences of Confederate volunteers and homefront supporters through four years of fighting, sacrifice, and the loss of 260,000 Confederate lives.

Northerners, too, fought for the principles of republican citizenship, charging that the South's secession imperiled free elections and majority rule. In his first Civil War message to Congress on July 4, 1861, Lincoln declared that "when ballots have fairly and constitutionally decided, there can be no successful appeal back to bullets." Believing that secession violated the sacred constitutional compact that had created the United States in 1787, the northern president appealed to the traditions of the nation's founders and summoned loyal citizens to save the Union. Northern patriotism prompted volunteer soldiers and civilians to battle through four years of fighting, sacrifice, and the loss of nearly 370,000 Union lives.

The bravery of those who fought and died would become legendary, embodying the power of self-governing peoples to wage wars of ideology. The Civil War became a "total" war—not just a clash of governments and armies, but of entire populations, affecting civilians and noncombatants as much as those who wore uniforms and fired weapons. Intangible factors, such as morale and loyalty, assumed new importance on battlefield and homefront, and the strength of will of government and military leaders on both sides often proved decisive. Total war also brought unexpected social consequences as vast armies crossed civilian terrain. Death seemed to be everywhere.

Although Confederate secessionists had seldom mentioned slavery as a reason for leaving the Union and few northerners had defined the war as an attack on that institution, the crisis forced the issue to center stage. As Union leaders waged total war, slavery seemed to give the South military advantages, and Lincoln decided to attack the institution to weaken the enemy. The result was a redefinition of the purposes of the war. By the time the war ended in 1865, the Union fought not only to restore the national government but also to emancipate the slaves. Thereafter, U.S. citizens would confront a different type of republi-

can government—no longer merely for white men, but for black men too. The Civil War would forever change the national identity.

Mobilizing for Victory

As the war began, each side had cause for optimism. With vastly larger numbers and potential military power, Union leaders expected a quick victory. Even if the Union could not win a decisive battle, northern strategists hoped to use the North's economic advantages to crush southern opposition. Adopting the so-called Anaconda plan, named for the deadly snake that strangled its victims, Union leaders aimed to choke southern trade by establishing coastal blockades, controlling the Mississippi river, and capturing the Confederate capital at Richmond. By causing economic hardships, the Union hoped to persuade southern leaders to abandon the fight. But the Anaconda plan required time to succeed, and time played into southern plans. To achieve its objectives, the Confederacy merely had to survive. Rather than invading enemy territory, the Confederates would adopt what President Davis called an "offensive defensive" strategy: beat back Union attacks and undermine the North's will to fight. Confederate optimism also expressed faith in the power of cotton. Believing that the European economy would stagnate without cotton exports, southerners expected England and France to assist the Confederacy. Within a year, it was clear that both sides had exaggerated their strengths; yet even in 1862 both believed that victory might be just around the corner.

Arousing the Citizenry

"War!" cried the poet Walt Whitman in 1861. "An armed race is advancing! the welcome for battle, no turning away." With the shots of Fort Sumter echoing in the land, Lincoln summoned 75,000

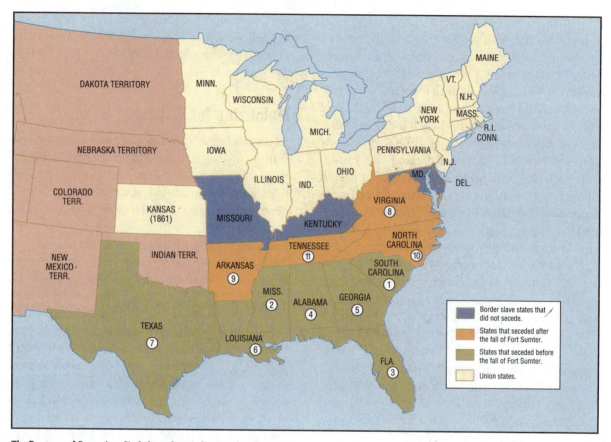

The Progress of Secession. Circled numbers indicate order of secession.

volunteers for 90-day duty, igniting patriotic fervor throughout the North. Enthusiastic communities soon organized local and state military units and proudly sent their sons to defend the Stars and Stripes. But northern mobilization ironically strengthened the Confederacy. Lincoln's call to arms prompted four more states—Virginia, Arkansas, Tennessee, and North Carolina—to secede from the Union. "Lincoln may bring his 75,000 troops against us," declared Confederate Vice President Alexander Stephens. "We fight for our homes. . . . We can call out a million . . . if need be, and when they are cut down we can call another, and still another, until the last man of the South finds a bloody grave." Southern women vowed that "none but the brave deserve the fair," and sent women's undergarments as a rebuke to men who were slow to enlist.

The strength of southern defiance surprised Lincoln, and the president soon called for more volunteers for three years of military service. The northern states rushed to fill their quotas. In 1861, volunteering became a male rite of passage on both sides; 18-year-olds were the largest age group during the first year of war. African Americans were still unwanted by either army.

With Virginia out of the Union, the Confederacy moved its capital from Montgomery to Richmond, barely 100 miles from Washington and close to Maryland, a "border" slave state, whose loyalty remained uncertain. When Massachusetts volunteers passed through Baltimore in April 1861, an anti-Union mob attacked the soldiers with rocks and rifle fire, provoking an armed response that left a dozen dead. Lincoln declared martial law, suspending the right of habeas corpus (which protected citizens from arbitrary arrest), and ordered the seizure of pro-secession leaders. Chief Justice Roger Taney ruled that the president was violating basic civil rights, but Lincoln insisted that the crisis demanded special executive powers and ignored a Court order to lift martial law. Military power kept Maryland in the Union. Lincoln also used troops to ensure loyalty of other border states, such as Kentucky and Missouri, though guerrilla warfare in those states indicated a deep division of opinion. Meanwhile, the Washington government encouraged the pro-Union mountainous portion of Virginia to become the separate state of West Virginia in 1863.

Economic and Diplomatic Issues

As the armies prepared for conflict, the Union held obvious material advantages. The North's population greatly exceeded the Confederacy's (22 million northerners to the South's 9 million whites, 4 million slaves, and 250,000 free blacks), and the North had more than four times as many white men of military age (18 to 45). Two-thirds of the nation's railroad lines lay in the North. The Union's industrial capacity showed even greater strength: 97 percent of the total firearms production, 96 percent of locomotives, 94 percent of iron, 94 percent of clothing, 90 percent of shoes. Even agricultural production was much greater in the North, except for cotton. This economic superiority inspired the Anaconda plan, the Union's primary military strategy to surround the southern states and strangle the Confederacy into submission. Yet southerners fought for their home territory. They believed that by prolonging the conflict, they could compel the North to abandon the fight.

Southern hopes also depended on economic power. Believing that cotton was "King," the Confederacy deliberately withheld exports of cotton to Britain and France to accentuate European dependence on southern agriculture and to persuade those nations to break the northern blockade of southern ports. Yet large surpluses from previous years enabled European textile manufacturers to remain in business—indeed, to earn greater profits than expected from the southern embargo and the consequent rise in cotton prices. Britain also had other sources for cotton in Egypt and India. Moreover, Britain remained dependent on U.S. grain production; 40 percent of Britain's wheat and flour came from northern farms.

Instead of choosing sides, Britain and France jointly declared neutrality, treating the Confederacy as an equal belligerent without granting diplomatic recognition or providing material aid. The ambiguous policy nearly led to hostilities in the fall of 1861, when a U.S. naval vessel intercepted two Confederate agents bound for Europe aboard the British ship *Trent*. Prudent apologies from the Lincoln administration avoided conflict, but the British continued to outfit southern warships, which preyed on northern shipping.

"The Red Business" Begins, 1861–1862

"Forward to Richmond," cried Horace Greeley's New York *Tribune* in the summer of 1861, as the Confederate congress prepared to meet in the southern capital. The first Union army moved into action in July amid so much optimism that civilians went out with picnic lunches to watch the battle. At Manassas Junction (also known as

Bull Run) in northern Virginia, 35,000 hastily trained Union soldiers charged 22,000 Confederates. So began what Whitman called "the red business." After nearly gaining a victory, Union forces collapsed under a flank attack, causing a terrified stampede all the way back to Washington. Union casualties (the killed, wounded, and missing) numbered nearly 2,900, and Confederate losses exceeded 1,900. "Times were too wild with excitement to stay in bed," exulted Mary Chesnut in Charleston, South Carolina. Meanwhile, in the North, "All is quiet and sad, and the mourners go about the streets," wrote nurse Clara Barton from Washington. A stunned Congress immediately summoned another half-million three-year recruits. "We now see the magnitude of the contest," admitted the chastened Senator John Sherman.

As volunteers joined Union regiments, Lincoln named General George McClellan to command the Army of the Potomac in an invasion of Virginia. A disciplined West Point graduate, McClellan transformed the raw recruits into soldiers by endless marching and drilling. But long preparations allowed the rebellion to continue, and Lincoln pleaded for action. Not until April 1862, nearly a year after the war began, did the 120,000 man Union army land on the Virginia peninsula, a logistical feat that required 400 ships and three weeks. Slowly McClellan inched toward Richmond. But the Union general exaggerated the size of the enemy and decided to wait for reinforcements.

Union soldiers loved McClellan for his professionalism and his caution. In the face of new rifled weapons, which fired expanding minié bullets with greater accuracy and speed than older weapons, frontal assaults would prove exceptionally deadly. But as McClellan hesitated, a Confederate army under Thomas "Stonewall" Jackson moved north through Virginia's Shenandoah valley, as if to cross the Potomac to attack Washington. Lincoln ordered

Civilians went out with picnic lunches to watch the battle.

reserve troops to meet Jackson, but the Confederates won tactical victories and eluded capture. Soon after, southern troops under Virginia's Robert E. Lee took the initiative, driving McClellan's Union forces into retreat in the Seven Days' Battles. Lincoln ordered McClellan to halt the campaign. A year's planning had brought 16,000 Union casualties, 20,000 Confederate.

While McClellan's army had prepared to invade Virginia, another Union army under General Ulysses S. Grant was fighting for control of the Mississippi valley. Victories in Tennessee early in 1862 forced the Confederates to retreat, but Union soldiers pursued them, finally meeting the Confederates at Shiloh, Tennessee, where two days of fighting in April left a combined total of 23,000 casualties. After the rebels withdrew, Grant marched west toward Memphis, gaining control of the great river from that city northward. Meanwhile, U.S. naval forces had entered the Mississippi from the south, seizing New Orleans in April 1862. But the middle stretch of the river remained in southern hands. Hoping to divide the Confederacy along the river, Union armies struggled to take the southern fortress at Vicksburg, Mississippi. Farther west, a Colorado militia defeated rebel troops in New Mexico.

Late in the summer of 1862, military action resumed in northern Virginia. In August, Confederate armies under Lee and Stonewall Jackson moved north to the second battle of Bull Run (Second Manassas), where they defeated Union forces. Another 25,000 men fell. Emboldened by victory, Lee carried the war into Union territory, advancing into Maryland in September 1862. A southern

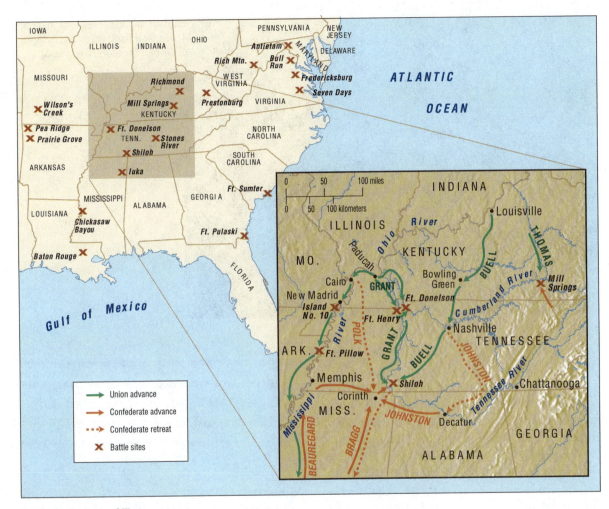

Civil War in the East and West

victory there might bring that border state into the Confederacy, weaken the northern will, or win British recognition of the southern nation. The ensuing battle at Antietam Creek became a bloodbath, claiming 23,000 casualties on the single deadliest day of the war, leaving bodies "thick as autumn leaves." McClellan's Union army came close to victory, but Lee managed to withdraw his troops to Virginia. Lee's failure to advance persuaded Britain and France to remain neutral.

Union armies still lacked a decisive victory. Two months later, at Fredericksburg, Virginia, they sustained another defeat. Union soldiers, including New York City's Irish regiment, were bled white by a series of uphill charges against entrenched infantry. "It will be a sad, sad Christmas by many an Irish hearthstone," wrote a Union officer. "It is well that war is so terrible," observed the victorious Lee, otherwise "we should grow too fond of it."

Scenes of battlefield carnage, such as this at the Battle of Bull Run, brought the war shockingly close to home.

A People's War

These early battles shocked combatants and civilians on both sides. "I shall never forget how awfully I felt on seeing for the first time a man killed in battle," reported one soldier. "I stared at his body, perfectly horrified! Only a few seconds ago that man was alive and well, and now he was lying on the ground, done for, forever!" That primal horror never stopped, recurred on every battlefield, and expressed an omnipresent sense of fear about the precariousness of survival. For some, facing battle became impossible. About 200,000 Union soldiers deserted the army (80,000 were caught) and 104,000 left Confederate ranks (21,000 were returned). Those who stayed often felt the same impulse to run, though they remained to fight. Union soldiers spoke often of the obligations of "duty"; Confederates mentioned the importance of "honor." "I never could rid myself of a sneaking desire to turn and run for all I was worth," admitted a sergeant from Connecticut, "but I wouldn't have run for a good deal more than

"Only a few seconds ago that man was alive and well, and now he was lying on the ground, done for, forever!"

I was worth." "Tell my father," said a mortally wounded North Carolina officer, "I died with my face to the enemy."

Field hospitals could do little to relieve the suffering. The standard medical treatment for wounded limbs was amputation, usually performed without anaesthetics. "The screams and groans of the poor fellows undergoing amputation are sometimes dreadful," said one soldier, "and then the sight of arms and legs surrounding these places, as they are thrown into great piles, is something one . . . can never forget." Because ambulance service was primitive, most casualties bled to death where they fell. Behind the lines, hospitals became death houses. Upon arriving at a Union hospital in Washington in 1862, the novelist Louisa May Alcott was struck first by the odor of rotten flesh. Lacking understanding of antiseptic treatment, medical aides inadvertently carried infection from patient to patient; often, second amputations had to be performed. Contagious diseases proliferated: dysentery, typhoid, malaria, even epidemics of mumps and measles ravaged the hospitals. Twice as many soldiers died of disease as from battle injuries. By 1865, the total number of dead was 620,000; the number of wounded reached a million, or 3.4 percent of the entire U.S. population.

Another casualty of war was the northern belief that victory depended merely on beating the rebel army. At the beginning, Lincoln called the war "a people's contest" that would determine "whether a constitutional republic . . . can, or cannot maintain its territorial integrity, against its own domestic foes." By emphasizing limited political objectives and affirming his willingness to protect slavery where it already existed, Lincoln hoped to coax the seceded states back into the Union. Ultimately, he believed, the decision depended on the southern citizenry, which accepted Confederate leadership, but might be persuaded to reject it.

The tragedy of warfare made a political compromise less likely. Increasingly, northern leaders saw the Confederacy not as a misguided political entity but as the enemy. "I gave up all idea of saving the Union except by complete conquest," Grant reported after the battle of Shiloh. As early as August 1861 Congress passed the first Confiscation act, which permitted the seizure of all property, including slaves, that could aid the military rebellion. This expedient measure allowed Union armies to use freed slaves in limited ways (as cooks, laborers, and laundry workers) but prudently avoided a direct attack on slavery per se.

During the first years of the war, Union armies did not forage widely in southern territory for food. Grant in the west and McClellan in the east worried about protecting their lines of supply. By the end of 1862, however, Grant had resolved "to consume everything that could be used to support or supply armies." Thereafter, wherever possible, Union soldiers would live off the land. In calculating the supplies needed by his troops, Grant began to study local maps together with 1860 census data to determine the economic resources of particular southern counties. This linking of civilian property and military policy, the assumption that southern citizens were responsible for their government's actions, reflected the shift to total war.

The War for Freedom

Although Lincoln hesitated to attack slavery, hoping that moderate policies would end the rebellion, Confederate stubbornness and military success encouraged the North to take stronger measures against a valuable southern resource. In small steps, the North extended its antislavery policies, restricting slavery in federal territories and allowing freed slaves and free blacks to serve in Union armies. Black military service, in turn, reinforced attacks on slavery as an institution. Even before the war was over, the northern Congress approved a Thirteenth Amendment to the Constitution and sent its antislavery provisions to the states for ratification. Thus the war for the Union became a war for freedom, redefining the conflict's political and moral issues and ultimately changing the definition of republican citizenship.

These developments did not necessarily alter public attitudes about racial differences. African Americans and Native Americans, to name the most prominent wartime examples, still confronted prejudice, discrimination, and violence in the North, which belied the promises of freedom. Yet the war irrevocably altered the position of black Americans, the first non-white racial group to become eligible for U.S. citizenship. This new northern version of republicanism would ultimately determine the national identity.

The Politics of Emancipation

Despite Lincoln's personal rejection of slavery, the president faced political obstacles to authorizing emancipation, especially the importance of keeping the border slave states—Delaware, Kentucky, Maryland, and Missouri—loyal to the Union. When General John C. Frémont, the Republican candidate for president in 1856, ordered the liberation of slaves owned by rebels in Missouri in 1861, Lincoln quickly overruled the order. Yet more radical Republicans in Congress felt fewer restraints. The first Confiscation Act, in 1861, not only permitted seizure of slaves working for the Confederacy but also prohibited slavery in the western territories and abolished slavery in Washington, D.C. The next year, Congress voted to prohibit the return of fugitive slaves to their former masters.

Meanwhile, abolitionists continued to press the president to take a bolder stand—on grounds of military advantage, if not political principle. "My paramount object . . . is to save the Union," Lincoln responded in 1862. "If I could save the Union without freeing *any* slave I would do it; and if I could save it by freeing *all* the slaves I would do it; and if I could save it by freeing some and leaving others alone I would also do that." Nevertheless, the president did persuade Congress to authorize government compensation to states that voluntarily abolished slavery, and he pleaded with members of congress from the border states to support a program of gradual emancipation. To ease the objections of whites to living among free blacks, Lincoln even proposed the colonization of African Americans to Haiti or Panama, though black leaders angrily rejected the idea.

> **"If I could save the Union without freeing *any* slave I would do it; and if I could save it by freeing *all* the slaves I would do it; and if I could save it by freeing some and leaving others alone I would also do that."**

It was African Americans themselves—slaves, ex-slaves, and free blacks—who influenced Lincoln and the North to change their policies. Whenever Union armies approached slave regions, some slaves felt emboldened to seek refuge and freedom behind Union lines. Northern leaders called these fugitives "contraband of war" and initially limited their use in the war effort. But as both armies demanded the full resources of civilian society, African Americans assumed greater importance in tipping the scales of war. Rather than permitting southern slaves to contribute to the rebellion, northern leaders began to use blacks to help the Union.

By 1862, Lincoln decided to announce a formal change of policy. Waiting until after the victory at Antietam in September 1862 (lest he appear too desperate), Lincoln issued a presidential proclamation, proposing to make all slaves in the rebellious states "forever free," unless those states returned to the Union by January 1, 1863. The president said nothing about the status of slaves in the loyal border states. Even that tentative step, according to a white eyewitness, brought "joy and thanksgiving" among northern African Americans. But many northern whites opposed emancipation, and Lincoln's critics advised "every white laboring man" to vote for Democrats. This anti-abolition sentiment in the North contributed to Democratic victories in the 1862 congressional elections.

Racist attitudes obviously pervaded the southern cause as well. In the words of Vice President Alexander Stephens, the Confederacy was dedicated to the proposition "that the negro is not equal to the white man; that slavery . . . is his natural and normal condition." Southern leaders made no effort to respond to Lincoln's preliminary emancipation offer. On New Year's Day 1863, therefore, the president's Emancipation Proclamation went into effect. "All night they tooted and tramped, fired crackers, sung 'Glory Hallelujah,'" reported Louisa May Alcott about Washington's black population. (In contrast, an indignant Jefferson Davis called the order the "most execrable measure recorded in the history of guilty man.") Yet Lincoln freed only those slaves in areas of rebellion—not in the border states, nor even in southern territory already held by Union troops. In other words, the Emancipation Proclamation did *not* free slaves in any area where the government could implement the policy. Keenly aware of the discrepancy, Republican radicals would continue to press for passage of a constitutional amendment to outlaw slavery throughout the nation.

Blacks Enter the Ranks

When the war began, many northern African Americans volunteered to fight, only to be turned away because it was a "white man's war." As one Union soldier explained, "The Southern people are rebels . . . but they are white, and God never intended a nigger to put white people down." Questioning the courage of black men, the War Department initially employed them as civilian workers, but not as fighters. Some African Americans did serve in the navy, but usually as noncombatants. The slaughter of war soon altered northern sentiments, if only for reasons of self-interest. "When this war is over and we have summed up the entire loss of life," wrote the governor of Iowa in 1862, "I shall not have any regrets if it is found that a part of the dead are niggers." Or as one northern Irish song put it, "I'll let Sambo be murdered instead of myself/on any day of the year."

By 1862, even before emancipation, Congress repealed a 1792 law that limited military service to white men and authorized the enlistment of black troops. During the fall of 1862, Lincoln permitted the formation of a regiment of freed slaves to serve under white officers on the Sea Islands off the South Carolina coast. After Lincoln issued the Emancipation Proclamation, the War Department began to raise regiments of black volunteers in the northern states. In 1864, Congress offered freedom to African American soldiers from the border states (which were not covered by the Emancipation Proclamation), and the next year extended that right to their families. By the war's end, about 15 percent of the entire northern black population served in Union armies. White officers who volunteered to lead these troops, many of whom came from principled abolitionist families, faced considerable ridicule. Most famous of the black regiments was the 54th Massachusetts. Northern states also hired agents to recruit freed slaves in the South, who served instead of local white volunteers.

Black soldiers faced special problems in the military. Of the 180,000 African Americans who joined the northern armies, 37,000 died, mostly from disease rather than bullets, a deathrate much higher than that of white soldiers. Military leaders often assigned blacks to manual labor and other unpleasant duties. Black recruits also received lower pay than white troops. Seven times the 54th Massachusetts protested that unequal distinction by refusing to accept any pay, eventually persuading Congress to change the policy, but only for blacks who had been free at the war's outset. African American complaints about discrimination in the ranks often brought harsh punishments, including charges of mutiny, for which blacks received physical discipline, imprisonment, even execution. Black volunteers believed nonetheless that they were fighting for the freedom of their people. "Once let the black man get upon his person the brass letters, U.S., let him get

On April 12, 1864, black soldiers who had already surrendered were wiped out by Confederates at Fort Pillow, Tennessee. General Nathan Bedford Forrest, who ordered the massacre, later became the head of the Ku Klux Klan. After the incident, "Remember Fort Pillow!" became a rallying cry for black troops.

an eagle on his button, and a musket on his shoulder," declared ex-slave Frederick Douglass, "and there is no power on earth which can deny that he has earned the right to citizenship." Indeed, African American military service transformed the nature of the war.

Given the chance to fight, black soldiers quickly proved their valor. In 1863, for example, the 54th Massachusetts advanced on Fort Wagner, South Carolina, in the face of withering fire—a military disaster that belied the myth of black cowardice. "I have no tears to shed over their graves," wrote the abolitionist Angelina Grimké Weld, "because I see that their heroism is working a great change in public opinion, forcing all men to see the sin and shame of enslaving such men." By the end of the war, African Americans constituted about 12 percent of the Union armies and a quarter of the Navy, and they earned innumerable citations for bravery.

The use of black troops brought condemnation from the Confederacy, and in 1863 the south-ern Congress authorized the execution of white Union officers who were captured while leading black troops. African American prisoners of war faced the death penalty for insurrection or a return to slavery. Lincoln responded by threatening to execute a Confederate prisoner for every Union prisoner killed, white or black, and to sentence a southern prisoner to hard labor for every black prisoner returned to slavery. Forced to moderate its official policy, the Confederacy still winked at atrocities committed against African Americans. In 1864, at Fort Pillow, Tennessee, to name the most notorious example, Confederate General Nathan Bedford Forrest permitted the killing of nearly 300 black Union soldiers who had already surrendered.

Nor did the courage shown by northern blacks persuade the Confederacy to enlist African Americans in their fight, at least until the war—and slavery—was virtually lost. Fearing a slave insurrection, southern leaders resisted changes in domestic life, relying on slaves to maintain the civilian economy. In 1864 the Confederate Congress agreed to accept blacks for noncombat assignments as teamsters, cooks, nurses, and laborers. But, despite severe manpower shortages, proposals to arm slaves with incentives of fighting for freedom drew hostile responses. "If slaves will make good soldiers," admitted one Georgia politician, "our whole theory of slavery is wrong." Not until the last month of the war did a desperate government offer emancipation in exchange for military service. Watching some "Confederate darkeys" on drill parade, a Virginia officer concluded, "this is but the beginning of the end."

War on Native Grounds

Both the U.S. government and the Confederacy competed for the support of Native Americans who had been expelled from their eastern lands during the 1820s and 1830s (see Chapters 8 and 9). Ironically, many Cherokee, Creek, Chickasaw, and Choctaw people owned African American slaves. They also felt an abiding hostility to the Washington government for forcing their removal from their homes. "Our geographical position, our social and domestic institutions, our feelings and sympathies, all attach us to our southern friends," declared the Chickasaw nation. But although Native leaders signed formal treaties with the Confederacy in 1861, significant numbers opposed those alliances and migrated elsewhere to preserve their neutrality.

Pro-Confederate Cherokees consulted oracle stones, engaged in war dances, and went into battle against Union forces in Missouri and Arkansas in 1861. Later, these Cherokees attacked the neutrals' encampments and drove them from the reservation. Fleeing to Kansas, Cherokee and Creek refugees endured extreme hardship without food, clothing, or shelter, and many joined the

> **Trader Myrick, who stated of the Sioux, "let them eat grass or their own dung," was found dead two weeks later with prairie grass stuffed in his mouth.**

Union armies against their Cherokee cousins. Despite such demonstrations of loyalty to the Union, the federal government treated all the southern groups as rebels. Forcing them to enter new treaties with the United States in 1865, the government ended slavery within the Native groups, granted tribal citizenship to former slaves, and compelled Native Americans to surrender about half their reservation land. During the four years of war, the western Cherokees lost more than a quarter of their population, dwindling to 15,000.

Northern tribes fared no better. During the 1850s, the federal government had forced the Santee Sioux of Minnesota to cede 24 million acres in exchange for annuities, reservation lands, and promises to establish mills, schools, and farms that would, in the words of the local Sioux agent, "make white men of them." But the annuity system was riddled with fraud, and crop failures aggravated the shortages caused by the war. By 1862, the Sioux faced mass starvation. Some broke into government warehouses and stole food; others pleaded for assistance. "If they are hungry," replied a trader named Myrick, "let them eat grass or their own dung." Two weeks later, the Sioux attacked local farmers; Myrick's body was found with prairie grass stuffed in his mouth.

The Sioux uprising terrified white Minnesotans, and uninformed Washington officials feared the influence of Confederate instigators. "Attend to the Indians," Lincoln telegraphed to Union generals, "necessity knows no law." Military leaders responded with promises to treat the Sioux "as maniacs or wild beasts." After skirmishing in the Minnesota woods, some Sioux fled to the Dakotas; most surrendered to face Union justice. In ten days' work, a military tribunal heard 392 cases and sentenced 303 to death. Lincoln commuted most sentences, except for cases of murder and rape. On the day after Christmas 1862, the government hanged thirty-eight Santee Sioux in the largest public execution in U.S. history. Soon afterward, Minnesotans grabbed Sioux lands and subsequently persuaded Congress to order removal of the peaceful Winnebagos to unfertile parts of the Dakotas. "Although we are now engaged in a great war between one another," said Lincoln with no trace of irony, "we are not as a race so much disposed to fight and kill one another as our red brethren."

Despite the government's preoccupation with the war, Washington continued to press the Plains Cheyenne and Arapahoe to abandon buffalo hunting for farming. As with the Sioux, shortages of food during the 1860s provoked a crisis of survival at the Sand Creek camp in the Colorado territory, and Cheyenne hunters began to raid local farms in 1864. When a rancher accused some Cheyennes of stealing livestock, the governor ordered a military attack on the unprotected village. When negotiations failed, a Colorado cavalry unit entered the Sand Creek camp. Firing cannons and rifles among sleeping people, the militia then attacked survivors with knives: castrating men, ripping open pregnant women, slaughtering children in the snow. Although a congressional committee later condemned the massacre, the federal government merely offered the survivors new treaties, exchanging claims in Colorado for promised reservations in Texas and Oklahoma. The Senate later changed the documents unilaterally to eliminate those promises. "I live in hopes," commented a Cheyenne leader; "but . . . it is hard for me to believe white men any more."

The War on the Home Front

As military casualties climbed to the hundreds of thousands, the sense of personal suffering and sacrifice moved from the battlefields to the homefronts on both sides. The war now involved whole societies, affecting civilian employment, local politics, and individual psychology. This private participation underscored the war's ideological passion; virtually no one could avoid taking sides. Yet the demand for civilian sacrifice affected groups unevenly, often accentuating social and economic divisions that had existed before the war. For the most part, civilian morale on both sides remained high, and the soldiers, Union and Confederate, believed that they were fighting for their families at home.

Facing the Death Toll

"News of the War!" exclaimed *Harper's Weekly* in 1862. "We all live on it. Few of us but would prefer our newspaper in these times to our breakfast." Total war involved not only mobilization of troops and industry but also of people's minds and beliefs. With homes everywhere containing the "vacant chair" of a son, father, or husband, civilians devoured newspapers for casualty lists, scoured correspondence from the campgrounds as soldiers reported gossip about their neighbors, and read avidly the descriptions of battle. "The only news I know," wrote the young Massachusetts poet Emily Dickinson,

> Is Bulletins all Day
> From Immortality

Newspaper circulation skyrocketed into the tens, even hundreds, of thousands for single issues, enabling enterprising publishers to boast about the advantages of this remarkable "advertising medium."

Winslow Homer drew this picture of a sharpshooter on picket duty.

Besides published information, civilians craved visual evidence of the war. Newspapers and magazines dispatched painters, such as the young Winslow Homer, to depict battle scenes and to sketch soldiers at rest. Mathew Brady's photographs of dead soldiers, exhibited in New York galleries, drew large crowds. "Minute as are the features of the dead," advised one newspaper, "you can, by bringing a magnifying glass to bear on them, identify not merely their general outline but actual expression." There was no romanticism about such details. A similar realism emerged in Civil War cemetery architecture. Although prewar "rural" cemeteries, such as Cambridge, Massachusetts's Mount Auburn, Chicago's Rose Hill, and Cincinnati's Spring Grove, used landscaping and statuary to evoke the naturalness of death, battlefield cemeteries, such as Gettysburg, appeared stark and impersonal, expressing an unvarnished egalitarianism. And Lincoln's famous eulogy for the dead at Gettysburg in November 1863 sought no higher meaning than the secular ends of the war. "We cannot hallow this ground," he said; the dead had already done that. Lincoln asked only that the living give the same devotion "to that cause" for which so many brave soldiers had died.

Citizens on both sides, however, believed fervently in the religious purposes of the war. Julia Ward Howe's "The Battle Hymn of the Republic," written in 1862, linked the northern cause to divine retribution, serving to rationalize total war. (Soldiers preferred less militant, sentimental songs, such as "Tenting Tonight" and "Just Before the Battle, Mother.") In 1864 alone, evangelicals distributed 6 million Christian books (such as *Come to Jesus*) as well as 1 million hymnals, 1 million Bibles, and 11 million tracts. Southern women also defined the war as a sacred cause, seeing the Confederacy as God's chosen nation and assuring soldiers that "piety will not make you effeminate or cowardly." Religious revivals spread through the Confederate ranks during seasons of military defeat, but Union armies experienced no major "awakenings." In his second inaugural address, Lincoln acknowledged the irony that both enemies "read the same Bible and pray to the same God, and each invokes His aid against the other." The president made the November harvest thanksgiving a national holiday in 1864, and that year the Treasury Department ordered all U.S. currency to bear the words "In God We Trust." Such evangelical imperatives inspired volunteers, civilian no less than soldiers.

Woman and the War

White women on both sides lamented their exclusion from the male adventure. "I never before wished I was a man," confessed a Tennessee woman. "Now I feel so keenly my weakness and dependence." Some 400 women managed to disguise themselves as men to enlist in the military; most were soon discovered and dismissed, though a few not before they were killed in action. More typically, women used their traditional skills to support the war, forming sewing and knitting societies to replenish supplies. Although northern textile manufacturers met the Union army's requirements, shortages of cloth in the Confederacy obliged southern women to make a virtue of wearing homespun outfits. "Our needles are now our weapons," explained one group.

Southern women often assumed the responsibilities of their absent husbands—taking over field work, running shops, and supervising slaves. Such role shifts brought identity problems for some; one wife and mother who assumed responsibility for 11 slaves admitted "I am so sick of trying to do a man's business when I am nothing but a poor contemptible piece of multiplying flesh." Others gladly took work in previously male occu-

Four hundred women disguised themselves as men to enlist in the military; most were soon discovered, a few not before they were killed in action.

pations, as teachers or as government clerks, inscribing tens of thousands of signatures on Confederate treasury bills. "No one said I was unladylike," remarked a volunteer nurse, "to climb into cattle cars . . . to feed those who cannot feed themselves." Yet most military nurses in the South were African American women and men, not white women.

Some northern women also found opportunities working for the philanthropic United States Sanitary Commission, which collected and distributed food, clothing, and medical supplies to the Union armies. By 1863, "Sanitary Fairs" appeared in northern cities, offering civilians evening entertainment while raising funds for the war. When the War Department appointed the humanitarian reformer Dorothea Dix to organize military hospitals and recruit female nurses in 1861, volunteers flocked to Washington. Dix supervised the selection and assignment of women nurses, taking pains to remind them to uphold their morality.

For many young women, the war provided escape from traditional female roles: "So sorry for the necessity," as the Massachusetts-born Clara Barton put it, "so glad for the opportunity." In 1863, for example, Cornelia Hancock, a 23-year old New Jersey Quaker volunteered to tend the wounded and soon confronted the terrible suffering and death. But she also reported discovering an inner resiliency and a feeling that "my past life was a myth." To her worried parents, she wrote,

"I feel like a new person. . . . I feel so erect." Although both Union and Confederate volunteers remained subordinate to male doctors and bureaucrats, the war released them from domestic roles and provided public tasks to fulfill. "We are changed by all this contact with terror," explained a northern nurse. Many Union nurses, such as Barton and Hancock, remained active reformers in the postwar years.

CONFLICTS IN THE CONFEDERACY

The Confederacy's martial spirit on the home front could not conceal cracks in the South's political consensus. Although the Confederate constitution described the southern government as a group of "sovereign and independent states," wartime pressure often forced the Richmond government to adopt policies that strengthened the central government, regardless of states' rights. Manpower shortages prompted the Confederacy to introduce military conscription in 1862, one year before the Union, but the laws permitted exemptions for slave overseers (requiring one white man for every twenty slaves) and allowed men who were drafted to hire substitutes. The cost of such replacements soon exceeded the reach of most people and brought complaints from poorer whites. Such inequities and favoritism toward slaveowners encouraged draft evasion and military desertions. Southern governors also resisted the use of state militia outside their state boundaries.

Although pre-war southern politicians had opposed the national government's support of economic development, such as tariffs and internal improvements, mobilization led the Confederacy to intervene directly in economic affairs. To improve transportation, the southern government gave subsidies for railroad construction and regulated the use of railroad equipment. Protective tariffs, long hated in the South and prohibited in the Confederate constitution, nonetheless served during wartime as a source of revenue. The Confederate government also supervised military production, even financing government-owned factories to manufacture gunpowder and munitions. To feed the Confederate army, the government "taxed" food production by seizing crops and claimed other goods-in-kind. Meanwhile, several states mandated limits in cotton acreage to encourage food production. Even so, wartime scarcity encouraged a huge inflation of food prices, and the resulting complaints from the homefront often triggered military desertions as soldiers worried about their families. In 1863, bread riots erupted in several southern cities as women stole loaves for their families. Jefferson Davis personally intervened in the Richmond riot, then persuaded newspapers and telegraph operators to censor the story lest it weaken southern morale.

The Northern Economy

The strength of the northern economy, by contrast, enabled the Union to mobilize industry and agriculture through capitalist incentives rather than government coercion. Such policies fit the Republican party agenda, which favored tariffs, national banking, internal improvements, and western settlement. With southern Democrats out of Congress, the Republican majority enacted laws that both supported the war and stimulated economic growth. The Tariff of 1861 raised duties on imports, not just for revenue purposes but also to protect northern industry. In 1862, Congress passed the Morrill Land Grant Act, giving the states public lands to support agricultural education and the "mechanical arts." The Homestead Act of 1862 offered free land to farmers who developed 160 acres and reduced the five-year residency requirements for war veterans. Envisioning a transcontinental railroad, Congress offered immense acreage to railroad companies to stimulate construction, though most development awaited the postwar years.

Other wartime financial legislation had tremendous social implications. To help finance the war, the Legal Tender Act of 1862 authorized the Treasury to issue paper currency (known as "Greenbacks"), which circulated to pay all taxes and debts except interest on government bonds. While facilitating public and private transactions, the currency steadily depreciated in value, nearly doubling the cost of living by 1865. Yet wealthy bondholders, whose interest payments came in hard specie, enjoyed great prosperity. To raise additional revenue, Congress also enacted the first federal income tax (3 percent for those earning over $800) as well as excise taxes, which affected all consumers, on almost every manufactured commodity.

Wartime demands proved a stimulus for most northern manufacturing. Although the absence of southern cotton weakened the textile industry, government purchases of uniforms, shoes, and munitions boosted production. In response to military needs, manufacturers created standard sizes for ready-to-wear clothing, which continued to be used after the war. Civilian workers also adopted what became "uniform" dress in business offices: jacket, pants, white linen shirt, and necktie. Shoes, manufactured on newly invented sewing machines, were made to fit either foot. Union officers also appreciated the advantages and prestige of personal timepieces, boosting the pocket watch industry. After battles, the watches became booty for thieves; as one looter explained, "where he is gone . . . time is nothing."

The war affected every aspect of economic development. Unable to ship their corn down the blockaded Mississippi River, farmers fed the corn to pigs and then brought the pigs to market. As the Union army consumed over half a billion pounds of packed meat during the war, Chicago stockyards emerged as the largest food processors in the nation. Meanwhile, the shortage of farm workers encouraged the mechanization of northern agriculture, and sales of farm implements soared. Coal, iron, and steel production also responded to enormous military demands.

Aggravating Social Tensions

Northern business prosperity contrasted with the condition of industrial workers, especially in the cities. As inflation sharply raised the price of goods (over 50 percent between 1862 and 1864), workers' wages lagged behind and their standard of living fell. Children, drawn into the labor force by the departure of soldiers, joined women at the bottom of the economic ladder. Women umbrella workers, for example, worked 16-hour shifts for wages of about $10 per day in today's currency. Seamstresses worked 14-hour days for the equivalent of $12.75 per week in today's money. Meanwhile, prison records showed a rise in the proportion of women and children charged with crimes relating to poverty; many were struggling relatives of absent soldiers.

Although labor unions greeted the war with patriotic enthusiasm, economic hardships ignited numerous labor disputes and strikes. Complicating these concerns was the northern Conscription Act of 1863, enacted over Democratic objections, which drafted "citizens" (not blacks) and permitted men to hire replacements for $300, about half a year's wages for unskilled workers. Passed just after Lincoln issued the Emancipation Proclamation, the law aroused indignation among workers who could not afford to pay for substitutes, hated the black exemption, and opposed the new war objective of freeing the slaves. Employers' use of African American strikebreakers intensified ethnic grievances. During an 1863 New York dock strike, predominantly Irish longshoremen used violence to clear black workers from the wharves.

These racial and class resentments exploded into riots in Manhattan in July 1863 when federal officials started the draft lottery. Enraged at the inequities, organized mobs disrupted the draft, burned factories, invaded the homes of abolitionists, and attacked men in business suits, presumably because they had paid their way out of military service. Angry mobs assaulted blacks indiscriminately—men, women, and children. Over 100 died during four days of street violence, requiring the use of Union troops to pacify the city.

The War of Conquest, 1863–1864

Despite growing frustration about the length of the war, both sides still fielded strong armies capable of winning tactical advantages that could lead to peace, if not victory. At the beginning of 1863, the Union's Army of the Potomac under "Fighting Joe" Hooker once again prepared to invade northern Virginia in hopes of capturing the Confederate capital. Against these forces, Confederates under Lee and Stonewall Jackson continued the offensive-defensive strategy to protect southern territory while striking opportunistically at northern units. Meanwhile, in the western theater, General Ulysses Grant advanced toward the Confederate fortress at Vicksburg, hoping to achieve Union control of the Mississippi River. This steady clash of military force had lasted for nearly two years, but in 1863 the Union began to break the Confederate defensive ring. The next year, despite heavy casualties, Union armies drove deeper into southern territory, steadily advancing against Confederate defenders. By the end of 1864, Union armies held Atlanta and were marching northward toward Charleston.

As the tide of battle turned, Union spirits rose. Although Lincoln had faced harsh criticism from anti-abolitionists, urban workers, and "peace" Democrats, the success of Union armies brought the Republican president and his party victories in the elections of 1864. By the time Lincoln pre-

sented his second inaugural address in March 1865, the war was nearly over. Already Congress had begun to debate postwar reconstruction of the Union. Questions about the status of ex-rebels and ex-slaves would shape the nation's politics for another decade. But the course of the war—the defeat of Confederate armies, the liberation of slaves—would determine the acceptable options. In fighting for the union, African Americans had established their claim to national citizenship.

Turning the Tide: Vicksburg and Gettysburg

In the spring of 1863, Union armies invaded northern Virginia, only to be stopped once again by Lee's tactical skills at Chancellorsville. But while the battle soured Union optimism, the South lost Stonewall Jackson, and Lee had still not tasted a clear victory. Nevertheless, the strategic stalemate in the eastern theater suggested the effectiveness of the offensive-defensive plan. Simultaneously, the Union failure to defeat Lee fueled criticism of Lincoln's leadership, and war-weary civilians denounced both the emancipation of slaves and the conscription of whites.

In the Mississippi valley, Union forces fared no better. Although the Confederate fortress at Vicksburg prevented Union control of the river, Grant used the Union navy to transport troops south of the fortress and then attacked from the east. Failing to conquer southern defenses, Grant established a siege that starved the post into surrender on July 4, 1863. The victory, followed by the capture of Port Hudson, gave the Union control of the river and split the western Confederacy (Louisiana, Arkansas, and Texas) from the eastern states. This part of the Anaconda strategy had finally prevailed.

Just days before Vicksburg fell, the Union's Army of the Potomac and the Confederacy's Army of Northern Virginia engaged in a ferocious battle at Gettysburg, Pennsylvania. During the siege at Vicksburg, Lee had proposed an invasion of the North, partly to demoralize the Union, partly to

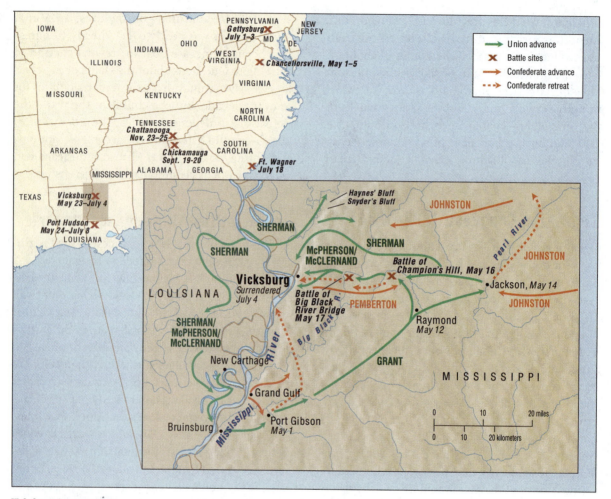

Vicksburg, Summer 1863

influence European opinion about assisting the South. In June 1863, as Grant was establishing his siege in Mississippi, Lee marched his army north through Maryland into Pennsylvania, finally encountering the Union army, now led by General George Meade, at Gettysburg. The ensuing battle epitomized the war's bitter fighting and foreshadowed its final outcome. For three days, outnumbered Confederate soldiers charged bravely into the blazing Union guns, until Lee had lost one-third of his army. Union troops suffered, too, but the North had more resources and men to sacrifice. Forced at last to retreat, Lee might have lost all his troops had the Union armies pursued more aggressively. Lee managed his escape, however, and the war went on.

War of Invasion

The Confederate hope that war weariness would persuade the North to seek a peaceful compromise was running out of time. By the end of 1863,

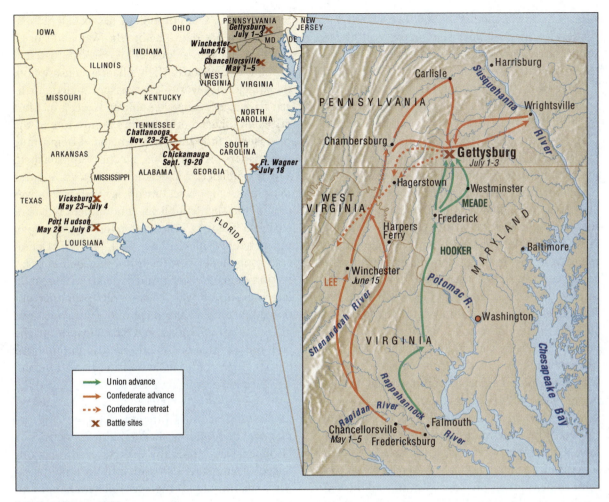

Union advance
Confederate advance
Confederate retreat
Battle sites

Gettysburg, Summer 1863

Union victories at Chattanooga, Tennessee, had opened the Confederacy for invasion. Preparing for a spring campaign, Lincoln promoted Grant to lead the Union armies and shifted him to the eastern sector, where the tough, resolute general would contend against the skillful Lee. The western command passed to William Tecumseh Sherman, whose sense of relentless discipline embodied the principles of total war. "The South has done her worst," he said to Grant, "now is the time for us to pile on our blows thick and fast."

Grant needed no encouragement. His goal was to defeat Lee's army in northern Virginia and capture the Confederate capital at Richmond. With 115,000 soldiers to Lee's 75,000, the Union general counted on numerical superiority to launch frontal attacks against Lee's weakened forces. In the Battle of the Wilderness in May 1864, Lee's armies benefited from the wooded terrain and inflicted 18,000 casualties, while losing 12,000. But this apparent Confederate victory failed to stop the Union advance. The fighting continued at Spotsylvania, where Grant lost another 18,000; Lee 12,000, but the result remained indecisive. Three weeks later, the armies clashed again at Cold Harbor, a vicious three-day battle in which Union forces sustained 7,000 losses in a single hour. Less than two weeks later, Grant attacked Lee at Petersburg, losing another 11,000 men. The six weeks' campaign cost the Union over 60,000 soldiers, while the Confederacy lost 37,000. By the fall of 1864, the two armies dug in for a long siege near Petersburg, Virginia.

Sherman, meanwhile, had begun to march from Tennessee to Atlanta, Georgia. "We have devoured the land," the general wrote to his wife. Killing farm animals for food, feeding their horses and mules from growing crops, looting and burning deserted buildings, Sherman's soldiers sent terror through the Confederacy. Southern women feared the pillage and spread rumors of rape. Northern soldiers generally proved respectful of white women, but freed slaves were sometimes targeted for sexual abuse. Indeed, Union courtesy toward whites permitted some southern women to step out of their traditional roles to act as spies or to insult the invading forces. Sometimes the tables were turned. When one Mississippi woman spat in the face of a Yankee prisoner, she did not expect him to return with Sherman's army; when he did, he reminded her of their previous meeting and burned her house to the ground. "Thus may it be with all who descend from their high pedestal of womanhood," said the arsonist. Whatever the limits of Union chivalry, by the summer of 1864 Sherman stood inside Atlanta, having caused 29,000 casualties and sustained 23,000. Meanwhile, General Philip Sheridan led Union forces through Virginia's Shenandoah valley, burning Confederate farms.

Seeking a Northern Consensus

"The cannon will not suffer any other sound to be heard for miles and for years around it," said the author Ralph Waldo Emerson during the battle of Spotsylvania. "Our chronology has lost all old distinctions in one date—before the War, and since." By 1864, the tremendous toll of war had frustrated civilians in the North. High inflation, conscription, the attack on slavery—these issues fueled northern grievances against Republican leadership. Most criticism focused on Lincoln's failure to end the bloodshed. "Stop the War," demanded Democratic newspapers as the 1864 election approached. When Confederate agents indicated a willingness to negotiate for peace, Lincoln sent representatives to talk. But the Republican commitment to emancipation, like the Confederacy's insistence on total independence, blocked any deal. Lincoln's Democratic opponents were themselves divided. A peace faction demanded an immediate armistice, but a larger group of "war" Democrats primarily opposed Lincoln's management of the war, violations of habeas corpus rights, and emancipation. In the end, the war Democrats prevailed and nominated former General McClellan to run against Lincoln.

During the campaign, Democrats invented the term *miscegenation* to refer to interracial sexual relations and accused Lincoln of advocating the practice. Republicans smeared Lincoln's critics as "Copperheads" (deadly snakes, easily camouflaged). Democrats also criticized the administration's inability to arrange prisoner exchanges. In prison hellholes like Georgia's Andersonville, Richmond's Libby, and Illinois's Camp Douglas, prisoners of war died like flies (30,000 Union; 26,000 Confederate). But Republicans rejected Confederate demands that African Americans be excluded from any prisoner returns. As with emancipation, Lincoln would not compromise the war's goals. Ultimately, it was the fortunes of war that determined the political outcome in November 1864. Bolstered by Sherman's victories in Georgia, the Republicans swept the presidential election. Lincoln won 55 percent of the popular vote, including 78 percent of the ballots cast by soldiers. The Republicans also carried both houses of Congress.

This Republican victory had vast political consequences. First, Lincoln treated the election as a mandate from the citizenry; he promptly urged the sitting lame-duck Congress, in which Democrats had substantial strength, to pass a constitutional amendment ending slavery throughout the nation. Only after intense administration pressure did enough Democrats agree to enact the Thirteenth Amendment in January 1865. Ratification by the states would be completed by the end of the year.

Amendment XIII (1865)

Section 1.
Neither slavery nor involuntary servitude, except as a punishment for crime whereof the party shall have been duly convicted, shall exist within the United States, or any place subject to their jurisdiction.

Section 2.
Congress shall have power to enforce this article by appropriate legislation.

Second, Lincoln had made a strategic decision during the campaign to choose a new vice-presidential running mate, Tennessee's Andrew Johnson, a lifelong Democrat and the only southern senator to remain in Washington after secession. Lincoln had brought Johnson aboard to strengthen his chances for reelection. But, as the postwar years would reveal, the new vice president did not share Lincoln's sympathy for the freed slaves nor accept Republican views of how best to reconstruct the shattered South.

The Confederacy Falls

"We cannot change the hearts of those people of the South," remarked Sherman as the war continued, "but we can make war so terrible and make them so sick of war that generations would pass away before they would again appeal to it." After burning large sections of Atlanta, Sherman's army commenced a devastating 280-mile march to the sea, destroying everything of military value on the way to Savannah. By January 1865, the seasoned troops were heading north toward South Carolina, birthplace of secession, and chanting, "Hail Columbia, happy land; if we don't burn you, I'll be damned." Columbia, South Carolina, fell in February, and Union soldiers, drunk on glory and confiscated whiskey, scribbled graffiti and "foul comments" on the public walls. The South had lost the power, though not the will, to fight.

"Fondly do we hope—fervently do we pray—that this mighty scourge of war may speedily pass away," said Lincoln in his second inaugural address in March 1865. As mass desertions weakened the remaining southern armies in Virginia, Grant finally turned Lee's flank at Petersburg. The Confederate government in Richmond abandoned the city, setting fires to prevent Union troops from capturing military supplies and records. Union cavalry prevented Lee's forces from escaping into North Carolina. At the village of Appomattox, the Confederate general reached the end of the fight. On April 9, 1865, Grant and Lee arranged a formal surrender. After a few weeks of mop-up skirmishing, the Civil War was over.

"No howling!" observed South Carolina's Mary Chesnut of the Confederate defeat. "Our poverty is made a matter of laughing. . . . Of the country, we try not to speak at all." Northerners could not contain their joy, nor forget, in Lincoln's words, "the loved and lost." To the victorious Union, Lincoln embodied the suffering and sacrifice of the war as he felt the strain of sending boys and men to their death, commuted sentences of deserters or Sioux warriors, and even lost a young son to malaria during his presidency. Yet Confederate loyalists remained bitter. Five days after Appomattox, while the president watched a play at

Ford's Theater in Washington, one unrepentant southern sympathizer, the actor John Wilkes Booth, crept behind Lincoln's seat and fired a bullet into the president's head.

The Unfinished War

The public mourning that followed Lincoln's assassination helped northern hearts recover from the horror of the war. As the president's black-draped funeral train moved on a 1600-mile journey from Washington through the nation's major cities to Springfield, Illinois, some 7 million citizens paused to pay homage (though municipal officials in New York, sharing the racist views that had prompted the draft riots, barred the city's African Americans from visiting the funeral cortege). Outside the ruined Confederacy, Lincoln's reputation rose to mythic heights; his name was placed on streets, counties, and towns; monuments were built in his honor; and his words were repeated so often that they became cliches. Southerners, by contrast, took solace in a cult of "the lost cause." Believing in the honor of secession and their defense of southern liberty, die-hard Confederates acknowledged only the superiority of Union power. "One thing I shall glory in to the latest hours of my life," wrote one Georgia woman. "We never yielded in the struggle until we were bound hand and foot and the heel of the despot was on our throats."

Conflicts between the North and the South thus endured, but the war had transformed the nation's political life. Until the Civil War, the noun "United States" was considered a plural phrase, but never so afterward. The defeat of secession had permanently altered the federal balance of power. Now a centralized government would determine constitutional rules of law, compelling the southern states to accept northern terms of recon-struction. To be sure, those conditions remained subject to debate. In 1864, Lincoln had vetoed a congressional plan of reconstruction, beginning a decade-long political struggle over the nature of the federal Union. After the war, moreover, Lincoln's Republican party would maintain a firm grip on national power and would continue to legislate policies that promoted industrial development. Republicans would demand justice for the former slaves. The war for freedom not only destroyed slavery but also killed the ante-bellum assumption that the government existed only to serve white people. In the end, the Civil War proved what Lincoln had only proposed in his Gettysburg Address of 1863: ". . . that government of the people, by the people, and for the people, shall not perish from the earth." The phrase would become a benchmark for postwar generations.

INFOTRAC® COLLEGE EDITION EXERCISES

For additional reading go to InfoTrac College Edition, your online research library at *http://web1.infotrac-college.com*.

Keyword search: Confederate states

Keyword search: Jefferson Davis

Keyword search: Fort Sumter

Keyword search: Civil War draft

Keyword search: Robert E. Lee

Keyword search: Emancipation Proclamation

Keyword search: Ulysses S. Grant

Keyword search: Appomattox

Keyword search: Lincoln assassination

ADDITIONAL READING

James M. McPherson, *Battle Cry of Freedom: The Civil War Era* (1988). A clear overview of the war's political, social, and military history.

Economic and Diplomatic Issues

Howard Jones, *Abraham Lincoln and a New Birth of Freedom: The Union and Slavery in the Diplomacy of the Civil War* (1999). This book places political and ideological issues in the international context.

A People's War

Gerald F. Linderman, *Embattled Courage: The Experience of Combat in the American Civil War* (1987). This study examines warfare from the perspective of the fighting soldiers; for ideological motives in the armies, see also James M. McPherson, *For Cause and Comrade: Why Men Fought in the Civil War* (1997).

Charles Royster, *The Destructive War: William Tecumseh Sherman, Stonewall Jackson, and the Americans* (1990). Analyzes the social and cultural implications of the Civil War's violence.

The Politics of Emancipation

William K. Klingaman, *Abraham Lincoln and the Road to Emancipation, 1861–1865* (2001). The author traces the president's growing commitment to ending slavery.

Leon F. Litwack, *Been in the Storm So Long: The Aftermath of Slavery* (1979). A superb account of southern African Americans carries the story into the era of reconstruction. See also an excellent anthology of contemporary documents in Ira Berlin and Leslie S. Rowlands, eds., *Families and Freedom: A Documentary History of African American Kinship in the Civil War Era* (1997).

Blacks Enter the Ranks

Joseph T. Glatthaar, *Forged in Battle: The Civil War Alliance of Black Soldiers and White Officers* (1990). This book discusses the experience of black Union soldiers and their white leaders; see also Christopher Looby, ed., *The Complete Civil War Journal of Thomas Wentworth Higginson* (1999).

War on Native Grounds

Philip Weeks, *Farewell, My Nation: The American Indian and the United States, 1820–1890* (1990). A succinct study of U.S.–Native American relations, the book's Civil War chapter offers an excellent summary.

The War on the Home Front

Phillip Shaw Paludan, *"A People's Contest": The Union and the Civil War, 1861–1865* (1988). A thorough survey of the war's impact on the North, summarizing recent scholarship.

Facing the Death Toll

Garry Wills, *Lincoln at Gettysburg: The Words That Remade America* (1992). This analysis of the Gettysburg Address places Lincoln in the context of 19th-century culture.

Women and the War

Drew Gilpin Faust, *Mothers of Invention: Women of the Slaveholding South in the American Civil War* (1996). This analysis takes a fresh look at how Confederate women responded to the military crisis.

Judith Ann Giesberg, *Civil War Sisterhood: The U.S. Sanitary Commission and Women's Politics in Transition* (2000). A study of middle-class northern women, this book links wartime activism with postwar reformism.

Conflicts in the Confederacy

Emory M. Thomas, *The Confederate Nation: 1861–1865* (1979). This volume provides a detailed survey of southern history; see also Gary W. Gallagher, *The Confederate War* (1997), which discusses the relationship between southern society and Confederate military strategy.

The Northern Economy

Iver Bernstein, *The New York City Draft Riots: Their Significance for American Society and Politics in the Age of the Civil War* (1990). This work provides an analysis of ethnic, economic and political tensions in the North.

15

Reconstructing the National Identity, 1865–1877

CHRONOLOGY

1865	Congress establishes Freedmen's Bureau
	Andrew Johnson succeeds slain President Lincoln
	Johnson issues amnesty proclamation
	States ratify Thirteenth Amendment
1865–1866	Southern states enact Black Codes
1866	Ku Klux Klan and vigilante groups appear in South
	Congress passes Civil Rights Act over Johnson's veto
	Women reformers organize American Equal Rights Association
1867	Congress passes Reconstruction Acts
	Farmers form Patrons of Husbandry
1868	House impeaches President Johnson; Senate votes acquittal
	States ratify Fourteenth Amendment
	Congress reseats southern representatives
	Fort Laramie treaty establishes Sioux reservation
	Ulysses S. Grant wins presidential election
1869	Transcontinental railroad completed in Utah
1870	States ratify Fifteenth Amendment
1871	Fire destroys Chicago; scandals topple New York Tweed Ring
1872	Grant defeats Liberal Republican Horace Greeley
1873	Wall Street panic precipitates economic downturn
	Slaughterhouse ruling limits enforcement of Fourteenth Amendment
1875	Congress passes Civil Rights Act
1876	Sioux warriors defeat U.S. cavalry at Little Big Horn
1877	Rutherford B. Hayes chosen president by electoral commission
	Hayes withdraws last federal troops from South

The boy was six or seven years old—he didn't know exactly the year of his birth—when he and his brother, sister, and mother, and all the other slaves on the Virginia plantation were summoned to the master's "big house" to hear the news of their freedom. "All was excitement and expectancy," recalled Booker T. Washington. The master's family stood or sat on the veranda, their faces clouded with sadness. A Union officer made a short speech, read aloud the Emancipation Proclamation, and advised the anxious slaves that they were free and could go where and when they pleased. Washington's mother, tears of joy streaming down her cheeks, leaned over her children, and kissed them tenderly. "For some minutes, there was great rejoicing, and thanksgiving, and wild scenes of ecstasy," Washington remembered. And then the former slaves retreated soberly to their cabins, feeling for the first time "the great responsibility of being free."

http://history.wadsworth.com

The metamorphosis of ex-slaves mirrored the transformation of the entire nation in 1865, as whites and blacks, southerners and northerners, faced a new sense of national identity. "The territorial, political, and historical oneness of the nation is now ratified by the blood of thousands of her sons," declared a new magazine, appropriately named *The Nation*, in 1865. In the same year, an Illinois editor boasted of "the mysterious but unmistakable homogeneity of [the] people." To be sure, such hyperbole ignored obvious disagreements about race, class, and gender. "Verily," observed the black abolitionist Frederick Douglass, "the work does not end with the abolition of slavery, but only begins."

A new sense of federal power now stimulated a vast quantity of national legislation. In the decade after 1865, the number of bills introduced to Congress tripled over the previous ten years, and the number of laws that were passed doubled. A growing federal bureaucracy—beginning with the Bureau of Statistics in 1866, the Department of Justice and the Weather Bureau in 1870, and the expanded 1870 national Census—greatly increased national record-keeping. Meanwhile, in 1866, the Western Union telegraph company, the nation's first major monopoly, knit together the strands of national communication.

If the Civil War produced an enlarged national government, the death of the Confederacy raised divisive questions about the definition of U.S. citizenship. Whom did the federal government now represent? How should the seceded states be "reconstructed" as members of the national Union? What was the legal status of ex-Confederates, and should all ex-rebels be treated alike? The end of slavery prompted additional questions about the status of ex-slaves and free blacks. Should African Americans be considered citizens? Should black women enjoy the status of black men? Should white women obtain the same privileges of citizenship as African American men?

These political questions touched the core of the national identity, forcing all Americans to consider their own status and rights. The Fourteenth Amendment, which gave citizenship to African Americans in 1868, introduced the word *male* into the U.S. Constitution for the first time, but ignored women like Elizabeth Cady Stanton, who demanded "government by . . . the whole people; for . . . the whole people." An Oregon newspaper carried the matter to a logical, and unpopular, conclusion: "If we make the African a citizen, we cannot deny the same right to the Indian and the Mongolian."

Public debate about citizenship did not necessarily affect the country's social and economic development. Indeed, the political nationalism expressed by leadership groups—party politicians, newspaper writers, businessmen, and their supporters at the polls—often contrasted with the concerns of political outsiders, such as immigrants, ex-slaves, women, and Native Americans, who experienced a contrary pattern of exclusion, separation, and persecution. Moreover, persistent local issues involving land use, economic development, or ethnic conflict often seemed more important to diverse communities than did the affairs debated in Washington, D.C.

The extraordinary economic growth after the Civil War, notably the completion of a transcontinental railroad, a burst in urbanization, and agricultural expansion at the expense of the Plains nations, distracted attention from political questions of citizenship, suffrage, and civil rights. And, because national politicians usually responded to the concerns of their separate constituencies, the lack of interest in the hinterlands about national politics made it difficult for leaders in Washington to fulfill the promises of equal rights for ex-slaves.

Yet by 1877, when the era of reconstruction ended, the contours of the national identity had assumed a new form, laying the basis for a multicultural government for future generations.

The Promise of Reconstruction

In 1865, the U.S. government had to determine the conditions for readmitting the seceded states into the Union and restoring political rights to ex-rebels. Even before the Civil War ended, President Abraham Lincoln had offered a general amnesty to Confederates, exempting only high political and military leaders, and proposed that as few as 10 percent of eligible voters, once they affirmed their loyalty to the Constitution, might create new state governments. Lincoln also indicated an interest in extending the vote to some southern blacks—at least those who were educated, had served in the Union army, and owned property. Yet Lincoln's plan was designed as much to encourage Confederate surrender as to restore the Union. More radical Republicans in Congress, concerned that Lincoln's easy terms for readmitting southern representatives would weaken their party's position, subsequently offered a stricter plan of reconstruction. As passed in the Wade-Davis bill of 1864, Congress demanded that a majority (not just 10 percent) of southern voters take "iron-clad" oaths of loyalty to the Union, repudiate Confederate debts, disenfranchise Confederate leaders, and accept the end of slavery. Lincoln considered these terms too rigid and refused to sign the bill into law.

After the Confederate surrender and Lincoln's assassination, the issue of reconstruction could no longer be avoided. The new president, Tennessee Democrat Andrew Johnson, distrusted the Republican-controlled Congress. Since the new Congress would not come into session until December 1865, the president initiated his own policies to restore the Union. Johnson's conciliatory approach to most ex-Confederates encouraged the southern states to pass discriminatory laws against the former slaves. Such disregard for black rights aroused criticism in the North, and congressional Republicans prepared to challenge the president's version of reconstruction.

At the end of the Civil War, moreover, the southern states were in a ruined condition. Damage to towns, fields, fences, and plantations had shattered the southern economy. Not only did investors lose the value of Confederate money, but the emancipation of 4 million slaves eliminated the basis of most southern wealth. The freed slaves, meanwhile, lost the minimal security and subsistence that slavery had provided. One month before the war ended, Congress had established the Bureau of Freedmen, Refugees, and Abandoned Land, known as the Freedmen's Bureau. The bureau's mission was to assist ex-slaves and poor whites with food, transportation, and legal advice; to help them obtain work or settle on abandoned lands; and to establish schools to prepare them to live independently. Such federal intervention in the realm of social welfare was unprecedented. Yet most ex-slaves did not await government instruction to explore their freedom. Indeed, African American initiatives in 1865 revealed so much passion for self-determination that white southerners became alarmed.

A Passion for Freedom

Freed slaves quickly asserted their independence. Many took new surnames that identified kinship and family connections; others took the last names of their former owners or of some famous personage. The desire for family ties prompted many

Former slaves who went to the Freedmen's Bureau could expect help with food, transportation, and legal advice; finding work or settling on abandoned lands; and schooling to prepare them to live independently.

ex-slaves to search for spouses, children, and parents who had been sold away during slavery. African Americans also endeavored to stabilize their family lives. In rural areas, where most blacks lived, married women tried to avoid field work, instead assuming domestic roles in their families. Black domestics who worked for whites chose to dwell at home, not with their employers. Such decisions reflected a deliberate effort to strengthen their own families, although poverty often forced them back into the labor force.

Whites encouraged ex-slaves to legalize their marriages, partly for reasons of morality, partly to relieve governments of responsibility for illegitimate children, and partly to enable public officials to enforce the legal responsibilities between husbands and wives for financial support. Formal marriage also gave black men the legal standing to protect their children against apprenticeship laws that permitted the seizure of minors who were without legal guardians to become wards of the state. Yet legal marriage raised new problems. Since state laws presumed that men were heads of the household, married black women, who had considerable family responsibility during slavery, now faced a state-imposed patriarchal family structure.

African Americans also departed from the white-controlled Christian churches of slavery days, effectively evading oversight of their spiritual lives. They now established independent congregations, usually within the Methodist or Baptist churches. In this way, freed African Americans continued to develop a distinct religious system that perpetuated African-derived styles of Christian worship services, such as singing, clapping, and call-and-response.

The abrupt independence of former slaves disrupted old assumptions about the social order. Former slaveholding women, once spared the drudgery of housework, discovered the "same old tune of washing, ironing and cooking . . . of being maids of all work." When young freed women appeared in public wearing stylish black veils, offended white women boycotted the fashion. Recognizing the importance of harnessing black labor to assure their own economic survival,

"I's free. Ain't wuf nuffin."

white landowners complained that "Negroes know nothing of the value of time," slept after sunrise, and demanded Saturdays without labor.

"Where shall Othello go?" remained, however, a serious question for one paternalistic planter, who doubted the ability of African Americans to survive on their own. "Poor elk—poor buffalo—poor Indian—poor Nigger—this is indeed a white man's country." Indeed, former slaves confronted a new and unfriendly world of economic relations. "I's free," observed one ex-slave. "Ain't wuf nuffin." Such vulnerability enabled unscrupulous whites to cheat the newly freed workers, refuse to pay wages, or commit violence against those who protested new forms of economic exploitation.

Johnson's Policy of Restoration

President Johnson's policy of "restoration" accentuated the problems of southern blacks. With Congress out of session in the spring of 1865, Johnson offered amnesty to southern rebels who agreed to a loyalty oath, restoring their property and political rights to all but the richest southern leaders. A second presidential proclamation called for the creation of new state governments, limiting the vote to pardoned white men; it also demanded ratification of the Thirteenth Amendment, which abolished slavery, as a condition for a state's readmission to the Union. When African American leaders like Frederick Douglass appealed to Johnson to extend voting rights to blacks, the former Tennessee slaveowner refused and defended white supremacy. Johnson also ordered the return of lands confiscated by the Union armies to pardoned ex-Confederates, even when freed slaves already inhabited those lands.

Johnson's views emboldened southern voters to elect ex-Confederates to draft new state constitutions. Rather than meet the president's conditions, moreover, the southern constitutional conventions hesitated to repudiate secession and the abolition of slavery. In addition, the first postwar southern governments sought to control the freed slaves by enacting restrictive laws known as "Black Codes." These laws gave African Americans minimal rights, such as the right to marry, own property, make contracts, bring lawsuits, and testify in court against other blacks. But the codes excluded African Americans from juries and the right to vote, rejected black testimony against whites, and provided more severe penalties for black criminals than for white ones.

The new codes limited the freedom of black workers. By defining black unemployment as vagrancy, southern laws permitted the courts to impose fines on idle blacks and to contract their labor to private citizens to repay the fines. Black children without adequate parental support could be apprenticed to businessmen and forced into involuntary labor. Some codes prohibited land ownership or leases, compelling ex-slaves to work for wages on other people's land. Black workers had to sign annual labor contracts or face high penalties, which could only be paid by additional labor. Although Freedmen's Bureau courts suspended some of these restrictions, military authorities endorsed the labor contracts both to protect blacks' rights and to assure economic stability. To African Americans and their northern sympathizers, the Black Codes seemed like a retreat toward reenslavement of black workers.

Congress Challenges Johnson

While the southern governments attempted to thwart political change, northern leaders prepared to enforce fundamental reforms. As the first postwar Congress convened in December 1865, the

Republican majority divided into two camps. The smaller group, called "Radicals," included Massachusetts's Charles Sumner and Ohio's Ben Wade in the Senate and Pennsylvania's Thaddeus Stevens in the House; this group believed fervently in protecting equal rights for all citizens, blacks as well as whites. The larger Republican wing, known as "Moderates," wanted assurances that secession and slavery were dead, but felt no commitment to black equality and hoped to cooperate with the president. But Johnson's generous amnesty, followed by the Black Codes, alarmed even Moderate Republicans, who assessed the newly elected southern representatives and refused to seat them.

Recognizing that southern whites were threatening the freedom of ex-slaves, Moderate Republicans supported Illinois Senator Lyman Trumbull's proposal to extend the term of the Freedmen's Bureau to offer federal protection for southern blacks. While promising to continue programs for education, supervision of labor contracts, and food and transportation for ex-slaves, the Freedmen's Bureau bill of 1866 also supported President Johnson's order restoring confiscated land to pardoned rebels and limited black settlement on other federal lands. Protection of black labor, not seizure of white-owned land, remained the Moderates' goal. In the end, the only pro-Confederates forced to surrender land to former slaves were the southern Native Americans in Indian territory. The subsequent Southern Homestead Act of 1866 merely offered undeveloped public lands for purchase by blacks and other Unionists, most of it too costly for former slaves. But even the Moderate version of the Freedmen's Bureau bill offended Johnson, who viewed any social aid to ex-slaves as a violation of constitutional limits on government authority. He vetoed the measure, and a stunned Congress initially failed to override the veto.

Moderate Republicans also sought to protect southern blacks by passing the Civil Rights bill of 1866, which disallowed discrimination in state laws. Congress limited this bill to those states that refused to guarantee civil rights to their own citizens. But Johnson vetoed the proposal as an unnecessary expansion of federal power. For the first time in U.S. history, Congress mustered two-thirds majorities to override a presidential veto of major legislation. By the summer of 1866, Congress also mustered the votes to pass the Freedmen's Bureau bill and override another presidential veto of the measure. This defiance of presidential leadership reflected growing resentment of Johnson's personal arrogance as well as his refusal to compromise with the congressional majority. The political rift would soon grow.

During the spring of 1866, Congress proceeded to draft a Fourteenth Amendment to the Constitution, establishing the citizenship of all people born or naturalized in the United States, which included blacks but not "Indians." This provision overturned the principles of the Dred Scott decision of 1857 (see Chapter 13). The Fourteenth Amendment also addressed the matter of black suffrage. With the end of slavery, southern states were no longer limited by the Three-Fifths Compromise to count black residents as a fraction of whites in apportioning representation in Congress; instead, southern blacks would count as whole persons, thus increasing southern representation. Republicans realized that white southerners would back Democratic candidates. To balance white voters, therefore, the proposed Amendment authorized congressional representation to be based on the number of "male" inhabitants allowed to vote, an effort to induce states to give the suffrage to black men. This provision was not necessarily popular in the northern states, of which only six gave black men the ballot. Eventually eight other northern states would vote on the issue of black suffrage, but it passed in only two, Iowa and Minnesota. Finally, the Fourteenth Amendment disqualified former

Confederate officials from holding office. Congress promptly sent the Fourteenth Amendment to the states for ratification. But of the former Confederate states, only Tennessee voted to ratify, stalling approval and angering Republican leaders.

The split between Congress and the president widened during the 1866 congressional elections. Seeking to build a coalition of Democrats and conservative Republicans, Johnson challenged the Republican majority, purging opponents from government jobs and embarking on an unprecedented—and unseemly—campaign tour that newspapers derided as the "Swing around the Circle." During the campaign, moreover, violent race riots by whites in Memphis and New Orleans revealed the terror that afflicted southern blacks. The violence undermined Johnson's political support and swept Republicans back into office.

Congressional Reconstruction

Frustrated by the South's refusal to ratify the Fourteenth Amendment, the new Republican-dominated Congress introduced its own program of reconstruction in 1867. Its aim was to end the Johnson-approved southern governments, whose representatives had still not been seated in Congress. The plan emerged in a series of Reconstruction acts, passed in 1867 over the Democratic president's vetoes. Denying the legality of the previous southern governments, Congress divided the South into five military districts to ensure enforcement of federal laws and established strict criteria for the election and admission of representatives to Congress. The measures required that black men be allowed to vote; took political rights from leading Confederates; required elected conventions to draft new state constitutions that would guarantee black male suffrage; mandated ratification of the Fourteenth Amendment; and, finally, allowed the election of state government officials and congres-sional representatives. In providing for reunion based on black suffrage, the act gave Republican leaders the possibility of countering white southern political power in Congress. Far more radical than the Fourteenth Amendment, congressional reconstruction brought black citizens directly into the nation's political structure.

Amendment XIV (1868)

Section 1.
All persons born or naturalized in the United States, and subject to the jurisdiction thereof, are citizens of the United States and of the state wherein they reside. No state shall make or enforce any law which shall abridge the privileges or immunities of citizens of the United States; nor shall any state deprive any person of life, liberty, or property, without due process of law; nor deny to any person within its jurisdiction the equal protection of the laws.

Section 2.
Representatives shall be apportioned among the several states according to their respective numbers, counting the whole number of persons in each state, excluding Indians not taxed. But when the right to vote at any election for the choice of electors for President and Vice President of the United States, Representatives in Congress, the executive and judicial officers of a state, or the members of the legislature thereof, is denied to any of the male inhabitants of such state, being twenty-one years of age, and citizens of the United States, or in any way abridged, except for participation in rebellion, or other crime, the basis of representation therein shall be reduced in the proportion which the number of such male citizens shall bear to the whole number of male citizens twenty-one years of age in such state.

Section 3.

No person shall be a Senator or Representative in Congress, or elector of President and Vice President, or hold any office, civil or military, under the United States, or under any state, who, having previously taken an oath, as a member of Congress, or as an officer of the United States, or as a member of any state legislature, or as an executive or judicial officer of any state, to support the Constitution of the United States, shall have engaged in insurrection or rebellion against the same, or given aid or comfort to the enemies thereof. But Congress may by a vote of two-thirds of each House, remove such disability.

Section 4.

The validity of the public debt of the United States, authorized by law, including debts incurred for payment of pensions and bounties for services in suppressing insurrection or rebellion, shall not be questioned. But neither the United States nor any state shall assume or pay any debt or obligation incurred in aid of insurrection or rebellion against the United States, or any claim for the loss or emancipation of any slave; but all such debts, obligations and claims shall be held illegal and void.

Section 5.

The Congress shall have power to enforce, by appropriate legislation, the provisions of this article.

The split between Johnson and Congress provoked a constitutional crisis. Hostile to congressional efforts to strengthen the power of southern blacks at the expense of whites, Johnson used his executive authority to grant thousands of pardons to ex-Confederates and to make appointments to undermine Congress's reconstruction program.

Republicans countered by enacting such laws as the Tenure of Office Act of 1867, which limited the president's right to dismiss executive officers. When Johnson defied that law by dismissing Secretary of War Edwin M. Stanton, a supporter of congressional reconstruction, Radical Republicans pushed for the president's impeachment.

After the House of Representatives voted to impeach Johnson for violating the Tenure of Office Act, the Senate held formal hearings in 1868. Although Johnson insisted that he had committed no crimes, he agreed privately to accept the Reconstruction acts. Moderate Republicans then became less hostile. The Senate finally voted 35–19 for conviction, but fell one vote short of the two-thirds majority necessary to remove the president from office. Johnson lost any hope of gaining reelection in 1868. Instead, Republicans backed war hero Ulysses S. Grant, who supported congressional reconstruction. Although politically inexperienced, Grant won the election.

Debating the Votes for Blacks and Women

As the presidential crisis ended in 1868, nearly all the southern states had adopted constitutions providing for black suffrage, ratified the Fourteenth Amendment, and returned delegates to Congress. But the 1868 elections underscored political trends that alarmed Republican leaders. First, in the southern states, violence against black voters showed that many whites did not accept the political settlements; second, in sixteen northern and border states where blacks were denied the suffrage, Democrats had made election gains. Republicans therefore proposed a Fifteenth Amendment, which prohibited both federal and state governments from interfering with suffrage on racial grounds. Although Democrats denounced this "most revolutionary measure," the Fifteenth Amendment actually threatened no existing power, for the proposed Amendment did not outlaw non-racial voting restrictions, such as literacy, education, or wealth, nor did it extend the franchise to women. Even so, western states, whose citizens were opposed to Chinese or Mexican voting, refused to ratify the Amendment.

Amendment XV (1870)

Section 1.
The right of citizens of the United States to vote shall not be denied or abridged by the United States or by any state on account of race, color, or previous condition of servitude.

Section 2.
The Congress shall have power to enforce this article by appropriate legislation.

Women reformers, such as Elizabeth Cady Stanton, Susan B. Anthony, Lucretia Mott, and Lucy Stone, had formed the American Equal Rights Association in 1866 to merge the campaigns for black and female voting. But a statewide referendum in Kansas in 1867 revealed that women's suffrage was even less popular than the black vote. Congress extended the franchise to African American men in Washington, D.C., but showed no interest in accommodating women's demands.

The language of the Fourteenth Amendment specifically referred to "male" voters. "On what principle of justice or courtesy," demanded Mrs. Stanton, "should woman yield her right of enfranchisement to the negro?" Furious that former Republican allies gave preeminence to African American men over Anglo Saxon women, some women appealed to racial prejudices in arguing against ratification of the proposed amendment. "American women of wealth, education, virtue and refinement," said Stanton, "do not wish the lower orders of Chinese, Africans, Germans and Irish . . . to make laws for . . . your daughters." Such opinions split the women's suffrage campaign into rival groups. Male reformers, such as Frederick Douglass, who publicly supported woman's suffrage, endorsed the Fifteenth Amendment, even though it omitted the women's vote. "Woman has a thousand ways by which she can attach herself to the ruling power of the land," Douglass explained to justify his position.

In 1868, reformers who opposed compromise formed the National Woman Suffrage Association, dedicated to passage of a Sixteenth Amendment for the women's vote. When Congress refused to consider the idea, some dissatisfied women decided to ignore male-only voting laws. In 1871 and 1872, hundreds of women attempted to cast ballots. One result was Susan B. Anthony's arrest and trial for illegal voting. In 1869, Mormon-dominated Utah granted women the franchise to strengthen conservative power, followed in 1870 by Wyoming, where the women's vote was seen as a moral force against social disorder. This growing awareness of women's potential power encouraged activists to seek reforms outside the ballot box. Although some groups continued to demand the vote, women reformers increasingly focused on social legislation, such as divorce reform, that would help women without changing the political system.

Reconstruction Comes to the South

The political environment in the southern states accentuated the economic problems faced by the freed slaves. Since southern blacks remained loyal to their Republican emancipators and southern whites clung to the Democratic party, state politics embodied fundamental racial conflicts. Hostile whites organized violent vigilante groups such as the Ku Klux Klan to keep blacks from voting, holding political office, or obtaining economic independence. Meanwhile, new state laws about marriage, apprenticeship, and land reinforced white economic supremacy. Such policies often worked against the interests of poor whites, who ironically identified with white leaders rather than with blacks who had similar problems. This oppression of southern blacks aroused northern criticism and justified the continuing presence of federal troops in the southern states. But northern interest in southern problems was easily distracted by other issues. Increasingly, southern blacks could challenge their status only at the peril of life and property.

Reconstruction Leadership

Congressional reconstruction initially disenfranchised ex-Confederates (about 15 percent of southern white men) and gave the vote to some 700,000 African Americans, thus assuring Republican majorities. Identifying with the party of Lincoln, blacks formed the majority of southern Republicans. Yet blacks constituted voting majorities in only five states. As the new state constitutions restored voting rights to most former Confederates (excluding only high ranking Confederate officers from holding public office), southern whites supported the Democratic party, with two significant exceptions.

One white group that supported the Republican party consisted of transplanted northerners, many of them ex-Union army officers or Freedmen's Bureau officials, who sought opportunity in the South. Democrats labeled this group *carpetbaggers,* implying that they were opportunists with no stake in southern society. A second group of southern Republicans had roots in the Whig party and favored regional economic development or came from nonslaveholding regions that had remained Unionist during the Civil War. Many were small farmers who opposed the restoration of

planter leadership. Their Democratic opponents called them *scalawags*—contemporary slang that meant "mean fellows" or "disgraces"—suggesting that these native-born southerners were betraying their region by supporting outsiders.

Despite the Democrats' negative views, southern Republicans formed complicated coalitions that transcended racial and class divisions. Although African Americans provided nearly 80 percent of the Republican vote, southern whites dominated officeholding, partly because of traditions of deference and partly to increase the party's appeal to white voters. Yet blacks participated actively in the political process, attending party conventions and holding local offices. By the end of Reconstruction in 1877, Republicans had sent 16 African Americans to Congress, including two Mississippi Senators, and elected nearly 700 blacks, most of them former slaves, to state government. Many more served in local government. Black officials, though always a minority among whites, enjoyed respect within black communities and ensured the basic fairness of government services.

Southern Politics and Economy

The Republican party's agenda in the South reflected the needs of its diverse constituency. Following the success of Freedmen's Bureau schools, and educational efforts by northern charitable organizations that sent teachers into the South, every southern state established a system of tax-supported public schools, which greatly increased literacy and provided primary education for a generation of African Americans. To be sure, the schools were usually poorly financed and racially segregated. Most southern states maintained segregated prisons, orphanages, and railroad cars, but Republican majorities legally ended discrimination in many public accommodations, such as streetcars and municipal employment, though such laws were not enforced.

Republican lawmakers also supported economic development. Democrats objected to growing state indebtedness and higher taxes, but shared the enthusiasm for certain public works, such as railroads. To attract private investment, the states eased restrictions on interest rates, donated public lands to factories, and enacted general incorporation laws. Yet northern capital remained scarce, largely because of better investment opportunities in the western states and in northern cities. Consequently, southern economic development rested on frail credit and bonds, and was further weakened by legislative bribery and graft. During the early 1870s, a national financial contraction pushed southern municipal and state governments toward bankruptcy, undermining public support of Republican policies.

Efforts to stimulate southern business hardly affected rural agriculture. Although the Union army had threatened rebels with land confiscation and sometimes allowed ex-slaves to work on confiscated lands, President Johnson restored most property to the original holders in 1865. Despite the help of northern philanthropists and the Freedmen's Bureau, very few ex-slaves ever managed to acquire their own holdings. Freed black workers thus had to find work on land owned by whites, often former slaveowners. Although landowners initially kept the paid workforce in large groups, or gangs, African Americans objected to the rigid supervision, which they associated with slavery. Instead, black field workers preferred smaller units, or squads, directed by a chosen leader.

Tensions arose frequently between white landowners and the black labor force. Freed slaves not only resisted strict supervision but also chose to work fewer hours than slavery had demanded, closer to the sunup-to-sundown schedule of white hired hands. In addition, women opted to work at home, rather than in the fields, and ex-slave children often left the fields to attend school. The result was a significant decline in labor productivity.

To regulate the freed labor force, the Freedmen's Bureau joined white planters in encouraging ex-slaves to sign annual labor contracts, usually exchanging specified work for wages. Since many former slaveowners resented paying for black labor, however, the system was subject to abuse. Blacks complained of nonpayment, or eviction for trifling offenses, after they had planted their crops. Meanwhile, failure to work at all opened blacks to charges of vagrancy and forced labor.

Eventually, a system evolved that was based on sharing the profits of land and labor. Two patterns emerged. The most common type was called *sharecropping*. In exchange for a year's labor, landowners provided food, supplies, tools, and seed, and paid workers with a portion of the crop (a "share") after the annual harvest was sold. The sharecropping system encouraged individual families to contract with landowners to grow specific crops. As family workers, rather than paid labor, women and children joined the men in fields. Although sharecroppers sometimes enjoyed independence from direct supervision, they remained workers, not tenants, and the crops belonged to the landowners, who settled accounts only after deducting expenses, including carrying charges, interest, and high markups. It was not uncommon for workers to obtain a smaller return than their cost of living during a year. Thus sharecroppers could easily become debtors and be obliged to work the next year under the same, or worse, terms to repay previous debts. The second, less common arrangement was called *tenant farming*. Farmers rented land for a specified sum and then repaid the landowner after the harvest. Tenants usually owned their own tools, farm animals, and seed, and were therefore less dependent on landowners and could plant what they wished.

African Americans who left the plantations for urban centers faced similar problems of protecting their independence. Housing segregation in southern towns forced blacks to live in crowded, unsanitary neighborhoods where epidemic diseases took their toll. In Nashville, Tennessee, for example, where many blacks inhabited shacks originally built for animals, the black mortality rate was double that of whites. Legal segregation of public facilities further restricted black activities. In cities like Atlanta, Richmond, and Nashville, however, ex-slaves found strength in numbers, forming community institutions, such as churches, schools, and burial societies. Religious organizations also founded teachers' training colleges, including Fisk and Atlanta Universities. Within a decade of emancipation, ex-slaves joined an older community of free blacks to build their own class system and cultural institutions within the larger segregated society.

Despite changes in labor practices, southern staple crops dominated the economy. With cotton the most valuable commodity per acre, southern farmers intensified production to cover wartime losses and the effects of a postwar drought. With payoffs based on the harvest sale prices, sharecropping also encouraged cotton production. In 1876, 60 percent of the black labor force was planting cotton. This emphasis on cotton undermined food production; the agricultural South actually had to import food from other regions.

High cotton prices suited the Republican agenda of stimulating economic development, especially investment in railroads to carry southern crops to market. Indeed, northern railroads saved Georgia's peach industry by bringing that perishable commodity more quickly to urban consumers. Atlanta, burned by Sherman's army during the Civil War, emerged as a rail center for southern commerce and soon became a model for other towns that vied for railroad lines. Republicans and Democrats alike supported government aid to railroads, giving tax breaks, public lands, and convict labor for private companies, while ignoring cases of bribery and corruption. Such practices greatly increased the states' debt, and left local governments vulnerable when the economy faltered in the early 1870s.

The penetration of railroads into the mountainous counties of the South, where nonslaveholding farmers had practiced subsistence agriculture before the Civil War, altered the small farm economy. As upcountry farmers turned to cotton to recover from wartime debts, postwar crop failures worsened their economic position. Using newly developed commercial fertilizers (delivered by railroads), planting fewer acres of corn and grains (and importing food from the Midwest by rail), and cultivating previously unproductive fields, small farmers became increasingly dependent on merchants' credit to obtain supplies and tools. "Nearly everybody has abandoned the ways of their fathers, and caught the cotton planting mania," lamented a Georgia newspaper. When cotton prices hit a plateau in the mid-1870s, overly specialized farmers went deeper into debt, often losing their land and becoming tenants or sharecroppers.

Poor farm workers, white and black alike, also lost an economic step when landowners began to demand fence laws in the 1870s to restrict open grazing on private property. In addition, seasonal game laws, designed to protect dwindling numbers of deer, fish, and birds, removed a significant source of nutrition for poorer families. When whites complained that blacks hunted singing birds that had "claims upon human sympathy, and are besides unfit for food," they were overlooking the importance of such dietary supplements. Despite common economic problems of rural poverty, abiding racial tensions between whites and blacks prevented political cooperation.

Rebuilding the National Economy

Amid the political and constitutional crises of Reconstruction, the country embarked on an era of unprecedented economic growth. Indeed, one reason for the weakness of the southern economy

The Western Territories, 1870

after the Civil War was that northern investors saw greater profits in western development. The great railroad boom, interrupted by the war, now moved to completion, linking eastern cities with western agriculture. Railroads, in turn, stimulated agricultural expansion, not only by more easily bringing southern cotton to northern markets and western food to southern cotton growers but also by encouraging an international migration of farmers into the western territories. Instead of joining the underpaid farm labor of the southern states, European and Chinese immigrants found opportunities in the West. Commercial farming also demanded organized markets for wholesale distribution, boosting the growth of rail centers like Chicago and Atlanta.

The creation of a national marketplace accentuated the problems of cultural outsiders. Just as the southern cotton economy limited the opportunities of former slaves and increased friction between landed whites and landless blacks, so postwar westward expansion brought battle-hardened federal troops into conflict with the Plains nations. While most citizens welcomed immigrants from Scandinavia and western Europe, anti-Asian sentiments provoked opposition to newcomers from China. Yet the preoccupation of post–Civil War Americans with issues of economic development deflected public interest from questions of Reconstruction and the rights of nonwhites. The politics of Washington—even the historic issues of the Civil War constitutional amendments—ultimately seemed less important to most people than did mundane local concerns.

Building a National Rail Network

"The whole country is opening up," exclaimed the hustler Colonel Sellers in Mark Twain's satire of post–Civil War greed, *The Gilded Age* (1874). "Slap down the rails and bring the land to market." Such rhetoric captured the national mood. Between 1862 and 1873, Congress gave 100 million acres of public land, plus $100 million of federal loans and bonds, to feed the railroad fever that doubled the length of the nation's tracks. Nearly $20 million of that sum lined the pockets of dishonest investors—and several congressmen who greased the wheels of public spending. But federal subsidies represented only a fraction of public investment. Small town boosters and ambitious farmers joined land speculators and politicians in endorsing railroad construction.

> **"Nothing so rapidly pushes forward the car of progress and civilization as the railroad locomotive."**

"Nothing . . . so rapidly pushes forward the car of progress and civilization," coaxed a Minneapolis newspaper, "as the railroad locomotive." Hoping that railroads would bring prosperity to isolated communities, boosters persuaded local governments to grant special tax advantages to encourage building. European investors also sank over $500 million (equivalent to $5 billion in today's money) into U.S. rail companies in the late 1860s. Such vast sums encouraged both speculation and corruption, as lobbyists appealed for public aid. The bubble finally burst in 1873 when Jay Cooke, the nation's leading railroad financier, failed to cover his overextended credit, precipitating a panic on Wall Street: "A monstrous yell," according to one observer. The Panic of 1873 brought the railroad boom to an abrupt halt.

Chinese Immigration

The construction of the transcontinental railroad epitomized the effort to create a national geography. "They are laying siege to Nature in her strongest citadel," declared a California newspaper in 1865 as workers of the Central Pacific began cutting roadbeds through the rugged high Sierra. With gold and silver mines attracting white laborers, western railroad builders set aside their prejudices and recruited Chinese immigrants. Using newly invented nitroglycerin, Chinese workers blasted through sheer rock, dug perilous snow tunnels, hung off mountain cliffs, and kept on laying track. "Their quiet efficiency," observed one employer, "was astounding." In 1868, U.S. ambassador

"Little Indian Boy, Step Out of the Way for the Big Engine," declared one promotional placard, demonstrating the railroads' lack of sympathy for the Plains peoples through whose lands they passed.

Anson Burlingame negotiated a treaty with China, expanding trade and permitting unrestricted immigration, which annually brought 18,000 Chinese workers into the country. Yet the 1790 Naturalization Act still prohibited Chinese from becoming U.S. citizens, and no politician endorsed extending the Fourteenth Amendment to cover Chinese settlers.

Chinese railroad workers also confronted racist violence, went on strike for equal pay, and demonstrated great technical skill, but their achievements earned little applause. Just before the symbolic golden spike linked the transcontinental railroad at Promontory Point, Utah, in May 1869, Chinese workers were moved out of camera range. After the completion of the major railroads, the Chinese found employment on California land reclamation projects; in San Francisco factories making shoes, cigars, or clothing; and as farmers specializing in Chinese vegetables and fruits. On the east coast, some businesses used Chinese as strikebreakers, fueling public hostility to "coolie"

labor. Whites resented Chinese competition, and the California Workingmen's party demanded their exclusion. By 1882, Congress voted to restrict most Chinese immigration.

Pacifying the Plains

The imperatives of railroad building also changed the government's relations with Native American inhabitants near the lines. Few railroad developers considered the Plains peoples anything but an obstacle. As new track extended onto the Plains, railroad crews became targets for warriors who resisted the invasion of their buffalo hunting grounds. General William Tecumseh Sherman, appointed in 1865 to command the U.S. Army between the Mississippi and the Rocky Mountains, quickly perceived a solution to the impending conflict. He proposed that the Sioux be moved to northern reservations and the Arapaho, Cheyenne, and Comanche peoples be pushed to the south, leaving a corridor for westward migrants. The policy required revisions of earlier treaties, but Sherman demanded cooperation. "The road must be built," he told the Lakota Sioux, "and you must not interfere with it."

U.S. peace commissioners opened negotiations to restrict the Sioux on the northern Plains, but the Army did not wait for their approval before building a line of forts along the Powder River, or Bozeman trail. Sioux leader Red Cloud then broke off talks and began to harass the outposts. In 1866, the Sioux lured an overeager cavalry contingent into an ambush and killed the entire force. General Sherman, well known for his advocacy of total warfare, vowed revenge, "even to their extermination." Moderate voices in Washington demanded a peaceful settlement, but skirmishing continued, and Red Cloud refused to negotiate until the Army abandoned the Powder River forts. In 1868, the U.S. government accepted that condition. The new treaty of Fort Laramie established the "Great Sioux Reservation" in western South Dakota, allowing unceded territory west of the reservation to be closed to whites, and permitted the Sioux to hunt in this region "so long as buffalo may range there in numbers sufficient to justify the chase."

Other Native American groups also signed reservation treaties, but the decentralized nature of tribal politics made compliance impossible. As Native warriors continued to attack white settlements, military leaders launched a winter campaign against the southern Cheyenne in 1868. Realizing that peaceful people would surely suffer, the Army found justification in the recent war against the Confederate South. "Did we cease to throw shells into Vicksburg or Atlanta because women and children were there?" asked General Philip Sheridan. The cavalry proceeded to attack the southern groups in north Texas, slaughtering indiscriminately and forcing survivors onto reser-

vations. When the Comanche leader Tosawi asked Sheridan, "Why am I and my people being tormented by you? I am a good Indian," the Civil War hero purportedly replied, "The only good Indians I ever saw were dead."

Whatever his exact words, Sheridan's deeds outraged humanitarian opinion, particularly among Quakers, who pleaded in Washington for a more benevolent policy. Such reformers hoped to eliminate the corruption associated with federal payments to the tribes. At the same time, Christian organizations hoped to "civilize" Native peoples by replacing their community orientation with an individualistic identity. These reformers urged instruction of English to undermine the "mythology and sorcery" of Native languages, which articulated an alternative world-view. To hasten the erosion of group loyalty, Congress ended the treaty-making relationship in 1871, thus transforming Native American *nations* into individual "wards" of the federal government. Instead of negotiating through Native leaders, Washington could now legislate directly for all its dependents.

Despite government efforts to confine the Plains peoples on reservations, inadequate government assistance forced them to hunt buffalo on the plains. To end such practices and establish tribal dependency on the government, U.S. leaders decided to destroy the plains' primary resource: the buffalo. Railroad companies hired hunters to shoot the animals by the thousands, using some to feed their workers but leaving most carcasses to rot. Upon encountering herds, railroad passengers would open the windows and commence firing. Cashing in on the fad, the Kansas Pacific introduced excursion trains for weekend sportsmen. When improvements in tanning techniques increased the value of buffalo hides after 1871, commercial hunters used fast-loading rifles to kill dozens of animals in mere minutes. The annual number of slaughtered buffalo reached 2.5 million

Upon encountering herds, railroad passengers would open the windows and commence firing.

in 1871 and exceeded 7 million by 1874. The hunters "are destroying the Indians' commissary," gloated General Sheridan. By 1876, the last of the great herds had vanished.

As long as buffalo remained on the northern Plains, the 1868 treaty gave the Sioux the right to hunt off their reservations. Four years later, the Northern Pacific railroad announced plans to construct a line through nonreservation territory. When federal officials requested a concession for the right-of-way, Sioux leaders refused to negotiate. But after a military survey discovered gold in the Black Hills, an area considered sacred by the Sioux, the government could not stop whites' invasion of Sioux lands. The Sioux still refused to cooperate, leading the War Department to announce a state of war. During the spring of 1876, the U.S. 7th Cavalry, under the command of George Armstrong Custer, rode into the Black Hills to enforce compliance. Encountering a party of Sioux and Cheyenne warriors near the Little Big Horn River, Custer attacked, only to be forced to retreat. The Oglala Sioux Crazy Horse then led an attack on Custer's troops, annihilating the regiment. The disastrous defeat intensified military resolve, and continuing warfare finally forced the Sioux to accept new treaties in 1878.

Farmers Settled the Plains

The military campaigns against the Plains peoples cleared U.S. claims to vast territories and accelerated railroad development. With immense acreage to sell and prospects of carrying western farm produce, the railroads encouraged settlement by European immigrants. Promising prosperity, the companies distributed promotional tracts in multiple languages (English, Swedish, Danish, Norwegian, and Dutch). Although the Homestead Act of 1862 offered free land to settlers, most farmers bought property from the railroads in order to live near the tracks and reduce their shipping costs. In farmhouse kitchens, one visitor noted in 1870, "the railway timetable hangs with the almanac." Despite rising land prices, the white population of the northern Plains (Minnesota, the Dakotas, Nebraska, Kansas) jumped from 300,000 in 1860 to over 2 million twenty years later. In 1870, Kansas farmers grew 17 million bushels of corn; by 1872, Minnesotans harvested 22 million bushels of wheat.

Kansas growers also competed with another railroad commodity: cattle. During the Civil War, Texas cowboys lost their export markets in New Orleans and held enormous herds by the war's end. As the Union Pacific railroad inched westward toward the town of Abilene, Kansas, local investors encouraged cattle drovers to bring their herds to the railhead there for shipment to urban markets. In 1867, 35,000 cows were shipped out of Abilene; one year later, the demand for cattle cars exceeded the supply.

The cattle industry soon collided with agricultural interests. Fearing that Texas cattle would spread disease, Kansas farmers imposed quarantine lines, known as "deadlines," to regulate the cattle trade. Farmers also demanded fence laws to protect their crops, but the shortage of trees made the cost of fencing prohibitive. In 1873, Congress passed the Timber Culture Act, offering free land for planting trees. In 1874, Nebraska's Governor J. Sterling Morton proposed a special day for tree planting, Arbor Day, which later became a legal holiday in many states. Meanwhile, the problem of fencing attracted widespread interest; in the decade after the Civil War, the federal Patent Office issued 800 new patents for fencing. Finally, in 1874, the introduction of barbed wire—flexible, cattle resistant, nearly invisible—provided the long-awaited solution. As the buffalo declined, fenced cattle took over the ranges, and intensive grazing eliminated the natural tall grasses. Prairie fires, a much-feared hazard of the Plains, disappeared.

Most settlers knew enough to expect periods of extreme heat and drought, but few anticipated the severe Plains weather that killed crops and livestock, and nothing presaged the grasshopper invasions of 1873 and 1874. "They came upon us in great numbers, in untold millions, in clouds upon clouds, until their fluttering wings looked like a sweeping snowstorm in the heavens, until their dark bodies covered everything green upon the earth," wrote a Wichita newspaper reporter. "In a few hours many fields that hung thick with long ears of golden maize were stripped bare of their value and . . . in their nakedness mocked the tiller of the soil."

Such disasters accentuated the fragility of farm life. Without adequate public assistance, growers formed cooperative groups to share information and marketing. In 1867, a Department of Agriculture official, Oliver H. Kelley, founded the Patrons of Husbandry, also known as the Grange. This network of social organizations, modeled on the Masons, claimed over 1 million members by the early 1870s. With the goal of protecting self-sufficient family farms, the Grange organized cooperative stores and grain elevators to eliminate the commercial middlemen, who seemed to be taking agricultural profits. Targeting bankers, merchants, and especially railroads, the Granger movement persuaded several midwestern states to prohibit discounts for large shippers or lower charges for long hauls than short trips, and to set maximum freight rates. These "Granger laws" on railroad pricing initially won approval from the Supreme Court in

Munn v. Illinois (1877), though later rulings prohibited states from regulating interstate commerce.

Organizing Urban Life

Rising agricultural production in the western states provided the stimulus for rapid urban expansion. After the Civil War, cities assumed a major role in building a national economy by importing raw produce and selling finished products. To contemporaries, the complexity of the urban economies encouraged comparisons to technological machinery; the burgeoning cities appeared immense, complicated, inhuman—and fast.

When Mrs. O'Leary's cow purportedly kicked over a kerosene lamp and ignited the great Chicago fire of 1871, the city's official weatherman described the ensuing firestorm as a "column of flame and smoke, which was [spinning] contrary to the hands of a watch." In the city, keeping time now depended less on clocks than on watches: portable, personal, pocket-held timepieces, which symbolized a new, speedier pace of urban life. "Atlanta is certainly a fast place in every sense of the word," remarked a local newspaper. Its residents "live fast and they die fast. They make money fast and they spend it fast. . . . The whole city seems to be running on wheels, and all of the inhabitants continually blowing off steam." The illusion of prosperity belied great disparities of urban wealth; most fatalities in the Chicago fire occurred in poor neighborhoods where flimsy construction and crowded conditions gave residents little time to escape. Afterwards, efforts to impose fire-resistant architecture failed because most residents lacked the resources to rebuild with anything but wood.

Newly invented steam-powered elevators offered the possibility of building vertically, but urban planners preferred geographical dispersal. To open new residential areas, New York City launched an elevated train system in 1868 and introduced an experimental subway two years later. San Francisco's

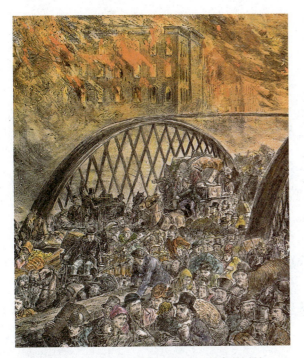

The Chicago Fire destroyed 17,000 buildings and left 100,000 residents—one-third of the city's population—homeless on October 8 and 9, 1871.

cable cars began running in 1873, stimulating residential construction on the city's hills. To ease health problems associated with urban congestion, New York adopted the Tenement House law in 1867, requiring improved ventilation, lighting, and sanitation in these multistoried residential buildings. Taking advantage of new streetcars, middle-class city dwellers were already fleeing to suburbs, where landscape architects introduced contour designs instead of rectangular streets.

The most dramatic urban developments remained commercial. For cattle, horses, pigs, and sheep, Chicago stood at the end of the line. The Union stockyards, begun in 1865, covered 100 acres, used three miles of troughs and half a million gallons of water to process tens of thousands of animals each day. The vast disassembly lines, notorious for their stench, and the introduction of refrigerated railcars in the 1860s, made Chicago the meat-packing center of the nation, if not the world.

New York's municipal development projects—street grading, dock renovations, and new transit lines—offered opportunities for a different kind of profiteering. Financed by municipal bonds instead of taxes, construction projects gave Mayor William Marcy "Boss" Tweed and his cronies an opportunity to dispense 60,000 patronage jobs while inflating the city debt by $60 million. The political organization, one contemporary boasted, "works with the precision of a well-regulated machine." Revelations of Tweed Ring graft in 1871 brought public outrage, and the corrupt mayor ended his days in prison. Yet municipal "machine" politics, supported by expensive public works projects, dominated the nation's cities well into the next century.

The End of Reconstruction

The creation of a national economy did not overcome ingrained traditions of local politics. Municipal government, county seats, and state legislatures remained the locus of power to resolve most economic issues. To be sure, post–Civil War citizens understood that the federal government had a responsibility to settle constitutional issues in the seceded states and to protect the rights of freed slaves. But after ratification of the Fourteenth and Fifteenth Amendments, preoccupation with economic development, together with the frustrations of supervising southern government, discouraged federal involvement in southern politics.

The Grant Years

In 1868, the Republican party nominated Civil War hero Ulysses S. Grant to run for president. His campaign slogan "Let Us Have Peace" characterized the climate of national politics. Although

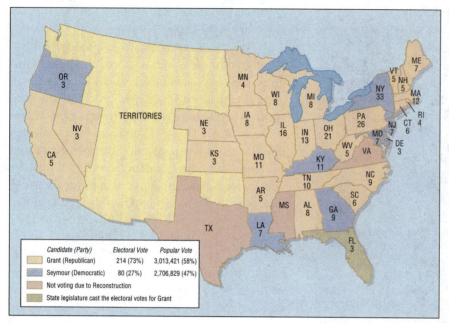

The Election of 1868

Candidate (Party)	Electoral Vote	Popular Vote
Grant (Republican)	214 (73%)	3,013,421 (58%)
Seymour (Democratic)	80 (27%)	2,706,829 (47%)
Not voting due to Reconstruction		
State legislature cast the electoral votes for Grant		

Democrats attacked Republican Reconstruction as a violation of constitutional principles, Civil War patriotism assured Republican majorities in the northern states and in the electoral college. Southern blacks also voted Republican. Yet, in 1868 Grant's popular majority was only 300,000. Despite his fine military leadership, moreover, the new president proved a poor administrator, appointing officials who would taint his tenure with scandal. Such political trouble further weakened public interest in a rigorous program of continued reconstruction.

Although Grant himself seemed above corruption, he remained loyal to cabinet officers, the vice president, and his personal secretary, even after their acceptance of bribes became public knowledge. The president's use of the spoils system to reward his supporters angered members of his own party, and Congress created a Civil Service Commission in 1871 to encourage appointments to public office on the basis of merit. Such reforms threatened the nation's party system, however, and political leaders allowed the commission to expire. Frustration with Grant's leadership finally inspired a party rebellion by self-styled "Liberal Republicans," who promised to provide government by "the best men." In 1872, the Liberal Republicans broke with Grant and nominated Horace Greeley, editor of the New York *Tribune,* for the presidency. Their criticism of "bayonet rule" in the South broadened their appeal among Democrats. But Grant, the Union hero, had the confidence of the North. In addition, the Republican platform favored women's rights, persuading women to campaign for the regular party. Grant easily won reelection.

Redeeming the South

Even before the Liberal Republican rebellion, Democrats had made major gains in the former Confederate states. As early as 1866, the violent Ku Klux Klan and other white vigilante groups had successfully intimidated Republican voters in areas where the political balance was uncertain. Congressional investigations led in 1871 to passage of the Ku Klux Klan Act and other enforcement laws, which made interference with civil and political rights a federal crime. Washington proceeded to prosecute hundreds of cases, and Grant sent federal troops to occupy violent areas. Such acts pacified the South, but accentuated the racial divide between the political parties. In 1872, Congress passed the Amnesty Act, which restored political rights to almost all ex-Confederates, excluding only 500 leading rebels from holding government office. Liberal Republicans worried that these new voters would back Democratic candidates and thus proposed "home rule," the removal of all federal troops from the South, to attract white voters to the Republican party.

"We must make the issue White and Black, race against race," countered a Virginia Democrat in 1873. "The position must be made so odious that no decent white man can support the radical [Republican] ticket and look a gentleman in the face." Calling themselves "Redeemers," Democrats appealed to white supremacy to disrupt the Republican coalition, and persuaded many white Republicans to vote Democratic. The Democrats also made major gains in the northern states. In the 1874 congressional elections, Democrats won control of House of Representatives for the first time since 1861. Thus Republicans lost their ability to coerce the South. Although the lame-duck Republican Congress passed the Civil Rights Act of 1875, outlawing racial discrimination in public places, enforcement required blacks to file legal complaints, a complicated procedure that seldom occurred. The law was virtually dead, even before the Supreme Court ruled it unconstitutional in 1883.

As conservative Democrats regained control of the southern states between 1869 and 1875, African Americans lost both white allies and national support. In states like Mississippi, whites used economic pressure and intimidation to bring carpetbaggers and scalawags into the Democratic party, while threatening blacks with violence to keep them from voting. Meanwhile, the second Grant administration gave patronage favors to southern Democrats; the Justice Department dropped civil rights cases; and the president refused to send troops to quell violence against black voters.

Such policies received sanction from the Supreme Court, which ruled in the *Slaughterhouse* cases of 1873 that the Fourteenth Amendment protected only national citizenship, not the rights that were traditionally monitored by the states. In 1876, the Court announced in *U.S. v. Cruickshank* that the new Amendments applied only to actions by the *states,* not private individuals, and thus restricted federal enforcement of civil rights laws. In addition, the Court held that the Fifteenth Amendment did not guarantee the right to vote. Although civil rights laws would remain on the books, white supremacy, racial segregation, and restrictions on black voting could now be imposed informally without risk of reprisal from the federal government.

The Compromise of 1877

The election of 1876, which pitted Ohio Republican Rutherford B. Hayes against New York Democrat Samuel J. Tilden, spelled the end of Reconstruction. Running on vague promises of political reform, neither candidate achieved a clear victory. Although Tilden led by 250,000 popular votes, his electoral college total of 184 fell one short of the necessary majority. Hayes could claim 165 electoral votes. Twenty disputed electoral votes remained in three southern states and Oregon. As inauguration day approached without a clear winner, Congress appointed an electoral committee to resolve the deadlock. Party loyalty continued to block a solution.

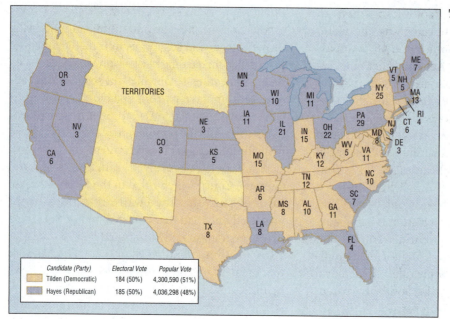

The Election of 1876

Candidate (Party)	Electoral Vote	Popular Vote
Tilden (Democratic)	184 (50%)	4,300,590 (51%)
Hayes (Republican)	185 (50%)	4,036,298 (48%)

Hayes finally agreed to a compromise in order to gain the contested southern electors. In exchange for the presidency, Republicans agreed to appoint a southerner to the cabinet, appropriate funds for public improvements in the South, and adopt a policy of noninterference in southern politics. Shortly after taking office, Hayes consummated the deal by removing the last federal troops from Louisiana and South Carolina, facilitating Democratic electoral victories in both states.

Although southern whites returned to political power and white property owners continued to control the southern economy, the constitutional changes made during Reconstruction had given African Americans a bedrock of civil rights, which, while often ignored, were never effaced. Racial prejudice against nonwhites certainly did not diminish, but racism no longer had legal sanction in the U.S. Constitution. Moreover, ex-slaves used the advantages of civil rights to build independent cultural institutions (families, churches, schools) that offered them some protection and autonomy. To be sure, many political outsiders were not content with the Reconstruction settlement and continued to demand equal rights. This dissatisfaction with second-class citizenship would flower in the civil rights movements of later generations.

The National Union

Pride in economic growth and progress, not the reconstruction of a national identity, set the tone of the hundredth anniversary celebrations of the Declaration of Independence. In 1876, Philadelphia opened a six-month Centennial Exposition that drew nearly 10 million spectators to celebrate the nation's historical development. Here the "progress of the age," in the words of the fair's promoters, could be seen in a panoply of in-

President Grant and the emperor of Brazil officially opened the Philadelphia Centennial Exhibition by starting the great Corliss engine in Machinery Hall.

ventions: the telephone, typewriter, electric light, Westinghouse's railroad air brake, Fleischmann's yeast, linoleum. All stood in wonder, even the poet Walt Whitman, before the 700-ton Corliss steam engine that silently powered the fair. Equally impressive was the 700-pound electric pendulum clock, which governed 26 other clocks precisely to the second. "Yes," said a visitor, "it is still in these things of iron and steel that the national genius most freely speaks." The promise of technology epitomized a dynamic vision of the future.

Visitors to the Centennial Exposition looked backward as well. Anthropological displays depicted the work of more primitive peoples who had first inhabited the continent, showing tipis and canoes, pottery and tools, and life-size figures made of wax and papier-mache, to contrast with the symbols of modern industry. Most observers lauded the change. "The red man," remarked the writer William Dean Howells, "as he appears in effigy and in photograph . . . is a hideous demon, whose malign traits can hardly inspire any emotion softer than abhorrence." African Americans were also seen at the fair, though they were not permitted to work on the construction projects that built the exposition, and a guidebook promised "a band of old-time plantation 'darkies' who will sing their quaint melodies and strum the banjo before visitors of every clime." Frederick Douglass was invited to sit on the dignitaries' platform, but was not permitted to speak.

The presence of foreign nationals (Chinese, Japanese, Egyptians, Turks, Spaniards) amused Philadelphia's visitors; boys and men pursued these strangers, hooting and shouting, according to one observer, "as if they had been animals of a strange species." A woman's pavilion, which had been added as "an afterthought," showed needlepoint, weaving, and power looms supervised by a "lady engineer." On July 4, five women reformers, including Susan B. Anthony and Elizabeth Cady Stanton, interrupted ceremonies to distribute copies of a Declaration of Rights for Women. It included demands that women be allowed to serve on juries and vote for government representatives, and that the word *male* be deleted from legal codes. Meanwhile, the public was fascinated by an off-limits side-show strip that featured "wild men of Borneo, and wild children of Australia, the fat woman . . . heavy enough to entitle her a place in Machinery Hall." Popular with the poor, a meeting point for "tramps, peddlers, and boot-blacks" as well as tipplers, prostitutes, and others labeled "pests and nuisances," the district was demolished by public order.

The Centennial Exposition thus embraced the contradictions of the national society: rich and poor, male and female, white and a rainbow of other colors. But, significantly, some groups were better represented than others. So it appeared within the nation's political system. In 1876, African Americans remained on the threshold of national citizenship; women, as the Fifteenth Amendment made manifest, were clearly excluded. Nor were Asians welcome: "The Chinese will not assimilate with our population," stated a Philadelphia newspaper in 1876. "From a plaything and curiosity [he] has become a vexing problem." Most citizens viewed Native Americans only as hostile, never more so than when the telegraph brought the shocking news that Custer's cavalry had been annihilated by the Sioux at the Little Big Horn. As the government celebrated a century of independence, the country remained culturally fragmented, the meaning of the past as uncertain as the shape of its future.

INFOTRAC® COLLEGE EDITION EXERCISES

For additional reading go to InfoTrac College Edition, your online research library at *http://web1.infotrac-college.com.*

Subject search: Ku Klux Klan, history
Keyword search: black codes
Subject search: Reconstruction
Keyword search: Fourteenth Amendment
Keyword search: Johnson impeachment
Keyword search: William Marcy Tweed

Keyword search: transcontinental railroad
Subject search: Ulysses S. Grant
Keyword search: Little Big Horn
Keyword search: Rutherford B. Hayes

ADDITIONAL READING

Eric Foner, *Reconstruction: America's Unfinished Revolution, 1863–1877* (1988). A comprehensive study of the era, this book illuminates the political struggles produced by the Civil War and the end of slavery.

Michael Perman, *Emancipation and Reconstruction: 1862–1879* (1987). This brief book summarizes the political and historiographical issues of the period.

John Brinckerhoff Jackson, *American Space: The Centennial Years, 1865–1876* (1972). This study explores the relationship of geography and culture.

Debating the Vote for Blacks and Women

Ellen Carol DuBois, ed., *Elizabeth Cady Stanton, Susan B. Anthony: Correspondence, Writings, Speeches* (1981). This collection of primary sources provides a good complement to DuBois's earlier book, *Feminism and Suffrage* (1978), which begins with pre–Civil War reformism.

Reconstruction Comes to the South

Laura F. Edwards, *Gendered Strife and Confusion: The Political Culture of Reconstruction* (1997). This book examines the effect of legal changes on southern domestic life.

Howard N. Rabinowitz, *Race Relations in the Urban South: 1865–1890* (1978). This social history of five southern cities should be supplemented by Leon F. Litwack's *Been In the Storm So Long* (1979), listed in Chapter 14.

Southern Politics and Economy

William Cohen, *At Freedom's Edge: Black Mobility and the Southern White Quest for Racial Control, 1861–1915* (1991). Analyzes African American labor opportunities and the prospects of postwar migration.

Steven Hahn, *The Roots of Southern Populism: Yeoman Farmers and the Transformation of the Georgia Upcountry, 1850–1890* (1983). This book examines economic changes among small farmers and their effect on social relations.

Building a National Rail Network

David Haward Bain, *Empire Express: Building the First Transcontinental Railroad* (1999). This narrative describes the vast technological undertaking.

Chinese Immigration

Sucheng Chan, *This Bittersweet Soil: The Chinese in California Agriculture, 1860–1910* (1986). This study moves beyond issues of discrimination to consider the forging of Chinese American communities.

Pacifying the Plains

Ralph K. Andrist, *The Long Death: The Last Days of the Plains Indians* (1964). This narrative describes U.S. policy toward the Plains nations.

Organizing Urban Life

Karen Sawislak, *Smoldering City: Chicagoans and the Great Fire, 1871–1874* (1995). Focusing on Chicago's calamity, the author analyzes the related social, economic, and political issues. See also William Cronon's *Nature's Metropolis* (1991), listed in previous chapters.

16

The Triumph of a National Marketplace, 1877–1893

CHRONOLOGY

1877	President Rutherford Hayes orders troops to end railroad strike
1878	Congress passes Bland-Allison Silver Act
1879	Philanthropists open Carlisle Indian School
1880	James Garfield wins presidential election
1881	Chester Arthur succeeds assassinated Garfield
	Booker T. Washington becomes head of Tuskegee Institute
1883	Congress passes Civil Service Reform Act
	Railroads introduce standard time zones
1884	Grover Cleveland elected first Democratic president since 1856
1886	Knights of Labor enroll over 700,000 members
	Bomb explodes in Chicago's Haymarket Square
	Samuel Gompers launches American Federation of Labor
1887	Congress passes Interstate Commerce and Dawes acts
1888	Benjamin Harrison defeats Cleveland for presidency
1890	Congress enacts Sherman Silver Purchase and Sherman Anti-Trust laws
	Kansas farmers form People's party (Populists)
	U.S. troops massacre Sioux at Wounded Knee, South Dakota
1892	Women's Christian Temperance Union claims 150,000 members
	Andrew Carnegie breaks steel strike at Homestead, Pennsylvania
	Cleveland defeats both Republicans and Populists
1893	World Columbian Exposition opens in Chicago
	Financial panic hits Wall Street

"The whole system of modern economic adminis- tration . . . has revolutionized the way of doing business all over the world," declared the rawboned businessman seated behind his massive oak desk. John D. Rockefeller, head of the nation's largest petroleum corporation, Standard Oil, swiveled in his chair to focus his steely gaze on his guest. "Individualism is gone, never to return," he went on. "The growth of a large business is merely a survival of the fittest, the working out of a law of nature and a law of God."

http://history.wadsworth.com

Rapid economic development after the Civil War brought the United States hurtling into the industrial age. The expansion of large manufacturing corporations like Standard Oil, the rise in the number of white-collar managers, and the mass distribution of national brand-name products transformed the country's economic activities. Along with industrial growth came other economic and social changes—urbanization, immigration, and increasing disparities of wealth—all of which affected people in every class and region. While some entrepreneurs rode the crest of industrialism to gain vast personal fortunes, and high school graduates found employment in the managerial system, skilled workers declined in status, rural people experienced a loss of independence, and almost all citizens faced a frightening, little-understood world of impersonal economic forces.

"The day of small things [is] past," wrote William Dean Howells in his novel *The Rise of Silas Lapham* (1885), "and I don't suppose it will ever come again in this country." Realizing that they now inhabited a national marketplace, business leaders, farmers, and urban workers struggled to gain control over their material condition and looked increasingly to the federal government to address their concerns. This realization that economic interests depended more on Washington than ever before reinforced a sense of belonging to a national community and sharing a national identity.

Building a Corporate Economy

As more industrialists, merchants, and agricultural producers participated in a national, even international, economy, older forms of business relationships based on character and personal contacts disappeared or became less important. Instead, corporation leaders embraced a new spirit of competition that intensified conflicts between rival companies and accentuated differences between employers and workers, merchants and farmers, landlords and tenants.

Successful corporate leaders like Rockefeller and steel magnate Andrew Carnegie justified their aggressive business practices by applying Charles Darwin's ideas of biological evolution to society. To these corporate titans, "social Darwinism" had a simple logic: survival of the fittest. Although many contemporaries denounced that doctrine of inevitability, the consequences of corporate growth were obvious. By 1890, the wealthiest 9 percent of the population controlled 71 percent of national wealth.

Corporate life opened economic opportunities for a new middle class of white-collar workers, but the widespread acceptance of impersonal business relations also provoked concerns about the survival of the less fortunate. Farmers and workers soon were organizing for self-protection and trying to influence government policies to preserve an economy of small producers. Economic changes also aroused anxieties about preserving a moral society, leading humanitarian social reformers to seek protection for the weak. These themes appeared in Mark Twain's classic *The Adventures of Huckleberry Finn* (1884)—the story of a youth seeking liberation from social rules and regulations—what Twain called "sivilization." In the end, escape proved impossible for Huck Finn, except in the realm of imagination: "I reckon I got to light out for the Territory ahead of the rest," says young Huck. "I been there before."

RAILROADS HERALD THE NEW ECONOMY

After the Civil War, a band of outlaws led by Jesse James achieved folk-hero status by attacking the most powerful corporate institution in the country: the railroads. The Missouri-based gang had committed audacious bank robberies and train hijackings, once robbing a bank while a political rally went on outside, but when the railroads hired equally murderous vigilantes to bring James to justice public sympathy shifted from the giant corporation to the local outlaws. A popular ballad expressed public sentiment: "Jesse James was a lad who killed many a man/He robbed the Glendale train/He took from the rich and he gave to the poor/He'd a hand and a heart and a brain." James was finally killed by a treacherous assassin, known ever afterward as "the dirty coward." But why did the public turn Jesse James into a hero?

Railroads set the pace of economic change after the Civil War and accentuated the problems of an industrial society. Between 1877 and 1890, U.S. trackage increased over 80,000 miles, creating a system that touched every corner of the nation and literally cut through the streets and neighborhoods of the nation's towns and cities. As railroads grew bigger, more small businesses and farmers became dependent on rates and schedules set by distant corporate leaders. Taxes and bonds to support railroad expansion fell heavily on local communities. Inextricably linked to the national economy, small producers perceived a threat to their economic and cultural independence. In this light, Jesse James appeared as the underdog, David confronting Goliath.

Railroad growth required immense capital resources, most of it from foreign investors. By 1893, thirty-three railroad companies, each worth at least $1 million, controlled 69 percent of the lines. The volume of traffic increased dramatically, with freight tripling to 700 million tons and passengers surpassing 500 million annually. Introducing uniform shipping procedures, such as a standard bill of lading that itemized freight, railroads could transport goods across multiple lines without pausing to unload and reship. Yet, with high fixed investments, railroad profits remained precarious. Facing "ruinous" competition, numerous companies organized "pools" to divide traffic and earnings while maintaining freight rates and fares. Such informal agreements were easy to violate, and unscrupu-

lous executives offered secret rebates to selected customers or simply refused to share incomes with rival companies.

As corporate cooperation failed, the railroads adopted another formula for reducing costs: dropping the wages of workers. "The great principle," explained one railroad executive, "was to earn more and to spend less." In July 1877, in the midst of an economic depression, the Baltimore & Ohio announced wage cuts of 10 percent. Workers in Martinsburg, West Virginia, called a strike to restore earnings and stopped the trains from running. When the state militia supported the strikers ("We are workmen first," said one) President Rutherford B. Hayes, who had recently removed federal troops from the South, now summoned U.S. soldiers to protect the B&O from "insurrection." Breaking through the workers' barricades, the army liberated the trains. The use of federal forces against the strikers incensed workers around the country. In Baltimore, rock-throwing protesters clashed with armed militia, leaving dead and wounded in the streets.

The Great Uprising

Labor tensions then exploded in Pittsburgh, where railroad workers struck against the nation's largest corporation, the Pennsylvania Railroad. Again, the local militia refused to attack the strikers, but the arrival of outside troops from Philadelphia precipitated pitched battles. Federal soldiers armed with machine guns finally restored civil order and railroad service. But strike fever spread around the country, causing labor walkouts and street violence in innumerable railroad towns.

In many cities, urban residents shared the workers' anger at the railroads. Daily railroad accidents on city streets threatened life and limb of ordinary citizens and contributed to a larger frustration at industrial changes. Taking advantage of the strikes, city workers and small businessmen joined in protests against the railroad companies. In Chicago, 20,000 workers attended a single protest demonstration, and the city's corporate leaders organized special armed police to prevent an uprising. Fifty workers died in the ensuing violence. In St. Louis, Socialists organized a peaceful general strike, bringing most business to a halt for a week. In San Francisco, protesting workers founded the Irish-led Workingmen's political party. This defense of labor rights in California also provoked attacks on Chinese workers. The cry "Chinese must go!" echoed from California to New York as white workers condemned the use of Asian immigrants. Congress responded by passing the Chinese Exclusion Act in 1882 that ended their legal immigration.

The "Great Uprising" of 1877 proved the strength, not of worker protest or labor unions but of corporate and federal power. As the federal War Department issued manuals for riot control, state governments passed legislation to reform the "National Guard." Backed by private business benefactors, states and cities constructed armories in urban centers and made provisions for a modern militia. Within twenty years, the National Guard comprised 100,000 volunteers, four times the size of the regular army; most officers came from the wealthier classes. Meanwhile, strike leaders lost their jobs, received fines and jail sentences, and faced blacklisting by employers to keep them from subsequent employment.

Standardizing Service

Victory over the railroad unions reduced labor costs but failed to resolve the financial risks of corporate competition. To manage their complicated assets and activities, railroad companies developed enormous bureaucracies, headed by salaried managers, who supervised both white-collar employees and the general work force. The notion that top executives were captains of industry reflected the military model of corporate structures: among railroad executives, many had learned the table of organization from their experience as Civil War generals. Most middle managers on the railroads were among the 8 percent of Americans who had graduated from high school.

To improve business efficiency, moreover, railroad leaders embraced standardization and technological innovation. Most citizens still lived by local sun time, but national corporations, especially those that used telegraph transmissions, saw the advantages of creating standard time. On Sunday, November 18, 1883, railroad executives unilaterally, with no federal laws or public support, ordered the adoption of four national time zones, eliminating the confusion of multiple local times. The time zones changed at places convenient for the railroads. Three years later, the companies converted all tracks to a uniform gauge, and soon afterward they introduced standardized air brakes and couplers.

Building Industrial Corporations

The growth of corporations that operated on a national level encouraged business leaders to adopt fundamental innovations in the way they managed their affairs. First, corporate expansion involved changes in the process of manufacturing whereby companies introduced new technologies and made production more efficient. A second stage brought innovations in management, including the establishment of formal lines of responsibility, improved accounting procedures, and overall coordination of operations. As a final stage, business leaders endeavored to stabilize and gain control of the flow of output, creating predictable markets to absorb production with maximum profits. Although corporate leaders like Rockefeller and Carnegie attributed their success to divine favor, their decisions demonstrated considerable business acumen, an

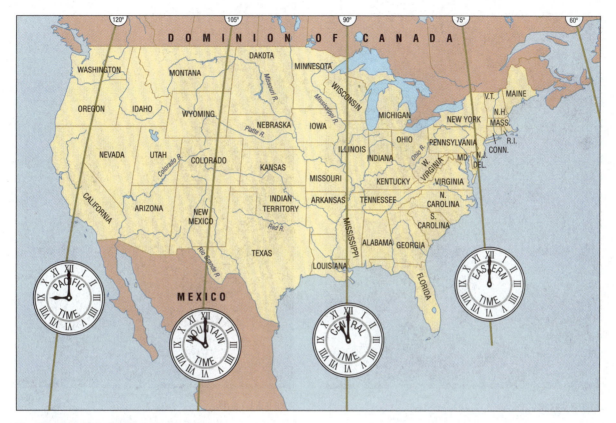

Time Zones Established by the Railroads, 1883

eye for details, and ceaseless, sometimes ruthless, calculation that focused exclusively on bottom-line values. Equally astute business leaders, with less stamina and audacity, showed less success.

Emphasizing Industrial Efficiency

Efforts to achieve industrial efficiency and lower labor costs encouraged technological inventions. By 1890, the federal government was issuing more than 25,000 patents each year. Within the steel industry alone, for example, the "Bessemer process" of manufacturing displaced iron production as the basic ingredient of railroad tracks and increased output from 30,000 tons in 1870 to 1.9 million tons in 1890. (Railroads accounted for 80 percent of all Bessemer steel sales.) Flaws in Bessemer steel soon led to the introduction of the open-hearth process, which tripled production and forged higher quality steel for machinery and structures. New technology, in turn, stimulated new plant design, making factories more efficient. For steel workers, changing manufacturing techniques had important economic consequences. By simplifying job tasks, new technologies demanded less employee judgment and permitted unskilled workers to perform more industrial jobs. The declining importance of skilled labor thus allowed industrial managers to establish work rules and regulate the pace of work.

Andrew Carnegie

John D. Rockefeller

The tremendous expansion of steel production required new techniques of corporate management. Drawing on his experiences as a railroad executive, Carnegie appointed other railroad leaders to run his business operations. Most important was the introduction of detailed accounting procedures to monitor daily costs of production throughout the system. Statistical data enabled careful evaluation of natural resources, worker output, and even the work of the company's managers. To standardize these details, typewriters appeared in business offices, creating a clear paper trail of business decisions and assessments of individual managerial performance. Since volume and speed enhanced profits, corporate leaders placed a high priority on eliminating waste and unused capac-

ity. One metal engineer, Frederick W. Taylor, became the nation's first industrial efficiency expert when he began to use a stopwatch to conduct time and motion studies of workers to determine the most efficient routines for each step of manufacture, and "Taylorism" became the watchword across the country.

The movement to centralize corporate administration culminated in the creation of Rockefeller's petroleum conglomerate, Standard Oil. Using the company's high-volume shipping to gain cuts in railroad rates, Rockefeller forced many competitors out of business and pressed others to accept uniform prices and production schedules. The introduction of long-distance crude oil pipelines in 1878 reduced transportation costs even further and

Bessemer converters at Andrew Carnegie's Pittsburgh steelworks in 1886

Automatic canning systems transformed several companies— Heinz pickles and ketchup, Campbell's soup, Borden's milk—into household names.

greatly expanded the industry's storage capacity. By then, Standard Oil controlled nearly 90 percent of the country's refined oil, two-thirds of which was exported overseas. High-volume production proved the key to profits. In 1885, Standard Oil's profits per gallon jumped from 53 cents to one dollar—but only if every plant produced 6,500 gallons per day. By controlling most of the nation's oil refineries, Rockefeller had created a horizontal monopoly.

The sprawling interstate oil empire depended on coordinated control and led Rockefeller simultaneously to create a vertical monopoly, one that controlled all aspects of the petroleum market from refining to distribution to sales. Rockefeller's associates transformed industrial finance by as-

signing their stockholdings to a single "trust" company, which then obtained power to centralize business decisions. With corporate headquarters in New York and special departments to coordinate suppliers, sales, transportation, and personnel, Standard Oil could dictate resource development and prices for the entire country. By 1890, monopolistic corporations also dominated other industries, including refining of sugar and cottonseed oil.

What pipelines did for oil, automated factories achieved in agriculture-based industries. The mass production of farm machinery, from improved plows to complicated threshers and binders, brought greater efficiency to agricultural production and encouraged crop specialization. The resulting huge harvests in turn stimulated industrial systems for processing and distribution. Tremendous quantities of wheat from the northern Plains, for example, inspired mass processing of grains, leading to mechanized flour mills in Minneapolis, which by 1890 produced over 7 million bushels of flour annually. Meanwhile, automatic canning systems transformed several companies (Heinz pickles and ketchup, Campbell's soup, Borden's milk) into household names. At a time when skilled hand labor could produce 3,000 cigarettes a day, the invention of continuous rolling machinery raised daily output to 120,000 cigarettes, paving the way for James Duke's American Tobacco Company. The craze for cigarettes not only supplanted the consumption of chewing tobacco and cigars, but also supported the Diamond Match Company,

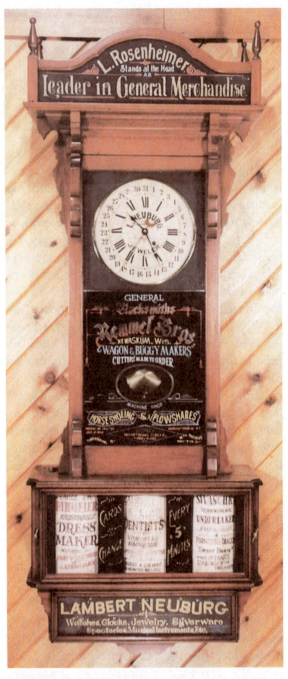

Even timepieces fell under the influence of advertising. This Sidney advertising clock was manufactured in the 1880s. It displays advertising from three different companies, and the three drums in its base revolved every five minutes to give a different message.

which made and boxed matches by the billions, dominating world markets.

The Birth of National Marketing

Improvements of mass production generated new approaches to corporate marketing. To assure reliable business relations, credit agencies, first formed before the Civil War, developed national networks to provide references for wholesalers and retailers. Equally innovative was the introduction of mass packaging to carry products to distant consumers. During the Civil War, the unavailability of southern cotton prompted northern manufacturers to find an alternative to packaging with cotton sacks. The result was the mass-produced paper bag, first patented in 1870, and followed by patents for cardboard in 1874 and paper box–making machinery in 1879.

Such packaging transformed the relationship between mass producers and individual consumers. Before the Civil War, manufacturers shipped in bulk to retailers who sold their products in smaller quantities to consumers, who in turn carried the goods home in their own containers. The new technologies allowed manufacturers to pre-package retail-size quantities of dry goods, which were sold by retailers merely by lifting packaged goods from their shelves. Manufacturers gained even more by establishing direct relations with consumers. In 1870, Congress passed the first law protecting product trademarks, encouraging producers to label their goods with brand names to ensure product recognition. "The man with the Quaker garb," the first cereal trademark, appeared on oats boxes, along with recipes that emphasized speed in preparation and testimonials of product purity. Henry Ward Beecher, pastor of the Plymouth Church in Brooklyn, lent his eloquence to Pear's Soap: "If cleanliness is next to Godliness, soap must be considered as a means of Grace, and a clergyman who recommends moral things should be willing to recommend soap. . . . I am willing to stand by every word in favor of [Pear's Soap] that I ever uttered. A man must be fastidious indeed who is not satisfied with it." Some manufacturers now linked new packaging to direct advertising. To market cigarettes, Duke's tobacco company spent nearly $1 million a year on boxtop premiums, prizes, and picture cards of professional athletes.

Technological improvements in printing and lithography also stimulated the development of a national marketplace. New national magazines, such as *Cosmopolitan, Ladies' Home Journal,* and *McClure's,* enabled advertisers to reach millions of readers throughout the country. Newspapers played a similar role. By 1891, Chicago boasted two dozen daily newspapers, some with multiple editions. While the Associated Press's telegraphic wire service brought world and national news into local communities, lower postal rates for reading matter allowed national magazines to carry feature stories and national brand advertising into middle class homes. As a result, national advertising revenues increased to $300 million, which was indicative of the competition among producers of cereals, patent medicines, baking powder, tobacco products, and soap.

Manufacturers relied on both wholesalers and a network of traveling salesmen ("drummers") to carry sample products to country stores. In 1872, Chicago's Montgomery Ward revolutionized the rural trade by introducing mail-order sales with such low prices that newspapers accused the company of fraud; fifteen years later, its 540-page catalog featured over 24,000 items. By then, the company needed 300 clerks to handle 750,000 mail orders annually. Sears, Roebuck entered the mail-order business in 1887, initially to sell watches.

For urban customers, the new department stores emerged as vast, seemingly limitless warehouses of choice. Offering varieties of products at fixed prices and a staff of service employees to facilitate selection of sizes and lines, dry-goods en-

trepreneurs like W. H. Macy in New York, John Wanamaker in Philadelphia, and Marshall Field in Chicago developed retail palaces to attract middle-class consumers. Automatic cash registers enabled sellers to track sales and inventory. With profits coming less from markups than from the rate of turnovers, department stores employed advertising agencies to promote their goods in mass circulation newspapers.

The Changing Face of Urban Life

The emergence of downtown department stores mirrored important changes in the urban landscape. By 1890, one-third of the U.S. population inhabited cities. Denver, Minneapolis, and Los Angeles blossomed overnight; Chicago and Philadelphia surpassed 1 million inhabitants; New York and Brooklyn together approached 2.5 million people. Rapid urbanization troubled conservatives, who saw danger lurking amidst the city's gaudy entertainment, luxury goods, and congested streets. "A feller has to look sharp in this city," the novelist Horatio Alger advised young men coming to the cities in his formula rags-to-riches adventure stories. While clergymen and business tycoons like Rockefeller and Carnegie touted the idea that hard work would bring success, Alger's fictional heroes usually achieved fortunes not by hard work, but from moral behavior and dumb luck. For most 19th-century city dwellers, however, virtue alone brought small rewards.

The attraction of cities reflected the increasingly obvious limitations of rural life. Frustrated by the lack of opportunity and equality, rural southern blacks migrated to southern cities or

"A feller has to look sharp in this city."

headed west. Too poor to purchase farms, they settled in small towns in Kansas and Nebraska. Whites had problems of their own. "Hard work and no holidays," one white youth described his reasons for abandoning rural life. "No books, no papers, no games, no young company." Hamlin Garland's fictional descriptions of farming in the 1880s, published as *Main-Travelled Roads* (1891), underscored "its sordidness, dullness, triviality, and its endless drudgeries."

After the perfection of the electric light bulb by Thomas Edison in 1879, cities quickly introduced central power plants to illuminate the night. Rural visitors were excited by new urban conveniences, such as electrically lit shopping emporiums, amusement arcades, and buildings with elevators (that so captivated tourists that they expected to pay for the rides!). Newcomers also explored the urban vice trades: gambling, alcohol, and prostitution so plentiful as to inspire guidebooks for the brave visitor. Pervasive corruption reinforced rural prejudices about city business practices. "She regards the question from the economic standpoint," explained one minister of a Chicago brothelkeeper. "Morals no more enter into her business than they do into the business of bulls and bears on the Stock Exchange." City residents dismissed such critics of modern life as backward "hayseeds."

Besides the rural migrants, industrial cities attracted 6 million immigrants from northern Europe between 1877 and 1890. Most came from Germany, then Britain, Ireland, and Scandinavia, countries where overpopulation and economic disadvantages led young adults to seek better working conditions. Familiarity with English enabled British and Irish immigrants to participate in local politics, where they formed political machines to distribute jobs and contracts.

By the 1880s, the first immigrants from southern and eastern Europe began to arrive in significant numbers. Russian Jews, facing anti-Semitic attacks, departed as families from their home-lands. Famine and epidemic diseases also encouraged emigration from southern Italy, though, unlike the Jews, many Italian immigrants were single men who planned to return home after saving money for their families. French Canadians crossed the border to find work in New England mills. Chinese immigrants, barred from the Pacific states, continued to settle in Hawaii, then an independent country. In 1884, the Japanese government first permitted Hawaiian sugar planters to import contract workers.

Having survived ten days to two weeks in abysmal shipboard conditions, immigrants spread rapidly around the country, working as unskilled railroad builders or as cheap agricultural labor. German farmers dotted the Plains. Scandinavian lumberjacks worked the virgin forests of Minnesota and the Pacific Northwest. Mining companies employed Welsh, Polish, and German labor. Ethnic differences and language barriers encouraged settlement in distinct communities or neighborhoods; ethnic lines generally appeared stronger than those of economic class.

While most ethnic minorities were newcomers, Hispanics in the Southwest, by contrast, experienced an economic invasion by Anglo settlers. As railroads reached New Mexico in the 1880s, Anglo land claimants and railroad land grants threatened Hispanic land holdings that preceded the Mexican War of 1846. Besides using U.S. courts to invalidate Mexican land rights, individual landowners destroyed the local pastoral economy based on grazing sheep on common lands. Resisting railroad domination, Hispanic vigilantes tore up the tracks, burned bridges, and ripped down fences that ruined their pastures. Such outlawry won wide community approval. Yet the disruption of traditional land use undermined the local, self-sustaining economy.

Most European immigrants settled in cities, forming the bedrock of urban industrial society. In 1880, 87 percent of Chicago's residents were

By eliminating horse-drawn vehicles, streetcars removed the stench of horse manure as well as the bodies of dead animals.

foreign born or children of immigrants; the proportion in Milwaukee, Detroit, New York, Cleveland, St. Louis, and San Francisco averaged over 80 percent. Living in ethnic neighborhoods, supporting foreign language newspapers, joining fraternal societies that provided places for meeting and entertainment and burial services, these transplanted workers sustained traditional customs while learning to survive in a new land.

Technology and Urban Geography

Dense population, together with expanding industrial and commercial activity, inflated the value of urban real estate, but technological innovation addressed problems of urban space. The introduction of steel-framed building designs permitted vertical construction, creating the first skyscrapers in Chicago in the 1880s. Imitated in other cities, ten-story buildings allowed corporations to move administrative staffs into a single headquarters, while electric lights permitted the clerical work force, still overwhelmingly male, to work late. Equally dramatic was the introduction of electric streetcars or trolleys, which altered commuting distances to places of work. By eliminating horse-drawn vehicles, streetcars also removed the stench of horse manure (ten pounds per animal per day) as well as the bodies of dead animals (15,000 overworked horses died in New York each year) from the streets of the city. In 1883, the opening of Brooklyn Bridge, linking Manhattan and Long Island, symbolized the era's technological achievements and, not incidentally, facilitated traffic between suburb and city.

The Brooklyn Bridge, designed and built by John and Washington Roebling, was both one of the greatest engineering feats of its era and an artistic triumph.

The new technologies quickly altered patterns of private residence. Seeking fresh air and tranquility, affluent corporate executives moved their families into homogeneous suburbs and rode the rail or trolley to downtown commercial buildings. Closer to town, small merchants, middle managers, skilled artisans, and the rising "white collar" employees lived in private homes, near clusters of stores, schools, and churches, and took streetcars to work. Members of this "new" middle class remained vulnerable to economic downturns that threatened their jobs and income. The poorest workers jammed themselves into central-city apartment buildings that were divided, subdivided, and partitioned. By 1890, a single Manhattan area of 45 blocks held 57,000 people. Responding to new building codes, landlords introduced the "dumbbell" tenement, typically a six-story building, with improved lighting and ventilation, but one toilet per floor, and no heat or hot water. Entire families sometimes crowded into single rooms. "The only grass that I could see," remarked one worker, "was the green paint on the walls."

Struggling for Workers' Rights

As mass production weakened the position of skilled workers, economic fluctuations created uncertainties of employment. Although industrialization brought higher real wages (mostly as a result of falling prices), the gains spread unevenly among the work force. Unskilled male laborers (averaging $1.50 per day for ten hours labor) struggled to cross the poverty line of $500 per year. To achieve minimal living standards, families required the additional labor of women and children, whose entry into the work force doubled between 1870 and 1890. White female workers avoided domestic service, preferring jobs as factory hands or outworkers in the needle trades. African American women, excluded from most industrial jobs, increasingly predominated in domestic service. African American women were twice as likely to be employed as white women. Despite the financial reasons for working, women's wages remained 75 percent of male rates, while children between the ages of 10 and 14 earned 50 percent or less.

All workers faced problems of job security. During the financial crisis of the 1870s, unemployment touched 30 percent of the Massachusetts labor force. About one-quarter of all workers lost their jobs for some period during every year of the late nineteenth century. Loss of employment also reflected occupational dangers. Each year, industrial accidents caused hundreds of thousands of injuries; by 1888, 100 workers died on the job each day, yet companies offered little if any compensation. State courts generally denied workers' damage claims, insisting that jobs came with risks and that workers shared responsibility with employers. Pervasive environmental hazards threatened the health of other workers; inside tenement sweatshops, lint, dust, and dirt spread tuberculosis ("sweaters' disease") and other infectious ailments. Sheer exhaustion took another toll. Although factory inspectors and government commissions deplored unhealthy working conditions, business leaders stressed the necessities of the marketplace.

The Knights of Labor Seek Reforms

The problems of industrial labor soon inspired movements for reform. Factory work was "an artificial and man-made condition, not God's arrangement and order," said the founder of the Noble and Holy Order of the Knights of Labor, formed in 1869 to benefit a group of tailors in Philadelphia. Hoping to represent all workers, regardless of occupation, the Knights of Labor endorsed broad plans for social reform, including temperance, education, and free land ownership. Unlike most unions, the Knights took the precaution of secrecy to prevent employer reprisals. Secrecy slowed the organization's growth until the great railroad strikes of 1877 demonstrated the power of collective action. Under the leadership of Terence Powderly, an Irish machinist, the Knights opened the union in 1881 to all "producers," those workers who actually made a product, but excluded nonproductive "parasites," such as lawyers, bankers, liquor sellers, and stockbrokers.

The Knights proceeded to organize diverse types of workers, including southern blacks, European immigrants, and women. This membership supported a multitude of reforms, some beneficial to all workers, some limited to particular ethnic groups or occupations. Among the Knights, self-interest sometimes supplanted a larger worker consciousness; sometimes the opposite was true. In Richmond, Virginia, for example, a Knights convention took a bold stand against "distinctions made by creed and color," only to arouse dangerous threats of retaliation by local racists. "They pointed at us with scorn and kept crying 'Nigger! Nigger!'" reported a North Carolina worker, "until the two words *nigger* and *Knight* became almost synonymous." Sharing prevailing anti-Chinese sentiments, the Knights opposed Asian immigration, supported boycotts of Chinese-made products, and tolerated organized violence against Chinese communities in the western states. The union also endorsed protests against the use of prisoners as unpaid workers. By the mid-1880s, the Knights claimed 15,000 local affiliates, representing some 750,000 workers.

This fledgling labor movement encountered stiff opposition from employers, who used police power and court decisions to crush strikes and contain dissent. A strike against the southwestern railroads failed in 1886 when owners refused to negotiate and forced the workers to return to work. That year, a New York court ruled against boycotts of specific businesses, undermining an effective labor weapon. Meanwhile, conflicts between organized labor and business leaders escalated as 40,000 Chicago workers, including some anarchists, struck for an eight-hour workday, and 80,000 paraded in support on May 1, 1886. Violence between strikers and police climaxed three days later at Haymarket Square. Just as a public meeting was ending, armed police attacked the crowd, and a bomb exploded, killing seven officers. After the riots ended, Chicago's industrial leaders encouraged the police to raid union halls, saloons, and private homes, leading to mass arrests, beatings, and the trial of eight anarchists for murder. Despite dubious evidence, all were convicted, and four radicals were hanged.

Trade Unionism Grows

Public outrage at the Haymarket violence, together with failed strikes, rapidly deflated the eight-hour movement. Although some radicals, such as immigrant anarchist Emma Goldman, now resolved to continue the fight against capitalism, most union workers disapproved of militant protest. Membership in the Knights of Labor rapidly declined. Instead, union workers identified with the more cautious economic agenda sponsored by the American Federation of Labor (AFL), founded in 1886 by cigarmaker Samuel Gompers. Ignoring the Knights' program of social reform, the AFL focused exclusively on workers' issues: higher wages, job security, and better working conditions. Unwilling to challenge the industrial order, but seeking a fair proportion of benefits, the union prudently built membership and strike funds before ordering walkouts. Strengthening the position of skilled workers at the expense of the unskilled, Gompers accepted race- and sex-segregated unions, which permitted disparities of pay within the same workplace.

Despite the AFL's caution and the decline of Knights' membership, organized workers continued to fight industrial corporations—not just about wages and hours, but for control of workplace rules and the legitimacy of unions. During the 1880s, some 10,000 strikes and lockouts disrupted normal business. Even the newly organized major-league baseball teams faced endless labor disputes. Baseball management and player unions agreed in the 1880s to ban African American athletes from what had been a racially integrated sport. But unions balked at salary caps and contracts that monitored the players' morality. "Players have been bought, sold and exchanged as though they were sheep instead of American citizens," protested a union manifesto. An independent Players League, formed in 1890, lacked sufficient capital to compete with established teams. The surviving owners then formed a twelve-team National League that controlled the sport to the end of the century.

The labor problems of skilled athletes seemed slight compared to the attacks on unskilled labor—none more dramatic than the struggles that erupted at Carnegie's Homestead steel plant near Pittsburgh, Pennsylvania, in 1892. By then, U.S. iron and steel manufacturing had surpassed Britain's output, largely through improvements in productivity based on technology, plant design, and labor efficiency. Nonetheless, when Carnegie's order to cut wages provoked worker protests, the company rejected collective bargaining, locked out the employees, and hired strikebreakers. As the steel company imported Pinkerton private police forces to protect the plant, idle steelworkers and their families—virtually the entire workers' community—fought pitched battles against the invasion of their occupational turf. After workers gained control of the city, the company persuaded the governor to send armed troops to suppress the uprising. Ultimately, Carnegie broke the union.

Reforming Industrial Society

Clashes between workers and industrialists focused on issues of wealth and power, but the spread of urban cultural values also challenged small-town, middle-class views of morality. As industrial employers enforced shop rules of efficiency, sobriety, and punctuality (the time clock was introduced in 1890), weary workers pursued leisure in a distinctive urban institution, the saloon. Urban saloons were themselves extensions of corporate competition among the nation's breweries. By the 1880s, British-backed breweries competed against established breweries owned by German American families such as Schlitz, Anheuser, and Busch, for the urban retail trade. To attract a worker clientele, the breweries paid for standard barroom fixtures, comfortable furniture, and free lunches for their customers.

Saloons thus emerged as a male enclave, where after-work drinking, singing, and joking provided inexpensive entertainment. "They all do what I would like to do now," admitted a New York health official. "They smoke a great deal; they drink considerable." Although kitchen taverns, run by wives and widows, had customarily allowed informal socializing among men and women, new licensing ordinances limited alcohol sales to public bars. Women, once central to drinking groups, became outsiders except as prostitutes, who could earn far more than any industrial worker.

Some women challenged the working man's leisure. "The rustle of women's wear attracted their attention," two Ohio men told a reporter about an incident in a saloon, "and looking up they saw what they thought was a crowd of a thousand ladies entering." At a time when the number of working women was doubling to 5 million, middle-class evangelical women organized a movement to defend what appeared as threats to their homes. During the 1870s, spontaneous protests against alcohol consumption spread through the small towns and cities of the Midwest, resulting in the formation of the Women's Christian Temperance Union (WCTU) in 1874. By 1892, the group claimed 150,000 dues-paying members; by contrast, the largest woman's suffrage organization enrolled 13,000.

Unlike other women's reform movements, such as the suffrage crusade, which welcomed male involvement, the WCTU was run entirely by women, headed after 1879 by Frances Willard. Many of these white middle-class reformers were

Artist John Sloan depicted the quieter side of saloon life in New York City.

graduates of the expanding women's colleges and state universities. By 1880, one-third of all college students were women, preparing to influence a larger community. "We stand here as a new Fact," exclaimed social worker Vida Scudder in 1890. "Our lives are in our hands." Yet the WCTU offered no direct challenge to male authority. The group's "manner," said Willard, "is not that of the street, the court, the mart or office; it is the manner of the home."

The WCTU's "home protection" campaign reflected important changes in domestic institutions. As economic necessity obliged more single women to enter the work force, the ability of young women to become homemakers declined. Three-quarters of all working women were under the age of 25, and 95 percent were unmarried. At a time when a single person's minimum weekly budget in Chicago was estimated at $9.70, the incomes of fe-

male factory workers averaged slightly more than $7, while women department store employees earned about $8. Worried about such independent women, middle-class reform groups like the Young Women's Christian Association (YWCA) promoted subsidized boardinghouses, but such assistance reached only a tiny proportion of female workers.

With more young women joining the work force, the average age at marriage crept upward (26 for men; 22 for women). Later marriages brought a drop in the national birthrate from over 7 per family at the beginning of the century to 4.24 in 1880 (and lower still for middle-class women). With fewer children to raise and more domestic servants to assist them, affluent women had more energy to devote to social concerns. One founder of the WCTU observed that the movement could not have begun a generation earlier when "woman was often no more than a slave

TABLE 16.1

Age of Consent, Selected States, 1886–1895

	1886 Age	1889 Age	1893 Age	1895 Age
Alabama	10	10	10	10
Arizona Territory	n.a.	14	18	18
Arkansas	n.a.	18	14	16
California	n.a.	10	10	14
Colorado	10	10	10	18
Delaware	7	n.a.	n.a.	7
District of Columbia		16	16	16
Florida	10	10	17	10
Indiana	n.a.	12	14	14
Kansas	10	18	18	18
Kentucky	12	12	16	12
Louisiana	12	18	n.a.	12
Maine	10	13	14	14
Massachusetts	10	14	14	16
Mississippi	12	10	n.a.	10
Missouri		12	14	18
Montana	10	10	n.a.	16
New York	10	16	16	18
North Carolina	10	10	10	10
Ohio	n.a.	14	n.a.	14
Oregon	n.a.	14	14	16
Pennsylvania	10	16	16	16
Tennessee	10	16	16	12
Texas	10	10	12	15
Wyoming	10	14	18	18

Sources: Benjamin DeCosta, "Age of Consent Laws, 1886," *Philanthropist,* February 1886, p. 5; Leila Robinson, "Age of Consent Laws, 1889," *Women's Journal,* April 6, 1889, p. 105; "Age of Consent Laws—1893," *Philanthropist,* June 1893, p. 8; and Helen Gardner, "Sound Morality," *Arena 14* (October 1895), 410.

to man." Challenging alcoholism and saloons focused attention on women's legal vulnerability. Since the law treated men as heads of household, men controlled family property and gained custody of children after divorces; women reformers well understood the economic risks of alcoholic husbands and fathers.

The women's purity crusade also targeted prostitution. At a time when the male medical profession advocated the licensing of "fallen women," two of the first women physicians, Elizabeth Blackwell and Caroline Wilson, led the campaign against the "double standard" that allowed men to have sexual relations with prostitutes without facing social criticism. Launching a department of social purity in 1885, the WCTU established "houses of refuge" for women seduced into prostitution and provided travelers' aid stations near railroad terminals to assist unescorted women. Focusing also on the sexual exploitation of children, WCTU reformers demanded a raising of the legal age of sexual consent. In 1886, twenty states permitted girls to marry at age 10; in Delaware the age was 7! Eight years later, only four states permitted marriage below the age of 14 (Table 16.1). Other legislation tried to protect children from abusive parents and to curtail hours of child labor.

The Crisis of Rural Society

The burdens of industrialization fell most visibly in the cities, but rural areas found no freedom from the commercial networks that linked the farm population to an international marketplace. On the Great Plains east of the Rocky Mountains, farmers settled on virgin fields with high hopes, only to confront a series of unexpected catastrophes, caused first by overproduction and market competition, then by droughts and agricultural collapse. Meanwhile, southern farmers faced equally bleak conditions. Despite vague promises made during the Civil War to transfer confiscated plantation land to freed slaves, 95 percent of the forfeited holdings were returned to their original owners. Unable to afford land of their own, poor whites and blacks entered into agreements with landowners to rent land as tenants or, more typically, to pay for the use of the land by sharing a portion of the next crop. Tenancy and sharecropping kept most southern farm families subordinate to a market-oriented credit system, a situation made catastrophic during the 1880s when international cotton prices fell and sharecroppers slipped into perennial debt.

The Hazards of Western Agriculture

For farmers on the Great Plains, railroads came first, both literally and financially. Long before growers cast their seeds in the ground, railroad promoters had disregarded warnings about the lack of adequate rainfall, suggesting that farming itself would improve the climate or that irrigation would solve problems of drought. The "bonanza" farm boom of the 1870s, during which mechanized agriculture brought immense yields, further overcame caution. Pushed by generous land offers from the railroads and liberal credit from eastern investors, 1 million farmers settled the northern Plains during the 1880s, gobbling acreage by the millions.

Settling on family-size holdings on "township" grids, these farmers entered the commercial world even before they planted a crop. Already they were indebted to bankers and merchants for machinery, land, and supplies to grow wheat and corn, and they faced interest payments as well as the cost of doing business with the railroads. Moreover, mechanized agriculture and improved transportation thrust American farmers into world markets at a time of growing competition and surplus production. Even when shipping costs fell, farming scarcely covered overhead expenses, particularly when international overproduction undermined the price of farm commodities in the 1880s. Wheat

sank from $1.19 a bushel to 49 cents; Kansas corn, once selling at 45 cents a bushel, fell to a dime. Farmers also confronted prolonged droughts that scorched the land from the Dakotas to Texas. Wheat yields plummeted from twenty bushels an acre to four. Heavily mortgaged for their property, farmers faced foreclosures and destitution: "Left," as one remarked, "with families on their hands—just their bare hands." Tens of thousands gave up and headed back east. Others joined cooperative groups for mutual aid. By 1890, frustrated farmers in Kansas organized the first People's party, later known as the Populists, to press for government assistance.

Economic Problems in the South

Like the western settlers, southern farmers confronted the hazards of commercial agriculture. Cotton production, ever the temptation to recover from debt, proved a poor ally. Because of a glut in international production, and competition from Egyptian growers, cotton prices sank from 11 cents a pound in 1875 to 9 cents in 1885 to under a nickel by 1894. "Competition may be the life of trade," remarked a southern grower in the 1880s, "but it is death to the farmer."

Sagging prices aggravated the burdens of a credit system based on sharecropping, which kept most farmers in debt to country stores and landlords. Borrowing for seed, fertilizer, and even the food that was no longer grown but imported by railroads, sharecroppers offered a portion of the future cotton harvest to obtain the necessities of life. Plagued by poverty, farm families suffered from malnutrition, inadequate clothing and shelter, and endemic diseases such as pellagra, rickets, and ringworm. A two-price retail system—one for cash, one for credit (with markups for food as high as 35 percent)—perpetuated debts and encouraged foreclosures. By 1890, about half of southern farms were operated not by owners, but by tenants and sharecroppers.

As southern farmers struggled for subsistence, a new breed of urban merchants and lawyers emerged in the 1880s to promote visions of a "New South." Seeking to attract northern investment, southern state legislatures offered economic incentives, such as tax reductions, waivers of government regulations, and convict labor to induce factory construction. Extractive industries (lumber mills, coal and iron mines, phosphate plants) benefited from generous sales of public lands, while Texas alone gave railroads more acreage than the size of Indiana. Gifts of contract labor were especially oppressive for young black men. Often arrested on frivolous charges, black prisoners were leased for a pittance to serve as virtual slave labor in horrible conditions. Annual convict death rates exceeded 10 percent. "One dies," explained an employer in 1883. "Get another."

Southern business promoters appeared oblivious to such oppression. "We have sown towns and cities in the place of theories," Atlanta *Constitution* editor Henry Grady assured New York investors in 1886, "and put business above politics." And southern industry did increase. In ten years, the railroad junction town of Birmingham, Alabama, boomed from 3,000 inhabitants to 26,000. Furniture and textile mill towns sprouted in the Carolina and Georgia piedmont, finding abundant cheap labor among impoverished tenant farmers. "They's more money at the mill," admitted one disillusioned worker, "but a better livin' on the farm." Meanwhile, southern state legislatures, responsive to landlords rather than to farm workers, passed laws that made minor agricultural theft a major crime and enacted fence laws that prohibited trespassing for hunting or fishing.

The Rise of Rural Protest Movements

To preserve their rural lives, farmers had joined the Patrons of Husbandry (the Grange) to provide mutual support. During the 1870s, organized farmers persuaded several states to enact so-called Granger laws to regulate the railroads. By the 1880s, rural poverty prompted southern farmers to form another protest group called the Farmers' Alliance. Under the leadership of Texas's Charles Macune, a self-educated doctor and lawyer, the Alliance advocated cooperative marketing to end farmers' dependence on local merchants who sold supplies at inflated rates and to eliminate middlemen who purchased cotton below market prices. Sending a troop of lecturers into rural hamlets and villages, the Alliance grew from 10,000 members in 1884 to 250,000 by 1888. "We are going to get out of debt," vowed one Georgia farmer, "and be free and independent people once more." But when the Alliance applied to southern bankers for credit to purchase supplies, business leaders refused any loans. Frustrated Alliance members began to demand government protection from "arrogant capitalists and powerful corporations."

Farmers' pleas for government assistance coincided with other political movements to expand the nation's money supply. Since 1865, the federal government had slowly redeemed the paper money ("Greenbacks") issued to finance the Civil War. Reducing currency contributed to the deflation of prices, but required debtors to repay loans at their face value. Poor farmers generally supported the Greenback movement, which advocated more paper money. But when they formed a third political party, the Greenbackers gained little support.

Another effort to attack deflation proposed adding silver to the money supply. The federal government historically coined both silver and gold at a ratio of sixteen to one. But western silver discoveries had weakened its value, and the government stopped using silver currency in 1873. Silver investors joined indebted farmers in appealing for the return of a silver currency. Claiming that the "crime of 1873" had caused the deflation of prices, these groups pressed Congress to pass the Bland Allison Act in 1878, requiring the Treasury to purchase and to coin silver as currency. The law failed to change the deflationary trend. By 1890, the free silver movement persuaded Congress to increase silver coinage under the Sherman Silver Purchase Act. That measure, bitterly contested by industrial leaders (who were known as "gold bugs"), would divide political parties in the next decade.

In 1890, these diverse strands of agrarian discontent came together in an expanded Farmers Alliance agenda. Meeting in an excited atmosphere in Ocala, Florida, angry farmers demanded a package of laws to reverse corporate control of the agricultural economy. The Alliance platform now proposed reduced tariffs, railroad regulation, free coinage of silver, a federal income tax, and direct election of senators (instead of by the state legislatures). Reformers also called for an innovative system of government warehouses (called "subtreasuries") to store crops until prices improved and to credit farmers with low-interest government loans to end dependence on unscrupulous merchants. This call for government action put the Alliance on the road to political insurgence. It also revealed that even impoverished rural citizens had developed a sense of national identity and looked to distant Washington for assistance. But, while western farmers were already marching into politics under the banner of the People's party in 1890, the southern Alliance resisted a break with the predominantly white Democratic party, which opposed government regulation of the economy.

Racial Hierarchy in the South

Members of the southern Farmers Alliance, well aware of the region's heritage of slavery, complained of "financial shackles that are infinitely more galling to Anglo-Saxon manhood." The southern Alliance accepted no African Americans. But the movement encouraged blacks to organize a parallel Colored Alliance, which by 1890 claimed about 250,000 members. African American farmers had much to lament about the southern credit system that reduced them to peonage. Yet protest activity carried grave risks. When a group of black cotton pickers called a walkout in eastern Arkansas, whites proceeded to murder the strikers. In 1890, however, the southern Alliance supported selected Democratic candidates, some of whom openly challenged the system of white supremacy. "You are kept apart that you may be separately fleeced of your earnings," Georgia's Tom Watson shouted to racially integrated crowds. Yet southern African Americans hesitated to desert the Republican party.

"We are in favor of granting and securing to the colored people all of their just rights," declared a Richmond newspaper, "but they must know that they are to behave themselves and *keep in their proper places*." Fear of African American political activity reinforced racial prejudices. Blacks continued to migrate into southern cities, partly for jobs, partly for better education for their young. But black schoolchildren learned to walk on the other side of the street from white students, and most African Americans found only the lowest paying jobs, as domestics for women and unskilled labor for men. When black women laundry workers went on strike for better wages in Atlanta in 1881, the municipal government legislated licensing fees, fines, and jail terms to end the walkout. Even the city zoo had separate walkways to keep spectators from observing animals together. The introduction of electric streetcars facilitated public segregation, since it became easier to run two cars at a time. Indeed, the first statewide segregation laws applied to seating on railroads, forbidding sale of first-class tickets to African Americans. Such limitations culminated during the next decade in restrictions on black voting through new poll taxes, literacy tests, and vague, selectively enforced education requirements.

In this increasingly closed racial climate, a select group of educated blacks created alternative institutions within segregation. At Nashville's Fisk University, for example, the Massachusetts-born William E. B. DuBois learned a classical curriculum, wrote essays on the problems of black identity, and prepared for Harvard University, where he studied sociology, history, and philosophy. For most southern blacks, academic learning remained unapproachable. Recognizing the limited opportunities for economic and social advancement, paternalistic northern philanthropists had introduced a program of industrial education at Hampton Institute in Virginia, where black students learned social skills such as cleanliness and manners. Most southern black leaders supported this limited advancement. "Stoop to conquer," advised a black newspaper in Richmond, Virginia. "You do the stooping and your children will do the conquering."

The most famous graduate of Hampton Institute was the ex-slave Booker T. Washington, who became the leading proponent of industrial education when he assumed leadership of Alabama's Tuskegee Institute in 1881. At a time when local whites feared that depressed conditions would encourage African American emigration, Washington educated rural blacks for work in small towns and farms. Emphasizing the virtues of hard work, self-improvement, and religious morality, Washington provided practical education for teachers and skilled artisans to facilitate adaptation to the southern economy. Instead of challenging racial discrimination, the "Wizard" of Tuskegee stressed accommodation to segregated life and repressed student protests against racism. After the Supreme Court overturned the Civil Rights Act of 1875, Washington drew an optimistic conclusion: "Brains, property, and character for the Negro," he said, "will settle the question of civil rights." This outlook appealed to northern benefactors, who supported Washington's educational programs and made him the most influential African American in the country.

Challenging the Native American Reservations

Among Washington's responsibilities at Hampton was the education of a unique student body: Kiowa and Cheyenne prisoners of war. After their capture by U.S. troops, young Plains warriors had been exiled to a federal camp in Florida, where a few committed suicide and others attracted the interest of northern philanthropists. Amazed at the Native Americans' ability to assimilate white customs, these reformers persuaded the government to assign "wild" students to the same program of uplift that prepared ex-slaves for menial labor. Under Washington's tutelage, Native American youth learned personal hygiene and etiquette, dancing and marching, and the rigorous discipline of clock time. Ironically, when Washington escorted one of his students to the national capital, the pupil dined comfortably in a segregated restaurant while the teacher had to wait outside.

The Native American experiment at Hampton coincided with growing concern about federal policy toward the reservation nations of the West. As white population settled the Plains, tribal holdings blocked the development of the region's natural resources—land, minerals, and timber. Efforts by Sioux, Nez Percé, and Apache warriors to escape reservation confinement and take up arms against white settlers reinforced reformers' pleas for change. "Everything an Indian does is in a circle," explained the Oglala holy man Black Elk about the deficiencies of the reservations, but the government "put us in these square boxes." Simultaneously, anthropologists and reformers stressed the possibility of eliminating both reservations and tribal "barbarism" by assimilating the people to "civilization."

"Kill the Indian, Save the Man" became the motto for change. Pressed by a coalition of humanitarian reformers and western developers, the federal government adopted a two-pronged effort to end the reservation system. Congress appropriated funds to establish off-reservation boarding schools to educate Native American children. Beginning at Pennsylvania's Carlisle Industrial Training School in 1879, the program enrolled 1,000 students by 1890 and opened federal schools on every reservation. Meanwhile, the government forced Native American groups to surrender their land, bringing millions of acres under federal control during the 1880s. Linking the two programs was the Dawes Act of 1887, which offered allotments of land (160 acres) to individual heads of family, thus breaking down common tribal land ownership, and promised U.S. citizenship to those who accepted. Surplus land could then be sold to whites.

Native Americans responded slowly to inducements of assimilation. Some withdrew into solitude and alcoholism; some circulated through white society, participating in popular circus entertainment, such as Buffalo Bill's Wild West Show. And some clung to the possibility of a cultural revival. During the late 1880s, a Paiute prophet named Wovoka described visions of resurrection based on a ceremonial ghost dance that would elevate ancestral spirits while permitting the death of whites. Appealing to desperate people, the ghost dance spread rapidly through the western nations, alarming federal authorities. Among the Sioux, "ghost shirts" promised protection from bullets. A combination of Native pride and white anxiety led to spontaneous vio-

> ## "A people's dream died there. There is no center any longer, and the sacred tree is dead."

lence, culminating in the massacre of 300 Sioux, mostly women and children, by U.S. troops at Wounded Knee, South Dakota, in 1890. "A people's dream died there," said Black Elk. "There is no center any longer, and the sacred tree is dead."

The Business of National Politics

Closer to the centers of national power in Washington, D.C., political leaders offered no resolution to the many social conflicts caused by the new industrial economy. Amidst rapid economic and social change, the government in Washington seemed mired in party squabbles. In 1880, political cartoonist Thomas Nast introduced the Republican elephant and the Democratic donkey to depict their laughable, mostly irrelevant differences. "All these years I have been dealing with ideas," complained President James Garfield soon after taking office in 1881, "and here I am considering all day whether A or B should be appointed to this or that office." Garfield's lament had dire personal consequences: a frustrated office-seeker shot and killed the president just four months after his inauguration. Passage of the Civil Service Reform Act of 1883, which mandated merit examinations for about 10 percent of federal jobs, hardly altered the political game. Garfield's successor, Chester A. Arthur, proved a master of party favoritism.

With a large and vigorous electorate—11 million eligible males and nearly 80 percent voter

The donkey and the elephant first became symbols of the Democratic and Republican parties when Thomas Nast gave them life, in cartoon form, in 1880.

turnouts—party competition kept elections close (Table 16.2) and emphasized rewards for the faithful. Between the Civil War and 1912, only in 1884 and 1892 did a Democratic candidate, Grover Cleveland, overcome Republican domination of the presidency. With only two exceptions during this period, however, Democrats controlled the House, while Republicans nearly always ran the Senate. Party passions also expressed ethnic loyalties. In the South, Democrats drew strength as the party of white supremacy; in the northern cities, immigrant voters supported Democratic political machines, which provided social services, jobs, and municipal contracts in exchange for votes. Republicans, especially strong in the Midwest, appealed to Protestant groups that favored government support of cultural uniformity, including prohibition, Sunday-closing laws, and opposition to foreign languages in public schools. Typically, Republican President Benjamin Harrison, elected between Cleveland's two terms,

formally recognized the Pledge of Allegiance to the flag in 1892.

Although women still lacked the right to vote, both parties appealed to female constituents to gain the support of their husbands and fathers. At a time when more women were working outside the household, Republicans described themselves as "the party of the home" and claimed that their support of high protective tariffs would protect jobs and incomes. Democrats, by contrast, appealed to women as consumers, arguing that lower tariffs would reduce domestic prices and help the family budget. Neither party made sincere efforts to support women's suffrage. Some women's rights advocates, such as Elizabeth Cady Stanton and Frances Willard, joined third-party movements, such as the Prohibition party because women participated equally in their campaigns. Most suffragists remained within the regular party organizations, ever hopeful and ever

TABLE 16.2

Margin of Victory in Presidential Elections, 1876–1892

Year	Total Republican and Democratic popular vote	Margin of victory	Margin of victory percentage
1876	9,412,860	251,476 (D)*	2.7
1880	8,899,409	9,457 (R)	0.1
1884	9,728,205	23,737 (D)	0.2
1888	10,985,634	95,096 (D)*	0.9
1892	10,748,448	365,516 (D)	3.4

*Republican electoral victory.

frustrated that a majority party would endorse their rights.

Regulating the Corporations

The balance of power between the major political parties caused enormous wrangling about railroads, corporations, and tariffs. The result was usually legislative compromise. After the Supreme Court reversed precedent in the *Wabash* case (1886), overturning the Granger laws and denying states the right to regulate interstate railroads, Congress faced complaints about freight rates that affected farmers, small-town merchants, and wholesalers. Meanwhile, railroad executives, seeking to simplify their business, preferred a single federal statute to replace multiple state laws. These diverse pressures led to passage of the Interstate Commerce Act in 1887, a landmark law that influenced subsequent federal regulation of business. Ordering that freight and passenger rates should be "reasonable and just," the law prohibited pooling between companies, blocked rebates

to favored shippers, and barred charging more for a short haul than a long haul over the same lines. The statute also created the Interstate Commerce Commission (ICC), the first federal regulatory agency, to supervise railroad operations. Yet with weak enforcement powers and the presence of industry supporters on the commission, the ICC served primarily to establish principles for uniform management.

Limited railroad regulation reflected widespread uncertainty about the value of corporate organizations. "Corporations tend to cheapen transportation, lessen the cost of production," explained Senator John Sherman, "and bring within reach of millions comforts and luxuries formerly enjoyed by thousands." Such blessings conflicted with fears of monopoly power and invasion of local economies. Yet, where pre–Civil War reformers described corporate power as "artificial" and "unnatural," the Supreme Court ruled in 1886 that associated stockholders (groups of individuals), and therefore the corporation itself, existed as a "natural entity," enjoying the same legal status as individual persons under the Constitution. Protection of Fifth and Fourteenth Amendment rights meant that corporations could not be deprived of property without "due process of law." In defining corporate property, the Court included not just material assets, such as factories, but intangible values, such as future earning power or consumer "good will." According to the Court, the Constitution protected the legal "right" of corporations to earn "reasonable" returns on investments, regardless of majority sentiments.

Efforts to control corporate power thus faced considerable legal difficulties. Several states tried to regulate giant trust companies by enacting antimonopoly laws, but these measures could not conflict with federal regulation of interstate commerce. In 1890, Congress responded to small-business pressure by passing the Sherman Anti-Trust Act, which outlawed business combinations "in restraint of trade." Lacking a regulatory process, the law depended on judicial interpretations of "reasonable" competition and was barely enforced before the 20th century.

Tariff policy also absorbed congressional attention. Republicans traditionally favored high protection, Democrats low. Following party lines, Congress passed the Republican-backed McKinley Tariff in 1890, raising import duties nearly 50 percent. Amidst the severe farm crisis, voters reacted angrily to the increased costs. With the southern Farmers Alliance backing reform Democrats and western farmers supporting Populist candidates, the 1890 off-year elections toppled Republican leadership in both houses of Congress.

The Populist Agenda of Reform

As farm incomes continued to fall, voters in the South and West became angered by the failure of the major party politicians to enact reforms. By 1892, the Populist movement was demanding national attention. "We meet in the midst of a na-

tion brought to the verge of moral, political, and material ruin," declared the Populist platform in 1892. "From the same prolific womb of governmental injustice we breed the two great classes—tramps and millionaires." Seeking to break the power of the entrenched parties, Populists struggled to forge an alliance between the Democratic South and the Republican Midwest, regions that had felt mutual distrust since the Civil War. Symbolizing the end of sectional discord, the new party nominated Union General James Weaver for the presidency and Confederate veteran James Field as his running mate. When the Democratic presidential challenger Grover Cleveland joined the Republican incumbent Benjamin Harrison in defending the gold standard, Populists found common ground in demanding the inflationary unlimited coinage of silver.

The Populist platform proposed drastic changes in the nation's political economy. These included government "subtreasury" warehouses for crops; public ownership of railroads, telegraphs, and telephones; a graduated income tax to shift the burden to wealthier classes; redistribution of railroad land grants to actual settlers and prohibition of foreign ownership of real estate; a one-term president, direct election of senators, the secret ballot, and statewide referenda and voter initiatives; and the eight-hour work day and legalization of labor boycotts.

With the fervor of a religious revival, the Populists prepared to fight the nation's political leadership, but the movement faced overwhelming obstacles. In the Midwest, habits of party voting, suspicion of southern Democrats, and disagreements about prohibition and women's suffrage undermined farmer solidarity. In the South, white and black farmers hesitated to cooperate, and Democratic candidates appealed openly to the region's racism to block an interracial alliance. Nor, despite the endorsement of organized labor unions, did

Populists address the needs of city voters. Indeed, urban radicals embraced reformer Henry George's proposal of supporting government with a single national tax on land, a way of penalizing city landlords but hardly a popular idea among the country's farmers.

Despite its disadvantages, the People's party could claim clear gains in 1892. It won over 1 million popular votes (8.5 percent of the total), twenty-two electoral votes, ten seats in the House, five in the Senate, three governorships, and nearly 1,500 state legislators. In the end, however, the Democrat Cleveland won the presidency with less than a majority of the votes. The Populists vowed to do better four years later.

White City/White Culture

Two months after Cleveland reentered the White House in 1893, the city of Chicago raised the curtain on the World's Columbian Exposition to mark the 400th anniversary of Columbus's historic voyage. Twelve million people visited the Fair to contemplate the architectural symmetry of 400 newly constructed buildings, fountains, and statuary that formed the "White City," made even more wondrous at night by 40,000 incandescent lightbulbs. Exhibitions celebrated the progress of civilized society and the fruits of technology, industry, and agriculture. The informal Midway spectacles, by contrast, introduced visitors to an adventurous, exotic world: the Ferris wheel, Chinese bazaars, and the naughty harem dancing of a woman named Little Egypt.

The Fair also depicted the limits of progress, though not always intentionally. The Women's Building, designed by Sophia Hayden, appeared, in the words of one artist, "like a man's ideal of woman—delicate, dignified, pure, and fair to look upon." While celebrating the domestic arts, the Fair hosted talks about women's history and politics. African Americans of either gender enjoyed no such welcome. Denied a building or hall, blacks organized a "Colored People's Day," during which Frederick Douglass called the Fair "a whited sepulcher." But the African American Nancy Green captured great attention cooking pancakes at a griddle, becoming the first living Aunt Jemima trademark. Native Americans (Navajos, Senecas, Penobscots, and Pueblos, among others), who had attended the Philadelphia Centennial of 1876 only as stuffed artifacts, appeared in flesh and blood. One white observer saw in them "a series of object lessons [showing] the development of . . . civilization." The director of the Carlisle Indian School objected that these specimens lacked the progressive character of his students and persuaded Fair directors to allow assimilated youth to demonstrate their "civilized" trades.

Triumph over the past aroused an ominous foreboding when historian Frederick Jackson Turner, a young professor at the University of Wisconsin, attended the American Historical Association's meeting at the Fair and read a paper called "The Significance of the Frontier in American History." Citing reports from the Superintendent of the Census for 1890, Turner announced that the western frontier of settlement, which had dominated the nation's history, no longer existed. Historians hailed this essay as a pioneering work of scholarship and agreed that the closing of the frontier constituted a crisis of national identity, the end of a culture of limitless expansion.

Other warnings underscored the historian's uneasy message. Just four days after the Fair opened, another Wall Street panic rocked the economy. By the time Turner voiced his concerns, thousands of businesses, including five major railroads, had failed, one-fifth of the nation's workers were unemployed, and the country stood at the brink of the worst economic disaster in its history. Amidst extraordinary industrial production, Americans faced the consequences of a national marketplace.

INFOTRAC® COLLEGE EDITION EXERCISES

For additional reading, go to InfoTrac College Edition, your online research library at *http://web1.infotrac-college.com.*

Keyword search: Andrew Carnegie

Keyword search: social Darwinism

Subject search: Haymarket

Subject search: AFL

Subject search: Populist Party

Keyword search: Wounded Knee

Subject search: Sherman Act

Keyword search: James Garfield

Keyword search: Grover Cleveland

ADDITIONAL READING

Building a Corporate Economy

Alan Trachtenberg, *The Incorporation of America: Culture and Society in the Gilded Age* (1982). A fine synthesis of the era, interweaving political, social, and cultural issues.

David O. Stowell, *Streets, Railroads, and the Great Strike of 1877* (1999). This brief book places railroad strikes in the context of urban economic development.

Emphasizing Industrial Efficiency

Alfred D. Chandler, Jr., *The Visible Hand: The Managerial Revolution in American Business* (1977). This book provides a detailed explanation of changing corporate business practices.

Ron Chernow, *Titan: The Life of John D. Rockefeller, Sr.* (1998). This biography depicts the personal decisions that led to the triumph of Standard Oil.

Paul Krause, *The Battle for Homestead, 1880–1892: Politics, Culture and Steel* (1992). Using Carnegie's steel plant as a case study, the book provides an analysis of the conflicts between labor and capital; for another study of workers' culture, see Madelon Powers, *Faces Along the Bar: Love and Order in the Workingman's Saloon, 1870–1920* (1998).

Olivier Zunz, *Making America Corporate: 1870–1920* (1990). A thoughtful analysis of corporate innovation, the book places economic change in a cultural context.

Reforming Industrial Society

Ruth Bordin, *Woman and Temperance: The Quest for Power and Liberty, 1873–1900* (1981). Focusing on the Women's Christian Temperance Union, the author links the temperance crusade to the women's rights movement.

Economic Problems in the South

Edward L. Ayers, *The Promise of the New South: Life after Reconstruction* (1992). A social history of the post–Civil War South, blending political, social, and cultural affairs.

Louis R. Harlan, *Booker T. Washington: The Making of a Black Leader, 1856–1901* (1972). This biography explores Washington's life within the framework of southern rural society.

Racial Hierarchy in the South

Leon F. Litwack, *Trouble in Mind: Black Southerners in the Age of Jim Crow* (1998). An analysis of the problems facing African Americans, depicting the violations of civil, political, and economic rights. For the status of Chinese Americans, see John Kuo Wei Tchen, *New York before Chinatown: Orientalism and the Shaping of American Culture* (1999).

Challenging the Native American Reservations

Frederick E. Hoxie, *A Final Promise: The Campaign to Assimilate the Indians, 1880–1920* (1984). A fine analysis of changing white attitudes toward the native tribes, which may be supplemented by the classic oral history, *Black Elk Speaks,* edited by John Niehardt.

The Business of National Politics

Rebecca Edwards, *Angels in the Machinery: Gender in American Party Politics from the Civil War to the Progressive Era* (1997). Describes the role of women in party affairs before they gained the vote.

The Populist Agenda of Reform

Robert C. McMath, Jr., *American Populism: A Social History, 1877–1898* (1993). A good synthesis of the farm protests, explaining the conflicts between southern and western interests.

White City/White Culture

James Gilbert, *Perfect Cities: Chicago's Utopias of 1893* (1991). Focusing on the Columbian Fair, the author analyzes urban values in an age of rapid change.

17

The Crisis of the 1890s

In 1893, the news in rural Wisconsin was not good. Mrs. Ira Ames "starved and froze to death"; her husband and seven children had been living "in a rickety shanty without fuel or food," and the youngest had died one week earlier. Workers at a nearby lumber mill rejected 10 percent wage cuts, forcing the business to close. With grain prices falling fast, wholesalers advised farmers to keep their produce off the market. In every town, banks and retail stores suspended operations. When the northern iron mines shut down, 15,000 people were left "in a helpless condition . . . [and] strong men were found weeping because their sick wives and helpless children had nothing to eat and next to nothing to wear." The number of unemployed "tramps" caused widespread fear. "Sometimes they come in large droves," complained a reporter. "Some of them are quite persistent and somewhat insolent in their methods of obtaining sustenance."

The economic downtown of the 1890s began with the withdrawal of British investments in U.S. railroads in 1893, but soon touched the entire economy, resulting in the failure of 600 banks, the closing of 15,000 businesses, and the loss of 3 million jobs, affecting more than 20 percent of the labor force. The ensuing economic depression brought immense personal suffering, provoked vicious labor disputes, and inspired pleas for government regulation of the economy.

The economic crisis emerged as the decade's primary political issue. Questions of money policy dominated the bitterly contested presidential election of 1896, which pitted the rural South and West against the urbanized and long settled agricultural areas of the Northeast. As voters turned out in record numbers, political leaders saw the election as a crucial turning point in the nation's history, a crisis about not only economic issues but also the national identity itself. Business leaders endorsed the Republican party and the gold standard, arguing that industrial growth and commercial development would bring national prosperity. Farmers and small business interests, by contrast, saw commerce and industrialism as a threat to preserving a nation of independent producers and lamented the growing presence of foreign immigrants. Such groups ultimately backed the Democrats and "free silver" as a way of preserving a democratic republic. The decisive triumph of business interests in 1896 capped that debate.

The return of prosperity the next year calmed political passions. Business leaders now focused on expanding the marketplace at home and abroad. New types of advertising stimulated domestic consumption and contributed to a redefinition of male and female roles. Meanwhile, the government pursued an aggressive foreign policy to stimulate U.S. trade in Asia and Latin America. By 1900, the nation's first overseas wars had brought the United States into the international arena.

Economic stability nonetheless offered limited gains to many social groups. Although women activists formed a vigorous social reform movement to improve the quality of urban life, the push for women's political rights faltered. During the 1890s, southern whites reentered the national mainstream and fought proudly for the Stars and Stripes; but southern blacks lost their political rights and confronted omnipresent discrimination. Native Americans faced new forms of government oppression, and their population dwindled to its lowest numbers, falling below half a million people at the turn of the century. Racist attitudes also dominated U.S. policy overseas, resulting in the creation of a colonial empire. Despite these obvious inequities, economic recovery after 1897 enabled political leaders to patch over the country's social divisions. By the end of the century, U.S. business was cultivating new markets around the world and heralding a new era of human progress.

The Economic Crisis Descends

The financial panic that hit Wall Street in 1893 caused instant failure for innumerable businesses, but few anticipated the broader social calamity that overwhelmed individual lives and brought a wave of suicides, insanity, and crime. Indeed, when a Chicago newspaper reported on the hundreds of homeless people who sought shelter every night in the city's jails, the headline offered a simple explanation for the disaster: "Hard Luck Stories."

Some religious leaders were more blunt: "No man in this land suffers from poverty," the Reverend Henry Ward Beecher told his affluent congregation in Brooklyn, "unless it be more than his fault—unless it be his sin." Yet in a world that attributed a person's success to "luck" or "character," the sudden economic downturn drove the unemployed to desperation. In Chicago, thousands of starving workers protested at the Columbian Exposition for jobs, food, and shelter. They wound up battling 350 club-wielding police and burning vacant fair buildings. To protect the city from tramps, police guarded the railroad stations and turned back unemployed rural laborers looking for work. Detroit's reform mayor Hazen Pingree hired the unemployed to construct city parks and allowed them to grow vegetables on empty lots. In every city, thousands camped out on municipal property and begged for private charity.

Workers Fight for Jobs

Competition for jobs and relief intensified ethnic conflicts. "There should be a law . . . to give a job to every decent man that's out of work," remarked an Irish woman who fed the unemployed in exchange for household chores. "And another law . . . to keep all them I-talians from coming in and taking the bread out of the mouths of honest people." In Brooklyn, Irish laborers fought in the streets against immigrant Italians and eastern European Jews. Several states passed laws barring foreign-born from public work. Although *The New York Times* criticized anti-Semitism, the paper warned against spreading radical literature in the Lower East Side, where "hatchet-faced, pimply, sallow-cheeked, rat-eyed young men of the Russian-Jew colony feed full." Amid economic struggles, the anti-immigrant, anti-Catholic American Protection Association, founded during the 1880s, won wide support in northern cities, often aligning with Republican political groups against pro-Democratic immigrants. In California, the arrival of the first Japanese contract laborers contributed to a well-developed anti-Asian movement.

As single young men took to the roads to find work, an Ohio businessman named Jacob Coxey organized the unemployed. Proposing a federal Good Roads law to employ workers on public

Political cartoonist William Allen Rogers spoofed the march from Ohio to Washington, D.C., of an army of workers led by Jacob Coxey. Upon reaching their goal, the leaders were arrested for trampling on the grass. Rogers's cartoon actually turned ridicule upon the "Original Coxey's Army"—industrialists who had been marching on the capital, with success, for years.

highways, Coxey summoned a march on Washington to press for legislation. On Easter Sunday 1894, 100 marchers departed for the national capital, swelling to 500 by the following month. In California, hundreds of idle workers, including the young writer Jack London, formed "industrial armies," snatched rides on the railroads, and headed east to join the protest. Political leaders in Washington had no desire to discuss this unprecedented demand for federal relief. When Coxey's "army" of 600 marchers entered the Capitol grounds, armed police dispersed the crowd and arrested Coxey for trespassing. Rather than bringing social reform, the protest highlighted widespread feelings of frustration and anger.

At Pullman, Illinois, where workers made railway sleeping cars and lived in company-owned homes, the government sent armed troops to quell labor protests. The crisis began when the Pullman Company slashed wages about 33 percent, but maintained its prices for rent, which was deducted from the employees' paychecks. Families were often left with a few pennies for food. When a workers' committee questioned the policy, Pullman fired the delegation. Recently, however, the American Railway Union, led by the popular organizer Eugene V. Debs, had won a strike against the Great Northern railroad in Minnesota and seen its membership rise to 150,000. Flexing its muscles, the union agreed to support the Pullman workers with a national boycott of Pullman sleeping cars.

As the workers' boycott halted the nation's rail service, Pullman officials conspired with federal officials to destroy the union. After the railroads hired strikebreakers to operate its plants, Attorney General Richard Olney, a former railroad lawyer, obtained a court injunction against the union on grounds that the strike interrupted delivery of the U.S. mail. President Cleveland then ordered federal troops to suppress the strike. The confrontation erupted in violence, leaving a dozen workers dead, scores wounded, and valuable property damaged.

Most newspapers depicted the strikers as insurrectionary "scum"—in the words of reporter Frederic Remington, a "malodorous crowd of anarchistic foreign trash." But most urban workers sympathized with the strikers. To weaken the labor protest, police arrested Debs on charges of conspiracy, wrecked his office, confiscated records, and, after he was released on bail, rearrested him for violating a legal injunction. The courts subsequently rejected the argument that workers had the right to strike in sympathy for fellow workers. In crushing the union, the railroads established a strict blacklist, blocking reemployment of 75 percent of the strikers. Debs received a six-month jail sentence, dur-

ing which he had an opportunity to read about socialism. He would help form the American Socialist party in 1901.

The Depression Dominates National Politics

Democrat Grover Cleveland had entered the White House on the eve of the depression. As a proponent of the gold standard, he attributed the drain of the nation's gold reserves, not to changing international investments, which removed European capital from U.S. businesses, or to overspeculation, but to the government's support of silver. After the Panic descended in 1893, Cleveland called a special session of Congress to repeal the Sherman Silver Purchase Act of 1890. The step succeeded only in focusing public attention on the country's money supply; it did nothing to stop the flow of gold to European banks. Consequently, the economy continued to decline. By 1895, Cleveland began to fear that the U.S. government would go bankrupt, and he summoned the richest Wall Street bankers, including J. P. Morgan, to save the gold standard. By extending loans to the federal government for discounted bonds, the financiers halted the gold drain, but for their efforts they made substantial profits in reselling U.S. securities. Cleveland's defense of gold infuriated many Democrats, who believed that "free silver" would encourage a monetary inflation and end the depression.

Efforts to alter tariff policy proved equally ineffective. Low-tariff Democrats believed that reducing trade barriers would improve the economy, but industrial lobbyists persuaded Congress to raise many rates. The resulting Wilson-Gorman tariff of 1894 made few reforms. The measure did include a federal income tax—2 percent for earnings over $4,000—but the next year the Supreme Court ruled that provision unconstitutional. "The present assault on capital is but the beginning," declared Court. "It will be the stepping-stone . . .

till our political contests will become a war of the poor against the rich; a war constantly growing in intensity and bitterness." Lest the Court's bias in that struggle appear unclear, the justices upheld the use of injunctions against strikers in the Debs case, disallowed state laws that limited women and children's labor to eight hours a day, and ruled that the Sherman Anti-Trust Act, which regulated interstate commerce, did not apply to manufacturing companies.

The fear of impending class warfare set the tone of electoral politics. In the 1894 congressional elections, depression problems led many voters to desert Cleveland and the Democrats. The Populist party, having gained many local victories in 1892, had hopes for success. In the South, agricultural poverty enabled them to attract new support among white farmers. But widespread fraud, together with pleas for white supremacy, enabled Democrats to remain in power throughout the South. In the western states, farmers still faced severe droughts and falling commodity prices, but silver mining interests flooded the campaign with "free silver" propaganda that emphasized monetary policy as a solution to farm problems. Yet even silver Democrats and Populists combined could not overcome the anti-Cleveland Republican majorities.

The Election of 1896

The presidential election of 1896 focused on the money issue, pitting supporters of the traditional gold standard against those demanding unlimited coinage of silver. The Republican party, dominated by eastern bankers like J. P. Morgan and industrialists like Mark Hanna, defended the gold standard and promised to restore financial stability, business prosperity, and economic growth. Party leaders nominated Ohio's William McKinley for the presidency, describing him as "the advance agent of prosperity." McKinley offered a simple

> **"You shall not press down upon the brow of labor this crown of thorns, you shall not crucify mankind upon a cross of gold."**

remedy for the nation's economic crisis, insisting that high protective tariffs, backed by a "sound" gold standard, would create business confidence, encourage foreign investment, and bring the "full and unrestricted labor of American workingmen."

The Democratic party, saddled with Cleveland's record, met in Chicago and quickly repudiated the gold standard. Armed with popular pamphlets like William Harvey's *Coin's Financial School,* which touted the virtues of silver as an antidote to the aristocratic gold, the free silver movement brought an evangelical zeal to the party convention. Silverites found the ideal candidate in the vigorous Nebraska politician William Jennings Bryan. Just 36 years old and a two-term veteran of Congress, the candidate spoke for "the plain people of this country" against the monied leadership of the cities. A magnificent speaker, Bryan defied Republicans who demanded the gold standard, spread his arms before a rapt audience, and proclaimed: "You shall not press down upon the brow of labor this crown of thorns, you shall not crucify mankind upon a cross of gold." With those words, Bryan accepted the Democratic nomination.

The third-party Populists, meeting in St. Louis one month later, held a shaky position. Obviously a minority party, their best hopes were in forming an alliance with the free-silver Democrats. But a fusion campaign behind Bryan would focus only on silver. The more radical Populist demands for government control of railroads and agricultural warehouses would have to be abandoned. Some Populists pleaded for an independent platform. But a majority approved endorsement of Bryan.

William Jennings Bryan

fight against the evils of silver and defined Bryan's Democrats as "social misfits who have almost nothing in common but opposition to the existing order and institutions." Playing on the fears of corporate leaders, Republican Marcus Hanna built a campaign war chest exceeding $4 million. The party proceeded to purchase hundreds of millions of leaflets, flyers, and advertising, as well as the train fares of tens of thousands of delegations (80,000 in one day) who were brought to visit McKinley's home in Canton, Ohio.

Such expensive tactics added a new dimension to presidential elections. Instead of appealing to traditional party loyalty, Hanna emerged as the first modern campaign manager by showing voters how the candidate stood on issues relating to their own self-interest. Election day proved the value of Republican money. With record-high voter participation, Bryan captured more than 6.5 million votes; but McKinley won by taking over half a million more. The Populists drew only 300,000 votes. Bryan carried the Democratic South, Rocky Mountain silver states, and the Great Plains—all rural areas afflicted by the depression—but he won nothing north of the Mason-Dixon line and east of the Mississippi River. McKinley captured the Midwest farm vote as well as the big cities, winning among middle-class conservatives, non-Irish immigrants, and urban labor. This victorious Republican coalition overturned the see-saw politics of the previous twenty years and built a national majority that would dominate political life until the next great depression of the 1930s forced another party realignment.

"We play Jonah," remarked Georgia's Tom Watson, "while they play the whale." As an assertion of principle, however, the Populists named Watson their vice-presidential candidate, offering voters a slight difference from Bryan's Democratic running mate, a wealthy shipbuilder from Maine.

The silver-voiced Bryan carried the crusade to the voters, traveling 18,000 miles by rail, presenting 600 speeches (over a dozen a day), and addressing 5 million people. He discussed farm prices, mortgage rates, and railroad regulation, but mostly he emphasized the silver issue. Bryan was "talking about silver all the time," said McKinley's campaign manager, "and that's where we've got him." Refusing to discuss other depression issues, Republicans defined the election as a

Reconstructing National Prosperity

The McKinley administration delivered on its conservative promises. In 1897, the Republican-led Congress sought to ensure business stability by passing the Dingley tariff, which raised import

The Election of 1896

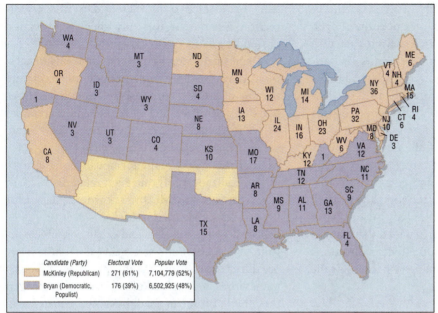

Candidate (Party)	Electoral Vote	Popular Vote
McKinley (Republican)	271 (61%)	7,104,779 (52%)
Bryan (Democratic, Populist)	176 (39%)	6,502,925 (48%)

duties to the highest levels yet. In 1900, the Currency Act established the gold standard as the basis of the national economy. By then, the expansion of foreign trade, together with the discovery of gold in Alaska, had eased the country's economic crisis. In an atmosphere of increasing prosperity, the presidential election of 1900 replayed the Bryan-McKinley contest, but without the zeal and the fear. Bryan continued to denounce industrial monopolies and corporate financiers. "I protest against all theories that enthrone money and debase mankind," he said. But McKinley and his new running mate, the former governor of New York, Theodore Roosevelt, promised voters a "full dinner pail." Once again, Republicans swamped the Democrats. By then, the Populists had disappeared from the scene. So, too, vanished an era of farmers' revolt.

As the economy recovered, business leaders drew important lessons from the recent depression. The huge number of business failures, large companies as well as small, demonstrated the dif-

ficulty of managing both capital and competition. Some large firms sought corporate stability by creating holding companies and trusts that controlled the stock of several companies and consequently could consolidate business policy for their companies. But the Sherman Anti-Trust Act of 1890 limited such cooperation by declaring illegal those business combinations that were "in restraint of trade." In the *Knight* case of 1895, however, the Supreme Court refined the law. That ruling distinguished manufacturing firms from commercial companies and ruled that single businesses were protected from anti-trust suits. Subsequent court decisions suggested, moreover, that holding companies, which consisted of more than one business, were *not* immune from anti-trust regulation. Corporate leaders now recognized that the best way to protect corporations from government interference was to merge their businesses completely, to form larger, single corporations.

Once the depression ended, corporate mergers increased rapidly, from 26 in 1896 and 69 in

1897 to more than 1,200 in 1899, resulting in fewer firms controlling a larger portion of each industry. Bankers and brokers, who invested in corporate consolidations, made profits by handling the exchange of corporate stock. "A radical change has been wrought into our business," explained the annual report of the National Biscuit Company, four years after a merger of three regional firms in 1898. Citing the efficiency of internal management, the advantages of acquiring raw materials in bulk, economizing manufacturing, and systematizing sales, the company boasted that these changes had "improv[ed] the quality of our goods and the condition in which they should reach the customer." Consolidated corporations thus claimed to dominate industry because of the superiority of their products.

The Emergence of Mass Marketing

The importance of bringing products to market and winning consumer loyalty emerged as another lesson of the 1890s depression. Despite four years of economic catastrophe, production had continued to expand, especially in retail trades. During the decade, the quantity of ready-to-wear clothing produced had doubled; so did the sale of luxury items like artificial jewelry; and the manufacture of pianos increased tenfold. But just as small producers complained about unfair competition from large industrialists, the decline of business in 1893 provoked widespread protests against the emergence of large retail department stores. Such shopping outlets differed from small stores by offering customers a wide variety of goods, including imported luxuries, multiple sizes, exotic styles, and delicacies. The big stores also threatened diverse local merchants, the butcher, grocer, shoemaker, jeweler, and florist. "The octopus," complained a small merchant in language usually reserved for railroad monopo-

lies, "has stretched out its tentacles in every direction, grasping in its slimy folds the specialist or one-line man."

Department stores enjoyed double advantages. First, they could purchase in bulk and accelerate the rate of product turnovers; second, large stores like Chicago's Marshall Field could afford premium prices for better property locations. "Real estate values," protested the Chicago city council, "have been unreasonably and enormously enhanced by the centralization [of] one giant retail district." In several states, small-business owners pushed for laws to tax department stores; some cities established special license fees and urban consumers organized boycotts. But when small New York retailers organized against the "encroachments" of department stores, a Wanamaker's executive challenged the inherent value of small business. "Small storekeepers," he declared, "belonged to a failing class." Indeed, within a few years, Field's Chicago department store employed nearly 10,000 workers who serviced a quarter of a million customers each day. By then, the return of business prosperity had eased the complaints of small merchants.

Large retailers focused on increasing the number of customers by introducing the concepts of fashion and constant change to encourage product turnover. Just half a century earlier, a potential buyer visited a local store, offering to exchange home-produced commodities for finished goods or bargaining over a cash price. By 1895, as one observer noted, "the expression `home-made'" [once a source of pride and praise] "is become a reproach."

The desirability of factory-made goods revealed not only the loss of traditional household skills—sewing, carpentry, the handicrafts—but also a new understanding of what consumption meant. In a classic study titled *The Theory of the Leisure Class* (1899), the Wisconsin-born economist Thorstein Veblen described consumer behavior as an effort to

The Denver Dry Goods Company boasted a shopping area "400 feet long," rivaling today's malls.

The Denver Dry Goods Co.,
Denver, Colo.

400 FEET LONG
CALIFORNIA ST., 16TH TO 16TH STREETS

achieve social status by purchasing selected commodities. According to Veblen, such "conspicuous consumption" enabled the wealthy to advertise their riches, while the less privileged, stimulated by envy and ambition, strove to earn the money to imitate the consumption patterns of their betters. "Nothing can be worn which is out of date," Veblen wrote of women's styles. "A new wasteful trinket or garment must constantly supersede the old one."

This emphasis on consumption mirrored a social outlook of "becoming." In religious terms, evangelicals stressed the importance of a "new birth" to bring sinners to salvation. During the late 19th century, revivalists like Chicago's Methodist Dwight Moody preached successfully in the busy cities, gaining converts among young adults. In economic terms, the opportunities of improving one's position served as a powerful magnet, drawing young people from the country to the cities. Theodore Dreiser, one of a new group of "realist" writers, depicted such youthful ambition, as well as the dangers of seduction on the urban frontier, in

> **"Each separate counter was a showplace of dazzling interest and attraction."**

his novel *Sister Carrie* (1900). Young Carrie, finding herself in one of Chicago's department stores, discovered that "Each separate counter was a showplace of dazzling interest and attraction . . . There was nothing there which she could not have used—nothing which she did not long to own. The dainty slippers and stockings, the delicately frilled skirts and petticoats . . . all touched her with individual desire, and she felt keenly the fact that not any of these things were in the range of her purchase."

In personal terms, the possibility of rebirth boosted a huge industry in patent medicine and cosmetics. Seductive peddlers, salesmen, and drug companies offered immense choices of magical cures and elixirs. In 1900, for example, "Mosko's

Silver" pills (perhaps echoing the free silver campaign) promised users "to feel young again, to realize the joyous sparkle of nerve life as it infuses the body with its growing vitality; to feel the magnetic enthusiasm of youthful ambition." Similar language defined the advantages of female clothing fashions.

Advertising and Image

In the amorphous space between the retailers' search for customers and the consumers' desire for personal improvement, a new breed of advertising experts offered to satisfy these interlocking economic needs. By 1900, professional advertising agencies and copywriters, not producers or retailers, had developed the marketing strategies and sales pitches that increasingly appeared in mass magazines and newspapers. Visual advertising, emphasizing color, graphic design, and corporate logos, demanded viewer attention. "Hot pictures," said one marketer, were better than "cold type." Similar advertising trends occurred in mail order catalogues and brochures, which featured seasonal sales, new products, and the excitement of change.

New printing techniques and the perfection of halftone photographic reproductions, together with screaming headlines and sensational stories, jolted the circulation of daily newspapers. Reporters like Jacob Riis wrote serial exposés of urban squalor, crime, and child labor, showing readers "how the other half lives." By the mid-1890s, Joseph Pulitzer's New York *World* and William Randolph Hearst's competing New York *Journal* reached a combined daily readership of 1 million. To boost revenue, such papers switched in 1894 from narrow columns of advertising to full-page display ads. Even marginally literate subscribers, who read the new comic strips, had no trouble understanding the visual images.

Professional advertisers rapidly rewrote the nation's economic script. Instead of assuming that a

Electric signs with flashing lights and colored bulbs added to the sparkle of urban night life, like Heinz's 45-foot green-bulb pickle in New York.

product would sell itself under the natural laws of supply and demand, advertisers transformed marketing from the sale of products to the invention of desires. As one woman professional remarked in 1899, "Without imagination, no wants. Without wants, no demand to have them supplied." Such appeals aimed to increase consumer demand at all levels of society. "We are not concerned with ability to pay," explained another woman advertiser, "but with the ability to want and choose." Advertising agencies perfected what they called "the pretty picture" to stimulate consumer imaginations. Both isolated rural families and urban tenement dwellers, who would not be expected to purchase such items, snipped out the illustrations to decorate otherwise bleak interiors of their homes. Commercial calendars replaced almanacs as monthly guides on the wall. For immigrant customers, visual advertising needed no English translations. Even the posh department stores introduced "bargain basements" to attract poorer customers downtown.

The burst of visual advertising altered the urban landscape. Using newly developed synthetic paints, outdoor billboards and product posters mushroomed on building walls and vacant lots. Electric signs with flashing lights and colored bulbs added to the sparkle of urban night life, but like Heinz's 45-foot green-bulb pickle in New York, the objective was not to amuse but to instill product identity. In 1900, the New York *Tribune* asked indignantly why parks should be surrounded by "fantastic boastings of boots and sauces and kidney specifics." Although some

Advertising cards were another way that businesses promoted their wares to an eager public. Here, J. & P. Coats heralds "the greatest thread and needle in the world" on one side of its card and offers customers an 1880 pocket calendar on the other.

complained that outdoor advertising contributed to "the desacration of . . . beautiful scenery," advertisers expressed no regrets. "The successful advertisement is obtrusive," said one marketer. "It continually forces itself upon the attention . . . . Everyone reads it involuntarily." At a time when pioneering psychologists like William James were exploring the human unconscious, commercial art linked aesthetic appeal to involuntary wishes.

Graphic designers also strove to bridge the gap between buyer and seller. Although pushcart peddlers crowded into immigrant neighborhoods and merchants shouted their wares on residential streets, downtown retailers designed lavish window displays to lure the customer inside. By 1900, the magazine read by professional window trimmers had reached a circulation of 10,000. Women's social purity groups frequently complained that mannequin window displays, which showed bare artificial limbs, were "immoral." But window designers justified such shock advertising because "even the male mind, naturally obtuse on such matters, is forced to marvel." Inside the stores, omnipresent mirrors and electric lighting enhanced the sense of opulent abundance.

Gender and Identity in the Corporate Age

In appealing to consumer desires, advertising helped to shape new images of male and female identity and contributed to the blurring of differing class and ethnic attitudes about gender roles. Introducing uniform standards of beauty and taste, epitomized in poster images of Charles Dana Gibson's "girls," advertisers could appeal to all spectators, including those considered "homely."

A later version of the Gibson girl, who says, "When I ventured to show myself at the Hotel Piazza, I created a sensation." Proclaimed her sisters, "When a man approaches, we do not tremble and droop our eyelids or gaze adoringly while he lays down the law . . . We're not a shy, retiring, uncomplaining generation. We're up to date and up to snuff, and every one of us is self-supporting."

Meanwhile, photographic displays of corsets, which bound the female form into hourglass figures, added a sexualized dimension to advertising and encouraged purchases. These changes in ideal shape coincided with the effort of insurance companies to develop tables of normal height, weight, and age, and to establish uniform standards of body size and health. Consequently, definitions of "manliness" also underwent change. Fat and flabbiness, instead of symbolizing comfortable prosperity, indicated "swollen, slothful ease." "The rich become effeminate, weak, and immoral," remarked one physician during the depression year of 1894, "and the lower classes, led on by their savage inclinations, undertake strikes, mobs, boycotts, and riots."

Creating a Youth Culture

Urban secondary school attendance doubled during the 1890s as 60 percent of native-born children began high school. Immigrant children remained in school at much lower rates. Partly because of depression conditions, most white children entered the work force around the age of 13, while 40 percent of African Americans were working at age 10. Two-thirds of all working women were unmarried. As young adults increasingly found jobs in corporate offices and retail sales, city life encouraged the formation of a distinct youth culture that was based on the purchase of recreational entertainment. While young men congregated in saloons, unmarried working women formed "pleasure clubs" to sponsor dances (known as "rackets"), social gatherings, and excursions to parks and beaches.

This leisure consumption emerged as the primary element of the urban youth culture. Clerical and sales jobs demanded standardized apparel, but in their leisure time, young women wore fashionable clothing and hairstyles. They also favored sexually charged "tough" dancing to live music and patronized penny arcades that featured slot machines, freak shows, and early motion pictures called "kinetoscopes." Unchaperoned social clubs initiated young people into adult roles as urban consumers.

Middle-class youth, by contrast, experienced more schooling and so postponed the transition into adulthood, entering a period of life that psychologists now called adolescence. Boys prepared

An 1879 quarterly calendar from *The Youth's Companion* that offers the motto "Right tastes for reading formed in youth are seeds of honor, virtue, truth."

for careers in the corporate sector by attending colleges and engineering schools to learn new technologies and commercial skills. A large literature of advice books also stressed the acquisition of knowledge and traits associated with "manliness" and "masculinity."

Aware of the declining birthrate among white Anglo-Saxon families, middle-class commentators worried about a decline of male virility. To conserve vitality, young men learned to avoid sex—"a great drain of nerve force," one youth noted in his 1898 diary, "and much useful time and energy would be more than wasted." The proposed remedy for young men, as Theodore Roosevelt put it in 1899, was "the strenuous life." The pursuit of self-discipline through aggressive sports like boxing and football would strengthen the warrior virtues and renew Anglo-Saxon vitality.

Middle-class women also faced new choices. As young women constituted a majority of secondary school students, opportunities for higher education increased in elite women's schools such as Vassar, Smith, and Wellesley, as well as in coeducational public universities founded after the Civil War.

Like their brothers, young women received medical advice to pursue healthy activity, such as uncorseted golf, tennis, and bicycling. Young women responded eagerly to a new fad for bicycle riding. In 1896, manufacturers built 1.2 million bicycles; four years later, the number reached 10 million. Women reformers like Frances Willard, head of the Women's Christian Temperance Union (WCTU), loved the bicycle as a "new implement of power." Male medical doctors worried, however, about the physical costs, warning that many a "healthy country girl" had lost the "bloom of youth" because bicycling produced sexual responses. Such fears typified medical treatment of women's sexual complaints. Gynecologists viewed female sexual desire as a disease, and surgeons operated to remove ovaries to eliminate unwanted feelings.

Women and Social Reform

The status of women typically changed after marriage. Although poor women often continued to work outside the home, pregnancy and childrearing kept most of them at home. Middle-class women also identified with the domestic household, where housewives cultivated the skills of consumption, forming 80 to 90 percent of department

A modest student's room at Illinois Women's College in 1909, showing a then-common electrical lamp and an assortment of family photos, as well as implying the woman's membership in a sorority.

Illinois Woman's College—Student's Room

store customers. Such women remained active in reform groups, such as the WCTU, which endorsed woman's suffrage and mothers' custody of children, but they presented no alternative to a life of domestic roles. Other women's groups, such as the General Federation of Women Clubs and the National Congress of Mothers, pushed for diverse measures, including government inspection of food, regulation of child labor, and infant health clinics. Although the male anti-alcohol movement welcomed women's support, it ignored the larger women's agenda in founding the single-issue Prohibition party in the 1880s and the Anti-Saloon League in 1893. By then, many conservative wives were leaving the WCTU to participate in the women's club movement,

which set aside reform activism altogether in favor of social recreation and self-improvement programs. African American women, who organized their own reformist clubs, found no welcome among white society matrons.

Meanwhile, as the leadership of the WCTU aged, younger women looked for other opportunities to find socially active roles. College-educated women usually faced one of three choices: marriage, a career of paid labor, or sheer drift. "A sense of her uselessness," in the words of Jane Addams, was the feeling of many female college graduates. Nearly half of those women never married; those who did married later in life and had fewer children. Career opportunities remained limited, though college women swelled the ranks of teachers and nurses. Rejecting both marriage and a career, the college-educated Addams entered a period of "nervous depression and sense of maladjustment," and she traveled to Europe to find meaning for her life. Her experiences were singular, but not unique. Addams's companion, Ellen Starr, shared her frustration. Together they hatched a plan that brought their lives (and many of their contemporaries, male and female) into a new movement for social reform.

Influenced by English reformers, Addams returned to Chicago in 1889 to launch a "settlement" community house, Hull House, in a poor immigrant neighborhood, with the purpose of educating, assimilating, and assisting struggling foreign families. The idea of voluntary social service reflected the values of "social gospel" Christianity, a religious movement that challenged social Darwinism and suggested that the reform of society would hasten personal redemption. The movement attracted middle-class college graduates, especially women, and led to the opening of settlement houses in most major cities, numbering over 100 by 1900. For immigrant neighbors, the settlements offered classes in English, nutrition, and healthcare, as well as cultural programs and lectures about current events. The settlement houses also provided midwife services and kindergartens for the busy mothers of the neighborhood and gave labor unions and ethnic groups a place to meet. For reformers like Addams, the settlements created a community—half domestic family, half college dormitory—which permitted same-sex friendships, sometimes called "Boston marriages," to flourish.

The settlement house movement involved reformers in political activities. The socialist Florence Kelley, who fled from an unhappy marriage to Hull House in 1891, joined working women to seek improvements of sweatshop conditions, limits on child and women's labor, and sanitation reforms to check the spread of smallpox in contaminated garments. The settlements also served as a training ground for college students, who came for a summer or a semester, and then devoted their careers to social welfare activities, such as juvenile court reform, public education, or healthcare. When working women in New York held mass protests against long hours and low pay in retail stores, middle-class reformers organized consumers' lobbies to press store managers for better working conditions. By 1899, Florence Kelley led the National Consumers' League in a "white list" campaign to persuade consumers to shop only in stores that treated employees fairly.

The commitment to social reform revitalized the woman's suffrage movement. In 1890, rival groups merged into the National American Woman Suffrage Association, headed by feminist pioneers Elizabeth Cady Stanton and Susan B. Anthony. While some pressed Congress to adopt a constitutional amendment, most women agitated on the local and state level, drawing a variety of middle-class supporters into the campaigns. In New York City, for example, reformers organized the Women's Municipal League, which campaigned for mayoral candidates who were opposed to graft and organized prostitution. Such activities drew middle-class women into the political process and stimulated pro-suffrage agitation. The Populists also welcomed women's participation and several women ran for public office as Populist candidates. In four western states (Wyoming, Utah, Colorado, Idaho) women already had the right to vote. In seeking the ballot, middle-class women often contrasted their superior education to illiterate male voters, black men, and immigrants, and denounced the inequities that favored men. These suffragists did not welcome African American women, who formed their own suffrage organizations. "The enfranchisement of women," explained one southern white suffragist, "would insure immediate and durable white supremacy, honestly attained."

Sexuality and Racial Conflict

Issues of sexual equality, though seldom expressed directly, remained central to problems of race. In 1892, three African American men, falsely accused by white business rivals of assaulting white women, were arrested, then taken from their jail in Memphis, Tennessee, and shot to death. That year, lynch mobs killed 241 African Americans, part of a racial reign of terror that affirmed white male power in the southern states. "Nobody in this section believes the old threadbare lie that Negro men assault white women," responded the black journalist Ida Wells. "If southern white men are not careful . . . , a conclusion will then be reached which will be very damaging to the moral reputation of their women." For speaking so candidly about white women's sexual complicity, Wells was run out of town. Moving to Chicago, the writer continued to campaign against lynching. Her pamphlets documented the false charges of black men raping white women and described the numerous "voluntary and clandestine" interracial contacts that made white men so hostile.

The myth of the omnipresent black rapist enabled whites to enforce their political power. In 1898, a mulatto newspaper editor of Wilmington, North Carolina, son of a former governor, casually reported on the eve of local elections that "poor white men are careless in the matter of protecting their women"; "the women of that race," he observed, "are not any more particular . . . with colored men, than are the white men with colored women." Enraged state Democrats quickly circulated 300,000 copies of the editorial, together with warnings against black voting, and stationed armed whites at the polls to keep blacks from casting ballots. Having intimidated black voters, a mob proceeded to burn the offending news-

paper office, killed 12 African Americans in the streets, and drove most propertied blacks from the city. The sexual exploitation of black women by white men, which no one denied, revealed the presumption of white male superiority. "It is not the same thing for a white man to assault a colored woman as for a colored man to assault a white woman," explained a South Carolina newspaper, "because the colored woman had no finer feelings nor virtue to be outraged."

Racial Segregation in the South

Racial segregation reinforced the political disenfranchisement of African Americans in the South. In 1890, Mississippi's constitution became the first to adopt specific rules to prevent black voting. Skirting the principles of the Fifteenth Amendment, the state approved a variety of measures to exclude blacks from suffrage. These laws included a poll tax, which required payment of a fee to vote, blocking the poorest of both races from voting; "grandfather" clauses, which allowed only citizens whose grandfathers had voted to exercise the franchise; "understanding" tests, which required voters to interpret constitutional texts and permitted local officials to judge their accuracy; and allwhite primary elections, which allowed "private" political parties to exclude non-whites. The effect was dramatic and drastic. "The political map of Mississippi no longer contains a black belt," cheered a Jackson newspaper in 1892. The idea spread to neighboring states. In Louisiana, African American voting fell 96 percent, from 130,000 registered voters to 5,000 between 1896 and 1900; in Alabama, only 1 percent of blacks qualified to vote; in Virginia, 5 percent; in Mississippi and Georgia, less than one-half of 1 percent. "Discrimination!" declared a Virginia politician in 1901. "Why, that is precisely what we propose . . . with a view to the elimination of every Negro voter who can be gotten rid of, legally."

As southern whites established rigid lines of racial division, the educator Booker T. Washington emerged as the primary spokesman of African American accommodation. Keenly aware of the dangers of challenging white supremacy, the head of Tuskegee Institute shrewdly juggled the need to calm white fears while seeking modest gains for frustrated blacks. Known to see good in every evil, even in slavery, Washington suggested that at least blacks "came out speaking the proud Anglo-Saxon tongue" and had learned "the habit of work." By teaching self-supporting crafts, such as carpentry and leather work, his curriculum tried to sustain black employment in the small towns of the South. In emphasizing manual labor rather than the liberal arts, Washington understood that was the only way he could obtain financial support from northern white philanthropists, and he suffered severe rebukes from them when he tried to make changes. At one Tuskegee commencement, the governor of Alabama angrily reminded the students that "this is a white man's country . . . , and we are going to make you keep your place. Understand that." When President McKinley visited Tuskegee in 1898, Washington received similar advice. "The soundness . . . of this institution," said the president, "is that those in charge . . . evidently do not believe in attaining the unattainable."

Although Washington secretly supported legal suits against segregation, his public poise earned the gratitude of moderate white leaders, who invited him to address the Cotton States Exposition in Atlanta in 1895. The moment was unprecedented; "a representative of Negro enterprise and Negro civilization," said the expositions sponsors, would address a mixed audience from a white man's platform. Washington told his hosts what they wanted to hear. "Cast down your bucket where you are," he advised the segregated throng, "making friends . . . of the people of all races by whom we are surrounded." The speaker extended his hand. "In all things that are purely social we can be as separate as the fingers," he said, "yet one as the hand in all things essential to mutual progress." This distinction between regional economic advancement (one hand) and rigid social separation (five fingers) offered no threat to white supremacy. The audience reacted with thunderous approval.

CHALLENGING RACIAL SEGREGATION

Not all southern blacks shared Washington's passivity. Generations of interracial mixing had produced a class of light-skinned African Americans, who fit neither category of "white" or "black" and called themselves "no-nation." In New Orleans, a French-speaking Creole elite resolved to challenge the rules of color by initiating a test case in 1892. Homer Plessy, one-eighth "Negro," deliberately entered a white railroad car to violate a law that mandated "equal but separate accommodations for the white and colored races." Arrested for the offense and convicted in Louisiana courts, Plessy carried his appeal to the U.S. Supreme Court. The Court's decision (*Plessy v. Ferguson*) upheld the principle of separate but equal in 1896. "If the civil and political rights of both races be equal," said the Court, "one cannot be inferior to the other." In rejecting Plessy's argument that segregation treated colored people as second-class citizens, the Court insisted that any resulting "badge of inferiority" existed only in black imaginations. Even Booker T. Washington dissented from that logic. "The colored people do not complain so much of the separation," he wrote, "as of the fact that the accommodations, with almost no exceptions, are not equal."

The *Plessy* case had lasting repercussions. Although the Court accepted segregation, the ruling did affirm the rights of African Americans to equal citizenship and equal facilities. Two years later, the Court would extend citizenship to U.S.-born children of Chinese immigrants, even though Asian-born residents were not permitted to become naturalized citizens. (Later still, the Court would rule that Chinese citizens were "colored" and so could be barred from white facilities.) These legal principles assumed great importance when U.S. power extended to colonial peoples in the Caribbean and Philippine islands, and the Court denied full rights of citizenship to some colored populations. By contrast, the protection of "equal" rights for African Americans provided the basis for overturning racial segregation half a century later, when the Court admitted that "separate" was inherently "unequal."

For the Harvard-educated intellectual, W. E. B. DuBois, the double standard of citizenship touched to the root of African American identity. In a profound essay, "Striving of the Negro People," first published the year after the *Plessy* ruling and reprinted in the classic volume *Souls of Black Folk* (1903), DuBois explored the idea of enforced "double-consciousness." "It is a peculiar sensation, this sense of always looking at one's self through the eyes of others," he confessed. "One ever feels his two-ness—an American, a Negro; two souls, two thoughts, two unreconciled strivings; two warring ideals in one dark body, whose dogged strength alone keeps it from being torn asunder." For DuBois, the resolution of racial identity was neither the acceptance of segregated inferiority, nor the search for integrated invisibility, but the perpetuation of the double vision. He wanted to be "both a Negro and an American, without being cursed and spit upon." Despite this defiance of racial accommodation, DuBois hesitated to break publicly with Booker T. Washington, even as he realized the impossibility of achieving fulfillment in a segregated world.

Racism and Native-Born Minorities

The limits of racial assimilation also disappointed those who defended the efforts of Native Americans to achieve equality. Native American land rights, designed by the Dawes Act of 1887 to ease the transition to white "civilization," conflicted with white expansionists who craved undeveloped real estate. In the southwest Indian Territory (renamed Oklahoma in 1907), squatters and "boomers" literally stampeded across Cheyenne and Arapaho territory to claim title to unalloted lands. In the Northwest, aggressive whites encroached on Puyallop property, persuading Congress to accelerate the breakup of tribal holdings. In numerous cases, the McKinley administration ignored fraudulent land seizures, while legislators lamented undue "pampering" of the Native nations. Treaty violations received legal sanction when the Supreme Court ruled that Congress had the right to legislate unilaterally.

The lack of political sympathy for Native American legal claims reflected both greed and prejudice. Professional anthropologists presented scientific doctrines that linked cultural advancement to race. "No amount of sentimentality" could save biologically inferior Native peoples, asserted the nation's first professor of anthropology. "To train the average Indian as a lawyer or a doctor," remarked the author of *The Winning of the West*, Theodore Roosevelt, "is . . . simply to spoil him." These theories of racial inferiority justified cutbacks in Native American education. Although the federal government gave $2 million to 200 public schools to educate Native children in 1895, federal policy soon responded to local protests against integrated schools. By 1900, nearly all Native American pupils attended segregated schools. Even so, many politicians doubted the value of "book knowledge," and McKinley's superintendent of Indian schools criticized an Oregon program for permitting piano lessons instead of teaching girls "cooking, sewing, and laundry work." "Let nature take its course," concluded one observer. "The Indian, poor devil, will presently die off."

Racial boundaries also created economic and social problems for the Southwest residents of Hispanic descent, whose lands were invaded by eastern-owned corporations and ambitious ranchers. Besides losing landholdings to U.S. claimants, Hispanic shepherds were restricted from scarce water resources. Increasingly dependent on merchants who extended credit and purchased wool, Spanish-speaking herders had to abandon communal grazing and enter an economic realm not different from cotton sharecropping. The depression of the 1890s led to a recalling of debts and high loss of property. Many turned to unskilled labor for the railroads and mining companies or became migrant farm workers in the expanding sugar-beet fields of Colorado. From an independent self-sustaining people, Southwest Hispanics formed the lowest levels of an expanding corporate economy.

The Road to Empire

The sense of Anglo-Saxon superiority, what an earlier generation called Manifest Destiny, reinforced interest in overseas expansion. Since the end of the Civil War, Protestant missionaries had visited "pagan" lands in Asia and the Pacific islands, seeking to uplift "backward" peoples. Political leaders also responded to economic and strategic interests. The depression of the 1890s underscored the importance of foreign markets to absorb surplus production. The United States had developed agricultural markets for cotton, wheat, and tobacco in Latin America, Europe, and Asia, but in 1894 U.S. manufacturing exports exceeded imports for the first time and continued to grow in subsequent years. Recognizing the importance of expanding international trade, naval strategist Alfred Thayer Mahan published a widely read book *The Influence of Sea Power upon History* (1890), which urged construction of a modern navy, building a canal through Central America, and the acquisition of overseas naval bases to protect U.S. commerce.

Commercial Expansion

This combination of interests brought the United States into competition with other national empires. In 1889, the desire for a naval base in the Samoan islands nearly provoked a war with Germany, which had similar imperial designs. Six years later, concern about British expansion in the Caribbean, close to the site of a future canal, ignited a bitter boundary dispute between Venezuela and British Guiana. Cleveland's Secretary of State Richard Olney invoked the Monroe Doctrine, forbidding European interference in the Western Hemisphere, and the administration threatened war. Britain, with a smaller stake in the region, ended the crisis by accepting arbitration.

The expanding sugar trade with the Hawaiian Islands also embroiled the nation in imperial politics in the Pacific. Responding to the growing power of U.S. sugar planters on the islands, native Hawaiians encouraged the new Queen Liliuokalani to challenge the rights of U.S. companies. The U.S. ambassador in Hawaii understood the danger: "Shall Asiatic or American civilization ultimately prevail here?" In 1893, U.S. residents of Hawaii fomented a rebellion and forced the Queen to withdraw. United States officials on the island then sent a treaty of annexation to Washington, but the Cleveland administration rebuffed the arrangement and Congress rejected ratification.

With the Queen tentatively restored to power, U.S. sugar interests faced competition from other expanding nations, particularly Japan. By 1894, 30,000 Japanese contract laborers, one-fifth of the islands' population, were working on Hawaii sugar plantations. Encouraged by the Japanese government, these mostly male workers came for high wages, hoping to return home to buy land. The Japanese presence alarmed pro-U.S. Hawaiians, who tried to block further emigration, but Japan responded angrily to the effort to stop immigration. Aware of the economic and strategic importance of Hawaii, U.S. leaders changed their position. When pro-U.S. Hawaiians proposed a new treaty of annexation in 1897, President McKinley reversed Cleveland's policy and urged ratification. Congress again buried the measure—but only until changing conditions impelled the annexation of the Hawaiian islands in 1898.

The Spanish-American War

That year, the United States went to war with Spain. For two decades, a Cuban independence movement had been engaged in brutal warfare against the Spanish empire. As casualties rose, U.S. newspapers, led by Hearst and Pulitzer in New York City, pressed the Cleveland administration to intervene on behalf of the rebels. This so-called yellow journalism reflected the growing power of the mass media to influence public opinion. But U.S. investments in Cuba barely reached $50 million, and the annual trade worth $100 million did not justify U.S. involvement. As the popular press reported the horrors of Spanish concentration camps and pleaded with Washington to declare war for Cuban independence, Cleveland refused to be swayed. His successor, McKinley, the last Civil War veteran to inhabit the White House, had no desire to seek glory in warfare. Even after newspapers published a letter from the Spanish ambassador scoffing at the president's weakness, McKinley tried to stifle the cry for war.

As political conditions in Cuba deteriorated and violence threatened U.S. interests, McKinley sent the battleship *Maine* to Havana to protect U.S. citizens. But a mysterious explosion destroyed the ship and claimed over 200 lives. The popular press shouted for war, and the motto "Remember the Maine!" rapidly turned the tide of political opinion. Recent examinations of the sunken hull suggest that the ship experienced an internal explosion, probably not attributable to Spanish mines. But contemporaries saw the explosion as evidence of Spain's inability to maintain peace and order in that strategic area. McKinley promptly delivered a war message in April 1898, and Congress responded by recognizing Cuban independence and authorizing military force to expel Spain from the island colony. As proof of the nation's honorable intentions, Congress passed an amendment, offered by Senator Henry Teller, disavowing any interest in making Cuba a territorial possession.

The summons to war aroused popular enthusiasm. For young volunteers like the writers Carl Sandberg and Sherwood Anderson, military service appeared as a rite of passage into maturity, just as their fathers' generation had forged an identity in the Union armies of the Civil War. Southerners, too, now found satisfaction fighting for the Stars and Stripes. "Nothing short of an archeological society will be able to locate Mason and Dixon's line after this," cheered one newspaper. African American soldiers, many veterans of service against the Plains nations, fought bravely on Cuban soil, winning five Medals of Honor. White officers praised their superiority in "holding together in the midst of danger." But the black soldiers experienced racist treatment in southern camps, and race riots erupted several times. In three separate incidents, white streetcar conductors killed black soldiers for refusing to sit in the rear. Citing black heroism in battle, Booker T. Washington protested the "cancer growing at the heart of the republic, that shall one day prove as dangerous as an attack from an army."

Military victory came easily in Cuba. Despite the obsolescence of U.S. weapons and poor preparations for the tropical climate, the troops encountered a weak Spanish adversary. The month-long war caused only 400 U.S. deaths in combat, though

Theodore Roosevelt with members of his Rough Riders. An outspoken imperialist during the 1890s, the future president saw the United States as an emerging world power.

Roosevelt's charge up San Juan Hill earned top billing in Buffalo Bill Cody's Wild West pageant, replacing the older saga of Custer's Last Stand.

over 5,000 soldiers eventually succumbed to yellow fever, malaria, and dysentery. The most celebrated fighter proved to be Theodore Roosevelt, who organized a cavalry unit known as the Rough Riders to show the valor of Anglo-Saxon warriors. Roosevelt's much-publicized charge up Cuba's San Juan Hill under a hail of bullets eventually earned top billing in Buffalo Bill Cody's Wild West pageant, replacing the older saga of Custer's Last Stand.

Despite promises of Cuban independence, U.S. forces remained on the island as an occupation army, improving sanitation and public health, but mostly to protect U.S. sugar investments. Three years after the fighting stopped, Congress adopted an amendment, sponsored by Senator Orville Platt, that provided for the withdrawal of U.S. troops, only after Cuba accepted limited sovereignty. These limitations included U.S. rights to intervene in Cuba's affairs and to construct a naval base at Guantanamo Bay. Although Cuban nationalists bitterly opposed those concessions, the U.S. military presence forced them to back down. During the next decade, those concessions justified U.S. military intervention twice to prevent attacks on sugar interests. Meanwhile, in Spain's other Caribbean colony, Puerto Ricans received rights of U.S. citizenship, though the territory obtained only nonvoting representation in Washington. In this way, the United States established its dominance in the Caribbean area.

Equally dramatic, and militarily more significant, the Pacific fleet under Admiral George Dewey destroyed the Spanish navy at Manila in the Philippines in a single day, and U.S. forces quickly occupied the capital. Spain, utterly defeated in war, accepted a forced treaty that granted Cuba independence, and gave the United States possession of the Philippines, Guam, and Puerto Rico for $20 million. What Secretary of State John Hay called "a splendid little war" had transformed the United States into a global power.

After defeating Spain in the Philippines, the United States (as in Cuba) refused to relinquish its economic and strategic position. Soon after the fighting ended, the half-Chinese Philippine nationalist, Emilio Aguinaldo, issued a declaration of independence and pleaded for U.S. recognition of Philippine sovereignty. Washington, however, had no intention of abandoning the island bases to the local people, whom U.S. Governor General William Howard Taft called "our little brown brothers," or to an imperial competitor like Japan.

Determined to expand U.S. power in the Pacific, McKinley offered Filipinos promises of "benevolent assimilation," but U.S. officials refused to negotiate with the independence movement, provoking a guerrilla uprising. U.S. forces then retaliated with terror tactics, including random murders, arson, water torture of prisoners, and starvation of civilians. The war dragged on for four years before military forces crushed the popular insurrection.

The war for empire unleashed widespread criticism at home. The Anti-Imperialist League claimed half a million members by 1899. Some of its supporters, like Jane Addams, were pacifists, appalled at the immorality of the struggle; some, like the German immigrant Carl Schurtz, protested the denial of self-government to colonial peoples; some, like union leader Samuel Gompers, feared that annexation of the Philippines would flood the labor market with cheap immigrant workers. In the Sen-

ate, southern Democrats denounced annexation of a dark-skinned, unassimilable race. Others resented wartime violations of domestic civil rights, such as the seizure of anti-war pamphlets by the Post Office.

Drawing a parallel with the destruction of small businesses by big corporations and retail giants, William James said the Filipinos were treated like a "pretty picture" and protested that the U.S. government acted with "the infernal adroitness of the great department store, which has reached perfect expertness in the art of killing silently . . . the neighboring small concern." To James, the real enemy of civic virtue was "bigness." Just as large corporations now dominated the national economy, so the expansion of empire heralded an era of impersonal relations, characterized by manipulation of pretty images and business accounting. The ideal of giving Cuba and the Philippines independence from Spanish oppression was now replaced by colonial subordination to U.S. power.

Entering the Global Arena

Critics of the expanding U.S. empire, though eloquent, remained a political minority. Congress gladly ratified the acquisition of new territories and underwrote the costs of war. The acquisition of the Philippines also stimulated interest in China, a vast potential marketplace already partitioned by competing European empires. In 1899 and 1900, Secretary of State John Hay sent formal letters to the governments of U.S. rivals in Asia (Britain, France, Germany, Japan, Russia, among others) to espouse an "Open Door" doctrine that advocated shared opportunity for world trade rather than local spheres of influence. Although no nation responded positively to this U.S. initiative, Washington proceeded as if the policy of unlimited trading rights was universal. In this way, the United States entered the global arena to stay and soon became a major player in world politics. An era that had begun amidst severe economic turmoil and depression came to an end with promises of economic expansion and a sense of international power. As the 20th century began, the nation's new catchword was "progress."

INFOTRAC® COLLEGE EDITION EXERCISES

For additional reading go to InfoTrac College Edition, your online research library at *http://web1.infotrac-college.com.*

Subject search: Pullman strike

Keyword search: William Jennings Brhan

Subject search: temperance

Subject search: settlement houses

Subject search: social gospel

Keyword search: Cady Stanton

Keyword search: DuBois

Keyword search: USS Maine

Keyword search: Rough Riders

Keyword search: Theodore Roosevelt

ADDITIONAL READING

Reconstructing National Prosperity

Jean Strouse, *Morgan: American Financier* (1999). This biography explores corporate finance during an era of unregulated banking.

The Emergence of Mass Marketing

William Leach, *Land of Desire: Merchants, Power and the Rise of a New American Culture* (1993). Describes marketing techniques in urban society.

Susan Porter Benson, *Counter Cultures: Saleswomen, Managers, and Customers in American Department Stores, 1890–1940* (1986). Focusing on retailing, this study links the concerns of women workers and consumers.

Advertising and Image

Jackson Lears, *Fables of Abundance: A Cultural History of Advertising in America* (1994). An analysis of cultural psychology and business ideas, this book places advertising in the context of corporate growth.

Women and Social Reform

Joanne J. Meyerowitz, *Women Adrift: Independent Wage Earners in Chicago, 1880–1930* (1988). Focusing on unmarried women, this study examines the risks and opportunities faced by young women on the urban frontier.

Kathy Peiss, *Cheap Amusements: Working Women and Leisure in Turn-of-the-Century New York* (1986). Depicting the lives of women workers, the book explores the new youth culture of cities.

Kathryn Kish Sklar, *Florence Kelley and the Nation's Work: The Rise of Women's Political Culture, 1830–1890* (1995). This study of the rise of social welfare work may be supplemented with Jane Addams's classic autobiography, *Twenty Years at Hull House* (1910).

Sexuality and Racial Conflict

Gail Bederman, *Manliness and Civilization: A Cultural History of Gender and Race in the United States, 1880–1917* (1995). This study places gender relations in the context of racial ideology.

Sarah Deutsch, *No Separate Refuge: Culture, Class, and Gender on an Anglo-Hispanic Frontier in the American Southwest, 1880–1940* (1987). This book offers a thorough social history of the impact of U.S. expansion on local communities of New Mexico.

The Spanish-American War

Robert L. Beisner, *Twelve against Empire: The Anti-Imperialists, 1898–1900* (1968). Focusing on well-known opponents of U.S. expansionism, the study illuminates dissatisfaction with prevailing trends.

Stuart Creighton Miller, *"Benevolent Assimilation": The American Conquest of the Philippines, 1898–1903* (1982). A searing account of territorial expansion, emphasizing the racist imperial context.

18

Industrial Society and Progressive Reform, 1900–1915

CHRONOLOGY

1900	Floods in Galveston, Texas prompt municipal reform
1901	Theodore Roosevelt succeeds assassinated President William McKinley
	Edwin Porter produces first intertitled movie, *Uncle Tom's Cabin*
1903	W.E.B. DuBois publishes *The Souls of Black Folk*
	Major-league baseball teams play first World Series
1906	Upton Sinclair exposes meatpacking industry in *The Jungle*
	Congress passes Pure Food and Drug Act
1908	Gentleman's Agreement restricts Japanese immigration
1910	Congress passes Mann Act to end white slave trade
	Activists organize the National Association for the Advancement of Colored People
1911	Ishi appears at Oroville, California
1912	Arizona and New Mexico enter the union
1913	Suffrage leaders organize protest parade in Washington, D.C.
	States ratify 17th Amendment for direct election of senators
	Congress passes first national anti-alcohol law
	Armory Show first exhibits abstract painting in the United States
1914	Margaret Sanger indicted for publicizing birth-control information

A curious stranger appeared one morning in August 1911 at a slaughterhouse in Oroville, California. Upon discovering him, employees at the slaughterhouse promptly informed the local sheriff that they had found "something out there," which turned out to be a starving, nearly naked man, estimated at 60 years of age, who spoke no known language. Identified as "an aboriginal Indian," he was soon handcuffed and taken to jail, where curiosity seekers saw "a pathetic figure crouched upon the floor." Neighboring Indians could make no sense of his language; "he was as strange to them as a visitor from another world." The jailers gave him a plate of hot beans and bread, as well as some refinements of modern civilization: doughnuts, an unloaded revolver, and a cigarette. What most aroused his curiosity and "greatest amazement" were the marks made on paper as reporters jotted their observations.

"He is without trace or taint of civilization," reported one witness, "but he is learning fast and seems to enjoy the process." So began the taming of the "wild" man. As the mysterious Native communicated through pantomime and experimented with "civilized food" (devouring unpeeled bananas and oranges, to the amusement of his captors) authorities summoned expert assistance, in the form of anthropologists from the University of California. The professors soon dressed the man in a blue shirt, overalls, and a straw hat, and took him by train to the celebrated anthropology museum in Berkeley for further examination. There the stranger posed for photographers, demonstrated his skill with bow and arrow, and delighted in his newly acquired pockets, which he filled with assorted scraps. Later, he would carry a pocket watch, which he wound each day to hear the ticking, but never tried to set to the "correct" time.

The learning experience went both ways. With the help of vocabulary lists from other tribal groups, the scholars determined that the stranger belonged to the Yahi people, and through additional conversation and sign language learned that the man's relatives, described as three "bucks" and a "squaw," had recently died. Apparently he was the last survivor of his band of people.

The man proceeded to narrate Yahi stories, indicating his spiritual beliefs. Observers described him as "childlike," noting his pleasure at blowing whistles, eating candy, or stroking a bright silver dollar. His first spoken English word was *money;* the second, *water.* Within a month, the anthropologists took the man to a San Francisco theater, where he watched costumed dancers from Brazil and appeared bewildered both by the performance and the bejeweled spectators. Commentators stressed his friendliness, sense of humor, and tranquility. But the stranger refused steadfastly to reveal his name, which was apparently a matter of spiritual privacy. At last, his guardians named him *Ishi* ("man" in his native tongue) and gave him living quarters in the museum and a job as a janitor. He soon demonstrated great skill "handling the broom, the mop, and the duster." During the ensuing months and years, this "greatest anthropological treasure" taught the curators how he had lived for sixty years in the world.

As Americans of the early 20th century contrasted the "natural" world of Ishi with their modern "civilization," they were equally struck by how much their own times were changing. "Never in the history of the world was society in so terrific flux as it is right now," wrote novelist Jack London, who had grown up in Oakland, California, a city near the Berkeley museum. "An unseen and fearful revolution is taking place in the fiber and structure of society." The omnipresence of change—population migrations, urban growth, new technologies, and corporate expansion—aroused both wonder and worry, optimism and fear, satisfaction and anxiety. As millions of immigrants struggled to master the rules of their new society, U.S.-born citizens questioned whether traditional institutions could handle the array of new problems. "There are no precedents to guide us," remarked the writer Walter Lippmann. "We have changed our environment more quickly than we know how to change ourselves."

By 1900, the problems of a new industrial society were inspiring a variety of reform movements that contemporaries called "progressivism." The word itself testified to a sense of forward movement, to a belief in change for the better. Yet the word included a multitude of meanings and contradictions. Some progressive reformers were idealistic, others were self-serving; some looked backward to a lost age, others hastened toward an improved future; some had specific legislative objectives, others sought to reshape the entire society. In the beginning, the progressive movement focused on local problems, such as city services (water supplies, the treatment of sewage), public utilities (regulating streetcars and electricity), and housing (urban congestion). Larger problems prompted some progressives to extend their activities to the state and national levels of government.

This chapter focuses on the social history of the progressive era, emphasizing the impact of

Ishi, the "wild man" who appeared one morning in August 1911 at a slaughterhouse in Oroville, California.

change on community life and values. The next chapter examines changes in the national economy and their impact on national policies and presidential politics. Yet, to contemporaries, the two aspects were inextricably linked. Whatever their particular causes and crusades, most progressives shared the belief that by improving their social and political environment, citizens could overcome the limitations of birth, race, and class. Common to these diverse impulses was a spirit of optimism—the belief that society *could* be improved—either by changes in individual lives, by group pressure, or by government laws. Indeed, enthusiasm for reform reflected the confidence that enlightened leaders had the obligation to

In 1890, a huge facility for the receipt of immigrants opened at Ellis Island in New York.

force progress, to marry moral justice to good government, and so to build a better world. In these commitments, progressivism became a key ingredient in the evolving national identity.

The Immigrant Experience

Since the 1880s, large numbers of foreign-born immigrants had landed on U.S. shores (see Chapter 16). Between 1900 and 1914, 13 million more arrived, bringing the nation's total population to nearly 100 million. What happened to the Native American, Ishi, serves as a microcosm of the immigrant experience—a learning process in which the newcomer came to understand elemental aspects of U.S. society and culture while simultaneously teaching his hosts about "strange" and "alien" values. From mutual misunderstandings,

the relationship evolved into friendly respect. And yet the interaction between "insider" and "outsider" appeared unequal. To native-born whites, the "immigrant" remained backward, simple, even innocent, a person in need of "uplifting" rather than acceptance. In other words, the national identity could be inclusive, rather than exclusive, but only on its own terms.

Ishi's experiences were surely singular, but the transition from "wild" to "civilized" paralleled the problems of millions of newcomers, who searched for understanding, safety, and security in a new environment. Names, for example, were a sensitive issue for immigrants, whose first encounters with U.S. officials often resulted in permanent misnaming. Like Ishi, immigrants from abroad experienced great fear at meeting the U.S. bureaucracy at the ports of entry, such as Ellis Island, near New York, a huge facility opened in 1890;

> **"Let no one believe that landing on the shores of 'the land of the free and the home of the brave' is a pleasant experience."**

Angel Island, in San Francisco Bay; or, the San Antonio border crossing in Texas. Although few were handcuffed and arrested, European immigrants faced frightening health inspections that resulted in about 20 percent being placed in temporary confinement or ordered back to their homelands. Asians, who were unwanted for racist reasons, sometimes remained in prisonlike barracks ("like the cages in the zoo," said one) for months, even years, before gaining admission to the country.

"Let no one believe that landing on the shores of 'the land of the free and the home of the brave' is a pleasant experience," wrote one newcomer, who compared the ordeal to "grinding machinery . . . which sifts, picks, and chooses, admitting the fit and excluding the weak and helpless." Immigrants with serious illnesses, even children, were sent back to Europe (at the shipping company's expense), separating families, sometimes forever. Even the welcoming food was different, as Ishi also discovered. Learning to peel a banana became a rite of passage, and later a form of stereotyped humor in comic strips, cartoons, and movies as characters "slipped" on misplaced banana peels.

This mass migration between 1880 and 1920 differed from earlier population movements to North America, though the diversity of newcomers requires cautious generalizations. Before 1890, most immigrants came from northern and western European countries, particularly Britain, Ireland, Germany, and Scandinavia. "New" immigrants migrated mainly from eastern, central, and southern Europe, spoke little English, professed Roman Catholic, Jewish, or Eastern Orthodox religions, and came from peasant or rural backgrounds.

Eastern European Jews, who were not permitted to own land in the countries of their birth, came with commercial and craft experience; two-thirds were skilled workers, and literate. Like the Irish a half-century earlier, Jewish immigrants fled religious and political persecution in Russia, Poland, and Austria-Hungary, and had no interest in returning to their homelands. They migrated as families or communities: half the adult Jewish immigrants were women; one quarter of the total comprised children. By contrast, other immigrants, such as Italians, Greeks, Slavs, Mexicans, and Japanese, came as temporary or seasonal workers, using their wages to support family members at home or saving funds to acquire land or businesses in the old country. Most were single, young men. As many as half returned to their native countries; some crossed the ocean many times or departed forever during economic downturns.

Forming Ethnic Communities

At a time when many U.S. citizens were leaving rural areas for opportunities in the cities, European immigrants joined the flow toward urban-industrial life. By 1910, a majority of residents of the nation's twelve largest cities were immigrants or the children of immigrants. Two million newcomers settled in New York City (though comprising only 40 percent of the city's total population). In San Francisco, three-quarters of all residents spoke a primary language other than English. Immigrant settlement also reflected occupational and environmental preferences. Slavic immigrants from Poland, for example, migrated to mining and industrial areas of the Northeast and Midwest, accepting hard work (with relatively good wages) because they expected to return to their homelands. Similarly, the mostly male

Italian immigrants preferred outdoor manual labor as construction workers (building New York's subways and bridges), seaboard fishermen, or farm workers in the California grape fields. Greeks and French Canadians entered the textile mills of New England, while Jewish tailors and retailers labored in the garment industry of New York.

The lure of employment, together with the practical and emotional difficulties of migration, encouraged newcomers to settle in ethnic clusters to preserve their languages, foods, and cultural traditions. For Catholic immigrants, parish churches provided a religious and social community, which offered charitable services, a parochial school system, hospitals, and cemeteries. But the dominance of English-speaking Irish clergymen and nuns, longer residents in the country and better assimilated than the new immigrants, pressed Polish, Italian, and Mexican Catholics to abandon their languages and customs. While many immigrants embraced rapid assimilation (for example, changing their names to "American" versions), others resented clerical pressure to abandon folk customs and participated in church services less frequently.

Ethnic groups of all nationalities built cultural institutions to protect and perpetuate community life. A variety of mutual aid societies included the Chinese Six Companies, reflecting the six regions where most immigrants originated; the Japanese "ken" groups, which celebrated holidays and offered relief assistance; the Jewish "landesman" organizations, which held picnics, made loans, and paid for funerals; and Italian "societas," whose dues-paying members received emergency aid. Foreign-language newspapers abounded, carrying news of the old world as well as advice on assimilation, such as proper dress and manners. Ethnic banks offered immigrants the security of doing business in native languages, and San Francisco's A. P. Gianinni turned the neighborhood

Bank of Italy into the largest bank in the world (renamed Bank of America).

Mass entertainment also reinforced ethnic lines, supporting Italian marionette performances, German music halls, and a flourishing Yiddish theater on New York's Lower East Side. Such ethnic fare competed with the native-produced stage entertainment, known as vaudeville, which consisted of musical programs, risqué comedy skits, and melodrama. Vaudeville's ethnic stereotypes and blackface parodies, based on earlier minstrel shows, enabled white newcomers to identify with the dominant culture.

For most European immigrants, the primary dilemma remained the balance between cultural preservation and the acceptance of mainstream national values. Irish immigrants of the mid-19th century assumed leadership in many multiethnic communities. By 1900, two-thirds of Irish Americans were citizens, with high voting rates that enabled them to dominate municipal politics. In cities of the Northeast, Irish police, firefighters, and civil servants traded political support to local bosses in exchange for public-service jobs. As second generation Irish attained higher education levels by 1900, nearly half held white-collar jobs, while Irish American women represented 20 percent of northern public school teachers. With skills in English, Irish women turned from domestic service to office and clerical trades.

Although the immigrant generation generally preserved its religion, custom, and language, public schools and civic leaders encouraged the immigrants' children to become "American." Adopting the English language, dress, and tastes, second-generation immigrants proved more adept than their parents in adjusting to the new culture. The settlement house movement, inspired by Jane Addams and Florence Kelley (see Chapter 17), often appealed to immigrant children to question the authority of their less-assimilated parents in matters of food, sanitation, and health. Younger immigrants thus guided their parents through the intricacies of urban life. Yet assimilation required real losses. "The very clothes I wore and the very food I ate," remarked a character in a Yiddish novel, "had a fatal effect on my religious habits."

Pacific Migration and the Problems of Race

Immigrants to the Pacific shores, who were marked by differences of complexion and physiology, encountered more obstacles to assimilation, but fewer conflicts about their ethnic identity. In the western states, racism reinforced the objections of those who feared Asian competition for jobs and business. By 1900, government restrictions of Chinese immigration had steadily reduced the Chinese American population to 90,000, half of whom resided in California, and the number continued to fall to 71,000 in 1910 and 60,000 in 1920. One immigrant who was confined at Angel Island lamented,

> We want to come to the Flowery Flag Nation but are barred;
> The Golden Gate firmly locked, without even a crack to crawl through.

Most Chinese Americans were men, single or married, but living without their wives and children, who had been left behind and could not by U.S. law accompany their fathers and husbands to America. In 1900, fewer than 5,000 Chinese women lived in the country, and those who were married were usually much younger than their Chinese husbands because older men could better afford to support a family. California law prohibited intermarriage with whites, but Chinese in New York often married whites. The great San Francisco earthquake of 1906, which destroyed the city's municipal records, enabled some Chinese men to claim naturalized citizenship. With

this loophole, many sponsored the immigration of so-called paper sons and women. But female migration from China remained minimal.

Although many Chinese continued to work on farms, most found jobs in cities like San Francisco, New York, and Boston, where "Chinatown" neighborhoods featured restaurants and laundries. These were considered women's occupations in China, but they provided the overwhelmingly male communities with reliable income. In this lonely male culture, many transplanted Chinese indulged in gambling, opium, and prostitution; yet most continued to send money to their distant families. When China's Sun Yat-sen visited the United States to gain support for his revolutionary movement against the imperial dynasty in China, he received financial aid from Chinese Americans. After his successful rebellion of 1911, many U.S. Chinese took the step of cutting their long "pig-tails" as a statement of support. Within segregated Chinese American communities, a thriving literary culture stimulated various literary forms, which blended Chinese folk styles with a distinct U.S. experience. The "Songs of Gold Mountain," some of which were published in 1911, expressed the sadness of men without families, protested injustices of racial prejudice, and affirmed dreams of success and a happy "homebound journey."

The experience of Japanese immigrants, who were also unwelcome on U.S. shores, reflected the advantages of family migration and a strong home country. As contract laborers, Japanese men and women had sailed to the Hawaiian islands to work on sugar plantations, becoming inexpensive field hands with hopes of returning home with their savings. These workers did not have to worry about learning new names; employers gave them "bangos," metal identification disks with numbers to wear around their necks, and thereafter called them by impersonal numbers. After the annexation of Hawaii in 1898, U.S. law prohibited contract labor,

> **The immigrant Japanese summoned "picture brides" from Japan—women known to their prospective husbands only by photographs.**

and many Japanese headed for the mainland. By 1910, U.S. Japanese outnumbered the Chinese, finding work as migratory farm labor, building railroads, or in canneries. In west coast cities like Los Angeles, San Francisco, and Seattle, Japanese merchants built a small business economy, called "Little Tokyo," to serve their communities.

Japanese immigration coincided with a boom in California agriculture, as extensive water projects increased fruit and vegetable production. By 1910, Japanese grew 70 percent of California's strawberry crop. With economic prosperity, the immigrant generation, known as *Issei*, summoned "picture brides" from Japan—women known to their prospective husbands only by photographs—and proceeded to parent a second generation of *Nisei*. Ethnic solidarity and mutual-aid groups provided a network of support, which included credit, insurance, and farm cooperatives.

Asian immigration aroused vocal opposition. "The Caucasian and Asiatic races are unassimilable," said California's Asiatic Exclusion League in denouncing the Japanese population. Goaded by anti-immigrant civic leaders, the San Francisco school board ordered the segregation of Asian students in 1906. When the government of Japan protested the insulting treatment of Japanese nationals and the violation of treaty agreements, the segregation order caused an international scandal. As an emerging world power, Japan demanded respect. President Theodore Roosevelt had recently won the Nobel Peace Prize for mediating the settlement of the Russo-Japanese War in 1905 and wished to extend a friendly policy to Japan. But he, too, worried about weakening the Anglo-Saxon race—in 1903 he warned about "race suicide"—and he had no desire to encourage Japanese immigration. Summoning San Francisco leaders to Washington, the president persuaded school officials to limit segregation to Korean and Chinese students (only 93 Japanese children were involved) and then proceeded to negotiate with Japan to curtail additional immigration. In 1908, the oddly named "Gentleman's Agreement" effectively ended Japanese immigration.

To the horror of white nativists, however, the arrangement permitted the continued immigration of picture brides and family members. The California legislature responded by denying land ownership to "aliens ineligible to citizenship." Since congressional law blocked Asians from becoming naturalized citizens, the state measure undercut the Japanese American agricultural economy. To bypass the law, Japanese parents bought property in the name of their U.S.-born children; others had to accept temporary leases, which discouraged investment. Racist hostility to Japanese Americans emerged in Cecil B. DeMille's silent film classic, *The Cheat* (1915), which presents interracial sexuality as an excuse for lynching. The failure of Japanese protests to alter such stereotypes or to end discriminatory laws indicated the strength of white prejudice and the powerlessness of the immigrant community, a situation that would affect Japanese American life for decades.

Crossing the Southwestern Borders

Opposition to Asian newcomers stimulated the migration of an alternative labor force from Mexico. During the last decades of the 19th century, U.S. railroad expansion south of the border had brought the Mexican economy into an international marketplace. The consolidation of agriculture to produce cash crops in Mexico disrupted small property holders, creating a landless population looking for work. By 1900, about 100,000 Mexicans inhabited the United States, mostly in the mining areas of southern Arizona or the ranches of south Texas, where vague national boundaries permitted frequent cross-migrations. The development of irrigation projects in the western states and the ensuing growth of fruit and vegetable production created a need for farm labor at the same time that changes in the Mexican economy caused a surplus labor supply.

Mexican immigrants were primarily young adult men who maintained close contact with their homes, sending money and often returning for periods of residence. Organized as contract laborers in violation of both U.S. and Mexican laws, these migrants passed freely through border crossings around El Paso with little interference from government officials. Before 1908, U.S. immigration officers did not even keep statistics on Mexican immigration. Thousands headed north each year, with about one-third settling permanently in the United States. Few single women participated in this migration, but married women and daughters found work both in the fields and in domestic service as laundry employees, cooks, and housekeepers. During the first decade of the century, the Mexican American population doubled to about 220,000 and doubled again in the ten years following the disruptive Mexican Revolution of 1910.

Assimilation, Identity, and Race

The presence of so many unassimilated immigrants aroused concern among white Protestant groups about the preservation of a national identity. "We no longer receive accessions from the best peoples," remarked a middle-class observer, "but from the mediocre and the worst." The novelist Henry James returned to his native New York in 1905 after a twenty-year absence in Europe, visited Ellis Island and the immigrant neighborhoods of the Lower East Side, and concluded that the alien population was "at home, really more at home . . . than they had ever in their lives been before." But instead of affirming ethnic pluralism, native-born leaders (as well as many immigrants) stressed assimilation as a homogenizing alternative. When the Jewish dramatist Israel Zangwell presented his play *The Melting Pot* to a Washington audience in 1908, no less an Anglo-Saxon warrior than Theodore Roosevelt praised the story's theme of the immigrant who "becomes completely Americanized."

Optimism about assimilation conflicted with prevailing theories of racial difference. Just as Roosevelt assumed the superiority of the Anglo-Saxon "race," many social scientists claimed that there was a hierarchy of racial types. Immigrants were "beaten men from beaten races," asserted the president of the Massachusetts Institute of Technology, while Madison Grant's influential book *The Passing of the Great Race* celebrated the "white man par excellence." Although Irish assimilation had reduced anti-Catholic sentiment, the rhetoric of race reinvigorated anti-Jewish prejudice. One historian asked seriously "whether the member of a parasitic race" had any rights "in a community to which he could hardly be said to belong." These ideas inspired political movements to curtail immigration.

Maintaining the Color Line

The problem of assimilating foreign immigrants illuminated older, home-grown issues of race. "Cannot the nation that has absorbed 10 million foreigners," asked the African American scholar W. E. B. DuBois, "absorb 10 million Negro Americans into that same political life at less cost than their unjust and illegal exclusion will involve?" Yet the same racist biology that affirmed the inferiority of Jews and Japanese, Mexicans and Mediterraneans, depicted the African American, in the words of one Mississippi politician, as "a lazy, lying, lustful animal"—a veritable "beast." Believing that biological race, not culture, separated blacks from whites, racial supremacists insisted that assimilation was futile. According to that logic, education of blacks served only "to spoil a good field hand and make an insolent cook."

In the South, where 80 percent of African Americans lived in 1910, politicians excluded blacks from voting, established rigid race segregation, and required demeaning social practices, such as insisting that blacks use rear doors and only their first names. In North Carolina, the court system mandated the use of two Bibles to segregate the swearing in of witnesses. Challenges to this system provoked deadly retaliation. Southern blacks learned to move around whites with extreme caution.

Northern blacks, given more legal rights and less overt hostility, still faced racial discrimination in housing, education, and employment. In organized sports, major league baseball had no black players; black jockeys lost their premier status; and black heavyweight boxer Jack Johnson had to wait years for a title fight. Nevertheless, a small northern African American elite attained higher education, participated in social and political clubs, and remained committed to improving the status of black citizens.

The political differences between South and North on matters of race precipitated a major split within the African American leadership. Booker T. Washington, respected by whites as the spokesman of the majority of blacks, stressed the importance of avoiding direct challenges to white power. This strategy won approval among northern philan-

thropists, who showered Washington's favored schools with funds, provided that blacks accepted their permanent inferiority. With such assumptions, President Roosevelt shocked the nation by inviting the black educator to dinner at the White House in 1901. Although respectable white leaders lambasted the president for this audacious step, Washington emerged as an important power broker for the black community, exerting great influence over government patronage.

The Harvard-educated DuBois took little satisfaction in Washington's ascent. "The problem of the twentieth century," he declared in his passionate manifesto *The Souls of Black Folk* (1903), "is the problem of the color line." Rejecting the compromises that demanded blacks accept inferior manual training and second-class citizenship, DuBois focused on "the talented tenth"—an African American leadership—that merited full equality. Breaking openly with Washington in 1905, DuBois and other northern blacks, such as the Boston newspaper publisher Monroe Trotter, called a meeting near Niagara Falls, on the Canadian side of the border because the delegates could not obtain hotel accommodations in Buffalo, New York. The Niagara group proceeded to issue a Declaration of Principles to disavow the impression that "the Negro American assents to inferiority."

Such protests scarcely affected rural blacks, who formed Washington's constituency, or touched white leaders who, at best, looked paternally at expressions of African American discontent. In 1906, President Roosevelt spoke publicly against lynching, but endorsed southern claims that black rapists typically provoked such violence. When black troops stationed at Brownsville, Texas, responded to racial harassment by shooting up the town in 1906, the president ordered blanket dishonorable discharges for the entire battalion, including six Medal of Honor winners, without addressing their guilt or innocence. That year, prominent southern politicians, such as the ex-Populist Tom Watson, played on anti-black feelings to win election, and 10,000 young whites in Atlanta, Georgia, went on a rampage, leaving two dozen African Americans dead in the streets. In 1908, the terror moved north into Springfield, Illinois, hometown of the martyred Abraham Lincoln, where allegations of a white woman's rape provoked mob violence that resulted in eight murders, beatings, and extensive property damage. "You shoot Negroes in Illinois, when they come into competition with your labor," the southern senator Ben Tillman told a northern audience, "as we shoot them in South Carolina, when they come in competition with us in matters of elections. You do not love them any better than we do."

Such outrages prompted northern black leaders and sympathetic whites to form a new organization, the National Association for the Advancement of Colored People (NAACP), in 1910. Aiming at middle-class blacks, assimilated Jews, and liberals of all stripes, the NAACP and its magazine, *The Crisis,* emerged as the dominant civil rights voice for the next half-century.

Social Change and the Progressive Spirit

Concern about the nation's racial identity reflected deeper anxieties about the immense changes occurring in urbanized industrial society. Not only did immigration produce a multicultural population, but the sheer density of the cities forced people in all classes to confront problems of poverty. Indeed, one of the central themes of utopian fiction at the turn of the century involved the regulation of overcrowded living conditions. During the 1890s, the settlement-house move-ment and appeals for moral reform drew on older Christian traditions of the social gospel and commitments to voluntary action (see Chapter 17). Activists like Jane Addams saw education and temperance as a way of uplifting the urban poor. Yet individual involvement could hardly solve the problems of industrial society.

By the early 20th century, a new breed of "progressive" reformers became concerned not only about isolated problems of poverty and crime but also with impersonal economic and social issues that afflicted masses of people. The progressives increasingly emphasized the importance of government action to improve society. Such efforts began in local communities and inspired political crusades for municipal reform. When social problems, such as contaminated food or narcotic abuse, involved multiple communities, reformers demanded state and national legislation. In calling for such reforms, progressives believed they were acting on behalf of the public good and a community of interests, but their efforts often overlooked the class and cultural bias of their proposed remedies. Emphasizing progressive values of efficiency, order, and social control, middle class reformers gained important legislation that curtailed political abuses and rationalized the political process. They showed less interest about (indeed, they often deplored) less rational issues of modern society involving sexuality, music, art, and the celebration of the "wild." Nevertheless, the spirit of progressivism was distinctive: it was optimistic and it demanded action.

Reforming the Cities

As the nation's urban population tripled in size between 1890 and 1920, congestion aggravated problems of housing, sanitation, and health. Diseases like tuberculosis and typhoid thrived in cities like New York, which pumped 500 million gallons of raw sewage into surrounding rivers every day, or in Chicago, where pollutants contaminated Lake Michigan. In 1900, whites had a life expectancy at birth of 48 years, nonwhites only 33 years. In the spirit of progressivism, New York City reformers began the century with a new tenement house law, requiring toilets and windows in every apartment, and by 1916 had enacted the first major zoning laws that limited the height and placement of tall buildings. Meanwhile, settlement-house workers instituted programs to instruct immigrants about household sanitation. In St. Louis, local women's groups led the fight for clean air, persuading city officials to impose penalties for smoke pollution, and organized a boycott of meat to protest adulterated food.

Such campaigns brought reformers into contact with city officials and quickly raised concern about political corruption. By the turn of the century, most municipal governments ran like political machines. In exchange for votes on election day, urban bosses provided constituents with important favors, such as patronage jobs in police and fire departments, food baskets and coal during times of unemployment, and legal assistance when small businesses or street peddlers operated without licenses. Meanwhile, the urban machines "taxed" companies that did business with the city—a form of "honest graft," in the words of one big-city boss—and awarded franchises and contracts for sewers, streetcars, and construction projects to favored companies. Such practices permitted utility companies to set high prices or provide shoddy services.

"The spirit of graft and lawlessness is the American spirit," warned journalist Lincoln Steffens in a popular exposé, The Shame of the Cities, first published in 1904. As reformers addressed problems of social services, crusading writers captured public attention by documenting the prevalence of political ills. In respectable magazines like McClure's and Collier's, journalists depicted networks of urban graft, prostitution, child labor, insurance fraud, and corporate greed. One series of articles, "The Treason of the Senate," explained how business interests manipulated state legislatures in the selection of U.S. senators. President Roosevelt denounced this style of journalism as "muckraking," claiming that the writers were more interested in exposing problems than in offering solutions. Yet the muckrakers considered the presidential insult a badge of honor. Upton Sinclair's fictional account of Chicago's meatpacking industry, The Jungle (1906), aroused public demands for government regulation of food and drug products. Protesting the impurity of canned goods and other meats, the press parodied a familiar rhyme:

> Mary had a little lamb,
> And when she saw it sicken,
> She shipped it off to Packingtown,
> And now it's labeled chicken.

Such outcries prompted, with Roosevelt's blessings, the first responsive national legislation in the Pure Food and Drug Act of 1906.

Complaints about water pollution, trolley car safety, and garbage collection brought reformers into the political arena. In growing cities such as Detroit, Cleveland, and St. Louis, middle-class reformers organized insurgent movements to change government leadership. Toledo's mayor Sam "Golden Rule" Jones, for example, introduced municipal ownership of utilities, set minimum wages for city employees, and launched a program of school and park construction. By 1915, two-thirds of the nation's municipal governments owned and regulated local water supplies. Urban reformers also won changes in government operations that replaced patronage positions with professional experts, such as public health officials, sanitary engineers, and city planners.

Seeking more efficient management of public affairs, city reformers innovated in government structures. In 1900, disastrous floods in Galveston, Texas, forced unprepared politicians to adopt a "commission" system of city government, similar to a corporation structure, whereby elected city commissioners rather than local aldermen administered municipal departments. By centralizing municipal operations, the Galveston plan broke with patronage politics, brought experts into administration, and improved public services. Hundreds of cities soon instituted similar systems. Urban reformers moved ballot boxes from saloons to public libraries and schools, created nonpartisan offices, and established residency requirements for voting.

Such movements invited the participation of women activists, who saw their quest for suffrage rights linked to government reform. In 1909, for example, suffragists acted as poll watchers in New York's mayoral election, despite warnings from male officials that they would be corrupted by the experience of visiting saloons. "We have lifted the veil, we have entered the holy of holies," boasted Harriot Stanton Blatch, daughter of the pioneering women's rights advocate Elizabeth Cady Stanton. Emboldened by such activity, suffragists formed coalitions between working women and wealthy female benefactors, organized public parades to protest disenfranchisement, and aggressively lobbied state legislatures for the vote.

Challenging the power of political bosses to select party candidates for public office, progressives in nearly every state introduced the direct primary to enable voters to choose electoral candidates. The cry for popular government increased pressure for the direct election of U.S. senators. This proposal was barely heard when suggested by the Populists in 1890, but now it inspired passage and ratification of the Seventeenth Amendment to the Constitution in 1913.

Amendment XVII (1913)

The Senate of the United States shall be composed of two Senators from each state, elected by the people thereof, for six years; and each Senator shall have one vote. The electors in each state shall have the qualifications requisite for electors of the most numerous branch of the state legislatures.

When vacancies happen in the representation of any state in the Senate, the executive authority of such state shall issue writs of election to fill such vacancies: Provided, that the legislature of any state may empower the executive thereof to make temporary appointments until the people fill the vacancies by election as the legislature may direct.

This amendment shall not be so construed as to affect the election or term of any Senator chosen before it becomes valid as part of the Constitution.

To enhance the responsiveness of government, progressives introduced other reforms that permitted voters to enact legislation. Implemented first in Oregon, the *initiative* enabled citizens to propose laws by petition and have them placed on statewide ballots for voter approval. Another innovation, the *referendum*, allowed the public to repeal legislation approved by elected representatives. With the right of *recall*, voters also obtained the power to remove elected representatives from office. These efforts at "direct democracy" assured power to numerical majorities, but gave advantages to well-financed groups that could organize the electorate.

While some progressive reformers, like Harriot Blatch and Leonora O'Reilly, consciously built political alliances across class lines, most progressives simply accepted the values and interests of their own middle-class groups. Thus their emphasis on creating efficient government sometimes came at the cost of weakening the power of immigrant and worker communities. The introduction of citywide elections, aimed at eliminating neighborhood bosses, depersonalized the political process and brought a sharp decline in voter participation. Similarly, the use of civil service examinations and the creation of government bureaucracies appealed to educated administrators, but simultaneously undermined informal loyalties to ethnic, family, and neighborhood groups.

Progressivism as Social Control

In assuming the superiority of middle-class values, progressive reformers believed that education could bridge the differences between economic classes and that public schools could act as instruments of cultural assimilation. Compulsory attendance laws brought higher enrollments in primary and secondary schools, tripling the percentage of high school graduates between 1900 and 1920. Urban school systems introduced kindergartens for younger children, giving educators, as one writer stated, "the earliest opportunity" to transform youngsters into "good American citizens." John Dewey, the era's most influential education theorist, envisioned public schools as institutions of socialization, teaching common democratic values. "The intermingling in the school of youth of different races, differing religions, and unlike customs," he wrote, "creates for all a new and broader environment" in which to construct a cooperative society.

Such idealism provided opportunities for women reformers to influence social policy. Progressive reformers like Florence Kelley assumed that women had special expertise on matters related to children. Together with other settlement house workers, like Lillian Wald, Kelley lobbied strenuously for the cre-

Progressive reformer Florence Kelley, who said "The noblest duty of the Republic is so cherishing all its children that they . . . may become self-governing citizens."

ation of a Children's Bureau in the newly created Department of Commerce and Labor. When approved by Congress in 1912, it became the first federal agency headed by a woman, Julia Lathrop. Women progressives pressed business to reduce child employment and lobbied for child labor laws, though federal courts ruled most of those restrictions unconstitutional. They also advocated a separate juvenile judicial system to give youthful delinquents alternatives to adult prisons.

To improve the quality of urban life, progressives promoted the construction of open spaces for leisure. Although middle-class neighborhoods included parks, poorer ethnic communities lacked such amenities. A turn-of-the-century survey of

"I can't go to the playgrounds now," complained one 11-year-old. "They get on my nerves with so many men and women around telling you what to do."

New York's Lower East Side found that most kids had never visited the spacious, but remote, Central Park. The Playground Association of America, founded by community and business leaders in 1906, lobbied for small parks, field houses, swimming pools, and athletic fields. By 1917, the number of cities with supervised recreational programs exceeded 500. Youngsters did not always welcome this "progress." "I can't go to the playgrounds now," complained one 11-year-old. "They get on my nerves with so many men and women around telling you what to do."

Adults, too, remained vulnerable to appeals for disciplined social behavior. Although working-class immigrants had customarily enjoyed public holidays as occasions for rowdy street gatherings and drunken fun, progressives instituted programs to promote "safe and sane" observation of civic festivities. Borrowing a tactic from the corporate world, Worcester, Massachusetts, officials issued sobriety warnings in ten languages, resulting in a calm celebration of the Fourth of July and the police chief's boast "It pays to advertise!" Sunday "blue" laws, which prohibited frivolous activity on the Sabbath, continued to limit leisure activities, particularly for people who worked six days a week. (Jewish businesses, closed for religious observance on Saturdays, suffered by enforcement of Sunday laws.) Professional baseball, featuring the first World Series in 1903, was banned on Sundays in many cities.

The progressive campaign to enforce public morality reinvigorated the movement to prohibit narcotics and alcohol. At the turn of the century, many over-the-counter patent medicines and soft drinks contained morphine, cocaine, and opium. (Coca-Cola had small amounts of cocaine until 1903.) As healthcare professionals adopted standard pharmaceutical practices within the American Medical Association, physicians joined social reformers in curbing access to addictive drugs. By 1914, the Harrison Narcotics Act limited drug use to medical purposes and required a prescription signed by a licensed physician.

Alcohol abuse remained a larger problem. As consumption increased 25 percent per capita in the decade after 1900, religious crusaders joined medical professionals, industrial employers, and progressive reformers in urging prohibition. The movement was particularly strong in the rural southern and western states, but prohibitionists also targeted the city saloon, patronized by working-class immigrants. In the South, white leaders stressed prohibition as a way of controlling black men. By 1907, two-thirds of southern counties voted to ban liquor sales; within the next two years, six states adopted prohibition. Lobbied heavily by the Anti-Saloon League, Congress permitted "dry" states to block the transportation of alcohol across state lines in 1913, a measure that foretold increasing restrictions in the future.

Other reformers saw danger lurking in new forms of mass entertainment. In 1905, the nation's first movie theater opened in Pittsburgh; by 1910, weekly movie attendance reached 26 million, and ten years later attendance had doubled. The appearance of motion pictures ("the movies," in popular slang) drew instant attention, not from the respectable middle classes, who preferred concerts and the theater, but from immigrant workers in the cities. "For a mere nickel," said one writer, explaining the trend, "the wasted man, whose life hereto has been toil and sleep, is kindled with wonder." Many early silent films addressed the contrast of wealth in the cities. In the movies, immigrant servant girls fell in love with affluent businessmen or envied the material possessions of their female employers. But most plot lines suggested that the classes were best kept separate and that fantasies of easy wealth should not be confused with social realities.

Although an older generation of foreign-born workers continued to patronize saloons, younger generations flocked to storefront theaters that offered continuous showings of short films. Often unable to understand English, foreigners had no trouble following the plots of silent films, relying on school-age children to translate the titles aloud. (The first movie to use intertitles to create a narrative flow was Edwin S. Porter's *Uncle Tom's Cabin,* 1902–1903). The immigrant community also produced the first movie entrepreneurs, many of them with experience in vaudeville or retail trades, who later founded the first studios in Hollywood, where real estate was cheaper and the weather suited to outdoor filming.

Crowded, noisy, suffused with the smells of foreign foods, the five-cent theaters, called "nickelodeons," awakened progressive concerns about moral depravity. "The very darkness of the room," warned Jane Addams, "is an added attraction to many young people, for whom the space is filled with the glamour of love making." Purity crusaders also objected to the images that flashed on the silver screen. Even primitive silent movies, such as a 60-second film, *The Kiss,* of 1896, appealed to forbidden interests. Porter's *The Great Train Robbery* (1905), the first full narrative story, startled audiences with shifts of locale and perspective, including a sudden murder. In 1912, New York suffragists collaborated with commercial filmmakers to produce *The Suffragette and the Man* and *What 8,000,000 Women Want,* romantic movies that advocated women's rights. Far more popular was *Traffic in Souls* (1913) which dealt with prostitution and attracted 30,000 viewers during its first week.

Middle-class critics, concerned about maintaining moral standards and good taste, recoiled from filmed images of sex and violence, and demanded official censorship. Other community leaders objected to movies with radical subjects, such as labor strikes. Such groups encouraged municipal officials to close offending movie theaters or ordered compulsory cutting of offensive scenes. (Among the casualties were the killing of Julius Caesar in the filmed Shakespeare play and images of hell in Faust.) To avoid harassment, the movie industry created its own censorship board, the first of many efforts to restrict movies to middle-class tastes.

Defining the New Woman

Insistence on moral censorship and social control reflected the increasing insecurities of urban middle-class families. Between 1880 and 1900, the white urban middle-class birth rate continued to fall from 4.24 children per family to 3.56 children (while rural and immigrant families remained larger). With less time needed for their children, middle-class women realized greater opportunities to enter the public sphere, not just as household consumers but as workers and social activists. At the same time, the nation experienced a rising divorce rate, which nearly doubled in the two decades after 1900. "Marriage is no longer the only vocation open to [a woman]," explained one college professor about the trend. "If marriage is a failure, she does not face the alternative of endurance or starvation." Yet, while married women refused to suffer in silence, marriage rates continued to rise.

For educated women, housewifery appeared as something like a profession. "Is it not pitiful, this army of incompetent wives?" commented an expert in the new field of home economics. As more middle-class women attended colleges, the art of housekeeping assumed an aura of "domestic science"; by 1916, 18,000 women had enrolled in home-economics programs at nearly 200 colleges. On coeducational campuses, this curriculum emerged as a scientific field for women, segregated by sex from the male sciences, but offering female educators a secure (if second-class) niche in faculty positions.

Educated experts, all of them women, produced a vast library of cookbooks, housekeeping guides, and etiquette manuals. Home-economics professionals viewed recipes as chemical formulas, insisted on accurate measurement with standard-sized cups and spoons, and demanded careful economy of household schedules, "just as a train does . . . like a clock." Viewing food purely as nutrition rather than flavor, one writer maintained in 1901 that "the test of good food is to have no reminder of it after eating."

Educated women revitalized the campaign to gain the vote and led a successful push for suffrage in the three Pacific states between 1910 and 1912. Failures in the Midwest slowed the movement, though membership in the National American Woman Suffrage Association (NAWSA) passed 75,000 after 1910. Influenced by the radical English suffrage movement, social worker Alice Paul advocated a national constitutional amendment and persuaded cautious suffrage leaders to stage a protest parade in Washington, D.C., in 1913, the day before the inauguration of president-elect Woodrow Wilson. The disruptive affair divided the suffrage movement into factions, magnifying the frustrations of failure.

Regulating Sexuality

"It's sex o'clock in America," announced a magazine in 1913, referring to "the chief topic of polite conversation." As city nightclubs and cabarets attracted a middle-class clientele, dancing, dating, and social mixing suggested a loosening of sexual propriety. "If the cabaret could talk," remarked *Variety,* "or the waiters tell all they know, the state would have to open a few extra courts to keep up with the rush for divorces." Young unmarried working women, who continued to enter the labor force in growing numbers, had broken with traditional courtship rules, allowing men to "treat" them to social events. Such relaxed attitudes disturbed progressive reformers. "The young men of the big cities today," observed one social worker in 1910, "are not gallantly paying the way of these girls for nothing." Yet surveys of sexual behavior showed that a high proportion of women remained virgins at marriage.

Men of all classes practiced less restraint. In the South, white men could initiate sexual activity around the age of 16 with a black woman, often through rape and sexual exploitation. Among city dwellers, men practiced a double standard of virtue by visiting prostitutes. To progressive reformers, the ease of sexual activity highlighted the hazards of urban life. Local vice commissions and federal investigators claimed to have discovered an international criminal syndicate that was importing prostitutes—a white slave trade—along with "the most bestial refinements of depravity."

Progressive reformers targeted the risks of spreading venereal diseases to innocent wives and customers. Yet, when the *Ladies Home Journal* ran an article on such diseases, 75,000 readers cancelled their subscriptions. Organized "social hygiene" experts joined religious crusaders in attacking prostitution and persuaded the government to ratify an international treaty barring prostitutes from entering the country. By 1910, prostitution had become the subject of overheated news stories, magazine articles, and movies, stimulating the appointment of investigating committees and the accumulation of expert testimony. The result was passage of the Mann Act of 1910, which prohibited the transportation of a woman across state lines for immoral purposes.

Few "slaves" were ever apprehended, but the law encouraged the Justice Department's newly formed Bureau of Investigation (later named the Federal Bureau of Investigation) to open field

Jack Johnson, the prizefighter, raised racist fears by appearing openly with the white woman with whom he was sharing his life.

offices throughout the country. The most famous Mann Act case of the era involved boxer Jack Johnson, the first African American heavyweight champion, whose public liaisons with white women offended authorities. Indicted under the law in 1913, Johnson left the country and held his championship fights abroad. He eventually served a one-year prison sentence. Meanwhile, as part of the anti-vice crusade, southern politicians persuaded Congress to prohibit the importation and interstate transportation of any films about prizefighting, lest viewers see a black man throttling a white. "No man descended from the old Saxon race," stated one representative, "can look upon that kind of [interracial] contest without abhorrence and disgust."

While progressive reformers attempted to control extramarital sexuality—adultery remained the prime grounds for divorce—regulation of reproduction aroused bitter divisions. At a time when the male medical profession established control of childbirth for middle-class women in antiseptic hospitals, working-class women continued to use midwives to deliver their children and to provide illegal abortions. The declining middle-class birth rate provided abundant evidence that educated women were practicing voluntary birth control. Sexual pleasure no longer appeared linked to reproduction.

Purity crusaders such as Anthony Comstock, who served as secretary for the private Society for the Suppression of Vice, viewed efforts to limit reproduction as immoral and lobbied for enforcement of anti–birth control laws. When reformer Margaret Sanger published a pamphlet titled *Family Limitation,* the federal government charged her with obscenity. Sanger fled the country in 1914 to avoid trial, but the anarchist Emma Goldman carried the birth control crusade on a national speaking tour. Sanger's subsequent opening of a birth control clinic in Brooklyn brought arrest, conviction, and a jail sentence. "A mutual and satisfied sexual act is of great benefit to the average woman," the unrepentant Sanger affirmed. "This is one of the great functions of contraceptives."

Taming the Wild

While sexual liberation alarmed Christian moralists, popular enthusiasm for modern music, dance, and art brought warnings of anarchy. Pianist Scott Joplin's ragtime music, with African-derived syncopated rhythms, impelled listeners to tap their feet and dance. Even the names of ragtime dances—Bullfrog Hop, Monkey Grind, Bunny Hug—implied sexually charged animalism. "The chief law of ragtime," responded one critic, "is to be lawless." The fad soon spread from smoky dance halls onto the nation's main streets. "Everything is being syncopated," reported one newspaper, "even conversation and political speeches."

The language of modern poetry also broke from conventional meters and rhymes, as writers like Ezra Pound, Edna St. Vincent Millay, and Amy Lowell experimented with new idioms, fresh rhythms, and common speech. Similarly, the visual arts now expressed a modern perspective. A new movement of realist painters, including John Sloan and George Bellows, whom critics denounced as the "Ashcan School," presented unvarnished images of industrial society. Most shocking was the exhibition of abstract paintings from Europe at New York City's Armory Show in 1913. Canvases by Pablo Picasso, Henri Matisse, and Marcel Duchamp forced spectators to confront the inherent irrationality of human perspective and the multiple meanings of social reality.

These disruptive signs of modernism coincided with a popular fascination at the tenuous balance between civilized order and natural wildness. Jack London's novel *The Call of the Wild* (1903) depicted Buck, a family dog transformed by the Alaskan Klondike into a member of a wolf pack, while Edgar Rice Burroughs's popular *Tarzan of the Apes* (1914) told of humans raised by animals. The fear of losing contact with wildlife and wilderness areas also inspired a flourishing back-to-nature movement among urban sophisticates. Urban department stores introduced pet departments so that middle-class customers could remain close to animals. Meanwhile, progressive reformers organized adult-supervised youth groups like the Boy Scouts and Camp Fire Girls, and President Roosevelt won popular acclaim for not shooting a cub bear on a hunting expedition (spawning a new industry for "teddy" bears). Kodak cameras promptly advertised wilderness treks for photography "hunters."

Roosevelt won popular acclaim for *not* shooting a cub bear on a hunting expedition.

This respect for wild nature encouraged Roosevelt to dedicate five national parks, sixteen national monuments, and fifty wildlife refuges as areas reserved from economic enterprise, setting precedents for the creation of the National Park Service in 1916.

Roosevelt's desire to protect the wild challenged business interests that advocated unlimited development of natural resources. Yet the progressive president insisted that conservation did not conflict with planned use of water, timber, and mineral resources to protect those treasures for future generations. Gifford Pinchot, head of the Forestry Department, shared the progressive belief in rational, efficient, and managed development. Mining and lumber companies complained about government interference, forcing Roosevelt to fight with Congress to reserve public lands. But true "preservationists," led by John Muir, founder of the Sierra Club, protested against *any* alteration of the natural world. Lamenting "ravaging commercialism" and "a perfect contempt for Nature," Muir led a futile fight to prevent the construction of the Hetch Hetchy reservoir to provide water for San Francisco. "Substituting a lake for the present swampy floor of the valley," replied Pinchot in the spirit of progressivism, "is altogether unimportant."

Failure to find a middle ground between the wild and the civilized undermined efforts either to protect or to assimilate the Native Americans who had survived wars of extermination and programs of forced education. Convinced by racial theorists that a Native American would never be more than "an adult child," Roosevelt's Commissioner of Indian Affairs declared that "nothing is gained by trying to undo nature's work." Rejecting the idea of "civilizing" Native peoples, the federal government shrank their curriculum to vocational training and acted as an employment agency for seasonal farm labor, which compensated workers at the rate of 89 cents per day. By such wage standards, Ishi did well, earning room and board as the anthropology museum janitor until he died of tuberculosis in 1916.

Toward a Progressive Society

Instead of lamenting the destruction of Native American societies or the difficulties of the immigrants' assimilation, most progressives celebrated the achievements of industrial civilization. To be sure, the proliferation of reform movements indicated widespread awareness of serious social problems. But even when their goals could not be achieved, progressives found solace in the very spirit of reformism, the willingness of reformers to try to make the world better. Meanwhile, national leaders in business and government focused on material dreams of economic development and, as we will see in the next chapter, fought political wars about how to regulate the vast, expanding corporate marketplace.

INFOTRAC® COLLEGE EDITION EXERCISES

For additional reading go to InfoTrac College Edition, your online research library at *http://web1.infotrac-college.com.*

Subject search: Ellis Island
Subject search: Angel Island
Subject search: nineteenth-century immigration
Subject search: Chinese Exclusion Act
Keyword search: Muckrakers
Keyword search: Lincoln Steffens
Keyword search: Upton Sinclair
Keyword search: Riis
Keyword search: Florence Kelley
Keyword search: Theodore Roosevelt

ADDITIONAL READING

Steven J. Diner, *A Very Different Age: Americans of the Progressive Era* (1998). A succinct social history, stressing the diverse responses to rapid change; see also John Whiteclay Chambers II, *The Tyranny of Change: America in the Progressive Era, 1900–1917* (1980).

Robert F. Heizer and Theodora Kroeber, eds., *Ishi, the Last Yahi: A Documentary History* (1979). These original documents tell the story of Ishi and his reception by anthropologists.

The Immigrant Experience

Alan M. Kraut, *The Huddled Masses: The Immigrant in American Society, 1880–1921* (1982). An overview of the immigrant experience, this study emphasizes the diversity among and within ethnic groups.

Pacific Immigration and the Problems of Race

Ronald Takaki, *Strangers from a Different Shore: A History of Asian Americans* (1989). A detailed history of Pacific immigration and the creation of ethnic communities, this work may be supplemented with the poetry in Marlon K. Hom's edition of *Songs of Gold Mountain* (1993).

Crossing the Southwestern Borders

George J. Sanchez, *Becoming Mexican American: Ethnicity, Culture, and Identity in Chicano Los Angeles, 1900–1945* (1993). This study explores Mexican migration and the formation of a distinct community and identity.

Maintaining the Color Line

David Levering Lewis, *W.E.B. DuBois: Biography of a Race, 1868–1919* (1993). This prize-winning biography offers an excellent analysis of African Americans in the progressive era.

Social Change and the Progressive Spirit

David Thelen, *Paths of Resistance: Tradition and Dignity in Industrializing Missouri* (1986). Focusing on a single state, the author explores public responses to economic development, linking such diverse topics as bank robbers and the music of ragtime.

Progressivism as Social Control

Steven A. Riess, *Sport in Industrial America: 1850–1920* (1995). This social-cultural history links the rise of mass sports to changes in urban life.

Roy Rosenzweig, *Eight Hours for What We Will: Workers and Leisure in an Industrial City, 1870–1920* (1983). Using Worcester, Massachusetts, the author explores issues involving saloons, playgrounds, and movies.

Stephen J. Ross, *Working-Class Hollywood: Silent Film and the Shaping of Class in America* (1998). A study of the depiction of labor in the movies, the book carries the story through the 1920s; see also Robert Sklar, *Movie-Made America: A Cultural History of American Movies* (1975).

Robert W. Snyder, *The Voice of the City: Vaudeville and Popular Culture in New York* (1989). This history of stage entertainment addresses questions of class and culture in the urban environment.

Defining the New Woman

Ellen Carol DuBois, *Harriot Stanton Blatch and the Winning of Woman Suffrage* (1997). This lively biography places women's political activities in the context of progressive reformism.

Robyn Muncy, *Creating a Female Dominion in American Reform: 1890–1935* (1991). This volume examines the role of professional women in shaping progressive social reforms.

Laura Shapiro, *Perfection Salad: Women and Cooking at the Turn of the Century* (1986). This book analyzes the home economics movement and changing views toward food and health.

Regulating Sexuality

John D'Emilio and Estelle B. Freedman, *Intimate Matters: A History of Sexuality in America* (1988). The chapters on the progressive era offer a lucid analysis of changing sexual attitudes and behavior.

Linda Gordon, *Woman's Body, Woman's Right: A Social History of Birth Control in America* (1976). A study of U.S. fertility patterns; several chapters explore the debate about birth control in the progressive era.

19

The Corporate Economy and Progressive Politics, 1901–1916

CHRONOLOGY

1901	Theodore Roosevelt succeeds President William McKinley
	United States Steel Company becomes billion-dollar corporation
	Eugene V. Debs launches Socialist Party of America
1903	Congress establishes Department of Commerce and Labor
	U.S. gains rights to build Panama Canal
1904	Supreme Court rules against Northern Securities monopoly
1905	Radicals organize Industrial Workers of the World
1908	Harvard University opens School of Business
1909	William Howard Taft elected president
	Congress passes Payne-Aldrich tariff
1910	Henry Ford opens Highland Park factory
1911	Triangle fire exposes workplace safety problems
	Supreme Court pronounces anti-trust "rule of reason"
1912	Woodrow Wilson defeats Taft, Roosevelt, and Debs for presidency
1913	Congress passes Underwood tariff and Federal Reserve Act
	States ratify 16th and 17th Amendments
1914	World War I begins in Europe
	Congress establishes Federal Trade Commission
	Ford introduces $5 day
1915	D.W. Griffith screens *The Birth of a Nation*
1916	Wilson reelected president

In order to teach immigrant workers the rules of industrial society, the International Harvester Company introduced an "English lesson" in 1912:

> I hear the whistle. I must hurry.
> I hear the five minute whistle.
> It is time to go into the shop.
>
> * * *
>
> I change my clothes and get ready to work.
> The starting whistle blows.
> I eat my lunch.
> It is forbidden to eat until then.
> The whistle blows at five minutes of starting time.
> I get ready to go to work.
> I work until the whistle blows to quit.
> I leave my place nice and clean.
> I put all my clothes in the locker.
> I must go home.

http://history.wadsworth.com

Learning to live one's life to the tune of whistles, bells, and time clocks—industrial discipline—was new not only to foreign immigrants but also to native-born producers, merchants, managers, and workers who were accustomed to more flexible routines. "The life of America is not the life it was . . . ten years ago," said Governor Woodrow Wilson of New Jersey in 1911. "We have changed our economic conditions from top to bottom, and . . . also the organization of our life." The transformation of the national economy—the consolidation of corporations and the reorganization of working conditions—introduced a range of economic issues that demanded public attention. In many industries, small businesses found themselves in competition with giant firms that could afford to cut prices, even below cost, to eliminate their rivals; then, with competition gone, they could exert monopolistic power in the marketplace. Changes in production, distribution, and marketing also created a broad class of consumers concerned about the prices, quality, and safety of basic household goods. Meanwhile, new workplace conditions forced employees to deal with an impersonal management system concerned about maximum efficiency. Feeling aggrieved by new management practices, workers organized labor unions and participated in strikes that often led to violence.

These changes aroused public interest in government regulation of the economy. During the first decades of the century, progressive reformers increasingly turned to the national level of government to demand congressional laws and presidential intervention to resolve business and labor disputes. Such appeals to Washington reflected not only the extensiveness of economic, social, and political problems but also a growing belief that the national government could and should intervene to resolve them. Indeed, the rise of progressivism stimulated a broader national outlook and reinforced the sense of national identity that could embrace, potentially at least, citizens in all social classes.

After 1901, presidents Theodore Roosevelt, William Howard Taft, and Woodrow Wilson addressed the problems of industrial society with specific political proposals. These ranged from federal rules against corporate consolidation (so-called "trust busting") to a hands-off (laissez-faire) approach that would permit business to do what it wanted. As discussed in the previous chapter, Congress passed national legislation to ensure quality standards of food and drugs and sought to control interstate commerce of alcohol and narcotics. By the end of Wilson's first term in 1916, a consensus about economic controls had inspired additional legislation governing the nation's banks and corporations. Such measures could not alleviate more general concerns about the social consequences of a corporate-dominated economy. "The standardized succeed," observed a leading economist. "The unstandardized leave town or drop into unmarked graves."

Inaugurating an Era of Economic Growth

One night in 1901, a manager of Andrew Carnegie's steel mills shook hands with banker J. P. Morgan, clinching a deal that led to the formation of the United States Steel Company, the country's first billion dollar business. The value of that single company was equivalent to 7 percent of the country's gross national product, or $400 billion in today's money. Such transactions underlined a growing concentration of corporate wealth. In the wave of business mergers that followed the depression of the 1890s (see Chapter 17), over 3,000 manufacturing companies had consolidated into a few hundred corporations (General Electric, U.S. Rubber, American Can Company, for example) that dominated entire industries. Economies of scale enabled big businesses to lower the costs of producing and marketing their goods. Businessmen also combined separate companies into conglomerates to centralize management and to make capital investment more efficient. Their goal was to maximize profits and to stabilize corporate earnings. Recognizing that consumer demand varied over time, investors sought to ensure predictable incomes at the highest possible levels by controlling the portion of the market that assured full and steady sales.

Solidifying the Corporate Economy

The emergence of large, coordinated corporations heralded a dramatic spurt in economic growth. Investments in manufacturing jumped from $8 billion in 1899 to nearly $21 billion fifteen years later, while the number of manufacturing workers increased to over 9 million. As the gross national product rose about 6 percent per year, national income surged over 30 percent. Major growth industries included steel, oil, and electricity. With manufacturing exports increasing rapidly, businesses built plants overseas, forming the first multinational manufacturing corporations.

Behind this economic expansion lay powerful banking institutions, led by Morgan and Rockefeller interests. In 1913, a congressional investigating committee reported that four financial groups dominated over 100 railroads, banks, insurance companies, and utilities, valued at over $22 billion. Some progressives warned that the concentration of banking wealth constituted a dangerous monopolistic "money trust." Although the nation's financial institutions remained competitive, fear of centralized banking led to demands for government oversight of the financial system. Critics noted that 70 individuals held fortunes worth at least $35 million or over 6 percent of the nation's wealth.

Business leaders made no apologies for their success. "The chief work of civilization is to eliminate chance," remarked one business executive, "and that can only be done by foreseeing and planning." The emphasis on efficient investment and management stimulated a demand for educated corporate executives who had broader skills than engineering and production. After 1900, colleges and universities introduced business courses into the curriculum, and in 1908 Harvard University's new School of Business offered the first master's degrees in business administration (MBAs). With courses in corporate finance, cost accounting, and management, the field of marketing moved from an entrepreneur's gut instinct to a subject of academic expertise.

The Business of Farming

Growing urban populations and expanding foreign markets created new demands for farm commodities, igniting a boom for farmers that ended the two-decade agricultural depression. Wheat jumped from 63 cents a bushel in 1901 to nearly a dollar eight years later; cotton climbed from 7 cents a pound to over a dime, and exports increased from 10 million to 16 million bales between 1900 and 1914. Meanwhile, federal legislation encouraged irrigation projects in California and the Southwest, increasing arable land for cotton and citrus trees while stimulating the consolidation of large holdings worked by Mexican American labor recruits. As the value of farm property doubled, so did agricultural income. Even though farm tenancy and sharecropping remained high in the South, labor shortages brought better farm wages.

All was not easy in rural regions. Although two-fifths of the nation's workers earned livings through farming, economists worried about rural depopulation and declining productivity. Farm output increased nearly 10 percent, but urban growth caused a greater demand for food. For the first time, the United States began to import such dietary staples as meat and grain. The resulting rise of farm prices contributed to a national inflation that undermined the income of city workers.

While wages rose 22 percent, food prices increased 37 percent.

Progressives looked to business for solutions to the farm problem. As urban-industrial society stressed virtues of punctuality and efficiency, reformers lamented the "tardiness" of farmers to adjust to modern conditions. "We must follow the lead of the manufacturer," advised one dairy farmer about selective breeding in 1912, "and develop more efficient types of animal machines." Worried about the declining farm population, President Roosevelt appointed a Commission on Country Life, which recommended rural public health programs, road building, and parcel-post service to counteract the "attractions of the modern city." Urging education to "uplift" rural areas, reformers preached the gospel of efficiency to youth farm clubs, encouraging stock-breeding, standardized crops, and home economics. "Perhaps they may send out some city women to teach us how to cook," objected one Wisconsin farm woman. "We will resent that." Programs for rural improvement culminated with passage of the Smith-Lever Act of 1914, which funded county farm agents to instruct farmers about "scientific" agriculture. The project aroused rural criticism and failed to improve farm productivity.

The Automobile Links the Farm and the City

The apparent crisis of rural life inspired, ironically, the most sophisticated patterns of industrial technology, the mass production of automobiles. As consumers, farmers applauded any improvements in transportation. They had lobbied successfully for the federal Post Office's Rural Free Delivery service, established in 1912, which eased the purchase of mechanical farm implements and domestic conveniences, such as sewing machines. Mechanized agriculture, in turn, encouraged larger holdings and accentuated rural isolation. But with the introduction of the automobile in the 1890s, country dwellers glimpsed new possibilities for mobility. Although some commentators insisted that "the cold and heartless" horseless carriage compared poorly to the "companionship of the horse," statistics proved an alternative sentiment in rural areas. In 1908, there were 20 million horses in the country and only 200,000 automobiles; four years later, the number of horses remained unchanged, while motorized cars approached 1 million. By 1915, there were 2.3 million cars on the road; five years later, ten times as many farmers drove cars as owned tractors (Table 19.1).

It was the Michigan farm boy Henry Ford who broadened rural horizons by building automobiles "for the great multitude." Although the automobile attracted mass interest, car manufacturers initially priced their vehicles for wealthier consumers—in rural areas for the "country doctor" who made house calls. In an era before installment buying, middle-class consumers were obliged to buy used cars. Poor people were left behind. Indeed, farmers often expressed their resentment of affluent urban drivers by bulldozing country roads. In the South, envy at automobile drivers targeted blacks, who were sometimes forced by violent whites to abandon their vehicles. Ford determined to keep auto prices low. Beginning with a Model N that sold for $600 in 1906, he offered farmers a sturdy, reliable vehicle made of "the best materials" and "the simplest designs that modern engineering can devise." Three years later, Ford's 20-horsepower Model T attracted over 10,000 customers at $850 per car; by 1911, Model T sales had tripled.

As ownership of autos increased, so did government regulation of driving. New York introduced the first speed law in 1901, mandating "reasonable and proper" speeds and later establishing maximum limits that varied from 6 to 20 miles per hour. Some communities, frustrated at speeding and "scorching," used stop watches to rig speed traps to punish fast drivers. New York also pioneered in auto registration laws, while Chicago had

TABLE 19.1

Motor Vehicle Sales and Registrations, 1900–1929 (in thousands)

| Year | Sales | | Registration | |
	Autos	Trucks and buses	Autos	Trucks
1900	4.1	—	8.0	—
1905	24.2	.7	77.4	1.4
1910	181.0	6.0	458.3	10.1
1915	895.9	74.0	2,332.4	158.5
1920	1,905.5	321.7	8,131.5	1,107.6
1925	3,735.1	530.6	17,481.0	2,569.7[a]
1929	4,455.1	881.9	23,120.8	3,674.5[b]

Source: U.S. Bureau of the Census, *Historical Statistics of the United States, Colonial Times to 1970* (Washington, D.C., 1975), p. 716.

[a]Bus registrations: 17.8.

[b]Bus registrations: 33.9.

Some communities used stop watches to rig speed traps.

the honor of beginning driver license testing. The annual eighteen-question hurdle focused on auto mechanics and driver responsibility. State regulation of commercial vehicles lagged behind, and the federal government declined on constitutional grounds to adopt national legislation. The Federal Highway Act of 1916 merely committed Washington to a $75 million road building program.

Establishing the Principles of Mass Production

Ford's determination to produce quality automobiles at low prices stimulated major industrial innovations. His strategy appeared simple: "The way to make automobiles," he said, "is to make one automobile just like another automobile." Thus a customer could buy a Ford car in any color—as long as it was black! Ford improved the standardization of interchangeable parts by developing complicated machine tools with low tolerance of error, thereby reducing the need for skilled labor to make last-minute adjustments to individual parts. Ford's factory technology assured uniform product quality and reliability. By 1906, Ford could deliver 100 cars a day.

After the introduction of the Model T and rising consumer demand, Ford's problems shifted from technology to labor. In 1908, the company employed 450 workers; five years later, Ford needed 14,000. The surge in employment reflected a drastic reduction in labor skills. Increasingly sophisticated factory machinery (capable, for example, of simultaneously drilling multiple holes in a single metal part) allowed a greater division of labor into small tasks. Influenced by efficiency experts like the celebrated Frederick W.

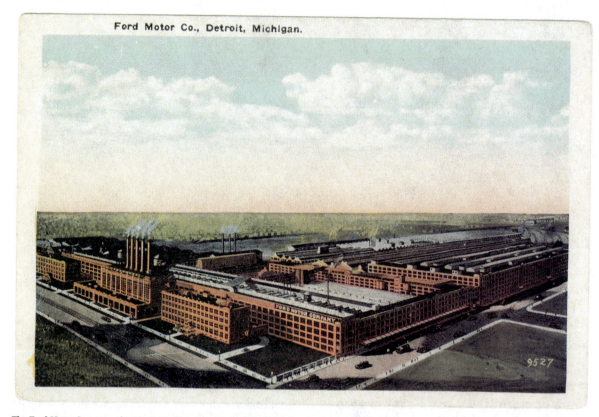

Ford Motor Co., Detroit, Michigan.

The Ford Motor Company plant in Detroit became the subject of a postcard, showing the facility in a bird's-eye view.

Taylor, who had introduced time and motion studies in the steel industry, Ford managers used stop watches to determine maximum times for separate operations and eliminate wasteful procedures. The company then replaced skilled workers with ordinary labor. Such workers could acquire proficiency with little training.

Ford's genius focused on accelerating the principles of mechanical production. After opening a large manufacturing plant in Highland Park, Michigan, in 1910, Ford installed machinery that pulled and lifted automobile components along a continuously moving line of production. Workers performed single tasks as the product passed their work station. Instead of giving piece-work incen-

tives, the machinery set the pace of work. The results seemed astounding. In the old factory, 28 men labored 9 hours a day to assemble 175 pistons; now 7 men worked 8 hours to produce 2,600. Ironically, skilled tasks shifted from the assembly line labor force to supervisors, foremen, inspectors, and clerks, who made sure the work proceeded without interruption.

The labor problem assumed a new form. While unskilled workers could learn and perform the simple operations of factory assembly, production figures remained lower than expected. The company attributed part of the problem to the ethnic origins of the labor force, causing language barriers that interfered with factory efficiency. In 1914, U.S.-born workers formed less than one-third of Ford employees; the remainder came from multiple nationalities of eastern and southern Europe. More serious were worker attitudes about factory labor. Two statistics reveal the result: 10 percent of the work force was absent on any day; on an annual basis, worker turnover (those who quit or were fired) reached 370 percent. To keep 14,000 workers steadily employed, Ford had to hire an extra 1,400 a day, 56,000 a year. Turnovers cost the company nearly $2 million per year.

Why did employees disappear? Mostly because time off gave workers a chance to relax, to extend the weekend into "Blue Monday," or to look for a better job elsewhere. Equally important were worker traditions of slowing the pace. Despite rigorous management oversight, workers saw no advantages to speed; however quick the pace, more work would follow. Company "speed kings" who tried to accelerate the schedule became targets of abuse and ultimately added to turnovers. Immigrant workers, who had to learn the regimen of factory production, gladly imitated the task rates of experienced employees.

To overcome worker resistance, Ford decided to offer positive incentives. Addressing the problem of long hours and small pay, the Ford company announced in 1914 a new program for selected workers—the $5 day for eight hours, twice the rate of prevailing wages. "No worker," said Ford, "will be discharged if we can help it, except for unfaithfulness or inefficiency." Those two conditions, however, illuminated the point of the program, which coincided with the creation of the company's sociological department to monitor worker compliance. Since union membership, ethnic allegiance, or personal habits could be construed as "unfaithfulness," Ford's personnel managers carefully screened the private lives of factory workers before approving participation in the $5 day. It

> **Ford's personnel managers carefully screened the private lives of factory workers. Days after announcing the program, the company fired nearly 900 Greek and Russian employees who had missed work to celebrate the Orthodox Christmas holiday.**

was no coincidence that just days after announcing the program, the company fired nearly 900 Greek and Russian employees who had missed work to celebrate the Orthodox Christmas holiday, which fell thirteen days after December 25. "If these men are to make their home in America," said a Ford official, "they should observe American holidays."

Ford's paternalism revealed other cultural aspects of the industrial ethic. The personnel department consisted of 200 white-collar men, who investigated the workers' private lives. Interviews with family members, neighbors, and landlords established a worker's thrift, social activities, and sex life. Since company policy required married women to leave their jobs, working women (mostly in the clerical force) were not considered heads of household and were ineligible for the $5 day. Male immigrants (but not native-born workers) had to show valid marriage certificates to enter the program. Such workers also had to demonstrate household cleanliness, frugality, temperance, and a willingness to learn English and "Americanized" manners in special company classes. The purpose of such education, according to a Ford official, was "to impress these men that they are, or should be, Americans, and that former racial, national, and linguistic differences are to be forgotten." Those who passed scrutiny enjoyed real wage benefits, and the turnover rate dropped from nearly 400 percent in 1913 to 16 percent in 1915.

The Principles of Mass Management

As Ford and other manufacturers soon discovered, supervision of the factory floor demanded an elaborate clerical force to keep accurate records and oversee business operations. And the white-collar work force, in turn, required its own supervision to function with maximum efficiency. In this way, the nation's office workers increased from 708,000 in 1900 to 1,524,000 in 1910 to 2,838,000 in 1920. To house this staff and keep down real estate overhead, corporations built their headquarters upwards. ("A skyscraper," said an architect in 1900, "is a machine that makes the land pay.") The tremendous expansion of downtown office buildings (Chicago alone added 1.5 million square feet of office space in 1910) indicated the surge of white-collar workers. Although Frederick Taylor's *Principles of Scientific Management* (1911) distinguished "brain work" from manual labor, management imposed rigorous rules of efficiency on office personnel. Time clocks measured employee punctuality, docking clerks for lateness and absence.

Principles of mass management invaded all levels of women's work. Women's occupational opportunities fell into a hierarchy of preferences, with the most educated becoming teaching and nursing professionals (along with a few doctors and lawyers). The hierarchy then descended to clerical work, followed by retail sales, factory assembly, and domestic services, the latter employing more women than any other. Within this hierarchy, racial segregation restricted the opportunities of nonwhites. In department stores, white women sold goods in the daytime; black women mopped the floors at night.

In all occupational sectors, women were increasingly supervised by male managers and pressed by demands for efficiency. For domestic

NEW YORK IN A FEW YEARS FROM NOW.
View from the Bay.

This cartoon correctly predicted the rising urban skylines. Here, the new skyscrapers dwarf the human scale.

workers, the introduction of electric vacuum cleaners and other appliances raised standards of cleanliness yet made no reduction in the work day. In lamp factories, to take an example from manufacturing, women started the day feeling slight electric shocks as they tested thirty-three bulbs per minute, but quickly lost that sensation in the race to make 6.5 cents per thousand. Department stores measured saleswomen's efficiency not only in retail dollars, but in the intangible public relations that induced a customer to return. In all these women's occupations, managers sought greater worker output with incentives and "welfare" bonuses that included rest rooms, cafeterias, credit unions, and medical assistance.

Clerical workers experienced peculiar restraints. The feminization of certain occupations highlighted the invisible principles of modern

In the language of business, a "typewriter" was both a machine and the person who used it; both acted as interchangeable parts to maximize office efficiency.

management. Just as Henry Ford refused to employ married women, both office managers and their employees assumed that marriage signaled the end of a woman's business career. "Miss Remington" (portrayed in typewriter advertisements as young, slender, and single) was "an idealized character," as the company stated, but therefore was a risk to business efficiency. Popular stereotypes, such as the 1902 movie *The Typewriter*, depicted women office workers as sexually active, both seductive and seducible, and consequently a threat to office propriety. To discourage problems, office buildings often had sex-segregated entrances, elevators, and lunchrooms. Mailrooms remained enclaves of male employees, but telephone operators were exclusively female—because men tended to curse.

The clustering of women as typist-stenographers underscored patterns of economic dependence. Since women accepted lower wages than men, managers obtained economic benefits by replacing male

Telephone operators were exclusively female—because men tended to curse.

typists with females. Unlike male clerks, women office workers took entry-level positions that were not steps to occupational advancement, but dead-end jobs. "Women stenographers are always women stenographers," remarked one male executive, "unless they get married." Interior office architecture reinforced those assumptions. After passing standardized typing tests, women typists worked at flat-topped desks, always visible to male supervisors, and often back-to-back with other clerks to minimize distractions. As members of a typing pool, secretaries responded to bells and buzzers, copied dictation from male executives, and acted, as one woman put it, like "human machines." Telephone operators felt similar pressures. "You become part of the machine," said one who dealt with 250–350 calls per hour.

The Grievances of Labor

Emphasis on industrial efficiency weighed heavily on the labor force. In one unexceptional case, a machinist who was caught looking out the factory window was punished by having his pay cut 25 cents a day for four months. Even without such discipline, wages remained low and trailed behind the inflationary trend. Although a 1906 study suggested that $600 per year was the minimum needed for subsistence, average annual nonfarm wages amounted to $508 for a 59-hour work week. Farm workers earned $255 per year; school teachers, mostly women, received $337. At least 10 million people lived below the poverty line. With rising consumer prices for food and fuel, the cost of living increased more than 20 percent during the first ten years of the century. After two decades of prosperity, two-thirds of the population owned just 5 percent of the national wealth in 1916.

Besides poverty, workers faced daily danger. One Saturday afternoon in March 1911, 500 Italian and Jewish women workers at the Triangle Shirtwaist Company in New York City heard a fire alarm just as they were preparing to go home. During a recent strike, the workers had complained that locked doors were dangerous, but owners feared that employees wanted free exits to sneak out of work. Now, as a raging fire blocked one passage and the locked doors refused to budge, the trapped women headed for the roof and windows, many plunging in terror to the concrete sidewalk below. Nearly 150 perished in the catastrophe. Eighty thousand workers marched in a somber funeral procession, and a subsequent investigation inspired laws for factory safety. The pro-suffrage Woman's Political Union linked the tragedy to women's need for political power. Leonora O'Reilly of the Women's Trade Union League advised workers that "the only way out is through the ballot and the only way to be sure of a good ballot is to cast it yourself."

The Triangle fire was dramatic, but not exceptional. Job-related deaths approached 20,000 per year, and another half million workers received serious or permanent injury. No statistician computed industrial illnesses caused by inhaled factory dust, chemical contaminants, or sheer exhaustion. Neither government nor private business provided compensation for work-related accidents or illness.

Industrial companies also exploited the labor of children, who earned a fraction of adult wages. "The most beautiful sight we see is the child at labor," said the founder of Coca-Cola. Entering the work force around age 13, nearly 2 million children between 10 and 15 were gainfully employed, and one-fifth of the nation's youth earned their own livings in 1913. Youngsters understood the importance of regular pay, and many saw the factory as a happier alternative to the regimen of school. Reformers like Florence Kelley of the National Consumer League persuaded department store managers to end night-time employment of children, and the Children's Bureau pressed for legal restrictions on child labor. But state laws usually permitted children of 12 to work ten hours a day, and the Supreme Court held federal limitations of child labor unconstitutional restraints of private contracts.

Efforts to limit the hours of women workers also provoked legal battles that created important precedents for the treatment of women in the public sphere. At the turn of the century, about 25 percent of the female work force (which totaled 5 million wage earners) had jobs in factories, but earned about half the wages of men. Believing that women's primary social function was motherhood, progressive reformers like Kelley pressed for laws that would limit the working hours of women to protect their health and enable them to fulfill maternal responsibilities. Other progressives believed that limits of women's labor would help male

The Triangle Factory fire, in which nearly 150 lives were lost, became such a tragedy because owners had locked the workers in to prevent them from sneaking off the job.

workers claim similar benefits. Business leaders opposed such laws as an interference of workers' rights to enter freely into labor contracts.

In 1908, the issue of women's work hours went to the Supreme Court in the case *Muller v. Oregon*. After hearing a sociological argument by progressive lawyer Louis Brandeis, which focused on contemporary statistical evidence rather than legal precedents, the Court ruled that "woman's physical structure and the performance of maternal functions place her at a disadvantage" and so justified special legal protections, including workday restrictions. Heralded as a "progressive" statement, the decision provided a constitutional rationale for limiting women's equality in the work force for the next six decades.

The availability of low-paid women and child labor enabled manufacturers to expand textile production throughout the South, particularly because male heads of household who were recruited from sharecropping or tenancy farm work

often had a hard time adjusting to industrial conditions. Dependent on the wages of children and women for survival, factory families resented efforts to restrict hours of labor. Southern customs also demanded segregated industries: cotton and furniture for whites, tobacco for blacks, a policy sometimes enforced by violence. Forced to live in segregated company housing without running water or toilets and to shop at overpriced company stores, southern factory workers earned paltry wages for 60-hour weeks.

Industrial expansion in the Southwest also benefited from the divisive multiethnic backgrounds of the labor force. When Rockefeller interests opened soft coal mines in southern Colorado, European immigrants joined Hispanics from northern New Mexico working underground. Emphasizing Americanization and labor discipline, the mine company's sociological department ignored ethnic cultures, except to play one group off another. But 9,000 mine workers bridged their differences in

1913–1914, calling a strike for shorter hours and safer conditions, and ending company control of community affairs. Evicted from company-owned housing, the miners built tent communities and continued picketing. Frustrated by worker defiance, the governor of Colorado ordered the National Guard to the community at Ludlow, where troops attacked the tent settlements and killed numerous residents, including eleven children. Despite public outrage, the company won the strike.

Organizing Union Power

The consolidation of corporate power, the return of prosperity, the burgeoning job market, and persistent inflation of prices—all encouraged working people to join unions to protect their economic position. Union membership jumped from 800,000 in 1900 to over 2 million in 1910, when it comprised over 12 percent of the labor force. Under the leadership of Samuel Gompers, the American Federation of Labor (AFL) attracted skilled craft workers by focusing on practical issues of wages, hours, and working conditions. This self-interested perspective avoided attacks on capitalism and business institutions, but insisted that labor had the right to organize and bargain collectively. Although labor had not gained an unambiguous right to strike, workers participated in over 3,000 walkouts in 1901, mostly over issues of union recognition. Unions achieved "very great good," conceded President Roosevelt that year, "when they combine insistence upon their own rights with law-abiding respect for the rights of others."

The AFL gained notable victories among coal miners and textile workers. But, in organizing skilled crafts, the federation ignored unskilled industrial workers and made minimal gestures to attract women and minorities. Rather, the union advocated a "family wage" to enable men to support their households. Although Gompers accepted labor involvement in politics and began after 1906 to endorse pro-labor candidates, the Federation rebuffed the socialist notion of working class alliances outside trade unionism. Opposed to foreign immigration as a threat to domestic wage rates, the AFL rejected Asian American union membership. When California farm workers formed the Japanese-Mexican Labor Association in 1903 and went on strike against wage cuts, the AFL refused to recognize the interracial union.

Some labor organizations adopted more militant positions. "The working class and the employing class have nothing in common," declared the nation's most radical union, the Industrial Workers of the World, whose members were known as "Wobblies." Spurred by charismatic western mine workers like the one-eyed Big Bill Haywood and songwriter-poet Joe Hill, as well as the legendary organizer Mother Jones, the IWW viewed negotiated labor contracts and political parties as unworthy piecemeal gains—"pie in the sky when you die," as one Wobbly song put it. Instead, the IWW demanded "direct action," including seizure of company property, sabotage, and violence to build a classless society of equals. By appealing to workers' families and cutting across ethnic lines, the Wobblies won followings among miners, loggers, seamen, and farm workers in the western states. In 1912, the IWW gained a dramatic victory among multiethnic textile strikers in Lawrence, Massachusetts. A subsequent strike, involving 18,000 silkworkers in Paterson, New Jersey, won support from New York intellectuals, including John Reed and Mabel Dodge, who organized a theatrical fund-raising pageant. But radical theater raised small funds, and the workers lost the strike.

The growth of labor unions provoked strong anti-union responses from business leaders. Launching an "open shop" campaign, the National Association of Manufacturers brought suits against striking unions for restraining trade in violation of the Sherman Anti-Trust Act of 1890.

Accepting such claims, courts issued injunctions that ended over 700 strikes during the first two decades of the century. Meanwhile, local police frequently intervened against picketers, using charges of "disorderly conduct" to harass strikers. Enlightened employers recognized the economic waste of work stoppages and supported efforts to avert strikes. By 1911, twenty-five states established mediation agencies, though their powers remained limited.

Employer blacklists, "yellow dog" contracts (which forced workers to disavow unions), and company spies further disrupted union activity. But the problems of organized labor also reflected the inherent values of workers themselves. Ethnic, racial, and cultural differences enabled employers to divide and conquer, most typically in the use of strikebreakers. The sexual segregation of certain occupations and gender prejudice—notions that married women could be dismissed or paid lower wages—further weakened labor solidarity. Such internal conflicts persisted because workers often refused to identify with class interests. Ever hopeful of upward mobility, employees typically rejected the status of permanent workers.

The Rise of Progressive Politics

Conflicts between organized labor and business reflected broader problems of managing an industrial economy. "Today," admitted one conservative executive, "almost all Americans are dependent upon the action of a great number of other persons mostly unknown." Massive corporations, mechanized workplaces, multinational wholesalers, and impersonal department stores overwhelmed the small business, the ordinary worker, and the average consumer. The loss of personal contact brought confusion and fear, but also a keen realization that economic power preyed on the most vulnerable citizens. "The trusts and the monopolies," said a Kansas City newspaper in 1901, "find their opportunities in the necessities of the people."

Frustrated by the reluctance of the major political parties to regulate the growth of big corporations, growing numbers of voters looked for remedies in socialism, which promised to make business subordinate to the interests of society. "While there is a lower class," declared Eugene V. Debs, the nation's most famous socialist, "I am in it." Founding the Socialist Party of America in 1901, Debs attracted diverse supporters, including German American municipal reformers in Milwaukee, Jewish garment workers on the Lower East Side, ex-Populists in Texas and Oklahoma, militant miners, loggers, and migrant workers in the West, and intellectuals like the writer Jack London. Such constituencies supported a thriving socialist press—newspapers, magazines, pamphlets—with combined circulation over 2 million. Running for president, Debs won 100,000 votes in 1900 and 400,000 in 1904. Although some radicals saw unions as instruments of social revolution, Debs's version stressed an agenda of workplace democracy and peaceful electoral politics. With a membership of 120,000 and a platform backing public ownership of utilities, the Socialist party won numerous elections on the local and state level and sent a single congressional representative to Washington in 1912.

The rise of political protest transcended the interests of a single class. Thus a strike of streetcar workers against a monopolistic franchise in St. Louis in 1900 burst into a citywide protest against high fares and poor schedules. Sympathy for striking teamsters against Chicago meatpackers in 1902 spread around the country, culminating in a national boycott of meat products. Muckraking revelations about Standard Oil's business practices by journalist Ida Tarbell, together with local grievances against the company, led to multiple state laws, legal suits, and federal investigations. In Wisconsin, Governor Robert La Follette tapped the state's university professors to draft legislation to regulate railroad rates. North Dakota farmers formed a protest Non-Partisan League in 1915. "If you put a lawyer, a banker, and an industrialist in a barrel and roll it downhill," one of the founders explained, "there'll always be a son-of-a-bitch on top."

Corporate Regulation and National Politics

When President William McKinley was shot to death by an anarchist assassin six months after his second inauguration in 1901, a close associate, Senator Mark Hanna, exclaimed: "Now look, that damned cowboy is president of the United States!" So Theodore Roosevelt, at 42 the youngest man ever to hold the nation's highest office, made his presidential debut. Born to wealth and privilege in New York, Roosevelt carried a lusty confidence, energy, and passion into Washington politics. Viewing the White House as a "bully pulpit," he emerged as an activist president, established a national agenda, drafted legislation, lobbied Congress and public opinion, and appealed for a public interest larger than the component parts. His outspoken approach to politics set important precedents for subsequent administrations, and his self-defined role as a political umpire strengthened the executive branch of government.

"The great corporations," said Roosevelt, addressing the most controversial subject of the age, "are the creatures of the State, and the State not only has the right to control them, but it is duty bound to control them." Yet the Republican president respected current economic trends—the nationalization of markets, demands for efficiency, consolidation of capital—which nourished giant business. He had no thought of dismantling these triumphs of capitalism. "These big aggregations are the inevitable development of modern industrialism," he explained, "and the effort to destroy them would be futile." But Roosevelt distinguished between good and bad corporations, and he feared

that ruthless capitalism would provoke worker anger, class conflict, and social upheaval. In 1902, the president dramatically intervened to end a strike in the anthracite coal fields by inviting both labor and management to the White House. When the union agreed to accept arbitration, but the mine owners refused, Roosevelt threatened federal seizure of the mines and thereby persuaded the mine companies to negotiate with the union. The ensuing strike settlement reinforced Roosevelt's presidential stature. The same year, the administration decided to prosecute a western rail monopoly, formed by Rockefeller, Morgan, and other railroad barons as the Northern Securities Company, for violations of the Sherman Anti-Trust Act.

These presidential actions made Roosevelt, in the words of one journalist, "the first political leader . . . to identify the national principle with the ideal of reform." Though a shocked Wall Street community attempted to negotiate with the White House, Roosevelt pushed the Northern Securities case to the Supreme Court, which ordered the break-up of the trust in 1904. The administration proceeded to file forty additional anti-trust suits, earning the president the reputation as a "trust-buster." More important, these cases strengthened the federal government's powers to regulate the national economy. But Roosevelt denied hostility to corporate bigness, per se. "This is an age of combination," he insisted.

Roosevelt's preference was not to destroy big business, but to regulate its actions. In 1903, he persuaded Congress to establish a cabinet-level Department of Commerce and Labor, including a Bureau of Corporations to investigate and recommend responsible business practices. Federal litigation served as a threat to force "gentleman's agreements" from companies like U.S. Steel and International Harvester. In 1903, Roosevelt signed the Elkins Act, which outlawed railroad rebates to favored customers and revived the Interstate Commerce Commission (ICC) to regulate railroad policy. The measure appealed to small shippers who resented discounts demanded by large corporations, but the policy also benefited the railroads, which did not have to pay the rebates.

By the 1904 elections, Roosevelt could boast about the "Square Deal" he embodied, and his decisive victory in the presidential election over a conservative Democrat reinforced his resolve. Pressing Congress to strengthen the ICC, the president signed the Hepburn Act of 1906, which gave that agency power to set maximum railroad rates and regulate pipelines. Conservative Republicans complained about government intervention in the economy; progressives, like LaFollette, criticized the lack of greater control. But Roosevelt's version of regulation prevented price gouging, while giving corporations assurances of economic stability. In the same spirit, the president supported the Pure Food and Drug Act and a meat inspection act (see Chapter 18) which both protected consumers and established standards more easily met by big companies. His conservation program (See Chapter 18) also balanced corporate development with public interests.

Roosevelt's ambitions to expand progressive legislation soon clashed with the conservative wing of the Republican party in Congress. After 1906, the lame-duck president lost his power to win reform legislation. Party leaders looked unkindly at his criticism of conservative judges who denied state worker compensation laws or voided restrictions on women's labor. A Wall Street stock-market crash in 1907 forced the White House to accommodate J. P. Morgan's demands for anti-trust relaxation in exchange for favorable financial policies. Such concessions then aroused criticism from the progressive wing of the Republican party. Roosevelt hoped to patch these party disagreements by supporting the conservative William Howard Taft to succeed him. During the 1908 election, the Democratic battle-horse, William Jennings Bryan, campaigned for the third time with the slogan "Shall the people rule?" But Taft carried the polls.

The Taft Administration

President Taft had different ideas from Roosevelt's. "The lesson must be learned," he said, "that there is only a limited zone within which legislation and governments can accomplish good." While Roosevelt departed on a prolonged hunting expedition to Africa, Taft looked no further than his predecessor's anti-trust policies. The new president proceeded to bring 150 suits and indictments against large corporations, infuriating Republican leaders in the business community.

Taft's anti-trust policies collapsed abruptly in 1911, when the Supreme Court modified its constitutional interpretations of the Sherman Act. In major cases involving the steel and tobacco industries, the Court enunciated a "rule of reason," which held that certain types of restraint of trade were reasonable and consequently legal. The decision put an end to indiscriminate trust-busting. "No such thing as reasonable or unreasonable crimes heretofore have been known in law," protested an anti-monopoly newspaper. The Court's position, not too different from Roosevelt's, meant that corporate growth would proceed, provided the companies avoided illegal or unfair policies.

The futility of Taft's anti-trust policy matched his failure to address tariff reform, further accentuating divisions within the Republican party. Progressives blamed high prices on the import duties established in the 1890s. Summoning a special session of Congress in 1909, Taft called for modest reductions, but quickly abandoned the fight when Republican conservatives demanded high duties. The Payne-Aldrich tariff actually raised rates on manufactured goods, imperiling agricultural exports. The president also waffled on a congressional dispute involving the party's Speaker of the House, finally favoring conservatives over reformers. Another controversy erupted when Taft failed to back Roosevelt's director of national forests, Gifford Pinchot, in a quarrel about the disposition of public lands. When Taft dismissed Pinchot in 1910, the insulted Roosevelt broke with the administration.

Big Sticks, Big Dollars

Roosevelt's motto, "Speak softly and carry a big stick," expressed the president's outlook toward global affairs, particularly involving the Caribbean nations and South America. An ardent expansionist during the war with Spain, Roosevelt had depicted military intervention among "barbarous" countries as "a most regrettable but necessary international police duty." As foreign trade extended economic and political interests overseas, global entanglements justified the development of a two-ocean navy and improved naval access between the nation's two coasts. Roosevelt believed that the United States had to build a canal through Panama to assure military superiority in the western hemisphere. Within two months of entering the White House, he negotiated with Britain to establish U.S. claims to the project.

Colombians, who claimed sovereignty over Panama, opposed Roosevelt's plans. Although the administration signed a treaty to build the canal, Colombia's senate rejected the agreement. Roosevelt then encouraged Panama's leaders to rebel from Colombia and sent U.S. warships to support the uprising. Once Panama won its independence, the president submitted the Hay-Buneau-Varilla treaty of 1903, which permitted construction of a U.S. canal and established a ten-mile wide Canal Zone. As military doctors learned to control the yellow fever and malaria that afflicted construction teams, the U.S. Army Corps of Engineers built a technological marvel: a fifty-mile ditch with giant locks to adjust water levels. The Panama Canal opened for business in 1914.

Roosevelt justified Big Stick diplomacy with what was called the Roosevelt Corollary to the Monroe Doctrine of 1823. Since then, the United

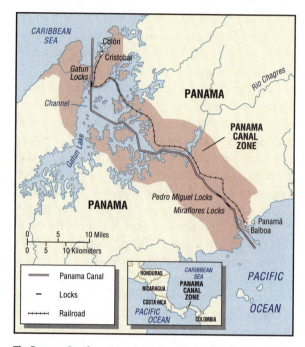

The Panama Canal

States had forbidden European intervention in the political affairs of the Western Hemisphere; consequently, said Roosevelt, the nation had an obligation to "keep order ourselves." When Venezuela refused to pay its debts to Britain and Germany, Washington intervened in the controversy to keep those nations from forcibly collecting Venezuelan assets and demanded an agreement through arbitration. Similar principles justified U.S. military intervention in the disputes of other Caribbean countries, including Cuba and the Dominican Republic. "What we will not permit the great powers of Europe to do," explained Roosevelt, "we will not permit any American republic to make it necessary for the great powers of Europe to do."

Roosevelt's strategic vision contrasted with the "dollar diplomacy" of his successor. Taft's goal was to substitute "dollars for bullets." Hoping to link U.S. and Latin American interests through economic relations, he encouraged corporate investments to develop resources, while stimulating the sale of manufactured goods to local elites. In Honduras and Costa Rica, for example, the United Fruit Company established huge banana plantations, dominating the local economies and government. By 1912, fully half of U.S. foreign investment was in Latin America. To protect these interests, the U.S. government intervened militarily in Honduras, Guatemala, and Haiti to overthrow unfriendly regimes or restore deposed leaders. U.S. troops remained in Nicaragua almost continuously from 1912 to 1933.

The Election of 1912

Taft's clumsy foreign policy was not the only reason he would be limited to a single term. By 1910, the entrenched Republican leadership, which had dominated national politics since 1897, faced challenges from progressive insurgents in both parties. The 1910 elections brought Democratic majorities to numerous state legislatures and to the House of Representatives for the first time since 1893. Ironically, conservatives in the previous congressional session had delayed passage of a graduated income tax by turning the measure into a constitutional amendment that required ratification by the states. With Democratic victories in 1910, the states eagerly endorsed the proposal, and the Sixteenth Amendment, providing for a federal income tax, eventually became law in 1913. The same impulse for progressive government inspired the Seventeenth Amendment for direct election of senators (see Chapter 18).

Amendment XVI (1913)

The Congress shall have power to lay and collect taxes on incomes, from whatever source derived, without apportionment among the several states, and without regard to any census of enumeration.

As congressional progressives formed a significant coalition, Taft's control of the Republican party weakened. In 1911, the La Follette wing organized the National Progressive Republican League to push for government reform and anticorruption measures, and to challenge the renomination of the president. Meanwhile, Theodore Roosevelt returned from the African jungles, furious at Taft's betrayals of his progressive agenda, and resolved to reenter the political arena. Unlike the conservative Taft, who wanted minimal government involvement in the economy, and unlike the progressive La Follette, who mistrusted corporate power, Roosevelt accepted a corporate economy, viewing steady government regulation as a way of controlling corporate excess.

Mixing genuine political differences with personal passion, Roosevelt turned the 1912 elections into a crusade. Touting his program of corporate progressivism as the "New Nationalism," the popular former president won numerous primary elections. But Taft controlled the party regulars and regained the Republican nomination. Roosevelt then led his followers from the convention hall to form a new political movement, the Progressive party. Embracing a platform that called for corporate regulation, worker protection (minimum wages, workmen's compensation, prohibition of child labor), woman's suffrage, and greater taxes on higher incomes, Roosevelt stood before a throng of 5,000 reformers to affirm their political mission. "We stand at Armegeddon," said the dynamic candidate, "and we battle for the Lord."

While the Republican party was splitting into Taft and Roosevelt factions, the Democrats rallied to another evangelical politician, New Jersey reform governor Woodrow Wilson. Southern born and bred, Wilson had earned a Ph.D. degree in government, served as president of Princeton University, and achieved national attention after the 1910 elections by defying the political bosses who had supported his campaign. As a newcomer to national politics, his position appeared ambiguous about the dominant issue of government regulation of business. Promising banking reform, tariff reductions, and dismantling "unreasonable" trusts, Wilson's "New Freedom" agenda appealed to small business interests and farmers in the South and West. "The men who understand the life of the country are the men on the make," said Wilson, "and not the men who are already made." Yet the Democratic candidate muted his anti-corporate stand to appeal to urban progressives. Like Roosevelt, he was not going to attack all big corporations. "If you want to cure men of joy riding," he explained, "you won't break up their automobiles, but catch the men . . . and see that these very useful and pleasant vehicles . . . are left for legitimate uses."

Against Taft, Roosevelt, and Wilson, the Socialist Eugene Debs added a fourth ingredient to the political soup. Although dedicated to working within the electoral system, the Socialist party supported government ownership of railroads, banks, and mines; unemployment insurance and old-age pensions; woman's suffrage; and limits on presidential terms and Supreme Court powers. Campaigning on a train called the "Red Special," Debs lacked both funds and a party organization. Yet the Socialists won numerous municipal elections and Debs captured over 900,000 votes, 6 percent of the electorate.

Socialism aside, the 1912 election brought no surprises. Taft, associated with incumbency, finished third; Roosevelt and the Progressive party came in second (it was the only time in U.S. history that a "third-party" candidate outpolled a major party presidential nominee). The Democratic Wilson, beneficiary of divided opponents, gained an electoral college landslide, but less than 42 percent of the total vote. Closer analysis showed that political patterns had scarcely changed. "Between the New Nationalism and the New Freedom," remarked one journalist, "was that fantastic imaginary gulf that always has existed between Tweedle-dum and Tweedle-

dee." Yet the 1912 elections provided a mandate for an activist government.

Legislating Wilson's New Freedom

Wilson, the scholar as president, followed Roosevelt's precedent and assumed bold leadership of his party agenda. He devised a legislative strategy, drafted bills, and wielded patronage power to gain passage of his program. The first president since John Adams to address Congress personally, Wilson also installed a direct telephone line to link the White House with Capitol Hill. The new president promptly summoned a special congressional session to revise the high protective tariff. Appealing to consumers, farmers, and shippers, the White House enforced strict party discipline to prevent legislative amendments that might weaken tariff reforms. The resulting Underwood tariff of 1913 represented the first significant reductions since the Civil War.

Lower import duties, however, meant reduced government revenues. With the Sixteenth Amendment ratified, Wilson pushed Congress to pass a graduated income tax in 1913, primarily a 1 percent rate against corporation incomes. Since the measure exempted the first $4,000 of family income, only 2 percent of the work force were affected. But in taxing the highest levels at rates reaching 7 percent, the measure established the progressive principle that the wealthy should bear a larger share of public expenditures. Although only 9 percent of the federal budget came from income taxes in 1916, the vast potential source of revenue laid precedents for future government expansion. Indeed, the new system of taxation would eventually bind nearly every working person to the federal government as taxpaying indirectly became an element of national citizenship.

Congressional revelations about the nation's financial establishment also prompted reforms of the national banking system. Keeping Congress

The Election of 1912

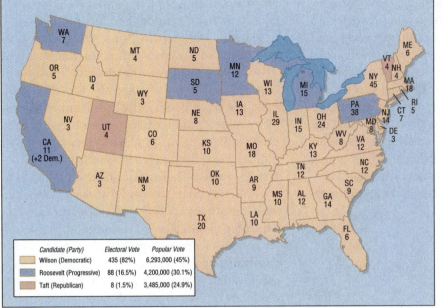

Candidate (Party)	Electoral Vote	Popular Vote
Wilson (Democratic)	435 (82%)	6,293,000 (45%)
Roosevelt (Progressive)	88 (16.5%)	4,200,000 (30.1%)
Taft (Republican)	8 (1.5%)	3,485,000 (24.9%)

in session during a hot Washington summer, Wilson cajoled passage of the Federal Reserve Act in 1913, creating financial institutions that continue to regulate the national economy. To accommodate anti–Wall Street feelings, the law established twelve regional banks, each controlled by local bankers. All private banks that operated nationally had to deposit part of their capital into their regional bank. These reserves provided inter-bank loans and backed the issue of paper money. To expand currency, the Federal Reserve could lower interest rates; to tighten money supplies, rates could be raised. Such decisions remained with the Federal Reserve Board, which was appointed by the president. In this way, public officials, not private bankers, regulated financial policy.

Wilson's willingness to protect private banking brought the administration closer to Roosevelt's vision of corporate progressivism. The Federal Trade Commission (FTC) Act of 1913 continued to narrow the differences between Wilson's New Freedom and Roosevelt's New Nationalism. Accepting the Supreme Court's "rule of reason," the law created the FTC as a regulatory agency, appointed by the president, to monitor commercial activities. Rather than institute anti-trust proceedings, the FTC issued restraining orders and negotiated with companies to win voluntary consent decrees to stop "unfair trade practices." Relying on corporate administrators, Wilson's FTC made little effort to restore business competition. Yet the White House also approved the Clayton Anti-Trust Act of 1914, which blocked blatant monopolistic tactics, such as price discrimination and overlapping of corporate directors among competing businesses. The measure also exempted labor unions and agricultural groups from anti-trust action.

This ambitious legislative package completed Wilson's primary agenda. But when the Republican party bounced back in the congressional elections of 1914, the Democratic president took pains to underscore his progressive credentials. In 1916,

Wilson stunned party leaders by nominating the controversial Louis Brandeis, a progressive Jewish lawyer, to the Supreme Court. Brandeis had built his reputation by attacking corporate inefficiency and by arguing in the *Muller* case that social benefits should outweigh constitutional precedents. Wilson bolstered his support among workers by signing laws regulating child labor (later ruled unconstitutional), seamen's working conditions, workers' compensation for federal employees, and eight-hour days for railroad employees. For farmers, Wilson endorsed rural credits and experimental programs.

The Limits of Progressivism

"What I have tried to do is get rid of any class legislation in this country," said Wilson in 1916. "The worst thing that could happen to America would be that she should be divided into groups and camps . . . that were at odds with one another." Wilson's ambitious progressive agenda enabled the minority party president to defeat Republican challenger Charles Evans Hughes by a slim margin in 1916. That victory came despite deep dissatisfaction with Wilson's foreign policy regarding World War I, which had been raging in Europe since 1914 (see Chapter 20). The president's electoral success thus underscored both his political talent and an underlying consensus about domestic issues. Yet these widely shared assumptions about politics and society illuminated the limits of progressive values.

Wilson's record on racial issues, for example, reflected the prejudices of his southern background. "It is like writing history with lightning," said Wilson in 1915 about a film he had just seen in the White House, "and my only regret is that it is all so terribly true." On the 50th anniversary of the Confederate surrender and the assassination of Abraham Lincoln, the nation's foremost filmmaker, D. W. Griffith, released a three-hour silent movie based on a popular racist novel *The Clansman,* which he retitled *The Birth of a Nation.* Drawing on President Wilson's earlier writings as a historian of Reconstruction, the film depicted African American men as violent rapists, best handled by lynch mobs and the Ku Klux Klan. Even the dying Booker T. Washington, who usually avoided public dissent, raised his voice in protest. As the NAACP showered complaints to politicians and pickets surrounded movie theaters, several cities banned or censored the film.

Wilson's endorsement of the movie dovetailed with his administration's policies about racial issues. One month after taking office, the postmaster general began to segregate employees in his department, encouraging other federal bureaucracies to adopt similar policies. In federal buildings, citizens now used segregated water fountains, rest rooms, and toilets. No black man was allowed to give dictation to a white secretary. Outside Washington, federal officials dismissed African American workers. "There are no Government positions for Negroes in the South," declared the Collector of Internal Revenue. "A Negro's place is in the cornfield." When an African American delegation visited the White House to challenge federal segregation, an enraged president abruptly terminated what he considered an "insulting" conversation.

Less viciously, the Wilson administration showed little regard for women's political rights. Annoyed by a suffrage protest in Washington the day before his inauguration, Wilson justified his silence on women's votes by claiming the Democratic platform had made no promises, then conceded that he was "tied to a conviction" that the states should legislate matters of suffrage. On immigration policy, Wilson raised no objections to a proposal to bar all newcomers of African descent (after considerable black lobbying, the idea was defeated in a congressional committee). But with an eye on the coming presidential contest, he did veto legislation in 1915 that would have required literacy tests for European immigrants. Two years later, he vetoed a second such measure, only to have it overridden by an exclusionist Congress.

The progressive leadership remained a white male preserve. Although reformers addressed economic inequities, fought corporate monopolies, and defended the rights of labor, ethnic grievances were seldom expressed, except by members of the aggrieved groups. Yet increasingly these cultural outsiders—immigrants, blacks, and women—made clear their refusal to disappear or become silent. As Wilson boasted about "the spirit of Progressive Democracy" in 1916, W. E. B. DuBois published an article on the nation's "lynching industry," concluding, ironically, "how peculiarly fitted the United States is for moral leadership of the world."

INFOTRAC® COLLEGE EDITION EXERCISES

For additional reading go to InfoTrac College Edition, your online research library at *http://web1.infotrac-college.com*.

Subject search: Henry Ford
Keyword search: Theodore Roosevelt
Keyword search: Frederick Taylor
Subject search: Taft
Keyword search: Woodrow Wilson

ADDITIONAL READING

The Automobile Links the Farm and the City

James J. Flink, *America Adopts the Automobile, 1895–1910* (1970). This illustrated history traces the social impact of automobiles.

Establishing the Principles of Mass Production

David Montgomery, *The Fall of the House of Labor: The Workplace, the State, and American Labor Activism, 1865–1925* (1987). From the perspective of workers, this study explores the effects of industrialization on U.S. jobs.

Stephen Meyer, III, *The Five Dollar Day: Labor Management and Social Control in the Ford Motor Company, 1908–1921* (1981). Based on company records, this study examines efforts to regulate workers' lives on and off the job.

The Principles of Mass Management

Lisa M. Fine, *The Souls of the Skyscraper: Female Clerical Workers in Chicago, 1870–1930* (1990). Using a single community, the author analyzes the emergence of sex segregation and efficiency in the office place; for contrast, see Susan Benson, *Counter Cultures*, listed in Chapter 17.

David M. Katzman, *Seven Days a Week: Women and Domestic Service in Industrializing America* (1978). This book provides a detailed analysis of women who worked for wages in other people's homes.

The Rise of Progressive Politics

Steven L. Piott, *The Anti-Monopoly Persuasion: Popular Resistance to the Rise of Big Business in the Mid-West* (1985). The author uses a series of local studies to document public frustration at corporate consolidation.

The Election of 1912

John Milton Cooper, *The Warrior and the Priest: Woodrow Wilson and Theodore Roosevelt* (1983). This dual biography examines the differences in politics and personality between the great presidential leaders.

David P. Thelen, *Robert M. LaFollette and the Insurgent Spirit* (1976). This brief biography examines the conflicts between progressive insurgents and mainstream politicians.

The Limits of Progressivism

Louis R. Harlan, *Booker T. Washington: The Wizard of Tuskegee, 1901–1915* (1983). The second volume of the biography, this work illuminates tensions within the African American leadership.

Robert Lang, ed., *The Birth of a Nation* (1994). This volume includes the entire script of the classic film and documents the ensuing controversy.

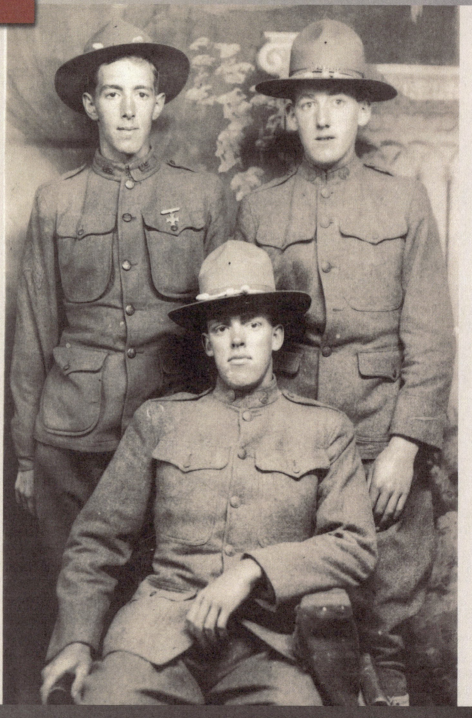

The Search for World Order, 1913–1920

May 7, 1915, a date that lived in public memory for an entire generation, brought shocking news. As the British ship *Lusitania* sailed within sight of the Irish coast, carrying a cargo of munitions as well as passengers, a German submarine fired a torpedo into its hull, sinking the vessel in eighteen minutes. Twelve hundred lives were lost, including 128 U.S. citizens. Militant leaders like Roosevelt denounced this "act of piracy" and demanded war. Secretary of State William Jennings Bryan, an avowed pacifist, pleaded for a neutral response. The horrified public glimpsed the prospect of war.

"There is such a thing," said President Woodrow Wilson, steering a middle course, "as a man being too proud to fight."

U.S. entry into the Great World War was still years away when national politicians in Washington began at the turn of the century to assume more responsibility to regulate economic affairs, and the federal government consequently intruded more into the lives of ordinary citizens. Progressive leaders tried to balance this growth of government power with political reforms, such as direct election of senators, attacks against corruption, and education of the electorate, but citizens were still discovering aspects of public life, such as income taxes, which earlier generations had not faced. At the same time, public interests increasingly extended beyond the country's territorial boundaries. International trade, worldwide investments, and rivalry among nations compelled the federal government to address more issues of foreign policy. Before the 20th century, international relations scarcely mattered to the general public. But the expansion of national power ended that isolation; no longer could the average citizen escape the implications of Washington's policies at home and abroad. By the second decade of the 20th century, the U.S. role in world affairs, though still a debated issue, had become an important aspect of the national identity.

U.S. involvement in international affairs followed from the expansion of overseas business. Continuing precedents set by Theodore Roosevelt and William Howard Taft, President Wilson frequently used military and economic power to protect U.S. interests in Latin America and Asia. After the outbreak of World War I in Europe in August 1914, Wilson struggled to maintain a neutral policy toward the warring parties (primarily Britain and its Allies versus Germany and the Central Powers). But he refused to sacrifice U.S. economic interests, and he allowed corporate leaders to invest heavily on the Allied side. Such connections ultimately fused the interests of the United States with those of the Allies. When Germany's submarine warfare directly threatened U.S. interests, Wilson abandoned neutrality and opted to enter the Allied camp. In leading the nation to war in April 1917, Wilson became the first U.S. president to assume a dominant role in world diplomacy. Yet his efforts to build a lasting peace collided with rival European interests and with a reluctant public at home.

U.S. entry into the war had important domestic consequences. As progressive leaders like Wilson endeavored to maximize industrial production for the war effort and sought to establish national unity, the federal government adopted programs to ensure business efficiency and to stifle dissent. Such policies made more citizens subject to government regulation than ever before—as soldiers, manufacturers, farmers, workers, and consumers. Women, African American men, and labor unionists took advantage of the wartime economy to improve their economic position, though most of their gains proved temporary. Political dissenters, by contrast, faced severe government repression, foreshadowing a postwar "red scare" and hostility to labor protest. Indeed, the domestic turmoil caused by the war stimulated a widespread desire to return to normal times, a mood that would set the tone of political life during the next decade.

Seeking U.S. Influence Overseas

"We created this nation," said President Wilson, "not to serve ourselves, but to serve mankind." Having embraced a progressive domestic policy of regulating business competition through government oversight (see Chapter 19), the president hoped to export an ideal world order based on principles of morality and self-restraint. He believed that negotiation, not military power, would assure international peace. Wilson's secretary of state, William Jennings Bryan, promptly initiated a program of signing treaties with over thirty nations, providing for mediation commissions to

America in the Caribbean, 1898–1930

settle disagreements. The desire to improve the human condition expressed both missionary idealism and assumptions of cultural superiority. "When properly directed," said Wilson with undisguised paternalism, "there is no people not fitted for self-government."

Interest in international stability reflected White House support of corporate expansion. The administration's low tariff policy stimulated foreign trade, while amendments to the Federal Reserve Act encouraged overseas investment. To boost foreign business, Congress increased the number of commercial attachés abroad. Between 1900 and 1915, U.S. exports doubled to $3 million, and foreign investments tripled to $3 billion. When the world war reduced the number of ships available for U.S. trade, Wilson sponsored legislation allowing the government to own and operate a commercial fleet. With presidential support,

Congress also lifted anti-trust restrictions on businesses involved in international trade. Such policies, Wilson told business leaders in 1914, supported the "righteous conquest of foreign markets."

Conflicts in Latin America

Washington matched economic expansion with military muscle. More than any other president, Wilson sent troops into foreign countries seven times, purportedly to stimulate "the development of constitutional liberty in the world." Like Roosevelt and Taft, Wilson saw the nations of Latin American as U.S. dependencies, protected from European exploitation by the Monroe Doctrine. Challenges to U.S. interests by local governments prompted the White House to send the Marines to assure friendly regimes in Nicaragua, Haiti, the

Dominican Republic, and Cuba. When German power expanded in the Danish West Indies, the administration pressed Denmark to sell those colonial possessions, renamed the Virgin Islands, to the United States in 1916. In wielding a big stick in the Caribbean, Wilson sought strategic influence to protect U.S. business, particularly after the Panama Canal opened in 1914, one month after World War I began in Europe.

Determined "to teach the South American republics to elect good men," Wilson reversed Taft's policy of supporting Mexico's General Victoriano Huerta, who had led a murderous rebellion, even though Huerta supported U.S. business interests. For the first time in U.S. history, Washington denied diplomatic recognition to an existing regime. "A government of butchers," said Wilson, did not represent the Mexican people. Instead, Wilson backed two rebel leaders, Venustiano Carranza and Pancho Villa, and ordered the Navy to occupy the port at Vera Cruz to prevent military supplies from reaching Huerta's army.

Sporadic fighting involving U.S. sailors nearly ignited formal warfare. As Huerta lost power, however, Carranza seized the government. But contrary to Wilson's plans, the new regime proposed land reforms that threatened U.S. oil interests. Unwilling to back Carranza, the president supported the faction led by Villa, who seemed more compliant. But when Carranza defeated Villa in 1915, Wilson switched sides and accepted Carranza's power. The frustrated Villa now cultivated Mexican resentment of U.S. interference. To embarrass Carranza, Villa attacked U.S. travelers in Mexico, then crossed the border in 1916 to burn the town of Columbus, New Mexico, killing over twenty people. The outraged Wilson appointed General John Pershing to lead a punitive expedition of 7,000 soldiers to capture Villa. But the chase failed, and Carranza demanded respect for Mexican sovereignty. Pressed by U.S. peace groups and worried about European affairs, Wilson ordered a graceless exit in 1917.

Upholding the Open Door in Asia

Efforts to blend missionary diplomacy and national interest complicated U.S. affairs in East Asia. Regarding China, Washington continued to uphold the Open Door policy, first announced in 1900, which insisted that all nations had an equal right to trade on the Asian mainland. Following the creation of a republican government in China in 1911, Wilson quickly extended diplomatic recognition and withdrew support of a multinational railroad project that imperiled Chinese sovereignty. Wilson's defense of the Open Door, however, worsened relations with Japan, which had emerged as an international power and desired to extend its influence in China. Already, anti-Japanese laws passed in California had angered the Japanese government (see Chapter 18). Although Japan formally protested the insult to Japanese Americans, the White House lacked the power, if not the desire, to overturn popular racist policies. Besides, as Wilson readily admitted to California politicians, he "only hoped . . . to offend the sensibilities of a friendly nation *as little as possible.*"

After war began in Europe, the rivalry with Japan intensified. Backing Britain and France against Germany, Japan proceeded to expel German interests from China and then staked claims to Germany's colonial possessions in the Mariana, Caroline, and Marshall islands. As Washington watched nervously, Japan presented China with twenty-one demands in 1915, claiming special trading privileges in Shantung and Manchuria, which threatened Chinese independence as well as the principles of the Open Door. Through diplomatic pressure, Wilson forced Japan to modify the demands. The president then encouraged

U.S. bankers to increase investment in China to challenge Japanese expansion. In 1917, the United States and Japan signed a treaty recognizing the Open Door, while acknowledging that Japan enjoyed "special interests" in Chinese affairs. The agreement forestalled conflict for a generation.

The United States in World War I

Quarrels about Open Door principles soon faded as violence increased in Europe after 1914. Sparked by the assassination of a Hapsburg prince, the European powers went to war to uphold a system of treaty alliances that divided the Allies (Britain, France, and Russia) and the Central Powers (Germany and Austria-Hungary) in the first general war since the age of Napoleon. Even worse, modern technology had produced new instruments of warfare (huge guns, poison gas, airplanes) that caused immense, horrible casualties. Distanced by 3,000 miles of ocean, U.S. observers initially scorned this resurgence of "savage tribes." Wilson announced a policy of U.S. neutrality and pleaded with the public to remain "neutral in fact as well as in name, impartial in thought as well as action." This position assumed that the United States had no interest in either side of the conflict. But as the war continued, Washington did take sides, though not always intentionally. The result, in any case, was to knit U.S. interests with those of the Allies.

The Problems of Neutrality

Wilson's proclamation of neutrality had ignored the obvious cultural and political commitments of diverse U.S. citizens to the warring countries. Nearly 9 million German Americans could not easily forget their heritage, nor could 5 million Irish Americans abandon their distrust of the British government, nor did 2 million Jewish immigrants forgive their former czarist oppressors. Collectively these groups formed a strong anti-Allied constituency. Many corporate leaders, by contrast, had close connections with British banks and supported the Allies. Within the administration, some policy makers expressed strong pro-British sentiments. Besides cultural traditions that linked Washington's leaders with Britain, the two nations had enjoyed diplomatic friendship since the 1890s. Britain's control of the only trans-Atlantic cable also gave the Allies an advantage in the propaganda war to sway public opinion. As German armies marched through neutral Belgium during the first weeks of war, British information depicted terrible German atrocities—killing of civilians, rape, looting, and arson, some of which was true, some not—as evidence of Germany's menace to civilization.

British mastery of the Atlantic sea lanes also directed the flow of commerce. Even before the outbreak of war, U.S. business with the Allies was four times greater than trade with the Central Powers. During the first two years of war, British and French purchases of war supplies and food jumped from $800 million to $3.2 billion, stimulating a boom in industry and agriculture. By contrast, a British naval blockade of German ports brought a sharp reduction of business, which dropped to merely $1 million in 1916. To cover U.S. losses caused by the blockade, Britain agreed to purchase all surplus goods and to make compensation after the war. Wilson did not protest these obvious violations of neutral rights.

"Money is the worst of contrabands," protested Secretary of State Bryan, who believed fervently in true neutrality; "it commands all other things." As the Allied governments ran short of cash in 1915, Wilson permitted U.S. bankers to extend enormous loans to Britain and France. "To maintain our prosperity," explained a cabinet official, "we must finance it." By 1917, Allied indebtedness to

"We are the mediating nation of the world. We . . . understand all nations."

The sinking of the British vessel *Lusitania* shocked the public, bringing fears of U.S. involvement in the world war.

U.S. financiers reached $2.5 billion, further interweaving U.S. national interests with those of the Allies. These economic ties limited Wilson's choices as the European rivals intensified the war. Republican critics, led by Theodore Roosevelt, demanded even more support of the Allies, but Wilson hoped that neutrality would enable the United States to preside at a permanent peace settlement that would replace national competition with unrestricted international trade. "We are the mediating nation of the world," said Wilson. "We . . . understand all nations."

To counter the British blockade, Germany introduced a new type of violent warfare, allowing submarines, known as U (for *untersee,* or "undersea") boats, to attack Allied shipping. Unlike surface vessels, which stopped military shipments through search and seizure and seldom threatened civilians, the submarine was too vulnerable to give advance warnings before attacking enemy shipping. In 1915, Germany announced a war zone around the British islands, threatening to sink ships that carried contraband goods. The White House quickly protested this "indefensible violation of neutral rights" and vowed to hold Germany accountable for the new policy. Although Wilson refused to advise citizens to avoid sailing into the war zones, the German embassy placed newspaper advertisements warning the public of potential dangers. The ads proved all too true in May 1915, when a German torpedo ripped into the *Lusitania.*

Overlooking other violations of neutral rights on the seas by Britain and the fact that the Lusitania was carrying contraband goods, the president sent Germany a stern protest, demanding an end to unrestricted submarine warfare. The bellicose Roosevelt considered the note proof of "abject cowardice and weakness." Bryan, indignant at Wilson's refusal to criticize Britain, resigned in protest. When neutralists in Congress proposed warning citizens to avoid travel in Europe, Wilson rejected any limitations of neutral rights. War passions rose, but Germany defused the crisis by agreeing to suspend military operations against passenger ships, though merchant vessels remained legitimate prey.

At a time when the European land armies were inflicting immense casualties—600,000 Germans died during the battle of Verdun (equivalent to total U.S. deaths in the Civil War); 20,000 British died during the first day of the battle of the

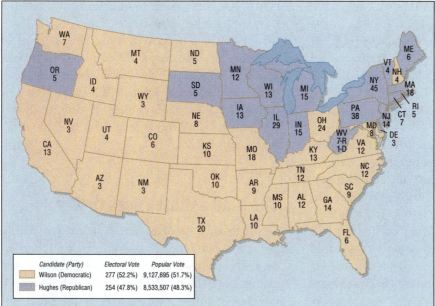

The Election of 1916

Candidate (Party)	Electoral Vote	Popular Vote
Wilson (Democratic)	277 (52.2%)	9,127,695 (51.7%)
Hughes (Republican)	254 (47.8%)	8,533,507 (48.3%)

Somme—U.S. complaints about neutral rights and civilian losses appeared as needless irritants to the warring powers. When the Allies began to arm merchant ships to attack submarines in 1916, Germany renewed the tactic of firing without warning and soon torpedoed the *Sussex,* causing injuries to several U.S. passengers. Wilson promptly issued an ultimatum, threatening to break diplomatic relations unless Germany abandoned indiscriminate attacks. Fearing U.S. intervention in the war, Germany retreated. The so-called *Sussex* pledge renounced unrestricted submarine warfare, provided that Britain ended the blockade of neutral shipping. "Any little German lieutenant," Wilson remarked, "can put us into war at any time by some calculated outrage."

The U.S. Arms for Peace

The crisis of neutral rights pushed the White House toward a program of national defense. "The world is on fire, and there is tinder every-

where," said Wilson as he toured the country during the winter of 1916 to win support for a $500 million military build-up. "America can not shut itself out from the rest of the world." Congress responded by increasing the size of the army and navy, extending federal control of the National Guard and creating the Reserve Officers' Training Corps (ROTC) on college campuses. The cost of the program would be financed by changes in the federal income tax, shifting the burden in a "progressive" direction to the higher income brackets.

As the 1916 presidential elections approached, however, Wilson resolved not to "turn America into a military camp." A strong progressive peace movement, involving reformers like Jane Addams, pleaded for neutrality. Within Congress, vocal midwestern progressives like Robert La Follette and George Norris represented farmers and small business groups that insisted the European war did not jeopardize national interests. Rural Democrats opposed military expenditures, and Socialists like Eugene Debs argued that only bankers profited from war. "I Didn't Raise My Boy to Be a Soldier," one of the most popular songs of the year, expressed widespread anti-war feelings. At the Democratic nominating convention, party delegates chanted the slogan "He Kept Us Out of War." With that message, the president squeaked to a reelection victory over Republican Charles Evans Hughes in 1916.

Emboldened by voter approval, Wilson attempted to lead the world to a negotiated peace. In December 1916, the president dispatched diplomatic messages to the major warring countries to request statements of peace terms. The result offered no hope of compromise; both sides still awaited a complete battlefield victory that would justify the terrible loss of life. Wilson nonetheless stood before the Senate in January 1917 to present an eloquent plan for "peace without victory." Seeking "not a balance of power, but a community of power," the president called for a peaceful global marketplace with freedom of the seas, mutual disarmament, and an international organization to preserve a world order. Wilson's moral vision provided no practical solutions to end the war, but he would offer even more grandiose ideas for a permanent world order the next year.

Even before Wilson's words echoed around the world, German leaders had rebuffed the idea of a negotiated settlement. Expecting to achieve victory before the United States would be provoked to enter the war, Germany announced a resumption of unlimited submarine warfare in January 1917. Wilson responded by breaking diplomatic relations with Germany. Yet the president hoped to maintain moral leverage in achieving a settlement by avoiding immediate confrontations. He waited a month before asking Congress to arm merchant ships and for discretionary power to conduct limited naval warfare. When anti-interventionists objected to such military action, Wilson sought public support by releasing a secret German message, the "Zimmerman Telegram" of 1915, that had been inter-

cepted by British agents. The document revealed a German promise, if the United States declared war, to assist Mexico in recovering the "lost provinces" of Texas, New Mexico, and Arizona. With this incendiary news, the House voted to arm U.S. ships, but Senate noninterventionists refused to be steamrolled, using a session-ending filibuster to thwart the president. Wilson then acted to arm the ships by executive order.

The United States Goes to War

During March 1917, the war came closer. "We are provincials no longer," said Wilson in his second inaugural address. In Russia, the overthrow of the czarist government inaugurated a constitutional government and so eliminated the potential embarrassment of the United States' becoming an ally of a despotic regime. In one day that month, German submarines sank three U.S. merchant ships; by the end of the month, 600,000 tons of Allied cargo lay on the Atlantic floor. From London, the U.S. ambassador warned that the Allies needed support to "prevent the collapse of world trade."

Responding to the momentum to declare war on Germany, noninterventionists urged Wilson to seek peaceful remedies through mediation or neutral patrols of the Atlantic sea lanes. "Do the American People Want War?" asked four anti-war writers in a full-page advertisement in the *New Republic*. Among the four was the young intellectual Randolph Bourne, who pleaded with the president to allow a public referendum before plunging the nation into war. Certainly Wilson understood that national opinion remained deeply divided. But the frustrations of diplomacy showed him the limits of moral persuasion. Only by becoming a participant in the war, he believed, could his voice, and U.S. interests, be heard.

Wilson decided to take the final step. "The world must be made safe for democracy," said

Wilson in his war message to Congress in April 1917. The representatives roared their approval. But Wilson himself wondered aloud why so many would cheer so fervently for a policy that would assure the death of so many thousands. Amidst passionate war fever, progressives like Norris denounced the financial arrangements that drew the nation into the Allied camp, and La Follette spoke for three hours in a tense, hushed atmosphere, pleading for restraint. After four days of angry argument, six senators and fifty representatives voted against the declaration of war. Among them was the pacifist Jeannette Rankin of Montana, the first woman to sit in Congress, who spoke with tears in her eyes: "I want to stand by my country," she said, "but I cannot vote for war."

Patriotism in Wartime

Wilson brought a progressive zeal to the war. Facing strong sentiment against U.S. involvement, the White House began by waging war to shape public opinion. By executive order, Wilson created the Committee on Public Information (CPI), headed by public-relations expert George Creel. More than a source of government information, the agency mixed news, propaganda, and advertising to harness public support for administration policy. Over the next year-and-a-half, the CPI maintained a staff of 150,000 workers and released 75 million pieces of print information to mold public opinion. In addition, the CPI selected 75,000 fast-talking "Four-Minute Men" to give brief patriotic speeches in local auditoriums and theaters. The committee also produced anti-German hate movies with titles like *The Prussian Cur,* as well as promotional films about *Our Colored Fighters* and *The American Indian Gets into the War Game.* (The Iroquois nation, refusing to recognize congressional sovereignty, voted independently to declare war on Germany.)

The committee also sponsored pro-war school programs from elementary level through college.

The press changed the German measles into "liberty measles," hamburger to "salisbury steak," and sauerkraut to "liberty cabbage."

It operated a censorship board to prevent export of suspect publications and films. It showered the country with posters and illustrated advertisements that depicted patriotic women as the vivacious "Lady Liberty" and "The Greatest Mother in the World," while showing the enemy as wild-eyed animals ("Destroy this Mad Brute!" "Halt the Hun!") Organizing huge pageants to promote the sale of government Liberty Bonds, a group of CPI motion picture "stars"—Charlie Chaplin, Mary Pickford, and Douglas Fairbanks—sold the war to an adoring public. Ethnic residents received special attention from CPI-backed "Loyalty Leagues," which distributed multilanguage editions of leaflets promoting "Americanization."

Demands for conformity did not necessarily require government attention. Espousing "100 percent Americanism," the pro-Allied press spontaneously changed the German measles into "liberty measles," hamburger to "salisbury steak," and sauerkraut to "liberty cabbage." More seriously, librarians stripped German-language books from the shelves; academic historians denounced pro-German accounts of the Middle Ages; and symphony orchestras stopped playing the music of Bach and Beethoven. The governor of Iowa forbade German speech in public. Communities boycotted German-owned shops, coerced neighbors to anglicize German names, and demanded demonstrations of loyalty through the purchase of bonds, flag-kissing rituals, and recitations of the Pledge of Allegiance. More than once, mobs attacked innocent German Americans, literally getting away with "patriotic murder."

Realizing that public pressure could not stifle dissent, the White House promoted repressive legislation. The Espionage Act of 1917 prohibited any action that discouraged military service or aided the enemy, including the mailing of "treasonable" material. With these provisions, the government proceeded to prosecute members of the Socialist party for calling the war a "crime against humanity." The post office also blocked the mailing of such antiwar periodicals as *The Masses* and foreign language newspapers. One movie producer received a ten-year prison sentence (later reduced to two) because his film *The Spirit of '76* showed British soldiers committing atrocities during the war for independence. When a Montana judge refused to convict a rancher who said that "Germany would whip the United States and he hoped so," Congress passed the Sedition Act of 1918. The law made it a crime to "utter, print, write, or publish any disloyal, profane, scurrilous or abusive language" about the institutions of government. Under these statutes, 1,500 people were arrested for criticizing public officials, questioning the military draft, or protesting taxes.

For giving an anti-war speech at the Socialist party convention in 1918, presidential candidate Eugene Debs received a ten-year sentence for sedition; he was still in jail two years later when he gained nearly 1 million votes. The government targeted the militant Industrial Workers of the World, raided their union halls around the country, and held hundreds in jail for months before staging trials that brought lengthy sentences. Refusing to recognize the courts, many Wobblies adopted a silent defense that assured conviction. Wartime orthodoxy also brought new immigration laws, establishing literacy requirements (passed over Wilson's veto in 1917) and permitting exclusion and deportation of anarchists.

"Free speech," wrote Supreme Court Justice Oliver Wendell Holmes in upholding the wartime suppression of civil liberties in 1919, "would not protect a man falsely shouting fire in a crowded theater and causing panic." In a unanimous ruling in the *Schenck* case, the Court allowed the government to restrict free speech (in this case, the mailing of anti-war pamphlets) in the face of "clear and present danger." The same court upheld the Debs conviction and the deportation of four Russian anarchists who had criticized U.S. intervention in the Soviet revolution.

Such legal restraints on dissent invited unprecedented harassment of political foes. Wilson's Department of Justice collaborated with a voluntary organization, the American Protective League (APL), which numbered 250,000 private citizens, who "investigated" and entrapped anyone deemed suspicious. At the Ford automobile factories in Detroit, for example, the APL reported pro-German attitudes to the sociological department and to the Justice Department's Bureau of Investigation. With such testimony, the Ford company dismissed suspected slow workers, labor union organizers, and employees reluctant to contribute to the Red Cross, YMCA, or liberty bond drives. Impersonating federal officers, APL operatives conducted interviews, tapped telephone lines, and intercepted mail. In September 1918, the Justice department deployed the APL in a spectacular four-day roundup of alleged draft dodgers ("slackers" in wartime slang) that netted from the streets of New York 50,000 men who lacked registration cards, though only 16,000 appeared to have violated the law.

Demands for political conformity endangered workers in all occupations. In Montana, local vigilantes seized an IWW organizer among the copper miners, dragged him behind a car until his body was broken, then hanged him from a bridge. During another copper strike in Bisbee, Arizona, in 1917, county officials rounded up 1,200 workers, one-third of them Spanish speaking, forced the men into empty boxcars, and shipped them to New

Mexico where they were abandoned in the desert for days before the army rescued them. In New York, a Columbia University psychology professor dared to write his congressional representative to criticize the draft; the university board of trustees used the letter to justify firing the dissident academic. Columbia's leading historian, Charles Beard, resigned in protest, but the influential philosopher and progressive educator John Dewey sadly accepted this perversion of progressive liberalism.

Efforts at social control gave legitimacy to the progressive purity crusade. By 1916, intense lobbying by the Anti-Saloon League had persuaded nineteen states to adopt prohibition. U.S. entry into the war bolstered the anti-alcohol movement. Linking "pro-Germanism" with the froth of German American beer, prohibitionists challenged the patriotism of the nation's brewers. Business leaders, long concerned about worker productivity, stressed the advantages of a sober labor force in wartime. "No drunken man," remarked a prohibitionist politician, "was ever efficient in civil or military life." Spurred by wartime food shortages, even nonprohibitionists saw advantages to saving grain. Responding to these arguments, Congress outlawed alcoholic beverages around military bases and then voted in 1917 to approve the Eighteenth Amendment to the Constitution, forbidding the sale of alcoholic beverages. With ratification by the states in 1919, the law closed the nation's saloons and bars, driving the liquor trade underground.

Amendment XVIII (1919)

Section 1.
After one year from the ratification of this article the manufacture, sale, or transportation of intoxicating liquors within, the importation thereof into, or the exportation thereof from the United States and all territory subject to the jurisdiction thereof for beverage purposes is hereby prohibited.

Section 2.
The Congress and the several states shall have concurrent power to enforce this article by appropriate legislation.

Section 3.
This article shall be inoperative unless it shall have been ratified as an amendment to the Constitution by the legislatures of the several states, as provided in the Constitution, within seven years from the date of the submission hereof to the states by the Congress.

Mustering the Troops

As the public sang George M. Cohan's popular interventionist tune "Over There," Wilson persuaded Congress to raise an army of conscripts, not volunteers, and signed the Selective Service Act in 1917. Many politicians worried whether the nation's eligible males would register. Adding community pressure to the force of law, the administration spiced the day of draft registration with the patriotic hoopla of parades, bands, and political speeches. Amidst the holiday spirit, 10 million men did their duty; fewer than a half million men failed to register. To be sure, pockets of resistance appeared around the country. Arizona Navajos fought off government agents who came to register them; Colorado Utes fled into the mountains; Wobblies everywhere stayed home. In Oklahoma, a tenant farmers' cooperative threatened to march on Washington to protest the draft, but the government suppressed the rebellion and prosecuted its leaders, who received five-year prison sentences. Many others grumbled, but the coercion of local draft boards and community patriotism easily filled the ranks. By the war's end, the draft had netted 3 million soldiers, while another 2 million volunteered for military service.

Public opinion also quashed pacifist sentiment, even among those opposed to war on religious grounds. Although 20,000 initially claimed conscientious objector status, most changed their minds. Indeed, the nation's most celebrated hero, Tennessee's Sergeant Alvin York, made the transition from pacifist to sharpshooter. Bona fide Quakers and Mennonites received nonmilitary assignments, but many suffered extreme torment for expressing their beliefs.

The draft law exempted noncitizen immigrants, but military leaders stressed the possibility of "de-hyphenating" the ethnic population through military service. Although many immigrants volunteered to fight for their new country, military policy complicated the results of their loyalty. To classify its recruits, the army introduced the first mass use of so-called intelligence quotient (IQ) testing. The resulting data demonstrated that education correlated with higher test scores. But evidence that immigrants from southern and eastern Europe performed poorly (because of lower education and language skills) led testers to conclude that these groups were innately inferior to those with an Anglo Saxon heritage. The tests thus contributed to postwar efforts to restrict immigration on racial or national grounds.

Southern political pressure persuaded the War Department to exclude black draftees. In the regular army, African American volunteers served in all-black units under white commanders. Black soldiers resented this second-class status. In one remarkable incident in 1917, racial discrimination in Houston, Texas, provoked black soldiers to attack the town, killing seventeen white civilians. The affair confirmed the worst southern nightmares. Military retribution followed quickly; thirteen African Americans were executed even before their appeals could be heard. Responding

to liberal pressure, the army then opened the draft to blacks and established a single training camp for African American officers. Military policy strictly limited promotions into the higher ranks.

For most "doughboys," as the unshaped soldiers were called, the war loomed as a "great adventure," in the words of Theodore Roosevelt, and most recruits viewed their experience as a rite of passage to find glory in a moral crusade to protect civilization from barbarism. The 20,000 women who served in the armed forces, mostly as nurses, also expressed the desire, as one put it, for "an experience of a lifetime." But to protect the soldiers' virtue and assure a healthy fighting force, the army endeavored to restrict the soldiers' access to liquor and to women. With government posters declaring "A German Bullet is Cleaner than a Whore" or "A Soldier who gets a dose is a Traitor!" the army adopted the progressive curriculum of the social-hygiene movement, advising troops to avoid prostitutes and venereal diseases. Military officials collaborated with civilian crusaders in rounding up women suspected of prostitution and closing red-light districts and brothels, even exporting the policy to France. When French Premier Georges Clemenceau offered to permit licensed prostitution to protect civilians from U.S. servicemen, one diplomat warned him to keep the idea from President Wilson "or he'll stop the war!"

Protecting unexposed recruits from harm sometimes proved impossible. Although the first U.S. troops sailed to France in June 1917, most did not cross the Atlantic until the next year. Their journey coincided with (indeed, accelerated) the worst disease epidemic of the century. Known as "Spanish" influenza, the illness struck rapidly, turning a healthy, vigorous person in just an hour or two into total helplessness, with fevers as high as 105°F and often leading to a fatal pneumonia. As troop movements spread the disease around the world, the deathrate soared, claiming over one-half million U.S. lives (20 million died worldwide). Doctors discovered that most fatal cases involved young adults, the age of many soldiers; in the end, 50,000 doughboys died of the flu—more than fell in battle.

Mobilizing the Home Front

Government orders for military supplies stimulated an enormous economic boom. "We are all making more money out of this war than the average human being ought to," admitted one steel executive. During the preparedness campaign of 1916, Wilson had created a Council of National Defense to ready U.S. industry for war. True to progressive principles, the administration relied on corporate leaders (plus union head Samuel Gompers) to bring "non-partisan" expertise into government affairs. After the United States entered the war, Wilson created a War Industries Board (WIB) to regulate production priorities, prices, and profits, a marriage of business and government that replaced free market conditions.

Under the leadership of financier Bernard Baruch, corporate executives served on government committees as "dollar-a-year men" (their official government salary) and negotiated contracts with private business, often in their own industries. Moral persuasion, rather than legal coercion, determined the terms of government procurement, but few objected to a system that assured generous profits. Indeed, the idea of "cost-plus" contracts (the government would pay all business costs *plus* a fixed profit) exceeded the short-term benefits. After a 1917 tax law allowed corporate advertising to be considered a tax-deductible expense, corporations spent more money on advertising than ever before, creating a precedent for business expenditures that continues today.

To stimulate agricultural production, both for wartime Allies and civilians, Wilson created the Food Administration, which ensured profitable markets for the nation's farmers. Headed by progres-

World War I posters appealed to women's patriotism and underscored their importance to the war effort.

sive mining engineer Herbert Hoover, the agency set high prices for agricultural goods to encourage production, then purchased the entire crop for domestic and foreign consumption. As harvests increased, farm incomes jumped 30 percent. Hoover coordinated these incentives with a public-relations campaign to encourage voluntary rationing and the cultivation of "victory gardens" by homeowners. Exhorting women to enlist as Kitchen Soldiers, wartime calendars demanded wheatless Mondays, meatless Tuesdays, and porkless Thursdays and Saturdays. Advertisements, posters, food wrappers, and movie cartoons urged people to be frugal, lean, and patriotic, a form of self-denial that avoided direct government coercion.

Centralized planning and management further regulated the national economy. To overcome massive transportation bottlenecks, the government assumed control of the railroads, establishing a Railroad Administration to coordinate the operations of competing companies. A separate Women's Service Section handled the problems of new women railroad employees. A government-run Fuel Administration provided coal for war industries and civilians, and occasionally ordered factory shutdowns and lower indoor temperatures to conserve energy.

Industrial efficiency justified new levels of standardization in manufacturing. For example, government specifications reduced the number of automobile tire sizes from 287 to 9, trimmed the number of typewriter spools from 150 to 5, and restricted the number of shoe colors to three—black, brown, or white. Standardized efficiency heralded a new system of daylight savings time that extended sunshine into the work day to save electricity and an estimated 1.25 million tons of fuel. Wartime efficiency also boosted consumer interest in wrist watches (portable time at a glance) that was encouraged by military issues of the novelty to all officers. Vaudeville comedians never failed to get a laugh by threatening to "slap you on the wrist watch." The $14 million watch industry became a mainstay of national advertising.

Wartime Benefits for Workers

Wartime prosperity quickly improved the economic position of the nation's workers. With government contracts guaranteeing profits, business simply passed extra labor costs to taxpayers and consumers. The war also curtailed immigration from Europe, ending the glut of foreign workers. Military conscription further reduced the labor

Government specifications reduced the number of automobile tire sizes from 287 to 9, typewriter spools from 150 to 5, and shoe colors to three—black, brown, or white.

supply. Taking advantage of the shortages, workers demanded better pay, fewer hours, and rights of collective bargaining. Business resistance, together with higher consumer prices, provoked a rising number of strikes. By 1917, over 4,200 walkouts involved more than 1 million workers. From this labor crisis, Gompers's American Federation of Labor (AFL) took the opportunity to achieve a long-desired respectability for unionized workers.

"No strikes," proclaimed the AFL, "which cannot be justified to the man risking his life on the firing line." Having given unconditional support for Wilson's preparedness campaign as well as the declaration of war, the British-born Gompers earned both presidential gratitude and an advisory role in shaping wartime labor policy. In 1917, the White House accepted a proposed Mediation Commission, which subsequently traveled around the country to settle labor disputes and incidentally conveyed government approval of the union movement. The creation of the National War Labor Board in 1918 reinforced this position. Endorsing conciliation rather than strikes or lockouts, the board recognized collective bargaining, a standard eight-hour day, equal pay for women, and the idea of a "living wage." In a few exceptional cases, refusal to cooperate with the Labor Board prompted government seizure of private business.

As union membership doubled to 5 million by 1920, the AFL emerged as a respectable partner

The wartime labor shortage enabled these women to take jobs welding bomb casings, but access to such "male" work stopped abruptly at the end of the war.

in industrial relations—a "business union" alternative to the more militant Socialists and Wobblies, who faced persecution for opposing the war. Gompers, who viewed radical labor as a threat to craft unionism, uttered no protest against the silencing of labor dissent. Nor did the AFL organize new members of the work force. As irrigation opened large acreage to plant cotton and sugar beets in the Southwest, large growers persuaded the federal government to eliminate immigration restrictions in 1917 in order to allow 70,000 Mexican "temporary" farm workers to enter the country. Landowners viewed the migrants, in the words of one grower, as "first-class labor, but number two men," and treated them accordingly. With the IWW's Agricultural Workers Order dead, no union existed to protest the farmworkers' paltry wages and poor living conditions. As African Americans left southern farms for northern cities,

moreover, the AFL accepted local race prejudice and did not recruit new members from the black labor pool.

The demand for labor presented women in all social classes with new opportunities. Although the war created fewer than 1 million new jobs, the departure of men into the army and the demand for military production enabled women to move to better-paying, previously male-only occupations. Wartime opportunities brought more white women into the manufacturing sector, while black women filled jobs vacated by white women and black men. To encourage women's labor, a federal agency, Women in Industry Service, lobbied for better working conditions, including limited night hours. Other government agencies established industrial training programs for women and issued orders requiring equal treatment of women in the workplace.

Despite such efforts, women workers usually confronted opposition from male labor unions and unorganized workers, who treated them, in the words of one woman clerk, as "either jokes or pets." Women usually received lower wages than men, and unions generally refused to support their claims of discrimination. Skilled workers not only felt threatened by female employees but also opposed the de-skilling of labor tasks into their component parts to make the jobs easier for women to perform. Nor did unions, employers, or the government interfere with obvious cases of sex discrimination and physical harassment. Black women were assigned to segregated, and lower-paid, jobs. Such problems sometimes prompted women to go on strike, though most walkouts failed to alter working conditions.

Few women's gains on the labor front lasted after the war ended. Most women industrial workers lost their jobs and got little support from the unions. "The same patriotism which induced women to enter industry," said one labor group, "should induce them to vacate their positions after the war." Although pre-war labor trends continued and the size of the female labor force steadily increased, women were forced to abandon such wartime occupations as streetcar conductors and machinists.

The Crusade for Women's Rights

Despite limited economic gains, women's political status changed dramatically in the climate of wartime mobilization. "We have made partners of the women in this war," said President Wilson in 1918. "Shall we admit them only to a partnership of suffering and sacrifice and toil?" Women's participation in the war effort had produced another presidential reversal. Initially contemptuous of women's right to vote, Wilson had come, by the war's end, to support a constitutional amendment providing for women's suffrage.

A dynamic woman's protest movement took credit for the president's metamorphosis. By 1916, nine western states permitted women's suffrage, but several large eastern states had rejected suffrage referenda to extend the ballot. In trying to overcome this resistance, the suffrage movement had split into two distinct and sometimes hostile camps. The first was the National American Woman Suffrage Association (NAWSA), a moderate organization headed by Carrie Chapman Catt. Proclaiming a so-called winning plan, NAWSA worked within the political system, focusing on state-by-state lobbying campaigns to persuade the separate legislatures to grant women the vote. The second camp, centering around the National Woman's Party, was led by the militant Alice Paul and Lucy Burns, and demanded an amendment to the Constitution that would supersede state laws. During the 1916 presidential campaign, pressure from these groups persuaded both major candidates to endorse woman's suffrage, but not the amendment. Believing that the party in power should be punished for its resistance, the more radical National Woman's party targeted the incumbent Democratic party. They parodied Wilson's 1916 slogan with the phrase "He Kept Us Out of Suffrage."

The war changed the political climate. Abandoning prewar pacifism, NAWSA's Catt thoroughly endorsed Wilson's military program and then contrasted the political loyalty of disenfranchised women with slackers, conscientious objectors, and pro-German men who enjoyed the vote. More bluntly, Paul's National Woman's party focused on the single issue of equal rights and dared to ask "Kaiser Wilson" to give them the same rights of self-determination for which the nation was fighting overseas. While NAWSA led a respectable lobbying crusade in Congress and the states, Paul brought a contingent of radicals to the White House gates in January 1917 and com-

THE END OF THE CLIMB

The triumph of women's suffrage inspired political cartoonists across the nation.

From Paul's militance, President Wilson finally came to appreciate the reasonableness of NAWSA's political agenda. Defining women's suffrage as "vital to the winning of the war," he appealed to Congress in 1918 to pass the suffrage amendment. As the House voted favorably, the feminists sitting in the gallery erupted in cheers and singing. But the Senate blocked the measure, and the radical protesters returned to the White House gates. Not until 1919 did the Senate vote its approval; the necessary thirty-six states finally ratified the Nineteenth Amendment, providing for women's suffrage, in 1920. The split between women moderates and radicals persisted for decades.

Amendment XIX (1920)

The right of citizens of the United States to vote shall not be denied or abridged by the United States or by any state on account of sex.

Congress shall have power to enforce this article by appropriate legislation.

menced a daily protest vigil to attract attention for the cause.

Paul's audacious behavior offended moderate suffragists like Catt and anti-suffrage conservatives who believed women were too irresponsible to vote. Yet Paul represented a new breed of women activists who called themselves "feminists." For such radicals, the vote was merely the first step toward full political equality. Although the White House demonstrations initially attracted only bemused comments, U.S. entry into the war ignited greater hostility because feminists seemed to threaten national unity. Harassed by spectators and arrested by Washington police for unlawful assembly, the suffragists refused to bend. Swelling the jails, they organized hunger strikes and taunted the government into committing outrageous forced feedings that swayed public opinion.

African Americans Close Ranks

Wartime opportunities also released southern farmers, whites as well as blacks, from landless poverty. As the ravaging boll weevil devoured cotton crops and war jobs cried for unskilled labor, southern tenants, sharecroppers, and field workers studied "the gourd" (the big dipper) in the night sky and made the journey north. For African Americans, the exodus promised freedom from racial oppression. Among southern blacks, an informal network of railroad workers, labor agents, and northern kin advertised the opportunities for economic betterment. "Leave the benighted land," summoned the *Chicago Defender,* a leading African American newspaper. "Get out of the South . . . . Come north, then, all you folks, both good and bad." Such advice resonated with generations of racial oppression. "Anywhere north will do [for] us," said one optimistic southern black, "and I suppose the worst place there is better than the best place here."

The movement began as a trickle in 1915, but reached floodtide proportions after U.S. entry into the war. By the war's end in 1918, over 300,000 African Americans, about 10 percent of the total southern black population, had embarked on a journey toward the promised land (Table 20.1). Most were young, unmarried, and male, and motivated not only by the prospect of jobs but also by the desire for liberation. When one Chicago-bound train crossed the Ohio River, the migrants literally stopped their watches, knelt in prayer, and sang the gospel hymn, "I Done Come out of the Land of Egypt with the Good News."

Chicago, Detroit, New York: These destinations looked like something less than the promised land as rural blacks struggled to reset their watches to the demands of urban living. Many found work at the bottom of the industrial ladder, in stockyards, steel mills, munitions factories, and railroad companies. Their wages were lower than whites' earnings, but still better than those they had earned in the South. By 1920, ten northern cities had black populations that exceeded 30,000; New York City had over 150,000 black residents.

In this new urban environment, transplanted southern blacks created lively cultural institutions and adapted to urban ways. Thriving African American churches, mostly Baptist and African Methodist Episcopal, offered emotional ballast, while the business-oriented Urban League helped newcomers find jobs. Such civic institutions promoted cultural uplift, recommending public cleanliness, decorum, and sobriety. But white property owners thrust blacks into crowded, high-rental slums, where poverty fed disease. In Chicago, death rates among African Americans were double those of

Table 20.1 Outmigration from the South, 1890–1930	Whites	Blacks
1890–1900	–30,000	–185,000
1900–1910	–69,000	–194,000
1910–1920	–663,000	–555,000
1920–1930	–704,000	–903,000

Source: Hope T. Eldridge and Dorothy S. Thomas, *Population Redistribution and Economic Growth,* Vol. 3 (Philadelphia: American Philosophical Society, 1964), 90.

whites, as was the proportion of stillbirths. In 1917, an NAACP lawsuit persuaded the Supreme Court to outlaw residential segregation by zoning, but whites enforced segregated neighborhoods by informal agreements and occasional bombings.

Racial violence continued to disrupt racially mixed communities. "The business of lynching Negroes is bad," admitted a Memphis newspaper in 1916. "The worst thing is that often the wrong Negro is lynched." Reacting to job competition from southern blacks in 1917, white workers in East St. Louis, Illinois, erupted in race warfare, killing dozens of African Americans and driving the black community from the city. Neither state nor federal officials seriously investigated this explosion, though 8,000 blacks marched silently down New York City's Fifth Avenue in protest. Well-publicized discrimination in the military kept race relations tense. Yet the nation's leading African American intellectual, W. E. B. DuBois, adopted a conciliatory position as the first U.S. troops sailed to war in Europe. By supporting the white man's war, DuBois hoped to share the spoils of self-determination. "Forget our special grievances," he declared. "Close ranks." Ironically, to avoid racial integration, the first black soldiers sent to Europe fought under the French command.

Artillery shells arrived as "a faraway moan that grows to a scream and then a roar like a train, followed by a groundshaking smash and a diabolical red light."

Being Over There

General John Pershing, dubious hero of the invasion of Mexico in 1916, led the American Expeditionary Forces (AEF) into France in 1917. But the doughboys needed additional training, and U.S. leaders kept most troops separated from other Allied armies, hoping to make a distinctive mark in battle. Twelve months after Congress declared war, only 350,000 men had prepared for action, and even these lacked training in tank warfare and trench assaults. U.S. forces depended upon Allied manufactures for most artillery and ammunition, drawing only 40 percent of military supplies from home. With the AEF unprepared for action, Germany seized the initiative, hoping to break French defenses before U.S. forces could affect the outcome of the war.

As German armies launched a spring offensive in March 1918, reaching within 50 miles of Paris, French General Ferdinand Foch assumed supreme command of the Allied forces, including U.S. troops. The AEF soon marched into defensive positions where enemy attacks seemed least likely to occur. Around Amiens, the doughboys saw their first limited fighting. A second German thrust in May brought the AEF into battle at Chateau-Thierry and Belleau Wood, where U.S. soldiers helped stop the German advances.

The war quickly lost the edge of glory. "To be in the front line," wrote one officer, "was to go hungry." Others suffered extreme "battle thirst," the effects of anxiety mixed with contaminated water. Gas attacks, which caused agonizing suffocation and blindness, added to the horror and suffering. Artillery shells arrived, reported one soldier, as "a faraway moan that grows to a scream and then a roar like a train, followed by a groundshaking smash and a diabolical red light." Such violence caused unexpected reactions. Soldiers' bodies shook convulsively, uncontrollably, while tears streamed from their eyes and involuntary shrieks burst from their chests. The reek of burned and rotting flesh stayed with them for years.

These early actions tested U.S. troops and contributed to the shifting tide of war. As fresh soldiers poured into France at a rate of 250,000 a month, the AEF became a growing military factor. By July 1918, the Allies could commence a counteroffensive, aimed at pushing back recent German advances. In the second battle of the Marne in July and August, a quarter of a million doughboys joined Allied armies in the fighting, and another 100,000 fought with the British to expel German units north of the Somme. With over a million U.S. soldiers in France, many still reeling from a fight with the flu, the AEF prepared for a major attack into the exhausted German ranks.

"It was zero hour," reported one officer as U.S. troops massed for action in September 1918, "and in one instant the entire front . . . was a sheet of flame, while the heavy artillery made the earth quake." Jumping into a 200-mile front in the Argonne Forest, nearly a million U.S. soldiers launched a seven-week offensive that pushed through rain and roiling mud toward the German border. The violence overwhelmed human capacities; thousands perished from sheer exhaustion. But the weary German army suffered more. By November, German leaders pleaded for a ceasefire. On the eleventh hour of the eleventh day of the eleventh month, the Great War finally came to an end. Soldiers rose to their feet and screamed for joy. But over 100,000 doughboys had died, half from disease.

For some U.S. troops, the war had not ended. One year before the Armistice on the western front, the radical Bolshevik party in Russia, led by V. I. Lenin, seized power and created the Soviet Union, dedicated to socialist principles. The Bolshevik regime soon signed a treaty with Germany and withdrew Russian participation from the war. The United States and the western Allies bitterly opposed the socialist revolution, fearing that the revolutionary spirit would spread to their own people. Following his Mexican precedent, Wilson refused to extend diplomatic recognition to the Soviet government. Then, as anti-Bolshevik Russian armies embarked on a civil war against the revolutionary regime, Allied leaders moved to topple the Soviet government and bring Russia back into the war against Germany.

During the summer of 1918, Wilson ordered a military expedition into Archangel in eastern Russia, to join French, British, and Japanese contingents in strengthening anti-Bolshevik forces. But U.S. soldiers saw little action, suffering the harsh weather until their withdrawal in 1919 and 1920. Besides demonstrating Allied hostility to socialism, the mission showed Wilson's commitment to multinational interventionism with strong nations cooperating for a moral world order.

Wilson Fights for a Permanent Peace

To forge a domestic consensus during wartime, Wilson appealed often for the end of partisan politics, but his attitude changed as the war entered its final stage and the 1918 congressional elections approached. Appealing for a Democratic majority, the president demanded endorsement of his personal plans for a treaty settlement. Ten months earlier, Wilson had presented Congress with a dramatic fourteen-point proposal to stabilize postwar European politics, guarantee democratic governments, and prevent the recurrence of war. Asserting the principle of "national self-determination," the president suggested a detailed remapping of Europe to reduce ethnic rivalries. He argued that disarmament, free trade, open treaties, and mediation, an international progressive agenda, would reduce the likelihood of future conflict. Finally, to enforce this world order, Wilson proposed the formation of a League of Nations to settle national differences.

Such grandiose plans required cooperation from all the warring countries. It also hinged on support from Wilson's partisan opponents at home. Yet Republican leaders questioned Wilson's plan to abandon the United States' unilateral foreign policy because it appeared to threaten the nation's independence. And despite Wilson's partisan campaign, Republicans carried the November 1918 elections. Nonetheless, he hoped to persuade European leaders to accept his proposals.

To maximize his influence at the treaty discussions, the president personally led the U.S. delegation to the Versailles Peace Conference in January 1919. Greeted by wildly cheering throngs wherever he traveled, Wilson expected his popularity to overcome national jealousy at the treaty table. He exaggerated his importance. Distorting Wilson's notion of self-determination, Allied diplomats chopped the Austrian, German, and Ottoman empires into new national units, often forcing rival ethnic groups into unstable alliances. Moreover, European leaders did not extend self-determination to Europe's colonies. Instead, the victorious Allies seized German colonies around the world and refused to relinquish their own imperial holdings. Vietnam's Ho Chi Minh, India's Mahatma Gandhi, and Pan-Africanists like Marcus Garvey and W. E. B. DuBois (who attended the conference to encourage decolonization) saw their hopes crushed.

Nor did Wilson prevent the Allies from imposing harsh judgments on Germany. Forcing the defeated nation to accept full responsibility for the war, the victors demanded $33 billion in reparations and restricted Germany's future military development. The heavy financial penalties, and the bitter pill of war guilt, denied Wilson's dream of a peace without victors. Yet Wilson accepted the unequal settlement because the treaty provided for a League of Nations to mediate world peace. "When the war psychosis has abated," he said hopefully, "it will not be difficult to settle all the disputes that baffle us now." Senate Republicans, excluded by the president from participating in the peace talks, had reason to question the president's confidence.

The heart of the controversy lurked in the treaty's Article 10, which established the principle of collective security. Under its terms, member nations would agree to act together to protect the independence of other nations against external aggression. The idea obliged all countries to fight wars voted by the League. Many considered the provision a threat to U.S. independence. In the Senate, one group of vehement "irreconcilables," fearing interminable foreign wars, announced unswerving opposition to the treaty. A second group of eastern Republicans, led by Henry Cabot Lodge, had no quarrel with international commitments, but objected to treaty limitations of Congress's right to declare war in the future. Motivated also by personal hatred of the president, Lodge proposed numerous amendments to weaken the treaty's obligations. Still a third group, known as "reservationists," embraced the League, but demanded elimination of Article 10.

Rather than negotiating with his adversaries, the angry president embarked on a strenuous national tour in September 1919 to muster public support for an unamended treaty. The effort proved tragically hopeless when Wilson collapsed from a stroke and returned to the White House half-paralyzed and unable to conduct official business. Strong of spirit, the broken leader refused to compromise when Lodge introduced an amended treaty for ratification. Ordering Democrats to vote against the revisions, Wilson allowed the modified treaty to fail twice on the Senate floor. There Wilson's dream died. In 1921, a joint congressional resolution formally ended the war. The United States never entered Wilson's League of Nations.

The Ashes of Peace

The retreat from internationalism left Wilson's Democratic party scarred and the nation divided. With the cancellation of war contracts and the return of soldiers to civilian life, unemployment soared, precipitating a wave of labor strikes and social violence. In 1919, over 3,600 strikes affected 4 million workers. Among these was a shipyard walkout in Seattle over wages that escalated into a peaceful city-wide general strike, though the mayor attributed the dispute to Russian revolutionaries and anarchists. When Boston's police chief dismissed unionized employees in 1919, the force went on strike, bringing on a wave of looting and violence. Massachusetts Governor Calvin Coolidge achieved national acclaim by breaking the strike with state troopers. That fall, the AFL sent over 350,000 steelworkers to strike against U.S. Steel, but management refused to negotiate and imported strikebreakers to defeat the union. Meanwhile, attacks on organized labor brought violent retaliation from Italian American anarchists, who targeted anti-union politicians with explosive bombs.

Attorney General A. Mitchell Palmer, who suddenly lost his front porch one night in 1919 when an anarchist bomb exploded, launched a federal attack on suspected radicals. Citing the wartime Sedition Act to justify government actions of questionable legality, Palmer determined to rid the country of political radicals. Initiating a well-publicized "Red Scare," the Department of Justice arbitrarily arrested thousands of labor agitators, socialists, and communists between November 1919 and March 1920. Although the government eventually deported about 500 aliens, including

Emma Goldman, most suspects were held without charges, treated to police brutality, then simply released. Sharing this anti-radical spirit, the New York legislature expelled five elected Socialists, and the House of Representatives refused to seat Milwaukee Socialist Victor Berger, despite his winning two elections. Meanwhile, twenty-eight states adopted sedition laws, which justified more arrests and the imposition of loyalty oaths on public employees. In the private sector, war veterans formed the American Legion in 1919 and undertook a "war of extermination," using violence to silence political critics.

Fury against political radicals was matched only by racial violence, which squashed DuBois's hope for achieving racial equality. During the first year of peace, lynch mobs murdered seventy-eight African Americans, including ten war veterans who died wearing military uniforms. Race riots erupted in dozens of communities across the nation, including Washington, D.C. Such outbursts were hardly new. But in northern cities, African Americans no longer appeared as passive victims.

At the war's end, DuBois called on African Americans for renewed militance to obtain equal rights. "We return," he wrote. "We return from fighting. We return fighting." When job competition in Chicago's stockyards provoked open warfare between the city's whites and blacks in 1919, war veterans of both races fired military weapons, and 38 died: 23 blacks, 15 whites. Frustrated by the failure of racial integration, northern blacks responded favorably to a new all-black organization, the Universal Negro Improvement Association, founded by the West Indian–born Marcus Garvey in 1916. Its goal was to affirm black self-sufficiency through independent economic and cultural institutions. The movement underscored a new racial pride. "If we must die," wrote the poet Claude McKay in the summer of 1919,

let it not be like hogs
Hunted and penned in an inglorious spot

Returning to Normalcy

The agony of blacks and "reds" meant little to the political leadership that shaped diplomacy, led wars, and conducted national elections. With the war finished, the League of Nations dead, and the labor movement buried, Democrats and Republicans focused on the spoils of party politics. Woodrow Wilson, though physically wrecked, toyed with seeking a third term, but his party would not have him. Attorney General Palmer had wasted his prominence with too many false arrests. The divided Democratic party found a candidate in Ohio's governor James Cox and chose an ambitious New Yorker and distant cousin of a previous president, Franklin D. Roosevelt, as his running mate. Still a minority party, the Democrats found little favor amidst the disillusionment of the peace.

"America's present need is not heroics but healing," advised the Republican candidate Warren G. Harding; "not nostrums but normalcy not revolution, but restoration." Sixteen million voters welcomed that rhetoric, ushering Harding and his running mate Calvin Coolidge to a landslide victory in every state outside the South. With that triumph, the nation turned from Wilsonian idealism to the matters of business. The Great War had transformed the nation's place in international affairs. For the first time, the United States stood not as a debtor nation, but a creditor to the world economy. Washington and Wall Street emerged from the war as capitals of finance and so, indirectly, of world stability. Yet, to Harding's pleasure, the largest chunk of national investment remained in domestic business. It was entirely fitting that the most popular book of the day was Sherwood Anderson's *Winesburg, Ohio* (1919), the story of insulated small town people, who perched precariously on the edge of a wider world that lured inhabitants outward or sent them scurrying home. To most U.S. citizens in 1920, the world remained a small place surrounded by temptations.

INFOTRAC® COLLEGE EDITION EXERCISES

For additional reading go to InfoTrac College Edition, your online research library at *http://web1.infotrac-college.com.*

Subject search: Pancho Villa

Subject search: Woodrow Wilson

Subject search: Huerta

Subject search: Carranza

Keyword search: World War I

keyword search: Versailles Treaty

Keyword search: Pershing

ADDITIONAL READING

The United States Goes to War

Robert H. Zieger, *America's Great War: World War I and the American Experience* (2000). A brief survey describing the controversies involving U.S. participation in the war.

David M. Kennedy, *Over Here: The First World War and American Society* (1980). An examination of the war's economic and social impact which places homefront policies in the progressive tradition.

Ronald Schaffer, *America in the Great War: The Rise of the War Welfare State* (1991). A series of well-integrated essays, analyzing the social, cultural, and political aspects of the war at home.

Patriotism in Wartime

Richard Polenberg, *Fighting Faiths: The Abrams Case, the Supreme Court, and Free Speech* (1987). Focusing on the wartime legal system, the author describes the treatment of political dissenters.

Leslie Midkiff DeBauche, *Reel Patriotism: The Movies and World War I* (1997). A study of the wartime movie industry.

Mustering the Troops

Edward M. Coffman, *The War To End All Wars: The American Military Experience in World War I* (1968). A detailed history of military affairs.

Wartime Benefits for Workers

Maurine Weiner Greenwald, *Women, War, and Work: The Impact of World War I on Women Workers in the United States* (1980). This book presents an analysis of women wartime workers.

The Crusade for Women's Rights

Christine A. Lunardini, *From Equal Suffrage to Equal Rights: Alice Paul and the National Woman's Party, 1910–1920* (1986). Emphasizing the role of radical suffragists, the book traces the fight for women's voting rights.

African Americans Close Ranks

James R. Grossman, *Land of Hope: Chicago, Black Southerners, and the Great Migration* (1989). Well-written and well-researched, this book traces the northern migration of southern blacks.

William M. Tuttle, Jr., *Race Riot: Chicago in the Red Summer of 1919* (1970). Carrying forward the story of the great migration, the author examines postwar racial violence.

Being Over There

Alfred W. Crosby, Jr., *Epidemic and Peace, 1918* (1976). This history of the influenza epidemic speculates about its political implications.

The Ashes of Peace

Paul Avrich, *Sacco and Vanzetti: The Anarchist Background* (1991). This study of Italian American anarchism illuminates the Red Scare, with implications for a celebrated legal case of the 1920s.

21

Colliding Cultures of the 1920s

"Nine-tenths of the American towns are so alike that it is the completest boredom to wander from one to another. Always, west of Pittsburgh, and often, east of it, there is the same lumber yard, the same railroad station, the same Ford garage, the same creamery, the same box-like houses and two-story shops. The new, more conscious houses are alike in their very attempts at diversity: the same bungalows, the same square houses of stucco or tapestry brick. The shops show the same standardized, nationally advertised wares; the newspapers of sections three thousand miles apart have the same 'syndicated features'; the boy in Arkansas displays just such a flamboyant ready-made suit as is found on just such a boy in Delaware, both of them iterate the same slang phrases from the same sporting-pages, and if one of them is in college and the other is a barber, no one may surmise which is which." (Sinclair Lewis, *Main Street*)

http://history.wadsworth.com

Main Street, namesake of Sinclair Lewis's bestselling novel of 1920, ". . . is the climax of civilization," said the author with tongue in cheek. As the federal census reported for the first time that a majority of citizens inhabited urban areas rather than the rural countryside, city slickers shared Lewis's snickering at the narrowness and bigotry of small town life. But the antipathy was mutual. In 1923, the phrase *Madison Avenue* entered the national vocabulary as shorthand for the New York–based advertising industry, which promoted new products and modern values to a nation of consumers. Awed by signs of industrial progress, traditionalists lamented the omnipresent invasion of commercial attitudes. "No people may remain free," warned a southern editor in 1923, "where money rules and morals rot."

As the economy recovered from a postwar depression in 1920–1921, manufacturing soared through the decade, bringing a 40 percent increase in the gross national product (GNP) to nearly $100 billion. After 1922, unemployment remained lower than 5 percent, and real wages increased 15 percent. New factory technology brought a dramatic 64 percent jump in productivity, resulting in a decline in the average length of the work week. The U.S. Steel company switched from two twelve-hour shifts per day to three of eight hours without sacrificing profits. As a result, the length of the average work week dropped from 46.3 hours in 1919 to 44.2 in 1929. "The man who builds a factory builds a temple," gloated presidential candidate Calvin Coolidge in 1924, "the man who works there worships there."

Optimism about industrial growth masked basic economic problems and severe inequalities of wealth. Better wages and shorter hours primarily benefited skilled white workers rather than the unskilled, who consisted largely of immigrants, African Americans, and poor white women. By 1929, the nation's wealthiest 1 percent controlled 30 percent of private assets, and half the population owned less than 5 percent of the nation's wealth. Put another way, the richest 0.1 percent of the population earned as much income in 1929 as the poorest 42 percent. During the heyday of corporate prosperity, basic industries, such as textiles, coal mining, and farming, faced disastrous economic dislocations, foreshadowing the economic crisis of the 1930s.

Nor did material advances for the middle classes satisfy a profound unease at the loss of idealism. In his novel *This Side of Paradise* (1920), F. Scott Fitzgerald announced that "all Gods [are] dead, all wars fought, all faiths in man shaken." The poet Ezra Pound lamented in 1920 that during the war so many had died

> For an old bitch gone in the teeth,
> For a botched civilization.

By the decade's end, the writer Ernest Hemingway had resolved to erase "the words sacred, glorious, and sacrifice," believing that amidst postwar prosperity there was "nothing sacred . . . no glory and the sacrifices were like the stockyards at Chicago." This self-defined Lost Generation of writers found sanctuary in Europe, where they looked with dismay at the shallow social ethics of both Main Street and Madison Avenue. Business insiders like advertising executive Bruce Barton saw no conflict between corporate ethics and spiritual values. His bestselling book of 1925, *The Man Nobody Knows,* described Jesus Christ as the ultimate salesman who "picked up twelve men from the bottom ranks of business and forged them into an organization that has conquered the world."

The "New Era" Roars Ahead

"His God was Modern Appliances," wrote Sinclair Lewis of the title character in *Babbitt,* a 1922 satire of small-business values in the Midwest. The business boom of the 1920s brought innovative production in electricity, chemistry, and consumer goods. But the key to prosperity depended upon mass consumption, and producers increasingly focused on marketing their wares. To entice consumers, advertising sold not only products but also images and symbols that attracted public attention. As a result, consumers bought more than they could afford, yet the economy showed basic structural weaknesses, continued inequality, and the stratification of real wealth.

Stimulating Middle-Class Consumption

Indicative of industrial growth during the 1920s, the number of private dwellings wired for electricity doubled to 17 million (60 percent of U.S. households), contributing to a tripling of electrical power consumption. To tap this expanding market, corporations like Westinghouse and General Electric built research and development laboratories to experiment with technology and create new consumer products. Meanwhile, the introduction of electric industrial machinery greatly increased worker productivity and reduced the cost of many goods. Manufacturers could now lure domestic customers to electric washing machines, toasters, refrigerators, vacuum cleaners, fans, and silent kitchen clocks.

Chemistry became a major growth industry. With immense wartime profits, the DuPont munitions company poured $40 million into related chemical ventures, developing synthetic fibers like rayon to replace cotton, cellophane to package consumer goods, and industrial dyes, paints, and lacquers. Innovative use of celluloid for sanitary treatment of war wounds led to the introduction of cellucotton absorbent napkins for women. "Today, with Kotex," read a typical advertisement, "you never need lose a single precious hour." Other chemical synthetics included dacron and acetates that were used for clothing, carpeting, and furniture, ovenproof Pyrex glass for home

This up-to-the-minute advertisement portrayed a modern woman with "bobbed" hair and an outfit featuring abstract designs. Note the assumption that women are responsible for clean and tidy homes.

kitchens, and anti-freeze solvents for automobile radiators.

DuPont's profits from chemistry contributed to a revolution in the automobile industry. Although the Ford Motor Company held its premiere status through 1925—turning out 9,000 Model Ts a day, one every second—DuPont investments in General Motors brought administrative efficiency and marketing innovations that drove Ford to the brink of bankruptcy. GM's new paint heralded the "garageless" car as well as multiple colors. Introducing a range of vehicles, from the cheaper Chevrolet to the more costly Pontiac, Oldsmobile, Buick, and Cadillac, GM priced cars to attract specific income brackets and encouraged frequent purchases to indicate a motorist's prosperity. The choice of annual models and accessories promoted stylistic obsolescence. By 1927, Ford belatedly closed his famous plant to retool a new Model A that could compete with GM's array of cars.

Automobile sales jumped from 2 million in 1919 to nearly 6 million ten years later, producing 23 million registered vehicles, more than the nation's total number of telephones. The industry's economic appetite seemed insatiable: Automobiles annually consumed 80 percent of the nation's rubber, 65 percent of leather upholstery, and 50 percent of plate glass, as well as 7 billion gallons of gasoline. Automobile parts accounted for one-third of the nation's total sales of durable goods during the decade. Yet, as early as 1926, some automobile executives realized that the industry was approaching a saturation point. Meanwhile, the demand for petroleum aroused fears that the nation faced imminent depletion of oil reserves, stimulating a risky speculative market until new discoveries of 28 billion gallons of underground oil promised to meet national needs for the next century.

State taxes on gasoline financed a wave of highway construction that absorbed $1 billion annually by 1929. Although skyscrapers soared above urban landscapes, Henry Ford predicted "the city is doomed." As asphalt roads spread from city centers, suburban communities mushroomed around every major city, growing at twice the rate of urban downtowns. Auto mobility stimulated a doubling of private housing construction, averaging nearly 1 million dwellings a year. Sprawling Los Angeles, with a population of 1.2 million by 1930, surpassed San Francisco and Seattle as the largest western city. Meanwhile, the first suburban shopping center opened in Kansas City in 1925. Fitzgerald's classic 1925 novel, *The Great Gatsby*, featured a flashy Rolls Royce, which linked the business world of Manhattan with the escapist leisure of East Egg, Long Island.

"Her voice was full of money," wrote Fitzgerald of the novel's glamorous heroine. But by the 1920s measuring wealth by standards of consumption overlooked the growing importance of credit purchases (Table 21.1). To offset seasonal sales of automobiles and stabilize monthly production, GM established a customer credit agency in 1919 to oversee installment purchases. By 1926, two-thirds of new cars were bought on credit. Other retailers followed with liberal credit policies, including personal charge accounts. In department stores, credit sales amounted to over half the total volume, and customers took advantage of charge accounts to return used merchandise, affecting as much as 15 percent of gross sales. For the first time, city banks opened consumer loan departments, permitting individuals to exceed budgets in making personal purchases. By 1929, 60 percent of all sales of cars, appliances, and furniture rested on private credit. Personal loans also financed the sale of investment stocks, as brokers gave generous terms for small down payments. Such paper prosperity, like expensive automobiles, fur coats, and diamond rings, no longer reflected a customer's actual worth.

Advertising Sets the Pace

Behind the burst of consumer spending echoed the voice of the mass advertising industry, whose revenues increased from $1.4 billion in 1919 to $3 billion ten years later. DuPont's new printing pigments brought color to magazine advertising as the *Saturday Evening Post* offered the first four-color pages to advertisers in 1926 at $11,000 per page. (That year, the *Post* also introduced an index of advertisers to match the editorial table of contents.) "Advertising isn't read much any more," explained one executive. "It is seen." Billboards, both in cities and the countryside, now aimed at drivers, not pedestrians. Visual attractions, such as photography and modern art, the

TABLE 21.1

Prices of Durable Goods Compared with Disposable Income, 1920–1928

Year	Annual Disposable Income per Household ($)	Product Advertised	Advertised Price(s) or Range of Prices ($)	Product Price as Percent of Annual Household Disposable Income
1920	2,914	Phonograph	25–2,500	0.9–86
		Vacuum sweeper	9–17.50	0.3–0.6
1922	2,312	Dodge auto	980	42.4
		Victrola	25–1,500	1.1–64.9
		Phonograph	65–775	2.8–33.5
		Diamond rings	31–435	1.3–18.8
1923	2,628	Dodge auto	880	33.5
		Piano	635 & up	24 & up
		Victrola	250 & 290	9.5 & 11.0
1925	2,621	Electric iron	7.50	0.3
		Radio	50–460	1.9–17.6
1926	2,727	Chevrolet auto	510–765	18.7–28.0
		Chrysler auto	1,075–1,275	39.4–46.8
		Electric vacuum	34.50 & 39	1.3 & 1.4
1928	2,620	Chevrolet auto	495–715	18.9–27.3
		Chrysler auto	1,040–1,655	39.7–63.2
		Piano	875 & up	33.4 & up
		Radio	77	1.3

Sources: Aggregate disposable income from "Number of Households," U.S. Bureau of the Census, *Historical Statistics*, Series A350, p. 43. Prices of durable goods from advertisements in October issues of *Ladies Home Journal*.

blurring of feature stories with paid commercials, and skywriting by chartered airplanes made advertisements appear as contemporary as the products they touted.

During the so-called New Era boom, advertisers appealed to the "new American tempo," a taut and busy pace that placed priorities on speed and efficiency. "Quick" became a popular virtue, as one columnist explained: "Quick lunches at soda fountain . . . quick cooking recipes . . . quick tabloid newspapers . . . quick news summaries . . . quicker novels . . . quick-drying furniture paint . . . quick-smoking

" I just paid the doctor another ten dollars on his bill."
"Oh goody, two more payments and the baby's ours."

The growth of modern consumer credit inspired cartoons like this one, which first appeared in *World's Work,* January 1926.

cigarettes . . . quick-service filling stations." Indicative of the obsession with timeliness was the reinvention of the word *deadline:* Once used as a measure of space (for instance, a line beyond which diseased cattle would be killed), during the 1920s the word became a measure of time. Advertising writers and journalists now had to deliver copy by a deadline; aging factory workers faced a deadline when they would be replaced by younger, more efficient hands. "These are times when the earth revolves twice as fast upon its axis," remarked a copywriter. "The three o'clock brunette is the four o'clock blonde. The spirit of the hour is, 'Cut it short or cut it out.'"

This self-consciousness about time conflicted with the seasonal world of rural life. In 1919, business leaders urged the federal government to ex-

"The spirit of the hour is, 'Cut it short or cut it out.'"

tend the use of wartime daylight savings time to allow more leisure (and consumption) in the cities. Rural constituents opposed this disrespect for "natural" or "God's time." "We might soon have laws passed attempting to dictate the volume of air a man should breath," warned one member of Congress, protesting the growth of federal power. After a bitter political fight, traditionalists managed to defeat the urban proposal.

The omnipresence of timekeeping stimulated a fad for watches with luminescent dials that would glow in the dark, a novelty first introduced for soldiers during the war. But women factory workers who pointed their brushes with their mouths to paint the dials with radium developed oral cancers, and the National Consumers League launched a campaign that ended the practice in 1927. Urban sophisticates also worried about the effects of time pressure on their health. "Life speeds up," said a laxative advertisement. "Yet this new pace is a strain." A variety of popular products offered remedies for "irregularity." Other products highlighted the perils of body odors, including the mythical "halitosis" that turned Listerine mouthwash into a household word.

When marketing surveys found that women accounted for 80 to 90 percent of all purchases for family use, advertisers set their targets on the middle class housewife. Sexual desire became the image of choice. One advertisement made the point explicitly: "The first duty of women is to attract." Accordingly, cosmetic sales increased from $17 million in 1914 to $121 million in 1925. Commercial images projected current styles of clothing, haircuts, and accessories, all of which changed seasonally and annually to demand constant repurchasing.

The Politics of Business

As business prospered, national politicians embraced the concerns of corporate leaders. Reacting to the federal economic regulations passed during the Progressive era and the world war, members of both political parties attacked such government activities and stressed private enterprise. Some criticized the growth of government bureaucracy to justify their opposition to social legislation, such as the abolition of child labor. Others complained about high taxes and thereby found reason to support tax cuts. Still others saw Bolshevism and "Reds" hiding behind programs for child healthcare. Many big-business executives objected to government regulation of Prohibition and joined the campaign to repeal the Eighteenth Amendment. Whatever their particular rhetoric, business leaders seldom questioned the principle that government should serve the interests of business.

The decade's three Republican presidents—Warren Harding, Calvin Coolidge, and Herbert Hoover—thus expressed the business values of their primary constituency. Harding's promise of "normalcy" during the 1920 election translated into the motto "less government in business and more business in government." To implement those views, Secretary of the Treasury Andrew Mellon, a wealthy industrialist and banker, introduced a program to reduce government spending in order to make cuts in corporate and high-bracket income taxes. To make up the lost government income, Mellon proposed raising the set fees and taxes that affected all consumers. As Congress repealed wartime excess profits taxes and lowered rates for personal incomes, he remarked: "I have never viewed taxation as a means of rewarding one class of taxpayers or punishing another."

Corruption in Government

Other Harding appointees adopted different strategies to enrich business associates and themselves. The head of the Veterans Bureau, for example, padded construction bills and sold federal property for a fraction of its value, robbing the government of $200 million. The genial Harding accepted the bureaucrat's resignation; only after the president's death did a Senate investigation lead to formal exposure and a prison sentence. Meanwhile, the attorney general sold jobs, pardons, and permits as well as protection for tax evaders and bootleggers. Though forced to resign in disgrace, the government's top lawyer burned incriminating documents to avoid a jail sentence.

Brooding on this corruption ("my God damn friends," Harding confided, "they're the ones that keep me walking the floor nights"), the president died suddenly of a stroke in 1923. Though mourned by the public, further revelations tarnished his reputation. Amidst widespread concern about the nation's oil reserves, senate investigators discovered that Secretary of the Interior Albert Fall had accepted bribes in exchange for oil leases on federal property at Teapot Dome, Wyoming. The courts eventually voided the contracts, and Fall went to jail. Such shady arrangements captured the speculative mood of New Era business. During the decade, the search for quick riches also led to fraudulent booms in real estate in Florida, silver mines in Nevada, stock transactions on Wall Street, and a numbers racket in Harlem.

Coolidge's Business

That the Republican party survived the Harding scandals to elect presidential successor Calvin

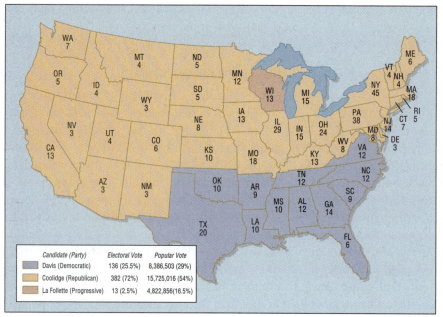

The Election of 1924

Candidate (Party)	Electoral Vote	Popular Vote
Davis (Democratic)	136 (25.5%)	8,386,503 (29%)
Coolidge (Republican)	382 (72%)	15,725,016 (54%)
La Follette (Progressive)	13 (2.5%)	4,822,856 (16.5%)

Coolidge in 1924 testified to voter acceptance of business values. With the slogan "Keep Cool with Coolidge," the Republican nominee (and president since Harding's death) reminded voters that "the chief business of the American people is business." His running mate was Charles Dawes, an international banker. Both Republicans represented old-stock Protestant values. As the incumbent, Coolidge benefited from the mood of prosperity and from contributions of business leaders who paid for his campaign.

The Democrats failed to mount an effective challenge because deep ideological splits within the party undermined any consensus. At the 1924 nominating convention in New York, one faction supported William McAdoo, a progressive critic of Wall Street, who supported Prohibition and refused to condemn the Ku Klux Klan. Another faction backed New York Governor Al Smith, a child of Catholic immigrants. The two groups, nearly equally balanced at the convention, rejected compromise. Instead, they battled over basic principles:

wets versus drys, Protestants versus immigrants, big cities versus rural southerners. It took 103 ballots before the Democrats nominated John Davis, a compromise candidate. The Wall Street lawyer hardly offered an alternative to Coolidge.

Criticism of the Republican leadership did come from a third candidate, the new Progressive party's Senator Robert La Follette of Wisconsin, who tried to revive the spirit of reform. "The great issue before the American people," declared the Progressive platform, "is control of government and industry by private monopoly." Such appeals attracted midwestern farmers and small business owners who viewed eastern bankers with suspicion. La Follette also drew support from urban ethnics and the AFL. But precisely because of his constituency, La Follette could not overcome the tinge of radicalism. In the final tally, Progressives won 16 percent of the popular vote; Democrats gained 24 percent; Coolidge captured 54 percent and swamped the electoral college. Yet fewer than half the country's eligible voters went to the polls.

The 1924 elections strengthened conservative Republicans in Congress and isolated the surviving progressives. Republican leaders thus faced little opposition in undermining pre-war progressive reforms. To protect industries from foreign competition, for instance, Congress raised tariffs rates to the highest levels, despite increasing prices for farmers and consumers. Mellon's tax revisions killed the progressive policy of placing larger burdens on the wealthy. Under Coolidge, the Federal Trade Commission tilted in a pro-business direction, limiting investigations of corporate practices and settling nearly all violations with informal consent agreements rather than through legal action. "The legitimate interests of business are in perfect harmony with the true interests of the public," explained the FTC chair in 1927.

Hoover and Trade Associations

The decade's most influential Republican leader was Secretary of Commerce Herbert Hoover, a self-made millionaire who had achieved fame by organizing the nation's wartime food program. Dedicated to private initiative, Hoover believed that voluntary cooperation by business could ensure corporate expansion and social prosperity. He encouraged business leaders to form trade associations within particular industries to include manufacturers, wholesalers, and retailers. Private businesses could share information, resolve disputes, and promote mutually beneficial marketing goals. By 1926, over 1,000 trade associations dotted the corporate landscape. Hoover's Commerce Department also promoted agricultural associations and persuaded Congress to exempt farm groups from anti-trust laws. The various trade associations formed a corps of political lobbying groups to influence the legislative process, drafting bills, providing "expert" witnesses, and lining up congressional votes.

Rather than object to such special interests, Republican leaders welcomed the business lobbies' advice and consent. Only "reactionaries and radicals," said Hoover in 1922, "would assume that all reform and human advance must come through government." Under Hoover's leadership, the Bureau of Standards provided companies with statistical information about production, inventories, and prices. Such neutral data, available to all businesses, promoted rational corporate planning. Through educational conferences, the bureau endorsed standardization of sizes, shapes, and styles of consumer products, such as bottles, canned goods, and durable appliances. Although constitutional precedents suggested that sharing information within trade groups violated anti-trust laws, the Supreme Court ruled in 1925 that such exchanges were legal, as long as no restraints of production or prices existed. The administration also created guidelines for commercial aviation and radio communications. "We are passing from a period of extremely individualistic action," said Hoover, "into a period of associational activities."

Mergers, Monopolies, and Chains

Amid the pro-business climate, corporate leaders initiated a wave of company mergers, resulting in the concentration of economic power in fewer hands. As 1,300 combines absorbed over 7,000 firms between 1919 and 1928, the Justice Department challenged just sixty transactions and chose to block only one. In several industries, such as aluminum, salt, sugar, and tropical fruits, monopolies established complete market control. Less than a handful of companies dominated petroleum, steel, copper, meat packing, and tobacco, while three firms made over 80 percent of U.S. automobiles. In food retailing, the Great Atlantic and Pacific Tea Company (A&P) operated 17,500 branch stores. Such business trends won ratification in several Supreme Court decisions, which accepted corporate consolidation as long as legal formalities were preserved.

Through chain stores, franchises, and national brand names, business concentration touched virtually every household in the country. By 1929, 1,500 companies controlled 70,000 retail outlets. In the largest cities, half of all retail sales flowed through chain stores and totaled 16 percent of the nation's business. By centralizing wholesale purchases and retail advertising, chain stores established an economic edge over smaller competitors. A&P's slogan, "Quality You Know by Name," evoked the familiarity of national brands that were backed by national advertising, packaged with recognized logos, and protected by factory quality control.

Foreign Trade Encourages Diplomatic Flexibility

Despite Republican criticism of government involvement in the economy, the party of business actively supported foreign trade and investment. Hoover's Commerce Department assisted oil companies in gaining concessions for refineries in Venezuela and the Persian Gulf area and helped rubber producers establish plantations in Brazil and the Dutch East Indies. During the decade, U.S. foreign investments doubled to $7.5 billion. In Latin America, corporations like United Fruit and the Guggenheim mining syndicate linked investments to trade and achieved sales of nearly $2 billion south of the border. Such economic expansion justified U.S. military intervention to ensure friendly regimes and protect U.S. corporations in the Dominican Republic, Honduras, and Nicaragua. When Mexico announced plans to nationalize mines and oil fields in 1927, however, the White House opted to negotiate a settlement that stabilized Standard Oil and banking investments without recourse to hostilities. In exchange for oil concessions, the United States backed the existing government against its dissidents.

Emphasizing diplomacy and free trade, Republican leaders hosted the Washington Arma-ments Conference in 1921–1922, which resulted in three treaties aimed at reducing the likelihood of war. Reflecting widely held anti-militarist feelings, the five major naval powers agreed to scrap 2 million tons of warships and accepted a fixed ratio of naval forces (5 for Britain and the United States, 3 for Japan, 1 for France and Italy) to preserve the existing balance of power. A second treaty committed the world powers to respect territorial possessions in the Pacific. Finally, the Nine-Power pact reaffirmed an Open Door policy in China and guaranteed existing territorial boundaries. Taken together, these agreements showed a practical interest in protecting international trade without requiring extensive military commitments. The aversion to military engagement culminated with the signing of the Kellogg-Briand peace pact in 1928, in which fifteen nations pledged to avoid war and adopt "pacific means" to settle disputes. Entirely symbolic, the treaty appealed to pacifist organizations without affecting national policy.

Foreign affairs focused primarily on protecting the U.S. dollar. Having rejected the Versailles treaty, Republican leaders felt no obligation to support France after Germany defaulted on reparation payments owed to the Allies. When France invaded Germany's Ruhr district in 1923 to force the payments, U.S. leaders insisted that France desist or immediately repay loans extended by Washington during the war. With such pressure, the United States forced France to renegotiate the German debt. U.S. bankers then proposed the "Dawes Plan" in 1924, which cut German obligations in half and encouraged the U.S. financial community to invest additional millions in loans to Germany. Praised as an enlightened alternative to French military action, the plan allowed bankers to support Germany's economic recovery, while extending over $1 billion in credit by 1930. Such programs demonstrated that the United States had become the world's leader in matters of

The refusal of businesses to negotiate with labor unions encouraged violent confrontations, as seen in this demonstration at Cleveland, Ohio, where strikers, encouraged by onlookers, throw stones at police.

finance and trade, but also indicated that the nation's political commitments lagged far behind.

Business Culture and the Worker

Corporate domination of the economy created the framework within which small businesses, farmers, and workers had to operate. Yet there were still significant pockets of resistance to a homogenized economy. Thus, despite the economic muscle of national franchises and chains, surveys of white working class and ethnic neighborhoods found little evidence of chain-store penetration. Unlike middle-class consumers, ethnic and working-class shoppers preferred to transact business (and share gossip) in their native language, to use products that preserved a cultural heritage, and to request personal services, such as credit and home delivery. Ethnic communities also supported local banks and insurance companies, even though such institutions were more risky.

One exception to this pattern involved urban African Americans. Having migrated to northern cities from rural areas, blacks generally lacked the capital to start their own businesses and resented their inability to find jobs in small white-run stores. Instead, northern blacks preferred to shop in anonymous chains and purchase national brands. By 1930, Harlem's blacks were organizing boycotts to pressure the chains to hire black workers.

The Problems of Labor

The strength of workers and ethnic communities underscored both their rejection of business values and their economic class differences. During a decade that celebrated the triumph of corporate efficiency and middle-class prosperity, workers faced a severe erosion of power. Having crushed the wave of labor strikes in 1919, corporate leaders further tamed the union movement during the postwar recession that brought high unemployment. When economic conditions improved in 1922, organized labor tried to recapture lost wages, but a series of large strikes in textiles, coal mining, and railroads resulted in disappointing failures.

Prosperity did bring wage increases, which soothed some labor unrest. Yet union membership did not increase, as it usually did during prosperous years—just the opposite. One reason lay in the conservative political climate of Washington. In 1921, the Supreme Court upheld the use of injunctions against striking steel workers and declared that picketing by more than one striker was illegal. Other rulings held unions responsible for triple damages and permitted the use of "yellow dog" contracts, in which workers were obliged to repudiate union membership. From 5 million in 1920, the number of organized workers dropped by one-third to 3.4 million in 1929. Meanwhile, more radical, largely ethnic workers, who supported the newly organized Workers, or Communist, party, faced arrest for conspiracy and were forced to pursue their activities underground.

Women workers also made limited advances during the decade. In 1930, one-third of all working women were still domestics, a majority of whom were foreign-born or African Americans. Another quarter of working women had factory jobs, which paid slightly more than half the wages of men. The major occupational change was in the rising proportion of women in clerical jobs, but women office workers still earned lower-than-average incomes. Although the number of college-educated women tripled, only one in four entered the labor force, and most took jobs in sex segregated fields, such as nursing, teaching, or social work. The decade also saw a rise in the proportion of married women who worked. But most working women were young and single and saw their careers as temporary, a situation that discouraged organized protest about workplace inequities.

Even for men, organized unionism became more difficult. Business leaders deliberately undermined labor unrest and unionization by making cosmetic concessions to workers' desires. "Slowly we are learning," remarked the head of General Electric, "that low wages for labor do not necessarily mean high profits for capital." Although poor working conditions in mining, steel, and textiles provoked fierce labor battles during the decade, corporate leaders understood that industrial peace offered mutual advantages and reduced the danger of more radical socialist remedies.

The so-called welfare capitalism, touted by business as the "American Plan," promised to eliminate labor disputes and curtail worker turnover by winning the wage earners' loyalty. In large companies, top management required shop foremen to attend leadership classes, where they learned to make employees efficient by persuasion rather than coercion. Companies installed centralized personnel departments, standardized job assignments and working conditions, and made promotions from within. Department stores introduced the wartime intelligence quotient (IQ) tests to screen prospective employees and hired psychiatrists and social workers to monitor worker behavior. Such social-science techniques sometimes backfired. Knowing they were subjects of management experiments, workers in time-and-motion studies used slow-down tactics to thwart the efficiency experts; in one North Carolina mill, workers threw their tester out the window.

Employers also used the tools of assimilation to overcome ethnic and class based loyalties. In factories, management intermixed ethnic groups to undermine the clannishness that weakened loyalty to the company. Treated as individuals, rather than part of a labor gang, workers faced supervisors alone. Mixing nationality groups also discouraged unionization. Meanwhile, to accelerate "Americanization" of immigrant workers, businesses introduced after-hours classes in English and civics. Company-sponsored social activities, such as sports teams, picnics, and Sunday excursions, further weakened attachments to the workers' home communities.

Business leaders also launched an "open shop" campaign to deflect workers' interest in unions. Company-run unions or employee councils created the illusion of labor participation in making work rules and grievance procedures; but, unlike the situation with collective bargaining, corporate budgets invariably determined work policies. Borrowing from Henry Ford's $5 day, businesses offered wage incentives to encourage individual productivity and added fringe benefits, such as paid vacations after a specified period of continuous employment. Other incentives included group life insurance, pension plans, medical services, and stock ownership. By 1929, nearly 1 million workers owned company stock. Most of it was miniscule in value but had dispersed widely enough so that monopolies like AT&T could claim to be "democratic" institutions, and the president of the Illinois Central railroad could state that "Main Street and not Wall Street . . . runs the railroads today." Such programs succeeded in reducing employee turnover and absence by half, while enhancing worker productivity. The number of strikes declined from 3,600 in 1919 to less than 1,000 a decade later. "American conditions," boasted a magazine editorial, "have just about wiped out the proletariat."

Sick Industries, Troubled Workers

Myopia, not utopia, explained such exaggerations. Despite impressive growth rates, mechanization of production created a labor surplus in textiles, mining, and agriculture. Faced with overproduction, relatively high wages, and competition from synthetic fibers, New England's historic textile mills disappeared, as one contemporary put it, "like wartime casualty lists." Although 1 million spindles were relocated to southern factories where wages were lower, even these mills suffered from surplus production, obliging most

employees to work part-time and families to pool their earnings. Similarly, half the nation's coal went unsold, forcing the closing of 3,000 mines and layoffs of three-quarters of bituminous mine workers. In both industries, employee anger and management arrogance produced violent strikes that were settled to the companies' advantage by military force.

The nation's farmers also showed few signs of prosperity. A tenfold increase in the number of tractors not only increased productivity, which stimulated surplus production, but also eliminated a large population of working horses and mules that had consumed 24 million acres of animal feed each year. Mechanized agriculture also demanded capital investments, for which farmers mortgaged their land. As European agriculture recovered from wartime devastation, farm exports declined and commodity prices fell precipitously. Midwestern droughts and southern boll weevils added to the farmers' afflictions. Larger agricultural businesses held sufficient capital to weather these problems. But by 1929, farm income had plunged drastically, and one-fifth of all holdings fell into bankruptcy. By 1929, 1 million farm families abandoned the land to find jobs in the cities.

As in the 19th-century agriculture crisis, farmers experimented with marketing cooperatives, winning congressional exemption from anti-trust laws and attracting half a million growers by 1923. Problems of capitalization and inexperience undermined the effort. In Congress, agrarian leaders formed a strong lobbying coalition, known as the Farm Bloc, which gained legislation for low-interest farm loans. The bloc also backed an elaborate plan involving federal price guarantees and sale of surplus produce overseas, known as the McNary-Haugen farm bill, which passed Congress twice. Coolidge believed the measure exceeded the responsibility of government and vetoed it both times. As agriculture poverty worsened in 1929,

Congress established the Federal Farm Board to purchase surplus production. But prices continued to plummet and the $500 million appropriation soon disappeared.

Citizenship and the National Identity

Amid the glamour of middle-class prosperity, an essayist suggested in 1925 that a person's "first importance to his country is no longer that of citizen but that of consumer." Such attitudes expressed the desire to minimize divisions within the national identity. At a time when Americanization programs and progressive educational curricula for immigrants' children strove to obliterate differences among ethnic, racial, and regional groups, advertisers and mass media emphasized the growing homogenization of a national culture. Yet efforts to blur social diversity often clashed with the interests of specific groups.

Nowhere was this issue more apparent, or complex, than in the dilemma faced by women activists after the ratification of the Nineteenth Amendment in 1920, which guaranteed female suffrage (see Chapter 20). Assumptions that women would act as a single political entity—a voting bloc comparable to the Farm Bloc or the labor lobby—rapidly disappeared as newly enfranchised women searched for a political agenda. Diversity typified their response. Just as the suffrage movement itself had splintered, activist women formed and joined a multitude of organizations, whose interests ranged from birth control and children's welfare to minority rights, cultural issues, and world peace.

Women as a group seldom convened on a single side of any political issue. Democrats and Republicans differed about their support of federal legislation; even feminists divided between those who demanded equal treatment in all aspects of public life and those who wanted to save special exemp-

tions for women in the workplace. Madison Avenue to the contrary, women and minority groups resisted homogenized categories and defended their interests as they defined them.

Women and Politics

Despite gaining the vote, women's rights of citizenship remained ambiguous. Earlier laws had denied native-born women who married noncitizens their birthright of citizenship and barred foreign-born women who married U.S. citizens from sharing their husband's status. Deprived of citizenship, such native-born women were treated as aliens and faced discrimination in public employment, including the teaching profession. Soon after women obtained the vote, at a time when politicians still thought they might vote as a bloc, Congress addressed the issue of citizenship. The resulting Cable Act of 1922 preserved the citizenship of native-born women, regardless of their spouse's status, and permitted foreign-born women to seek citizenship individually. Yet the law perpetuated inequities. If a woman's spouse was ineligible for citizenship (that is, an Asian man) the native-born wife lost her citizenship for the duration of the marriage.

Citizenship did not necessarily give women other political rights. Since the Nineteenth Amendment spoke only of voting, states moved at various speeds to allow women to serve on juries. After a New Jersey all-woman jury served honorably in 1920, the judge promised to summon similar panels in the future, except in cases of slander, "where they might be forced to hear bad language." Some states forbade women jurors for another thirty years. Numerous states convened special legislative sessions to allow women to register to vote in 1920, but a few established residency requirements that prevented female participation that year. Other states denied women's right to hold public office. Some quickly enacted appropriate constitutional changes, but Oklahoma waited until 1942 before giving women that right.

Equal rights, in any case, did not translate into political power. "Beneath the veneer of courtesy . . . accorded women," remarked New York's Eleanor Roosevelt in 1928, "there is a widespread male hostility . . . against sharing with them any actual control." When the major suffragist organizations disbanded in 1920, women activists formed the nonpartisan League of Women Voters to educate citizens about political issues. Ironically, women's enfranchisement coincided with a general decline of all voting. Partly the result of the conservative climate that discouraged political activism, and partly due to the lack of passionate contemporary issues, women entered the voting booth slowly and usually voted in patterns similar to their spouses'.

Most women activists participated in politics through private voluntary organizations, but some did seek election to public office. Women found electoral success in local and county governments, especially as elected school officials. By 1929, 149 women were serving as state legislators, and two were governors (both succeeded their husbands). But out of a total of nearly 10,000 elected state legislators, their numbers were tiny. Indeed, those few who moved close to national party leaders, such as New York's Belle Moskowitz, who worked for Al Smith, exercised power behind the scenes.

Women reformers did succeed in preserving a progressive legacy by persuading Congress to address the health problems of mothers and children. Concerned about the nation's high infant-mortality rate, especially in rural areas, the federal government's Children's Bureau, headed by Julia Lathrop, advocated legislation to provide medical information and assistance to the nation's mothers. Drawing support from women activists in the newly formed Women's Joint Congressional Committee, the Children's Bureau organized a lobbying campaign that led Congress to enact the Sheppard-Towner Maternity and Infant Protection Act in

Eleanor Rooosevelt was a progressive reformer who championed the rights of minorities, aiding the political campaigns of her husband, Franklin D. Roosevelt, during the 1920s.

1921. The law provided welfare aid to new mothers and required states to provide matching funds for health education. Health professionals, mostly women, created informational programs and medical services, such as home visits, that reached households in every state and contributed to a drop in rural infant mortality. Yet conservative groups and male medical professionals still objected to federally funded welfare. Despite lobbying by women reformers, Congress refused to renew the program, and the nation's first major social welfare assistance ended in 1929.

Political differences also divided progressive women about how to define their rights in the public sector. Reformers had long advocated special legislation to protect female workers from harsh working conditions. The Supreme Court's

Muller decision of 1908 (see Chapter 19) had accepted the idea that women's physical differences merited special consideration. In light of women's equal suffrage, however, the Court reversed itself in the *Adkins* case of 1922, claiming that gender differences had almost reached "the vanishing point" and overturned a law providing minimum wages for female employees. Progressives denounced the ruling and proposed constitutional amendments to reverse the decision.

Feminists like Alice Paul and the National Woman's party rejected such tactics. Rather than pursuing issues that presumed the differences of gender, Paul advocated the end to all legal discrimination and proceeded to draft an Equal Rights Amendment (ERA) that was introduced to Congress in 1923. The measure drew passionate opposition not only from conservative men and women but also from a generation of women social reformers who had struggled for specialized legislation to protect women from exploitation in a free market. Organizations like the Women's Trade Union League opposed the idea, as did the women's leadership in the Children's Bureau. Congress allowed the proposal to die, though the issue remained on the national agenda for decades.

Proposed Amendment (1923)

- Men and women shall have equal rights throughout the United States and every place subject to jurisdiction.
- Congress shall have power to enforce this article by appropriate legislation.

Citizenship and Native American Rights

Problems about defining women's citizenship paralleled federal relations with Native American people living on tribal reservations. Although two-thirds of them were citizens, they remained legal dependents of the federal government (specifically, the Interior Department's Indian Bureau) and they lacked the right to elect representatives or to challenge federal policy in the courts. Reservation inhabitants were thus vulnerable to public schemes to take their lands. Harding's secretary of the interior, guilty of the Teapot Dome crimes, announced a plan permitting outsiders to seize valuable irrigated property from the Pueblo nations in New Mexico. Land disputes nearly led to armed battles, but with the support of Santa Fe intellectuals, such as Mabel Dodge, D. H. Lawrence, and Mary Austin, the Pueblos persuaded Congress to defeat the proposal. The Interior Department then announced plans to permit oil and gas leasing on reservation property, but the newly formed American Indian Defense Association beat back that challenge.

To protect Native Americans from legal attacks, reformers proposed universal citizenship, observing that the "vague" rights of the past usually meant "greater profits for someone else." Not all Native people wanted U.S. citizenship, fearing further destruction of their cultural heritage as well as loss of their protected status as government wards. Already reservation land holdings had shrunk to 50 million acres, one-third of which were leased to non-Native people. Finally, Congress voted in 1924 to extend citizenship to all Native Americans. But, as was the case for women, state governments defined Native citizenship as a limited right. New Mexico and Arizona, with large Native American populations, continued to bar their right to vote. Meanwhile, federal and state governments restricted religious freedom, prohibiting the sun dance (deemed immoral and disruptive), the ceremonial use of peyote and other intoxicants, and the extravagant giving away of property, known as *potlatch*. In one memorable six-day extravaganza in 1921, one chief gave away 4 motor boats; 24 canoes; 3 pool tables; thousands of blankets, dresses, and shawls; violins; guitars; washtubs; basins; sewing machines; record players; and more. Although government reports challenged these restrictions, federal officials refused to alter bureau policy.

Immigration and the New Citizens

Concern about cultural boundaries also affected immigration policy. Typical of a growing national obsession with the influx of foreigners, the 1920 census eliminated the distinction between "mulatto" and "Negro" (all people of African descent were to be considered the same) and introduced the category "children of the foreign born." "We are being made a dumping ground for the human wreckage of the war," warned a congressional leader. Despite the 1917 Immigration Act's mandated literacy test, the end of the world war had prompted a resurgence of immigration. As eastern European Jews fled from violent episodes of persecution, known as *pogroms,* the number of new arrivals exceeded 50,000 per month. By 1921, Harding endorsed an Emergency Quota Act, which restricted the number of immigrants and gave preference to northern Europeans.

Although ethnic communities flourished in the cities, and second-generation ethnics were rapidly adopting mainstream values, the nation's political leaders continued to worry about the deterioration of their race. "Biological laws," said Coolidge, "tell us that certain divergent people will not mix or blend." In 1924, Congress voted to refine immigration restrictions in the National Origins Act. The law established permanent quotas based on the place of origin of the newcomers. A complicated formula, reflecting the prevailing ethnic and race prejudices, allotted 70 percent of the quota to English, Germans, and Irish, and gave the balance to southern and eastern European nationalities, effectively shrinking admission from those regions.

Business groups, which historically supported the entry of cheap labor, raised few objections to the measure. By the 1920s, mechanization and electricity had greatly increased worker productivity, limiting the ability of industry to absorb new workers. Thus immigration restrictions encouraged businesses to improve labor relations to avoid turnovers and walkouts. And while the new law narrowed immigration, 4 million newcomers still entered the country during the decade. After 1926, for the first time in U.S. history, a majority of immigrants were women. Usually young and increasingly married, these women differed from the pre-war transient labor force that intended to return to their native lands. Planning to become permanent residents, these women gave stability to ethnic communities.

No quotas applied to Asian immigrants; the 1924 law simply barred all aliens who were ineligible for citizenship. Two years earlier, the Supreme Court had ruled in the *Ozawa* case that Japanese were ineligible for citizenship on legislative grounds dating to 1790: they were not white. Formal protests from the Japanese government, ostensibly a U.S. ally, made no difference. "The mingling of Asiatic blood with European or American blood," explained political commentator Franklin D. Roosevelt, "produces, in nine cases out of ten, the most unfortunate results." Several western states passed alien land laws, forbidding residents ineligible for citizenship from owning real property; state laws also barred intermarriage between Asians and whites. In 1927, the Supreme Court extended the 1896 *Plessy* doctrine (see Chapter 17) to block Chinese pupils, as members of "colored races," from attending white schools in Mississippi.

The desire for cheap agricultural labor also led Congress to eliminate immigration quotas within the Western Hemisphere. Attracted by jobs in sugar beet fields and cotton plantations of the Southwest, over 700,000 Mexican farm workers entered the country during the decade, doubling the Mexican American population to 1.5 million. Poorly paid and seasonally unemployed, migrant farm workers endured harsh working conditions and substandard living arrangements. In urban areas, residential segregation and poverty caused high infant mortality, including an epidemic of bubonic plague in Los Angeles. But barriers to European immigration opened jobs in the industrial sector. Chicago's Mexican community, consisting mostly of young single men, jumped from 1,200 in 1920 to 19,000 ten years later. Exploited in the dirtiest and lowest-paid jobs, Mexicans saw themselves as transients, exhibiting the lowest rate of naturalized citizenship of all immigrant groups.

Within all ethnic enclaves, cultural minorities struggled with issues of identity and assimilation. Members of the Jewish community moved away from Orthodox religion and joined the more-assimilated Conservative or Reform congregations. Some rejected organized religion altogether, stimulating a poignant immigrant literature that included Abraham Cahan's *The Rise of David Levinsky* (1917), Anna Yezierka's *Bread Givers* (1925), and Mike Gold's *Jews Without Money* (1930). Such novels expressed the dilemmas of rejecting heritage amid the opportunities of a new country. Catholic immigrants also worried about the loss of heritage. Polish, Italian, and Mexican immigrants often opposed meltingpot programs within the Catholic church and supported foreign-language classes that preserved ethnic literacy. But while first-generation immigrants depended on community support, children born in America learned English in public schools, copied fashions from middle-class magazines, and found recreation in mainstream sports, music, and movies.

Ethnic politics also became tamer. The repressive Red Scare of 1919–1920 greatly weakened radical groups and drove the ethnic-based Communist party underground. When a New York City high school student published a poem disparaging the U.S. government in the Communist *Daily Worker,* he received a six-month jail sentence for obscenity.

Meanwhile, the Socialist party moderated its rhetoric and focused primarily on quadrennial appeals for presidential votes. Contemporaries focused more attention on the trial of two Italian American anarchists, Nicola Sacco and Bartolomeo Vanzetti, for bank robbery and murder. Despite nationwide mass protests and appeals for clemency for these immigrants, the two were convicted and executed in 1927, reminding other ethnic workers of the perils of radical dissent.

Living in a Black Metropolis

African Americans seldom assimilated into white society. In the southern states, the wave of lynching that followed the war prompted whites in Atlanta to form a Commission on Interracial Cooperation, a biracial group that sponsored educational programs and campaigned for state laws against lynching. More vocally, the NAACP organized a national campaign to persuade Congress to enact a federal anti-lynching law. In 1921, President Harding endorsed the proposal, asking Congress "to wipe the stain of barbaric lynching from the banner of a free and orderly representative democracy." The House passed the bill, but southern senators used a filibuster to kill the measure.

Such proposals contributed to an easing of racial violence, and the number of lynching cases declined. But southern blacks continued to move into northern cities. As nearly 1 million African Americans formed dense communities in Harlem and Chicago's South Side, however, job prospects steadily declined. The labor surplus placed blacks at the lowest economic levels: last hired, first fired. Organized labor showed no interest in recruiting them. Though declared unconstitutional by the Supreme Court in 1917, residential segregation continued to push newcomers into unhealthy tenements. Such illegalities received presidential approval. Opposing "every suggestion of social equality," Harding announced, "Racial amalgamation there cannot be."

Amid poverty, illiteracy, and high mortality rates, many African Americans heeded the call of the Caribbean-born prophet Marcus Garvey, who advocated self-sufficiency, self-betterment, and black pride. "Up you mighty Race!" he exhorted. "No more fear, no more cringing, no more syco-phantic begging and pleading." Attracting an en-thusiastic following in northern cities, Garvey's Universal Negro Improvement Association (UNIA) offered blacks practical assistance such as medical aid and death benefits. But the movement went fur-ther, inviting blacks to participate as stockholders and employees in diverse black enterprises, includ-ing groceries, restaurants, a doll factory, a news-paper, and the spectacular Black Star steamship line which engaged in international commerce.

The UNIA's mission was not merely profit; it also included a sense of racial pride and a revital-ization of interest in the African heritage. Garvey's preaching resonated with the spirituality of Africa, the common culture and destiny, he said, of all black people. As African Americans re-sponded to this cultural identity, the UNIA founded 700 branches in thirty-eight states, in-cluding the South, and 200 overseas. Within three years, Garvey claimed 2 million followers. Yet capital shortages and mismanagement doomed the business aspect of his program.

Garvey also offended integrationists by cele-brating racial separation. His much-publicized meeting with leaders of the Ku Klux Klan made many enemies among northern blacks, including the NAACP's DuBois and A. Philip Randolph, or-ganizer of the Brotherhood of Sleeping Car Porters. Young blacks organized a "Garvey Must Go" campaign. Meanwhile, the FBI, hostile to black nationalism, infiltrated the UNIA and found evidence to indict its leader. Convicted of mail fraud in 1923 for issuing fraudulent stock, Gar-

vey served two years in prison before being de-ported in 1927. His exile ended the movement, but left a strong legacy of black nationalism.

Garvey's meteoric ascent illuminated a crav-ing for racial identity that inspired northern blacks to celebrate their cultural vitality in a movement known as the "Harlem Renaissance." Writers like Langston Hughes, Sterling Brown, and Zora Neale Hurston used poetry, prose, songs, and art to affirm pride in African American humanity, concluding (in Hughes's words): "We know we are beautiful. And ugly, too." The 1925 anthology, *The New Negro,* edited by black critic Alain Locke, embodied a cultural manifesto. It was Harlem's "spiritual coming of age," said Locke, not typical, but "prophetic." Five years later, *The New York Times* announced a typo-graphical change that revealed a changing climate among northern whites: hereafter, the newspaper would capitalize the *N* in *Negro* "as an act of recognition of racial self-respect for those who have been generations in 'the lower case.'"

Discovering the Jazz Age

Through the language of African America beat the drums of spirituals, blues, and jazz, music of polyrhythm, syncopation, and improvisation that captivated a younger generation. Trumpeter Louis Armstrong, pianist Duke Ellington, and vocalist Bessie Smith lured white audiences into smoky ball-rooms, many of them rigorously segregated. The names of the most famous night spots, Harlem's Cotton Club, Chicago's Plantation, and Los Ange-les's Club Alabam, had southern associations, in-dicative of their regional roots.

Not everyone applauded the new music. Critic H. L. Mencken detected only the "sound of rivet-ing," while another writer suggested that if Beethoven returned from the dead "he would

This sheet music cover from "Under the Harlem Moon" captures the vibrant energy of the Harlem Renaissance.

thank heaven for his deafness." But many white musicians like Bix Beiderbecke, turned to jazz as religious converts, finding in the complex mixtures of tonality and beat an emotional intensity that transcended formal western music. Matched with southern black dancing, the Charleston, lindy, and jitterbug recently brought North, jazz bands expressed the fast tempo of modern life.

Inventing Modern Media

Most listeners discovered jazz through the newest medium of mass communication: the radio. Wireless telegraphy had existed as a form of coded transmission since the 1890s, but the broadcast of the 1920 election returns by a Pittsburgh sta-

tion awakened public interest. By 1923, half a million home radios were receiving broadcasts from 600 stations; seven years later, the audience exceeded 12 million households, 40 percent of the nation. Though initially treated as a free medium, subject to the whims of broadcasters who competed for airwaves, radio transmission required federal licensing after 1927. The merger of local stations into national networks rationalized the commercial benefits and encouraged homogenization of programming.

"Radio," announced a Westinghouse manufacturer, "provided [salesmen] with a latch key to nearly every home." For the first time, advertisers could purchase, not space but time, and commercial sponsors became dictators of what audiences heard. Broadcasters preferred popular music, rather than high-brow symphonies or jazz. Light dance tunes, such as "Yes, We Have No Bananas" or George Gershwin's "Someone to Watch over Me," appealed to family audiences that hovered around the early radio sets. As white musicians, like Paul Whiteman, embraced African American sounds, the search for mass audiences tamed the solos, slowed the tempo, and sanitized the lyrics. More palatable to middle-class listeners were familiar black stereotypes—the witless, lazy, ne'er-do-wells personified in the most popular radio program of the decade, "The Amos 'n' Andy Show." Performed by two southern whites, the weekly comedy depicted the travails of black migrants in Chicago, endlessly mystified by city life.

Movies, Talkies, and Celebrities

Cities had an endless potential for chaos. In an unforgettable image of controlled anarchy, the actor Harold Lloyd hung by the hands of a clock high above the city streets in the movie *Safety Last* (1923). The scene typified the comedy genre in the era of silent films. Working-class viewers, many unfamiliar with English, howled as subtle actors like Lloyd, Buster Keaton, and Charlie Chaplin satirized sexual hypocrisy, bureaucratic pomposity, and formal manners. Yet even when movies scoffed at upper-class pretension, most pictures reaffirmed an implicit class system. Cross-class marriages worked as comedies, not as dramas.

As the Hollywood industry consolidated into eight studios, which made 90 percent of U.S. films and controlled distribution through national theater chains, movie producers sought to attract middle-class audiences with romantic themes and sexual display. Cecil B. DeMille's *Old Wives for New* (1918) and *The Affairs of Anatol* (1921) teased spectators with immoral opportunities, while ultimately upholding the sanctity of marriage. DeMille's famous bathtub scenes, released at a time when more people owned cars than indoor bathtubs, gave viewers glimpses of partly undressed actresses while celebrating values of lavish consumption.

Even in the country's "Middletown" (Muncie, Indiana, the site of a classic sociological study by Helen and Robert Lynd), movies and sex went together. Advertisements for the 1925 film *Alimony* promised "brilliant men, beautiful jazz babies, champagne baths, midnight revels, petting parties in the purple dawn, all ending in one terrific smashing climax that makes you gasp." As women became a larger part of movie audiences, increasing from 60 percent in 1920 to 83 percent in 1927, movies contributed to a culture of middle-class consumption. Screen actors' behavior became the model for the mass audience; their clothing, cosmetics, and hairstyles showed women how to transform themselves. Hollywood also imported European actors, such as Rudolph Valentino and Greta Garbo, to imply sexual promiscuity without offending middle-class tastes. (Similarly, European women appeared in tobacco advertising to flaunt female smoking.)

The introduction of sound films, the "talkies," with Warner Brothers' *The Jazz Singer* in 1927, required expensive remodeling of movie theaters

"Brilliant men, beautiful jazz babies, champagne baths, midnight revels, petting parties in the purple dawn, all ending in one terrific smashing climax that makes you gasp."

and added a touch of class to the industry. Ironically, that pathbreaking movie underscored Hollywood's paradoxical stand about issues of ethnicity and race. Almost all black roles in 1920s films placed blacks as maids and butlers who served rich whites. The major exceptions were black-made "race" movies, especially the films of Oscar Micheaux, which showed more realistic descriptions of black life. *The Jazz Singer,* by contrast, required white actor Al Jolson to put on blackface makeup as he made the transition from an orthodox Jewish boy to an assimilated "American" entertainer. While perpetuating familiar stereotypes, early sound movies stressed the values of cultural assimilation, at least for whites. Ethnic actors adopted "American" stage names, spoke without accents, and minimized their particular cultures.

The mass media (movies, radio, slick magazines) ballyhooed the age of celebrity. Hollywood "stars" appealed to consumer fantasies, embodying a lifestyle of wealth, leisure, and self-indulgence. Equally romantic were the premier athletes of mass spectator sports, self-made heroes whose personal exploits defied the anonymity of modern life. With the stroke of a bat, Babe Ruth's home runs transformed baseball into a game of sudden power, while breakaway runs by Illinois halfback Red Grange defied the regimentation of college football.

Most famous was aviator Charles Lindbergh, whose solo flight across the Atlantic in 1927 grabbed media attention on two continents and brought 2 million people to a tickertape parade at New York's Broadway. His personal feat spoke to a vanishing world that praised character, ingenuity, skill, and persistence—virtues still cherished, but increasingly blanketed by corporate identity, routinized work, and homogenized culture. In Lindbergh the public created a singular hero who flourished amid millions of anonymous spectators. He symbolized both pioneer individualism and modern machinery, a man of the past and the future.

The Conservative Backlash

"The Jazz Age" was Fitzgerald's tag for the era. But when the *Ladies Home Journal* denounced "unspeakable jazz" in 1921, the issue was not about music but the image of "youths of both sexes . . . with limbs intertwined and torso in contact." As the birthrate continued to decline (4.3 per family in 1920) and divorces doubled, moralists confronted a new openness about sex. Surveys found that women born after 1900 were twice as likely to indulge in premarital intercourse than their mothers. Among college women, petting and dating appeared nearly universal, though intercourse was reserved for one's future mate. "None of the Victorian mothers," wrote Fitzgerald, "had any idea how casually their daughters were accustomed to be kissed."

The corruption of traditional values emerged as a major issue not only in mass media and fiction but also in political life. Fear of "moaning" saxophones led to the passage of 60 municipal laws banning jazz from public dance halls. Purity crusaders pressed for the censorship of Hollywood films, leading the movie industry to appoint Harding's postmaster general, Will Hays, with authority to oversee the content of motion pictures. Literary defiance of conventional morality, such as Theodore Dreiser's *An American Tragedy* (1925), resulted in outright banning in Boston. Meanwhile, anti-alcohol enthusiasts fumed at the failure to enforce Prohibition. Although ethnic gangsters like Al

Capone built empires by controlling bootlegging, gambling, and prostitution, federal authorities hesitated to challenge the local patronage networks that protected illegal business. Many blamed the sins of the age on unassimilated immigrants; others saw a Catholic conspiracy designed to weaken the country's moral fiber. "One flag, one school, one Bible," became a nativist motto.

Fears of a foreign conspiracy dovetailed with a hatred of modern, secular ideas. Convinced that a new generation had lost the true faith, Protestant "fundamentalists" denounced deviations from the scriptural word. When Tennessee banned the teaching of Darwinian evolution as a defiance of the Book of Genesis, the American Civil Liberties Union backed biology teacher John Scopes in testing the law's constitutionality. In the "monkey trial" of 1925, the first court proceeding broadcast by radio, the old morality confronted modernity when populist William Jennings Bryan defended a literal interpretation of the Bible, while atheist attorney Clarence Darrow spoke for the defense. After weighty public addresses, the jury took eight minutes to convict Scopes. But when Bryan died five days later, the cosmopolitan press claimed that God had made a final judgment in favor of evolution.

The Resurgent Ku Klux Klan

Nothing appeared so whimsical to the Knights of the Ku Klux Klan. "One by one," remarked the order's imperial wizard, "all our traditional moral standards went by the boards. The sacredness of our Sabbath, of our homes, of chastity, and finally even of our right to teach our children in our own schools." D. W. Griffith's *Birth of a Nation* had stimulated the rebirth of the KKK (see Chapter 19), and by the mid-1920s the secret society could claim 5 million members, including half a million women who formed an auxiliary group. Originating in the Deep South, but spreading to northern states like Indiana and Oregon, the Klan

The Election of 1928

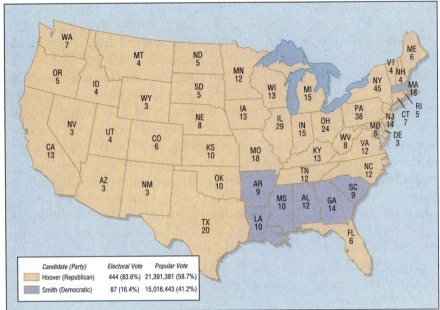

Candidate (Party)	Electoral Vote	Popular Vote
Hoover (Republican)	444 (83.6%)	21,391,381 (58.7%)
Smith (Democratic)	87 (16.4%)	15,016,443 (41.2%)

looked to a mythical past of Anglo Saxon Protestant purity, allegedly despoiled by foreign-born aliens, especially Jews and Catholics, and disrespectful blacks. Elaborate nighttime initiation rites transformed "alien" outsiders into "naturalized" citizens of the KKK. Members defended Prohibition, immigration restriction, and public education, while waging war against ethnic deviants and moral offenders with economic boycotts, political intimidation, and raw violence.

Comprising respectable, lower-middle-class churchgoers, Klan men and women expressed dissatisfaction at social changes beyond their control. Unable to regulate the lives of youth and women, the KKK assailed dance halls, bootlegging, and sexual immorality, patrolling back roads at night to catch and punish couples violating social custom. The Georgia Klan claimed to receive twenty letters a week from women appealing for "justice" against wandering or violent spouses. Anti-Semitic speeches referred typically to conspiracies of in-

ternational financiers who threatened small-town economies or seduced innocent women with promises of money. The Klan's anti-Catholic tirades warned about the perversions of parochial schools and the dishonesty of urban voting machines. Violence against blacks upheld a traditional paternal order and reminded white women of their dependence on male power. Yet ironically, scandals within the Klan involving sexual attacks on women and financial corruption weakened the organization's following by mid-decade.

The Election of 1928

The Klan remained a presence, if not a force, in the presidential election of 1928, which pitted Protestant Republican Herbert Hoover against Catholic Democrat Al Smith. With the theme song "The Sidewalks of New York," Smith embodied for his opponents the dreaded alien loose in the land. He was an outspoken "wet" against prohibition, had a Catholic heritage, and retained connections to Manhattan's Tammany Hall political machine. Hoover, by contrast, spoke the language of small-town capitalism, stressing values of individual initiative, voluntary cooperation, and self-made success, even as he represented the interests of big corporations.

Recognizing the cultural stakes in the election, women joined the contest in unprecedented numbers, though gender issues apparently had no effect on their voting. Subsequent analysis found that the most decisive factor was religion. Smith carried heavily Catholic Massachusetts and Rhode Island, but several states in the solid Democratic South deserted the party. With 58 percent of the popular vote, Hoover dominated the electoral college 444 to 87. Yet Smith's campaign brought the white ethnic constituency into the Democratic party, and for the first time since 1892 Democrats carried the nation's twelve largest urban areas. The country was "not yet dominated by its great cities," crowed a Minnesota newspaper. "Main Street is still the principal thoroughfare of the nation." But the operative word was *yet*: Smith's urban tallies foreshadowed a transformation of political power.

Optimism on the Verge of Disaster

As the nation prepared for the Hoover presidency, prosperity submerged the conflicts of culture. Careful economic analysis might have revealed basic structural weakness, such as the decline of home building, low farm prices, and high unemployment in textiles and mining. But most corporate and political leaders lacked any incentive to examine those problems. Their world focused not so much on the economy of production as on the fruits of consumption; and, if there was color in their world, it was not the white and black of racial identity and ethnic purity, but the multicolored advertisements of their magazines.

In 1928, the country's leaders could indulge in the confidence that had driven the election of Herbert Hoover. "We in America today are nearer to the final triumph over poverty than ever before in the history of any land," the candidate had boasted. Although there was "no guarantee [of] . . . a job for every man," he said, "that is the primary purpose of the policies we advocate." Meanwhile, filmmaker King Vidor released one of the last silent pictures, *The Crowd*, in 1928, a movie that epitomized the decade's economic transformation. Rejecting the boredom of corporate conformity, the film's hero (born on the Fourth of July, 1900) finds ultimate joy as part of a theatrical audience laughing mindlessly (and identically) in a world of pure commercial entertainment. In less than a year, even that illusion of national satisfaction would be shattered.

INFOTRAC® COLLEGE EDITION EXERCISES

For additional reading go to InfoTrac College Edition, your online research library at *http://web1.infotrac-college.com*.

Keyword search: Lost Generation
Keyword search: Gertrude Stein
Keyword search: Marcus Garvey
Subject search: NAACP history
Keyword search: Harlem Renaissance
Keyword search: Nineteenth Amendment
Keyword search: Prohibition
Keyword search: Ku Klux Klan
Subject search: Washington Conference
Keyword search: Coolidge
Keyword search: Herbert Hoover

ADDITIONAL READING

Lynn Dumenil, *The Modern Temper: American Culture and Society in the 1920s* (1995). An excellent work of synthesis, this book deflates the myths of the "roaring twenties" and focuses on the transformation of progressivism; for a political summation, see also David J. Goldberg, *Discontented America: The United States in the 1920s* (1999).

Robert S. Lynd and Helen Merrell Lynd, *Middletown: A Study in Contemporary American Culture* (1929). This pioneering survey of life in Muncie, Indiana, remains an exciting primary source of the era.

Advertising Sets the Pace

Roland Marchand, *Advertising the American Dream: Making Way for Modernity, 1920–1940* (1985). Carefully reasoned and well-illustrated, the study provides an overview of the advertising industry's principles; see also the same author's *Creating the Corporate Soul: The Rise of Public Relations and Corporate Imagery in American Big Business* (1998).

Business Culture and the Worker

David A. Horowitz, *Beyond Left and Right: Insurgency and the Establishment* (1997). Surveying political dissenters through the 20th century, the chapters on the 1920s focus on anti-corporate values and movements.

Women and Politics

Nancy F. Cott, *The Grounding of Modern Feminism* (1987). This volume analyzes the problems facing feminists after the suffrage victory; see also the later chapters of Robyn Muncy, *Creating a Female Dominion in American Reform*, listed in Chapter 18.

Immigration and the New Citizens

Lizabeth Cohen, *Making a New Deal: Industrial Workers in Chicago, 1919–1939* (1990). Exploring tensions between ethnic labor and business, this book links issues of the 1920s with the turmoil of the next decade.

Mark Reisler, *By the Sweat of their Brow: Mexican Immigrant Labor in the United States, 1900–1940* (1976). This detailed study of Mexican American immigrants provides a solid introduction and may be supplemented by George Sanchez's *Becoming Mexican American*, listed in Chapter 18.

Living in a Black Metropolis

Ann Douglas, *Terrible Honesty: Mongrel Manhattan in the 1920s* (1995). This book explores New York's cultural diversity and transformation; see also David Levering Lewis, *When Harlem Was in Vogue* (1981).

David Levering Lewis, *W.E.B. DuBois: The Fight for Equality and the American Century* (2000). From the vantage of the NAACP's major spokesman, the author traces racial controversies through the decade.

Judith Stein, *The World of Marcus Garvey: Race and Class in Modern Society* (1986). This analysis of black nationalism explains the rise and fall of the Garvey movement.

Discovering the Jazz Age

Kathy Ogren, *The Jazz Revolution: Twenties America and the Meaning of Jazz* (1989). A study of music and society, the book traces the public's response to the new sound.

Paula S. Fass, *The Damned and the Beautiful: American Youth in the 1920s* (1977). Examining college campus life, the author illuminates cultural values and generational conflict.

Wanda M. Corn, *The Great American Thing: Modern Art and National Identity, 1915–1935* (1999). A study of fine art, this book traces the cultural context of innovation; see also the Hayward Gallery's *Rhapsodies in Black: Art of the Harlem Renaissance* (1997).

Movies, Talkies, and Celebrities

Sumiko Higashi, *Cecil B. DeMille and American Culture: The Silent Era* (1994). Focusing on a leading filmmaker, this volume explores social themes in silent films; see also Scott Eyman, *The Speed of Sound: Hollywood and the Talkie Revolution* (1997).

The Conservative Backlash

Nancy Maclean, *Behind the Mask of Chivalry: The Making of the Second Ku Klux Klan* (1994). Analyzing the Klan's social roots, the book links the movement to anti-modern discontents; see also Kathleen M. Blee, *Women of the Klan: Racism and Gender in the 1920s* (1991).

Hard Times, 1929–1939

CHRONOLOGY

"A young girl who went around with Ellen tells about seeing her last evening back of a café downtown, outside the kitchen door, kicking, showing her legs so that the cook came out and gave her some food and some men gathered in the alley and threw small coins on the ground for a look at her legs . . . .

'I guess she'll go on the street now,' a thin woman says faintly, and no one takes the trouble to comment further. Like every commodity now the body is difficult to sell and girls say you're lucky if you get fifty cents."
(Meridel Le Sueur, *Women on the Breadlines,* 1932)

When Herbert Hoover presented his inauguration address in March 1929, no one contested his claim that the country had "reached a higher degree of comfort and security than ever existed before in the history of the world" and that the United States had achieved "liberation from widespread poverty." Four years later, the president's economic outlook (his very name!) had become laughingstock for millions of distressed citizens who named their collections of cardboard shelters "Hooverville" and called their newspapers, used for body insulation, "Hoover blankets." By then, the Great Depression had destroyed earnings and incomes, undermined slogans about hard work and thrift, and challenged personal and national images of success and self-confidence. "With the present breakdown," wrote essayist Edmund Wilson in 1931, "we have come to the end of something." The nation had stopped in its tracks.

The vast economic crisis could be traced to structural problems of the previous decade. High war debts and lagging foreign trade, agricultural overproduction, "sick industries," and the uneven distribution of income—all contributed to the downturn. But the collapse of stock prices in October 1929 punctured the balloon of inflated optimism. After the Crash, the situation rapidly worsened, bringing suffering for millions of citizens—homelessness, joblessness, forced uprooting, and psychological trauma.

Adding to public despair was the inability of economic experts, government agencies, or even common sense to provide solutions to the crisis. Hoover's rhetorical advice failed to improve the economy, and the president reluctantly accepted federal responsibility to alleviate widespread poverty. But administration remedies remained haphazard and insufficient, and the depression deepened.

By 1932, desperate voters demanded change and turned expectantly to the Democratic presidential candidate Franklin D. Roosevelt. Possessing no simple answer to the crisis, Roosevelt spoke generally of a "New Deal" and then, after his election, developed a legislative package of labor laws, social-welfare reforms, and increased government services. The New Deal eased some economic problems, but Roosevelt's policies never achieved full recovery. The depression did not end until the country began to mobilize for World War II (see Chapter 23). The New Deal's political legacy proved more durable, creating broader federal powers, a larger government bureaucracy, and greater acceptance of cultural minorities into the national family.

The Echoing Crash

The Wall Street Crash of 1929 did not *cause* the depression; that resulted from long-term economic weaknesses. But the abrupt drop in stock prices in 1929 undermined investment and destroyed economic initiative. For the previous four years, promises of prosperity had inspired a rising wave of financial investment. Total stock-market values in 1925 amounted to $27 billion; by October 1929, the figure had reached $87 billion. Yet stock prices rose twice as fast as industrial production. Instead of buying stocks in anticipation of increasing corporate growth and product sales, investors purchased shares in hopes of reselling the stock at higher prices. Generous marketing offers encouraged speculators to buy stocks on credit (or "margin") sometimes for as little as 10 percent of face value. Stockbrokers earned commissions on the full value, while investors used the discounted stock as collateral for additional purchases, which added to the speculative spiral. As long as stock traders expected prices to rise, everyone profited, despite inflated numbers and the shaky economic foundation of basic industries.

Panic on Wall Street

In October 1929, investor confidence wavered. As the Federal Reserve Board moved to cool speculation by raising interest rates, creditors began to recall loans and demand full payment for stocks bought on margin. To settle accounts, investors quickly sold overpriced stocks, taking heavy losses. On "Black Thursday," October 24, 1929, 13 million shares changed hands, bringing record-breaking declines worth $3 billion (about $24 billion in today's money). Leading bankers attempted to stop the flow of funds by making large purchases. But on "Black Tuesday," October 29, 1929, the bottom fell out of the market, as panic selling hit Wall Street and values plummeted $14 billion. When President Hoover announced that the economy was "sound and prosperous," investors ignored him. By mid-November, stock prices dropped $30 billion, 40 percent of the total value, and the trend continued. By 1932, $74 billion of investor wealth had disappeared.

As the Wall Street crash signaled a loss of confidence in economic growth, the sudden shrinkage of capital investment compounded structural weaknesses in the economy. Through the Roaring Twenties, pockets of unemployment appeared in coal mining, cotton manufacturing, shipbuilding, and railroads. Even in successful industries, higher productivity ran ahead of wage increases. During the decade, the richest 1 percent of the population controlled more than one-third of personal wealth and increased its share of national earnings from 12 to 19 percent. Middle-class consumption depended on credit; 60 percent of retail sales came on the installment plan. And three-fifths of U.S. families earned only enough to cover necessities. Residential construction and automobile sales began to slide in 1927. As consumer spending dropped, inventories of unsold merchandise nearly quadrupled, from $500 million in 1928 to $1.8 billion the next year.

The Debt Crisis Deepens

The weakness of the nation's banking system aggravated the financial crisis. Low farm prices—partly the result of overproduction, partly from the lack of European markets—created large debts in the form of bank mortgages. Unable to collect payments, small banks failed with alarming frequency (over 500 per year through the 1920s). Meanwhile, larger banks had invested in the stock market, extending credit that would never be repaid. The spiderweb of credit also snared U.S. banks in the problems of Europe. As the world's major creditor nation, the United States collected war debts from the world war Allies, who in turn financed those payments from war reparations taken from the defeated powers. When Germany lacked capital to make payments, U.S. banks advanced credit to keep the money flowing. But as the stock market crash reduced available capital, international debts remained unpaid. In 1930, the Hoover administration revised the schedule of foreign loan repayments and the next year issued a moratorium on debt collection. But the collapse of the European banking system in 1931 drained additional capital from U.S. money markets. When anxious depositors tried to rescue their savings, 6,000 banks closed their doors, taking $20 billion from customers.

As personal savings vanished in a maze of international accounting, the lack of credit and customers accelerated business failures. "We are going through a period when character and courage are on trial," said Hoover, pleading for renewed business confidence. To protect farm prices and domestic industry, the president ignored the advice of economists and signed the high Hawley-Smoot tariff in 1930, raising rates to the highest levels in U.S. history, further inflating prices and retarding consumer purchases. With equally poor insight, the Federal Reserve Board raised interest rates in 1931, thinking to deter speculation, but actually shrinking the money supply. Despite presidential bromides and business "Buy Now" campaigns, production found fewer outlets. Between 1929 and 1932, the gross national product dropped 45 percent, and foreign exports slid by two-thirds. By 1932, over 100,000 firms had declared bankruptcy.

The Crisis of Unemployment

Unemployment soared. Even before the Crash, 1.5 million workers sat idle. Two months later, jobless levels touched 3 million. By the next winter, 4 to 5 million were out of work; the year after that, 8 million were unemployed; by 1933, 13 million had lost their jobs, representing 25 percent of the labor force. Even during years of "recovery," unemployment was 11.4 million in 1934; 10.6 million in 1935; and 9 million in 1936. During the winter of 1937–1938, joblessness rose again, exceeding 10 million, or 19 percent of the work force. In 1940, as the nation mobilized for war, the unemployment rate was still nearly 15 percent.

Statistics sketch only the surface of suffering: they did not include "unemployables," such as the disabled or single mothers with children, who struggled to find jobs in normal times; they did not include former full-time workers who now labored part time at reduced wages. The statistics did not include the small armies of transients—at least 1 million (including 200,000 children)—who lived in hobo "jungles" on the outskirts of towns or slept beneath bridges and on park benches, or rode freight trains to warm-weather states and then returned to wherever they had started. Such people

> "It's an awful sensation to have nothing to eat. . . . Fear and defeat sit in you . . . . actual fear of the evening coming down, of the night, of the grocery man."

did not stay in one place long enough to be counted in unemployment figures. Nor did statistics count dependents of the jobless: family members who lived on someone else's earnings.

Survival could no longer be taken for granted. To cut household expenses, families adopted cheaper lifestyles and substituted labor (usually women's labor) for cash, turning to homemade clothes, home baked bread, and home preserved produce. Inadequate nutrition brought a rash of childhood ailments, such as rickets, pellagra, gum inflammation, and tooth decay. And countless people went hungry—"always half-starved," as one young man reported, "and therefore irritable." Government authorities admitted that thousands died of starvation each year. "It's an awful sensation to have nothing to eat," observed the Minnesota writer Meridel Le Sueur. "Fear and defeat sit in you . . . actual fear of the evening coming down, of the night, of the grocery man."

Despair reflected traditional values of individualism, the sense of personal responsibility for success and failure. President Hoover, himself a self-made man, warned in 1931 that public relief programs would undermine the national "character" and destroy "the roots of self-government." The crisis ultimately ignited social protest movements, but the remarkable thing was that most people, unable to understand or accept the power of impersonal economic forces, blamed themselves for their failures, not the economic system. "Depression," a word the White House preferred

Unemployed workers, some still wearing the clothes of middle-class respectability, obtain free food in a New York soup kitchen, 1931.

to more alarming synonyms like "panic" or "crisis," assumed a psychological dimension. "First, indifference," is the way one suddenly unemployed editor described his changing state of mind. "Next, reassuring faith; third, galling bitterness; fourth, morbidity." When the Apple Shippers Association offered apples on credit, unemployed people appeared on every street corner in every city selling apples for a nickel, stark evidence of self-sufficiency and desperation. (The Census Bureau classified apple sellers "employed.")

Families in Crisis

Insecurity toppled society's normal balance. "Around fifty," remarked an unemployed writer, "a man loses nerve . . . , the nerve it takes to ask a stranger for a job." Middle-aged men proved less employable than their wives and children, who accepted lower wages or took sex-segregated jobs as maids, waitresses, and sales clerks. Such men lost both their self-esteem and their status in the household. To children, maternal authority often replaced a father's preeminence. Psychologists reported higher rates of male sexual impotence. Wives also took the opportunity to resist unwanted demands. "The women punished the men for not bringing home the bacon by withholding themselves sexually," said a psychiatrist who worked with unemployed miners.

Married women faced their own disadvantages. Although 25 percent of all women worked outside the home, and the proportion of married women who worked increased 50 percent during the decade, public opinion expressed disapproval of working wives. Over 80 percent told a Gallup poll in 1936 that they opposed women working if their husbands had a job. Companies routinely restricted married women's employment, even though few men worked in "female" occupations. A survey of

1,500 public school districts found that 77 percent did not hire married women, and over 60 percent dismissed women teachers who married. The federal government also fired 1,600 married women and, to avoid cheating, ruled in 1933 that women employees had to take their husband's name. Prohibiting more than one member of a family from working in civil-service jobs, government dismissed women, who usually earned less than their spouses. Justifications for such policies ranged from spreading jobs among men to restoring women's place in the home. Meanwhile, as white women took more domestic jobs, the percentage of black women in the labor force declined.

The precariousness of social relations opened a realm for commercial exploitation. Taking advantage of public despair and the fear of failure, advertisers adopted scare tactics to promote inexpensive merchandise such as soap, packaged groceries, and cosmetics. Cutbacks in advertising budgets revived cheaper black-and-white photographs, which replaced the vivid colors of the 1920s and cast a gloomy appearance on depression-era faces. "A serious business handicap," one bench sitter discovered, could be relieved by softer toilet tissue, while mouthwash merchandisers warned that "sometimes very little may turn the scales against us." Although disposable incomes dropped 26 percent between 1929 and 1933, the most successful industries were pharmaceuticals (including personal hygiene products) and tobacco, which now appealed more openly to women.

Seeking Relief

At the beginning of the economic crisis, the newly poor turned to private charity—family, friends, neighbors, religious groups, and other community institutions. Shoppers requested credit from local merchants; tenants skipped their rent (often bringing calamity to shopkeepers and landlords who depended on neighborhood patrons). In every city, soup lines and bread lines abounded. By 1932, private assistance in Chicago increased over 700 percent, covering two-thirds of all relief expenditures. As local communities struggled to aid the growing lists of needy people, however, business failures weakened the very contributors who supported such charities. At a time when deposit insurance did not exist, the collapse of small ethnic banks spelled personal disaster. "There were no disorders," said a newspaper about the failure of an African American–run bank. "Instead, there was a deathlike pall that hung over those who had entrusted their life savings."

Public charity could offer limited assistance. Few states even had welfare programs. In most places, relief remained the responsibility of municipal or county governments and aimed to help specific groups, such as mothers with small children, the disabled, and the ill. The emergency overwhelmed local resources, and increasing property-tax delinquency reduced available funds. At a time when 300,000 were unemployed in New York, the city provided temporary jobs for one-tenth of the needy. State governments contributed additional assistance, but could never meet the demand. In some areas, officials denied assistance to African Americans, Mexican Americans, and other "alien" groups. By 1932, cities as large as Detroit and Buffalo announced bankruptcy.

Beginning Federal Assistance

After the 1930 elections returned Democratic majorities to Congress, Hoover overcame his scruples about providing federal aid to the unemployed. In 1931, the White House proposed a $2 billion public works program, the most expensive federal program until that time, and proceeded to construct buildings, bridges, and dams (including the Colorado River project later named for the president). Hoover also approved additional funding for the Federal Farm Board, created in 1929 be-

"No president," said Hoover, "must ever admit that he has been wrong."

fore the Crash, to purchase cotton and wheat surpluses. But as global markets continued to shrink and farm prices fell, Washington abandoned the program in 1931, $500 million in debt.

As the economy remained stalled and banks failed, Hoover supported inflationary measures to stimulate business expansion. In 1931, he signed a Home Loan law to provide assistance for mortgage companies to promote home ownership. In 1932, the president endorsed the Norris-La-Guardia Act, a concession to organized labor, which prohibited the use of court injunctions to end strikes, picketing, and boycotts. Most innovative was the creation of the Reconstruction Finance Corporation (RFC) in 1932, the first federal agency to confront depression issues. By making government credit available to banks, insurance companies, railroads, and other private corporations, the measure intended to expand business activity. Such funds saved numerous banks from collapse. But, while consumer purchasing power remained weak, business saw little reason to use the government's 6 percent loans to invest in productive expansion. After Congress amended the RFC to permit loans for state and local governments, the agency extended assistance for public works projects and for direct relief to the states. Yet the administration spent these funds slowly, believing that recovery depended on business confidence. "No president," said Hoover, "must ever admit that he has been wrong."

A Worsening Farm Crisis

Hoover had initiated innovative programs, including the use of federal funds for public works jobs, but his emphasis on business interests and voluntary solutions brought limited improvements. One-third of the nation's workers were still farmers and now faced extreme hardship. Farm prices had fallen through the 1920s, and the depression cut sales another 30 percent, even below the cost of production for oats, barley, corn, and hogs. Cotton slid from 18 cents a pound in 1929 to 5 cents in 1933; "$2 wheat" sold for a quarter; milk dipped to 2 cents a quart. Land values dropped by half between 1920 and 1930, and half again five years later. By 1930, one-half the nation's farmers were not landowners, but tenants; the proportion in the southern states was higher, reaching 70 percent in Mississippi. By 1932, one-half of midwestern farmers faced foreclosure on their mortgages. "We are a sick and sorry people," an Indiana woman wrote to Washington.

Overproduction remained the prime problem for farmers, compounded by the decline of foreign markets. Environmental disasters accentuated their plight. Across the Great Plains, from Texas to the Dakotas, perennial drought choked the growing crops that withered and died, while plagues of grasshoppers gobbled the shriveled dwarfs. Then blistering heat ate into the over-tilled soil, drying earth to dust and leaving the land vulnerable to scorching winds. In a single day in 1934, western winds lifted 350 million tons of topsoil ("soil drifting like snow," reported a county official) and darkened the skies of cities as distant as Boston, New York, and Washington. Small pigs suffocated in the dust. In the cotton regions of Texas and Oklahoma, infestations of boll weevils added to the afflictions.

The farm crisis prompted radical proposals. In 1931, Louisiana Governor Huey Long suggested that cotton states coordinate a moratorium on all planting for a year, allowing prices to recover. To individualistic farmers, the idea sounded like dictatorship ("alien to the American system," said one newspaper) and the plan died. Reaching out

In a single day, western winds lifted 350 million tons of topsoil, darkening the skies of cities as distant as Boston, New York, and Washington. Small pigs suffocated in the dust.

to desperate tenant farmers in Alabama, the Communist party helped organize the mostly black Share Croppers Union in 1931 to demand food advances, fair contracts, and reduced interest payments that had created a system of peonage. Poor whites refused to collaborate openly across race lines, though some lent secret support. White landlords fought back with violence and a corrupt legal system to crush the protest.

In the Midwest, dairy farmers organized the Farm Holiday Association in 1932 to get better prices. Barricading highways to stop delivery of milk, small producers dumped their barrels into the ditches. Rural violence against noncompliant farmers captured national headlines, but the movement accomplished few economic gains. More practical were efforts to stop mortgage foreclosures, as community pressure, backed by threats of violence, forced county sheriffs to accept low bids and return farm property to their original owners.

Frustration at an unresponsive government also provoked a dramatic march on Washington in 1932 by veterans of the world war, the so-called Bonus Expeditionary Force, which demanded early payment of bonuses for war service that Congress had already approved. To preserve a balanced budget, Hoover rejected the idea, but when sympathetic congressmen introduced legislation, 20,000 veterans journeyed to Washington to press for its passage. Living in shantytowns while Congress debated, many refused to depart when the measure failed. Viewing this resistance as evidence of insurrection, the president ordered the army to evict the protesters. General Douglas MacArthur exceeded Hoover's instruction, and his armed troops set fire to the veterans' encampment, fired tear gas, wielded bayonets, and left 100 wounded. Although conservatives praised the president for ending the protest, a larger public perceived Hoover as indifferent to the plight of ordinary citizens.

Attacking the Chain Stores

The feeling of economic powerlessness rejuvenated popular opposition to large, impersonal retail businesses that benefited from depression conditions. Taking advantage of business weakness and consumer poverty, chain stores increasingly invaded areas usually dominated by small shops, attracting customers with lower prices, standard brands (backed by national advertising), and self-service aisles that reduced overhead. By 1931, chain stores controlled 45 percent of retail grocery sales and 18 percent of all retail transactions. Moreover, with labor costs down, the cheapness of renovations encouraged chains to enter new territory, imperiling mom-and-pop stores, which teetered on failure.

In 1930, armed veterans attacked an A&P chain store in Ohio to protest the market's unpatriotic failure to close for the Armistice Day holiday. By 1931, 300 anti-chain organizations and two dozen anti-chain newspapers were defending the individual merchant, "the natural man," against "an unnatural monster" that threatened small business. When the Supreme Court ruled in 1931 that government could raise taxes on chains, twenty-six states passed such legislation, as well as laws prohibiting below-cost sales. Although government studies concluded that consumers preferred lower prices, the anti-chain movement underscored the precarious position of local merchants. The success of the chains, by contrast, foreshadowed the concentration of retail business among fewer companies.

Economic Crisis and Race

Although community interests often drew neighbors together to resist outside threats like chain stores, hard times exacerbated racial conflicts and accentuated problems among cultural minorities. The census of 1930, for example, introduced a new category of "race": *Mexican,* which comprised 640,000 people. The word allowed no distinction between aliens and citizens, between residents born in Mexico or in the United States. That year, President Hoover named this group as a contributor to the depression: "They took jobs away from American citizens," he said. The statement fueled white resentment of Mexican American workers in the western states. Meanwhile, in northern cities, such as Chicago and Baltimore, African Americans faced disproportionate unemployment. In 1931, the black-led National Urban League protested against employers who fired blacks to reduce white unemployment.

Problems of Ethnic Identity

Even as Hoover declared that foreign-born workers "took" jobs from citizens, Mexican American farm hands in California earned 14 cents an hour. They, too, experienced high rates of unemployment, and many moved to Denver or Los Angeles to find work or relief. But urban jobs also disappeared, and companies often replaced Mexicans with white workers. Mexican American unemployment ran twice as high as for whites. Government relief agencies treated aliens and citizens alike and routinely denied Mexicans welfare benefits or pub-

lic works jobs. In Colorado, the governor ordered the National Guard to patrol the New Mexico state border to turn back Hispanics, including U.S. citizens. Responding to this prejudicial atmosphere, the Hoover administration joined state and local officials in supporting voluntary repatriation to Mexico as well as the arbitrary roundup of suspected aliens. During the 1930s, one-third of all Mexican Americans—at least 400,000 people, half of whom were U.S. citizens—were transported to Mexico, regardless of their legal status.

Japanese Americans faced similar problems of citizenship and ethnic identity. The Japanese American Citizens League, founded by second-generation *Nisei* in 1930, organized fifty chapters with 6,000 members to promote self-help and assimilation. Eligible as citizens to vote, they founded Democratic political clubs and advocated legislation to outlaw discrimination. Yet, some Japanese residents, proud of their homeland's emergence as a world power, registered their children as citizens of Japan. Racial prejudice limited Japanese occupational mobility, but ironically insulated the community from depression hardships. Japanese businesses and farms operated on a small scale and served local communities, while ethnic charity helped the needy.

The Chinatowns of New York and San Francisco offered similar havens for local relief. Although economic hardship pressed rural Chinese to move into cities, the Chinese American economy was self-sustaining and faced little competition from whites. Indeed, a major growth industry of the decade was tourism (rising to third place among the nation's businesses) and the Chinatowns cultivated an "Oriental" image to attract customers. (To accommodate the national passion for desserts, a Chinese noodle worker invented the fortune cookie with a printed proverb inside.) As unemployment worsened, urban Chinese participated in protest demonstrations, forcing government officials to acknowledge their claims for relief. Like Japanese *Nisei,* U.S.-born Chinese felt the double pull of cultures, anxious to become Americanized yet denied access to education, jobs, or social life. At the same time, the outbreak of war between Japan and China in 1931 heightened Chinese cultural awareness. "If you were Chinese American," one recalled, "you certainly felt the fate of China was important."

For Filipinos, who migrated from the U.S. territory as agricultural workers, the economic crisis brought enduring political consequences. Perceived as a threat to white jobs and to white women, the largely male Filipino community faced widespread discrimination and laws that prohibited intermarriage with whites. Such policies, a California publisher declared, protected the nation "against the peaceful penetration of another colored race." This racism revealed curious contradictions. In 1933, a California court ruled that Filipinos were not "Mongolian," but were "Malay," and thus were not covered by the state's interracial marriage ban. A different racial logic led the U.S. Supreme Court to rule that Filipinos were ineligible for citizenship. As U.S. territorial residents, however, Filipinos enjoyed unrestricted entry to the mainland. That was one reason why in 1934 Congress passed the Tydings-McDuffie Act, which established the Philippine Islands as a commonwealth and promised independence in ten years. The measure protected domestic sugar producers from Philippine competition and permitted restrictions of Filipino immigration. By classifying Filipinos as aliens, the law also excluded them from federal welfare rolls.

African Americans in the Depression

As the depression reinforced cultural divisions, African Americans confronted racially based economic restrictions. Amidst high unemployment, even traditional "Negro" jobs disappeared in the South. Desperate whites became garbage collectors, street sweepers, bellhops, and elevator operators. In northern cities, black unemployment reached levels that were twice, even three times, as high as for whites. Yet because southern states deprived African Americans of welfare benefits, the migration to the North continued, though at a reduced rate. During the decade, 400,000 blacks made the journey, then faced the difficulties of living in tenement squalor.

Black voters had supported the Republicans in 1928. That year, Republican Oscar DePriest of Chicago became the first northern African American elected to Congress, indicative of the emerging political power of urban blacks. Yet racial discrimination pervaded the federal government. When DePriest's secretary was denied entry into the congressional restaurant, the Republican representative protested, only to have a House committee uphold the ban. As a Quaker, President Hoover did invite the black leader to the White House, the first such social visit since Theodore Roosevelt hosted Booker T. Washington. But the president appointed few blacks to federal jobs, excluded them from public works, and segregated African American Gold Star Mothers, whose sons had died in the World War, on the voyage to France to dedicate a memorial. When Hoover nominated a racist judge to the Supreme Court, the NAACP joined a coalition of dissenters that blocked the appointment.

Southern blacks faced continuing racial violence. "Whenever a negro crosses this dead line between the white and negro races," said an Alabama congressman, "and places his black hand on a white woman, he deserves to die." Few paid attention, then, when, after an interracial fight aboard a freight train, an Alabama sheriff rounded up nine African American youths, jailed them in Scottsboro, and charged them with raping two white women. An all-white jury soon found them guilty; within three days, a judge sentenced them to death. When news of the trial reached Communist party headquarters in New York, the radical group denounced the legal frame-up and sent lawyers south to appeal the ruling. "There is terror in Alabama" became a slogan of protest that echoed in northern cities. As the case proceeded through the legal system (eventually the Supreme Court would reverse the convictions on grounds that blacks were excluded from the juries), the Scottsboro case inspired a national movement to make lynching a federal crime. Southern politicians prevented such laws.

Mr. Roosevelt Goes to Washington

The despair of the Great Depression translated into a culture of fear. Racial conflict expressed one aspect of economic anxiety, as competition for jobs inflamed older hatred and distrust. Fear also took more benign forms. It encouraged smaller families, inspired popular entertainment, and ultimately shaped the country's political discourse. President Hoover tried to ease public anxiety by speaking confidently about recovery and urging a resumption of normal business. Yet few voters believed him when he stated in 1932 that "no one has starved" or that relief was "just around the corner." As the 1932 elections approached, fear emerged as a central theme: fear of unemployment, starvation, eviction; fear of the future; fear of the unknown.

A Culture of Fear

Economic insecurity forced young people to postpone marriage, sometimes forever. As the age of marriage rose, family fertility rates declined. From 21 live births per 1000 in 1929, the average fell to 18 in 1933, below the replacement level for the first time in U.S. history. Necessity reinforced a movement for educated birth control. During the decade, all states but Massachusetts and Connecticut permitted the sale of contraceptives, and in 1936 the Supreme Court (in *U.S. v. One Package of Japanese Pessaries*) lifted federal bans on dissemination of birth-control information. Meanwhile, an underground abortion industry prospered, serving tens of thousands of women each year (and annually claiming an estimated 10,000 lives). But fewer children did not alleviate family fears. A new genre of commercial advertisements reminded parents that undernourished children failed at school.

Fear also inspired comedy. In 1931, market researchers discovered that adults liked to read comic strips, heralding an era of advertising cartoons that fattened newspaper funny pages and popularized the humanized farm animals that inhabited the Walt Disney studios. Disney's cartoons bridged the sentimentalized rural world of barnyard creatures and the sophisticated technologies that created seamless animation. Mickey Mouse, the magical rodent introduced in 1928, survived amidst chaos, showing a world that was unbalanced, disordered, ever on the brink of destruction—and yet always saved and restored by the wand of fantasy and wish fulfillment. (By contrast, the mass-produced, $1.33 Mickey Mouse watches that appeared in 1933 fell apart with startling frequency and stayed broken.)

Hollywood's 1933 horror epic, *King Kong*, began on a depression relief line and ended with the recently completed Empire State Building, the world's tallest skyscraper and symbol of modern technology, falling apart. But Superman, another cartoon immigrant of the decade, invented by two high school students in Cleveland, regularly made things right by transforming the mortal Clark Kent into a man of steel. Comic books became the teenage rage. By the end of the decade, *Superman* was distributed in newspapers with a combined circulation of 20 million. And in the peak depression year, 1933, the country's most popular tune was Disney's "Who's Afraid of the Big Bad Wolf?" from the cartoon *The*

Franklin D. Roosevelt takes the presidential oath of office on March 4, 1933, minutes before assuring the citizenry that "the only thing we have to fear is fear itself." FDR's predecessor, Herbert Hoover, stands at the far right.

Three Little Pigs, a parable of the work ethic that literally whistled in the face of paralyzing fear.

The Election of 1932

Governor Franklin D. Roosevelt of New York had triumphed over physical paralysis after a polio attack in 1921 left him crippled. He concealed his infirmity from the public, lest it undermine his image as a strenuous leader. Instead, he spoke about his determination to end the economic crisis, one way or another. "The country demands bold, persistent experimentation," said Roosevelt as he campaigned for the Democratic presidential nomination in 1932. "It is common sense to take a method and try it. If it fails, admit it frankly and try another. But above all, try something." Roosevelt's charismatic promise earned him the Demo-cratic nomination. As a symbol of his willingness to break precedents, the candidate flew to the party's convention in Chicago and pledged "a new deal for the American people."

Hoover was the wounded Republican candidate. Despite his efforts to end the depression, the president was identified with protecting the interests of business over the poor. "The sole function of government," he stated during the campaign, "is to bring about a condition of affairs favorable to . . . private enterprise." Roosevelt's campaign rhetoric remained vague and contradictory, but unlike Hoover, he made clear his belief in a government commitment "to prevent the starvation or dire want of any of its fellow men and women." Although born to old wealth (he was a distant cousin of Theodore Roosevelt), he embraced the problems of the disadvantaged and promised change.

"FDR, the Man of the Hour," a 1932 campaign clock showing Roosevelt standing—without crutches—at the helm of the ship of state.

ern blacks comprised only 3 percent of the electorate, their ballots hardly affected the outcome.

Four months elapsed between election day in November 1932 and the presidential inauguration the following March. (Not until February 1933 did the states ratify the Twentieth Amendment, moving the presidential inauguration to January 20.) Meanwhile, Hoover held the reins of power, and a frustrated country watched its economic circumstances worsen. In January 1933, highly publicized senate hearings about the stock market crash revealed scandalous examples of corporate tax dodging and corruption, further eroding confidence in the business elite. Another bank panic followed, as depositors raced to withdraw their funds from shaky institutions. Stock prices again slipped. In the last weeks of his administration, Hoover urged the president-elect to issue a statement of support to bolster business confidence. But Roosevelt had no desire to be tied to policies of the past. By the time he took the oath of office, the nation's banking system was on the edge of collapse.

Amendment XX (1933)

Section 1.
The terms of the President and Vice President shall end at noon on the 20th day of January, and the terms of Senators and Representatives at noon on the 3d day of January, of the years in which such terms would have ended if this article had not been ratified; and the terms of their successors shall then begin.

Section 2.
The Congress shall assemble at least once in every year, and such meeting shall begin at noon on the 3d day of January, unless they shall by law appoint a different day.

Voters responded to the differences between the candidates. With over 57 percent of the popular vote, Roosevelt gained a decisive victory, and his coattails carried large Democratic majorities into both houses of Congress. More fully than Al Smith four years earlier, Roosevelt solidified the support of urban ethnic voters, who formed the basis of a new Democratic coalition that would last for four decades. Unlike Smith, the candidate expressed no quarrels with conservative southern Democratics and held the "solid South." Yet precisely because African Americans saw southern Democrats as their oppressors, blacks remained loyal to the Republican party. At a time when most southern blacks could not vote and north-

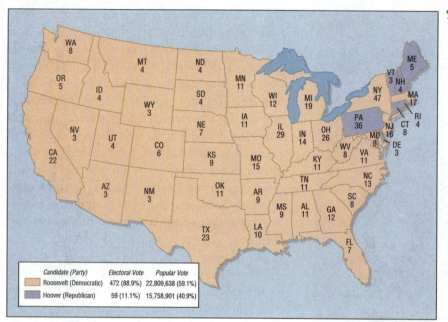

The Election of 1932

Candidate (Party)	Electoral Vote	Popular Vote
Roosevelt (Democratic)	472 (88.9%)	22,809,638 (59.1%)
Hoover (Republican)	59 (11.1%)	15,758,901 (40.9%)

Section 3.

If, at the time fixed for the beginning of the term of the President, the President elect shall have died, the Vice President elect shall become President. If a President shall not have been chosen before the time fixed for the beginning of his term, or if the President elect shall have failed to qualify, then the Vice President elect shall act as President until a President shall have qualified; and the Congress may by law provide for the case wherein neither a President elect nor a Vice President elect shall have qualified, declaring who shall then act as President, or the manner in which one who is to act shall be selected, and such person shall act accordingly until a President or Vice President shall have qualified.

Section 4.

The Congress may by law provide for the case of the death of any of the persons from whom the House of Representatives may choose a President whenever the right of choice shall have devolved upon them, and for the case of the death of any of the persons from whom the Senate may choose a Vice President whenever the right of choice shall have devolved upon them.

Section 5.

Sections 1 and 2 shall take effect on the 15th day of October following the ratification of this article.

Section 6.

This article shall be inoperative unless it shall have been ratified as an amendment to the Constitution by the legislatures of three-fourths of the several states within seven years from the date of its submission.

Launching the New Deal

Roosevelt's first inaugural speech soothed the public's anxieties. "The only thing we have to fear is fear itself—nameless, unreasoning, unjustified terror which paralyzes needed efforts to convert retreat into advance." Promising "vigorous action," the president immediately summoned a special session of Congress "to wage a war against the emergency." Within a week, the White House received half a million letters of congratulation, and personal letters to the president continued to arrive at the rate of 8,000 a day.

Roosevelt's words, his voice carried by radio, provided a sense of confidence and security. He proved to be a master of the media. During his long presidency, Roosevelt held 998 press conferences (two per week on average) and more than two dozen radio "fireside chats" to keep the public informed about his ideas and policies. He spoke as a friend of the common citizen. His portrait, cut from newspapers and magazines, appeared on the walls of millions of private homes. "He is at once God and their intimate friend," wrote the journalist Martha Gellhorn in 1934. "He knows them all by name, knows their little town and mill, their little lives and problems. And though everything else fails, he is there, and will not let them down."

Roosevelt's vision of recovery demanded broad federal powers. Recognizing that state and local governments could not meet the economic crisis, the White House introduced a range of innovative measures—the so-called alphabet soup of reform agencies FERA, CWA, PWA, CCC, NYA, NRA, NIRA, and WPA—that accepted federal responsibility for rebuilding the economy. Yet, the long list of New Deal laws exaggerated the president's commitment to a single strategy or program. Rather, Roosevelt's genius lay in his flexibility—his attachment to a policy only if it worked—and his pragmatic willingness to move in several directions at once. Not merely a political program, the New Deal constituted a political attitude, an improvisational style, that sought real remedies and strove to restore confidence in government. Even before

"He is at once God and their intimate friend . . . . he is there, and will not let them down."

the inauguration, Congress took the first step of change by passing a constitutional amendment to repeal prohibition. Whatever the benefits of alcohol, politicians expected rising taxes on booze to help support federal spending.

Amendment XXI (1933)

Section 1.
The eighteenth article of amendment to the Constitution of the United States is hereby repealed.

Section 2.
The transportation or importation into any state, territory, or possession of the United States for delivery or use therein of intoxicating liquors, in violation of the laws thereof, is hereby prohibited.

Section 3.
This article shall be inoperative unless it shall have been ratified as an amendment to the Constitution by conventions in the several states, as provided in the Constitution, within seven years from the date of the submission hereof to the states by the Congress.

The Bank Holiday

Once in office, Roosevelt ordered the closing of all banks (a "bank holiday," he announced) to stop the run on shaky institutions. Three days later, the administration unveiled the Emergency Banking Act, which assured federal scrutiny of all banks and provided government assistance for weaker institutions. Within another two days,

Congress approved the measure, hardly bothering with the details. Three days after that, Roosevelt's voice resonated on a Sunday night radio broadcast, the first "fireside chat" in which the president explained his policies directly to 60 million listeners. Easing public concerns, the speech brought immediate success. When banks opened the following Monday, deposits exceeded withdrawals. The financial panic had passed.

The White House then turned to regulation of the banking system. At Roosevelt's instigation, Congress soon passed the Glass-Steagall Act of 1933, which separated commercial banking from investment banking to limit potential speculation with savers' funds. The law also created the Federal Deposit Insurance Corporation (FDIC) to provide government guarantees of bank deposits, a program that still protects individual savers up to a certain sum. Meanwhile, in response to congressional investigations of corruption and "insider trading" that contributed to the Wall Street Crash, the Securities Act of 1933 required formal reporting of stock information and held corporate officials responsible for illegal activities. Congress also created the Securities and Exchange Commission in 1934 to oversee stock trading practices.

Aiding the Unemployed

Having established plans to regulate the financial system, the New Deal turned to problems of personal misery, initiating programs to aid the 15 million unemployed, the 30 million families without economic support, and homeowners facing 1,000 foreclosures a day. The Home Owners Loan Corporation, created in 1933, offered government bonds to refinance mortgages and saved over 1 million residences from default. Passage of the Federal Emergency Relief Administration in 1933 pumped $500 million to state and municipal governments to aid the jobless. The FERA offered direct federal funds for relief for the first time in U.S. history, eventually dispersing $4 billion in stipends and work projects to 20 million people. As unemployment persisted into the winter of 1933–1934, the Civil Works Administration hired 4 million idle workers to undertake public construction projects. Linking government money to work programs countered criticism that the New Deal squandered public funds, and the service restored citizen morale: workers were helping themselves.

New Deal relief programs formally disallowed discrimination on the basis of race or religion, though loopholes and vague enforcement provisions often undermined such objectives. The inconsistency reflected the power of southern Democrats, who shaped and enacted New Deal legislation in Congress and demanded the preservation of a racial hierarchy. Secretary of the Interior Harold Ickes, formerly an officer of the NAACP, fought to implement the nondiscrimination goal by requiring public works contractors to allocate a minimal percentage of jobs to skilled and unskilled African Americans. One black youth remembered that PWA, the acronym of the Public Works Administration, translated as "Poppa's working again." Few New Deal administrators were as aggressive as Ickes in gaining compliance. In many programs, especially in southern states, discrimination prevailed, providing blacks with lower wages, worse jobs, and proportionally fewer positions. Even when the president's wife, Eleanor Roosevelt, advised him of such problems, Roosevelt placed priority on enacting New Deal reforms and chose not to offend southern leaders.

Amid mass unemployment, the nation's youth—21 million between the ages of 16 and 24—formed, in the words of one contemporary, "a generation robbed of time and opportunity." To assist young unmarried workers, the New Deal introduced the Civilian Conservation Corps in 1933, a program that intertwined publicly funded jobs with environmental reconstruction. Hiring 2.5 million young men (there were virtually no projects for women), the CCC embarked on reforestation, land reclamation, and other ecological efforts. Operated as a quasi-military program, the corps introduced urban youth to outdoor life, stressed communal discipline, and attacked problems of soil erosion and flood control. As in the Army, black youths were kept in segregated camps. The program's manual labor projects offered relatively few job skills suitable for the regular economy.

Helping Rural Areas

More ambitious programs for environmental management followed the creation of the Tennessee Valley Authority in 1933. Twice blocked by Republican leaders in the 1920s, TVA was responsible for constructing nine dams in a seven-state region along the Tennessee River to provide flood control, reservoirs, and electrical power for nitrate factories and rural customers. As an independent public corporation, the agency employed environmental experts to plan resource use, soil conservation, and reforestation. Criticized as a government invasion of private industry, the agency served as a yardstick to set utility rates, brought benefits of electricity to isolated customers, and stimulated private investment.

The Agricultural Adjustment Act of 1933, a key measure aimed at rehabilitating the farm economy, tried to ease falling commodity prices. Using the theory that reduced farm output would end surpluses and thus raise prices, the measure offered government price supports for basic crops such as cotton, wheat, and corn, but awarded subsidies to farmers who lowered production. "Kill every third pig," proposed the AAA. "Plow every third row under." In 1933 the program financed the slaughter of 6 million pigs and uprooted 25 percent of the

nation's cotton crop. Such waste drew wide criticism, particularly because the program benefited big farms more than small and accelerated the concentration of production in fewer farms. In any case, the Supreme Court soon ruled that the special taxes levied to finance the program were unconstitutional. The 1936 Soil Conservation Act, which took land out of cultivation for environmental reasons, eventually offered a constitutionally acceptable alternative.

The reduction of cotton planting produced disastrous results for southern tenant farmers, most of whom were blacks. Although the AAA provided for cash awards to farmers who abandoned their crops, white landlords seldom transferred government payments to the tenants. Forced from their lands by the federal program, southern blacks suffered without adequate relief. Distressed sharecroppers in Arkansas formed the Southern Farm Tenants Union (SFTU) in 1934 and eventually gained 30,000 members throughout the South. Landlords retaliated with additional evictions and violence. Efforts by New Deal liberals to require stricter supervision of government payments met resistance from conservatives in Congress and the administration. In 1935, Roosevelt created the Resettlement Administration to educate farmers about land use and ease problems of tenancy, but made few gains. By 1937, a new agency, the Farm Security Administration, attempted to help landless farmers, but lacked funding to make significant improvements. A group of FSA photographers, including Dorothea Lange and Walker Evans, brought the plight of southern farmers to national attention with their black-and-white photographs of rural poverty.

In the midwestern states, New Deal assistance for drought-whipped farmers offered too little and came too late. In scenes etched indelibly in John Steinbeck's novel *The Grapes of Wrath* (1939), hundreds of thousands abandoned the parched

After years of economic and environmental calamity, artist Ben Shawn's 1936 poster suggested that the Resettlement Administration would help both people and their land.

land. For half a million migrants from the Oklahoma "dust bowl," California seemed like the land of opportunity, but farm work was scarce. Replacing deported Mexicans in the fields, midwestern migrants endured extreme poverty as produce pickers, faced cultural discrimination as unwanted "Okies," and fought losing battles to improve their wages. Their psychological burdens were omnipresent. "What did one do for an address?" worried an uprooted woman from the

Dakotas. "Without a mailing address, how did a person even know who she was?"

Seeking Industrial Recovery

In the nation's cities, the problems of industrial recovery seemed equally unsolvable. The New Deal's National Industrial Recovery Act of 1933 offered a two-pronged approach to boost industrial development. Under the Public Works Administration, the federal government allocated money for major building programs (bridges, tunnels, dams) not so much to make jobs as to stimulate production and manufacturing. The law created the National Recovery Administration to supervise business cooperation within industries to achieve standard prices and practices. The NRA granted companies immunity from anti-trust laws and allowed each industry to draft self-regulating codes that included production, prices, and wages. New Deal reformers, led by Secretary of Labor Frances Perkins, the first woman to hold a cabinet position, introduced a federal ban on child labor as well as "Section 7a," which affirmed the right of workers to organize unions for collective bargaining.

Unveiled with slogans ("We Do Our Part") and "Blue Eagle" product stickers, the NRA coordinated voluntary corporate agreements within virtually every industry. But a maze of competing interest groups overwhelmed government administrators and undermined efforts to stimulate recovery. For example, the NRA allowed companies to set prices, which were usually inflated, thus conflicting with efforts to strengthen purchasing power and outraging consumers. Small-business owners criticized price fixing by large corporations, and both groups evaded labor guarantees and refused wage hikes. Meanwhile, corporate managers decried government interference in private enterprise. Such grievances reduced to a simple complaint: industrial codes restricted competition and kept prices high, undermining economic expansion. These issues became moot when the Supreme Court ruled in the *Schechter* case of 1935 that the law exceeded Congress's power to regulate business within separate states. "A horse and buggy definition of interstate commerce," protested Roosevelt. But NRA had already failed to revive the economy.

Critics, Visionaries, and the Second New Deal

The 1934 elections returned a Democratic majority to Congress, but slow economic recovery discouraged Roosevelt's supporters and nourished dissident movements hostile to the New Deal. The persistence of poverty inspired demands for more radical reforms, including welfare programs, unemployment insurance, and federal regulation of business. At the same time, business leaders fumed at reforms already enacted. Instead of viewing Roosevelt as a defender of capitalism, corporate conservatives saw the New Deal intruding on their right to set prices or negotiate with workers. By 1935, moreover, several key New Deal programs, such as AAA and NIRA, were facing legal challenges that would soon lead the Supreme Court to declare them unconstitutional. Ideology aside, the White House worried most about ending the depression. As Roosevelt looked uncertainly toward the next presidential election, he decided to embark on a new legislative agenda—what historians have called the Second New Deal.

Radicals and Reactionaries

Many social reformers welcomed the New Deal as a step toward creating a regulated economy that would benefit all segments of society, but continuing economic problems undermined confidence in Roosevelt's remedies. At the same time, the rise

of dictatorships in Europe—Benito Mussolini's fascist regime in Italy and the 1933 appointment of Nazi Party chancellor Adolf Hitler in Germany—propelled radical groups such as the Communist party to form a "Popular Front" coalition to oppose the spread of fascism, militarism, and state-backed racism. Insisting that communism was "twentieth-century Americanism," the Communist party appealed to second-generation ethnics whose parents had been born in Europe, as well as to radical progressives who decried the power of big business. When urban landlords evicted nonpaying tenants, leaving impoverished renters stranded with their personal belongings on the streets, members of the Young Communist League broke open the locked doors, carried furniture inside, and restored electrical services, thus providing shelter until the sheriff arrived with new eviction orders. The Communist party's agenda included federal unemployment insurance and racial justice. By 1934, the party had 50,000 members, half of whom were unemployed.

Other radical movements, most of them marginal, proliferated around the country. In the Midwest, Farmer-Labor parties gained state approval of mortgage relief, tax reductions, and welfare. In California, socialist Upton Sinclair nearly won the governorship in 1934 on a platform "End Poverty in California" (EPIC), which called for government operation of idle factories. And a retired physician, Dr. Francis Townsend, captured national attention with a revolving pension plan that proposed to give $200 a month to retired people over age 60 provided they spent the entire sum each month. The scheme promised to stimulate consumer spending and cut unemployment by encouraging early retirement, though most politicians understood the plan would bankrupt the treasury.

Beyond these radical proposals, a variety of New Deal critics expressed frustration at the failure of recovery and threatened Roosevelt's popularity, but never for long. One flash in the pan was Father Charles Coughlin, a Catholic priest who broadcast a weekly radio show from Royal Oak, Michigan. Initially a Roosevelt supporter, Coughlin lavished venom on the nation's "banksters" who, he told his 40 million listeners, "want your farm, your business, your job, your cheap wheat, and your high debts." Pretending he had the president's backing, Coughlin organized a lobbying network called the National Union for Social Justice, and preached a mishmash of currency and banking reforms. Roosevelt ignored the sermons. When the priest directly criticized the president, his audience shriveled. But Coughlin's ability to arouse urban white ethnics and small-business owners showed an abiding suspicion of the flawed remedies coming from Washington.

"Every Man a King" was the message of another Roosevelt rival, Louisiana's self-styled "Kingfish," Huey Long. Attacking "the chain banks in Wall Street," the southern Democrat revived Populist critiques of remote financial conspirators and vowed to redistribute the nation's wealth by taxing millionaires out of existence. Elected to the Senate, Long broke with the Democratic leadership, and by 1935 was organizing 27,000 "Share Our Wealth" clubs around the country. Like Townsend and Coughlin, Long drew support not from destitute workers, but from marginal farmers, local business owners, and lower-middle-class town leaders who clung precariously to small amounts of property and respectability. Roosevelt worried about Long's challenge and ordered a public opinion poll to measure his strength, one of the newer applications of market research in the 1930s. Before the campaign began, a personal enemy shot Long dead in the Louisiana state capitol in 1935.

Corporate conservatives also attacked the New Deal. Believing the federal regulations that protected labor unions were a threat to private enterprise, business groups like the National Association of Manufacturers sponsored expensive advertising campaigns to weaken Roosevelt's popularity. In institutional advertising, large businesses like DuPont not only touted their products, but defended a capitalist system that ensured, in the corporation's famous tag line, "Better Living." In 1934, big business conservatives organized the American Liberty League, a bipartisan political group whose primary purpose was to unseat Roosevelt in 1936. Its leading spokesman was Al Smith, the former Democratic candidate, who attacked the New Deal for instigating class hatred. Such charges threatened the New Deal coalition in the next election, prompting the president to consider new measures.

Unveiling a Second New Deal

As dissidents attacked his policies, Roosevelt took the initiative in 1935, offering a reinvigorated program to assist the unemployed. The $5 billion Works Progress Administration, established in 1935, offered jobs to 3.5 million recipients to rebuild the nation's infrastructure. By the time the WPA closed its doors in 1943, it had built 572,000 miles of rural highways, 78,000 bridges, 8,000 parks, 350 airports, 67,000 miles of city streets, and 40,000 public buildings, including post offices, sewer systems, and other civic facilities. To win support from southern Democrats who controlled Congress, the measure established eligibility tests for employment, which were administered by local governments; placed ceilings on jobs for women; and often paid below-market wages. For the first time, the federal government offered support for unemployed artists, writers, musicians, and other intellectuals. Such funding inspired a renaissance of local history projects, including detailed interviews with ex-slaves, public murals that depicted regional themes, folk-song anthologies, theatrical productions, travel guides, and educational activities. Meanwhile, the new National Youth Administration offered vocational training and stipends to needy high school and college students.

Moving beyond relief measures to issues of social welfare, Roosevelt also presented the Social Security Act of 1935, a landmark law that provided the first federal unemployment insurance and old-age pensions. Funded by payroll taxes on both employers and workers, the measure had a deflationary effect by removing deductions from circulation. But, by taxing wages, Roosevelt ensured that "no damn politician" would dare to dismantle the system. To appease southern congressional leaders, the law exempted domestics and farm workers—the lowest-paid occupations, most often held by racial minorities. One-year residence requirements excluded migrant workers. The law's Aid for Dependent Children program set means and moral requirements for eligible mothers. Such limitations reflected prevailing political sentiments that viewed nonwhites and women heads of family as second-class citizens. Nonetheless, Social Security represented a bold departure of policy by acknowledging federal responsibility for public welfare.

The CIO Organizes Industrial Workers

The Roosevelt administration also acted to protect workers' rights within labor unions. After the Supreme Court invalidated NIRA in 1935, the president endorsed Senator Robert Wagner's National Labor Relations Act, which confirmed workers' rights to join unions and to bargain collectively through representatives and outlawed such anti-union business practices as spying and blacklisting. The law created the National Labor Relations Board to supervise union elections, investigate charges of unfair labor practices, and order legal remedies. To mollify conservatives in Congress, the new law did not cover farm workers, domestics, or

public employees. But union leaders called the legislation the "magna carta" of labor relations, a defense of labor rights that had been challenged in courts and Congress for a century.

Organized labor moved swiftly to benefit from New Deal protection. Although union membership had sagged during the early depression, major strikes erupted in California agriculture, on the New York and San Francisco waterfronts, among Minneapolis truckdrivers and midwestern auto workers. These confrontations provoked deadly violence that reflected worker militance and corporate hostility to unionization. Yet the AFL, which was primarily committed to protecting skilled workers, remained uninterested in industrial unionism, which involved all workers regardless of their tasks within a single industry. "Organize the unorganized," pleaded John L. Lewis, head of the mine workers. Determined to start unions for unskilled workers, Lewis, together with other industrial unionists, pressed for the formation of the Congress of Industrial Organizations (CIO) in 1935 to mobilize worker dissatisfaction in basic industries such as steel, automobiles, and rubber.

Rubber workers in Akron, Ohio, the nation's tire capital, did not wait for CIO leadership to assert their rights. Angered at arbitrary dismissals, thousands of employees at the Goodyear plant went on strike, ultimately organizing an eleven-mile-long picket line to surround the vast factories. Arming themselves with weapons, striking workers confronted the company's "goon" squads and city police to defend their jobs. The strike brought limited economic gains, but the union had shown its power.

In 1936, the CIO's auto workers introduced a new weapon, the "sit-down strike." When General Motors refused to recognize their union, the workers called a strike *inside* the factory and refused to leave the premises. The sit-down strike had clear advantages: employers could not easily introduce strikebreakers, nor could they retake the plants without damaging their property. When the Roosevelt administration and the recently elected Democratic governor refused to sanction violence against the strikers, the car maker was obliged to negotiate a settlement.

Union victories in rubber and automobiles set precedents for sit-downs in other industries, such as steel. Yet management did not always capitulate. Private and local police forces often attacked strikers and their families; workers sometimes died for their principles. In 1937, labor unions called nearly 5,000 strikes and claimed victory in 80 percent. By the time the Supreme Court outlawed sit-downs in 1939, union membership had tripled from 3 million in 1932 to nearly 10 million and achieved solid footing in major industries.

Revising Native American Policy

White House sympathy for the dispossessed also brought changes in Native American policies. Choosing the anthropologist John Collier to head the Interior department's Indian Bureau, the administration backed programs that respected traditional tribal cultures. Overturning precedents, Collier fought for Native American religious freedom, including peyote ceremonies, and curtailed the presence of Christian missionaries who sought to win converts.

Such positions brought criticism from church groups as well as from assimilated Native Americans who rejected tribal ways and considered the New Deal's defense of collective land ownership "communistic." These pressure groups forced modification of federal policy. The 1934 Indian Reorganization Act abandoned the 19th-century allotment programs, which had permitted individual ownership of tribal lands and had reduced Native American holdings by millions of acres. Although some nations, such as the southwestern

Navajo, refused to participate in new programs, Collier's insistence that Native Americans share responsibility for legislation constituted an important shift in federal policy.

Building the Second Roosevelt Administration

As the 1936 election approached, voters understood that the single most important issue was Roosevelt himself. The New Deal had created a multitude of enemies. Corporate leaders who opposed social welfare, higher taxes, and federal power bristled at his name ("that man," they said)—to them he seemed to embody the threat of class warfare. To lead the campaign against big government, Republicans nominated Kansas Governor Alfred Landon. Two-thirds of the nation's newspaper publishers endorsed the Republican candidate. Public opinion polls, still in their infancy, predicted a Republican victory.

Roosevelt welcomed the hatred he attracted. Insisting that he had ably defended capitalism and private property, he offered no apology for remedying the system's "injustices and inequities." His constituents needed no persuasion. By 1936, the growing number of unionized workers embraced the New Deal's protection, and a young generation of white ethnic city dwellers, many voting for the first time, turned to the Democratic party. Among the poorest citizens, Roosevelt captured 80 percent of the vote.

The city vote, first won for the Democrats by Al Smith in 1928, now became a bastion of Democratic power. Notwithstanding its abiding concern about maintaining the color line and states' rights, even the solid South held steady for Roosevelt, despite conservative disapproval of growing federal power. With over 60 percent of the popular vote—and all the electoral votes except for those of Maine and Vermont—Roosevelt car-

The Election of 1936

ried the 1936 election. His coalition of support would dominate national politics for the next two generations.

A New Deal for African Americans

"Abraham Lincoln Is Not a Candidate in the Present Election," the Baltimore *African American* reminded its readers in 1936. Four years earlier, blacks had remained loyal to the party of Lincoln because southern Democrats remained virulent racists. In administering New Deal relief programs, southern leaders had cruelly manipulated the rules to disqualify needy blacks. By his second campaign, however, Roosevelt had claims on black voters. His wife, Eleanor Roosevelt, had emerged as an influential partisan of equal rights, and she often persuaded the president to approve civil rights measures when they did not imperil his economic agenda. When forced to reduce her staff for economy reasons, Mrs. Roosevelt chose

to dismiss white workers because they would more easily find new jobs than blacks. Secretary Ickes desegregated federal offices and rejected racial discrimination in public relief. Major African American authors such as Zora Neal Hurston, Richard Wright, and Ralph Ellison published their first works in WPA publications. By opening New Deal relief programs to African Americans, the administration created enduring loyalties among black voters. In 1934, a majority of northern blacks voted Democratic in the congressional elections.

Obliged to southern congressmen for their support of the New Deal, Roosevelt moved cautiously on civil-rights issues. Although he appointed numerous blacks to government positions, the president dared not challenge southern leaders by supporting a federal anti-lynching bill. Not until a mob killed some white prisoners in California did the president publicly denounce lynching, which, he said, was "a vile form of collective murder." But

Roosevelt would go no further, even keeping his wife from speaking in favor of anti-lynching bills that failed on several occasions to pass in Congress.

In 1936, Roosevelt appealed directly to black voters. African American delegates attended a desegregated Democratic National Convention for the first time, and black reporters sat in a racially integrated press box. African Americans responded by voting for Roosevelt's reelection, forming a crucial ingredient in the new Democratic coalition. Subsequently, Roosevelt appointed the first black judge to the federal bench. And, in an important protest in 1939, Eleanor Roosevelt defied the Daughters of the American Revolution, who had barred black contralto Marian Anderson from singing in Washington's Constitution Hall, by promoting a concert on the steps of the Lincoln Memorial. In 1940, the administration approved a postage stamp honoring Booker T. Washington, the first black to appear on a stamp. Such gestures did not eliminate racial discrimination, but demonstrated a commitment to racial justice.

The Limits of Presidential Power

The second Roosevelt landslide offered the prospect of further reform, but ironically aroused strong counterforces that weakened the president's ability to control congressional majorities. Even before his second inauguration in 1937, Roosevelt had triggered a political backlash among southern Democrats. As key New Deal legislation, including Social Security and the Wagner Act, faced legal challenges in the courts, the president feared that the Supreme Court might overthrow his program, just as it earlier had rejected the AAA and NIRA. In the wake of his election victory, Roosevelt abruptly proposed to eliminate the judicial roadblock by reorganizing the highest Court. To rejuvenate "overworked" judges, the plan called for the appointment of additional justices, one for each incumbent over the age of 70. Since Roosevelt would appoint the new judges, he expected to guarantee a pro–New Deal majority.

The "court-packing" scheme aroused indignation among conservatives, both Democrats and Republicans, and reinforced fears of excessive presidential power. The issue never came to a vote, perhaps because Roosevelt's threat of reform persuaded several older justices to retire. Then, as controversial cases came for legal review in 1937, the Court upheld state minimum wage laws as well as Social Security and the Wagner Act. These decisions, together with Roosevelt's appointment of liberal judges, protected the New Deal, affirmed federal power, and set precedents for an activist judiciary. But in igniting conservative anger, the White House had strengthened an alliance of its enemies.

Another Economic Crisis

Roosevelt's political defeat coincided with disaster in his economic program. Worried about continuing federal deficits and believing that a slight dip in unemployment indicated the end of the depression, the president had ordered cutbacks in public work and relief programs just as the new Social Security payroll taxes reduced take-home pay. To the president's amazement, the economy entered a severe slump in 1937. Industrial production suddenly fell 40 percent, corporate profits dropped 80 percent, and unemployment jumped to 11 million, 20 percent of the work force. Fully four years after taking office, the president had failed to understand, much less resolve, the economic crisis.

Although uncertain about the causes of the downturn, Roosevelt understood the potential political calamity for his administration. With emergency appropriations in 1938, federal billions poured into WPA, PWA, and other relief agencies, eventually easing the crisis. In choosing this policy of deficit spending, Roosevelt avoided the more radical alternative of funding government spending with higher business taxes or imposing greater regulations over business prices and profits. Instead, he opted for a fiscal policy that boosted consumer spending rather than restructuring the nation's economy. In this sense, the second New Deal preserved the capitalist system. Yet the failure of industrial recovery remained a puzzle and a yoke for the president.

Congressional conservatives of both parties continued to attack the New Deal. Roosevelt's proposal to reorganize the executive branch brought new cries of impending dictatorship. In 1938, the House of Representatives established a committee to investigate "un-American" activities, opening public hearings on communism, labor organizers, and civil rights agitation. Congress did approve housing legislation for slum clearance, passed the Fair Labor Standards Act that established minimum wages and maximum hours (initially 40 cents an hour in a 40-hour week), banned child labor, and extended assistance to farmers. But a strong anti–New Deal coalition continued to weaken presidential proposals and reduce relief appropriations. In the 1938 congressional elections, Roosevelt confronted his opponents and targeted conservative Democrats for defeat. But his efforts to "purge" the party backfired as Republicans gained new seats in Congress and anti-Roosevelt Democrats returned to office. Two months later, Roosevelt's State of the Union address scarcely touched domestic issues. The era of reform had ended.

The New Deal proved to be a watershed in U.S. history. Although based on precedents from the Hoover administration and although significantly flawed by its inability to restore prosperity, Roosevelt's presidency broke new ground in stabilizing economic and social relations. In the short run, Washington provided essential economic assistance for millions of people, helped restore farm incomes to destitute families, and enabled displaced workers to keep their homes. Other measures had lasting effects. The regulation of the stock market and federal insurance of the banking system, for example, protected investors, large and small, from losing their life's savings because of reckless or illegal speculation. Other New Deal laws, including NIRA, the National Labor Relations Act, and the Fair Labor Standards Act, gave guarantees to labor unions that protected workers from arbitrary employers and ended child labor. The Social Security Act, though offering far less to workers than programs of other industrialized countries, established unprecedented minimum standards to assist the elderly, the disabled, and the needy.

Such legislation set the foundations of social and economic policy for the remainder of the century. What the New Deal did not accomplish—or even attempt—is equally revealing. Roosevelt accepted the principles of the capitalist economy and never proposed a redistribution of wealth. He made no effort to seize private property, even when the banking system verged on total collapse. Nor did the New Deal attack the political system of states' rights, permitting state and local institutions to survive, though they perpetuated racial and economic inequities. Roosevelt's reforms thus worked within an established framework, supporting the structure of power, even as it put a human face on government assistance to a desperate generation.

The Legacy of Crisis

The waning of the New Deal by 1940 reflected growing concern about world affairs. As war erupted in Europe and Asia, a resurgence of patriotic themes appeared in fiction, popular culture, and the mass media. Margaret Mitchell's immensely popular novel *Gone With the Wind* (1937) celebrated a Civil War heritage of triumph over adversity, while poets, playwrights, and filmmakers lauded Abraham Lincoln for his compassionate politics. Frank Capra's Hollywood trilogy, *Mr. Deeds Goes to Town* (1936), *Mr. Smith Goes to Washington* (1939), and *Meet John Doe* (1941) praised the virtues of common people, common sense, common cause. The depression also promoted the art of documentary realism, as Farm Security Administration photographers and *Life* magazine portrayed the ordeal of ordinary citizens.

Franklin Delano Roosevelt embodied this national culture. In his radio broadcasts and press conferences, the president spoke earnestly to a broad public, weaving together not only a political coalition but also a sense of national purpose. The appointment of Jews and Catholics to federal office, the lesser but unprecedented recognition of African Americans and women, and his sympathy for the poor and the needy, illuminated a larger commitment to democratic pluralism. No longer did a president merely tolerate cultural outsiders. In a world increasingly challenged by totalitarian politics, Roosevelt defended a society of multiple faiths, diverse ethnic groups, and conflicting economic needs.

These enlarged commitments justified the expansion of federal power. As the national budget tripled between 1932 and 1939 and government doubled in size, Washington became a presence in ordinary lives. Even people who were dependent on federal relief lamented and often criticized the power of New Deal managers who formulated policy, established regulations, and built an administrative bureaucracy—all those "alphabet" agencies that became a national joke and a tax burden. To be sure, many citizens remained beyond the purview of government: sharecroppers, migrant workers, domestics, Asian and Hispanic minorities. But acceptance of government responsibility

for social welfare stood as an enduring legacy of the Great Depression and the New Deal.

INFOTRAC® COLLEGE EDITION EXERCISES

For additional reading go to InfoTrac College Edition, your online research library at *http://web1.infotrac-college.com*.

Keyword search: Great Depression

Keyword search: New Deal

Keyword search: court packing

Keyword search: Social Security Act

Keyword search: Wagner Act

ADDITIONAL READING

Roger Biles, *A New Deal for the American People* (1991). This book offers a concise analysis of the depression decade. For a fuller narrative, see David M. Kennedy, *Freedom from Fear* (1999).

Caroline Bird, *The Invisible Scar* (1966). Written during the prosperous 1960s, the book examines the depression's cultural legacy.

Families in Crisis

Linda Gordon, *Pitied But Not Entitled: Single Mothers and the History of Welfare, 1890–1935* (1994). Chapters on the making of social security policy depict the limited political power of women during the decade.

Susan Ware, *Holding Their Own: American Women in the 1930s* (1982). A survey of women's history, this book ranges from policy issues to popular culture.

A Worsening Farm Crisis

Catherine McNicol Stock, *Main Street in Crisis: The Great Depression and the Old Middle Class on the Northern Plains* (1992). Focusing on farm problems, the book describes the economic and cultural crisis.

James Curtis, *Mind's Eye, Mind's Truth: FSA Photography Reconsidered* (1989). A meticulous study of depression photographs, the book depicts underlying assumptions of New Deal imagery.

Mr. Roosevelt Goes to Washington

George McJimsey, *The Presidency of Franklin Delano Roosevelt* (2000). A thorough study of New Deal policies, this book includes good bibliographies of recent scholarship. For a White House perspective, see Blanche Wiesen Cook, *Eleanor Roosevelt: 1933–1938* (1999).

Radicals and Reactionaries

Alan Brinkley, *Voices of Protest: Huey Long, Father Coughlin, and the Great Depression* (1982). Exploring anti–New Deal sentiment, the author explains the rise and fall of Roosevelt's critics; for corporate dissidents, see, William L. Bird, Jr., *"Better Living": Advertising, Media and the New Vocabulary of Business Leadership, 1935–1955* (1999).

Helping Rural Areas

James N. Gregory, *American Exodus: The Dust Bowl Migration and Okie Culture in California* (1989). Looking afresh at the people of Steinbeck's fiction, the author provides a social history of uprooted farmers.

A New Deal for African Americans

Robin D. G. Kelley, *Hammer and Hoe: Alabama Communists during the Great Depression* (1990). Describing radical politics in the South, the author examines the issues of race and class.

Nancy J. Weiss, *Farewell to the Party of Lincoln: Black Politics in the Age of FDR* (1983). This book studies the New Deal's relationships with blacks, emphasizing economic benefits in gaining black support.

Problems of Ethnic Identity

Vicki L. Ruiz, *Cannery Women/Cannery Lives: Mexican Women, Unionization, and the California Food Processing Industry, 1930–1950* (1987). Based partly on oral history, this study links ethnic identity and labor protest; see also Lizabeth Cohen, *Making a New Deal*, listed in Chapter 21.

Devra Weber, *Dark Sweat, White Gold: California Farm Workers, Cotton, and the New Deal* (1994). Focusing on Mexican American farm workers, this study reveals the New Deal's limited benefits.

Judy Young, *Unbound Feet: A Social History of Chinese Women in San Francisco* (1995). A study of assimilation and ethnic identity, chapters on the depression illuminate the problems of Asian immigrants.

The Legacy of Crisis

Studs Terkel, *Hard Times: An Oral History of the Great Depression* (1970). A widely quoted work, this anthology tells the stories of ordinary people.

23

A. C.-5

Keep 'Em

Flying!

BOMBER

The War against Fascism, 1931–1945

"Yes, Ma, this is a case where sons must go against their mothers' wishes for the sake of their mothers themselves," wrote Hyman Katz to his Jewish mother in New York in 1937. "I am fighting against those who establish an inquisition like that of their ideological ancestors several centuries ago, in Spain."

http://history.wadsworth.com

Katz was one of 3,000 American volunteers who defied a State Department ban on travel to Spain to take up arms to defend the elected government from its military enemies. These young men and women, who called themselves the "Abraham Lincoln Brigade," came from nearly every state in the union and from all walks of life. Many were college students, dropouts, or unemployed; some were artists, writers, or professionals; others were manual workers, union organizers, and veterans of depression-era labor wars. The brigade was the first fully integrated army in U.S. history and included 90 African Americans, several Native Americans, and 3 Asian Americans. A corps of doctors and nurses provided medical care. "For the first time in history," another volunteer wrote home to his parents, "for the first time since Fascism began systematically throttling and rending all we hold dear—we are getting the opportunity to fight back." Six weeks later, the young soldier lay dead on a Spanish battlefield, one of 800 American idealists who gave their lives in the Spanish Civil War to stop the spread of militarism.

While young volunteers in the Lincoln Brigade fought and died in Spain, the U.S. government stood aloof from the war. Following the lead of Britain and France, President Franklin D. Roosevelt adopted a policy of "non-intervention," hoping to keep the nation from becoming embroiled in European conflict. By contrast, Germany's Adolf Hitler and Italy's Benito Mussolini openly aided the military rebels in Spain, and German air forces outraged international opinion by bombing civilians, prompting Pablo Picasso's most famous painting, *Guernica*. The Spanish Republic fell in 1939. Six months later, the same German pilots who had bombed Guernica were flying over Poland on September 1, 1939, firing the first shots of World War II. Roosevelt admitted that U.S. neutrality in Spain had been a mistake.

Roosevelt's response to the Spanish Civil War reflected the limitations of depression diplomacy. As world trade tumbled by 25 percent and total U.S. exports dropped 50 percent between 1929 and 1933, New Deal leaders believed that the way to end the depression and restore prosperity was to sell the nation's industrial and agricultural surplus overseas. But other countries, such as Britain, Germany, and Japan, equally cursed by the depression, had similar goals. The economic crisis thus accentuated international rivalry.

Meanwhile, Italy, Germany, and Japan, which were later known as the Axis powers, sought military solutions to their economic and political problems. Their militarism ultimately threatened U.S. security. Roosevelt sought to protect U.S. interests by challenging the expansion of the Axis powers, but his pro-internationalist position confronted widespread anti-intervention sentiments from political leaders and many others who opposed foreign entanglements.

During the Spanish Civil War, Washington refused to intervene on either side of the conflict, but by the end of the decade, the outbreak of World War II in Europe and Asia demanded a reevaluation of U.S. neutrality. Despite considerable contrary opinion, Roosevelt reluctantly led the nation toward war. As the country mobilized its military resources, industrial production soared, unemployment fell, and wartime prosperity at last ended the Great Depression. Yet, as the United States assumed world leadership, international relations increasingly affected domestic programs. Military needs, for example, determined industrial priorities, and the government strove to preserve peace between business and labor. The result was a government bureaucracy that aroused new concerns about presidential power, huge military budgets, and corporate influence in Washington.

Depression and World Affairs

During the 1932 election, Roosevelt argued that the primary problem facing the economy was not production of goods, but their consumption. "A mere builder of more industrial plants . . . is as likely to be a danger as a help," said Roosevelt. "Our task now is not . . . producing more goods. It is the soberer, less dramatic business . . . of seeking to reestablish foreign markets for our surplus production, of meeting the problem of underconsumption." Even though his predecessor, Herbert Hoover, had agreed to participate in a world economic conference to stabilize the international gold standard, Roosevelt abandoned the policy. Instead, to stimulate exports, he permitted a devaluation of the dollar in 1933.

The White House then persuaded Congress to pass the Reciprocal Trade Agreement Act of 1934, which ended a tradition of high protective tariffs and authorized reductions by as much as 50 percent. "Foreign markets must be regained," said Roosevelt, "if producers are to rebuild a full and enduring domestic prosperity." Secretary of State Cordell Hull proceeded to negotiate mutual tariff reductions with 14 nations by 1936—boosting U.S. exports by 40 percent, but still one-third below 1929 levels. In another precedent-breaking step, Roosevelt extended diplomatic recognition to the Communist-led Soviet Union in 1933, hoping to increase U.S. trade, though expectations proved overly optimistic and the political relationship remained mutually mistrustful.

The Good Neighbor Policy and the Open Door

Washington also strengthened economic ties with Latin America as part of the "Good Neighbor" policy. To build friendly commercial relations, the Hoover administration had quietly repudiated unilateral intervention in Latin American politics. Depression conditions encouraged Roosevelt to continue that policy. Secretary Hull's tariff reductions doubled U.S. trade south of the border. Roosevelt completed the removal of U.S. Marines from Latin America in 1933 and rejected the use of troops in Cuba when the collapse of world sugar prices provoked a rebellion. Instead, the administration exerted diplomatic pressure to support a friendly regime, then signed a treaty with Cuba that ended the 1901 Platt Amendment (see Chapter 19), but tightened U.S. influence over the island economy. In 1936, the White House formally renounced military intervention, conceding that "no state has the right to intervene in the internal or external affairs of another."

The priority on foreign trade intensified U.S. competition with Japan for influence on the Asian mainland. In China, the rise of a Nationalist movement under Chiang Kai-shek threatened Russian and Japanese economic interests in Manchuria. Japan responded in 1931 by sending military forces into the northern province and creating a client state, known as Manchukuo, as a permanent sphere of influence. U.S. trade with China remained a small fraction of its dealings with the more industrialized Japan. But violation of the traditional open-door policy in China appeared to be a dangerous precedent for limiting economic growth. Hoover's Secretary of State Henry Stimson issued a statement, known as the Stimson Doctrine, which refused to recognize the Japanese conquest of Manchuria. Japan ignored the statement and attacked other Chinese cities.

Such issues evoked small public response. "The American people," commented a Philadelphia newspaper, "don't give a hoot in a rain barrel about who controls North China." This intellectual gap, the difference in perception between policy making leaders and ordinary citizens, explained the

Manchuria, 1931

lack of support for administration objectives. To most Americans, Asia and Europe seemed remote; they *were* remote, even to immigrants and children of immigrants who had recently reached U.S. shores. Only exceptional individuals outside government—international business leaders, for example, or volunteers in the Lincoln Brigade—anticipated the implications of U.S. diplomacy.

Facing Facism in Europe

The global economic crisis aggravated political tensions that remained in Europe from the end of the World War. A decade before Roosevelt's election, a nationalist movement known as *fascism* had enabled Benito Mussolini to seize power in Italy. Mussolini's fascist government rejected democratic principles, glorifying militarism and the power of the state. But, as a weak nation, Italy was a small threat to peace. In Germany, by contrast, the Depression created severe social stress that permitted another fascist movement, national socialism (*nazism*), to achieve power in 1933. Under the leadership of Adolf Hitler, Nazi Germany embarked on a program of rearmament, partly to affirm its stature as a first-class power and partly to alleviate mass unemployment.

Distanced by the Atlantic Ocean, U.S. policy makers saw less a military threat in fascism than a dangerous commercial rivalry. With a goal of achieving economic independence, the Nazi regime subsidized German industry and directly challenged U.S. trade in Europe and Latin America. Offering special credit arrangements, Germany attempted to undercut Hull's reciprocal treaties and discriminated against U.S. trade. Between 1934 and 1936, German exports to Latin America doubled, while U.S. sales to Germany fell over 50 percent. As the trade war continued, German competition forced the State Department to acknowledge Latin American interests. When Mexico seized U.S. oil holdings in 1938, for example, Washington had to reject military intervention and persuade U.S. oil companies to accept negotiated compensation. Meanwhile, Germany's growing power in central Europe—its seizure of Austria and parts of Czechoslovakia in 1938—interfered with U.S. business.

Government leaders were less troubled on hearing stories about Nazi brutality. Although the mass arrest of German union leaders, communists, Jews, and political dissidents disturbed members of the administration, Washington raised no protest against Nazi racial policy. Hitler's proclamation of the so-called Nuremberg Laws of 1935, which stripped German Jews of their citizenship, alarmed religious and cultural leaders and prompted protests against allowing the 1936 Olympics to be held in Berlin. The games went on, but millions of Americans cheered when African American track star Jesse Owens won gold medals that flouted Nazi theories of the "master race." Not until November 1938, on *Kristallnacht*, the night that Nazi terrorists attacked Jewish synagogues, businesses, and private homes, did Americans perceive the menace of Germany's racial program. Even then, the White House refused to relax immigration laws to assist Jewish refugees.

Creating a Policy of Neutrality

As Germany repudiated the Versailles treaty of 1919 and invaded the demilitarized Rhineland, Mussolini threatened war in Ethiopia in 1934 to avenge a minor insult and restore Italy's imperial status. The next year, Japan announced plans to increase its navy in violation of the 1922 Washington agreements, ignoring U.S. and British objections. These moves aroused concern about another world war. In the United States, public interest in pacifism and global disarmament increased. Remembering the failure of Woodrow Wilson's "war to end all war," college students organized campus strikes to demand cuts in military budgets and signed the British "Oxford Pledge," vowing never to serve in foreign wars.

In Congress, a vocal nonintervention coalition urged legislation to ensure U.S. neutrality, whenever a war erupted. Hoping to eliminate business incentives to go to war, anti-interventionists tried to block economic entanglements with foreign powers, especially the trade and credit arrangements that had drawn the nation into war in 1917. North Dakota's Gerald P. Nye opened a sensational Senate investigation of the munitions industry in 1934, dominating headlines for a year with revelations of corporate profiteering during the last war. The so-called merchants of death had profited, said Nye, "while millions died." Amidst Depression suspicion of business leaders, the public feared that financial ties to Europe would embroil the nation in another needless war.

Congressional efforts to restrict foreign entanglements conflicted with Roosevelt's desire to maintain presidential control of overseas arms sales. But the public supported strict neutrality laws, and in August 1935 Congress passed the first Neutrality act. Trying to avoid the issues that had led the country into the last war, the law imposed a mandatory embargo on arms sales to warring countries, established federal licensing of munitions dealers, and restricted private travel on ships operated by belligerent nations. The loss of presidential flexibility troubled Roosevelt, who warned that the law "might drag us into war instead of keeping us out."

Moral Embargoes and Revised Neutrality Laws

When Italy invaded Ethiopia five weeks later, Roosevelt grappled with limited options, but few Americans believed the conflict involved national interests. In a purely symbolic gesture, the president proposed a "moral embargo" on the shipment of oil to Italy, an idea ignored by U.S. petroleum companies. Mussolini promptly signed a treaty of alliance with Hitler in 1936. Meanwhile, Congress passed a second Neutrality act in 1936, banning loans and credits to warring nations, tightening the embargo on arms shipments, but allowing presidential discretion in deciding when a state of war existed.

"We are not isolationists," a frustrated Roosevelt had said during the 1936 election campaign, "except insofar as we seek to isolate ourselves completely from war." The outbreak of the Spanish

Civil War (1936–1939) had brought no change in U.S. policy. Although public opinion polls showed majority support for the embattled Spanish Republic, the president instead listened to business leaders, who warned that socialists in Spain threatened U.S. interests. In the election year, Roosevelt also worried about alienating Catholic voters who supported the military rebellion against the anti-clerical left-wing government. While Germany and Italy tested new weapons in Spain, the White House blocked arms shipments to both sides.

Trade embargoes, aimed to ensure neutrality, had the negative effect of limiting exports that promised to restore domestic prosperity. Responding to commercial pressure, Congress enacted a new Neutrality act in 1937. This law permitted the sale of nonmilitary products to warring countries, but included two key provisions: nations at war had to pay for the shipments in cash (to avoid the credit ties that had linked munitions manufacturers to the Allies in 1917); and the shipments had to be made in non-U.S. vessels (to protect neutral rights at sea). In signing the law, Roosevelt recognized that "cash and carry" benefited nations with large gold reserves and strong navies: Britain and France, not Germany.

The first test of the law came when Japan resumed military action against China in 1937. Appealing to regional hostility toward European colonialism, Japan offered a "Greater East Asia Co-Prosperity Sphere," involving an Asian-only marketplace for Chinese resources and Japanese industrial products. By excluding U.S. business, the plan defied the principles of the Open Door. Roosevelt resolved to assist China. He did so by refusing to acknowledge that a state of war existed between Japan and China, thus evading the embargoes required by the Neutrality act. Instead, the administration extended credits to China and permitted the sale of munitions used to resist Japan. Such finesse enabled the White House to

> ## "It's a terrible thing to look over your shoulder when you are trying to lead—and to find no one there."

preserve flexibility, but U.S. aid to China remained minimal.

Hoping to awaken citizen awareness, the president spoke publicly in 1937 against the "epidemic of world lawlessness" and proposed a "quarantine" against aggressor nations. The dramatic speech provoked interest, but editorial responses were mixed. "It's a terrible thing to look over your shoulder when you are trying to lead," said Roosevelt, "and to find no one there." After Japanese aircraft bombed U.S. vessels in China in late 1937, an indignant public urged a boycott of Japanese goods, but Roosevelt avoided conflict in Asia by accepting Japan's diplomatic apology and payment for damages. Presidential caution expressed the sentiments of Congress. The House of Representatives came within eleven votes of supporting a constitutional amendment that would have required a national referendum before the country could declare war.

Roosevelt's policies followed those of Britain and France. When Hitler demanded portions of Czechoslovakia inhabited by ethnic Germans, Roosevelt endorsed the Allies' policy of appeasement, which surrendered to German demands at the Munich Conference of 1938. But the president also initiated a program of military rearmament to strengthen national defense. As Germany seized the remainder of Czechoslovakia in 1939 and threatened Poland, Roosevelt sought revision of the Neutrality laws to permit weapons sales to the Allies, but he lacked the votes in Congress. After Germany attacked Poland in September 1939, drawing Britain and France into World War II,

Roosevelt could do no more than declare U.S. neutrality. "But," he added in a radio address to the public, "I cannot ask that every American remain neutral in thought as well."

The Failure of Neutrality

U.S. sympathies lay with the Allies. German aggression evoked memories of the First World War, and Nazi racism repelled many citizens. Yet the Roosevelt administration refused to intervene to save European Jews facing persecution. Responding to widespread anti-Semitism in the United States, State Department officials did not even fill the quota of legal German immigrants, closing the door to desperate Jewish refugees. Roosevelt eventually relaxed some restrictions, permitting about 250,000 Jews (including the physicist Albert Einstein) to enter the country between 1933 and 1944. More typical was the plight of 900 Jews aboard the steamship *St. Louis* in 1939, who failed to gain admission and were forced to return to Europe, where many would later perish in the Nazi Holocaust.

Roosevelt focused on strengthening ties with the Allies. After the outbreak of World War II, the president summoned a special session of Congress to repeal the arms embargo, opening a strenuous national debate about neutrality. "What the majority of the American people want," remarked a perceptive magazine editor, "is to be as unneutral as possible without getting into war." Despite strong opposition from anti-interventionists, Congress revised the Neutrality act in 1939 and permitted belligerent nations to purchase military supplies on a cash-and-carry basis. Although the rules still restricted U.S. ships from entering war zones, most citizens understood that the policy effectively placed the United States in the Allied camp.

As German armies conquered Scandinavia, the Low Countries, and France during the spring of 1940, Roosevelt criticized "the illusion that we are remote and isolated." Although noninterventionists replied that there was no chance of Germany invading the Western Hemisphere, the administration warned of Germany's growing economic power and the threat to domestic stability. The shocking defeat of France in June 1940 increased pro-Allied sympathy. Congress followed with $17 billion for naval construction and defense. Meanwhile, the president established a secret research committee to consider new weapons, including Einstein's suggestion of an atomic bomb.

Foreign Policy and Roosevelt's Third Term

During the summer of 1940, dramatic air battles over Britain underscored the power of the German war machine. As German planes bombed British cities and submarines sank Allied shipping, Prime Minister Winston Churchill requested U.S. naval assistance. Roosevelt responded in 1940 with an executive order that transferred fifty U.S. destroyers to Britain in exchange for British bases in the Western Hemisphere. According to Roosevelt, the destroyer-base deal did not require congressional approval.

Britain's dire situation now provoked a major domestic debate about foreign policy. Noninterventionists condemned the destroyer deal as an example of excessive presidential power. But internationalists had already captured the Republican party and nominated the Wall Street lawyer Wendell Willkie for the presidency. Willkie approved the destroyer swap and accepted Roosevelt's proposals for military preparedness. Frustrated noninterventionists then formed the America First Committee and soon enrolled 800,000 members to lobby against U.S. commitments to the Allies. By then, Roosevelt had announced his candidacy for a third term.

With both presidential nominees supporting military conscription in 1940, Congress passed

In 1940, radio broadcasts by CBS reporter Edward R. Murrow depicted the terror of the air bombings of Britain to anxious listeners in the United States.

the first peacetime draft in U.S. history. Yet Roosevelt avoided running ahead of public opinion. "Your boys," he assured voters on the eve of the election, "are not going to be sent into any foreign wars." The next week, Roosevelt captured 55 percent of the popular vote, to become the only president to serve more than two terms.

Proposing Lend-Lease

The electoral mandate of November 1940 overcame Roosevelt's caution. In a post-election fireside chat, he described the country as "the great arsenal of democracy" and urged more aid for the Allied

cause. In his 1941 State of the Union address, the president endorsed "Four Freedoms" for which, he said, the Allies fought: freedom of speech, freedom of worship, freedom from want, freedom from fear. Roosevelt advocated support of Britain, not with manpower but with "weapons of defense." Within a week, the White House unveiled the new "Lend-Lease" program, which would authorize the president to sell, transfer, exchange, lend, or lease military equipment and other commodities to any country "whose defense the president deems vital to the defense of the United States." Once again, Congress and the public engaged in a bitter debate about presidential power and obligations to the Allies. Anti-interventionists warned of impending warfare, but Congress passed the measure in March 1941, offering $7 billion to assist Britain, China, and other Allies. After Germany invaded the Soviet Union in June, Roosevelt extended Lend-Lease to the communist ally.

Lend-Lease ended the illusion of U.S. neutrality. Meeting privately with Prime Minister Churchill in 1941, Roosevelt endorsed the so-called Atlantic Charter, a statement of Anglo American "common principles," which included the right of national self-determination, freedom of the seas, equal access to raw materials and markets, and a system of international security. Meanwhile, the president extended the "neutral zone" halfway across the Atlantic, enabling the Navy to escort Lend-Lease material safely to Allied recipients. In an executive agreement with the Danish government-in-exile, Roosevelt established U.S. bases in Greenland.

By the summer of 1941, U.S. convoys protected Allied shipping to Iceland, close to German submarine operations. Noninterventionists warned against provoking German retaliation, and in August Congress voted to renew the draft law by only one vote. In September, the U.S. destroyer *Greer* exchanged fire with a German submarine. Roosevelt now ordered U.S. ships to "shoot on sight" any German vessels in the neutral zone. "It is time," he said, "to stop being deluded by the romantic notion that the Americas can go on living happily and peacefully in a Nazi-dominated world." By November, Congress allowed armed merchant ships to enter the war zone. Roosevelt now waited for Germany to rise to the challenge.

Japan Joins the Axis

Unimpressed by the U.S. military potential, Hitler did not worry about drawing the country into open hostilities. But, ironically, German victories in Europe—the conquest of France and the Netherlands and the invasion of the Soviet Union in 1941—altered the balance of power in Asia and opened opportunities for Japanese expansion. Seeking the natural resources of southeast Asia (rubber, oil, tin), Japan threatened the French, Dutch, and British colonies.

Roosevelt resolved to protect British interests in the region. Exerting economic pressure, Washington terminated the existing U.S.-Japanese trade agreement and placed an embargo on sales of aviation gasoline and scrap iron to Japan in 1940. After Japan moved troops into northern Indochina, the president halted the sale of high-grade iron and steel, but allowed export of certain petroleum products. By increasing economic pressure, Roosevelt hoped to end Japanese advances, but in 1940 Japan signed a military assistance pact with Germany and Italy.

Standing at a crossroads, Japan and the United States opened formal diplomatic negotiations in 1941, but neither side would compromise its policies. While the U.S. Open Door policy required Japan to withdraw from Indochina and China before restoring full trade, Japan's Co-Prosperity program demanded special privileges on the Asian mainland. When Japan marched into southern Indochina in July 1941, Washington froze Japan's U.S. assets, limiting Japan's ability to purchase goods. Japan now had to choose between continuing expansionist policies to obtain oil from Dutch and British possessions or to call an embarrassing retreat. For Japanese militarists, there was no choice. Even by their own estimates, they knew Japan could not win a war with the United States. But they expected Roosevelt to pursue a "Europe-first" strategy, giving Japan time to build military forces while German armies decided the future peace.

The United States Goes to War

On Sunday, December 7, 1941—a day Roosevelt said would "live in infamy"—Japan attacked the U.S. naval base at Pearl Harbor in the territory of Hawaii. Catching the base by surprise, Japanese airplanes damaged and sank battleships and cruisers lying at anchor, destroyed 200 aircraft, and claimed 3,500 casualties. "You cannot escape the clutch of fear at your heart," the president's wife, Eleanor Roosevelt, told a radio audience that night. "And yet," she said, "the certainty of what we have to meet will make you rise above those fears." The next day, 60 million radio listeners heard the president address Congress, announcing a state of war with Japan and promising to lead the country to "absolute victory." With the single dissenting vote by Montana's pacifist Representative Jeannette Rankin (who also voted against war in 1917), Congress formally declared war against Japan. Still, Roosevelt did not challenge the neutralists by requesting a war vote against Germany and Italy. Instead, both fascist nations declared war against the United States on December 11, enabling Congress to reciprocate.

"Every single man, woman, and child," said Roosevelt as he led the nation into war, "is a partner in the most tremendous undertaking of our

The military used Navajo "code talkers" whose language could not be deciphered by the enemy.

American history." Mobilization first involved the building of armies and navies to wage war. Sixteen million men and women entered the armed services. These included 700,000 African Americans who served in segregated units; nearly 300,000 women volunteers, most of whom worked in administrative and clerical jobs behind the battle lines; and 25,000 Native Americans, including the Navajo "code talkers" whose language could not be deciphered by the enemy. For white ethnic soldiers, military service proved a great homogenizing factor. Soldiers served, not with hometown units but with strangers, and the term used for the ordinary recruit, "G.I." (short for "Government Issue"), suggested their interchangeability. The most popular wartime graffiti, "Killroy Was Here," would be written by thousands of anonymous men.

Military service proved to be anything but interchangeable. Only one-eighth of U.S. soldiers participated in combat and experienced the horror of what front-line journalist Ernie Pyle described as "fear beyond fear, misery to the point of numbness, a look of surpassing indifference to anything anybody can do to you." Bill Mauldin's grim cartoons of "dogfaces" Willie and Joe testified to the agony and pride of those who did the fighting. By contrast, military officials generally considered African Americans unqualified for combat, assigning most to behind-the-lines duty involving manual labor. A squadron of black pilots, the "Tuskegee Airmen," eventually earned combat distinction, as did small groups of ground troops in Europe, but African Americans in uniform served in a segregated army. For most soldiers, random factors—geography, age,

Fresh, spirited American troops, flushed with victory, are bringing in thousands of hungry, ragged, battle-weary prisoners. (News item)

Cartoonist Bill Mauldin depicted the steady courage, pride, and humor of ordinary G.I.s who fought in the war. Here he responded to an upbeat news item by showing the reality of weary "dogfaces" trudging through the rain.

training, or dumb luck—determined one's military assignment. To explain how the system worked, GIs used another acronym, SNAFU—"situation normal, all fouled up."

Strategy for Victory

The ill-defined word *victory* served as the nation's primary military objective. One year after Pearl Harbor, public-opinion polls found that one-third of the nation had no idea of U.S. policy goals. But even before the fighting began in 1941, Roosevelt opted for a Europe-first strategy. Perceiving Germany as the greater menace to U.S. interests, Washington leaders treated the war in the Pacific as a holding action, more dramatic than events across the Atlantic, but ultimately winnable through superior U.S. arms. Although the public clamored for revenge against Japan, Roosevelt never wavered from his plan.

After Pearl Harbor, the nation watched bitterly as Japanese forces advanced in the Pacific. One week after the war began U.S. troops surrendered at Guam, and a week after that capitulated at Wake Island. In the winter and spring of 1942, Japanese armies seized the Dutch East Indies, captured Singapore, and overran the Solomon and Gilbert Islands. In the Philippines, U.S. soldiers clung to bases at Corregidor and Bataan until starved and pounded into submission. In 1942, General Douglas MacArthur abandoned the Philippines, but vowed to return and fight again. The Japanese then forced survivors to march, as prisoners of war, fifty-five miles to squalid camps. Thousands died in captivity. Such atrocities inflamed anti-Japanese opinion and justified the waging of total warfare against the Asian foe. Yet by the late spring of 1942, Japanese forces had spread across the south Pacific, preparing to strike at Australia and New Zealand.

Island Hopping Toward Japan

The initial assault on Pearl Harbor had failed to cripple aircraft carriers and shore installations. By the spring of 1942, the Navy was prepared to strike back. A quickly assembled Pacific fleet sailed west from Hawaii and engaged Japanese naval forces in the Battle of the Coral Sea, inflicting heavy losses on the enemy. Just weeks later, at Midway naval air forces demonstrated the effectiveness of air power by sinking seven Japanese carriers, cruisers, and destroyers. These victories halted Japanese expansion in the south Pacific.

By mid-1942, U.S. troops, fighting with Australians and New Zealanders, commenced a brutal war of island-hopping, aiming toward Japan. The invasion of Japanese-held islands brought fierce and deadly warfare. It took six months for the Marines to drive the enemy from Guadalcanal, finally succeeding early in 1943. Allied forces then moved northward through the Solomon Islands, Tarawa, the Gilberts, the Marshalls, and the Marianas. In 1944, MacArthur fulfilled his promise to the Philippines ("I shall return") and led U.S. troops in recapturing Manila in February 1945.

As Allied forces moved closer to Japan, the Marines encountered terrific fighting at Guam, Iwo Jima, and Okinawa in 1945, destroying enemy resistance but at very high cost. Military leaders worried that Japanese warriors might fight a suicidal war to prevent an invasion of the home islands. Meanwhile, each advance northward brought Japanese targets within air range. In 1942, General James Doolittle led the first raids over Tokyo, a morale-boosting attack that served warning of what would follow. By 1944, U.S. bombers brought the war to Japan's civilian population, targeting both factories and residential areas. Under the command of General Curtis LeMay, U.S. planes dropped incendiary bombs that created intense firestorms. In a single night in March 1945, the firebombing of Tokyo ignited a holocaust that claimed 100,000 lives. Americans accepted these attacks as appropriate punishment of a savage enemy. Military leaders aimed to weaken Japanese resistance before a planned invasion to be timed to follow after the defeat of Germany.

Building the Grand Alliance

Military strategy in Europe was linked more delicately to international power relations. The "Big Three"—Roosevelt, Churchill, and Stalin—fought a common enemy, but also defended their separate

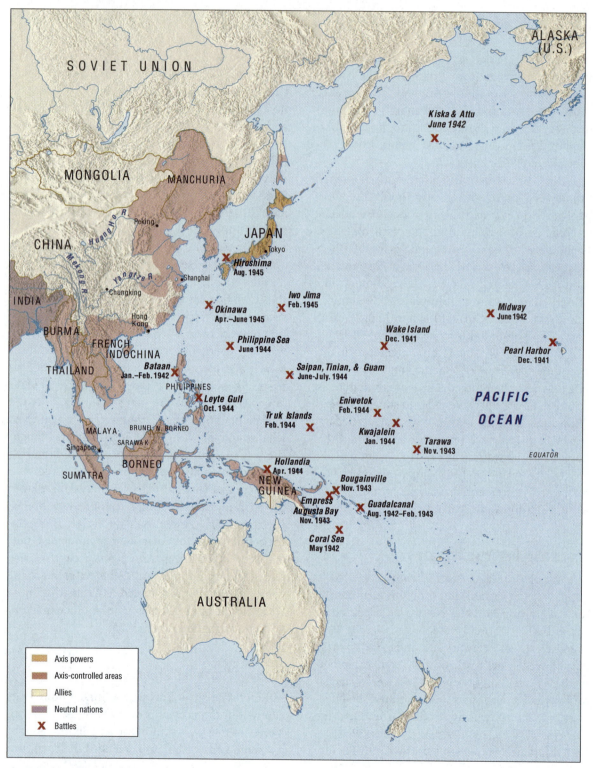

The Pacific Theater, 1941–1945

national objectives, which were not always compatible. In a series of high-level meetings, beginning with a conference between Roosevelt and Churchill at Casablanca in 1942 and another attended by all three in Teheran in 1943, Allied leaders learned to cooperate and patch over many of their differences. In 1942, for instance, Roosevelt and Churchill gave assurances to Stalin by vowing to fight for an "unconditional surrender" of the enemy. Roosevelt's military advisors criticized the phrase because it might harden enemy resistance and undermine future negotiations, but Roosevelt still hoped for Soviet support in the war against Japan.

The Big Three never lost sight of their differing national interests. Confronting the most brutal Nazi warfare, Stalin demanded extensive Allied aid and the quick opening of a second front in western Europe to disperse enemy forces. Stalin also wanted postwar guarantees to protect the Soviet Union from future invasions. Meanwhile, Britain fought defensively, hoping to preserve the Empire and trade advantages within the Commonwealth, the Mediterranean, and the Middle East. For his part, Roosevelt wanted a quick victory, preferring to expend economic resources to save U.S. lives, and looked to a postwar Open Door policy to replace both British and Soviet economic spheres.

While Stalin pleaded for a second front, U.S. strategists led by Generals George C. Marshall and Dwight D. Eisenhower prepared a concentrated build-up of forces in Britain prior to an invasion of the continent. Gaining air superiority over Europe, Allied air forces mercilessly bombed German factories, cities, and transportation routes, punishing civilians and preparing for amphibious landings in France. Meanwhile, U.S. and British troops invaded North Africa in 1942, eliminating German threats to Middle East oil and setting the stage for an invasion of Italy. In 1943, the western Allies attacked Sicily and Italy, overcoming Italian resistance and signing a negotiated treaty. But German armies entered Italy and fiercely resisted Allied advances into 1945.

While U.S. troops fought in the Mediterranean area, Eisenhower amassed his forces in Britain for the largest invasion in history. Allied armies included 2.9 million soldiers, 10,000 aircraft, 53,000 ships, and 1,100 landing craft. On D-Day, June 6, 1944, they moved into action, landing at dawn on the beaches of Normandy, France. Overcoming tough German resistance, the Allies began the race to meet Russian armies somewhere in Germany. "The German is beaten," wrote journalist Ernie Pyle in August, "and he knows it." Despite brutal fighting, including a winter counteroffensive in the Battle of the Bulge, the vastly superior Allied armies moved steadily toward the German border. By the beginning of 1945, political leaders saw that victory was only months away.

Allied leaders jockeyed to control the terms of peace. The Big Three met again in February 1945 at Yalta to negotiate the postwar political settlement. Concerned about the Japanese enemy, Roosevelt gratefully accepted Stalin's promise to enter the Pacific war 90 days after the German surrender. The Allies also agreed to partition Germany into occupied zones. More difficult to resolve was the status of Poland, the nation whose invasion had started the war. Stalin, whose country had suffered the most, losing more than 20 million lives, demanded control of the Polish government to ensure protection from another invasion. Roosevelt and Churchill reluctantly conceded Soviet claims, though the western powers persuaded Stalin to hold free elections in Poland. The agreement underscored the facts of geopolitics. The Soviets already occupied most of eastern Europe and had a larger stake in determining the postwar settlement of the region.

The Big Three also agreed to form a postwar United Nations (U.N.). Unlike Woodrow Wilson's failed League of Nations to which neither the United States nor the Soviet Union had belonged,

The European Theater, 1942–1944

The "Big Three" in Yalta—Roosevelt, Stalin, and Churchill.

Allied leaders accepted a superior role in the new organization. Roosevelt called them the "Four Policeman": the United States, Soviet Union, Britain, and China. Each nation (and later France, too) could protect its national interest through the veto power in the U.N. Security Council. Meeting in San Francisco in April 1945, big powers and little nations proceeded to forge the U.N. agreements. Unlike Wilson, Roosevelt built bipartisan congressional support for U.S. participation in the international body. The president also endorsed international economic agreements—the creation of the International Monetary Fund and the World Bank in 1944—to stabilize postwar trade and investment. Fearing a return of depression conditions, Roosevelt wanted an economic world order to protect U.S. exports.

Mobilizing the Home Front

Roosevelt's mastery of diplomacy—his ability to improvise and adjust plans—matched his skill in mobilizing homefront resources. Although the president had faced considerable opposition to war preparations before Pearl Harbor, he created an administrative apparatus and defense program that enabled the country to mobilize rapidly. The attack at Pearl Harbor had not scratched the nation's mighty industrial potential. During 1941, federal defense expenditures had boosted arms production over 200 percent. Moreover, with federal subsidies, private business had strong incentives to switch to war production; of $26 billion spent to mobilize factories, Washington paid two-thirds of the cost. The results were astounding. By the end of 1942, the United States was making more war materiel than all its enemies combined. By the war's end in 1945, U.S. factories had built over 5,000 merchant ships, 100,000 tanks, 300,000 airplanes, 2.4 million military trucks, 41 billion rounds of ammunition, and 6 million tons of bombs.

To oversee this vast industrial expansion, the president created another alphabet soup of federal agencies, including the War Production Board (WPB) and the Office of War Mobilization (OWM), which set production priorities and allocated resources. The rise of small bureaucracies—draft boards, rationing agencies, civil defense groups—quadrupled the size of federal civilian employment, reaching nearly 4 million by 1945. Meanwhile, corporate executives, such as Sears, Roebuck's Donald Nelson, served in "dollar-a-year" positions to administer the "cost-plus" contracts that guaranteed business profits. "If you . . . go to war . . . in a capitalist country," explained Secretary of War Henry Stimson, "you have to let business make money . . . or business won't work." Incentives, not coercion, goaded industry into action.

With federal wartime expenditures exceeding $320 billion, double the total government outlay since the founding of the republic in 1789, the nation's gross national product jumped from $91 billion in 1939 to $166 billion in 1945. Washington preferred to award contracts to larger corporations capable of filling huge orders. By 1943, just 100 companies received 70 percent of wartime business; meanwhile, half a million small businesses disappeared, many of them absorbed by 1,600 wartime corporate mergers. Benefiting from tax rebates and suspension of anti-trust actions, government contractors acquired vast commercial assets at a fraction of cost. The federal government also supported research and development in private business and universities, financing pioneering work in jet propulsion, digital electronic computers, and atomic energy. The top-secret "Manhattan Project" to build the atomic bomb required 120,000 workers and $2 billion at thirty-seven facilities around the country.

This successful cooperation between big business and the federal government had important consequences for the postwar economy. Accepting the government's ability to regulate economic issues, most corporate leaders no longer defended a laissez-faire (no government) free-enterprise system. And, with growing confidence in business leaders, liberal political leaders no longer pressed for government planning. Here lay the basis for the postwar "military-industrial complex," in which government policy underwrote corporate prosperity and labor unions gained economic security in exchange for acceptance of management leadership.

Labor Goes to War

The mobilization of wartime labor not only absorbed the 7 million unemployed of 1939 (17 per-

cent of the work force), but attracted other previously underemployed workers, such as teenagers, the elderly, women, and minorities. Other workers came from rural areas, as 17 percent of the farm population migrated into the military or took urban jobs. With the federal government pumping $70 billion into shipbuilding, aircraft factories, and other war industries in the western states, 7 million people headed across the Mississippi, half of them landing on the Pacific coast. Such departures were more than offset by agricultural mechanization. The Department of Agriculture estimated that tractors, chemical fertilizers, and land consolidation improved productivity by 25 percent. To ease shortages of railroad and farm hands in the Southwest, Washington also recruited Mexican contract workers, creating the *bracero* (manual labor) program to import 200,000 temporary workers.

Labor shortages also brought new groups into the industrial economy. Displaced by mechanized agriculture and seeking war jobs, 750,000 African Americans continued the historic migration from the southern states, and over 300,000 arrived in California, where jobs abounded. But not necessarily for blacks. "It is against company policy to employ [Negroes] as aircraft workers . . . regardless of their training," said one manufacturer, who did suggest their employment as janitors.

Challenging such prejudices, A. Philip Randolph, head of the mostly black Brotherhood of Sleeping Car Porters, demanded federal action to end discrimination in war employment. At a private meeting with the president, Randolph threatened to bring 100,000 protesters to Washington. "We loyal Negro Americans," declared the March on Washington Movement, "demand the right to work and fight for our country." Roosevelt dared not confront southern political leaders or the military by desegregating the army. But the threat of a demonstration in Washington persuaded him to create the Fair Employment Practices Commission (FEPC) in 1941 to investigate cases of racial discrimination. For the next four years, the FEPC settled numerous disputes, though southern businesses successfully avoided its jurisdiction. Meanwhile, 40,000 Native Americans left tribal reservations for war-related work.

Women also seized new opportunities for jobs. Though constituting 25 percent of the work force in 1940, women contended with employer and middle-class bias that criticized working wives and mothers. Wartime necessity overcame such scruples, attracting over 6 million new women workers between 1941 and 1944, a 57 percent increase. As civil-service employment soared, white women flocked into office work, increasing their numbers by 2 million between 1940 and 1944, about half of whom worked for the federal government. African American women, overwhelmingly domestic workers before the war, moved into industrial occupations, though pay scales remained below those of white women and men. By 1945, women comprised 36 percent of the civilian labor force.

Despite government regulations that mandated equal pay, working women faced widespread discrimination. When women took traditional male jobs, some companies reclassified the work as "female" to reduce wage scales permanently. The government's Office of War Information (OWI) organized job campaigns, asking women to replace men at war, turning characters like "Rosie the Riveter" into homefront legends—but such propaganda did not alter the view that mothers belonged at home. The largest numbers of new workers were aged between 14 to 19 and 35 to 44, outside the prime childbearing years. Even then, government advertising emphasized that women's employment should be temporary, until men returned from military service. While 75 percent of women workers indicated a desire to remain in the work force after the war, government, industry, and labor cooperated to restore jobs to returning veterans.

Women's work also threatened traditional family relations. As industrial production created jobs, the nation's marriage rate increased dramatically from 73 per thousand in 1939 to 93 per thousand in 1942. Birthrates followed the curve upwards, nine to ten months later (Table 23.1). Yet, population migration and family separation raised anxieties about family stability. Coinciding with the baby boom was a rise in illegal abortions, causing 17 percent of maternal deaths in pregnancy. Often noted was the rise in wartime divorces. Newspapers also headlined rising rates of teenage delinquency (mostly for sexual promiscuity), and pundits blamed working mothers for disrupting parental authority.

Labor shortages strengthened the position of unions, whose ranks grew by 40 percent to 13 million during the war. Just after Pearl Harbor, leaders of the major unions pledged a no-strike policy for the war's duration, but workers' desire for wage increases produced constant turmoil. Although the War Manpower Commission (WMC) presided over labor disputes, workers declared independence by changing jobs and skipping work. In 1944, the turnover rate in manufacturing reached 82 percent. Workers also objected to wage freezes. To prevent inflation, the government had established cost-of-living standards that tried to keep wage hikes to 15 percent of prewar levels, but these limits did not apply to overtime. Between 1941 and 1945, hourly wages increased 24 percent, but weekly earnings jumped 70 percent. Federal rules also mandated union "maintenance of membership," which obliged virtually every war-related worker to join a union.

Despite the benefits of wartime jobs, rank-and-file workers frequently declared unauthorized "wildcat" strikes to protest work rules. Most were settled quickly. The most serious wartime strike

TABLE 23.1

The Wartime Marriage and Baby Boom

Year	Marriage rate (per 1000 unmarried women over 15)	Total marriages	Birthrate (women, 15–44)	Total births
1939	73.0	1,404,000	77.6	2,466,000
1940	82.8	1,596,000	79.9	2,559,000
1941	88.5	1,696,000	83.4	2,703,000
1942	93.0	1,772,000	91.5	2,989,000
1943	83.0	1,577,000	94.3	3,104,000
1944	76.5	1,452,000	88.8	2,939,000
1945	83.6	1,613,000	85.9	2,858,000

Source: U.S. Census Bureau, *Historical Statistics of the United States, Bicentennial Edition* (Washington, DC: U.S. Government Printing Office, 1975), Part I, 49, 64.

occurred in 1943 when John L. Lewis's United Mineworkers threatened the entire coal-based economy by calling strikes for better wages. To avoid disruptions, Roosevelt pressured mine owners to meet the union demands. Angered by labor's independence, a more conservative Congress responded in 1943 by enacting, over Roosevelt's veto, the Smith-Connally Labor Act, which imposed 30-day cooling off periods before strikes, prohibited walkouts in war industries, and banned union contributions to political parties. The legislation set the tone of postwar labor policy, but failed to reduce the frequency of wartime labor strife.

Consumer Culture on the Homefront

As full employment fattened workers' paychecks, the administration attempted to check inflation by creating the Office of Price Administration (OPA), perhaps the most unpopular federal agency. Backed by the Anti-Inflation Act of 1942, the OPA froze agricultural prices, wages, and rents, and managed to limit consumer price increases to 2 percent during the last two years of the war. More controversial was the agency's rationing program of scarce resources, which required consumers to use government stamps to make certain purchases. Restricted products included canned goods (because of tin shortages), rubber, gasoline, coffee, sugar, meat, butter, and fuel oil. Consumers with cash could bypass these rules in an expensive illegal black market. Government scrap campaigns (the collection of used tires, tin cans, and kitchen fat) served less to recycle resources than to boost patriotic morale.

To pay for the war, the Revenue Act of 1942 raised corporate taxes to 40 percent and excess profits taxes to 90 percent, though both were lowered in practice through rebates and low mortgage programs. For personal incomes, the highest brackets paid over 90 percent in taxes, but the law broadened the tax base by reaching the lowest-paid as well. As the number of taxpayers increased from 4 million to 28 million, tax collection loomed as a new bureaucratic problem. Instead of paying taxes in April for the previous year's earnings, the law added an anti-inflationary program of payroll withholding for the current year. But the prospect of withholding 1943 income taxes at the same time 1942 taxes were due raised additional objections. The popular solution was to forgive most 1942 taxes. The government also organized massive bond sales both to raise money and reduce the quantity of cash in circulation to fight inflation. As in World War I, popular entertainers, such as radio singer Kate Smith, band leader Duke Ellington, and actress Carole Lombard (who died in a 1943 plane crash) led popular campaigns to sell war bonds, which absorbed $150 billion from consumer savings.

Although wartime workers earned more than ever before, rising incomes did not always generate greater purchasing power. After the government ordered automobile manufacturers to shift production to tanks and airplanes, for example, consumers faced only a used car market and gas rationing. Extra earnings often went into personal savings accounts, waiting for later opportunities for consumption. Homefront advertising tantalized consumers with pictures of refrigerators, washing machines, automobiles, even private airplanes—but only for "tomorrow," after the war. Meanwhile, patriotic slogans and victory jingles linked household purchases to winning the war. "Your first duty is your beauty," said one cosmetics manufacturer; "morale on the homefront is the woman's job." Corporate advertising focused on defending the free-enterprise system.

For immediate gratification, consumers bought cheap entertainment, such as newly introduced pa-perback books (with small print and thin pages to save paper); went to the movies (weekly ticket sales exceeded 80 million); or danced the lindy hop and jitterbug to five-cent jukebox records. Among the melody hits were "We'll Have to Slap the Dirty Jap," "Goodbye Mama, I'm Off to Yoka-hama," and "Don't Sit under the Apple Tree with Anyone Else but Me." Radio programming endorsed patriotic themes and broadcast marathons to sell bonds. One radio series called "Freedom's People," sponsored by the federal government's Office of Education, focused directly on issues of racial justice. Meanwhile, the Office of War Information (OWI) developed popular documentary films, such as *The Negro Soldier* (1944) and Frank Capra's series *Why We Fight* (1942–1945), which provided an official version of the war.

The Hollywood motion picture industry also rallied to the flag, offering sentimental fare that glorified military prowess, praised Allies, demonized enemies, and inspired domestic sacrifice. Movies like *Casablanca* (1943) became classics by personalizing the struggle. Tearjerkers like *Since You Went Away* (1944) depicted the sacrifices of homefront families, and musicals like *Meet Me in St. Louis* (1944) juxtaposed nostalgia with fears of domestic upheaval. Such images enabled the movie industry to attain the highest box office returns ever.

Whatever the medium—films, radio, mass magazines, or advertising—ethnic stereotypes prevailed, helping to define public perceptions of the war and its purposes. The familiar Europeans (Jew, Irish, Italian, Pole) formed the typical all-American combat battalion, usually under the leadership of an Anglo Protestant officer, and sometimes even included African Americans, despite military racial segregation. Chinese and Filipino Americans, who served in the military in disproportionately high numbers, entered the official meltingpot and appeared as dedicated patriots in movies and advertising. In 1943, Filipinos in the military became eligible for citizenship for the first time. That year, Congress repealed the Chinese Exclusion Act of 1882, established a small quota for immigration, and permitted Chinese residents to become citizens.

Friendly images of Italian and German civilians reinforced government policy. Roosevelt adopted a lenient attitude toward the 600,000 Italian Americans who had not filed for citizenship. Although a few hundred pro-Mussolini "enemy aliens" were confined in prison camps, a presidential order issued on Columbus Day 1942 removed the enemy stigma and eased requirements for naturalized citizenship. Similarly, the White House strove to avoid the anti-German hysteria that accompanied World War I. Following government policy, Hollywood films distinguished Nazis from other Germans, while the war's most popular cartoon, Walt Disney's *Der Fuehrer's Face* (1942), incited audiences to yell at the Nazi leader. The Japanese enemy, often placed in jungle settings, emerged as evil incarnate, a racial caricature and a violent foe. Meanwhile, the controversial Soviet allies assumed heroic stature in numerous productions, though public opinion remained wary about communist objectives.

The Politics of Wartime

As government power increasingly impinged on business, labor, and consumer activity, political leaders in both parties lamented the growing federal bureaucracy. With the passing of mass unemployment, a conservative majority in Congress voted to dismantle the depression-era agencies— WPA, CCC, NYA, and HOLC. In 1943, Roosevelt had to admit that "Dr. New Deal" had become "Dr. Win the War." Yet the president hesitated to abandon a liberal agenda, and he opened the 1944 election year by proposing an "economic bill of rights" for all citizens. With 1 million veterans already home, Roosevelt supported the Serviceman's Readjustment Act, known as the G.I. Bill of Rights, which would provide unemployment insurance, social security, home loans, and education benefits to ease the transition to civilian life and prop up consumer spending.

During the 1944 election, Republicans made government bureaucracy a campaign issue. Their presidential candidate, the moderate Thomas Dewey, contrasted his youthfulness with Roosevelt's age and exhaustion. In language that foreshadowed a postwar red scare, his running mate, Ohio's John Bricker, charged that communism was "worming . . . into our national life [and taking] a strangle hold . . . through the control of the New Deal." Roosevelt could ignore such allegations, but in his own party Democratic conservatives forced him to drop the liberal Vice President Henry Wallace from the campaign. Roosevelt turned to Missouri Senator Harry S Truman, who had earned a reputation for investigating waste and corruption in wartime production. With the war and foreign policy the major issues, Roosevelt won 55 percent of the popular vote, achieving a fourth presidential term.

Establishing Political Conformity

Despite party competition, a wartime consensus continued to marginalize unconventional political, religious, and ethnic groups. Under the guise of protecting national security, Roosevelt had requested J. Edgar Hoover's Federal Bureau of Investigation to conduct surveillance of fascist and communist organizations as early as 1936. After the war began, the FBI extended investigations to

The War against Fascism, 1931–1945 | **541**

include propaganda "opposed to the American way of life" as well as agitators who provoked "class hatred." Such objectives allowed federal agents to monitor the NAACP and other reform groups. Military counterintelligence even bugged hotel rooms used by Eleanor Roosevelt. Although the Communist party endorsed U.S. participation in the war after 1941, the FBI clumped communists with fascists in a secret custodial detention plan to arrest "dangerous" suspects during a national emergency.

The Smith Act in 1940 made it a crime to propose the overthrow of the government by force and enabled the administration to prosecute fascist groups, such as the pro-Nazi Silver Shirts. Roosevelt's attorney general also cited the Espionage Act of 1917 to enjoin Father Charles Coughlin's "Christian Front" from mailing its anti-Semitic magazine and persuaded Catholic leaders to silence the radio priest. Meanwhile, federal interpretation of draft laws limited "conscientious objectors" to those who believed in God. A few Native American nations, such as the Hopi and Seminole, refused to cooperate with the draft, but the largest group of objectors were Jehovah's Witnesses, who rejected *any* killing. Although 35,000 conscientious objectors accepted some alternative service to war, more than 5,000 pacifists, mostly Jehovah's Witnesses, went to jail, serving sentences averaging over four years.

The Incarceration of Japanese Americans

Japanese Americans also discovered limited protection of their civil rights. Shocked by Pearl Harbor and Japanese victories in the Pacific, many West Coast journalists falsely reported that Japanese Americans had conspired with the Japanese enemy and planned additional subversion at home. When no such attacks occurred, California

Roosevelt issued an executive order in 1942 calling for the internment of the 110,000 Japanese Americans living on the West Coast.

Attorney General Earl Warren used this evidence of loyalty as counterproof: "We are just being lulled into a false sense of security," he told a congressional committee.

President Roosevelt responded to such claims by issuing Executive Order 9066 in 1942, requiring the internment of the 110,000 Japanese Americans living on the West Coast, two-thirds of whom were U.S. citizens by birth. By contrast, the territory of Hawaii, with a much larger Japanese American population and the target of the first Japanese bombs, experienced no panic and continued to rely on local Japanese to mobilize for war. The difference revealed the power of racism, which was much stronger on the mainland. "It's a question of whether the white man lives on the Pacific or a brown man," stated one California farmer eager to eliminate Japanese American competitors. Military leaders shared those sentiments: "A Jap's a Jap," remarked the regional commanding general.

"Has the Gestapo come to America?" responded one angry *Nisei* citizen. Forced to sell all their property at a fraction of its value and transported to ten concentration camps in remote parts of the country, most Japanese Americans stoically accepted exile as proof of their loyalty. As administered by the government's War Relocation Authority, which called the prisoners "colonists," the camps were bleak, primitive, and terrifying. Surrounded by armed guards and barbed wire fences, inhabiting drafty tar-paper covered barracks, obliged to share mess halls, showers, and toilets with strangers, Japanese Americans grappled with the shame and pride of their ethnic identity.

The sense of injustice divided Japanese American communities. When the U.S. military recruited a Japanese American battalion in 1943, 1,200 volunteers proudly formed the "Fighting 442nd" Division, becoming the most decorated combat unit in Europe. Ironically, these soldiers eventually participated in the liberation of Nazi concentration camps, where the horrors of racism were blatantly exposed. But fifteen times as many of the Japanese Americans refused to cooperate with U.S. loyalty tests, and 8,000 opted to return to Japan after the war. In the 1944 *Korematsu* case, the Supreme Court upheld the relocation program on the basis of military necessity, but subsequently ruled in the *Endo* case (1944) that citizens could not be detained after their loyalty had been established. Yet Roosevelt delayed closing the internment camps for five months, believing that the release of Japanese Americans would hurt his reelection chances in 1944. Postwar litigation continued until 1988, when Congress approved monetary compensation for surviving Japanese Americans. Not until 2000 did the government bestow Medals of Honor on deserving Japanese American soldiers.

African Americans' Double-V Campaign

African Americans found themselves in a two-front war. Richard Wright's explosive 1940 novel *Native Son* depicted an omnipresent rage at racial injustice that explained why many African Americans supported the Japanese over their own white oppressors. In contrast to African American leaders in World War I, who agreed to "close ranks" in hopes of future benefits, black leaders of World War II endorsed a "Double V" campaign seeking immediate victory over racism at home. Within

the military, segregation extended to Red Cross blood ("colored" and "white") and separate, usually unequal mess halls and recreational facilities. Despite proven valor, the Army awarded no Congressional Medals of Honor to blacks, though six African Americans, including a veteran of the Lincoln Brigade, finally received such medals in 1997. At one base, black athlete Jackie Robinson was court martialed (and acquitted) for refusing to sit in the back of a bus. Such discrimination brought endless complaints, and serious race riots involving military weapons, but only occasional reforms.

"As we . . . defend democracy from foreign attack," declared a 15-year-old high school student, Martin Luther King, Jr., "let us . . . give fair play and free opportunity for all people." Attacking segregation in employment, housing, and education, the NAACP increased membership ninefold to 450,000, while the newly formed Congress of Racial Equality (CORE) used sit-down tactics to integrate lunch counters and public facilities in northern cities. But northern whites resented the presence and economic threat of black workers, especially migrants from the South. In Detroit, white mobs rioted in 1942 to stop racial mixing in a federally funded housing project, and factory workers organized hate strikes to prevent employment of black women. The next year, Detroit exploded in a two-day race riot, one of 242 racial battles in 47 cities that disrupted the home front. In Philadelphia, white trolley-car workers went on strike to protest a government integration order, leading federal authorities to summon armed troops to operate the transit system.

Defending Minority Cultures

When African, Mexican, and Filipino American youth adopted baggy "zoot suits" and pompadour haircuts as a fashion uniform, whites targeted the flamboyant style to assert their disapproval. Responding to rumors that Hispanic gang members had attacked a sailor in Los Angeles, white servicemen started a four-day riot against Mexican Americans in 1943, that was climaxed by slashing trousers and stripping the victims. Native Americans faced similar indignities. In 1944, fifty tribes organized the National Congress of American Indians to protect treaty rights and federal benefits. Yet in 1945, Arizona and New Mexico still refused to accept Native American voting rights. Meanwhile, white political conservatives argued that Native Americans no longer needed federal protection and called for the termination of tribal governments.

Despite such racial antagonism, World War II proved a turning point in racial attitudes, stimulating greater toleration and acceptance of ethnic diversity. Within the military, ministers, priests, and rabbis upheld interdenominational equality. In 1943, the Supreme Court pointed to Nazi excesses to explain why Jehovah's Witnesses need not be compelled to salute the flag. The next year, the Court denied the legality of the white primary, which had disenfranchised African Americans in the southern states. By 1944, Roosevelt established the War Refugee Board to facilitate the admission of displaced Jews. Such government acts obviously did not change private prejudices, but public policy altered the limits of acceptable behavior and represented a large step toward acceptance of a multicultural society. The discovery of appalling Nazi death camps in 1945 underscored the evils of home-grown racism.

Toleration of sexual differences remained more ambiguous. Prior to World War II, both the military and civilian society had punished homosexual crimes of "sodomy." But the large number of psychiatric cases after World War I persuaded the Selective Service Administration to institute pre-induction psychiatric evaluations for new recruits. Among the grounds for excluding personnel were "homosexual proclivities." Such vague criteria allowed most gays and lesbians to enter the military (only about 5,000 were formally rejected), but the screening program established a precedent for considering homosexuals unfit for service. During wartime, same sex barracks enabled gays and lesbians to form personal and community attachments, which often extended into off-base relationships. Yet exposure of homosexuality usually led to bad, or "blue," discharges, which cost individuals their veterans' benefits. Such policies simply extended civilian attitudes and standards.

The End of the War

By the spring of 1945, the possibility of establishing a lasting peace seemed imminent, though world leaders still grappled with many unresolved questions. How would Germany be forever neutralized? Would the Soviets permit democratic governments and capitalist institutions in Eastern Europe? Which faction, Nationalist or Communist, would dominate postwar China? Which nation would control eastern Asia? What would be the status of European colonies in Asia and Africa? Roosevelt hoped that a spirit of negotiation and compromise would settle the details, but he understood that the Allies did not have an equal stake in every area of the world. Confident in his diplomatic skill, the president often accepted ambiguity as the best solution. But, before he could obtain final agreements on these sensitive matters of foreign policy, Roosevelt died suddenly of a stroke on April 12, 1945.

Truman's Truce

News of the president's death stunned the nation, shocking no one more than Vice President Harry

S Truman, who told reporters he felt like a load of hay had just fallen on his head. The former Missouri senator had no diplomatic experience, little information about Roosevelt's postwar plans, and a cantankerous personality. Yet, within one month, the new president faced the delicate issues that came with Germany's surrender on May 8, 1945 (V-E Day). Although Roosevelt had accepted the vague language of diplomatic agreements, Truman adopted a rigid stand against Soviet claims in Poland and flexed U.S. economic power against Britain and the Soviet Union to gain political advantages. Meanwhile, the president confronted the secret issue of using the new atomic bomb against Japan.

While war continued in the Pacific, the Allies tried to sustain an atmosphere of compromise at a meeting in Potsdam, Germany, in July 1945. Once again, Stalin promised to fulfill his agreement at Yalta to send troops against Japan, but that leverage, which had been so important half a year earlier, had lost its importance. During the conference, Truman learned of the successful test of an atomic bomb at Alamogordo, New Mexico. Soviet assistance now appeared less urgent to defeat Japan. With growing self-confidence, Truman urged Stalin to establish democratic governments in eastern Europe. The Soviet leader viewed the request as a betrayal of the Allies' agreements at Yalta and refused to budge. Although the Allies still agreed at Potsdam to partition Germany, they postponed other questions to a subsequent meeting.

Victory in the Pacific

By the summer of 1945, Japan's position seemed hopeless. Facing constant bombings and an Allied invasion, Japanese diplomats made secret inquiries about negotiating a truce. The United States, insisting on an unconditional surrender, made no response. Military plans to drop an atomic bomb on a Japanese city proceeded with limited discussion. To be sure, some members of the scientific community that developed the bomb, led by the refugee physicist Leo Szilard, questioned the use of such weapons against civilians. But Truman saw no need to delay a weapon that might end the war immediately and save the lives of U.S. soldiers. The atomic bomb also offered political advantages, in that victory would not require the intervention of Soviet forces in east Asia. Perhaps, too, the White House hoped to demonstrate the superiority of U.S. weapons to the truculent Soviet ally.

Truman issued a final ultimatum to Japan. Then he allowed military plans to proceed. On August 6, 1945, a B-29 airplane dropped a single atomic bomb on Hiroshima, instantly destroying the city and taking over 100,000 lives. The destructive power of the bomb had exceeded scientific expectations. Three days later, as promised at Yalta, the Soviet Union declared war on Japan. That day, another B-29 dropped a second atomic bomb and destroyed the city of Nagasaki. A stunned Japanese government now pleaded for peace, asking only for the preservation of their sacred Emperor. When Truman accepted that condition on August 14, 1945 (V-J Day), World War II came to a close.

The Price of Victory

The violence of the war—atomic bombs, concentration camps, military casualties in the millions—shocked the world. U.S. casualties included over 400,000 dead and 800,000 wounded, but were a fraction of other countries' losses. Yet the face of this war, broadcast in newsreels and magazine photographs, horrified the imagination. In a final

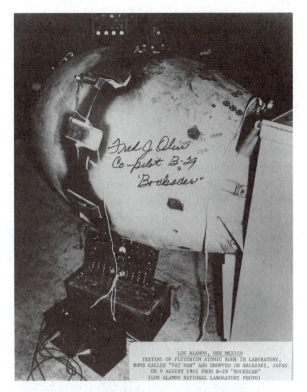

The atomic bomb nicknamed "Fat Man," in testing at the Los Alamos, New Mexico, lab before it was dropped on Nagasaki on August 9, 1945. The photograph bears the signature of Colonel Fred J. Olivi, copilot of the B-29 bomber "Bockscar," which dropped the bomb.

others. The Allies later used the Nuremberg principles against Japanese war criminals.

Instead of limiting wartime violence, however, World War II ironically extended the limits of acceptable casualties. The bombing of civilians, so outrageous in China and Spain in the 1930s, became the normal course of war. The use of atomic weapons made all life on the planet precarious and tentative. Even chemical advances, such as the wartime development of the pesticide DDT, paid no heed to human costs and environmental consequences. And the hope for a lasting peace appeared extremely fragile. During the founding conference of the United Nations in San Francisco in 1945, a 27-year-old navy war hero reported the proceedings from the "serviceman's viewpoint," noting the growing rift between the United States and Britain as opposed to the Soviet Union. "It is this distrust—which is becoming deeper," wrote the young John F. Kennedy, "that is causing grave and considerable discouragement." Despite such disappointment, the United States appeared in 1945 as the strongest power in the world, and almost all its citizens agreed that the nation could never again evade its collective responsibilities to uphold world peace. By 1945, global power had become an inextricable part of the national identity.

act of solidarity, the Allies convened an International Military Tribunal at Nuremberg, Germany, in August 1945 to bring Nazi war criminals to justice. Shockingly graphic evidence of atrocities and genocide led the Allied judges to reach important agreements about international crimes. Their rulings mandated that individuals remained accountable for their actions, and they defined specific acts as crimes against humanity. After formal legal proceedings, the Allied courts ordered the execution of selected Nazis and the imprisonment of

INFOTRAC® COLLEGE EDITION EXERCISES

For additional reading go to InfoTrac College Edition, your online research library at *http://web1.infotrac-college.com*.

Keyword search: Lincoln Brigade

Keyword search: Francisco Franco

Keyword search: Benito Mussolini

Subject search: Hitler

Keyword search: Good Neighbor Policy

Subject search: FDR

Keyword search: United Nations

Keyword search: Bastogne

Subject search: Pearl Harbor

Subject search: Okinawa

Subject search: D Day

Keyword search: Russian Front

Subject search: Japanese internment

Subject search: Harry Truman

Subject search: Hiroshima

ADDITIONAL READING

Peter N. Carroll, *The Odyssey of the Abraham Lincoln Brigade: Americans in the Spanish Civil War* (1994). Following the lives of U.S. volunteers, the book links radical politics of the 1930s with anti-fascism.

The United States Goes to War

Patrick J. Hearden, *Roosevelt Confronts Hitler: America's Entry into World War II* (1987). Emphasizing economic issues, the author places foreign policy in the depression context.

Doris Kearns Goodwin, *No Ordinary Time: Franklin and Eleanor Roosevelt: The Home Front in World War II* (1994). This narrative history gives a White House perspective on the war.

Strategy for Victory

Michael S. Sherry, *The Rise of American Air Power: The Creation of Armageddon* (1987). A provocative analysis of bombing strategies, the book explores political, social, and moral issues.

Mobilizing the Home Front

John J. Jeffries, *Wartime America: The World War II Home Front* (1996). This volume provides a brief overview of wartime issues.

William M. Tuttle, Jr., *"Daddy's Gone to War": The Second World War in the Lives of America's Children* (1993). The author depicts the war's impact on children and their parents.

The Politics of Wartime

Alan Brinkley, *The End of Reform: New Deal Liberalism in Recession and War* (1995). Tracing the demise of New Deal programs, the book illuminates political change on the home front.

Labor Goes to War

Maureen Honey, *Creating Rosie the Riveter: Class, Gender, and Propaganda during World War II* (1984). This book analyzes changing images and roles of women in the war.

Consumer Culture on the Home Front

William L. Bird, Jr. and Harry R. Rubenstein, *Design for Victory: World War II Posters on the American Home Front* (1998). This brief illustrated volume places wartime posters in a political perspective.

Thomas Doherty, *Projections of War: Hollywood, American Culture, and World War II* (1993). This book analyzes the political and social views of Hollywood movies.

Library of America, *Reporting World War II: American Journalism, 1938–1946* (1995). An outstanding two-volume anthology of wartime reportage, the book includes articles depicting the war at home and abroad.

The Incarceration of Japanese Americans

Richard Drinnon, *Keeper of Concentration Camps: Dillon S. Myer and American Racism* (1987). The book exposes the prejudices of Japanese internment and links wartime policies to programs for Native Americans.

African Americans' Double-V Campaign

Mary Penick Motley, *The Invisible Soldier: The Experience of the Black Soldier, World War II* (1975). A fascinating oral history, depicting the pervasive discrimination in the military.

Patricia Sullivan, *Days of Hope: Race and Democracy in the New Deal Era* (1996). Beginning with the Depression, the author examines the political context for African Americans seeking racial justice.

Defending Minority Cultures

Allan Berube, *Coming Out under Fire: Gay Men and Women in World War II* (1990). Based in part on interviews with veterans and psychiatrists, the book is a pioneering study of homosexuals and the military.

24

HOW to SURVIVE ATOMIC ATTACK

ALL ABOUT FALLOUT
Radiation Levels of Safety, Danger and Death
Protection Against Fallout
Decontamination Procedures

LATEST RADIATION DETECTION INSTRUMENTS
Description, Cost and Operation

HOW TO:
Build a Basement Shelter
Build an Underground Shelter
Stock and Store Food and Water

LIVING IN THE SHELTER
Games and Activities

New Pre-Fab Underground Shelter

SPECIAL! The Horror of an Atomic Explosion—
Photos of HIROSHIMA and NAGASAKI—
Nuclear Shock Wave Destruction

50¢

Cold War Society, 1945–1952

CHRONOLOGY

One of my classmates . . . muttered something and pointed outside the window, saying, "A B-29 is coming." . . . Looking in the direction that he was pointing . . . [all] I can remember was a pale lightning flash for two or three seconds . . . It was awful, awful. . . . I was trapped under the debris and I was in terrible pain. . . . Then, I heard about ten of my surviving classmates singing our school song. . . . I could hear sobs. Someone was calling his mother. But those who were still alive were singing the school song for as long as they could. . . . We thought that someone would come and help us. . . . But nobody came to help . . . , and we stopped singing one by one. In the end, I was singing alone. Then I started to feel fear creeping in. . . . Finally I cleared the things around my head. And with my head sticking out of the debris, I realized the scale of the damage. The sky over Hiroshima was dark. Something like a tornado or a big fireball was storming throughout the city. . . . I found one of my classmates lying alive. . . . It is hard to tell, his skull was cracked open, his flesh was dangling out from his head. He had only one eye left, and it was looking right at me. . . . I held his hand, then he started to reach for his notebook in his chest pocket, so I asked him, . . . "You want me to take this along to hand it over to your mother?" He nodded. . . . still I could hear him crying out, . . . "Mother, Mother." (Yoshitaka Kawamoto, 13 years old on August 6, 1945, and 0.8 kilometers away from the hypocenter)

"Whatever elation there is in the world today," observed magazine columnist Norman Cousins at the moment of the Allied victory in 1945, "is severely tempered by . . . a primitive fear . . . of forces man can neither channel nor comprehend." Overnight, the atomic bombing of Japan had opened a new world of mysterious power, prospects of extinction, and "primordial apprehensions." Next to the Bomb lay more mundane, but very real, reasons to worry. Despite gestures of cooperation, the United States and the Soviet Union had failed to reach agreement about the future of Germany and Eastern Europe. In addition, the conversion to a peacetime economy was causing considerable disruption—shortages, inflation, layoffs, and strikes—that aroused fears of a return to depression conditions.

These unexpected concerns contributed to a mood of frustration. The Washington bureaucracy, instead of vanishing after the war, remained to preside over the uncertain peace. When the loss of wartime work and runaway inflation prompted labor unions to organize a rash of postwar strikes, consumers objected to the inconveniences, and business leaders demanded legislation to restrict worker protests. Just as the federal government was claiming more power than ever before, dissent about Truman's foreign policy raised allegations about the loyalty of certain citizens. Postwar Hollywood movies captured these murmurings with an anxious, claustrophobic style called *film noir* ("dark film"), which included *Detour* (1945), *They Live by Night* (1949), and *D.O.A.* (1950). "Seldom," remarked radio commentator Edward R. Murrow, "has a war ended leaving the victors with such a sense of uncertainty and fear, with such a realization that the future is obscure and that survival is not assured."

Concern about diplomatic disputes and social disorder in war-torn Europe encouraged President Harry Truman to challenge Soviet threats around the world. Depicting the global situation as extremely perilous, he prepared the nation for another war, this time against the former U.S. ally. This unexpected reversal, from anticipations of peace to preparations for war, demanded a strong domestic consensus. Appealing for bipartisan support, Truman used national security issues to justify an anti-communist crusade at home.

Although the administration worried that pressure for political conformity might stifle civil liberties, the undeclared war at home and abroad, the so-called Cold War, excused government vigilance against opposition. This warlike attitude set the tone of national politics as the public confronted dramatic social and economic changes. Despite international worries and fear of communism, the country now entered an era of startling population growth, economic expansion, social mobility, and broad prosperity. Preoccupied by such private issues, voters permitted party leaders to define the political agenda.

The Era of Prosperity Begins

For the young adults of the postwar generation, including over 10 million veterans of the armed services, concern about politics and foreign policy was offset by the prospect of unprecedented opportunities. The men and women who had fought in the war yearned for economic security and stability. They intended, in the words of a popular song of 1945, "to make up for lost time." They wanted children and families, homes and jobs, and steady incomes to purchase furniture and automobiles. Workers and business leaders alike initially worried that without military spending the economy might nosedive into another depression. But the Servicemen's Readjustment Act of 1944 (G.I.

Bill) provided an economic cushion for veterans, and unspent wartime savings helped to jump-start the postwar economy (see Chapter 23). Inspired by advertising that envisioned a society of mass consumers, veterans dreamed not only of material comfort but also of social mobility, the possibility of moving from working-class status into the middle classes.

Ethnic Identity in Postwar Society

The optimism of the postwar generation reflected both economic opportunities and a belief in social equality, at least for whites. This generation came of age during the depression and the war. Many were children of immigrants, first- or second-generation citizens, and residents of urban areas. Their parents had first identified with the Democratic party in 1928 by voting for the unsuccessful Catholic candidate Al Smith, then by supporting Franklin D. Roosevelt's New Deal. The Democratic party had reciprocated by providing federal assistance during hard times and by appointing Catholics, Jews, and African Americans to government positions. Such advancement still aroused prejudices among conservative groups who worried about preserving white Protestant values, but during the war the Roosevelt administration had refused to inflame ethnic antagonism, except against Japanese Americans. Multiethnic combat platoons, depicted so gallantly in Hollywood movies, enabled white ethnics, blacks, Mexican Americans, Native Americans, and Chinese Americans to demonstrate their loyalty to the republic.

"I am not a Polack," screamed one war veteran, Stanley Kowalski (played by Marlon Brando), in Tennessee Williams's theatrical masterpiece of 1947, A Streetcar Named Desire. "People from Poland are Poles, not Polacks. But what I am is a one-hundred-percent American, born and raised in the greatest country on earth and proud as hell of it, so don't ever call me a Polack." Other postwar Hollywood films, such as *Gentleman's Agreement* (1947) and *Crossfire* (1947), attacked anti-Semitism and discrimination against white ethnic groups. In higher education, arbitrary quotas based on race, religion, and ethnicity still restricted academic admissions, but major universities now made token appointments of ethnic minorities, much as the U.S. Supreme Court had Jewish and Catholic "seats." The Catholic Cardinal Francis Spellman described his hatred of atheistic communism not as a religious position, "but as an American in defense of my country."

Minorities Seek Civil Rights

Nonwhite ethnic groups now cited their wartime patriotism to claim full political rights. "If in the trenches of Europe and the Pacific we were equal and we demonstrated our loyalty and love for the Stars and Stripes," declared a Mexican American group in San Antonio, Texas, "then in civil life we also desire equality." The NAACP cited the wartime "death struggle against the apostles of racism" in persuading the U.S. Supreme Court to prohibit segregation in interstate bus travel in 1946. That year, Congress passed the Indian Claims Commission Act, permitting Native American nations to sue the federal government for past violations of treaty rights—"An example," said South Dakota Senator Karl Mundt, "for all the world to follow in its treatment of minorities." To be sure, the commission proved slow to assist the claimants, but in 1948 a federal court upheld Native American voting rights in all states.

Appeals for ethnic acceptance coincided with an effort to remedy legal injustices. Mexican American veterans formed the GI Forum to protect their claims to Veterans Administration benefits and a veritable lawyers' meltingpot (including the NAACP, American Jewish Congress, and Japanese American Citizens League) supported the League of United

Latin American Citizens (LULAC) in successfully suing to end segregation in California's public schools. In 1948, California courts ruled that laws barring interracial marriages were unconstitutional, and the U.S. Supreme Court rejected the state's alien land laws that had prevented Asians from owning real estate. Anti-discrimination laws were not always enforced, but principles of racial and ethnic equality were now firmly established.

Other forms of racial discrimination persisted. In the southern states, politicians showed no shame in affirming racial divisions. "Negro soldiers disgraced the flag," Mississippi's James Eastland told the Senate in 1945. "I assert that the Negro race is an inferior race." But now these attitudes did not go unchallenged. Returning black veterans, such as Medgar Evers, defied local custom by seeking to vote. Armed mobs often blocked their efforts. Yet, in Mississippi, African American voter registration climbed from 2,000 in 1940, to 2,500 in 1946, to 5,000 one year later—a striking increase even if the total amounted to 1 percent of the eligible number. When Mississippi Senator Theodore Bilbo, an outspoken racist, won reelection in 1946, the NAACP mobilized black veterans and labor organizations to block his seating, although Bilbo's death halted the proceedings.

Other African Americans voted with their feet. At the end of the 1940s, 70 percent of Mississippi's blacks had less than a seventh-grade education (only 2 percent had completed high school), and annual per pupil expenditures for blacks totaled $32.55, compared to $122.93 for whites. Median family incomes for Mississippi whites exceeded $1,600; for blacks $601. As the mechanization of agriculture reduced the need for farm workers, rural blacks departed from the southern states in increasing numbers. During the 1940s, the outmigration of southern blacks reached 1.6 million. By the end of the decade, the southern share of the nation's African American population dropped from 77 percent to 68 percent, while the propor-

With a portrait of Abraham Lincoln on the wall behind them, Brooklyn Dodgers general manager Branch Rickey signed second baseman Jackie Robinson to a major league contract, breaking the "color line" that had excluded African Americans since the 1890s.

tion of the Northeast grew to 13 percent, the Midwest to 15 percent, and the West to 4 percent.

In northern cities, African Americans confronted distinct problems of adjustment. "In the South everyone knew you," explained Ralph Ellison in his novel of the black migration, *The Invisible Man* (1952), "but coming North was a jump into the unknown . . . . You could actually make yourself anew." The first thing Ellison's ambitious character did was buy a watch to keep up with the northern pace. Rural blacks brought with them a preference for evangelical religion and a musical style called the blues. Yet northern blacks earned lower wages than comparable whites, and residential segregation caused higher rents. In the climate of postwar toleration, African Americans demanded changes, including open housing laws and better employment opportunities. In 1947, the interracial Congress of Racial Equality (CORE) organized sit-in protests at northern lunch counters to force desegregation, and launched an integrated "freedom ride" on interstate buses in the South to test compliance with Supreme Court rulings. In

North Carolina, local officials sentenced the riders to a month on the chain gang. The integration of major-league baseball by Brooklyn Dodger second-baseman Jackie Robinson in 1947 gave blacks something to cheer about, but the athlete continued to face discrimination on and off the field.

Challenges to southern segregation drew grisly responses. When one black veteran voted in a Georgia primary election in 1946, he was shot dead. A revival of the Ku Klux Klan brought other incidents of floggings, gang beatings, and murder. Southern police seldom brought the accused to trial; when they did, all-white juries voted acquittal. The 17-year-old Martin Luther King, Jr., a sophomore at Atlanta's Morehouse College, gained public attention with a letter to the editor. "We want and are entitled to the basic rights and opportunities of American citizens," he declared, including "the same courtesy and good manners that we ourselves bring to all human relations." In Mississippi, local blacks bravely organized a boycott of gas stations that lacked "colored" toilets, but dared not attack prevailing "separate but equal" arrangements. A visiting sociologist noted, however, that the younger blacks listened to songs that derided white supremacy.

Outbreaks of racial violence infuriated President Truman, particularly because many victims were war veterans. In addition, he realized the importance of protecting his liberal New Deal constituency in the northern cities. In 1946, Truman responded by creating a Committee on Civil Rights, charged with making recommendations to ease racial tensions. The resulting report, *To Secure These Rights,* released in 1947, announced that "the time for action is now." Describing the moral, economic, and international repercussions of racial inequality, the commission recommended enforcement of civil rights laws, expanded black suffrage, and an end to segregation.

With White House support, the Supreme Court ruled in 1947 that racial discrimination in housing was unconstitutional. One Mississippi congressman warned that the decision would "destroy the value of property owned by . . . loyal Americans." But Truman applauded the ruling and promptly introduced a civil rights legislative program that included an end to the discriminatory poll tax, a federal anti-lynching law, a permanent Fair Employment Practices Commission, and a civil rights commission to oversee federal law enforcement. The package died in Congress. In the 1948 election year, Truman delivered some of his promises through executive action, ordering the end of racial discrimination in federal employment and prohibiting segregation in the armed forces. The military did not rush to comply with the order.

The Prospect of Social Mobility

Although business leaders worried at the war's end that a combination of labor agitation and government regulation would undermine the free enterprise system, class conflict proved less threatening than predicted. "The saving grace of the American social system," explained *Life* magazine in 1949, "is that our social positions are not fixed artificially . . . . The phenomenon of social 'mobility'—the opportunity to move rapidly upward through the levels of society—is the distinguishing characteristic of U.S. democracy." Such optimism ignored frustrations associated with a corporate economy. Arthur Miller's drama *Death of a Salesman* (1949) depicted the difficulty of upward mobility and its illusory benefits. "It's a measly manner of existence," the salesman's son observed about middle-class security, "to suffer fifty weeks of the year for the sake of a two-week vacation, when all you really desire is to be outdoors, with your shirt off." Yet many war veterans eagerly embraced those rewards of material comfort and security.

Criticism of conformity would become a cliché of postwar society, but after fifteen years of economic deprivation and wartime controls, the postwar generation craved economic advancement. Such aspirations fueled a postwar boom in consumer goods. Meanwhile, large corporations, which had earned huge wartime profits and obtained generous government allowances to reconvert to civilian markets, dominated the expanding economy. At the war's end, corporate leaders feared that cutbacks in military production would cause severe economic dislocations. In 1946, Congress debated a Full Employment bill that would commit the federal government to intervene to ensure sufficient jobs. Conservatives considered the measure socialistic, believing that government planning would destroy capitalism. "Christian freedom will give way to atheistic slavery, cooperation to coercion," warned one aviation executive in 1946, "and the dead hand of bureaucracy will close the throttle on progress." Congress then deleted the word *full* before enacting the Employment Act of 1946. The law created a presidential Council of Economic Advisers and endorsed the principle of government regulation through spending policies and tax incentives to maximize jobs and ensure stability.

Birth of the Baby Boom

Early signs of a postwar boom arrived exactly nine months after V-J Day, when hospitals reported an abrupt rise in the nation's birthrate. During the 1940s, U.S. mothers delivered 32 million babies, a 25 percent increase over the previous decade. Although hasty wartime marriages produced a sharp rise in divorces in 1946, that year's 2.2 million marriages doubled the prewar annual high. By 1950, two-thirds of all men and women over the age of fifteen were married, the highest proportion in U.S. history.

The rising marriage rate showed another demographic trend: couples were marrying at a younger age. Between 1940 and 1950, the median age of marriage for women dropped from 21.5 to 20.3; the age for men dipped from 24.3 to 22.8. Early marriages lengthened the time of marital fertility. As the average age of mothers at the time of their first births fell from 23 to 21, and for their second births from 27 to 24, the number of children per family rose to 3.2. This birth boom crossed economic classes and ethnic groups; the average number of children per black family was slightly higher than for whites. The rise of hospital births contributed to a drop in infant mortality. So did the introduction of wartime wonder drugs such as penicillin. Yet the number of families with five or more children declined, and the average age of mothers at the birth of their last child remained about 30.

This new generation of parents, younger than former heads of household, welcomed childrearing advice that rejected tradition. "Trust yourself" was the motto offered by the number one bestselling book of the postwar decade, Dr. Benjamin Spock's *Baby and Child Care* (1946). Whereas the previous generation had raised their children by rigid time tables, Spock encouraged parents to respect the individuality of their offspring. Such permissiveness took more parental time. But the pediatrician's practical wisdom coincided with a new emphasis on women's domestic roles. A 1945 survey found that most brides wanted four children.

Women Return to the Work Force

As reconversion to a civilian economy saw the percentage of working women drop from 36 percent in 1945 to 29 percent in 1947, marriage assumed new importance. "Women have many careers but only one vocation—motherhood," announced an article in the *Atlantic Monthly*. "The independent woman is a contradiction in terms," explained the popular psychology of *Modern Woman: The Lost Sex* (1947); indeed, "the more educated a woman is, the greater chance there is of sexual disorder." Popular Hollywood movies, such as *Mildred Pierce* (1945) and *The Snake Pit* (1949), reinforced the idea that nondomestic women made bad role models for their daughters or were psychologically disturbed.

This cult of domesticity discouraged the pursuit of independent careers. Surveys found that women attended college not to acquire professional skills but to meet husbands. Two-thirds of all college women failed to complete their degree requirements. Such patterns reflected the widespread belief that men would be breadwinners, women their domestic supporters. Destined for motherhood, coeds with C averages seemed "more likely to succeed," according to *Good Housekeeping*. These assumptions did not extend to nonwhites. The majority of African American women workers still held unskilled jobs that lacked minimum wages, overtime pay, or social security benefits.

The limits on women's economic independence received legal sanction. In 1947, the Supreme Court ruled that women did not have a constitutional right to serve on juries; other federal decisions supported state laws that restricted the rights of married women to work or obtain credit. In 1948, the Court upheld a Michigan law that prohibited women from getting licenses to tend bars unless they were the wives or daughters of tavern keepers. "Motherhood cannot be amended," applauded *The New York Times* when Congress defeated the Equal Right Amendment in 1946. Officials of the government's Women's Bureau also opposed changing labor laws that gave special protection to women, fearing that they would face the same work demands as men.

Following the initial layoffs of 1945–1946, however, women's employment rebounded quickly, returning to wartime levels by 1950. These women workers did not fit the historical pattern of being young and unmarried. Rather, women who entered the work force after 1945 tended to be older; increasingly they were mothers with school-age children. Unlike prewar society, in which working women were usually poor, more women workers were coming from the middle class. Indeed, since real wages (discounting for inflation) did not return to wartime levels until 1955, more households depended on two-income adults. Meanwhile, women headed 7 percent of all households in 1950, and these were among the poorest in the country. That was because almost all "women's" occupations (secretarial, sales, domestic) paid lower wages. Nevertheless, women's growing participation in the work force of the 1950s defied the ideology of domesticity and set precedents for the future.

Women who stayed on the homefront faced economic problems as consumers. But only occasionally did housewives organize protests, such as meat boycotts, to win lower prices. Women's political activity showed little cohesion. Throughout the postwar decade, women, as women, had

little political identity. The short fiction of Tillie Olsen, collected in the volume *Tell Me a Riddle* (1962), depicted the struggles of time-pressed working mothers, but her writing stands as a poignant exception to the era's absence of a feminist perspective.

Veterans' Benefits and Postwar Prosperity

The limits of women's opportunity contrasted with that of men. By 1950, the G.I. Bill had enabled 2.3 million veterans (nearly all of them men) to attend schools of higher education on federal scholarships. Such government grants sparked the expansion of academic institutions by financing building construction, by opening branch campuses and night schools, and by giving scholarships that stimulated a doubling of college diplomas awarded during the 1940s. Meanwhile, the proportion of women on campuses dropped from 34 percent in the 1920s to 20 percent; their share of doctorates declined from 16 percent to 10 percent. However, married veterans successfully lobbied Congress to increase living allowances, which also subsidized marriage and the baby boom, while reinforcing the importance of higher education for postwar careers.

The G.I. Bill also helped solve the most pressing problem of postwar society, the shortage of adequate housing. Since the Great Depression, residential construction had virtually ceased, forcing veterans and their families to accept substandard quarters. Congress grappled with public-housing legislation for cities, one of the few New Deal issues to survive the war. But anti-government conservatives, led by Republican Senator Joseph R. McCarthy, and private builders like William Levitt, denounced public housing as "communistic." Although Congress eventually passed the Housing Act of 1949, provisions for slum clearance and construction of low-cost units never received sufficient funding. Instead, private builders like Levitt took advantage of low-

Aerial view of Levittown, New York, the creation of William Levitt, who took advantage of low-interest federal loans to purchase land in the suburbs and then used mass-production techniques to build private developments.

interest federal loans to purchase land in city suburbs for construction of private developments, such as Long Island's "Levittown."

Using mass-production techniques, including standard blueprints, prefabricated parts, and specialized labor teams, Levitt appealed to veterans by building simple, functional houses for under $8,000. The G.I. Bill made such homes affordable by eliminating down payments and extending 30-year loans backed by the Veterans Administration and the Federal Housing Administration (FHA). Federal tax deductions for home mortgages subsidized private housing. For the first time in U.S. history, most of the nation's families owned their own residence. The FHA, mortgage bankers, and private builders like Levitt also adopted guidelines that excluded nonwhites from many communities.

As white families moved to the suburbs, automobiles became a middle-class necessity. Car registrations jumped from 26 million in 1945 to 40 million in 1950. The introduction of the high-compression (high-octane-burning) V-8 engine in 1949 Cadillacs set the standard for a thriving car culture featuring large vehicles that traded fuel efficiency for horsepower. Although gas prices remained low, the automobile caused greater dependence on foreign petroleum and worsened environmental pollution. In 1947, journalist John Gunther had praised Los Angeles as a clean city; ten years later, auto exhaust had created a perpetual smog.

Middle-class consumers also fueled a demand for durable goods (refrigerators, washing machines, furniture), which they paid for with wartime savings, thus preventing an economic downturn when war production stopped in 1945. Four years later, one architect observed that "the automobile [had] emancipated the consumer but not the merchant." Seeking to recapture their former customers, downtown department stores began to open branch stores in the suburbs, paving the way to the first shopping malls during the 1950s. Indeed, the need for a suburban infrastructure stimulated a boom in commercial construction, as newly formed communities built schools, hospitals, municipal offices, and shopping facilities.

The search for upward social mobility stimulated population movement to the western states. Following wartime trends, growth in the oil industry attracted job seekers to Texas, while openings in aircraft production and electronics drew workers to California. Continuation of the wartime *bracero* (manual labor) program also brought 200,000 Mexican migrant laborers north of the border by 1947 (half of them in California) as well as a substantial number of illegal immigrants. The introduction of inexpensive air travel sped the arrival of Puerto Ricans, whose numbers on the U.S. mainland rose from 50,000 in 1930 to nearly 250,000 by 1950. These migration patterns shifted the country's population center further west and created new types of ethnic diversity.

Making Peace with Organized Labor

With the war over, organized labor dropped the no-strike pledge and sought to recover losses of purchasing power caused by rising prices. The result was a series of crippling strikes in key industries such as automobiles, steel, and railroad transport. In 1946, 4.6 million workers (more than 10 per cent of the labor force) participated in work stoppages. Such militance alarmed business leaders, particularly in small companies that faced competition. Larger corporations, by contrast, could afford to pass on costs to consumers. During the auto workers strike, the White House pressured General Motors to concede regular cost-of-living adjustments (COLAs) to offset inflation. Such agreements, later imitated in other big-business industries, provided worker stability during the postwar boom.

Peace with organized labor also involved government intervention. When John L. Lewis's coal miners called a strike in the winter of 1946, threatening widespread disruptions, President Truman took the union to court, challenging its

right to strike and forcing the mine workers to resume negotiations. Angered by labor militance, a conservative Congress passed the Taft-Hartley Act of 1947, a landmark law that restricted the right to strike. Truman vetoed the measure, showing his sympathy for unions as part of the Democratic coalition. But a Republican Congress overrode the veto. The law established the ground rules of postwar labor relations to the present day.

Under the Taft-Hartley Act, the president could seek court injunctions against strikes and obtain cooling-off periods during which federal mediators would try to negotiate settlements. Spontaneous wildcat strikes, secondary boycotts, and general strikes involving nonworkers became illegal. The law also permitted states to enact "right to work" measures, which undermined mandatory union membership ("closed shops"). In addition, the law prohibited members of the Communist party to hold union offices, regardless of their election by the membership. (In 1949, the CIO would expel 11 communist-led unions.) Such provisions sought to prevent strikes that caused economic disruption, public inconvenience, or threatened business control of the workplace. Union leaders vowed to see the law repealed.

Building a Cold War Political Consensus

Postwar economic issues soon entered the political arena. In 1946, the Republican campaign slogan "Had enough?" addressed the frustrations of strikes, inflation, and the failure of government regulations to end consumer shortages. Voters also resented the administration's inability to reach a settled peace with the Soviet Union. The campaign was bitter and ugly. Republican Senator Robert Taft said the Democrats were "divided between Communism and Americanism," a taint that would plague national politics for a decade, but was indicative of the troubled mood. In 1946, Republicans carried both houses of Congress for the first time in twenty years and captured a majority of state governorships. The election brought a new generation of politicians to Washington—war veterans like Massachusetts's John F. Kennedy, California's Richard M. Nixon, and Wisconsin's Joseph McCarthy, who would influence the political landscape for three decades and more.

As the conservative Republican-controlled 80th Congress swept into office in 1947, Truman proved to be a loyal New Dealer and a shrewd opponent. Still dwarfed by the long shadow of his predecessor, the president lacked the suave, genial style that had charmed Roosevelt's supporters and enraged his critics. Blunt and brusque, Truman nonetheless demonstrated considerable political finesse. He would achieve legislative success, win election in his own right, and leave an indelible mark on U.S. foreign policy. When Republicans dismissed the president as an "ordinary American," presidential advisor Jonathan Daniels called the words "a snob phrase invented by those who, after Roosevelt's death, hoped to minimize the presidency." One consequence of that attitude was passage of the 22nd Amendment in 1951, prohibiting a president from serving more than two terms.

Amendment XXII (1951)

Section 1.
No person shall be elected to the office of the President more than twice, and no person who has held the office of President, or acted as President, for more than two years of a term to which some other person was elected President shall be elected to the office of the President more than once. But this article shall not apply to any person holding the office of President when this article was proposed by the Congress, and shall not prevent any person who may be holding the office of President, or acting as President, during the term within which this article becomes operative from holding the office of President or acting as President during the remainder of such term.

Section 2.
This article shall be inoperative unless it shall have been ratified as an amendment to the Constitution by the legislatures of three-fourths of the several states within seven years from the date of its submission to the states by the Congress.

Truman's 1947 State of the Union message showed no retreat from the New Deal. His ambitious agenda included anti-trust laws, farm supports, streamlining the military, national health insurance, and civil rights. But as conservative southern Democrats aligned themselves with the Republican majority, the president faced strong opposition. When Truman nominated David Lilienthal, a liberal Jewish New Deal manager, to head the civilian-controlled Atomic Energy Commission (AEC), which oversaw top-secret programs, Republican leader Taft condemned the candidate as "soft on . . . Communism." The feisty Truman chose to fight such slurs. "It is a matter of principle," he noted, "and we cannot let the peanut politicians ruin a good man." Moderate Republicans like Arthur Vandenberg refused to follow Taft, and the president won an important victory.

Launching the Anti-Communist Crusade

The question of whether the White House was hard or soft on communism soon changed the face of national politics. The inability to reach agreements with the Soviet Union about the political status of Germany and Eastern Europe frustrated government leaders who hoped to establish global peace based on multilateral cooperation and free trade. Disappointed by the continued bickering between the two powers, politicians in both parties blamed communist influence in government for undermining negotiations. An emerging anti-communist consensus thus targeted two interrelated threats. First, many opposed Soviet expansion in Eastern Europe and feared further aggression; second, they believed that domestic spies, leftists, or "fellow travelers" were undertaking subversive activities at home. Such perceptions now made Communism the litmus test of all political discussion. To be anti-communist justified a multitude of political positions, including opposition to public housing and civil rights; to propose social reforms raised a red flag of subversion.

By 1947, President Truman had been arguing with Soviet diplomats for nearly two years. Premier Josef Stalin, notorious for his ruthless treatment of dissidents, had determined to prevent future invasions of his country by installing friendly communist governments on his country's borders in Eastern Europe and Asia. To Washington, Soviet domination of its neighboring countries seemed to repeat German aggression of the 1930s. Moreover, U.S. leaders believed that domestic prosperity and world peace depended on free trade between nations and democratic governments. Otherwise, economic crises might precipitate the same competitive conditions that had caused World War II.

"We must face the fact," Truman advised Congress in 1945, "that peace must be built on power as well as upon good will and good deeds." While continuing negotiations with the Soviets about Germany and Eastern Europe, the administration proceeded to construct a strategy to ensure national security. Through a series of bilateral treaties, the United States established military

bases from the Azores in the Atlantic to Okinawa in the Pacific. Following prewar promises, Congress granted independence to the Philippine Islands in 1946, but prudently reserved military positions to keep troops in the Pacific. More secretly, the government tried to gain control of the world's uranium resources, the key ingredient for building atomic weapons. Washington also exported humanitarian aid and surplus food, hoping to ease postwar economic hardships that might lure neutral governments into the communist bloc. For similar reasons, rebuilding the Western European economy became a high priority. "Peace, freedom, and world trade are indivisible," said Truman. "We must not go through the Thirties again."

Frustrated by Soviet stubbornness and emboldened by the monopoly of atomic weapons, Truman refused to "baby" the former ally, admitting at the end of 1945 that "another war is in the making." The president did not object when former British Prime Minister Winston Churchill visited in 1946 and denounced the Soviet "iron curtain" that had descended across Europe. Public criticism of Churchill's speech surprised the White House; a war-weary country had no heart for another conflict. But in 1946, the military staged dramatic atomic bomb tests at Bikini atoll in the Pacific, demonstrating the power of such weapons and a commitment to remain vigilant.

"Fear advertising no long carries the old punch in selling mouthwashes," remarked a *New York Times* critic, "but it still works fine to sell a national policy." By the end of 1947, the AEC had established a public relations branch to soothe public fears about atomic energy. Yet the tremendous popular interest in science fiction (peopled by atom-smashing scientists and their mutants) and a new fascination with unidentified flying objects (UFOs) suggested an underlying anxiety about modern technology. "Science no longer

> ## "Science no longer means primarily the promise of a more abundant life; it means the atomic bomb."

means primarily the promise of a more abundant life," noted *Scientific American* in 1950. "It means the atomic bomb."

Containing Soviet Influence

Despite fears of another war, Truman's advisors saw no alternative than to challenge Soviet influence in Eastern Europe. In 1946, Moscow ambassador George F. Kennan transmitted an 8,000-word analysis (the "Long Telegram"), which depicted the Soviet state as a government "committed fanatically" to undermining "the internal harmony of our society" and threatening the international order. Emphasizing the futility of negotiations, Kennan advocated a tough policy aimed at "long-term patient, and vigilant containment" of communist expansion. The United States, in other words, must be prepared to prevent the inevitable Soviet aggression that could occur anywhere at any time. Reiterated by administration leaders, "containment" became the watchword of Truman's policy.

By 1947, the president stood at a crossroads. In February, the British government informed Washington that economic problems prevented continued support for the Greek monarchy in its war against communist guerrillas. Warning that Greece and Turkey might slip into the Soviet sphere of influence, the British urged U.S. intervention to block a communist victory. Truman's advisors endorsed immediate action, yet the public showed no enthusiasm for foreign entanglements. Senator Vandenberg, chair of the foreign relations committee, recommended that Truman "scare hell out of the American people."

The president promptly summoned a special session of Congress in March 1947 to announce what became known as the "Truman Doctrine." "Every nation must choose between alternative ways of life," Truman stated in tense, dramatic language. Warning that the freedom of the entire world was at stake, the president depicted communist nations marching toward world conquest. He concluded by requesting $400 million of economic and military assistance for Greece and Turkey. Critics like Taft challenged such global responsibilities and questioned support of undemocratic governments. But public opinion, alarmed by presidential statements, backed the White House, and Congress overwhelmingly approved Truman's proposal. Such peacetime commitments reaffirmed the nation's unwillingness to return to "isolationist" policies of the 1930s.

"There is no use pretending . . . that for $400 million we have bought peace," admitted Vandenberg. "It is merely a down payment." The administration revealed the next installment a month later when Secretary of State George C. Marshall presented the 1947 Harvard University commencement address. Recognizing that economic unsettledness invited communist expansion, Marshall proposed a program of economic aid to rebuild war-torn Europe. "Our policy is directed not against any country or doctrine," he stated, "but against hunger, poverty, desperation and chaos." The price tag of this European Recovery Program reached $17 billion. Such expenditures supported the export of U.S. goods and services, including farm surpluses, and so boosted the domestic economy. When budget conscious Republicans questioned this subsidy to big business (already three-quarters of the federal budget went to military spending and foreign aid), the White House responded by emphasizing the anti-communist benefits of the program. Persuaded by that logic, Congress approved the Marshall Plan in 1948.

"There are today many Communists in America. They are everywhere—in factories, offices, butcher shops, on street corners, in private businesses—and each carries with him the germs of death for society."

Anti-Communism on the Home Front

Warnings about the communist menace also influenced Truman's domestic programs. In 1945, the discovery of a Soviet spy ring in Canada and the leaking of secret government reports gave credibility to charges of communist subversion. Recently opened archives suggest that Soviet spies did indeed operate within the atomic bomb project, but probably accelerated Soviet science by months rather than years. Although Truman believed "we have far too many sane people" to worry about communism, he responded to Republican allegations by creating a commission on government employee loyalty to develop federal guidelines to screen undesirables. The move did not calm the Republicans. With the seating of the 80th Congress in 1947, the House Committee on Un-American Activities (HUAC), first created in 1938, opened investigations of communist influence in government, schools, labor unions, and the motion picture industry. Two months later, nine days after enunciating the Truman Doctrine, the president announced a federal employee loyalty program, calling for the scrutiny of all government workers and ordering dismissal of employees for whom there were "reasonable grounds" for suspicion of disloyalty.

Truman's efforts to contain the Republican anti-communist crusade by launching his own investigations fed the very fears he tried to remove.

Under the administration's loyalty program, the FBI and the Civil Service Commission began investigating 2 million federal employees—and eventually surveyed over 5 million people. As a result, several thousand government workers resigned their jobs and 212 were dismissed; none were charged with espionage. To handle the administrative work, the FBI budget jumped from $35 million in 1947 to $53 million three years later. Truman also ordered the attorney general to compile a list of subversive organizations, of which he named seventy-eight in 1947. (Eventually the list would total 254 groups.) Membership in such "front" organizations, which allegedly had ties to the Communist party, invited FBI investigations, job harassment, and subpoenas to appear before government investigating agencies.

"There are today many Communists in America," Truman's attorney general declared in 1949. "They are everywhere—in factories, offices, butcher shops, on street corners, in private businesses—and each carries with him the germs of death for society." In fact, the Communist party boasted a peak membership of 75,000 at a time when the Soviet Union was a wartime ally. Even then, the public suspected Soviet intentions. But hostilities with the Soviet Union intensified fears of another war. In 1947, the news media focused attention on HUAC's examination of communists in Hollywood. When ten screenwriters and producers refused to testify about their political associations on the basis of the First Amendment, Congress voted them in contempt, a crime that brought the "Hollywood 10" year-long prison terms. Later witnesses learned to invoke the Fifth Amendment against self-incrimination as a defense against these inquiries. Meanwhile, the Hollywood studios attempted to stifle further investigations by establishing an industry blacklist against other suspected radicals. More sensational was HUAC's 1948 investigation of charges that

Screenwriter Dalton Trumbo, one of the Hollywood Ten targeted by the House Un-American Activities Committee (HUAC), declared as he left the witness stand, "This is the beginning of American concentration camps." Congress subsequently voted Trumbo (and the other "unfriendly" witnesses) in contempt for refusing to testify to the committee. Each received a one-year prison sentence.

State Department official Alger Hiss, seemingly a paragon of respectability, had passed secret documents to the Soviet Union. Hiss's dramatic perjury trial fed public fears about traitors in government and catapulted HUAC Republican Richard Nixon into prominence.

Such cases established a connection between the Soviet enemy and domestic communism, a connection that often appeared hazy and unproven, but risky to national security. In 1949, the Justice Department indicted top leaders of the U.S. Communist party for conspiring to advocate the overthrow of the government by force; their conviction two years later led to arrests of other party leaders, and some communists went "underground" to avoid arrest. In addition, many states followed Washington's lead by instituting loyalty investigations and requiring loyalty oaths from public employees, such as police, firefighters, teachers, librarians, and even public-school students who desired a diploma. Such programs extended into the private sector, as businesses fired suspected radicals and demanded oaths from employees.

The fear of domestic communism reflected less a danger of subversion (nearly all criminal allegations referred to the period before 1945 when the Soviet Union was an ally) than it did the deeper anxieties of the postwar era. "Red Fascism" was FBI Director J. Edgar Hoover's definition of communism—a totalitarian, atheistic threat to democracy, religion, and private initiative. Yet the image of a soulless communist society, popularized in magazines and Hollywood films like *Red Menace* (1949), awakened concerns about domestic society, the fear that big government, corporate business, and impersonal economic forces were limiting free expression and individual choice. Many believed that government bureaucrats, not accountable to the electorate, were shaping the nation's future. "Our problem is not outside ourselves. Our problem is within ourselves," declared Republican presidential candidate Thomas Dewey in 1948. "Spiritually, we have yet to find the means to put together the world's broken pieces, to bind up its wounds, to make a good society."

Mobilizing for War in Peacetime

The sense of national emergency moved the administration to prepare for war by reorganizing the armed services. To streamline military decisions, the National Security Act of 1947 unified the military branches, including the Air Force, within a new civilian-led Department of Defense; established a rotating Joint Chiefs of Staff; and created the National Security Council (NSC) and Central Intelligence Agency (CIA), answerable only to the president. The law centralized military policy within the White House and permitted budgetary exemptions that authorized secret programs independent of congressional oversight.

In planning military strategy, Truman had limited options. The Atomic Energy Act of 1946 provided for civilian, not military, control of nuclear weapons, and the Atomic Energy Commission moved slowly to develop an arsenal. In 1947, the United States had only two atomic bombs in operating condition. Yet the rapid demobilization of military forces after the war reflected public dissatisfaction with an expensive standing army; U.S. ground forces could never match the size of the Soviet army. To assure military credibility with the least impact on the federal budget, Truman opted in 1948 for an air–atomic bomb strategy, hoping that atomic weapons and a large air force would deter Soviet power. According to a White House report, "other nations will hesitate to attack us or our vital interests because of the violence of the counterattack they would have to face." But, since

Stalin believed that atomic bombs without a conventional army could not achieve victory, the strategy did not prove as menacing as Truman hoped.

Implementing the air-atomic program required a gigantic expansion of the military budget. Budget-cutting Republicans showed little enthusiasm for Truman's military package. But when communists seized control of Soviet-occupied Czechoslovakia in 1948, the administration saw tangible evidence of aggression through internal subversion. The Soviet Union had "destroyed the independence and democratic character of a whole series of nations," the president told a tense joint session of Congress. Responding to the crisis, Congress voted to fund the Marshall Plan, approved the military draft, and authorized $3.5 billion, more than the president requested, for military programs.

"Will Russia move first?" the president asked his advisors in 1948. News from Germany was ominous. The Allies had temporarily divided both Germany and its capital, Berlin, into zones of occupation. But Berlin sat within the Soviet zone. When the Western Allies abandoned efforts to reach agreement with Stalin and made plans to bring Germany into the western alliance, the Soviet Union blockaded access to Berlin in 1948. Washington now prepared for war, and Truman ordered an airlift of food and supplies to the surrounded city. The world waited nervously. The risky operation lasted for 11 months before the Soviets ended the blockade.

Strengthening Global Alliances

The policy of containment defined U.S. policy around the world. Since World War II, Washington had supported the Nationalist Chiang Kai-shek regime against communist rivals led by Mao Zedong. By 1948, the State Department concluded that Chiang's corrupt government could not survive, and Truman decided to curtail involvement in the civil war. But congressional conservatives, pressured by a vocal "China Lobby," voted to support the Chiang government, thus aligning the United States with the anti-communist dictatorship.

As the Chinese civil war proceeded, the administration anticipated Chiang's defeat by strengthening ties to Japan, the recently defeated enemy, as a noncommunist ally in the Pacific. In addition, since Washington viewed all communist regimes as part of a worldwide conspiracy, the State Department rejected overtures from Vietnam's guerrilla leader, Ho Chi Minh, who appealed for assistance in the war against the French colonial government. Washington was primarily interested in keeping France in the anti-communist coalition in Europe and refused to assist Vietnamese rebels. The United States also backed anti-communist regimes in Korea and the Philippines and secretly funded anti-communist political parties in Italy and France. Closer to home, the United States built alliances in Latin America, sponsoring the Organization of American States in 1948, which provided for collective defense.

The Cold War and the 1948 Elections

The international crisis strengthened the president's domestic hand. Thwarted by Soviet resistance to U.S. foreign policy, Truman showed no tolerance for dissent within his administration. He clashed publicly with Henry Wallace, his chief rival to the Roosevelt legacy. Wallace had served as New Deal secretary of agriculture, Roosevelt's third term vice president, and Truman's secretary of commerce, and now opposed the president's foreign policy. When Wallace warned in 1946 that the United States had "no more business in the *political* affairs of Eastern Europe than Russia had in the *political* affairs of Latin America, western Europe, and the United States," Truman fired his

cabinet secretary. "The Reds, phonies, and the 'parlor pinks,'" the president exclaimed, "seem to be banded together and are becoming a national danger."

The fiasco prepared Truman for the 1948 presidential campaign. After Wallace entered the contest as an independent Progressive party candidate, Truman used the international crisis to depict his critic as a communist dupe. Moreover, when the State Department debated whether to recognize the new state of Israel in 1948, Truman's insistence that the United States act promptly raised his standing among Jewish voters. The president still faced fissures within the New Deal coalition. During the 1948 Democratic convention, the alliance between northern liberals and southern conservatives cracked open on the issue of civil rights. "The time has arrived," declared Minneapolis Mayor Hubert Humphrey, "for the Democratic party to get out of the shadow of states rights, and walk forthrightly into the bright sunshine of human rights."

The adoption of a strong civil rights platform infuriated southern delegates, who bolted from the convention. Three days later, these "Dixiecrats" formed the States Rights party and nominated South Carolina's Strom Thurmond for president. Truman never wavered in his support of civil rights. In 1948, he became the first presidential candidate to campaign in Harlem, and he kept black voters within the Democratic fold. Loyal southern Democrats, such as Texas Senate candidate Lyndon B. Johnson, openly attacked the civil rights plank.

Confident of victory, the Republican party nominated Dewey and his running mate, California Governor Earl Warren. Muffling conservative delegates, Republicans endorsed social security, civil rights, and housing legislation. Truman called their bluff. Summoning a special session of Congress on July 26 ("turnip day" in Missouri, he reminded his farm constituency) the president

Truman holding up the famous incorrect headline. The instant fame of this photograph expressed widespread delight at the failure of political "experts" to understand the ordinary voter.

dared the 80th Congress to enact the Republican program. Congress adjourned without taking action. Truman had another weapon. Taking off on a spirited whistle-stop cross-country rail campaign, the incumbent blasted the "do-nothing" Congress.

"Give 'em hell, Harry!" became the Democratic cry. When Wallace insisted that the president exaggerated the Soviet menace and boldly defied racial segregation as he campaigned in the South, Truman could dismiss him as a radical. Dewey, the Republican candidate, was largely silent on matters of foreign policy because he shared Truman's views. Yet public-opinion polls showed Dewey leading the race. On election eve, the conservative *Chicago Tribune* went to press with the predictable headline: DEWEY DEFEATS TRUMAN.

The next day, the president held the newspaper aloft and gloated. Truman beat Dewey by 2 million votes, 303–189 in the electoral college. Thurmond carried the Deep South (thirty-four electoral votes), while Wallace polled slightly more than 1 million votes, half of them in New York, and zero in the electoral college. The Democrats swept both houses of Congress. Wallace's weak showing proved the miniscule influence of communists in U.S. politics. Moreover, the president ran stronger than Roosevelt had in 1940 and 1944 among white ethnics, particularly Catholics and union members. Indeed, white ethnics who identified with their kin in Europe felt outrage at communist assaults on religion in their homelands and applauded Truman's opposition to Soviet expansion. In 1948, the New Deal coalition had held, and the president looked forward to resuming the liberal agenda.

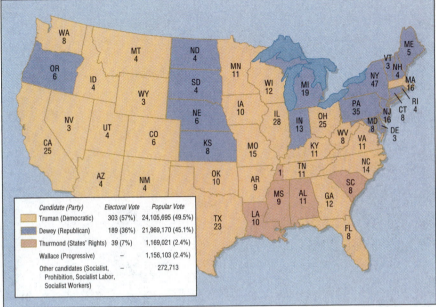

Candidate (Party)	Electoral Vote	Popular Vote
Truman (Democratic)	303 (57%)	24,105,695 (49.5%)
Dewey (Republican)	189 (36%)	21,969,170 (45.1%)
Thurmond (States' Rights)	39 (7%)	1,169,021 (2.4%)
Wallace (Progressive)	–	1,156,103 (2.4%)
Other candidates (Socialist, Prohibition, Socialist Labor, Socialist Workers)	–	272,713

"Every segment of our population and every individual," Truman told the 81st congress in 1949, "has a right to expect from our government a fair deal." With Democratic majorities in Congress, the president presented an ambitious legislative program, known as the Fair Deal, including increases in minimum wages and social security, national health insurance, aid to education, and repeal of the Taft-Hartley law. Yet Truman underestimated the true congressional majority, a conservative coalition of southern Democrats and midwestern Republicans opposed to his programs. The program would languish in Congress and then fade from public interest for another two decades. In its place, anti-communism would emerge as the top domestic priority.

Solidifying the Western Alliance

Anti-communism also dominated discussion of foreign policy. In 1949, Truman signed the North Atlantic Treaty Organization (NATO) pact, which committed the country to military intervention to protect western Europe, including the newly created West German state. The agreement, the first peacetime military pact in U.S. history, precipitated angry congressional debate. Although the Senate ratified the treaty, Congress refused to allocate funds to implement U.S. obligations. At stake was the question of U.S. overseas responsibilities, the same issue that had divided the country in 1941. Despite wartime commitments to the United Nations and support of the Truman Doctrine, a vocal minority questioned open-ended promises to defend foreign allies.

At this moment of political stalemate, Truman received ominous news that drastically changed the political climate. In September 1949, the president announced that the Soviet Union had exploded an atomic bomb, breaking the U.S. monopoly of that ultimate weapon. The shock quickly ended the NATO quarrel; within a week,

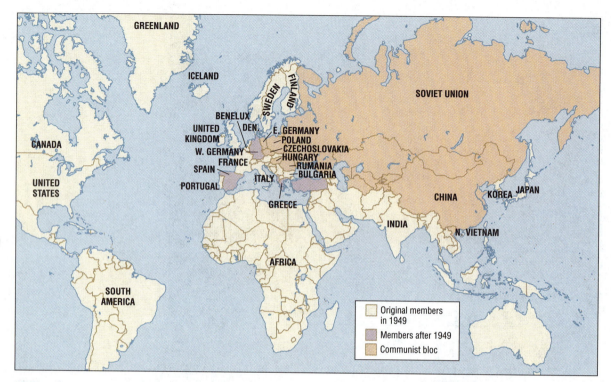

NATO

Congress voted the necessary funds. The nation girded for another world war. Two months later, Mao Zedong's communist armies brought the Chinese civil war to an end on the mainland, and Chiang's Nationalist regime fled to the island of Taiwan.

As the 1940s drew to a close, the public faced new and terrible fears about communist expansion. Even though the 1948 elections showed the political insignificance of the Communist party, conservatives expressed concern about un-American spies and traitors. Truman's policy of containment—essentially, a defensive strategy that responded to communist initiatives—offered no foreseeable resolution of international tensions. Two days after the president announced the Soviet atomic bomb test, evangelist Billy Graham opened a religious revival in Los Angeles, personalizing the risk of the Cold War. "We must be prepared for *any* eventuality at *any* time," the missionary intoned, echoing White House rhetoric. "Time is desperately short . . . prepare to meet thy God." Worried citizens wondered how the country had moved so quickly from the optimism of peace in 1945 to the edge of atomic war against the Soviet Union.

The Rise of Joseph R. McCarthy

"Five years after a world war has been won, men's hearts should anticipate a long peace," remarked Wisconsin's Senator Joseph R. McCarthy. Instead, the country was embroiled in a "final, all-out battle between communistic atheism and Christianity." The date was February 9, 1950, just five months after the Soviet bomb test, two months after China's Communists drove the Nationalists to Taiwan, one month after a jury convicted former State Department official Alger Hiss of perjury for denying he had given government documents to the communists, and six days after British police arrested scientist Klaus Fuchs for passing atomic secrets to the Soviet Union. Standing before a meeting of the Women's Republican Club in Wheeling, West Virginia, McCarthy drew the critical connection between the Cold War overseas and the crisis at home. Holding up a sheet of paper, the burly ex-Marine, who spoke in a shrill and piercing voice, announced that he held in his hands a list of 205 names of known Communists "who nevertheless are still working and shaping policy in the State Department."

The news landed like a bombshell, seemingly demonstrating how the Truman administration had "lost" both China and the atomic bomb monopoly and had led the country to the most dangerous moment in its history. According to McCarthy, homegrown communist agents and spies (in the senator's lexicon, "rats," "skunks," and "vermin") had betrayed the nation. With reporters pursuing the flamboyant senator on a speaking tour, the number of alleged communists changed daily as McCarthy manipulated the media and raised controversy about the charges. The Wisconsin senator proved a genius at publicity, linking his name inextricably to the era as he touched public anxieties. "McCarthyism," as the domestic anti-communist crusade was labeled, addressed the fear that Soviet agents had infiltrated the government and subverted U.S. policy. McCarthy's accusations against government officials also expressed public discomfort at the expansion of a federal bureaucracy that was not responsible to the voters. A crude and boisterous personality, McCarthy attacked the "pompous . . . striped pants" elite who formulated foreign policy.

"The bright young men who are born with silver spoons in their mouths," said McCarthy, "have been the worst."

Protecting Internal Security

As McCarthy hurled charges of communists in government in 1950, the FBI arrested two New York party members, Julius and Ethel Rosenberg, for passing atomic bomb secrets to the Soviet Union during World War II. Despite the Rosenbergs' insistence of their innocence, thin evidence of their guilt, and international protests against the ensuing trial, their conviction lent credence to McCarthy's accusations; two presidents refused to give them clemency, and both were electrocuted in 1953. The Rosenberg case, like the Hiss conviction, reinforced the belief that communists were not merely political radicals but agents of the Soviet Union.

Such fears prompted Congress to pass the Internal Security Act, sponsored by Nevada Senator Patrick McCarran, in 1950. The law required communists to register with the federal government, barred them from working in defense industries or obtaining passports, and created a Subversive Activities Control Board to monitor the activities of communist-front organizations. The McCarran Act also included a measure, sponsored by senate liberals, authorizing the president to declare a national emergency and permitting the arrest of suspected dissidents even without their committing illegal acts. Truman vetoed the bill, warning that "government stifling of free expression of opinion is a long step toward totalitarianism." Congress soon overrode the veto.

As accusations of communist infiltration gained public support, Truman attempted to deflect criticism by establishing more rigorous standards for removing alleged subversives. In 1951, a new executive order permitted the dismissal of federal employees *not* on "reasonable grounds," but when there was "reasonable doubt" about their loyalty; the burden of proving innocence or guilt thus shifted from the accuser to the accused. Among the 3,000 government employees who were fired or resigned under Truman were dozens of homosexuals or "sex perverts" who were deemed security risks because enemy agents could blackmail them.

Fears of "un-American" influences also brought amendments to federal immigration policy. Concerned about "hard-core indigestible blocs which . . . are our deadly enemies," Congress passed the McCarran-Walter Act in 1952. The law reaffirmed the national origins system of restricting immigration, limited newcomers from Communist countries, and allowed the president to expel suspected subversives. Meanwhile, the HUAC reopened investigation of Hollywood in 1951, grabbing headlines by forcing prominent actors to affirm their political loyalty or face blacklisting. While criticizing such witch hunts, the White House contributed to the climate of fear. In 1950, Truman created the Federal Civil Defense Administration, which distributed 16 million copies of the booklet, *Survival under Atomic Attack*. Amid such anxieties, Hollywood produced a series of science-fiction thrillers, including *The Thing* (1951), which ended with the advice: "Watch the Skies!"

This sense of living under siege permeated White House policy. In January 1950, a month before McCarthy's Wheeling speech, Truman ordered the Atomic Energy Commission to proceed with development of a hydrogen superbomb. Soon afterward, Mao Zedong's People's Republic of China signed a mutual-assistance pact with the Soviet Union. Both nations extended diplomatic recognition to Vietnam's anti-French rebels led by Ho Chi Minh. That spring, the president's National Security Council proposed a comprehensive policy document known as NSC-68. Following the logic of "containment," the paper depicted the Soviet Union "animated by a new fanatic faith" and determined "to impose its absolute authority over the rest of the world." NSC-68 recommended quadrupling the national defense budget, which was already reaching $13 billion a year. In Congress, soaring military expenses aroused opposition to international commitments.

Police Action in Korea

Caution about military budgets vanished with the outbreak of the Korean War on June 25, 1950. Without warning, armed forces from communist North Korea crossed the 38th parallel into South Korea, seeking to achieve national unification under communist leadership. Although newly released documents suggest that North Korea instigated the invasion, Truman believed that the Soviet Union had ordered the attack. Backed by a United Nations resolution (which passed because the Soviets were boycotting Security Council meetings to protest the U.N.'s rejection of communist China), the president did not wait for congressional approval. Instead, he ordered a "police action" and sent U.S. troops into action to defend South Korea. Public opinion overwhelmingly supported the president's emergency decision to "draw the line" against communist aggression. Sixteen United Nations allies joined the war effort, but the United States provided most of the materiel costs. The Supreme Commander, General Douglas MacArthur, received orders directly from Washington.

As North Korean forces moved rapidly southward in Soviet-built tanks, U.S. troops held a defensive perimeter around the port of Pusan and managed to stop the invading army. After hard fighting in the summer heat, the U.N. allies turned the tide, forcing the North Koreans into retreat. When the war began, Truman wanted only to restore the South Korean boundary at the 38th par-

The War in Korea

allel. But when General MacArthur executed a brilliant amphibious landing at Inchon and drove North Korean troops beyond that dividing line, the president authorized further advances. With the 1950 elections approaching, Truman hoped to silence Republican critics by defeating the Communist enemy. MacArthur promised that the soldiers would be home by Christmas.

As the autumn offensive carried U.N. forces toward the Yalu river that separated Korea from

China, Mao Zedong saw a threat to his own country and ordered Chinese troops into action. In bitter winter conditions, Communist forces smashed the U.N. lines, seizing thousands of U.S. prisoners and driving the Allied armies into retreat below the 38th parallel. Amid talk of using atomic bombs, Truman exercised restraint, and MacArthur managed to stabilize the battle lines around the original political boundary. But the general expressed frustration at this "limited" war and urged an attack on China.

Truman's preference for a negotiated settlement led MacArthur to criticize the president's "no-win" policy. Angered by this public insubordination, the commander-in-chief fired MacArthur in 1951. Public opinion overwhelmingly sympathized with the general, who returned home to ticker tape parades and a rare appearance before a joint session of Congress. Yet the difficulty of winning the war also gave support to a negotiated treaty. As military action stopped, peace talks to end the stalemate began in 1951, but dragged on for another two years. By then, 2 million U.S. soldiers served in Korea, including 54,000 who died there.

A New Balance of Power

The Korean war had an enduring impact on global strategy. Despite congressional doubts about rising military expenditures, the crisis justified the permanent military buildup recommended in NSC-68. As the size of the armed services doubled to 3.5 million, the annual defense budget increased over fourfold to $60 billion. Although the United States had twenty times the number of atomic weapons as the Soviet Union, Truman continued to build the nuclear arsenal. Yet, by 1953, both powers successfully tested the new hydrogen bomb. To bolster U.S. allies in Western Europe, Truman supported the rearming of Germany, easing French fears by agreeing to station U.S. troops in Europe, the first peacetime standing army overseas.

Washington also increased military assistance to France to suppress the Vietnam liberation movement, linking U.S. interests to colonialism in Indochina. To further stabilize the western Pacific, the United States signed a new treaty with Japan, restoring control of the home islands, but allowing U.S. bases on Okinawa. Other alliances built a ring of defenses against Communist expansion. By 1952, the fascist nations of World War II—Germany, Japan, Italy, and Spain—had become anti-Communist allies; the former Allies, China and the Soviet Union, were now the enemies. Meanwhile, huge military budgets demanded a larger federal bureaucracy and a homefront mentality that encouraged political consensus. Many now questioned Truman's fitness to lead the nation in another global war.

INFOTRAC® COLLEGE EDITION EXERCISES

For additional reading go to InfoTrac College Edition, your online research library at *http://web1.infotrac-college.com.*

Keyword search: Cold War
Subject search: Harry Truman
Subject search: Marshall Plan
Keyword search: NATO
Keyword search: Warsaw Pact
Subject search: Korean War
Keyword search: civil rights movement
Keyword search: Joseph McCarthy
Keyword search: Alger Hiss
Keyword search: Rosenberg case

ADDITIONAL READING

David McCulloch, *Truman* (1992). The author provides a well-written, sympathetic biography of Harry Truman and his times.

The Era of Prosperity Begins

George Lipsitz, *Rainbow at Midnight: Labor and Culture in the 1940s* (1994). The author describes the impact of World War II on economic, social, and cultural forces, emphasizing the changes of the 1940s.

William Graebner, *The Age of Doubt: American Thought and Culture in the 1940s* (1991). A study of cultural and intellectual history, this brief volume emphasizes the relationship between ideas and social issues.

Ethnic Identity in Postwar Society

Richard Polenberg, *One Nation Divisible: Class, Race, and Ethnicity in the United States since 1938* (1980). The book's postwar chapters link the era's social trends to Cold War assumptions.

Minorities Seek Civil Rights

Jules Tygiel, *Baseball's Great Experiment: Jackie Robinson and His Legacy* (1983). Based partly on oral history, the author depicts the integration of major league baseball.

Veterans' Benefits and Postwar Prosperity

Rosalyn Baxandall and Elizabeth Ewen, *Picture Windows: How the Suburbs Happened* (2000). This volume places postwar housing issues in a historical context.

Building a Cold War Political Consensus

Gary A. Donaldson, *Truman Defeats Dewey* (1999). A good analysis of postwar politics; see also Greg Mitchell's *Tricky Dick and the Pink Lady: Richard Nixon vs. Helen Gahagan Douglas—Sexual Politics and the Red Scare, 1950* (1998).

Richard J. Hogan, *A Cross of Iron: Harry S Truman and the Origins of the National Security State, 1945–1954* (1998). This book provides the political and ideological context of postwar foreign policy decisions.

Mobilizing for War in Peacetime

Paul Boyer, *By the Bomb's Early Light: American Thought and Culture at the Dawn of the Atomic Age* (1985). Focusing on the atomic bomb, the author provides a sensitive analysis of postwar values and assumptions.

Melvyn P. Leffler, *A Preponderance of Power: National Security, the Truman Administration, and the Cold War* (1992). A balanced, thorough account of the major issues of U.S. foreign policy.

The Rise of Joseph R. McCarthy

Ellen Schrecker, *Many Are the Crimes: McCarthyism in America* (1998). A fine summation of anti-communism, the book describes the pattern of government repression.

Victor S. Navasky, *Naming Names* (1980). Examining anti-communist congressional hearings, the author explores the moral issues facing the Hollywood film industry.

25

A Troubled Consensus, 1952–1960

CHRONOLOGY

1952	Dwight D. Eisenhower defeats Adlai Stevenson
1953	U.S. signs armistice in Korea
	CIA topples Iran government
1954	TV networks broadcast Army-McCarthy hearings
	Eisenhower rejects intervention in Vietnam
	AEC lifts security clearance of J. Robert Oppenheimer
	Brown decision overturns public-school segregation
	CIA intervenes in Guatemala
	Senate votes to censure Joseph McCarthy
1955	*Brown* II orders desegregation with "deliberate speed"
	Rosa Parks' arrest spurs bus boycott in Montgomery
1956	Eisenhower defeats Stevenson for second term
	Allan Ginsberg publishes *Howl*
1957	Congress passes modest Civil Rights Act
	Eisenhower orders troops to Little Rock high school
	Soviet Union launches Sputnik
1958	Congress creates National Aeronautics and Space Administration (NASA)
1960	African American students begin sit-in protests
	Soviets shoot down U-2 spy plane

In February 1954, the young minister Martin Luther King, Jr., delivered a sermon at the Second Baptist Church in Detroit about the importance of "rediscovering lost values." "Automobiles and subways, televisions and radios, dollars and cents, can *never* be substitutes for God," he preached, as the vocal congregation cheered him on. King insisted that he had devoted his life "to something eternal and absolute. Not to these little gods that . . . that can give us a few Cadillac cars and Buick convertibles, as nice as they are, that are in style today and out of style three years from now . . . . but [to] the God who threw up that great cosmic light, that gets up early in the morning in the eastern horizon, who paints its technicolor across the blue, something that man could never make."

As King's sermon showed, the symbols of consumer prosperity—Cadillacs and Buicks, TVs, and radios—pervaded postwar society. But, amid such prosperity, the public also confronted terrible fears of mass death and often looked to the "eternal and absolute" for understanding and solace. By 1952, public schools around the country were requiring pupils to wear dogtags with name, address, and blood type to help identify the bodies of atomic-war victims. "I cannot tell you when or where the attack will come," said President Harry Truman, but "we must be ready." As the 1952 elections approached, such advice aggravated public frustration. The stalemated Korean war had drained lives and money and a presidential freeze on wartime wages and prices angered voters. Despite numerous laws, executive orders, and criminal investigations, the communist peril appeared omnipresent, relentless, and terrifying. Although Congress appropriated $3 billion for civilian bomb shelters, officials acknowledged that less than 1 percent of the public would be protected.

The Cold War nevertheless prompted government spending that contributed to unprecedented domestic prosperity. As the gross national product (GNP, the total value of goods and services) increased by 250 percent between 1945 and 1960, and per capita income jumped by 35 percent, consumers could now purchase household items that were considered luxuries just a decade before. For the expanding middle class, refrigerators, television sets, automobiles, washing machines, and even private residences appeared as family necessities. With the baby boom continuing until its peak in 1957, manufacturers produced a wide array of children's products, which, because of high consumer demand, soon became national fads. These included Davy Crockett coonskin hats, plastic hula hoops, and chlorophyll toothpaste.

The economic boom reflected advances in technology that reduced the cost of agricultural and industrial production. More plentiful tractors and other farm machinery, while contributing to the decline of the rural population, kept down the prices of food and fibers and boosted the national standard of living. Manufacturing improvements lowered the cost of industrial products, including cars, electronics, and petrochemicals. Corporate prosperity in turn led to rising wages (including union-won cost-of-living increases) and ensured an expanding domestic market. Equally important, the United States continued to dominate world trade as Western Europe and Japan imported food and industrial goods.

Cold War policies reinforced the growth of big-business corporations. As international crises necessitated a stronger defense posture, leaders in both parties saw no alternative to large military budgets and a growing federal bureaucracy; thus, the Cold War created closer relationships between the Pentagon and corporate military contractors. Such economic patterns weakened the position of small business, which shared the Cold War outlook but enjoyed less influence among policy makers. Yet the growth of corporate management created more jobs for white-collar workers. During this decade of prosperity, a growing proportion of working-class children graduated from high school, attended college, and looked for careers as managers of the service economy.

While the growth of a corporate-dominated economy troubled small-business interests that suffered from competition, individualists also expressed concern when companies like IBM boasted that "our training makes our men interchangeable." Many social commentators lamented the effects of corporate life on domestic institutions: the rising divorce rate, increasing numbers of women in the work force, and intergenerational conflict, especially the emergence of a distinctive adolescent youth culture and its associated problems of "juvenile delinquency." Still others criticized the exclu-

IBM boasted that "our training makes our men interchangeable."

sion of racial minorities from economic opportunity. Dissatisfaction with corporate values thus reached diverse groups—political liberals and small entrepreneurs; intellectuals, writers, and artists concerned about the impersonality of big organizations; and a burgeoning youth culture that questioned the materialistic values of postwar society. Yet, during the 1950s, the Cold War climate kept the lid on most dissent.

Republicans Come to Washington

The crisis atmosphere in foreign affairs undermined support for the Democratic leadership. Criticized for failing to win the Cold War, Truman had no taste for another term. He suggested giving the Democratic nomination to General Dwight D. Eisenhower, hero of World War II and head of the NATO command in Europe. Ike was certainly interested in the White House, but the seemingly apolitical military leader proved to be a Republican. His lack of clear party credentials became an electoral asset. World War II veterans saw him as a man above party labels.

Eisenhower's candidacy in 1952 sparked a bitter struggle within the Republican party about its own identity. Conservative, largely midwestern Republicans opposed costly government programs and overseas commitments; their preferred candidate was Ohio Senator Robert Taft. Eastern big-business interests, however, demanded an internationalist foreign policy to protect overseas investment and trade and, unlike Taft, they accepted some New Deal domestic programs, such as social security, to stabilize economic growth at home. These corporate leaders backed Eisenhower, who won the nomination. To balance the slate, Republicans chose conservative California Senator Richard M. Nixon as vice-presidential candidate. Meanwhile, the Democrats nominated the cerebral Adlai Stevenson, governor of Illinois, to run for president. But Stevenson was saddled by the problems of Truman's incumbency, allowing Republicans to develop a simple formula to depict the nation's ills—K1C2: Korea, communism, and corruption.

Stevenson's campaign suffered less because of political issues than from a new ingredient in presidential politics, the role of personal images. Eisenhower, the first presidential candidate to make television commercials, projected a soldierly self-confidence that the public craved. His military experience promised to end the Korean conflict, and his commitment to NATO showed no retreat in Europe, yet the candidate avoided the extreme anti-communism associated with Senator Joseph McCarthy. Instead, Eisenhower permitted Nixon to act as the party's militant anti-communist. Nixon, once a member of the House Committee on Un-American Activities (HUAC), called Stevenson "Adlai the appeaser." When newspapers reported that the vice-presidential nominee had obtained secret campaign funds, Eisenhower considered removing him from the ticket. Nixon adopted a novel defense, appearing on television to appeal to voters over the heads of party leaders.

The outcome of the election was decisive. Eisenhower's landslide—55 percent of the popular vote, 442 to 89 in the electoral college—saw the Republicans carry four southern states, the first crack in the Democrats' solid South since the Catholic Al Smith ran in 1928. Eisenhower also dented the New Deal coalition in the cities, gaining votes among white ethnics, Catholics, and blacks, and bringing a slight Republican majority

Richard Nixon's celebrated "Checkers" speech—so named because the candidate referred sentimentally to the gift of a cocker spaniel named Checkers—revealed the power of the new television medium and the importance of projecting a favorable political "image."

to both houses of Congress (though the death of a senator soon restored the Democrats' edge). Yet voting statistics revealed that the popular Ike drew more support than other Republicans, including McCarthy. The Cold War crisis abroad and anti-communist campaigns at home had narrowed the differences between the parties.

Eisenhower's presidential style encouraged political consensus. Comfortable with corporate administrative procedures, he filled cabinet positions with business leaders and lawyers. Although he opposed the idea of big government, Ike accepted minimal levels of social security. In 1953, he established the Department of Health, Education and Welfare and appointed as secretary Olveta Culp Hobby, the second woman to hold a cabinet office. As a career army officer, Eisenhower endorsed military superiority, including an increase of nuclear weaponry. But he frequently rejected pressure to resort to arms and warned of the domestic perils of large military budgets. "I just don't believe you can buy one hundred percent security in every little corner of the world," he said in 1954.

Confronting the Red Scare

Despite his popularity, Eisenhower continued to face pressure from more extreme anti-communists. To head off attacks from McCarthy, the president replaced Truman's loyalty program (see Chapter 24) with new standards in 1953. Instead of limiting the grounds for dismissing government employees to cases of disloyalty or subversion, Eisenhower's executive order permitted dismissal on the basis of more general charges, such as a person's holding beliefs that were merely inconsistent "with the interests of national security." These criteria led the Atomic Energy Commission in 1954 to lift the security clearance of physicist J. Robert Oppen-

The Election of 1952

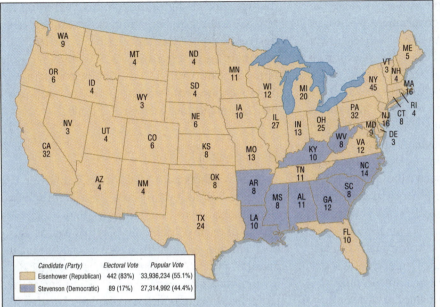

Candidate (Party)	Electoral Vote	Popular Vote
Eisenhower (Republican)	442 (83%)	33,936,234 (55.1%)
Stevenson (Democratic)	89 (17%)	27,314,992 (44.4%)

heimer, head of the team that built the first atomic bomb, because of his opposition to the hydrogen bomb project. The scientist's associations with communists threatened to embarrass the administration, and his "willful disregard of the normal and proper obligations of society" undermined the rigid demands of public conformity.

As federal panels screened the civil service to eliminate "security risks," standards of loyalty proved slippery and constitutional protections disappeared. "Of course, the fact that a person believes in racial equality doesn't *prove* that he's a Communist," admitted the chair of one federal committee, "but it certainly makes you look twice, doesn't it? You can't get away from the fact that racial equality is part of the Communist line." Under such guidelines, Eisenhower dismissed over 2,000 employees during his first year in office. Since the proceedings did not involve criminal charges, the Supreme Court ruled that employees were not entitled to due process under the law. Another ruling upheld the right of private businesses to fire employees who were members of the Communist party.

The Army-McCarthy Hearings

The White House loyalty program aimed to save Washington from communist subversion, but even Eisenhower's patriotism gave him no protection from Senator McCarthy. As chair of the subcommittee on government operations, the senator opened public hearings in 1953 to investigate communist influence in the State Department's Voice of America radio network and the U.S. Information Agency. His scattered attacks alarmed the executive branch, leading the State Department to purge "subversive" books from government libraries overseas. Eisenhower hesitated to intercede; "I will not get into the gutter with that guy," he said. But when McCarthy accused the Army of harboring "Communist conspirators," the president claimed "executive privilege" to deny the Senate access to government witnesses. "We are defeating ourselves," Eisenhower warned, "if we use methods that do not conform to the American sense of justice."

Indicative of McCarthy's prominence, all three television networks chose to broadcast his investigations of Army security procedures in 1954, giving the public a 36-day spectacle of the senator's hostile treatment of witnesses. McCarthy's approval ratings rapidly dropped from 50 percent to 34 percent. Having accused the previous Democratic administrations of "twenty years of treason," he now added an additional year, implicating Eisenhower as a communist accomplice. Embarrassed by such allegations, the Democratic-led Senate moved, at last, to silence the Republican demagogue. Voting to censure McCarthy for bringing the upper house into "dishonor and disrepute," the Senate effectively destroyed his political power. McCarthy remained in office until his death three years later of alcoholism.

Though he lent his name to the era, McCarthy was not solely responsible for anti-communist excesses. Just as the campaign preceded his rise in 1950, so the political repression continued after his fall. HUAC, for example, questioned over 600 witnesses in labor unions, churches, and the entertainment industry. The Subversive Activities Control Board held extensive hearings about organizations placed on the attorney general's list of alleged subversive groups. In 1954, congressional liberals, including Minnesota's Hubert Humphrey, supported the Communist Control Act that denied the party constitutional protections. Meanwhile, the FBI proceeded with secret surveillance and detention plans to monitor suspects and leak government files. In 1956, FBI Director Hoover created the unauthorized Counter Intelligence Program (COINTELPRO), allowing illegal wiretaps, bugs, and burglaries ("black bag" jobs) to disrupt various dissenting groups, including the NAACP. Such government harassment helped to destroy the U.S. Communist party. In 1957, its members numbered only 3,500. By then, the Supreme Court ruled in the *Yates* case that proof of subversion required not merely revolutionary beliefs but specific subversive actions.

Waging the Cold War

Despite conflicts with McCarthy, Eisenhower saw the Cold War as a moral struggle and he stressed the importance of unrelenting vigilance against a powerful enemy. "Freedom is pitted against slavery; lightness against the dark," he said in his inaugural speech. "A soldier's pack is not so heavy a burden as a prisoner's chains." Such certainties simplified foreign policy making but obscured important issues of national security. As Eisenhower's secretary of state John Foster Dulles admitted, "Our people can understand, and will support, policies which can be explained and understood in moral terms. But policies merely based on carefully calculated expediency could never be explained and would never be understood." Such cynicism not only encouraged dishonesty toward the public but also limited international flexibility.

Eisenhower's military program reflected this rigidity. Unveiling a strategy known as "massive retaliation" in 1953, the administration threatened to use atomic weapons against the Kremlin in Moscow to deter Soviet advances in any part of the world. To bring an end to the Korean war, the White House issued a not-so-subtle threat to initiate atomic warfare unless the communists resumed negotiations. Coincidentally, the sudden death of Soviet leader Josef Stalin in 1953 created concerns in China about other issues, prompting a renewal of peace talks in Korea. In June 1953, the two sides agreed to a truce that left the Korean peninsula divided into two countries.

The administration's "New Look" in military policy emphasized atomic weapons and air power, a program that was popular because it reduced the size of conventional forces and permitted cuts in the military budget. Yet the principles of massive retaliation raised the stakes of Cold War conflict and extended commitments around the world. When China attacked islands off the coast of Taiwan in 1955, Eisenhower prepared for an atomic attack. The threat persuaded China to retreat. (A similar crisis three years later again raised global tensions, but passed without conflict.) Meanwhile, the nations of Europe divided into armed camps: the NATO alliance in western Europe versus the Soviet Union's satellite nations in eastern Europe.

Nearly every issue of international relations would be defined by this bipolar stalemate. Although Eisenhower presented a dramatic "atoms for peace" speech to the United Nations in 1953, the plan would have preserved U.S. nuclear superiority and found no favor in Moscow. The two superpowers did agree to a summit meeting in Geneva in 1955, which was hailed by the international press as a "thaw" in the Cold War, but the former allies could not resolve issues of a divided Germany or mutual disarmament. In Asia, Eisenhower continued the policy of anti-communist containment, giving billions of dollars of military and economic aid to South Korea, Taiwan, the Philippines, and French colonial forces in Indochina. In 1955, these commitments were formalized in the South East Asia Treaty Organization (SEATO), a military alliance that was never invoked.

The CIA's Secret Wars

Total warfare against communism justified a secret foreign policy. Although Eisenhower avoided direct clashes with the Soviet Union, the Central Intelligence Agency (CIA), headed by Allen Dulles (brother of the secretary of state) controlled a top-secret multibillion-dollar budget that was exempt from congressional oversight. Initially created to gather intelligence, the CIA under Eisenhower pursued covert warfare beyond formal diplomacy. CIA-backed raids from Taiwan against the Chinese mainland, for example, hardly affected the Cold War, but when China complained, Washington denied responsibility—not only to the Chinese government but also to the U.S. public.

Using the CIA, Eisenhower advanced U.S. objectives in the developing nations of the "Third World" without seeking congressional approval. Twice the CIA succeeded in overthrowing governments deemed unfriendly by administration leaders. When a nationalist government in Iran attempted to end western control of local oil reserves in 1953, Eisenhower refused to negotiate with the Iranians. Instead, the CIA engineered a rebellion, which reinstalled the hereditary Shah of Iran. Bringing the Shah's government into the anti-communist alliance with additional military and economic aid, Washington protected the investments of U.S. petroleum companies. Similarly, the United States blocked efforts by Guatemala's land reformers to nationalize property held by the United Fruit Company in 1954. Claiming that the reformers endorsed "international communism," Eisenhower allowed the CIA to organize a mercenary army that proceeded to overthrow Guatemala's government. Afterward, the United States supported a military regime that used anti-communism as an excuse to repress peasant land reformers and labor unions.

Crisis in Indochina

The belief that communism represented a monolithic enemy, and that all communists took orders from the Kremlin, embroiled the United States in the anti-colonial war in Vietnam that was led by

"You have a row of dominos set up, you knock over the first one, and what will happen to the last one is the certainty that it will go over very quickly."

the pro-communist Ho Chi Minh. Following the outbreak of the Korean conflict, Washington financed 80 percent of France's costs to suppress the rebellion, partly to oppose the insurgents, partly to ensure French support of anti-communism in western Europe. By 1954, France faced total defeat in Vietnam. As Vietnamese guerrillas surrounded the French base at Dien Bien Phu, France appealed to Eisenhower for military assistance.

Although the White House approved CIA missions to support the garrison, the president refused to commit ground forces without approval from Congress or the European allies, and neither would support U.S. intervention. Yet Eisenhower worried about the strategic consequences of a French defeat. To the press, he presented what became known as the "domino theory" to justify involvement in the region: "You have a row of dominos set up," said Ike. "You knock over the first one, and what will happen to the last one is the certainty that it will go over very quickly." Translated into geopolitical terms, Eisenhower warned that a communist victory in Indochina would imperil not only southeast Asia but also affect the economic and military security of Japan and the Philippines.

Eisenhower's unwillingness to intervene in Vietnam forced the French to surrender in 1954. Democratic Senate Majority Leader Lyndon B. Johnson chastised the White House for "such a stunning reversal." Thereafter, Vietnam virtually disappeared from U.S. news reports. Yet Eisen-

hower had no intention of accepting a communist victory. Although France recognized the separation of Indochina into three countries—Laos, Cambodia, and Vietnam—and accepted a temporary division of Vietnam at the 17th parallel, Washington refused to sign the ensuing Geneva Accords of 1954 and instead initiated a secret war against the Vietnamese victors. Rejecting national elections that would have created a single Vietnamese nation, Eisenhower backed a separate South Vietnamese government headed by Ngo Dinh Diem and sent over $1 billion of aid to the anti-communist dictator. By 1959, Diem's repression had triggered another guerrilla revolt, creating an unsettled political upheaval that Eisenhower passed on to his successors.

The Domestic Consensus

The prevailing anti-Communist crusade blurred many differences between the major political parties. Because of the congressional seniority system, those representatives and senators with the longest tenures in office became committee chairmen. In the southern states, most blacks could not vote, and the Democrats maintained a one-party system that ensured the reelection of the same men to political office. Consequently, southern Democrats controlled the congressional leadership. Most were politically conservative and had no quarrel with Eisenhower's foreign policy, nor did they question the importance of destroying communism.

Both parties also shared a commitment to balanced budgets, allowing slight expansion of social security to include self-employed workers, modest public-housing legislation, and the generous Interstate Highway Act of 1956, which was justified on grounds of national security. Compromise dictated the resolution of debates about minimum wages, but federal legislation ignored the poorest

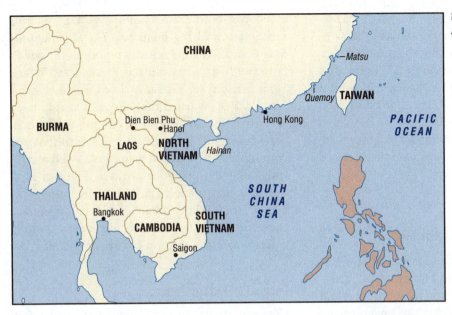

Southeast Asia after the Geneva Accords of 1954

workers, including domestics, who were usually women and racial minorities. Talk of national health insurance drew warnings of communism. Health, Education, and Welfare Secretary Hobby opposed the free distribution of the new Salk polio vaccine to poor children in 1955, calling the idea "socialized medicine . . . by the back door."

Besides communism, the most bitter domestic disputes focused on energy policy—a not inconsiderable issue in this age of high-octane internal combustion engines, rising commercial aviation (in 1958, the Boeing 707 initiated jet travel), and mounting obligations of military defense. Conservative Republicans and southern Democrats favored state control of offshore oil deposits—both on principles of states' rights and because state legislatures were easier to control. Liberals preferred federal administration to regulate oil reserves. Under Eisenhower, the states' faction prevailed. The White House also supported the Atomic Energy Act of 1954, which permitted the first private operation of nuclear reactors to gen-

erate electrical power. Efforts failed to dismantle the Tennessee Valley Authority—the great symbol of the New Deal's public ownership of electricity—but conservatives blocked similar projects in other regions.

"Moderation," concluded the Democratic presidential contender Adlai Stevenson in 1956, "is the spirit of the times." A cautious Democratic party, hoping to win southern electoral votes, avoided taking a stand on issues of racial segregation and embraced Eisenhower's Cold War agenda. Learning that radioactive fallout from nuclear tests might contaminate the nation's food, Stevenson proposed a moratorium on these military experiments. He also suggested that a voluntary army replace peacetime conscription. On both military issues, however, Eisenhower appeared as the preeminent expert. "The butchers of the Kremlin," remarked Vice President Nixon, "would make mincemeat of Stevenson."

The great Republican handicap in 1956 appeared to be Eisenhower's health. A recent heart attack reminded voters that, by the end of his second term, Ike would be the oldest man to serve as the nation's chief executive. But the president's robust smile overcame public doubts. With 58 percent of the popular vote, Eisenhower took all but seven states, but other Republicans ran poorly, and the Democrats held majorities in both houses of Congress. Eisenhower's personality had prevailed, but the political balance in Washington expressed the country's centrist mood.

Creating a Corporate Culture

The assumption that communists served as agents of a foreign power justified loyalty oaths, criminal punishment of noncompliant witnesses, and attacks on civil liberties. But the image of the communist menace also revealed concern about changes occurring *within* U.S. society. "The average Communist," said one of the government's "expert" witnesses on the subject, "no matter how much his desire for integrity, tends to become a puppet." J. Edgar Hoover described communists, "body and soul," as the "property" of the party. Communists were "no longer individuals," suggested a third expert, "but robots . . . chained in an intellectual and moral slavery." Lacking human emotions, regimented and humorless, the stereotyped communist appeared as a soulless entity without imagination or free will. Such images appeared in the haunting 1956 Hollywood movie *Invasion of the Body Snatchers,* in which small-town citizens became a mindless army devoted to an alien race.

Fear of personality loss emerged as a major theme in popular sociology. In the influential book *The Lonely Crowd* (1950), Harvard's David Reisman argued that middle-class citizens had lost an internal gyroscope and now measured their self-worth by conforming to other people's standards. Numerous books—William Whyte's examination of big business, *The Organization Man* (1956); Vance Packard's report on the advertising industry, *The Hidden Persuaders* (1957); Sloan Wilson's novel, *The Man in the Gray Flannel Suit* (1955)—warned that corporate capitalism, seemingly the archenemy of communist bureaucracy, demanded a stultifying conformity from corporate executives and managers as well as clerical staff and blue-collar workers. The new middle class, said sociologist C. Wright Mills in his classic study *White Collar* (1951), had become a "new proletariat." Indeed, the distinction "white-collar" implied a uniform civilian dress code.

Corporate Expansion

Concern about corporate power mirrored economic trends that were closely tied to the Cold War. During the Eisenhower presidency, the federal government spent $350 billion on military contracts, mostly with big corporations. By 1960, 38 percent of the labor force worked for corporations with over 500 employees, while only 16 percent were self-employed. The expanding West Coast aircraft industry, for example, employed 1.25 million workers by 1959, while electronics enjoyed an annual growth rate of 15 percent and became the fifth largest industry by the end of the decade.

The relationship between big business and government troubled the nation's preeminent Cold Warrior. "We have been compelled to create a permanent armaments industry of vast proportions," complained Eisenhower when he left office. "We annually spend on military security alone more than the net income of all United States corporations." The Cold War had thus created the very bureaucratic apparatus (Eisenhower called it "the military-industrial complex") that conservatives, entrepreneurs, and individualists rejected in the communist state. Despite large military expenditures, moreover, economic recessions and unemployment (from 3 to 8 percent annually after the Korean war) produced persistent uncertainty.

Even without government expenditures, corporate growth reflected a burst of consumer spending for domestic purposes. Having exhausted wartime savings to purchase durable products such as automobiles and appliances, consumers shifted after 1950 to buy disposable goods and services, such as insurance, entertainment, and travel. Planned obsolescence by auto manufacturers encouraged car owners to replace vehicles every other year, while men's fashions now began to copy women's styles by changing annually. The Diner's Club credit card, introduced in 1950 as a perquisite for business executives, set a trend for spending with borrowed money. (Not until the 1970s could married women obtain personal credit lines.) Installment credit jumped from $4 billion in 1954 to $43 billion in 1960.

Stimulating the consumer binge, advertising became a boom industry, promoting consumer disposables such as tobacco, beverages, and home furnishings. Ever-rising sales of televisions (by 1955, 65 percent of the nation's homes owned a set) encouraged national advertising of products available throughout the country. Local manufacturers increasingly had trouble competing with national brands. The number of breweries dropped from 450 in 1950 to 170 ten years later. Local newspapers and radio stations lost revenue to the new electronic medium.

Advertising heralded the arrival of a new service economy. "Fewer individuals manipulate *things*," observed sociologist C. Wright Mills; "more handle *people* and *symbols*." As consumers spent money for insurance, utilities, auto repair, travel, and entertainment, the number of occupations in service industries passed the number of

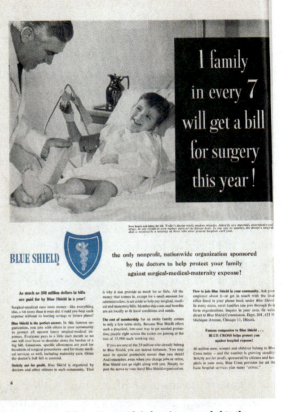

Insurance, one of the era's growth industries, appealed to the parents of the baby boomers.

jobs in manufacturing for the first time in 1956. Part of a long historical trend that saw technology replacing blue-collar work, the post-industrial society also witnessed the expansion of government employment. During the 1950s, state and municipal jobs increased by 52 percent, mostly in white-collar work. By 1960, 8.5 million employees received government paychecks.

Work and Gender

The growth of service-sector jobs had an important impact on domestic life and gender roles. As women continued to enter the work force in rising numbers, nearly 40 percent of all adult women were employed by 1960. With an average age of 41, most working women were married, and many had school-age children. Their opportunities remained limited: most women found jobs in sex-segregated, nonunionized occupations such as nursing, sales, and secretarial work. By 1960, 10 percent of U.S. families were headed by women, but these households had median incomes half the amount of those headed by men. Yet a survey of employed women found that nearly half worked because of financial responsibilities. African American women had a higher rate of employment than whites, but over one-third worked as private household servants, and black women typically earned about half as much as white women.

The entry of women into service-sector jobs mirrored other social trends. Women's growing financial independence paralleled—if it did not cause—a rising rate of divorce. In 1940, 26 percent of all marriages ended in divorce; in 1960, 39 percent did, part of a long historical trend. The increase in the number of working wives and mothers also changed the nation's eating habits. With larger refrigerators and freezers to store food, working women increasingly purchased frozen foods and pre-made meals, such as the "TV dinner," which made its debut in 1954. More families also turned to fast-food franchises such as McDonald's, which debuted in 1958.

Women's desire for working careers contradicted the prevailing media ideology of domesticity. The great sex goddess of 1950s films, Marilyn Monroe, devoted considerable plot time, in movies like *How to Marry a Millionaire,* to finding a spouse. In 1954, *McCall's* magazine invented the term *togetherness,* depicting the ideal male as the family breadwinner and the perfect woman as a wife, mother, and homemaker. Indeed, the most popular television comedy of the decade, *I Love Lucy,* consistently scorned the housewife's efforts

The American dream? A pleased husband brings home his mannequin-like new wife from a shopping spree at Ohrbach's.

to find success outside the home. Yet laughter belied the tensions of family life. Situation comedies named *The Honeymooners* and *Father Knows Best* complemented televised commercials that showed an unending battle of the sexes. Family problems created growing business for professional psychiatrists, whose clientele shifted in the postwar decade from hospitalized cases of mental illness to milder forms of "neurosis" and "maladjustment." Pharmaceutical tranquilizers became the treatment of choice.

The family tensions of the 1950s reflected an uneasiness about the emergence of new gender roles. Since most jobs in the service sector did not depend on physical strength, some male white-collar workers sought validation of their masculine ideal through selected consumption. They drove big cars with elongated tail fins, engaged more in extramarital sex, and purchased hedonistic items such as whiskey, music, and clothing that they saw advertised in new male magazines like *Playboy*. When the Philip Morris tobacco company re-targeted the sale of Marlboro cigarettes from women to men in the mid-1950s, advertisers discovered that the most successful image in reaching male consumers was a tattooed cowboy—the so-called Marlboro Man, who symbolized untrammeled individualism. By the end of the decade, this male prototype emerged as the hero of the television programs with the highest viewer ratings. Adult westerns—"Gunsmoke," "Have Gun Will Travel," and "Maverick"—had titles that celebrated an independent, nonconforming man with a gun, the very opposite of the organization men who ran successful corporations.

While married men identified with the disappearing cowboy, married women embraced consumer products that also transformed their public images. "Does she . . . or doesn't she?" asked Shirley Polykoff, the only woman copywriter at one major advertising agency in 1956. Despite the embarrassment of her male colleagues, who tried to censor the phrase, her question did not directly relate to sex. At a time when only 7 percent of the nation's women dared to dye their hair (mostly actresses, models, and prostitutes), the Clairol company boldly answered Polykoff's double-edged question: "Hair color so natural only her hairdresser knows for sure." The slogan changed women's appearance. Within a decade, nearly half of all U.S. women were regularly coloring their hair, boosting the industry's annual sales from $25 million to $200 million. Most followed the dictum of another Marilyn Monroe hit, *Gentlemen Prefer Blondes* (1953), and chose lighter shades.

Actor James Dean epitomized the brooding rebellion of a younger generation that rejected the materialism of their society. Dean starred with Natalie Wood in the 1955 film *Rebel Without a Cause*.

Youth, Sexuality, and Religion

Changing gender relations sometimes troubled the young. "You're tearing me apart," screamed actor James Dean, the offspring of an unhappy marriage in the 1955 movie *Rebel Without a Cause*. As Hollywood productions showed young people seeking domestic stability, the first generation of "teenagers" (the word entered the common vocabulary at the end of World War II) found their own anti-establishment voice through the music of rock 'n' roll. Blending African American rhythm-and-blues with white country and gospel, the new music arrived with Bill Haley's "Rock Around the Clock" in 1954. Flaunting sexual gyrations, a seductive grin, and defiant lyrics, the sideburned Elvis Presley became a cult figure with songs like "Don't Be Cruel" and "All Shook Up." The nation's youth created a thriving multibillion-dollar marketplace for teenage products such as records, cosmetics, and clothing. Sexual expression remained under wraps, more implied than practiced, though the rate of premarital intercourse continued to rise. For less-defiant youth, singer Pat Boone and television's *American Bandstand* offered a tamer, "clean" version of rock 'n' roll.

Among adults, by contrast, nontraditional sexual behavior created a powerful, if hidden, undertow in middle-class values. Publication of Dr. Alfred Kinsey's two-volume study of sexual behavior revealed a wide disparity between professed values of chastity and actual practices. Nearly all men and 50 percent of the women interviewed acknowledged premarital intercourse; half the men and a quarter of the women had extramarital sexual relations; 37 percent of the men and 13 percent of the women confessed at least one post-adolescent homosexual contact (though Kinsey's prisoner respondents may have inflated the statistics). Increasingly, such sexual activity was piercing the veil of secrecy.

A revitalized purity crusade attempted to stifle explicit forms of sexual expression, but antagonists to censorship of sex now prompted a defense of civil liberties. Despite conservative criticism of sexually charged fiction, the bestselling novels of the late 1950s—Grace Metallious's *Peyton Place* (1957) and Vladimir Nabokov's *Lolita* (1958)—attracted millions of respectable readers. Acknowledging changing public values, the Supreme Court outlawed literary censorship on the basis of First Amendment rights, and thus allowed the sale of such classics as D. H. Lawrence's *Lady Chatterley's Lover* and Henry Miller's *Tropic of Cancer.* Yet both the motion picture and television industries maintained rigid codes against nudity, obscenity, and sexual expression. State and local law generally treated homosexual behavior as criminal. To protect themselves from police harassment, gay men formed the Mattachine Society in 1951 and lesbians organized the Daughters of Bilitis in 1955, laying the basis for a gay and lesbian rights movement.

Middle-class acceptance of sexual expression ironically coincided with a renaissance of interest in organized religion. Perhaps as a response to wartime crises and to the social upheaval that accompanied population movement, church membership in all denominations surged upward between 1940 and 1960, from 64 million to 115 million, increasing from 50 percent to 63 percent of the population. As part of the Cold War against atheistic communism, Congress added the words "under God" to the Pledge of Allegiance in 1954. Bestselling writers like the Reverend Norman Vincent Peale offered a theology of common sense, more a secular reassurance than a promise of salvation. Yet preachers like Billy Graham held numerous revivals that struck an evangelical chord. Such revivalist values would soon support the greatest civil rights movement of the century.

Poverty amid Affluence

The affluence of middle-class culture obscured pockets of poverty that afflicted a wide variety of citizens. Regardless of race and region, among the poorest Americans were those over the age of 65, many driven from the work force by mandatory retirement rules but lacking adequate pensions. In 1960, more than half the nation's elderly had annual incomes below $3,000—not enough, according to a Senate report, for "decent housing, proper nutrition, adequate medical care . . . , or necessary recreation." Although the number of retirees eligible for social-security benefits increased fivefold during the 1950s, public assistance proved inadequate. This poverty reinforced popular stereotypes in movies and television that old people were incompetent, frail, and senile.

The Rural Poor

News commentator Edward R. Murrow shattered the myth of national abundance with a 1960 Thanksgiving Day broadcast about rural poverty called *Harvest of Shame*. In 1959, nearly 2 million farm workers, most of them whites, earned less than $3,000. Typically, the nation's migrant farmhands inhabited housing without electricity or running water, lacked legal protection against unfair wages and arbitrary pay deductions, and were unable to educate their children in public schools or obtain government assistance. Instead, they formed a rootless population that followed seasonal crops with little opportunity for economic improvement.

In the western states, Mexican American farm workers faced additional problems of racial discrimination. Often failing to distinguish native-born citizens from immigrants, the federal government initiated "Operation Wetback," which resulted in the deportation of 3 million Mexican Americans between 1951 and 1954. "The beet workers go home empty-handed," protested one southwestern civil-rights group, "but we are sure of what will be waiting for them next year—the old barns and chicken coop without windows or screens . . . and the ditches where they get their drinking water."

Problems of Racial Minorities

Poorest of all were Native Americans, whose mortality rates were three times higher than the national average. On reservations, unemployment exceeded 70 percent among Montana's Blackfeet and 86 percent among Mississippi's Choctaws. Encouraged by the government's Bureau of Indian Affairs, about 100,000 Native Americans migrated to cities, where for the first time many lived with electricity and indoor plumbing. But only an estimated 3,000 found permanent work. Most took seasonal, low-paying, unskilled jobs; others had no work at all. Separated from their traditional cultures, these urban newcomers abandoned religious rituals and ceased to speak their own languages, with the result that many Native languages have since become extinct. But poverty and isolation also encouraged a countermigration to the reservations; perhaps as many as two-thirds of urban dwellers returned to their homes.

Complicating problems of Native American identity was the federal government's program of "termination." Designed to end dependence on federal funds and to encourage assimilation, Congress attempted to dissolve tribal structures, disburse collective assets among individual residents, and terminate federal responsibility for the reservations. Between 1953 and 1960, over 100 Native American nations lost their federal protection, which affected over 1 million acres and 12,000 individuals. Assimilated people often welcomed removal of government oversight, but most Native groups resisted the changes. Among Wisconsin's Menominee nation, for example, termination ended federal contracts to purchase tribal-owned lumber, and new taxes reduced their profits further. Forced to sell corporate lands for survival, the Menominees lost rights to fish and hunt (as well as their homes), and low incomes resulted in the closing the local hospital. Such problems, hovering over all Native groups, produced a strong anti-termination movement that would alter government policies in the next decade.

Chinese Americans also experienced disproportionate poverty. Despite the tourist glamour of urban Chinatowns, Chinese American men had annual incomes that were 60 percent of white men's, while Chinese American women earned only 40 percent of what white women did. Unemployment rates were twice as high as for whites, and more than one-third of all Chinese American families lived below the official poverty line. They also had high rates of tuberculosis and suicide. Such problems reflected not only poverty but also a long history of segregated living plus the disproportionate number of single elderly men in Chinese communities. By contrast, assimilated Japanese, with a higher percentage of native-born citizens, more frequently gained middle-class status.

Postwar city life also intensified the problems of African Americans and Puerto Ricans, who arrived in northern cities just as white families were moving to the suburbs. By 1960, half the nation's blacks lived in central cities, where service jobs enabled about 40 percent to achieve middle-income status. But urban-renewal projects eliminated many residential buildings, which were often replaced by office space, parking lots, highways, and commercial units. The loss of residential space caused rents to climb, claiming a larger portion of nonwhite incomes.

In New York City, 80 percent of the Puerto Rican residents earned less than the government's "modest but adequate" standard of living. African American men earned about 70 percent of white male incomes; African American women earned about half of white women's incomes (which was only 60 percent of that of white men). With more jobs moving to the suburbs, urban newcomers found employment in the unskilled or semiskilled sectors, largely in service work as waiters, janitors, practical nurses, and housekeepers. The rate of unemployment among black adults (10 per-

cent) and black teenagers (24 percent) was twice as high as that for whites.

The Origins of the Civil Rights Movement

At a time when cold warriors extolled political democracy against Soviet dictatorship and corporate leaders celebrated capitalism over communism, African Americans bitterly recognized the injustices of second-class citizenship. By the 1950s, economic inequality, racial discrimination, and political weakness had created a volatile mix of frustration, anger, and a determination to seek changes. The result was the emergence of a dynamic civil rights movement that sought racial equality. Its agenda was initially cautious and legalistic. Civil rights activists demanded that equal-protection laws be enforced, that unequal laws be eliminated as unconstitutional, and that all citizens be held to a single standard of justice. They believed that such legal reforms would ultimately resolve other social problems such as poverty.

A Segregated Society

In 1952, seventy years after the federal government began keeping statistics of lynchings, the nation's annual total for the first time amounted to zero and stayed zero for the next two years. Yet, in the southern states, local law (plus custom and threat) kept the races strictly divided. In Texas, the state prohibited interracial boxing matches; in Alabama, a white woman could not nurse a black man in a hospital. "Colored" and "white" identified water fountains, laundries, parks, and beaches in the South. Six states forbade white and black prisoners from being chained together; eleven states obliged blacks to ride in the back of buses and streetcars; seventeen states required black and white children to attend segregated schools. In California and the Southwest, school segregation included Mexican Americans. In northern and western states, residential patterns, which were based on economic class, discrimination, or informal prejudice, maintained de facto (status quo, and nonlegal) segregation of public schools.

After 1953, Eisenhower tackled problems of racial segregation in federal jurisdiction. Responding to pressure from Republican moderates and Harlem's African American representative, Adam Clayton Powell, he ordered the completion of desegregation in the armed forces, integrated civilian jobs in government naval yards, and opened public facilities such as movie theaters and public schools in Washington, D.C. Yet Eisenhower's sole black appointee in the White House, E. Frederick Morrow, a public relations expert, was required always to have two secretaries in his office, lest he be seen alone with a white woman. African American voters appreciated these tokens of improvement and gave Ike 5 percent more support in 1956 than four years earlier. Meanwhile, a Mexican American civil-rights organization persuaded the Supreme Court to rule in May 1954 that the equal protection principles of the Fourteenth Amendment—in this case dealing with discrimination on juries—applied not only to "blacks" but to "white" Mexican Americans.

Challenging Separate but Equal

Justification of segregation derived from the Supreme Court's *Plessy* decision of 1896 (see Chapter 17), which had ruled that the Fourteenth Amendment did not prohibit racial segregation as long as separate facilities, such as railroads and public schools, provided equal services. Abundant evidence showed, however, that southern

> **Eisenhower's sole black appointee was required always to have two secretaries in his office, lest he be seen alone with a white woman.**

states provided far less funding for black schools than for whites, paid lower teacher salaries for blacks, mandated the use of textbooks discarded by white schools, and permitted school buildings used by blacks to deteriorate.

After World War II, the NAACP's chief legal counsel, Thurgood Marshall, initiated a series of suits to desegregate postgraduate schools. Arguing that separate institutions in these situations were not equal, Marshall persuaded the U.S. Supreme Court to order the desegregation of such schools. Similar logic led the Court to outlaw public-school segregation for Mexican American children in Texas and California. By 1950, Marshall shifted his legal strategy to argue that segregation itself, not merely unequal schools, was unconstitutional. Although the *Plessy* ruling held that segregation did not convey a "badge of inferiority," Marshall used psychological testimony that indicated "prejudice and segregation have definitely detrimental effects" on student development.

In the historic decision, *Brown v. Board of Education of Topeka,* delivered on May 17, 1954, by Eisenhower's newly appointed chief justice, Earl Warren, a unanimous Supreme Court overturned the constitutionality of school segregation. In public education, said the Court, "'separate but equal' has no place. Separate educational facilities are inherently unequal." The ruling challenged nearly a century of racial segregation and foreshadowed fundamental changes in the country's race relations.

Encouraged by the *Brown* case, Thurgood Marshall forecast the integration of all public schools in five years and the complete collapse of segregation by the centennial of the Emancipation Proclamation in 1963. Eisenhower, who personally disliked the Court's decision, expressed less optimism. He reminded the public that the "final battle against intolerance is to be fought—not in the chambers of any legislature—but in the hearts of men." Mississippi Senator James Eastland had no doubts about changing people's hearts and minds: "You are not required to obey any court which passes out such a ruling," he told his constituents. "In fact, you are obliged to defy it."

Responding to these conflicting pressures, the Supreme Court issued a second decree in 1955 (known as *Brown* II), which ordered compliance with the desegregation order, not immediately but "with all due deliberate speed," and passed responsibility to monitor compliance to federal district courts, which were dominated by segregationist judges. Through that legal loophole marched an army of southern politicians dedicated to maintaining segregation. The southern white motto became: "massive resistance." Southern legislatures made voter registration more difficult, harassed civil-rights groups (several states outlawed the NAACP), and permitted police spying against African American activists.

Outside the legal system, white community leaders formed "citizens councils," which used their economic power to punish blacks who tried to vote or register their children in integrated schools. Boycotts of black business, dismissal of employees, refusal of credit, and eviction of tenants forced many African American families to flee the South. In addition, a revived Ku Klux Klan used violence and terror to crush political change. A wave of bombings targeted black churches, Jewish synagogues, and integrated schools. When 14-year-old Emmett Till, a Chicago youth visiting relatives in Mississippi, whistled at a white woman in 1955, local Klansmen kidnapped and killed him. Photographs of his mutilated body outraged the black community and liberal whites. Despite eyewitness testimony, an all-white jury acquitted the accused killers. Eisenhower declined to use federal authority against local officials.

Black Protest, White Resistance, Federal Action

African Americans did not wait for Washington to take action. A new national crusade began dramatically in December 1955, when one NAACP activist in Montgomery, Alabama, seamstress Rosa Parks, made herself a test case by refusing to surrender her bus seat to a white passenger. After her arrest, supporters organized a boycott of city buses to press for desegregation. As African Americans formed the "Montgomery Improvement Association," they chose as their spokesman a newly appointed minister who held a Ph.D. degree in theology: Martin Luther King, Jr. "There comes a time when people get tired of being trampled over by the iron feet of oppression," King told a tense overflow crowd that attended a mass meeting at his church.

The bus boycott lasted for weeks, then months. King infused the movement with the principles of nonviolent protest that were derived from Christian biblical texts and from Mahatma Gandhi's nonviolent, anti-colonial resistance in India. As King taught nonviolence, protesters would not retaliate against their attackers but would offer forgiveness; by loving their enemies, they would arouse the conscience of their persecutors and other sympathetic people. Such a strategy demanded immense self-discipline and courage in the face of omnipresent violence. Baptist ministers like King played prominent roles in the crusade, but the movement was mass-based

Montgomery, Alabama, police fingerprint Rosa Parks after her arrest for refusing to give up her seat to a white person on a segregated bus.

and dependent on the personal commitment of individual participants.

The Montgomery boycott unified the black community, but it required a Supreme Court decision in December 1956, one year after Rosa Parks' arrest, before municipal officials accepted desegregation. Meanwhile, other southern communities defended traditions of segregation. In 1956, 101 southern congressmen announced a Declaration of Constitutional Principles, what was called a "Southern Manifesto," that denied the power of the federal government to order desegregation in the states. Several states even repealed compulsory education laws in order to validate closing integrated schools and passed anti-treason legislation that made criticism of state government a crime. A combination of legal resistance and mounting violence produced clear results: in some southern states, the number of eligible black voters *declined*. Hoping to attract African American support, the administration proposed legislation to protect voting rights, but southerners killed the bill in the Senate.

"Give us the ballot," pleaded Martin Luther King, Jr., "and we will no longer have to worry the federal government about our rights." In 1957, on the third anniversary of the *Brown* ruling, 30,000 protesters made a "prayer pilgrimage" to the nation's capital to demand civil rights legislation. Once again, the administration endorsed laws to protect voting rights. So did Senate Majority Leader Lyndon Johnson, previously a Texas segregationist, who now sought to broaden his national influence. Persuading southern senators to abandon filibuster threats in exchange for a weak bill, Johnson won approval of the first civil rights law since Reconstruction. The 1957 Civil Rights Act created a Civil Rights Commission and authorized the Justice Department to seek injunctions against interference with the right to vote. Enforcement powers remained limited. Three years later, only 25 percent of eligible African Americans could vote. Another civil rights law, passed in 1960, did not strengthen federal power.

Youth and Desegregation

In the wake of the *Brown* ruling, the civil rights movement moved beyond legislative halls into the streets. Each autumn, as African American schoolchildren attempted to enter desegregated schools, local officials and angry crowds conspired to block pupil integration. The crisis climaxed in September 1957, when Arkansas Governor Orval Faubus rejected a federal court order and mobilized the National Guard to prevent the integration of Central High School in Little Rock. Eisenhower preferred to ignore the issue. But news pictures of hysterical mobs barring nine students from attending the school showed blatant violations of federal law and embarrassed the president. "Law cannot be flouted with impunity," said Eisenhower as he federalized the National Guard and sent armed paratroopers to enforce the court order. Amid howling mobs, bomb threats, and year-long harassment, federal soldiers guarded the school building. The next year, Faubus closed the school rather than integrate, though judicial orders later opened the system. Similar mob violence erupted throughout the southern states. By 1960, less than 1 percent of southern African American children attended integrated schools.

"We must believe that a prejudiced mind can be changed," insisted Dr. King. Seeking to reach the conscience of white supremacists, religious activists organized the Southern Christian Leadership Conference (SCLC) in 1957, adopting the motto "To Redeem the Soul of America." Advocating nonviolent civil disobedience, the move-

ment sought through public displays of racial injustice to compel law-abiding people to confront the evils of racism. The strategy especially appealed to a younger generation, educated in southern cities after World War II, who rejected second-class citizenship. The emergence of independent nations in Africa, beginning with Ghana in 1957, evoked identification with an African heritage and inspired interest in political change.

Through the late 1950s, civil rights protest accepted the rule of law, appealing for court decisions, congressional legislation, and executive action. The debate seldom addressed de facto segregation outside the South. One exception was Lorraine Hansberry's compelling drama, *A Raisin in the Sun* (1959), which focused on the problems of a Chicago family plagued by racism and "ghetto-itis." Liberal cities, like New York, enacted anti-discrimination housing laws, but enforcement was difficult and slow.

By 1960, frustration at the pace of change brought new tactics to the movement. That winter, four African American freshman at North Carolina Agricultural and Technical (A&T) College in Greensboro decided to violate segregation laws to force a political confrontation. Entering a Woolworth's store, the four sat down at the segregated lunch counter. Refused service, the students remained seated. Other customers subjected them to taunts and violence but the perpetrators were not arrested. The next day, more students returned; within a week the sit-in movement had spread through the South, targeting shopping centers, theaters, and other public facilities. Some businesses quietly accepted integration; others became scenes of confrontation that reinvigorated the protest movement. Two months later, SCLC's Ella Baker helped black and white undergraduates organize another civil rights group, the Student Non-Violent Coordinating Committee (SNCC), which instigated further protest in the next decade.

Renewing Partisan Conflict

As the grandfatherly Eisenhower presided over the strongest military power on earth, the continuing Cold War, which appeared to be a permanent national emergency, demanded civic discipline that often weakened the very freedoms the nation defended. Democratic victories in the congressional elections of 1956 emboldened liberals like Minnesota's Hubert Humphrey to seek a new domestic agenda. Partly a partisan attack against the Republican administration, partly an effort to preserve New Deal reformism, partly a move away from the southern-dominated congressional leadership, Senate Democrats presented a liberal legislative package in 1957 that included civil rights, public housing, and unemployment insurance. Although few proposals became law, the ideas ignited a major political debate between the two parties.

Republicans were also questioning the price of Cold War vigilance. When Eisenhower unveiled a $73.3 billion budget in 1957, calling for the largest peacetime expenditures in history, administration conservatives warned that the package would cause another depression. Never happy with large federal budgets, the president invited Congress to make cuts. Democrats took the opportunity to embarrass the White House. Yet the reduction of government expenses slowed economic growth, bringing a decline in industrial production and increased unemployment by 1958. Congress quickly restored federal spending and halted the downturn. But the so-called Eisenhower recession weakened the president's standing and added to budgetary deficits.

Waging Peace

In "waging the peace," as Eisenhower later described his Cold War presidency, the White House viewed national security as a legitimate justification for executive actions that concealed policy from citizen scrutiny. When public anxiety about atomic radiation spread through the press in 1953, Eisenhower advised the Atomic Energy Commission to keep the people "confused" about potential hazards. As atomic bomb testing rained fallout through the western states, the AEC steadfastly denied any danger to public health; legal cases in the 1990s suggested otherwise.

Despite frequent televised broadcasts of massive nuclear-bomb explosions, the White House kept the public uninformed about the country's tremendous buildup of a military arsenal. New weapons included the miniaturization of thermonuclear warheads that fit onto supersonic missiles, the stationing of intermediate-range missiles in western Europe, and the construction of intercontinental ballistic missiles (ICBMs) that could carry nuclear payloads to the Soviet Union in minutes. By the end of the decade, a large popular literature depicted the terrors and risks of nuclear warfare. Nevil Shute's *On the Beach* (1957) and Walter Miller's *A Canticle for Leibowitz* (1959) forecast the annihilation of civilization, a prospect that no longer seemed like science fiction. Such feelings inspired the first public demonstrations against continued nuclear testing, civil-defense drills, and the international arms race.

Eisenhower also deceived the public about his handling of the Soviet threat, fearing that revelations would compromise the nation's intelligence apparatus. Concerned about a surprise nuclear attack, the president proposed an "open skies" program in 1955 that would permit inspection flights over each country. When the Soviet Union rejected the plan, Eisenhower implemented the project anyway, in secret, violating Soviet air space. Beginning in 1956, the CIA organized high-flying reconnaissance flights by U-2 airplanes to photograph Soviet military installations and locate potential targets. The U-2 took air samples to measure radioactive fallout and tested Soviet radar defenses. Such information proved extremely useful, enabling the Pentagon to reduce military programs and save over $2 billion.

The Space Race

While U.S. spy flights remained secret, the Soviet Union found another way to penetrate American air space. On October 4, 1957, Moscow stunned the world by announcing the successful launch of the first artificial earth satellite, "Sputnik." Circling the globe from outer space while transmitting a steady electronic beep that awed citizens of earth, Sputnik demonstrated the power of Soviet rocketry, the possibility of missile warfare, and aerial surveillance of U.S. defenses. Aware of the nation's growing missile capabilities, Eisenhower felt no panic at the news, and he permitted the U-2s to continue tracking Soviet activities. When civilian pilots reported sightings of mysterious aircraft, the CIA offered vague explanations about weather phenomena, misleading the public and contributing to conspiracy theories about UFOs. Meanwhile, in the broad light of network television, the Navy's effort to launch a Vanguard rocket fizzled on the ground. By early 1958, the Army's Jupiter rocket launched the first U.S. satellite, a 30-pounder that Soviet leaders scorned as a "grapefruit."

Responding to Soviet advances, Eisenhower appointed a White House science advisory committee consisting of academic scientists, who for the first time could give the president authoritative information about technological issues. High on their agenda was the question of whether remote equipment could adequately monitor Soviet nuclear testing. Mustering public support for a space program, Congress created the National Aeronautics and Space Administration (NASA) in 1958 to oversee civilian space exploration and doubled the funding of research and development for missiles and satellites. In 1959, NASA unveiled Project Mercury, introducing the first seven "astronauts," who would try to beat the Soviet "cosmonauts" in the "space race." Congress also funded the National Defense Education Act in 1958 to encourage the study of math and science and stimulate students to enter the field of teaching.

Chilling the Cold War

The shock waves of Sputnik reverberated with fresh Soviet threats. As U.S. and Soviet bomb tests reached megaton levels, Soviet leader Nikita Khrushchev demanded that the former Allied powers officially sign peace treaties with both East and West Germany and depart from Berlin. But Eisenhower refused to alter the European balance of power and warned the Soviets not to overestimate "Western weakness." Both superpowers spoke publicly of World War III. But neither Khrushchev nor Eisenhower wanted war, and in 1958 the two leaders agreed to engage in personal diplomacy to ease tensions and order a suspension of nuclear bomb tests.

Grievances still abounded, not least being the Soviet willingness to support the new communist regime in Cuba led by Fidel Castro. Angered by Castro's agrarian reforms, which nationalized U.S. corporate property, Eisenhower retaliated with economic sanctions against Cuba's sugar exports and ordered the CIA to begin planning an invasion of the island to overthrow the communist regime. Despite this aggressive response, there were positive signs that the thaw in international relations might continue. By 1958, both Soviet and U.S. scientists agreed that distant seismographs could adequately monitor nuclear testing, eliminating the need for controversial onsite inspections. As Eisenhower and Khrushchev prepared for a summit meeting in Paris in 1960, both

The charismatic Fidel Castro established a revolutionary government in Cuba in 1959 and proceeded to offend U.S. leaders by nationalizing corporate property.

powers anticipated that friendly negotiations could result in a lasting nuclear test ban and possibly even the first stages of disarmament.

Such optimism vanished with news of a plane crash in May 1960: a Soviet missile had shot down a U-2 spy plane. Washington denied the charge, claiming that a weather plane had strayed off course. Khrushchev answered by producing the surviving pilot, Francis Gary Powers, as proof of U.S. intrigue. Eisenhower, publicly embarrassed by the fiasco, struggled to recover his diplomatic position. To deny responsibility for the flight would enable Eisenhower to escape Russian scorn but would open the president to election-year charges that he had lost control of his administration.

Eisenhower reluctantly accepted his responsibility. "It is a distasteful but vital necessity," he said, reminding the public of the need to be vigilant against surprise attacks. Yet the president's honesty ruined the summit conference; Khrushchev refused to negotiate.

The U-2 fiasco underscored the frustrations of Cold War policy. Eisenhower's clumsy diplomacy had thwarted hopes of ending nuclear competition. Worse, the president of the United States, who for eight years had endeavored to rise above party conflict, had lied both to the Soviet Union and to U.S. citizens about sensitive issues of war and peace—and been caught. White House secrecy on grounds of the national security suggested that federal power was no longer accountable to the public. The problem—what the media would later call the "credibility gap" between the government and the citizenry—undermined the consensus that controlled U.S. politics during the 1950s.

Dissenting from the Consensus

Outside the political arena, seeds of discontent began to blossom in painting, music, literature, and popular culture. After World War II, a dynamic group of "abstract expressionist" painters (Jackson Pollack, Willem de Kooning, Mark Rothko) used bold nonrepresentational color and line that forced viewers to find their own meanings in the works. Larry Rivers's blurry version of *Washington Crossing the Delaware* (1953) snorted at old-fashioned patriotism. New forms of bebop jazz, played by saxophonist Charlie Parker and trumpeters Dizzy Gillespie and Miles Davis, expressed a frantic energy that defied musical restraints and transcended iambic lyrics.

Bebop sounds echoed in the rhythm of "Beat" poetry. "I saw the best minds of my generation destroyed by madness," asserted the poet Allan Ginsberg in 1955, reading his poem "Howl" in

San Francisco. Long, open lines, reminiscent of Walt Whitman, scorned a sterile, materialist society and condemned "the scholars of war" who had created "demonic industries" and "monstrous bombs." Like Whitman, the bearded Ginsberg celebrated a mystical spiritualism, but also the human body, mind-expanding drugs, and homosexual experience. The book's appearance in San Francisco brought police censorship on grounds of obscenity, leading to a well-publicized trial and acquittal in 1957. Other Beat writers, including Jack Kerouac, William Burroughs, and Gary Snyder, played at the borderline between religious vision and psychological collapse. Their work celebrated spontaneity and nonconformity; they glorified psychic exploration, raw experience, and visionary insight. The Beats would provide direct links to counterculture forms in the next decade.

On more popular levels, contemporary humor, articulated in a jazz soloist style by stand-up comedians like Lenny Bruce, Mort Sahl, and Dick Gregory, bitterly satirized middle-class prejudices and conventional politics. Mainstream media labeled them subversive and sick. Meanwhile, high school students discovered a new range of irrationality in the aptly named *Mad* magazine, which targeted the pillars of society: family, religion, chastity, and advertising. Such dissidence expressed explosive fires burning beneath the facade of corporate tranquility.

The Legacy of the Cold War Consensus

The excitement of artists, musicians, poets, and comedians made slight contact with the political establishment. Critics of middle-class conformity, civil rights activists, rock 'n' roll lyricists, and Beat poets scarcely altered the status quo, but their dis-

contents testified to the myopia of the national leadership. By 1960, the United States had waged the Cold War against a communist enemy that purportedly threatened every aspect of national life. Yet victory was nowhere in sight. Worse, the vigilance demanded by the endless conflict seemed to be numbing the nation's democratic idealism.

The same Cold War that terrorized the homefront had fueled a decade of tremendous economic growth. As Washington pumped billions of dollars into defense budgets, nearly 10 percent of all domestic jobs depended on federal spending. Eisenhower himself warned, in 1960, that the resulting military-industrial complex had created a self-perpetuating momentum: cold warriors believed that no expense was too great for national security; conversely, any reductions in military spending would disrupt the nation's defense and imperil domestic prosperity. Such logic justified the administration's refusal to divert federal funds to address other issues of social concern such as poverty, education, or aid to the elderly. Thus Cold War prosperity continued to spread unevenly, leaving fully 20 percent of the people impoverished. Those who did not share in the middle-class affluence remained largely invisible to the Republican leadership. Such groups would surface in the next decade, however, providing further evidence of the limits of the Cold War consensus.

INFOTRAC® COLLEGE EDITION EXERCISES

For additional reading go to InfoTrac College Edition, your online research library at *http://web1.infotrac-college.com*.

Keyword search: Dwight Eisenhower

Keyword search: John Foster Dulles

Keyword search: National Security Act

Keyword search: Brown decision
Subject search: Central High School
Subject search: space race

ADDITIONAL READING

Republicans Come to Washington

Stephen E. Ambrose, *Eisenhower* (1984). This detailed
biography describes national politics from the White
House perspective. For a contrasting view, see Blanche
Weisen Cook, *The Declassified Eisenhower* (1981).

Confronting the Red Scare

Jeff Broadwater, *Eisenhower and the Anti-Communist
Crusade* (1992). This study of domestic policies
stresses Ike's moderation and flexibility.

Waging the Cold War

Gordon H. Chang, *Friends and Enemies: The United
States, China, and the Soviet Union: 1948–1972* (1990).
Based on fresh archival material, this study places U.S.
policy in the context of Sino-Soviet conflict.

Walter Lafeber, *America, Russia, and the Cold War*
(1985). A balanced study of foreign policy issues.

Crisis in Indochina

James R. Arnold, *The First Domino: Eisenhower, the
Military, and America's Intervention in Vietnam* (1991).
The author provides a balanced analysis of U.S. policy
in Asia.

Work and Gender

Jessica Weiss, *To Have and to Hold: Marriage, the Baby
Boom, and Social Change* (2000). This sociological
study places postwar families in historical perspective;
see also Elaine Tyler May, *Homeward Bound: American
Families in the Cold War Era* (1988).

Peter Biskind, *Seeing Is Believing: How Hollywood
Taught Us to Stop Worrying and Love the Fifties* (1983).

An analysis of popular films, the book illuminates hidden tensions within the domestic consensus.

Lynn Spigel, *Make Room for TV: Television and the
Family Ideal in Postwar America* (1992). Looking at
social values and television programming, the book
explores the impact of the newest mass medium on
social life.

The Origins of the Civil Rights Movement

Pete Daniel, *Lost Revolutions: The South in the 1950s*
(2000). A study of postwar southern society, the book
examines economic change, popular culture, and race
relations.

Challenging Separate but Equal

Richard Kluger, *Simple Justice* (1976). A thorough history of *Brown v. Board of Education,* this book places
the legal ruling in social context. See too the brief
biography, Douglas Brinkley, *Rosa Parks* (2000).

Black Protest, White Resistance, Federal Action

Taylor Branch, *Parting the Waters: America in the King
Years, 1954–1963* (1988). A full study of the civil
rights movement, emphasizing the role of Martin
Luther King, Jr.

Clayborne Carson, ed., *The Papers of Martin Luther
King, Jr.: Birth of a New Age* (1997). The third volume
of King's personal correspondence highlights the
Montgomery boycott.

The Space Race

Walter A. McDougall, *The Heavens and the Earth: A
Political History of the Space Age* (1985). Comparing
Soviet and U.S. support of science and technology, the
author presents a detailed analysis of the space race.

Dissenting from the Consensus

Daniel Belgrad, *The Culture of Spontaneity: Improvisation
and the Arts in Postwar America* (1998). A study of ideas,
the book emphasizes dissident movements of the 1950s.

26

Advancing a Liberal Agenda, 1960–1963

CHRONOLOGY

1960   African American students use sit-in protests against segregation

Congress passes a modest Civil Rights Act

John F. Kennedy narrowly defeats Richard Nixon

1961   CORE begins "Freedom Rides"

Cuba's Fidel Castro thwarts U.S. invasion at Bay of Pigs

Kennedy starts Peace Corps

U.S. sends military advisors to Vietnam

1962   Astronaut John Glenn circles the earth

Joseph Heller publishes *Catch 22*

Young radicals form Students for a Democratic Society (SDS)

James Meredith integrates University of Mississippi

Soviet missiles provoke Cuban nuclear crisis

1963   Betty Friedan publishes *The Feminine Mystique*

Rachel Carson publishes *Silent Spring*

Kurt Vonnegut publishes *Cat's Cradle*

SCLC organizes protests in Birmingham

Congress passes Equal Pay Act

Civil rights leaders summon March on Washington

U.S. supports coup against South Vietnam's Ngo Dinh Diem

Sniper kills Kennedy in Dallas

"Somehow the mood is beginning to change," wrote liberal essayist Arthur M. Schlesinger, Jr., at the dawn of the 1960s. "People—not everyone by a long way, but enough to disturb the prevailing mood—seem to seek a renewal of conviction, a new sense of national purpose."

Norman Mailer, author of the acclaimed novel *The Naked and the Dead* (1948), saw in 1960 that the country stood at a critical crossroads. "Americans have been leading a double life, and our history has moved on two rivers, one visible, one underground," he wrote in an essay about the 1960 Democratic party convention. "There has been a history of politics which is concrete, factual, practical and unbelievably dull . . . ; and there is a subterranean river of untapped, ferocious, lonely desires, that concentration of ecstasy and violence which is the dream life of the nation."

By then, an energetic youth culture, nourished on rock 'n' roll, was looking critically at middle class values, breaking taboos, and creating what observers would later call "the sexual revolution." The times, affirmed Bob Dylan, the decade's premier songwriter-poet, were "a-changin'."

http://history.wadsworth.com

No politician appeared to contain the cultural contradictions of the age. The 1960 presidential election, pitting Vice President Richard M. Nixon against Massachusetts Senator John F. Kennedy, expressed cautious expectations. For the first time, both candidates were born in the 20th century; both served as Navy officers during World War II and both promised to lead the nation to a "new frontier." Yet neither candidate questioned the structure of postwar society or the vigorous pursuit of the Cold War. Nor, despite Schlesinger's optimism, did an overwhelming majority of citizens seek social change or cultural renewal. As the generation that fought in World War II approached middle age and prepared their baby boomers for college and corporate jobs, few anticipated the birth of the most tumultuous decade of the century.

By 1960, a generation younger than Mailer and Schlesinger, Kennedy and Nixon, was beginning to come of age. The baby boomers were still too young to affect the country's political culture. But a slightly older age group—the children born just before World War II, who included guitarist-singer Bob Dylan, student activist Tom Hayden, novelist Ken Kesey, and essayist Susan Sontag—attempted to bridge the two rivers of 20th-century American culture. They wrote both about the sober politics of power and, in Mailer's words, "the dream life of the nation." Their efforts would challenge the prevailing political and cultural consensus, and by the end of the decade would inspire a previously unimagined conflict of values among many dissident groups.

Kennedy's New Frontier

The charisma of a young politician ignited the new decade. "The American people are tired of the drift of our national course," said presidential contender Kennedy. In contrast to the grandfatherly Eisenhower, who at 70 was then the oldest man to hold the nation's highest office, the 42-year-old Kennedy possessed a movie star's glamour, a Harvard education, his banker father's wealth, and a sharp Irish wit, managing to conceal serious chronic illnesses that imperiled his longevity. In the Senate, Kennedy attacked Eisenhower for creating a "missile gap" between U.S. and Soviet weapons. "This is not a call for despair," said Kennedy. "It is a call for action." In his acceptance speech to the Democratic party, the candidate proclaimed the coming of a New Frontier.

Kennedy's most formidable obstacle to election was his religion. The first Roman Catholic presidential candidate since Al Smith had lost in 1928, Kennedy confronted widespread religious bigotry. His chief rival for the Democratic nomination, liberal Hubert Humphrey, used the theme song "Give Me That Old Time Religion" during the Democratic primary in largely Protestant West Virginia, and Protestant ministers in both parties warned of the perils of Catholic leadership. But the candidate also benefited from the changing political climate after World War II, which accepted equal rights for white ethnics. Facing the religious issue directly, Kennedy demanded his birthright as a citizen. In the end, however, ethnic prejudices prevailed. Kennedy would win a high proportion of Catholic voters, but lose even more votes among Protestants—with the single exception of Protestant African Americans.

Civil rights played a small but significant role in the 1960 contest. As the student-led sit-in protests spread in 1960 from Greensboro, North Carolina, through the segregated South, both parties competed for black votes. Vice President Nixon, riding Eisenhower's coattails, hoped to restore African Americans to the Republican ranks and endorsed a civil rights plank in the party platform. But Nixon feared offending white voters and avoided any formal commitments, even denying his loose ties to the NAACP. Kennedy, by contrast, identified with the idealism of African American protest. "It is in the American tradition to stand up for one's rights," he remarked in a cultivated dismissal of race prejudice, "even if the new way is to sit down."

Only once in the campaign did issues of race move to the forefront. Three weeks before the election, Martin Luther King, Jr., joined other blacks in trying to desegregate a restaurant in Atlanta, Georgia, and was arrested for trespassing. After refusing bail, King was sent to jail, a dangerous situation that alarmed his supporters. Kennedy then made a much-publicized telephone call to calm the minister's wife, Coretta Scott King, and Kennedy aides worked behind the scenes to gain King's release. Evangelical African Americans, who otherwise expressed suspicion of Kennedy's Catholic religion, now turned to the Democratic leader. In the end, blacks would give Kennedy about 70 percent of their votes.

Religion assumed such importance in 1960 because the differences between the candidates appeared so slight. Both Nixon and Kennedy endorsed the Cold War, quibbling only about whether the United States should intervene militarily to keep the tiny islands, Quemoy and Matsu, near Taiwan, from capture by communist China. Nixon took credit for the Eisenhower era of prosperity; Kennedy said "We can do better." Rather than becoming a battle over issues, the campaign focused on four nationally televised debates that drew 100 million viewers. Paying more attention to the candidates' images (their physical appearance and gestures), viewers rated Kennedy the more appealing. (Radio audiences preferred Nixon.) Moreover, in contrast to past political commercials that showed "talking heads" exclusively, Kennedy's campaign introduced

For the first time, electronic images significantly influenced voters' decisions.

a dynamic montage of photographic displays backed by popular music and the voice of singer Frank Sinatra. For the first time, electronic images significantly influenced voters' decisions.

These intangible factors became important because the balloting was so close. Kennedy's popular majority amounted to 118,000 votes—one-tenth of 1 percent. His vice-presidential running mate, Texas's Lyndon Johnson, barely carried his home state. In Illinois, the party's small majority probably resulted from voting fraud in Chicago. Kennedy also trailed congressional Democrats, who retained majorities in both houses. Yet southern Democrats, who now chaired 10 of 17 committees in the Senate, and 13 of 21 in the House, favored few domestic reforms. They would subsequently join Republicans in blocking many administration proposals.

Celebrating Technology

Kennedy's sophisticated television style—calm, cool, detached—mirrored his enthusiasm for technological management, detached analysis, and cold reason. Scorning "passionate movements," which had aroused political debate in the past, the president insisted that government involved "technical problems [,] . . . administrative problems," which required rational solutions. Secretary of Defense Robert S. McNamara, former head of the Ford Motor Company, epitomized the new leadership. To supervise the soaring Pentagon budgets, McNamara introduced bottom-line "cost-benefit"

The televised presidential debates portrayed Nixon in the worst possible light. His heavy five o'clock shadow and pasty makeup, in contrast to Kennedy's image of self-confidence, may have lost him as many as 4 million votes.

accounting to establish procurement priorities and military strategies. Rejecting Eisenhower's "massive retaliation," Kennedy opted for "flexible response," which included a rapid buildup of missiles and nuclear warheads, as well as conventional weapons for "brushfire" wars, and the creation of an elite Special Forces ("Green Berets") for guerrilla action. Meanwhile, the miniaturization of technology had restored U.S. preeminence in the missile war.

Inheriting Eisenhower's "space race" with the Soviet Union, Kennedy called for a human landing on the moon by the end of the decade. "No single space project," he exhorted, "will be more impressive to mankind." As the space agency developed plans for Project Mercury's circumnavigation of the earth, federal appropriations increased

fivefold to $5 billion, amounting to 78 percent of federal-funded research and development programs. After NASA launched two suborbital flights in 1961, astronaut John Glenn circled the earth three times in 1962, boosting public confidence in the space program. "This is the new ocean," said Kennedy, and he demanded that the country be "second to none." Yet, while the media celebrated the glamor of space adventure, government expenditures served primarily military functions, including ballistic missiles, intelligence satellites, and global communications. Nevertheless, the administration defended private ownership of federally funded communications systems and defeated an anti-corporation filibuster by senators seeking to strengthen federal oversight of the communications industry.

The Election of 1960

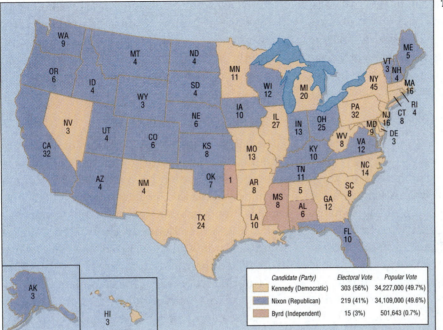

Candidate (Party)	Electoral Vote	Popular Vote
Kennedy (Democratic)	303 (56%)	34,227,000 (49.7%)
Nixon (Republican)	219 (41%)	34,109,000 (49.6%)
Byrd (Independent)	15 (3%)	501,643 (0.7%)

Waging War on New Frontiers

The success of the space program boosted public morale in the global competition against the communist powers. Kennedy's militant inaugural speech had focused entirely on foreign policy. Describing the nation at "its hour of maximum danger," the president pledged to "pay any price, bear any burden, meet any hardship, support any friend, oppose any foe to assure the survival and the success of liberty." Such absolute commitments showed a cold warrior's willingness to accept, if necessary, "mankind's final war." Accordingly, under Kennedy the Cold War would reach new levels of international tension and terror, and yet remain cloaked in the rhetoric of liberal idealism.

"Ask not what your country can do for you," advised Kennedy in his inaugural address. "Ask what

> **"Ask not what your country can do for you. Ask what you can do for your country."**

you can do for your country." Tapping the idealism of the nation's youth, the president announced the creation of a Peace Corps in 1961. By bringing technology, capitalism, and education to poorer countries around the world, citizen volunteers would engage in "a mission of freedom" in the struggle against communist influence. The president's Food for Peace program exported surplus agricultural goods to feed the world's poor, sustaining 93 million people per day by 1963. Kennedy also unveiled "a new alliance for progress" to provide technical assistance and capital investment in Latin America. Such programs revealed a mixture of benevolence and self-interest, boosting both political prestige and international trade. Despite glowing presidential language, these policies deliberately did not challenge the existing social or political inequality of third world countries.

Kennedy versus Castro

U.S. promises of economic assistance to Latin America challenged the revolutionary promises of communism, particularly those of the socialist regime installed by Fidel Castro in Cuba in 1959. Just before leaving office, Eisenhower had broken diplomatic relations with the Castro government and had instructed the CIA to plan a military attack against Cuba, just 90 miles from the Florida coast. Kennedy supported both policies. By 1961, the president recommended a business boycott and prohibited the importation of Cuban sugar. Three months after taking office, Kennedy endorsed plans for an invasion of the island by CIA-trained Cuban exiles at the Bay of Pigs on the southern coast of Cuba, but he withheld formal military assistance. He also concealed his intentions from the public. When the attack began in April 1961, poor planning and tactical failures brought disaster as the Cuban army thwarted the invasion and took many Cuban American prisoners.

The president accepted responsibility for the failed invasion, but expressed no remorse for the Big Stick operation. Summarizing the administration's Cold War logic, he declared, "We are opposed around the world by a monolithic and ruthless conspiracy that relies primarily on covert means for expanding its sphere of influence." Such assumptions justified lying to the press and the public about U.S. policy toward Cuba. "Every democracy," the president told a conference of journalists, "recognizes the necessary restraints of national security." Kennedy approved other secret CIA operations against Castro, including consulting with professional gangsters to assassinate the Cuban leader. Such tactics misled the public and drew Cuba closer to the Soviet orbit.

Contesting with Khrushchev

The failure of the Bay of Pigs invasion weakened Kennedy's efforts to negotiate the Cold War in Europe. Shortly after his inauguration, the president had persuaded Congress to approve additional military funding to strengthen his diplomatic position. But when Kennedy confronted Premier Khrushchev in Vienna that spring, the arms buildup intensified their mutual mistrust. Instead of resolving differences about the division of Germany, both leaders returned home to resume military development. Kennedy asked Congress for larger military appropriations, called up the military reserves, and extended the draft. As the White House requested funds to construct bomb shelters in anticipation of nuclear war, Khrushchev ordered the erection of a fortified barrier separating East and West Berlin.

Kennedy soon tested Soviet resolve. Responding to Khrushchev's threat, the president ordered 1,500 battle-ready soldiers to move from West Germany into West Berlin. The world waited anxiously for a military showdown. Khrushchev made no move, but soon afterward he lifted the deadline for settling the Berlin question. Yet Khrushchev also announced the resumption of nuclear bomb testing, and Kennedy saw "no other choice" but to do the same.

This confrontation between the nuclear powers aroused new concerns. For the first time since the beginning of the Cold War in the 1940s, a multitude of peace organizations, including the National Committee for a Sane Nuclear Policy (SANE) and the Student Peace Union, pleaded with the administration for restraint. Yet Washington intensified Soviet concerns by revealing that U.S. intelligence had discovered their military weakness. Neither side would consider disarmament, which might alter what Kennedy called "the uncertain balance of terror."

The Cuban Missile Crisis

Fear of nuclear weakness now set the world on the road to genuine catastrophe. Responding to Castro's pleas for support, and to check U.S. nuclear superiority, Soviet troops began to build bases in Cuba in the summer of 1962 for missiles with a striking range of 2,000 miles, capable of reaching most Atlantic cities and the Panama Canal. The Soviets also introduced nearly 100 nuclear warheads, most attached to tactical rockets with a range of twenty miles, though the United States did not learn of their existence until the 1990s. By the fall of 1962, U-2 surveillance planes had discovered the missile sites. Contrary to Soviet assurances to Washington, these missiles were not defensive weapons, but offensive missiles that could be deployed against North American targets.

To analyze the options, Kennedy summoned an emergency planning committee, which included McNamara, Secretary of State Dean Rusk, Attorney General Robert Kennedy, U.N. Ambassador Adlai Stevenson, and members of the Joint Chiefs of Staff. Their discussions, which were secretly tape-recorded and published in the 1990s, revealed the high stakes of nuclear diplomacy. Some policy makers advocated an immediate military attack aimed at Cuba or Moscow; others recommended removing U.S. missiles from Turkey as a way of reaching a negotiated settlement. Many feared that a confrontation in Cuba would explode into a nuclear holocaust. Underlying all the choices was a belief that Soviet weapons in the Western Hemisphere imperiled the nation's security and were not acceptable.

As the president's advisors contemplated actions that could lead to nuclear war, their comments revealed anxiety as well as rational calculation. One civil defense expert explained to Kennedy that Soviet missiles made 92 million citizens vulnerable to attack, but shelters might protect only 40 million. Later, the president asked an obvious but embarrassing question: If the Soviet Union already possessed intercontinental missiles capable of destroying the entire Western Hemisphere, what difference did the Cuban missiles make? "They've got enough to blow us up anyway." The answer had to do not with military power, but with the image of power and the effects of that image on international relations with other countries. "This is a political struggle as much as military," said Kennedy. Capitulation to Khrushchev in Cuba, one advisor explained, "did not substantially alter the strategic balance of power *in fact*," but changed the balance "*in appearance*; and in matters of national will and world leadership . . . such appearances contribute to reality."

Kennedy broke the news to the public in a dramatic television address in October 1962. "We will not . . . risk the cost of worldwide nuclear war in which the fruits of victory would be ashes in our mouth," he vowed, "but neither will we shrink from that risk at any time it must be faced." As the superpowers prepared for a nuclear war, the president ordered a naval blockade around Cuba to prevent the landing of additional weapons. Surprised by Kennedy's militant response, Khrushchev rushed to defuse the crisis. "Only a madman," he wrote to the president, "can believe that armaments are the principal means in the life of a society." When Kennedy agreed privately to remove U.S. missiles in Turkey and to permit Castro to remain in power, Khrushchev retreated publicly, ordering the removal of Soviet missiles from Cuba.

The world breathed a sigh of relief. But while Kennedy claimed to have achieved a great diplomatic victory, the White House breached the agreement and supported efforts to remove Castro through secret means, including assassination.

The missile crisis—the closest brush with nuclear war in history—convinced both superpowers to limit needless confrontations. The installation of a hotline telephone as a means of instant communications between Washington and Moscow aimed at stopping an accidental war. Meanwhile, a political split between the Soviet Union and China altered the international picture. As the People's Republic prepared for its first nuclear bomb test, both Khrushchev and Kennedy hoped to minimize the Chinese threat. Although the Soviets still refused to permit on-site inspections in their country to verify compliance with a test ban, Kennedy learned that satellite photography and seismographic data provided sufficient protections.

"We all inhabit this same planet. We all breathe the same air," said Kennedy in a bold speech at American University in June 1963, in which he announced his willingness to sign a treaty banning atmospheric tests of nuclear weapons. "We all cherish our children's future. And we all are mortal." He pleaded to make the world "safe for diversity." Three months later, the Senate ratified the document, the first limitation of the nuclear arms race, though underground testing continued and the nuclear arsenal of both powers continued to grow.

Competing for the Third World

Although traditional diplomacy sometimes resolved superpower conflicts, Kennedy believed that global supremacy depended on increasing U.S. influence among the smaller nations of the world. "The great battlefield for the defense and expansion of freedom," he remarked in 1961, "is the whole southern half of the globe . . . the lands of the rising peoples." Yet, in this so-called Third World, U.S. multinational corporations conducted business primarily with local elites who dominated their countries. As increasing exports of military weapons and supplies to foreign governments helped the economy maintain a positive balance of payments and international trade, these materials often served to strengthen undemocratic regimes. Corporate leaders showed no interest in the majority population of the developing nations. When their impoverished people demanded social reform or economic improvements, Third World leaders typically adopted Cold War language and blamed the protests on communist subversion (just as southern governors would claim that civil rights protests were communist-inspired).

The Cold War perspective had blinded post–World War II presidents to the local causes of social unrest in the third world. Thus the State Department blamed China and the Soviet Union for instigating the Korean war, misunderstanding the primary role of North Korean nationalists. In the Philippines, the United States treated the indigenous Huk revolutionaries as Moscow's puppets and supported the anti-communist but undemocratic government. In the Middle East, Washington viewed nationalist movements as communist threats to vital oil reserves. Like his predecessors, Kennedy saw nationalist trends in Latin America and Asia as incipient communist attacks, which were, as he put it in 1961, "nibbling away" at the borders of freedom.

Making Commitments in Vietnam

Having failed to overthrow the Castro government in Cuba, Kennedy resolved to stop communist expansion in southeast Asia. In 1961, the White House managed to reach agreement with the Soviets to establish a neutral regime in Laos. But the administration proved less flexible in managing the continuing crisis in Vietnam. By 1961, the United States was supporting a separate South Vietnamese government led by the Catholic Ngo Dinh Diem and opposing the North Vietnamese communist government led by Ho Chi Minh. Diem welcomed U.S. military assistance in the war against communism, but rejected pressure for land reform or political democracy. Hostile to all dissidents—both the communist National Liberation Front, known as the Viet Cong, and noncommunist Buddhist priests—Diem ran a dictatorship that disregarded democratic rights.

By 1961, the Viet Cong were increasing attacks against the government in Saigon, ultimately seeking the national unification promised by the 1954 Geneva Accords (see Chapter 25). Diem requested additional military assistance. Unwilling to commit conventional forces, the White House responded in 1961 by sending military "advisors" to instruct the South Vietnamese army and Green Berets to engage in "counterinsurgency" actions. Public interest in Vietnam remained minimal. Few newspapers had foreign correspondents in the area; not until September 1963 did television network news increase from fifteen minutes to half an hour to allow coverage of such "secondary" stories.

Kennedy never doubted that his true opponents in Vietnam were in the Kremlin and Beijing and that communist "aggression" had to be stopped in southeast Asia. Although he did not entirely share Eisenhower's domino theory (that the fall of one Asian nation to communism would topple the others), he believed it was essential to stop communism in Vietnam, lest such a defeat weaken U.S. credibility in other nations. As U.S.

involvement escalated from 750 soldiers in 1961 to over 16,000 two years later, the number of military actions increased. Yet a clear victory seemed uncertain. To undermine Viet Cong support in the countryside, military advisors introduced in 1962 the "strategic hamlet" plan, which required concentration of the peasant population into barbed wire encampments (one presidential advisor called it "accelerated urbanization") to prevent their contact with anti-Diem guerrillas. But the strategy could not isolate the omnipresent Viet Cong, and otherwise loyal peasants objected to the forced uprooting.

The Kennedy administration expressed frustration at Diem's failure to wage an aggressive war against the Viet Cong or to initiate social reforms to weaken the enemy's support. But for public consumption, Washington insisted that the military effort was succeeding. "Every quantitative measure we have," boasted Secretary McNamara, "shows we're winning this war." Yet State Department reports of 30,000 of the enemy killed in 1962 exceeded the estimated size of the Viet Cong army at the beginning of the war. Such self-deceptions were not accidental. Kennedy wanted neither to be accused by Republicans of losing the war in Asia nor to become embroiled in a repetition of a Korean-style stalemate. When *New York Times* reporter David Halberstam described obvious failures of military policy, Kennedy personally asked the nation's most prestigious newspaper to give the journalist another assignment.

By 1963, the Viet Cong insurgents, who took strategic orders and military assistance from North Vietnam, were increasing terrorist attacks in South Vietnam's villages and cities. Meanwhile, South Vietnam's Buddhists were protesting Diem's political oppression. Tensions exploded in Saigon when South Vietnamese troops fired on a crowd of anti-government protesters. To embarrass the Diem

During the Kennedy presidency, Secretary of Defense Robert McNamara ably defended U.S. military commitments in Vietnam.

Buddhist priests publicly set themselves afire in filmed political suicides that shocked world opinion.

regime, Buddhist priests publicly set themselves afire in filmed political suicides that shocked world opinion. Washington pleaded with South Vietnam's leader to initiate political reform to strengthen the anti-communist cause. Diem ignored those pleas. Yet given the Cold War agenda, Kennedy could not abandon the embattled nation. "For us to withdraw from that effort," the president explained, "would mean a collapse not only of South Vietnam but Southeast Asia. So we are going to stay there."

Nevertheless, the administration also feared that Diem might institute private negotiations with North Vietnam and seek a truce that would keep him in power. Worried that the government of South Vietnam would abandon the war and jeopardize U.S. prestige, the administration made secret plans to replace the Diem leadership. With U.S. backing, a group of South Vietnamese army officers staged a coup d'etat against Diem, killing the dictator on November 2, 1963.

Although Kennedy approved a change of power in Saigon, the murder of Diem stunned him. But it did not change his policy toward the war. Although the president had announced the withdrawal of 1,000 troops by the end of the year and declared that the U.S. commitment in Vietnam would end in 1965, Kennedy was merely expressing the false optimism that encouraged intervention in the first place. One week after Diem's death, Washington cabled the new government in Saigon, "we cannot envision any points that would be negotiable." In other words, Washington would not accept a political compromise with Vietnam's communists. Twelve days later, in what would have been Kennedy's last speech in Dallas, the president's words read: "Our assistance to . . . nations can be painful, risky and costly, as is true in Southeast Asia today. But we dare not weary of the task." Subsequent claims that Kennedy was planning to end the war in Vietnam—or that such "plans" led to his murder—are not supported by the historical record.

Creating the Domestic Agenda

Kennedy's bold initiatives in global affairs contrasted with his caution about domestic policy. When he entered office in 1961, opinion polls found that 42 percent of the public wished for moderate policies, 24 percent wanted a conservative agenda, and 23 percent preferred liberal proposals. This midstream consensus limited political innovation. Moreover, with southern Democrats holding the reins of power in Congress, Kennedy lacked the votes to overcome the political inertia. "There is no sense in raising hell," he remarked, "and then not being successful."

During the 1960 primary in West Virginia, Kennedy had discovered extreme poverty, and he was prepared to offer remedies. By 1962, Michael Harrington's book *The Other America* had increased public awareness of the nation's poor. According to Harrington, 20 percent of the population, consisting of racial minorities, rural whites, and the elderly, inhabited a "culture of poverty." Influenced by this work, Kennedy proposed the creation of an Area Development Agency to stimulate construction of new factories and jobs in depressed regions, such as the mountainous parts of West Virginia and Kentucky that are known as Appalachia. The idea of area redevelopment also extended to fifty-six Native American reservations, where residents hoped that federal funds would replace the economic losses caused by the termination of tribal government (see Chapter 25).

Hopes for a federal anti-poverty program were largely unfulfilled. Although Congress approved Kennedy's proposal, funding remained insufficient to create many jobs. The total in West Virginia reached a mere 350 by 1963. On reservation lands, corporations typically negotiated 99-year leases for natural resources that effectively ended additional federal assistance to residents. Native Americans derided the program as "termination by corporation." Committed to balanced budgets, Congress did not consider poverty a federal concern.

Kennedy's liberal Council of Economic Advisers nevertheless pressed for fiscal reform to stimulate economic development. Following the ideas of British economist John Maynard Keynes, Kennedy's economists, led by Walter Heller, proposed tax cuts to stimulate consumer spending. At a time of increasing federal expenditures for military purposes, a reduction of taxes deliberately created an unbalanced budget. Kennedy initially resisted the idea. But, by 1963, he proposed a program of "deficit spending," calling for nearly $14 billion of tax cuts on individual incomes, as well as reforms to shift the tax burden to people with higher incomes. Passed by Congress the next year, the program stimulated a 7 percent boost in the gross national product, encouraged business investment to increase productivity, and lowered unemployment. In a triumph of liberal ideology, corporate profits jumped 57 percent between 1960 and 1964, apparently demonstrating the government's ability to manage economic growth.

Rights for Blacks and Women

Kennedy's willingness to offer innovative tax policies did not extend to the more contentious issues of civil rights. Despite campaign promises to address problems of discrimination, the president hesitated to challenge the southern leadership in Congress. While running for office, he had criticized Eisenhower for failing to end segregated housing "with the stroke of a pen." When Kennedy did not act on the issue, civil rights activists sent pens to the White House to remind him of his promises, but the president rejected desegregation by executive order. He did use executive powers to create a presidential Committee on Equal Employment Opportunity, thus bypassing its opponents in Congress. Headed by Vice President Lyndon Johnson, the committee tried to end discrimination in work done under government contract, relying on voluntary compliance of contractors. The committee seldom punished violations. Kennedy, meanwhile, appeased southern Democrats with patronage appointments, federal construction jobs, and price supports for cotton.

The White House also gave more government jobs to African Americans than had previous presidents, and permitted blacks to work outside the area of race relations. Among Kennedy's appointees was NAACP counsel Thurgood Marshall, who was named to a federal appellate court; the Senate judiciary committee held up confirmation for a year. African Americans also circulated in Kennedy social activities. The president's brother, Attorney General Robert F. Kennedy, resigned from New York's private Metropolitan Club when it refused his request to admit blacks and Jews. Such symbolic gestures showed the administration's sympathies but did not alter federal policy.

Kennedy paid even less attention to women's rights; he simply did not perceive the changes in women's economic status or the contemporary sexual revolution as political issues. Kennedy appointed no women to his cabinet. But in response to the important changes in women's social posi-

tion since World War II, the president in 1962 appointed a special Commission on the Status of Women, made the elderly Eleanor Roosevelt honorary chair, and requested recommendations for new government policies. The commission proceeded to address the political ramifications of women's new roles in postwar society.

By 1960, 40 percent of adult women were members of the work force, a statistic that was steadily increasing. To be sure, women earned 60 percent of male incomes, worked in sex-segregated jobs, and seldom exercised corporate power. Yet women's educational levels were also rising, as was the age of marriage. After the introduction of the birth control pill in 1960, women obtained greater freedom to have sexual relations without risk of pregnancy. The "new woman," explained the bestselling book *Sex and the Single Girl* (1962), by *Cosmopolitan* editor Helen Gurley Brown, "took the pill and lived in an apartment with a double bed." Increased sexual activity gave some women a sense of independence, although many feminists later argued that sexual liberation often led to exploitation in a society where women still operated at considerable social and economic disadvantage. Meanwhile, married women showed deep dissatisfaction with the lack of choices in their lives. Betty Friedan's manifesto *The Feminine Mystique* (1963) expressed the frustrations of married middle-class women who wanted, beyond marriage and motherhood, meaningful careers.

Discovering remedies proved more controversial. The National Woman's party had first proposed an equal rights amendment to the Constitution during the 1920s and still supported federal laws that would guarantee full equality for both sexes. Like earlier presidents, however, Kennedy listened more to the government's Women's Bureau, which opposed any erosion of labor laws that specifically protected women in the workplace. And when the

Betty Friedan achieved national fame with the publication of *The Feminine Mystique* in 1963. Three years later, she helped found the National Organization for Women.

presidential commission on the Status of Women endorsed provisions for legal equality without regard for sex in 1963, the White House took no steps to implement its proposals. In 1963, Congress did pass the Equal Pay Act, mandating equal compensation for equal work, but the law exempted many jobs and lacked enforcement powers. Congress also ignored the prevailing sex segregation of employment, such as the classification of secretarial (female) work as less important that management (male) work, thus obscuring definitions of "equal work."

Kennedy's minimal interest in the problems of women and blacks reflected the political weakness of both groups. Without women's organized power, the president had no trouble ignoring inequality. On issues of civil rights, Kennedy hoped to limit government intervention to enforce voting rights passed by Congress in 1957 and 1960 (see Chapter 25). Yet his respect of southern white power led Kennedy to appoint segregationist judges to the very federal courts that were responsible for upholding civil rights laws as well as implementation of the *Brown* decision.

Civil Rights Protest

Indignant at Kennedy's indifference, African Americans initiated new forms of nonviolent protest. The principles of civil disobedience aimed not only to awaken the conscience of southern racists but also to arouse the passive leadership in Washington. In 1961, the Congress of Racial Equality (CORE), led by James Farmer, announced a program of "freedom rides" on public buses in the southern states to defy segregation rules in interstate travel. The protests would soon capture national attention.

Although informers told the FBI of impending trouble, Director J. Edgar Hoover issued no warnings to the imperiled riders. In Anniston and Birmingham, Alabama, local police conveniently disappeared just as the integrated buses arrived, allowing violent mobs to attack the civil rights activists. One white Justice Department aide who tried to intervene was beaten unconscious.

Coming on the eve of a presidential summit conference with Soviet leader Nikita Khrushchev, the violence proved an embarrassment to the administration. Kennedy's first reaction was to demand an end to the protest. But freedom riders followed their own conscience and continued their travels. The president then ordered federal marshals to protect the contingent and obtained court injunctions against further interference. Meanwhile, the Justice Department persuaded the Interstate Commerce Commission to issue orders prohibiting segregation in interstate travel.

Even with the spotlight of national media and presidential rhetoric, civil rights protests did not always succeed. In 1961, leaders of the Student Non-Violent Coordinating Committee (SNCC, pronounced "snick") issued desegregation demands in Albany, Georgia, and invited Dr. King to lend publicity to the campaign. Despite non-violent protest tactics, the white Albany leadership avoided public brutality but arrested dozens of protesters, including King, and kept displays of violence outside camera range. "Mind over matter," the local police chief told the activists. "I don't mind and you don't matter." Youthful SNCC leaders resented King's refusal to become more militant. President Kennedy's efforts to encourage negotiations brought no changes. "Even the government," commented one black woman, "is a white man." After a year's protest, the Albany campaign had failed, leaving a bitter generation gap within the civil rights movement.

African American initiatives, countered by southern white obstruction, kept issues of segregation in the spotlight. In 1962, a 28-year-old black Air Force veteran named James Meredith won a court order to attend the all-white University of Mississippi. But the state governor, Ross Barnett, refused to accept the federal order and accused civil rights protesters of communist subversion. Such a threat was surely imaginary, but to the extent that states' rights southern leaders saw big government in Washington changing their society, the perception was apt. The civil

rights movement, backed by military power, indeed threatened to topple the old social order.

Kennedy followed Eisenhower's precedent at Little Rock, federalized the National Guard, and ordered federal marshals to escort Meredith onto the campus at Oxford, Mississippi. An angry mob of students and racists staged a night of violence, setting fires, throwing rocks, and shooting. Two journalists were killed the day Meredith entered the university. Kennedy tried to limit federal involvement to legal protection, yet he recognized that southerners retreated before federal power and that many whites opposed the racist leadership.

SNCC's campaign to register African American voters in the deep South underscored the dangers of civil rights activity. Funded by wealthy northern white foundations and labor unions, SNCC's Voter Education Project aimed to replace literacy tests, which restricted black voting, with universal suffrage. The idea provoked constant local violence, including beatings, bombings, arson, and murder.

Unwilling to enter a legal battle about federal jurisdiction in local criminal proceedings, the administration offered little protection for the civil rights activists. SNCC then accused the federal government of participating in the murderous conspiracy. About Kennedy's inertia, said one black activist, "we lost two years because we admired him." Pressured by northern liberals, Kennedy finally introduced a civil rights bill in February 1963. The measure would make interference with voting rights a federal crime, increase federal funds for school desegregation, and expand the enforcement powers of the Civil Rights Commission.

Birmingham and the Civil Rights Crisis

"We are committed to achieving true equality of opportunity," said Kennedy in 1963, in his first open avowal of the civil rights crusade, "because it is right." By then, African American leaders demanded the dismantling of the entire system of public segregation. "We have reached the point of no return," said Martin Luther King, Jr., as he led the Southern Christian Leadership Conference (SCLC) in a civil rights campaign into Birmingham, Alabama in 1963. The objective was to desegregate the city's downtown business district. Entertainer Harry Belafonte helped enlarge SCLC's bail fund to underwrite the large number of expected arrests. Dr. King was one of the first thrown into jail. During three days of solitary confinement—from Good Friday to Easter Sunday—the minister wrote his poignant "Letter from a Birmingham Jail," in which he articulated the philosophy of nonviolent civil disobedience. Civil rights demonstrators "are not the creators of tension," he declared. "We merely bring to the surface the hidden tension that is already alive. We bring it out in the open, where it can be seen and dealt with."

Released on bail, King directed the crusade to desegregate Birmingham's department stores, where, for instance, African Americans could not try on the clothes they purchased. As noisy nonviolent demonstrators paraded in the streets, police chief Eugene "Bull" Connor ordered mass arrests, which filled the local jails. The SCLC leadership feared that the Birmingham protest might fail, as the Albany Movement had waned the previous year, for want of volunteers to make such sacrifices. Civil rights leaders then turned to the future, selecting recruits among African American children, some as young as six. As the youngsters marched bravely through the streets, police attacked them with high-pressure fire hoses, billy clubs, and German shepherds. National television broadcast these violent images around the country, and the public conscience

shuddered. That month, Alabama Governor George Wallace stood in the doorway of a registration building on the University of Alabama campus, defying, futilely, a federal order to admit black students.

"We face . . . a moral crisis as a country and as a people," Kennedy advised a somber television audience in June 1963. In a passionate but restrained address, the president explained that the issues were "as old as the Scriptures and . . . as clear as the Constitution." He pleaded with white voters to face the self-deception that the country had "no class or caste system, no ghettos, no master race except with respect to Negroes," and he dismissed the logic of asking blacks to "be content with . . . patience and delay." The time had come for change, said Kennedy. As the president introduced a new civil rights bill, he declared that "race has no place in American life or law." That night, a member of the Mississippi Ku Klux Klan murdered civil rights leader Medgar Evers.

The March on Washington

Kennedy's civil rights proposal called for the desegregation of public accommodations, federal authority to sue to integrate public schools, improvement of black employment opportunities, and protection of voting rights. As Congress considered the measure, black leaders proposed a March on Washington to lobby for equal rights and jobs. Fearing that public disturbances might jeopardize the legislation, Kennedy summoned civil rights leaders to the White House to discourage further demonstrations.

The president was not eager for the meeting, believing it would anger southern Democrats. "It's like having [Karl] Marx coming to the White House," he remarked. On a stroll through the Rose Garden with Dr. King, the president warned the civil rights leader that he was under FBI surveillance and advised him to end his relationship with a white supporter who once had been a member of the Communist party. Such candor suggested Kennedy's commitment to civil rights, but it also demonstrated the lingering power of McCarthyism and the precarious position of liberal politicians. King, for his part, proceeded to end his relationship with the tainted friend. Yet civil rights leaders also rebuffed Kennedy's efforts to cancel the mass demonstration.

On August 28, 1963, the diverse civil rights leadership brought 250,000 demonstrators to Washington to affirm support for Kennedy's bill. "I have a dream," King cried to the fervent crowd, "that the sons of former slaves and the sons of former slaveowners will be able to sit together at the table of brotherhood." Another speaker, SNCC's John Lewis, angrily criticized Kennedy for failing to protect civil rights workers and condemned the administration's "immoral compromises" with racist politicians; but Lewis agreed that the passage of civil rights laws should be followed by "the community of love, peace, and true brotherhood."

More militant African American leaders, such as the Black Muslim nationalist Malcolm X, had no opportunity to speak, because the demonstration's organizers still believed in the possibility of harmonious racial integration. But growing numbers of African Americans shared Malcolm X's frustration and impatience. Much depended on how whites responded to black demands for equality. Yet just one month after the March on Washington, a bomb exploded in the basement of a black church in Birmingham, killing four young girls. White police and the FBI made no effort to apprehend the perpetrators. As Congress debated the civil rights laws, leaders of both races questioned the possibility of peaceful integration. Responding to the public mood, the major news media—newspapers, network television and weekly magazines—

A 1966 Gallup opinion poll found that a majority of the public disputed the Warren Commission findings.

began to focus on racism, not as a southern problem but as a national crisis. Many blacks doubted that the white majority would voluntarily seek a solution. "A revolutionary," said Malcolm X defiantly, "is a black nationalist."

Death of a President

Despite the skepticism of many black leaders, the White House continued to push for civil rights legislation, though the president would not live to see the results. On a political trip to Dallas, Texas, to solidify the Democratic party for the next presidential election, Kennedy was shot and killed by sniper fire on November 22, 1963. Police soon arrested Lee Harvey Oswald, once a defector to the Soviet Union, who denied his guilt. But before the accused assassin could testify in court, a local mobster named Jack Ruby killed Oswald while the accused was in police hands. These surprising events created an aura of mystery about the killings and added to public suspicions about politics in the 1960s. Kennedy's successor, Lyndon Johnson, appointed a blue-ribbon committee, headed by Chief Justice Earl Warren, to investigate the murders. The Warren Report, issued just before the 1964 election, stated that Oswald was a "loner" and had killed Kennedy for personal motives. But confusing evidence and conflicting eyewitness accounts sustained public belief in a larger conspiracy. A 1966 Gallup opinion poll found that a majority of the public disputed the Warren Commission findings; but paradoxically, the same majority opposed a reopening of the case.

A Nation Mourns

The assassination, and the ceremonial funeral that followed, froze the country. Anyone old enough to remember the moment could tell exactly what he or she was doing when the news of Kennedy's shooting disrupted the day's activities. Whatever one's political opinion of Kennedy, the patriotic symbolism, the endless television coverage (for three days the networks cancelled all commercial advertising), and the confrontation with violent death brought the public together in a shared emotional experience. Surveys later found that 92 percent of the entire nation learned of the killing within two hours, and millions watched the same broadcasts as the nation laid its president to rest and were watching on television when Ruby murdered Oswald in a Dallas police station.

The mass mourning magnified Kennedy's stature. His grave at Arlington National Cemetery, marked by an eternal flame, became a shrine. Instantly manufactured Kennedy memorabilia—charms, jewelry, photographs, and books—abounded, as stunned citizens purchased commemorative icons of the late president. Yet 1963 Christmas sales were unusually low, reflecting the country's psychological depression. Governments named and renamed public buildings after the dead president. The space center at Cape Canaveral became Cape Kennedy (and, in a geopolitical reversal, became Canaveral again during the Nixon administration). As the nation grappled with public grief, mere politics paled by comparison. Kennedy had created in death what had eluded him in life: a broad cultural consensus that transcended the differences of party politics.

A New Generation

The Kennedy assassination constituted a unique collective experience that idealized the slain president's importance, but the traumatic events especially influenced the attitudes of the younger generation then coming of age. Kennedy's exhortation to "ask what you can do for your country" had inspired a generation of students to volunteer for the Peace Corps, embark on a civil rights crusade, or enlist in the military. Yet the new generation, born and raised in the shadow of atomic bombs and nuclear showdowns, also responded to more ambiguous questions about the country's identity during the 1960s. Kennedy's death inspired feelings of patriotism, but its violence underscored the fragile and perilous condition of human life in the nuclear age.

It was Kennedy's own contemporaries, the generation that fought in World War II, who first questioned the suicidal logic of the Cold War and the nuclear arms race. Replying indirectly to Kennedy's militant rhetoric, novelist Joseph Heller's immensely popular satire *Catch 22* (1962) challenged the validity of any patriotic sacrifices. "What is a country?" he asked. The answer was not merely a joke. "A country is a piece of land surrounded on all sides by boundaries, usually unnatural." The fifty or sixty countries that had recently engaged in a world war, said Heller, "can't *all* be worth dying for"; more to the point, he contended, "anything worth dying for is worth living for." Although a World War II veteran and a generation older than the baby boomers, Heller captured an enthusiastic following among college students by deriding the sheer craziness of a warfare mentality. Survival, not cataclysm, was the novelist's testament for the next generation.

Such dissent percolated through the popular culture during the Kennedy presidency. Like Heller, the novelist Kurt Vonnegut used satire to express his objections to the Cold War consensus. A German-held prisoner of war during World War II, Vonnegut had survived the Allied fire-bombings of Dresden in 1945 and dreaded the prospect of nuclear annihilation. His novel *Cat's Cradle* (1963) attracted a cult following on college campuses. "That's the trouble with the world," he said of the character who invented the atomic bomb: "too many people in high places . . . are stone-cold dead." He, too, repudiated patriotism, suggesting that God's creation "ignores national, institutional, occupational, familial, and class boundaries." Many Hollywood motion pictures continued to glorify the nation's nuclear arsenal (in *A Gathering of Eagles* [1963], for example). But filmmaker Stanley Kubrick, who worked in self-imposed exile in England, attacked the folly of nuclear warfare in his immensely popular satire, *Dr. Strangelove or: How I Learned to Stop Worrying and Love the Bomb* (1964).

These pungent anti-war statements mirrored the feelings of growing numbers of young adults who recoiled from the idea of nuclear confrontation. "We may be the last generation in the experiment with living," declared Tom Hayden in the "Port Huron Statement," the founding document of the radical group Students for a Democratic Society (SDS). Hayden's manifesto attacked the militaristic status quo that had made the Department of Defense "the world's largest single organization." Yet despite the numbing effects of the Cold War, Hayden maintained that a new generation of students was "breaking the crust of apathy."

This generation also embraced the emerging science of ecology, sympathizing with Rachel Carson's bestselling study *Silent Spring* (1963), which warned about the chemical dangers to the natural environment. During the Cuban missile crisis, 21-year-old folk singer–guitarist Bob Dylan wrote "A Hard Rain's Gonna Fall," an anthem against cataclysmic warfare. He later explained that "every line of it is actually the start of a whole song but . . . I thought I wouldn't have enough time alive to write all those songs so I put all I could into this one."

Young adults who experienced the shock of a presidential assassination well understood the vulnerability of human life.

Another young writer who attacked the deadliness of bureaucratic conformity was Ken Kesey. As an employee in the psychiatric ward of a Veterans Administration hospital in California, he had experimented with mind-altering drugs. In his 1963 novel, *One Flew over the Cuckoo's Nest*, Kesey reversed the distinction between madness and sanity, and described impersonal institutions as a threat to human freedom. Kesey, too, developed a mass following during the decade. Susan Sontag wrote for a more esoteric audience, but her literary essays also criticized the overintellectualization of cultural life. She urged audiences "to recover the senses" and allow themselves to experience art and life as they found it. She, too, wrote about images of atomic holocaust and the related anxieties of dehumanization.

These commentators protested against the loss of authentic experiences and pleaded for a human dimension in social institutions. They stressed feelings over-rationality, and humor over reason. Significantly, these Kennedy-era dissidents—Hayden, Dylan, Kesey, and Sontag—were *not* baby boomers born after World War II. Rather, they were slightly older, and their democratic idealism argued strenuously against the stultifying values of American life.

Such incipient change did not belong exclusively to political pundits and cultural critics. Among the most innovative segments of society during the Kennedy era was the nation's advertising industry. With the new decade, Madison Avenue executives introduced what became know as "the creative revolution," a change in management style that relaxed the business atmosphere and encouraged nonconformity, irreverence, authenticity, and humor. "You start out by hiring people who are creative, then give them room to do what they want," advised George Lois, a Greek American who founded one of the most successful agencies of the decade. "We try to hire people who will disagree with us." Like Lois, many of the advertising innovators were white ethnics, the children of immigrants, who brought an outsider's perspective to contemporary trends. Advertising not only touted corporate products but also shaped the outlook of the nation's consumer culture. In this way, the manufacture of public images for products, presidents, and social trends changed what Sontag called the "sensibility" of the times; advertising, in other words, helped invent the nuances and voices that made the 1960s a distinctive decade.

The Myth of "The Sixties"

Kennedy's assassination appeared as a watershed in the history of the decade, a turning point that changed the character of society and culture. Vowing to uphold the slain president's commitment to civil rights legislation, a grieving nation overwhelmingly embraced the principles of racial justice and supported federal laws against segregation. This vision of equal rights appealed especially to the nation's youth. As the first baby boomers turned 18 in 1964 (part of the 24 million youngsters who reached adulthood in the 1960s), the idealism that had attracted only a small minority during the Kennedy years gained strength in numbers. The new generation endorsed other social trends of a liberal nature, including birth control, sexual expressiveness, and greater equality for women. Horrified by visions of nuclear annihilation, this generation rejected the Cold War imperatives that saw communism as so totally evil as to justify nuclear warfare. Most important, the youth

of the 1960s questioned the overriding rationalism of corporate life and its related demands of self-discipline, conformity, and hard work. Instead, they asserted counter values of self-expression, nonconformity, and sheer pleasure.

Because young people were so numerous in the 1960s (in 1969, the nation's median age was still below 30), the new generation stamped its character on the entire decade, creating an enduring image of the Sixties as a time of liberation. But such generalizations ignore three important social groups. First, not all young people supported social change. In 1960, over 100 delegates from forty-four colleges and universities gathered at the estate of conservative leader William F. Buckley and founded Young Americans for Freedom (YAF). "In this time of moral and political crisis," these young conservatives denounced an activist federal government, endorsed a free "market economy," and demanded victory in the war against communism. Besides such outspoken conservatives, probably a majority of young adults accepted the social status quo or were sufficiently apolitical that they ignored questions of social reform.

Second, as we have seen in the Kennedy era, the most powerful members of society belonged to an older generation and largely supported existing policies, including an aggressive pursuit of the Cold War. This older, established generation dominated the nation's political and economic life through the decade. Finally, as the 1960 election demonstrated, the adult population was itself divided about equally between conservatives who rejected change and liberals who supported some reforms. Most adults wanted a middle position. These three overlapping groups—conservative youth, established adults, and cautious moderates—did not capitulate to demands of youthful idealists and reformers. Indeed, it was the intense quarrels among these groups that set the tone of the Sixties.

Thus the central conflicts of the decade were not neatly divided between the young and the old, but were fought between conservatives and liberals. At a time when only people over age 21 had the right to vote, the younger generation had much less political influence than its numbers implied. Yet if the 1960s began with a Kennedy-Nixon political consensus, the decade ended with the most polarized political situation since the Civil War. By then, the baby boomers—mere teenagers when Kennedy was killed—had become a significant political force.

INFOTRAC® COLLEGE EDITION EXERCISES

For additional reading go to InfoTrac College Edition, your online research library at *http://web1.infotrac-college.com.*

Subject search: John F. Kennedy

Subject search: Castro

Subject search: Vietnam War

Subject search: SNCC

Subject search: Martin Luther King

ADDITIONAL READING

David Farber, *The Age of Great Dreams: America in the 1960s* (1994). A clear and balanced overview of the decade. See also Maurice Isserman and Michael Kazin, *American Divided: The Civil War of the 1960s* (2000), and Edward P. Morgan, *The 60s Experience: Hard Lessons about Modern America* (1991).

Allen J. Matusow, *The Unraveling of America: A History of Liberalism in the 1960s* (1984). Examining national politics, the book describes the rise and fall of a liberal consensus.

Waging War on New Frontiers

David Halberstam, *The Best and the Brightest* (1972). This journalistic study of the Kennedy leadership re-

mains an excellent source for understanding policy decisions.

Contesting with Khrushchev

Michael R. Beschloss, *The Crisis Years: Kennedy and Khrushchev, 1960–1963* (1991). A thorough discussion of Kennedy's foreign policy, describing the Cold War crisis and diplomacy.

The Cuban Missile Crisis

Ernest R. May and Philip D. Zelikow, eds., *The Kennedy Tapes: Inside the White House during the Cuban Missile Crisis* (1997). These transcriptions of tape-recorded conversations underscore the high stakes of presidential policy.

Making Commitments in Vietnam

David Kaiser, *American Tragedy: Kennedy, Johnson, and the Origins of the Vietnam War* (2000). This detailed account of foreign policy contrasts Kennedy's skepticism about Vietnam with Johnson's militance.

Fredrik Logevall, *Choosing War: The Lost Chance for Peace and the Escalation of War in Vietnam* (1999). The early chapters of this book focus on Kennedy's Vietnam policy.

Neil Sheehan, *A Bright and Shining Lie: John Paul Vann and America in Vietnam* (1988). Exploring the early stages of the Vietnam war, the author describes the conflict between official policy and realities in the field.

Rights for Blacks and Women

Cynthia Harrison, *On Account of Sex: The Politics of Women's Issues, 1945–1968* (1988). Focusing on disagreements within the women's movement, the author views the changes of the 1960s in a longer perspective.

Civil Rights Protest

Taylor Branch, *Pillar of Fire: America in the King Years, 1963–65* (1998). This detailed volume depicts the intense passion involved in the civil rights movement and links personal stories to the historical context. See also Robert Weisbrot, *Freedom Bound: A History of America's Civil Rights Movement* (1990).

Death of a President

Gerald L. Posner, *Case Closed: Lee Harvey Oswald and the Assassination of JFK* (1993). A thorough discussion of the Kennedy assassination, this volume sets to rest a variety of conspiracy theories.

A New Generation

Larry Dobrow, *When Advertising Tried Harder: The Sixties, the Golden Age of Advertising* (1984). This well-illustrated volume describes the changes in Madison Avenue's style.

Gerald Howard, ed., *The Sixties* (1982). This anthology of contemporary essays offers a good introduction to cultural issues.

27

Disputing the National Agenda, 1963–1968

CHRONOLOGY

Five days after Kennedy was killed, the somber President Lyndon B. Johnson stood before a hushed joint session of Congress and spoke hoarsely to the grief-stricken nation: "Everything I have," he said, "I would give gladly not to be here today." For days, Johnson had worked the telephones, pleading with Kennedy's friends and appointees to support the new administration. Now, as the nation searched for direction, he invoked the memory of the slain president and appealed to citizens in all parties to accept his leadership. Although Johnson lacked the charm of his predecessor, he possessed superior political skills and he made the best of the tragic assassination to complete Kennedy's unfinished business. "Let us continue," he urged.

At a moment when the civil rights bill appeared stuck in a congressional committee, Johnson declared that passage of the measure was his top priority. "No memorial," he said, "could more eloquently honor President Kennedy's memory." Later, he would present the nation with his dream of the "Great Society," a package of legislative proposals that promised to revitalize the

American dream. "The Great Society rests on abundance and liberty for all," he said. "It demands an end to poverty and racial injustice, to which we are totally committed in our time. But that is just the beginning."

As a young politician, Johnson had embraced Franklin D. Roosevelt's New Deal, and now he wanted the federal government to meet the needs of the poorest citizens. Assuming presidential leadership, he soon introduced an elaborate program that would expand federal responsibility for social welfare. By showing that the United States could provide equal rights for all and could eliminate poverty, such domestic goals would also reinforce U.S. foreign policy in its competition with communism. Thus Johnson would continue Kennedy's militant foreign policy, making fresh commitments to preserve U.S. interests in southeast Asia. With tremendous personal energy, Johnson steered this liberal agenda for domestic reform and international intervention through a supportive Democratic-controlled Congress.

But Johnson's activist proposals soon confronted two powerful counterforces. First, strong conservative groups in Congress opposed White House efforts to increase federal spending for social welfare and questioned the limited war in Vietnam. Clustered among southern Democrats and northern Republicans, these congressional conservatives resisted Johnson's liberal agenda. Second, the younger generation did not necessarily share Johnson's enthusiasm for enlarged government power and objected vocally to the expanding war. Although many young adults expressed no quarrel with Johnson (perhaps a majority remained uninterested in political affairs), a significant proportion, especially on college campuses, opposed White House policies in Vietnam. Many challenged the principles of modern government: bureaucracy, executive leadership, and social control. Johnson's legislative agenda would soon arouse irreconcilable opposition.

Conflicts between liberals and conservatives, between political leaders and the younger generation, marked the 1960s as a decade of turmoil. Johnson's ability to manipulate public grief for Kennedy initially brought liberal advances. But issues like civil rights and the Vietnam war raised the cost of government and demanded public sacrifice. For two years, Johnson successfully minimized dissent by embracing both military expenditures and domestic spending, a policy known as "guns and butter." Yet the financial burdens on government alarmed corporate leaders and social conservatives. Meanwhile, a youthful anti-war movement organized mass demonstrations against White House foreign policy. As the murmur of dissent spread throughout the land, Johnson's consensus vaporized in bitter fights, both in Washington and in local communities as citizens debated the merits of both domestic welfare programs and the war in Asian jungles. By the time Johnson left office in 1969, the country was embroiled in the worst domestic crisis since the Civil War.

Defining the Liberal Agenda

Lyndon Baines Johnson was primarily a political animal. He had served as a Texas representative during Roosevelt's New Deal, a Senate majority leader under Eisenhower, and a vice president frustrated by the powerlessness of his office. Johnson resolved to use his presidency to fulfill a liberal agenda of social welfare and civil rights. After persuading Kennedy's top advisors to remain in office, the president demonstrated his legislative genius by pressing Congress to pass domestic programs that allowed the federal government to manage economic policy and promote racial integration. Despite severe criticism from political conservatives in both parties, Johnson proceeded to build a consensus that gave him a

landslide victory in 1964 and paved the way for his "Great Society." Focusing on these domestic priorities, few Johnson supporters reacted to the growing entanglement in the war in Vietnam.

A Liberal Economy

Convinced that federal tax policy could accelerate economic growth, Democrats formally rebuffed the principle of balanced budgets in favor of deficit spending. Kennedy's initial proposal had stalled before a skeptical Congress, but three months after taking office Johnson persuaded Congress to pass the Revenue Act of 1964. The law, which reduced corporate and personal income taxes, boosted the economy toward unprecedented growth. By encouraging investment in technological innovations, such as electronic circuitry to monitor manufacturing, and modern office equipment such as copy machines, the tax cut stimulated industrial productivity and corporate profits. Moreover, as the gross national product jumped 7 percent in a single year, economic expansion brought higher tax revenues, which reduced the federal deficit by one-third to just $4 billion in 1966.

Government management of the economy triggered business prosperity, but not for all companies and taxpayers. Large corporations continued to receive a disproportionate share of federal contracts for military and space programs, and 71 percent of manufacturing profits went to the country's 400 largest companies. Multinational corporations fared especially well. As U.S. investment in Europe doubled during the decade, the value of overseas plants rose, and exports surged. Dominating international manufacturing of machines, electronics, and chemicals, U.S. companies also controlled three-quarters of the world's oil supplies. High corporate earnings rewarded the wealthy few. In 1966, the richest fifth of U.S. families received over 45 percent of the nation's income, while the lowest fifth earned less than 4 percent.

Legislating the Great Society

Johnson had obtained substantial personal wealth from ownership of Texas TV and radio stations that had benefited from federal licenses, but because he had risen from poverty the new president felt a strong obligation to assist the less fortunate. His State of the Union address in 1964 was the first since the end of World War II to focus almost exclusively on domestic issues. Believing that better education, medical care, job training, and racial equality would transform the lives of ordinary citizens, Johnson declared "unconditional war on poverty" and proposed creation of the Great Society. Lobbying Congress and the business community aggressively, Johnson soon signed the Economic Opportunity Act of 1964. The law created the Office of Economic Opportunity (OEO), established the Jobs Corps to provide work training for youth, sent volunteers into needy communities to provide social services, gave support for nutrition programs such as school lunches and food stamps, and funded regional development projects in poverty areas. As part of the measure, the Community Action Program (CAP) mandated "participatory democracy" to bring the poor directly into the government planning process, a controversial idea that threatened the power of elected local leaders. Meanwhile, a Headstart program gave preschool support to children of the poor. And, as Johnson often exclaimed, these federal projects were just the first step on the road to social justice.

Civil Rights for Blacks and Women

Johnson also engineered passage of Kennedy's pending civil-rights bill. As southern Democrats, including the president's closest allies in the Sen-ate, threatened to filibuster the proposal, Johnson appealed to northern Republicans to vote to end further discussion and bring the controversial measure to a full vote. To reinforce the moral point, Johnson offered his supporters federal patronage and government contracts. Key Republicans took the bait, and with this Republican support, northern senators finally broke southern resistance.

The Civil Rights Act of 1964 mandated the end of segregation in all public accommodations and schools, legally dooming the principle of separate but equal and ending the long era of segregated institutions. The landmark measure also demanded equal job opportunities in nearly all businesses and labor unions and established the Equal Employment Opportunity Commission (EEOC) to assure compliance. Liberals celebrated legislation that promised to end racial discrimination and establish a legal environment that disallowed overt prejudice. Opponents of increased federal power such as Arizona Senator Barry Goldwater condemned the law's intrusion into the private sector, and southern politicians such as Alabama Governor George Wallace called the law a communist threat to a free society. Both Goldwater and Wallace soon entered the 1964 presidential contest to challenge Johnson's programs.

As political leaders discussed racial equality, a little-noticed clause in the Civil Rights Act extended the rights of women. During the congressional debates, the conservative Virginia Representative Howard Smith noticed that the original bill forbade discrimination because of "race, color, religion, or national origin," and he decided to remedy an obvious omission by adding the word "sex." Smith's motives remain unclear. Some subsequently suggested that he introduced the category of sex to assure defeat of the entire bill; others claimed that he merely wished to give white women the same protections proposed for black men and women. Whatever his intent, women representatives supported the amendment. "We want this crumb of equality," said one Republican woman, "to correct something that goes back . . . to the Dark Ages." With such support, Smith's amendment passed both houses of Congress.

Extending civil rights protections to women brought mixed results. The newly established EEOC instituted several suits for equal pay, and the federal civil service ordered equal health benefits for women workers. Meanwhile, several state governments passed laws for equal pay, granted married women rights to own property independent of their husbands (and thus to obtain personal credit cards), and modified rules that limited women's right to serve on juries. But the EEOC hesitated to change long-established customs of sexual segregation in the workplace. For example, the Commission still permitted separate male and female help-wanted advertisements in newspapers, thus enabling employers to limit job opportunities by gender. The federal agency also refused to challenge labor laws that mandated special protection for women workers, such as limited hours of work and exemption from arduous work assignments.

Frustrated by the government's caution, leading women reformers, including author Betty Friedan, in 1966 created a public lobbying group, the National Organization for Women (NOW), to pressure the federal government to end sex discrimination in employment and to relieve problems of working women. NOW's agenda included federal support of childcare centers, maternity leave, and legal abortion, but its greatest impact came in the area of employment. Pressured by NOW, the EEOC ruled in 1968 that airlines could not fire female flight attendants (then known as "stewardesses") merely because they married or passed age 32. That year, the EEOC also banned sex discrimination in employment advertising.

As an older generation of women expanded the realm of economic rights, a younger generation of feminists pressed for equality within the civil rights movement. Women's participation in political protest had offered no protection of sex. Despite a rhetoric of southern chivalry, women activists faced equal violence, risk, and punishment. Yet within organizations like the Student Non-Violent Coordinating Committee (SNCC) and Students for a Democratic Society (SDS), these women received second-class assignments as clerical support, food providers, and sex mates, rather than leadership positions. When activists Casey Hayden and Mary King drafted a "SNCC Position Paper" in 1964, comparing "male superiority" to "white supremacy," SNCC's Stokely Carmichael quipped that "the only position for women . . . is prone."

The failure of radical men to recognize women's equality provoked the first demands for "women's liberation." Other women activists began attacking so-called sexist institutions. In 1968, radical feminists from New York's WITCH (Women's International Terrorist Conspiracy from Hell) organized protests at the Miss America pageant and tossed "instruments of torture" (girdles, brassieres, hair curlers) into a "freedom trash can." By the decade's end, multigenerational women's groups were laying the basis for a national feminist revival.

The Election of 1964

The liberal agenda soon ignited conservative opposition. "We just delivered the South to the Republican party," President Johnson remarked as he signed the Civil Rights Act in 1964. Furious at Washington's attack on state laws, southern Democrats abandoned Johnson to back Barry Goldwater, an outspoken conservative opposed to federal regulation, big government, and social security. His supporters showed no interest in the civil rights movement or racial equality. Only fourteen black delegates participated in the Republican National Convention.

President Johnson's voice-over for the "Daisy Field" ad said, "These are the stakes.... We must either love each other, or we must die." Then the male voice returned, to urge a vote for Johnson: "The stakes are too high for you to stay at home."

"Extremism in defense of liberty is no vice," proclaimed Goldwater in accepting the Republican nomination. "Moderation in the pursuit of justice is no virtue." Playing on voter fears of social change—rising crime, political corruption, civil rights protest, and desegregation—the candidate promised "I will give you back your freedom." Young conservatives on college campuses, entering politics for the first time, responded to Goldwater's attack on federal bureaucracy and his defiance of the party's "eastern establishment." The candidate also advocated a militant foreign policy, suggesting the use of nuclear weapons in Vietnam, or merely "to lob one into the men's room of the Kremlin." To portray Goldwater as irresponsible, Johnson responded with the era's most vivid political commercial, shown only once on television. In it, a little girl picks petals from a daisy as a male voice counts down from ten to one, the screen turns black, and an atomic bomb explodes into a huge mushroom cloud.

Johnson also faced opposition within the Democratic party. "The involuntary servitude act of 1964" was George Wallace's term for federal civil rights legislation. "I think we are going to continue to have segregation in Alabama," said the governor, "as they have in most states in the union." Entering Democratic primaries in the northern states, Wallace exploited white working-class resentment of civil rights agitation, and of apparent benefits given to blacks at their expense. In South Milwaukee, 3,000 voices joined to sing "Dixie"—in Polish. Wallace captured 33 percent of the vote in the Wisconsin primary, 29 percent in Indiana, 43 percent in Maryland. The media called the phenomenon "white backlash." But Wallace could not stop the Johnson bandwagon. The frustrated governor could only hurl condemnations at the "faceless, spineless, power-hungry theorists and black-robed judicial anarchists" who had thwarted him. He vowed to run for president again.

In South Milwaukee, 3,000 voices joined to sing "Dixie"—in Polish.

Democrats versus Freedom Democrats

Without the solidly Democratic South, Johnson struggled to preserve the New Deal coalition of urban white ethnics, blacks, and organized labor. The racial divide remained the weakest link. Although the Kennedy administration had encouraged SNCC's activists to work within the political system by registering black voters in the South, legal complications and local violence thwarted the effort. Facing southern opposition and hoping to provoke federal support, SNCC invited northern college students to volunteer for "Freedom Summer" in 1964, to register black voters in Mississippi. Appealing to youthful idealism, the project nevertheless involved deadly risks. As 700 white students converged on Mississippi, white supremacists retaliated with bombings, arson, beatings, mass arrests, and the murder of civil rights volunteers. The courageous civil rights workers continued to organize "Freedom Schools" to teach blacks literacy, civics, and political radicalism. In the end, about 1,500 African Americans faced county registrars and qualified to vote; they and others learned, in the words of Mississippi activist Fannie Lou Hamer, that "white folks are human."

Despite limited gains, a delegation of SNCC workers and new black voters, self-named as the Mississippi Freedom Democratic party, claimed to represent 80,000 voters and journeyed to the Democratic National Convention in 1964 with hopes of unseating the regular all-white delegation. Johnson wanted no part of the plan. Fearing that the rebellion would cost him white votes throughout the country, the president offered only token representation to the dissident blacks. Just as Fannie Lou Hamer was presenting dramatic televised testimony about violations of her constitutional rights, including a beating by white police, Johnson demanded network airtime that preempted the broadcast. Although the president attempted to ease black complaints by choosing the liberal Hubert Humphrey as his vice-presidential running mate, frustrated African American delegates felt humiliation, indignation, and bitterness at Johnson's tactics. Meanwhile, the white Mississippi delegation, already inclined to support Goldwater, departed from the convention.

The Johnson-Humphrey ticket promised a politics of consensus, defending the commitment to racial equality and economic betterment as a citizen's basic right. Compared to Goldwater, the Democrats appeared to offer a moderate, nonaggressive foreign policy. Although the president secretly made plans to escalate the war in Vietnam and obtained congressional authorization to bomb the north, Johnson publicly denied interest in widening the war and criticized those who wished "American boys to do the job that Asian boys should do."

Such language soothed voter fears. The Democrats attracted 43 million votes—61 percent of the electorate, the largest margin in U.S. history. Even though Johnson lost five states in the Deep South, the northern Democratic coalition of union workers and ethnic minorities held firm. Not only did he win among urban white ethnics, but despite his insults to Mississippi blacks, Johnson carried more than 90 percent of the African American vote. With two-to-one majorities in both houses of Congress, Johnson no longer needed white southern support to continue his program.

Rise and Fall of a Great Society

Backed by a landslide mandate, Johnson initiated a legislative agenda comparable in scope and

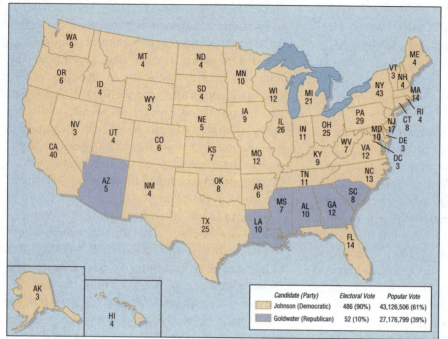

The Election of 1964

Candidate (Party)	Electoral Vote	Popular Vote
Johnson (Democratic)	486 (90%)	43,126,506 (61%)
Goldwater (Republican)	52 (10%)	27,176,799 (39%)

achievement to Roosevelt's New Deal. As in 1933, a Democratic Congress followed the president's bidding. A package of new laws extended federal assistance to a multitude of needy groups—the young and the old, foreign born and racial minorities, low-income families and starving artists. The liberal commitment to federal spending reflected not only optimistic faith in legislative reform, but also an undeniable generosity of spirit. The Great Society expressed the era's economic confidence and raised public expectations of improvement to even higher levels.

Enacting the Great Society

Johnson's Great Society began by aiding the youngest citizens. As baby boomers swamped the public schools, the Elementary and Secondary Education Act of 1965 offered federal funds to assist schools and linked this assistance to the number of low-income families in each district. Designed to enhance educational opportunity for underprivileged children, federal money came with long strings tied to Washington. To qualify for grants, school districts had to demonstrate "good faith" compliance with racial desegregation. When some local authorities attempted to skirt these requirements, federal orders tightened the guidelines for acceptable progress. In this way, the federal budget served to impose national standards, primarily in the area of racial balance. With federal funding for education reaching $10 billion by the end of the decade, conservatives protested the loss of local control over public schools.

The Great Society also moved to remedy the disadvantages—and fears—of old age. Linking federal assistance for health care to the social security program, the Medicare Act of 1965 provided hospital and nursing home care for people over 65, obtaining funds through payroll deductions. The law covered most doctors' fees, though a strong lobby by the American Medical Association made participation in Medicare voluntary. In addition, the law provided "Medicaid" assistance to states that provided health services for people of all ages. These programs cushioned the problems of retirement and old age. Yet federal money also stimulated a rapid rise in medical costs, as hospitals and doctors increased the quantity of medical intervention and inflated their prices. Within one decade, rising hospital costs erased the monetary advantages of government assistance for most patients.

Great Society legislation reflected the era's optimistic spirit about government's ability to improve individual lives. During 1965, Johnson's agenda added an imposing list of legislative accomplishments (Table 27.1). The Appalachian Assistance program, funded at $1 billion, brought federal road projects into that depressed area. A federal housing law, calling for nearly $8 billion, gave rental assistance to low-income families. Creating the Department of Housing and Urban Development (HUD), Johnson appointed sociologist Robert Weaver to head the agency; he was the first African American to join a presidential cabinet. Another $1 billion funded the Demonstration Cities and Metropolitan Development Act to support urban renewal. Congress also established the National Endowments for the Arts and the Humanities to underwrite cultural projects and academic research. Johnson's proposals gained 58 percent congressional support in 1964, 69 percent in 1965, and 56 percent in 1967.

Perhaps the most enduring legacy of the Great Society addressed the problems of noncitizens, foreigners seemingly outside the reach of federal law. Since the 1920s, immigration policy had perpetuated a hierarchical view of national origins, welcoming newcomers from northern Europe while discriminating against eastern Europeans, Asians, and Africans. The liberal 1960s repudiated these racial assumptions. The Immigration Act of 1965 limited admissions to 300,000 per year but discarded quotas based on nationality. Instead, the law favored immigration of relatives of U.S. citizens and those who possessed special skills helpful to economic growth. Few initially realized the consequences of these changes, but the surge of immigration from Latin America and Asia would transform the United States into a multicultural society.

Legal Reform and Voting Rights

While Congress enacted social reforms, a liberal Supreme Court, headed by Chief Justice Earl Warren, issued a multitude of constitutional rulings that expressed the prevailing sentiment for equal rights. In the landmark 1962 decision *Baker v. Carr,* the Court held that political apportionment in state government had to guarantee each voter equal weight in determining results; this meant that sparsely populated rural regions could not exercise more power than crowded urban districts. That year, the justices upheld the separation of church and state (*Murray v. Corlett*) by prohibiting prayers and Bible-reading in public schools. Several cases involving police arrests (*Escobedo,* 1964 and *Miranda,* 1966) protected the rights of suspects and defendants to due process of law, including the right to remain silent and to obtain legal counsel. The high court also overturned state laws that barred racial intermarriage; denied state requirements that voters demonstrate literacy in English; protected newspapers from libel suits filed by public figures; and permitted busing pupils to facilitate the desegregation of schools.

Congress also passed, and the state legislatures ratified, the Twenty-Fourth Amendment to

TABLE 27.1

Accomplishments of the 89th Congress

THE FIRST SESSION

1. Medicare
2. Elementary and Secondary Education
3. Higher Education
4. Farm Bill
5. Department of Housing and Urban Development
6. Omnibus Housing Act (including rent supplements, and low and moderate income housing)
7. Social Security Increases
8. Voting Rights
9. Immigration Bill
10. Older Americans Act
11. Heart Disease, Cancer, and Stroke Research and Facilities
12. Law Enforcement Assistance Act
13. National Crime Commission
14. Drug Controls
15. Mental Health Research and Facilities
16. Health Professions Education
17. Medical Library Facilities
18. Vocational Rehabilitation
19. Inter-American Bank Fund Increases
20. Stepping Up the War Against Poverty
21. Arts and Humanities Foundation
22. Appalachia
23. Highway Beautification
24. Air Pollution (auto exhausts and research)
25. Water Pollution Control (water quality standards)
26. High-speed Ground Transportation
27. Extension and Strengthening of MDTA
28. Presidential Disability and Succession
29. Child Health Medical Assistance
30. Regional Development

TABLE 27.1

Accomplishments of the 89th Congress *(continued)*

THE SECOND SESSION

1. The Department of Transportation
2. Truth in Packaging
3. Demonstration Cities
4. Funds for Rent Supplements
5. Funds for Teacher Corps
6. Asian Development Bank
7. Water Pollution (Clean Rivers)
8. Food for Peace
9. March Anti-Inflation Package
10. Narcotics Rehabilitation
11. Child Safety
12. Vietnam Supplemental
13. Foreign Aid Extension
14. Traffic Safety
15. Highway Safety
16. Public Health Service Reorganization
17. Community Relations Service Reorganization
18. Water Pollution Control Administration Reorganization
19. Mine Safety
20. Allied Health Professions Training
21. International Education
22. Child Nutrition
23. Bail Reform
24. Civil Procedure Reforms
25. Tire Safety
26. Protection for Savers (increase in Federal Insurance for savings accounts)
27. The GI Bill
28. Minimum Wage Increase
29. Urban Mass Transit
30. Elementary and Higher Education Funds

Source: Lawrence F. O'Brien and Joseph A. Califano, Jr., "Final Report to President Lyndon B. Johnson on the 89th Congress," *Public Papers of the Presidents of the United States: Lyndon B. Johnson,* Vol. 2 (Washington, Government Printing Office, 1967), 1193–94.

Police violence at Selma, Alabama, shocked the country and stimulated passage of the Voting Rights Act of 1965.

the Constitution in 1964, outlawing the poll taxes that had prevented African American participation in southern elections. Just as southern white politicians perceived another federal attack on states' rights, the voter registration issue exploded into a national crisis when African Americans began a voter campaign in Selma, Alabama, in 1965 and Governor Wallace encouraged local officials to block their efforts. Martin Luther King and the Southern Christian Leadership Conference responded by organizing nonviolent demonstrations. Weeks of arbitrary arrests and beatings climaxed on "Bloody Sunday," March 7, 1965, when state police attacked a peaceful march of civil-rights demonstrators. As television networks broadcast scenes of police violence, public outrage mounted, and the president decided to intervene directly. Calling a joint session of Congress, Johnson demanded federal laws to protect voting rights for all citizens, ending his dramatic speech with words taken directly from the civil rights movement: "All of us . . . must overcome the crippling legacy of bigotry and injustice," said the first southern president since Woodrow Wilson, "and we *shall* overcome."

Amendment XXIV (1964)

Section 1.
The right of citizens of the United States to vote in any primary or other election for President or Vice President, for electors for President or Vice President, or for Senator or Representative in Congress, shall not be denied or abridged by the United States or any state by reason of failure to pay any poll tax or other tax.

Section 2.
The Congress shall have power to enforce this article by appropriate legislation.

The Voting Rights Act of 1965 transformed the political landscape. Attacking the power of local elites, who for a century had denied the political rights of African Americans, the law banned literacy tests as a qualification for voting and authorized federal examiners to register voters in states that practiced discrimination. As federal power weakened local government in the South, African Americans entered the political arena in rising numbers. In 1966, federal examiners registered more than 400,000 new African American voters; two years later, more than 1 million southern blacks had won the right to vote. Black voting did not eliminate the racial divide—just the opposite. As southern African Americans enlisted in the Democratic party, southern whites searched for another political port. Many turned to George Wallace; others became Republicans. Either way, for the first time since Reconstruction, party politics were flourishing in the southern states.

The decade's other constitutional changes produced more peaceful democratic reforms. In 1961, ratification of the Twenty-Third Amendment to the Constitution gave residents of the nation's capital in the District of Columbia the right to vote for presidential and vice-presidential electors, though not for congressional representation. Following the assassination of Kennedy, the Twenty-Fifth Amendment, ratified in 1967, established new lines of presidential succession, reducing the importance of party continuity and substituting principles of public choice. Under the amendment, the vice president would be succeeded, not by appointive officers of the cabinet, who traditionally shared the president's party position, but by elected leaders in Congress, who frequently came from another party. Both constitutional changes, adopted without significant public debate, addressed issues of representative government and, like the Twenty-Fourth Amendment, tightened connections between leaders and voters.

Amendment XXIII (1961)

Section 1.
The District constituting the seat of government of the United States shall appoint in such manner as the Congress may direct:

A number of electors of President and Vice President equal to the whole number of Senators and Representatives in Congress to which the District would be entitled if it were a state, but in no event more than the least populous state; they shall be in addition to those appointed by the states, but they shall be considered, for the purposes of the election of President and Vice President, to be electors appointed by a state; and they shall meet in the District and perform such duties as provided by the twelfth article of amendment.

Section 2.
The Congress shall have power to enforce this article by appropriate legislation.

Amendment XXV (1967)

Section 1.
In case of the removal of the President from office or of his death or resignation, the Vice President shall become President.

Section 2.
Whenever there is a vacancy in the office of the Vice President, the President shall nominate a Vice President who shall take office upon confirmation by a majority vote of both Houses of Congress.

Section 3.
Whenever the President transmits to the President pro tempore of the Senate and the Speaker of the House of

Representatives his written declaration that he is unable to discharge the powers and duties of his office, and until he transmits to them a written declaration to the contrary, such powers and duties shall be discharged by the Vice President as Acting President.

Section 4.

Whenever the Vice President and a majority of either the principal officers of the executive departments or of such other body as Congress may by law provide, transmit to the President pro tempore of the Senate and the Speaker of the House of Representatives their written declaration that the President is unable to discharge the powers and duties of his office, the Vice President shall immediately assume the powers and duties of the office as Acting President.

Thereafter, when the President transmits to the President pro tempore of the Senate and the Speaker of the House of Representatives his written declaration that no inability exists, he shall resume the powers and duties of his office unless the Vice President and a majority of either the principal officers of the executive department or of such other body as Congress may by law provide, transmit within four days to the President pro tempore of the Senate and the Speaker of the House of Representatives their written declaration that the President is unable to discharge the powers and duties of his office. Thereupon Congress shall decide the issue, assembling within forty-eight hours for that purpose if not in session. If the Congress, within twenty-one days after receipt of the latter written declaration, or, if Congress is not in session, within twenty-one days after Congress is required to assemble, determines by two-thirds vote of both Houses that the President is unable to discharge the powers and duties of his office, the Vice President shall continue to discharge the same as Acting President; otherwise, the President shall resume the powers and duties of his office.

Racial Discontent

Passage of a liberal political agenda, including protection of civil rights, enabled racial minorities to challenge longstanding traditions of segregation and discrimination. Coinciding with an era of prosperity, civil rights laws permitted minority groups to improve their levels of wealth, education, and political power. But the realization that racial prejudice persisted and that severe economic and social problems continued to afflict racial minorities created growing frustration within African American communities. Disillusioned by unfulfilled promises of equality, many young black activists rejected the white leadership that controlled the country's political agenda. Decrying the failure of liberal reform, African Americans, Mexican Americans, Native Americans, and other minorities simultaneously affirmed the value of a distinct cultural identity. Such assertions of racial pride indicated growing self-confidence, yet at the same time alienated many white allies. Demands for political power and cultural autonomy thus accentuated racial differences and contributed to a climate of mistrust and antagonism that ultimately destroyed Johnson's liberal consensus.

From "Negro" to "Black"

When George Wallace lost a state election in 1958, he claimed to have been "out-niggered" by his opponent. As African Americans demanded equal rights and self-respect during the 1960s, such language receded from public conversation, even in the South. In a liberal culture, the acceptable adjective to describe persons of African descent was no longer the white standard of "colored." Instead, the biologically neutral and capitalized word *Negro* (derived from the Spanish for "black"), along with *Caucasian* and *Mongolian*, came to signify the three "races" of human beings.

In 1966 heavyweight boxing champion Cassius Clay renamed himself Muhammed Ali, part of a trend among young African Americans to affirm a distinct cultural identity.

Yet Malcolm X had observed that the Spanish word for "blacks" represented a legacy of the slave trade and consequently demeaned people of African ancestry. Moreover, while Martin Luther King, SNCC activists, and Democratic politicians promoted a racially neutral country, black separatist groups, such as Elijah Mohammed's Nation of Islam, known popularly as the "Black Muslims," emphasized the cultural advantages of *not* disappearing into a racial meltingpot.

Although Malcolm X subsequently rejected the Nation of Islam, he remained skeptical of cultural integration. "We must recapture our heritage and our identity," he said in 1964. "We must launch a Cultural Revolution to unbrainwash an entire people." His assassination in 1965, apparently by black political opponents, thwarted his plans to build an African American political movement, but his posthumously published *Autobiography of Malcolm X* (1966) gave intellectual sustenance to younger blacks dissatisfied with liberal reforms. To a new generation of activists, the word *Negro* denoted cultural subservience, for which the substitution *Black* (capitalized) represented an expression of cultural independence. Many young blacks then followed Malcolm X's lead and adopted Muslim names to replace their "slave" names. Meanwhile, in 1967 the U.S. Geological Survey ordered all government maps to remove disparaging references to African and Asian Americans; accordingly, 143 geographic places labeled "Nigger" became "Negro" and twenty-six places called "Jap" became "Japanese."

Assertions of African American identity did not immediately threaten liberal reforms. Upholding the commitment to political equality, Johnson appointed many blacks to government offices, including the former NAACP attorney Thurgood Marshall, who became the first African American to serve on the U.S. Supreme Court, in 1967. The previous year, Massachusetts elected the first African American Senator since Reconstruction. Although Daniel Moynihan's 1965 Labor Department report on African American families ignited controversy by suggesting that female-headed households and high birthrates among single black women indicated a dysfunctional family structure, African American families made major economic advances during the decade. In the five years after 1964, black families' median income increased by one-third, and the ratio between black and white family incomes improved from 54 to 61 percent. Government statistics showed that the proportion of black families living in poverty declined from 48 percent in 1959 to 28 percent in 1969.

Fire in the Ghettos

Progress for middle-class blacks contrasted with persistent problems among the poor. By 1965, nearly half the country's African Americans lived outside the southern states, where relative economic improvement still left them in poverty. As northern industries and white city dwellers moved to the suburbs and to sunbelt states in the Southwest, African Americans entered city centers at a time of economic decline. In 1968, the rate of black unemployment was three times that of whites. Residential discrimination by landlords and banks contributed to overcrowded ghetto conditions, and public-housing construction remained a fraction

Chicago's Aid to Dependent Children program allowed only 21 cents per meal—the cost of packaged macaroni and powdered cheese or a loaf of sliced bread.

of legislative promises. "The projects are hideous," wrote the black novelist James Baldwin of public housing, "cheerless as a prison." Welfare assistance remained inadequate. Chicago's Aid to Dependent Children program allowed only 21 cents per meal— the cost of packaged macaroni and powdered cheese or a loaf of sliced bread.

Heightened expectations, unfulfilled promises, and continuing grievances about economic injustice and police brutality created a volatile mix in central cities. Five days after Johnson signed the Voting Rights Act in 1965, Los Angeles's black ghetto in Watts exploded. As young blacks chanted "Burn, baby, burn," 50,000 African Americans rioted for six days, looting shops, setting fires, and battling police. The spontaneous rebellion startled the country, but foreshadowed even more racial violence in subsequent years. When Martin Luther King, Jr., led an open housing campaign into Chicago's suburban communities in 1966, angry whites denounced the crusade and met the marchers with violence. In 1967, another long, hot summer saw Newark, New Jersey, and Detroit, Michigan, go up in flames, in the most notorious of over 100 neighborhood riots that spread around the country. Pitting local blacks against white shopkeepers, and street fighters against police and national guardsmen, the racial violence antagonized whites and undermined the liberal civil rights movement.

After pouring billions into anti-poverty programs, the bewildered president appointed a National Advisory Commission on Civil Disorders, headed by Illinois Governor Otto Kerner, to explain the failure of government assistance to ease racial tensions. The Kerner report of 1968 hardly soothed the liberal conscience. Blaming "white racism" for sustaining explosive conditions (slums, poverty, joblessness, inadequate schools, and police brutality), the commission warned that "our nation is moving toward two societies, one black, one white—separate but unequal." The investigation advised massive federal spending for housing, jobs, and welfare, as well as an attack on de facto school segregation in northern cities. But by then the white backlash had undermined Democratic initiatives. After 1966, the federal anti-poverty agency OEO received half its projected budget, and Senate filibusters killed housing reforms.

Affirming Black Identity

Frustration at the failure of liberal reform provoked fundamental changes within the nation's African American communities. In 1966, James Meredith, the black student who had integrated the University of Mississippi four years earlier, embarked on a personal protest march through Mississippi to call attention to racial discrimination. A sniper's bullet soon felled him, exposing intense white hostility to racial integration. Civil rights leaders, including Dr. King, rushed to Mississippi to continue Meredith's walk. But SNCC's Stokely Carmichael scoffed at nonviolent demonstrations and now demanded "Black Power." The strident slogan expressed many facets of black desires: a political movement to lobby government; economic self-sufficiency, including jobs and black-owned business; and cultural nationalism. Media attention focused primarily on black anger and the rejection of an integrated civil rights movement. When SNCC expelled white members, integrationists like Hubert Humphrey and King chided young blacks for destroying the civil rights coalition.

While black cultural nationalists celebrated Afro hairstyles, soul food, and a Christmas-season holiday named "Kwanzaa," inner-city youth in Oakland, California, organized the Black Panther Party for Self-Defense to challenge police brutality and seek political remedies. Led by streetwise Bobby Seale and Huey Newton, the Black Panthers won notoriety for violent confrontations with the police and dramatized their right to bear arms by "occupying" the California legislature while carrying loaded rifles. They also gained intellectual respectability from Eldridge Cleaver's prison-written bestseller *Soul on Ice* (1968), which analyzed the psychological aspects of white racism. Cleaver became the Panthers' minister of information.

By 1968, the Black Panthers presented a ten-point program that demanded jobs, housing, and education. The group also started local health clinics and a school breakfast program for black children. But Panther militancy and alleged criminality alarmed white authorities. The FBI and local police around the country adopted extralegal measures to immobilize the leadership through raids, arrests, and brutality. Other assertions of Black Power brought angry racial confrontations. At the international Olympic Games in Mexico City in 1968, medal-winning U.S. black athletes wore black socks and raised their fists in the Black Power salute during the playing of the national anthem, a gesture that offended many whites and reinforced the white backlash.

Awakening Racial Identities

The Black Power movement stimulated other ethnic minorities to seek political expressions of cultural identity and fair treatment. Government statistics found Hispanics even poorer than blacks: half of New Mexico's Hispanics lived below the poverty line; in Los Angeles, with a Mexican American community approaching 1 million, Hispanic unemployment exceeded black rates. Although the Johnson administration added 2,000 Mexican Americans to federal job rolls, a 24 percent increase, none sat on the president's Equal Employment Opportunity Commission (EEOC). "We are America's invisible minority," protested Mexican American activists in 1966. The Mexican American Political Association began picketing at California post offices to protest discrimination in government employment.

While established Mexican American political groups, such as the GI Forum and the League of United Latin American Citizens (LULAC), lobbied the president for political patronage, a younger generation affirmed their identity as "Chicanos" and staged more militant demonstrations. In 1968, 15,000 Mexican American students walked out of Los Angeles public schools to protest the failure of the city's bilingual education program. When Johnson visited El Paso, Texas, in 1967, radical protesters carried signs that read: "Don't Ask Rich Mexicans to Talk for the Poor." Media attention focused on a national boycott of California grapes, led by Cesar Chavez, the charismatic leader of the United Farm Workers. Adopting the nonviolent strategy of Dr. King, Chavez appealed for justice to gain improvements for Mexican American migrant workers. Assertions of Chicano pride also encouraged an outpouring of cultural activity, such as Luis Valdez's militant theatrical productions Teatro Campesino. In Denver, Rodolfo "Corky" Gonzalez helped organize "La Raza Unida" (The United Race) to demand equal rights, economic opportunity, and a bilingual culture.

Similar militancy and cultural resurgence revitalized Native American politics. Adopting civil rights tactics, several groups in Washington state organized "fish-in" demonstrations to challenge court rulings that violated older treaty agreements giving Native peoples the right to use public lands. Eventually, they persuaded the Supreme Court to overturn state laws. In New Mexico, the Taos Pueblo refused federal compensation for seizure of the sacred Blue Lake and eventually won a government reversal. Vine DeLoria's book *Custer Died for Your Sins* (1969) stood as a public manifesto for Native American political and cultural rights.

These protests culminated in demands to end the postwar federal policy to terminate all tribal governments (see Chapter 25). Endorsing Native American demands for self-determination, President Johnson announced a new national policy of "maximum choice" in 1968 to allow Native Americans to maintain their independence. That year, Congress passed the Indian Civil Rights Act, which required tribal consent before a state could claim jurisdiction over reservations. Proclaiming "Red Power," young activists established the American Indian Movement (AIM) in 1968, setting the stage for militant action in the next decade.

The Rise of the Youth Movement

Assertions of cultural independence by racial minorities coincided with the emergence of a dynamic youth culture, whose main strength lay in its numbers. As the most densely populated age group, the maturing baby boomers held considerable cultural, economic, and political influence. To be sure, this young generation, born and raised amid postwar prosperity, identified affluence and consumption as part of its birthright; it therefore remained vulnerable to the marketing strategies devised by a new breed of Madison Avenue advertisers. Yet this generation also articulated distinctive attitudes about social relations, political rights, and U.S. policy. Although many baby boomers, perhaps even a majority, had no quarrel with the status quo and defended traditional institutions, a significant proportion became involved in public affairs and contributed to the

"It took me a long time to get young, and I'm proud of it."

ferment surrounding racial politics and the war in Vietnam.

The Culture of the Boomers

For teenagers raised on the pulse beat of rock 'n' roll, music and dance defined a distinctive sensibility. During the gloomy winter that followed the Kennedy assassination, the arrival of four long-haired "Beatles" from Liverpool, England, brought a spark of vitality to the youth culture. Nourished on electric-guitar performers like Elvis Presley, sixties teenagers screamed hysterically as the Beatles mixed familiar rock 'n' roll rhythms with almost-innocent lyrics, such as "I wanna hold your hand." "Everybody else thought they were for the teeny-boppers," remarked the era's finest lyricist, Bob Dylan, "I knew they were pointing the direction where music had to go." Attaching his guitar to electric amplifiers in 1965, Dylan outraged folk-music purists who despised the new technology. But by intertwining politically conscious lyrics and a grainy vocal style, Dylan reached a mass audience with his first popular success, "Like a Rolling Stone" (1965). "It took me a long time to get young," said Dylan, "and I'm proud of it." Other popular rock groups—the Supremes, Temptations, and Rolling Stones—produced a hard-driving "soul" beat that made people dance. Unlike earlier generations, sixties youth did not dance as couples to measured steps, but rather embarked on free-form movement with or without partners.

Sixties rock music mirrored the new generation's sexual liberation, which appeared as unsubtle as the Rolling Stones' 1965 song title "Let's Spend the Night Together." By mid-decade, college students were successfully challenging the centuries-old principle of *in loco parentis* (in the place of the parent), which had permitted college deans and administrators to establish curfews and limit visits between the sexes. Academic dress codes fell, just as the craze for British fashion introduced the miniskirt, unisex blue jeans, and long hair. Surveys found that the age of first sexual experience became lower each year and that the frequency of sexual intercourse increased within all social classes. The availability of birth-control pills eased the separation of sexuality from marriage. Yet unwanted pregnancies also increased. Each year, an estimated half-million young adult women obtained an illegal abortion; thousands died from malpractice and self-induced injuries. California became the first state to legalize abortions in 1967.

As sexual behavior changed, standards relaxed about nudity, obscenity, and artistic expression. Supreme Court rulings ended censorship of literary works and permitted sexual displays (provided they had some redeeming social value), and Hollywood movies began to allow uncensored speech and nudity. By 1968, the film industry had adopted a new code that graded movies, to advise viewers to censor themselves. Meanwhile, theatrical productions such as *Hair* flaunted public nudity, and *Playboy* magazine claimed a readership of 3 million.

Television remained a bastion of conventional morality, though programs increasingly used humor to exploit sexual subjects. Less restrictive, ironically, were televised commercials and print advertisements that perfected sexually arousing imagery to sell products. In mass-advertising campaigns, the typical woman was no longer a motherly housewife who drove a Ford station wagon, but a single swinger like the pouty blonde Danish model who, to the tune "The Stripper," cooed "Take it off, take it all off!" in a shave-cream commercial that oozed with sexual desire. By the end of the decade, the search for customers also prompted the appearance of racial minorities in mainstream advertising.

Indicative of the influence of the youth movement, commercial advertising now appealed to a youth-defined mass culture of all ages. With the age group 13 to 22 possessing discretionary spending power worth $25 billion a year, much was at stake. Many products, such as soft drinks, cigarettes, and toiletries, aimed directly at young consumers, inviting them to identify with their peers. More commonly, advertisers urged older consumers to buy products that would enable *them* to identify with the young. Thus, for example, men's fashions linked images of youthful rebellion with turtleneck shirts, bright-colored ties, and pastel suits. Moreover, as Madison Avenue celebrated the rising generation, advertising joined the attack on established institutions, introducing irreverent language that made fun of conventional behavior, including advertising itself. Even this "hip" advertising often perpetuated racial stereotypes (for example, describing Mexican Americans as "bandits"). Such images prompted boycott campaigns by minority groups. Women appeared primarily as objects of sexual desire.

The openness of sexual imagery mirrored a broader sexual revolution and a new acceptance of the human body. In 1965, Dr. William Masters and Virginia Johnson published a startling book, *Human Sexual Response*. Based on carefully observed clinical experiments, the study found that most women reached sexual climax through clitoral stimulation and seemed to possess greater orgasmic capacity than men. The findings undermined the idea that women were "naturally" passive as sexual partners or that they even needed men for sexual gratification. Such clinical data, widely disseminated in popular magazines, encouraged greater experimentation. The divorce rate, often attributed to sexual incompatibility, skyrocketed to the highest levels in history (Table 27.2).

Table 27.2	
Divorces of Existing Marriages per Thousand New Marriages, 1910–1980	
Year	**Divorces per thousand new marriages**
1910	83
1920	171
1930	196
1940	264
1945	485
1950	385
1955	377
1960	393
1965	479
1966	499
1967	523
1968	584
1969	639
1970	708
1975	1,036
1980	1,189

Source: U.S. Bureau of the Census, *Statistical Abstract of the United States* (Washington, DC: U.S. Government Printing Office, 1982).

Drugs and the Counterculture

The younger generation also found communal identity in the use of drugs. Marijuana and psychedelic LSD (lysergic acid diethylamide, or "acid") promised visionary mind expansion that altered perceptions of reality. Harvard psychologists Timothy Leary and Richard Alpert, using government-provided LSD to experiment with brain chemistry, claimed to have discovered a new consciousness. After their dismissal from academia for unprofessional conduct in disseminating LSD in 1963, the two emerged as mentors for drug-induced liberation, becoming famous for advising the younger generation, in Leary's motto, to "Turn on, tune in, drop out." Meanwhile, aiming to shock a befuddled citizenry into cultural rebellion, novelist Ken Kesey gathered a menage of "Merry Pranksters," who embarked on a cross-country odyssey aboard a multi-colored school bus with its destination labeled "FARTHER." In San Francisco, the group organized "acid trips" or "happenings" where drugged participants enjoyed free concerts by groups like Jefferson Airplane, the Grateful Dead, and Janis Joplin's Big Brother and the Holding Company.

By 1967, a new breed of cultural rebel, the "hippie," had turned San Francisco into a mecca for the media-hyped "Summer of Love." Living in communal crash pads, fed by collective groups like the Diggers, celebrated by alternative "counterculture" newspapers such as *The Oracle,* the hippies celebrated communal values of "natural living," sexual freedom, and sharing. The hippie fad climaxed during the summer of 1969, when 400,000 people converged at the Woodstock rock festival in rural New York and proclaimed the "Age of Aquarius." By then, corporate record companies controlled the rock industry, raking in earnings of $1 billion a year. Meanwhile, Hollywood invented its own cultural rebels, grossing millions in movies that celebrated alienated youth: *Bonnie and Clyde* (1967), *The Graduate* (1967), and *Easy Rider* (1969). True hippies organized rural communes and departed to live on the land.

The Politics of Alienation

"I've got nothing, Ma, to live up to," sang Dylan of his generation's despair at the nation's authority figures. While cultural rebellion satisfied apolitical middle-class youth, activist college students supported a "New Left" politics to challenge social injustice. In the South, young African Americans in SNCC questioned the nonviolent strategy of their mentors. Meanwhile, the radical Students for a Democratic Society (SDS) identified the educated young—not the Marxist working class—as the vanguard of social protest against racism, poverty, and militarism.

College students increasingly saw themselves as victims of an oppressive society. When administrators at the University of California at Berkeley refused to allow political organizing on campus in 1964, students spontaneously created the Free Speech Movement to demand their rights to organize as citizens. As campus administrators fought to preserve their power, students went on strike to force change. "There is a time when the operation of the machine becomes so odious, makes you so sick at heart," declared student leader Mario Savio, "that . . . you've got to put your bodies upon the gears and upon the wheels . . . and you've got to make it stop." Some campus protests, most notoriously at San Francisco State and Columbia University, led to violent confrontations with the police in 1968.

The conflict of generational values ultimately reflected disagreement about the most pressing political issue of the decade: the war in Vietnam. As the military draft compelled young men to serve in an unpopular war, the so-called generation gap became the focus of anger and anguish. Frustrated by political voicelessness, the nation's youth demanded greater political participation. Indeed, a generation that once hailed Kennedy's Peace Corps as an opportunity to serve their country now asserted its own political agenda, seeking "Peace Now!" Mainstream politicians in both parties recoiled at such dissent, criticized "extremists," and promised voters that they would heal the nation's wounds.

Lyndon Johnson's War

Cultural conflict of the 1960s remained inseparable from the crisis of authority caused by the Vietnam

"There's Money Enough To Support Both Of You —
Now, Doesn't That Make You Feel Better?"

Cartoonist Herblock captured the tension between funding both the
war in Vietnam and the Great Society at home.

war. President Johnson understood the interweaving of civil disorder and foreign affairs, the
competition for Treasury dollars by Great Society
programs and military targets. "The Great Society
had the chance to grow into a beautiful woman,"
Johnson later told an interviewer. "She'd be so big
and beautiful that the American people couldn't
help but fall in love with her." The president understood the price of unfaithfulness. "If I left the
woman I really loved—the Great Society—in
order to get involved with that bitch of a war on
the other side of the world, then I would lose
everything at home." Yet that is what Johnson did.
His choice of metaphors revealed a Cold Warrior's

attitude toward women. In Johnson's eyes, Vietnam obliged him to prove his masculinity. In any
case, by escalating the war, Johnson abandoned
the liberal agenda.

The connection between domestic issues and
Vietnam reverberated in the military statistics.
Since the Korean war, the armed services had reflected the liberal promise of racial integration,
apparently allowing blacks and other minorities
to serve without prejudice. But 80 percent of U.S.
soldiers in Vietnam came from working-class
backgrounds, and ethnic minorities comprised a
disproportionate share of battle casualties. In the
mid-1960s, 23 percent of the combat dead were
African Americans (only later, after the military
responded to such inequities, did the ratio become proportionate to the African American population, about 11 percent); merely 2 percent of
black soldiers served as officers. Meanwhile, the
military classified Hispanics as "Caucasians" and
thus had no statistics about their service, though
it appears that Mexican Americans won a disproportionate number of Medals of Honor and had
higher casualty rates. The most common name on
the Vietnam War Memorial would be Johnson, a
name used by both whites and blacks, but the second most common was Rodriguez. "One of the
tragedies of war," observed Mexican American
folk singer Joan Baez, an anti-war activist, "is that
the poor people of every nationality are the ones
who carry most of the guns, suffer, fight, and die."

Ironically, despite the Pentagon's emphasis on
statistics, the army kept poor records about the
number of women who served in Vietnam. Ap-
proximately 11,000 women participated in the
war, including some 7,000 Army nurses. Others
had noncombatant roles, such as clerks and or-
derlies. Since the use of helicopters reduced the
time between the injury of a soldier and his treatment to less than three hours, the nurses dealt
closely with the dead and dying, as well as with
severely wounded patients. Their 12-hour work

shifts, six days a week, left them little time to cope with the omnipresent sense of loss. Like combat soldiers, many nurses experienced enduring psychological problems associated with posttraumatic stress disorder (PTSD).

Committing to War

Johnson and his advisors justified such sacrifices by stressed the responsibility of the United States to defend the "free world" from communist aggression. Moreover, their view of the Vietnam war reflected the Cold War consensus that saw a Soviet hand behind every international conflict. "Surrender anywhere," said Johnson in 1964, "threatens defeat everywhere." When a reform group in the Dominican Republic attempted to seize power from the Army in 1965, for example, Johnson promptly ordered the Marines to suppress the uprising, claiming that communists had organized the revolt. He worried not only about political defeat overseas but also about the potential effect on domestic politics. Fearing that conservatives would attack him for "losing" Vietnam, Johnson vowed not "to be the president who saw Southeast Asia go the way China went."

Although as a presidential candidate in 1964 Johnson assured voters that he wanted "no wider war," the administration had already initiated hostile actions against North Vietnam and planned additional military escalation that would begin after the election. One series of operations involved intelligence overflights, dropping propaganda leaflets, and commando raids by South Vietnamese soldiers. The president also approved increased military stockpiles in Thailand and the Philippines, the deployment of tactical personnel and equipment in the region, and destroyer patrols along the coast of North Vietnam in the Gulf of Tonkin. In July 1964, Johnson announced that U.S. forces in Vietnam would increase from 16,000 to 23,000.

Such provocation brought a North Vietnamese response in August 1964. As the destroyer Maddox gathered intelligence in the Tonkin Gulf, three North Vietnamese patrol boats attacked the vessel, causing minor damage. Nervous radar operators subsequently reported a second attack, though it apparently never occurred. After using the hotline to Moscow for the first time to assure the Soviets of his limited objectives, Johnson ordered an air attack on North Vietnam. He then used the incident to present Congress with a previously written joint resolution authorizing the president to take "all necessary measures . . . to prevent further aggression" in Vietnam. The 1964 Tonkin Gulf Resolution, granting the commander-in-chief discretionary power to lead the nation into war, passed the House unanimously and the Senate with only the dissenting votes of Oregon's Wayne Morse and Alaska's Ernest Gruening. The resolution served two purposes: first, it quieted Republican critics about Johnson's handling of Vietnam and showed others that he was the more restrained presidential candidate; second, it gave Johnson approval for the post-election escalation. "Like grandma's nightshirt," said Johnson, "it covered everything."

After the November election, the White House continued its plans to escalate the war. Fearing that the politically divided government of South Vietnam lacked the resolve to fight for its self-preservation, Johnson looked for an excuse to justify U.S. intervention. The Viet Cong provided an opportunity in February 1965 by attacking the U.S. base at Pleiku. National Security Advisor McGeorge Bundy observed soon afterward that "Pleikus are streetcars," by which he meant that such pretexts for intervention came along all the time; if you missed one, another would soon appear.

Johnson now ordered Operation Rolling Thunder—air strikes against North Vietnam. White House claims that the air war was merely retaliatory deceived the public about the regular sustained bombings that raised the military stakes and committed the nation to a long war. Enemy anti-aircraft fire increased the loss of life and planes; captured pilots would suffer torment and misery as prisoners of war. Inaccurate targeting brought rising civilian casualties. To guard the U.S. air base at Danang, moreover, Johnson ordered Marines into Vietnam in March 1965. These were the first U.S. ground troops in the war. The White House consulted neither Congress nor the South Vietnamese government. The next month, Washington approved offensive "combat deployment."

At Johnson's instructions, these military decisions were kept secret from the press and public, lest they arouse criticism. In April 1965, Johnson presented a speech at Johns Hopkins University expressing interest in "unconditional discussions" and offered North Vietnam development aid to build dams and power plants in the Mekong Delta in exchange for accepting a separate South Vietnamese government. "We want nothing for ourselves," said Johnson, "only that the people of South Vietnam be allowed to guide their own country." That single uncompromising *only* constituted the primary fallacy of Johnson's policy—that South Vietnam was a "country" and that Vietnam's communists were not nationalists but agents of international communism. Johnson's position precluded any negotiated settlement.

Escalating Military Action

Taking a lesson from the Korean War, U.S. policy makers rejected an invasion north of the 17th parallel, lest it provoke China to intervene. Yet, by the end of 1965, the number of U.S. air attacks passed 70,000 strikes, including B-52 "carpet" bombings that unleashed immense tonnage from invisible heights. Meanwhile, General William Westmoreland, the chief military commander in Vietnam, requested additional ground forces to eliminate the guerrilla armies that operated inside South Viet-

nam. Counting on superior technology (defoliants, helicopters, weapons), Westmoreland ordered search-and-destroy missions that would engage the secretive enemy in combat, then expose them to additional firepower from the air. Numerically, the plan seemed to work. When U.S. troops fought the enemy, the ratio of Viet Cong casualties to American often exceeded 10 to 1, though military body counts always appeared dubious to civilian observers. Body counts also encouraged soldiers to shoot first, ask questions later, which sometimes resulting in the indiscriminate killing of civilians. Yet jungle warfare enabled the enemy to initiate 80 percent of combat actions, using elements of surprise and an amazing hidden tunnel system to minimize losses. Even at 10 to 1 ratios, the United States could not win such a war of attrition.

"We must continue to raise the price of aggression," said Johnson as he ordered bombings against enemy supply lines and factories near Hanoi and the port of Haiphong. To encourage peace negotiations, the president halted the bombing during the 1966 Christmas holidays and sent ambassadors to world capitals. But by refusing to accept communist representation in South Vietnam, White House conditions prevented serious discussion. Some military leaders suggested using nuclear weapons in Vietnam, but Johnson knew that world opinion opposed such tactics and feared Soviet or Chinese retaliation. With nearly half a million U.S. forces in Vietnam at the end of 1967, Westmoreland promised "light at the end of the tunnel." Defense Secretary Robert McNamara, chief architect of U.S. war policy, no longer believed the military calculations; without taking his doubts public, he resigned in late 1967.

The Cost of War

The war created an immense economic burden— $20 billion a year by 1967. Unwilling to abandon

U.S. helicopters airlift members of the 2nd Battalion, 14th Infantry Regiment from the Filhol rubber plantation to a new staging area during a search-and-destroy mission. Such technological warfare could not defeat an elusive enemy.

the Great Society, which Johnson had said was "the woman I really loved," the president did not ask Congress for wartime taxes. Economies in government spending and minor tax changes enabled the White House to conceal the full cost of the war. This guns-and-butter policy created swollen federal budget deficits, jumping from $3.8 billion in 1966 to $8.7 billion in 1967 to $25.2 billion in 1968. Deficit spending stimulated inflation. As the consumer price index increased 5 percent in 1968, rising prices slowed economic growth, weakened the dollar overseas, and undermined foreign trade. By the time Congress forced the president to accept higher taxes in 1968, the nation's economy was severely wounded.

Johnson's war policy collapsed in 1968. As U.S. forces concentrated tremendous firepower to protect a Marine outpost at Khe Sanh from enemy encirclement, the Viet Cong and North Vietnamese regulars launched coordinated attacks against every major city in South Vietnam during the Tet holiday season in January 1968. Catching U.S. and

South Vietnam troops by surprise, enemy soldiers entered the U.S. embassy compound in Saigon. Elsewhere, the Viet Cong attacked military targets and South Vietnam's civil administration, killing political foes and local leaders. Yet, by exposing the guerrilla armies to counterattack, the Tet offensive had suicidal consequences. Although South Vietnam's armies took the opportunity to eliminate domestic rivals, such as anti-regime Buddhists and other dissenters accused of being Viet Cong sympathizers, the street battles also claimed an estimated 32,000 Viet Cong troops and virtually eliminated enemy forces based in South Vietnam.

During the Tet offensive, U.S. soldiers suffered 4,000 killed, 20,000 wounded, and the 8 to 1 ratio over enemy casualties suggested a tactical victory. But the political importance of Tet was its proof of enemy resilience and determination. Westmoreland's promise of an imminent victory seemed foolish, if not dishonest, and his request for another 206,000 troops underscored the difficulty ahead. Tet showed that the enemy had merely *to*

The War in Vietnam

U.S. and South Vietnamese troop movements

Major North Vietnamese supply routes into South Vietnam

CHINA

NORTH VIETNAM

•Dien Bien Phu

LAOS

✕ Hanoi
U.S. air raids late 1960s, 1972

✕ *Gulf of Tonkin Incident Aug. 1964*

Gulf of Tonkin

Hainan

•Vientiane

DEMILITARIZED ZONE

17TH PARALLEL DEMARCATION LINE
(GENEVA ACCORDS, 1954)

Invasion of Laos Feb. 6–March, 1971

Hue ✕ *Tet Offensive Jan. 30–Feb. 1968*

•Da Nang

THAILAND

✕ *My Lai Massacre March 16, 1968*

HO CHI MINH TRAIL

CAMBODIA

SOUTH VIETNAM

South China Sea

Invasion of Cambodia April 29–June 29, 1970

Phnom Penh•

Saigon
✕ *Tet Offensive Jan. 30–March 7, 1968*
Surrender of South Vietnam, 1975

MEKONG DELTA

Gulf of Thailand

0   100   200 miles

0   100   200 kilometers

exist to prevent U.S. forces from winning the war. The battle also indicated the weakness of South Vietnam's military posture; without U.S. assistance, a stable government could not endure. Three years of military action and political propaganda had failed to pacify the country.

Mounting Opposition to the War

As military action escalated, so did opposition to the war. In 1965, just weeks after Johnson ordered the bombing of North Vietnam, 20,000 protesters traveled to Washington to denounce U.S. military aggression. Acknowledging that administration leaders were not evil men, SDS leader Paul Potter asked "what kind of system . . . allows 'good' men to make those kinds of decisions?" As the military draft affected college students, anti-war "teach-ins" and protest demonstrations sprouted on most major campuses.

Opposition to the war reflected more than expediency. Enlightened by the civil rights movement and mistrustful of political leaders, a younger generation questioned participation in a technological war to defend a third-world government that could hardly claim to uphold democratic principles. The war also raised moral issues about who would serve, and possibly die, and who would not. Of the 30 million young adult men eligible for military service during the 1960s, only 10 percent entered the armed services and went to Vietnam. Others, such as college students and skilled professionals, received deferments and exemptions. Even in Vietnam, a disproportionate share of educated whites avoided combat assignments.

"Hell, no, we won't go!" became a familiar chant on college campuses. "Girls say yes to boys who say no" became a nonfeminist voice of support. Some young men burned their draft cards and refused induction, thousands fled to Canada, and thousands more deserted the armed forces. In

"Hell, no, we won't go!"

October 1967, stop-the-draft protests in Oakland, California, near the University of California's Berkeley campus, provoked street battles between 20,000 demonstrators and local police. That month, the National Mobilization Against the War attracted ten times as many protesters to march at the Pentagon. Norman Mailer's prize-winning "novel-as-history" *The Armies of the Night* (1968) analyzed the fervor of anti-war dissent and concluded that the younger generation hated political authority "because the authority lied."

Countering Dissent

Opposition to the war blended with other moral issues. Working-class families denounced a draft system that deferred students and middle-class professionals. When heavyweight boxing champion Muhammed Ali sought deferment as a Muslim minister, boxing officials took away his title. SNCC became the first civil rights group to condemn the war. "The bombs in Vietnam explode at home," proclaimed Martin Luther King, Jr., as he joined the anti-war crusade in 1967. "We are willing to make the Negro 100 percent of a citizen in warfare, but reduce him to 50 percent of a citizen on American soil." Catholic conscientious objectors led attacks against draft boards, mounting a "resistance" movement and defiling draft records with blood.

To silence anti-war critics, the FBI and military intelligence organized secret attacks on pacifist groups and gathered information on the personal behavior of thousands of citizens. Convinced that political dissent was inspired by communists, President Johnson ordered the CIA to conduct domestic surveillance—a violation of the CIA charter.

Operation CHAOS investigated thousands of dissenters, even "suspicious" members of Congress, but located no foreign involvement in the anti-war movement. Johnson rejected the report.

The expansion of anti-war action fueled a conservative backlash. As civil disorder destroyed the domestic consensus, Republicans parlayed issues of "law and order" to make large gains in the 1966 elections. By 1968, ghetto rioting, student rebellions, and anti-war demonstrations built a groundswell of worry about crime and the erosion of patriotism. "A bearded professor . . . thinks he knows how to settle the Vietnam war," Governor George Wallace ridiculed dissenters, but "hasn't got enough sense to park his bicycle straight." Wallace announced the formation of the American Independent party to launch a presidential campaign based on repeal of civil rights laws and victory in Vietnam. Meanwhile, Johnson's Democratic party split into "hawk" and "dove" factions. As AFL-CIO unions backed the president, the civil rights wing looked for alternative candidates. The liberal consensus was unraveling.

The Passions of 1968

The Tet offensive demoralized a war-weary nation. Minnesota Senator Eugene McCarthy, a political maverick who detested the war, astonished political regulars by winning 42 percent of the vote in the New Hampshire Democratic primary in March 1968. The upset spurred New York Senator Robert Kennedy to announce his own candidacy against the man who had succeeded his brother. As the anti-war candidates prepared for a season of primary contests, Johnson removed Westmoreland from military command in Vietnam and summoned his highest-level advisors to appraise the continuing war. The previous November, this prestigious elite had endorsed the escalation of bombing. Now they expressed doubts. As military victory appeared more distant, the "wise men" warned that unless the war gained full citizen support, including war taxes and a balanced budget, the declining value of the dollar overseas would imperil foreign trade and domestic stability.

Johnson weighed their advice and then faced the nation. In a dramatic televised speech in March 1968, the president outlined a new initiative for peace in Vietnam. Agreeing for the first time to negotiate with the Viet Cong, he announced a suspension of bombing of North Vietnam and pleaded for a diplomatic settlement. Then Johnson added an unexpected postscript to his speech: he would not seek reelection in 1968. The war, and its domestic consequences, had eroded his power.

Season of Assassination

Four days later, on the same day that North Vietnam agreed to begin peace talks in Paris, a sniper killed Martin Luther King, Jr., in Memphis, Tennessee. The murder brought a mixture of shock, sadness, despair, and rage, and provoked angry blacks to riot in dozens of cities around the country. Although the nonviolent King had planned a Poor People's March to the capital that spring, his death distracted attention from the anti-poverty agenda. In a final gesture to the slain leader, Congress passed the Open Housing Act, prohibiting racial discrimination in the sale and rental of 80 percent of the nation's dwellings and offered $5 billion in mortgage and rent subsidies. But the post-assassination violence added to public concern about law and order, giving conservatives a strong political weapon.

While anti-war liberals McCarthy and Kennedy competed for the Democratic nomination, Vice President Hubert Humphrey ran as Johnson's candidate. The lively primary season ended abruptly in Los Angeles in June, when a Palestinian opposed to Kennedy's pro-Israel position murdered the senator

The Election of 1968

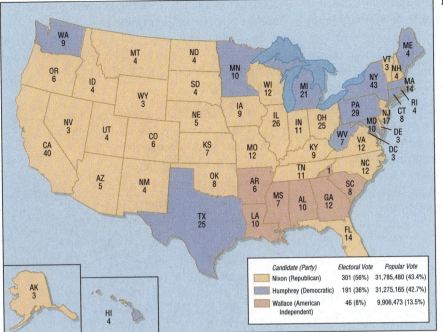

Candidate (Party)	Electoral Vote	Popular Vote
Nixon (Republican)	301 (56%)	31,785,480 (43.4%)
Humphrey (Democratic)	191 (36%)	31,275,165 (42.7%)
Wallace (American Independent)	46 (8%)	9,906,473 (13.5%)

just minutes after his victory in California. His televised funeral—like those of his brother and Dr. King—underscored the fragility of political succession. Democratic regulars rallied behind Humphrey, while anti-war activists went to the Democratic National Convention in Chicago that summer to demand a peace candidate. The city's Democratic leadership refused to tolerate such dissent. Denying parade permits to the protesters, Chicago police attacked the demonstrators in what a presidential investigation later called a "police riot." Television cameras zeroed in on the carnage in the streets while the convention's support of Humphrey and the war played to a missing audience.

The Bitter Campaign

Democratic chaos contrasted with the smooth and orderly revival of Republican candidate Richard Nixon. Promising to "end the war and win the peace in the Pacific," the former vice president projected the image of a "new Nixon," dedicated to global restraint and reassertion of U.S. power. Yet his political advertising focused entirely on domestic issues: the fear of crime in the streets, violent anti-war demonstrations, and the loss of patriotism. "We're going to build this country up so that no one will dare use the U.S. flag for a doormat again," vowed Nixon. His vice-presidential choice, Maryland Governor Spiro Agnew, had earned notoriety for condemning civil rights and anti-war demonstrators. As Nixon promised to "bring people together," the Republican slogan—"This time, vote as if your whole world depended on it"—underscored the perilous mood. Appealing to "forgotten Americans"—the lower-middle class of urban white ethnics, blue-collar workers, and southern whites—Nixon targeted groups that had voted Democratic ever since the New Deal.

In an October surprise, Johnson announced a complete cessation of bombing in Vietnam, and Humphrey's voter ratings suddenly improved. But Johnson's incumbency contributed too many handicaps. In November, Nixon won election by seven-tenths of a percentage point. Wallace, who hoped at best to throw the election into the House of Representatives, took 13.5 percent of the popular total and 45 electoral votes in the South. Nixon carried the rest of the South (except Texas) and everything west of the Mississippi. Only in the Northeast did Humphrey preserve the alliance of unions, blacks, Jews, and Catholics.

The War Continues

Nixon's election triumph reflected public anxiety and anger about political turmoil, social division, and the younger generation's attack on moral standards. Yet the anti-authoritarian youth movement, which celebrated peace, civil rights, sex, rock, and drugs, scarcely affected the outlook of the political leadership. None of the 1968 presidential aspirants—not even the dove-ish "Clean Gene" McCarthy—favored social reform or the cessation of the war without protecting the corporate leadership and U.S. primacy in international affairs.

Although the media highlighted extremes of dissent, the political process continued to operate with minimal disruption. While voters looked to Nixon to reestablish respect for "law and order," therefore, a large segment of the younger generation refused to acknowledge his political authority. As the Republicans entered the White House, the U.S. death toll in Vietnam passed 30,000; more than half a million U.S. soldiers still carried weapons in that embattled country. The causes of political discontent remained volatile and undiminished. Under Nixon, the war would continue both in Vietnam and at home.

INFOTRAC® COLLEGE EDITION EXERCISES

For additional reading go to InfoTrac College Edition, your online research library at *http://web1.infotrac-college.com.*

Keyword search: Lyndon Johnson

Subject search: Great Society

Subject search: Tonkin Gulf

Keyword search: Tet Offensive

Subject search: Martin Luther King assassination

Keyword search: Bobby Kennedy

Subject search: Nixon

ADDITIONAL READING

Irving Bernstein, *Guns or Butter: The Presidency of Lyndon Johnson* (1996). The author provides a detailed analysis of domestic politics, but see also Doris Kearns's biographical portrait *Lyndon Johnson and the American Dream* (1976).

Robert Dallek, *Flawed Giant: Lyndon Johnson and his Times, 1961–1973* (1998). The second of a two-volume biography, this work focuses on Washington politics and presidential motivations.

Civil Rights for Blacks and Women

Clayborne Carson, *In Struggle: SNCC and the Black Awakening of the 1960s* (1981). This book analyzes black student protest and the decision to exclude white participation. See also the related titles listed in Chapter 26.

Sara Evans, *Personal Politics: The Root of Women's Liberation in the Civil Rights Movement and the New Left* (1979). Drawing on oral histories, the author links the emerging women's movement to political activism on other fronts.

Affirming Black Identity

William L. Van DeBurg, *New Day in Babylon: The Black Power Movement and American Culture, 1965–1975* (1992). This study examines the debates about black identity and the transformation of black culture since the mid-1960s.

Awakening Racial Identities

Julie Leininger Pycior, *LBJ and Mexican Americans: The Paradox of Power* (1997). Placing Johnson's relations with Mexican Americans in the context of Texas politics, the book examines political issues during the Johnson presidency. For a collection of related sources, see George Mariscal, *Aztlan and Vietnam: Chicano and Chicana Experiences of the War* (1999).

The Culture of the Boomers

Thomas Frank, *The Conquest of Cool* (1997). This study of advertising discusses changing images and ideology during the 1960s.

Nick Bromell, *Tomorrow Never Knows: Rock and Psychedelics in the 1960s* (2000). The author stresses the power of music and drugs in awakening cultural dissent.

The Politics of Alienation

Rebecca E. Klatch, *A Generation Divided: The New Left, the New Right, and the 1960s* (1999). A sociological study, the book depicts the polarization of politics among the younger generation.

Lyndon Johnson's War

Christian G. Appy, *Working-Class War: American Combat Soldiers in Vietnam* (1993). Based partly on oral histories, the book analyzes the problems and culture within the military in Vietnam.

Winnie Smith, *American Daughter Gone to War* (1992). A nurse's memoir, this book provides a haunting account of the medical side of the war.

Marilyn B. Young, *The Vietnam Wars, 1945–1990* (1991). This book offers an excellent overview of U.S. policy in Vietnam. For a different perspective, see George L. Herring, *America's Longest War* (1996). See also Logevall's *Choosing War,* cited in Chapter 26.

Mounting Opposition to the War

Tom Wells, *The War Within: America's Battle over Vietnam* (1994). This book presents a detailed analysis of the anti-war movement.

The Bitter Campaign

Joe McGinniss, *The Selling of the President: 1968* (1969). This contemporary account of the Nixon campaign includes examples of television advertisements.

28

The "Imperial Presidency" of Richard Nixon, 1969–1974

CHRONOLOGY

1969	Richard Nixon takes office; Spiro Agnew is vice president
	Secret bombings begin in Cambodia
	President announces "Vietnamization"
	Anti-war movement stages Moratorium Day protests
1970	Nixon orders attacks in Cambodia
	Students killed at Kent State, Jackson State
	Congress defeats Family Assistance Plan
1971	Nixon orders attacks in Laos
	The New York Times publishes the Pentagon Papers
	President establishes wage-price freeze
	Congress passes Equal Rights Amendment
1972	Nixon visits People's Republic of China
	U.S. agrees to SALT treaty with Soviet Union
	Plumbers arrested at Watergate
	Nixon defeats George McGovern in landslide
1973	Paris treaty formally ends Vietnam war
	Roe v. Wade decision upholds abortion rights
	Senate opens Watergate investigations
	OPEC establishes oil embargo
	Agnew resigns; Gerald Ford chosen vice president
	Congress passes War Powers Act
1974	Nixon resigns as president; Ford succeeds him

"After a period of confrontation," said Richard Nixon in his inaugural address in 1969, "we are entering an era of negotiation." Vietnam was still the main issue of political contention. Suggesting a willingness to reach accommodation with his critics, the president held out hopes of ending the war and restoring tranquility at home. But about such sensitive matters, Nixon preferred in public statements to say less rather than more, fearing that debate would arouse further criticism and undermine his diplomatic position. His speech made no reference to his "secret plan" to end the war. Instead, the new president asked for time—six months perhaps—to obtain the elusive truce. Meanwhile, he asked the frustrated citizenry to "lower our voices . . . so that our words can be heard as well as our voices." At that very moment, however, anti-war demonstrators were holding counter-inauguration protests across the street from the White House.

The Vietnam debate would set the tone of the country's political life for the next six years. The conflicts of cultures that had brewed throughout the decade—divisions between the generations, between men and women, between blacks and whites, between pro-war hawks and anti-war doves—touched a multitude of social issues. Many respectable middle-class groups, such as Women's Strike for Peace and Another Mother for Peace, had participated in the anti-war movement, but media and presidential attention targeted the more dissident youth. "Drugs, crime, campus revolts, racial discord, draft resistance—on every hand," Nixon told a college audience in South Dakota that spring, "we find old standards violated, old values discarded, old principles ignored." Yet while decrying this loss of "fundamental values," the president tended to take positions that aggravated, rather than relieved, political tensions. "I understand that there . . . continues to be opposition to the war in Vietnam," Nixon conceded. "However, under no circumstances will I be affected by it."

During his first term in office, Nixon's ignoring the anti-war movement enabled him to make important diplomatic agreements with the communist superpowers, altering the balance of world power and reducing U.S. involvement in Vietnam. But the president's reluctance to face dissent also led him to violate principles of law and constitutional government with equal aloofness. Nixon's suspicion of the media soon threatened basic rights of free speech and due process as well. Within half a decade, the candidate who had promised in 1968 to "bring us together" opened chasms of hostility that nearly destroyed the nation's political foundations.

Seeking "Peace with Honor"

The central issue of Nixon's presidency proved to be Nixon himself. Believing that international affairs, especially in Vietnam, were the country's

> **Developing what he called the "Madman Theory," Nixon posed as a world leader who would do *anything* to force the enemy to negotiate.**

major problem, Nixon assumed primary responsibility for directing foreign policy. Although his erudite National Security Advisor, Henry Kissinger, sometimes shared the spotlight with him, the president kept his subordinate on a tight rein. Nixon had built a reputation as a tough, though volatile, politician and he tried to use this image to diplomatic advantage. Developing what he called the "Madman Theory," Nixon posed as a world leader who would do *anything* to force the enemy to negotiate. He also embraced Kissinger's theory of "linkage," which held all international affairs to be interrelated, especially in dealings with communist powers. Cooperation in one aspect of diplomacy (for example, easing trade relations with the Soviet Union) had to be linked to other issues, such as restraints on nuclear weapons. Moreover, Nixon and Kissinger viewed themselves as realists and had little regard for what they viewed as idealism, legalism, or political morality.

This mix of personality, ideology, and politics directed Nixon's approach to ending the war in Vietnam. Like his Democratic predecessors, Nixon remained committed to preserving an independent, noncommunist government in South Vietnam. But, unlike Lyndon Johnson, he recognized the limits of exerting U.S. power to achieve that goal, and he understood the impatience of his own citizenry. He would not unilaterally quit the war; according to public opinion polls, few people demanded an abrupt departure. But he hoped to use promises of withdrawing U.S. troops from Vietnam to persuade the enemy to accept a compromise political solution and to quiet dissent at home.

Nixon exchanges toasts with Zhou Enlai during his historic trip to The People's Republic of China.

Nixon called his solution to Vietnam "peace with honor," a euphemism for a military retreat that would not be called a defeat. Unlike Johnson, who had feared that withdrawal from Vietnam would provoke Republicans to attack the president for losing Southeast Asia to the communists, Nixon had established an anti-communist reputation that protected him from such criticism. His policies thus operated on two levels. First, he would use military force to demonstrate to the enemy U.S. resolution in Vietnam, hoping to advance peace talks that would preserve South Vietnam as an independent country. Second, and paradoxically, Nixon would begin to withdraw U.S. troops from Vietnam to ease domestic dissent, reduce the cost of the war, and encourage South Vietnam to create a viable anti-communist government. This willingness to pursue an innovative foreign policy did not indicate any sympathy for the growing anti-war movement—just the opposite. In fact, to strengthen his diplomatic hand, Nixon refused to tolerate dissent on the homefront. As a result, tensions between the

White House and the anti-war public increased, and political debate became more polarized. In the end, Nixon's aggressive war policies sharpened the country's political differences.

Nixon Expands the War

To stifle signs of weakness that might encourage the enemy to avoid negotiations, Nixon initiated an aggressive military policy in Vietnam. When North Vietnam greeted the new administration in 1969 with a three-week offensive that included shelling South Vietnamese cities and claimed 1,100 U.S. combat deaths, Washington answered with a "pacification" operation involving crop burning, population removal, defoliation of jungles, and heavy bombings. In April 1969, the 33,641 U.S. war dead in Vietnam exceeded the total of the Korean war. The next month, the battle of "Hamburger Hill" illustrated the frustrations of search-and-destroy military operations. As paratroopers made ten frontal assaults against enemy positions, soldiers for the first time challenged military orders and threatened mutiny. Then, after taking the hill with heavy losses, the troops were withdrawn because the position had no intrinsic military value.

Nixon's initial policy also veered in secret, riskier directions. Responding to intelligence reports that North Vietnam's military headquarters were based in Cambodia, Nixon ordered Operation Breakfast, a sustained bombing campaign of that neutral country that was designed to eliminate communist sanctuaries. To avoid arousing anti-war protest, Nixon demanded absolute secrecy, permitting an elaborate system of false reporting to disguise the bombing missions. Nevertheless, *New York Times* reporter William Beecher learned of the operation, probably from enemy sources, for whom the attacks were hardly secret. Upon reading the news item, Nixon and Kissinger ordered wiretaps of the journalist and any administration officials who might have leaked information. These secret activities, both the bombings and the wiretaps, represented the president's first steps outside the law. Nixon's road to Watergate began in Southeast Asia.

As for bombing Cambodia (which included Operations Lunch, Snack, Dessert, and Dinner to become Operation Menu), the attacks failed to destroy North Vietnamese forces, who merely moved deeper into the country. During the ensuing 14-month period, B-52 planes dropped 103,921 tons of bombs in Cambodia (an enormous amount, but still less than half the total tonnage dropped there by 1973). This indiscriminate bombing undermined Cambodia's political leadership, contributing to the rise of the sadistic Khmer Rouge regime that murdered millions of Cambodians during the next decade.

Seeking Negotiations

Despite the peace talks that had begun in Paris in 1968, Nixon, like Johnson, refused to accept communist participation in South Vietnam's government. Kissinger explained that a political compromise in Vietnam would destroy U.S. credibility as an anti-communist ally and weaken U.S. influence around the world. While maintaining a rigid position in Vietnam, Nixon and Kissinger believed that agreement with the Soviet Union and China to stabilize the nuclear arms race might also bring peace in Vietnam. Adopting Kissinger's principle of linkage, the idea that negotiations should not focus on single issues but embrace all elements of disagreement, Nixon believed that the world's great powers—not North Vietnam or the Viet Cong—held the secret to peace. Soon after taking office, Nixon began to use private channels to reach the major communist adversaries. He was surprised to learn that they had less influence in Hanoi, the capital of North Vietnam, than he had thought.

Nixon also learned that diplomatic negotiations would take longer than expected, and he feared that delay would arouse further dissent at home. Thus the president developed a strategic policy to intensify the war while reducing troop commitments. He unveiled the new strategy, which he called "Vietnamization," in 1969. Under the plan, the United States would strengthen South Vietnam's military forces, thus permitting a gradual but steady withdrawal of U.S. troops from that embattled country. To be sure, Nixon refused to be bound to a rigid timetable, hoping to encourage North Vietnam to negotiate. And to keep the pressure on the enemy, he ordered continued bombing of enemy camps in South Vietnam and Cambodia. Yet peace negotiations in Paris remained stalemated. While Nixon insisted on mutual withdrawal of North Vietnamese and U.S. troops and the preservation of a noncommunist government in South Vietnam, Hanoi's diplomats demanded immediate U.S. withdrawal and free elections, including communists, in South Vietnam.

Despite winning no concessions from Hanoi and despite South Vietnam's angry objections to troop withdrawals, the president ordered the departure of 25,000 ground forces in the fall of 1969 and steadily increased the number until 110,000 had departed Vietnam by the following spring. To quiet his domestic critics, Nixon proposed changes in the military draft laws. Replacing rules that had kept men eligible for service until age 26, the White House backed a one-year lottery system and the elimination of educational deferments that favored more-affluent men. Such measures anticipated the creation of an all-volunteer army.

The Anti-War Movement and the Silent Majority

Unaware of the secret bombings in Cambodia or of Kissinger's secret conversations with North Vietnam, congressional Democrats denounced the war, and anti-war sentiment grew around the country. On October 15, 1969, the New Mobilization Committee to End the War organized a Moratorium Day protest, attracting hundreds of thousands of dissenters in major cities. Public-opinion polls showed majority support for choosing a specific date to withdraw all U.S. forces from Vietnam. This pressure helped persuade Nixon to postpone plans to increase the bombing in Vietnam, but the president refused to acknowledge such concessions. Instead, he enraged anti-war activists by spending Moratorium Day watching televised football.

Nixon waited two weeks to reply to the demonstrations. Then, in an angry and influential televised rebuttal to the anti-war movement, the president insisted that street demonstrators and petitioners who opposed the war constituted only a "vocal minority" and that a much larger group of citizens, which he called "the silent majority," supported White House policy. Escalating the rhetorical war, Nixon refused to make conciliatory gestures, as Vice President Spiro Agnew proceeded to attack both the anti-war movement and the national media that focused on public dissent. "A spirit of national masochism prevails," Agnew declared, "encouraged by an effete corps of impudent snobs who characterize themselves as intellectuals."

Amid this angry national debate, the public now learned of a military engagement that had occurred eighteen months earlier at the village of My Lai, during which U.S. soldiers had killed about 500 Vietnamese civilians. The atrocity underscored the moral ambiguities of the U.S. presence in Vietnam. Anti-war demonstrators saw the tragedy as evidence of military racism, a failure to distinguish allies from enemies, civilians from soldiers. Yet the Viet Cong's guerrilla tactics, which included hiding among the civilian population, shared responsibility for human error. Although the military justice system eventually convicted Lieutenant William Calley for the crime, no higher officers were ever charged and Nixon later reduced Calley's sentence.

The My Lai massacre indicated other problems of military morale. With the White House talking about troop withdrawals, the draftees who served in Vietnam often lacked the discipline of volunteer professionals. U.S. combat soldiers typically served twelve months in Vietnam, and "short-termers"— those who would soon be rotated home—were often reluctant to take unnecessary initiative. Moreover, like their siblings at home, Vietnam soldiers experimented with marijuana, opium, and heroin (though seldom in battle situations), which became a serious problem. As on the homefront, racial tensions escalated. So did desertion rates and cases of "fragging" (attempts by enlisted men to kill their superiors). In Vietnam, the most commonly seen graffito became the peace symbol.

The Cambodia Incursion

Polarization of opinion about the war had created a volatile atmosphere on the homefront. But by early 1970 new draft laws, troop withdrawals, and optimism about Vietnamization permitted political passions to cool. As peace talks remained stalled, Nixon wanted to pressure North Vietnam to hasten negotiations. To demonstrate that Vietnamization did not indicate a weakening of commitments, he chose a bold military initiative in the spring of 1970.

"We are not a weak people," said Nixon as he ordered attacks on North Vietnamese troops based in Cambodia. Destabilized by U.S. bombing, Cambodia's neutral regime had recently been overthrown by an anti-communist leadership. Nixon saw an opportunity to eradicate the enemy headquarters that had escaped destruction during the previous year of bombing. He also hoped that the expansion of the war would persuade North Vietnam to negotiate a truce. Anxious about this decision, the president repeatedly watched the movie *Patton* (1970), the story of America's toughest general in World War II, to bolster his confidence.

Insisting that "the world's most powerful nation" could not act "like a pitiful, helpless giant," Nixon announced, in a tense televised address in April 1970, the decision to launch an attack in Cambodia. To justify this escalation of the war into a neutral country (he called it an "incursion," not an invasion) the president again resorted to rhetorical sleight-of-hand. "It is not our power but our will and character that is being tested," he emphasized. At a time when the White House boasted of the success of Vietnamization, however, congressional doves in both parties denounced the unexpected expansion of the war. "Presidential assurances," editorialized *The New York Times,* "can no longer be accepted."

The War Hits Home

Kent State University in northeastern Ohio now emerged as a flashpoint of the nation's raging controversies. In recent years, campus activists had of-fended the local community by endorsing new values of sexual expression, counterculture styles, and anti-war politics. Town residents complained that movie theaters favored sex-related films and no longer featured "family" subjects; local women criticized college "girls [who] sleep around." Most of all, Kent's residents despised the unpatriotic tone of anti-war rallies. "Authority, law and order," said one woman, "are the backbone of our society."

Nixon's Cambodia speech touched the nerve endings of the country's divided communities. On May 1, 1970, 300 students at Kent State ripped out the pages of the Constitution from the back of their U.S. history textbooks, dug a hole in the lawn, and solemnly buried the document, charging that Nixon had killed the laws of the land. Over the weekend, Kent students rioted in the streets and burned the campus Reserve Officer Training Corps (ROTC) center, a symbol of the military's presence in campus life. Ohio Governor James Rhodes sent the national guard to restore order. As students prepared for a noontime campus rally, military authorities demanded their dispersal. Greeted by jeers and rocks, the guard suddenly opened fire. Within minutes, four students lay dead, and nine more were seriously wounded. Some had been protesting the war; others were merely heading for class. Ten days later, police shootings at a dormitory at Mississippi's Jackson State College left two African American students dead.

The killing of college students appeared as shocking as the deaths in Vietnam and proved to be equally polarizing. On campuses around the country, students spontaneously organized strikes to protest "business as usual." Nixon and Agnew replied with warnings instead of condolences. A national opinion poll found that 58 percent blamed the students for the violence and half supported the invasion of Cambodia. But surveys that focused on student opinion found 76 percent demanding "basic changes in the system." A presi-

The famous photograph that captured the nation's horror and disbelief at the shooting deaths of four students during an anti–Vietnam War protest at Kent State University in Ohio.

dential commission investigating campus unrest that summer concluded that the Kent State murders were "unnecessary, unwarranted, and inexcusable," while those at Jackson State were "unreasonable" and "unjustified." Agnew called the findings "pabulum for the permissivists."

Diplomatic Adjustments and Political Confrontation

As public opinion split, so Washington politics divided. Two cabinet officers publicly dissented from presidential policy. One month after Kent State, the Senate repealed the 1964 Tonkin Gulf resolution, the prime legislative sanction for the war, though the House narrowly backed the president. Other "end the war" resolutions that were introduced to Congress produced flamboyant prose but political deadlock. Congress did establish a 60-day limit to the Cambodian operation, and at that deadline U.S. troops departed, having failed to locate or destroy the elusive communist headquarters. Afterwards, U.S. and South Vietnamese pilots treated Cambodia as a "free fire zone," indiscriminately bombing that country. Yet North Vietnamese troops and supplies continued to flow through Cambodia to South Vietnam along the Ho Chi Minh Trail.

The effort to defeat the enemy in Cambodia had failed, and negotiations remained stalled. Despite doubts about South Vietnam's military proficiency, the president subtly altered U.S. terms for peace. By the end of 1970, Washington no longer demanded mutual withdrawal of North Vietnamese forces from the South in exchange for a U.S. departure. Instead, Nixon proposed a ceasefire in place. Meanwhile, scheduled troop withdrawals continued. Rather than facilitating negotiations, the shift in goals stiffened North Vietnam's resolve.

By 1971, "peace with honor" seemed a distant prospect. To break the diplomatic deadlock, Nixon ordered an attack inside Laos, another neutral country, in the spring of 1971. According to plans, South Vietnamese ground forces, supported by U.S. air power, would demonstrate the success of Vietnamization by blocking the Ho Chi Minh Trail, the primary supply route from North Vietnam to the Viet Cong. Instead, South Vietnam's overmatched soldiers took heavy losses and withdrew after six weeks without accomplishing their mission. The costly operation highlighted the failure of Vietnamization, and peace talks remained ineffective. Nevertheless, Nixon announced that the South Vietnamese troops fought "in a superior way." He promptly ordered the withdrawal of another 100,000 U.S. troops, bringing the total withdrawn to 365,000.

Anti-war protests increased at home. In May 1971, several thousand members of the Vietnam Veterans Against the War encamped in Washington, then in a dramatic gesture threw away their medals. The next week, hundreds of thousands of protesters poured into the capital. As demonstrators blocked commuter traffic, the administration ordered mass arrests, which the courts subsequently held to be illegal.

Nixon faced additional political pressure in 1971 with the publication of the so-called Pentagon Papers, a secret study begun by Johnson's Secretary of Defense Robert McNamara to chronicle U.S. involvement in Vietnam. Leaked to the press by former National Security officer Daniel Ellsberg, the 7,000-page document revealed a long history of presidential deception that added fuel to the anti-war movement. Although not implicated in the report, Nixon attempted to halt its publication, only to be rebuffed by the Supreme Court. Enraged by this violation of presidential secrecy, Nixon ordered Ellsberg indicted for releasing the documents. The president also took another step across the legal line. Determined to

crush Ellsberg as a warning against other administration "leaks," Nixon authorized a group of "Plumbers" to uncover private information about his critic. Their first target was Ellsberg's psychiatrist; from personal medical files they hoped to learn information to discredit the critic. In the summer of 1971, the Plumbers burglarized the doctor's offices but found nothing of value.

Bombing for Peace

By the end of 1971, the diplomatic stalemate in Vietnam had hardly changed. Although Vietnamization had greatly reduced the number of U.S. forces in the country, North Vietnam had proportionately less reason to make concessions. Hoping to break the deadlock, Nixon told a television audience early in 1972 that the two countries had been engaging in secret diplomacy for two years. "Nothing is served by silence," he said, "when it enables the other side to imply possible solutions publicly that it has already flatly rejected privately." Such candor endeavored to stop the spread of anti-war sentiment.

North Vietnam responded to Nixon in February 1972 by launching the heaviest ground offensive since Tet 1968. Nixon quickly escalated the war, ordering B-52 raids against Hanoi and Haiphong Harbor. Directing bombing against selected sites, the president resolved to force North Vietnam to resume negotiations. Instead, the offensive continued.

Nixon raised the stakes. "The bastards have never been bombed like they are going to be bombed," he remarked privately. Ordering a naval blockade of North Vietnam, the president approved the mining of Haiphong Harbor, the port used by Soviet vessels, and increased B-52 raids against targets in North Vietnam. Because of the simultaneous warming of relations with the Soviet Union and China, public opinion supported the president's decision. The immense destruction succeeded in persuading North Vietnam to resume diplomatic discussions. Hoping to reach agreement before the 1972 elections, both sides now made major concessions, leading to what was called a "leopard spot" arrangement. Rather than seeking to preserve South Vietnam as a non-communist entity, which had been the U.S. objective since 1954, Nixon agreed to allow North Vietnamese forces to remain in South Vietnam in those areas currently held by their armies.

The compromise settlement implied that the Vietnamese civil war would continue, without the participation of U.S. troops, even after the signing of a formal ceasefire. By October 1972, a political settlement seemed imminent. The only stumbling block was to persuade the government of South Vietnam to accept the terms. Nixon offered the U.S. ally extensive economic and military assistance, and Kissinger dared to declare, just five days before the 1972 election, that "peace is at hand." But to Nixon's dismay, South Vietnam refused to accept a settlement that would ensure its ultimate demise.

The Paris Peace Treaty

After Nixon's reelection, negotiations stalled again. Without revealing that the primary objections to the settlement came from South Vietnam, the frustrated president now ordered the most massive air attack of the war against North Vietnam. In just ten days, during the 1972 Christmas season, B-52 bombers unloaded 36,000 tons of explosives—more than the entire tonnage dropped in North Vietnam between 1969 and 1971—and hit military targets around Hanoi as well as, inadvertently, a nearby civilian hospital. Staggered by the bombing, North Vietnam quickly resumed negotiations. With terms largely accepted the previous October, the talks moved quickly.

In January 1973, three days after Nixon's second inauguration, and half a day after the death of Lyndon Johnson, the Paris peace treaty ended the nation's longest war. The agreement provided for an immediate cease fire, the exchange of all prisoners of war, and the prompt withdrawal of U.S. military forces. At the last moment, Nixon took the precaution of rushing economic and military aid to South Vietnam. He reclassified military advisors as civilian employees and established a military command inside the U.S. embassy in Saigon. The political settlement recognized both the existing South Vietnamese government in Saigon and a Provisional Revolutionary Government (representing North Vietnam and the Viet Cong) as co-equals, each remaining in the portions of Vietnam they controlled. And so, without direct U.S. participation, the Vietnam civil war continued until April 1975, when North Vietnam overran Saigon, claimed victory, and established a single government for Vietnam.

Coming Home

"There was no dancing in the streets, no honking of horns, no champagne," the press reported the day after the treaty was signed. In the dozen years since President Kennedy had sent military advisors to Vietnam, the war had taken its toll: 58,000 U.S. dead, 150,000 wounded, some 2,000 missing in action, $140 billion from the U.S. Treasury—as well as millions of Vietnamese on both sides who were killed, maimed, and tormented. Blood was not the only price paid by U.S. soldiers. Under the military's rotation system, most soldiers served for one year and returned home, not with their unit but as individuals. Some faced hostility from anti-war activists, but most confronted an indifferent society, grateful only to have avoided similar duty.

"It isn't peace," observed one veteran, "and there is no honor." For Vietnam veterans, problems of readjustment abounded, common enough to be given the medical label *posttraumatic stress*

"It isn't peace, and there is no honor."

disorder, or *PTSD.* Reliving nightmares of combat and fear, veterans typically experienced depression, guilt, anger, self-deprecation, and distrust of authority. Between 1968 and 1974, unemployment rates for all Vietnam veterans were 22 percent, for nonwhite veterans 50 percent, much higher than national averages. Some suffered from medical symptoms resulting from exposure to Agent Orange, a toxic defoliant used widely in Vietnam. Others had acquired drug addictions in Vietnam which, when identified, led to less than honorable discharges. Among married veterans, 38 percent separated from their wives within six months of returning home. The veterans' suicide rate was 24 percent higher than for their age peers. To protest a system that had punished them unfairly, some veterans joined anti-war groups, but most suffered in silence. Political leaders showed little sympathy for their problems, nor did politicians approve giving amnesty to draft evaders or military deserters, a position that was supported by most citizens.

The Limits of Power

The retreat from Vietnam in 1973 underscored the limits of national power. In his 1961 inaugural address, Kennedy had vowed to "pay any price" to defend freedom anywhere in the world. Nixon's second inaugural speech in January 1973 spoke more cautiously: "The time has passed when America will make every other nation's conflict our own, or make every other nation's future our responsibility, or presume to tell the people of other nations how to manage their own affairs." The president did not mean that U.S. internationalism had ceased. His administration would continue to intervene directly and covertly in countries, such as Chile, that established socialist governments. But the idea that U.S. military power and wealth could dictate world affairs had suffered a stunning setback in Vietnam.

The continuing war in southeast Asia also forced a redefinition of presidential power. The Paris treaty had not ended the air war in Cambodia, and when Congress passed a measure prohibiting expenditures for those actions, Nixon vetoed the bill. The federal separation of powers about declaring war now approached a constitutional deadlock. (See U.S. Constitution, Article I, Section 8, and Article II, Section 2.) Each branch of government claimed the right to control basic military policy. Amid angry accusations of betraying U.S. allies in southeast Asia, Congress and the White House agreed to a tentative compromise, permitting the Cambodian bombing to continue but only for a limited time.

Congress then moved to affirm its constitutional right to declare war. Ever since Harry Truman used the Cold War emergency to order a "police action" in Korea, presidents had sent troops near and far without direct legislative consent. The War Powers Act of 1973, passed over Nixon's veto, now required that a presidential commitment of military forces without formal congressional approval be limited to sixty days. Under the law, the White House retained considerable independence to send U.S. troops overseas, but post-Vietnam presidents had to acknowledge the collateral power of Congress in war situations.

Détente and the Stabilization of Power

Nixon's retreat in Vietnam reflected not only domestic pressures but also a new perception of the global balance of power. During the 1960s, the Soviet Union had achieved a nuclear arsenal of approximate equality with that of the United States, creating an international order based on what was called Mutual Assured Destruction (MAD). Neither power could launch a nuclear attack without facing equally destructive retaliation. Meanwhile, China had entered the nuclear club, and ideological disagreements divided the two communist nations. Nixon and Kissinger saw the communist split as an opportunity to reshape the Cold War from a system of endless confrontation to a peaceful and stable arena for mutual benefit. Global strategists described such a transition as *détente,* an easing of tensions.

Opening China

As a rigid Cold Warrior in the 1940s and 1950s, Nixon had supported the political isolation of the communist People's Republic of China. But as president, he understood that normal relations with the People's Republic would put pressure on the Soviet Union to approach the United States. He also hoped that China would encourage North Vietnam to negotiate for peace. Using back channels of diplomacy, Nixon indicated his willingness to improve relations between the two nations.

Small gestures, such as China's invitation to the U.S. ping pong team in 1971 and a lifting of U.S. trade restrictions, showed a gradual lessening of conflict. Even U.S. warfare in Vietnam seemed less a threat to détente, the relaxation of tension. The administration learned that China would not intervene in Vietnam, as it had in Korea, as long as the United States did not invade North Vietnam. Nixon also realized that China could not persuade Hanoi to negotiate. But the main source of contention remained the status of Taiwan, the island to which the anti-communist Chinese had fled in 1949 (see Chapter 24). When Nixon indicated that the United States would reject Taiwan's claim to be the sole government of China, the door to normal relations opened wide.

The announcement of Nixon's visit to the People's Republic of China in 1972 stunned the world. Although some conservatives decried the betrayal of Taiwan, the meeting of heads of state merely accepted the global reality. In the Shanghai communiqué of 1972, the two powers agreed to maintain the political balance in Asia. Each reaffirmed support for opposite sides in Korea and agreed to treat Taiwan as an "internal" problem to be settled by the rival Chinese governments. Nixon promised to remove U.S. troops from Taiwan at some unspecified date. The United States also dropped its opposition to the People's Republic's representation in the United Nations Security Council, and in 1973 the two nations exchanged diplomatic missions. Ironically, the normalization of relations with China had undermined the logic of the Vietnam war. Communist power no longer appeared as a monolithic threat to U.S. interests in Asia.

Negotiating SALT

Overtures to China facilitated agreements with the Soviet Union, part of Nixon's triangulated strategy to establish a permanent world order. Anxious to stabilize the nuclear arms race, the White House pushed for Strategic Arms Limitations Talks (SALT), particularly involving new technologies, such as anti-ballistic missiles (ABMs). By 1969, the United States had significant superiority in two of the three key aspects of nuclear strategy: more long-range bombers and more nuclear submarines, whereas Moscow had slightly more intercontinental ballistic missiles (ICBMs). The proposed SALT treaty would not reduce that balance of force, but would limit future developments. It did not address the issue of multiple warheads (MIRVs), in which the United States had a technological lead. To sweeten negotiations, Nixon offered to sell surplus grain to the Soviet Union to alleviate its serious agricultural shortages. By 1972, lower-level diplomats had settled most of these matters. Following his visit to China, therefore, Nixon journeyed to Moscow to assure Kremlin leaders that détente with China did not threaten the Soviet state and to formalize the SALT agreement.

Assuming that both sides already possessed sufficient weapons to preserve the MAD strategy, the SALT treaty limited construction of defensive ABMs (both parties realized that such systems would not work) and stopped the installation of new ICBM launchers. SALT did not reduce the size of nuclear arsenals, nor prevent expansion of the number of warheads and other delivery systems. In other agreements, however, the two superpowers agreed to ban nuclear weapons from the ocean floors and to improve their hotline communications in the event of accidents. The stabilization of strategic weapons thus reduced the likelihood of superpower confrontation. Areas of conflict moved to the sidelines of power, to conflicts in the Middle East and Africa, where the nuclear powers continued to compete for influence.

Home Front Politics

Although Nixon gave top priority to the Vietnam war and its diplomatic repercussions, military policy also raised budgetary issues that affected domestic programs. President Johnson's reluctance to increase taxes to finance the war had triggered inflationary pressures, which in turn led Congress to curtail Great Society spending (see Chapter 27). Nixon thus inherited serious financial strains as well as the political consequences of diminished government spending. At the same time, however, federal budget cuts seemed to benefit Republicans by causing divisions within the traditional Democratic coalition of white ethnics and northern blacks. Republicans hoped to take

advantage of the rift to strengthen Nixon's support in 1972. The resulting intensification of domestic debate made party conflict more bitter and combative. Seeking to destroy his political rivals, Nixon crossed the line of normal politics by authorizing illegal activities against the Democratic party. The results would poison his second term in office.

Problems of Economic Stability

The cost of the Vietnam war had disastrous consequences for the domestic economy. Through the late 1960s, federal budget deficits stimulated inflation and weakened the balance of trade. Nixon's willingness to sell grain to the Russians in 1972 was no act of charity. Although the president had promised to cut federal spending, the war remained an enormous drain as troop reductions in Vietnam were offset by expensive military operations. In addition, the administration hesitated to slash domestic programs that the public supported. Most of the potential savings made possible by Vietnamization had already been committed to domestic programs such as Social Security and Medicare. During Nixon's first term, federal spending jumped from $194.6 billion in 1969 to $250 billion four years later.

Without budget cuts, the Federal Reserve Board tried to check inflation by raising interest rates to the highest levels since the eve of the Great Depression in 1929. But a tight money policy retarded business investment and increased unemployment. And, to the surprise of many economists and politicians, inflation continued to rise. To describe the situation in 1970, Democrats introduced the term *stagflation*—the worst of both worlds, stagnation and inflation. As Democratic party leader Lawrence O'Brien put it, "All the things that should go up— the stock market, corporate profits, real spendable income, productivity—go down, and all the things that should go down—unemployment, prices, interest rates—go up."

Although Nixon resisted appeals to order federal regulation of prices and wages, the White House used persuasion to obtain rollbacks in steel prices and to freeze wages in the construction industry. But 1971 saw inflation and unemployment rise together. For the first time since 1893, the country had a deficit in international trade. In midsummer 1971, Nixon abruptly reversed course. By presidential order, the "New Economic Policy" required a 90-day freeze on wages, prices, and profit margins. To stimulate business, the president took the dollar off the international gold standard, ordered a 10 percent tariff surcharge, and removed excise taxes to boost automobile sales. Although unemployment remained 6 percent, the inflation rate dipped nearly in half to 3.2 percent.

Nixon then extended the controls into 1972 and devalued the dollar 11 percent. By reducing the cost of U.S. goods overseas, the adjustment boosted exports of agricultural products. Sales of high-technology weapons also surged, especially to the oil-rich Middle East, where the Arab nations were preparing for war. Thanks to détente, sales to China leaped from $5 million in 1970 to $1 billion in 1973. Yet corporate profits spread unevenly. Auto sales plummeted by 7 million cars in 1973, and the Lockheed aviation giant faced bankruptcy. The domestic economy remained shaky.

The Politics of Recession

Economic problems haunted Nixon's political efforts to gain support among white urban workers. Although that group was liberal on economic issues such as Medicare, it remained conservative on social issues such as drug use, pornography, campus protests, and racial unrest. Many resented that government benefits like welfare were given to inner-city blacks. As parents of children who

fought disproportionately in Vietnam, white workers also shared the president's contempt for the anti-war movement and the role of college-educated students in challenging traditional values. When New York's Mayor John Lindsay lowered flags at city hall to commemorate the four dead students at Kent State in 1970, construction workers forcibly re-raised the banner and then attacked nearby students.

A delighted president invited the head of the construction workers' union, Peter Brennan, to the White House to defend old-fashioned patriotism and later appointed him Secretary of Labor. It was this cadre of "hard-hats" that Nixon and Agnew had in mind when they celebrated "the silent majority" during the 1970 campaign. As a counterpoint to the four-letter words used by street protesters, Nixon asked these ordinary Americans to use another four-letter word: the *vote*. Vote the hard hats did, but not for Republicans. Rhetoric alone failed to rally the urban working class, which because of economic problems remained loyal to the Democratic party in 1970.

Anger among urban white ethnics also reflected hostility to federal racial policies. As Great Society programs of the 1960s increased welfare assistance to northern blacks, white workers objected to special treatment that excluded their own interests. In an effort to force integration in the building trades, for example, Nixon unveiled the "Philadelphia Plan" in 1970, requiring that a portion of federally funded projects hire nonwhite workers. The plan aimed to overcome generations of discrimination in the construction industry's labor unions. But jobs for blacks took away work from whites already teetering on calamity. That year, 30 percent of the nation's construction workers experienced unemployment, 10 percent for more than four months. The militant rhetoric of Black Power hardly increased sympathy from workers who felt their own loss of economic power.

The frustrations of working life emerged in 1970 as the centerpiece of the most popular television program of the decade, Norman Lear's *All in the Family,* which featured Carroll O'Connor as the enraged blue-collar worker Archie Bunker and Jean Stapleton as his repressed but witty wife Edith. Embodying the white backlash, Bunker condemned the changes of a lifetime, attacking diverse ethnic minorities, homosexuals, and liberals. Other characters on the program challenged Bunker's opinions, turning this "family" into a political battleground. For the first time television dared show undisguised bigotry, inspiring a larger debate about the subterranean anger that afflicted the nation's working people.

In real life, the root of working-class anger was economic. Because television emphasized humor, viewers never saw Archie at work or appreciated the toll of industrial life on unskilled labor. In 1970, workplace accidents reached 27,000 per day, causing 55 deaths each day, or 14,200 a year. Congress passed the Occupational Safety and Health Act (OSHA) in 1970, but enforcement powers remained weak. Meanwhile, younger blue-collar workers, influenced by the values of the 1960s youth culture, questioned the meaninglessness of most jobs. Studs Terkel's classic oral history *Working* (1973) detailed the frustrations of most occupations. Indeed, when the Pentagon established an all-volunteer army, recruiting posters appealed to widespread discontent: "If your job puts you to sleep, try one of ours." The difficulties of working-class life intensified racial competition for scarce jobs, and many white workers viewed Archie Bunker as a mouthpiece of their own resentments.

Although Republicans attracted few black voters, Nixon supported existing federal programs to ease the job crisis in the cities. With the approach of his first "long hot summer" (the season of urban violence), the president assigned emergency funds to the Department of Housing and Urban Development (HUD) to rebuild riot-torn neighborhoods and provide low-income housing. Federal rent subsidies leaped from $1 million in 1969 to $3 billion four years later. The Office of Economic Opportunity (OEO) created job programs for black youth to relieve unemployment rates that exceeded 30 percent. Meanwhile, Congress quadrupled the food stamp program, which helped both the urban poor and struggling midwestern farmers. Similarly, the president promoted a new Office of Minority Business Enterprise to help black entrepreneurs by tripling the number of loans to black-operated companies, increasing federal contracts, and sponsoring minority investment programs. But small business development remained undercapitalized. In 1972, only twenty-six black-owned companies had annual sales over $5 million.

The economic crisis among minorities reflected a long historical trend, beginning with the loss of agricultural jobs in the South after World War II and the steady migration of blacks and other groups into northern cities, where sufficient jobs did not exist. Expenditures by the Social Security program's Aid to Families with Dependent Children (AFDC) showed the economic impact on the federal government. Between 1960 and 1970, the number of people receiving AFDC funds jumped from 3 million to 8.4 million. Half of all female-headed families received AFDC funds in 1970. By 1972, one-ninth of all U.S. children, including one-third of all black children, received welfare assistance. Federal rules discouraged recipients from taking lower-paying jobs, discriminated against the working poor, and indirectly encouraged single parents to remain unmarried. The perception that welfare mothers had no incentive to work contributed to the white backlash.

Nixon's view of the situation boiled down to two words: "welfare mess." In 1969, Nixon's chief domestic advisor, Daniel Patrick Moynihan, proposed a new Family Assistance Plan (FAP) to replace AFDC. The FAP would give every family of four a guaranteed income of $1,600, while tax incentives would allow recipients to keep portions of additional earnings. Congressional conservatives opposed outright income payments and liberals considered the proposed minimum payments too small. Although the measure passed the House in 1970, the controversial bill died in the Senate. Nixon felt no incentive to offer subsequent welfare reforms.

Nixon's Southern Strategy

Having received slight support from African American voters in 1968, Nixon felt little incentive to endorse black political demands. Adopting the words of the civil rights anthem "We Shall Overcome," his inaugural address summoned "black and white together" to achieve full racial equality. Yet the Republican president had no intention of endangering his support among white southerners, many of whom rejected federal court orders to desegregate public schools. Fifteen years after the *Brown* decision, 68 percent of southern black children still attended segregated schools. Under Johnson, the Department of Health, Education, and Welfare (HEW) had advanced integration by threatening to deny federal funds for noncomplying schools.

The president had other priorities, and he allowed his foreign-policy agenda to weaken the federal government's commitment to racial desegregation. Hoping to persuade the Soviet Union to accept the SALT proposals, the White House wanted Congress to approve the construction of an anti-ballistic missile system (ABMs) to use as a bargaining chip. But congressional liberals opposed the missiles and Nixon needed southern votes in Congress to proceed with the ABMs. In exchange for the missiles, Nixon traded desegregation in Mississippi. Responding to pressure from southern representatives, the administration opted not to enforce court orders to integrate schools at once, but instead filed legal suits opposing the use

of school busing to speed desegregation. That process served to delay implementation and transferred responsibility for desegregation to the courts rather than the presidency.

In 1971, however, the Supreme Court ruled in the *Swann* case that busing was both constitutional and necessary to end segregated schools. After southern school districts lost the legal fight, fewer than 14 percent of black students attended all-black schools. But in what became an accelerating trend, white students now enrolled in private schools to avoid desegregation. Realizing that the school busing issue would emerge in the next presidential election, Nixon condemned the Court's decision and appealed for a congressional moratorium of mandatory school transportation programs. Meanwhile, Attorney General John Mitchell testified against extending the 1965 Voting Rights Act, which had expanded the African American electorate.

Nixon also moved to reverse the liberal trend within the judicial system. With the retirement of Chief Justice Earl Warren in 1969, the president resolved to appoint "strict constructionist" judges who would minimize social change. The nomination of the conservative Warren Burger gained easy approval of the Senate. But when Nixon proposed South Carolina's Clement Haynsworth to fill a second vacancy, investigators uncovered an anti-labor, pro-segregationist record as well as rulings reflecting a conflict of interests. The Senate rejected the choice. Nixon dismissed the decision as "vicious character assassination" and nominated Florida's G. Harrold Carswell, a less distinguished judge who had once campaigned on a segregationist platform, castigated civil rights lawyers from the bench, and blocked desegregation of a public golf course. When the Senate rejected this candidate as well, Nixon scored political points in the South by condemning what he called "regional discrimination." African American leaders in turn condemned White House cynicism. Finally, Nixon nominated Minnesota moderate Harry Blackmun, and the dispute ended.

The Politics of Sex and Gender

Nixon's relations with racial minority groups expressed deliberate political objectives (the southern strategy, for example, or his disdain for liberalism), but the administration's position on gender issues reflected mere indifference. As more women entered the work force and participated in a feminist revival that demanded equal rights, the White House attempted to harness a political force that it scarcely understood. "I want a woman to be a woman," the president remarked in 1970, leading Washington columnist Jack Anderson to suggest that "millions of women" interpreted the president to mean "a woman's place is in the home." To be sure, Nixon appointed more women to government office than Kennedy and Johnson had—3.5 percent of his total appointments—and he created the President's Task Force on Women's Rights and Responsibilities in 1969. But his well-publicized personal attitudes remained unsympathetic to the feminist agenda. "Let me make one thing perfectly clear," said Nixon, "I wouldn't want to wake up next to a lady pipe fitter."

Based on the values of the civil rights movement and the counterculture of the 1960s, feminists entered the mainstream political arena after 1970. That year, on the fiftieth anniversary of women's suffrage, tens of thousands of women participated in public demonstrations to demand an array of reforms, including abortion rights, publicly financed childcare, and equal opportunity in education and employment. In 1971, such activists as Bella Abzug, Betty Friedan, and Gloria Steinem organized the National Women's Political Caucus to press for political changes in both parties, though they would become more influential among Democrats.

Responding to the growing number of working women, the Democratic Congress approved federal funding for childcare centers in 1971. Nixon vetoed the measure, arguing that "communal approaches to childrearing" threatened "family-centered traditions." But he did sign the Equal Employment Opportunity Act of 1972, which strengthened equal-pay laws, prohibited discrimination in educational programs that received federal money, and extended the power of the EEOC to prohibit job discrimination based on sex. Compliance often required lengthy litigation, but these laws established the basis for equal opportunity in white-collar management jobs and education, including women's sports programs. Congress also approved, and Nixon supported, the Equal Rights Amendment (ERA), which stated that "equality of rights shall not be denied or abridged . . . on account of sex." Within two years, 33 states—just five short of the necessary three-quarters for ratification—endorsed the measure.

As the ERA gained approval in the states, local legislatures engaged in intense debates about legalizing abortion. By 1973, fourteen states had approved that procedure. Because the issue primarily affected the local levels of government, Washington politicians could avoid choosing sides. But the issue suddenly captured national attention when the Supreme Court ruled in the landmark case *Roe v. Wade* in 1973 that women had a constitutional right to abortion during the first trimester of pregnancy. Angered by federal intervention in "domestic" affairs, conservatives began to demand that Congress enact restrictions on abortions. The question of abortion rights, linked increasingly to the ERA, emerged as the most controversial social issue of the decade.

Equally inflammatory, though less widespread, was the issue of gay and lesbian rights. The sexual revolution of the 1960s had accelerated the emergence of a gay culture in most large cities and universities. Still considered an illegal activity, homosexual behavior often prompted police harassment. But when New York City police raided the Stonewall Tavern in Greenwich Village in 1969, the homosexual patrons spontaneously fought back, igniting a street rebellion to defend their rights. Having emerged from the homosexual closet, gays and lesbians proceeded to build a political movement to seek equal rights.

This "gay pride" movement drew on earlier civil rights protests to affirm the value of alternative lifestyles. Lesbian women also became an open presence in the feminist movement. Yet few political leaders wanted to be associated with gay rights. When one of Nixon's potential judicial nominees suggested that the Constitution did not prohibit same-sex marriage, Nixon replied, "There goes a Supreme Court justice! I can't go *that* far."

Hostility to gay rights, abortions, and the ERA illuminated the fundamental challenges raised by the gender liberation movements. Not only did feminists, lesbians, and gays demand changes in public policy, but they simultaneously attacked the conventional roles of domestic life as well as public images in advertising and the arts. By the 1970s, these gender liberation movements forced a reappraisal of the presumed male standards of society. At a time, for example, when nearly half the student population on the nation's college campuses were women, but only 10 percent of the faculty were, what did it mean that department heads were universally titled "Chairman"? The entire society soon grappled with the need to invent gender-neutral language.

Feminists also challenged traditional assumptions that men were heads of households. Widespread marital dissatisfaction had stimulated the passage of liberalized divorce laws, which in turn sent the divorce rate skyrocketing. But the principle of legal equality for women clashed with the reality of their economic inequality. Inadequate alimony and child support payments typically resulted in a decline of economic status for divorced women, while the economic position of divorced men improved. Popular novels, written by women like Joan Didion, Alix Kates Shulman, Erica Jong, and Alice Adams, focused on the midlife crisis of female identity when marriages failed. Equally important, for the first time most young women, like young men, faced choices involving both marriage and careers.

The Election of 1972

In this context of emerging feminism, the newly founded *Ms.* magazine ranked the presidential candidates of 1972, giving highest marks to Senator George McGovern. After the violence at the 1968 Democratic convention in Chicago, the South Dakota liberal had initiated procedural reforms that opened the Democratic party to greater representation by women, minorities, and youth. Between 1968 and 1972, the proportion of women delegates to the Democratic convention increased from 13 percent to 38 percent; participation of blacks tripled from 5 percent to 15 percent; and the number of people under age 30 increased from 2.6 percent to 23 percent. As an anti-war liberal, McGovern hoped to benefit by the ratification of the Twenty-Sixth Amendment in 1971, which made this election the first in which 18-year-olds could vote.

Amendment XXVI (1971)

Section 1.
The right of citizens of the United States, who are 18 years of age or older, to vote, shall not be denied or abridged by the United States or any state on account of age.

Section 2.
The Congress shall have the power to enforce this article by appropriate legislation.

McGovern faced formidable obstacles. Although the South Dakotan attracted the party's liberal leadership, Alabama's George Wallace, the former American Independent candidate, had returned to the Democratic party, presenting himself as an anti-government populist. With the slogan "Send 'Em a Message," the southern politician appealed to voter frustration about economic woes, the continuing war, and court-ordered school busing. Wallace ran well among northern urban whites and in the South. But in the Maryland primary, five bullets from an assassin's pistol ended his bid, leaving Wallace paralyzed in a wheelchair.

McGovern prevailed at the Democratic convention. Old-line Democrats, more familiar with white ethnic urban machines, scarcely recognized the party's new leadership. Statistics confirmed the impression: 39 percent held postgraduate degrees; 31 percent earned over $25,000 (equivalent to about $100,000 in current dollars). Yet even with delegates stacked in his favor, McGovern's support wavered. Feminists were outraged when the candidate refused to support an abortion plank, and many joined the Democratic Black Caucus in backing Brooklyn's African American candidate, Shirley Chisholm, the first woman to run for president. McGovern managed to carry the convention and proceeded to appeal for party unity with the theme "Come Home America."

Reelecting the President

Nixon had no trouble finding his way home. The president's extraordinary success in foreign affairs (opening China, the SALT accord) demonstrated his international stature. Troop withdrawals, mixed with the bombing in Vietnam, attracted mainstream voters. In the role of chief executive, Nixon tried to appear untainted by mere party politics. Outside the White House, none suspected that the president's men had committed "dirty tricks" against Democratic candidates—distributing phony campaign literature, spying, and wiretapping. When police in Washington, D.C., arrested a team of burglars at the Democratic headquarters in the Watergate building in June 1972, voters accepted the administration's dismissal of the incident as "a third-rate burglary." The Republican nominating convention was a carefully rehearsed affair; Nixon faced no rivals. As novelist Norman Mailer reported, the purpose of the convention was to create an image of a convention.

The president's acceptance speech swept away the nation's troubles into the past tense: "There was Vietnam—so bloody, so costly, so bitterly divisive. . . . At home our horrified people watched our cities burn, crime burgeon, campuses dissolve into chaos . . . . Working men and women found their living standards fixed or falling, the victim of inflation." Denying that these problems had occurred during his own administration, Nixon asked for "Four More Years!" To attract northern white ethnics, the president canceled his Philadelphia Plan to integrate construction work, demanded a moratorium on school busing, denounced abortion, and reaffirmed "peace with honor." Nixon also manipulated federal economic policies to improve the political climate. Ordering executive departments to increase spending, the president approved lower interest rates to stimulate business and cut unemployment. It was "good for the country," Nixon told his cabinet, and "might help us politically."

The result was a presidential landslide. Destroying the New Deal coalition, Nixon carried white ethnics, Catholics, labor unions, white-collar professionals, and the once-solid South, losing only among Jews, the Spanish-speaking, and African Americans. In sum, the president captured 60.7 percent of the popular vote and won every electoral ballot, except those of Massachusetts and Washington, D.C. Yet Democrats retained strong majorities in both houses of Congress, indicative of increased voter ticket-splitting as issues rather than party la-

The Election of 1972

Candidate (Party)	Electoral Vote	Popular Vote
Nixon (Republican)	520 (96.7%)	47,169,911 (60.7%)
McGovern (Democratic)	17 (3.1%)	29,170,383 (37.5%)
Hospers (Libertarian)	1 (0.2%)	3,673 (–)
Schmitz (American)	–	1,099,482 (1.4%)

bels influenced political behavior. Also notable was the steady slip in presidential voter turnout from 63.8 percent of eligible voters in 1960 to 55.7 percent in 1972. In the aftermath of Nixon's victory, few listened when the losing candidate charged Nixon with "deliberate deceptions" and "sinister plots."

Nixon's Second Term

With Democrats controlling Congress, Nixon's second administration accentuated differences between the executive and legislative branches. Debate focused on policy matters, such as the president's proposal to reduce federal spending for social welfare programs. But these political issues led to deeper conflicts involving the president's constitutional relationship with Congress. Nixon's claims of "executive privilege" to deny Congress access to White House documents and testimony intro-

duced questions of accountability. Did the White House have the right to impound (that is, not spend) expenditures voted by Congress? Congressional investigation of the recent election campaign also suggested serious violations of federal law. To what extent could the president transact business in secret? Did Congress have the right to scrutinize presidential conversations? The scandals associated with the Watergate break-in brought the nation to a major constitutional crisis.

Debating Government Spending

"The time has come," said Nixon in his second inaugural speech, "to turn away from the condescending policies of paternalism." With the election over, the administration announced a retrenchment in federal spending to reduce budget deficits and fight inflation. Nixon demanded cuts for hospital construction, public housing, education, and scientific research. Such reductions most seriously affected minority citizens (15.4 percent of the nation consisting of African Americans, the Spanish-speaking, and American Indians) whose median income was 54 percent that of whites.

Democrats denounced the White House position. When Congress proceeded to approve funds for HEW's Office of Economic Opportunity, however, Nixon claimed a presidential right to impound those appropriations. The Democrats took the issue into the federal courts, which eventually ruled against the president. Nixon then appointed a temporary head of OEO with instructions to dismantle the agency. When courts ruled that action illegal, Nixon simply made no budget requests for OEO. Yet Nixon's effort to reduce the government's economic role had calamitous effects. The abrupt lifting of wage and price controls in 1973 brought runaway inflation, especially in food prices, and consumers organized a nationwide boycott of meat.

The Price of Oil

While battling with Congress about domestic spending, Nixon's efforts to control inflation collapsed completely after the outbreak of the Yom Kippur war between the Arab nations and Israel in 1973. By providing military assistance to the Israeli ally, Washington provoked the Arab nations to retaliate. In 1973, the Arab-dominated Organization of Petroleum Exporting Countries (OPEC) halted shipments of oil to the United States, Western Europe, and Japan. This oil embargo, which lasted for five months, underscored the country's economic vulnerability. In half a year, the domestic price of oil leaped 367 percent, setting off an inflationary spiral throughout the economy and causing unemployment as factories were forced to shut down.

The nation's dependence on oil imports reflected corporate decisions to maximize profits while conserving domestic petroleum reserves.

With oil consumption increasing from 9.7 million barrels a day in 1960 to 16.2 million barrels in 1974, the proportion of imported petroleum jumped from 19 percent to 38 percent. Now, with prices suddenly skyrocketing, the oil companies reaped 57 percent higher profits over the previous year. Nixon soon announced "Project Independence," a long-term program to achieve energy self-sufficiency based on conservation and the use of nuclear power. Goaded by the crisis, the White House and Congress buried their differences to impose emergency conservation measures. These involved lowering thermostats in homes and businesses to 68 degrees, reducing air travel by 10 percent, cutting speed limits to 55, and establishing winter daylight savings time. Yet the sudden, unexpected, and mandatory changes in daily life dampened public confidence in government policy; foreign power had brought the country to its knees.

Energy conservation immediately reduced jobs, causing unemployment to jump above 5 percent. Blue-collar workers felt the sting first, but joblessness spread quickly into the white-collar sector. Traditionally "safe" jobs, such as teaching, became more precarious. Responding to declining economic opportunities, college enrollments declined, and college students increasingly switched majors from the humanities and social sciences to more marketable subjects like business administration. Rising fuel costs also aggravated inflation. Between 1973 and 1974, wholesale prices leaped 14 percent. A 1967 consumer dollar was now worth 68 cents. In the face of energy shortages and economic downturns, the president emerged as a target for public frustration and anger.

Discovering Campaign Crimes

Money was at the heart of Nixon's problems. In 1971, his supporters organized a Committee to Re-Elect the President (CRP, pronounced "creep") and formed 400 "dummy" corporations to collect and disburse secret campaign contributions. With $55 million raised from corporate donors, many of them expecting beneficial treatment from Washington, CRP paid in cash to finance the "dirty tricks" campaign against the Democrats, including the break-in of their headquarters at the Watergate complex to attach electronic listening devices to the party's telephones. Evidence at the crime site linked the burglars to the White House "Plumbers," who conducted other illegal acts for the president. The CRP commenced an immediate cover-up, using cash payments to buy silence from the criminals. It would take two years before the public learned that Nixon personally participated in some of these illegal decisions, ordering aides to interfere with an FBI investigation of Watergate payments.

Several separate investigations thwarted the cover-up. The first occurred in the pages of the *Washington Post,* as two reporters, Carl Bernstein and Bob Woodward, located an administration source—the so-called Deep Throat—who revealed information linking the White House to the crimes. A second investigation emerged within the federal courts. When the seven burglars arrested at Watergate pleaded guilty in their criminal trial to avoid testifying about their employers, Judge John Sirica used maximum sentencing to encourage one of the defendants, former CIA operative James McCord, to admit receiving "political pressure" from Republican party leaders.

Democratic politicians had a special interest in discovering the attack on their party's offices and launched a third investigation. A Select Senate Committee, chaired by North Carolina's Sam Ervin, opened televised hearings in 1973. White House attorney John Dean mesmerized the nation with details about the Plumbers as well as the existence of a White House "enemies list" that was passed to the Internal Revenue Service (IRS) for audits. As such information became public, Nixon

fired the four highest advisors on his staff: Dean, H.R. Haldeman, John Ehrlichman, and Attorney General Richard Kleindeist. Hoping to insulate himself from further congressional investigation, he appointed Elliot Richardson, "a man of incomparable integrity," to head the Justice Department, and authorized him to appoint an independent special prosecutor to deal with the Watergate case. Richardson then chose Archibald Cox to head the investigation.

The case took an astounding turn in 1973 when a White House aide casually revealed the existence of a secret tape-recording system in the White House Oval Office. Realizing that the tapes held vital evidence, both Special Prosecutor Cox and Senator Ervin demanded specific recordings. Nixon refused, arguing that the separation of powers and executive privilege protected the confidentiality of presidential conversations. Federal courts rejected Nixon's claim and ordered that the tapes be transferred to the courts. When Cox proceeded to subpoenae additional tapes, Nixon ordered Attorney General Richardson to fire Cox; but when Richardson refused and resigned, Nixon fired his replacement, the deputy attorney general, for also refusing. Finally, Solicitor General Robert Bork assumed the office of attorney general and executed the order. This so-called Saturday Night Massacre imperiled constitutional government. Tremendous public outrage forced Nixon to retreat, and he reluctantly submitted some of the recordings. Yet some tapes appeared to be missing; others had blank spots caused by manual erasures.

Unraveling the Executive Branch

Amid these jurisdictional fights, Nixon and Vice President Agnew encountered troubles with the IRS. Under investigation for receiving kickbacks in exchange for government contracts in Maryland, Agnew chose to plead "no contest" rather than face criminal proceedings and resigned from office.

Agnew's departure further undermined public confidence in the administration. Following the new succession scheme of the Twenty-Fifth Amendment, Nixon nominated House Republican leader Gerald Ford of Michigan for the vice presidency, and Congress quickly approved the appointment. Soon afterward, the IRS challenged Nixon's tax deductions for donations of his own vice-presidential papers, prompting the president to declare: "I am not a crook!" The IRS subsequently reported that Nixon owed $450,000 for illegally changing the date of a gift of documents to the National Archives. Meanwhile, a grand jury indicted former top presidential advisors for perjury and obstructing justice. "There are animals crashing around in the forest," said one Republican leader. "I can hear them, but I can't see them." With the conspiracy widening, the House of Representatives voted 406–4 in February 1974 to authorize the Judiciary Committee to commence impeachment proceedings.

The constitutional deadlock soon reached another crisis when Warren Burger's Supreme Court unanimously ordered the president to submit the missing subpoenaed tapes. Already the president had released an edited transcription of his tape-recorded conversations, a 1,309-page document that revealed Nixon's profanity and pettiness. Now the unedited tapes exposed the "smoking gun"—evidence of Nixon's complicity in the Watergate cover-up. In May 1974 the House Judiciary committee, chaired by New Jersey's Peter Rodino, commenced formal impeachment proceedings, while special Watergate prosecutor Leon Jaworski, who had replaced Cox, appealed to the Supreme Court to obtain the original tape recordings. In July, the high Court ruled against Nixon's claim of executive privilege and ordered release of the tapes. Two days later, the House Judiciary committee began to vote on the articles of impeachment, with strong majorities charging the president with obstructing justice, abusing his powers of office, and violating congressional subpoenas. Two other proposed articles of impeachment—concealing the bombing of Cambodia and filing fraudulent tax returns—did not pass in the committee. But as the full House of Representatives prepared to vote formal impeachment charges, Nixon decided to avoid a final trial in the Senate. In August 1974, the president resigned from office and passed executive leadership to his appointed vice president, Gerald Ford.

A Loss of Public Confidence

The rise and fall of Richard Nixon involved more than a morality play about politics. During the prolonged Watergate controversy, the public glimpsed behind the curtain of politics to see the inner workings of power. Amid the multitude of players—White House aides, Senate investigators, CIA operators, campaign donors—it was difficult to follow the plot lines or to understand connections between corporate contributors and congressional votes or executive orders. But, even while politicians and the media praised the workings of the nation's legal system, the public recognized that Nixon's evils were only slightly exceptional.

Other presidents had perpetrated similar scandalous behavior. Why had Nixon been forced to resign? First, he had been caught committing crimes within the legal system itself—that is, attempting to obstruct justice—and had been forced to acknowledge that no person was above the law. Second, he had attacked his most powerful political enemy: the Democratic party itself. Third, he had repeatedly demonstrated a personal arrogance in denying his culpability, which offended ordinary citizens. Finally, some of his crimes were directly linked to the Vietnam war (wiretapping news reporters, burglarizing Ellsberg's psychiatrist) and his personal failings seemed to embody the nation's deeper weakness, the loss of global power as seen in the defeat in Southeast Asia and the oil embargo. Instead of standing as a man in control of his country's destiny, Nixon appeared as a frustrated weakling.

As the disgraced president departed from Washington, faith in the nation's political system plummeted. "We assume that politicians are without honor," remarked feminist poet Adrienne Rich. "We read their statements trying to crack the code. The scandals of their politics: not that men in high places lie, only that they do so with such indifference, so endlessly, still expecting to be believed."

INFOTRAC® COLLEGE EDITION EXERCISES

For additional readings go to InfoTrac College Edition, your online research library at *http://web1.infotrac-college.com*.

Keyword search: Kissinger

Subject search: Nixon

Subject search: Kent State

Subject search: Nixon resignation

ADDITIONAL READING

Stephen E. Ambrose, *Nixon: Triumph of a Politician, 1962–1972* (1989). The second of a three-volume biography, the book provides a presidential perspective on political events.

Melvin Small, *The Presidency of Richard Nixon* (1999). This detailed political history is a good place to start and includes an extensive bibliography.

Seeking "Peace with Honor"

Jeffrey Kimball, *Nixon's Vietnam War* (1998). Focusing on foreign policy, this volume places Nixon's strategies in an international context. See also Larry Berman, *No Peace, No Honor: Nixon, Kissinger, and Betrayal in Vietnam* (2001).

Robert S. Litwak, *Détente and the Nixon Doctrine: American Foreign Policy and the Pursuit of Stability,* *1969–1976* (1984). An analysis of foreign policy, emphasizing the relationship between big power diplomacy and Vietnam.

Nixon Expands the War

William Shawcross, *Sideshow: Kissinger, Nixon, and the Destruction of Cambodia* (1979). This volume presents a journalist's exposé of the effects of bombing on Cambodia.

The Anti-War Movement and the Silent Majority

Rhodri Jeffrey-Jones, *Peace Now! American Society and the Ending of the Vietnam War* (1999). Focusing on anti-war advocates, the author explores the role of students, labor unions, African Americans, and women.

Coming Home

Paul Starr, *The Discarded Army* (1973). A contemporary account of the problems facing Vietnam veterans.

The Politics of Recession

Richard Krickus, *Pursuing the American Dream: White Ethnics and the New Populism* (1976). An analysis of workers and politics, examining issues of class and ethnicity.

Allen J. Matusow, *Nixon's Economy: Booms, Busts, Dollars, and Voters* (1998). An analysis of economic policy, this book describes the political context.

The Politics of Sex and Gender

Ruth Rosen, *The World Split Open: How the Modern Women's Movement Changed America* (2000). The author describes the "second wave of feminism" and its impact throughout society.

Discovering Campaign Crimes

Carl Bernstein and Bob Woodward, *All the President's Men* (1975). This journalistic survey lends freshness to the unraveling Watergate case.

Stanley I. Kutler, *The Wars of Watergate: The Last Crisis of Richard Nixon* (1990). This book provides a thorough discussion of presidential crime, but see also the relevant Watergate tapes in Stanley I. Kutler, *Abuse of Power: The New Nixon Tapes* (1997).

An Age of Limits: The 1970s

Televisions around the world began broadcasting grainy, indistinct images of the gray lunar surface on July 20, 1969. Glued to their screens, viewers hungrily awaited a first glimpse of human beings emerging from the Apollo 11 spacecraft's landing module. Then there was movement, a heavily suited figure, light as a balloon, moving down the lander's steps to the moon's yielding surface. "That's one small step for a man," crackled the voice of astronaut Neil Armstrong, in what he must have known were words that would ring throughout history, "one giant leap for mankind."

As the astronaut proceeded to plant a motionless U.S. flag on the dusty lunar surface, viewers at home were astonished to see the blue planet Earth hanging delicately on the horizon, distanced from the explorer by a gulf of space. The image became an icon of the 1970s—dramatic evidence of daring space technology, but also clear demonstration that the third planet was humankind's only habitat. The earth was our spaceship in the universe.

http://history.wadsworth.com

The startling view of the earth in cold isolation ignited public interest in the science of ecology, a word derived from the Greek *oikos,* meaning "house," and sparked concern about the earth's natural environment. Half a year later, on January 1, 1970, President Richard Nixon's first official act of the 1970s was to sign the Environmental Protection Act, which created the Environmental Protection Agency and mandated environmental impact studies for all government projects. The growing awareness of ecological limits mirrored a new sense of geopolitics in the years after the Vietnam war, the Watergate scandals, and the Middle East oil embargoes. Although few doubted that the United States possessed insuperable nuclear arsenals and controlled the world's strongest industrial potential, the inability to impose the country's will on North Vietnam or the Arab oil empires exposed unexpected, and dangerous, national weakness. And just as Vietnam and Watergate revealed the failure of political leadership, Nixon's successors, Presidents Gerald Ford and Jimmy Carter, inherited persistent problems of economic stagnation and faltering foreign trade. Inflation, unemployment, and energy shortages became chronic troubles. In addition, repeated incidents of political corruption marred public perceptions of Washington politics.

The result was a crisis of national identity. As the country celebrated its 200th birthday on July 4, 1976, public opinion polls uncovered a marked loss of faith in the nation's major institutions. One survey found that 69 percent of respondents believed that "the country's leaders have consistently lied to the people." Another poll measured a decline of public confidence in corporations, from 55 percent in 1966 to 16 percent ten years later. This despair contrasted with the holiday spirit that accompanied the Bicentennial. "It was a people's day," noted political reporter Elizabeth Drew. But "the good feeling one observed," she said, "comes out of confidence in our country, as distinguished from confidence in our government." As the national leadership lost credibility, more citizens across the political spectrum turned to cultural politics and community movements to express political concerns. By the end of the 1970s, resurgent optimism was challenging the politics of limits, and the country supported politicians who promised to reassert world leadership.

The Politics of Cultural Conflict

Public frustration with government intensified the already explosive issue of cultural politics. Since the mid-1960s, ethnic, gender, and social identity had assumed political dimensions, as racial minorities and white majorities, feminists and gays, young and old, demanded a political voice and competed for government favor. Economic recession and energy shortages accentuated these divisions. Equally important, a new moral tone entered political contests. First apparent in the civil rights movement and the Vietnam war debates, moral values dominated discussion of abortion laws, gay rights, and efforts to legislate equality through affirmative action programs. Such moral issues polarized politics and undermined pragmatic compromises. Public arenas served less to achieve political consensus than to underscore the fragmentation of interests and goals.

The Limits of Black Progress

Cultural conflicts worsened in this era of recession, because the economic slowdown aggravated problems among the poorest people, particularly racial minorities. Although more African Americans than ever before were achieving middle-class status, a majority of the nation's blacks were simultaneously sinking deeper into poverty. Since the 1960s, educated middle-class blacks had approached closer economic equality with comparable whites, and black women's income nearly equaled white women's earnings. A rising proportion of African Americans obtained white-collar and professional occupations, and the number of black elected officials increased from 103 in 1964 to 1,469 in 1970 and 4,311 in 1977. Yet in urban areas, African American joblessness continued at twice the rate of white unemployment. Census surveys found that in male-headed households, family incomes improved through the decade but remained 20 percent lower than in white male-headed households. By 1980, however, women, who had much lower incomes than men, headed 40 percent of black families, while white women headed only 12 percent of their families. Because of wage disparities and the availability of only part-time work, women headed two-thirds of black families living in poverty. In sum, 31 percent of blacks and over 50 percent of black children resided in households below the government's poverty line.

Urban poverty aggravated racial tensions. As more affluent whites departed city neighborhoods for the suburbs, city centers became minority enclaves and public schools became de facto segregated. Seeking to create a racial mix in northern schools, federal courts ordered the merger of urban and suburban school districts and mandatory busing, but white suburbanites opposed such programs, and the Supreme Court ultimately rejected that remedy in 1974. Meanwhile, in southern school districts white enrollments increasingly shifted to private schools to avoid integration. The burden of integrating public schools thus moved to urban centers, where residents were poorer than in the suburbs. In South Boston and Louisville, Kentucky, court-ordered busing provoked violent protests from whites who resented government interference in neighborhood schools and opposed forced racial integration. By the end of the decade, school districts throughout the nation were successfully challenging mandatory busing.

Whites also attacked affirmative action programs designed to remedy past discrimination.

When the University of California at Davis's medical school denied admission to Allan Bakke, while accepting minority applicants with lower grades, he carried the case against "reverse discrimination" to the Supreme Court in 1978. In a split 5–4 decision, the Court tried to thread a middle course by denying the legality of statistical race quotas, yet by an equally narrow vote ruled that racial factors could be considered in admission standards. These ambiguities satisfied neither side, reflecting the blurred public opinion on the issue. The next year, the Court retreated in another case, called "the blue-collar Bakke," by rejecting a challenge to affirmative action in employment. Such litigation would continue for the next twenty years, contributing to African American mistrust of civil rights promises while angering whites about special privileges for minorities.

The Resurgence of Native American Activism

As African American activism shifted in the 1970s from street protests to legal battles, Native American leaders also saw the courts as an opportunity for political victories. For members of the militant American Indian Movement (AIM), the decade began with the protest occupation of Alcatraz Island in San Francisco Bay that focused national attention on the historic violation of Native American treaty rights. Targeting the Bureau of Indian Affairs (BIA), AIM leaders led a protest march called the "Trail of Broken Treaties" to Washington, D.C., in 1972 to demand recognition of Native sovereignty. Although the federal government agreed to consider the complaints, AIM's militancy aroused criticism from entrenched reservation leaders who benefited from BIA patronage. When the government rejected radical claims in 1973, AIM leaders occupied the village of Wounded Knee, South Dakota, site of the 1890 massacre, to protest both federal indifference to poverty, health, and welfare issues and corruption among some reservation leaders. After a tense 70-day standoff, marked by violence and bloodshed, a compromise agreement provided for the election of local leaders.

Native American activists discovered another potent issue in the federal giveaway of underground natural resources. Pushed for centuries into the country's poorest areas, reservation residents found during the energy crisis that their lands held 5 percent of the nation's untapped oil and natural gas, 30 percent of its uranium, and one-third of the western states' coal. Complaining that the BIA allowed corporations to pay token royalties to the tribes, the Northern Cheyennes and Crows of Montana won the right to renegotiate leasing agreements. Taking a lesson from OPEC, the mineral-rich tribes in 1975 organized the Council of Energy Reserve Tribes (CERT), a consortium of twenty-five nations led by Navajo Peter MacDonald. Other legal action restored treaty rights elsewhere, including the return of millions of acres of land to the Passamaquoddys and Penobscots in Maine; fishing rights to the Chippewas and Ottawas who lived near the Great Lakes; and half the annual salmon catch on Puget Sound in Washington. Such assertions of tribal rights involved a larger rebirth of Native American culture. As novelists like Leslie Marmon Silko and Gerald Vizenor produced literary work with a distinctive perspective, a younger generation established linguistic mentor programs to keep alive religious beliefs and Native American languages facing extinction.

The Growth of Immigrant Communities

New immigrant groups from Latin America and Asia also emerged to seek political rights and assert their cultural identity. During the 1970s, the nation's Hispanic population nearly doubled. Two-thirds came from Mexico, comprising 10 million legal immigrants and several million "undocu-mented aliens." As a relatively young group with a high birthrate, the Hispanic population grew faster than national averages. Yet unemployment remained 45 percent higher than for whites, and nearly one-quarter lived below the government standard of poverty. Nevertheless, Hispanic communities in California, Texas, and the Southwest organized effective civil rights groups to protest discrimination in education and employment and supported a thriving Latino cultural revival, with distinctive music, theater, fiction, and poetry. Meanwhile, in Florida, half a million exiles from Cuba built a prosperous bilingual community with considerable influence in local politics. Stridently anti-communist, Cuban Americans would influence U.S. policy toward the Castro regime for the next three decades.

With Los Angeles becoming the nation's largest port of entry for immigrants, people from the Philippines, Taiwan, Korea, Indochina, and India totaled 40 percent of the nation's new arrivals. Benefiting from the 1965 immigration law that gave priority to family members of U.S. residents (see Chapter 26), a large proportion of Asian immigrants were women—the wives, widowed mothers, and children of earlier immigrants. Many settled in Hawaii and the inner-city neighborhoods of Los Angeles, San Francisco, and New York, finding employment in low-wage service and garment work. Older Asian ethnic groups, originally from China and Japan but possessing English-language skills, now made their mark in academia. Chinese American writings, such as Maxine Hong Kingston's prizewinning *The Woman Warrior* (1976), expressed the conflicts of ethnic identity, and mainstream audiences began to discover these works.

The Conflicts of Feminist Politics

Cultural politics focusing on sex and gender crossed ethnic lines as women fulfilled the promises of the 1960s civil rights movement in education, employment, and family life. Women now gained headlines with notable "firsts": the first women's studies programs, the first women's athletic departments, the first women umpires, referees, and presidential candidates. After Congress passed the Equal Rights Amendment (ERA) in 1972 and sent the measure to the states for ratification (see Chapter 28), other federal policies extended women's economic rights. At a time when more than half the nation's women participated in the labor force, the Equal Employment Opportunity Commission (EEOC) set a powerful precedent by ordering the giant AT&T corporation to adopt a policy of affirmative action. The ruling awarded back pay to women and minorities who had been denied advancement because of past "discriminatory practices." Later in the decade, feminist lawyers successfully challenged sexual abuse on the job. Catherine MacKinnon's influential book *The Sexual Harassment of Working Women* (1979) brought the problem to public light, and by 1980 the EEOC added sexual harassment as a category of legal discrimination.

Other forms of sexual violence also became suspect. Prior to the women's liberation movement, rape had been an underreported crime, as victims shamefully avoided exposure. But in 1970, essayist Susan Griffin published an influential article in the left-wing *Ramparts* magazine suggesting that rape did not involve the satisfaction of "natural" male desires, but rather functioned to suppress women's independence. As feminists became more vocal about rape, the legal system treated the crime more seriously. In several celebrated cases (one involving a black prisoner in North Carolina, another a battered Hispanic), the courts acquitted women who killed their rapists. Spurred by growing feminist protests, legal authorities also began to treat domestic violence, including marital rape, as a criminal offense. Feminists now opened shelters for battered wives and joined conservative women in protesting pornography as an incitement to sexual violence.

Several Supreme Court rulings further altered the constitutional framework of women's legal rights. During the 1970s, a series of sex-discrimination cases gave women full equality before the law. According to the high Court, women could not be barred from jury duty; seniority and social security benefits could not favor men over women; and men and women had to enjoy the same legal age of majority. "No longer is the female destined solely for the home and the rearing of the family," the Court declared, "and only the male for the marketplace in the world of ideas." Meanwhile, Congress passed the Equal Credit Opportunity Act in 1974, giving all married women the right to obtain credit in their own names. By 1977, federal funds sponsored the National Women's Conference in Houston, Texas, a gathering of 20,000 women charged with identifying "the barriers that prevent women from participating fully and equally in all aspects of national life." The convention endorsed comprehensive reforms, ranging from childcare centers to gay rights.

The success of the women's liberation movement ironically aroused anti-feminist critics, including conservative women. In many state legislatures, the ERA encountered strong opposition. Conservative groups, led by Phyllis Schlafly's Stop-ERA coalition, publicized the seeming threat to male-headed households. Warning that the amendment would deprive women of financial support, child custody rights, protection in employment, and exemption from military service, Schlafly spearheaded a grassroots movement that stopped the ERA in its tracks. Despite endorsement by both national parties, the ERA never obtained the necessary three-quarters of the states to become a constitutional amendment.

Equally controversial was the response to the 1973 Supreme Court ruling in *Roe v. Wade*,

The stigma of divorce undermined the political aspirations of Nelson Rockefeller, but few mentioned that Ronald Reagan had been married twice.

declaring that women had a constitutional right to abortion. Despite federal law and opinion polls that found a majority favoring women's right to abortion without the "veto power" of their husbands, diverse anti-abortion groups, including the Catholic church, fundamentalist Protestants, and political conservatives, pressed to reverse federal policy. In 1976, Illinois Representative Henry Hyde successfully sponsored legislation forbidding Medicare funds for abortions. After the Supreme Court upheld the measure, Congress passed additional laws restricting federal expenditures to terminate pregnancy. As the number of abortions continued to increase annually, the issue remained a volatile topic, pitting right-to-life protesters against feminists and civil libertarians.

Redefining Family and Community Relations

The tensions of cultural politics reflected not only ethnic diversity and feminist demands but also fundamental changes in society's most basic institution: the family. As national divorce rates continued to climb, doubling between 1966 and 1976, opinion surveys found growing acceptance of marital separation on grounds of incompatibility. Numerous states enacted "no-fault" divorce laws, easing legal separations. Divorce no longer had moral and political repercussions. During the

1960s, the stigma of divorce had undermined the political aspirations of New York Governor Nelson Rockefeller, but few even mentioned that Republican presidential candidate Ronald Reagan had been married twice.

New Family Demographics

Rising divorce rates coincided with a sharp drop in the nation's marriage rate, which reached a historic low of ten marriages per thousand in 1975. In this decade of economic recession, young adults increasingly delayed their weddings. By 1980, the average age of first marriage was 22.1 for women and 24.6 for men, a full year higher than in 1975 and nearly two years higher than in the 1950s. Such trends lowered the national birthrate, which dropped from 18.4 per thousand in 1970 to 14.8 per thousand at mid-decade. Among married women in their twenties, the rate of childlessness was so high that demographers speculated that a generation of liberated women had forsaken childbearing forever. By 1980, however, the birthrate began to increase, especially among women over 30. With the new medical technology of sonograms and amniocentesis, combined with the legality of abortion (in case of negative genetic findings), and a 100 percent increase in the number of cesarian deliveries, women had merely delayed their first babies until launching their careers or finding second spouses. The census also found that 80 percent of divorced men and women remarried within three years.

By the mid-1970s, the government's yardstick of a "typical" household—a working father, housewife mother, and two children—represented only 7 percent of all U.S. families. During the decade, the number of single-person households increased 60 percent, comprising nearly one-quarter of all domiciles by 1980. Some of these statistics indicated the longevity of elderly individuals, especially widows who maintained independent households, but the number of single people under 35 also increased 200 percent. The rising population of unmarried young adults, the baby boomers, had strong effects on the marketplace, ranging from the expansion of "singles" food products to higher rents for small-sized urban apartments and burgeoning sales of domestic pets and pet foods.

Families in Change

The proliferation of divorce, cohabitation, and remarriage produced new attitudes toward family institutions. Fully 40 percent of all children born in the 1970s spent some time in single-parent households, 90 percent of them headed by women. The number of households with couples who lived together without marriage tripled to 1.6 million, one-quarter of which contained children. These relationships required no legal "divorce," but one-third eventually resulted in marriage, and an estimated one-third endured outside the law. Although most states did not recognize cohabitation, unmarried status gained wide acceptance. Even conservative family films like *Rocky* (1975) showed unmarried couples living together without making moral judgments. In 1977, the federal government waived marriage rules in public housing without stirring controversy. Couples also gained legal protection in a celebrated 1977 "palimony" case involving actor Lee Marvin, when California courts held that a live-in mate had similar rights to a legal spouse.

Changing family relations reflected the pressures of a tightening economy. At this time of recession, the major growth industries (food, health, and business services, which provided 40 percent of all new jobs between 1973 and 1980) were traditionally "women's work." Such positions involved only part-time employment at minimum wages, limited advancement, and no unionization. That was why women earned only a fraction of male incomes. Moreover, since only 40 percent of the nation's jobs produced sufficient income to support a family, married women with children had to take available jobs, regardless of their qualifications.

By the end of the decade, half of all mothers and 43 percent of women with preschool-age children were working. Childcare now emerged as another growth industry dominated by women. Families who could not afford childcare left their youngsters unsupervised. Surveys found that most children watched an estimated 12,000 to 16,000 hours of television by age 16. The rising number of working mothers changed the nation's consumption habits, as stores stayed open later to accommodate working shoppers. The appearance of new consumer conveniences, such as microwave ovens, takeout meals, and mail order catalogues, facilitated tasks formerly done by housewives.

Contributing to alternative family styles was the rising number of homosexuals who lived openly as couples. Estimated at 5 percent of the population, gays increasingly came out of the closet to acknowledge their sexual identity and lifestyle. In 1973, the American Psychiatric Association formally declassified homosexuality as a "mental disorder" and endorsed full civil rights for gays. Feminists at the National Women's Conference supported lesbian rights as a basic demand. On Father's Day 1977, President Jimmy Carter spoke publicly about extending civil rights to homosexuals, but many religious leaders still perceived homosexuality as immoral and pressed for local legislation to repeal their civil rights protections. Political contests in Miami, St. Paul, and Seattle put the issues in a national spotlight. When voters in California faced an initiative to ban homosexuals from teaching, even conservatives like ex-Governor Reagan criticized such infringements on personal privacy. These political battles brought mixed results, leaving a legacy of

The explosion of city wall grafitti—spray-painted tagging—affirmed group identity with local turf.

mutual hostility and mistrust that would influence political opinion to the end of the century.

A New Youth Culture

The transformation of family values particularly affected young adults. Following the sexual revolution of the 1960s, 80 percent of teenage males and 65 percent of teenage females experienced sexual intercourse, with an average age of initiation at 16. By 1980, teenage pregnancies exceeded 1 million a year, a more than 10 percent increase in five years. Teenagers accounted for nearly half a million abortions, one-third of the U.S. total. (Women between ages 20 and 24 accounted for half the total.) But one-fifth of teenagers gave birth out of wedlock, and 87 percent of these kept their babies. For young unmarried mothers, economic opportunities remained limited, contributing to a cycle of poverty.

Young adults of the 1970s formed a distinctive youth culture that pulled in two directions. The first type could be seen in Hollywood's 1977 hit, *Saturday Night Fever,* which portrayed the limited opportunities of working-class youth but suggested the possibility of improvement through self-discipline, hard work, and consumer spending. Finding expression in "disco" music, such as Norma Jeane's "(I Just Can't Wait Till) Saturday," the style supported a $4 billion entertainment industry for music, clothing, and cosmetics as a remedy for boring, dead-end, minimum-wage jobs.

The second type of youth culture appeared in movies like *The Warriors* and *Boulevard Nights* (both 1977), which depicted the futility of economic ambition and glorified ethnic gang territoriality. Closer to the reality of inner city life, these movies celebrated violence and vandalism and were banned in some cities. Contrary to disco's high fashions, the alternative youth culture adopted a style that flaunted tough street life, including the wearing of safety pins, chains, and ripped clothing. Instead of disco's choreographed dancing, it involved nondance pogo steps to "punk rock" and "new wave" music. Performers like Elvis Costello, Tom Robinson, and Pink Floyd sang lyrics that depicted schools as institutions of "thought control" and used language banned from the airwaves.

The New Elderly and a Search for Roots

The vitality of youth culture ironically paralleled a new exuberance for old age. As life expectancy for white men reached 69.5 and for white women 77.2 (African Americans averaged nearly five years less), the over-65 population increased 20 percent during the 1970s. This growing longevity resulted partly from advances in medical technology, such as magnetic resonance imaging (MRI), CT scans, and heart surgery. It also reflected changes in lifestyle, such as increased physical activity and dietary care. Nearly half of the elderly lived with spouses in independent households, and 25 percent lived alone. To avoid losing their economic independence or pension benefits, widows and widowers often shared living arrangements outside marriage. In better health than earlier generations, the new elderly resented enforced retirement and successfully pressed Congress in 1978 to raise the age of mandatory retirement from 65 to 70.

Older citizens also formed political lobby groups, such as the American Association of Retired Persons (AARP), which quadrupled its membership to 12 million, and the more radical Gray Panthers, founded by Maggie Kuhn in 1970. Sheer numbers forced a reconsideration of traditional stereotypes about old age. Abandoning popular images of senility, incompetence, and ill health, the mass media (television, movies, advertising) increasingly portrayed the serious problems of aging. "Old age is not illness," wrote 70-year-old author May Sarton in 1978. "It is a timeless ascent."

"Old age is not illness. It is a timeless ascent."

Interest in ancestry boosted a remarkable enthusiasm for genealogy and popular history. Alex Haley's family history *Roots* (1976) told the story of an African American family from slavery days to the present, becoming an instant bestseller. As an 8-day television series, the saga attracted at least 130 million viewers—more than half the country's population saw at least one show—and inspired interest in oral history and other historical subjects. Historical documentary films, often produced by women filmmakers who were excluded from Hollywood's mainstream, presented forgotten aspects of women's history, such as union organizing during the 1930s (*Harlan County*, 1977) and the workers' homefront in World War II (*Rosie the Riveter*, 1978).

The growing respect for public history reversed liberal enthusiasm for urban renewal and the demolition of old buildings, instead demanding historical preservation. Architectural renovation became an element in city planning and neighborhood restoration. These types of popular history moved the subject of history away from the study of elite groups, who left behind written records, to those whose legacy consisted of artifacts and the spoken word. Together with the interest in ethnic and minority history, the change in perspective altered the content of standard U.S. history courses to include the lives of ordinary citizens. Outside the classroom, a popular fad for nostalgia emerged in movies, television programs, fashions, and advertising, as marketers repackaged the past to sell commercial products.

An Era of Presidential Weakness

The interest in community history and ethnic roots reflected a new politics of limits. Frustrated by Vietnam, Watergate, and presidential incompetence, the public expressed a deepening distrust of the national leadership. Angered by Nixon's illegal activities, voters perceived his successor, Gerald Ford, as a caretaker president, holding office merely until the next elections. Ford's inability to solve economic problems and a faltering foreign policy ensured a Democratic victory in 1976. Yet Ford's successor, President Jimmy Carter, faced the same domestic and international problems and seemed equally unable to solve them. He, too, became a one-term president. The weakness of Nixon's successors further undermined public confidence in the federal government. Rather than looking to Washington for political solutions, voters saw the federal government as the source of their problems. Liberals and conservatives alike believed that government could provide only limited answers to economic and social issues, and stressed the importance of strengthening community institutions to meet public needs.

The Presidency of Gerald Ford

In the aftermath of Watergate, Nixon's handpicked successor, Gerald Ford, bore the brunt of public anger and confusion. A former congressional representative from Michigan, the unelected president described himself as "a Ford, not a Lincoln," and projected images not of power and resolution but of simple calm. "Our national nightmare is over,"

". . . a Ford, not a Lincoln . . ."

he declared upon taking office. After the turbulence of Watergate, the public welcomed the prospect of normal politics. Yet economic problems, crisis diplomacy, and poor management soon tossed the president into choppy political seas.

Ford brought his troubles on himself. One month after replacing the impeached Nixon, the new president abruptly terminated investigation of the Watergate crimes by granting his predecessor a complete pardon. Overnight, Ford's popularity ratings plunged from 72 percent to 49 percent. Although the president subsequently appeared before a House investigating committee to deny any secret deals with Nixon, the magnanimous gesture ended up tarnishing his reputation. Ford drew more criticism for nominating billionaire Nelson Rockefeller as his vice president. After the Democratic Congress confirmed the choice, two unelected officials headed the executive branch of government.

Following the scandals, Congress passed campaign finance reforms that limited donations, established income tax check-offs to underwrite elections, and required the disclosure of campaign contributors. The Supreme Court later weakened the law by ruling that personal spending was a free speech right that could not constitutionally be abridged. Bitterness over Watergate brought huge Democratic victories in the 1974 congressional elections. Equally significant, voter participation dropped to 38 percent, the lowest since World War II.

Ford endeavored to continue Nixon's foreign policies of détente, relying on Secretary of State Henry Kissinger to negotiate additional SALT agreements to balance nuclear strength with the

Soviet Union. Yet when Ford met Soviet leader Leonid Brezhnev at Helsinki in 1975 and formally recognized the Soviet military presence in Eastern Europe, presidential policy offended powerful opponents. Republican conservatives objected to any concessions to communist expansion, and congressional Democrats protested Soviet restrictions on Jewish emigration to Israel. Instead of easing relations between the superpowers, summit diplomacy accentuated controversy about foreign policy and prevented any slowing of the nuclear arms race.

Asserting Congressional Power

Mistrust of presidential leadership encouraged Congress to seek greater control of foreign policy. Following passage of the 1973 War Powers Act (see Chapter 28), legislators moved to regulate the CIA by requiring the White House to report secret overseas activity to Congress "in a timely fashion." But when Ford sought approval for CIA intervention in a civil war in Africa's Angola in 1975, Congress refused to fund the operation, despite the prior intervention of Soviet and Cuban forces. Congressional leaders also opened public hearings into previous CIA conduct, exposing agency involvement in foreign assassination plots, including efforts to kill Cuba's Fidel Castro. Investigations also revealed covert actions to sabotage the elected Marxist government in Chile in 1973, though executive secrecy prevented further prosecution.

Efforts to restrain overseas intervention culminated in Congress's refusal to provide emergency military aid to South Vietnam in 1975. As North Vietnam's forces moved rapidly toward South Vietnam's capital, congressional leaders in both parties agreed only to assist the evacuation of remaining U.S. advisors and key South Vietnamese personnel. In April, the last helicopter rose from the roof of the U.S. embassy. The operation transported

120,000 South Vietnamese allies, the first of half a million refugees from Indochina who would make the United States their home. The long war—despite $150 billion in costs, millions of Vietnamese casualties, and 58,000 U.S. deaths—now ended in political and military defeat.

Two weeks earlier, the Communist Khmer Rouge had seized power in Cambodia. Just after the fall of Saigon this revolutionary government captured a U.S. merchant ship, *Mayaguez,* off shore. In a final display of U.S. resolve in southeast Asia, Ford ordered military forces to recover the vessel. Coming just as Cambodia released the ship, the attack cost more lives than would have been saved. Yet the administration used the fiasco to assert its continuing commitment in the region.

"Let no adversary believe that our difficulties mean a slackening of our national will," said President Ford, affirming the country's international responsibilities. Yet the final defeat of South Vietnam in 1975 underscored fundamental changes in U.S. power since the beginnings of the Cold War. Although the world's superpowers still had to reckon with U.S. military might, Washington could no longer wield power unilaterally in small countries. Together with a lingering anti-war movement at home, the limits of U.S. power overseas awakened a new era of anti-interventionism. Conservatives like Reagan bristled at this change, warning of the consequences of a "Vietnam syndrome." But many citizens welcomed the retreat from unrestrained internationalism. Unlike the isolationism associated with the 1930s, the new perspective accepted U.S. responsibility for confronting global conflict and negotiating on behalf of U.S. allies, but it drew strict lines at military intervention.

Inflation, Recession, and "Disaster"

Washington's inability to control events in Vietnam mirrored the crisis of economic instability at home. During the month that Ford took office, wholesale prices jumped nearly 4 percent, the second highest monthly increase since 1946; simultaneously, unemployment rose, the Gross National Product fell, housing construction shrank, and the country's international trade deficit reached a new high. Responding to the recession, the Democratic Congress appropriated funds for public schools, housing, and mass transit, and raised the minimum wage. Ford instead focused on inflation, seeking to curb consumer spending with special surtaxes. Sporting a lapel button with the motto "WIN" ("Whip Inflation Now"), the president pleaded for voluntary restraint to stop rising prices, exhorting citizens to "clean up your plate when you leave the table." Such advice accomplished nothing.

"The state of the union," the president admitted in his first annual address, "is not good." Amidst angry disagreements between Ford and Congress about appropriate remedies, the economy appeared uncontrollable. With the White House determined to slow inflation by reducing government spending and with Congress supporting expenditures to create jobs and stimulate domestic consumption, legislative stalemates forced a compromise. Rising energy costs aggravated economic problems. Although Ford supported the use of nuclear energy and synthetic fuels to ease dependence on imported oil, shortage of capital during the recession limited those options. Congress finally approved a gradual deregulation of oil prices and ended tax breaks for petroleum corporations.

To stabilize access to Middle East resources, the president encouraged Kissinger to embark on "shuttle diplomacy," whirlwind trips between Israel and the Arab nations to seek a peaceful settlement, but their historic quarrels appeared unbridgeable. Meanwhile, Congress approved the Metric Conversion Act, hoping to increase exports by allowing U.S. corporations to produce industrial components according to the decimal measurements of the metric system. Such long-term remedies underscored the decline of U.S. economic power and the need to accommodate Third World markets. At home, a budgetary crisis brought the city of New York nearly to bankruptcy, forcing the federal government to offer assistance to the welfare-burdened metropolis. Indicative of the public mood was the popularity of a new genre of Hollywood movies—"disaster" films like the 1975 box office hit *Jaws,* which depicted the perilous condition of ordinary life and the inability of corrupt officials to solve community problems.

The Election of 1976

Distrust of the political leadership set the tone of the 1976 elections. Twice in a single month, Ford escaped injury in separate incidents when two women failed in assassination attempts. Within the Republican party, Ford faced strong competition from conservative Ronald Reagan, who condemned détente with the Soviet Union and criticized the decline of U.S. influence in the Third World. Ford managed to gain the nomination by an eyelash and chose Kansas Senator Robert Dole as his running mate. Yet despite his incumbency, the president sought election as an opponent of federal power, calling for "less government, less spending, less inflation."

As the party out of power, the Democrats also ran against Washington politics. Jimmy Carter, the soft-spoken former governor of Georgia, adopted the slogan "Jimmy Who?" to appeal to an electorate frustrated by professional politicians. Gaining support from African American church leaders, Carter used his born-again Christian background to attract

The Election of 1976

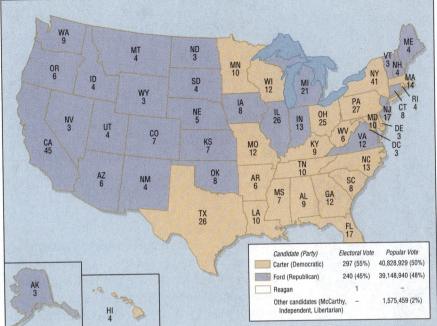

Candidate (Party)	Electoral Vote	Popular Vote
Carter (Democratic)	297 (55%)	40,828,929 (50%)
Ford (Republican)	240 (45%)	39,148,940 (48%)
Reagan	1	–
Other candidates (McCarthy, Independent, Libertarian)	–	1,575,459 (2%)

white southerners who had deserted the Democratic party for Nixon in the previous two elections. Focusing the campaign on the issue of public trust, the Democrats benefited by continuing anger over Watergate. In the final tally, Ford won a majority of the white male vote and swept the western states. But Carter rebuilt the New Deal coalition, carrying union workers in the Northeast, African Americans, and middle-class liberals as well as the South. The Democratic victory had its limits. The electoral college vote was the closest since 1916, and voter participation dropped below 55 percent.

Carter's Crisis of Leadership

"We have learned that 'more' is not necessarily 'better,'" said Carter in his inaugural address, "that

even our great nation has recognized limits, and that we can neither answer all questions nor solve all problems." Carter's effort to lower public expectations reflected his limited political options. First, the nation's economic troubles—an annual inflation rate of 6 percent and unemployment at nearly 7 percent—could not easily be legislated away. As President Ford had discovered, simultaneous inflation and unemployment demanded conflicting remedies either by cutting federal deficits or by increasing government spending, not both. Second, Carter's political inexperience and his reluctance to burden his administration with Washington professionals weakened his ability to persuade Congress to adopt any program.

Through no fault of his own, Carter confronted a fiercely independent Congress. Following Watergate, a new breed of young Democrats forced a

In sharp contrast to the "imperial presidency" of Richard Nixon, Jimmy Carter and his family insisted on walking to the inaugural ceremonies.

TABLE 29.1	
Unemployment Rates, 1976–1980	
1976	7.5%
1977	9.0%
1978	6.0%
1979	5.8%
1980	7.0%

Source: *Economic Report of the President* (Washington, DC: U.S. Government Printing Office, 1988).

break-up of the old congressional seniority system that gave power to party leaders who chaired a few committees (see Chapter 25). During the Carter presidency, a survey of internal congressional voting found the lowest level of party loyalty since 1940. Finally, a number of congressional scandals, involving bribery, kickbacks, alcoholism, and sexual promiscuity, eroded confidence in the political leadership. "For some citizens," remarked Carter, "the government has become like a foreign country."

A Faltering Economy

The economy emerged as Carter's major domestic concern. Although the president promised to "discipline" government spending, inflationary pressures reflected broader economic problems that caused a sharp drop in productivity. Instead of investing to modernize factories, manufacturers built plants overseas, acquired existing companies, or simply delayed decisions in the face of inflation. Declining productivity meant higher costs for business and rising prices. In addition, cost-of-living increases that were built into labor and business contracts demanded a steady escalation of costs and prices. Meanwhile, higher interest rates, aimed at fighting inflation, raised the cost of capital and further discouraged new investment. Such factors weakened U.S. competition in foreign trade, causing a decline in steel, automobile, and electronics sales.

Inflation remedies also conflicted with domestic demands to resolve unemployment (Table 29.1). Despite White House efforts to curtail federal spending, Congress passed a $4 billion emergency public works law in 1977 and debated the Humphrey-Hawkins full employment bill that would make the federal government an employer of last resort (Table 29.2). The latter measure increased conflicts within the Democratic party. Having earned African American voting support in 1976, Carter fulfilled campaign promises by

TABLE 29.2

Federal Social Welfare Expenditures, 1976–1980 (rounded billions of dollars)

1976	$197.0 b
1978	$239.7 b
1980	$302.6 b

Source: *Statistical Abstract of the United States* (Washington, DC: U.S. Government Printing Office, 1987).

TABLE 29.3

Imports and Exports, 1976–1980 (billions of dollars)

1976	$123.5 b	$115.2 b
1978	$174.8 b	$143.7 b
1980	$244.9 b	$220.6 b

Source: *Statistical Abstract of the United States* (Washington, DC: U.S. Government Printing Office, 1987).

appointing blacks and other minorities to federal judgeships (increasing the percentage of black federal judges from 4 percent in 1977 to 9 percent in 1981). He also awarded government contracts to minority-owned companies and approved settlement of job discrimination cases. But the president's weak support for full-employment measures infuriated the Congressional Black Caucus and organized labor. Although Congress enacted Humphrey-Hawkins in 1978, Carter gained little credit in the black community.

To stimulate business competitiveness, Carter reduced government regulation of key industries, such as airlines, trucking, communications, and banking, waiving restraints that dated to the New Deal. Yet the administration also backed agricultural price supports for large wheat growers, aided the ailing steel industry, and rushed to assist the failing Chrysler Corporation, the nation's tenth largest business. As low productivity and foreign competition (Table 29.3) drove the automaker toward bankruptcy in 1979, the White House supported a $1.5 billion loan guarantee to keep Chrysler solvent. Carter also endorsed legislation to protect the environment from unlimited economic development, agreeing to regulate strip mining, to establish a "Superfund" to finance the cleanup of chemical contamination,

and to reserve federal lands in Alaska from future development.

Another Energy Crisis

The nation's economic problems remained closely tied to rising energy prices. The hard winter of 1977 brought record snowfalls, subzero temperatures, factory closings, and the layoff of 1.6 million workers. "Face the fact," said Carter. "The energy shortage is permanent." In April, the president presented a detailed energy program to a somber nation. Describing the energy crisis as "the moral equivalent of war," Carter proposed a tax package to penalize energy waste and to reduce dependence on foreign oil through frugality and energy conservation. The petroleum industry responded by demanding government deregulation to stimulate oil production. Amid these mixed pressures, Congress approved the creation of a cabinet-level Department of Energy, but debated for nineteen months before passing the National Energy Act in 1978. The law made few concessions to conservation or alternative energy. Instead, Congress opted for gradual decontrol of oil prices, giving business an incentive to increase production, but including windfall profits taxes to allow rebates for poor consumers.

694 | WE THE PEOPLE: A Brief American History

The energy picture darkened in 1979. The outbreak of civil war against the Shah of Iran sharply curtailed world oil production, and the Organization of Petroleum Exporting Countries (OPEC) announced a 14.5 percent price increase. Stung by this inflationary policy, Carter asked consumers to conserve fuel by driving less, honoring the 55-mph speed limit, and lowering thermostats. As an unhappy public accommodated these restrictions, another shock occurred when the nuclear power plant at Three Mile Island, Pennsylvania, overheated perilously. Although technicians averted a cataclysmic meltdown, the emergency demonstrated inherent problems with nuclear energy, not least the high cost of building and maintaining reactor cores. Such problems underscored U.S. dependence on petroleum. Yet Congress rejected a mandatory oil rationing plan, and gasoline shortages produced higher prices and enormous traffic lines as customers waited at the pumps. Then, three months later, OPEC ordered another price hike of 50 percent.

With rising fuel costs pushing inflation into double digits, the Federal Reserve Board raised prime interest rates from 15 percent in 1979 to more than 20 percent the next year. Carter watched helplessly as the economy faltered. The president's approval rating plummeted from 75 percent at the beginning of his term to below 25 percent in mid-1979. Frustrated and bewildered by the economic crisis, Carter canceled a major energy policy address that summer and withdrew to the presidential retreat at Camp David to consult with leading politicians and community leaders about the state of the nation.

Then in a televised broadcast in July 1979, the president addressed the public about what he called the "crisis of confidence" that threatened the "social and political fabric." Depicting a decline of traditional values ("hard work, strong families, close-knit communities, and our faith in God"), Carter criticized Washington politicians for failing to respond to the crisis. The White House then introduced another package of energy legislation, emphasizing the use of conservation and synthetic fuels. But when a numbed public failed to respond, Congress delayed action until 1980, allowing oil decontrol and nuclear safety measures to substitute for alternative policies.

The Politics of Limits

Frustrated by the inadequacies of federal programs to resolve energy shortages, economic problems, or cultural enmity, local activists increasingly focused on neighborhood, municipal, or state government to achieve political goals. During the mid-1970s, anti-nuclear activists around the country started protest movements, such as New England's Clamshell Alliance, to oppose the construction of nuclear reactors to produce electricity. California Governor Jerry Brown, a former Catholic seminarian, embraced the philosophy that "small is beautiful." Respectful of natural limits to growth, such community populists proposed renewable energy sources such as solar power, recycling programs, and small-scale technology. Focusing on the miniaturization of technology in telephone systems, computers, and word processors, futurist Alvin Toffler predicted the emergence of a society based on the self-sufficient "electronic cottage."

More potent attacks on government came from militant conservatives, many of whom identified with the political aspirations of former California governor Ronald Reagan. Although Presidents Nixon, Ford, and Carter acknowledged the role of government in providing social security and health benefits for the elderly, environmental protection, and equal civil rights for all citizens, growing antigovernment opinion challenged federal interference in economic and social affairs. But, where local populists attempted to mandate greater corporate responsibility to communities, the emerging "New Right" demanded a free marketplace to set utility rates, energy costs, and social programs.

Unlike community populists, the New Right also appealed to religious conservatives by condemning changes in social values. Opposing gun control, abortion, homosexuality, pornography, and the ERA, conservatives advocated a society based on family, church, and the work ethic. Backed by popular media preachers, so-called televangelists, who included Jerry Falwell and his "Moral Majority," the new conservatives mobilized an electronic church that by 1980 reached 2 million contributing viewers "to work for pro-God, pro-family policies in government." Such groups proved strongest in the Sunbelt states of the South and Southwest.

The New Right and the community populists shared a growing suspicion about the misuse of government power. Indicative of the public mood, California voters in 1978 approved a controversial popular initiative, Proposition 13, which placed sharp restrictions on property taxes, despite resulting cuts in public education, libraries, and other social services. In a similar spirit, Congress passed the Revenue Act of 1978, which reduced capital gains taxes, a measure favored by two-thirds of those polled, even though the law benefited only 2 percent of the taxpayers. Support of such tax cuts reflected the growing strength of anti-government politics and a widening mistrust of professional politicians and government bureaucrats to define the nation's political agenda. These attitudes revealed the bitter legacy of Vietnam, Watergate, energy crises, and flawed presidential authority.

A Vacillating Foreign Policy

Carter's domestic problems mirrored his persistent reversals of foreign policy. With the Vietnam war over, the president promised reductions in defense spending and continuation of détente. Rejecting the Cold War arms race during his first year in office, the president canceled production of the B-1 bomber, halted research on a nuclear radiation bomb, blocked reopening of the military draft, and proposed troop withdrawals from South Korea. The White House also surprised the country by extending formal diplomatic recognition to the People's Republic of China in 1979 and terminating the mutual defense treaty with Taiwan. Conservative Republicans attacked the president for abandoning an old ally, viewing the policy as a further sign of global weakness. Following Kissinger's precedents, the administration also negotiated a second strategic arms limitations treaty (SALT II) with the Soviet Union, signing an agreement in 1979 to stabilize the continuing growth of long-range missiles, bombers, and nuclear warheads and to allow satellite technology to monitor compliance.

When militant cold warriors criticized his proposals, however, Carter's position wavered. He canceled plans to remove troops from South Korea, backed research for a "stealth" bomber, and called the Soviet Union a menace to world peace. "We must remember," said a retreating Carter in 1979, "that not every instance of the firm application of the power of the United States is a potential Vietnam." The quest for détente with the Soviet Union collapsed completely in the 1980 election year. While congressional liberals criticized SALT II for failing to halt the nuclear arms race, conservatives blasted the president for limiting U.S. power. Carter then endorsed a larger nuclear submarine fleet, requested funds for a mobile missile system that would be less vulnerable to Soviet attack, and supported compulsory "national service" for men and women.

The Soviet invasion of Afghanistan in 1979 provoked greater presidential militancy. Facing bitter conservative criticism in his reelection bid, Carter could not afford to appear weak or irresolute. He promptly ordered an embargo on high-technology exports to the Soviet Union, demanded a world boycott of the 1980 Olympics scheduled for Moscow, and asked the Senate to postpone consideration of SALT II. Fearing the Soviets were moving toward Persian Gulf oil fields, the president issued what was called "the Carter Doctrine," defining the region as a "vital" interest. Carter then requested a 25 percent increase of military spending during the next five years. This military buildup contrasted with Carter's initial posture of seeking to reduce the arms race, raising questions about his credibility.

Accommodating the Third World

Carter fared better in implementing foreign policy changes with Third World nations, but remained vulnerable to conservative criticism. Placing "human rights" at the center of diplomatic relations, Carter criticized apartheid (racial segregation) in white supremacist South Africa, refused to recognize Rhodesia (Zimbabwe) until the white minority allowed black political participation, and became the first president to visit black Africa. More boldly, Carter defied conservative outrage to complete negotiations of the 1978 Panama Canal treaties that provided for the transfer of the Canal Zone to Panama in 2000. Determined to stop the treaties in the senate, conservative leaders, such as Ronald Reagan and political strategist Richard Viguerie, mounted a massive grassroots campaign involving the early use of direct-mail and telemarketing techniques to build a conservative resurgence. The White House won treaty ratification by a single vote, eliminating the most obvious symbol of U.S. militarism in the Western Hemisphere. Carter's disavowal of big-stick tactics altered the U.S. position in Nicaragua. When rebels attacked the undemocratic dictatorship in 1979, the White House refused to aid the doomed regime.

Carter's commitment to peaceful negotiations climaxed in his brokering an agreement that ended thirty years of conflict between Egypt and Israel. Inviting the leaders of both countries to Camp David in 1978, Carter led them toward a framework for peace that promised to stabilize the Middle East. Yet his failure to consult with Palestinian leaders limited the accomplishment. Carter eased criticism by supplying U.S. allies in the Middle East with military aid. But the White House could not persuade Israel to withdraw from territory claimed by Palestine. Middle East nationalism precluded a political settlement, but Carter reduced the risk of U.S. military involvement and built alliances with oil-producing allies such as Saudi Arabia.

Carter's unexpected confrontation with radical nationalism in Iran, however, spelled disaster. Ever since the CIA-backed coup d'état of 1953 (see Chapter 25), U.S. presidents had supported the oil-rich Shah of Iran as an anti-communist ally. Even Carter's demand for international "human rights" made exceptions for the Shah's infamous regime. When fundamentalist Muslim leaders seized power in Teheran in 1979, Washington's continuing support of the Shah undermined normal relations with Iran. In the shift of governments, the United States lost access to Iran's oil, lost $7 billion in cancelled arms contracts, and lost sensitive listening posts to monitor Soviet missiles.

Despite deteriorating relations, the nation and the world were shocked when Iranian militants seized the U.S. embassy in Teheran, captured sixty hostages, and demanded that the United States return the exiled Shah, who was receiving medical treatment in New York. As angry street crowds chanted "Death to Carter," Iran's revolutionaries paraded the blindfolded hostages and burned U.S. flags in humiliating scenes that were rebroadcast on television for a year. Carter showed great restraint, hoping to save the hostages, but conservatives charged that U.S. prestige had reached its lowest point since World War II.

The Election of 1980

The fiasco in Iran dominated the 1980 presidential contest as liberals and conservatives alike criticized the president for failing to show moral leadership at a time of national crisis. Challenged for the Democratic nomination by Massachusetts's Senator Edward Kennedy, the president reignited Cold War issues, including the Soviet invasion of Afghanistan and higher military spending, to win a chance for a second term. But the same militarism played into the hands of Carter's chief Republican opponent, ex-Governor Reagan. As television news daily broadcast the ritualistic humiliation of U.S. hostages in Iran, Republicans scoffed at presidential weakness and the resulting loss of national pride. "Our allies are losing confidence in us," said Reagan, as the nations of Western Europe ignored Carter's appeal to boycott the Moscow Olympics, "and our adversaries no longer respect us."

A televised debate between the candidates attracted 100 million viewers and crystallized the ideological issues. Carter, who defended his record, expressed a worldview of limits. "We have demanded that the American people sacrifice," he admitted, "and they have done very well." Reagan, the genial ex–movie star who had led the screen actors' union during the anti-communist crusades of the 1940s and 1950s, appeared relaxed and friendly, hardly the right-wing ideologue depicted by Democrats. "Ask yourself," he advised voters, "are you better off than you were four years ago?" By election day, the answer was obvious. With inflation exceeding 12 percent, interest rates passing 15 percent, unemployment hitting 8 million people, and real wages declining 3 percent in the previous twelve months, voters abandoned the Democrats in droves.

"This isn't an election," remarked political analyst Elizabeth Drew, "it's an earthquake." Carter at-

As those at home watched the blindfolded American hostages on television daily, they bedecked the trees at home with yellow ribbons, symbols based on the popular song "Tie a Yellow Ribbon 'Round the Old Oak Tree," expressing hope of a speedy homecoming.

tracted 41 percent of the popular vote. A third-party candidate, the moderate Republican John Anderson, took 7 percent. Reagan carried 51 percent and swamped Carter in the electoral college (489-49). He also led Republicans to their first majority in the Senate since 1953, while gaining 33 seats in the House of Representatives and four additional governorships. Like Richard Nixon, Reagan broke the New Deal coalition by winning among Jews, Catholics, and union members. But indicative of growing splits between ethnic groups,

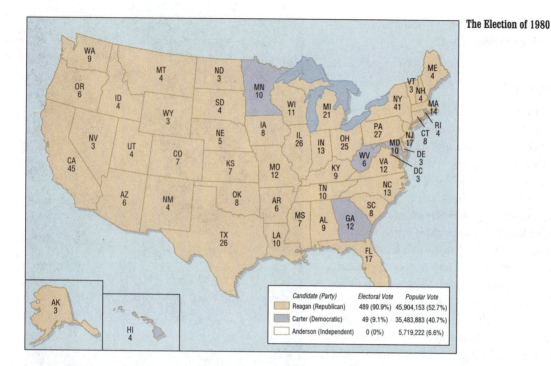

The Election of 1980

Candidate (Party)	Electoral Vote	Popular Vote
Reagan (Republican)	489 (90.9%)	45,904,153 (52.7%)
Carter (Democratic)	49 (9.1%)	35,483,883 (40.7%)
Anderson (Independent)	0 (0%)	5,719,222 (6.6%)

African Americans and Hispanics remained overwhelmingly Democratic. Women voters divided nearly evenly between the parties. Yet voting participation in 1980 showed a continuing decline, falling to 52.3 percent of the eligible electorate, suggesting dissatisfaction with the presidential choices, if not the structure of national power.

Rejecting the Era of Limits

The primary issue of the 1980 election reflected not merely economic grievances or international turmoil. The choice involved nothing less than the national identity. Frustrated by the collapse of political leadership—the defeat in Vietnam, endless scandals of Washington politics, energy shortfalls, and economic chaos—voters refused to accept a political world of limits. "People who talk about an age of limits," said Reagan, "are really talking about their own limitations, not America's." Rather than seeking new answers for the future, the public found comfort and inspiration in the nation's past. Ronald Reagan, the oldest man ever elected president, promised to lead the country back to the promised land. "It is time for us to realize," said Reagan as he assumed office, "that we are too great a nation to limit ourselves to small dreams."

INFOTRAC® COLLEGE EDITION EXERCISES

For additional readings go to InfoTrac College Edition, your online research library at *http://web1.infotrac-college.com.*

Subject search: Gerald Ford

Subject search: Apollo 11

Subject search: Jimmy Carter

Keyword search: Camp David Accords
Subject search: Iran hostage
Subject search: Panama Canal
Keyword search: Afghanistan Soviet
Subject search: Ronald Reagan

ADDITIONAL READING

Peter N. Carroll, *It Seemed Like Nothing Happened: America in the 1970s* (1982). A survey of social, cultural, and political history, emphasizing creative alternatives by out-groups.

The Limits of Black Progress

Ronald P. Formisano, *Boston against Busing: Race, Class, and Ethnicity in the 1960s and 1970s* (1991). A detailed study of racial conflict in South Boston, this book examines the struggles between liberals and conservatives.

J. Harvie Wilkinson III, *From Brown to Bakke* (1979). A study of judicial rulings, examining the legal context of affirmative action.

The Conflicts of Feminist Politics

Donald G. Mathews and Jane Sherron De Hart, *Sex, Gender, and the Politics of ERA* (1990). This book depicts the rise and fall of the Equal Rights Amendment. See also Ruth Rosen, *The World Split Open*, listed in Chapter 28.

The Presidency of Gerald Ford

John Robert Greene, *The Presidency of Gerald Ford* (1995). This volume offers a detailed analysis of White House policies.

Carter's Crisis of Leadership

Burton I. Kaufman, *The Presidency of James Earl Carter, Jr.* (1993). A sympathetic account of Carter's goals and policies.

A Faltering Economy

Anthony S. Campagna, *Economic Policy in the Carter Administration* (1995). Analyzing the decade's economic crises, the author places Carter's policies in the context of his predecessors.

The Politics of Limits

Harry C. Boyte, *The Backyard Revolution* (1980). This book gives an optimistic appraisal of community activists and the new populism.

Alan Crawford, *Thunder on the Right: The "New Right" and the Politics of Resentment* (1980). This critical study examines the rise of conservatism and its political support of Ronald Reagan.

A Vacillating Foreign Policy

David Skidmore, *Reversing Course: Carter's Foreign Policy, Domestic Politics, and the Failure of Reform* (1996). The book emphasizes the impact of partisan politics on international relations.

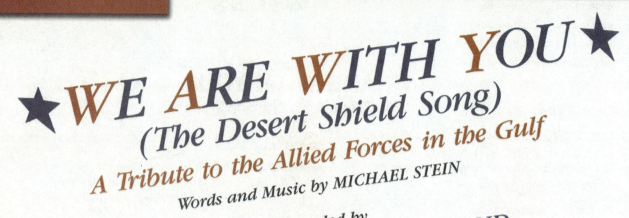

30

★WE ARE WITH YOU★
(The Desert Shield Song)
A Tribute to the Allied Forces in the Gulf
Words and Music by MICHAEL STEIN

Recorded by
THE UNITED STATES NAVY BAND

Politics in a Multicultural Society, 1981–2001

CHRONOLOGY

1981	Ronald Reagan inaugurated
	Congress passes Economic Recovery Act
	Physicians first identify AIDS epidemic
1982	Deep recession raises unemployment
1984	Reagan wins in landslide over Walter Mondale
1986	Congress passes Immigration Reform and Tax Reform laws
	Iran-Contra scandals surface
1987	U.S. and Soviet Union sign INF arms limitation treaty
1988	George H.W. Bush elected president
1989	Berlin Wall comes down
1990	Congress passes Americans with Disabilities Act
1991	Operation Desert Storm drives Iraq from Kuwait
	U.S. and Soviet Union sign START arms reduction treaty
	Bush nominates Clarence Thomas to Supreme Court
1992	Bill Clinton defeats Bush reelection bid
1993	Congress approves North American Free Trade Agreement
1994	Republicans propose "Contract with America"
1995	U.S. brokers Balkan settlement at Dayton, Ohio
	Budget impasse closes federal government
1996	Congress enacts Welfare Reform Act
	Clinton defeats Robert Dole; Republicans carry Congress
1998–1999	Clinton impeachment trial
2000	George W. Bush wins contested election for president
2001	World Trade Center attacked

Twenty years after Ronald Reagan's landslide victory, voters went to the polls on November 7, 2000, expecting resolution of the closest presidential contest in over a century. Early that night, the pollsters announced that the Democratic candidate, Vice President Al Gore, had won the state of Florida and, with that victory, the election as well. Several hours later, the pollsters changed their minds, awarding Florida to the Republican candidate, Texas Governor George W. Bush. Gore soon telephoned his concession to the apparent winner. But then Democrats began to question the Florida tally. Gore retracted his concession, prompting further recounts that delayed the outcome for another six weeks.

The long battle over the presidential election of 2000 revealed just how evenly divided the country's political culture had become. Not only was the voting extremely close—Bush, the winner of the electoral contest, had lost the popular vote—but the polarization of opinion had also created an unbridgeable chasm between Democrats and Republicans, between liberal and conservative policies, even between members of the

http://history.wadsworth.com

supposedly neutral judicial branch of government. The impossibility of reaching a compromise, which for six weeks appeared as an ultimate political gridlock, reflected partisan antagonisms that had been building for twenty years, since the election of Ronald Reagan in 1980.

In 1981, the newly elected president, Ronald Reagan, embodied the triumph of a reinvigorated conservatism. On Inauguration Day, the government of Iran waited for the noon hour in Washington, D.C.—the moment of Reagan's oath taking—to release the embassy hostages, who had been held for more than a year. With happy news in the air, Reagan's inaugural speech reaffirmed U.S. commitments overseas, suggesting that Carter's foreign policy had suffered from military weakness as well as from a loss of national will. The new president vowed to restore U.S. prestige. Primarily, however, Reagan focused on the country's economic ills—inflation, unemployment, low productivity—and promised prosperity by rejecting government regulation. "In this present crisis," he said, pointing toward what became known as the "Reagan Revolution," "government is not the solution to our problem." Instead, the Republican leader pledged to "reverse the growth of government which [has] . . . grown beyond the consent of the governed."

Reagan's anti-government position set the stage for the next two decades of national politics. After Republicans enacted major tax cuts and budget reductions, the resulting limitations of public resources accentuated social divisions and cultural conflicts as competing interest groups fought for government support. Such competition polarized political life, creating a volatile electorate and intensified partisan conflict. Leadership demanded craft and compromise, an ability to balance political divisions, which ironically increased public distrust of elected officials. Although voter participation continued to fall in most elections, frustrated citizens flooded Congress with ever-larger numbers of letters to express their political views; 92 million "voted" this way in 1981. Yet public dissatisfaction with national politics meant that neither Republicans nor Democrats could establish a durable majority. Reagan's vice president, George Bush, would easily succeed to the White House in 1988, achieve unprecedented heights of popularity in 1991, then tumble in the polls and fail to win reelection the next year.

The shifting balance of power in Washington further undermined citizens with the weakest voices and the least influence in the increasingly expensive political process. As business enjoyed two decades of growth and profits, a homeless population appeared in every city, straining community resources for welfare and medical aid. Meanwhile, the real income of wage earners steadily declined, and white-collar managers faced layoffs caused by "downsizing" businesses. When the economy improved in the mid-1990s, corporations maintained strict accountability of the labor force, a key to the economy's improved productivity. But the hours of nonunionized labor increased, averaging an estimated 50 to 60 hours per week. Moreover, census bureau statistics showed that, as median incomes rose in the mid-1990s, the disparities of income also increased.

Persisting economic problems accentuated other issues involving race and gender. The conservative majority that elected Reagan in 1980 supported a social agenda that sought to restrict abortions, to relax rules separating church and state (thus permitting prayers in public schools and government subsidies to religious education), and to stifle the rights of homosexuals. Yet Congress, the courts, and public opinion (as measured in innumerable polls) showed little support for such policies. Conservatives also opposed affirmative action programs that aimed to compensate for past dis-

crimination of racial minorities and women. During the 1980s, disputes about these issues remained in the courts, but by the end of the century, voter initiatives successfully challenged preferences for minority groups. Meanwhile, a tremendous surge of immigration from Latin America, the Caribbean, and Asia, together with a strengthening of the African American middle class, produced a more complex multicultural society than ever before. Women in all groups also benefited by laws and litigation that banned job discrimination and sexual harassment in the workplace.

Such changes often intensified conflict between political and social groups. White male workers in all classes, for example, now faced competition for jobs and new rules for appropriate behavior. In 1998, the Supreme Court ruled that sexual harassment extended to same-sex situations. A new legal environment also protected the rights of the elderly and the physically impaired. Yet equality of opportunity did not typically overcome traditions of discrimination and disadvantage. Racial minorities remained disproportionately at lower economic levels and suffered greater problems associated with poverty.

In education, employment, and community life, therefore, conflicts of lifestyles and values continued to disrupt the civic peace. "We have grown into an experiment in democratic diversity," declared President Bill Clinton as he began his second term in 1997; but amid "abiding bigotry and intolerance," he admitted, "we are not there yet." As the 21st century began, "We the People" remained fragmented, if not hostile; anxious, if not embattled; and politically frustrated, if not enraged. And yet an anti-government consensus, marked by suspicion of politicians, legislation, and international agreements, only affirmed the republic's basic principles of self-government, political responsibility, and the private rights of individuals.

Reagan's personal hero was President Calvin Coolidge, who had said that the business of America was business.

Reagan's Conservative Agenda

The Republican leadership that took office in 1981 expressed less interest in social change than it did in reducing federal power. On the homefront, the administration vigorously pursued anti-government economic policies, demanding major tax reductions and smaller appropriations for social programs. "The idea has been established," said Reagan, "that almost every service that someone might need in life ought to be provided by the government. . . . We reject that notion." Instead, the president believed that business, freed from government restraint, would restore prosperity and create an economic environment for individual opportunity. He declared that his personal hero was President Calvin Coolidge, who had said that the business of America was business.

Republican foreign policy, meanwhile, aimed at establishing military supremacy in a world divided not only by Cold War superpowers but also by regional powers that resisted U.S. interference. Although the White House demanded large cuts for domestic spending, Reagan refused to consider reductions of military appropriations and instead accelerated the arms buildup initiated by President Carter. Such priorities reflected an ideological desire for military superiority, not any new threats to international peace. Yet Congress, and to a lesser extent the voting public, accepted budgetary imbalances and resulting foreign-trade problems to demonstrate a resurgence of U.S. power. Only then, said Reagan, could the United States maintain its national identity as a "city on a hill."

Confronting the Soviet Union

Contrasting U.S. moral superiority with the "evil empire" of the Soviet Union, Reagan sought to negotiate from strength. At his urging, Congress increased military spending by one-third, adding hundreds of billions each year to the budget. Alarmed by the rapid expansion of the nuclear arsenal, a grassroots peace movement mushroomed around the country to demand a nuclear freeze. In 1982, one anti-nuclear rally at New York's Central Park attracted over 500,000 protesters, the largest political demonstration in the nation's history. But the president continued to escalate the nuclear arms race, proposing in 1983 the Strategic Defense Initiative, a system of laser weapons that would target enemy missiles from outer space. Although many defense experts derided the proposal as "Star Wars," both technologically improbable and inordinately expensive, the president clung to the scheme. Reagan also approved the stationing of nuclear missiles in NATO countries in Europe.

To intensify confrontation with the Soviet Union, the administration endorsed an unofficial "Reagan Doctrine," which promoted anti-Soviet activities in Third World countries, including the Middle East, Afghanistan, and Nicaragua. By treating regional conflicts as extensions of the Cold War with Moscow, the White House assumed that the communist menace was monolithic (not fragmented by separate national interests) but underestimated the role of nationalism as a separate global force. When civil war erupted in Lebanon in 1982, Reagan sent the Marines as part of a peacekeeping force to counter apparent Soviet influence. The U.S. presence angered Muslim factions, who retaliated by bombing the Marine base in 1983.

With over 200 killed, Reagan withdrew U.S. forces, offering no explanation of the mission's objectives.

Reagan continued to respond aggressively to communist influence elsewhere. Learning that left-wing radicals had staged a coup d'état in tiny Grenada, an island nation in the Caribbean, the president ordered a military invasion to oust the pro-Cuban communist leaders. Although the political gains appeared slight, the president touted the adventure as a rejection of post-Vietnam anti-interventionism. Reagan also persuaded Congress to allow military aid in Angola and backed the anti-Soviet faction.

"If Central America were to fall," said Reagan in 1983, "our credibility would collapse, our alliances would crumble." Reversing Carter's human rights agenda, Washington supported the military government in El Salvador, sending weapons and supplies and training Salvadorian security forces in anti-guerrilla terror tactics. Simultaneously, the administration challenged the legality of Salvadoran refugees who sought sanctuary in the United States. In Nicaragua, the White House broke relations with the leftist Sandinista regime and ordered the CIA to assist the "Contra" rebels who fomented civil war. The president described the guerrillas as "the moral equivalent of the founding fathers." Despite Reagan's popularity, however, 19 major opinion polls between 1983 and 1988 found that only 20 to 40 percent of the public favored assistance to the Contras. Although Congress waffled on supporting the fighting in Nicaragua, public pressure finally forced an end to funding the war in 1985. Yet Reagan would imperil his own power by ignoring the law.

Cutting Domestic Spending

Reagan's high military and foreign policy budgets clashed with his domestic goals. Vowing to "get government off our backs," Reagan determined to reduce federal authority by cutting government funds at their source. Soon after taking office, he proposed the largest tax cut in history, including both personal income and corporate profits. Embracing the theory of "supply-side" economics, which suggested that tax reductions would stimulate investment, create jobs, and improve productivity, the White House promised that prosperity would "trickle down" from business to workers. As House Democrats attacked "Reaganomics," the president benefited by an unexpected calamity. When an assassin's bullets nearly killed him in 1981, public sympathy extended from Reagan to his agenda. His tax plan also satisfied middle-class workers, who had seen inflation undermine their purchasing power while driving their incomes into higher tax brackets.

Congress proceeded to pass the Economic Recovery Tax Act in 1981, reducing personal income taxes by 25 percent. The law reversed federal tax policy that had existed since the Great Depression, establishing instead a "regressive" system that shifted the burdens from the higher- to the lower-income groups. Most benefits went to the wealthiest individuals, whose rates dropped from 70 to 50 percent. Lower corporate taxes also assisted taxpayers with money to invest. Between 1979 and 1983, the incomes of the top 5 percent of U.S. households increased by 29 percent, and they received one-fifth of all national income. At the same time, increases in social security contributions reduced the real earnings of most workers. Meanwhile, unemployment rates jumped from 6 percent in 1982 to 9.6 percent in 1983.

Deregulating Business

Reagan's program also accelerated the deregulation of business begun during the Carter administration. As corporate mergers and stock takeovers increased, eliminating such long-established companies as Gulf Oil, Hughes Aircraft, and Nabisco, the administration relaxed enforcement of anti-monopoly laws designed to encourage competition. Responding to his business constituency rather than to union leaders, Reagan curtailed the authority of the Occupational Safety and Health Administration (OSHA) in 1981. And when 12,000 air traffic controllers protested working conditions in the newly deregulated airline industry by going on strike in 1981, the president summarily fired the strikers and broke their union. "Dammit, the law is the law," said Reagan, "and the law says that they cannot strike. If they strike, they quit their jobs." The mass dismissal sent a strong warning to all unions, reinforcing the private sector's determination to reduce labor costs in an era of growing global competition.

Arguing that environmental protection laws raised business costs and weakened competition abroad, the administration eased enforcement of air and water pollution standards, although environmental groups successfully lobbied Congress to override presidential vetoes of clean water laws and hazardous waste cleanups. When Secretary of the Interior James Watt leased offshore oil and gas rights and proposed to sell timber from national parks, environmentalists mounted a conflict-of-interest campaign that forced Watts to resign in 1983. Other environmental administrators faced criminal charges for collusion with industrial polluters. Corporate denial of energy shortages persuaded Reagan to reverse windfall profits taxes on oil companies and to end government funding of research for alternative energy sources. Despite wide public disapproval of these policies, Reagan avoided criticism when foreign oil producers independently cut prices in 1983.

Deregulation of the banking industry fed the era's entrepreneurial spirit. The Banking Act of 1982 extended financial deregulation by raising limits on interest rates and permitting savings-and-loan associations to offer commercial services. Bankers gained a freer hand in offering loans, encouraging riskier investments in commercial real estate such as shopping malls. When Texas oil prices fell and real-estate values plummeted in California and the Southwest in the mid-1980s, however, bankruptcy among savings institutions skyrocketed. Much of the loss was protected by federally funded insurance, which was supported by public taxes. After Reagan left office in 1989, Congress voted to cover multibillion-dollar losses in the savings industry, adding to taxpayer support of the deregulated financiers.

Reducing Government Assistance

Underlying Reagan's financial policies lay the expectation that lower taxes and a smaller regulatory bureaucracy would reduce available government funds and thus terminate the so-called binge of spending since the New Deal for social welfare, health, education, and environmental protection. Although Reagan was obliged to accept some tax increases between 1982 and 1984, by 1986 an estimated $750 billion of potential tax revenue had failed to reach the government treasury. The effect of these budget policies was a sharp recession in 1982, which undermined the working poor. Convinced that inflation remained a more severe problem, Reagan endorsed higher interest rates and a smaller money supply, which lowered the rate of inflation from over 10 percent in 1981 to 3.2 percent in 1983. But at the same time, such policies dropped the GNP by 2.1 percent and resulted in over 50,000 business failures, including the largest number of bank and farm closures since the Great Depression, and over 10 percent unemployment, affecting over 10 million workers.

Since older voters had overwhelmingly supported Reagan, the White House refused to alter politically sensitive social security benefits, but the administration reduced allocations for food stamps, job training, health care, and aid to low-income students. Most severely affected by the recession were blue-collar male workers, whose manufacturing jobs disappeared overseas. Only 60 percent found new jobs—about half at lower pay. For white men with only high school education, the slowdown created enduring insecurities. For the first time, more women than men enrolled in college, more than 50 percent of married women worked, and white men constituted less than half the nation's work force. "Part of the unemployment is not as much recession," said a defensive president in 1982, "as it is the great increase of the people going into the job market, and—ladies, I'm not picking on anyone—" he quipped, "but . . . because of the increase in women who are working today." Reagan thus deflected responsibility for his policies and drove a wedge within the Democratic constituency of women and blue-collar workers. But in 1982, Democrats won victories in congressional districts with high rates of unemployment.

By 1983, however, a combination of military spending and lower interest rates rejuvenated the economy. As net corporate profits rose and disposable incomes reached the highest levels in 20 years, unemployment eased, though over 7.5 percent of the work force remained idle. For most working families, average household income declined in real dollars between 1979 and 1987 by about 5 percent, except when another adult also found a job. But relative to the recent recession, voters perceived a clear improvement of their status.

The Election of 1984

Reagan's reelection was never in doubt. The Republican slogan, "We Brought America Back," appealed to visions of economic growth and prosperity, but the key element of the party's message was the president himself. Despite an ineffective foreign

policy and the 1982 recession, Reagan's charisma enabled him to rise above partisan conflict. His personal popularity far exceeded support for the positions he took, including defense spending, opposition to abortions, and support of the white supremacist government in South Africa. Democratic opponents called him the "Teflon" president, because nothing bad stuck to his image. Reagan benefited, too, by the Republican war chest of financial contributions, much larger than Democrats raised.

Democrats also suffered from internal divisions, testifying to the collapse of the New Deal coalition of southern whites, northern white ethnics and union workers, and racial minorities. As well-organized evangelical groups supported conservative positions on abortion, school prayer, affirmative action, and gun control, white southern majorities now voted Republican. Meanwhile, organized labor, which had represented over 30 percent of the work force in the 1960s, now spoke for only 16 percent of workers (a percentage that declined to 13.5 by the end of the century). Blue-collar male workers bitterly resented the party's support of affirmative action programs for minorities and women. African Americans, Hispanics, and Jews remained at the Democratic core, but could scarcely offset other defections.

African American civil rights leader Jesse Jackson further challenged party regulars by organizing a "rainbow" coalition among poorer voters and sought the Democratic nomination. The old Democratic alliance against big business was crumbling, but with strong AFL-CIO support, Carter's former vice president, Walter Mondale, won the party's nomination. The Democratic candidate soon undermined his own position by insisting candidly that Reagan's imbalanced budgets could be remedied only by tax increases, a position hardly popular in the anti-government climate.

Mondale sought women voters by selecting New York Representative Geraldine Ferraro as his running mate, the first major party nomination of a woman. The novelty barely affected the outcome. Riding the crest of prosperity, the Reagan-Bush ticket won 59 percent of the popular vote and carried every electoral district except Minnesota and Washington, D.C. Reagan ran well among both the elderly and the young and gained a majority of women voters. He took only 36 percent of the labor union constituency. Democrats retained their only elected majority in the House of Representatives, but southern Democrats, known as "boll weevils," often followed the Republican lead.

Protecting Outsiders

With its largely white constituency and the uneven balance of power in Washington, the victorious Republican leadership reduced the government's commitment to civil rights for racial minorities and women. Put on the defensive, Congress and the courts struggled to limit presidential initiatives. In 1982, for example, Congress ignored the threat of a presidential veto to extend the Voting Rights Act for twenty-five years. When Reagan's Justice Department moved to overturn school busing for racial integration and curtail affirmative action in employment, the appointive Civil Rights Commission protested, leading the president to fire Carter's appointees. Federal courts ruled the dismissal illegal, but the White House effectively gutted the liberal agency. The Supreme Court also rejected administration efforts to permit tax-exempt status for racially segregated private schools, though other rulings weakened civil-rights enforcement. Not until 1988 did Congress muster the votes to override a presidential veto and pass the Civil Rights Restoration Act, which denied government funds to any organization that practiced discrimination of race, sex, or age.

Immigration and Ethnic Tensions

National policy toward immigrant groups reflected a similar mix of conservative ideology and pragmatic accommodation of multicultural changes. As 6 million immigrants entered the country during the 1980s, half of them from Asia and about 40 percent from Latin America and the Caribbean, conservative Republicans worried about preserving the nation's "unity and political stability." The administration worried especially about an estimated 3 to 5 million illegal aliens, mostly from Mexico, but including refugees from war-torn Central America. Rejecting old policies of mass deportation, Congress passed the Immigration Reform and Control Act of 1986, which offered legal status to undocumented aliens already in the country, provided that they formally registered with authorities. Amnesty for the resident population then justified strict sanctions against future illegal immigrants and outlawed their employment. Although immigrant groups protested the law, the measure greatly boosted the number of naturalized citizens.

Shifting immigration patterns changed the country's social and cultural composition. West Coast cities like Los Angeles, San Francisco, and Seattle became home to large numbers of Asians from the Philippines, Korea, China, Thailand, Indochina, and India. Sunbelt areas in Florida, Texas, and southern California attracted Hispanic immigrants. The traditional trilogy of Protestant-Catholic-Jew now had to accommodate 4 million members of Eastern Orthodox denominations, 4 million Mormons, more than 2 million Muslims (only a fraction of whom were U.S.-born Black Muslims), and growing numbers of Hindus and Buddhists. In addition, high birthrates made Hispanic Americans the fastest growing population in the country. The 1990 census reported that 14 percent of the nation's households spoke languages other than English.

With a median age in the late twenties, most immigrants found low-wage jobs in the service sector and in textile manufacturing, while foreign-born professionals provided skilled labor in health care, engineering, and science. Competition for jobs sometimes aroused a nativist backlash and ethnic rivalry. In the mid-1980s, African Americans in Los Angeles and New York organized boycotts against Korean shopkeepers, while violence flared between native-born whites and Hispanics, Vietnamese, and Laotians in several cities. Older resident groups organized English-only movements, leading twenty-three states to declare English their official language by 1995. Most of the laws were never enforced, and Arizona's was declared unconstitutional. More extremist groups, such as the Ku Klux Klan and the Aryan Nation, demanded an end to immigration, and liberal groups like the Sierra Club discussed immigration restrictions to control population growth. Yet assimilated immigrants successfully entered the corporate economy, sent their children to prestigious schools, and elected growing numbers of representatives to Congress. By 2000, nearly 10 percent of all residents were foreign born; according to the Census Department this was the highest proportion in U.S. history.

The Politics of Gender and Sex

Feminist leaders faced an uphill struggle in Reagan's Washington, but achieved significant advances despite the president's limited interest in women's rights. The 1980 Republican platform had denounced the Equal Rights Amendment (ERA), contributing to the failure of the constitutional proposal in 1982. Anti-ERA leaders like Phyllis Schlafly saw their victory as a way of sparing women from wartime combat. Yet by the decade's end, Republican leaders had integrated women into the armed forces. In 1981, Reagan appointed Sandra Day O'Connor as the first woman on the Supreme Court and gave cabinet positions to three women. Following the Republican platform, the president publicly opposed abortion rights, but he gave no support to a proposed constitutional prohibition of the procedure. The first divorced man to be president, Reagan also approved new laws easing collection of child support payments and allowing divorced and widowed women to qualify for their spouse's pensions. Most feminist gains came on the state level of government with passage of laws against domestic violence, sexual harassment, and unequal pay. By 1989, women representatives comprised 17 percent of the state legislatures and nearly 6 percent of the House of Representatives.

Dependent on a strong and vocal evangelical constituency, Republicans opposed expanding the rights of homosexuals. Gay men and lesbians in the military service faced criminal punishment and expulsion not only for sexual *behavior* but also for merely disclosing their sexual orientation. Local governments also debated gay civil rights measures, though regional attitudes affected the outcomes. Thriving gay communities emerged throughout the country, supporting bookstores, health centers, entertainment groups, and academic research. Gay characters routinely appeared in mainstream Hollywood movies and, less frequently, on television. By 1987, gays and lesbians attracted half a million demonstrators to Washington, D.C., in an affirmation of gay pride.

Anti-gay prejudice escalated with the outbreak of the epidemic known as AIDS (acquired immune deficiency syndrome). First noted in 1978, the disease had caused over 1,000 deaths by 1983. Transmitted by semen and blood, AIDS devastated the

To religious conservatives, AIDs appeared as a divine punishment for sinful behavior.

gay male population as well as hemophiliacs and intravenous drug abusers (the latter mostly among racial minorities). To religious conservatives, the outbreak appeared as a divine punishment for sinful behavior. Republican leaders responded slowly to the health crisis, declining to increase funding for research. Only when fellow actor Rock Hudson died in 1985 did Reagan, and much of the public, acknowledge the seriousness of the epidemic. Meanwhile, gay activists organized grass-roots lobby groups, founded community health and hospice centers, and mounted educational campaigns for "safe sex" that slowed the epidemic. By 1990, the death toll approached 100,000, and twice that number showed signs of the disease, but the rate of infection had begun to decline.

The political weakness of cultural outsiders—racial minorities, feminists, and gays—increased the role of the judiciary in protecting their legal rights. Yet the preponderance of Republican-appointed judges (by the time Reagan left office, he had appointed half the federal judiciary) shifted the courts in a conservative direction. In 1987, Reagan's nomination to the Supreme Court of ultra-conservative Robert Bork, the Nixon appointee who had executed the "Saturday Night Massacre" in 1973 (see Chapter 28), aroused bitter opposition as a coalition of liberal groups fought to preserve a judicial balance. Bork's defeat, a blow to Reagan's second-term influence, barely sustained a Court majority in favor of abortion rights. But in a controversial case involving gay equality, the Supreme Court ruled in 1986 that privacy rights did not protect homosexuals from a Georgia anti-sodomy law. Gay rights in the workplace remained an unsettled legal issue. Other rulings weakened affirmative action programs and in labor cases moved the burden of proof from employers to employees.

The Collapsing Conservative Consensus

Reagan's landslide reelection in 1984 reflected voter satisfaction with economic recovery and preservation of Cold War strength. But continuing budget imbalances and rising economic competition overseas threatened U.S. trade and jobs. For the first time since 1913, the U.S. became in 1984 a debtor nation with a negative balance of trade and payments. Meanwhile, international conflicts failed to fit the Republicans' anti-Soviet view of world affairs. In Central America, the second-term president blundered and damaged his image. Nor did unequal prosperity resolve deeper social tensions about race, ethnicity, and gender. By the 1988 election, national politics expressed a worsening polarization between antagonistic social groups.

Budgetary Deficits and Economic Weakness

Although Republican leaders espoused a free-market economy with minimal government interference, Reagan responded to a powerful constituency of older Americans and continued to support federal aid to retired people. Expenditures for Social Security increased by one-third, and Medicare costs nearly doubled. In addition, the White House endorsed an expensive five-year agricultural measure for farm price supports, government purchase of dairy surpluses, and subsidies of farm incomes. Following scandals in the Environmental Protection Agency, the president approved $8.5 billion for a toxic cleanup Superfund. Congress also overrrode a veto to pass a clean water law that cost $18 billion. And all parties approved a multibillion-dollar bailout of bankrupt savings-and-loan associations.

Without new taxes, these domestic expenditures, together with a 41 percent increase in military appropriations, saw the federal budget deficit leap from $90 billion in 1982 to $220 billion in 1985. But when Congress enacted legislation to mandate deficit-reduction targets and automatic spending cuts, the Supreme Court ruled the law unconstitutional. The White House and Congress then agreed to the Tax Reform Act of 1986, which further reduced income taxes at the highest brackets from 50 to 28 percent and slashed corporate taxes from 48 to 34 percent. But, in a concession to Democrats, the measure also eliminated taxes for the lowest incomes, raised capital gains rates, and reduced business deductions. Rather than solving the budget crisis, the compromise indicated a tightening gridlock in partisan politics.

As the budget deficit continued to soar, the federal government was forced to borrow larger sums to finance the debt, raising interest rates to attract foreign investors. During half a decade, the national debt doubled to $2 trillion. Capital imports meant that foreign consumers had fewer dollars to spend on U.S. exports. The dollar became more expensive, making imports cheaper. Two economic results followed: first, many U.S. multinational corporations closed their plants at home and shifted production overseas, taking away thousands of domestic jobs; second, foreign competitors dumped products on U.S. markets at below domestic production costs. The trade deficit with Japan alone amounted to $50 billion in 1987, mostly in electronics, computer chips, and automobiles. Overall, the yearly international trade deficit jumped from $36 billion in 1980 to $170 billion in 1987. Reagan at last set aside free trade rhetoric and accepted new tariff protections, including the right to retaliate against unfair foreign trade practices.

While international finance fueled a surging stock market, entrepreneurs invested not in manufacturing plants but also in corporate takeovers and buyouts, building fortunes in stocks and junk bonds. The abrupt collapse of stockmarket prices in October 1987 belied White House optimism about the economy. Other evidence underscored the paradox of prosperity. For the working middle class, the loss of manufacturing jobs had brought a drop in real hourly wages from $9.50 in 1978 to $8 by 1990. Median household income, which was slightly below $30,000, fell $1,000 in real dollars since the mid-1970s. Only the highest 20 percent of the population, which earned above $80,000 per year, avoided loss or stagnation of earnings. The departure of jobs overseas also aggravated inner-city poverty, reinforcing an illegal economy based on crime, drugs, and prostitution. Homelessness abounded in every major city.

The Iran-Contra Scandals

Economic calamity infuriated the voting public much less than White House involvement in illegal activities associated with the Iran-Contra scandals. After criticizing President Carter for failing to gain release of hostages held in Iran, Reagan vowed never to negotiate with terrorists or bargain for hostages. Yet when pro-Iran terrorist groups in Lebanon seized U.S. hostages, including a CIA agent, administration officials agreed to trade military weapons to gain their release, using Israel as an intermediary to disguise the transaction from the public. That deception was not illegal. But National Security Council officials, including Colonel Oliver North, then used the profits from that transaction to fund the Contra rebels in Nicaragua, in violation of congressional prohibitions of support for the guerrilla war. The subterfuge broke into the headlines in 1986 when a Nicaraguan soldier shot down a CIA aircraft on an illegal mission.

This poster depicting an unflattering image of President Ronald Reagan with a terse message deploring his Iran-Contra actions was slapped up on a graffiti-covered wall.

News of the secret operation outraged public opinion, crashing Reagan's approval ratings. A blue-ribbon panel, headed by former Texas Senator John Tower, cleared Reagan of direct complicity in 1987, but the report depicted a president who "did not seem to be aware" of policy decisions and their implications. Subsequent congressional investigations, spotlighting an unrepentant Colonel North, revealed that top administration leaders had knowingly created the illegal operation and deliberately conducted foreign policy outside the purview of their government. The destruction of incriminating public records underscored high-level corruption and led to guilty pleas and convictions of seven officials, though North's was later reversed on a technicality. In 1992, Reagan's successor, President George Bush, pardoned six accomplices.

Thaw in the Cold War

Evidence of Reagan's wavering leadership was outweighed by unexpected changes in world power relations. Although the president had refused to initiate arms control talks with the Soviet Union, the emergence of a new leader in Moscow, the cosmopolitan Mikhail Gorbachev, brought opportunities for easing international tensions. Pressed by the weakness of the militarized Soviet economy, Gorbachev introduced economic reforms in 1985 to decentralize government oversight and agreed to reduce the number of Soviet missiles (intermediate nuclear forces, or INF) in Europe. In 1985, Reagan met with Gorbachev at Geneva, in the first of four summit negotiations that resulted in the signing of an INF treaty in 1987. The high cost of nuclear competition had eroded the Soviet economy, persuading Gorbachev to curtail military expansion. "We are going to do something terrible to you Americans," one Soviet official quipped. "We are going to deprive you of an enemy." In the public eye, Ronald Reagan received credit for ending the Cold War.

The presidency of Ronald Reagan remains a controversial subject. Conservative writers con-

> ### "We are going to do something terrible to you Americans; we are going to deprive you of an enemy."

tinue to praise his moral vision and leadership. According to this view, tax cuts and deregulation of business inspired investment, stimulated corporate growth, and brought five years of prosperity. Such commentators credit expanded military budgets for the collapse of Soviet power and the administration for achieving victory in the Cold War. Critics of Reagan, by contrast, lament the social costs of mounting budget deficits and national debt. Citing the increase of economic inequality, they criticize the hypocritical bailout of savings-and-loan institutions and wasteful military expenditures. Reagan's indifference to matters of social justice—civil rights, for example—underscored a vague administrative style that encouraged the Iran-Contra fiasco. In the end, Reagan's personal popularity still contrasts with wider disapproval of the policies he endorsed.

The Rise and Fall of George Bush

"We don't need radical new directions," said Vice President George Bush as he campaigned to succeed Reagan in 1988. "We don't need to remake society—we just need to remember who we are." Thus Bush ran on Reagan's record, confident in the existing Republican majority. Yet, as a longtime public servant and office holder, once head of the CIA and a former ambassador to China, Bush did not share Reagan's distrust of government. Moreover, the Texas Republican had stronger commitments to the party's social agenda, opposing abortions, favoring school prayers, rejecting affirmative action, and taking pride in his membership in the National Rifle Association, which lobbied against gun control. A decorated World War II pilot, Bush had strong credentials as a Cold Warrior. He chose as his running mate the boyish Indiana Senator James Danforth Quayle to strengthen his ties to the party's right wing.

The Election of 1988

The Democrats had less confidence than Bush about who they were. The party's initial frontrunner, former Colorado Senator Gary Hart, appealed to middle-class liberals but had to withdraw when accused of marital infidelity. Jesse Jackson developed a second campaign, focusing on populist issues of jobs, corporate irresponsibility, and equality for minorities and women. The African American Jackson would win one-third of the primary vote, but appeared too divisive for white ethnic workers. The party's nomination went to Massachusetts Governor Michael Dukakis, a centrist candidate who focused on tax issues, education, health insurance, and a balanced budget. Those issues would play a small role in the election.

Emboldened by their evangelical supporters, the Republicans appealed to white southerners and middle-class suburbanites by stressing a social agenda based on "family" values, law and order, and patriotism. By contrast, Republicans depicted Dukakis as a flawed liberal. "He is out of the mainstream," said Bush. "Do we want this country to go that far left?" Citing the governor's veto of a law that would have required students to recite the Pledge of Allegiance daily, Bush visited flag factories to imply his opponent's disloyalty. Even more emotional were Bush's attacks on Dukakis's 1976 veto of a Massachusetts law banning prisoner furloughs. Televised Republican commercials depicted the case of Willie Horton, an African American felon who had raped a white woman while on prison leave, and blamed Dukakis's liberalism as "soft on crime." Bush did make a single campaign pledge: "Read my lips. No new taxes!" The promise would later return to haunt him.

With such appeals, Republicans captured the conservative, evangelical vote and won majorities among young adults and women. Bush's greatest support came from white males, who gave him a 63 percent margin, solidifying Republican strength among southerners and suburbanites. Despite a weak presidential campaign, however, Democrats gained seats in the Senate and House, suggesting the nonideological motivation of the electorate. Indeed, most 1988 victors could be counted not by their party affiliations but by their incumbency. With corporate campaign contributions exceeding $30 million, sitting representatives had strong advantages over their challengers.

"What I don't want to do," said Bush, in explaining his political outlook, "is make the situation worse." Coming to the presidency without an activist agenda, Reagan's successor emphasized continuity of policies and a willingness to compromise with opponents. Preferring voluntary reform rather than government regulation, Bush promoted a "Points of Light" program, each day recognizing individual citizens or groups for advancing "the ethic of community service." Such gestures substituted for presidential concern about economic decline and Republican eagerness to reduce welfare expenses.

The End of the Cold War

Bush's best opportunities came in the area of foreign policy. As Soviet leader Gorbachev moderated communist policies in the Soviet Union, citizens in the satellite nations of Eastern Europe (Czechoslovakia, East Germany, Hungary, Poland, Yugoslavia, and the Baltic states of Estonia, Latvia, and Lithuania) felt freer to reject the repressive

In 1989 the Berlin Wall, longstanding symbol of the division between East and West, was toppled.

and bureaucratic communist leadership. When East Germany opened its borders with the West in 1989, Germans from both sides joyously destroyed the Berlin Wall, for twenty-eight years a symbol of seemingly irreconcilable differences. By 1990, Germany was reunified and Soviet power in Eastern Europe was drastically reduced.

During the perilous political upheavals in Eastern Europe, Bush cautiously ignored Democratic demands for a more activist role and tried to encourage Soviet reform without provoking a reactionary backlash against Gorbachev. To bolster the

Soviet leader's position against hard-line communists, Bush extended trade benefits to Moscow in exchange for easing Soviet emigration barriers against Jews. Summit meetings between Bush and Gorbachev also led to agreements restricting production of chemical weapons in 1990. The next year, the two powers signed an unprecedented Strategic Arms Treaty (START), which not only limited nuclear deployment but also mandated reductions of existing arsenals, mostly short-range nuclear weapons. After Gorbachev resigned in 1992, effectively dissolving the Soviet Union into its separate republics, Bush continued negotiations with Russian leader Boris Yeltsin. Their 1993 START II agreement drastically reduced global tension by calling for the gradual elimination of all land-based nuclear missiles.

The implosion of the Soviet empire not only eliminated the nation's primary adversary, but ironically also created a vacuum at the center of U.S. foreign policy. For nearly half a century, the anti-communist crusade had shaped the nation's international relations. How would the United States respond? To be sure, Washington had traditionally regarded Latin America and the Caribbean as a special sphere of influence and continued to treat Cuba as a hostile nation. Yet Bush also accepted a brokered peace settlement in Nicaragua in 1990 and oversaw a treaty agreement that ended a 12-year civil war in El Salvador in 1992. In other parts of the world, the eruption of regional discord no longer demanded a U.S. presence. Both President Bush and his successor, Bill Clinton, showed reluctance to pursue unilateral policies overseas and instead attempted to build coalitions and alliances with other countries. When the disintegration of Yugoslavia produced civil war between Serbian Christians and Bosnian Muslims, Washington cooperated closely with European allies to impose sanctions on Serbia and to deliver food and medical supplies to besieged Sarajevo.

The removal of the communist threat also affected U.S. relations with its allies. Countries like El Salvador and Colombia had used anti-communism as a way of obtaining military support from Washington. Now they emphasized warring against other enemies, the so-called international drug cartels. This shift in emphasis led Bush to alter relations with Panama's leader, Manuel Noriega, long a beneficiary of CIA payments for supporting anti-communist policies in Cuba and Nicaragua. After a U.S. grand jury indicted Noriega for drug dealing, Bush ordered 24,000 troops to invade Panama in 1989 to seize the leader and bring him for trial in Florida. Although popular at home and in Panama, the invasion, seen as a resurgence of big-stick diplomacy, brought criticism from the Organization of American States, which voted 20-1 to condemn U.S. intervention.

War in the Persian Gulf

Bush proved more skillful in orchestrating a united coalition against Iraq's aggressive ruler, Saddam Hussein. When Iraq invaded oil-rich Kuwait in 1990 and moved troops to the Saudi Arabia border, threatening world access to vital oil reserves, the White House used the United Nations to build alliances with 30 countries, including the Soviet Union and several Arab governments. This coalition demanded that Iraq withdraw to previous borders or face military attack. Meanwhile, the president proceeded with military plans known as Desert Shield and Desert Storm. Under the leadership of General Colin Powell, appointed by Bush as the first African American to head the Joint Chiefs of Staff, and General Norman Schwartzkopf, 540,000 U.S. troops and 160,000 Allied forces headed toward a confrontation with the Iraqi army, which was dug into the Kuwaiti desert.

As U.N. troops prepared for war in 1991, Bush appealed for congressional support under the War

At the end of the Gulf War the vast oil fields of the Persian Gulf were left aflame. Iraq's leaders, who had set the fires, remained in power to imperil peace in the region.

Powers Act, provoking impassioned debate about U.S. military intervention. "No Blood for Oil," the slogan of scattered anti-war groups, reflected the ambiguities of supporting undemocratic Middle Eastern regimes to protect U.S. economic interests in the Persian Gulf. Yet public opinion and Congress supported the president. Giving Iraq ample opportunities to enter negotiations, Bush finally ordered the invasion in 1991, commencing a six-week air and missile attack that hit Iraqi military installations and the civilian population in Bagh-

dad. Although Saddam Hussein had predicted victory in "the mother of all battles," 70,000 bombing sorties together with a 300-mile wide ground assault far exceeded Iraq's military defenses. Four days after the invasion began, Bush told the world that "our military objectives are met." U.S. troops had suffered 146 combat deaths.

"We've kicked the Vietnam syndrome once and for all," the president exclaimed, referring to public reluctance to support military intervention overseas. Yet Bush appeared reluctant to increase U.S. casualties, provoke Arab nationalism, or continue a war that might become unpopular. Ordering Allied forces to establish defensive perimeters and no-flight zones around Iraq, the White House ended military operations before overthrowing Saddam Hussein's regime. "It hasn't been a clean end," Bush admitted. Yet the war had successfully defended U.S. strategic interests and had woven a multinational coalition that included the Soviet Union. "A new partnership of nations has begun," the president boasted. "A new world order can emerge."

Partisan Politics and Domestic Policy

Bush's calculated development of multinational support overseas contrasted with a passive approach toward domestic policy. His administration could count few legislative accomplishments. Unlike Reagan, Bush accepted government regulation of environmental standards and approved the Clean Air Act of 1990, which established strict criteria to reduce toxic emissions from power plants and automobiles. Yet Bush threatened to veto any measure that included unemployment compensation for workers displaced by the law. The president also endorsed the bipartisan Americans with Disabilities Act of 1990, which prohibited job discrimination against the handicapped and required that public accommodations be accessible to citizens with disabilities.

Less willingly, Bush signed the Civil Rights Act of 1991, which assisted women and minorities in challenging employment discrimination.

Rather than initiating legislation, Bush made his mark by blocking congressional bills with his veto powers. Forty-four times the White House rebuffed bills approved by majorities (ten of them involving cases of abortion rights) and only once, on a bill regulating the cable television industry, did Congress find the necessary two-thirds vote to override the president. Bush's veto record testified to deep partisan divisions in the legislative process: a refusal to compromise on issues involving unemployment benefits, family and medical leave for workers, campaign finance reform, or civil rights.

In 1990, a Bush veto of a temporary appropriation measure, designed to keep the government running while a final budget was negotiated, resulted in the closing of several federal departments, including the National Park Service. The shutdown proved an embarrassment for both parties and infuriated the public. Government gridlock increased public support of a line-item veto that would allow a president merely to reject a portion of pending legislation rather than the entire bill. Yet Congress had rejected such constitutional changes since the Nixon administration and continued to oppose the idea during the Republican incumbency.

Partisan conflict between the White House and Congress triggered several impassioned controversies, which ultimately weakened Bush's hopes for reelection. The first followed from Bush's flag-waving campaign, when the president urged Congress to approve a constitutional amendment banning flag burning. Unwilling to alter basic First Amendment rights, Congress defused the controversy by instead passing a law to that effect. Later the Supreme Court ruled the law unconstitutional on First Amendment grounds.

A second controversy resulted from the president's efforts to move federal courts in a conservative direction. Like Reagan and other predecessors, Bush nominated judges who shared his political outlook; by the end of his term, the two Republican presidents had appointed fully three-fourths of the federal bench. But when Bush nominated the conservative African American Clarence Thomas to succeed the retiring liberal Thurgood Marshall on the Supreme Court in 1991, he unwittingly opened a national furor about related charges of sexual harassment. During Senate hearings on the nomination, one of Thomas's former employees, law professor Anita Hill, charged the nominee with sexual harassment. Three days of nationally televised hearings and simultaneous public debate exposed deep divisions in the country about the persistence of racial and gender discrimination. Infuriated by Hill's treatment, twelve women members of Congress marched from the House to the Senate, protesting unequal treatment of women in public life. When the Senate voted to confirm the Thomas appointment anyway, feminists announced that 1992 would become "the year of the woman," and a record number of forty-six women ran for Congress.

The flag amendment and the Thomas nomination outraged liberal opinion, but what doomed Bush's political future involved his betrayal of conservatives. Having promised "no new taxes," Bush by 1990 confronted a $3.2 trillion national debt and impending budget deficits exceeding $200 billion. When the economy entered a recession in 1990, the loss of federal tax revenues accentuated the imbalance. Legislation passed in 1985 mandated huge cuts in domestic and military spending. Forced to take action, Bush agreed with Democrats to accept higher taxes if Congress reduced deficit spending. The deal outraged conservatives, who blasted Bush for breaking his word.

The legislation also failed to abate a deepening economic recession. As annual trade deficits reached $150 billion and budget shortfalls approached $300 billion, the nation's unemployment rate jumped above 7 percent. Voters blamed leaders in both parties. Indicative of the public mood in 1992 was ratification of the Twenty-Seventh Amendment, preventing members of Congress from raising their salaries without first giving voters a chance to remove them from office. Sensing the drift of the political winds, ninety-one members of the House, more incumbents than ever before, decided not to seek reelection in 1992.

Amendment XXVII (1992)

No law varying the compensation for the services of the Senators and Representatives shall take effect until an election of Representatives shall have intervened.

A Democratic Alternative

Bush carried his dismal economic record into the 1992 contest. Ironically, the previous year's victory in Iraq had diminished foreign policy as a campaign issue, except in the negative sense that Saddam Hussein remained in power. Moreover, the end of the Cold War had failed to produce an expected "peace dividend" that would bolster domestic spending or permit further tax cuts. Other political problems reflected persistent ideological differences among diverse groups. As militant Christian organizations blocked access to abortion clinics, the Supreme Court in 1992 upheld congressional restrictions on federal funding of abortions and state-mandated waiting periods. Conservatives attacked the National Endowment of the Arts for supporting homoerotic art and threatened to gut the agency's budget unless projects conformed to "the general standard of decency."

In 1992, racial divisions also shocked the country. After an all-white jury acquitted Los Angeles police in a videotaped beating of black motorist Rodney King, furious African Americans staged four days of violence against whites and Asian immigrants, leaving fifty dead and $1 billion of property destroyed. No president could be blamed for such problems. Yet a 1992 Gallup poll found that, although 73 percent of the public expressed satisfaction with their personal lives, only 24 percent approved the state of the nation.

The Election of 1992

Democratic candidate William Jefferson "Bill" Clinton offered a strong challenge to Republican leadership. At 45, the Arkansas governor was a mid-life baby boomer, a generation younger than Bush, and appealed to an electorate looking for change. Paired with another southern running mate, Tennessee's Albert Gore, the Democrat faulted Bush for allowing the deficit to run unchecked, causing rising unemployment for white-collar workers, and watching welfare rolls climb without offering alternatives for jobs. Clinton benefited, too, by the presence of a maverick third-party candidate, self-made billionaire H. Ross Perot, who organized the Reform party and attacked entrenched politicians. Perot appealed primarily to independent voters frustrated by government gridlock and to small business interests troubled by trade deficits, a constituency that normally voted Republican.

A Democratic slogan, "It's the economy, stupid!" focused attention on Bush's worst problem. Clinton adopted a moderate position, rejecting Republican trickle-down economics but also denying tax-and-spend liberal solutions. On social and economic issues, Clinton cultivated a centrist position that broadened his constituency, even in the conservative South. For example,

The Election of 1992

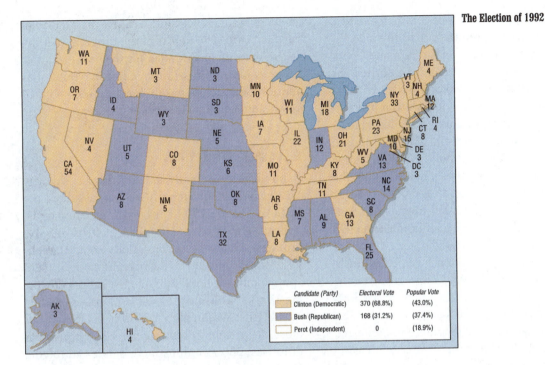

Candidate (Party)	Electoral Vote	Popular Vote
Clinton (Democratic)	370 (68.8%)	(43.0%)
Bush (Republican)	168 (31.2%)	(37.4%)
Perot (Independent)	0	(18.9%)

while praising Supreme Court rulings that protected abortion rights and supporting gay rights, he endorsed the death penalty, opposed racial quotas, proposed "workfare" for the needy, and demanded a stronger interventionist foreign policy. Appealing, in short, to "the forgotten middle class," Clinton built an electoral consensus based on moderate change.

With voter turnout increasing for the first time in 30 years, Democrats won a decisive victory in the electoral college, though the popular voting statistics—43 percent for Clinton, 37 percent for Bush, and 19 percent for Perot—hardly provided a clear mandate. Although Democrats held small majorities in Congress and the number of elected women, African Americans, and Hispanics increased, conservatives retained power in both parties. "Most everybody is for change in gen-

> **"Most everybody is for change in general, and then against it in particular."**

eral," remarked Clinton during his first term, "and then against it in particular."

A Moderate Domestic Agenda

Once elected, Clinton fulfilled campaign promises to give government jobs to people who "looked like America," and he chose more women, African Americans, and Hispanics than his predecessors. Maya Angelou, an African American poet, celebrated this multicultural constituency in her poem, "Good Morning, America," which she read at the president's inauguration. Clinton also appointed the second woman on the Supreme Court, Ruth Bader Ginsberg, a feminist who shifted the judicial balance in favor of abortion. By executive order, Clinton also reversed Republican prohibitions on abortions in the military and lifted restrictions on fetal medical research. Yet his proposed acceptance of homosexuals in the military drew fierce bipartisan conservative attacks, forcing the president to retreat. A compromise policy, "Don't ask, don't tell," satisfied neither liberals nor conservatives, and the discharges of homosexuals in the military continued unabated.

Moderate social policies, once vetoed by Bush, did find acceptance. In 1993, Congress passed the Family and Medical Leave Act, allowing workers to take unpaid absence for family emergencies. The president also signed several long-contested measures, including the Motor Voter bill, easing voting registration for licensed drivers; the Brady bill, first proposed after the botched Reagan assassination attempt, which required a waiting period before the purchase of handguns; a National Service Plan that enabled college students to finance tuition with community service; and higher minimum wages and tax credits for low-income workers. Even these centrist measures aroused anti-government feelings.

Confrontation between Clinton and Congress truly exploded over a proposed reform of the nation's healthcare system. As the White House tried to make healthcare a basic right of all citizens, an administration panel chaired by the president's wife, Hilary Rodham Clinton, delivered a proposal that mixed government regulation and private insurance. The plan promised to extend medical insurance to 40 million uncovered citizens. But diverse critics, including the insurance and health industries, campaigned against the complicated program, warning that higher taxes and government bureaucracy would weaken the quality of medical care. The defeat of the program in 1994 left the president wounded for the next elections. Later in his administration, Clinton would offer more moderate proposals for a patients' bill of rights and health insurance for children.

A Conservative Revival

Republican conservatives, led by House Minority Leader Newt Gingrich of Georgia, assumed the initiative in the 1994 congressional campaigns, appealing to widespread public distrust of government. That year, opinion polls found that eligible voters, by a 65–22 percent margin, said "public officials don't care much what people like me think," and only 19 percent believed they could "trust Washington to do what is right all or most of the time." Frustrated by unkept political promises, 350 Republican candidates adopted a "Contract with America," vowing to vote for mandatory term limits, a balanced budget amendment, welfare reform, strict law enforcement, "pro-family" legislation, and a strong national defense. With only 38 percent of the electorate voting, Republicans achieved solid majorities in both houses of Congress for the first time in forty years. The new House Speaker Gingrich proclaimed "a historic election," but voting analysis showed that victory went to the better-financed candidates in 85 percent of the races.

As the Republican House moved to implement the conservative Contract, party leaders encountered the same obstacles that had earlier blocked presidential initiatives. The House passed a constitutional amendment demanding a balanced budget by 2002, but twice the measure fell short in the Senate. Another constitutional proposal to limit congressional terms failed to obtain a two-thirds majority. Clinton waited until 1996 to approve the line-item veto, a measure historically favored by the executive branch but ultimately held unconstitutional by the courts. When Congress approved major budget cuts for Medicare, Medicaid, education, and the environment in 1995, the White House countered with strong vetoes. Refusing to compromise, Republicans permitted the government to suspend operations twice in 1995, disrupting Social Security payments and other public agencies. Public opinion overwhelmingly sided with the president.

Forced to accept bipartisan domestic policies, Congress and the White House sought middle ground as the 1996 elections approached. A new health law permitted workers to transfer insurance from job to job and provided tax breaks for the self-employed. In 1996, Clinton accepted the Welfare Reform Act, which returned aid programs to the states through block grants, curtailed the historic Aid for Dependent Children (AFDC) program, limited lifetime welfare aid to five years, and required most welfare recipients to surrender assistance in two years with or without a job. The measure also blocked funds for legal resident aliens who were not citizens. In the face of liberal criticism, Clinton insisted the program would incorporate welfare recipients into the economy, and he promised to eliminate obvious inequities. The continuation of the economic boom enabled unemployment rates to reach their lowest points since the 1960s, easing criticism of federal welfare cuts.

Cautious Interventionism Overseas

Clinton's foreign policy continued Bush's cautious interventionism. Although Clinton had criticized his predecessor for failing to press for democratic reforms in China, the Democratic president also ignored Chinese political repression to promote U.S. trade. Similarly, Clinton embraced Bush's post–Cold War policies toward the Russian re-

publics, offering economic assistance to encourage stability and extend nuclear disarmament. The administration continued Bush's isolation of Iraq, enforcing United Nations economic sanctions and no-fly zones, even mobilizing military forces on several occasions to protect international inspection of Iraqi weapons.

Clinton made few overseas commitments, carefully seeking coalitions to justify intervention. In Somalia, a U.N. food relief mission embroiled U.S. forces in civil war in 1993, forcing Clinton to order a larger military expedition, but only to achieve a more orderly withdrawal. When terrorists bombed U.S. embassies in Kenya and Tanzania in 1998, Clinton ordered retaliatory bombing against suspected terrorist bases, but made no policy changes. An uneasy peace also persisted in the Middle East, despite U.S. efforts to mediate a settlement. Secretary of State Madeline Albright, the first woman to hold that position, walked the same shaky tightrope as her male predecessors.

In the disintegrated Yugoslavia, Clinton married U.S. policy to U.N. peacekeeping efforts, allowing NATO air strikes to thwart genocidal "ethnic cleansing" by Serbs. In 1995, the president pressed the rival factions to meet at Dayton, Ohio, where they signed a peace treaty. The agreement required U.S. troops to participate in a NATO police force. When Serbian nationalists initiated genocidal attacks against Muslims in Kosovo in 1999, Clinton encouraged a NATO coalition to bomb Serbian forces and cities. The strategy demonstrated NATO's military power and forced the Serbs to compromise. No U.S. lives were lost. But, as in Iraq, U.S. policy checked nationalist aggression without resolving the local conflicts. That prudent position expressed the nation's limited commitment to overseas conflicts, a middle point between the old isolationism and militant Cold War interventionism.

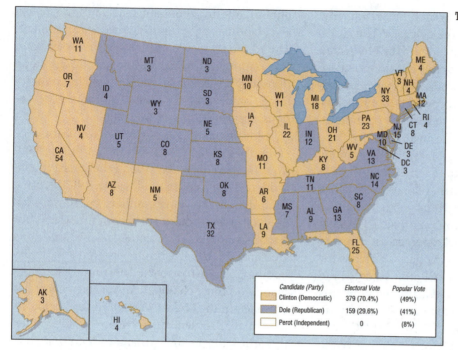

The Election of 1996

Candidate (Party)	Electoral Vote	Popular Vote
Clinton (Democratic)	379 (70.4%)	(49%)
Dole (Republican)	159 (29.6%)	(41%)
Perot (Independent)	0	(8%)

Boosting Foreign Trade

Clinton's pragmatic foreign policy reflected a high priority on encouraging foreign trade. The president fought a bitter internal war with Democratic liberals to win congressional approval of the North American Free Trade Agreement (NAFTA) in 1993, a measure that eliminated trade barriers with Mexico and Canada but threatened domestic jobs. The next year, Clinton gained Senate ratification of the General Agreement on Trade and Tariffs (GATT), which stimulated tariff reductions with over 100 countries. Although a pro-labor bloc warned that these agreements jeopardized occupational safety laws, environmental protection, and domestic wages, Clinton insisted that free trade promoted U.S. exports and created new jobs. Although foreign sales contributed to the booming economy, especially in electronics ex-

ports, opponents of unregulated trade rallied at the World Trade Organization meeting in Seattle in 1999 to demand protection of workers and the environment. The ensuing violence underscored deep divisions about the social responsibility of multinational corporations. Yet to maximize foreign trade with communist-led China, Clinton overlooked violations of human rights and allegations of espionage. In 2000, Congress enacted the China Trade Act, affirming the century-old idea of the Open Door policy (see Chapter 18) by lifting trade restrictions with that country.

Partisan Divisions

In 1996, Clinton ran for reelection as a cautious moderate, allowing voter surveys to dictate his political positions. Republicans passed over extreme conservatives like Patrick Buchanan to nominate Kansas Senator Robert Dole, a career politician known for insider maneuvering and support of the conservative social agenda. Polls showed considerable disagreement about issues like abortion and gun control, leading Clinton to focus on the economy. Benefiting by prosperity, especially tremendous growth in the computer industry, a bullish stock market, and high employment statistics, the administration promised better education, job training, and support of the Internet (the "information superhighway"). Although half the eligible electorate stayed home, Clinton took 49 percent of the popular vote to Dole's 41 percent and Perot's 8 percent and carried seven of the eight largest states. Women preferred Clinton over Dole, 54–38 percent; men split evenly. But once again the election divided power between the parties: the Democrats held the White House, Republicans controlled both houses of Congress.

Domestic prosperity enabled the Clinton administration to survive a multitude of personal problems. Like President Reagan, Clinton cultivated the media in what appeared to be a permanent reelection campaign, speaking above political critics directly to a public less interested in specific issues than in presidential assurances of stability and leadership. Scandals that preceded Clinton's presidential tenure (charges of sexual harassment by former Arkansas employees, dubious bank loans, and the alleged Whitewater real estate frauds) failed to weaken his popularity, as measured in opinion polls. When news of the president's improprieties with a female White House aide, Monica Lewinsky, surfaced in 1998, Clinton's personal ratings actually rose. "It's almost impossible not to be charmed by him," remarked one presidential aide, "and it's almost impossible not to be disappointed by him."

The Clinton sex scandal revealed the president's obvious duplicity and nearly destroyed his admin-

> **"It's almost impossible not to be charmed by him, and it's almost impossible not to be disappointed by him."**

istration. The political issues remained transparently partisan. When the special independent prosecutor, Kenneth Starr, charged that Clinton had lied to a grand jury about a sexual affair and had allegedly tried to sway witness testimony, the House of Representatives voted on strict party lines to impeach the president. It was only the second time such a step had been taken. (The first case involved President Andrew Johnson in 1867.) Charged with perjury and obstruction of justice, President Clinton faced prosecution by Republican House managers in the Senate. In 1999, the Senate voted acquittal of both charges. Clinton formally apologized to the country for his moral failings and paid punitive fines for contempt of court. The independent prosecutor later cleared the Clintons of the Whitewater charges.

Beyond the political issues, the impeachment case illustrated broader changes in the country's social values and a range of new assumptions about public life. These included the belief that sexual harassment in the workplace was no longer a joke but a crime (thus lending credence to Clinton's female accusers). The case also showed a tacit acceptance of extramarital sex by consenting adults (not only by Clinton and Lewinsky, but also by several of their Republican critics who admitted such relationships; some then resigned from office and some did not). The investigation also presumed that public figures had no rights of privacy, and Republicans allowed the most intimate sexual details to become public knowledge.

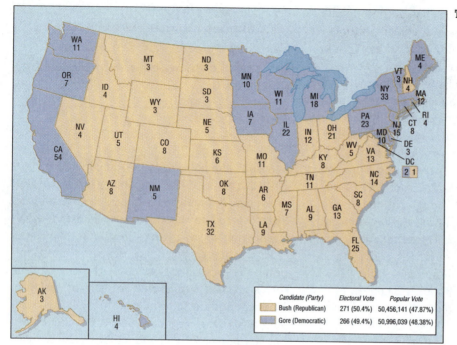

The Election of 2000

Candidate (Party)	Electoral Vote	Popular Vote
Bush (Republican)	271 (50.4%)	50,456,141 (47.87%)
Gore (Democratic)	266 (49.4%)	50,996,039 (48.38%)

The shifting legal and political strategies of the case confirmed a widespread belief that elected officials routinely lie to the public and that media images and "spin" dominated political discussion. Despite these revelations, Clinton remained securely in office and no political leader proposed remedies for the future. The Clinton affair thus stood in the mainstream of society and politics, not as an aberration of normal affairs of state.

Election 2000

Because the Twenty-Second Amendment barred Clinton from seeking a third term, the impeachment trial had no clear effect on the ensuing presidential election. Vice President Albert Gore, stressing his environmental record and economic prosperity, easily gained the Democratic nomination. Texas Governor George W. Bush, son of Clinton's predecessor, offered what he called "compassionate conservatism." Three televised debates between Bush and Gore blurred the differences between the candidates on matters of policy, as each tried to avoid taking a stand that might offend voters. Public images, "character," and party labels, not issues, would decide the outcome. Meanwhile, arch-conservatives backed the Reform party's Patrick Buchanan and had slight effect on the election, except to confuse some balloting in Florida. But anti-corporation environmentalists, who supported the Green party's Ralph Nader, nibbled into Gore's base and surely contributed to the outcome in Florida, where the election hinged on a few hundred votes.

After the polls closed on November 7, 2000, voting analysis showed clear distinctions in the support base of each of the candidates. In geo-

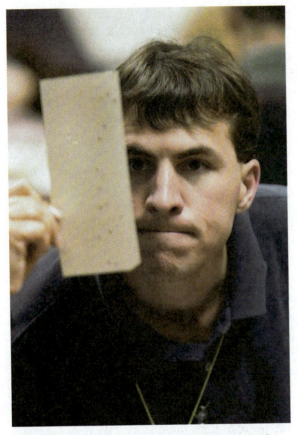

Recounting the votes of the 2000 presidential election in Florida. The process went on until the U.S. Supreme Court ordered it stopped, declaring George W. Bush the victor.

male Protestant vote, while Gore attracted religious and racial minorities and women. In cultural terms, then, Gore appealed to a pluralistic, diversified constituency, while Bush attracted those from a small-town, homogeneous communities.

But the most important difference between the candidates was party identity. Whatever the country's ideological splits, the election hinged on the eleven electoral votes of Florida, where a variety of polling devices had produced a significant undercount of actual voting. Although the initial tally gave Bush a lead of several hundred votes, Democrats demanded selected recounts to ensure a more accurate tally. Republicans promptly challenged the recount procedure. The Florida judiciary, dominated by Democrats, rejected the Republican protest, leading Bush's supporters to appeal to the United States Supreme Court. On the nation's highest judicial body, Republicans outnumbered Democrats 5–4. And, by that margin, the Court ordered an end to the Florida recount, effectively awarding that state's electoral votes to Bush.

graphic terms, the Democratic Gore carried most metropolitan areas with multicultural populations, including the states of the Northeast, upper Midwest, and Pacific coast. The Republican Bush won the South and Great Plains. In demographic terms, Gore garnered the votes of women, especially among college educated women. Bush won the white male vote, particularly in the suburbs, rural areas, and towns with fewer than 50,000 inhabitants. In sum, Bush took 63 percent of the white

Dilemmas of a Multicultural Society

The narrowness of the presidential election of 2000 expressed a bitter political divide that had characterized national politics for twenty years. During the 1990s, political polarization—disagreements between Republicans and Democrats, between conservatives and liberals, between Congress and the Executive—had created a balance of power in Washington, forcing the last three presidents of the twentieth century to seek centrist positions to accommodate their political opponents. Meanwhile, the nation as a whole (as distinct from the government) grappled with equally complex divisions of race, ethnicity, class, and gender.

While government leaders created political gridlock, half the country's eligible voters remained outside the political process altogether—indifferent, alienated, or enraged by party politics. Right-wing extremists even formed armed militia groups, waging private wars against the Internal Revenue Service, the FBI, and other federal agencies. In an act of domestic terrorism, militants retaliated for a government attack on a religious cult in Waco by bombing the federal building in Oklahoma City in 1995. More citizens than ever lived outside the law. Although federal statistics showed that annual crime rates fell during the decade, the United States housed more prisoners—1.72 million or 2.8 percent of the adult population—than any other country in the world. Nearly half of all African American males spent time inside the criminal justice system. After serving their terms, ex-felons were typically denied the right to vote.

Most political struggle remained legal but appeared strident and polarized. When the conservative Patrick Buchanan addressed the Republican National Convention in 1992, he described a country at war with itself. "It is a cultural war," he stated, "as critical to the kind of nation we shall be as the Cold War itself." No party or social group had a clear claim on righteousness. In 1997, for example, the Southern Baptist Convention voted to boycott Walt Disney productions to protest the media company's alleged advocacy of "homosexuality, infidelity, and adultery." Yet that year the Census Bureau reported that the percentage of households occupied by married couples declined from 60.8 percent in 1980 to 53.7 percent in 1995, and the number of households occupied by unmarried couples continued to rise.

Irreconcilable differences proliferated in communities around the country. In Louisiana, for instance, a local school board established a policy in 1992 to rename every school named after a slave-owner. "Why," asked a civil rights leader, "should African Americans want their kids to pay respect . . . to someone who enslaved their ancestors?" As a result, the name of George Washington, supposedly the Father of the country, was effaced from selected buildings. Native Americans from Minnesota to California demanded new names for places called "squaw." "It's a white term imposed on the Indians," said an ethnographer, defining the word as slang for female genitalia. In such cases, local whites protested "political correctness" and fought to retain their own nomenclature for geographic sites.

At stake were more fundamental questions of group identity. Bitter debates about affirmative action appeared around the country as voters, legislators, and courts increasingly rejected numerical quotas or advantages for racial and ethnic minorities. Political power would settle most disputes. But popular referenda, legislation, and court rulings could not mask essential cultural differences.

While ethnic groups debated place names and affirmative action programs, political leaders grappled with the cultural contradictions of the larger society. President Clinton found answers in the realm of time and history. "We may not share a common past," he declared in his 1997 State of the Union address, "but surely we share a common future." Looking backward to one's roots, he conceded, might be essential for a strong personal and group identity, but a sense of community—a national identity—also depended on foresight. "America is more than a place," said the last president of the twentieth century. America, he said, "is an idea, the most powerful idea in the history of nations. We are now the bearers of that idea into a new world." As the nation entered a new millenium, "We the People" remained the bearers of history—of roots, traditions, and meaning. And with that history, we, the people, carried what Clinton's successor, President George W.

Not long into his administration, George W. Bush faced an unprecedented challenge, one that would prompt him to declare that eliminating the threat of global terrorism would be the main goal of his administration. After the September 11, 2001, terrorist assault on New York's World Trade Center and the Pentagon, the complexity of identifying friend and foe in the post–Cold War world, as well as the importance of building international coalitions, became palpable.

Bush, called "an unfolding promise," that "no insignificant person was ever born."

Enduring Freedom

In his inaugural address of 2001, the second President Bush had admitted to the American people, "Sometimes our differences run so deep it seems we share a continent but not a country." Scarcely nine months after making that speech, the president faced a cheering crowd in Sacramento, California, and retracted his statement, underscoring the profound and fundamental changes in political opinion that followed the surprise terrorist attacks on September 11, 2001: at New York City's World Trade Center; the Pentagon in Washington, D.C.; and other suspected targets. Coming at a time when the national and world economy had entered a period of decline, the sudden destruction of the nation's proud symbols of internationalist involvement forced the country to confront aggressive enemies who threatened not only human life and material goods but also the structures that knit together economic, political, and social life. The result was an outpouring of patriotic commitment with expressions of community spirit, charity, and benevolence that dwarfed earlier partisan strife and interest politics. "Since September 11," said Bush in ordering Operation Enduring Freedom, U.S. military strikes against terrorist bases in Afghanistan, "an entire generation of young Americans has gained new understanding of the value of freedom and its cost in duty and in sacrifice."

This transformation of national mood and purpose also altered U.S. global strategies. Like his two immediate predecessors, the elder Bush and Clinton, the president immediately scrapped his unilateral foreign policy and moved to strengthen alliances with nations around the world, including some he had earlier characterized as competitors on the global stage. Although the White House had initially spoken about canceling U.S. participation in the ABM missile ban treaty agreement of 1970 and thereby had provoked criticism from allies in Western Europe as well as Russia and China, the global war against terrorism prompted Russian leaders to seek cooperation with the United States, including acceptance of new nuclear defense arrangements. Similarly, the Bush administration quickly reversed its confrontational approach to China. Although the two powers had recently exchanged public criticism about U.S. military surveillance in China and Chinese suppression of civil rights, both nations promised to face the terrorist peril as allies. Dozens of other countries shared intelligence information and offered assistance in the war against terrorism. As with the emergence of a domestic consensus, international differences about environmentalism, globalization, and nuclear disarmament were put on the back burner while a shocked and troubled world tried to eliminate a terrorist foe that threatened biological and chemical catastrophe.

Symbols of national unity permeated the landscape. Flags, sidewalk shrines in front of fire stations and churches, and patriotic hymns paid homage to the thousands who had died on September 11 and to those embarking on a dangerous global war. Such patriotism had emerged in earlier wars, but this time the embattled national identity was uniquely inclusive. Although, in the first days after the attacks, a few angry individuals committed violent acts against Arab Americans, the Bush administration took pains to distinguish the Islamic followers of Afghanistan's Taliban government and the terrorist Osama bin Laden (whom the president called "evildoers") from law-abiding Muslim Americans and other Arab groups. Japanese Americans and other minorities insisted on repudiating the racist domestic policies that had accompanied U.S. involvement in earlier world wars.

Issues of economic sacrifice remained more problematic. As terror attacks disrupted business, Congress approved billions of dollars to aid the airline industry but ignored many workers who faced unemployment. Yet rising federal expenditures for military activities also promised to produce more jobs and reinvigorate the homefront economy. Beyond such material concerns, the national mood remained solemn and uncertain, even as political and economic leaders urged a return to normalcy. Unlike an armed battalion, the terrorist enemy struck deviously, used civilian technologies and fought not so much for territory or military position as to establish a war of nerves. This war for freedom, the president advised, demanded not only military might and personal sacrifice, but also an enduring patience.

INFOTRAC® COLLEGE EDITION EXERCISES

For additional readings go to InfoTrac College Edition, your online research library at *http://web1.infotrac-college.com*.

Subject search: Reagan

Keyword search: Iran-Contra

Subject search: George Bush

Subject search: Gulf War

Subject search: Noriega

Subject search: Gorbachev

Keyword search: Bill Clinton

Keyword search: impeachment

ADDITIONAL READING

William C. Berman, *America's Right Turn: From Nixon to Bush* (1994). A good political survey, emphasizing problems of constituency loyalty.

Reagan's Conservative Agenda

John W. Sloan, *The Reagan Effect: Economics and Presidential Leadership* (1999). This book explores the political context of Reagan's economic program.

Garry Wills, *Reagan's America: Innocents at Home* (1987). This trenchant analysis of Reagan's life explores the cultural background of his popularity.

Immigration and Ethnic Tensions

David M. Reimers, *Unwelcome Strangers: American Identity and the Turn against Immigration* (1998). This book describes efforts to change immigration policy in the 1990s.

The Politics of Gender and Sex

Susan Faludi, *Backlash: The Undeclared War against American Women* (1991). Focusing on mass media and popular culture, this book explores how the conservative era shaped attitudes and policies toward women.

The Iran-Contra Scandals

Christian Smith, *Resisting Reagan: The U.S. Central America Peace Movement* (1996). Focusing on opponents of U.S. policy in Central America, this book explores the social context of political dissidents.

David Thelen, *Becoming Citizens in the Age of Television: How Americans Challenged the Media and Seized Political Initiative During the Iran-Contra Debate* (1996). Using citizen correspondence to Congress, the author studies shifts in democratic values.

The Rise and Fall of George Bush

Herbert S. Parmet, *George Bush: The Life of a Lone Star Yankee* (1997). This political biography presents a chronological narrative of the Bush presidency; for a more topical analysis, see David Mervin, *George Bush and the Guardianship Presidency* (1996).

A Democratic Alternative

Stanley Allen Renshon, *High Hopes: The Clinton Presidency and the Politics of Ambition* (1996). The author examines Clinton's temperament, values, and approach to leadership.

A Conservative Revival

Dan Balz and Ronald Brownstein, *Storming the Gates: Protest Politics and the Republican Revivial* (1996). The authors present a fine journalistic analysis of conservative politics, culminating in the elections of 1994.

Boosting Foreign Trade

David M. Lampton, *Same Bed, Different Dreams: Managing U.S.-China Relations, 1989–2000* (2001). The author discusses the context of post-Cold War diplomacy with China.

Partisan Divisions

Richard A. Posner, *An Affair of State: The Investigation, Impeachment, and Trial of President Clinton* (1999). A lawyer's analysis of the Clinton scandals, this book provides a balanced discussion of the legal and political issues.

The Declaration of Independence*

In Congress, July 4, 1776.

A Declaration by the Representatives of the United States of America, in General Congress assembled.

When in the Course of human Events, it becomes necessary for one People to dissolve the Political Bonds which have connected them with another, and to assume among the Powers of the Earth, the separate and equal Station to which the Laws of Nature and of Nature's God entitle them, a decent Respect to the Opinions of Mankind requires that they should declare the causes which impel them to the Separation.

We hold these Truths to be self-evident, that all Men are created equal, that they are endowed by their Creator with certain unalienable Rights, that among these are Life, Liberty, and the Pursuit of Happiness—That to secure these Rights, Governments are instituted among Men, deriving their just Powers from the Consent of the Governed, that whenever any Form of Government becomes destructive of these Ends, it is the Right of the People to alter or to abolish it, and to institute new Government, laying its Foundation on such Principles, and organizing its Powers in such Forms, as to them shall seem most likely to effect their Safety and Happiness. Prudence, indeed, will dictate that Governments long established should not be changed for light and transient Causes; and accordingly all Experience hath shewn, that Mankind are more disposed to suffer, while Evils are sufferable, than to right themselves by abolishing the Forms to which they are accustomed. But when a long Train of Abuses and Usurpations, pursuing invariably the same Object, evinces a Design to reduce them under absolute Despotism, it is their Right, it is their Duty, to throw off such Government, and to provide new Guards for their future Security. Such has been the patient Sufferance of these Colonies; and such is now the Necessity which constrains them to alter their former Systems of Government. The History of the present King of Great Britain is a History of repeated Injuries and Usurpations, all having in direct Object the Establishment of an absolute Tyranny over these States. To prove this, let facts be submitted to a candid World.

He has refused his Assent to Laws, the most wholesome and necessary for the public Good.

He has forbidden his Governors to pass Laws of immediate and pressing Importance, unless suspended in their Operation till his Assent should be obtained; and when so suspended, he has utterly neglected to attend to them.

He has refused to pass other Laws for the Accommodation of large Districts of People, unless those People would relinquish the Right of Representation in the Legislature, a Right inestimable to them, and formidable to Tyrants only.

---

*The spelling, capitalization, and punctuation of the original have been retained here.

He has called together Legislative Bodies at Places unusual, uncomfortable, and distant from the Depository of their Public Records, for the sole Purpose of fatiguing them into Compliance with his Measures.

He has dissolved Representative Houses repeatedly, for opposing with manly Firmness his Invasions on the Rights of the People.

He has refused for a long Time, after such Dissolutions, to cause others to be elected; whereby the Legislative Powers, incapable of Annihilation, have returned to the People at large for their exercise; the State remaining in the mean time exposed to all the Dangers of Invasion from without, and Convulsions within.

He has endeavoured to prevent the Population of these States; for that Purpose obstructing the Laws for Naturalization of Foreigners; refusing to pass others to encourage their Migration hither, and raising the Conditions of new Appropriations of Lands.

He has obstructed the Administration of Justice, by refusing his Assent to Laws for establishing Judiciary Powers.

He has made Judges dependent on his Will alone, for the Tenure of their offices, and the Amount and payments of their Salaries.

He has erected a Multitude of new Offices, and sent hither Swarms of Officers to harass our People, and eat out their Substance.

He has kept among us, in times of Peace, Standing Armies, without the consent of our Legislatures.

He has affected to render the Military independent of, and superior to the Civil Power.

He has combined with others to subject us to a Jurisdiction foreign to our Constitution, and unacknowledged by our Laws; giving his Assent to their Acts of pretended Legislation:

For quartering large Bodies of Armed Troops among us:

For protecting them, by a mock Trial, from Punishment for any Murders which they should commit on the Inhabitants of these States:

For cutting off our Trade with all Parts of the World:

For imposing Taxes on us without our Consent:

For depriving us, in many cases, of the Benefits of Trial by Jury:

For transporting us beyond Seas to be tried for pretended Offences:

For abolishing the free System of English Laws in a neighbouring Province, establishing therein an arbitrary Government, and enlarging its Boundaries, so as to render it at once an Example and fit Instrument for introducing the same absolute Rule into these Colonies:

For taking away our Charters, abolishing our most valuable Laws, and altering fundamentally the Forms of our Governments:

For suspending our own Legislatures, and declaring themselves invested with Power to legislate for us in all Cases whatsoever.

He has abdicated Government here, by declaring us out of his Protection and waging War against us.

He has plundered our Seas, ravaged our Coasts, burnt our towns, and destroyed the Lives of our People.

He is, at this Time, transporting large Armies of foreign Mercenaries to compleat the works of Death, Desolation, and Tyranny, already begun with circumstances of Cruelty and Perfidy, scarcely paralleled in the most barbarous Ages, and totally unworthy the Head of a civilized Nation.

He has constrained our fellow Citizens taken Captive on the high Seas to bear Arms against their Country, to become the Executioners of their Friends and Brethren, or to fall themselves by their Hands.

He has excited domestic Insurrections amongst us, and has endeavoured to bring on the Inhabitants of our Frontiers, the merciless Indian Savages, whose known Rule of Warfare is an undistinguished Destruction, of all Ages, Sexes and Conditions.

In every state of these Oppressions we have Petitioned for Redress in the most humble Terms: Our repeated Petitions have been answered only by repeated Injury. A Prince, whose Character is thus marked by every act which may define a Tyrant, is unfit to be the Ruler of a free People.

Nor have we been wanting in Attentions to our British Brethren. We have warned them from Time to Time of Attempts by their Legislature to extend an unwarrantable Jurisdiction over us. We have reminded them of the Circumstances of our Emigration and Settlement here. We have appealed to their native Justice and Magnanimity, and we have conjured them by the Ties of our common Kindred to disavow these Usurpations, which would inevitably interrupt our Connections and Correspondence. They too have been deaf to the Voice of Justice and of Consanguinity. We must, therefore, acquiesce in the Necessity, which denounces our Separation, and hold them, as we hold the rest of Mankind, Enemies in War, in Peace, Friends.

We, therefore, the Representatives of the UNITED STATES OF AMERICA, in General Congress Assembled, appealing to the Supreme Judge of the World for the Rectitude of our Intentions, do, in the Name, and by Authority of the good People of these Colonies, solemnly Publish and Declare, That these United Colonies are, and of Right ought to be, Free and Independent States; that they are absolved from all Allegiance to the British Crown, and that all political Connection between them and the State of Great Britain, is and ought to be totally dissolved; and that as Free and Independent States, they have full Power to levy War, conclude Peace, contract Alliances, establish Commerce, and to do all other Acts and Things which Independent States may of right do. And for the support of this declaration, with a firm Reliance on the Protection of divine Providence, we mutually pledge to each other our Lives, our Fortunes, and our sacred Honor.

Constitution of the United States of America*

We the people of the United States, in Order to form a more perfect Union, establish Justice, insure domestic Tranquility, provide for the common defence, promote the general Welfare, and secure the Blessings of Liberty to ourselves and our posterity, do ordain and establish this Constitution for the United States of America.

Article I

Section 1. All legislative Powers herein granted shall be vested in a Congress of the United States, which shall consist of a Senate and House of Representatives.

Section 2. The House of Representatives shall be composed of Members chosen every second Year by the People of the several States, and the Electors in each State shall have the Qualifications requisite for Electors of the most numerous Branch of the State Legislature.

No person shall be a Representative who shall not have attained to the Age of twenty-five Years, and been seven Years a Citizen of the United States, and who shall not, when elected, be an Inhabitant of that State in which he shall be chosen.

Representatives and direct [Taxes][1] shall be apportioned among the several States which may be included within this Union, according to their respective Numbers [which shall be determined by adding to the whole Number of free Persons, including those bound to Service for a Term of Years, and excluding Indians not taxed, three fifths of all other Persons].[2] The actual Enumeration shall be made within three Years after the first Meeting of the Congress of the United States, and within every subsequent Term of ten Years, in such Manner as they shall by Law direct. The Number of Representatives shall not exceed one for every thirty Thousand, but each State shall have at Least one Representative; and until such enumeration shall be made, the State of New Hampshire shall be entitled to chuse three, Massachusetts eight, Rhode Island and Providence Plantations one, Connecticut five, New-York six, New Jersy four, Pennsylvania eight, Delaware one, Maryland six, Virginia ten, North Carolina five, South Carolina five, and Georgia three.

When vacancies happen in the Representation from any State, the Executive Authority thereof shall issue Writs of Election to fill such Vacancies.

The House of Representatives shall chuse their Speaker and other Officers; and shall have the sole Power of Impeachment.

---

*The spelling, capitalization, and punctuation of the original have been retained here. Brackets indicate passages that have been altered by amendments to the Constitution.

1. Modified by the Sixteenth Amendment.
2. Modified by the Fourteenth Amendment.

Section 3. The Senate of the United States shall be composed of two Senators from each State [chosen by the Legislature thereof],[3] for six Years; and each Senator shall have one Vote.

Immediately after they shall be assembled in Consequence of the first Election, they shall be divided as equally as may be into three Classes. The Seats of the Senators of the first Class shall be vacated at the Expiration of the second year, of the second Class at the Expiration of the fourth Year, and of the third Class at the Expiration of the sixth Year, so that one third may be chosen every second Year [and if Vacancies happen by Resignation, or otherwise, during the Recess of the Legislature of any State, the Executive thereof may make temporary Appointments until the next Meeting of the Legislature, which shall then fill such Vacancies.][4]

No Person shall be a Senator who shall not have attained to the Age of thirty Years, and been nine Years a Citizen of the United States, and who shall not, when elected, be an Inhabitant of that State for which he shall be chosen.

The Vice President of the United States shall be President of the Senate, but shall have no Vote, unless they be equally divided.

The Senate shall chuse their other Officers, and also a President pro tempore, in the Absence of the Vice President, or when he shall exercise the Office of President of the United States.

The Senate shall have the sole Power to try all Impeachments. When sitting for that Purpose, they shall be on Oath or Affirmation. When the President of the United States is tried, the Chief Justice shall preside: And no Person shall be convicted without the Concurrence of two thirds of the Members present.

Judgment in Cases of Impeachment shall not extend further than to removal from Office, and disqualification to hold and enjoy any Office of honor, Trust or Profit under the United States; but the Party convicted shall nevertheless be liable and subject to Indictment, Trial, Judgment and Punishment, according to Law.

Section 4. The Times, Places and Manner of holding Elections for Senators and Representatives, shall be prescribed in each State by the Legislature thereof; but the Congress may at any time by Law make or alter such Regulations, except as to the Places of chusing Senators.

[The Congress shall assemble at least once in every Year, and such Meeting shall be on the first Monday in December, unless they shall by Law appoint a different Day.][5]

Section 5. Each House shall be the Judge of the Elections, Returns and Qualifications of its own Members, and a Majority of each shall constitute a Quorum to do Business; but a smaller Number may adjourn from day to day, and may be authorized to compel the Attendance of absent Members, in such Manner, and under such Penalties as each House may provide.

Each House may determine the Rules of its Proceedings, punish its Members for disorderly Behaviour, and, with the Concurrence of two thirds, expel a Member.

Each House shall keep a Journal of its Proceedings, and from time to time publish the same, excepting such Parts as may in their Judgment require Secrecy; and the Yeas and Nays of the Members of either House on any question shall, at the Desire of one fifth of those present, be entered on the Journal.

Neither House, during the Session of Congress, shall, without the Consent of the other, adjourn for more than three days, nor to any other Place than that in which the two Houses shall be sitting.

3. Repealed by the Seventeenth Amendment.
4. Modified by the Seventeenth Amendment.

5. Changed by the Twentieth Amendment.

Section 6. The Senators and Representatives shall receive a Compensation for their Services, to be ascertained by Law, and paid out of the Treasury of the United States. They shall in all Cases, except Treason, Felony and Breach of the Peace, be privileged from Arrest during their Attendance at the Session of their respective Houses, and in going to and returning from the same; and for any Speech or Debate in either House, they shall not be questioned in any other Place.

No Senator or Representative shall, during the Time for which he was elected, be appointed to any civil Office under the Authority of the United States, which shall have been created, or the Emoluments whereof shall have been encreased during such time; and no Person holding any Office under the United States, shall be a Member of either House during his Continuance in Office.

Section 7. All Bills for raising Revenue shall originate in the House of Representatives; but the Senate may propose or concur with Amendments as on other Bills.

Every Bill which shall have passed the House of Representatives and the Senate, shall, before it become a Law, be presented to the President of the United States; If he approves he shall sign it, but if not he shall return it, with his objections to that House in which it shall have originated, who shall enter the Objections at large on their Journal, and proceed to reconsider it. If after such Reconsideration two thirds of that House shall agree to pass the Bill, it shall be sent, together with the Objections, to the other House, by which it shall likewise be reconsidered, and if approved by two thirds of that House, it shall become a Law. But in all such Cases the Votes of both Houses shall be determined by yeas and Nays, and the Names of the Persons voting for and against the Bill shall be entered on the Journal of each House respectively. If any Bill shall not be returned by the President within ten Days (Sundays excepted) after it shall have been presented to him, the Same shall be a Law, in like Manner as if he had signed it, unless the Congress by their Adjournment prevent its Return, in which Case it shall not be a Law.

Every Order, Resolution, or Vote to which the Concurrence of the Senate and House of Representatives may be necessary (except on a question of Adjournment) shall be presented to the President of the United States; and before the Same shall take Effect, shall be approved by him, or being disapproved by him, shall be repassed by two thirds of the Senate and House of Representatives, according to the Rules and Limitations prescribed in the Case of a Bill.

Section 8. The Congress shall have Power To lay and collect Taxes, Duties, Imposts and Excises, to pay the Debts and provide for the common Defence and general Welfare of the United States; but all Duties, Imposts and Excises shall be uniform throughout the United States;

To borrow Money on the credit of the United States;

To regulate Commerce with foreign Nations, and among the several States, and with the Indian Tribes;

To establish a uniform Rule of Naturalization, and uniform Laws on the subject of Bankruptcies throughout the United States;

To coin Money, regulate the Value thereof, and of foreign Coin, and fix the Standard of Weights and Measures;

To provide for the Punishment of counterfeiting the Securities and current Coin of the United States.

To establish Post Offices and post Roads;

To promote the Progress of Science and useful Arts, by securing for limited Times to Authors and Inventors the exclusive Right to their respective Writings and Discoveries;

To constitute Tribunals inferior to the supreme Court;

To define and punish Piracies and Felonies committed on the high Seas, and Offences against the Law of Nations;

To declare War, grant Letters of Marque and Reprisal, and make Rules concerning Captures on Land and Water;

To raise and support Armies, but no Appropriation of Money to that Use shall be for a longer Term than two Years;

To provide and maintain a Navy;

To make Rules for the Government and Regulation of the land and naval Forces;

To provide for calling forth the Militia to execute the Laws of the Union, suppress Insurrections and repel Invasions;

To provide for organizing, arming, and disciplining the Militia, and for governing such Part of them as may be employed in the Service of the United States, reserving to the States respectively, the Appointment of the Officers, and the Authority of training the Militia according to the discipline prescribed by Congress;

To exercise exclusive Legislation in all Cases whatsoever, over such District (not exceeding ten Miles square) as may, by Cession of particular States, and the Acceptance of Congress, become the Seat of the Government of the United States, and to exercise like Authority over all Places purchased by the Consent of the Legislature of the State in which the Same shall be, for the Erection of forts, Magazines, Arsenals, dockYards, and other needful Buildings;—And

To make all Laws which shall be necessary and proper for carrying into Execution the foregoing Powers, and all other Powers vested by this Constitution in the Government of the United States, or in any Department or Officer thereof.

Section 9. The Migration or Importation of such Persons as any of the States now existing shall think proper to admit, shall not be prohibited by the Congress prior to the Year one thousand eight hundred and eight, but a Tax or duty may be imposed on such Importation, not exceeding ten dollars for each Person.

The Privilege of the Writ of Habeas Corpus shall not be suspended, unless when in Cases of Rebellion or Invasion the public Safety may require it.

No Bill of Attainder or ex post facto Law shall be passed.

[No Capitation, or other direct, Tax shall be laid, unless in Proportion to the Census or Enumeration herein before directed to be taken.][6]

No Tax or Duty shall be laid on Articles exported from any State.

No Preference shall be given by any Regulation of Commerce or Revenue to the Ports of one State over those of another; nor shall Vessels bound to, or from, one State, be obliged to enter, clear, or pay Duties in another.

No Money shall be drawn from the Treasury, but in Consequence of Appropriations made by Law; and a regular Statement and Account of the Receipts and Expenditures of all public Money shall be published from time to time.

No Title of Nobility shall be granted by the United States; and no Person holding any Office or Profit or Trust under them, shall, without the Consent of the Congress, accept of any present, Emolument, Office, or Title, of any kind whatever, from any King, Prince, or foreign State.

Section 10. No state shall enter into any Treaty, Alliance, or Confederation; grant Letters of Marque and Reprisal; coin Money; emit Bills of Credit; make any Thing but gold and silver Coin a Tender in Payment of Debts; pass any Bill of Attainder, ex post facto Law, or Law impairing the Obligation of Contracts, or grant any Title of Nobility.

6. Modified by the Sixteenth Amendment.

No State shall, without the Consent of the Congress, lay any Imposts or Duties on Imports or Exports, except what may be absolutely necessary for executing its inspection Laws; and the net Produce of all Duties and Imposts, laid by any State on Imports or Exports, shall be for the Use of the Treasury of the United States; and all such Laws shall be subject to the Revision and Controul of the Congress.

No State shall, without the Consent of Congress, lay any duty of Tonnage, keep Troops, or Ships of War in time of Peace, enter into any Agreement or Compact with another State, or with a foreign Power or engage in War, unless actually invaded, or in such imminent Danger as will not admit of delay.

Article II

Section 1. The executive Power shall be vested in a President of the United States of America. He shall hold his Office during the Term of four Years, and, together with the Vice President, chosen for the Same Term, be elected, as follows.

Each State shall appoint, in such Manner as the Legislature thereof may direct, a Number of Electors, equal to the whole Number of Senators and Representatives to which the State may be entitled in the Congress; but no Senator or Representative, or Person holding an Office of Trust or Profit under the United States, shall be appointed an Elector.

[The Electors shall meet in their respective States, and vote by Ballot for two Persons of whom one at least shall not be an Inhabitant of the same State with themselves. And they shall make a List of all the Persons voted for, and of the Number of Votes for each; which List they shall sign and certify, and transmit sealed to the Seat of the Government of the United States, directed to the President of the Senate. The President of the Senate shall, in the Presence of the Senate and House of Representatives, open all the Certificates, and the Votes shall then be counted. The Person having the greatest Number of Votes shall be the President, if such Number be a Majority of the whole Number of Electors appointed; and if there be more than one who have such Majority, and have an equal Number of Votes, then the House of Representatives shall immediately chuse by Ballot one of them for President; and if no Person have a Majority, then from the five highest on the List the said House shall in like Manner chuse the President. But in chusing the President, the Votes shall be taken by States, the Representation from each State having one Vote; A quorum for this Purpose shall consist of a Member or Members from two thirds of the States, and a Majority of all the states shall be necessary to a Choice. In every Case, after the Choice of the President, the Person having the greatest Number of Votes of the Electors shall be the Vice President. But if there should remain two or more who have equal Votes, the Senate shall chuse from them by Ballot the Vice President.][7]

The Congress may determine the Time of chusing the Electors, and the Day on which they shall give their Votes; which Day shall be the same throughout the United States.

No person except a natural born Citizen, or a Citizen of the United States, at the time of the Adoption of this Constitution, shall be eligible to the Office of President; neither shall any Person be eligible to that Office who shall not have attained to the Age of thirty five Years, and been fourteen Years a Resident within the United States.

7. Changed by the Twelfth Amendment.

[In Case of the Removal of the President from Office, or of his Death, Resignation, or Inability to discharge the Powers and Duties of the said Office, the same shall devolve on the Vice President, and the Congress may by Law provide for the Case of Removal, Death, Resignation or Inability, both of the President and Vice President, declaring what Officer shall then act as President, and such Officer shall act accordingly, until the Disability be removed, or a President shall be elected.][8]

The President shall, at stated Times, receive for his Services, a Compensation, which shall neither be encreased nor diminished during the Period for which he shall have been elected, and he shall not receive within that Period any other Emolument from the United States, or any of them.

Before he enter on the Execution of his Office, he shall take the following Oath or Affirmation:— "I do solemnly swear (or affirm) that I will faithfully execute the Office of President of the United States, and will to the best of my Ability, preserve, protect and defend the constitution of the United States."

Section 2. The President shall be Commander in Chief of the Army and Navy of the United States, and of the Militia of the several States, when called into the actual Service of the United States; he may require the Opinion, in writing, of the principal Officer in each of the executive Departments, upon any Subject relating to the Duties of their respective Offices, and he shall have Power to grant Reprieves and Pardons for Offences against the United States, except in Cases of Impeachment.

He shall have Power, by and with the Advice and Consent of the Senate, to make Treaties, provided two thirds of the Senators present concur;

and he shall nominate, and by and with the Advice and Consent of the Senate, shall appoint Ambassadors, other public Ministers and Consuls, Judges of the supreme Court, and all other Officers of the United States, whose Appointments are not herein otherwise provided for, and which shall be established by Law; but the Congress may by Law vest the Appointment of such inferior Officers, as they think proper, in the President alone, in the Courts of Law, or in the Heads of Departments.

The President shall have Power to fill up all Vacancies that may happen during the Recess of the Senate, by granting Commissions which shall expire at the end of their next Session.

Section 3. He shall from time to time give to the Congress Information of the State of the Union, and recommend to their Consideration such Measures as he shall judge necessary and expedient; he may, on extraordinary Occasions, convene both Houses, or either of them, and in Case of Disagreement between them, with Respect to the Time of Adjournment, he may adjourn them to such Time as he shall think proper; he shall receive Ambassadors and other public Ministers; he shall take Care that the Laws be faithfully executed, and shall Commission all the Officers of the United States.

Section 4. The President, Vice President and all civil Officers of the United States, shall be removed from Office on Impeachment for, and Conviction of, Treason, Bribery, or other high Crimes and Misdemeanors.

Article III

Section 1. The judicial Power of the United States, shall be vested in one supreme Court, and

---

8. Modified by the Twenty-fifth Amendment.

in such inferior Courts as the Congress may from time to time ordain and establish. The Judges, both of the supreme and inferior Courts, shall hold their Offices during good Behaviour, and shall, at stated Times, receive for their Services, a Compensation, which shall not be diminished during their Continuance in Office.

Section 2. The judicial Power shall extend to all Cases, in Law and Equity, arising under this Constitution, the Laws of the United States, and Treaties made, or which shall be made, under their Authority;—to all Cases affecting Ambassadors, other public Ministers and Consuls;—to all Cases of admiralty and maritime Jurisdiction;—to Controversies to which the United States shall be a Party;—to Controversies between two or more States;—[between a State and Citizens of another State;]9—between Citizens of different States,—between Citizens of the same State claiming Lands under Grants of different States, [and between a state, or the Citizens thereof, and foreign States, Citizens or Subjects.]10

In all cases affecting Ambassadors, other public Ministers and Consuls, and those in which a State shall be Party, the supreme Court shall have original Jurisdiction. In all the other Cases before mentioned, the supreme Court shall have appellate Jurisdiction, both as to Law and Fact, with such Exceptions, and under such Regulations as the Congress shall make.

The Trial of all Crimes, except in Cases of Impeachment, shall be by Jury; and such Trial shall be held in the State where the said Crimes shall have been committed; but when not committed within any State, the Trial shall be at such Place or Places as the Congress may by Law have directed.

Section 3. Treason against the United States, shall consist only in levying War against them, or in adhering to their Enemies, giving them Aid and Comfort. No Person shall be convicted of Treason unless on the Testimony of two Witnesses to the same overt Act, or on Confession in open Court.

The Congress shall have Power to declare the Punishment of Treason, but no Attainder of Treason shall work Corruption of Blood, or Forfeiture except during the Life of the Person attainted.

Article IV

Section 1. Full Faith and Credit shall be given in each State to the public Acts, Records, and judicial Proceedings of every other State. And the Congress may by general Laws prescribe the Manner in which such Acts, Records and Proceedings shall be proved, and the Effect thereof.

Section 2. The Citizens of each State shall be entitled to all Privileges and Immunities of Citizens in the several States.

A Person charged in any State with Treason, Felony, or other Crime, who shall flee from Justice, and be found in another State, shall on Demand of the executive Authority of the State from which he fled, be delivered up, to be removed to the State having Jurisdiction of the Crime.

[No Person held to Service or Labour in one State under the Laws thereof, escaping into another, shall, in Consequence of any Law or Regulation therein, be discharged from such Service or Labour, but shall be delivered up on Claim of the Party to whom such Service or Labour may be due.]11

---

9. Modified by the Eleventh Amendment.
10. Modified by the Eleventh Amendment.

11. Repealed by the Thirteenth Amendment.

Section 3. New States may be admitted by the Congress into this Union; but no new State shall be formed or erected within the Jurisdiction of any other State; nor any State be formed by the Junction of two or more States, or Parts of States, without the Consent of the Legislatures of the States concerned as well as of the Congress.

The Congress shall have Power to dispose of and make all needful Rules and Regulations respecting the Territory or other Property belonging to the United States; and nothing in this Constitution shall be so construed as to Prejudice any Claimes of the United States, or of any particular State.

Section 4. The United States shall guarantee to every State in this Union a Republican Form of Government, and shall protect each of them against Invasion, and on Application of the Legislature, or of the Executive (when the Legislature cannot be convened) against domestic Violence.

Article V

The Congress, whenever two thirds of both Houses shall deem it necessary, shall propose Amendments to this Constitution, or on the Application of the Legislatures of two thirds of the several States, shall call a Convention for proposing Amendments, which, in either Case, shall be valid to all Intents and Purposes, as Part of this Constitution, when ratified by the Legislatures of three fourths of the several States, or by Conventions in three fourths thereof, as the one or the other Mode of Ratification may be proposed by the Congress; Provided that no Amendment which may be made prior to the Year One thousand eight hundred and eight shall in any Manner affect the first and fourth Clauses in the Ninth Section of the first Article; and that no State, without its Consent, shall be deprived of its equal Suffrage in the Senate.

Article VI

All Debts contracted and Engagements entered into, before the Adoption of this Constitution, shall be as valid against the United States under this Constitution, as under the Confederation.

This Constitution, and the laws of the United States which shall be made in Pursuance thereof; and all Treaties made, or which shall be made, under the Authority of the United States, shall be the supreme Law of the Land; and the Judges in every State shall be bound thereby, any Thing in the Constitution or Laws of any State to the Contrary notwithstanding.

The Senators and Representatives before mentioned, and the Members of the several State Legislatures, and all executive and judicial Officers, both of the United States and of the several States, shall be bound by Oath or Affirmation, to support this Constitution; but no religious Text shall ever be required as a Qualification to any Office or public Trust under the United States.

Article VII

The Ratification of the Conventions of nine States, shall be sufficient for the Establishment of this constitution between the States so ratifying the Same.

Done in Convention by the Unanimous Consent of the States present the Seventeenth Day of September in the Year of our Lord one thousand seven hundred and Eighty seven and of the Independence of the United States of America the Twelfth. IN WITNESS whereof we have hereunto subscribed our Names.

Go. WASHINGTON
Presid't. and deputy from Virginia

Attest
William Jackson
Secretary

Delaware
Geo. Read
Gunning Bedford jun
John Dickinson
Richard Basset
Jaco. Broon

Massachusetts
Nathaniel Gorham
Rufus King

Connecticut
Wm. Saml. Johnson
Roger Sherman

New York
Alexander Hamilton

New Jersey
Wh. Livingston
David Brearley
Wm. Paterson
Jona. Dayton

Pennsylvania
B. Franklin
Thomas Mifflin
Robt. Morris
Geo. Clymer
Thos. FitzSimons
Jared Ingersoll

James Wilson
Gouv. Morris

Virginia
John Blair
James Madison Jr.

North Carolina
Wm. Blount
Richd. Dobbs Spaight
Hu. Williamson

South Carolina
J. Rutledge
Charles Cotesworth
Pinckney
Charles Pinckney
Pierce Butler

Georgia
William Few
Abr. Baldwin
New Hampshire
John Langdon
Nicholas Gilman

Maryland
James McHenry
Dan of St. Thos. Jenifer
Danl. Carroll

Amendment I[12]

Congress shall make no law respecting an establishment of religion, or prohibiting the free exercise thereof; or abridging the freedom of speech, or of the press; or the right of the people peace-

12. The first ten amendments were passed by Congress on September 25, 1789, and were ratified on December 15, 1791.

ably to assemble, and to petition the Government for a redress of grievances.

Amendment II

A well regulated militia, being necessary to the security of a free State, the right of the people to keep and bear arms, shall not be infringed.

Amendment III

No Soldier shall, in time of peace be quartered in any house, without the consent of the owner, nor in time of war, but in a manner to be prescribed by law.

Amendment IV

The right of the people to be secure in their persons, houses, papers, and effects, against unreasonable searches and seizures, shall not be violated, and no warrants shall issue, but upon probable cause, supported by oath or affirmation, and particularly describing the place to be searched, and the persons or things to be seized.

Amendment V

No person shall be held to answer for a capital, or otherwise infamous crime, unless on a presentment or indictment of a Grand Jury, except in cases arising in the land or naval forces, or in the militia, when in actual service in time of war or public danger; nor shall any person be subject for the same offence to be twice put in jeopardy of life or limb; nor shall be compelled in any criminal case to be a witness against himself, nor be deprived of life, liberty, or property, without due process of law; nor shall private property be taken for public use, without just compensation.

Amendment VI

In all criminal prosecutions, the accused shall enjoy the right to a speedy and public trial, by an impartial jury of the State and district wherein the crime shall have been committed, which district shall have been previously ascertained by law, and to be informed of the nature and cause of the accusation; to be confronted with the witnesses against him; to have compulsory process for obtaining witnesses in his favor, and to have the assistance of counsel for his defence.

Amendment VII

In Suits at common law, where the value in controversy shall exceed twenty dollars, the right of trial by jury shall be preserved, and no fact tried by a jury, shall be otherwise reexamined in any Court of the United States, than according to the rules of the common law.

Amendment VIII

Excessive bail shall not be required, nor excessive fines imposed, nor cruel and unusual punishments inflicted.

Amendment IX

The enumeration in the Constitution, of certain rights, shall not be construed to deny or disparage others retained by the people.

Amendment X

The powers not delegated to the United States by the Constitution, nor prohibited by it to the States, are reserved to the States respectively, or to the people.

Amendment XI
(Ratified February 7, 1795)

The Judicial power of the United States shall not be construed to extend to any suit in law or equity, commenced or prosecuted against one of the United States by Citizens of another State, or by Citizens or Subjects of any Foreign State.

Amendment XII
(Ratified June 15, 1804)

The Electors shall meet in their respective states, and vote by ballot for President and Vice-President, one of whom, at least, shall not be an inhabitant of the same state with themselves; they shall name in their ballots the person voted for as President, and in distinct ballots the person voted for as Vice President, and they shall make distinct lists of all persons voted for as President, and of all persons voted for as Vice-President, and of the number of votes for each, which lists they shall sign and certify, and transmit sealed to the seat of the government of the United States, directed to the President of the Senate;—The President of the Senate shall, in the presence of the Senate and House of Representatives, open all the certificates and the votes shall then be counted;—The person having the greatest number of votes for President, shall be the President, if such number be a majority of the whole number of Electors appointed; and if no person have such majority, then from the persons having the highest numbers not exceeding three on the list of those voted for as President, the House of Representatives shall choose immediately, by ballot, the President. But in choosing the President, the votes shall be taken by states, the representation from each state having one vote; a quorum for this purpose shall consist of a member or members from two-thirds of the states, and a majority of all the states shall be necessary to a choice. [And if the House of Representatives shall not choose a President whenever the right of choice shall devolve upon them, before the fourth day of March next following, then the Vice-President shall act as President, as in the case of the death or other constitutional disability of the President.][13]—The person having the greatest number of votes as Vice-President, shall be the Vice-President, if such number be a majority of the whole number of Electors appointed, and if no person have a majority, then from the two highest numbers on the list, the Senate shall choose the Vice-President; a quorum for the purpose shall consist of two-thirds of the whole number of Senators, and a majority of the whole number shall be necessary to a choice. But no person constitutionally ineligible to the office of President shall be eligible to that of Vice-President of the United States.

Amendment XIII
(Ratified on December 6, 1865)

Section 1. Neither slavery nor involuntary servitude, except as a punishment for crime whereof the party shall have been duly convicted, shall exist within the United States, or any place subject to their jurisdiction.

Section 2. Congress shall have power to enforce this article by appropriate legislation.

Amendment XIV
(Ratified on July 9, 1868)

All persons born or naturalized in the United States, and subject to the jurisdiction thereof, are citizens of the United States and of the State wherein they reside. No State shall make or enforce any law which shall abridge the privileges or immunities of citizens of the United States; nor shall any State deprive any person of life, liberty, or property, without due process of law; nor deny to any person within its jurisdiction the equal protection of the laws.

Section 2. Representatives shall be apportioned among the several States according to their respective numbers, counting the whole number of persons in each State, excluding Indians not taxed. But when the right to vote at any election for the choice of electors for President and Vice President of the United States, Representatives in Congress, the Executive and Judicial officers of a State, or the members of the Legislature thereof, is denied to any of the male inhabitants of such State, being [twenty-one][14] years of age, and citizens of the United States, or in any way abridged, except for participation in rebellion, or other crime, the basis of representation therein shall be reduced in the proportion which the number of such male citizens shall bear to the whole number of male citizens twenty-one years of age in such State.

Section 3. No person shall be a Senator or Representative in Congress, or elector of President and Vice President, or hold any office, civil or military, under the United States, or under any State, who having previously taken an oath, as a member of Congress, or as an officer of the United States, or as a member of any State legislature, or as an executive or judicial officer of any State, to support the Constitution of the United States, shall have engaged in insurrection or rebellion against the same, or given aid or comfort to the enemies thereof. But Congress may by a vote of two-thirds of each House, remove such disability.

---

13. Changed by the Twentieth Amendment.

14. Changed by the Twenty-sixth Amendment.

Section 4. The validity of the public debt of the United States, authorized by law, including debts incurred for payment of pensions and bounties for services in suppressing insurrection or rebellion, shall not be questioned. But neither the United States nor any State shall assume or pay any debt or obligation incurred in aid of insurrection or rebellion against the United States, or any claim for the loss or emancipation of any slave, but all such debts, obligations and claims shall be held illegal and void.

Section 5. The Congress shall have power to enforce, by appropriate legislation, the provisions of this article.

Amendment XV
(Ratified on February 3, 1870)

Section 1. The right of citizens of the United States to vote shall not be denied or abridged by the United States or by any State on account of race, color, or previous condition of servitude.

Section 2. The Congress shall have power to enforce this article by appropriate legislation.

Amendment XVI
(Ratified on February 3, 1913)

The Congress shall have power to lay and collect taxes on incomes, from whatever source derived, without apportionment among the several States, and without regard to any census or enumeration.

Amendment XVII
(Ratified on April 8, 1913)

The Senate of the United States shall be composed of two Senators from each State, elected by the people thereof, for six years; and each Senator shall have one vote. The electors in each State shall have the qualifications requisite for electors of the most numerous branch of the State legislatures.

When vacancies happen in the representation of any State in the Senate, the executive authority of such State shall issue writs of election to fill such vacancies: *Provided,* That the legislature of any State may empower the executive thereof to make temporary appointments until the people fill the vacancies by election as the legislature may direct.

This amendment shall not be so construed as to affect the election or term of any Senator chosen before it becomes valid as part of the Constitution.

Amendment XVIII
(Ratified on January 16, 1919)

Section 1. After one year from the ratification of this article the manufacture, sale, or transportation of intoxicating liquors within, the importation thereof into, or the exportation thereof from the United States and all territory subject to the jurisdiction thereof for beverage purposes is hereby prohibited.

Section 2. The Congress and the several States shall have concurrent power to enforce this article by appropriate legislation.

Section 3. This article shall be inoperative unless it shall have been ratified as an amendment to the Constitution by the legislatures of the several States, as provided in the Constitution, within seven years from the date of the submission hereof to the States by the Congress.[15]

Amendment XIX
(Ratified on August 18, 1920)

The right of citizens of the United States to vote shall not be denied or abridged by the United States or by any State on account of sex.

---

15. The Eighteenth Amendment was repealed by the Twenty-first Amendment.

Congress shall have power to enforce this article by appropriate legislation.

Amendment XX
(Ratified on January 23, 1933)

Section 1. The terms of the President and Vice President shall end at noon on the 20th day of January, and the terms of Senators and Representatives at noon on the 3rd day of January, of the years in which such terms would have ended if this article had not been ratified, and the terms of their successors shall then begin.

Section 2. The Congress shall assemble at least once in every year, and such meeting shall begin at noon on the 3rd day of January, unless they shall by law appoint a different day.

Section 3. If, at the time fixed for the beginning of the term of the President, the President elect shall have died, the Vice President elect shall become President. If a President shall not have been chosen before the time fixed for the beginning of his term, or if the President elect shall have failed to qualify, then the Vice President elect shall act as President until a President shall have qualified; and the Congress may by law provide for the case wherein neither a President elect nor a Vice President elect shall have qualified, declaring who shall then act as President, or the manner in which one who is to act shall be selected, and such person shall act accordingly until a President or Vice President shall have qualified.

Section 4. The Congress may by law provide for the case of the death of any of the persons from whom the House of Representatives may choose a President whenever the rights of choice shall have devolved upon them, and for the case of the death of any of the persons from whom the Senate may choose a Vice President whenever the right of choice shall have devolved upon them.

Section 5. Sections 1 and 2 shall take effect on the 15th day of October following the ratification of this article.

Section 6. This article shall be inoperative unless it shall have been ratified as an amendment to the Constitution by the legislatures of three-fourths of the several States within seven years from the date of its submission.

Amendment XXI
(Ratified on December 5, 1933)

Section 1. The eighteenth article of amendment to the Constitution of the United States is hereby repealed.

Section 2. The transportation or importation into any State, Territory, or possession of the United States for delivery or use therein of intoxicating liquors, in violation of the laws thereof, is hereby prohibited.

Section 3. This article shall be inoperative unless it shall have been ratified as an amendment to the Constitution by conventions in the several States, as provided in the Constitution, within seven years from the date of the submission hereof to the States by the Congress.

Amendment XXII
(Ratified on February 27, 1951)

No person shall be elected to the office of the President more than twice, and no person who has held the office of President, or acted as President, for more than two years of a term to which some other person was elected President shall be elected to the office of the President more than once. But this Article shall not apply to any person holding the office of President when this Article was proposed by the Congress, and shall not prevent any person who may be holding the office of President, or acting as President, during the term within which this Article becomes operative from holding the office of President or acting as President during the remainder of such term.

Amendment XXIII
(Ratified on March 29, 1961)

Section 1. The District constituting the seat of Government of the United States shall appoint in such manner as the Congress may direct:

A number of electors of President and Vice President equal to the whole number of Senators and Representatives in Congress to which the District would be entitled if it were a State, but in no event more than the least populous State; they shall be in addition to those appointed by the States, but they shall be considered, for the purposes of the election of President and Vice President, to be electors appointed by a State; and they shall meet in the District and perform such duties as provided by the twelfth article of amendment.

Section 2. The Congress shall have power to enforce this article by appropriate legislation.

Amendment XXIV
(Ratified on January 23, 1964)

Section 1. The right of citizens of the United States to vote in any primary or other election for President or Vice President, for electors for President or Vice President, or for Senator or Representative in Congress, shall not be denied or abridged by the United States or any State by reason of failure to pay any poll tax or other tax.

Section 2. The Congress shall have power to enforce this article by appropriate legislation.

Amendment XXV
(Ratified on February 10, 1967)

Section 1. In case of the removal of the President from office or of his death or resignation, the Vice President shall become President.

Section 2. Whenever there is a vacancy in the office of the Vice President, the President shall nominate a Vice President who shall take office upon confirmation by a majority vote of both Houses of Congress.

Section 3. Whenever the President transmits to the President pro tempore of the Senate and the Speaker of the House of Representatives his written declaration that he is unable to discharge the powers and duties of his office, and until he transmits to them a written declaration to the contrary, such powers and duties shall be discharged by the Vice President as Acting President.

Section 4. Whenever the Vice President and a majority of either the principal officers of the executive departments or of such other body as Congress may by law provide, transmit to the President pro tempore of the Senate and the Speaker of the House of Representatives their written declaration that the President is unable to discharge the powers and duties of his office, the Vice President shall immediately assume the powers and duties of the offices as Acting President.

Thereafter, when the President transmits to the President pro tempore of the Senate and the Speaker of the House of Representatives his written declaration that no inability exists, he shall resume the powers and duties of his office unless the Vice President and a majority of either the principal officers of the executive department or of such other body as Congress may by law provide, transmit within four days to the President pro tempore of the Senate and the Speaker of the House of Representatives their written declaration that the President is unable to discharge the powers and duties of his office. Thereupon Congress shall decide the issue, assembling within forty-eight hours for that purpose if not in session. If the Congress, within twenty-one days after receipt of the latter written declaration, or, if Congress is not in session, within twenty-one days after Congress is required to assemble, determines by two-thirds vote of both Houses that the President is unable to discharge the powers and duties of his office, the Vice President shall continue to discharge the same as Acting President; otherwise; the President shall resume the powers and duties of his office.

Amendment XXVI
(Ratified on July 1, 1971)

Section 1. The right of citizens of the United States, who are eighteen years of age or older, to vote shall not be denied or abridged by the United States or by any State on account of age.

Section 2. The Congress shall have the power to enforce this article by appropriate legislation.

Amendment XXVII
(Ratified on May 7, 1992)

No law, varying the compensation for the services of the Senators and Representatives, shall take effect, until an election of Representatives shall have intervened.

Presidential Elections, 1789–2000

Year	President	Vice President	Party of President	Election Year	Winner's Electoral College Vote %	Winner's Popular Vote %
1789–1797	George Washington	John Adams	None	(1789)	*	No popular vote
				(1793)	*	No popular vote
1797–1801	John Adams	Thomas Jefferson	Fed	(1797)	*	No popular vote
1801–1809	Thomas Jefferson	Aaron Burr (to 1805)	Dem-R	(1801)	HR*	No popular vote
		George Clinton (to 1809)		(1805)	92.0	No popular vote
1809–1817	James Madison	George Clinton (to 1813)	Dem-R	(1809)	69.7	No popular vote
		Elbridge Gerry (to 1817)		(1813)	59.0	No popular vote
1817–1825	James Monroe	Daniel D. Tompkins	Dem-R	(1817)	84.3	No popular vote
				(1821)	99.5	No popular vote
1825–1829	John Quincy Adams	John C. Calhoun	Nat R	(1824)	HR	39.1**
1829–1837	Andrew Jackson	John C. Calhoun (to 1833)	Dem	(1828)	68.2	56.0
		Martin Van Buren (to 1837)		(1832)	76.6	54.5
1837–1841	Martin Van Buren	Richard M. Johnson	Dem	(1836)	57.8	50.9
1841	William H. Harrison	John Tyler	Whig	(1840)	79.6	52.9
1841–1845	John Tyler	(No VP)	Whig	(1840)	—	52.9
(1845–1849)	James K. Polk	George M. Dallas	Dem	(1844)	61.8	49.6

*Electoral College system before the Twelfth Amendment (1804). The original Constitutional provisions called for the person with the second highest total Electoral College vote to be the Vice President.

**Received fewer popular votes than an opponent. HR: Election decided in House of Representatives.

Year	President	Vice President	Party of President	Election Year	Winner's Electoral College Vote %	Winner's Popular Vote %
1849–1850	Zachary Taylor	Millard Fillmore	Whig	(1848)	56.2	47.3
1850–1853	Millard Fillmore	(No VP)	Whig		—	—
1853–1857	Franklin Pierce	William R. King	Dem	(1852)	85.8	50.9
1857–1861	James Buchanan	John C. Breckinridge	Dem	(1856)	58.8	45.6
1861–1865	Abraham Lincoln	Hannibal Hamlin (to 1865)	Rep	(1860)	59.4	39.8
		Andrew Johnson (1865)		(1864)	91.0	55.2
1865–1869	Andrew Johnson	(No VP)	Rep		—	—
1869–1877	Ulysses S. Grant	Schuyler Colfax (to 1873)	Rep	(1868)	72.8	52.7
		Henry Wilson (to 1877)		(1872)	81.9	55.6
1877–1881	Rutherford B. Hayes	William A. Wheeler	Rep	(1876)	50.1	47.9**
1881	James A. Garfield	Chester A. Arthur	Rep	(1880)	58.0	48.3
1881–1885	Chester A. Arthur	(No VP)	Rep		—	—
1885–1889	Grover Cleveland	Thomas A. Hendricks	Dem	(1884)	54.6	48.5
1889–1893	Benjamin Harrison	Levi P. Morton	Rep	(1888)	58.1	47.8**
1893–1897	Grover Cleveland	Adlai E. Stevenson	Dem	(1892)	62.3	46.0
1897–1901	William McKinley	Garret A. Hobart (to 1901)	Rep	(1896)	60.6	51.0
		Theodore Roosevelt (1901)		(1900)	64.7	51.7
1901–1909	Theodore Roosevelt	(No VP, 1901–1905)	Rep		—	—
		Charles W. Fairbanks (1905–1909)		(1904)	70.6	56.4
1909–1913	William Howard Taft	James S. Sherman	Rep	(1908)	66.4	51.6
1913–1921	Woodrow Wilson	Thomas R. Marshall	Dem	(1912)	81.9	41.9
				(1916)	52.2	49.3
1921–1923	Warren G. Harding	Calvin Coolidge	Rep	(1920)	76.1	60.3
1923–1929	Calvin Coolidge	(No VP, 1923–1925)	Rep		—	—
		Charles G. Dawes (1925–1929)		(1924)	71.9	54.0
1929–1933	Herbert Hoover	Charles Curtis	Rep	(1928)	83.6	58.2
1933–1945	Franklin D. Roosevelt	John N. Garner (1933–1941)	Dem	(1932)	88.9	57.4
		Henry A. Wallace (1941–1945)		(1936)	98.5	60.8
		Harry S Truman (1945)		(1940)	84.6	54.7
				(1944)	81.4	53.4

*Electoral College system before the Twelfth Amendment (1804). The original Constitutional provisions called for the person with the second highest total Electoral College vote to be the Vice President.

**Received fewer popular votes than an opponent. HR: Election decided in House of Representatives.

Year	President	Vice President	Party of President	Election Year	Winner's Electoral College Vote %	Winner's Popular Vote %
1945–1953	Harry S. Truman	(No VP, 1945–1949)	Dem		—	—
		Alban W. Barkley		(1948)	57.1	49.5
1953–1961	Dwight D. Eisenhower	Richard M. Nixon	Rep	(1952)	83.2	55.1
				(1956)	86.1	57.4
1961–1963	John F. Kennedy	Lyndon B. Johnson	Dem	(1960)	58.0	49.7
1963–1969	Lyndon B. Johnson	(No VP, 1963–1965)	Dem		—	—
		Hubert H. Humphrey (1965–1969)		(1964)	90.3	61.6
1969–1974	Richard M. Nixon	Spiro T. Agnew	Rep	(1968)	55.9	43.4
		Gerald R. Ford (appointed)		(1972)	96.7	60.7
1974–1977	Gerald R. Ford	Nelson A. Rockefeller (appointed)	Rep		—	—
1977–1981	Jimmy Carter	Walter Mondale	Dem	(1976)	55.2	50.1
1981–1989	Ronald Reagan	George Bush	Rep	(1980)	90.9	50.7
				(1984)	97.4	59.8
1989–1993	George Bush	J. Danforth Quayle	Rep	(1988)	79.0	53.4
1993–2001	William J. Clinton	Albert Gore	Dem	(1992)	68.8	43.2
				(1996)	70.4	49.9
2001–	George W. Bush	Richard Cheney	Rep	(2000)	50.3	48**

*Electoral College system before the Twelfth Amendment (1804). The original Constitutional provisions called for the person with the second highest total Electoral College vote to be the Vice President.

**Received fewer popular votes than an opponent. HR: Election decided in House of Representatives.

Source for election data: Svend Peterson, *A Statistical History of American Presidential Elections.* New York: Frederick Ungar Publishing, 1963. Updates: Richard Scammon, *America Votes* 19. Washington D.C.: Congressional Quarterly, 1991; *Congressional Quarterly Weekly Report,* Nov. 7, 1992, p. 3552.

Abbreviations:

Dem = Democratic

Dem-R = Democratic-Republican

Fed = Federalist

Dem-J = Jacksonian Democrats

Nat R = National Republican

Rep = Republican

Union = Unionist

Presidential Administrations

President	Vice President	Secretary of State	Secretary of Treasury
George Washington 1789–1797	John Adams 1789–1797	Thomas Jefferson 1789–1794 Edmund Randolph 1794–1795 Timothy Pickering 1795–1797	Alexander Hamilton 1789–1795 Oliver Wolcott 1795–1797
John Adams 1797–1801	Thomas Jefferson 1797–1801	Timothy Pickering 1797–1800 John Marshall 1800–1801	Oliver Wolcott 1797–1801 Samuel Dexter 1801
Thomas Jefferson 1801–1809	Aaron Burr 1801–1805 George Clinton 1805–1809	James Madison 1801–1809	Samuel Dexter 1801 Albert Gallatin 1801–1809
James Madison 1809–1817	George Clinton 1809–1813 Elbridge Gerry 1813–1817	Robert Smith 1809–1811 James Monroe 1811–1817	Albert Gallatin 1809–1814 George Campbell 1814 Alexander Dallas 1814–1816 William Crawford 1816–1817
James Monroe 1817–1825	Daniel D. Tompkins 1817–1825	John Quincy Adams 1817–1825	William Crawford 1817–1825

Secretary of War	Secretary of Navy	Postmaster General	Attorney General
Henry Knox 1789–1795		Samuel Osgood 1789–1791	Edmund Randolph 1789–1794
Timothy Pickering 1795–1796 James McHenry 1796–1797		Timothy Pickering 1791–1795 Joseph Habersham 1795–1797	William Bradford 1794–1795 Charles Lee 1795–1797
James McHenry 1797–1800 Samuel Dexter 1800–1801	Benjamin Stoddert 1798–1801	Joseph Habersham 1797–1801	Charles Lee 1797–1801
Henry Dearborn 1801–1809	Benjamin Stoddert 1801 Robert Smith 1801–1809	Joseph Habersham 1801 Gideon Granger 1801–1809	Levi Lincoln 1801–1805 John Breckinridge 1805–1807 Caesar Rodney 1807–1809
William Eustis 1809–1813 John Armstrong 1813–1814 James Monroe 1814–1815 William Crawford 1815–1817	Paul Hamilton 1809–1813 William Jones 1813–1814 Benjamin Crowninshield 1814–1817	Gideon Granger 1809–1814 Return Meigs 1814–1817	Caesar Rodney 1809–1811 William Pinkney 1811–1814 Richard Rush 1814–1817
George Graham 1817 John C. Calhoun 1817–1825	Benjamin Crowninshield 1817–1818 Smith Thompson 1818–1823 Samuel Southard 1823–1825	Return Meigs 1817–1823 John McLean 1823–1825	Richard Rush 1817 William Wirt 1817–1825

President	Vice President	Secretary of State	Secretary of Treasury	Secretary of War
John Quincy Adams 1825–1829	John C. Calhoun 1825–1829	Henry Clay 1825–1829	Richard Rush 1825–1829	James Barbour 1825–1828 Peter B. Porter 1828–1829
Andrew Jackson 1829–1837	John C. Calhoun 1829–1833 Martin Van Buren 1833–1837	Martin Van Buren 1829–1831 Edward Livingston 1831–1833 Louis McLane 1833–1834 John Forsyth 1834–1837	Samuel Ingham 1829–1831 Louis McLane 1831–1833 William Duane 1833 Roger B. Taney 1833–1834 Levi Woodbury 1834–1837	John H. Eaton 1829–1831 Lewis Cass 1831–1837 Benjamin Butler 1837
Martin Van Buren 1837–1841	Richard M. Johnson 1837–1841	John Forsyth 1837–1841	Levi Woodbury 1837–1841	Joel R. Poinsett 1837–1841
William H. Harrison 1841	John Tyler 1841	Daniel Webster 1841	Thomas Ewing 1841	John Bell 1841
John Tyler 1841–1845		Daniel Webster 1841–1843 Hugh S. Legaré 1843 Abel P. Upshur 1843–1844 John C. Calhoun 1844–1845	Thomas Ewing 1841 Walter Forward 1841–1843 John C. Spencer 1843–1844 George M. Bibb 1844–1845	John Bell 1841 John C. Spencer 1841–1843 James M. Porter 1843–1844 William Wilkins 1844–1845
James K. Polk 1845–1849	George M. Dallas 1845–1849	James Buchanan 1845–1849	Robert J. Walker 1845–1849	William L. Marcy 1845–1849
Zachary Taylor 1849–1850	Millard Fillmore 1849–1850	John M. Clayton 1849–1850	William M. Meredith 1849–1850	George W. Crawford 1849–1850
Millard Fillmore 1850–1853		Daniel Webster 1850–1852 Edward Everett 1852–1853	Thomas Corwin 1850–1853	Charles M. Conrad 1850–1853
Franklin Pierce 1853–1857	William R. King 1853–1857	William L. Marcy 1853–1857	James Guthrie 1853–1857	Jefferson Davis 1853–1857

Secretary of Navy	Postmaster General	Attorney General	Secretary of Interior
Samuel Southard 1825–1829	John McLean 1825–1829	William Wirt 1825–1829	
John Branch 1829–1831 Levi Woodbury 1831–1834 Mahlon Dickerson 1834–1837	William Barry 1829–1835 Amos Kendall 1835–1837	John M. Berrien 1829–1831 Roger B. Taney 1831–1833 Benjamin Butler 1833–1837	
Mahlon Dickerson 1837–1838 James K. Paulding 1838–1841	Amos Kendall 1837–1840 John M. Niles 1840–1841	Benjamin Butler 1837–1838 Felix Grundy 1838–1840 Henry D. Gilpin 1840–1841	
George E. Badger 1841	Francis Granger 1841	John J. Crittenden 1841	
George E. Badger 1841 Abel P. Upshur 1841–1843 David Henshaw 1843–1844 Thomas Gilmer 1844 John Y. Mason 1844–1845	Francis Granger 1841 Charles A. Wickliffe 1841–1845	John J. Crittenden 1841 Hugh S. Legaré 1841–1843 John Nelson 1843–1845	
George Bancroft 1845–1846 John Y. Mason 1846–1849	Cave Johnson 1845–1849	John Y. Mason 1845–1846 Nathan Clifford 1846–1848 Isaac Toucey 1848–1849	
William B. Preston 1849–1850	Jacob Collamer 1849–1850	Reverdy Johnson 1849–1850	Thomas Ewing 1849–1850
William A. Graham 1850–1852 John P. Kennedy 1852–1853	Nathan K. Hall 1850–1852 Sam D. Hubbard 1852–1853	John J. Crittenden 1850–1853	Thomas McKennan 1850 A. H. H. Stuart 1850–1853
James C. Dobbin 1853–1857	James Campbell 1853–1857	Caleb Cushing 1853–1857	Robert McClelland 1853–1857

President	Vice President	Secretary of State	Secretary of Treasury	Secretary of War
James Buchanan 1857–1861	John C. Breckinridge 1857–1861	Lewis Cass 1857–1860 Jeremiah S. Black 1860–1861	Howell Cobb 1857–1860 Philip F. Thomas 1860–1861 John A. Dix 1861	John B. Floyd 1857–1861 Joseph Holt 1861
Abraham Lincoln 1861–1865	Hannibal Hamlin 1861–1865 Andrew Johnson 1865	William H. Seward 1861–1865	Salmon P. Chase 1861–1864 William P. Fessenden 1864–1865 Hugh McCulloch 1865	Simon Cameron 1861–1862 Edwin M. Stanton 1862–1865
Andrew Johnson 1865–1869		William H. Seward 1865–1869	Hugh McCulloch 1865–1869	Edwin M. Stanton 1865–1867 Ulysses S. Grant 1867–1868 John M. Schofield 1868–1869
Ulysses S. Grant 1869–1877	Schuyler Colfax 1869–1873 Henry Wilson 1873–1877	Elihu B. Washburne 1869 Hamilton Fish 1869–1877	George S. Boutwell 1869–1873 William A. Richardson 1873–1874 Benjamin H. Bristow 1874–1876 Lot M. Morrill 1876–1877	John A. Rawlins 1869 William T. Sherman 1869 William W. Belknap 1869–1876 Alphonso Taft 1876 James D. Cameron 1876–1877
Rutherford B. Hayes 1877–1881	William A. Wheeler 1877–1881	William M. Evarts 1877–1881	John Sherman 1877–1881	George W. McCrary 1877–1879 Alexander Ramsey 1879–1881
James A. Garfield 1881	Chester A. Arthur 1881	James G. Blaine 1881	William Windom 1881	Robert T. Lincoln 1881
Chester A. Arthur 1881–1885		F. T. Frelinghuysen 1881–1885	Charles J. Folger 1881–1884 Walter Q. Gresham 1884 Hugh McCulloch 1884–1885	Robert T. Lincoln 1881–1885
Grover Cleveland 1885–1889	T. A. Hendricks 1885	Thomas F. Bayard 1885–1889	Daniel Manning 1885–1887 Charles S. Fairchild 1887–1889	William C. Endicott 1885–1889

Secretary of Navy	Postmaster General	Attorney General	Secretary of Interior	Secretary of Agriculture
Isaac Toucey 1857–1861	Aaron V. Brown 1857–1859 Joseph Holt 1859–1861 Horatio King 1861	Jeremiah S. Black 1857–1860 Edwin M. Stanton 1860–1861	Jacob Thompson 1857–1861	
Gideon Welles 1861–1865	Horatio King 1861 Montgomery Blair 1861–1864 William Dennison 1864–1865	Edward Bates 1861–1864 James Speed 1864–1865	Caleb B. Smith 1861–1863 John P. Usher 1863–1865	
Gideon Welles 1865–1869	William Dennison 1865–1866 Alexander Randall 1866–1869 William M. Evarts 1868–1869	James Speed 1865–1866 Henry Stanbery 1866–1868 O. H. Browning 1866–1869	John P. Usher 1865 James Harlan 1865–1866	
Adolph E. Borie 1869 George M. Robeson 1869–1877	John A. J. Creswell 1869–1874 James W. Marshall 1874 Marshall Jewell 1874–1876 James N. Tyner 1876–1877	Ebenezer R. Hoar 1869–1870 Amos T. Akerman 1870–1871 G. H. Williams 1871–1875 Edwards Pierrepont 1875–1876 Alphonso Taft 1876–1877	Jacob D. Cox 1869–1870 Columbus Delano 1870–1875 Zachariah Chandler 1875–1877	
R. W. Thompson 1877–1881 Nathan Goff, Jr. 1881	David M. Key 1877–1880 Horace Maynard 1880–1881	Charles Devens 1877–1881	Carl Schurz 1877–1881	
William H. Hunt 1881	Thomas L. James 1881	Wayne MacVeagh 1881	S. J. Kirkwood 1881	
William E. Chandler 1881–1885	Thomas L. James 1881 Timothy O. Howe 1881–1883 Walter Q. Gresham 1883–1884 Frank Hatton 1884–1885	B. H. Brewster 1881–1885	Henry M. Teller 1881–1885	
William C. Whitney 1885–1889	William F. Vilas 1885–1888 Don M. Dickinson 1888–1889	A. H. Garland 1885–1889	L. Q. C. Lamar 1885–1888 William F. Vilas 1888–1889	Norman J. Colman 1889

President	Vice President	Secretary of State	Secretary of Treasury	Secretary of War	Secretary of Navy
Benjamin Harrison 1889–1893	Levi P. Morton 1889–1893	James G. Blaine 1889–1892 John W. Foster 1892–1893	William Windom 1889–1891 Charles Foster 1892–1893	Redfield Procter 1889–1891 Stephen B. Elkins 1891–1893	Benjamin F. Tracy 1889–1893
Grover Cleveland 1893–1897	Adlai E. Stevenson 1893–1897	Walter Q. Gresham 1893–1895 Richard Olney 1895–1897	John G. Carlisle 1893–1897	Daniel S. Lamont 1893–1897	Hilary A. Herbert 1893–1897
William McKinley 1897–1901	Garret A. Hobart 1897–1899 Theodore Roosevelt 1901	John Sherman 1897–1898 William R. Day 1898 John Hay 1898–1901	Lyman J. Gage 1897–1901	Russell A. Alger 1897–1899 Elihu Root 1899–1901	John D. Long 1897–1901
Theodore Roosevelt 1901–1909	Charles Fairbanks 1905–1909	John Hay 1901–1905 Elihu Root 1905–1909 Robert Bacon 1909	Lyman J. Gage 1901–1902 Leslie M. Shaw 1902–1907 George B. Cortelyou 1907–1909	Elihu Root 1901–1904 William H. Taft 1904–1908 Luke E. Wright 1908–1909	John D. Long 1901–1902 William H. Moody 1902–1904 Paul Morton 1904–1905 Charles J. Bonaparte 1905–1906 Victor H. Metcalf 1906–1908 T. H. Newberry 1908–1909
William H. Taft 1909–1913	James S. Sherman 1909–1913	Philander C. Knox 1909–1913	Franklin MacVeagh 1909–1913	Jacob M. Dickinson 1909–1911 Henry L. Stimson 1911–1913	George von L. Meyer 1909–1913
Woodrow Wilson 1913–1921	Thomas R. Marshall 1913–1921	William J. Bryan 1913–1915 Robert Lansing 1915–1920 Bainbridge Colby 1920–1921	William G. McAdoo 1913–1918 Carter Glass 1918–1920 David F. Houston 1920–1921	Lindley M. Garrison 1913–1916 Newton D. Baker 1916–1921	Josephus Daniels 1913–1921
Warren G. Harding 1921–1923	Calvin Coolidge 1921–1923	Charles E. Hughes 1921–1923	Andrew W. Mellon 1921–1923	John W. Weeks 1921–1923	Edwin Denby 1921–1923
Calvin Coolidge 1923–1929	Charles G. Dawes 1925–1929	Charles E. Hughes 1923–1925	Andrew W. Mellon 1923–1929	John W. Weeks 1923–1925	Edwin Denby 1923–1924

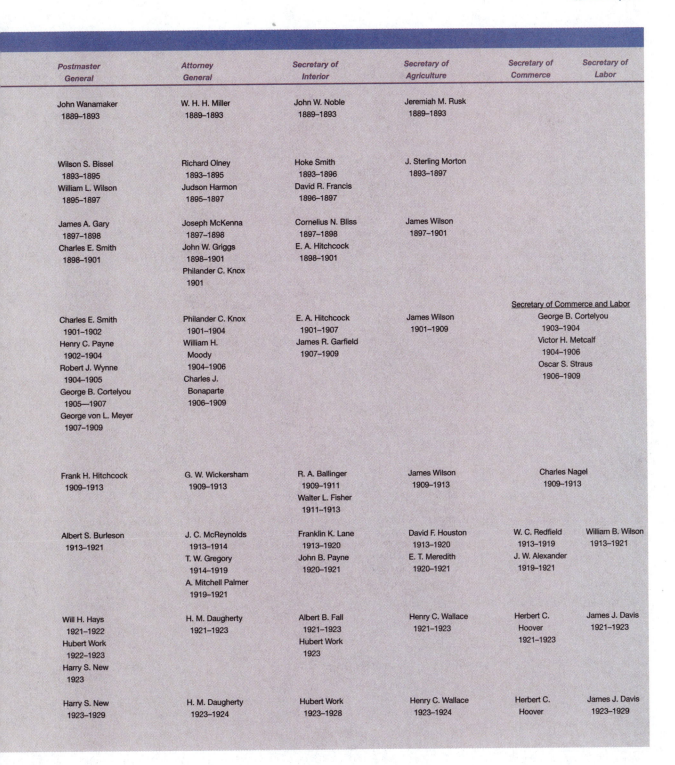

Postmaster General	Attorney General	Secretary of Interior	Secretary of Agriculture	Secretary of Commerce	Secretary of Labor
John Wanamaker 1889–1893	W. H. H. Miller 1889–1893	John W. Noble 1889–1893	Jeremiah M. Rusk 1889–1893		
Wilson S. Bissel 1893–1895 William L. Wilson 1895–1897	Richard Olney 1893–1895 Judson Harmon 1895–1897	Hoke Smith 1893–1896 David R. Francis 1896–1897	J. Sterling Morton 1893–1897		
James A. Gary 1897–1898 Charles E. Smith 1898–1901	Joseph McKenna 1897–1898 John W. Griggs 1898–1901 Philander C. Knox 1901	Cornelius N. Bliss 1897–1898 E. A. Hitchcock 1898–1901	James Wilson 1897–1901		
Charles E. Smith 1901–1902 Henry C. Payne 1902–1904 Robert J. Wynne 1904–1905 George B. Cortelyou 1905—1907 George von L. Meyer 1907–1909	Philander C. Knox 1901–1904 William H. Moody 1904–1906 Charles J. Bonaparte 1906–1909	E. A. Hitchcock 1901–1907 James R. Garfield 1907–1909	James Wilson 1901–1909	Secretary of Commerce and Labor George B. Cortelyou 1903–1904 Victor H. Metcalf 1904–1906 Oscar S. Straus 1906–1909	
Frank H. Hitchcock 1909–1913	G. W. Wickersham 1909–1913	R. A. Ballinger 1909–1911 Walter L. Fisher 1911–1913	James Wilson 1909–1913	Charles Nagel 1909–1913	
Albert S. Burleson 1913–1921	J. C. McReynolds 1913–1914 T. W. Gregory 1914–1919 A. Mitchell Palmer 1919–1921	Franklin K. Lane 1913–1920 John B. Payne 1920–1921	David F. Houston 1913–1920 E. T. Meredith 1920–1921	W. C. Redfield 1913–1919 J. W. Alexander 1919–1921	William B. Wilson 1913–1921
Will H. Hays 1921–1922 Hubert Work 1922–1923 Harry S. New 1923	H. M. Daugherty 1921–1923	Albert B. Fall 1921–1923 Hubert Work 1923	Henry C. Wallace 1921–1923	Herbert C. Hoover 1921–1923	James J. Davis 1921–1923
Harry S. New 1923–1929	H. M. Daugherty 1923–1924	Hubert Work 1923–1928	Henry C. Wallace 1923–1924	Herbert C. Hoover	James J. Davis 1923–1929

President	Vice President	Secretary of State	Secretary of Treasury	Secretary of War	Secretary of Navy	Postmaster General	Attorney General
Calvin Coolidge 1923–1929	Charles G. Dawes 1925–1929	Frank B. Kellogg 1925–1929		Dwight F. Davis 1925–1929	Curtis D. Wilbur 1924–1929		Harlan F. Stone 1924–1925 John G. Sargent 1925–1929
Herbert C. Hoover 1929–1933	Charles Curtis 1929–1933	Henry L. Stimson 1929–1933	Andrew W. Mellon 1929–1932 Ogden L. Mills 1932–1933	James W. Good 1929 Patrick J. Hurley 1929–1933	Charles F. Adams 1929–1933	Walter F. Brown 1929–1933	J. D. Mitchell 1929–1933
Franklin Delano Roosevelt 1933–1945	John Nance Garner 1933–1941 Henry A. Wallace 1941–1945 Harry S Truman 1945	Cordell Hull 1933–1944 E. R. Stettinius, Jr. 1944–1945	William H. Woodin 1933–1934 Henry Morgenthau, Jr. 1934–1945	George H. Dern 1933–1936 Harry H. Woodring 1936–1940 Henry L. Stimson 1940–1945	Claude A. Swanson 1933–1940 Charles Edison 1940 Frank Knox 1940–1944 James V. Forrestal 1944–1945	James A. Farley 1933–1940 Frank C. Walker 1940–1945	H. S. Cummings 1933–1939 Frank Murphy 1939–1940 Robert Jackson 1940–1941 Francis Biddel 1941–1945
Harry S Truman 1945–1953	Alben W. Barkley 1949–1953	James F. Byrnes 1945–1947 George C. Marshall 1947–1949 Dean G. Acheson 1949–1953	Fred M. Vinson 1945–1946 John W. Snyder 1946–1953	Robert P. Patterson 1945–1947 Kenneth C. Royall 1947	James V. Forrestal 1945–1947	R. E. Hannegan 1945–1947 Jesse M. Donaldson 1947–1953	Tom C. Clark 1945–1949 J. H. McGrath 1949–1952 James P. McGranery 1952–1953
				Secretary of Defense James V. Forrestal 1947–1949 Louis A. Johnson 1949–1950 George C. Marshall 1950–1951 Robert A. Lovett 1951–1953			
Dwight D. Eisenhower 1953–1961	Richard M. Nixon 1953–1961	John Foster Dulles 1953–1959 Christian A. Herter 1957–1961	George M. Humphrey 1953–1957 Robert B. Anderson 1957–1961	Charles E. Wilson 1953–1957 Neil H. McElroy 1957–1961 Thomas S. Gates 1959–1961		A. E. Summerfield 1953–1961	H. Brownell, Jr. 1953–1957 William P. Rogers 1957–1961
John F. Kennedy 1961–1963	Lyndon B. Johnson 1961–1963	Dean Rusk 1961–1963	C. Douglas Dillon 1961–1963	Robert S. McNamara 1961–1963		J. Edward Day 1961–1963 John A. Gronouski 1961–1963	Robert F. Kennedy 1961–1963
Lyndon B. Johnson 1963–1969	Hubert H. Humphrey 1965–1969	Dean Rusk 1963–1969	C. Douglas Dillon 1963–1965 Henry H. Fowler 1965–1968 Joseph W. Barr 1968–1969	Robert S. McNamara 1963–1968 Clark M. Clifford 1968–1969		John A. Gronouski 1963–1965 Lawrence F. O'Brien 1965–1968 W. Marvin Watson 1968–1969	Robert F. Kennedy 1963–1965 N. deB. Katzenbach 1965–1967 Ramsey Clark 1967–1969

Secretary of Interior	Secretary of Agriculture	Secretary of Commerce	Secretary of Labor	Secretary of Health, Education and Welfare	Secretary of Housing and Urban Development	Secretary of Transportation
Roy O. West 1928–1929	Howard M. Gore 1924–1925 W. J. Jardine 1925–1929	1923–1928 William F. Whiting 1928–1929				
Ray L. Wilbur 1929–1933	Arthur M. Hyde 1929–1933 Roy D. Chapin 1932–1933	Robert P. Lamont 1929–1932 William N. Doak 1930–1933	James J. Davis 1929–1930			
Harold L. Ickes 1933–1945	Henry A. Wallace 1933–1940 Claude R. Wickard 1940–1945	Daniel C. Roper 1933–1939 Harry L. Hopkins 1939–1940 Jesse Jones 1940–1945 Henry A. Wallace 1945	Frances Perkins 1933–1945			
Harold L. Ickes 1945–1946 Julius A. Krug 1946–1949 Oscar L. Chapman 1949–1953	C. P. Anderson 1945–1948 C. F. Brannan 1948–1953	W. A. Harriman 1946–1948 Charles Sawyer 1948–1953	L. B. Schwellenbach 1945–1948 Maurice J. Tobin 1948–1953			
Douglas McKay 1953–1956 Fred Seaton 1956–1961	Ezra T. Benson 1953–1961	Sinclair Weeks 1953–1958 Lewis L. Strauss 1958–1961	Martin P. Durkin 1953 James P. Mitchell 1953–1961	Oveta Culp Hobby 1953–1955 Marion B. Folsom 1955–1958 Arthur S. Flemming 1958–1961		
Stewart L. Udall 1961–1963	Orville L. Freeman 1961–1963	Luther H. Hodges 1961–1963	Arthur J. Goldberg 1961–1963 W. Willard Wirtz 1962–1963	A. H. Ribicoff 1961–1963 Anthony J. Celebrezze 1962–1963		
Stewart L. Udall 1963–1969	Orville L. Freeman 1963–1969	Luther H. Hodges 1963–1965 John T. Connor 1965–1967 Alexander B. Trowbridge 1967–1968 C. R. Smith 1968–1969	W. Willard Wirtz 1963–1969	Anthony J. Celebrezze 1963–1965 John W. Gardner 1965–1968 Wilbur J. Cohen 1968–1969	Robert C. Weaver 1966–1968 Robert C. Wood 1968–1969	Alan S. Boyd 1966–1969

President	Vice President	Secretary of State	Secretary of Treasury	Secretary of Defense	Postmaster General	Attorney General	Secretary of Interior	Secretary of Agriculture
Richard M. Nixon 1969–1974	Spiro T. Agnew 1969–1973 Gerald R. Ford 1973–1974	William P. Rogers 1969–1973 Henry A. Kissinger 1973–1974	David M. Kennedy 1969–1970 John B. Connally 1970–1972 George P. Schultz 1972–1974 William E. Simon 1974	Melvin R. Laird 1969–1973 Elliot L. Richardson 1973 James R. Schlesinger 1973–1974	Winton M. Blount 1969–1971	John M. Mitchell 1969–1972 Richard G. Kleindienst 1972–1973 Elliot L. Richardson 1973 William B. Saxbe 1974	Walter J. Hickel 1969–1971 Rogers C. B. Morton 1971–1974	Clifford M. Hardin 1969–1971 Earl L. Butz 1971–1974
Gerald R. Ford 1974–1977	Nelson A. Rockefeller 1974–1977	Henry A. Kissinger 1974–1977	William E. Simon 1974–1977	James R. Schlesinger 1974–1975 Donald H. Rumsfeld 1975–1977		William B. Saxbe 1974–1975 Edward H. Levi 1975–1977	Rogers C. B. Morton 1974–1975 Stanley K. Hathaway 1975 Thomas D. Kleppe 1975–1977	Earl L. Butz 1974–1976
Jimmy Carter 1977–1981	Walter F. Mondale 1977–1981	Cyrus R. Vance 1977–1980 Edmund S. Muskie 1980–1981	W. Michael Blumenthal 1977–1979 G. William Miller 1979–1981	Harold Brown 1977–1981		Griffin Bell 1977–1979 Benjamin R. Civiletti 1979–1981	Cecil D. Andrus 1977–1981	Robert Bergland 1977–1981
Ronald W. Reagan 1981–1989	George H. Bush 1981–1989	Alexander M. Haig, Jr. 1981–1982 George P. Shultz 1982–1989	Donald T. Regan 1981–1985 James A. Baker 1985–1988 Nicholas F. Brady 1988–1989	Caspar W. Weinberger 1981–1987 Frank C. Carlucci 1987–1989		William French Smith 1981–1985 Edwin Meese 1985–1988 Richard Thornburgh 1988–1989	James G. Watt 1981–1983 William P. Clark 1983–1985 Donald P. Hodel 1985–1989	John R. Block 1981–1986 Richard E. Lyng 1986–1989
George H. Bush 1989–1993	J. Danforth Quayle 1989–1993	James A. Baker 1989–1992 Lawrence S. Eagleburger 1992–1993	Nicholas F. Brady 1989–1993	Richard Cheney 1989–1993		Richard Thornburgh 1989–1990 William Barr 1990–1993	Manuel Lujan 1989–1993	Clayton Yeutter 1989–1990 Edward Madigan 1990–1993
William Clinton 1993–2001	Albert Gore 1993–2001	Warren M. Christopher 1993–1996 Madeleine K. Albright 1997–2001	Lloyd Bentsen 1993–1994 Robert E. Rubin 1994–1999 Lawrence H. Summers 1999–2001	Les Aspin 1993–1994 William J. Perry 1994–1996 William S. Cohen 1997–2001		Janet Reno 1993–2001	Bruce Babbitt 1993–2001	Mike Espy 1993–1994 Dan Glickman 1995–2001
George W. Bush 2001–	Richard B. Cheney 2001–	Gen. Colin L. Powell 2001–	Paul H. O'Neill 2001–	Donald H. Rumsfeld 2001–		John Ashcroft 2001–	Gale A. Norton 2001–	Ann M. Veneman 2001–

Secretary of Commerce	Secretary of Labor	Secretary of Health, Education and Welfare	Secretary of Housing and Urban Development	Secretary of Transportation	Secretary of Energy	Secretary of Veterans Affairs
Maurice H. Stans 1969–1972 Peter G. Peterson 1972 Frederick B. Dent 1972–1974	George P. Shultz 1969–1970 James D. Hodgson 1970–1973 Peter J. Brennan 1973–1974	Robert H. Finch 1969–1970 Elliot L. Richardson 1970–1973 Caspar W. Weinberger 1973–1974	George W. Romney 1969–1973 James T. Lynn 1973–1974	John A. Volpe 1969–1973 Claude S. Brinegar 1973–1974		
Frederick B. Dent 1974–1975 Rogers C. B. Morton 1975 Elliot L. Richardson 1975–1977	Peter J. Brennan 1974–1975 John T. Dunlop 1975–1976 W. J. Usery 1976–1977	Caspar W. Weinberger 1974–1975 Forrest D. Matthews 1975–1977	James T. Lynn 1974–1975 Carla A. Hills 1975–1977	Claude S. Brinegar 1974–1975 William T. Coleman 1975–1977		
Juanita Kreps 1977–1981	F. Ray Marshall 1977–1981	Joseph Califano 1977–1979 Patricia Roberts Harris 1979–1980	Patricia Roberts Harris 1977–1979 Moon Landrieu 1979–1981	Brock Adams 1977–1979 Neil E. Goldschmidt 1979–1981	James R. Schlesinger 1977–1979 Charles W. Duncan, Jr. 1979–1981	

		Secretary of Health and Human Services	Secretary of Education			
		Patricia Roberts Harris 1980–1981	Shirley M. Hufstedler 1980–1981			
Malcolm Baldridge 1981–1987 C. William Verity, Jr. 1987–1989	Raymond J. Donovan 1981–1985 William E. Brock 1985–1987 Ann Dore McLaughlin 1987–1989	Richard S. Schweiker 1981–1983 Margaret M. Heckler 1983–1985 Otis R. Bowen 1985–1989	Terrell H. Bell 1981–1985 William J. Bennett 1985–1988 Lauro Fred Cavazos 1988–1989	Samuel R. Pierce, Jr. 1981–1989	Drew Lewis 1981–1983 Elizabeth H. Dole 1983–1987 James H. Burnley 1987–1989	James B. Edwards 1981–1982 Donald P. Hodel 1982–1985 John S. Harrington 1985–1989
Robert Mosbacher 1989–1991 Barbara Franklin 1991–1993	Elizabeth Dole 1989–1990 Lynn Martin 1992–1993	Louis Sullivan 1989–1993	Lamar Alexander 1990–1993	Jack Kemp 1989–1993	Samuel Skinner 1989–1990 Andrew Card 1990–1993	James Watkins 1989–1993	Edward J. Derwinski 1989–1993
Ronald H. Brown 1993–1996 William M. Daley 1997–2000 Norman Y. Mineta 2000–2001	Robert B. Reich 1993–1996 Alexis M. Herman 1997–2001	Donna E. Shalala 1993–2001	Richard W. Riley 1993–2001	Henry G. Cisneros 1993–1996 Andrew M. Cuomo 1997–2001	Federico F. Peña 1993–1996 Rodney E. Slater 1997–2001	Hazel O'Leary 1993–1996 Federico F. Peña 1997–1998 Bill Richardson 1998–2001	Jesse Brown 1993–1997 Togo D. West, Jr.[2] 1998–2001
Donald L. Evans 2001–	Elaine L. Chao 2001–	Tommy G. Thompson 2001–	Roderick R. Paige 2001–	Melquiades R. Martinez 2001–	Norman Y. Mineta 2001–	Spencer Abraham 2001–	Anthony Principi 2001–

PHOTO CREDITS